WRITING SAMPLES

Writing samples in this book show you representative types of writing about literature—from initial notes to a revised, final research paper. Reading these samples along with their commentary should help you understand what is expected when your instructor asks you to write about the literature you are reading.

Marking Up Texts for Writing Ideas

Annotation and notes on Linda Brewer's "20/20" (p. 18)

Notes on Raymond Carver's "Cathedral" (p. 47)

Reading notes on *Trifles* (p. 788)

Response Papers

Response Paper on Raymond Carver's "Cathedral" (p. 50)

Names in "On Her Loving Two Equally" (p. 502)

Response Paper on W. H. Auden's "Stop all the clocks, cut off the telephone" (p. 562)

Essays

A Narrator's Blindness in Raymond Carver's "Cathedral" (p. 53)

How Setting Reflects Emotions in Anton Chekhov's "The Lady with the Dog" (p. 207)

Multiplying by Dividing in Aphra Behn's "On Her Loving Two Equally" (p. 505)

Philip Larkin's "Church Going" (p. 651)

A Journey of Sisterhood in Susan Glaspell's *Trifles* (p. 796)

Comparative Essay

Out-Sonneting Shakespeare: An Examination of Edna St. Vincent Millay's Use of the Sonnet Form (p. 680)

Research Essay

"Only a Girl"? Gendered Initiation in Alice Munro's "Boys and Girls" (p. 1340)

CRITICAL APPROACHES

This short guide to important critical approaches briefly explains the tools that professional critics and theorists employ when they write about literature.

Emphasis on the Text (p. 1354)

New Criticism

Structuralism

Poststructuralism

Deconstruction

Narrative Theory

Emphasis on the Source (p. 1362)

Biographical Criticism

Psychoanalytic Criticism

Emphasis on the Receiver (p. 1368)

Reader-Response Criticism

Historical and Ideological Criticism (p. 1370)

Marxist Criticism

Feminist Criticism

Gender Studies and Queer Theory

African American and Ethnic Literary Studies

New Historicism

Cultural Studies

Postcolonial Criticism and Studies of World Literature

THE NORTON INTRODUCTION TO

LITERATURE

PORTABLE TWELFTH EDITION

KELLY J. MAYS

UNIVERSITY OF NEVADA, LAS VEGAS

 W. W. NORTON & COMPANY   New York, London

W. W. Norton & Company has been independent since its founding in 1923, when William Warder Norton and Mary D. Herter Norton first published lectures delivered at the People's Institute, the adult education division of New York City's Cooper Union. The firm soon expanded its program beyond the Institute, publishing books by celebrated academics from America and abroad. By mid-century, the two major pillars of Norton's publishing program—trade books and college texts—were firmly established. In the 1950s, the Norton family transferred control of the company to its employees, and today—with a staff of four hundred and a comparable number of trade, college, and professional titles published each year—W. W. Norton & Company stands as the largest and oldest publishing house owned wholly by its employees.

Editor: Sarah Touborg
Associate Editor: Ariella Foss
Project Editor: Katie Callahan
Assistant Editor: Rachel Taylor
Manuscript Editor: Jude Grant
Managing Editor, College: Marian Johnson
Managing Editor, College Digital Media: Kim Yi
Production Manager: Ashley Horna
Media Editor: Carly Fraser Doria
Media Editorial Assistant: Ava Bramson
Marketing Manager, Literature: Kimberly Bowers
Design Director: Rubina Yeh
Book Designer: Jo Anne Metsch
Photo Editor: Ted Szczepanski
Photo Research: Julie Tesser
Permissions Manager: Megan Schindel
Permissions Clearer: Margaret Gorenstein
Composition: Westchester Book Group
Manufacturing: LSC Communications—Crawfordsville

Permission to use copyrighted material is included in the permissions acknowledgments section of this book, which begins on page A16.

Library of Congress Cataloging-in-Publication Data

Names: Mays, Kelly J., editor.
Title: The Norton introduction to literature / [edited by] Kelly J. Mays.
Description: Portable twelfth edition. | New York : W. W. Norton & Company, 2016. |
    Includes bibliographical references and index.
Identifiers: LCCN 2016016295 | ISBN 9780393938937 (pbk.)
Subjects: LCSH: Literature—Collections.
Classification: LCC PN6014 .N67 2016c | DDC 808—dc23 LC record available at
    https://lccn.loc.gov/2016016295

W. W. Norton & Company, Inc., 500 Fifth Avenue, New York, N.Y. 10110

www.wwnorton.com

W. W. Norton & Company Ltd., 15 Carlisle Street, London W1D 3BS

4   5   6   7   8   9   0

Contents

Contents Arranged by Topic   xix
Preface for Instructors   xxxiii
Introduction   1
    What Is Literature?   1
    What Does Literature Do?   3
    JOHN KEATS, *On First Looking into Chapman's Homer*   4
    What Are the Genres of Literature?   5
    Why Read Literature?   7
    Why Study Literature?   10

Fiction

FICTION: READING, RESPONDING, WRITING   12

    ANONYMOUS, *The Elephant in the Village of the Blind*   14
    READING AND RESPONDING TO FICTION   16
    LINDA BREWER, *20/20*   17
        SAMPLE WRITING: *Annotation and Notes on "20/20"*   18
    MARJANE SATRAPI, *The Shabbat* (from *Persepolis*)   21
    WRITING ABOUT FICTION   32
    RAYMOND CARVER, *Cathedral*   33
        SAMPLE WRITING: WESLEY RUPTON, *Reading Notes on Raymond Carver's "Cathedral"*   47
        SAMPLE WRITING: WESLEY RUPTON, *Response Paper on Raymond Carver's "Cathedral"*   50
        SAMPLE WRITING: BETHANY QUALLS, *A Narrator's Blindness in Raymond Carver's "Cathedral"*   53

UNDERSTANDING THE TEXT   57

1 **PLOT**   57
    JACOB AND WILHELM GRIMM, *The Shroud*   60

JAMES BALDWIN, *Sonny's Blues*   66

JOYCE CAROL OATES, *Where Are You Going, Where Have You Been?*   94

2   **NARRATION AND POINT OF VIEW**   110

EDGAR ALLAN POE, *The Cask of Amontillado*   115

ERNEST HEMINGWAY, *Hills Like White Elephants*   122

JAMAICA KINCAID, *Girl*   127

3   **CHARACTER**   130

TONI MORRISON, *Recitatif*   138

AUTHORS ON THEIR WORK: Toni Morrison   155

DAVID FOSTER WALLACE, *Good People*   156

4   **SETTING**   164

ITALO CALVINO, from *Invisible Cities*   166

ANTON CHEKHOV, *The Lady with the Dog*   171

AMY TAN, *A Pair of Tickets*   186

JUDITH ORTIZ COFER, *Volar*   203

SAMPLE WRITING: STEVEN MATVIEW, *How Setting Reflects Emotions in Anton Chekhov's "The Lady with the Dog"*   207

5   **SYMBOL AND FIGURATIVE LANGUAGE**   213

NATHANIEL HAWTHORNE, *The Birth-Mark*   219

EDWIDGE DANTICAT, *A Wall of Fire Rising*   234

6   **THEME**   249

AESOP, *The Two Crabs*   249

STEPHEN CRANE, *The Open Boat*   254

YASUNARI KAWABATA, *The Grasshopper and the Bell Cricket*   275

READING MORE FICTION   279

TONI CADE BAMBARA, *The Lesson*   279

AUTHORS ON THEIR WORK: Toni Cade Bambara   286

KATE CHOPIN, *The Story of an Hour*   287

LOUISE ERDRICH, *Love Medicine*   289

WILLIAM FAULKNER, *A Rose for Emily*   308

CHARLOTTE PERKINS GILMAN, *The Yellow Wallpaper*   316

JAMES JOYCE, *Araby*   330

FRANZ KAFKA, *A Hunger Artist*   336

JHUMPA LAHIRI, *Interpreter of Maladies*   344

GABRIEL GARCÍA MÁRQUEZ, *A Very Old Man with Enormous Wings: A Tale for Children*   362

HERMAN MELVILLE, *Bartleby, the Scrivener: A Story of Wall Street*   368

ALICE MUNRO, *Boys and Girls*   400

FLANNERY O'CONNOR, *A Good Man Is Hard to Find*   412

TILLIE OLSEN, *I Stand Here Ironing*   426

DAVID SEDARIS, *Jesus Shaves*   433

JOHN UPDIKE, *A & P*   437

AUTHORS ON THEIR WORK: John Updike   443

EUDORA WELTY, *Why I Live at the P.O.*   444

JUNOT DÍAZ, *Wildwood*   455

Poetry

POETRY: READING, RESPONDING, WRITING   476

DEFINING POETRY   477

LYDIA DAVIS, *Head, Heart*   478

AUTHORS ON THEIR CRAFT: Billy Collins   480

POETIC SUBGENRES AND KINDS   481

EDWIN ARLINGTON ROBINSON, *Richard Cory*   482

THOMAS HARDY, *The Ruined Maid*   483

WILLIAM WORDSWORTH, [*I wandered lonely as a cloud*]   485

FRANK O'HARA, *Poem* [*Lana Turner has collapsed*]   486

PHILLIS WHEATLEY, *On Being Brought from Africa to America*   487

EMILY DICKINSON, [*The Sky is low—the Clouds are mean*]   488

BILLY COLLINS, *Divorce*   488

BRUCE SPRINGSTEEN, *Nebraska*   489

ROBERT HAYDEN, *A Letter from Phillis Wheatley* 490

RESPONDING TO POETRY 492

APHRA BEHN, *On Her Loving Two Equally* 493

WRITING ABOUT POETRY 501

SAMPLE WRITING: *Response Paper on Names in "On Her Loving Two Equally"* 502

SAMPLE WRITING: *Multiplying by Dividing in Aphra Behn's "On Her Loving Two Equally"* 505

UNDERSTANDING THE TEXT 509

7 SPEAKER: WHOSE VOICE DO WE HEAR? 509

NARRATIVE POEMS AND THEIR SPEAKERS 509

X. J. KENNEDY, *In a Prominent Bar in Secaucus One Day* 509

SPEAKERS IN THE DRAMATIC MONOLOGUE 511

ROBERT BROWNING, *Soliloquy of the Spanish Cloister* 511

THE LYRIC AND ITS SPEAKER 514

MARGARET ATWOOD, *Death of a Young Son by Drowning* 515

AUTHORS ON THEIR CRAFT: Billy Collins and Sharon Olds 516

WILLIAM WORDSWORTH, *She Dwelt among the Untrodden Ways* 517

DOROTHY PARKER, *A Certain Lady* 518

POEMS FOR FURTHER STUDY 519

WALT WHITMAN, [*I celebrate myself, and sing myself*] 519

LANGSTON HUGHES, *Ballad of the Landlord* 519

E. E. CUMMINGS, [*next to of course god america i*] 520

GWENDOLYN BROOKS, *We Real Cool* 521

LUCILLE CLIFTON, *cream of wheat* 521

ELIZABETH BISHOP, *Exchanging Hats* 522

8 SITUATION AND SETTING: WHAT HAPPENS? WHERE? WHEN? 524

SITUATION 525

RITA DOVE, *Daystar* 525

LINDA PASTAN, *To a Daughter Leaving Home* 526

THE CARPE DIEM POEM 527

JOHN DONNE, *The Flea* 527

ANDREW MARVELL, *To His Coy Mistress* 528

SETTING 530

MATTHEW ARNOLD, *Dover Beach* 530

THE OCCASIONAL POEM 532

MARTÍN ESPADA, *Litany at the Tomb of Frederick Douglass* 532
    AUTHORS ON THEIR WORK: Martín Espada 533

ONE POEM, MULTIPLE SITUATIONS AND SETTINGS 534

LI-YOUNG LEE, *Persimmons* 534

ONE SITUATION AND SETTING, MULTIPLE POEMS 537

CHRISTOPHER MARLOWE, *The Passionate Shepherd to His
    Love* 537

SIR WALTER RALEIGH, *The Nymph's Reply
    to the Shepherd* 538

ANTHONY HECHT, *The Dover Bitch* 539

POEMS FOR FURTHER STUDY 540

NATASHA TRETHEWEY, *Pilgrimage* 540

KELLY CHERRY, *Alzheimer's* 541

JUDITH ORTIZ COFER, *The Latin Deli: An Ars Poetica* 542

ADRIENNE SU, *Escape from the Old Country* 543

9 **THEME AND TONE** 546

TONE 546

W. D. SNODGRASS, *Leaving the Motel* 547

THEME 548

MAXINE KUMIN, *Woodchucks* 549

ADRIENNE RICH, *Aunt Jennifer's Tigers* 550
    AUTHORS ON THEIR WORK: Adrienne Rich 551

THEME AND CONFLICT 552

ADRIENNE SU, *On Writing* 553
    AUTHORS ON THEIR WORK: Adrienne Su 554

POEMS FOR FURTHER STUDY 554

WILLIAM BLAKE, *London* 554

PAUL LAURENCE DUNBAR, *Sympathy*   555

W. H. AUDEN, [*Stop all the clocks, cut off the telephone*]   556

SHARON OLDS, *Last Night*   556

KAY RYAN, *Repulsive Theory*   557

SIMON J. ORTIZ, *My Father's Song*   558

ROBERT HAYDEN, *Those Winter Sundays*   559

MARTÍN ESPADA, *Of the Threads That Connect the Stars*   560

SAMPLE WRITING: STEPHEN BORDLAND, *Response Paper on W. H. Auden's "Stop all the clocks, cut off the telephone"*   562

10 LANGUAGE: WORD CHOICE AND ORDER   566

PRECISION AND AMBIGUITY   566

SARAH CLEGHORN, [*The golf links lie so near the mill*]   566

MARTHA COLLINS, *Lies*   567

DENOTATION AND CONNOTATION   567

WALTER DE LA MARE, *Slim Cunning Hands*   568

THEODORE ROETHKE, *My Papa's Waltz*   569

WORD ORDER AND PLACEMENT   570

SHARON OLDS, *Sex without Love*   572

POEMS FOR FURTHER STUDY   573

GERARD MANLEY HOPKINS, *Pied Beauty*   573

WILLIAM CARLOS WILLIAMS, *The Red Wheelbarrow*   574

This Is Just to Say   574

KAY RYAN, *Blandeur*   574

A. E. STALLINGS, *Shoulda, Woulda, Coulda*   575

11 PICTURING: VISUAL IMAGERY AND FIGURES OF SPEECH   577

RICHARD WILBUR, *The Beautiful Changes*   578

LYNN POWELL, *Kind of Blue*   579

METAPHOR   580

WILLIAM SHAKESPEARE, [*That time of year thou mayst in me behold*]   580

LINDA PASTAN, *Marks*   582

PERSONIFICATION   582

EMILY DICKINSON, [*Because I could not stop for Death—*] 583

SIMILE AND ANALOGY 583

ROBERT BURNS, *A Red, Red Rose* 584

TODD BOSS, *My Love for You Is So Embarrassingly* 585

ALLUSION 585

AMIT MAJMUDAR, *Dothead* 586

PATRICIA LOCKWOOD, *What Is the Zoo for What* 587

POEMS FOR FURTHER STUDY 589

WILLIAM SHAKESPEARE, [*Shall I compare thee to a summer's day?*] 589

ANONYMOUS, *The Twenty-Third Psalm* 589

JOHN DONNE, [*Batter my heart, three-personed God*] 590

RANDALL JARRELL, *The Death of the Ball Turret Gunner* 590

12 SYMBOL 592

THE INVENTED SYMBOL 593

JAMES DICKEY, *The Leap* 593

THE TRADITIONAL SYMBOL 595

EDMUND WALLER, *Song* 596

DOROTHY PARKER, *One Perfect Rose* 597

THE SYMBOLIC POEM 598

WILLIAM BLAKE, *The Sick Rose* 598

POEMS FOR FURTHER STUDY 599

JOHN KEATS, *Ode to a Nightingale* 599

ROBERT FROST, *The Road Not Taken* 602

HOWARD NEMEROV, *The Vacuum* 603

ADRIENNE RICH, *Diving into the Wreck* 603

ROO BORSON, *After a Death* 606

BRIAN TURNER, *Jundee Ameriki* 606

AUTHORS ON THEIR WORK: Brian Turner 607

13 THE SOUNDS OF POETRY 609

RHYME 609

ONOMATOPOEIA, ALLITERATION, ASSONANCE,
AND CONSONANCE   611

ALEXANDER POPE, from *The Rape of the Lock*   612

SOUND POEMS   613

HELEN CHASIN, *The Word* Plum   613
KENNETH FEARING, *Dirge*   614
ALEXANDER POPE, *Sound and Sense*   615

POETIC METER   618

SAMUEL TAYLOR COLERIDGE, *Metrical Feet*   620
ANONYMOUS, [*There was a young girl from St. Paul*]   623
ALFRED, LORD TENNYSON, from *The Charge of the Light
Brigade*   623
JANE TAYLOR, *The Star*   624
ANNE BRADSTREET, *To My Dear and Loving Husband*   625
JESSIE POPE, *The Call*   626
WILFRED OWEN, *Dulce et Decorum Est*   627

POEMS FOR FURTHER STUDY   628

WILLIAM SHAKESPEARE, [*Like as the waves make
towards the pebbled shore*]   628
GERARD MANLEY HOPKINS, *Spring and Fall*   628
WALT WHITMAN, *Beat! Beat! Drums!*   629
KEVIN YOUNG, *Ode to Pork*   630

14 INTERNAL STRUCTURE   633

DIVIDING POEMS INTO "PARTS"   633

PAT MORA, *Sonrisas*   633

INTERNAL VERSUS EXTERNAL OR FORMAL "PARTS"   635

GALWAY KINNELL, *Blackberry Eating*   635

LYRICS AS INTERNAL DRAMAS   636

SEAMUS HEANEY, *Punishment*   636
SAMUEL TAYLOR COLERIDGE, *Frost at Midnight*   639
SHARON OLDS, *The Victims*   641

MAKING ARGUMENTS ABOUT STRUCTURE   642

POEMS WITHOUT "PARTS"   642

WALT WHITMAN, *I Hear America Singing* 643

POEMS FOR FURTHER STUDY 644

WILLIAM SHAKESPEARE, [*Th' expense of spirit in a waste of shame*] 644

PERCY BYSSHE SHELLEY, *Ode to the West Wind* 645

PHILIP LARKIN, *Church Going* 647

AUTHORS ON THEIR WORK: Philip Larkin 649

SAMPLE WRITING: LINDSAY GIBSON, *Philip Larkin's "Church Going"* 651

15 **EXTERNAL FORM** 655

STANZAS 655

TRADITIONAL STANZA FORMS 656

RICHARD WILBUR, *Terza Rima* 657

TRADITIONAL VERSE FORMS 658

FIXED FORMS OR FORM-BASED SUBGENRES 659

TRADITIONAL FORMS: POEMS FOR FURTHER STUDY 659

DYLAN THOMAS, *Do Not Go Gentle into That Good Night* 659

NATASHA TRETHEWEY, *Myth* 660

ELIZABETH BISHOP, *Sestina* 661

CIARA SHUTTLEWORTH, *Sestina* 662

E. E. CUMMINGS, [*l(a*] 663

[*Buffalo Bill's*] 663

CONCRETE POETRY 664

GEORGE HERBERT, *Easter Wings* 664

THE SONNET: AN ALBUM 666

HENRY CONSTABLE, [*My lady's presence makes the roses red*] 668

WILLIAM SHAKESPEARE, [*My mistress' eyes are nothing like the sun*] 669

[*Not marble, nor the gilded monuments*] 669

[*Let me not to the marriage of true minds*] 670

JOHN MILTON, [*When I consider how my light is spent*] 670

WILLIAM WORDSWORTH, *Nuns Fret Not* 671

ELIZABETH BARRETT BROWNING, *How Do I Love Thee?* 672

CHRISTINA ROSSETTI, *In an Artist's Studio* 672

EDNA ST. VINCENT MILLAY, *[What lips my lips have kissed, and where, and why]* 673

    [Women have loved before as I love now] 673

    [I, being born a woman and distressed] 674

    [I will put Chaos into fourteen lines] 674

ROBERT FROST, *Range-Finding* 675

    Design 675

GWENDOLYN BROOKS, *First Fight. Then Fiddle.* 676

GWEN HARWOOD, *In the Park* 676

BILLY COLLINS, *Sonnet* 677

HARRYETTE MULLEN, *Dim Lady* 677

    SAMPLE WRITING: MELISSA MAKOLIN, *Out-Sonneting Shakespeare: An Examination of Edna St. Vincent Millay's Use of the Sonnet Form* 679

READING MORE POETRY 685

JULIA ALVAREZ, *"Poetry Makes Nothing Happen"?* 685

ANONYMOUS, *Sir Patrick Spens* 686

W. H. AUDEN, *In Memory of W. B. Yeats* 687

    Musée des Beaux Arts 689

BASHŌ, *[A village without bells—]* 690

    [This road—] 690

WILLIAM BLAKE, *The Lamb* 690

    The Tyger 691

    Chimney Sweeper 692

ROBERT BROWNING, *My Last Duchess* 692

SAMUEL TAYLOR COLERIDGE, *Kubla Khan* 694

BILLY COLLINS, *Introduction to Poetry* 695

COUNTEE CULLEN, *Yet Do I Marvel* 696

E. E. CUMMINGS, *[in Just—]* 696

EMILY DICKINSON, *[I dwell in Possibility—]* 697

    [I stepped from Plank to Plank] 698

    [My Life had stood—a Loaded Gun—] 698

[A narrow Fellow in the Grass] 699
[Tell all the truth but tell it slant—] 699
[Wild Nights—Wild Nights!] 700
JOHN DONNE, The Canonization 700
[Death, be not proud] 702
Song 702
A Valediction: Forbidding Mourning 703
PAUL LAURENCE DUNBAR, We Wear the Mask 704
T. S. ELIOT, The Love Song of J. Alfred Prufrock 705
ROBERT FROST, Home Burial 709
Stopping by Woods on a Snowy Evening 712
ANGELINA GRIMKÉ, Tenebris 713
SEAMUS HEANEY, Digging 713
GERARD MANLEY HOPKINS, God's Grandeur 714
The Windhover 715
LANGSTON HUGHES, Harlem 715
I, Too 716
BEN JONSON, On My First Son 716
JOHN KEATS, Ode on a Grecian Urn 717
To Autumn 718
ETHERIDGE KNIGHT, [Eastern guard tower] 720
[The falling snow flakes] 720
[Making jazz swing in] 720
Hard Rock Returns to Prison from the Hospital
for the Criminal Insane 720
CLAUDE MCKAY, The Harlem Dancer 721
The White House 722
PAT MORA, Elena 722
Gentle Communion 723
LINDA PASTAN, love poem 724
MARGE PIERCY, Barbie Doll 724
SYLVIA PLATH, Daddy 725
Lady Lazarus 727
EDGAR ALLAN POE, The Raven 730
EZRA POUND, In a Station of the Metro 733
The River-Merchant's Wife: A Letter 733

DUDLEY RANDALL, *Ballad of Birmingham* 734

ADRIENNE RICH, *At a Bach Concert* 735

History 736

PERCY BYSSHE SHELLEY, *Ozymandias* 737

WALLACE STEVENS, *Anecdote of the Jar* 737

The Emperor of Ice-Cream 738

ALFRED, LORD TENNYSON, *Tears, Idle Tears* 739

Ulysses 739

DEREK WALCOTT, *A Far Cry from Africa* 741

WALT WHITMAN, *Facing West from California's Shores* 742

A Noiseless Patient Spider 743

RICHARD WILBUR, *Love Calls Us to the Things of This World* 743

WILLIAM CARLOS WILLIAMS, *The Dance* 744

WILLIAM WORDSWORTH, [*The world is too much with us*] 745

[*A slumber did my spirit seal*] 745

W. B. YEATS, *All Things Can Tempt Me* 745

Easter 1916 746

The Lake Isle of Innisfree 748

Leda and the Swan 749

The Second Coming 749

BIOGRAPHICAL SKETCHES: POETS 751

Drama

DRAMA: READING, RESPONDING, WRITING 768

READING DRAMA 768

SUSAN GLASPELL, *Trifles* 771

RESPONDING TO DRAMA 784

SAMPLE WRITING: *Annotation of* Trifles 784

SAMPLE WRITING: *Reading Notes* 788

WRITING ABOUT DRAMA 792

SAMPLE WRITING: JESSICA ZEZULKA, Trifles *Plot Response Paper* 794

SAMPLE WRITING: STEPHANIE ORTEGA, *A Journey of Sisterhood* 796

UNDERSTANDING THE TEXT 800

16 ELEMENTS OF DRAMA 800
HENRIK IBSEN, *A Doll House* 812
AUGUST WILSON, *Fences* 873
AUTHORS ON THEIR WORK: August Wilson 935

READING MORE DRAMA 936

LORRAINE HANSBERRY, *A Raisin in the Sun* 936
JANE MARTIN, *Two Monologues from* Talking With . . . 1013
ARTHUR MILLER, *Death of a Salesman* 1018
AUTHORS ON THEIR WORK: Arthur Miller 1100
WILLIAM SHAKESPEARE, *Hamlet* 1101
SOPHOCLES, *Antigone* 1211

WRITING ABOUT LITERATURE 1248

17 BASIC MOVES: PARAPHRASE, SUMMARY, AND DESCRIPTION 1250

18 THE LITERATURE ESSAY 1255

19 THE WRITING PROCESS 1279

20 THE LITERATURE RESEARCH ESSAY 1295

21 QUOTATION, CITATION, AND DOCUMENTATION 1308

22 SAMPLE RESEARCH ESSAY
SARAH ROBERTS, *"Only a Girl"? Gendered Initiation in Alice Munro's "Boys and Girls"* 1340

CRITICAL APPROACHES 1352

GLOSSARY A1

Permissions Acknowledgments A16
Index of Authors A26
Index of Titles and First Lines A30
Index of Literary Terms A36

Contents Arranged by Topic

CRIME & PUNISHMENT

JAMES BALDWIN, *Sonny's Blues* 66

SUSAN GLASPELL, *Trifles* 771

SEAMUS HEANEY, *Punishment* 636

LANGSTON HUGHES, *Ballad of the Landlord* 519

ETHERIDGE KNIGHT, *[Eastern guard tower]* 720
[The falling snow flakes] 720
Hard Rock Returns to Prison from the Hospital for the Criminal Insane 720

MAXINE KUMIN, *Woodchucks* 549

HERMAN MELVILLE, *Bartleby, the Scrivener* 368

JOYCE CAROL OATES, *Where Are You Going, Where Have You Been?* 94

FLANNERY O'CONNOR, *A Good Man Is Hard to Find* 412

EDGAR ALLAN POE, *The Cask of Amontillado* 115

WILLIAM SHAKESPEARE, *Hamlet* 1101

SOPHOCLES, *Antigone* 1211

BRUCE SPRINGSTEEN, *Nebraska* 489

CROSS-CULTURAL ENCOUNTERS/JOURNEYS

ANONYMOUS, *The Elephant in the Village of the Blind* 14

MARGARET ATWOOD, *Death of a Young Son by Drowning* 515

TONI CADE BAMBARA, *The Lesson* 279

LINDA BREWER, *20/20* 17

ANTON CHEKHOV, *The Lady with the Dog* 171

JUDITH ORTIZ COFER, *The Latin Deli: An Ars Poetica* 542

STEPHEN CRANE, *The Open Boat* 254

JUNOT DÍAZ, *Wildwood* 455

ROBERT FROST, *The Road Not Taken* 602

ROBERT HAYDEN, *A Letter from Phillis Wheatley* 490

SEAMUS HEANEY, *Punishment* 636

JAMES JOYCE, *Araby* 330

JHUMPA LAHIRI, *Interpreter of Maladies* 344

LI-YOUNG LEE, *Persimmons* 534

AMIT MAJMUDAR, *Dothead* 586

GABRIEL GARCÍA MÁRQUEZ, *A Very Old Man with Enormous Wings* 362

PAT MORA, *Sonrisas* 633

FLANNERY O'CONNOR, *A Good Man Is Hard to Find* 412

ADRIENNE RICH, *Diving into the Wreck* 603

DAVID SEDARIS, *Jesus Shaves* 433

ADRIENNE SU, *Escape from the Old Country* 543

AMY TAN, *A Pair of Tickets* 186

ALFRED, LORD TENNYSON, *Ulysses* 739

NATASHA TRETHEWEY, *Pilgrimage* 540

BRIAN TURNER, *Jundee Ameriki* 606

DEREK WALCOTT, *A Far Cry from Africa* 741

PHILLIS WHEATLEY, *On Being Brought from Africa to America* 487

WALT WHITMAN, *Facing West from California's Shores* 742

DEATH/MORTALITY/MOURNING

MARGARET ATWOOD, *Death of a Young Son by Drowning* 515

W. H. AUDEN, [*Stop all the clocks, cut off the telephone*] 556

W. H. AUDEN, *In Memory of W. B. Yeats* 687

ROO BORSON, *After a Death* 606

KATE CHOPIN, *The Story of an Hour* 287

LYDIA DAVIS, *Head, Heart* 478

WALTER DE LA MARE, *Slim Cunning Hands* 568

JAMES DICKEY, *The Leap* 593

EMILY DICKINSON, [*Because I could not stop for Death—*] 583

JOHN DONNE, [*Death, be not proud*] 702

A Valediction: Forbidding Mourning 703

LOUISE ERDRICH, *Love Medicine* 289

WILLIAM FAULKNER, *A Rose for Emily* 308

KENNETH FEARING, *Dirge* 614

ROBERT FROST, *Home Burial* 709

JACOB AND WILHELM GRIMM, *The Shroud*   60

SEAMUS HEANEY, *Punishment*   636

GERARD MANLEY HOPKINS, *Spring and Fall*   628

RANDALL JARRELL, *The Death of the Ball Turret Gunner*   590

BEN JONSON, *On My First Son*   716

JOHN KEATS, *Ode on a Grecian Urn*   717

    Ode to a Nightingale   599

    To Autumn   718

MAXINE KUMIN, *Woodchucks*   549

PAT MORA, *Gentle Communion*   723

HOWARD NEMEROV, *The Vacuum*   603

WILFRED OWEN, *Dulce et Decorum Est*   627

SYLVIA PLATH, *Lady Lazarus*   727

EDGAR ALLAN POE, *The Raven*   730

DUDLEY RANDALL, *Ballad of Birmingham*   734

ADRIENNE RICH, *Aunt Jennifer's Tigers*   550

MARJANE SATRAPI, *The Shabbat*   21

WILLIAM SHAKESPEARE, *Hamlet*   1101

    [That time of year thou mayst in me behold]   580

PERCY BYSSHE SHELLEY, *Ozymandias*   737

SOPHOCLES, *Antigone*   1211

ALFRED, LORD TENNYSON, *Tears, Idle Tears*   739

DYLAN THOMAS, *Do Not Go Gentle into*

    That Good Night   659

NATASHA TRETHEWEY, *Myth*   660

    Pilgrimage   540

BRIAN TURNER, *Jundee Ameriki*   606

WILLIAM WORDSWORTH, *[A slumber did my spirit seal]*   745

    She Dwelt among the Untrodden Ways   517

W. B. YEATS, *Easter 1916*   746

GENDER

ELIZABETH BISHOP, *Exchanging Hats*   522

ROBERT BROWNING, *My Last Duchess*   692

JUNOT DÍAZ, *Wildwood*   455

JOHN DONNE, *The Flea*   527

RITA DOVE, *Daystar*   525

WILLIAM FAULKNER, *A Rose for Emily* 308

CHARLOTTE PERKINS GILMAN, *The Yellow Wallpaper* 316

SUSAN GLASPELL, *Trifles* 771

LORRAINE HANSBERRY, *A Raisin in the Sun* 936

THOMAS HARDY, *The Ruined Maid* 483

GWEN HARWOOD, *In the Park* 676

SEAMUS HEANEY, *Punishment* 636

HENRIK IBSEN, *A Doll House* 812

X. J. KENNEDY, *In a Prominent Bar in Secaucus One Day* 509

JAMAICA KINCAID, *Girl* 127

ANDREW MARVELL, *To His Coy Mistress* 528

CLAUDE MCKAY, *The Harlem Dancer* 721

EDNA ST. VINCENT MILLAY, *[I, being born a woman and distressed]* 674

PAT MORA, *Elena* 722

HARRYETTE MULLEN, *Dim Lady* 677

ALICE MUNRO, *Boys and Girls* 400

TILLIE OLSEN, *I Stand Here Ironing* 426

LINDA PASTAN, *Marks* 582

MARGE PIERCY, *Barbie Doll* 724

SYLVIA PLATH, *Daddy* 725

ADRIENNE RICH, *Aunt Jennifer's Tigers* 550

   Diving into the Wreck 603

   History 736

CHRISTINA ROSSETTI, *In an Artist's Studio* 672

WILLIAM SHAKESPEARE, *[My mistress' eyes are nothing like the sun]* 669

SOPHOCLES, *Antigone* 1211

AUGUST WILSON, *Fences* 873

HOME/FAMILY/CHILDHOOD

AESOP, *The Two Crabs* 249

JAMES BALDWIN, *Sonny's Blues* 66

TONI CADE BAMBARA, *The Lesson* 279

ELIZABETH BISHOP, *Sestina* 661

JUDITH ORTIZ COFER, *Volar* 203

SAMUEL TAYLOR COLERIDGE, *Frost at Midnight* 639

EDWIDGE DANTICAT, *A Wall of Fire Rising* 234

JUNOT DÍAZ, *Wildwood* 455

RITA DOVE, *Daystar* 525

LOUISE ERDRICH, *Love Medicine* 289

MARTÍN ESPADA, *Of the Threads That Connect
    the Stars* 560

ROBERT FROST, *Home Burial* 709

LORRAINE HANSBERRY, *A Raisin in the Sun* 936

GWEN HARWOOD, *In the Park* 676

ROBERT HAYDEN, *Those Winter Sundays* 559

SEAMUS HEANEY, *Digging* 713

BEN JONSON, *On My First Son* 716

JAMES JOYCE, *Araby* 330

JAMAICA KINCAID, *Girl* 127

LI-YOUNG LEE, *Persimmons* 534

JANE MARTIN, *Handler* [*from* Talking With . . .] 1013

ARTHUR MILLER, *Death of a Salesman* 1018

PAT MORA, *Elena* 722

    Gentle Communion 723

TONI MORRISON, *Recitatif* 138

ALICE MUNRO, *Boys and Girls* 400

SHARON OLDS, *The Victims* 641

TILLIE OLSEN, *I Stand Here Ironing* 426

SIMON J. ORTIZ, *My Father's Song* 558

LINDA PASTAN, *Marks* 582

    To a Daughter Leaving Home 526

SYLVIA PLATH, *Daddy* 725

THEODORE ROETHKE, *My Papa's Waltz* 569

SOPHOCLES, *Antigone* 1211

AMY TAN, *A Pair of Tickets* 186

EUDORA WELTY, *Why I Live at the P.O.* 444

AUGUST WILSON, *Fences* 873

ILLNESS/DISABILITY/AGING

JAMES BALDWIN, *Sonny's Blues* 66

RAYMOND CARVER, *Cathedral* 33

KELLY CHERRY, *Alzheimer's* 541

T. S. ELIOT, *The Love Song of J. Alfred Prufrock* 705

LOUISE ERDRICH, *Love Medicine* 289

WILLIAM FAULKNER, *A Rose for Emily* 308

CHARLOTTE PERKINS GILMAN, *The Yellow Wallpaper* 316

NATHANIEL HAWTHORNE, *The Birth-Mark* 219

GERARD MANLEY HOPKINS, *Spring and Fall* 628

X. J. KENNEDY, *In a Prominent Bar in Secaucus One Day* 509

JANE MARTIN, *French Fries [from* Talking With . . .] 1016

JOHN MILTON, *[When I consider how my light is spent]* 670

TONI MORRISON, *Recitatif* 138

WILFRED OWEN, *Dulce et Decorum Est* 627

WILLIAM SHAKESPEARE, *[That time of year though mayst in me behold]* 580

ALFRED, LORD TENNYSON, *Ulysses* 739

DYLAN THOMAS, *Do Not Go Gentle into That Good Night* 659

INITIATION

TONI CADE BAMBARA, *The Lesson* 279

JUNOT DÍAZ, *Wildwood* 455

JAMES JOYCE, *Araby* 330

JAMAICA KINCAID, *Girl* 127

ALICE MUNRO, *Boys and Girls* 400

JOYCE CAROL OATES, *Where Are You Going, Where Have You Been?* 94

JOHN UPDIKE, *A & P* 437

LANGUAGE

HELEN CHASIN, *The Word* Plum 613

JUDITH ORTIZ COFER, *The Latin Deli: An Ars Poetica* 542

SAMUEL TAYLOR COLERIDGE, *Metrical Feet* 620

MARTHA COLLINS, *Lies* 567

EMILY DICKINSON, *[Tell all the truth but tell it slant—]* 699

GALWAY KINNELL, *Blackberry Eating* 635

JHUMPA LAHIRI, *Interpreter of Maladies* 344

LI-YOUNG LEE, *Persimmons* 534

PATRICIA LOCKWOOD, *What Is the Zoo for What* 587

PAT MORA, *Elena*   722

HARRYETTE MULLEN, *Dim Lady*   677

LINDA PASTAN, *Marks*   582

ALEXANDER POPE, *Sound and Sense*   615

LYNN POWELL, *Kind of Blue*   579

DAVID SEDARIS, *Jesus Shaves*   433

A. E. STALLINGS, *Shoulda, Woulda, Coulda*   575

DEREK WALCOTT, *A Far Cry from Africa*   741

LITERATURE & OTHER ARTS

JULIA ALVAREZ, "*Poetry Makes Nothing Happen*"?   685

W. H. AUDEN, *In Memory of W. B. Yeats*   687

   Musée des Beaux Arts   689

JAMES BALDWIN, *Sonny's Blues*   66

WILLIAM BLAKE, *The Tyger*   691

GWENDOLYN BROOKS, *First Fight. Then Fiddle.*   676

ROBERT BROWNING, *My Last Duchess*   692

JUDITH ORTIZ COFER, *The Latin Deli: An Ars Poetica*   542

SAMUEL TAYLOR COLERIDGE, *Kubla Khan*   694

   Metrical Feet   620

BILLY COLLINS, *Introduction to Poetry*   695

   Sonnet   677

MARTHA COLLINS, *Lies*   567

EMILY DICKINSON, [*I dwell in Possibility—*]   697

SEAMUS HEANEY, *Digging*   713

FRANZ KAFKA, *A Hunger Artist*   336

JOHN KEATS, *Ode on a Grecian Urn*   717

   On First Looking into Chapman's Homer   4

GALWAY KINNELL, *Blackberry Eating*   635

ETHERIDGE KNIGHT, [*Making jazz swing in*]   720

LI-YOUNG LEE, *Persimmons*   534

CLAUDE MCKAY, *The Harlem Dancer*   721

EDNA ST. VINCENT MILLAY, [*I will put Chaos into fourteen lines*]   674

HARRYETTE MULLEN, *Dim Lady*   677

ALEXANDER POPE, *Sound and Sense*   615

ADRIENNE RICH, *Aunt Jennifer's Tigers*   550

    At a Bach Concert   735

CHRISTINA ROSSETTI, *In an Artist's Studio*   672

WILLIAM SHAKESPEARE, [*Shall I compare thee to a summer's day?*]   589

    [*My mistress' eyes are nothing like the sun*]   669

    [*Not marble, nor the gilded monuments*]   669

PERCY BYSSHE SHELLEY, *Ozymandias*   737

WALLACE STEVENS, *Anecdote of the Jar*   737

ADRIENNE SU, *On Writing*   553

JANE TAYLOR, *The Star*   624

WALT WHITMAN [*I celebrate myself, and sing myself*]   519

WALT WHITMAN, *Beat! Beat! Drums!*   629

WALT WHITMAN, *I Hear America Singing*   643

RICHARD WILBUR, *Terza Rima*   657

WILLIAM CARLOS WILLIAMS, *The Dance*   744

WILLIAM WORDSWORTH, *Nuns Fret Not*   671

W. B. YEATS, *All Things Can Tempt Me*   745

NATURE/THE NATURAL ENVIRONMENT

MARGARET ATWOOD, *Death of a Young Son by Drowning*   515

WILLIAM BLAKE, *The Lamb*   690

    London   554

    The Tyger   691

SAMUEL TAYLOR COLERIDGE, *Frost at Midnight*   639

STEPHEN CRANE, *The Open Boat*   254

E. E. CUMMINGS, [*l(a*]   663

EMILY DICKINSON, [*A narrow Fellow in the Grass*]   699

    [*The Sky is low—the Clouds are mean*]   488

PAUL LAURENCE DUNBAR, *Sympathy*   555

ROBERT FROST, *Design*   675

    Range-Finding   675

    Stopping by Woods on a Snowy Evening   712

NATHANIEL HAWTHORNE, *The Birth-Mark*   219

SEAMUS HEANEY, *Digging*   713

GERARD MANLEY HOPKINS, *God's Grandeur*   714

    Pied Beauty   573

    The Windhover   715

YASUNARI KAWABATA, *The Grasshopper and the Bell Cricket* 275

JOHN KEATS, *Ode to a Nightingale* 599

To Autumn 718

GALWAY KINNELL, *Blackberry Eating* 635

ETHERIDGE KNIGHT, *[The falling snow flakes]* 720

MAXINE KUMIN, *Woodchucks* 549

CHRISTOPHER MARLOWE, *The Passionate Shepherd to His
Love* 537

GABRIEL GARCÍA MÁRQUEZ, *Old Man with Wings* 362

ALICE MUNRO, *Boys and Girls* 400

SIMON J. ORTIZ, *My Father's Song* 558

LYNN POWELL, *Kind of Blue* 579

SIR WALTER RALEIGH, *The Nymph's Reply to the Shepherd* 538

KAY RYAN, *Blandeur* 574

Repulsive Theory 557

PERCY BYSSHE SHELLEY, *Ode to the West Wind* 645

WALLACE STEVENS, *Anecdote of the Jar* 737

WALT WHITMAN, *A Noiseless Patient Spider* 743

RICHARD WILBUR, *The Beautiful Changes* 578

WILLIAM WORDSWORTH, *[I wandered lonely as a cloud]* 485

W. B. YEATS, *The Lake Isle of Innisfree* 748

RACE/CLASS

ANONYMOUS, *Sir Patrick Spens* 686

JAMES BALDWIN, *Sonny's Blues* 66

TONI CADE BAMBARA, *The Lesson* 279

WILLIAM BLAKE, *The Chimney Sweeper* 692

SARAH CLEGHORN, *[The golf links lie so near the mill]* 566

LUCILLE CLIFTON, *cream of wheat* 521

JUDITH ORTIZ COFER, *Volar* 203

COUNTEE CULLEN, *Yet Do I Marvel* 696

EDWIDGE DANTICAT, *A Wall of Fire Rising* 234

PAUL LAURENCE DUNBAR, *Sympathy* 555

We Wear the Mask 704

MARTÍN ESPADA, *Litany at the Tomb of Frederick Douglass* 532

WILLIAM FAULKNER, *A Rose for Emily* 308

ANGELINA GRIMKÉ, *Tenebris* 713

LORRAINE HANSBERRY, *A Raisin in the Sun*   936
THOMAS HARDY, *The Ruined Maid*   483
ROBERT HAYDEN, *A Letter from Phillis Wheatley*   490
LANGSTON HUGHES, *Ballad of the Landlord*   519
   Harlem   715
   I, Too   716
X. J. KENNEDY, *In a Prominent Bar in Secaucus One Day*   509
CLAUDE MCKAY, *The White House*   722
ARTHUR MILLER, *Death of a Salesman*   1018
TONI MORRISON, *Recitatif*   138
FLANNERY O'CONNOR, *A Good Man is Hard to Find*   412
TILLIE OLSEN, *I Stand Here Ironing*   426
DUDLEY RANDALL, *Ballad of Birmingham*   734
EDWARD ARLINGTON ROBINSON, *Richard Cory*   482
DEREK WALCOTT, *A Far Cry from Africa*   741
PHILLIS WHEATLEY, *On Being Brought from Africa to
   America*   487
AUGUST WILSON, *Fences*   873

RELIGION/MYTH

ANONYMOUS, *The Twenty-Third Psalm*   589
MATTHEW ARNOLD, *Dover Beach*   530
WILLIAM BLAKE, *The Lamb*   690
   The Tyger   691
ROBERT BROWNING, *Soliloquy of the Spanish Cloister*   511
SAMUEL TAYLOR COLERIDGE, *Frost at Midnight*   639
COUNTEE CULLEN, *Yet Do I Marvel*   696
JOHN DONNE, *[Batter my heart, three-personed God]*   590
LOUISE ERDRICH, *Love Medicine*   289
GEORGE HERBERT, *Easter Wings*   664
GERARD MANLEY HOPKINS, *God's Grandeur*   714
   Pied Beauty   573
   The Windhover   715
PHILIP LARKIN, *Church Going*   647
AMIT MAJMUDAR, *Dothead*   586
GABRIEL GARCÍA MÁRQUEZ, *A Very Old Man with Enormous
   Wings*   362

JANE MARTIN, *Handler* [*from* Talking With . . .] 1013

JOHN MILTON, [*When I consider how my light is spent*] 670

SYLVIA PLATH, *Lady Lazarus* 727

ADRIENNE RICH, *Diving into the Wreck* 603

DAVID SEDARIS, *Jesus Shaves* 433

ALFRED, LORD TENNYSON, *Ulysses* 739

DAVID FOSTER WALLACE, *Good People* 156

RICHARD WILBUR, *Love Calls Us to the Things of This World* 743

WILLIAM WORDSWORTH, [*The world is too much with us*] 745

W. B. YEATS, *Leda and the Swan* 749

   The Second Coming 749

ROMANTIC LOVE & RELATIONSHIPS

W. H. AUDEN, [*Stop all the clocks, cut off the telephone*] 556

APHRA BEHN, *On Her Loving Two Equally* 493

TODD BOSS, *My Love for You Is So Embarrassingly* 585

ANNE BRADSTREET, *To My Dear and Loving Husband* 625

ELIZABETH BARRETT BROWNING, *How Do I Love Thee?* 672

ROBERT BROWNING, *My Last Duchess* 692

ROBERT BURNS, *A Red, Red Rose* 584

ANTON CHEKHOV, *The Lady with the Dog* 171

KATE CHOPIN, *The Story of an Hour* 287

BILLY COLLINS, *Divorce* 488

HENRY CONSTABLE, [*My lady's presence makes the roses red*] 668

EMILY DICKINSON, [*Wild Nights—Wild Nights!*] 700

JOHN DONNE, *The Canonization* 700

   The Flea 527

T. S. ELIOT, *The Love Song of J. Alfred Prufrock* 705

LOUISE ERDRICH, *Love Medicine* 289

SUSAN GLASPELL, *Trifles* 771

NATHANIEL HAWTHORNE, *The Birth-Mark* 219

ANTHONY HECHT, *The Dover Bitch* 539

ERNEST HEMINGWAY, *Hills Like White Elephants* 122

HENRIK IBSEN, *A Doll House* 812

JAMES JOYCE, *Araby* 330

YASUNARI KAWABATA, *The Grasshopper and the Bell Cricket* 275

CHRISTOPHER MARLOWE, *The Passionate Shepherd to His Love*   537

ANDREW MARVELL, *To His Coy Mistress*   528

EDNA ST. VINCENT MILLAY, [*I, being born a woman and distressed*]   674

[*What lips my lips have kissed, and where, and why*]   673

[*Women have loved before as I love now*]   673

HOWARD NEMEROV, *The Vacuum*   603

SHARON OLDS, *Last Night*   556

Sex without Love   572

The Victims   641

DOROTHY PARKER, *A Certain Lady*   518

One Perfect Rose   597

LINDA PASTAN, *love poem*   724

EZRA POUND, *The River-Merchant's Wife: A Letter*   733

SIR WALTER RALEIGH, *The Nymph's Reply to the Shepherd*   538

ADRIENNE RICH, *Aunt Jennifer's Tigers*   550

CHRISTINA ROSSETTI, *In an Artist's Studio*   672

WILLIAM SHAKESPEARE, [*Let me not to the marriage of true minds*]   670

[*My mistress' eyes are nothing like the sun*]   669

[*Shall I compare thee to a summer's day?*]   589

CIARA SHUTTLEWORTH, *Sestina*   662

W. D. SNODGRASS, *Leaving the Motel*   547

A. E. STALLINGS, *Shoulda, Woulda, Coulda*   575

DAVID FOSTER WALLACE, *Good People*   156

EDMUND WALLER, *Song*   596

AUGUST WILSON, *Fences*   873

WAR/HISTORY

WILLIAM BLAKE, *London*   554

E. E. CUMMINGS, [*next to of course god america i*]   520

EDWIDGE DANTICAT, *A Wall of Fire Rising*   234

MARTÍN ESPADA, *Litany at the Tomb of Frederick Douglass*   532

ROBERT FROST, *Range-Finding*   675

SEAMUS HEANEY, *Punishment*   636

RANDALL JARRELL, *The Death of the Ball Turret Gunner*   590

WILFRED OWEN, *Dulce et Decorum Est*   627

JESSE POPE, *The Call*   626

ADRIENNE RICH, *History*   736

MARJANE SATRAPI, *The Shabbat*   21

AMY TAN, *A Pair of Tickets*   186

NATASHA TRETHEWEY, *Pilgrimage*   540

BRIAN TURNER, *Jundee Ameriki*   606

DEREK WALCOTT, *A Far Cry from Africa*   741

WALT WHITMAN, *Beat! Beat! Drums!*   629

RICHARD WILBUR, *Terza Rima*   657

W. B. YEATS, *Easter 1916*   746

   The Second Coming   749

Preface for Instructors

Like its predecessors, this Portable Twelfth Edition of *The Norton Introduction to Literature* offers in a single volume a complete course in reading literature and writing about it. A teaching anthology focused on the actual tasks, challenges, and questions typically faced by students and instructors, *The Norton Introduction to Literature* offers practical advice to help students transform their first impressions of literary works into fruitful discussions and meaningful critical essays, and it helps students and instructors together tackle the complex questions at the heart of literary study.

The Norton Introduction to Literature has been revised with an eye to providing a book that is as flexible and as useful as possible—adaptable to many different teaching styles and individual preferences—and that also conveys the excitement at the heart of literature itself.

FEATURES OF *THE NORTON INTRODUCTION TO LITERATURE*

Although this Portable Twelfth Edition contains much that is new or refashioned, the essential features of the text have remained consistent over many editions:

Diverse selections with broad appeal

Because readings are the central component of any literature class, my most important task has been to select a rich array of appealing and challenging literary works. Among the 37 stories, 204 poems, and 7 plays in *The Norton Introduction to Literature*, readers will find selections by well-established and emerging voices alike, representing a broad range of times, places, cultural perspectives, and styles. The readings are excitingly diverse in terms of subject and style as well as authorship and national origin. In selecting and presenting literary texts, my top priorities continue to be quality as well as pedagogical relevance and usefulness. I have integrated the new with the old and the experimental with the canonical, believing that contrast and variety help students recognize and respond to the unique features of any literary work. In this way, I aim to help students and instructors alike approach the unfamiliar by way of the familiar (and vice versa).

Helpful and unobtrusive editorial matter

As always, the instructional material before and after each selection avoids dictating any particular interpretation or response, instead highlighting essential terms and concepts in order to make the literature that follows more accessible to student readers. Questions and writing suggestions help readers apply general concepts to specific readings in order to develop, articulate, refine, and defend their own responses. As in all Norton anthologies, I have annotated the works with a light hand, seeking to be informative but not interpretive.

An introduction to the study of literature

To introduce students to fiction, poetry, and drama is to open up a complex field of study with a long history. The Introduction addresses many of the questions that students may have about the nature of literature as well as the practice of literary criticism. By exploring some of the most compelling reasons for reading and writing about literature, much of the mystery about matters of method is cleared away, and I provide motivated students with a sense of the issues and opportunities that lie ahead as they study literature. As in earlier editions, I continue to encourage student fascination with particular authors and their careers, expanding upon the featured "Authors on Their Work."

Thoughtful guidance for writing about literature

The Portable Twelfth Edition integrates opportunities for student writing at each step of the course, highlighting the mastery of skills for students at every level. "Reading, Responding, Writing" sections at the beginning of each genre unit, including a thoroughly revised opener to the poetry unit, offer students concrete advice about how to transform careful reading into productive and insightful writing. Sample questions for each work or about each element (e.g., "Questions about Character") provide exercises for answering these questions or for applying new concepts to particular works, and examples of student writing demonstrate how a student's notes on a story or poem may be developed into a response paper or an organized critical argument. New essays bring the total number of examples of student writing to thirteen.

The constructive, step-by-step approach to the writing process is thoroughly demonstrated in several chapters called "Writing about Literature." As in the chapters introducing concepts and literary selections, the first steps presented in the writing section are simple and straightforward, outlining the basic formal elements common to essays—thesis, structure, and so on. Following these steps encourages students to approach the essay both as a distinctive genre with its own elements and as an accessible form of writing with a clear purpose. From here, I walk students through the writing process: how to choose a topic, gather evidence, and develop an argument; the methods of writing a research essay; and the mechanics of effective quotation and responsible citation and documentation in accordance with the dramatically revamped eighth edition of the *MLA Handbook* (2016). New, up-to-date material on using the Internet for research has been included. Also featured is a sample research paper that has been annotated to call attention to important features of good student writing.

Even more resources for student writers are available at the free student website, LitWeb, described below.

A sensible and teachable organization

The accessible format of *The Norton Introduction to Literature*, which has worked so well for teachers and students for many editions, remains the same. Each genre is approached in three logical steps. Fiction, for example, is introduced by "Fiction: Reading, Responding, Writing," which treats the purpose and nature of fiction, the reading experience, and the steps one takes to begin writing about fiction. This feature is followed by the six-chapter section called "Understanding the Text," which concentrates on the genre's key elements. "Reading More Fiction," the final component in the Fiction section, is a reservoir of additional readings for independent study or a different approach. The Poetry and Drama sections, in turn, follow exactly the same organizational format as Fiction.

The book's arrangement allows movement from narrower to broader frameworks, from simpler to more complex questions and issues, and mirrors the way people read—wanting to learn more as they experience more. At the same time, no chapter or section depends on any other, so that individual teachers can pick and choose which chapters or sections to assign and in what order. A new, alternate table of contents organizes literary selections by topic, facilitating comparison across, as well as within genres.

NEW TO THE PORTABLE TWELFTH EDITION

Twenty-seven new selections and a new topical table of contents

There are four new stories, twenty-two new poems, and one new play in this Twelfth Edition of *The Norton Introduction to Literature*. You will find new selections from popular and canonical writers such as August Wilson,

Toni Cade Bambara, Philip Larkin, Lucille Clifton, Langston Hughes, and William Blake, as well as works by exciting new authors such as Junot Díaz, Kevin Young, Patricia Lockwood, Todd Boss, and Adrienne Su. A new, alternate table of contents organizes literary selections by topic, facilitating comparison across, as well as within, genres.

Significantly improved writing pedagogy and up-to-date guidance on citation and documentation

Recent editions of *The Norton Introduction to Literature* greatly expanded and improved the resources for student writers, including thorough introductions to each genre in "Reading, Responding, Writing," broadened online materials, and new student essays. The chapters on Writing about Literature have been completely revised to demonstrate more by example; to focus on the essential moves involved in writing and interpretation, as well as the most frequently assigned types of writing; and to guide students carefully through the new approach to citation and documentation introduced in the latest eighth edition of the *MLA Handbook* (2016). Throughout the volume, writing prompts and suggestions have also been revised, while new samples of student writing bring the total to thirteen.

STUDENT RESOURCES

LitWeb (digital.wwnorton.com/litweb)

Improved and expanded, this free resource offers tools that help students read and write about literature with skill and understanding:

- New Pause & Practice exercises expand on the "Writing about Literature" chapters and offer additional opportunities to practice effective writing. Seven exercises, each tied to a specific writing skill, test students on what they know, provide instruction both text and video for different learning styles, assess students on what they've learned, and give them an opportunity to apply newly strengthened skills.
- In-depth workshops feature fifty-five often-taught works from the text, all rooted in the guidance given in the "Reading, Responding, Writing" chapters. These workshops have been updated an expanded for the Twelfth Edition and include rich embedded media to show students how literature connects with the world around them.
- Self-grading multiple-choice quizzes on sixty of the most widely taught works offer instant feedback designed to hone students' close-reading skills.

INSTRUCTOR RESOURCES

Instructor's Manual

This thorough guide offers in-depth discussions of nearly all the works in the anthology as well as teaching suggestions and tips for the writing-intensive literature course.

Coursepacks for learning management systems

Available for all major learning management systems (including Blackboard, Angel, Moodle), this free and customizable resource makes the features of LitWeb and plus the Writing about Literature video series and other material available to instructors within the online framework of their choice.

Teaching Poetry: A Handbook of Exercises for Large and Small Classes (Allan J. Gedalof, University of Western Ontario)

This practical handbook offers a wide variety of innovative in-class exercises to enliven classroom discussion of poetry. Each of these flexible teaching exercises includes straightforward step-by-step guidelines and suggestions for variation.

Play DVDs

DVDs of most of the plays in the anthology are available to qualified adopters. Semester-long Netflix subscriptions are also available.

To obtain any of these instructional resources, please contact your local Norton representative.

ACKNOWLEDGMENTS

In working on this book, I have been guided by teachers and students in my own and other English departments who have used this textbook and responded with comments and suggestions. Thanks to such capable help, I am hopeful that this book will continue to offer a solid and stimulating introduction to the experience of literature.

This project continually reminds me why I follow the vocation of teaching literature, which after all is a communal rather than a solitary calling. Since its inception, *The Norton Introduction to Literature* has been very much a collaborative effort. I am grateful for the opportunity to carry on the work begun by the late Carl Bain and Jerome Beaty, whose student I will always be. And I am equally indebted to my wonderful colleagues Paul Hunter and Alison Booth. Their wisdom and intelligence have had a profound effect on me, and their stamp will endure on this and all future editions of this book. I am thankful to Alison especially for the erudition, savvy, grace, and humor she brought to our partnership.

Thanks also to Jason Snart, of the College of Dupage, for his work preparing the online resources for students. As more and more instructors have integrated online materials into their teaching, users of this book have benefited from his experienced insight into teaching writing and literature, as well as his thoughtful development of exercises, quizzes, videos and more. I would also like to thank Carly Fraser Doria, emedia editor for the Twelfth Edition, as well as Kimberly Bowers, marketing manager for both the Eleventh and Twelfth Editions.

In putting together the Twelfth Edition, I have accrued many debts to friends and colleagues and to users of the Eleventh Edition who reached out to point out its mistakes, as well as successes. I am grateful for their generosity and insight, as I also am that of my wise and patient editors, Spencer Richardson-Jones, Sarah Touborg, and Ariella Foss. But I am also peculiarly aware this edition of more enduring and personal debts as well, which I hope it's not entirely out of place to honor here—to my mother, Lola Mays, who died in the very midst of this book's making, and to both my sister, Nelda Mays, and my husband and in-house editor, Hugh Jackson, without whom I'm not sure I would have made it through that loss, this book, or anything else. To them, much love, much thanks.

The Norton Introduction to Literature continues to thrive because so many teachers and students generously take the time to provide valuable feedback and suggestions. Thank you to all who have done so. This book is equally your making.

At the beginning of planning for the Twelfth Edition, my editors at Norton solicited the guidance of hundreds of instructors via in-depth reviews and a Web-hosted survey. The response was impressive, bordering on overwhelming; it was also immensely helpful. Thank you to those provided extensive written commentary: Julianne Altenbernd (Cypress College), Troy Appling (Florida Gateway College), Christina Bisirri (Seminole State College), Jill Channing (Mitchell Community College), Thomas Chester (Ivy Tech), Marcelle Cohen (Valencia College), Patricia Glanville (State College of Florida), Julie Gibson (Greenville Tech), Christina Grant (St. Charles Community College), Lauren Hahn (City Colleges of Chicago), Zachary Hyde (Valencia College), Brenda Jernigan (Methodist University), Mary Anne Keefer (Lord Fairfax Community College), Shari Koopman (Valencia College), Jessica Rabin (Anne Arundel Community

College), Angela Rasmussen (Spokane Community College), Britnee Shandor (Lanier Technical College), Heidi Sheridan (Ocean County College), Jeff Tix (Wharton Jr. College), Bente Videbaek (Stony Brook University), Patrice Willaims (Northwest Florida State College), and Connie Youngblood (Blinn College).

Thanks also to everyone who responded to the survey online:

Sue Abbotson (Rhode Island College), Emory Abbott (Georgia Perimeter College), Mary Adams (Lincoln College-Normal), Julie Altenbernd (Cypress College), Troy Appling (Florida Gateway College), Marilyn Judith Atlas (Ohio University), Unoma Azuah (Lane College), Diann Baecker (Virginia State University), Aaron Barrell (Everett Community College), Craig Barrette (Brescia University), John Bell (American River College), Monica Berlin (Knox College), Mary Anne Bernal (San Antonio College), Jolan Bishop (Southeastern Community College), Randall Blankenship (Valencia College), Margaret Boas (Anne Arundel Community College), Andrew Bodenrader (Manhattanville College), James Borton (Coastal Carolina University), Ethel Bowden (Central Maine Community College), Amy Braziller (Red Rocks Community College), Jason Brown (Herkimer County Community College), Alissa Burger (SUNY Delhi), Michael Burns (Spokane Community College), Ryan Campbell (Front Range Community College), Anna Cancelli (Coastal Carolina Community College), Vanessa Canete-Jurado (Binghamton University), Rebecca Cash (SUNY Adirondack), Kevin Cavanaugh (Dutchess Community College), Emily Chamison (Georgia College & State University), Jill Channing (Mitchell Community College), Thomas Chester (Ivy Tech), Ann Clark (Jefferson Community College), Thomas Coakley (Mount Aloysius College), Susan Cole (Albert Magnus College), Tera Joy Cole (Idaho State University), Vicki Collins (University of South Carolina Aiken), Jonathan Cook (Durham Technical Community College), Beth Copeland (Methodist University), Bill Corby (Berkshire Community College), James Crowley (Bridgewater State University), Diane D'Amico (Allegheny College), Susan Dauer (Valencia College), Emily Dial-Driver (Rogers State University), Lorraine DiCicco (University of Western Ontario), Christina Devlin (Montgomery College), Jess Domanico (Point University), William Donovan (Idaho State University), Bonnie Dowd (Montclair State University), Douglas Dowland (Ohio Northern University), Justine Dymond (Springfield College), Jason Evans (Prairie State College), Richard Farias (San Antonio College), Karen Feldman (Seminole State College), V. Ferretti (Westmoreland County Community College), Bradley Fest (University of Pittsburgh), Glynn-Ellen Fisichelli (Nassau Community College), Colleen Flanagan (Seminole State College of Florida), Michael Flynn (University of North Dakota), Matthew Fullerty (Chowan University), Robert

Galin (University of New Mexico at Gallup), Margaret Gardineer (Felician College), Jan Geyer (Hudson Valley Community College), Seamus Gibbons (Bergen Community College), Eva Gold (Southeastern Louisiana University), Melissa Green (Ohio University Chillicothe), Frank Gruber (Bergen Community College), Lauren Hahn (City Colleges of Chicago), Rob Hale (Western Kentucky University), Nada Halloway (Manhattanville College), Melody Hargraves (St. Johns River State College), Elizabeth Harlan (Northern Virginia Community College), Stephanie Harzewski (University of New Hampshire), Lance Hawvermale (Ranger College), Catherine Heath (Victoria College), Beth Heim de Bera (Rochester Community and Technical College), Natalie Hewitt (Hope International University), Melissa Hoban (Blinn College), Charles Hood (Antelope Valley College), Trish Hopkins (Community College of Vermont), Spring Hyde (Lincoln College), Tammy Jabin (Chemeketa Community College), Kim Jacobs-Beck (University of Cincinnati Clermont College), Brenda Jerrigan (Methodist University), Kathy Johnson (SUNY Cobleskill), Darlene Johnston (Ohio Northern University), Kimberly Kaczorowski (University of Utah), Maryellen Keefe (SUNY Maritime College), Mary Anne Keefer (Lord Fairfax Community College), Caroline Kelley (Bergen Community College), Tim Kelley (Northwest-Shoals Community College), Mary Catherine Killany (Robert Morris University), Amy Kolker (Black Hawk College), Beth Kolp (Dutchess Community College), Shari Koopman (Valencia College), Jill Kronstadt (Montgomery College), Liz Langemak (La Salle University), Audrey Lapointe (Cuyamaca College), Dawn Lattin (Idaho State University), Richard Lee (Elon University), Nancy Lee-Jones (Endicott College), Sharon Levy (Northampton Community College), Erika Lin (George Mason University), Clare Little (Embry-Riddle Aeronautical University), Paulette Longmore (Essex County College), Carol Luther (Pellissippi State Community College), Sean McAuley (North Georgia Technical College), Sheila McAvey (Becker College), Kelli McBride (Seminole State College), Jim McWilliams (Dickinson State University), Vickie Melograno (Atlantic Cape Community College), Agnetta Mendoza (Nashville State Community College), David Merchant (Louisiana Tech University), Edith Miller (Angelina College), Benjamin Mitchell (Georgia College & State University), James Norman (Bridgewater State University), Angelia Northrip-Rivera (Missouri State University), James Obertino (University of Central Missouri), Elaine Ostry (SUNY Plattsburg), Michelle Paulsen (Victoria College), Russell Perkin (Saint Mary's University), Katherine Perry (Georgia Perimeter College), Thomas Pfister (Idaho State University), Gemmicka Piper (University of Iowa), Michael Podolny (Onondaga Community College), Wanda Pothier-Hill (Mt.

Wachusett Community College), Gregg Pratt (SUNY Adirondack, Wilton Campus), Jonathan Purkiss (Pulaski Technical College), Jessica Rabin (Anne Arundel Community College), Elizabeth Rambo (Campbell University), Angela Rasmussen (Spokane Community College), Rhonda Ray (East Stroudsburg University), Janet Red Feather (Normandale Community College), Joan Reeves (Northeast Alabama Community College), Matthias Regan (North Central College), Elizabeth Rescher (Richard Bland College), Stephanie Roberts (Georgia Military College), Paul Robichaud (Albert Magnus College), Nancy Roche (University of Utah), Mary Rohrer-Dann (Pennsylvania State University), Michael Rottnick (Ellsworth Community College), Scott Rudd (Monroe Community College), Ernest Rufleth (Louisiana Tech University), Frank Rusciano (Rider University), Michael Sarabia (University of Iowa), Susan Scheckel (Stony Brook University), Lori Schroeder (Knox College), Britnee Shandor (Lanier Technical College), Jolie Sheffer (Bowling Green State University), Olympia Sibley, (Blinn College), Christine Sizemore (Spelman College), Chris Small (New Hampshire Technical Institute), Katherine Smit (Housatonic Community College), Whitney Smith (Miami University), Jason Snart (College of Dupage), John Snider (Montana State University- Northern), Shannon Stewart (Costal Carolina University), Susan St. Peters (Riverside City College), Michael Stubbs (Idaho State University), Patrice Suggs (Craven Community College), Joseph Sullivan (Marietta College), Heidi L. Sura (Kirtland Community College), David Susman (York County Community College), Fred Svoboda (University of Michigan), Taryne Taylor (University of Iowa), Nancy Thompson (Community College of Vermont), Rita Treutel (University of Alabama at Birmingham), Keja Valens (Salem State University), Diana Vecchio (Widener University), Bente Videbaek (Stony Brook University), Donna Waldron (Campbell University), Kent Walker (Brock University), Brandi Wallace (Wallace Community College), Valerie Wallace (City Colleges of Chicago), Maureen Walters (Vance-Granville Community College), Megan Walsh (St. Bonaventure University), Kimberly Ward (Campbell University), Catherine Welter (University of New Hampshire), Jeff Westover (Boise State University), Kathy Whitaker (East Georgia State College), Bruce Wigutow (Farmingdale State College), Jessica Wilkie (Monroe Community College), Leigh Williams (Dutchess Community College), Jenny Williams (Spartanburg Community College), Patrice Williams (Northwest Florida State College), Gregory Wilson (St. John's University), Mark WIlson (Southwestern Oregon Community College), Rita Wisdom (Tarrant County College), Martha Witt (William Paterson University), Robert Wiznura (Grant MacEwan University), Jarrell Wright (University of Pittsburgh), Kelly Yacobucci

(SUNY Cobleskill), Kidane Yohannes (Burlington County College), Brian Yost (Texas A&M University), Connie Youngblood (Blinn College), Susan Youngs (Southern New Hampshire University), and Jason Ziebart (Central Carolina Community College).

THE NORTON INTRODUCTION TO

LITERATURE

PORTABLE TWELFTH EDITION

Introduction

In the opening chapters of Charles Dickens's novel *Hard Times* (1854), the aptly named Thomas Gradgrind warns the teachers and pupils at his "model" school to avoid using their imaginations. "Teach these boys and girls nothing but Facts. Facts alone are wanted in life," exclaims Mr. Gradgrind. To press his point, Mr. Gradgrind asks "girl number twenty," Sissy Jupe, the daughter of a circus performer, to define a horse. When she cannot, Gradgrind turns to Bitzer, a pale, spiritless boy who "looked as though, if he were cut, he would bleed white." A "model" student of this "model" school, Bitzer gives exactly the kind of definition to satisfy Mr. Gradgrind:

> Quadruped. Graminivorous. Forty teeth, namely, twenty-four grinders, four eyeteeth, and twelve incisive. Sheds coat in spring; in marshy countries, sheds hoofs.

Anyone who has any sense of what a horse is rebels against Bitzer's lifeless picture of that animal and against the "Gradgrind" view of reality. As these first scenes of *Hard Times* lead us to expect, in the course of the novel the fact-grinding Mr. Gradgrind learns that human beings cannot live on facts alone; that it is dangerous to stunt the faculties of imagination and feeling; that, in the words of one of the novel's more lovable characters, "People must be amused." Through the downfall of an exaggerated enemy of the imagination, Dickens reminds us why we like and even *need* to read literature.

WHAT IS LITERATURE?

But what is literature? Before you opened this book, you probably could guess that it would contain the sorts of stories, poems, and plays you have encountered in English classes or in the literature section of a library or bookstore. But why are some written works called *literature* whereas others are not? And who gets to decide? *The American Heritage Dictionary of the English Language* offers a number of definitions for the word *literature*, one of which is "imaginative or creative writing, especially of recognized artistic value." In this book, we adopt a version of that definition by focusing on fictional stories, poems, and plays—the three major kinds (or **genres**) of "imaginative or creative writing" that form the heart of literature as it has been taught in schools and universities for over a century. Many of the works we have chosen to include are already ones "of recognized artistic value" and thus belong to what scholars call the **canon**, a select, if much-debated and ever-evolving, list of the most highly and widely esteemed works. Though quite a few of the literary texts we include are simply too new to have earned that status, they, too, have already drawn praise, and some have even generated controversy.

Certainly it helps to bear in mind what others have thought of a literary work. Yet one of this book's primary goals is to get you to think for yourself, as well as communicate with others, about what "imaginative writing" and "artistic value" are or might be and thus about what counts as literature. What makes a story or poem different from an essay, a newspaper editorial, or a technical manual? For that matter, what makes a published, canonical story like Herman Melville's BARTLEBY, THE SCRIVENER both like and unlike the sorts of stories we tell each other every day? What about so-called *oral literature*, such as the fables and folktales that circulated by word of mouth for hundreds of years before they were ever written down? Or published works such as comic strips and graphic novels that rely little, if at all, on the written

word? Or Harlequin romances, television shows, and the stories you collaborate in making when you play a video game? Likewise, how is Shakespeare's poem MY MISTRESS' EYES ARE NOTHING LIKE THE SUN both like and unlike a verse you might find in a Hallmark card or even a jingle in a mouthwash commercial?

Today, literature departments offer courses in many of these forms of expression, expanding the realm of literature far beyond the limits of the dictionary definition. An essay, a song lyric, a screenplay, a supermarket romance, a novel by Toni Morrison or William Faulkner, and a poem by Walt Whitman or Emily Dickinson—each may be read and interpreted in *literary ways* that yield insight and pleasure. What makes the literary way of reading different from pragmatic reading is, as scholar Louise Rosenblatt explains, that it does not focus "on what will remain [. . .] *after* the reading—the information to be acquired, the logical solution to a problem, the actions to be carried out," but rather on "what happens *during* [. . .] reading." The difference between pragmatic and literary reading, in other words, resembles the difference between a journey that is only about reaching a destination and one that is just as much about fully experiencing the ride.

In the pages of this book, you will find cartoons, an excerpt from a graphic novel, song lyrics, folktales, and stories and plays that have spawned movies. Through this inclusiveness, we do not intend to suggest that there are no distinctions among these various forms of expression or between a good story, poem, or play and a bad one; rather, we want to get you thinking, talking, and writing both about what the key differences and similarities among these forms are and what makes one work a better example of its genre than another. Sharpening your skills at these peculiarly intensive and responsive sorts of reading and interpretation is a primary purpose of this book and of most literature courses.

Another goal of inclusiveness is simply to remind you that literature doesn't just belong in a textbook or a classroom, even if textbooks and classrooms are essential means for expanding your knowledge of the literary terrain and of the concepts and techniques essential to thoroughly enjoying and understanding a broad range of literary forms. You may or may not be the kind of person who always takes a novel when you go to the beach or secretly writes a poem about your experience when you get back home. You may or may not have taken a literature course (or courses) before. Yet you already have a good deal of literary experience and even expertise, as well as much more to discover about literature. A major aim of this book is to make you more conscious of how and to what end you might use the tools you already possess and to add many new ones to your tool belt.

WHAT DOES LITERATURE DO?

One quality that may well differentiate stories, poems, and plays from other kinds of writing is that they help us move beyond and probe beneath abstractions by giving us concrete, vivid particulars. Rather than talking *about* things, they bring them to life for us by *representing* experience, and so they *become* an experience for us—one that engages our emotions, our imagination, and all of our senses, as well as our intellects. As the British poet and critic Matthew Arnold put it more than a century ago, "The interpretations of science do not give us this intimate sense of objects as the interpretations of poetry give it; they appeal to a limited faculty, and not to the whole man. It is not Linnaeus [. . .] who gives us the true sense of animals, or water, or plants, who seizes their secret for us, who makes us participate in their life; it is Shakespeare [. . .] Wordsworth [. . .] Keats."

To test Arnold's theory, compare the *American Heritage Dictionary's* rather dry definition of *literature* with the following poem, in which John Keats describes his first encounter with a specific literary work—George Chapman's translation of the *Iliad* and the *Odyssey*, two **epics** by the ancient Greek poet Homer.

JOHN KEATS
On First Looking into Chapman's Homer[1]

Much have I traveled in the realms of gold,
And many goodly states and kingdoms seen;
Round many western islands have I been
Which bards in fealty to Apollo[2] hold.
5 Oft of one wide expanse had I been told
That deep-browed Homer ruled as his demesne;
Yet did I never breathe its pure serene[3]
Till I heard Chapman speak out loud and bold:
Then felt I like some watcher of the skies
10 When a new planet swims into his ken;[4]
Or like stout Cortez[5] when with eagle eyes
He stared at the Pacific—and all his men
Looked at each other with a wild surmise—
Silent, upon a peak in Darien.

1816

1. George Chapman's were among the most famous Renaissance translations of Homer; he completed his *Iliad* in 1611, his *Odyssey* in 1616. Keats wrote the sonnet after being led to Chapman by a former teacher and reading the *Iliad* all night long.
2. Greek god of poetry and music. *Fealty:* literally, the loyalty owed by a vassal to his feudal lord.
3. Atmosphere.
4. Range of vision; awareness.
5. Actually, Balboa; he first viewed the Pacific from Darien, in Panama.

Keats makes us *see* literature as a "wide expanse" by greatly developing this **metaphor** and complementing it with **similes** likening reading to the sighting of a "new planet" and the first glimpse of an undiscovered ocean. More important, he shows us what literature means and why it matters by allowing us to share with him the subjective experience of reading and the complex sensations it inspires—the dizzying exhilaration of discovery; the sense of power, accomplishment, and pride that comes of achieving something difficult; the wonder we feel in those rare moments when a much-anticipated experience turns out to be even greater than we had imagined it would be.

It isn't the definitions of words alone that bring this experience to life for us as we read Keats's poem, but also their sensual qualities—the way the words look, sound, and even feel in our mouths because of the particular way they are put together on the page. The sensation of excitement—of a racing heart and mind—is reproduced *in* us as we read the poem. For example, notice how the lines in the middle run into each other, but then Keats forces us to slow down at the poem's end—stopped short by that dash and comma in the poem's final lines, just as Cortez and his men are when they reach the edge of the known world and peer into what lies beyond.

WHAT ARE THE GENRES OF LITERATURE?

The conversation that is literature, as well as the conversation about literature, invites all comers, requiring neither a visa nor a special license of any kind. Yet literary studies, like all disciplines, has developed its own terminology and its own systems of classification. Helping you understand and effectively use both is a major focus of this book; especially important terms appear in bold throughout and are defined in a glossary at the back.

Some essential literary terms are common, everyday words used in a special way in the conversation about literature. A case in point, perhaps, is the term *literary criticism*, as well as the closely related term *literary critic*. Despite the usual connotations of the word *criticism*, literary criticism is called *criticism* not because it is negative or corrective but rather because those who write criticism ask searching, analytical, "critical" questions about the works they read. Literary criticism is both the process of interpreting and commenting on literature and the result of that process. If you write an essay on the play *Hamlet*, the poetry of John Keats, or the development of the short story in the 1990s, you engage in literary criticism, and by writing the essay, you've become a literary critic.

Similarly, when we classify works of literature, we use terms that may be familiar to you but have specific meanings in a literary context. All academic disciplines have systems of classification, or taxonomies, as well as jargon. Biologists, for example, classify all organisms into a series of ever-smaller, more specific categories: *kingdom, phylum* or *division, class, order, family, genus,* and *species.* Classification and comparison are just as essential in the study of literature. We expect a poem to work in a certain way, for example, when we know from the outset that it *is* a poem and not, say, a factual news report or a short story. And—whether consciously or not—we compare it, as we read, to other poems we've read in the past. If we know, further, that the poem was first published in eighteenth-century Japan, we expect it to work differently from one that appeared in the latest *New Yorker*. Indeed, we often choose what to read, just as we choose what movie to see, based on the "class" or "order" of book or movie we like or what we are in the mood for that day—horror or comedy, action or science fiction.

As these examples suggest, we generally tend to categorize literary works in two ways: (1) on the basis of contextual factors, especially historical and cultural context—that is, when, by whom, and where it was produced (as in *nineteenth-century literature, the literature of the Harlem Renaissance, American literature,* or *African American literature*)—and (2) on the basis of formal textual features. For the latter type of classification, the one we focus on in this book, the key term is *genre*, which simply means, as the *Oxford English Dictionary* tells us, "A particular style or category of works of art; esp. a type of literary work characterized by a particular form, style, or purpose."

Applied rigorously, *genre* refers to the largest categories around which this book is organized—**fiction**, **poetry**, and **drama** (as well as **nonfiction** prose). The word *subgenre* applies to smaller divisions within a genre, and the word *kind* to divisions within a subgenre. *Subgenres* of fiction include the **novel**, the **novella**, and the **short story**. *Kinds* of novels, in turn, include things like the **bildungsroman** or the epistolary novel. Similarly, important subgenres of nonfiction include the essay, as well as **biography** and autobiography; a memoir is a particular kind of autobiography, and so on.

However, the terms of literary criticism are not so fixed or so consistently, rigorously used as biologists' are. You will often see the word *genre* applied both much more narrowly—referring to the novel, for example, or even to a kind of novel such as the epistolary novel or the historical novel.

The way we classify a work depends on which aspects of its form or style we concentrate on, and categories may overlap. When we divide fiction, for example, into the subgenres novel, novella, and short story, we take the length of the works as the salient aspect. (Novels are much longer than short stories.) But other fictional subgenres—detective fiction, **gothic fiction**, **historical fiction**, science fiction, and even **romance**—are based on the types of **plots**, **characters**, **settings**, and so on that are customarily featured in these works. These latter categories may include works from all the other, length-based categories. There are, after all, gothic novels (think Stephenie Meyer), as well as gothic short stories (think Edgar Allan Poe).

A few genres even cut across the boundaries dividing poetry, fiction, drama, and nonfiction. A prime example is **satire**—any literary work (whether poem, play, fiction, or nonfiction) "in which prevailing vices and follies are held up to ridicule" (*Oxford English Dictionary*). Examples of satire include poems such as Alexander Pope's *Dunciad* (1728); plays, movies, and television shows, from Molière's *Tartuffe* (1664) to Stanley Kubrick's *Dr. Strangelove* (1964) to *South Park* and *The Daily Show*; works of fiction like Jonathan Swift's *Gulliver's Travels* (1726) and Voltaire's *Candide* (1759); and works of nonfiction such as Swift's "A Modest Proposal" (1729) and Ambrose Bierce's *The Devil's Dictionary* (1906). Three other major genres that cross the borders between fiction, poetry, drama, and nonfiction are **parody**, **pastoral**, and romance.

Individual works can thus belong simultaneously to multiple generic categories or observe some **conventions** of a genre without being an example of that genre in any simple or straightforward way. The Old English poem *Beowulf* is an **epic** and, because it's written in verse, a poem. Yet because (like all epics) it narrates a story, it is also a work of fiction in the more general sense of that term.

Given this complexity, the system of literary genres can be puzzling, especially to the uninitiated. Used well, however, classification schemes are among the most essential and effective tools we use to understand and enjoy just about everything, including literature.

WHY READ LITERATURE?

Because there has never been and never will be absolute, lasting agreement about where exactly the boundaries between one literary genre and another should be drawn or even about what counts as literature at all, it might be more useful from the outset to focus on *why* we look at particular forms of expression.

Over the ages, people have sometimes dismissed *all* literature or at least certain genres as a luxury, a frivolous pastime, even a sinful indulgence. Plato famously banned poetry from his ideal republic on the grounds that it tells beautiful lies that "feed and water our passions" rather than our reason. Thousands of years later, the influential eighteenth-century philosopher Jeremy Bentham decried the "magic art" of literature as doing a good deal of "mischief" by "stimulating our passions" and "exciting our prejudices." One of Bentham's contemporaries—a minister—blamed the rise of immorality, irreligion, and even prostitution on the increasing popularity of that particular brand of literature called the novel.

Today, many Americans express their sense of literature's insignificance by simply not reading it: The 2004 government report *Reading at Risk* indicates that less than half of U.S. adults read imaginative literature, with the sharpest declines occurring among the youngest age groups. Even if they very much enjoy reading on their own, many contemporary U.S. college students nonetheless hesitate to study or major in literature for fear that their degree won't provide them with marketable credentials, knowledge, or skills.

Yet the enormous success of *The Hunger Games* trilogy and the proliferation of reading groups are only two of many signs that millions of people continue to find both reading literature and discussing it with others to be enjoyable, meaningful, even essential activities. English thrives as a major at most colleges and universities, almost all of which require undergraduates majoring in other areas to take at least one course in literature. (Perhaps that's why you are reading this book!) Schools of medicine, law, and business are today *more* likely to require their students to take literature courses than they were in past decades, and they continue to welcome literature majors as applicants, as do many corporations. So why do so many people read and study literature, and why do schools encourage and even require students to do so? Even if we know what literature is, what does it *do* for us? What is its value?

There are, of course, as many answers to such questions as there are readers. For centuries, a standard answer has been simply that imaginative literature provides a unique brand of "instruction and delight." John Keats's ON FIRST LOOKING INTO CHAPMAN'S HOMER illustrates some of the many forms such delight can take. Some kinds of imaginative writing offer us the delight of immediate escape, but imaginative writing that is more difficult to read and understand than a Harry Potter or Twilight novel offers escape of a different and potentially more instructive sort, liberating us from the confines of our own time, place, and social milieu, as well as our habitual ways of thinking, feeling, and looking at the world. In this way, a story, poem, or play can satisfy our desire for broader experience—including the sorts of experience we might be unable or unwilling to endure in real life. We can learn what it might be like to grow up on a Canadian fox farm or to clean ashtrays in the Singapore airport. We can travel back into the past, experiencing war from the perspective of a soldier watching his comrade die or of prisoners suffering in a Nazi labor camp. We can journey into the future or into universes governed by entirely different rules than our own. Perhaps we yearn for such knowledge because we can best come to understand our own identities and outlooks by leaping over the boundaries that separate us from other selves and worlds.

Keats's friend and fellow poet Percy Bysshe Shelley argued that literature increases a person's ability to make such leaps, to "imagine intensely and comprehensively" and "put himself in the place of another and of many othe[r]" people in order "to be greatly good." Shelley meant "good" in a moral sense, reasoning that the ability both to accurately imagine and to truly *feel* the human consequences of our actions is the key to ethical behavior. But universities and professional schools today also define this "good" in distinctly pragmatic ways. In virtually any career you choose, you will need to interact positively and productively with both coworkers and clients, and in today's increasingly globalized world, you will need to learn to deal effectively and empathetically with people vastly different from yourself. At the very least, literature written by people from various backgrounds and depicting various places, times, experiences, and feelings will give you some understanding of how others' lives and worldviews may differ from your own—or how they may be very much the same.

Similarly, our rapidly changing world and economy require intellectual flexibility, adaptability, and ingenuity, making ever more essential the human knowledge, general skills, and habits of mind developed through the study of literature. Literature explores issues and questions relevant in any walk of life. Yet rather than offering us neat or comforting solutions and answers, literature enables us to experience difficult situations and human conundrums in all their complexity and to look at them from various points of view. In so doing, it invites us sometimes to question conventional thinking and sometimes to see its wisdom, even as it helps us imagine altogether new possibilities.

Finally, literature awakens us to the richness and complexity of language—our primary tool for engaging with, understanding, and shaping the world around us. As we read more and more, seeing how different writers use language to help us feel their joy, pain, love, rage, or laughter, we begin to recognize the vast range of possibilities for self-expression. Writing and discussion in turn give us invaluable practice in discovering, expressing, and defending our own nuanced, often contradictory thoughts about both literature and life. The study of literature enhances our command of language and our sensitivity to its effects and meanings in every form or medium, providing interpretation and communication skills especially crucial in our information age. By learning to appreciate and articulate what the language of a story, poem, a play, or an essay does to us and by considering how it affects others, we also learn much about what we can do with language.

What We Do With Literature: Three Tips

1. *Take a literary work on its own terms.* Adjust to the work; don't make the work adjust to you. Be prepared to hear things you do not want to hear. Not all works are about your ideas, nor will they always present emotions you want to feel. But be tolerant and listen to the work first; later you can explore the ways you do or don't agree with it.

2. *Assume there is a reason for everything.* Writers do make mistakes, but when a work shows some degree of verbal control it is usually safest to assume that the writer chose each word carefully; if the choice seems peculiar, you may be missing something. Try to account for everything in a work, see what kind of sense you can make of it, and figure out a coherent pattern that explains the text as it stands.

3. *Remember that literary texts exist in time, and times change.* Not only the meanings of words, but whole ways of looking at the universe vary in different ages. Consciousness of time works two ways: Your knowledge of history provides a context for reading the work, and the work may modify your notion of a particular age.

WHY STUDY LITERATURE?

You may already feel the power and pleasure to be gained from a sustained encounter with challenging reading. Then why not simply enjoy it in solitude, on your own free time? Why take a course in literature? Literary study, like all disciplines, has developed its own terminology and its own techniques. Some knowledge and understanding of both can greatly enhance our personal appreciation of literature and our conversations with others about it. Literature also has a context and a history, and learning something about them can make all the difference in the amount and kind of pleasure and insight you derive from literature. By reading and discussing different genres of literature, as well as works from varied times and places, you may well come to appreciate and even love works that you might never have discovered or chosen to read on your own or that you might have disliked or misunderstood if you did.

Most important, writing about works of literature and discussing them with your teachers and other students will give you practice in analyzing literature in greater depth and in considering alternative views of both the works themselves and the situations and problems the works explore. A clear understanding of the aims and designs of a story, poem, or play never falls like a bolt from the blue. Instead, it emerges from a process that involves trying to put into words *how* and *why* this work had such an effect on you and, just as important, responding to what others say or write about it. Literature itself is a vast, ongoing, ever-evolving conversation in which we most fully participate when we enter into actual conversation with others.

As you engage in this conversation, you will notice that interpretation is always variable, always open to discussion. A great diversity of interpretations might suggest that the discussion is pointless. On the contrary, that's when the discussion gets most interesting. Because there is no single, straight, paved road to an understanding of a literary text, you can explore a variety of blazed trails and less-traveled paths. In sharing your own interpretations, tested against your peers' responses and guided by your instructor's or other critics' expertise, you will hone your skills at both interpretation and communication. After the intricate and interactive process of interpretation, you will find that the work has changed when you read it again. What we do with literature alters what it does to us.

FICTION

James Baldwin

FICTION
Reading, Responding, Writing

Stories are a part of daily life in every culture. Stories are what we tell when we return from vacation or survive an accident or illness. They help us make sense of growing up or growing old, of a hurricane or a war, of the country and world we live in. In conversations, a story may be invited by the listener ("What did you do last night?") or initiated by the teller ("Guess what I saw when I was driving home!"). We assume such stories are true, or at least that they are meant to describe an experience honestly. Of course, many of the stories we encounter daily, from jokes to online games to television sitcoms to novels and films, are intended to be **fiction**—that is, stories or narratives about imaginary persons and events. Every story, however, whether a news story, sworn testimony, idle gossip, or a fairy tale, is always a version of events told from a particular perspective (or several), and it may be incomplete, biased, or just plain made up. As we listen to others' stories, we keep alert to the details, which make the stories rich and entertaining. But we also need to spend considerable time and energy making sure that we accurately interpret what we hear: We ask ourselves who is telling the story, why the story is being told, and whether we have all the information we need to understand it fully.

Even newspaper articles, which are supposed to tell true stories—the facts of what actually happened—may be open to such interpretation. Take as an example the following article, which appeared in the *New York Times* on January 1, 1920:

ACCUSED WIFE KILLS HER ALLEGED LOVER

Cumberland (Md.) Woman Becomes Desperate When Her Husband Orders Her from Home.

Special to The New York Times.

CUMBERLAND, Md., Dec. 31.—Accused by her husband of unfaithfulness, Mrs. Kate Uhl, aged 25, this morning stabbed to death Bryan Pownall, who she alleged was the cause of the estrangement with her husband, Mervin Uhl.

Mrs. Uhl, who is the mother of three children, denies her husband's charge of misconduct with Pownall, asserting that the latter forced his attentions on her by main physical strength against her will.

The stabbing this morning came as a dramatic sequel to the woman's dilemma after she had been ordered to leave her home. Mrs. Uhl summoned Pownall after her husband had gone to work this morning, and according to her story begged him to tell her husband that she, Mrs. Uhl, was not to blame. This Pownall refused to do, but again tried to make love to her, Mrs. Uhl said. When Pownall sought to kiss her Mrs. Uhl seized a thin-bladed butcher knife and stabbed the man to the heart, she admitted.

The report's appearance in a reliable newspaper; its identification of date, location, and other information; and the legalistic adjectives "accused" and "alleged" suggest that it strives to be accurate and objective. But given the distance between us and the events described here, it's also easy to imagine this chain of events being recounted in a play, murder mystery, Hollywood film, or televised trial. In other words, this news story is still fundamentally a *story*. Note that certain points of view are better represented than others and certain details are highlighted, as might be the case in a novel or short story. The news item is based almost entirely on what Kate Uhl asserts, and even the subtitle, "Woman Becomes Desperate," plays up the "dramatic sequel to the woman's dilemma." We don't know what Mervin Uhl said when he allegedly accused his wife and turned her out of the house, and Bryan Pownall, the murdered man, never had a chance to defend himself. Presumably, the article reports accurately the husband's accusation of adultery and the wife's accusation of rape, but we have no way of knowing whose accusations are true.

Our everyday interpretation of the stories we hear from various sources—including other people, television, newspapers, and advertisements—has much in common with the interpretation of short stories such as those in this anthology. In fact, you'll probably discover that the processes of reading, responding to, and writing about stories are already somewhat familiar to you. Most readers already know, for instance, that they should pay close attention to seemingly trivial details; they should ask questions and find out more about any matters of fact that seem mysterious, odd, or unclear. Most readers are well aware that words can have several meanings and that there are alternative ways to tell a story. How would someone else have told the story? What are the storyteller's perspective and motives? What is the context of the tale—for instance, when is it supposed to have taken place and what was the occasion of telling it? These and other questions from our experience of everyday storytelling are equally relevant in reading fiction. Similarly, we can usually tell in reading a story or hearing it whether it is supposed to make us laugh, shock us, or provoke some other response.

TELLING STORIES: INTERPRETATION

Everyone has a unique story to tell. In fact, many stories are about this difference or divergence among people's interpretations of reality. A number of the stories in this anthology explore issues of storytelling and interpretation.

Consider a well-known tale, THE ELEPHANT IN THE VILLAGE OF THE BLIND, a Buddhist story over two thousand years old. Like other stories that have been transmitted orally, this one exists in many versions. Here's one way of telling it:

The Elephant in the Village of the Blind

Once there was a village high in the mountains in which everyone was born blind. One day a traveler arrived from far away with many fine things to sell and many tales to tell. The villagers asked, "How did you travel so far and so high carrying so much?" The traveler said, "On my elephant." "What is an elephant?" the villagers asked, having never even heard of such an animal in their remote mountain village. "See for yourself," the traveler replied.

The elders of the village were a little afraid of the strange-smelling creature that took up so much space in the middle of the village square. They could hear it breathing and munching on hay, and feel its slow, swaying movements disturbing the air around them. First one elder reached out and felt its flapping ear. "An elephant is soft but tough, and flexible, like a leather fan." Another grasped its back leg. "An elephant is a rough, hairy pillar." An old woman took hold of a tusk and gasped, "An elephant is a cool, smooth staff." A young girl seized the tail and declared, "An elephant is a fringed rope." A boy took hold of the trunk and announced, "An elephant is a water pipe." Soon others were stroking its sides, which were furrowed like a dry plowed field, and others determined that its head was an overturned washing tub attached to the water pipe.

At first each villager argued with the others on the definition of the elephant, as the traveler watched in silence. Two elders were about to come to blows about a fan that could not possibly be a pillar. Meanwhile the elephant patiently enjoyed the investigations as the cries of curiosity and angry debate mixed in the afternoon sun. Soon someone suggested that a list could be made of all the parts: the elephant had four pillars, one tub, two fans, a water pipe, and two staffs, and was covered in tough, hairy leather or dried mud. Four young mothers, sitting on a bench and comparing impressions, realized that the elephant was in fact an enormous, gentle ox with a stretched nose. The traveler agreed, adding only that it was also a powerful draft horse and that if they bought some of his wares for a good price he would be sure to come that way again in the new year.

. . .

The different versions of such a tale, like the different descriptions of the elephant, alter its meaning. Changing any aspect of the story will inevitably change how it works and what it means to the listener or reader. For example, most versions of this story feature not an entire village of blind people (as this version does), but a small group of blind men who claim to be wiser than their sighted neighbors. These blind men quarrel endlessly because none of them can see; none can put together all the evidence of all their senses or all the elephant's various parts to create a whole. Such traditional versions of the story criticize people who are too proud of what they think they know; these versions imply that sighted people would know better what an elephant is. However, other versions of the tale, like the one above, are set in an imaginary "country" of the blind. This setting changes the emphasis of the story from the errors of a few blind wise men to the value and the insufficiency of *any* one person's perspective. For though it's clear that the various members of the community in this version will never agree entirely on one interpretation of (or story about) the elephant, they do not let themselves get bogged down in endless dispute. Instead they compare and combine their various stories and "readings" in order to form a more satisfying, holistic understanding of the wonder in their midst. Similarly, listening to others' different interpretations of stories, based on their different perspectives, can enhance your experience of a work of literature and your skill in responding to new works.

Just as stories vary depending on who is telling them, so their meaning varies depending on who is responding to them. In the elephant story, the villagers pay attention to what the tail or the ear feels like, and then they draw on comparisons to what they already know. But ultimately, the individual interpretations of the elephant depend on what previous experiences each villager brings to bear (of pillars, water pipes, oxen, and dried mud, for example), and also on where (quite literally) he or she stands in relation to the elephant. In the same way, readers participate in re-creating a story as they interpret it. When you read a story for the first time, your response will be informed by other stories you have heard and read as well as your expectations for this kind of story. To grapple with what is new in any story, start by observing one part at a time and gradually trying to understand how those parts work together to form a whole. As you make sense of each new piece of the picture, you adjust your expectations about what is yet to come. When you have read and grasped it as fully as possible, you may share your interpretation with other readers, discussing different ways of seeing the story. Finally, you might express your reflective understanding in writing—in a sense, telling *your* story about the work.

Questions about the Elements of Fiction

- Expectations: What do you expect?
  - from the title? from the first sentence or paragraph?
  - after the first events or interactions of characters?
  - as the **conflict** is resolved?

(continued on next page)

(continued)

- What happens in the story? (See ch. 1.)
  - Do the characters or the situation change from the beginning to the end?
  - Can you summarize the **plot**? Is it a recognizable kind or **genre** of story?
- How is the story narrated? (See ch. 2.)
  - Is the **narrator** identified as a character?
  - Is it narrated in the past or present tense?
  - Is it narrated in the first, second, or third person?
  - Do you know what every character is thinking, or only some characters, or none?
- Who are the **characters**? (See ch. 3.)
  - Who is the **protagonist**(s) (hero, heroine)?
  - Who is the **antagonist**(s) (villain, opponent, obstacle)?
  - Who are the other characters? What is their role in the story?
  - Do your expectations change with those of the characters, or do you know more or less than each of the characters?
- What is the **setting** of the story? (See ch. 4.)
  - When does the story take place?
  - Where does it take place?
  - Does the story move from one setting to another? Does it move in one direction only or back and forth in time and place?
- What do you notice about how the story is written?
  - What is the **style** of the prose? Are the sentences and the vocabulary simple or complex?
  - Are there any **images, figures of speech**, or **symbols**? (See ch. 5.)
  - What is the **tone** or mood? Does the reader feel sad, amused, worried, curious?
- What does the story mean? Can you express its **theme** or themes? (See ch. 6.)
  - Answers to these big questions may be found in many instances in your answers to the previous questions. The story's meaning or theme depends on all its features.

READING AND RESPONDING TO FICTION

When imaginary events are acted out onstage or onscreen, our experience of those events is that of being a witness to them. In contrast, prose fiction, whether oral or written, is relayed to us by someone. Reading it is more like hearing what happened after the fact than witnessing it before our very eyes. The teller, or **narrator**, of fiction addresses a listener or reader, often referred to as the audience. How much or how little we know about the characters and what they say or do depends on what a narrator tells us.

You should read a story attentively, just as you would listen attentively to someone telling a story out loud. This means limiting distractions and interruptions; you should take a break from social networking and obtrusive music. Literary prose, as well as poetry, works with the sounds as well as meanings of words, just as film works with music and sound as well as images. Be prepared to mark up the text and to make notes.

While reading and writing, you should always have a good college-level dictionary on hand so that you can look up any unfamiliar terms. In the era of the Internet it's especially easy to learn more about any word or concept, and doing so can help enrich your reading and writing. Another excellent resource is the *Oxford English Dictionary*, available in the reference section of most academic libraries or on their websites, which reveals the wide range of meanings words have had over time. Words in English always have a long story to tell because over the centuries so many languages have contributed to our current vocabulary. It's not uncommon for meanings to overlap or even reverse themselves.

The following short short story is a contemporary work. As in "The Elephant in the Village of the Blind," this narrator gives us a minimal amount of information, merely observing the characters' different perceptions and interpretations of things they see during a cross-country car trip. As you read the story, pay attention to your expectations, drawing on your personal experience as well as such clues as the title; the characters' opinions, behavior, and speech; specifics of setting (time and place); and any repetitions or changes. When and how does the story begin to challenge and change your initial expectations? You can use the questions above to guide your reading of any story and help you focus on some of its important features.

LINDA BREWER
20/20

B y the time they reached Indiana, Bill realized that Ruthie, his driving companion, was incapable of theoretical debate. She drove okay, she went halves on gas, etc., but she refused to argue. She didn't seem to know how. Bill was used to East Coast women who disputed everything he said, every step of the way. Ruthie stuck to simple observation, like "Look, cows." He chalked it up to the fact that she was from rural Ohio and thrilled to death to be anywhere else.

She didn't mind driving into the setting sun. The third evening out, Bill rested his eyes while she cruised along making the occasional announcement.

"Indian paintbrush. A golden eagle."

Miles later he frowned. There was no Indian paintbrush, that he knew of, near Chicago.

5   The next evening, driving, Ruthie said, "I never thought I'd see a Bigfoot in real life." Bill turned and looked at the side of the road streaming innocently out behind them. Two red spots winked back—reflectors nailed to a tree stump.

"Ruthie, I'll drive," he said. She stopped the car and they changed places in the light of the evening star.

"I'm so glad I got to come with you," Ruthie said. Her eyes were big, blue, and capable of seeing wonderful sights. A white buffalo near Fargo. A UFO above Twin Falls. A handsome genius in the person of Bill himself. This last vision came to her in Spokane and Bill decided to let it ride.

1996

* * *

SAMPLE WRITING: ANNOTATION AND NOTES ON "20/20"

Now re-read the story, along with the brief notes one reader made in the margins, based on the questions in the box on pages 15 and 16. The reader then expanded these annotations into longer, more detailed notes. These notes could be organized and expanded into a response paper on the story. Some of your insights might even form the basis for a longer essay on one of the elements of the story.

20/20

Like "20/20 hindsight" or perfect vision? Also like the way Bill and Ruthie go 50/50 on the trip, and see things in two different ways.

Bill's doubts about Ruthie. Is he reliable? Does she "refuse" or not "know how" to argue? What's her view of him?

Bill's keeping score; maybe Ruthie's nicer, or has better eyesight. She notices things.

By the time they reached Indiana, Bill realized that Ruthie, his driving companion, was incapable of theoretical debate. She drove okay, she went halves on gas, etc., but she refused to argue. She didn't seem to know how. Bill was used to East Coast women who disputed everything he said, every step of the way. Ruthie stuck to simple observation, like "Look, cows." He chalked it up to the fact that she was from rural Ohio and thrilled to death to be anywhere else.

She didn't mind driving into the setting sun. The third evening out, Bill rested his eyes while she cruised along making the occasional announcement.

"Indian paintbrush. A golden eagle."

Miles later he frowned. There was no Indian paintbrush, that he knew of, near Chicago.

The next evening, driving, Ruthie said, "I never thought I'd see a Bigfoot in real life." Bill turned and looked at the side of the road streaming innocently out behind them. Two red spots winked back—reflectors nailed to a tree stump.

"Ruthie, I'll drive," he said. She stopped the car and they changed places in the light of the evening star.

"I'm so glad I got to come with you," Ruthie said. Her eyes were big, blue, and capable of seeing wonderful sights. A white buffalo near Fargo. A UFO above Twin Falls. A handsome genius in the person of Bill himself. This last vision came to her in Spokane and Bill decided to let it ride.

Margin notes:

Repetition, like a folk tale: 2nd sunset drive, 3rd time she speaks. Not much dialogue in story.

Bill's only speech. Turning point: Bill sees something he doesn't already know.

Repetition, like a joke, in 3 things Ruthie sees.

Story begins and ends in the middle of things: "By the time," "let it ride."

Initial Impressions

Plot: begins in the middle of action, on a journey. *Narration*: past tense, third person. *Setting*: Indiana is a middling, unromantic place.

Paragraph 1

Narration and Character: Bill's judgments of Ruthie show that he prides himself on arguing about abstract ideas; that he thinks Ruthie must be stupid; that they didn't know each other well and aren't suited for a long trip together. Bill is from the unfriendly East Coast; Ruthie, from easygoing, dull "rural Ohio." *Style*: The casual language—"okay" and "etc."—sounds like Bill's voice, but he's not the narrator. The vague "etc." hints that Bill isn't really curious about her. The observation of cows sounds funny, childlike, even stupid. But why does he have to "chalk it up" or keep score?

Paragraph 2

Plot and Character: This is the first specific time given in the story, the "third evening": Ruthie surprises the reader and Bill with more than dull "observation."

(continued on next page)

(continued)

Paragraph 4

Style, Character, Setting, and Tone: Dozing in the speeding car, Bill is too late to check out what she says. He frowns (he doesn't argue) because the plant and the bird can't be seen in the Midwest. Brewer uses a series of place names to indicate the route of the car. There's humor in Ruthie's habit of pointing out bizarre sights.

Paragraph 5

Character and Setting: Bigfoot is a legendary monster living in Western forests. Is Ruthie's imagination getting the better of Bill's logic? "Innocently" personifies the road, and the reflectors on the stump wink like the monster; Bill is finally looking (though in hindsight). The scenery seems to be playing a joke on him.

Paragraph 6

Plot and Character: Here the characters change places. He wants to drive (is she hallucinating?), but it's as if she has won. The narration (which has been relying on Bill's voice and perspective) for the first time notices a romantic detail of scenery that Ruthie doesn't point out (the evening star).

Paragraph 7

Character and Theme: Bill begins to see Ruthie and what she is capable of. What they see *is* the journey these characters take toward falling in love, in the West where things become unreal. *Style:* The long "o" sounds and images in "A white buffalo near Fargo. A UFO above Twin Falls" (along with the words Ohio, Chicago, and Spokane) give a feeling for the wildness (notice the Indian place names). The outcome of the story is that they *go far* to Fargo, see double and fall in love at Twin Falls—see and imagine wonderful things in each other. They end up with perfectly matched vision.

READING AND RESPONDING TO GRAPHIC FICTION

You may approach any kind of narrative with the same kinds of questions that have been applied to 20/20. Try it on the following chapter of Marjane Satrapi's *Persepolis*. This best-selling graphic novel, or graphic memoir, originally written in French and now a successful film, relates Satrapi's own experience as a girl in Iran through her artwork and words. *Persepolis* begins with a portrait of ten-year-old Satrapi, wearing a black veil, in 1980. The Islamic leaders of Iran had recently imposed religious law, including mandatory head coverings for schoolgirls. On September 22, 1980, Iraq invaded Iran, beginning a conflict that lasted until 1988, greatly affecting Satrapi's childhood in Tehran (once known as Persepolis). The Iran-Iraq War was a precursor of the Persian Gulf War of 1990–91 and the Iraq War, or Second Gulf War, that began in 2003.

This excerpt resembles an illustrated short story, though it is closely based on actual events. How do the images contribute to expectations, narration (here, telling and showing), characterization, plot, setting, style, and themes? Read (and view) with these questions in mind and a pencil in hand. Annotating or taking notes will guide you to a more reflective response.

MARJANE SATRAPI
(b. 1969)

The Shabbat

As the granddaughter of Nasreddine Shah, the last Quadjar emperor of Iran, Iranian-born Marjane Satrapi is a princess by birth and a self-declared pacifist by inclination. Only ten years old at the time of the 1979 Islamist revolution, she was reportedly expelled at age fourteen from her French-language school after hitting a principal who demanded she stop wearing jewelry. Fearing for her safety, Satrapi's secularist parents sent her to Vienna, Austria, where she would remain until age eighteen, when she returned to Iran to attend college. After a brief marriage ended in divorce, Satrapi moved to France in 1994, where her graphic memoir, *Persepolis*, was published to great acclaim in 2000. Subsequently translated into numerous languages, it appeared in the United States as *Persepolis: The Story of a Childhood* (2003) and *Persepolis 2: The Story of a Return* (2004). A 2007 animated movie version was nominated for an Academy Award in 2008. Satrapi's other works are *Embroideries* (2005), which explores Iranian women's views of sex and love through a conversation among Satrapi's female relatives; *Chicken with Plums* (2006), which tells the story of both the 1953 CIA-backed Iranian coup d'état and the last days of Satrapi's great-uncle, a musician who committed suicide; and several children's books.

THE SHABBAT

TO KEEP US FROM FORGETTING THAT WE WERE AT WAR, IRAQ OPTED FOR A NEW STRATEGY...

I HEARD THEY'RE GOING TO USE BALLISTIC MISSILES AGAINST US.

WHAT ARE YOU SAYING? WE'RE NOT AT WAR WITH THE SOVIET UNION. I DON'T BELIEVE THE IRAQIS HAVE WEAPONS LIKE THAT.

FROM THE IRAQI BORDER TO TEHRAN IT'S THOUSANDS OF MILES. MISSILES THAT CAN GO THAT FAR COST A FORTUNE!

WELL, THAT'S WHAT THE RUMORS SAY!

WE IRANIANS ARE OLYMPIC CHAMPIONS WHEN IT COMES TO GOSSIP.

SHE'S RIGHT. WE LOVE TO EXAGGERATE.

YOU SEEM TO HAVE THE OPPOSITE SYMPTOM.

WHY DO YOU SAY THAT?

EVEN WHEN YOU SEE SOMETHING WITH YOUR OWN EYES, YOU NEED CONFIRMATION FROM THE BBC.

MY NATURAL OPTIMISM JUST LEADS ME TO BE SKEPTICAL.

Shabbat: Sabbath (Hebrew).

MOM'S PESSIMISM SOON WON OUT OVER DAD'S OPTIMISM. IT TURNED OUT THAT THE IRAQIS DID HAVE MISSILES. THEY WERE CALLED "SCUDS" AND TEHRAN BECAME THEIR TARGET.

WHEN THE SIRENS WENT ON, IT MEANT WE HAD THREE MINUTES TO KNOW IF THE END HAD COME.

WE'RE NOT GOING TO THE BASEMENT?

IT WOULDN'T MAKE ANY DIFFERENCE!!

CONSIDERING THE DAMAGE THEY DO, WHETHER WE'RE IN THE BASEMENT OR ON THE ROOF, IT'S THE SAME THING.

THE THREE MINUTES SEEMED LIKE THREE DAYS. FOR THE FIRST TIME, I REALIZED JUST HOW MUCH DANGER WE WERE IN.

BOOM!!

I DON'T WANT TO DIE!

YOU WON'T DEAR. I PROMISE YOU!

NOW THAT TEHRAN WAS UNDER ATTACK, MANY FLED. THE CITY WAS DESERTED. AS FOR US, WE STAYED. NOT JUST OUT OF FATALISM. IF THERE WAS TO BE A FUTURE, IN MY PARENTS' EYES, THAT FUTURE WAS LINKED TO MY FRENCH EDUCATION. AND TEHRAN WAS THE ONLY PLACE I COULD GET IT.

SOME PEOPLE, MORE CIRCUMSPECT, TOOK SHELTER IN THE BASEMENTS OF BIG HOTELS, WELL-KNOWN FOR THEIR SAFETY. APPARENTLY, THEIR REINFORCED CONCRETE STRUCTURES WERE BOMBPROOF.

ONE EXAMPLE WAS OUR NEIGHBORS, THE BABA-LEVYS. THEY WERE AMONG THE FEW JEWISH FAMILIES THAT HAD STAYED AFTER THE REVOLUTION. MR. BABA-LEVY SAID THEIR ANCESTORS HAD COME THREE THOUSAND YEARS AGO, AND IRAN WAS THEIR HOME.

...THEIR DAUGHTER NEDA WAS A QUIET GIRL WHO DIDN'T PLAY MUCH, BUT WE WOULD TALK ABOUT ROMANCE FROM TIME TO TIME.

...ONE DAY A BLOND PRINCE WITH BLUE EYES WILL COME AND TAKE ME TO HIS CASTLE...

OH YEAH! ME TOO!

SO LIFE WENT ON...

The Shah: the shah, or king, of Iran was deposed in 1979, the beginning of what was soon known as the Islamic Revolution under the leadership of Ayatollah Ruholla Khomeini (1900–89). An ayatollah is a high-ranking cleric in the Shia branch of Islam to which most Iranians adhere.

FASTER! PLEASE HURRY...

A CROWD HAD GATHERED IN FRONT OF MY STREET! THE BOMB HAD HIT MY STREET!

MA'AM, WHICH BUILDING WAS HIT?

APPARENTLY, IT EXPLODED AT THE END OF THE STREET.

MY BUILDING AND THE BABA-LEVY'S WERE AT THE END OF THE STREET.

LET ME THROUGH.

ONE CHANCE IN TWO THAT IT WAS OUR BUILDING.

PLEASE, LET ME THROUGH.

YOU CAN'T GO BEYOND THIS POINT!

...I LIVE HERE...

AND HE LET ME THROUGH.

I DIDN'T WANT TO LOOK UP. I LOOKED AT MY TREMBLING LEGS. I COULDN'T GO FORWARD, LIKE IN A NIGHTMARE.

LET THEM BE ALIVE. LET THEM BE ALIVE. LET THEM...

MARJI

MARJI!

MOM!

YOU'RE ALL RIGHT? DAD'S ALL RIGHT? GRANDMA'S ALL RIGHT?

EVERYONE'S OK. I WAS THE ONLY ONE HOME.

OH, MOM.

...

WHERE DID IT HIT?

THE BABA-LEVY'S HOUSE.

AT LEAST THEY WEREN'T HOME!

...

MOM, THEY WEREN'T, RIGHT?

WELL, I DON'T KNOW. IT'S SATURDAY, YOU KNOW.

I KNOW IT'S SATURDAY. SO?

SATURDAY IS THE JEWISH SABBATH. WHEREVER THEY ARE, JEWS ARE SUPPOSED TO GO HOME.

...YOU THINK THAT...?

IT'S TRUE THAT THEY WEREN'T VERY OBSERVANT. I THINK YOU'RE RIGHT. THEY MUST HAVE STAYED AT THE HILTON.

YOU KNOW THE TAPE I PUT ON THE WINDOWS? IT WORKED PERFECTLY. ALL THE WINDOWS ARE BROKEN, BUT THERE'S NOT A PIECE OF BROKEN GLASS IN THE HOUSE!

I COULD TELL THAT MY MOTHER WAS TRYING TO CHANGE THE SUBJECT.

WHEN WE WALKED PAST THE BABA-LEVY'S HOUSE, WHICH WAS COMPLETELY DESTROYED, I COULD FEEL THAT SHE WAS DISCREETLY PULLING ME AWAY. SOMETHING TOLD ME THAT THE BABA-LEVYS HAD BEEN AT HOME. SOMETHING CAUGHT MY ATTENTION.

I SAW A TURQUOISE BRACELET. IT WAS NEDA'S. HER AUNT HAD GIVEN IT TO HER FOR HER FOURTEENTH BIRTHDAY...

THE BRACELET WAS STILL ATTACHED TO... I DON'T KNOW WHAT...

NO SCREAM IN THE WORLD COULD HAVE RELIEVED MY SUFFERING AND MY ANGER.

2000

KEY CONCEPTS

As you read, respond to, and write about fiction, some key terms and concepts may be useful in comparing or distinguishing different kinds of stories. Stories may be oral rather than written down, and they may be of different lengths. They may be based on true stories or completely invented. They may be written in verse rather than prose, or they may be created in media other than the printed page.

STORY AND NARRATIVE

Generally speaking, a *story* is a short account of an incident or series of incidents, whether actual or invented. The word is often used to refer to an entertaining tale of imaginary people and events, but it is also used in phrases like "the *story* of my life"—suggesting a true account. The term **narrative** is especially useful as a general concept for the substance rather than the form of what is told about persons and their actions. A story or a tale is usually short, whereas a narrative may be of any length from a sentence to a series of novels and beyond.

Narratives in Daily Life

Narrative plays an important role in our lives beyond the telling of fictional stories. Consider the following:

- Today, sociologists and historians may collect *personal narratives* to present an account of society and everyday life in a certain time or place.
- Since the 1990s, the practice of *narrative medicine* has spread as an improved technique of diagnosis and treatment that takes into account the patient's point of view.
- There is a movement to encourage *mediation* rather than litigation in divorce cases. A mediator may collaborate with the couple in arriving at a shared perspective on the divorce; in a sense, they try to agree on the story of their marriage and how it ended.
- Some countries have attempted to recover from the trauma of genocidal ethnic conflict through *official hearings of testimony* by victims as well as defendants. South Africa's Truth and Reconciliation Commission is an example of this use of stories.

ORAL NARRATIVE AND TALES

We tend to think of stories in their written form, but many of the stories that we now regard as among the world's greatest, such as Homer's *Iliad* and the

Old English epic *Beowulf*, were sung or recited by generations of storytellers before being written down. Just as rumors change shape as they circulate, oral stories tend to be more fluid than printed stories. Traditionally oral **tales** such as fairy tales or folktales may endure for a very long time yet take different forms in various countries and eras. And it's often difficult or impossible to trace such a story back to a single "author" or creator. In a sense, then, an oral story is the creation of a whole community or communities, just as oral storytelling tends to be a more communal event than reading.

Certain recognizable signals set a story or tale apart from common speech and encourage us to pay a different kind of attention. Children know that a story is beginning when they hear or read "Once upon a time . . . ," and traditional oral storytellers have formal ways to set up a tale, such as *Su-num-twee* ("listen to me"), as Spokane storytellers say. "And they lived happily ever after," or simply "The End," may similarly indicate when the story is over. Such conventions have been adapted since the invention of printing and the spread of literacy.

FICTION AND NONFICTION

The word *fiction* comes from the Latin root *fingere* 'to fashion or form.' The earliest definitions concern the act of making something artificial to imitate something else. In the past two centuries, *fiction* has become more narrowly defined as "prose narrative about imaginary people and events," the main meaning of the word as we use it in this anthology.

Genres of Prose Fiction by Length

A **novel** is a work of prose fiction of about forty thousand words or more. The form arose in the seventeenth and early eighteenth centuries as prose romances and adventure tales began to adopt techniques of history and travel narrative as well as memoir, letters, and biography.

A **novella** is a work of prose fiction of about seventeen thousand to forty thousand words. The novella form was especially favored between about 1850 and 1950, largely because it can be more tightly controlled and concentrated than a long novel, while focusing on the inner workings of a character.

A **short story** is broadly defined as anywhere between one thousand and twenty thousand words. One expectation of a short story is that it

(continued on next page)

> *(continued)*
>
> may be read in a single sitting. The modern short story developed in the mid-nineteenth century, in part because of the growing popularity of magazines.
>
> A **short short story**, sometimes called "flash fiction" or "micro-fiction," is generally not much longer than one thousand words and sometimes much shorter. There have always been very short fictions, including parables and fables, but the short short story is an invention of recent decades.

In contrast with fiction, **nonfiction** usually refers to *factual* prose narrative. Some major nonfiction genres are history, biography, and autobiography. In film, documentaries and "biopics," or biographical feature films, similarly attempt to represent real people, places, and events. The boundary between fiction and nonfiction is often blurred today, as it was centuries ago. So-called true crime novels such as Truman Capote's *In Cold Blood* (1966) and novelized biographies such as Colm Tóibín's *The Master* (2004), about the life of the novelist Henry James, use the techniques of fiction writing to narrate actual events. Graphic novels, with a format derived from comic books, have become an increasingly popular medium for memoirs. (Two examples are Art Spiegelman's *Maus* [1986, 1991] and Marjane Satrapi's *Persepolis*.) Some Hollywood movies and TV shows dramatize real people in everyday situations or contexts, or real events such as the assassination of President John F. Kennedy. In contrast, **historical fiction**, developed by Sir Walter Scott around 1815, comprises prose narratives that present history in imaginative ways. Such works of prose fiction adhere closely to the facts of history and actual lives, just as many "true" life stories are more or less fictionalized.

The fiction chapters in this volume present a collection of prose works— mostly short stories—almost all of which were printed within the author's lifetime. Even as you read the short prose fiction in this book, bear in mind the many ways we encounter stories or narrative in everyday life, and consider the almost limitless variety of forms that fiction may take.

WRITING ABOUT FICTION

During your first reading of any story, you may want to read without stopping to address each of the questions on pages 15 and 16. After you have read the whole piece once, re-read it carefully, using the questions as a guide. It's always interesting to compare your initial reactions with your later ones. In fact, a paper may focus on comparing the expectations of readers (and characters) at the beginning of a story to their later conclusions. Responses to fiction may come in unpredictable order, so feel free to address the questions as they arise. Looking at how the story is told and what happens to which characters may lead to observations on expectations or setting. Consideration of setting and style can help explain the personalities, actions, mood, and effect of the story, which can lead to well-informed ideas about the meaning of the whole. But any one of the questions, pursued further, can serve as the focus of more formal writing.

Following this chapter are three written responses to Raymond Carver's short story CATHEDRAL. First, read the story and make notes on any features that you find interesting, important, or confusing. Then look at the notes and response paper by Wesley Rupton and the essay by Bethany Qualls, which show two different ways of writing about "Cathedral."

RAYMOND CARVER
(1938–88)
Cathedral

Born in the logging town of Clatskanie, Oregon, to a working-class family, Raymond Carver married at nineteen and had two children by the time he was twenty-one. Despite these early responsibilities and a lifelong struggle with alcoholism, Carver published his first story in 1961 and graduated from Humboldt State College in 1963. He published his first book, *Near Klamath*, a collection of poems, in 1968 and thereafter supported himself with visiting lectureships at the University of California at Berkeley, Syracuse University, and the Iowa Writer's Workshop, among other institutions. Described by the *New York Times* as "surely the most influential writer of American short stories in the second half of the twentieth century"; credited by others with "reviving what was once thought of as a dying literary form"; and compared to such literary luminaries as Ernest Hemingway, Stephen Crane, and Anton Chekhov, Carver often portrays characters whom one reviewer describes as living, much as Carver long did, "on the edge: of poverty, alcoholic self-destruction, loneliness." The author himself labeled them the sort of "good people," "doing the best they could," who "filled" America. Dubbed a "minimalist" due to his spare style and low-key plots, Carver himself suffered an early death, of lung cancer, at age fifty. His major short-story collections include *Will You Please Be Quiet, Please?* (1976), *What We Talk about When We Talk about Love* (1983), and the posthumously published *Call if You Need Me* (2001).

This blind man, an old friend of my wife's, he was on his way to spend the night. His wife had died. So he was visiting the dead wife's relatives in Connecticut. He called my wife from his in-laws'. Arrangements were made. He would come by train, a five-hour trip, and my wife would meet him at the station. She hadn't seen him since she worked for him one summer in Seattle ten years ago. But she and the blind man had kept in touch. They made tapes and mailed them back and forth. I wasn't enthusiastic about his visit. He was no one I knew. And his being blind bothered me. My idea of blindness came from the movies. In the movies, the blind moved slowly and never laughed. Sometimes they were led by seeing-eye dogs. A blind man in my house was not something I looked forward to.

That summer in Seattle she had needed a job. She didn't have any money. The man she was going to marry at the end of the summer was in officers' training school. He didn't have any money, either. But she was in love with the guy, and he was in love with her, etc. She'd seen something in the paper: HELP WANTED—*Reading to Blind Man*, and a telephone number. She phoned and went over, was hired on the spot. She'd worked with this blind man all summer. She read stuff to him, case studies, reports, that sort of thing. She helped him organize his little office in the county social-service department. They'd become good friends, my wife and the blind man. How do I know these things? She told me. And she told me something else. On her last day in the office, the blind man asked if he could touch her face. She agreed to this. She told me he touched his fingers to every part of her face, her nose—even her neck! She never forgot it. She even tried to write a poem about it. She was always trying to write a poem. She wrote a poem or two every year, usually after something really important had happened to her.

When we first started going out together, she showed me the poem. In the poem, she recalled his fingers and the way they had moved around over her face. In the poem, she talked about what she had felt at the time, about what went through her mind when the blind man touched her nose and lips. I can remember I didn't think much of the poem. Of course, I didn't tell her that. Maybe I just don't understand poetry. I admit it's not the first thing I reach for when I pick up something to read.

Anyway, this man who'd first enjoyed her favors, the officer-to-be, he'd been her childhood sweetheart. So okay. I'm saying that at the end of the summer she let the blind man run his hands over her face, said goodbye to him, married her childhood etc., who was now a commissioned officer, and she moved away from Seattle. But they'd kept in touch, she and the blind man. She made the first contact after a year or so. She called him up one night from an Air Force base in Alabama. She wanted to talk. They talked.

He asked her to send him a tape and tell him about her life. She did this. She sent the tape. On the tape, she told the blind man about her husband and about their life together in the military. She told the blind man she loved her husband but she didn't like it where they lived and she didn't like it that he was a part of the military-industrial thing. She told the blind man she'd written a poem and he was in it. She told him that she was writing a poem about what it was like to be an Air Force officer's wife. The poem wasn't finished yet. She was still writing it. The blind man made a tape. He sent her the tape. She made a tape. This went on for years. My wife's officer was posted to one base and then another. She sent tapes from Moody AFB, McGuire, McConnell, and finally Travis, near Sacramento, where one night she got to feeling lonely and cut off from people she kept losing in that moving-around life. She got to feeling she couldn't go it another step. She went in and swallowed all the pills and capsules in the medicine chest and washed them down with a bottle of gin. Then she got into a hot bath and passed out.

But instead of dying, she got sick. She threw up. Her officer—why should he have a name? he was the childhood sweetheart, and what more does he want?—came home from somewhere, found her, and called the ambulance. In time, she put it all on a tape and sent the tape to the blind man. Over the years, she put all kinds of stuff on tapes and sent the tapes off lickety-split. Next to writing a poem every year, I think it was her chief means of recreation. On one tape, she told the blind man she'd decided to live away from her officer for a time. On another tape, she told him about her divorce. She and I began going out, and of course she told her blind man about it. She told him everything, or so it seemed to me. Once she asked me if I'd like to hear the latest tape from the blind man. This was a year ago. I was on the tape, she said. So I said okay, I'd listen to it. I got us drinks and we settled down in the living room. We made ready to listen. First she inserted the tape into the player and adjusted a couple of dials. Then she pushed a lever. The tape squeaked and someone began to talk in this loud voice. She lowered the volume. After a few minutes of harmless chitchat, I heard my own name in the mouth of this stranger, this blind man I didn't even know! And then this: "From all you've said about him, I can only conclude—" But we were interrupted, a knock at the door, something, and we didn't ever get back to the tape. Maybe it was just as well. I'd heard all I wanted to.

Now this same blind man was coming to sleep in my house.

"Maybe I could take him bowling," I said to my wife. She was at the draining board doing scalloped potatoes. She put down the knife she was using and turned around.

"If you love me," she said, "you can do this for me. If you don't love me, okay. But if you had a friend, any friend, and the friend came to visit, I'd make him feel comfortable." She wiped her hands with the dish towel.

"I don't have any blind friends," I said.

10   "You don't have *any* friends," she said. "Period. Besides," she said, "goddamn it, his wife's just died! Don't you understand that? The man's lost his wife!"

I didn't answer. She'd told me a little about the blind man's wife. Her name was Beulah. Beulah! That's a name for a colored woman.

"Was his wife a Negro?" I asked.

"Are you crazy?" my wife said. "Have you just flipped or something?" She picked up a potato. I saw it hit the floor, then roll under the stove. "What's wrong with you?" she said. "Are you drunk?"

"I'm just asking," I said.

15   Right then my wife filled me in with more detail than I cared to know. I made a drink and sat at the kitchen table to listen. Pieces of the story began to fall into place.

Beulah had gone to work for the blind man the summer after my wife had stopped working for him. Pretty soon Beulah and the blind man had themselves a church wedding. It was a little wedding—who'd want to go to such a wedding in the first place?—just the two of them, plus the minister and the minister's wife. But it was a church wedding just the same. It was what Beulah had wanted, he'd said. But even then Beulah must have been carrying the cancer in her glands. After they had been inseparable for eight years—my wife's word, *inseparable*—Beulah's health went into a rapid decline. She died in a Seattle hospital room, the blind man sitting beside the bed and holding on to her hand. They'd married, lived and worked together, slept together—had sex, sure—and then the blind man had to bury her. All this without his having ever seen what the goddamned woman looked like. It was beyond my understanding. Hearing this, I felt sorry for the blind man for a little bit. And then I found myself thinking what a pitiful life this woman must have led. Imagine a woman who could never see herself as she was seen in the eyes of her loved one. A woman who could go on day after day and never receive the smallest compliment from her beloved. A woman whose husband could never read the expression on her face, be it misery or something better. Someone who could wear makeup or not—what difference to him? She could, if she wanted, wear green eye-shadow around one eye, a straight pin in her nostril, yellow slacks and purple shoes, no matter. And then to slip off into death, the blind man's hand on her hand, his blind eyes streaming tears—I'm imagining now—her last thought maybe this: that he never even knew what she looked like, and she on an express to the grave. Robert was left with a small insurance policy and half of a twenty-peso Mexican coin. The other half of the coin went into the box with her. Pathetic.

So when the time rolled around, my wife went to the depot to pick him up. With nothing to do but wait—sure, I blamed him for that—I was having a drink and watching the TV when I heard the car pull into the drive. I got up from the sofa with my drink and went to the window to have a look.

I saw my wife laughing as she parked the car. I saw her get out of the car and shut the door. She was still wearing a smile. Just amazing. She went around to the other side of the car to where the blind man was already starting to get out. This blind man, feature this, he was wearing a full beard! A beard on a blind man! Too much, I say. The blind man reached into the back seat and dragged out a suitcase. My wife took his arm, shut the car door, and, talking all the way, moved him down the drive and then up the steps to the front porch. I turned off the TV. I finished my drink, rinsed the glass, dried my hands. Then I went to the door.

My wife said, "I want you to meet Robert. Robert, this is my husband. I've told you all about him." She was beaming. She had this blind man by his coat sleeve.

The blind man let go of his suitcase and up came his hand. 20

I took it. He squeezed hard, held my hand, and then he let it go.

"I feel like we've already met," he boomed.

"Likewise," I said. I didn't know what else to say. Then I said, "Welcome. I've heard a lot about you." We began to move then, a little group, from the porch into the living room, my wife guiding him by the arm. The blind man was carrying his suitcase in his other hand. My wife said things like, "To your left here, Robert. That's right. Now watch it, there's a chair. That's it. Sit down right here. This is the sofa. We just bought this sofa two weeks ago."

I started to say something about the old sofa. I'd liked that old sofa. But I didn't say anything. Then I wanted to say something else, small-talk, about the scenic ride along the Hudson. How going *to* New York, you should sit on the right-hand side of the train, and coming *from* New York, the left-hand side.

"Did you have a good train ride?" I said. "Which side of the train did you 25 sit on, by the way?"

"What a question, which side!" my wife said. "What's it matter which side?" she said.

"I just asked," I said.

"Right side," the blind man said. "I hadn't been on a train in nearly forty years. Not since I was a kid. With my folks. That's been a long time. I'd nearly forgotten the sensation. I have winter in my beard now," he said. "So I've been told, anyway. Do I look distinguished, my dear?" the blind man said to my wife.

"You look distinguished, Robert," she said. "Robert," she said. "Robert, it's just so good to see you."

30 My wife finally took her eyes off the blind man and looked at me. I had the feeling she didn't like what she saw. I shrugged.

I've never met, or personally known, anyone who was blind. This blind man was late forties, a heavy-set, balding man with stooped shoulders, as if he carried a great weight there. He wore brown slacks, brown shoes, a light-brown shirt, a tie, a sports coat. Spiffy. He also had this full beard. But he didn't use a cane and he didn't wear dark glasses. I'd always thought dark glasses were a must for the blind. Fact was, I wished he had a pair. At first glance, his eyes looked like anyone else's eyes. But if you looked close, there was something different about them. Too much white in the iris, for one thing, and the pupils seemed to move around in the sockets without his knowing it or being able to stop it. Creepy. As I stared at his face, I saw the left pupil turn in toward his nose while the other made an effort to keep in one place. But it was only an effort, for that eye was on the roam without his knowing it or wanting it to be.

I said, "Let me get you a drink. What's your pleasure? We have a little of everything. It's one of our pastimes."

"Bub, I'm a Scotch man myself," he said fast enough in this big voice.

"Right," I said. Bub! "Sure you are. I knew it."

35 He let his fingers touch his suitcase, which was sitting alongside the sofa. He was taking his bearings. I didn't blame him for that.

"I'll move that up to your room," my wife said.

"No, that's fine," the blind man said loudly. "It can go up when I go up."

"A little water with the Scotch?" I said.

"Very little," he said.

40 "I knew it," I said.

He said, "Just a tad. The Irish actor, Barry Fitzgerald? I'm like that fellow. When I drink water, Fitzgerald said, I drink water. When I drink whiskey, I drink whiskey." My wife laughed. The blind man brought his hand up under his beard. He lifted his beard slowly and let it drop.

I did the drinks, three big glasses of Scotch with a splash of water in each. Then we made ourselves comfortable and talked about Robert's travels. First the long flight from the West Coast to Connecticut, we covered that. Then from Connecticut up here by train. We had another drink concerning that leg of the trip.

I remembered having read somewhere that the blind didn't smoke because, as speculation had it, they couldn't see the smoke they exhaled. I thought I knew that much and that much only about blind people. But this blind man smoked his cigarette down to the nubbin and then lit another one. This blind man filled his ashtray and my wife emptied it.

When we sat down at the table for dinner, we had another drink. My wife heaped Robert's plate with cube steak, scalloped potatoes, green beans. I buttered him up two slices of bread. I said, "Here's bread and butter for you." I swallowed some of my drink. "Now let us pray," I said, and the blind man lowered his head. My wife looked at me, her mouth agape. "Pray the phone won't ring and the food doesn't get cold," I said.

We dug in. We ate everything there was to eat on the table. We ate like 45 there was no tomorrow. We didn't talk. We ate. We scarfed. We grazed that table. We were into serious eating. The blind man had right away located his foods, he knew just where everything was on his plate. I watched with admiration as he used his knife and fork on the meat. He'd cut two pieces of meat, fork the meat into his mouth, and then go all out for the scalloped potatoes, the beans next, and then he'd tear off a hunk of buttered bread and eat that. He'd follow this up with a big drink of milk. It didn't seem to bother him to use his fingers once in a while, either.

We finished everything, including half a strawberry pie. For a few moments, we sat as if stunned. Sweat beaded on our faces. Finally, we got up from the table and left the dirty plates. We didn't look back. We took ourselves into the living room and sank into our places again. Robert and my wife sat on the sofa. I took the big chair. We had us two or three more drinks while they talked about the major things that had come to pass for them in the past ten years. For the most part, I just listened. Now and then I joined in. I didn't want him to think I'd left the room, and I didn't want her to think I was feeling left out. They talked of things that had happened to them—to them!—these past ten years. I waited in vain to hear my name on my wife's sweet lips: "And then my dear husband came into my life"—something like that. But I heard nothing of the sort. More talk of Robert. Robert had done a little of everything, it seemed, a regular blind jack-of-all-trades. But most recently he and his wife had had an Amway distributorship, from which, I gathered, they'd earned their living, such as it was. The blind man was also a ham radio operator. He talked in his loud voice about conversations he'd had with fellow operators in Guam, in the Philippines, in Alaska, and even in Tahiti. He said he'd have a lot of friends there if he ever wanted to go visit those places. From time to time, he'd turn his blind face toward me, put his hand under his beard, ask me something. How long had I been in my present position? (Three years.) Did I like my work? (I didn't.) Was I going to stay with it? (What were the options?) Finally, when I thought he was beginning to run down, I got up and turned on the TV.

My wife looked at me with irritation. She was heading toward a boil. Then she looked at the blind man and said, "Robert, do you have a TV?"

The blind man said, "My dear, I have two TVs. I have a color set and a black-and-white thing, an old relic. It's funny, but if I turn the TV on, and I'm always turning it on, I turn on the color set. It's funny, don't you think?"

I didn't know what to say to that. I had absolutely nothing to say to that. No opinion. So I watched the news program and tried to listen to what the announcer was saying.

50   "This is a color TV," the blind man said. "Don't ask me how, but I can tell."

"We traded up a while ago," I said.

The blind man had another taste of his drink. He lifted his beard, sniffed it, and let it fall. He leaned forward on the sofa. He positioned his ashtray on the coffee table, then put the lighter to his cigarette. He leaned back on the sofa and crossed his legs at the ankles.

My wife covered her mouth, and then she yawned. She stretched. She said, "I think I'll go upstairs and put on my robe. I think I'll change into something else. Robert, you make yourself comfortable," she said.

"I'm comfortable," the blind man said.

55   "I want you to feel comfortable in this house," she said.

"I am comfortable," the blind man said.

After she'd left the room, he and I listened to the weather report and then to the sports roundup. By that time, she'd been gone so long I didn't know if she was going to come back. I thought she might have gone to bed. I wished she'd come back downstairs. I didn't want to be left alone with a blind man. I asked him if he wanted another drink, and he said sure. Then I asked if he wanted to smoke some dope with me. I said I'd just rolled a number. I hadn't, but I planned to do so in about two shakes.

"I'll try some with you," he said.

"Damn right," I said. "That's the stuff."

60   I got our drinks and sat down on the sofa with him. Then I rolled us two fat numbers. I lit one and passed it. I brought it to his fingers. He took it and inhaled.

"Hold it as long as you can," I said. I could tell he didn't know the first thing.

My wife came back downstairs wearing her pink robe and her pink slippers.

"What do I smell?" she said.

"We thought we'd have us some cannabis," I said.

65   My wife gave me a savage look. Then she looked at the blind man and said, "Robert, I didn't know you smoked."

He said, "I do now, my dear. There's a first time for everything. But I don't feel anything yet."

"This stuff is pretty mellow," I said. "This stuff is mild. It's dope you can reason with," I said. "It doesn't mess you up."

"Not much it doesn't, bub," he said, and laughed.

My wife sat on the sofa between the blind man and me. I passed her the number. She took it and toked and then passed it back to me. "Which way is this going?" she said. Then she said, "I shouldn't be smoking this. I can hardly keep my eyes open as it is. That dinner did me in. I shouldn't have eaten so much."

"It was the strawberry pie," the blind man said. "That's what did it," he 70 said, and he laughed his big laugh. Then he shook his head.

"There's more strawberry pie," I said.

"Do you want some more, Robert?" my wife said.

"Maybe in a little while," he said.

We gave our attention to the TV. My wife yawned again. She said, "Your bed is made up when you feel like going to bed, Robert. I know you must have had a long day. When you're ready to go to bed, say so." She pulled his arm. "Robert?"

He came to and said, "I've had a real nice time. This beats tapes, 75 doesn't it?"

I said, "Coming at you," and I put the number between his fingers. He inhaled, held the smoke, and then let it go. It was like he'd been doing it since he was nine years old.

"Thanks, bub," he said. "But I think this is all for me. I think I'm beginning to feel it," he said. He held the burning roach out for my wife.

"Same here," she said. "Ditto. Me, too." She took the roach and passed it to me. "I may just sit here for a while between you two guys with my eyes closed. But don't let me bother you, okay? Either one of you. If it bothers you, say so. Otherwise, I may just sit here with my eyes closed until you're ready to go to bed," she said. "Your bed's made up, Robert, when you're ready. It's right next to our room at the top of the stairs. We'll show you up when you're ready. You wake me up now, you guys, if I fall asleep." She said that and then she closed her eyes and went to sleep.

The news program ended. I got up and changed the channel. I sat back down on the sofa. I wished my wife hadn't pooped out. Her head lay across the back of the sofa, her mouth open. She'd turned so that her robe had slipped away from her legs, exposing a juicy thigh. I reached to draw her robe back over her, and it was then that I glanced at the blind man. What the hell! I flipped the robe open again.

"You say when you want some strawberry pie," I said.   80

"I will," he said.

I said, "Are you tired? Do you want me to take you up to your bed? Are you ready to hit the hay?"

"Not yet," he said. "No, I'll stay up with you, bub. If that's all right. I'll stay up until you're ready to turn in. We haven't had a chance to talk. Know

what I mean? I feel like me and her monopolized the evening." He lifted
his beard and he let it fall. He picked up his cigarettes and his lighter.
"That's all right," I said. Then I said, "I'm glad for the company."
85   And I guess I was. Every night I smoked dope and stayed up as long as
I could before I fell asleep. My wife and I hardly ever went to bed at the
same time. When I did go to sleep, I had these dreams. Sometimes I'd
wake up from one of them, my heart going crazy.

Something about the church and the Middle Ages was on the TV. Not
your run-of-the-mill TV fare. I wanted to watch something else. I turned to
the other channels. But there was nothing on them, either. So I turned back
to the first channel and apologized.

"Bub, it's all right," the blind man said. "It's fine with me. Whatever you
want to watch is okay. I'm always learning something. Learning never
ends. It won't hurt me to learn something tonight. I got ears," he said.

We didn't say anything for a time. He was leaning forward with his head
turned at me, his right ear aimed in the direction of the set. Very discon-
certing. Now and then his eyelids drooped and then they snapped open
again. Now and then he put his fingers into his beard and tugged, like he
was thinking about something he was hearing on the television.

On the screen, a group of men wearing cowls was being set upon and
tormented by men dressed in skeleton costumes and men dressed as devils.
The men dressed as devils wore devil masks, horns, and long tails. This
pageant was part of a procession. The Englishman who was narrating the
thing said it took place in Spain once a year. I tried to explain to the blind
man what was happening.

90   "Skeletons," he said. "I know about skeletons," he said, and he nodded.

The TV showed this one cathedral. Then there was a long, slow look at
another one. Finally, the picture switched to the famous one in Paris, with
its flying buttresses and its spires reaching up to the clouds. The camera
pulled away to show the whole of the cathedral rising above the skyline.

There were times when the Englishman who was telling the thing
would shut up, would simply let the camera move around over the cathedrals. Or else the camera would tour the countryside, men in fields walking
behind oxen. I waited as long as I could. Then I felt I had to say something.
I said, "They're showing the outside of this cathedral now. Gargoyles. Little
statues carved to look like monsters. Now I guess they're in Italy. Yeah,
they're in Italy. There's paintings on the walls of this one church."

"Are those fresco paintings, bub?" he asked, and he sipped from his drink.

I reached for my glass. But it was empty. I tried to remember what I
could remember. "You're asking me are those frescoes?" I said. "That's a
good question. I don't know."

The camera moved to a cathedral outside Lisbon. The differences in ⁹⁵
the Portuguese cathedral compared with the French and Italian were not
that great. But they were there. Mostly the interior stuff. Then something
occurred to me, and I said, "Something has occurred to me. Do you have
any idea what a cathedral is? What they look like, that is? Do you follow
me? If somebody says cathedral to you, do you have any notion what they're
talking about? Do you know the difference between that and a Baptist
church, say?"

He let the smoke dribble from his mouth. "I know they took hundreds
of workers fifty or a hundred years to build," he said. "I just heard the man
say that, of course. I know generations of the same families worked on a
cathedral. I heard him say that, too. The men who began their life's work
on them, they never lived to see the completion of their work. In that wise,
bub, they're no different from the rest of us, right?" He laughed. Then his
eyelids drooped again. His head nodded. He seemed to be snoozing. Maybe
he was imagining himself in Portugal. The TV was showing another cathedral now. This one was in Germany. The Englishman's voice droned on.
"Cathedrals," the blind man said. He sat up and rolled his head back
and forth. "If you want the truth, bub, that's about all I know. What I just
said. What I heard him say. But maybe you could describe one to me? I
wish you'd do it. I'd like that. If you want to know, I really don't have a
good idea."

I stared hard at the shot of the cathedral on the TV. How could I even
begin to describe it? But say my life depended on it. Say my life was being
threatened by an insane guy who said I had to do it or else.

I stared some more at the cathedral before the picture flipped off into
the countryside. There was no use. I turned to the blind man and said, "To
begin with, they're very tall." I was looking around the room for clues. "They
reach way up. Up and up. Toward the sky. They're so big, some of them,
they have to have these supports. To help hold them up, so to speak. These
supports are called buttresses. They remind me of viaducts, for some reason. But maybe you don't know viaducts, either? Sometimes the cathedrals
have devils and such carved into the front. Sometimes lords and ladies.
Don't ask me why this is," I said.

He was nodding. The whole upper part of his body seemed to be moving back and forth.

"I'm not doing so good, am I?" I said.   100

He stopped nodding and leaned forward on the edge of the sofa. As
he listened to me, he was running his fingers through his beard. I wasn't
getting through to him, I could see that. But he waited for me to go on just
the same. He nodded, like he was trying to encourage me. I tried to think
what else to say. "They're really big," I said. "They're massive. They're built

of stone. Marble, too, sometimes. In those olden days, when they built cathedrals, men wanted to be close to God. In those olden days, God was an important part of everyone's life. You could tell this from their cathedral-building. I'm sorry," I said, "but it looks like that's the best I can do for you. I'm just no good at it."

"That's all right, bub," the blind man said. "Hey, listen. I hope you don't mind my asking you. Can I ask you something? Let me ask you a simple question, yes or no. I'm just curious and there's no offense. You're my host. But let me ask if you are in any way religious? You don't mind my asking?"

I shook my head. He couldn't see that, though. A wink is the same as a nod to a blind man. "I guess I don't believe in it. In anything. Sometimes it's hard. You know what I'm saying?"

"Sure, I do," he said.

105   "Right," I said.

The Englishman was still holding forth. My wife sighed in her sleep. She drew a long breath and went on with her sleeping.

"You'll have to forgive me," I said. "But I can't tell you what a cathedral looks like. It just isn't in me to do it. I can't do any more than I've done."

The blind man sat very still, his head down, as he listened to me.

I said, "The truth is, cathedrals don't mean anything special to me. Nothing. Cathedrals. They're something to look at on late-night TV. That's all they are."

110   It was then that the blind man cleared his throat. He brought something up. He took a handkerchief from his back pocket. Then he said, "I get it, bub. It's okay. It happens. Don't worry about it," he said. "Hey, listen to me. Will you do me a favor? I got an idea. Why don't you find us some heavy paper? And a pen. We'll do something. We'll draw one together. Get us a pen and some heavy paper. Go on, bub, get the stuff," he said.

So I went upstairs. My legs felt like they didn't have any strength in them. They felt like they did after I'd done some running. In my wife's room, I looked around. I found some ballpoints in a little basket on her table. And then I tried to think where to look for the kind of paper he was talking about.

Downstairs, in the kitchen, I found a shopping bag with onion skins in the bottom of the bag. I emptied the bag and shook it. I brought it into the living room and sat down with it near his legs. I moved some things, smoothed the wrinkles from the bag, spread it out on the coffee table.

The blind man got down from the sofa and sat next to me on the carpet.

He ran his fingers over the paper. He went up and down the sides of the paper. The edges, even the edges. He fingered the corners.

115   "All right," he said. "All right, let's do her."

He found my hand, the hand with the pen. He closed his hand over my hand. "Go ahead, bub, draw," he said. "Draw. You'll see. I'll follow along with you. It'll be okay. Just begin now like I'm telling you. You'll see. Draw," the blind man said.

So I began. First I drew a box that looked like a house. It could have been the house I lived in. Then I put a roof on it. At either end of the roof, I drew spires. Crazy.

"Swell," he said. "Terrific. You're doing fine," he said. "Never thought anything like this could happen in your lifetime, did you, bub? Well, it's a strange life, we all know that. Go on now. Keep it up."

I put in windows with arches. I drew flying buttresses. I hung great doors. I couldn't stop. The TV station went off the air. I put down the pen and closed and opened my fingers. The blind man felt around over the paper. He moved the tips of his fingers over the paper, all over what I had drawn, and he nodded.

"Doing fine," the blind man said. 120

I took up the pen again, and he found my hand. I kept at it. I'm no artist. But I kept drawing just the same.

My wife opened up her eyes and gazed at us. She sat up on the sofa, her robe hanging open. She said, "What are you doing? Tell me, I want to know."

I didn't answer her.

The blind man said, "We're drawing a cathedral. Me and him are working on it. Press hard," he said to me. "That's right. That's good," he said. "Sure. You got it, bub. I can tell. You didn't think you could. But you can, can't you? You're cooking with gas now. You know what I'm saying? We're going to really have us something here in a minute. How's the old arm?" he said. "Put some people in there now. What's a cathedral without people?"

My wife said, "What's going on? Robert, what are you doing? What's 125 going on?"

"It's all right," he said to her. "Close your eyes now," the blind man said to me.

I did it. I closed them just like he said.

"Are they closed?" he said. "Don't fudge."

"They're closed," I said.

"Keep them that way," he said. He said, "Don't stop now. Draw." 130

So we kept on with it. His fingers rode my fingers as my hand went over the paper. It was like nothing else in my life up to now.

Then he said, "I think that's it. I think you got it," he said. "Take a look. What do you think?"

But I had my eyes closed. I thought I'd keep them that way for a little longer. I thought it was something I ought to do.

"Well?" he said. "Are you looking?"

135   My eyes were still closed. I was in my house. I knew that. But I didn't feel like I was inside anything.

"It's really something," I said.

1983

SAMPLE WRITING: READING NOTES

Wesley Rupton wrote the notes below with the "Questions about the Elements of Fiction" in mind (pp. 15–16). As you read these notes, compare them to the notes you took as you read CATHEDRAL. Do Rupton's notes reveal anything to you that you didn't notice while reading the story? Did you notice anything he did not, or do you disagree with any of his interpretations?

Notes on Raymond Carver's "Cathedral"

What do you expect?

- Title: The first words are "this blind man," and those words keep being repeated. Why not call it "The Blind Man" or "The Blind Man's Visit"?
- The threatening things the husband says made me expect that he would attack the blind man. I thought the wife might leave her husband for the blind man, who has been nicer to her.
- When they talk about going up to bed, and the wife goes to "get comfortable" and then falls asleep, I thought there was a hint about sex.

What happens in the story?

- Not that much. It is a story about one evening in which a husband and wife and their guest drink, have dinner, talk, and then watch TV.
- These people have probably drunk two bottles of hard liquor (how many drinks?) before, during, and after a meal. And then they smoke marijuana.
- In the final scene, the two men try to describe and draw cathedrals that are on the TV show. Why cathedrals? Though it connects with the title.
- The husband seems to have a different attitude at the end: He likes Robert and seems excited about the experience "like nothing else in my life up to now."

How is the story narrated?

- It's told in first person and past tense. The husband is the narrator. We never get inside another character's thoughts. He seems to be telling someone about the incident, first saying the blind man was coming, and then filling in the background about his wife and the blind man, and then telling what happens after the guest arrives.
- The narrator describes people and scenes and summarizes the past; there is dialogue.
- It doesn't have episodes or chapters, but there are two gaps on the page, before paragraph 57 and before paragraph 88. Maybe time passes here.

Who are the characters?

- Three main characters: husband, wife, and blind man (the blind man's own wife has just died, and the wife divorced her first husband). I don't think we ever know the husband's or wife's names. The blind man, Robert, calls him "bub," like "buddy." They seem to be white, middle-class Americans. The wife is lonely and looking for meaning. The blind man seems sensitive, and he cares about the poetry and tapes.
- The husband is sort of acting out, though mostly in his own mind. Asking "Was his wife a Negro?" sounds like he wants to make fun of black or blind people. His wife asks, "Are you drunk?" and says that he has no friends; I thought he's an unhappy man who gets drunk and acts "crazy" a lot and that she doesn't really expect him to be that nice.
- It sounds like these people have plenty of food and things, but aren't very happy. They all sound smart, but the narrator is ignorant, and he has no religion. All three characters have some bad or nervous habits (alcohol, cigarettes, drugs; insomnia; suicide attempt; divorce).

What is the setting and time of the story?

- Mostly in the house the evening the blind man arrives. But after the intro there's a kind of flashback to the summer in Seattle ten years ago (par. 2). The story about the visit starts again in paragraph 6, and then the wife tells the husband more about the blind man's marriage—another flashback in paragraph 16. In paragraph 17, "the time rolled around" to the story's main event. After that, it's chronological.
- We don't know the name of the town, but it seems to be on the U.S. East Coast (five hours by train from Connecticut [par. 1]). It can't be

too long ago or too recent either: They mention trains, audiotapes, color TV, no Internet. No one seems worried about food or health the way they might be today.

- I noticed that travel came up in the story. Part of what drives the wife crazy about her first husband is moving around to different military bases (par. 4). In paragraph 46, Robert tells us about his contact with ham radio operators in places he would like to visit (Guam, Alaska). The TV show takes Robert and the narrator on a tour of France, Italy, and Portugal.

What do you notice about how the story is written?

- The narrator is irritating. He repeats words a lot. He uses stereotypes. He seems to be informally talking to someone, as if he can't get over it. But then he sometimes uses exaggerated or bored-sounding phrases: "this man who'd first enjoyed her favors," "So okay. I'm saying . . . married her childhood etc." (par. 4). His style is almost funny.

- Things he repeats: Paragraphs 2 and 3: "She told me" (3 times), "he could touch her face . . . he touched his fingers to every part of her face . . ." (and later "touched her nose" and "they'd kept in touch"). "She even tried to write a poem . . . always trying to write a poem" (and 4 more times "poem"). The words "talk," "tape," "told" are also repeated.

What does the story mean? Can you express its theme or themes?

- The way the narrator learns to get along with the blind man must be important. The narrator is disgusted by blind people at first, and at the end he closes his eyes on purpose.

- I think it makes a difference that the two men imagine and try to draw a cathedral, not a flower or an airplane. It's something made by human beings, and it's religious. As they mention, the builders of cathedrals don't live to see them finished, but the buildings last for centuries. It's not like the narrator is saved or becomes a great guy, but he gets past whatever he's afraid of at night, and he seems inspired for a little while. I don't know why the wife has to be left out of this, but probably the husband couldn't open up if he was worrying about how close she is to Robert.

SAMPLE WRITING: RESPONSE PAPER

A response paper may use a less formal organization and style than a longer, more formal essay, but it should not just be a summary or description of the work. Indeed, a response paper could be a step on the way to a longer essay. You need not form a single thesis or argument, but you should try to develop your ideas and feelings about the story through your writing. The point is to get your thoughts in writing without worrying too much about form and style.

Almost everything in the following response paper comes directly from the notes above, but notice how the writer has combined observations, adding a few direct quotations or details from the text to support claims about the story's effects and meaning. For ease of reference, we have altered the citations in this paper to refer to paragraph numbers. Unless your instructor indicates otherwise, however, you should always follow convention by instead citing page numbers when writing about fiction.

Rupton 1

Wesley Rupton
Professor Suarez
English 170
6 January 2017

Response Paper on Raymond Carver's "Cathedral"

Not much happens in Raymond Carver's short story "Cathedral," and at first I wondered what it was about and why it was called "Cathedral." The narrator, the unnamed husband, seems to be telling someone about the evening that Robert, a blind friend of his wife, came to stay at their house, not long after Robert's own wife has died. After the narrator fills us in about his wife's first marriage and her relationship with the blind man, he describes what the three characters do that evening: they drink a lot of alcohol, eat a huge dinner that leaves them "stunned" (par. 46), smoke marijuana, and after the wife falls asleep the two men watch TV.

A show about cathedrals leads the husband to try to describe what a cathedral looks like, and then the men try to draw one together. The husband seems to have a different attitude at the end: he likes Robert and seems excited about an experience "like nothing else in my life up to now" (par. 131).

The husband's way of telling the story is definitely important. He is sort of funny, but also irritating. As he makes jokes about stereotypes, you start to dislike or distrust him. When he hears about Robert's wife, Beulah, he asks, "Was his wife a Negro?" (par. 12) just because her name sounds like a black woman's name to him. In three paragraphs, he flashes back to the time ten years ago when his wife was the blind man's assistant and the blind man

> asked if he could touch her face. . . . She told me he touched his fingers to every part of her face. . . . She even tried to write a poem about it. . . .
>
> . . . In the poem, she recalled his fingers . . . over her face. In the poem, she talked about what she had felt . . . when the blind man touched her nose and lips. (pars. 2-3)

The narrator seems to be going over and over the same creepy idea of a man feeling his wife's face. It seems to disgust him that his wife and the blind man communicated or expressed themselves, perhaps because he seems incapable of doing so. When his wife asks, "Are you drunk?" and says that he has no friends, I got a feeling that the husband is an unhappy man who gets drunk and acts "crazy" a lot and that his wife doesn't really expect him to be very nice (pars. 8-13). He's going to make fun of their guest (asking a blind man to go bowling). The husband is sort of acting out, though he's mostly rude in his own mind.

There's nothing heroic or dramatic or even unusual about these people (except that one is blind). The events take place in a house somewhere in an American suburb and not too long ago. Other than the quantity of alcohol and drugs they consume, these people don't do anything unusual, though the blind man seems strange to the narrator. The ordinary setting and plot make the idea of something as grand and old as a European cathedral come as a surprise at the end of the story. I wondered if part of the point is that they desperately want to get out of a trap they're in. I noticed that travel came up in the story. Part of what drove the wife crazy with her first husband was moving around to different military bases (par. 4).

In paragraph 46, Robert tells us about his contact with ham radio operators in places he would like to visit (Guam, Alaska). The TV show takes Robert and the narrator on a tour of France, Italy, and Portugal.

The way the narrator changes from disliking the blind man to getting along with him must be important to the meaning of the story. After the wife goes up to "get comfortable," suggesting that they might go to bed, the story focuses on the two men. Later she falls asleep on the sofa between them, and the narrator decides not to cover up her leg where her robe has fallen open, as if he has stopped being jealous. At this point the narrator decides he is "glad for the company" of his guest (par. 84). The cooperation between the two men is the turning point. The narrator is disgusted by blind people at first, and at the end he closes his eyes on purpose. The two men try to imagine something and build something together, and Robert is coaching the narrator. Robert says, "let's do her," and then says, "*You're* doing fine" (pars. 115, 118; emphasis added). I think it makes a difference that they imagine and draw a cathedral, not a flower or a cow or an airplane. It's something made by human beings, and it's religious. I don't think the men are converted to believing in God at the end, but this narrow-minded guy gets past whatever he's afraid of at night and finds some sort of inspiring feeling. I don't know why the wife has to be left out, but probably the husband couldn't open up if he was worrying about how close she is to Robert.

The ideas of communicating or being in touch and travel seem connected to me. I think that the husband tries to tell this story about the cathedral the way his wife tried to write a poem. The narrator has had an exciting experience that gets him in touch with something beyond his small house. After drawing the cathedral, the narrator says that he "didn't feel like I was inside anything" (par. 135). Though I still didn't like the narrator, I felt more sympathy, and I thought the story showed that even this hostile person could open up.

Work Cited

Carver, Raymond. "Cathedral." *The Norton Introduction to Literature*, edited by Kelly J. Mays, portable 12th ed., W. W. Norton, 2017, pp. 33-46.

SAMPLE WRITING: ESSAY

Bethany Qualls wrote the following first draft of an essay analyzing character and narration in Carver's CATHEDRAL. Read this paper as you would one of your peers' papers, looking for opportunities for the writer to improve her presentation. Is the tone consistently appropriate for academic writing? Does the essay maintain its focus? Does it demonstrate a steady progression of well-supported arguments that build toward a strong, well-earned conclusion? Is there any redundant or otherwise unnecessary material? Are there ideas that need to be developed further? For a critique and revision of this essay's conclusion, see ch. 18, "The Literature Essay," in the Writing about Literature section of this book.

(For ease of reference, we have altered the citations in this essay to refer to paragraph numbers. Unless your instructor indicates otherwise, however, you should always follow convention by instead citing page numbers when writing about fiction. For more on citation, please refer to ch. 21.)

Qualls 1

Bethany Qualls
Professor Netherton
English 301
16 January 2017

A Narrator's Blindness in Raymond Carver's "Cathedral"

A reader in search of an exciting plot will be pretty disappointed by Raymond Carver's "Cathedral" because the truth is nothing much happens. A suburban husband and wife receive a visit from her former boss, who is blind. After the wife falls asleep, the two men watch a TV program about cathedrals and eventually try to draw one. Along the way the three characters down a few cocktails and smoke a little pot. But that's about as far as the action goes. Instead of focusing on plot, then, the story really asks

---

us to focus on the characters, especially the husband who narrates the story. Through his words even more than his actions, the narrator unwittingly shows us why nothing much happens to him by continually demonstrating his utter inability to connect with others or to understand himself.

The narrator's isolation is most evident in the distanced way he introduces his own story and the people in it. He does not name the other characters or himself, referring to them only by using labels such as "this blind man," "his wife," "my wife" (par. 1), and "the man [my wife] was going to marry" (par. 2). Even after the narrator's wife starts referring to their visitor as "Robert," the narrator keeps calling him "the blind man." These labels distance him from the other characters and also leave readers with very little connection to them.

At least three times the narrator notices that this habit of not naming or really acknowledging people is significant. Referring to his wife's "officer," he asks, "why should he have a name? he was the childhood sweetheart, and what more does he want?" (par. 5). Moments later he describes how freaked out he was when he listened to a tape the blind man had sent his wife and "heard [his] own name in the mouth of this . . . blind man [he] didn't even know!" (par. 5). Yet once the blind man arrives and begins to talk with the wife, the narrator finds himself "wait[ing] in vain to hear [his] name on [his] wife's sweet lips" and disappointed to hear "nothing of the sort" (par. 46). Simply using someone's name suggests an intimacy that the narrator avoids and yet secretly yearns for.

Also reinforcing the narrator's isolation and dissatisfaction with it are the awkward euphemisms and clichés he uses, which emphasize how disconnected he is from his own feelings and how uncomfortable he is with other people's. Referring to his wife's first husband, the narrator says it was he "who'd first enjoyed her favors" (par. 4), an antiquated expression even in 1983, the year the story was published. Such language reinforces our sense that the narrator cannot speak in language that is meaningful or heartfelt, especially when he tries to talk about emotions. He describes his wife's feelings for her first husband, for example, by using generic language and then just trailing off entirely: "she was in love with the guy, and he was in love with her, etc." (par. 2). When he refers to the blind man and his wife as "inseparable," he points out that this is, in fact, his "wife's word," not one that he's come up with (par. 16). And even when he admits that he would like to hear his wife talk about him (par. 46), he speaks in language that seems to come from books or movies rather than the heart.

Once the visit actually begins, the narrator's interactions and conversations with the other characters are even more awkward. His discomfort with the very idea of the visit is obvious to his wife and to the reader. As he says in his usual deadpan manner, "I wasn't enthusiastic about his visit" (par. 1). During the visit he sits silent when his wife and Robert are talking and then answers Robert's questions about his life and feelings with the shortest possible phrases: "How long had I been in my present position? (Three years.) Did I like my work? (I didn't.)" (par. 46). Finally, he tries to escape even that much involvement by simply turning on the TV and tuning Robert out.

Despite Robert's best attempt to make a connection with the narrator, the narrator resorts to a label again, saying that he "didn't want to be left alone with a blind man" (par. 57). Robert, merely "a blind man," remains a category, not a person, and the narrator can initially relate to Robert only by invoking the stereotypes about that category that he has learned "from the movies" (par. 1). He confides to the reader that he believes that blind people always wear dark glasses, that they never smoke (par. 43), and that a beard on a blind man is "too much" (par. 18). It follows that the narrator is amazed about the connection his wife and Robert have because he is unable to see Robert as a person like any other. "Who'd want to go to such a wedding in the first place?" (par. 16), he asks rhetorically about Robert's wedding to his wife, Beulah.

Misconceptions continue as the narrator assumes Beulah would "never receive the smallest compliment from her beloved," since the compliments he is thinking about are physical ones (par. 16). Interestingly, when faced with a name that is specific (Beulah), the narrator immediately assumes that he knows what the person with that name must be like ("a colored woman," par. 11), even though she is not in the room or known to him. Words fail or mislead the narrator in both directions, as he's using them and as he hears them.

There is hope for the narrator at the end as he gains some empathy and forges a bond with Robert over the drawing of a cathedral. That process seems to begin when the narrator admits to himself, the reader, and Robert that he is "glad for [Robert's] company" (par. 84) and, for the first time, comes close to disclosing the literally nightmarish loneliness of his life. It culminates in a moment of physical and emotional intimacy that the narrator admits is "like nothing else in my life up to now" (par. 131)—a moment in which discomfort with the very idea of blindness gives way to

Qualls 4

an attempt to actually experience blindness from the inside. Because the narrator has used words to distance himself from the world, it seems fitting that all this happens only when the narrator *stops* using words. They have a tendency to blind him.

However, even at the very end it isn't clear just whether or how the narrator has really changed. He does not completely interact with Robert but has to be prodded into action by him. By choosing to keep his eyes closed, he not only temporarily experiences blindness but also shuts out the rest of the world, since he "didn't feel like [he] was inside anything" (par. 135). Perhaps most important, he remains unable to describe his experience meaningfully, making it difficult for readers to decide whether or not he has really changed. For example, he says, "It was like nothing else in my life up to now" (par. 131), but he doesn't explain why this is true. Is it because he is doing something for someone else? Because he is thinking about the world from another's perspective? Because he feels connected to Robert? Because he is drawing a picture while probably drunk and high? There is no way of knowing.

It's possible that not feeling "inside anything" (par. 135) could be a feeling of freedom from his own habits of guardedness and insensitivity, his emotional "blindness." But even with this final hope for connection, for the majority of the story the narrator is a closed, judgmental man who isolates himself and cannot connect with others. The narrator's view of the world is one filled with misconceptions that the visit from Robert starts to slowly change, yet it is not clear what those changes are, how far they will go, or whether they will last.

Qualls 5

Work Cited

Carver, Raymond. "Cathedral." *The Norton Introduction to Literature,* edited by Kelly J. Mays, portable 12th ed., W. W. Norton, 2017, pp. 33–46.

Understanding the Text

1 PLOT

At its most basic, every story is an attempt to answer the question *What happened?* In some cases, this question is easy to answer. J. R. R. Tolkien's *The Lord of the Rings* trilogy (1954–55) is full of battles, chases, and other heart-stopping dramatic action; Mark Twain's *Adventures of Huckleberry Finn* (1884) relates Huck and Jim's adventures as they travel down the Mississippi River. Yet if we ask what happens in other works of fiction, our initial answer might well be, "Not much." In one of the most pivotal scenes in Henry James's novel *The Portrait of a Lady* (1881), for example, a woman enters a room, sees a man sitting down and a woman standing up, and beats a hasty retreat. Not terribly exciting stuff, it would seem. Yet this event ends up radically transforming the lives of just about everyone in the novel. "On very tiny pivots do human lives turn" would thus seem to be one common message—or **theme**—of fiction.

All fiction, regardless of its subject matter, should make us ask, *What will happen next?* and *How will all this turn out?* And responsive readers of fiction will often pause to answer those questions, trying to articulate just what their expectations are and how the story has shaped them. But great fiction and responsive readers are often just as interested in questions about *why* things happen and about *how* the characters' lives are affected as a result. These *how* and *why* questions are likely to be answered very differently by different readers of the very same fictional work; as a result, such questions will often generate powerful essays, whereas mainly factual questions about what happens in the work usually won't.

PLOT VERSUS ACTION, SEQUENCE, AND SUBPLOT

The term **plot** is sometimes used to refer to the events recounted in a fictional work. But in this book we instead use the term **action** in this way, reserving the term *plot* for the way the author sequences and paces the events so as to shape our response and interpretation.

The difference between action and plot resembles the difference between ancient chronicles that merely list the events of a king's reign in chronological order and more modern histories that make a meaningful sequence out of those events. As the British novelist and critic E. M. Forster put it, "The king died and then the queen died" is not a plot, for it has not been "tampered with." "The queen died after the king died" describes the same events, but the order in which they are reported has been changed. The reader of the first sentence focuses on the king first, the reader of the second on the queen. The second sentence, moreover, subtly encourages us to speculate about *why* things happened, not just *what* happened and *when*: Did the queen die *because* her husband did? If so, was her death the result of her grief? Or was she murdered by a rival who saw the king's death as the perfect opportunity to get rid of her, too? Though our two sentences describe the same action, each has quite a different focus, emphasis, effect, and meaning thanks to its *sequencing*—the precise order in which events are related.

Like chronicles, many fictional works do relate events in chronological order, starting with the earliest and ending with the latest. Folktales, for example, have this sort of plot. But fiction writers have other choices; events need not be recounted in the particular order in which they happened. Quite often, then, a writer will choose to mix things up, perhaps opening a story with the most recent event and then moving backward to show us all that led up to it. Still other stories begin somewhere in the middle of the action or, to use the Latin term, *in medias res* (literally, "in the middle of things"). In such plots, events that occurred before the story's opening are sometimes presented in **flashbacks**. Conversely, a story might jump forward in time to recount a later **episode** or event in a **flashforward**. **Foreshadowing** occurs when an author merely gives subtle clues or hints about what will happen later in the story.

Though we often talk about *the* plot of a fictional work, however, keep in mind that some works, especially longer ones, have two or more. A plot that receives significantly less time and attention than another is called a **subplot**.

PACE

In life, we sometimes have little choice about how long a particular event lasts. If you want a driver's license, you may have to spend a boring hour or two at the motor vehicle office. And much as you might prefer to relax and enjoy your lunch, occasionally you have to scarf it down in the ten minutes it takes you to drive to campus.

One of the pleasures of turning experiences into a story, however, is that doing so gives a writer more power over them. In addition to choosing the order in which to recount events, the writer can also decide how much time and attention to devote to each. *Pacing*, or the duration of particular episodes— especially relative to each other and to the time they would have taken in real life—is a vital tool of storytellers and another important factor to consider in analyzing plots. In all fiction, pace as much as sequence determines focus and emphasis, effect and meaning. And though it can be very helpful to differentiate between "fast-paced" and "slow-paced" fiction, all effective stories contain both faster and slower bits. When an author slows down to home in on a particular moment and scene, often introduced by a phrase such as "Later that evening . . ." or "The day before Maggie fell down . . . ," we call this a **discriminated occasion**. For example, the first paragraph of Linda Brewer's 20/20 quickly and generally refers to events that occur over three days. Then Brewer suddenly slows down, pinpointing an incident that takes place on "[t]he third evening out. . . ." That episode consumes four paragraphs of the story, even though the action described in those paragraphs accounts for only a few minutes of Bill and Ruthie's time. Next the story devotes two more paragraphs to an incident that occurs "[t]he next evening." In the last paragraph, Brewer speeds up again, telling us about the series of "wonderful sights" Ruthie sees between Indiana and Spokane, Washington.

CONFLICTS

Whatever their sequence and pace, all plots hinge on at least one **conflict**—some sort of struggle—and its resolution. Conflicts may be *external* or *internal*. External conflicts arise between characters and something or someone outside themselves. Adventure stories and films often present this sort of conflict in its purest form, keeping us poised on the edge of our seats as James

Bond struggles to outwit and outfight an arch-villain intent on world domination or destruction. Yet external conflicts can also be much subtler, pitting an individual against nature or fate, against a social force such as racism or poverty, or against another person or group of people with a different way of looking at things (as in "20/20"). The cartoon on page 59 presents an external conflict of the latter type and one you may well see quite differently than the cartoonist does.

Internal conflicts occur when a character struggles to reconcile two competing desires, needs, or duties, or two parts or aspects of himself: His head, for instance, might tell him to do one thing, his heart another. Often, a conflict is simultaneously external and internal, as in the following brief folktale, in which a woman seems to struggle simultaneously with nature, with mortality, with God, and with her desire to hold on to someone she loves versus her need to let go.

JACOB AND WILHELM GRIMM
The Shroud

There was once a mother who had a little boy of seven years old, who was so handsome and lovable that no one could look at him without liking him, and she herself worshipped him above everything in the world. Now it so happened that he suddenly became ill, and God took him to himself; and for this the mother could not be comforted, and wept both day and night. But soon afterwards, when the child had been buried, it appeared by night in the places where it had sat and played during its life, and if the mother wept, it wept also, and, when morning came, it disappeared. As, however, the mother would not stop crying, it came one night, in the little white shroud in which it had been laid in its coffin, and with its wreath of flowers round its head, and stood on the bed at her feet, and said, "Oh, mother, do stop crying, or I shall never fall asleep in my coffin, for my shroud will not dry because of all thy tears which fall upon it." The mother was afraid when she heard that, and wept no more. The next night the child came again, and held a little light in its hand, and said, "Look, mother, my shroud is nearly dry, and I can rest in my grave." Then the mother gave her sorrow into God's keeping, and bore it quietly and patiently, and the child came no more, but slept in its little bed beneath the earth.

1812

. . .

THE FIVE PARTS OF PLOT

Even compact and simple plots, like that of THE SHROUD, have the same five parts or phases as lengthy and complex plots: (1) exposition, (2) rising action, (3) climax or turning point, (4) falling action, and (5) conclusion or resolution. The following diagram, named Freytag's pyramid after the nineteenth-century German scholar Gustav Freytag, maps out a typical plot structure:

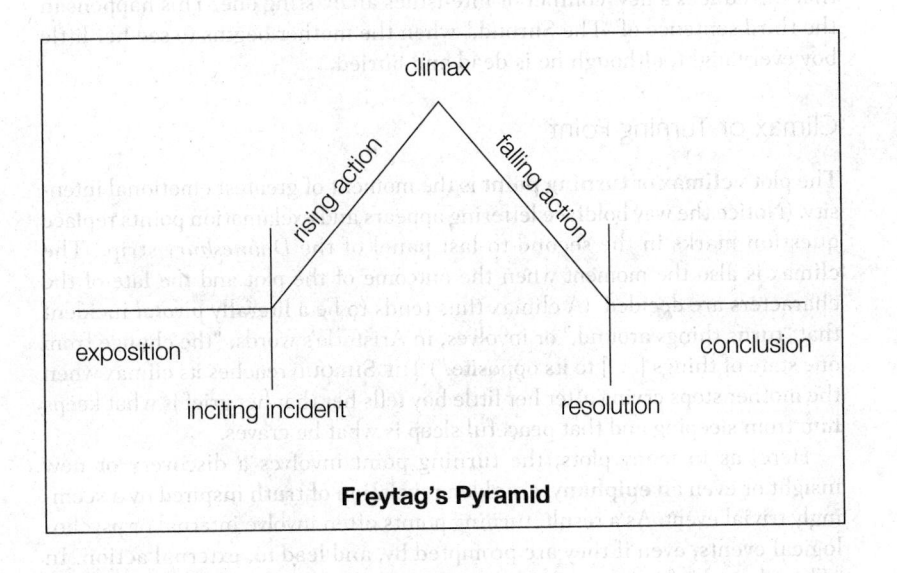

Freytag's Pyramid

Exposition

The first part of the plot, called the **exposition**, introduces the characters, their situations, and, usually, a time and place, giving us all the basic information we need to understand what is to come. In longer works of fiction, exposition may go on for paragraphs or even pages, and some exposition may well be deferred until later phases of the plot. But in our examples, the exposition is all up-front and brief: Trudeau's first panel shows us a teacher (or at least his words), a group of students, and a classroom; the Grimms' first sentence introduces a mother, her young son, and the powerful love she feels for him.

Exposition usually reveals some source or seed of potential conflict in the initial situation, of which the characters may be as yet unaware. In Trudeau's cartoon, the contrast between the talkative teacher, who expects "independent thought" from those in his class, and the silent, scribbling students suggests a conflict in the making. So, too, does the Grimms' statement that the mother "worshipped" her boy "above everything" else in a world in which nothing and no one lasts forever.

Rising Action

By suggesting a conflict, exposition may blend into the second phase of the plot, the **rising action**, which begins with an **inciting incident** or *destabilizing event*—that is, some action that destabilizes the initial situation and incites open conflict, as does the death of the little boy in the second sentence of the folktale. Typically, what keeps the action rising is a **complication**, an event that introduces a new conflict or intensifies an existing one. This happens in the third sentence of "The Shroud," when the mother begins to see her little boy every night, although he is dead and buried.

Climax or Turning Point

The plot's **climax** or **turning point** is the moment of greatest emotional intensity. (Notice the way boldface lettering appears and exclamation points replace question marks in the second-to-last panel of the *Doonesbury* strip.) The climax is also the moment when the outcome of the plot and the fate of the characters are decided. (A climax thus tends to be a literally *pivotal* incident that "turns things around," or involves, in Aristotle's words, "the change from one state of things [. . .] to its opposite.") THE SHROUD reaches its climax when the mother stops crying after her little boy tells her that her grief is what keeps him from sleeping and that peaceful sleep is what he craves.

Here, as in many plots, the turning point involves a discovery or new insight or even an **epiphany**, a sudden revelation of truth inspired by a seemingly trivial event. As a result, turning points often involve internal or psychological events, even if they are prompted by, and lead to, external action. In "The Shroud," for instance, the mother's new insight results in different behavior: She "wept no more."

Sometimes, though, critics differentiate between the story's climax and the **crisis** that precedes and precipitates it. In "The Shroud," for example, these critics would describe the crisis as the moment when the son confronts the mother with information that implicitly requires her to make a choice, the climax as the moment when she makes it. This distinction might be especially helpful when you grapple with longer works of fiction in which much more time and action intervenes between the crisis and the climax.

Falling Action

The **falling action** brings a release of emotional tension and moves us toward the resolution of the conflict or conflicts. This release occurs in "The Shroud" when the boy speaks for the second and last time, assuring his mother that her more peaceful demeanor is giving him peace as well.

In some works of fiction, resolution is achieved through an utterly unexpected twist, as in "Meanwhile, unknown to our hero, the marines were just on the other side of the hill," or "Susan rolled over in bed and realized the whole thing had been just a dream." Such a device is sometimes called a **deus ex machina**. (This Latin term literally means "god out of a machine" and derives from the ancient theatrical practice of using a machine to lower onto the stage a god who solves the problems of the human characters.)

Conclusion

Finally, just as a plot begins with a situation that is later destabilized, so its **conclusion** presents us with a new and at least somewhat stable situation— one that gives a sense of closure because the conflict or conflicts have been resolved, if only temporarily and not necessarily in the way we or the characters had expected. In "The Shroud," that resolution comes in the last sentence, in which the mother bears her grief "quietly and patiently" and the child quietly sleeps his last sleep. The final *Doonesbury* panel presents us with a situation that is essentially the reverse of the one with which the strip begins—with the teacher silently slumped over his podium, his students suddenly talking to each other instead of scribbling down his words. Many plots instead end with a situation that outwardly looks almost identical to the one with which they began. But thanks to all that has happened between the story's beginning and its end, the final "steady state" at which the characters arrive can never be exactly the same as the one in which they started. A key question to ask at the end of a work of fiction is precisely why, as well as how, things are different.

Some fictional works may also include a final section called an **epilogue**, which ties up loose ends left dangling in the conclusion proper, updates us on what has happened to the characters since their conflicts were resolved, and/or provides some sort of commentary on the story's larger significance. (An epilogue is thus a little like this paragraph, which comes after we have concluded our discussion of the five phases of plot but still feel that there is one more term to deal with.)

A Note on *Dénouement*

In discussions of plot, you will very often encounter the French word **dénouement** (literally, "untying," as of a knot). In this anthology, however, we generally try to avoid using *dénouement* because it can be, and often is, used in three different, potentially contradictory ways—as a synonym for *falling action*; as a synonym for *conclusion* or *resolution*; and even as a label for a certain kind of epilogue.

Plot Summary: An Example and an Exercise

Although any good **plot summary** should be a relatively brief recounting (or *synopsis*) of what happens in a work of fiction, it need not necessarily tell what happens in the same order that the work itself does. As a result, many a plot summary is in fact more like an action summary in the sense that we define the terms *action* and *plot* in this book. But unless you have a good reason for reordering events, it is generally a good idea to follow the plot. The following plot summary of Raymond Carver's CATHEDRAL does just that:

> The narrator is annoyed to learn that his wife's old friend Robert, a blind man who once employed her as a reader, is coming to visit the couple. The wife has corresponded with her friend for years via cassette tapes, describing the details of her early marriage, divorce, and remarriage to her husband, the narrator. Uncomfortable with the prospect of having a blind person in his home, the narrator is surprised by Robert's appearance and behavior: his booming voice and full beard are not what he expected, and he eats, drinks, and smokes marijuana with relish. After dinner the three watch television. After the narrator's wife has fallen asleep, a program about cathedrals begins. The narrator asks Robert if he knows what cathedrals look like or represent, and Robert, admitting that he does not, asks the narrator to draw one. With Robert's hand lying on top of his own, the narrator traces roofs, spires, arches, and even people. Eventually Robert instructs the narrator to close his eyes and continue drawing. The narrator reports that this experience was like nothing else in my life up to now. (From "Raymond Carver: 'Cathedral,'" *Characters in Twentieth Century Literature*, Book Two [Gale Research, 1995].)

Now try this yourself: Choose any of the stories in this anthology and write a one-paragraph plot summary. Then, in a paragraph or two, reflect on your choices about which details to include, which to omit, and how to order them (especially if you've deviated from the plot). What does your summary imply about the story's focus, meaning, and significance? Now repeat the exercise, summarizing the story in a different way and then reflecting on the significance and effect of the changes you've made.

Alternatively, try the same exercise with a friend who has also read the story: Each of you should write your own summary; then exchange them and (separately or together) write a few paragraphs comparing your summaries and reflecting on the significance of the similarities and differences.

COMMON PLOT TYPES

If most plots are essentially variations on the same five-part pattern, some plots have even more features in common. As you think back over the fiction you have read and the movies you have seen (not to mention the video games you have played), you might be surprised to discover just how many of their plots involve a quest—a character or characters' journey to find something or someone that seems, at least at first, of tremendous material or spiritual value. Traditionally, that requires a literal journey, the challenge being not only to find and acquire the object but also to return home with it. Such quests occur often in folktales and are a **convention** of chivalric **romance** and **epic**, in which the questing heroes are often men of high rank sent on their quests by someone with even greater power—a god, a wizard, a prophet, a king. And many works of modern fiction—from James Joyce's ARABY to Tolkien's *Lord of the Rings* to William Gibson's science-fiction classic *Neuromancer* (1984)—depend for their full effect on our knowledge of the conventions of traditional quest plots.

Many fictional works both ancient and modern also (or instead) follow patterns derived from the two most important and ancient forms (or subgenres) of drama—**tragedy** and **comedy**. Tragic plots, on the one hand, trace a downward movement centering on a character's fall from fortune into misfortune and isolation; they end unhappily, often with death. Comedic plots, on the other hand, tend to end happily, often with marriage or some other act of social integration and celebration.

. . .

As you read the stories in this chapter, or any other work of fiction, think about what sets each one apart when it comes to plot; how each uses variations on common plot conventions; how each generates, fulfills, and often frustrates our expectations about the action to come; and how each uses sequence, pace, and other techniques to endow action with both emotional charge and meaning. When it comes to action and plot, every good story holds its own surprises and offers a unique answer to the nagging question *What happened?*

Questions about Plot

- Read the first few paragraphs and then stop. What potential for conflict do you see here? What do you expect to happen in the rest of the story?
- What is the inciting incident or destabilizing event? How and why does this event destabilize the initial situation?
- How would you describe the conflict that ultimately develops? To what extent is it external, internal, or both? What, if any, complications or secondary conflicts arise?
- Where, when, how, and why does the story defy your expectations about what will happen next? What in this story—and in your experience of other stories—created these expectations?
- What is the climax or turning point? Why and how so?
- How is the conflict resolved? How and why might this resolution fulfill or defy your expectations? How and why is the situation at the end of the story different from what it was at the beginning?
- Looking back at the story as a whole, what seems especially significant and effective about its plot, especially in terms of the sequence and pace of the action?
- Does this plot follow any common plot pattern? Is there, for example, a quest of any kind? Or does this plot follow a tragic or comedic pattern?

JAMES BALDWIN
(1924–87)
Sonny's Blues

For much of his life, James Baldwin was a leading literary spokesman for civil rights and racial equality in America. Born in New York City but long a resident of France, he first attracted critical attention with two extraordinary novels, *Go Tell It on the Mountain* (1953), which draws on his past as a teenage preacher in the Fireside Pentecostal Church, and *Giovanni's Room* (1956), which deals with the anguish of being black and homosexual in a largely white and heterosexual society. Other works include the novels *Another Country* (1962) and *If Beale Street Could Talk* (1974), the play *Blues for Mr. Charlie* (1964), and a story collection, *Going to Meet the Man* (1965). Baldwin is perhaps best remembered as a perceptive and eloquent essayist, the author of *Notes of a Native Son* (1955), *Nobody Knows My Name* (1961), *The Fire Next Time* (1963), *No Name in the Street* (1972), and *The Price of a Ticket* (1985).

read about it in the paper, in the subway, on my way to work. I read it, and I couldn't believe it, and I read it again. Then perhaps I just stared at it, at the newsprint spelling out his name, spelling out the story. I stared at it in the swinging lights of the subway car, and in the faces and bodies of the people, and in my own face, trapped in the darkness which roared outside.

It was not to be believed and I kept telling myself that, as I walked from the subway station to the high school. And at the same time I couldn't doubt it. I was scared, scared for Sonny. He became real to me again. A great block of ice got settled in my belly and kept melting there slowly all day long, while I taught my classes algebra. It was a special kind of ice. It kept melting, sending trickles of ice water all up and down my veins, but it never got less. Sometimes it hardened and seemed to expand until I felt my guts were going to come spilling out or that I was going to choke or scream. This would always be at a moment when I was remembering some specific thing Sonny had once said or done.

When he was about as old as the boys in my classes his face had been bright and open, there was a lot of copper in it; and he'd had wonderfully direct brown eyes, and great gentleness and privacy. I wondered what he looked like now. He had been picked up, the evening before, in a raid on an apartment downtown, for peddling and using heroin.

I couldn't believe it: but what I mean by that is that I couldn't find any room for it anywhere inside me. I had kept it outside me for a long time. I hadn't wanted to know. I had had suspicions, but I didn't name them, I kept putting them away. I told myself that Sonny was wild, but he wasn't crazy. And he'd always been a good boy, he hadn't ever turned hard or evil or disrespectful, the way kids can, so quick, so quick, especially in Harlem. I didn't want to believe that I'd ever see my brother going down, coming to nothing, all that light in his face gone out, in the condition I'd already seen so many others. Yet it had happened and here I was, talking about algebra to a lot of boys who might, every one of them for all I knew, be popping off needles every time they went to the head.[1] Maybe it did more for them than algebra could.

I was sure that the first time Sonny had ever had horse,[2] he couldn't have been much older than these boys were now. These boys, now, were living as we'd been living then, they were growing up with a rush and their heads bumped abruptly against the low ceiling of their actual possibilities. They were filled with rage. All they really knew were two darknesses, the darkness of their lives, which was now closing in on them, and the darkness of the movies, which had blinded them to that other darkness, and in

---

1. Lavatory.
2. Heroin.

which they now, vindictively, dreamed, at once more together than they were at any other time, and more alone.

When the last bell rang, the last class ended, I let out my breath. It seemed I'd been holding it for all that time. My clothes were wet—I may have looked as though I'd been sitting in a steam bath, all dressed up, all afternoon. I sat alone in the classroom a long time. I listened to the boys outside, downstairs, shouting and cursing and laughing. Their laughter struck me for perhaps the first time. It was not the joyous laughter which—God knows why—one associates with children. It was mocking and insular, its intent was to denigrate. It was disenchanted, and in this, also, lay the authority of their curses. Perhaps I was listening to them because I was thinking about my brother and in them I heard my brother. And myself.

One boy was whistling a tune, at once very complicated and very simple, it seemed to be pouring out of him as though he were a bird, and it sounded very cool and moving through all that harsh, bright air, only just holding its own through all those other sounds.

I stood up and walked over to the window and looked down into the courtyard. It was the beginning of the spring and the sap was rising in the boys. A teacher passed through them every now and again, quickly, as though he or she couldn't wait to get out of that courtyard, to get those boys out of their sight and off their minds. I started collecting my stuff. I thought I'd better get home and talk to Isabel.

The courtyard was almost deserted by the time I got downstairs. I saw this boy standing in the shadow of a doorway, looking just like Sonny. I almost called his name. Then I saw that it wasn't Sonny, but somebody we used to know, a boy from around our block. He'd been Sonny's friend. He'd never been mine, having been too young for me, and, anyway, I'd never liked him. And now, even though he was a grown-up man, he still hung around that block, still spent hours on the street corners, was always high and raggy. I used to run into him from time to time and he'd often work around to asking me for a quarter or fifty cents. He always had some real good excuse, too, and I always gave it to him. I don't know why.

10   But now, abruptly, I hated him. I couldn't stand the way he looked at me, partly like a dog, partly like a cunning child. I wanted to ask him what the hell he was doing in the school courtyard.

He sort of shuffled over to me, and he said, "I see you got the papers. So you already know about it."

"You mean about Sonny? Yes, I already know about it. How come they didn't get you?"

He grinned. It made him repulsive and it also brought to mind what he'd looked like as a kid. "I wasn't there. I stay away from them people."

"Good for you." I offered him a cigarette and I watched him through the smoke. "You come all the way down here just to tell me about Sonny?" "That's right." He was sort of shaking his head and his eyes looked strange,   15 as though they were about to cross. The bright sun deadened his damp dark brown skin and it made his eyes look yellow and showed up the dirt in his kinked hair. He smelled funky. I moved a little away from him and I said, "Well, thanks. But I already know about it and I got to get home."

"I'll walk you a little ways," he said. We started walking. There were a couple of kids still loitering in the courtyard and one of them said good-night to me and looked strangely at the boy beside me.

"What're you going to do?" he asked me. "I mean, about Sonny?"

"Look. I haven't seen Sonny for over a year, I'm not sure I'm going to do anything. Anyway, what the hell *can* I do?"

"That's right," he said quickly, "ain't nothing you can do. Can't much help old Sonny no more, I guess."

It was what I was thinking and so it seemed to me he had no right to   20 say it.

"I'm surprised at Sonny, though," he went on—he had a funny way of talking, he looked straight ahead as though he were talking to himself—"I thought Sonny was a smart boy, I thought he was too smart to get hung."

"I guess he thought so too," I said sharply, "and that's how he got hung. And how about you? You're pretty goddamn smart, I bet."

Then he looked directly at me, just for a minute. "I ain't smart," he said. "If I was smart, I'd have reached for a pistol a long time ago."

"Look. Don't tell *me* your sad story, if it was up to me, I'd give you one." Then I felt guilty—guilty, probably, for never having supposed that the poor bastard *had* a story of his own, much less a sad one, and I asked, quickly, "What's going to happen to him now?"

He didn't answer this. He was off by himself some place.   25

"Funny thing," he said, and from his tone we might have been discussing the quickest way to get to Brooklyn, "when I saw the papers this morning, the first thing I asked myself was if I had anything to do with it. I felt sort of responsible."

I began to listen more carefully. The subway station was on the corner, just before us, and I stopped. He stopped, too. We were in front of a bar and he ducked slightly, peering in, but whoever he was looking for didn't seem to be there. The juke box was blasting away with something black and bouncy and I half watched the barmaid as she danced her way from the juke box to her place behind the bar. And I watched her face as she laughingly responded to something someone said to her, still keeping time to the music. When she smiled one saw the little girl, one sensed the doomed, still-struggling woman beneath the battered face of the semi-whore.

"I never *give* Sonny nothing," the boy said finally, "but a long time ago I come to school high and Sonny asked me how it felt." He paused, I couldn't bear to watch him, I watched the barmaid, and I listened to the music which seemed to be causing the pavement to shake. "I told him it felt great." The music stopped, the barmaid paused and watched the juke box until the music began again. "It did."

All this was carrying me some place I didn't want to go. I certainly didn't want to know how it felt. It filled everything, the people, the houses, the music, the dark, quicksilver barmaid, with menace; and this menace was their reality.

30   "What's going to happen to him now?" I asked again.

"They'll send him away some place and they'll try to cure him." He shook his head. "Maybe he'll even think he's kicked the habit. Then they'll let him loose"—he gestured, throwing his cigarette into the gutter. "That's all."

"What do you mean, that's *all*?"

But I knew what he meant.

"I *mean*, that's *all*." He turned his head and looked at me, pulling down the corners of his mouth. "Don't you know what I mean?" he asked, softly.

35   "How the hell *would* I know what you mean?" I almost whispered it, I don't know why.

"That's right," he said to the air, "how would *he* know what I mean?" He turned toward me again, patient and calm, and yet I somehow felt him shaking, shaking as though he were going to fall apart. I felt that ice in my guts again, the dread I'd felt all afternoon; and again I watched the barmaid, moving about the bar, washing glasses, and singing. "Listen. They'll let him out and then it'll just start all over again. That's what I mean."

"You mean—they'll let him out. And then he'll just start working his way back in again. You mean he'll never kick the habit. Is that what you mean?"

"That's right," he said, cheerfully. "*You* see what I mean."

"Tell me," I said at last, "why does he want to die? He must want to die, he's killing himself, why does he want to die?"

40   He looked at me in surprise. He licked his lips. "He don't want to die. He wants to live. Don't nobody want to die, ever."

Then I wanted to ask him—too many things. He could not have answered, or if he had, I could not have borne the answers. I started walking. "Well, I guess it's none of my business."

"It's going to be rough on old Sonny," he said. We reached the subway station. "This is your station?" he asked. I nodded. I took one step down. "Damn!" he said, suddenly. I looked up at him. He grinned again. "Damn it if I didn't leave all my money home. You ain't got a dollar on you, have you? Just for a couple of days, is all."

All at once something inside gave and threatened to come pouring out of me. I didn't hate him any more. I felt that in another moment I'd start crying like a child.

"Sure," I said. "Don't sweat." I looked in my wallet and didn't have a dollar, I only had a five. "Here," I said. "That hold you?"

He didn't look at it—he didn't want to look at it. A terrible, closed look 45 came over his face, as though he were keeping the number on the bill a secret from him and me. "Thanks," he said, and now he was dying to see me go. "Don't worry about Sonny. Maybe I'll write him or something."

"Sure," I said. "You do that. So long."

"Be seeing you," he said. I went on down the steps.

And I didn't write Sonny or send him anything for a long time. When I finally did, it was just after my little girl died, and he wrote me back a letter which made me feel like a bastard.

Here's what he said:

Dear brother, 50
    You don't know how much I needed to hear from you. I wanted to write you many a time but I dug how much I must have hurt you and so I didn't write. But now I feel like a man who's been trying to climb up out of some deep, real deep and funky hole and just saw the sun up there, outside. I got to get outside.
    I can't tell you much about how I got here. I mean I don't know how to tell you. I guess I was afraid of something or I was trying to escape from something and you know I have never been very strong in the head (smile). I'm glad Mama and Daddy are dead and can't see what's happened to their son and I swear if I'd known what I was doing I would never have hurt you so, you and a lot of other fine people who were nice to me and who believed in me.
    I don't want you to think it had anything to do with me being a musician. It's more than that. Or maybe less than that. I can't get anything straight in my head down here and I try not to think about what's going to happen to me when I get outside again. Sometime I think I'm going to flip and *never* get outside and sometime I think I'll come straight back. I tell you one thing, though, I'd rather blow my brains out than go through this again. But that's what they all say, so they tell me. If I tell you when I'm coming to New York and if you could meet me, I sure would appreciate it. Give my love to Isabel and the kids and I was sure sorry to hear about little Gracie. I wish I could be like Mama and say

the Lord's will be done, but I don't know it seems to me that trouble is the one thing that never does get stopped and I don't know what good it does to blame it on the Lord. But maybe it does some good if you believe it.

Your brother,
Sonny

Then I kept in constant touch with him and I sent him whatever I could and I went to meet him when he came back to New York. When I saw him many things I thought I had forgotten came flooding back to me. This was because I had begun, finally, to wonder about Sonny, about the life that Sonny lived inside. This life, whatever it was, had made him older and thinner and it had deepened the distant stillness in which he had always moved. He looked very unlike my baby brother. Yet, when he smiled, when we shook hands, the baby brother I'd never known looked out from the depths of his private life, like an animal waiting to be coaxed into the light.

"How you been keeping?" he asked me.
55 "All right. And you?"
"Just fine." He was smiling all over his face. "It's good to see you again."
"It's good to see you."
The seven years' difference in our ages lay between us like a chasm: I wondered if these years would ever operate between us as a bridge. I was remembering, and it made it hard to catch my breath, that I had been there when he was born; and I had heard the first words he had ever spoken. When he started to walk, he walked from our mother straight to me. I caught him just before he fell when he took the first steps he ever took in this world.
"How's Isabel?"
60 "Just fine. She's dying to see you."
"And the boys?"
"They're fine, too. They're anxious to see their uncle."
"Oh, come on. You know they don't remember me."
"Are you kidding? Of course they remember you."
65 He grinned again. We got into a taxi. We had a lot to say to each other, far too much to know how to begin.
As the taxi began to move, I asked, "You still want to go to India?"
He laughed. "You still remember that. Hell, no. This place is Indian enough for me."
"It used to belong to them," I said.
And he laughed again. "They damn sure knew what they were doing when they got rid of it."

Years ago, when he was around fourteen, he'd been all hipped on the
idea of going to India. He read books about people sitting on rocks, naked,
in all kinds of weather, but mostly bad, naturally, and walking barefoot
through hot coals and arriving at wisdom. I used to say that it sounded to
me as though they were getting away from wisdom as fast as they could. I
think he sort of looked down on me for that.

"Do you mind," he asked, "if we have the driver drive alongside the
park? On the west side—I haven't seen the city in so long."

"Of course not," I said. I was afraid that I might sound as though I were
humoring him, but I hoped he wouldn't take it that way.

So we drove along, between the green of the park and the stony, lifeless
elegance of hotels and apartment buildings, toward the vivid, killing streets
of our childhood. These streets hadn't changed, though housing projects
jutted up out of them now like rocks in the middle of a boiling sea. Most of
the houses in which we had grown up had vanished, as had the stores from
which we had stolen, the basements in which we had first tried sex, the
rooftops from which we had hurled tin cans and bricks. But houses exactly
like the houses of our past yet dominated the landscape, boys exactly like
the boys we once had been found themselves smothering in these houses,
came down into the streets for light and air and found themselves encircled
by disaster. Some escaped the trap, most didn't. Those who got out always
left something of themselves behind, as some animals amputate a leg and
leave it in the trap. It might be said, perhaps, that I had escaped, after all, I
was a school teacher; or that Sonny had, he hadn't lived in Harlem for years.
Yet, as the cab moved uptown through streets which seemed, with a rush,
to darken with dark people, and as I covertly studied Sonny's face, it came
to me that what we both were seeking through our separate cab windows
was that part of ourselves which had been left behind. It's always at the
hour of trouble and confrontation that the missing member aches.

We hit 110th Street and started rolling up Lenox Avenue. And I'd known
this avenue all my life, but it seemed to me again, as it had seemed on the
day I'd first heard about Sonny's trouble, filled with a hidden menace
which was its very breath of life.

"We almost there," said Sonny.

"Almost." We were both too nervous to say anything more.

We live in a housing project. It hasn't been up long. A few days after it was
up it seemed uninhabitably new, now, of course, it's already rundown. It
looks like a parody of the good, clean, faceless life—God knows the people
who live in it do their best to make it a parody. The beat-looking grass
lying around isn't enough to make their lives green, the hedges will never
hold out the streets, and they know it. The big windows fool no one, they
aren't big enough to make space out of no space. They don't bother with

the windows, they watch the TV screen instead. The playground is most popular with the children who don't play at jacks, or skip rope, or roller skate, or swing, and they can be found in it after dark. We moved in partly because it's not too far from where I teach, and partly for the kids; but it's really just like the houses in which Sonny and I grew up. The same things happen, they'll have the same things to remember. The moment Sonny and I started into the house I had the feeling that I was simply bringing him back into the danger he had almost died trying to escape.

Sonny has never been talkative. So I don't know why I was sure he'd be dying to talk to me when supper was over the first night. Everything went fine, the oldest boy remembered him, and the youngest boy liked him, and Sonny had remembered to bring something for each of them; and Isabel, who is really much nicer than I am, more open and giving, had gone to a lot of trouble about dinner and was genuinely glad to see him. And she's always been able to tease Sonny in a way that I haven't. It was nice to see her face so vivid again and to hear her laugh and watch her make Sonny laugh. She wasn't, or, anyway, she didn't seem to be, at all uneasy or embarrassed. She chatted as though there were no subject which had to be avoided and she got Sonny past his first, faint stiffness. And thank God she was there, for I was filled with that icy dread again. Everything I did seemed awkward to me, and everything I said sounded freighted with hidden meaning. I was trying to remember everything I'd heard about dope addiction and I couldn't help watching Sonny for signs. I wasn't doing it out of malice. I was trying to find out something about my brother. I was dying to hear him tell me he was safe.

"Safe!" my father grunted, whenever Mama suggested trying to move to a neighborhood which might be safer for children. "Safe, hell! Ain't no place safe for kids, nor nobody."

80   He always went on like this, but he wasn't, ever, really as bad as he sounded, not even on weekends, when he got drunk. As a matter of fact, he was always on the lookout for "something a little better," but he died before he found it. He died suddenly, during a drunken weekend in the middle of the war, when Sonny was fifteen. He and Sonny hadn't ever got on too well. And this was partly because Sonny was the apple of his father's eye. It was because he loved Sonny so much and was frightened for him, that he was always fighting with him. It doesn't do any good to fight with Sonny. Sonny just moves back, inside himself, where he can't be reached. But the principal reason that they never hit it off is that they were so much alike. Daddy was big and rough and loud-talking, just the opposite of Sonny, but they both had—that same privacy.

Mama tried to tell me something about this, just after Daddy died. I was home on leave from the army.

This was the last time I ever saw my mother alive. Just the same, this picture gets all mixed up in my mind with pictures I had of her when she was younger. The way I always see her is the way she used to be on a Sunday afternoon, say, when the old folks were talking after the big Sunday dinner. I always see her wearing pale blue. She'd be sitting on the sofa. And my father would be sitting in the easy chair, not far from her. And the living room would be full of church folks and relatives. There they sit, in chairs all around the living room, and the night is creeping up outside, but nobody knows it yet. You can see the darkness growing against the windowpanes and you hear the street noises every now and again, or maybe the jangling beat of a tambourine from one of the churches close by, but it's real quiet in the room. For a moment nobody's talking, but every face looks darkening, like the sky outside. And my mother rocks a little from the waist, and my father's eyes are closed. Everyone is looking at something a child can't see. For a minute they've forgotten the children. Maybe a kid is lying on the rug, half asleep. Maybe somebody's got a kid in his lap and is absent-mindedly stroking the kid's head. Maybe there's a kid, quiet and big-eyed, curled up in a big chair in the corner. The silence, the darkness coming, and the darkness in the faces frighten the child obscurely. He hopes that the hand which strokes his forehead will never stop—will never die. He hopes that there will never come a time when the old folks won't be sitting around the living room, talking about where they've come from, and what they've seen, and what's happened to them and their kinfolk.

But something deep and watchful in the child knows that this is bound to end, is already ending. In a moment someone will get up and turn on the light. Then the old folks will remember the children and they won't talk any more that day. And when light fills the room, the child is filled with darkness. He knows that every time this happens he's moved just a little closer to that darkness outside. The darkness outside is what the old folks have been talking about. It's what they've come from. It's what they endure. The child knows that they won't talk any more because if he knows too much about what's happened to *them,* he'll know too much too soon, about what's going to happen to *him.*

The last time I talked to my mother, I remember I was restless. I wanted to get out and see Isabel. We weren't married then and we had a lot to straighten out between us.

There Mama sat, in black, by the window. She was humming an old 85 church song, *Lord, you brought me from a long ways off.* Sonny was out somewhere. Mama kept watching the streets.

"I don't know," she said, "if I'll ever see you again, after you go off from here. But I hope you'll remember the things I tried to teach you."

"Don't talk like that," I said, and smiled. "You'll be here a long time yet."
She smiled, too, but she said nothing. She was quiet for a long time.
And I said, "Mama, don't you worry about nothing. I'll be writing all the
time, and you be getting the checks. . . ."

"I want to talk to you about your brother," she said, suddenly. "If anything happens to me he ain't going to have nobody to look out for him."

90   "Mama," I said, "ain't nothing going to happen to you *or* Sonny. Sonny's
all right. He's a good boy and he's got good sense."

"It ain't a question of his being a good boy," Mama said, "nor of his having good sense. It ain't only the bad ones, nor yet the dumb ones that gets
sucked under." She stopped, looking at me. "Your Daddy once had a brother,"
she said, and she smiled in a way that made me feel she was in pain. "You
didn't never know that, did you?"

"No," I said, "I never knew that," and I watched her face.

"Oh, yes," she said, "your Daddy had a brother." She looked out of the
window again. "I know you never saw your Daddy cry. But *I* did—many a
time, through all these years."

I asked her, "What happened to his brother? How come nobody's ever
talked about him?"

95   This was the first time I ever saw my mother look old.

"His brother got killed," she said, "when he was just a little younger than
you are now. I knew him. He was a fine boy. He was maybe a little full of
the devil, but he didn't mean nobody no harm."

Then she stopped and the room was silent, exactly as it had sometimes
been on those Sunday afternoons. Mama kept looking out into the streets.

"He used to have a job in the mill," she said, "and, like all young folks,
he just liked to perform on Saturday nights. Saturday nights, him and your
father would drift around to different places, go to dances and things like
that, or just sit around with people they knew, and your father's brother
would sing, he had a fine voice, and play along with himself on his guitar.
Well, this particular Saturday night, him and your father was coming home
from some place, and they were both a little drunk and there was a moon
that night, it was bright like day. Your father's brother was feeling kind of
good, and he was whistling to himself, and he had his guitar slung over his
shoulder. They was coming down a hill and beneath them was a road that
turned off from the highway. Well, your father's brother, being always kind
of frisky, decided to run down this hill, and he did, with that guitar banging and clanging behind him, and he ran across the road, and he was making water behind a tree. And your father was sort of amused at him and he
was still coming down the hill, kind of slow. Then he heard a car motor
and that same minute his brother stepped from behind the tree, into the
road, in the moonlight. And he started to cross the road. And your father

started to run down the hill, he says he don't know why. This car was full of white men. They was all drunk, and when they seen your father's brother they let out a great whoop and holler and they aimed the car straight at him. They was having fun, they just wanted to scare him, the way they do sometimes, you know. But they was drunk. And I guess the boy, being drunk, too, and scared, kind of lost his head. By the time he jumped it was too late. Your father says he heard his brother scream when the car rolled over him, and he heard the wood of that guitar when it give, and he heard them strings go flying, and he heard them white men shouting, and the car kept on a-going and it ain't stopped till this day. And, time your father got down the hill, his brother weren't nothing but blood and pulp."

Tears were gleaming on my mother's face. There wasn't anything I could say.

"He never mentioned it," she said, "because I never let him mention it   100 before you children. Your Daddy was like a crazy man that night and for many a night thereafter. He says he never in his life seen anything as dark as that road after the lights of that car had gone away. Weren't nothing, weren't nobody on that road, just your Daddy and his brother and that busted guitar. Oh, yes. Your Daddy never did really get right again. Till the day he died he weren't sure but that every white man he saw was the man that killed his brother."

She stopped and took out her handkerchief and dried her eyes and looked at me.

"I ain't telling you all this," she said, "to make you scared or bitter or to make you hate nobody. I'm telling you this because you got a brother. And the world ain't changed."

I guess I didn't want to believe this. I guess she saw this in my face. She turned away from me, toward the window again, searching those streets.

"But I praise my Redeemer," she said at last, "that He called your Daddy home before me. I ain't saying it to throw no flowers at myself, but, I declare, it keeps me from feeling too cast down to know I helped your father get safely through this world. Your father always acted like he was the roughest, strongest man on earth. And everybody took him to be like that. But if he hadn't had me there—to see his tears!"

She was crying again. Still, I couldn't move. I said, "Lord, Lord, Mama,   105 I didn't know it was like that."

"Oh, honey," she said, "there's a lot that you don't know. But you are going to find out." She stood up from the window and came over to me. "You got to hold on to your brother," she said, "and don't let him fall, no matter what it looks like is happening to him and no matter how evil you gets with him. You going to be evil with him many a time. But don't you forget what I told you, you hear?"

"I won't forget," I said. "Don't you worry, I won't forget. I won't let nothing happen to Sonny."

My mother smiled as though she was amused at something she saw in my face. Then, "You may not be able to stop nothing from happening. But you got to let him know you's *there*."

Two days later I was married, and then I was gone. And I had a lot of things on my mind and I pretty well forgot my promise to Mama until I got shipped home on a special furlough for her funeral.

110 And, after the funeral, with just Sonny and me alone in the empty kitchen, I tried to find out something about him.

"What do you want to do?" I asked him.

"I'm going to be a musician," he said.

For he had graduated, in the time I had been away, from dancing to the juke box to finding out who was playing what, and what they were doing with it, and he had bought himself a set of drums.

"You mean, you want to be a drummer?" I somehow had the feeling that being a drummer might be all right for other people but not for my brother Sonny.

115 "I don't think," he said, looking at me very gravely, "that I'll ever be a good drummer. But I think I can play a piano."

I frowned. I'd never played the role of the oldest brother quite so seriously before, had scarcely ever, in fact, *asked* Sonny a damn thing. I sensed myself in the presence of something I didn't really know how to handle, didn't understand. So I made my frown a little deeper as I asked: "What kind of musician do you want to be?"

He grinned. "How many kinds do you think there are?"

"Be *serious*," I said.

He laughed, throwing his head back, and then looked at me. "I *am* serious."

120 "Well, then, for Christ's sake, stop kidding around and answer a serious question. I mean, do you want to be a concert pianist, you want to play classical music and all that, or—or what?" Long before I finished he was laughing again. "For Christ's *sake*, Sonny!"

He sobered, but with difficulty. "I'm sorry. But you sound so—*scared!*" and he was off again.

"Well, you may think it's funny now, baby, but it's not going to be so funny when you have to make your living at it, let me tell you *that*." I was furious because I knew he was laughing at me and I didn't know why.

"No," he said, very sober now, and afraid, perhaps, that he'd hurt me, "I don't want to be a classical pianist. That isn't what interests me. I mean"—he paused, looking hard at me, as though his eyes would help me to understand, and then gestured helplessly, as though perhaps his hand would help—"I mean, I'll have a lot of studying to do, and I'll have to study *everything*, but, I mean, I want to play *with*—jazz musicians." He stopped. "I want to play jazz," he said.

Well, the word had never before sounded as heavy, as real, as it sounded that afternoon in Sonny's mouth. I just looked at him and I was probably frowning a real frown by this time. I simply couldn't see why on earth he'd want to spend his time hanging around nightclubs, clowning around on bandstands, while people pushed each other around a dance floor. It seemed—beneath him, somehow. I had never thought about it before, had never been forced to, but I suppose I had always put jazz musicians in a class with what Daddy called "good-time people."

"Are you *serious*?" 125

"Hell, *yes*, I'm serious."

He looked more helpless than ever, and annoyed, and deeply hurt.

I suggested, helpfully: "You mean—like Louis Armstrong?"[3]

His face closed as though I'd struck him. "No. I'm not talking about none of that old-time, down-home crap."

"Well, look, Sonny, I'm sorry, don't get mad. I just don't altogether get it, 130 that's all. Name somebody—you know, a jazz musician you admire."

"Bird."

"Who?"

"Bird! Charlie Parker![4] Don't they teach you nothing in the goddamn army?"

I lit a cigarette. I was surprised and then a little amused to discover that I was trembling. "I've been out of touch," I said. "You'll have to be patient with me. Now. Who's this Parker character?"

"He's just one of the greatest jazz musicians alive," said Sonny, sullenly, 135 his hands in his pockets, his back to me. "Maybe *the* greatest," he added, bitterly, "that's probably why *you* never heard of him."

"All right," I said, "I'm ignorant. I'm sorry. I'll go out and buy all the cat's records right away, all right?"

"It don't," said Sonny, with dignity, "make any difference to me. I don't care what you listen to. Don't do me no favors."

I was beginning to realize that I'd never seen him so upset before. With another part of my mind I was thinking that this would probably turn

---

3. New Orleans–born trumpeter and singer (1901–71); by the 1950s, his music would have seemed old-fashioned to a jazz aficionado.
4. Charlie ("Bird") Parker (1920–55), brilliant saxophonist and jazz innovator; working in New York in the mid-1940s, he developed, with Dizzy Gillespie and others, the style of jazz called "bebop." He was a narcotics addict.

out to be one of those things kids go through and that I shouldn't make it seem important by pushing it too hard. Still, I didn't think it would do any harm to ask: "Doesn't all this take a lot of time? Can you make a living at it?"

He turned back to me and half leaned, half sat, on the kitchen table. "Everything takes time," he said, "and—well, yes, sure, I can make a living at it. But what I don't seem to be able to make you understand is that it's the only thing I want to do."

140   "Well, Sonny," I said gently, "you know people can't always do exactly what they *want* to do—"

"*No*, I don't know that," said Sonny, surprising me. "I think people *ought* to do what they want to do, what else are they alive for?"

"You getting to be a big boy," I said desperately, "it's time you started thinking about your future."

"I'm thinking about my future," said Sonny, grimly. "I think about it all the time."

I gave up. I decided, if he didn't change his mind, that we could always talk about it later. "In the meantime," I said, "you got to finish school." We had already decided that he'd have to move in with Isabel and her folks. I knew this wasn't the ideal arrangement because Isabel's folks are inclined to be dicty[5] and they hadn't especially wanted Isabel to marry me. But I didn't know what else to do. "And we have to get you fixed up at Isabel's."

145   There was a long silence. He moved from the kitchen table to the window. "That's a terrible idea. You know it yourself."

"Do you have a *better* idea?"

He just walked up and down the kitchen for a minute. He was as tall as I was. He had started to shave. I suddenly had the feeling that I didn't know him at all.

He stopped at the kitchen table and picked up my cigarettes. Looking at me with a kind of mocking, amused defiance, he put one between his lips. "You mind?"

"You smoking already?"

150   He lit the cigarette and nodded, watching me through the smoke. "I just wanted to see if I'd have the courage to smoke in front of you." He grinned and blew a great cloud of smoke to the ceiling. "It was easy." He looked at my face. "Come on, now. I bet you was smoking at my age, tell the truth."

I didn't say anything but the truth was on my face, and he laughed. But now there was something very strained in his laugh. "Sure. And I bet that ain't all you was doing."

5. Snobbish, bossy.

He was frightening me a little. "Cut the crap," I said. "We already decided that you was going to go and live at Isabel's. Now what's got into you all of a sudden?"

"*You* decided it," he pointed out. "*I* didn't decide nothing." He stopped in front of me, leaning against the stove, arms loosely folded. "Look, brother. I don't want to stay in Harlem no more, I really don't." He was very earnest. He looked at me, then over toward the kitchen window. There was something in his eyes I'd never seen before, some thoughtfulness, some worry all his own. He rubbed the muscle of one arm. "It's time I was getting out of here."

"Where do you want to *go*, Sonny?"

"I want to join the army. Or the navy, I don't care. If I say I'm old 155 enough, they'll believe me."

Then I got mad. It was because I was so scared. "You must be crazy. You goddamn fool, what the hell do you want to go and join the *army* for?"

"I just told you. To get out of Harlem."

"Sonny, you haven't even finished *school*. And if you really want to be a musician, how do you expect to study if you're in the *army*?"

He looked at me, trapped, and in anguish. "There's ways. I might be able to work out some kind of deal. Anyway, I'll have the G.I. Bill when I come out."

"*If* you come out." We stared at each other. "Sonny, please. Be reason- 160 able. I know the setup is far from perfect. But we got to do the best we can."

"I ain't learning nothing in school," he said. "Even when I go." He turned away from me and opened the window and threw his cigarette out into the narrow alley. I watched his back. "At least, I ain't learning nothing you'd want me to learn." He slammed the window so hard I thought the glass would fly out, and turned back to me. "And I'm sick of the stink of these garbage cans!"

"Sonny," I said, "I know how you feel. But if you don't finish school now, you're going to be sorry later that you didn't." I grabbed him by the shoulders. "And you only got another year. It ain't so bad. And I'll come back and I swear I'll help you do *whatever* you want to do. Just try to put up with it till I come back. Will you please do that? For me?"

He didn't answer and he wouldn't look at me.

"Sonny. You hear me?"

He pulled away. "I hear you. But you never hear anything *I* say." 165

I didn't know what to say to that. He looked out of the window and then back at me. "OK," he said, and sighed. "I'll try."

Then I said, trying to cheer him up a little, "They got a piano at Isabel's. You can practice on it."

And as a matter of fact, it did cheer him up for a minute. "That's right," he said to himself. "I forgot that." His face relaxed a little. But the worry, the thoughtfulness, played on it still, the way shadows play on a face which is staring into the fire.

But I thought I'd never hear the end of that piano. At first, Isabel would write me, saying how nice it was that Sonny was so serious about his music and how, as soon as he came in from school, or wherever he had been when he was supposed to be at school, he went straight to that piano and stayed there until suppertime. And, after supper, he went back to that piano and stayed there until everybody went to bed. He was at the piano all day Saturday and all day Sunday. Then he bought a record player and started playing records. He'd play one record over and over again, all day long sometimes, and he'd improvise along with it on the piano. Or he'd play one section of the record, one chord, one change, one progression, then he'd do it on the piano. Then back to the record. Then back to the piano.

170   Well, I really don't know how they stood it. Isabel finally confessed that it wasn't like living with a person at all, it was like living with sound. And the sound didn't make any sense to her, didn't make any sense to any of them— naturally. They began, in a way, to be afflicted by this presence that was living in their home. It was as though Sonny were some sort of god, or monster. He moved in an atmosphere which wasn't like theirs at all. They fed him and he ate, he washed himself, he walked in and out of their door; he certainly wasn't nasty or unpleasant or rude, Sonny isn't any of those things; but it was as though he were all wrapped up in some cloud, some fire, some vision all his own; and there wasn't any way to reach him.

At the same time, he wasn't really a man yet, he was still a child, and they had to watch out for him in all kinds of ways. They certainly couldn't throw him out. Neither did they dare to make a great scene about that piano because even they dimly sensed, as I sensed, from so many thousands of miles away, that Sonny was at that piano playing for his life.

But he hadn't been going to school. One day a letter came from the school board and Isabel's mother got it—there had, apparently, been other letters but Sonny had torn them up. This day, when Sonny came in, Isabel's mother showed him the letter and asked where he'd been spending his time. And she finally got it out of him that he'd been down in Greenwich Village, with musicians and other characters, in a white girl's apartment. And this scared her and she started to scream at him and what came up, once she began—though she denies it to this day—was what sacrifices they were making to give Sonny a decent home and how little he appreciated it.

Sonny didn't play the piano that day. By evening, Isabel's mother had calmed down but then there was the old man to deal with, and Isabel herself. Isabel says she did her best to be calm but she broke down and started crying. She says she just watched Sonny's face. She could tell, by watching him, what was happening with him. And what was happening was that they penetrated his cloud, they had reached him. Even if their fingers had been a thousand times more gentle than human fingers ever are, he could hardly help feeling that they had stripped him naked and were spitting on that nakedness. For he also had to see that his presence, that music, which was life or death to him, had been torture for them and that they had endured it, not at all for his sake, but only for mine. And Sonny couldn't take that. He can take it a little better today than he could then but he's still not very good at it and, frankly, I don't know anybody who is.

The silence of the next few days must have been louder than the sound of all the music ever played since time began. One morning, before she went to work, Isabel was in his room for something and she suddenly realized that all of his records were gone. And she knew for certain that he was gone. And he was. He went as far as the navy would carry him. He finally sent me a postcard from some place in Greece and that was the first I knew that Sonny was still alive. I didn't see him any more until we were both back in New York and the war had long been over.

He was a man by then, of course, but I wasn't willing to see it. He came 175 by the house from time to time, but we fought almost every time we met. I didn't like the way he carried himself, loose and dreamlike all the time, and I didn't like his friends, and his music seemed to be merely an excuse for the life he led. It sounded just that weird and disordered.

Then we had a fight, a pretty awful fight, and I didn't see him for months. By and by I looked him up, where he was living, in a furnished room in the Village, and I tried to make it up. But there were lots of other people in the room and Sonny just lay on his bed, and he wouldn't come downstairs with me, and he treated these other people as though they were his family and I weren't. So I got mad and then he got mad, and then I told him that he might just as well be dead as live the way he was living. Then he stood up and he told me not to worry about him any more in life, that he *was* dead as far as I was concerned. Then he pushed me to the door and the other people looked on as though nothing were happening, and he slammed the door behind me. I stood in the hallway, staring at the door. I heard somebody laugh in the room and then the tears came to my eyes. I started down the steps, whistling to keep from crying, I kept whistling to myself, *You going to need me, baby, one of these cold, rainy days.*

I read about Sonny's trouble in the spring. Little Grace died in the fall. She was a beautiful little girl. But she only lived a little over two years. She died of polio and she suffered. She had a slight fever for a couple of days, but it didn't seem like anything and we just kept her in bed. And we would certainly have called the doctor, but the fever dropped, she seemed to be all right. So we thought it had just been a cold. Then, one day, she was up, playing, Isabel was in the kitchen fixing lunch for the two boys when they'd come in from school, and she heard Grace fall down in the living room. When you have a lot of children you don't always start running when one of them falls, unless they start screaming or something. And, this time, Gracie was quiet. Yet, Isabel says that when she heard that *thump* and then that silence, something happened to her to make her afraid. And she ran to the living room and there was little Grace on the floor, all twisted up, and the reason she hadn't screamed was that she couldn't get her breath. And when she did scream, it was the worst sound, Isabel says, that she'd ever heard in all her life, and she still hears it sometimes in her dreams. Isabel will sometimes wake me up with a low, moaning, strangling sound and I have to be quick to awaken her and hold her to me and where Isabel is weeping against me seems a mortal wound.

I think I may have written Sonny the very day that little Grace was buried. I was sitting in the living room in the dark, by myself, and I suddenly thought of Sonny. My trouble made his real.

One Saturday afternoon, when Sonny had been living with us, or anyway, been in our house, for nearly two weeks, I found myself wandering aimlessly about the living room, drinking from a can of beer, and trying to work up courage to search Sonny's room. He was out, he was usually out whenever I was home, and Isabel had taken the children to see their grandparents. Suddenly I was standing still in front of the living room window, watching Seventh Avenue. The idea of searching Sonny's room made me still. I scarcely dared to admit to myself what I'd be searching for. I didn't know what I'd do if I found it. Or if I didn't.

180   On the sidewalk across from me, near the entrance to a barbecue joint, some people were holding an old-fashioned revival meeting. The barbecue cook, wearing a dirty white apron, his conked[6] hair reddish and metallic in the pale sun, and a cigarette between his lips, stood in the doorway, watching them. Kids and older people paused in their errands and stood there, along with some older men and a couple of very tough-looking women who watched everything that happened on the avenue, as though they owned it, or were maybe owned by it. Well, they were watching this, too. The revival was being carried on by three sisters in black, and a brother. All they had were their voices and their Bibles and a tambourine. The brother was testifying[7] and while he testified two of the sisters stood together, seeming to say, amen, and the third sister walked around with the tambourine outstretched and a couple of people dropped coins

---

6. Processed: straightened and greased.
7. Publicly professing belief.

into it. Then the brother's testimony ended and the sister who had been taking up the collection dumped the coins into her palm and transferred them to the pocket of her long black robe. Then she raised both hands, striking the tambourine against the air, and then against one hand, and she started to sing. And the two other sisters and the brother joined in. It was strange, suddenly, to watch, though I had been seeing these meetings all my life. So, of course, had everybody else down there. Yet, they paused and watched and listened and I stood still at the window. *"Tis the old ship of Zion,"* they sang, and the sister with the tambourine kept a steady, jangling beat, *"it has rescued many a thousand!"* Not a soul under the sound of their voices was hearing this song for the first time, not one of them had been rescued. Nor had they seen much in the way of rescue work being done around them. Neither did they especially believe in the holiness of the three sisters and the brother, they knew too much about them, knew where they lived, and how. The woman with the tambourine, whose voice dominated the air, whose face was bright with joy, was divided by very little from the woman who stood watching her, a cigarette between her heavy, chapped lips, her hair a cuckoo's nest, her face scarred and swollen from many beatings, and her black eyes glittering like coal. Perhaps they both knew this, which was why, when, as rarely, they addressed each other, they addressed each other as Sister. As the singing filled the air the watching, listening faces underwent a change, the eyes focusing on something within; the music seemed to soothe a poison out of them; and time seemed, nearly, to fall away from the sullen, belligerent, battered faces, as though they were fleeing back to their first condition, while dreaming of their last. The barbecue cook half shook his head and smiled, and dropped his cigarette and disappeared into his joint. A man fumbled in his pockets for change and stood holding it in his hand impatiently, as though he had just remembered a pressing appointment further up the avenue. He looked furious. Then I saw Sonny, standing on the edge of the crowd. He was carrying a wide, flat notebook with a green cover, and it made him look, from where I was standing, almost like a schoolboy. The coppery sun brought out the copper in his skin, he was very faintly smiling, standing very still. Then the singing stopped, the tambourine turned into a collection plate again. The furious man dropped in his coins and vanished, so did a couple of the women, and Sonny dropped some change in the plate, looking directly at the woman with a little smile. He started across the avenue, toward the house. He has a slow, loping walk, something like the way Harlem hipsters walk, only he's imposed on this his own half-beat. I had never really noticed it before.

I stayed at the window, both relieved and apprehensive. As Sonny disappeared from my sight, they began singing again. And they were still singing when his key turned in the lock.

"Hey," he said.

"Hey, yourself. You want some beer?"

185 "No. Well, maybe." But he came up to the window and stood beside me, looking out. "What a warm voice," he said.

They were singing *If I could only hear my mother pray again!*

"Yes," I said, "and she can sure beat that tambourine."

"But what a terrible song," he said, and laughed. He dropped his notebook on the sofa and disappeared into the kitchen. "Where's Isabel and the kids?"

"I think they went to see their grandparents. You hungry?"

190 "No." He came back into the living room with his can of beer. "You want to come some place with me tonight?"

I sensed, I don't know how, that I couldn't possibly say no. "Sure. Where?"

He sat down on the sofa and picked up his notebook and started leafing through it. "I'm going to sit in with some fellows in a joint in the Village."

"You mean, you're going to play, tonight?"

"That's right." He took a swallow of his beer and moved back to the window. He gave me a sidelong look. "If you can stand it."

195 "I'll try," I said.

He smiled to himself and we both watched as the meeting across the way broke up. The three sisters and the brother, heads bowed, were singing *God be with you till we meet again.* The faces around them were very quiet. Then the song ended. The small crowd dispersed. We watched the three women and the lone man walk slowly up the avenue.

"When she was singing before," said Sonny, abruptly, "her voice reminded me for a minute of what heroin feels like sometimes—when it's in your veins. It makes you feel sort of warm and cool at the same time. And distant. And—and sure." He sipped his beer, very deliberately not looking at me. I watched his face. "It makes you feel—in control. Sometimes you've got to have that feeling."

"Do you?" I sat down slowly in the easy chair.

"Sometimes." He went to the sofa and picked up his notebook again. "Some people do."

200 "In order," I asked, "to play?" And my voice was very ugly, full of contempt and anger.

"Well"—he looked at me with great, troubled eyes, as though, in fact, he hoped his eyes would tell me things he could never otherwise say—"they *think* so. And *if* they think so—!"

"And what do *you* think?" I asked.

He sat on the sofa and put his can of beer on the floor. "I don't know," he said, and I couldn't be sure if he were answering my question or pursuing his thoughts. His face didn't tell me. "It's not so much to *play.* It's to *stand* it, to be able to make it at all. On any level." He frowned and smiled: "In order to keep from shaking to pieces."

"But these friends of yours," I said, "they seem to shake themselves to pieces pretty goddamn fast."

"Maybe." He played with the notebook. And something told me that I 205 should curb my tongue, that Sonny was doing his best to talk, that I should listen. "But of course you only know the ones that've gone to pieces. Some don't—or at least they haven't *yet* and that's just about all *any* of us can say." He paused. "And then there are some who just live, really, in hell, and they know it and they see what's happening and they go right on. I don't know." He sighed, dropped the notebook, folded his arms. "Some guys, you can tell from the way they play, they on something *all* the time. And you can see that, well, it makes something real for them. But of course," he picked up his beer from the floor and sipped it and put the can down again, "they *want* to, too, you've got to see that. Even some of them that say they don't—*some*, not all."

"And what about you?" I asked—I couldn't help it. "What about you? Do *you* want to?"

He stood up and walked to the window and I remained silent for a long time. Then he sighed. "Me," he said. Then: "While I was downstairs before, on my way here, listening to that woman sing, it struck me all of a sudden how much suffering she must have had to go through—to sing like that. It's *repulsive* to think you have to suffer that much."

I said: "But there's no way not to suffer—is there, Sonny?"

"I believe not," he said and smiled, "but that's never stopped anyone from trying." He looked at me. "Has it?" I realized, with this mocking look, that there stood between us, forever, beyond the power of time or forgiveness, the fact that I had held silence—so long!—when he had needed human speech to help him. He turned back to the window. "No, there's no way not to suffer. But you try all kinds of ways to keep from drowning in it, to keep on top of it, and to make it seem—well, like *you*. Like you did something, all right, and now you're suffering for it. You know?" I said nothing. "Well you know," he said, impatiently, "why *do* people suffer? Maybe it's better to do something to give it a reason, *any* reason."

"But we just agreed," I said, "that there's no way not to suffer. Isn't it 210 better, then, just to—take it?"

"But nobody just takes it," Sonny cried, "that's what I'm telling you! *Everybody* tries not to. You're just hung up on the *way* some people try—it's not *your* way!"

The hair on my face began to itch, my face felt wet. "That's not true," I said, "that's not true. I don't give a damn what other people do, I don't even care how they suffer. I just care how *you* suffer." And he looked at me.

"Please believe me," I said, "I don't want to see you—die—trying not to
suffer."

"I won't," he said flatly, "die trying not to suffer. At least, not any faster
than anybody else."

"But there's no need," I said, trying to laugh, "is there? in killing
yourself."

215   I wanted to say more, but I couldn't. I wanted to talk about will power
and how life could be—well, beautiful. I wanted to say that it was all
within; but was it? or, rather, wasn't that exactly the trouble? And I wanted
to promise that I would never fail him again. But it would all have
sounded—empty words and lies.

So I made the promise to myself and prayed that I would keep it.

"It's terrible sometimes, inside," he said, "that's what's the trouble. You
walk these streets, black and funky and cold, and there's not really a living
ass to talk to, and there's nothing shaking, and there's no way of getting it
out—that storm inside. You can't talk it and you can't make love with it, and
when you finally try to get with it and play it, you realize *nobody's* listening.
So *you've* got to listen. You got to find a way to listen."

And then he walked away from the window and sat on the sofa again,
as though all the wind had suddenly been knocked out of him. "Sometimes
you'll do *anything* to play, even cut your mother's throat." He laughed and
looked at me. "Or your brother's." Then he sobered. "Or your own." Then:
"Don't worry. I'm all right now and I think I'll *be* all right. But I can't
forget—where I've been. I don't mean just the physical place I've been, I
mean where I've *been*. And *what* I've been."

"What have you been, Sonny?" I asked.

220   He smiled—but sat sideways on the sofa, his elbow resting on the
back, his fingers playing with his mouth and chin, not looking at me. "I've
been something I didn't recognize, didn't know I could be. Didn't know
anybody could be." He stopped, looking inward, looking helplessly young,
looking old. "I'm not talking about it now because I feel *guilty* or anything
like that—maybe it would be better if I did, I don't know. Anyway, I can't
really talk about it. Not to you, not to anybody," and now he turned and
faced me. "Sometimes, you know, and it was actually when I was most *out*
of the world, I felt that I was in it, that I was *with* it, really, and I could
play or I didn't really have to *play*, it just came out of me, it was there. And
I don't know how I played, thinking about it now, but I know I did awful
things, those times, sometimes, to people. Or it wasn't that I *did* anything
to them—it was that they weren't real." He picked up the beer can; it was
empty; he rolled it between his palms: "And other times—well, I needed a
fix, I needed to find a place to lean, I needed to clear a space to *listen*—

and I couldn't find it, and I—went crazy, I did terrible things to *me*, I was terrible *for* me." He began pressing the beer can between his hands, I watched the metal begin to give. It glittered, as he played with it like a knife, and I was afraid he would cut himself, but I said nothing. "Oh well. I can never tell you. I was all by myself at the bottom of something, stinking and sweating and crying and shaking, and I smelled it, you know? *my* stink, and I thought I'd die if I couldn't get away from it and yet, all the same, I knew that everything I was doing was just locking me in with it. And I didn't know," he paused, still flattening the beer can, "I didn't know, I still *don't* know, something kept telling me that maybe it was good to smell your own stink, but I didn't think that *that* was what I'd been trying to do—and—who can stand it?" and he abruptly dropped the ruined beer can, looking at me with a small, still smile, and then rose, walking to the window as though it were the lodestone rock. I watched his face, he watched the avenue. "I couldn't tell you when Mama died—but the reason I wanted to leave Harlem so bad was to get away from drugs. And then, when I ran away, that's what I was running from—really. When I came back, nothing had changed, *I* hadn't changed, I was just—older." And he stopped, drumming with his fingers on the windowpane. The sun had vanished, soon darkness would fall. I watched his face. "It can come again," he said, almost as though speaking to himself. Then he turned to me. "It can come again," he repeated. "I just want you to know that."

"All right," I said, at last. "So it can come again. All right."

He smiled, but the smile was sorrowful. "I had to try to tell you," he said.

"Yes," I said. "I understand that."

"You're my brother," he said, looking straight at me, and not smiling at all.

"Yes," I repeated, "yes. I understand that."   225

He turned back to the window, looking out. "All that hatred down there," he said, "all that hatred and misery and love. It's a wonder it doesn't blow the avenue apart."

We went to the only nightclub on a short, dark street, downtown. We squeezed through the narrow, chattering, jampacked bar to the entrance of the big room, where the bandstand was. And we stood there for a moment, for the lights were very dim in this room and we couldn't see. Then, "Hello, boy," said the voice and an enormous black man, much older than Sonny or myself, erupted out of all that atmospheric lighting and put an arm around Sonny's shoulder. "I been sitting right here," he said, "waiting for you."

He had a big voice, too, and heads in the darkness turned toward us.

Sonny grinned and pulled a little away, and said, "Creole, this is my brother. I told you about him."

230   Creole shook my hand. "I'm glad to meet you, son," he said, and it was clear that he was glad to meet me *there*, for Sonny's sake. And he smiled, "You got a real musician in *your* family," and he took his arm from Sonny's shoulder and slapped him, lightly, affectionately, with the back of his hand.

"Well. Now I've heard it all," said a voice behind us. This was another musician, and a friend of Sonny's, a coal-black, cheerful-looking man, built close to the ground. He immediately began confiding to me, at the top of his lungs, the most terrible things about Sonny, his teeth gleaming like a lighthouse and his laugh coming up out of him like the beginning of an earthquake. And it turned out that everyone at the bar knew Sonny, or almost everyone; some were musicians, working there, or nearby, or not working, some were simply hangers-on, and some were there to hear Sonny play. I was introduced to all of them and they were all very polite to me. Yet, it was clear that, for them, I was only Sonny's brother. Here, I was in Sonny's world. Or, rather: his kingdom. Here, it was not even a question that his veins bore royal blood.

They were going to play soon and Creole installed me, by myself, at a table in a dark corner. Then I watched them, Creole, and the little black man, and Sonny, and the others, while they horsed around, standing just below the bandstand. The light from the bandstand spilled just a little short of them and, watching them laughing and gesturing and moving about, I had the feeling that they, nevertheless, were being most careful not to step into that circle of light too suddenly; that if they moved into the light too suddenly, without thinking, they would perish in flame. Then, while I watched, one of them, the small black man, moved into the light and crossed the bandstand and started fooling around with his drums. Then—being funny and being, also, extremely ceremonious—Creole took Sonny by the arm and led him to the piano. A woman's voice called Sonny's name and a few hands started clapping. And Sonny, also being funny and being ceremonious, and so touched, I think, that he could have cried, but neither hiding it nor showing it, riding it like a man, grinned, and put both hands to his heart and bowed from the waist.

Creole then went to the bass fiddle and a lean, very bright-skinned brown man jumped up on the bandstand and picked up his horn. So there they were, and the atmosphere on the bandstand and in the room began to change and tighten. Someone stepped up to the microphone and announced them. Then there were all kinds of murmurs. Some people at the bar shushed others. The waitress ran around, frantically getting in the last orders, guys and chicks got closer to each other, and the lights on the bandstand, on the quartet, turned to a kind of indigo. Then they all looked different there. Creole looked about him for the last time, as though he were making certain that all his chickens were in the coop, and then he— jumped and struck the fiddle. And there they were.

All I know about music is that not many people ever really hear it. And even then, on the rare occasions when something opens within, and the music enters, what we mainly hear, or hear corroborated, are personal, private, vanishing evocations. But the man who creates the music is hearing something else, is dealing with the roar rising from the void and imposing order on it as it hits the air. What is evoked in him, then, is of another order, more terrible because it has no words, and triumphant, too, for that same reason. And his triumph, when he triumphs, is ours. I just watched Sonny's face. His face was troubled, he was working hard, but he wasn't with it. And I had the feeling that, in a way, everyone on the bandstand was waiting for him, both waiting for him and pushing him along. But as I began to watch Creole, I realized that it was Creole who held them all back. He had them on a short rein. Up there, keeping the beat with his whole body, wailing on the fiddle, with his eyes half closed, he was listening to everything, but he was listening to Sonny. He was having a dialogue with Sonny. He wanted Sonny to leave the shoreline and strike out for the deep water. He was Sonny's witness that deep water and drowning were not the same thing—he had been there, and he knew. And he wanted Sonny to know. He was waiting for Sonny to do the things on the keys which would let Creole know that Sonny was in the water.

And, while Creole listened, Sonny moved, deep within, exactly like 235 someone in torment. I had never before thought of how awful the relationship must be between the musician and his instrument. He has to fill it, this instrument, with the breath of life, his own. He has to make it do what he wants it to do. And a piano is just a piano. It's made out of so much wood and wires and little hammers and big ones, and ivory. While there's only so much you can do with it, the only way to find this out is to try; to try and make it do everything.

And Sonny hadn't been near a piano for over a year. And he wasn't on much better terms with his life, not the life that stretched before him now. He and the piano stammered, started one way, got scared, stopped; started another way, panicked, marked time, started again; then seemed to have found a direction, panicked again, got stuck. And the face I saw on Sonny I'd never seen before. Everything had been burned out of it, and, at the same time, things usually hidden were being burned in, by the fire and fury of the battle which was occurring in him up there.

Yet, watching Creole's face as they neared the end of the first set, I had the feeling that something had happened, something I hadn't heard. Then they finished, there was scattered applause, and then, without an instant's warning, Creole started into something else, it was almost sardonic, it was *Am I Blue*.[8] And, as though he commanded, Sonny began to play. Something began to happen. And Creole let out the reins. The dry, low, black man said something awful on the drums, Creole answered, and the drums talked back. Then the horn insisted, sweet and high, slightly detached perhaps, and Creole listened, commenting now and then, dry, and driving, beautiful and calm and old. Then they all came together again, and Sonny was part of the family again. I could tell this from his face. He seemed to have found, right there beneath his fingers, a damn brand-new piano. It seemed that he couldn't get over it. Then, for a while, just being happy with Sonny, they seemed to be agreeing with him that brand-new pianos certainly were a gas.

Then Creole stepped forward to remind them that what they were playing was the blues. He hit something in all of them, he hit something in me, myself, and the music tightened and deepened, apprehension began to beat the air. Creole began to tell us what the blues were all about. They were not about anything very new. He and his boys up there were keeping it new, at the risk of ruin, destruction, madness, and death, in order to find new ways to make us listen. For, while the tale of how we suffer, and how we are delighted, and how we may triumph is never new, it always must be heard. There isn't any other tale to tell, it's the only light we've got in all this darkness.

And this tale, according to that face, that body, those strong hands on those strings, has another aspect in every country, and a new depth in every generation. Listen, Creole seemed to be saying, listen. Now these are Sonny's blues. He made the little black man on the drums know it, and the bright, brown man on the horn. Creole wasn't trying any longer to get Sonny in the water. He was wishing him Godspeed. Then he stepped back, very slowly, filling the air with the immense suggestion that Sonny speak for himself.

240   Then they all gathered around Sonny and Sonny played. Every now and again one of them seemed to say, amen. Sonny's fingers filled the air with life, his life. But that life contained so many others. And Sonny went all the way back, he really began with the spare, flat statement of the opening phrase of the song. Then he began to make it his. It was very beautiful because it wasn't hurried and it was no longer a lament. I seemed to hear with what burning he had made it his, and what burning we had yet to make it ours, how we could cease lamenting. Freedom lurked around us and I understood, at last, that he could help us to be free if we would listen, that he would never be free until we did. Yet, there was no battle in

8. A favorite jazz standard, brilliantly recorded by Billie Holiday.

his face now, I heard what he had gone through, and would continue to go through until he came to rest in earth. He had made it his: that long line, of which we knew only Mama and Daddy. And he was giving it back, as everything must be given back, so that, passing through death, it can live forever. I saw my mother's face again, and felt, for the first time, how the stones of the road she had walked on must have bruised her feet. I saw the moonlit road where my father's brother died. And it brought something else back to me, and carried me past it, I saw my little girl again and felt Isabel's tears again, and I felt my own tears begin to rise. And I was yet aware that this was only a moment, that the world waited outside, as hungry as a tiger, and that trouble stretched above us, longer than the sky.

Then it was over. Creole and Sonny let out their breath, both soaking wet, and grinning. There was a lot of applause and some of it was real. In the dark, the girl came by and I asked her to take drinks to the bandstand. There was a long pause, while they talked up there in the indigo light and after awhile I saw the girl put a Scotch and milk on top of the piano for Sonny. He didn't seem to notice it, but just before they started playing again, he sipped from it and looked toward me, and nodded. Then he put it back on top of the piano. For me, then, as they began to play again, it glowed and shook above my brother's head like the very cup of trembling.[9]

1957

QUESTIONS

1. SONNY'S BLUES begins *in medias res*. What does Baldwin achieve by beginning the story as he does? How does the order in which events are related later in the story affect your experience of reading it and interpreting its meaning?
2. What external conflict(s) is (or are) depicted in the story? What internal conflict(s)? How are they resolved?
3. James Baldwin famously avowed that "[i]t is only in his music [. . .] that the Negro in America has been able to tell his story," and music of various kinds features prominently in SONNY'S BLUES. Note all the times when music is mentioned, as well as all the varieties of music. What story seems to be told both *through* and *about* music in SONNY'S BLUES?

9. See Isaiah 51.17, 22–23: "Awake, awake, stand up, O Jerusalem, which hast drunk at the hand of the Lord the cup of his fury; thou hast drunken the dregs of the cup of trembling, and wrung them out. [. . .] Behold, I have taken out of thine hand the cup of trembling, even the dregs of the cup of my fury; thou shalt no more drink it again: But I will put it into the hand of them that afflict thee [. . .] ."

JOYCE CAROL OATES
(b. 1938)
Where Are You Going, Where Have You Been?

A remarkably, even uniquely, prolific writer of short stories, poems, novels, and nonfiction, Joyce Carol Oates was born in Lockport, New York. Daughter of a tool-and-die designer and his wife, she submitted her first novel to a publisher at fifteen and a few years later became the first person in her family to graduate from high school, later earning a BA from Syracuse University (1960) and an MA from the University of Wisconsin (1961). The recipient of countless awards, including a National Book Award for the novel *them* (1969), the O. Henry Special Award for Continuing Achievement (1970, 1986), a Pushchart Prize (1976), and at least four lifetime achievement awards, Oates taught for over thirty-five years at Princeton University, retiring in 2014. Her recent novels include *Little Bird of Heaven* (2009), *Mudwoman* (2012), *Daddy Love* and *The Accursed* (2013), and *Carthage* (2014). A new short-story collection, *High Crime Area: Tales of Darkness and Dread*, came out in 2012, one year after her memoir *A Widow's Story*.

For Bob Dylan

Her name was Connie. She was fifteen and she had a quick, nervous giggling habit of craning her neck to glance into mirrors or checking other people's faces to make sure her own was all right. Her mother, who noticed everything and knew everything and who hadn't much reason any longer to look at her own face, always scolded Connie about it. "Stop gawking at yourself. Who are you? You think you're so pretty?" she would say. Connie would raise her eyebrows at these familiar old complaints and look right through her mother, into a shadowy vision of herself as she was right at that moment: she knew she was pretty and that was everything. Her mother had been pretty once too, if you could believe those old snapshots in the album, but now her looks were gone and that was why she was always after Connie.

"Why don't you keep your room clean like your sister? How've you got your hair fixed—what the hell stinks? Hair spray? You don't see your sister using that junk."

Her sister, June, was twenty-four and still lived at home. She was a secretary in the high school Connie attended, and if that wasn't bad enough—

with her in the same building—she was so plain and chunky and steady that Connie had to hear her praised all the time by her mother and her mother's sisters. June did this, June did that, she saved money and helped clean the house and cooked and Connie couldn't do a thing, her mind was all filled with trashy daydreams. Their father was away at work most of the time and when he came home he wanted supper and he read the newspaper at supper and after supper he went to bed. He didn't bother talking much to them, but around his bent head Connie's mother kept picking at her until Connie wished her mother was dead and she herself was dead and it was all over. "She makes me want to throw up sometimes," she complained to her friends. She had a high, breathless, amused voice that made everything she said sound a little forced, whether it was sincere or not.

There was one good thing: June went places with girl friends of hers, girls who were just as plain and steady as she, and so when Connie wanted to do that her mother had no objections. The father of Connie's best girl friend drove the girls the three miles to town and left them at a shopping plaza so they could walk through the stores or go to a movie, and when he came to pick them up again at eleven he never bothered to ask what they had done.

They must have been familiar sights, walking around the shopping plaza 5 in their shorts and flat ballerina slippers that always scuffed on the sidewalk, with charm bracelets jingling on their thin wrists; they would lean together to whisper and laugh secretly if someone passed who amused or interested them. Connie had long dark blond hair that drew anyone's eye to it, and she wore part of it pulled up on her head and puffed out and the rest of it she let fall down her back. She wore a pullover jersey top that looked one way when she was at home and another way when she was away from home. Everything about her had two sides to it, one for home and one for anywhere that was not home: her walk, which could be childlike and bobbing, or languid enough to make anyone think she was hearing music in her head; her mouth, which was pale and smirking most of the time, but bright and pink on these evenings out; her laugh, which was cynical and drawling at home—"Ha, ha, very funny,"—but high-pitched and nervous anywhere else, like the jingling of the charms on her bracelet.

Sometimes they did go shopping or to a movie, but sometimes they went across the highway, ducking fast across the busy road, to a drive-in restaurant where older kids hung out. The restaurant was shaped like a big bottle, though squatter than a real bottle, and on its cap was a revolving figure of a grinning boy holding a hamburger aloft. One night in midsummer they ran across, breathless with daring, and right away someone leaned out a car window and invited them over, but it was just a boy from high school they didn't like. It made them feel good to be able to ignore him. They went up through the maze of parked and cruising cars to the bright-lit, fly-infested restaurant, their faces pleased and expectant as if they were entering a sacred building that loomed up out of the night to give them what haven and blessing they yearned for. They sat at the counter and crossed their legs at the ankles, their thin shoulders rigid with excitement, and listened to the music that made everything so good: the music was always in the background, like music at a church service; it was something to depend upon.

A boy named Eddie came in to talk with them. He sat backward on his stool, turning himself jerkily around in semicircles and then stopping and turning back again, and after a while he asked Connie if she would like something to eat. She said she would so she tapped her friend's arm on her way out—her friend pulled her face up into a brave, droll look—and Connie said she would meet her at eleven across the way. "I just hate to leave her like that," Connie said earnestly, but the boy said that she wouldn't be alone for long. So they went out to his car, and on the way Connie couldn't help but let her eyes wander over the windshields and faces all around her, her face gleaming with a joy that had nothing to do with Eddie or even this place; it might have been the music. She drew her shoulders up and sucked in her breath with the pure pleasure of being alive, and just at that moment she happened to glance at a face just a few feet away from hers. It was a boy with shaggy black hair, in a convertible jalopy[1] painted gold. He stared at her and then his lips widened into a grin. Connie slit her eyes at him and turned away, but she couldn't help glancing back and there he was, still watching her. He wagged a finger and laughed and said, "Gonna get you, baby," and Connie turned away again without Eddie noticing anything.

She spent three hours with him, at the restaurant where they ate hamburgers and drank Cokes in wax cups that were always sweating, and then down an alley a mile or so away, and when he left her off at five to eleven only the movie house was still open at the plaza. Her girl friend was there, talking with a boy. When Connie came up, the two girls smiled at each other and Connie said, "How was the movie?" and the girl said, "You should know." They rode off with the girl's father, sleepy and pleased, and Connie couldn't help but look back at the darkened shopping plaza with its big empty parking lot and its signs that were faded and ghostly now, and over at the drive-in restaurant where cars were still circling tirelessly. She couldn't hear the music at this distance.

Next morning June asked her how the movie was and Connie said, "So-so."

---

1. Older car, often in poor condition.

She and that girl and occasionally another girl went out several times a   10
week, and the rest of the time Connie spent around the house—it was summer vacation—getting in her mother's way and thinking, dreaming about
the boys she met. But all the boys fell back and dissolved into a single face
that was not even a face but an idea, a feeling, mixed up with the urgent
insistent pounding of the music and the humid night air of July. Connie's
mother kept dragging her back to the daylight by finding things for her to do
or saying suddenly, "What's this about the Pettinger girl?"

And Connie would say nervously, "Oh, her. That dope." She always
drew thick clear lines between herself and such girls, and her mother was
simple and kind enough to believe it. Her mother was so simple, Connie
thought, that it was maybe cruel to fool her so much. Her mother went
scuffling around the house in old bedroom slippers and complained over
the telephone to one sister about the other, then the other called up and the
two of them complained about the third one. If June's name was mentioned
her mother's tone was approving, and if Connie's name was mentioned it
was disapproving. This did not really mean she disliked Connie, and actually Connie thought that her mother preferred her to June just because she
was prettier, but the two of them kept up a pretense of exasperation, a sense
that they were tugging and struggling over something of little value to
either of them. Sometimes, over coffee, they were almost friends, but something would come up—some vexation that was like a fly buzzing suddenly
around their heads—and their faces went hard with contempt.

One Sunday Connie got up at eleven—none of them bothered with
church—and washed her hair so that it could dry all day long in the sun.
Her parents and sister were going to a barbecue at an aunt's house and Connie said no, she wasn't interested, rolling her eyes to let her mother know
just what she thought of it. "Stay home alone then," her mother said
sharply. Connie sat out back in a lawn chair and watched them drive
away, her father quiet and bald, hunched around so that he could back the
car out, her mother with a look that was still angry and not at all softened
through the windshield, and in the backseat poor old June, all dressed
up as if she didn't know what a barbecue was, with all the running yelling
kids and the flies. Connie sat with her eyes closed in the sun, dreaming
and dazed with the warmth about her as if this were a kind of love, the
caresses of love, and her mind slipped over onto thoughts of the boy she
had been with the night before and how nice he had been, how sweet it
always was, not the way someone like June would suppose but sweet, gentle, the way it was in movies and promised in songs; and when she opened
her eyes she hardly knew where she was, the backyard ran off into weeds
and a fencelike line of trees and behind it the sky was perfectly blue and

still. The asbestos "ranch house"[2] that was now three years old startled her—it looked small. She shook her head as if to get awake.

It was too hot. She went inside the house and turned on the radio to drown out the quiet. She sat on the edge of her bed, barefoot, and listened for an hour and a half to a program called *XYZ Sunday Jamboree*, record after record of hard, fast, shrieking songs she sang along with, interspersed by exclamations from "Bobby King": "An' look here, you girls at Napoleon's— Son and Charley want you to pay real close attention to this song coming up!"

And Connie paid close attention herself, bathed in a glow of slow-pulsed joy that seemed to rise mysteriously out of the music itself and lay languidly about the airless little room, breathed in and breathed out with each gentle rise and fall of her chest.

15   After a while she heard a car coming up the drive. She sat up at once, startled, because it couldn't be her father so soon. The gravel kept crunching all the way in from the road—the driveway was long—and Connie ran to the window. It was a car she didn't know. It was an open jalopy, painted a bright gold that caught the sunlight opaquely. Her heart began to pound and her fingers snatched at her hair, checking it, and she whispered, "Christ, Christ," wondering how she looked. The car came to a stop at the side door and the horn sounded four short taps, as if this were a signal Connie knew.

She went into the kitchen and approached the door slowly, then hung out the screen door, her bare toes curling down off the step. There were two boys in the car and now she recognized the driver: he had shaggy, shabby black hair that looked crazy as a wig and he was grinning at her.

"I ain't late, am I?" he said.

"Who the hell do you think you are?" Connie said.

"Toldja I'd be out, didn't I?"

20   "I don't even know who you are."

She spoke sullenly, careful to show no interest or pleasure, and he spoke in a fast, bright monotone. Connie looked past him to the other boy, taking her time. He had fair brown hair, with a lock that fell onto his forehead. His sideburns gave him a fierce, embarrassed look, but so far he hadn't even bothered to glance at her. Both boys wore sunglasses. The driver's glasses were metallic and mirrored everything in miniature.

"You wanta come for a ride?" he said.

Connie smirked and let her hair fall loose over one shoulder.

---

2. Style of long, one-story houses common in suburban neighborhoods built between the 1940s and 1980s. *Asbestos:* fireproof building material once used in roofs and siding, but now known to be toxic.

"Don'tcha like my car? New paint job," he said. "Hey."

"What?" 25

"You're cute."

She pretended to fidget, chasing flies away from the door.

"Don'tcha believe me, or what?" he said.

"Look, I don't even know who you are," Connie said in disgust.

"Hey, Ellie's got a radio, see. Mine broke down." He lifted his friend's 30 arm and showed her the little transistor radio the boy was holding, and now Connie began to hear the music. It was the same program that was playing inside the house.

"Bobby King?" she said.

"I listen to him all the time. I think he's great."

"He's kind of great," Connie said reluctantly.

"Listen, that guy's *great*. He knows where the action is."

Connie blushed a little, because the glasses made it impossible for her 35 to see just what this boy was looking at. She couldn't decide if she liked him or if he was a jerk, and so she dawdled in the doorway and wouldn't come down or go back inside. She said, "What's all that stuff painted on your car?"

"Can'tcha read it?" He opened the door very carefully, as if he were afraid it might fall off. He slid out just as carefully, planting his feet firmly on the ground, the tiny metallic world in his glasses slowing down like gelatine hardening, and in the midst of it Connie's bright-green blouse. "This here is my name, to begin with," he said. ARNOLD FRIEND was written in tarlike black letters on the side, with a drawing of a round, grinning face that reminded Connie of a pumpkin, except it wore sunglasses. "I wanta introduce myself. I'm Arnold Friend and that's my real name and I'm gonna be your friend, honey, and inside the car's Ellie Oscar, he's kinda shy." Ellie brought his transistor radio up to his shoulder and balanced it there. "Now, these numbers are a secret code, honey," Arnold Friend explained. He read off the numbers 33, 19, 17 and raised his eyebrows at her to see what she thought of that, but she didn't think much of it. The left rear fender had been smashed and around it was written, on the gleaming gold background: DONE BY CRAZY WOMAN DRIVER. Connie had to laugh at that. Arnold Friend was pleased at her laughter and looked up at her. "Around the other side's a lot more—you wanta come and see them?"

"No."

"Why not?"

"Why should I?"

"Don'tcha wanta see what's on the car? Don'tcha wanta go for a ride?" 40

"I don't know."

"Why not?"

"I got things to do."

"Like what?"

45   "Things."

He laughed as if she had said something funny. He slapped his thighs. He was standing in a strange way, leaning back against the car as if he were balancing himself. He wasn't tall, only an inch or so taller than she would be if she came down to him. Connie liked the way he was dressed, which was the way all of them dressed: tight faded jeans stuffed into black, scuffed boots, a belt that pulled his waist in and showed how lean he was, and a white pullover shirt that was a little soiled and showed the hard small muscles of his arms and shoulders. He looked as if he probably did hard work, lifting and carrying things. Even his neck looked muscular. And his face was a familiar face, somehow; the jaw and chin and cheeks slightly darkened because he hadn't shaved for a day or two, and the nose long and hawklike, sniffing as if she was a treat he was going to gobble up and it was all a joke.

"Connie, you ain't telling the truth. This is your day set aside for a ride with me and you know it," he said, still laughing. The way he straightened and recovered from his fit of laughing showed that it had been all fake.

"How do you know what my name is?" she said suspiciously.

"It's Connie."

50   "Maybe and maybe not."

"I know my Connie," he said, wagging his finger. Now she remembered him even better, back at the restaurant, and her cheeks warmed at the thought of how she had sucked in her breath just at the moment she passed him—how she must have looked to him. And he had remembered her. "Ellie and I come out here especially for you," he said. "Ellie can sit in back. How about it?"

"Where?"

"Where what?"

"Where're we going?"

55   He looked at her. He took off the sunglasses and she saw how pale the skin around his eyes was, like holes that were not in shadow but instead in light. His eyes were like chips of broken glass that catch the light in an amiable way. He smiled. It was as if the idea of going for a ride somewhere, to someplace, was a new idea to him.

"Just for a ride, Connie sweetheart."

"I never said my name was Connie," she said.

"But I know what it is. I know your name and all about you, lots of things," Arnold Friend said. He had not moved yet but stood still leaning back against the side of his jalopy. "I took a special interest in you, such a pretty girl, and found out all about you—like I know your parents and sister are gone somewheres and I know where and how long they're going to be gone, and I know who you were with last night, and your best girl friend's name is Betty. Right?"

He spoke in a simple lilting voice, exactly as if he was reciting the words to a song. His smile assured her that everything was fine. In the car Ellie turned up the volume on his radio and did not bother to look around at them.

"Ellie can sit in the backseat," Arnold Friend said. He indicated his 60 friend with a casual jerk of his chin, as if Ellie did not count and she should not bother with him.

"How'd you find out all that stuff?" Connie said.

"Listen: Betty Schultz and Tony Fitch and Jimmy Pettinger and Nancy Pettinger," he said in a chant. "Raymond Stanley and Bob Hutter—"

"Do you know all those kids?"

"I know everybody."

"Look, you're kidding. You're not from around here." 65

"Sure."

"But—how come we never saw you before?"

"Sure you saw me before," he said. He looked down at his boots, as if he was a little offended. "You just don't remember."

"I guess I'd remember you," Connie said.

"Yeah?" He looked up at this, beaming. He was pleased. He began to 70 mark time with the music from Ellie's radio, tapping his fists lightly together. Connie looked away from his smile to the car, which was painted so bright it almost hurt her eyes to look at it. She looked at that name, ARNOLD FRIEND. And up at the front fender was an expression that was familiar— MAN THE FLYING SAUCERS. It was an expression kids had used the year before but didn't use this year. She looked at it for a while as if the words meant something to her that she did not yet know.

"What're you thinking about? Huh?" Arnold Friend demanded. "Not worried about your hair blowing around in the car, are you?"

"No."

"Think I maybe can't drive good?"

"How do I know?"

"You're a hard girl to handle. How come?" he said. "Don't you know 75 I'm your friend? Didn't you see me put my sign in the air when you walked by?"

"What sign?"

"My sign." And he drew an X in the air, leaning out toward her. They were maybe ten feet apart. After his hand fell back to his side the X was still in the air, almost visible. Connie let the screen door close and stood perfectly still inside it, listening to the music from her radio and the boy's blend together. She stared at Arnold Friend. He stood there so stiffly relaxed, pretending to be relaxed, with one hand idly on the door handle as if he was keeping himself up that way and had no intention of ever moving again. She recognized most things about him, the tight jeans that showed his thighs and buttocks and the greasy leather boots and the tight shirt, and even that slippery friendly smile of his, that sleepy dreamy smile that all the boys used to get across ideas they didn't want to put into words. She recognized all this and also the singsong way he talked, slightly mocking, kidding, but serious and a little melancholy, and she recognized the way he tapped one fist against the other in homage to the perpetual music behind him. But all these things did not come together.

She said suddenly, "Hey, how old are you?"

His smile faded. She could see then that he wasn't a kid, he was much older—thirty, maybe more. At this knowledge her heart began to pound faster.

80   "That's a crazy thing to ask. Can'tcha see I'm your own age?"

"Like hell you are."

"Or maybe a coupla years older. I'm eighteen."

"Eighteen?" she said doubtfully.

He grinned to reassure her and lines appeared at the corners of his mouth. His teeth were big and white. He grinned so broadly his eyes became slits and she saw how thick the lashes were, thick and black as if painted with a black tarlike material. Then, abruptly, he seemed to become embarrassed and looked over his shoulder at Ellie. "*Him*, he's crazy," he said. "Ain't he a riot? He's a nut, a real character." Ellie was still listening to the music. His sunglasses told nothing about what he was thinking. He wore a bright-orange shirt unbuttoned halfway to show his chest, which was a pale, bluish chest and not muscular like Arnold Friend's. His shirt collar was turned up all around and the very tips of the collar pointed out past his chin as if they were protecting him. He was pressing the transistor radio up against his ear and sat there in a kind of daze, right in the sun.

85   "He's kinda strange," Connie said.

"Hey, she says you're kinda strange! Kinda strange!" Arnold Friend cried. He pounded on the car to get Ellie's attention. Ellie turned for the first time and Connie saw with shock that he wasn't a kid either—he had a fair, hairless face, cheeks reddened slightly as if the veins grew too close to the surface of his skin, the face of a forty-year-old baby. Connie felt a wave of dizziness rise in her at this sight and she stared at him as if waiting for something to change the shock of the moment, make it all right again. Ellie's lips kept shaping words, mumbling along with the words blasting in his ear.

"Maybe you two better go away," Connie said faintly.

"What? How come?" Arnold Friend cried. "We come out here to take you for a ride. It's Sunday." He had the voice of the man on the radio now. It was the same voice, Connie thought. "Don'tcha know it's Sunday all day? And honey, no matter who you were with last night, today you're with Arnold Friend and don't you forget it! Maybe you better step out here," he said, and this last was in a different voice. It was a little flatter, as if the heat was finally getting to him.

"No. I got things to do."

"Hey." ⁹⁰

"You two better leave."

"We ain't leaving until you come with us."

"Like hell I am—"

"Connie, don't fool around with me. I mean—I mean, don't fool *around*," he said, shaking his head. He laughed incredulously. He placed his sunglasses on top of his head, carefully, as if he was indeed wearing a wig, and brought the stems down behind his ears. Connie stared at him, another wave of dizziness and fear rising in her so that for a moment he wasn't even in focus but was just a blur standing there against his gold car, and she had the idea that he had driven up the driveway all right but had come from nowhere before that and belonged nowhere and that everything about him and even about the music that was so familiar to her was only half real.

"If my father comes and sees you—" ⁹⁵

"He ain't coming. He's at a barbecue."

"How do you know that?"

"Aunt Tillie's. Right now they're—uh—they're drinking. Sitting around," he said vaguely, squinting as if he was staring all the way to town and over to Aunt Tillie's backyard. Then the vision seemed to get clear and he nodded energetically. "Yeah. Sitting around. There's your sister in a blue dress, huh? And high heels, the poor sad bitch—nothing like you, sweetheart! And your mother's helping some fat woman with the corn, they're cleaning the corn—husking the corn—"

"What fat woman?" Connie cried.

"How do I know what fat woman, I don't know every goddamn fat woman ¹⁰⁰ in the world!" Arnold Friend laughed.

"Oh, that's Mrs. Hornsby. . . . Who invited her?" Connie said. She felt a little light-headed. Her breath was coming quickly.

"She's too fat. I don't like them fat. I like them the way you are, honey," he said, smiling sleepily at her. They stared at each other for a while through the screen door. He said softly, "Now, what you're going to do is this: you're going to come out that door. You're going to sit up front with me and Ellie's going to sit in the back, the hell with Ellie, right? This isn't Ellie's date. You're my date. I'm your lover, honey."

"What? You're crazy—"

"Yes. I'm your lover. You don't know what that is but you will," he said. "I know that too. I know all about you. But look: it's real nice and you couldn't ask for nobody better than me, or more polite. I always keep my word. I'll tell you how it is, I'm always nice at first, the first time. I'll hold you so tight you won't think you have to try to get away or pretend anything because you'll know you can't. And I'll come inside you where it's all secret and you'll know you can't. And I'll come inside you where it's all secret and you'll give in to me and you'll love me—"

105   "Shut up! You're crazy!" Connie said. She backed away from the door. She put her hands up against her ears as if she'd heard something terrible, something not meant for her. "People don't talk like that, you're crazy," she muttered. Her heart was almost too big now for her chest and its pumping made sweat break out all over her. She looked out to see Arnold Friend pause and then take a step toward the porch, lurching. He almost fell. But, like a clever drunken man, he managed to catch his balance. He wobbled in his high boots and grabbed hold of one of the porch posts.

"Honey?" he said. "You still listening?"

"Get the hell out of here!"

"Be nice, honey. Listen."

"I'm going to call the police—"

110   He wobbled again and out of the side of his mouth came a fast spat curse, an aside not meant for her to hear. But even this "Christ!" sounded forced. Then he began to smile again. She watched this smile come, awkward as if he was smiling from inside a mask. His whole face was a mask, she thought wildly, tanned down to his throat but then running out as if he had plastered makeup on his face but had forgotten about his throat.

"Honey—? Listen, here's how it is. I always tell the truth and I promise you this: I ain't coming in that house after you."

"You better not! I'm going to call the police if you—if you don't—"

"Honey," he said, talking right through her voice, "honey. I'm not coming in there but you are coming out here. You know why?"

She was panting. The kitchen looked like a place she had never seen before, some room she had run inside but that wasn't good enough, wasn't going to help her. The kitchen window had never had a curtain, after three years, and there were dishes in the sink for her to do—probably—and if you ran your hand across the table you'd probably feel something sticky there.

115   "You listening, honey? Hey?"

"—going to call the police—"

"Soon as you touch the phone I don't need to keep my promise and can come inside. You won't want that."

She rushed forward and tried to lock the door. Her fingers were shaking. "But why lock it," Arnold Friend said gently, talking right into her face. "It's just a screen door. It's just nothing." One of his boots was at a strange angle, as if his foot wasn't in it. It pointed out to the left, bent at the ankle. "I mean, anybody can break through a screen door and glass and wood and iron or anything else if he needs to, anybody at all, and specially Arnold Friend. If the place got lit up with a fire, honey, you'd come runnin' our into my arms, right into my arms an' safe at home—like you knew I was your lover and'd stopped fooling around. I don't mind a nice shy girl but I don't like no fooling around." Part of those words were spoken with a slight rhythmic lilt, and Connie somehow recognized them—the echo of a song from last year, about a girl rushing into her boyfriend's arms and coming home again—

Connie stood barefoot on the linoleum floor, staring at him. "What do you want?" she whispered.

"I want you," he said.

"What?"   120

"Seen you that night and thought, that's the one, yes sir. I never needed to look anymore."

"But my father's coming back. He's coming to get me. I had to wash my hair first—" She spoke in a dry, rapid voice, hardly raising it for him to hear.

"No, your daddy is not coming and yes, you had to wash your hair and you washed it for me. It's nice and shining and all for me. I thank you, sweetheart," he said with a mock bow, but again he almost lost his balance. He had to bend and adjust his boots. Evidently his feet did not go all the way down; the boots must have been stuffed with something so that he would seem taller. Connie stared out at him and behind him at Ellie in the car, who seemed to be looking off toward Connie's right, into nothing. Then Ellie said, pulling the words out of the air one after another as if he were just discovering them, "You want me to pull out the phone?"

"Shut your mouth and keep it shut," Arnold Friend said, his face red from   125 bending over or maybe from embarrassment because Connie had seen his boots. "This ain't none of your business."

"What—what are you doing? What do you want?" Connie said. "If I call the police they'll get you, they'll arrest you—"

"Promise was not to come in unless you touch that phone, and I'll keep that promise," he said. He resumed his erect position and tried to force his shoulders back. He sounded like a hero in a movie, declaring something important. But he spoke too loudly and it was as if he was speaking to someone behind Connie. "I ain't made plans for coming in that house where I don't belong but just for you to come out to me, the way you should. Don't you know who I am?"

"You're crazy," she whispered. She backed away from the door but did not want to go into another part of the house, as if this would give him permission to come through the door. "What do you . . . you're crazy, you . . ."

"Huh? What're you saying, honey?"

130   Her eyes darted everywhere in the kitchen. She could not remember what it was, this room.

"This is how it is, honey: you come out and we'll drive away, have a nice ride. But if you don't come out we're gonna wait till your people come home and then they're all going to get it."

"You want that telephone pulled out?" Ellie said. He held the radio away from his ear and grimaced, as if without the radio the air was too much for him.

"I toldja shut up, Ellie," Arnold Friend said, "you're deaf, get a hearing aid, right? Fix yourself up. This little girl's no trouble and's gonna be nice to me, so Ellie keep to yourself, this ain't your date—right? Don't hem him in on me, don't hog, don't crush, don't bird dog, don't trail me," he said in a rapid, meaningless voice, as if he were running through all the expressions he'd learned but was no longer sure which of them was in style, then rushing on to new ones, making them up with his eyes closed. "Don't crawl under my fence, don't squeeze in my chipmunk hole, don't sniff my glue, suck my Popsicle, keep your own greasy fingers on yourself!" He shaded his eyes and peered in at Connie, who was backed against the kitchen table. "Don't mind him, honey, he's just a creep. He's a dope. Right? I'm the boy for you and like I said, you come out here nice like a lady and give me your hand, and nobody else gets hurt, I mean, your nice old bald-headed daddy and your mummy and your sister in her high heels. Because listen: why bring them in this?"

"Leave me alone," Connie whispered.

135   "Hey, you know that old woman down the road, the one with the chickens and stuff—you know her?"

"She's dead!"

"Dead? What? You know her?" Arnold Friend said.

"She's dead—"

"Don't you like her?"

140   "She's dead—she's—she isn't here anymore—"

"But don't you like her, I mean, you got something against her? Some grudge or something?" Then his voice dipped as if he was conscious of a rudeness. He touched the sunglasses perched up on top of his head as if to make sure they were still there. "Now, you be a good girl."

"What are you going to do?"

"Just two things, or maybe three," Arnold Friend said. "But I promise it won't last long and you'll like me the way you get to like people you're close to. You will. It's all over for you here, so come on out. You don't want your people in any trouble, do you?"

She turned and bumped against a chair or something, hurting her leg, but she ran into the back room and picked up the telephone. Something roared in her ear, a tiny roaring, and she was so sick with fear that she could do nothing but listen to it—the telephone was clammy and very heavy and her fingers groped down to the dial but were too weak to touch it. She began to scream into the phone, into the roaring. She cried out, she cried for her mother, she felt her breath start jerking back and forth in her lungs as if it was something Arnold Friend was stabbing her with again and again with no tenderness. A noisy sorrowful wailing rose all about her and she was locked inside it the way she was locked inside this house.

After a while she could hear again. She was sitting on the floor with her 145
wet back against the wall.

Arnold Friend was saying from the door, "That's a good girl. Put the phone back."

She kicked the phone away from her.

"No, honey. Pick it up. Put it back right."

She picked it up and put it back. The dial tone stopped.

"That's a good girl. Now, you come outside." 150

She was hollow with what had been fear but what was now just an emptiness. All that screaming had blasted it out of her. She sat, one leg cramped under her, and deep inside her brain was something like a pinpoint of light that kept going and would not let her relax. She thought, I'm not going to see my mother again. She thought, I'm not going to sleep in my bed again. Her bright-green blouse was all wet.

Arnold Friend said, in a gentle-loud voice that was like a stage voice, "The place where you came from ain't there anymore, and where you had in mind to go is canceled out. This place you are now—inside your daddy's house—is nothing but a cardboard box I can knock down anytime. You know that and always did know it. You hear me?"

She thought, *I have got to think. I have got to know what to do.*

"We'll go out to a nice field, out in the country here where it smells so nice and it's sunny," Arnold Friend said. "I'll have my arms tight around you so you won't need to try to get away and I'll show you what love is like, what it does. The hell with this house! It looks solid all right," he said. He ran his fingernail down the screen and the noise did not make Connie shiver, as it would have the day before. "Now, put your hand on your heart, honey. Feel that? That feels solid too but we know better. Be nice to me, be sweet like you can because what else is there for a girl like you but to be sweet and pretty and give in?—and get away before her people get back?"

155   She felt her pounding heart. Her hand seemed to enclose it. She thought for the first time in her life that it was nothing that was hers, that belonged to her, but just a pounding, living thing inside this body that wasn't really hers either.

"You don't want them to get hurt," Arnold Friend went on. "Now, get up, honey. Get up all by yourself."

She stood.

"Now, turn this way. That's right. Come over here to me.—Ellie, put that away, didn't I tell you? You dope. You miserable creepy dope," Arnold Friend said. His words were not angry but only part of an incantation. The incantation was kindly. "Now, come out through the kitchen to me, honey, and let's see a smile, try it, you're a brave, sweet little girl and now they're eating corn and hot dogs cooked to bursting over an outdoor fire, and they don't know one thing about you and never did and honey, you're better than them because not a one of them would have done this for you."

Connie felt the linoleum under her feet; it was cool. She brushed her hair back out of her eyes. Arnold Friend let go of the post tentatively and opened his arms for her, his elbows pointing in toward each other and his wrists limp, to show that this was an embarrassed embrace and a little mocking, he didn't want to make her self-conscious.

160   She put out her hand against the screen. She watched herself push the door slowly open as if she was back safe somewhere in the other doorway, watching this body and this head of long hair moving out into the sunlight where Arnold Friend waited.

"My sweet little blue-eyed girl," he said in a half-sung sigh that had nothing to do with her brown eyes but was taken up just the same by the vast sunlit reaches of the land behind him and on all sides of him—so much land that Connie had never seen before and did not recognize except to know that she was going to it.

1966

QUESTIONS

1. At what specific points in the story do your expectations about "where you are going" change? Why and how so? How might these shifts in your expectations relate to Connie's?
2. To what extent is the major conflict in Oates's story external (between Connie and Arnold, Connie and her family, Connie and her milieu)? To what extent is it internal (within Connie herself)? Why might she act as she does at the story's end? What happens next, or does it matter?
3. Both Connie and Arnold Friend more than once suggest that he is, or should be, familiar to her. Aside from the fact she has seen him at least once before, why and how does he seem familiar? Why might that familiarity be significant,

or how might it shape your sense of who Arnold is or what he might represent in the story?

SUGGESTIONS FOR WRITING

1. Write an essay comparing the way any two of the stories in this chapter handle the traditional elements of plot: exposition, rising action, climax, falling action, conclusion. Consider especially how plot elements contribute to the overall artistic effect.
2. Many stories depict events out of chronological order. For example, SONNY'S BLUES makes liberal use of flashbacks. Select any story from this anthology, and write an essay discussing the significance of sequence.
3. Write an essay that explores the central conflict in any one of the stories in this chapter. What is the nature of the conflict? When, where, and how does it develop or become more complicated as the story unfolds? How is it resolved at the end of the story? Why and how is that resolution satisfying?

2 NARRATION AND POINT OF VIEW

When we read fiction, our sense of who is telling us the story is as important as what happens. Unlike drama, in which events are acted out in front of us, fiction is always mediated or represented to us by someone else, a **narrator**. Often a reader is very aware of the **voice** of a narrator telling the story, as if the words are being spoken aloud. Commonly, stories also reveal a distinct angle of vision or perspective from which the characters, events, and other aspects are viewed. Just as the verbal quality of narration is called the voice, the visual angle is called the **focus**. Focus acts much as a camera does, choosing the direction of our gaze, the framework in which we see things. Both voice and focus are generally considered together in the term **point of view**. To understand how a story is narrated, you need to recognize both voice and focus. These in turn shape what we know and care about as the plot unfolds, and they determine how close we feel to each character.

A story is said to be from a character's point of view, or a character is said to be a focal or focalizing character, if for the most part the action centers on that character, as if we see with that character's eyes or we watch that character closely. But the effects of narration certainly involve more than attaching a video camera to a character's head or tracking wherever the character moves. What about the spoken and unspoken words? In some stories, the narrator is a character, and we may feel as if we are overhearing his or her thoughts, whereas in other stories the narrator takes a very distant or critical view of the characters. At times a narrator seems more like a disembodied, unidentified voice. Prose fiction has many ways to convey speech and thought, so it is important to consider voice as well as focus when we try to understand the narration of a story.

Besides focus and voice, point of view encompasses more general matters of value. A story's narrator may explicitly endorse or subtly support whatever a certain character values, knows, or seeks, even when the character is absent or silent or unaware. Other narrators may treat characters and their interests with far more detachment. At the same time, the **style** and **tone** of the narrator's voice—from echoing the characters' feelings to mocking their pretentious speech or thoughts to stating their actions in formal diction—may convey clues that a character or a narrator's perspective is limited. Such discrepancies or gaps between vision and voice, intentions and understandings, or expectations and outcomes generate **irony**.

Sometimes the point of view shifts over the course of a narrative. Or the style of narration itself may even change dramatically from one section to another. Bram Stoker's novel *Dracula* (1897), for example, is variously narrated through characters' journals and letters, as well as newspaper articles.

The point of view varies according to the narrator's position in the story and the grammatical person (for example, first or third) the narrative voice assumes. These elements determine who is telling the story, whom it is about, and what information the reader has access to.

TYPES OF NARRATION

Third-Person Narration

A *third-person narrator* tells an unidentified listener or reader what happened, referring to all characters using the pronouns *he, she,* or *they*. Third-person narration is virtually always external, meaning that the narrator is not a character in the story and does not participate in its action. Even so, different types of third-person narration—omniscient, limited, and objective—provide the reader with various amounts and kinds of information about the characters.

An *omniscient* or *unlimited narrator* has access to the thoughts, perceptions, and experiences of more than one character (often of several), though such narrators usually focus selectively on a few important characters. A *limited narrator* is an external, third-person narrator who tells the story from a distinct point of view, usually that of a single character, revealing that character's thoughts and relating the action from his or her perspective. This focal character is also known as a **central consciousness**. Sometimes a limited narrator will reveal the thoughts and feelings of a small number of the characters in order to enhance the story told about the central consciousness. (Jane Austen's novel *Emma* [1815] includes a few episodes from Mr. Knightley's point of view to show what he thinks about Emma Woodhouse, the focal character, and her relationships.) Finally, an *objective narrator* does not explicitly report the characters' thoughts and feelings but may obliquely suggest them through the characters' speech and actions. Stories with objective narrators consist mostly of dialogue interspersed with minimal description.

First-Person Narration

Instead of using third-person narration, an author might choose to tell a story from the point of view of a *first-person narrator*. Most common is first-person singular narration, in which the narrator uses the pronoun *I*. The narrator may be a major or minor character within the story and therefore is an *internal narrator*. Notice that the first-person narrator may be telling a story mainly about someone else or about his or her own experience. Sometimes the first-person narrator addresses an **auditor**, a listener within the fiction whose possible reaction is part of the story.

One kind of narrator that is especially effective at producing irony is the *unreliable narrator*. First-person narrators may unintentionally reveal their flaws as they try to impress. Or narrators may make claims that other characters or the audience know to be false or distorted. Some fictions are narrated by villains, insane people, fools, liars, or hypocrites. When we resist a narrator's point of view and judge his or her flaws or misperceptions, we call that narrator unreliable. This does not mean that you should dismiss everything such a narrator says, but you should be on the alert for ironies.

Less common is the first-person plural, where the narrator uses the pronoun *we*. The plural may be used effectively to express the shared perspective of a community, particularly one that is isolated, unusually close-knit, or highly regulated. Elizabeth Gaskell's classic short novel *Cranford* (1853) is a good example. The narrator is a young woman who visits a community of genteel widows and spinsters in the English village of Cranford and describes their customs. At one point, a visitor arrives, Lady Glenmire, and all of Cranford society is in awe of her aristocratic rank and title. At an evening party, "We were all very silent at first. We were thinking what we could talk about, that should be high enough to interest My Lady. There had been a rise in the price of sugar, which, as preserving-time was near, was a piece of intelligence to all our housekeeping hearts, and would have been the natural topic if Lady Glenmire had not been by. But we were not sure if the Peerage ate preserves" (that is, whether aristocrats ate fruit jam). The high price of sugar doesn't seem "high enough" in another sense for a high-ranked guest to talk about.

The narrator of Cranford does refer to herself as "I" and sometimes addresses the reader as "you." The narrative perspective and voice is rather similar in Kazuo Ishiguro's *Never Let Me Go* (2005), a novel that also portrays an isolated group that follows regulated customs. At a boarding school, a student, Polly, suddenly questions one of the rules: "*We* all went silent. Miss Lucy [the teacher] didn't often get cross, but when she did, *you* certainly knew about it, and we thought for a second Polly was for it [would be punished]. But then we saw Miss Lucy wasn't angry, just deep in thought. *I* remember feeling furious at Polly for so stupidly breaking the unwritten rule, but at the same time, being terribly excited about what answer Miss Lucy might give" (emphasis added). Ishiguro's narrator, like Gaskell's, resorts to different narrative perspectives and voices to represent the experience of both a community and an individual in it.

Second-Person Narration

Like narrators who refer to themselves as "we" throughout a work of fiction, *second-person narrators* who consistently speak to *you* are unusual. This technique has the effect of turning the reader into a character in the story. Jay

McInerney, for example, in his novel *Bright Lights, Big City* (1984) employs the second-person voice, creating an effect similar to conversational anecdotes. But second-person narratives can instead sound much like instructional manuals or "how-to" books or like parents or other elders speaking to children.

TENSE

Along with the grammatical "person," the verb tense used has an effect on the narration of a story. Since narrative is so wrapped up in memory, most stories rely on the past tense. In contemporary fiction, however, the present tense is also frequently used. The present tense can lend an impression of immediacy, of frequent repetition, or of a dreamlike or magical state in which time seems suspended. An author might also use the present tense to create a conversational tone. Rarely, for a strange prophetic outlook, a narrator may even use the future tense, predicting what *will* happen.

NARRATOR VERSUS IMPLIED AUTHOR

As you discover how a story is being narrated, by whom, and from what point of view, how should you respond to the shifting points of view, tones of voice, and hints of critical distance or irony toward characters? Who is really shaping the story, and how do you know what is intended? Readers may answer the question "Who is telling this story?" with the name of the author. It is more accurate and practical, however, to distinguish between the narrator who presents the story and the flesh-and-blood author who wrote it, even when the two are hard to tell apart. If you are writing an essay about a short story, you do not need to research the biography of the author or find letters or interviews in which the author comments on the writing process or the intended themes of the work. This sort of biographical information may enrich your study of the story (it can be a good critical approach), but it is not *necessary* to an understanding of the text. And yet if you only consider the narrator when you interpret a story, you may find it difficult to account for the effects of distance and irony that come from a narrator's or a character's limitations. Many critics rely on the concept of the *implied author*, not to be confused with either the flesh-and-blood person who wrote the work or the narrator who relates the words to us. Most of the time, when we ask questions about the "author" of a work, we are asking about its implied author, the perspective and values that govern the whole work, including the narrator.

Why not ignore the idea of the narrator or the implied author? What's wrong with writing an essay about *Great Expectations* (1860–61) in which you refer only to the author, Charles Dickens? After all, his name is on the title page, and we know that Pip's coming-of-age story has some autobiographical aspects. Yet from the first sentence of the novel it is clear that someone besides Charles Dickens is telling the story: Pip, the first-person narrator. "My father's family name being Pirrip, and my Christian name Philip, my infant tongue could make of both names nothing longer or more explicit than Pip. So, I called myself Pip, and came to be called Pip." The reader sympathizes with Pip, the focal character-narrator, as an abused child, but he is also flawed and makes mistakes, as Pip himself realizes when he has grown up and tells the story of his own life. The reader understands Pip's errors through the subtle guidance of the implied author who created the narrator and shaped the plot and other characters. How useful or accurate would it be to attribute Pip's character and experience to the real Charles Dickens? The facts of the flesh-and-blood author's life and his actual personality differ widely from the novel's character, which in turn may differ from what Charles Dickens himself consciously intended. Hence the value of referring to a narrator and an implied author of a work of fiction. In critical essays, these concepts help us discover what even the most detailed biography might never pin down: Who in fact was Charles Dickens, and what did he actually intend in *Great Expectations*?

Reading a story, we know that it consists of words on a page, but we imagine the narrator speaking to us, giving shape, focus, and voice to a particular history. At the same time, we recognize that the reader should not take the narrator's words as absolute truth, but rather as effects shaped by an implied author. The concept of the implied author helps keep the particulars of the real author's (naturally imperfect) personality and life out of the picture. But it also reminds us to distinguish between the act of writing the work and the imaginary utterance of "telling" the story: The narrator is *neither* the real nor the implied author.

Questions about Narration and Point of View

- Does the narrator speak in the first, second, or third person?
- Is the story narrated in the past or present tense? Does the verb tense affect your reading of it in any way?
- Does the narrator use a distinctive vocabulary, style, and tone, or is the language more standard and neutral?
- Is the narrator identified as a character, and if so, how much does he or she participate in the action?
- Does the narrator ever seem to speak to the reader directly (addressing "you") or explicitly state opinions or values?
- Do you know what every character is thinking, or only some characters, or none?
- Does the narrative voice or focus shift during the story or remain consistent?
- Do the narrator, the characters, and the reader all perceive matters in the same way, or are there differences in levels of understanding?

Because our responses to a work of fiction are largely guided by the designs and values implied in a certain way of telling the story, questions about narration and point of view can often lead to good essay topics. You might start by considering any other choices the implied author might have made and how these would change your reading of the story. As you read the stories in this chapter, imagine different voices and visions, different narrative techniques, in order to assess the specific effects of the particular types of narration and point of view. How would each story's meaning and effects change if its narrative voice or focus were different? Can you show the reader of your essay how the specific narration and point of view of a story contribute to its significant effects?

EDGAR ALLAN POE
(1809–49)
The Cask of Amontillado

Orphaned before he was three, Edgar Poe was adopted by John Allan, a wealthy Richmond businessman. Poe received his early schooling in Richmond and in England before a brief, unsuccessful stint at the University of Virginia. After serving for two years in the army, he was appointed to West Point in 1830 but expelled within the year for cutting classes. Living in Baltimore with his grandmother, aunt, and cousin Virginia (whom he married in 1835, when she was thirteen), Poe eked out a precarious living as an editor; his keen-edged reviews earned him numerous literary enemies. His two-volume *Tales of the Grotesque and Arabesque* received little critical attention when published in 1839, but his poem "The Raven" (1845) made him a literary celebrity. After his wife's death of tuberculosis in 1847, Poe, already an alcoholic, became increasingly erratic; two years later he died mysteriously in Baltimore.

The thousand injuries of Fortunato I had borne as I best could, but when he ventured upon insult I vowed revenge. You, who so well know the nature of my soul, will not suppose, however, that I gave utterance to a threat. *At length* I would be avenged; this was a point definitively settled—but the very definitiveness with which it was resolved precluded the idea of risk. I must not only punish but punish with impunity. A wrong is unredressed when retribution overtakes its redresser. It is equally unredressed when the avenger fails to make himself felt as such to him who has done the wrong.

It must be understood that neither by word nor deed had I given Fortunato cause to doubt my good will. I continued, as was my wont, to smile in his face, and he did not perceive that my smile *now* was at the thought of his immolation.

He had a weak point—this Fortunato—although in other regards he was a man to be respected and even feared. He prided himself upon his connoisseurship in wine. Few Italians have the true virtuoso spirit. For the most part their enthusiasm is adopted to suit the time and opportunity, to practice imposture upon the British and Austrian *millionaires*. In painting and gemmary, Fortunato, like his countrymen, was a quack, but in the matter of old wines he was sincere. In this respect I did not differ from him materially;—I was skilful in the Italian vintages myself, and bought largely whenever I could.

It was about dusk, one evening during the supreme madness of the carnival season, that I encountered my friend. He accosted me with excessive warmth, for he had been drinking much. The man wore motley. He had on a tight-fitting parti-striped dress,[1] and his head was surmounted by the conical cap and bells. I was so pleased to see him that I should never have done wringing his hand.

5   I said to him—"My dear Fortunato, you are luckily met. How remarkably well you are looking to-day. But I have received a pipe[2] of what passes for Amontillado, and I have my doubts."

"How?" said he. "Amontillado? A pipe? Impossible! And in the middle of the carnival!"

"I have my doubts," I replied; "and I was silly enough to pay the full Amontillado price without consulting you in the matter. You were not to be found, and I was fearful of losing a bargain."

"Amontillado!"

"I have my doubts."

10   "Amontillado!"

"And I must satisfy them."

"Amontillado!"

"As you are engaged, I am on my way to Luchresi. If any one has a critical turn it is he. He will tell me——"

"Luchresi cannot tell Amontillado from Sherry."

15   "And yet some fools will have it that his taste is a match for your own."

"Come, let us go."

"Whither?"

"To your vaults."

---

1. Fortunato wears a jester's costume (i.e., motley), not a woman's dress.
2. Large cask.

"My friend, no; I will not impose upon your good nature. I perceive you have an engagement. Luchresi———"

"I have no engagement;—come." 20

"My friend, no. It is not the engagement, but the severe cold with which I perceive you are afflicted. The vaults are insufferably damp. They are encrusted with nitre."[3]

"Let us go, nevertheless. The cold is merely nothing. Amontillado! You have been imposed upon. And as for Luchresi, he cannot distinguish Sherry from Amontillado."

Thus speaking, Fortunato possessed himself of my arm; and putting on a mask of black silk and drawing a *roquelaire*[4] closely about my person, I suffered him to hurry me to my palazzo.

There were no attendants at home; they had absconded to make merry in honour of the time. I had told them that I should not return until the morning, and had given them explicit orders not to stir from the house. These orders were sufficient, I well knew, to insure their immediate disappearance, one and all, as soon as my back was turned.

I took from their sconces two flambeaux,[5] and giving one to Fortu- 25
nato, bowed him through several suites of rooms to the archway that led into the vaults. I passed down a long and winding staircase, requesting him to be cautious as he followed. We came at length to the foot of the descent, and stood together upon the damp ground of the catacombs of the Montresors.

The gait of my friend was unsteady, and the bells upon his cap jingled as he strode.

"The pipe," said he.

"It is farther on," said I; "but observe the white web-work which gleams from these cavern walls."

He turned towards me, and looked into my eyes with two filmy orbs that distilled the rheum of intoxication.

"Nitre?" he asked, at length. 30

"Nitre," I replied. "How long have you had that cough?"

"Ugh! ugh! ugh!—ugh! ugh! ugh!—ugh! ugh! ugh!—ugh! ugh! ugh!— ugh! ugh! ugh!"

My poor friend found it impossible to reply for many minutes.

"It is nothing," he said, at last.

"Come," I said, with decision, "we will go back; your health is precious. 35
You are rich, respected, admired, beloved; you are happy, as once I was.

---

3. Potassium nitrate (saltpeter), a white mineral often found on the walls of damp caves and used in gunpowder.
4. Man's heavy, knee-length cloak.
5. That is, two torches from their wall brackets.

You are a man to be missed. For me it is no matter. We will go back; you will be ill, and I cannot be responsible. Besides, there is Luchresi——"

"Enough," he said; "the cough is a mere nothing; it will not kill me. I shall not die of a cough."

"True—true," I replied; "and, indeed, I had no intention of alarming you unnecessarily—but you should use all proper caution. A draught of this Medoc[6] will defend us from the damps."

Here I knocked off the neck of a bottle which I drew from a long row of its fellows that lay upon the mould.

"Drink," I said, presenting him the wine.

40   He raised it to his lips with a leer. He paused and nodded to me familiarly, while his bells jingled.

"I drink," he said, "to the buried that repose around us."

"And I to your long life."

He again took my arm, and we proceeded.

"These vaults," he said, "are extensive."

45   "The Montresors," I replied, "were a great and numerous family."

"I forget your arms."

"A huge human foot d'or,[7] in a field azure; the foot crushes a serpent rampant whose fangs are imbedded in the heel."

"And the motto?"

"*Nemo me impune lacessit.*"[8]

50   "Good!" he said.

The wine sparkled in his eyes and the bells jingled. My own fancy grew warm with the Medoc. We had passed through long walls of piled skeletons, with casks and puncheons[9] intermingling, into the inmost recesses of the catacombs. I paused again, and this time I made bold to seize Fortunato by an arm above the elbow.

"The nitre!" I said; "see, it increases. It hangs like moss upon the vaults. We are below the river's bed. The drops of moisture trickle among the bones. Come, we will go back ere it is too late. Your cough——"

"It is nothing," he said; "let us go on. But first, another draught of the Medoc."

I broke and reached him a flaçon of De Grâve. He emptied it at a breath. His eyes flashed with a fierce light. He laughed and threw the bottle upwards with a gesticulation I did not understand.

55   I looked at him in surprise. He repeated the movement—a grotesque one.

6. Like De Grâve (below), a French wine.
7. Of gold.
8. No one provokes me with impunity (Latin).
9. Large casks.

"You do not comprehend?" he said.

"Not I," I replied.

"Then you are not of the brotherhood."

"How?"

"You are not of the masons."[1]   60

"Yes, yes," I said; "yes, yes."

"You? Impossible! A mason?"

"A mason," I replied.

"A sign," he said, "a sign."

"It is this," I answered, producing from beneath the folds of my *roquelaire*   65
a trowel.

"You jest," he exclaimed, recoiling a few paces. "But let us proceed to
the Amontillado."

"Be it so," I said, replacing the tool beneath the cloak and again offering
him my arm. He leaned upon it heavily. We continued our route in search
of the Amontillado. We passed through a range of low arches, descended,
passed on, and descending again, arrived at a deep crypt, in which the
foulness of the air caused our flambeaux rather to glow than flame.

At the most remote end of the crypt there appeared another less spacious. Its walls had been lined with human remains, piled to the vault
overhead, in the fashion of the great catacombs of Paris. Three sides of this
interior crypt were still ornamented in this manner. From the fourth side
the bones had been thrown down, and lay promiscuously upon the earth,
forming at one point a mound of some size. Within the wall thus exposed
by the displacing of the bones, we perceived a still interior crypt or recess,
in depth about four feet, in width three, in height six or seven. It seemed
to have been constructed for no especial use within itself, but formed
merely the interval between two of the colossal supports of the roof of the
catacombs, and was backed by one of their circumscribing walls of solid
granite.

It was in vain that Fortunato, uplifting his dull torch, endeavoured to
pry into the depth of the recess. Its termination the feeble light did not
enable us to see.

"Proceed," I said; "herein is the Amontillado. As for Luchresi——"   70

"He is an ignoramus," interrupted my friend, as he stepped unsteadily
forward, while I followed immediately at his heels. In an instant he had
reached the extremity of the niche, and finding his progress arrested by
the rock, stood stupidly bewildered. A moment more and I had fettered
him to the granite. In its surface were two iron staples, distant from each

1. Masons or Freemasons, an international secret society condemned by the Catholic Church.
Montresor means by *mason* one who builds with stone, brick, etc.

other about two feet, horizontally. From one of these depended a short chain, from the other a padlock. Throwing the links about his waist, it was but the work of a few seconds to secure it. He was too much astounded to resist. Withdrawing the key I stepped back from the recess.

"Pass your hand," I said, "over the wall; you cannot help feeling the nitre. Indeed, it is *very* damp. Once more let me *implore* you to return. No? Then I must positively leave you. But I will first render you all the little attentions in my power."

"The Amontillado!" ejaculated my friend, not yet recovered from his astonishment.

"True," I replied; "the Amontillado."

75   As I said these words I busied myself among the pile of bones of which I have before spoken. Throwing them aside, I soon uncovered a quantity of building stone and mortar. With these materials and with the aid of my trowel, I began vigorously to wall up the entrance of the niche.

I had scarcely laid the first tier of the masonry when I discovered that the intoxication of Fortunato had in great measure worn off. The earliest indication I had of this was a low moaning cry from the depth of the recess. It was *not* the cry of a drunken man. There was then a long and obstinate silence. I laid the second tier, and the third, and the fourth; and then I heard the furious vibration of the chain. The noise lasted for several minutes, during which, that I might hearken to it with the more satisfaction, I ceased my labours and sat down upon the bones. When at last the clanking subsided, I resumed the trowel, and finished without interruption the fifth, the sixth, and the seventh tier. The wall was now nearly upon a level with my breast. I again paused, and holding the flambeaux over the mason-work, threw a few feeble rays upon the figure within.

A succession of loud and shrill screams, bursting suddenly from the throat of the chained form, seemed to thrust me violently back. For a brief moment I hesitated, I trembled. Unsheathing my rapier, I began to grope with it about the recess; but the thought of an instant reassured me. I placed my hand upon the solid fabric of the catacombs and felt satisfied. I reapproached the wall. I replied to the yells of him who clamoured. I re-echoed, I aided, I surpassed them in volume and in strength. I did this, and the clamourer grew still.

It was now midnight, and my task was drawing to a close. I had completed the eighth, the ninth and the tenth tier. I had finished a portion of the last and the eleventh; there remained but a single stone to be fitted and plastered in. I struggled with its weight; I placed it partially in its destined position. But now there came from out the niche a low laugh that erected the hairs upon my head. It was succeeded by a sad voice, which I had difficulty in recognizing as that of the noble Fortunato. The voice said—

"Ha! ha! ha!—he! he! he!—a very good joke, indeed—an excellent jest.
We will have many a rich laugh about it at the palazzo—he! he! he!—over
our wine—he! he! he!"

"The Amontillado!" I said.   80

"He! he! he!—he! he! he!—yes, the Amontillado. But is it not getting
late? Will not they be awaiting us at the palazzo—the Lady Fortunato and
the rest? Let us be gone."

"Yes," I said, "let us be gone."

"For the love of God, Montresor!"

"Yes," I said, "for the love of God!"

But to these words I hearkened in vain for a reply. I grew impatient. I   85
called aloud—

"Fortunato!"

No answer. I called again—

"Fortunato!"

No answer still. I thrust a torch through the remaining aperture and let
it fall within. There came forth in return only a jingling of the bells. My
heart grew sick; it was the dampness of the catacombs that made it so. I
hastened to make an end of my labour. I forced the last stone into its position; I plastered it up. Against the new masonry I re-erected the old ram-
part of bones. For the half of a century no mortal has disturbed them. *In
pace requiescat!*[2]

1846

QUESTIONS

1. What can the reader infer about Montresor's social position and character
   from hints in the text? What evidence does the text provide that Montresor is
   an unreliable narrator?
2. Who is the auditor, the "You," addressed in the first paragraph of THE CASK OF
   AMONTILLADO? When is the story being told? Why is it being told? How does
   your knowledge of the auditor and the occasion influence the effect the story
   has on you?
3. What devices does Poe use to create and heighten the suspense in the story?
   Is the outcome ever in doubt?

2. May he rest in peace (Latin).

ERNEST HEMINGWAY
(1899–1961)
Hills Like White Elephants

Among the most distinctively American of writers, even if he rarely wrote about America, Ernest Hemingway grew up in an upscale Chicago suburb, but he spent his summers on Lake Walloon in northern Michigan. Here, his physician father nurtured his love of hunting and fishing. Hemingway graduated from high school just two months after the United States entered World War I. Forbidden to enlist by his parents and uninterested in college, he worked as a reporter for the *Kansas City Star* before volunteering as a Red Cross ambulance driver. Badly wounded on the Italian front, he returned to the States and to journalism. Then, in 1921, he moved to Paris, entering the famed expatriate circle that included Ezra Pound, Gertrude Stein, and F. Scott Fitzgerald. Two volumes of stories, *In Our Time* (1925) and *Men without Women* (1927), and two major novels, *The Sun Also Rises* (1926) and *A Farewell to Arms* (1929), established Hemingway's international reputation as both a masterful literary craftsman and a chief spokesman for the "Lost Generation," while later, less critically acclaimed books on topics such as bullfighting (*Death in the Afternoon*, 1932) and big-game hunting (*Green Hills of Africa*, 1935) helped confirm his status as an almost mythic figure, patron saint of what the *New York Times* called a "cult" of daring and danger. Hemingway supported the Loyalists in the Spanish Civil War—the subject of his novel *For Whom the Bell Tolls* (1940); served as a war correspondent during World War II; and survived two plane crashes and four marriages. Severely depressed and suffering an array of physical ailments, he took his own life shortly before his sixty-second birthday, only a few years after earning both a Pulitzer—for *The Old Man and the Sea* (1952)—and a Nobel (1954).

The hills across the valley of the Ebro[1] were long and white. On this side there was no shade and no trees and the station was between two lines of rails in the sun. Close against the side of the station there was the warm shadow of the building and a curtain, made of strings of bamboo beads, hung across the open door into the bar, to keep out flies. The American and the girl with him sat at a table in the shade, outside the building. It was

---

1. River in northern Spain.

very hot and the express from Barcelona would come in forty minutes. It stopped at this junction for two minutes and went on to Madrid.

"What should we drink?" the girl asked. She had taken off her hat and put it on the table.

"It's pretty hot," the man said.

"Let's drink beer."

"Dos cervezas," the man said into the curtain.   5

"Big ones?" a woman asked from the doorway.

"Yes. Two big ones."

The woman brought two glasses of beer and two felt pads. She put the felt pads and the beer glasses on the table and looked at the man and the girl. The girl was looking off at the line of hills. They were white in the sun and the country was brown and dry.

"They look like white elephants," she said.

"I've never seen one," the man drank his beer.   10

"No, you wouldn't have."

"I might have," the man said. "Just because you say I wouldn't have doesn't prove anything."

The girl looked at the bead curtain. "They've painted something on it," she said. "What does it say?"

"Anis del Toro. It's a drink."

"Could we try it?"   15

The man called "Listen" through the curtain. The woman came out from the bar.

"Four reales."[2]

"We want two Anis del Toro."

"With water?"

"Do you want it with water?"   20

"I don't know," the girl said. "Is it good with water?"

"It's all right."

"You want them with water?" asked the woman.

"Yes, with water."

"It tastes like licorice," the girl said and put the glass down.   25

"That's the way with everything."

"Yes," said the girl. "Everything tastes of licorice. Especially all the things you've waited so long for, like absinthe."

"Oh, cut it out."

"You started it," the girl said. "I was being amused. I was having a fine time."

2. Spanish coins.

30   "Well, let's try and have a fine time."

"All right. I was trying. I said the mountains looked like white elephants. Wasn't that bright?"

"That was bright."

"I wanted to try this new drink. That's all we do, isn't it—look at things and try new drinks?"

"I guess so."

35   The girl looked across at the hills.

"They're lovely hills," she said. "They don't really look like white elephants. I just meant the coloring of their skin through the trees."

"Should we have another drink?"

"All right."

The warm wind blew the bead curtain against the table.

40   "The beer's nice and cool," the man said.

"It's lovely," the girl said.

"It's really an awfully simple operation, Jig," the man said. "It's not really an operation at all."

The girl looked at the ground the table legs rested on.

"I know you wouldn't mind it, Jig. It's really not anything. It's just to let the air in."

45   The girl did not say anything.

"I'll go with you and I'll stay with you all the time. They just let the air in and then it's all perfectly natural."

"Then what will we do afterward?"

"We'll be fine afterward. Just like we were before."

"What makes you think so?"

50   "That's the only thing that bothers us. It's the only thing that's made us unhappy."

The girl looked at the bead curtain, put her hand out and took hold of two of the strings of beads.

"And you think then we'll be all right and be happy."

"I know we will. You don't have to be afraid. I've known lots of people that have done it."

"So have I," said the girl. "And afterward they were all so happy."

55   "Well," the man said, "if you don't want to you don't have to. I wouldn't have you do it if you didn't want to. But I know it's perfectly simple."

"And you really want to?"

"I think it's the best thing to do. But I don't want you to do it if you don't really want to."

"And if I do it you'll be happy and things will be like they were and you'll love me?"

"I love you now. You know I love you."

"I know. But if I do it, then it will be nice again if I say things are like 60
white elephants, and you'll like it?"

"I'll love it. I love it now but I just can't think about it. You know how I
get when I worry."

"If I do it you won't ever worry?"

"I won't worry about that because it's perfectly simple."

"Then I'll do it. Because I don't care about me."

"What do you mean?"   65

"I don't care about me."

"Well, I care about you."

"Oh, yes. But I don't care about me. And I'll do it and then everything
will be fine."

"I don't want you to do it if you feel that way."

The girl stood up and walked to the end of the station. Across, on the 70
other side, were fields of grain and trees along the banks of the Ebro. Far
away, beyond the river, were mountains. The shadow of a cloud moved
across the field of grain and she saw the river through the trees.

"And we could have all this," she said. "And we could have everything
and every day we make it more impossible."

"What did you say?"

"I said we could have everything."

"We can have everything."

"No, we can't."   75

"We can have the whole world."

"No, we can't."

"We can go everywhere."

"No, we can't. It isn't ours anymore."

"It's ours."

"No, it isn't. And once they take it away, you never get it back."   80

"But they haven't taken it away."

"We'll wait and see."

"Come on back in the shade," he said. "You mustn't feel that way."

"I don't feel any way," the girl said. "I just know things."   85

"I don't want you to do anything that you don't want to do—"

"Nor that isn't good for me," she said. "I know. Could we have another
beer?"

"All right. But you've got to realize—"

"I realize," the girl said. "Can't we maybe stop talking?"

They sat down at the table and the girl looked across at the hills on the 90
dry side of the valley and the man looked at her and at the table.

"You've got to realize," he said, "that I don't want you to do it if you don't want to. I'm perfectly willing to go through with it if it means anything to you."

"Doesn't it mean anything to you? We could get along."

"Of course it does. But I don't want anybody but you. I don't want any one else. And I know it's perfectly simple."

"Yes, you know it's perfectly simple."

95   "It's all right for you to say that, but I do know it."

"Would you do something for me now?"

"I'd do anything for you."

"Would you please please please please please please please stop talking?"

He did not say anything but looked at the bags against the wall of the station. There were labels on them from all the hotels where they had spent nights.

100   "But I don't want you to," he said, "I don't care anything about it."

"I'll scream," the girl said.

The woman came out through the curtains with two glasses of beer and put them down on the damp felt pads. "The train comes in five minutes," she said.

"What did she say?" asked the girl.

"That the train is coming in five minutes."

105   The girl smiled brightly at the woman, to thank her.

"I'd better take the bags over to the other side of the station," the man said. She smiled at him.

"All right. Then come back and we'll finish the beer."

He picked up the two heavy bags and carried them around the station to the other tracks. He looked up the tracks but could not see the train. Coming back, he walked through the barroom, where people waiting for the train were drinking. He drank an Anis at the bar and looked at the people. They were all waiting reasonably for the train. He went out through the bead curtain. She was sitting at the table and smiled at him.

"Do you feel better?" he asked.

110   "I feel fine," she said. "There's nothing wrong with me. I feel fine."

1927

QUESTIONS

1. Find the first indication in HILLS LIKE WHITE ELEPHANTS that the two main characters are not getting along. What is the first clue about the exact nature of their conflict? Why are they going to Madrid? Why do the characters (and the author) refrain from speaking about it explicitly?

2. Point of view includes what characters see. Notice each use of the word "look." What does each person in the story look at, and what does each person seem to understand or feel? Is there anything in the story that none of these people would be able to see or know? How do the different kinds of observation add to the effect of the story?

3. Research the phrase "white elephant." What is the significance of this phrase in the story's title?

JAMAICA KINCAID
(b. 1949)
Girl

Raised in poverty by her homemaker mother and carpenter stepfather on the small Caribbean island of Antigua, Elaine Potter Richardson was sent to the United States to earn her own living at age seventeen, much like the protagonists of her first novels, *Annie John* (1983) and *Lucy* (1990). Working as an au pair and receptionist, she earned her high-school equivalency degree and studied photography at the New School for Social Research in New York and, briefly, Franconia College in New Hampshire. Returning to New York, she took the name of a character in a George Bernard Shaw play, at least in part out of resentment toward her mother, with whom she had once been very close. After a short stint as a freelance journalist, Kincaid worked as a regular contributor to the *New Yorker* from 1976 until 1995, in 1979 marrying its editor's son, composer Allen Shawn, with whom she would eventually move to Bennington, Vermont and raise two children. "Girl," her first published story, appeared in the *New Yorker* in 1978 and was later republished in her first collection, *At the Bottom of the River* (1983). Subsequent novels include *The Autobiography of My Mother* (1996), paradoxically the least autobiographical of her books; *Mr. Potter* (2002), a fictionalized account of her efforts to understand the biological father she never knew; and *See Now Then* (2013). Kincaid's equally impressive nonfiction includes *My Brother* (1997), a memoir inspired by her youngest brother's death from AIDS, and *A Small Place* (1988), an essay exploring the profound economic and psychological impact of Antigua's dependence on tourism. Divorced in 2002, Kincaid is currently Professor of African and African American Studies in Residence at Harvard.

ash the white clothes on Monday and put them on the stone heap; wash the color clothes on Tuesday and put them on the clothesline to dry; don't walk barehead in the hot sun; cook pumpkin fritters in very hot sweet oil; soak your little cloths right after you take them off; when buying cotton to make yourself a nice blouse, be sure that it doesn't have gum on it, because that way it won't hold up well after a wash; soak salt fish overnight before you cook it; is it true that you sing benna[1] in Sunday school?; always eat your food in such a way that it won't turn someone else's stomach; on Sundays try to walk like a lady and not like the slut you are so bent on becoming; don't sing benna in Sunday school; you mustn't speak to wharf-rat boys, not even to give directions; don't eat fruits on the street—flies will follow you; *but I don't sing benna on Sundays at all and never in Sunday school*; this is how to sew on a button; this is how to make a buttonhole for the button you have just sewed on; this is how to hem a dress when you see the hem coming down and so to prevent yourself from looking like the slut I know you are so bent on becoming; this is how you iron your father's khaki shirt so that it doesn't have a crease; this is how you iron your father's khaki pants so that they don't have a crease; this is how you grow okra—far from the house, because okra tree harbors red ants; when you are growing dasheen, make sure it gets plenty of water or else it makes your throat itch when you are eating it; this is how you sweep a corner; this is how you sweep a whole house; this is how you sweep a yard; this is how you smile to someone you don't like too much; this is how you smile to someone you don't like at all; this is how you smile to someone you like completely; this is how you set a table for tea; this is how you set a table for dinner; this is how you set a table for dinner with an important guest; this is how you set a table for lunch; this is how you set a table for breakfast; this is how to behave in the presence of men who don't know you very well, and this way they won't recognize immediately the slut I have warned you against becoming; be sure to wash every day, even if it is with your own spit; don't squat down to play marbles— you are not a boy, you know; don't pick people's flowers—you might catch something; don't throw stones at blackbirds, because it might not be a blackbird at all; this is how to make a bread pudding; this is how to make doukona;[2] this is how to make pepper pot; this is how to make a good medicine for a cold; this is how to make a good medicine to throw away a child before it even becomes a child; this is how to catch a fish; this is how to throw back a fish you don't like, and that way something bad won't fall on you; this is how to bully a man; this is how a man bullies you; this is how to love a man, and if this doesn't work there are other ways, and if they don't work don't feel too bad about giving up; this is how to spit up

---

1. Caribbean folk-music style.
2. Spicy pudding, often made from plantain and wrapped in a plantain or banana leaf.

in the air if you feel like it, and this is how to move quick so that it doesn't fall on you; this is how to make ends meet; always squeeze bread to make sure it's fresh; *but what if the baker won't let me feel the bread?*; you mean to say that after all you are really going to be the kind of woman who the baker won't let near the bread?

1983

QUESTIONS

1. Describe the focus, or focalization, in GIRL. Do we see what one person sees or observe one person in particular? Describe the voice of the narrator in GIRL. Who is the "you"? How do the focus and voice contribute to the reader's response to the story?
2. Look closely at the indications of time in the story. What actions take place at certain times? Does any event or action happen only once? Is there a plot in GIRL? If so, how would you summarize it?
3. The instructions in GIRL have different qualities, as if they come from different people or have different purposes. Why are two phrases in italics? Can you pick out the phrases that are more positive from the girl's point of view? Are there some that seem humorous or ironic?

SUGGESTIONS FOR WRITING

1. Write an essay analyzing the worldview and values of the narrator of GIRL, as they are implied by her instructions to the girl. What, to her, does it mean to be a good "girl," and why is it so important to be one?
2. Carry a notebook or record yourself for a day or two, and note any stories you tell or hear, such as in daydreams, in conversation, on the phone, through e-mail or texts. Consider what makes stories. Your transcripts may be short and may consist of memories, observations about your own character or those of people around you, plans, or predictions about the future. Choose two of your notes and modify them into plot summaries (no more than a paragraph each), using the first or the third person, the present or the past tense. Add a note about whether a full version of each story should give the inner thoughts of one or more characters, and why.
3. Hemingway's HILLS LIKE WHITE ELEPHANTS offers a detached perspective on relationships between men and women at the time the story was published. The story is narrated in a specific style and tone, relying on repetition of some ordinary phases (e.g., "you've got to realize"). Write an essay on the story, in which you show how the voice (style and tone) of the narration and the point of view help convey the text's perspective on contemporary sexual relationships.
4. Choose any story in this anthology and write a response paper exploring how its effect and meaning are shaped by its narration.
5. Write a parody of THE CASK OF AMONTILLADO set in modern times, perhaps on a college campus ("A Keg of Bud"?). Or write your own short story, "Boy," modeled on Jamaica Kincaid's GIRL. Use either your own point of view or that of an unwelcome adviser.

CHARACTER

Robert Buss, *Dickens' Dream* (1870)

In the unfinished watercolor *Dickens' Dream*, the nineteenth-century writer peacefully dozes while above and around him float ghostly images of the hundreds of characters that people his novels and, apparently, his dreams. This image captures the undeniable fact that characters loom large in the experience of fiction, for both its writers and its readers. Speaking for the former, Elie Wiesel describes a novelist like himself as practically possessed by characters who "force the writer to tell their stories" because "they want to get out." As readers of fiction, we care about *what* happens and *how* mainly because it happens *to* someone. Indeed, without a "someone," it is unlikely that anything would happen at all.

It is also often a "someone," or the *who* of a story, that sticks with us long after we have forgotten the details of what, where, and how. In this way, characters sometimes seem to take on a life of their own, to float free of the texts where we first encounter them, and even to haunt us. You may know almost nothing about Charles Dickens, but you probably have a vivid sense of his characters Ebenezer Scrooge and Tiny Tim from *A Christmas Carol* (1843).

A **character** is any personage in a literary work who acts, appears, or is referred to as playing a part. Though *personage* usually means a human being, it doesn't have to. Whole genres or subgenres of fiction are distinguished, in part, by the specific kinds of nonhuman characters they conventionally feature, whether alien species and intelligent machines (as in science fiction), animals (as in fables), or elves and monsters (as in traditional fairy tales and modern fantasy). All characters must have at least some human qualities, however, such as the ability to think, to feel pain, or to fall in love.

Evidence to Consider in Analyzing a Character: A Checklist

- the character's name
- the character's physical appearance
- objects and places associated with the character
- the character's actions
- the character's thoughts and speech, including
  - content (what he or she thinks or says)
  - timing (when he or she thinks or says it)
  - phrasing (how he or she thinks or says it)
- other characters' thoughts about the character
- other characters' comments to and about the character
- the narrator's comments about the character

HEROES AND VILLAINS VERSUS PROTAGONISTS AND ANTAGONISTS

A common term for the character with the leading male role is **hero**, the "good guy," who opposes the **villain**, or "bad guy." The leading female character is the **heroine**. Heroes and heroines are usually larger than life, stronger or better than most human beings, sometimes almost godlike. They are characters that a text encourages us to admire and even to emulate, so that the words *hero* and *heroine* can also be applied to especially admirable characters who do not play leading roles.

In most modern fiction, however, the leading character is much more ordinary, not so clearly or simply a "good guy." For that reason, it is usually more appropriate to use the older and more neutral terms *protagonist* and *antagonist* for the leading character and his or her opponent. These terms do not imply either the presence or the absence of outstanding virtue or vice.

The claim that a particular character either is or is not heroic might well make a good thesis for an essay, whereas the claim that he is or is not the protagonist generally won't. You might argue, for instance, that Montresor (in Poe's THE CASK OF AMONTILLADO) or Ebenezer Scrooge (in Dickens's *A Christmas Carol*) is a hero, but most readers would agree that each is his story's protagonist. Like most rules, however, this one admits of exceptions. Some stories do leave open to debate the question of which character most deserves to be called the *protagonist*. In SONNY'S BLUES, for example, Sonny and his brother are equally central.

Controversial in a different way is a particular type of protagonist known as an **antihero**. Found mainly in fiction written since around 1850, an antihero, as the name implies, possesses traits that make him or her the opposite of a traditional hero. An antihero may be difficult to like or admire. One early and influential example of an antihero is the narrator-protagonist of Fyodor Dostoevsky's 1864 Russian-language novella *Notes from the Underground—* a man utterly paralyzed by his own hypersensitivity. More familiar and recent examples are Homer and Bart Simpson.

It would be a mistake to see the quality of a work of fiction as dependent on whether we find its characters likable or admirable, just as it would be wrong to assume that an author's outlook or values are the same as those of the protagonist. Often, the characters we initially find least likable or admirable may ultimately move and teach us the most.

MAJOR VERSUS MINOR CHARACTERS

The *major* or *main characters* are those we see more of over time; we learn more about them, and we think of them as more complex and, frequently, as more "realistic" than the *minor characters*, the figures who fill out the story. These major characters can grow and change, too, sometimes defying our expectations.

Yet even though minor characters are less prominent and may seem less complex, they are ultimately just as indispensable to a story as major characters. Minor characters often play a key role in shaping our interpretations of, and attitudes toward, the major characters, and also in precipitating the changes that major characters undergo. For example, a minor character might function as a **foil**—a character that helps by way of contrast to reveal the unique qualities of another (especially main) character.

Questions about minor characters can lead to good essay topics precisely because such characters' significance to a story is not immediately apparent. Rather, we often have to probe the details of the story to formulate a persuasive interpretation of their roles.

FLAT VERSUS ROUND AND STATIC VERSUS DYNAMIC CHARACTERS

Characters that act from varied, often conflicting motives, impulses, and desires, and who seem to have psychological complexity, are said to be *round characters*; they can "surprise convincingly," as one critic puts it. Simple, one-dimensional characters that behave and speak in predictable or repetitive (if sometimes odd) ways are called *flat*. Sometimes characters seem round to us because our impression of them evolves as a story unfolds. Other times, the characters themselves—not just our impression of them—change as a result of events that occur in the story. A character that changes is *dynamic*; one that doesn't is *static*. Roundness and dynamism tend to go together. But the two qualities are distinct, and one does not require the other: Not all round characters are dynamic; not all dynamic characters are round.

Terms like *flat* and *round* or *dynamic* and *static* are useful so long as we do not let them harden into value judgments. Because flat characters are less complex than round ones, it is easy to assume they are artistically inferior; however, we need only to think of the characters of Charles Dickens, many of whom are flat, to realize that this is not always the case. A truly original flat character with only one or two very distinctive traits or behavioral or verbal tics will often prove more memorable than a round one. Unrealistic as such characters might seem, in real life you probably know at least one or two people who can always be counted on to say or do pretty much the same thing every time you see them. Exaggeration can provide insight, as well as humor. Dickens's large gallery of lovable flat characters includes a middle-aged man who constantly pulls himself up by his own hair and an old one who must continually be "fluffed up" by others because he tends to slide right out of his chair. *South Park*'s Kenny is little more than a hooded orange snowsuit and a habit of dying in ever more outrageous ways only to come back to life over and over again.

STOCK CHARACTERS AND ARCHETYPES

Flat characters who represent a familiar, frequently recurring type—the dumb blond, the mad scientist, the inept sidekick, the plain yet ever-sympathetic best friend—are called *stock characters* because they seem to be pulled out of a stockroom of familiar, prefabricated figures. Characters that recur in the myths and literature of many different ages and cultures are instead called **archetypes**, though this term also applies to recurring elements other than characters (such as actions or symbols). One archetypal character is the trick-ster figure that appears in the guise of Brer Rabbit in the Uncle Remus stories, the spider Anansi in certain African and Afro-Caribbean folktales, the coyote in Native American folklore, and, perhaps, Bugs Bunny. Another such charac-ter is the **scapegoat**.

READING CHARACTER IN FICTION AND LIFE

On the one hand, we get to know characters in a work of fiction and try to understand them much as we do people in real life. We observe what they own and wear, what they look like and where they live, how they carry them-selves and what expressions flit across their faces, how they behave in vari-ous situations, what they say and how they say it, what they don't say, what others say about them, and how others act in their presence. Drawing on all that evidence and on our own past experience of both literature and life, we try to deduce characters' motives and desires, their values and beliefs, their strengths and weaknesses—in short, to figure out what makes them tick and how they might react if circumstances changed. In our daily lives, being able to "read" other people in this way is a vital skill, one that we may well hone by reading fiction. The skills of observation and interpretation, the enlarged experience and capacity for empathy, that we develop in reading fiction can help us better navigate our real world.

On the other hand, however, fictional characters are not real people; they are imaginary personages crafted by authors. Fiction offers us a more orderly and expansive world than the one we inhabit every day—one in which each person, gesture, and word is a meaningful part of a coherent, purposeful design—one in which our responses to people are guided by a narrator and, ultimately, an author; one in which we can sometimes crawl inside other people's heads and know their thoughts; one in which we can get to know murderers and ministers, monsters and miracle workers—the sorts of people (or personages) we might be afraid, unwilling, or simply unable to meet or spend time with in real life.

In other words, fictional characters are the products not of nature, chance, or God, but of careful, deliberate **characterization**—the art and technique of representing fictional personages. In analyzing character, we thus need to consider not only who a character is and what precisely are his or her most important traits, motivations, and values, but also precisely how the text shapes our interpretation of, and degree of sympathy or admiration for, the charac-ter; what function the character serves in the narrative; and what the char-acter might represent.

This last issue is important because all characters, no matter how indi-vidualized and idiosyncratic, ultimately become meaningful to us only if they represent something beyond the story, something bigger than themselves—a type of person, a particular set of values or way of looking at the world, a human tendency, a demographic group. When you set out to write about a character, consider how the story would be different without the character and what the author says or shows us through the character.

Direct and Indirect Characterization: An Example and an Exercise

The following conversation appears in the pages of a well-known nineteenth-century novel. Even without being familiar with this novel, you should be able to discern a great deal about the two characters that converse in this scene simply by carefully attending to what each says and how each says it. As you will see, one of the things that differentiates the two speakers is that they hold conflicting views of "character" itself:

"In what order you keep these rooms, Mrs Fairfax!" said I. "No dust, no canvas coverings: except that the air feels chilly, one would think they were inhabited daily."

"Why, Miss Eyre, though Mr Rochester's visits here are rare, they are always sudden and unexpected; and as I observed that it put him out to find everything swathed up, and to have a bustle of arrangement on his arrival, I thought it best to keep the rooms in readiness."

"Is Mr Rochester an exacting, fastidious sort of man?"

"Not particularly so; but he has a gentleman's tastes and habits, and he expects to have things managed in conformity to them."

"Do you like him? Is he generally liked?"

"O yes; the family have always been respected here. Almost all the land in this neighbourhood, as far as you can see, has belonged to the Rochesters time out of mind."

"Well, but leaving his land out of the question, do you like him? Is he liked for himself?"

"I have no cause to do otherwise than like him; and I believe he is considered a just and liberal landlord by his tenants: but he has never lived much amongst them."

"But has he no peculiarities? What, in short, is his character?"

"Oh! his character is unimpeachable, I suppose. He is rather peculiar, perhaps: he has travelled a great deal, and seen a great deal of the world, I should think. I daresay he is clever: but I never had much conversation with him."

(continued on next page)

(continued)

"In what way is he peculiar?"

"I don't know—it is not easy to describe—nothing striking, but you feel it when he speaks to you: you cannot be always sure whether he is in jest or earnest, whether he is pleased or the contrary; you don't thoroughly understand him, in short—at least, I don't: but it is of no consequence, he is a very good master."

• What facts about the two speakers can you glean from this conversation? What do you infer about their individual outlooks, personalities, and values?
• What different definitions of the word *character* emerge here? How would you describe each speaker's view of what matters most in the assessment of character?

This scene—from Charlotte Brontë's *Jane Eyre* (1847)—demonstrates the first of the two major methods of presenting character—*indirect characterization* or showing (as opposed to *direct characterization* or telling). In this passage Brontë simply *shows* us what Jane (the narrator) and Mrs. Fairfax say and invites us to infer from their words who each character is (including the absent Mr. Rochester), how each looks at the world, and what each cares about.

Sometimes, however, authors present characters more directly, having narrators *tell* us what makes a character tick and what we are to think of him or her. Charlotte Brontë engages in both direct and indirect characterization in the paragraph of *Jane Eyre* that immediately follows the passage above. Here, Jane (the narrator) tells the reader precisely what she thinks this conversation reveals about Mrs. Fairfax, even as she reveals more about herself in the process:

This was all the account I got from Mrs Fairfax of her employer and mine. There are people who seem to have no notion of sketching a character, or observing and describing salient points, either in persons or things: the good lady evidently belonged to this class; my queries puzzled, but did not draw her out. Mr Rochester was Mr Rochester in her eyes; a gentleman, a landed proprietor—nothing more: she inquired and searched no further, and evidently wondered at my wish to gain a more definite notion of his identity.

• How does Jane's interpretation of Mrs. Fairfax compare to yours?
• How and why might this paragraph corroborate or complicate your view of Jane herself?

Characters, Conventions, and Beliefs

Just as fiction and the characters that inhabit it operate by somewhat different rules than do the real world and real people, so the rules that govern particular fictional worlds and their characters differ from one another. As the critic James Wood argues,

> our hunger for the particular depth or reality level of a character is tutored by each writer, and adapts to the internal conventions of each book. This is how we can read W. G. Sebald one day and Virginia Woolf or Philip Roth the next, and not demand that each resemble the other. [. . . Works of fiction] tend to fail not when the characters are not vivid or "deep" enough, but when the [work] in question has failed to teach us how to adapt to its conventions, has failed to manage a specific hunger for its own characters, its own reality level.

Works of fiction in various subgenres differ widely in how they handle characterization. Were a folktale, for example, to depict more than a few, mainly flat, archetypal characters; to make us privy to its characters' thoughts; or to offer up detailed descriptions of their physiques and wardrobes, it would cease both to be a folktale and to yield the particular sorts of pleasures and insights that only a folktale can. By the same token, readers of a folktale miss out on its pleasures and insights if they expect the wrong things of its characters and modes of characterization.

But even within the same fictional subgenre, the treatment of character varies over time and across cultures. Such variations sometimes reflect profound differences in the way people understand human nature. Individuals and cultures hold conflicting views of what produces personality, whether innate factors such as genes, environmental factors such as upbringing, supernatural forces, unconscious impulses or drives, or a combination of some or all of these. Views differ as well as to whether character is simply an unchanging given or something that can change through experience, conversion, or an act of will. Some works of fiction tackle such issues head on. But many others—especially from cultures or eras different from our own—may raise these questions for us simply because their modes of characterization imply an understanding of the self different from the one we take for granted.

We can thus learn a lot about our own values, prejudices, and beliefs by reading a wide array of fiction. Similarly, we learn from encountering a wide array of fictional characters, including those whose values, beliefs, and ways of life are vastly different from our own.

⋅ ⋅ ⋅

The stories in this chapter differ widely in terms of the number and types of characters they depict and the techniques they use to depict them. In their pages, you will meet a range of diverse individuals—some complex and compelling, some utterly ordinary—struggling to make sense of the people around them just as you work to make sense of them and, through them, yourself.

Questions about Character

- Who is the protagonist, or might there be more than one? Why and how so? Which other characters, if any, are main or major characters? Which are minor characters?
- What are the protagonist's most distinctive traits, and what is most distinctive about his or her outlook and values? What motivates the character? What is it about the character that creates internal and/or external conflict?
- Which textual details and moments reveal most about this character? Which are most surprising or might complicate your interpretation of this character? How is your view of the character affected by what you *don't* know about him or her?
- What are the roles of other characters? Which, if any, functions as an antagonist? Which, if any, serves as a foil? Why and how so? How would the story as a whole (not just its action or plot) be different if any of these characters disappeared? What points might the author be raising or illustrating through each character?
- Which of the characters, or which aspects of the characters, does the text encourage us to sympathize with or to admire? to view negatively? Why and how so?
- Does your view of any character change over the course of the story, or do any of the characters themselves change? If so, when, how, and why?
- Does characterization tend to be indirect or direct in the story? What kinds of information do and don't we get about the characters, and how does the story tend to give us that information?

TONI MORRISON
(b. 1931)

Recitatif[1]

Born in Lorain, Ohio, a steel town on the shores of Lake Erie, Chloe Anthony Wofford was the first member of her family to go to college, graduating from Howard University in 1953 and earning an MA from Cornell. She taught at both Texas Southern University and at Howard before becoming an editor at Random House, where she worked for nearly twenty years. In such novels as *The Bluest Eye* (1969), *Sula* (1973), *Song of Solomon* (1977), *Beloved* (1987), and *Paradise* (1998), Morri-

---

1. In classical music such as opera, a vocal passage that is sung in a speechlike manner.

son traces the problems and possibilities faced by black Americans struggling with slavery and its aftermath in the United States. More recent work includes her eighth novel, *Love* (2003); two picture books for children co-authored with her son, Slade—*The Bog Box* (1999) and *Book of Mean People* (2002); a book for young adults, *Remember: The Journey to School Integration* (2004); and *What Moves at the Margin: Selected Nonfiction* (2008). In 1993, Morrison became the first African American author to win the Nobel Prize for Literature.

My mother danced all night and Roberta's was sick. That's why we were taken to St. Bonny's. People want to put their arms around you when you tell them you were in a shelter, but it really wasn't bad. No big long room with one hundred beds like Bellevue.[2] There were four to a room, and when Roberta and me came, there was a shortage of state kids, so we were the only ones assigned to 406 and could go from bed to bed if we wanted to. And we wanted to, too. We changed beds every night and for the whole four months we were there we never picked one out as our own permanent bed.

It didn't start out that way. The minute I walked in and the Big Bozo introduced us, I got sick to my stomach. It was one thing to be taken out of your own bed early in the morning—it was something else to be stuck in a strange place with a girl from a whole other race. And Mary, that's my mother, she was right. Every now and then she would stop dancing long enough to tell me something important and one of the things she said was that they never washed their hair and they smelled funny. Roberta sure did. Smell funny, I mean. So when the Big Bozo (nobody ever called her Mrs. Itkin, just like nobody ever said St. Bonaventure)—when she said, "Twyla, this is Roberta. Roberta, this is Twyla. Make each other welcome." I said, "My mother won't like you putting me in here."

"Good," said Bozo. "Maybe then she'll come and take you home."

How's that for mean? If Roberta had laughed I would have killed her, but she didn't. She just walked over to the window and stood with her back to us.

"Turn around," said the Bozo. "Don't be rude. Now Twyla. Roberta. When you hear a loud buzzer, that's the call for dinner. Come down to the first floor. Any fights and no movie." And then, just to make sure we knew what we would be missing, "*The Wizard of Oz.*"

Roberta must have thought I meant that my mother would be mad about my being put in the shelter. Not about rooming with her, because

5

---

2. Large New York City hospital best known for its psychiatric wards.

as soon as Bozo left she came over to me and said, "Is your mother sick too?"

"No," I said. "She just likes to dance all night."

"Oh," she nodded her head and I liked the way she understood things so fast. So for the moment it didn't matter that we looked like salt and pepper standing there and that's what the other kids called us sometimes. We were eight years old and got F's all the time. Me because I couldn't remember what I read or what the teacher said. And Roberta because she couldn't read at all and didn't even listen to the teacher. She wasn't good at anything except jacks, at which she was a killer: pow scoop pow scoop pow scoop.

We didn't like each other all that much at first, but nobody else wanted to play with us because we weren't real orphans with beautiful dead parents in the sky. We were dumped. Even the New York City Puerto Ricans and the upstate Indians ignored us. All kinds of kids were in there, black ones, white ones, even two Koreans. The food was good, though. At least I thought so. Roberta hated it and left whole pieces of things on her plate: Spam, Salisbury steak—even jello with fruit cocktail in it, and she didn't care if I ate what she wouldn't. Mary's idea of supper was popcorn and a can of Yoo-Hoo. Hot mashed potatoes and two weenies was like Thanksgiving for me.

10   It really wasn't bad, St. Bonny's. The big girls on the second floor pushed us around now and then. But that was all. They wore lipstick and eyebrow pencil and wobbled their knees while they watched TV. Fifteen, sixteen, even, some of them were. They were put-out girls, scared runaways most of them. Poor little girls who fought their uncles off but looked tough to us, and mean. God did they look mean. The staff tried to keep them separate from the younger children, but sometimes they caught us watching them in the orchard where they played radios and danced with each other. They'd light out after us and pull our hair or twist our arms. We were scared of them, Roberta and me, but neither of us wanted the other one to know it. So we got a good list of dirty names we could shout back when we ran from them through the orchard. I used to dream a lot and almost always the orchard was there. Two acres, four maybe, of these little apple trees. Hundreds of them. Empty and crooked like beggar women when I first came to St. Bonny's but fat with flowers when I left. I don't know why I dreamt about that orchard so much. Nothing really happened there. Nothing all that important, I mean. Just the big girls dancing and playing the radio. Roberta and me watching. Maggie fell down there once. The kitchen woman with legs like parentheses. And the big girls laughed at her. We should have helped her up, I know, but we were scared of those girls with lipstick and eyebrow pencil. Maggie couldn't talk. The kids said

she had her tongue cut out, but I think she was just born that way: mute. She was old and sandy-colored and she worked in the kitchen. I don't know if she was nice or not. I just remember her legs like parentheses and how she rocked when she walked. She worked from early in the morning till two o'clock, and if she was late, if she had too much cleaning and didn't get out till two-fifteen or so, she'd cut through the orchard so she wouldn't miss her bus and have to wait another hour. She wore this really stupid little hat—a kid's hat with ear flaps—and she wasn't much taller than we were. A really awful little hat. Even for a mute, it was dumb—dressing like a kid and never saying anything at all.

"But what about if somebody tries to kill her?" I used to wonder about that. "Or what if she wants to cry? Can she cry?"

"Sure," Roberta said. "But just tears. No sounds come out."

"She can't scream?"

"Nope. Nothing."

"Can she hear?"   15

"I guess."

"Let's call her," I said. And we did.

"Dummy! Dummy!" She never turned her head.

"Bow legs! Bow legs!" Nothing. She just rocked on, the chin straps of her baby-boy hat swaying from side to side. I think we were wrong. I think she could hear and didn't let on. And it shames me even now to think there was somebody in there after all who heard us call her those names and couldn't tell on us.

We got along all right, Roberta and me. Changed beds every night, got 20
F's in civics and communication skills and gym. The Bozo was disappointed in us, she said. Out of 130 of us state cases, 90 were under twelve. Almost all were real orphans with beautiful dead parents in the sky. We were the only ones dumped and the only ones with F's in three classes including gym. So we got along—what with her leaving whole pieces of things on her plate and being nice about not asking questions.

I think it was the day before Maggie fell down that we found out our mothers were coming to visit us on the same Sunday. We had been at the shelter twenty-eight days (Roberta twenty-eight and a half) and this was their first visit with us. Our mothers would come at ten o'clock in time for chapel, then lunch with us in the teachers' lounge. I thought if my dancing mother met her sick mother it might be good for her. And Roberta thought her sick mother would get a big bang out of a dancing one. We got excited about it and curled each other's hair. After breakfast we sat on the bed watching the road from the window. Roberta's socks were still wet. She washed them the night before and put them on the radiator to dry. They hadn't, but she put them on anyway because their tops were so pretty—

scalloped in pink. Each of us had a purple construction-paper basket that we had made in craft class. Mine had a yellow crayon rabbit on it. Roberta's had eggs with wiggly lines of color. Inside were cellophane grass and just the jelly beans because I'd eaten the two marshmallow eggs they gave us. The Big Bozo came herself to get us. Smiling she told us we looked very nice and to come downstairs. We were so surprised by the smile we'd never seen before, neither of us moved.

"Don't you want to see your mommies?"

I stood up first and spilled the jelly beans all over the floor. Bozo's smile disappeared while we scrambled to get the candy up off the floor and put it back in the grass.

She escorted us downstairs to the first floor, where the other girls were lining up to file into the chapel. A bunch of grown-ups stood to one side. Viewers mostly. The old biddies who wanted servants and the fags who wanted company looking for children they might want to adopt. Once in a while a grandmother. Almost never anybody young or anybody whose face wouldn't scare you in the night. Because if any of the real orphans had young relatives they wouldn't be real orphans. I saw Mary right away. She had on those green slacks I hated and hated even more now because didn't she know we were going to chapel? And that fur jacket with the pocket linings so ripped she had to pull to get her hands out of them. But her face was pretty—like always, and she smiled and waved like she was the little girl looking for her mother—not me.

25   I walked slowly, trying not to drop the jelly beans and hoping the paper handle would hold. I had to use my last Chiclet because by the time I finished cutting everything out, all the Elmer's was gone. I am left-handed and the scissors never worked for me. It didn't matter, though; I might just as well have chewed the gum. Mary dropped to her knees and grabbed me, mashing the basket, the jelly beans, and the grass into her ratty fur jacket.

"Twyla, baby. Twyla, baby!"

I could have killed her. Already I heard the big girls in the orchard the next time saying, "Twyyyyyla, baby!" But I couldn't stay mad at Mary while she was smiling and hugging me and smelling of Lady Esther dusting powder. I wanted to stay buried in her fur all day.

To tell the truth I forgot about Roberta. Mary and I got in line for the traipse into chapel and I was feeling proud because she looked so beautiful even in those ugly green slacks that made her behind stick out. A pretty mother on earth is better than a beautiful dead one in the sky even if she did leave you all alone to go dancing.

I felt a tap on my shoulder, turned, and saw Roberta smiling. I smiled back, but not too much lest somebody think this visit was the biggest thing that ever happened in my life. Then Roberta said, "Mother, I want you to meet my roommate, Twyla. And that's Twyla's mother."

I looked up it seemed for miles. She was big. Bigger than any man and on her chest was the biggest cross I'd ever seen. I swear it was six inches long each way. And in the crook of her arm was the biggest Bible ever made.

Mary, simple-minded as ever, grinned and tried to yank her hand out of the pocket with the raggedy lining—to shake hands, I guess. Roberta's mother looked down at me and then looked down at Mary too. She didn't say anything, just grabbed Roberta with her Bible-free hand and stepped out of line, walking quickly to the rear of it. Mary was still grinning because she's not too swift when it comes to what's really going on. Then this light bulb goes off in her head and she says "That bitch!" really loud and us almost in the chapel now. Organ music whining; the Bonny Angels singing sweetly. Everybody in the world turned around to look. And Mary would have kept it up—kept calling names if I hadn't squeezed her hand as hard as I could. That helped a little, but she still twitched and crossed and uncrossed her legs all through service. Even groaned a couple of times. Why did I think she would come there and act right? Slacks. No hat like the grandmothers and viewers, and groaning all the while. When we stood for hymns she kept her mouth shut. Wouldn't even look at the words on the page. She actually reached in her purse for a mirror to check her lipstick. All I could think of was that she really needed to be killed. The sermon lasted a year, and I knew the real orphans were looking smug again.

We were supposed to have lunch in the teachers' lounge, but Mary didn't bring anything, so we picked fur and cellophane grass off the mashed jelly beans and ate them. I could have killed her. I sneaked a look at Roberta. Her mother had brought chicken legs and ham sandwiches and oranges and a whole box of chocolate-covered grahams. Roberta drank milk from a thermos while her mother read the Bible to her.

Things are not right. The wrong food is always with the wrong people. Maybe that's why I got into waitress work later—to match up the right people with the right food. Roberta just let those chicken legs sit there, but she did bring a stack of grahams up to me later when the visit was over. I think she was sorry that her mother would not shake my mother's hand. And I liked that and I liked the fact that she didn't say a word about Mary groaning all the way through the service and not bringing any lunch.

Roberta left in May when the apple trees were heavy and white. On her last day we went to the orchard to watch the big girls smoke and dance by the radio. It didn't matter that they said, "Twyyyyyla, baby." We sat on the ground and breathed. Lady Esther. Apple blossoms. I still go soft when I smell one or the other. Roberta was going home. The big cross and the big Bible was coming to get her and she seemed sort of glad and sort of not. I thought I would die in that room of four beds without her and I knew Bozo had plans to move some other dumped kid in there with me. Roberta promised to write every day, which was really sweet of her because she couldn't read a lick so how could she write anybody. I would have drawn pictures and sent them to her but she never gave me her address. Little by little she faded. Her wet socks with the pink scalloped tops and her big serious-looking eyes—that's all I could catch when I tried to bring her to mind.

35   I was working behind the counter at the Howard Johnson's on the Thru-way just before the Kingston exit. Not a bad job. Kind of a long ride from Newburgh,[3] but okay once I got there. Mine was the second night shift—eleven to seven. Very light until a Greyhound checked in for breakfast around six-thirty. At that hour the sun was all the way clear of the hills behind the restaurant. The place looked better at night—more like shelter—but I loved it when the sun broke in, even if it did show all the cracks in the vinyl and the speckled floor looked dirty no matter what the mop boy did.

It was August and a bus crowd was just unloading. They would stand around a long while: going to the john, and looking at gifts and junk-for-sale machines, reluctant to sit down so soon. Even to eat. I was trying to fill the coffee pots and get them all situated on the electric burners when I saw her. She was sitting in a booth smoking a cigarette with two guys smothered in head and facial hair. Her own hair was so big and wild I could hardly see her face. But the eyes. I would know them anywhere. She had on a powder-blue halter and shorts outfit and earrings the size of bracelets. Talk about lipstick and eyebrow pencil. She made the big girls look like nuns. I couldn't get off the counter until seven o'clock, but I kept watching the booth in case they got up to leave before that. My replacement was on time for a change, so I counted and stacked my receipts as fast as I could and signed off. I walked over to the booth, smiling and wonder-ing if she would remember me. Or even if she wanted to remember me. Maybe she didn't want to be reminded of St. Bonny's or to have anybody know she was ever there. I know I never talked about it to anybody.

I put my hands in my apron pockets and leaned against the back of the booth facing them.

"Roberta? Roberta Fisk?"

She looked up. "Yeah?"

40   "Twyla."

She squinted for a second and then said, "Wow."

"Remember me?"

"Sure. Hey. Wow."

---

3. City on the Hudson River north of New York City.

"It's been a while," I said, and gave a smile to the two hairy guys.

"Yeah. Wow. You work here?"   45

"Yeah," I said. "I live in Newburgh."

"Newburgh? No kidding?" She laughed then a private laugh that included the guys but only the guys, and they laughed with her. What could I do but laugh too and wonder why I was standing there with my knees showing out from under that uniform. Without looking I could see the blue and white triangle on my head, my hair shapeless in a net, my ankles thick in white oxfords. Nothing could have been less sheer than my stockings. There was this silence that came down right after I laughed. A silence it was her turn to fill up. With introductions, maybe, to her boyfriends or an invitation to sit down and have a Coke. Instead she lit a cigarette off the one she'd just finished and said, "We're on our way to the Coast. He's got an appointment with Hendrix." She gestured casually toward the boy next to her.

"Hendrix? Fantastic," I said. "Really fantastic. What's she doing now?"

Roberta coughed on her cigarette and the two guys rolled their eyes up at the ceiling.

"Hendrix. Jimi Hendrix, asshole. He's only the biggest—Oh, wow. Forget it."   50

I was dismissed without anyone saying goodbye, so I thought I would do it for her.

"How's your mother?" I asked. Her grin cracked her whole face. She swallowed. "Fine," she said. "How's yours?"

"Pretty as a picture," I said and turned away. The backs of my knees were damp. Howard Johnson's really was a dump in the sunlight.

James is as comfortable as a house slipper. He liked my cooking and I liked his big loud family. They have lived in Newburgh all of their lives and talk about it the way people do who have always known a home. His grandmother is a porch swing older than his father and when they talk about streets and avenues and buildings they call them names they no longer have. They still call the A & P[4] Rico's because it stands on property once a mom and pop store owned by Mr. Rico. And they call the new community college Town Hall because it once was. My mother-in-law puts up jelly and cucumbers and buys butter wrapped in cloth from a dairy. James and his father talk about fishing and baseball and I can see them all together on the Hudson in a raggedy skiff. Half the population of Newburgh is on welfare now, but to my husband's family it was still some upstate paradise of a time long past. A time of ice houses and vegetable

---

4. Supermarket, part of a chain originally known as the Great Atlantic and Pacific Tea Company, in business from 1859 to 2015.

wagons, coal furnaces and children weeding gardens. When our son was born my mother-in-law gave me the crib blanket that had been hers.

55 But the town they remembered had changed. Something quick was in the air. Magnificent old houses, so ruined they had become shelter for squatters and rent risks, were bought and renovated. Smart IBM[5] people moved out of their suburbs back into the city and put shutters up and herb gardens in their backyards. A brochure came in the mail announcing the opening of a Food Emporium. Gourmet food it said—and listed items the rich IBM crowd would want. It was located in a new mall at the edge of town and I drove out to shop there one day—just to see. It was late in June. After the tulips were gone and the Queen Elizabeth roses were open everywhere. I trailed my cart along the aisle tossing in smoked oysters and Robert's sauce and things I knew would sit in my cupboard for years. Only when I found some Klondike ice cream bars did I feel less guilty about spending James's fireman's salary so foolishly. My father-in-law ate them with the same gusto little Joseph did.

Waiting in the check-out line I heard a voice say, "Twyla!"

The classical music piped over the aisles had affected me and the woman leaning toward me was dressed to kill. Diamonds on her hand, a smart white summer dress. "I'm Mrs. Benson," I said.

"Ho. Ho. The Big Bozo," she sang.

For a split second I didn't know what she was talking about. She had a bunch of asparagus and two cartons of fancy water.

60 "Roberta!"

"Right."

"For heaven's sake. Roberta."

"You look great," she said.

"So do you. Where are you? Here? In Newburgh?"

65 "Yes. Over in Annandale."

I was opening my mouth to say more when the cashier called my attention to her empty counter.

"Meet you outside." Roberta pointed her finger and went into the express line.

I placed the groceries and kept myself from glancing around to check Roberta's progress. I remembered Howard Johnson's and looking for a chance to speak only to be greeted with a stingy "wow." But she was waiting for me and her huge hair was sleek now, smooth around a small, nicely shaped head. Shoes, dress, everything lovely and summery and rich. I was dying to know what happened to her, how she got from Jimi Hendrix to

---

5. The International Business Machine Corporation, which had its executive headquarters in Poughkeepsie, New York.

Annandale, a neighborhood full of doctors and IBM executives. Easy, I thought. Everything is so easy for them. They think they own the world. "How long," I asked her. "How long have you been here?" "A year. I got married to a man who lives here. And you, you're married 70 too, right? Benson, you said." "Yeah. James Benson." "And is he nice?" "Oh, is he nice?" "Well, is he?" Roberta's eyes were steady as though she really meant the question and wanted an answer. "He's wonderful, Roberta. Wonderful." 75 "So you're happy." "Very." "That's good," she said and nodded her head. "I always hoped you'd be happy. Any kids? I know you have kids." "One. A boy. How about you?" "Four." 80 "Four?" She laughed. "Step kids. He's a widower." "Oh." "Got a minute? Let's have a coffee." I thought about the Klondikes melting and the inconvenience of going 85 all the way to my car and putting the bags in the trunk. Served me right for buying all that stuff I didn't need. Roberta was ahead of me. "Put them in my car. It's right here." And then I saw the dark blue limousine. "You married a Chinaman?" "No," she laughed. "He's the driver." "Oh, my. If the Big Bozo could see you now." 90 We both giggled. Really giggled. Suddenly, in just a pulse beat, twenty years disappeared and all of it came rushing back. The big girls (whom we called gar girls—Roberta's misheard word for the evil stone faces described in a civics class) there dancing in the orchard, the ploppy mashed potatoes, the double weenies, the Spam with pineapple. We went into the coffee shop holding on to one another and I tried to think why we were glad to see each other this time and not before. Once, twelve years ago, we passed like strangers. A black girl and a white girl meeting in a Howard Johnson's on the road and having nothing to say. One in a blue and white triangle waitress hat—the other on her way to see Hendrix. Now we were behaving like sisters separated for much too long. Those four short months were nothing in time. Maybe it was the thing itself. Just being there, together. Two little girls who knew what nobody else in the world knew—how not to ask questions. How to believe what had to be believed. There was politeness in that reluctance and generosity as well. Is your mother sick too? No, she dances all night. Oh—and an understanding nod.

We sat in a booth by the window and fell into recollection like veterans.

"Did you ever learn to read?"

"Watch." She picked up the menu. "Special of the day. Cream of corn soup. Entrées. Two dots and a wriggly line. Quiche. Chef salad, scallops . . ."

95   I was laughing and applauding when the waitress came up.

"Remember the Easter baskets?"

"And how we tried to *introduce* them?"

"Your mother with that cross like two telephone poles."

"And yours with those tight slacks."

100   We laughed so loudly heads turned and made the laughter harder to suppress.

"What happened to the Jimi Hendrix date?"

Roberta made a blow-out sound with her lips.

"When he died I thought about you."

"Oh, you heard about him finally?"

105   "Finally. Come on, I was a small-town country waitress."

"And I was a small-town country dropout. God, were we wild. I still don't know how I got out of there alive."

"But you did."

"I did. I really did. Now I'm Mrs. Kenneth Norton."

"Sounds like a mouthful."

110   "It is."

"Servants and all?"

Roberta held up two fingers.

"Ow! What does he do?"

"Computers and stuff. What do I know?"

115   "I don't remember a hell of a lot from those days, but Lord, St. Bonny's is as clear as daylight. Remember Maggie? The day she fell down and those gar girls laughed at her?"

Roberta looked up from her salad and stared at me. "Maggie didn't fall," she said.

"Yes, she did. You remember."

"No, Twyla. They knocked her down. Those girls pushed her down and tore her clothes. In the orchard."

"I don't—that's not what happened."

120   "Sure it is. In the orchard. Remember how scared we were?"

"Wait a minute. I don't remember any of that."

"And Bozo was fired."

"You're crazy. She was there when I left. You left before me."
"I went back. You weren't there when they fired Bozo."
"What?"   125
"Twice. Once for a year when I was about ten, another for two months
when I was fourteen. That's when I ran away."
"You ran away from St. Bonny's?"
"I had to. What do you want? Me dancing in that orchard?"
"Are you sure about Maggie?"
"Of course I'm sure. You've blocked it, Twyla. It happened. Those girls   130
had behavior problems, you know."
"Didn't they, though. But why can't I remember the Maggie thing?"
"Believe me. It happened. And we were there."
"Who did you room with when you went back?" I asked her as if I
would know her. The Maggie thing was troubling me.
"Creeps. They tickled themselves in the night."
My ears were itching and I wanted to go home suddenly. This was all   135
very well but she couldn't just comb her hair, wash her face and pretend
everything was hunky-dory. After the Howard Johnson's snub. And no
apology. Nothing.
"Were you on dope or what that time at Howard Johnson's?" I tried to
make my voice sound friendlier than I felt.
"Maybe, a little. I never did drugs much. Why?"
"I don't know; you acted sort of like you didn't want to know me then."
"Oh, Twyla, you know how it was in those days: black—white. You
know how everything was."
But I didn't know. I thought it was just the opposite. Busloads of blacks 140
and whites came into Howard Johnson's together. They roamed together
then: students, musicians, lovers, protesters. You got to see everything at
Howard Johnson's and blacks were very friendly with whites in those days.
But sitting there with nothing on my plate but two hard tomato wedges
wondering about the melting Klondikes it seemed childish remembering
the slight. We went to her car, and with the help of the driver, got my stuff
into my station wagon.
"We'll keep in touch this time," she said.
"Sure," I said. "Sure. Give me a call."
"I will," she said, and then just as I was sliding behind the wheel, she
leaned into the window. "By the way. Your mother. Did she ever stop
dancing?"
I shook my head. "No. Never."
Roberta nodded.   145
"And yours? Did she ever get well?"
She smiled a tiny sad smile. "No. She never did. Look, call me, okay?"

"Okay," I said, but I knew I wouldn't. Roberta had messed up my past somehow with that business about Maggie. I wouldn't forget a thing like that. Would I?

Strife came to us that fall. At least that's what the paper called it. Strife. Racial strife. The word made me think of a bird—a big shrieking bird out of 1,000,000,000 B.C. Flapping its wings and cawing. Its eye with no lid always bearing down on you. All day it screeched and at night it slept on the rooftops. It woke you in the morning and from the *Today* show to the eleven o'clock news it kept you an awful company. I couldn't figure it out from one day to the next. I knew I was supposed to feel something strong, but I didn't know what, and James wasn't any help. Joseph was on the list of kids to be transferred from the junior high school to another one at some far-out-of-the-way place and I thought it was a good thing until I heard it was a bad thing. I mean I didn't know. All the schools seemed dumps to me, and the fact that one was nicer looking didn't hold much weight. But the papers were full of it and then the kids began to get jumpy. In August, mind you. Schools weren't even open yet. I thought Joseph might be frightened to go over there, but he didn't seem scared so I forgot about it, until I found myself driving along Hudson Street out there by the school they were trying to integrate and saw a line of women marching. And who do you suppose was in line, big as life, holding a sign in front of her bigger than her mother's cross? MOTHERS HAVE RIGHTS TOO! it said.

150   I drove on, and then changed my mind. I circled the block, slowed down, and honked my horn.

Roberta looked over and when she saw me she waved. I didn't wave back, but I didn't move either. She handed her sign to another woman and came over to where I was parked.

"Hi."

"What are you doing?"

"Picketing. What's it look like?"

155   "What for?"

"What do you mean, 'What for?' They want to take my kids and send them out of the neighborhood. They don't want to go."

"So what if they go to another school? My boy's being bussed too, and I don't mind. Why should you?"

"It's not about us, Twyla. Me and you. It's about our kids."

"What's more *us* than that?"

160   "Well, it is a free country."

"Not yet, but it will be."

"What the hell does that mean? I'm not doing anything to you."

"You really think that?"

"I know it."

"I wonder what made me think you were different."   165

"I wonder what made me think you were different."

"Look at them," I said. "Just look. Who do they think they are? Swarming all over the place like they own it. And now they think they can decide where my child goes to school. Look at them, Roberta. They're Bozos."

Roberta turned around and looked at the women. Almost all of them were standing still now, waiting. Some were even edging toward us. Roberta looked at me out of some refrigerator behind her eyes. "No, they're not. They're just mothers."

"And what am I? Swiss cheese?"

"I used to curl your hair."   170

"I hated your hands in my hair."

The women were moving. Our faces looked mean to them of course and they looked as though they could not wait to throw themselves in front of a police car, or better yet, into my car and drag me away by my ankles. Now they surrounded my car and gently, gently began to rock it. I swayed back and forth like a sideways yo-yo. Automatically I reached for Roberta, like the old days in the orchard when they saw us watching them and we had to get out of there, and if one of us fell the other pulled her up and if one of us was caught the other stayed to kick and scratch, and neither would leave the other behind. My arm shot out of the car window but no receiving hand was there. Roberta was looking at me sway from side to side in the car and her face was still. My purse slid from the car seat down under the dashboard. The four policemen who had been drinking Tab in their car finally got the message and strolled over, forcing their way through the women. Quietly, firmly they spoke. "Okay, ladies. Back in line or off the streets."

Some of them went away willingly; others had to be urged away from the car doors and the hood. Roberta didn't move. She was looking steadily at me. I was fumbling to turn on the ignition, which wouldn't catch because the gearshift was still in drive. The seats of the car were a mess because the swaying had thrown my grocery coupons all over it and my purse was sprawled on the floor.

"Maybe I am different now, Twyla. But you're not. You're the same little state kid who kicked a poor old black lady when she was down on the ground. You kicked a black lady and you have the nerve to call me a bigot."

The coupons were everywhere and the guts of my purse were bunched   175
under the dashboard. What was she saying? Black? Maggie wasn't black.

"She wasn't black," I said.

"Like hell she wasn't, and you kicked her. We both did. You kicked a black lady who couldn't even scream."

"Liar!"

"You're the liar! Why don't you just go on home and leave us alone, huh?"

180   She turned away and I skidded away from the curb.

The next morning I went into the garage and cut the side out of the carton our portable TV had come in. It wasn't nearly big enough, but after a while I had a decent sign: red spray-painted letters on a white background—AND SO DO CHILDREN ****. I meant just to go down to the school and tack it up somewhere so those cows on the picket line across the street could see it, but when I got there, some ten or so others had already assembled—protesting the cows across the street. Police permits and everything. I got in line and we strutted in time on our side while Roberta's group strutted on theirs. That first day we were all dignified, pretending the other side didn't exist. The second day there was name calling and finger gestures. But that was about all. People changed signs from time to time, but Roberta never did and neither did I. Actually my sign didn't make sense without Roberta's. "And so do children what?" one of the women on my side asked me. Have rights, I said, as though it was obvious.

Roberta didn't acknowledge my presence in any way and I got to thinking maybe she didn't know I was there. I began to pace myself in the line, jostling people one minute and lagging behind the next, so Roberta and I could reach the end of our respective lines at the same time and there would be a moment in our turn when we would face each other. Still, I couldn't tell whether she saw me and knew my sign was for her. The next day I went early before we were scheduled to assemble. I waited until she got there before I exposed my new creation. As soon as she hoisted her MOTHERS HAVE RIGHTS TOO I began to wave my new one, which said, HOW WOULD YOU KNOW? I know she saw that one, but I had gotten addicted now. My signs got crazier each day, and the women on my side decided that I was a kook. They couldn't make heads or tails out of my brilliant screaming posters.

I brought a painted sign in queenly red with huge black letters that said, IS YOUR MOTHER WELL? Roberta took her lunch break and didn't come back for the rest of the day or any day after. Two days later I stopped going too and couldn't have been missed because nobody understood my signs anyway.

It was a nasty six weeks. Classes were suspended and Joseph didn't go to anybody's school until October. The children—everybody's children—soon got bored with that extended vacation they thought was going to be so great. They looked at TV until their eyes flattened. I spent a couple of mornings tutoring my son, as the other mothers said we should. Twice I opened a text from last year that he had never turned in. Twice he yawned in my face. Other mothers organized living room sessions so the kids would keep up. None of the kids could concentrate so they drifted back to *The Price Is Right* and *The Brady Bunch*.[6] When the school finally opened there were fights once or twice and some sirens roared through the streets every once in a while. There were a lot of photographers from Albany. And just when ABC was about to send up a news crew, the kids settled down like nothing in the world had happened. Joseph hung my HOW WOULD YOU KNOW? sign in his bedroom. I don't know what became of AND SO DO CHILDREN ****. I think my father-in-law cleaned some fish on it. He was always puttering around in our garage. Each of his five children lived in Newburgh and he acted as though he had five extra homes.

I couldn't help looking for Roberta when Joseph graduated from high school, but I didn't see her. It didn't trouble me much what she had said to me in the car. I mean the kicking part. I know I didn't do that, I couldn't do that. But I was puzzled by her telling me Maggie was black. When I thought about it I actually couldn't be certain. She wasn't pitch-black, I knew, or I would have remembered that. What I remember was the kiddie hat, and the semicircle legs. I tried to reassure myself about the race thing for a long time until it dawned on me that the truth was already there, and Roberta knew it. I didn't kick her; I didn't join in with the gar girls and kick that lady, but I sure did want to. We watched and never tried to help her and never called for help. Maggie was my dancing mother. Deaf, I thought, and dumb. Nobody inside. Nobody who would hear you if you cried in the night. Nobody who could tell you anything important that you could use. Rocking, dancing, swaying as she walked. And when the gar girls pushed her down, and started roughhousing, I knew she wouldn't scream, couldn't—just like me—and I was glad about that.

We decided not to have a tree, because Christmas would be at my mother-in-law's house, so why have a tree at both places? Joseph was at SUNY New Paltz and we had to economize, we said. But at the last minute, I changed my mind. Nothing could be that bad. So I rushed around town looking for a tree, something small but wide. By the time I found a place, it was snowing and very late. I dawdled like it was the most important purchase in the world and the tree man was fed up with me. Finally I chose one and had it tied onto the trunk of the car. I drove away slowly because the sand trucks were not out yet and the streets could be murder at the beginning of a snowfall. Downtown the streets were wide and rather empty except for a cluster of people coming out of the Newburgh Hotel. The one hotel in town that wasn't built out of cardboard and Plexiglas. A party, probably.

185

6. Television sitcom popular in the 1970s. *The Price Is Right*: television game show popular in the 1970s.

The men huddled in the snow were dressed in tails and the women had on furs. Shiny things glittered from underneath their coats. It made me tired to look at them. Tired, tired, tired. On the next corner was a small diner with loops and loops of paper bells in the window. I stopped the car and went in. Just for a cup of coffee and twenty minutes of peace before I went home and tried to finish everything before Christmas Eve.

"Twyla?"

There she was. In a silvery evening gown and dark fur coat. A man and another woman were with her, the man fumbling for change to put in the cigarette machine. The woman was humming and tapping on the counter with her fingernails. They all looked a little bit drunk.

"Well. It's you."

190 "How are you?"

I shrugged. "Pretty good. Frazzled. Christmas and all."

"Regular?" called the woman from the counter.

"Fine," Roberta called back and then, "Wait for me in the car."

She slipped into the booth beside me. "I have to tell you something, Twyla. I made up my mind if I ever saw you again, I'd tell you."

195 "I'd just as soon not hear anything, Roberta. It doesn't matter now, anyway."

"No," she said. "Not about that."

"Don't be long," said the woman. She carried two regulars to go and the man peeled his cigarette pack as they left.

"It's about St. Bonny's and Maggie."

"Oh, please."

200 "Listen to me. I really did think she was black. I didn't make that up. I really thought so. But now I can't be sure. I just remember her as old, so old. And because she couldn't talk—well, you know, I thought she was crazy. She'd been brought up in an institution like my mother was and like I thought I would be too. And you were right. We didn't kick her. It was the gar girls. Only them. But, well, I wanted to. I really wanted them to hurt her. I said we did it, too. You and me, but that's not true. And I don't want you to carry that around. It was just that I wanted to do it so bad that day—wanting to is doing it."

Her eyes were watery from the drinks she'd had, I guess. I know it's that way with me. One glass of wine and I start bawling over the littlest thing.

"We were kids, Roberta."

"Yeah. Yeah. I know, just kids."

"Eight."

205 "Eight."

"And lonely."

"Scared, too."

She wiped her cheeks with the heel of her hand and smiled. "Well, that's all I wanted to say."

I nodded and couldn't think of any way to fill the silence that went from the diner past the paper bells on out into the snow. It was heavy now. I thought I'd better wait for the sand trucks before starting home.

"Thanks, Roberta." 210

"Sure."

"Did I tell you? My mother, she never did stop dancing."

"Yes. You told me. And mine, she never got well." Roberta lifted her hands from the tabletop and covered her face with her palms. When she took them away she really was crying. "Oh shit, Twyla. Shit, shit, shit. What the hell happened to Maggie?"

1983

QUESTIONS

1. At the end of RECITATIF, how do Twyla's and Roberta's explorations of the "truth" of what they had seen at St. Bonny's many years earlier affect your sense of the "truth" of later episodes in the story? Is either Twyla or Roberta more reliable than the other?

2. At what point in the story do you first begin to make assumptions about the race and class of the two main characters, Twyla and Roberta? Why? Do you change your mind later in the story? When and why so—or not? What is the significance of Morrison's choice both to withhold information about the characters' race and class and to have Twyla narrate the story?

3. How does the relationship between Twyla and Roberta evolve over the course of the story?

AUTHORS ON THEIR WORK

TONI MORRISON (B. 1931)

From "Toni Morrison: The Art of Fiction CXXXIV" (1993)*

MORRISON: Faulkner in *Absalom, Absalom!* spends the entire book tracing race, and you can't find it. No one can see it, even the character who *is* black can't see it. [. . .] Do you know how hard it is to withhold that kind of information but hinting, pointing all of the time? And then to reveal it in order to say that it is *not* the point anyway? It is technically just astonishing. As a reader you have been forced to hunt for a drop of black blood that means everything and nothing. The insanity of racism.

* * *

MORRISON: [. . .] I wrote a story entitled "Recitatif," in which there are two little girls in an orphanage, one white and one black. But the reader doesn't know which is white and which is black. I use class codes, but no racial codes.

INTERVIEWER: Is this meant to confuse the reader?

MORRISON: Well, yes. But to provoke and enlighten. I did that as a lark. What was exciting was to be forced as a writer not to be lazy and rely on obvious codes. Soon as I say, "Black woman . . ." I can rest on or provoke predictable responses, but if I leave it out then I have to talk about her in a complicated way—as a person.

*"Toni Morrison: The Art of Fiction CXXXIV." Interview by Elisa Schappell with Claudia Brodsky Lacour. *The Paris Review*, no. 128, Fall 1993, www.theparisreview .org/interviews/1888/the-art-of-fiction-no-134-toni-morrison.

DAVID FOSTER WALLACE
(1962–2008)
Good People

Born in Ithaca, New York, to a philosophy professor and an English teacher, David Foster Wallace has been dubbed an "outrageously gifted novelist" and "the genius of his generation," as well as a "recovering smart aleck" and "a decent, decent man." A philosophy and English major at Amherst College, he contemplated a career in math before—at age twenty-four—earning an MFA from the University of Arizona and publishing his first novel, *The Broom of the System* (1987). His subsequent work includes short-story collections like *Brief Interviews with Hideous Men* (1999) and *Oblivion* (2006), as well as wide-ranging nonfiction, some of which appears in *A Supposedly Fun Thing I'll Never Do Again* (1997) and *Consider the Lobster and Other Essays* (2006). At over a thousand pages and with almost four hundred footnotes, his most famous novel, *Infinite Jest* (1996), intertwines several narratives set in a near-future in which years are named by their corporate sponsors ("Year of the Whopper") and New England is a giant toxic-waste dump. Included on *Time's* list of the hundred best novels published since 1923, it also helped earn Wallace a MacArthur "genius grant."

Wallace described his own goal as "morally passionate, passionately moral fiction" that might help readers "become less alone inside." Though admired as much for its humor as its bulk and complexity, his fiction often dwells on what he

called "an ineluctable part of being a human"—"suffering." Thou
battled depression, his 2008 suicide shocked and saddened fans
ers around the world. The story "Good People," first published in 2007, ultı...
became part of *The Pale King* (2011), the unfinished novel he left behind.

They were up on a picnic table at that park by the lake, by the edge of
the lake, with part of a downed tree in the shallows half hidden by
the bank. Lane A. Dean, Jr., and his girlfriend, both in bluejeans and
button-up shirts. They sat up on the table's top portion and had their
shoes on the bench part that people sat on to picnic or fellowship together
in carefree times. They'd gone to different high schools but the same
junior college, where they had met in campus ministries. It was springtime,
and the park's grass was very green and the air suffused with honeysuckle and lilacs both, which was almost too much. There were bees, and
the angle of the sun made the water of the shallows look dark. There had
been more storms that week, with some downed trees and the sound of
chainsaws all up and down his parents' street. Their postures on the picnic table were both the same forward kind with their shoulders rounded
and elbows on their knees. In this position the girl rocked slightly and
once put her face in her hands, but she was not crying. Lane was very
still and immobile and looking past the bank at the downed tree in the
shallows and its ball of exposed roots going all directions and the tree's
cloud of branches all half in the water. The only other individual nearby
was a dozen spaced tables away, by himself, standing upright. Looking at
the torn-up hole in the ground there where the tree had gone over. It was
still early yet and all the shadows wheeling right and shortening. The girl
wore a thin old checked cotton shirt with pearl-colored snaps with the
long sleeves down and always smelled very good and clean, like someone
you could trust and care about even if you weren't in love. Lane Dean had
liked the smell of her right away. His mother called her *down to earth* and
liked her, thought she was good people, you could tell—she made this
evident in little ways. The shallows lapped from different directions at
the tree as if almost teething on it. Sometimes when alone and thinking
or struggling to turn a matter over to Jesus Christ in prayer, he would find
himself putting his fist in his palm and turning it slightly as if still playing and pounding his glove to stay sharp and alert in center. He did not
do this now; it would be cruel and indecent to do this now. The older individual stood beside his picnic table—he was at it but not sitting—and
looked also out of place in a suit coat or jacket and the kind of men's hat
Lane's grandfather wore in photos as a young insurance man. He

appeared to be looking across the lake. If he moved, Lane didn't see it. He looked more like a picture than a man. There were not any ducks in view.

One thing Lane Dean did was reassure her again that he'd go with her and be there with her. It was one of the few safe or decent things he could really say. The second time he said it again now she shook her head and laughed in an unhappy way that was more just air out her nose. Her real laugh was different. Where he'd be was the waiting room, she said. That he'd be thinking about her and feeling bad for her, she knew, but he couldn't be in there with her. This was so obviously true that he felt like a ninny that he'd kept on about it and now knew what she had thought every time he went and said it—it hadn't brought her comfort or eased the burden at all. The worse he felt, the stiller he sat. The whole thing felt balanced on a knife or wire; if he moved to put his arm up or touch her the whole thing could tip over. He hated himself for sitting so frozen. He could almost visualize himself tiptoeing past something explosive. A big stupid-looking tiptoe, like in a cartoon. The whole last black week had been this way and it was wrong. He knew it was wrong, knew something was required of him that was not this terrible frozen care and caution, but he pretended to himself he did not know what it was that was required. He pretended it had no name. He pretended that not saying aloud what he knew to be right and true was for her sake, was for the sake of her needs and feelings. He also worked dock and routing at UPS, on top of school, but had traded to get the day off after they'd decided together. Two days before, he had awakened very early and tried to pray but could not. He was freezing more and more solid, he felt like, but he had not thought of his father or the blank frozenness of his father, even in church, which had once filled him with such pity. This was the truth. Lane Dean, Jr., felt sun on one arm as he pictured in his mind an image of himself on a train, waving mechanically to something that got smaller and smaller as the train pulled away. His father and his mother's father had the same birthday, a Cancer. Sheri's hair was colored an almost corn blond, very clean, the skin through her central part pink in the sunlight. They'd sat here long enough that only their right side was shaded now. He could look at her head, but not at her. Different parts of him felt unconnected to each other. She was smarter than him and they both knew it. It wasn't just school—Lane Dean was in accounting and business and did all right; he was hanging in there. She was a year older, twenty, but it was also more— she had always seemed to Lane to be on good terms with her life in a way that age could not account for. His mother had put it that she *knew what it is she wanted*, which was nursing and not an easy program at Peoria Junior College, and plus she worked hostessing at the Embers and had bought her own car. She was serious in a way Lane liked. She had a cousin that died when she was thirteen, fourteen, that she'd loved and been close with. She only talked about it that once. He liked her smell and her downy arms and the way she exclaimed when something made her laugh. He had liked just being with her and talking to her. She was serious in her faith and values in a way that Lane had liked and now, sitting here with her on the table, found himself afraid of. This was an awful thing. He was starting to believe that he might not be serious in his faith. He might be somewhat of a hypocrite, like the Assyrians in Isaiah,[1] which would be a far graver sin than the appointment—he had decided he believed this. He was desperate to be good people, to still be able to feel he was good. He rarely before now had thought of damnation and Hell—that part of it didn't speak to his spirit—and in worship services he more just tuned himself out and tolerated Hell when it came up, the same way you tolerate the job you've got to have to save up for what it is you want. Her tennis shoes had little things doodled on them from sitting in her class lectures. She stayed looking down like that. Little notes or reading assignments in Bic in her neat round hand on the rubber elements around the sneaker's rim. Lane A. Dean, looking now at her inclined head's side's barrettes in the shape of blue ladybugs. The appointment was for afternoon, but when the doorbell had rung so early and his mother'd called to him up the stairs, he had known, and a terrible kind of blankness had commenced falling through him.

He told her that he did not know what to do. That he knew if he was the salesman of it and forced it upon her that was awful and wrong. But he was trying to understand—they'd prayed on it and talked it through from every different angle. Lane said how sorry she knew he was, and that if he was wrong in believing they'd truly decided together when they decided to make the appointment she should please tell him, because he thought he knew how she must have felt as it got closer and closer and how she must be so scared, but that what he couldn't tell was if it was more than that. He was totally still except for moving his mouth, it felt like. She did not reply. That if they needed to pray on it more and talk it through, then he was here, he was ready, he said. The appointment could get moved back; if she just said the word they could call and push it back to take more time to be sure in the decision. It was still so early in it— they both knew that, he said. This was true, that he felt this way, and yet he also knew he was also trying to say things that would get her to open

1. Perhaps a reference to Isaiah 36, in which the Assyrians promise to save the kingdom of Judah if its king will trust and surrender to them rather than relying on God. Later chapters describe Assyria's fall as punishment for their hubris.

up and say enough back that he could see her and read her heart and know what to say to get her to go through with it. He knew this without admitting to himself that this was what he wanted, for it would make him a hypocrite and liar. He knew, in some locked-up little part of him, why it was that he'd gone to no one to open up and seek their life counsel, not Pastor Steve or the prayer partners at campus ministries, not his UPS friends or the spiritual counselling available through his parents' old church. But he did not know why Sheri herself had not gone to Pastor Steve—he could not read her heart. She was blank and hidden. He so fervently wished it never happened. He felt like he knew now why it was a true sin and not just a leftover rule from past society. He felt like he had been brought low by it and humbled and now did believe that the rules were there for a reason. That the rules were concerned with him person-ally, as an individual. He promised God he had learned his lesson. But what if that, too, was a hollow promise, from a hypocrite who repented only after, who promised submission but really only wanted a reprieve? He might not even know his own heart or be able to read and know himself. He kept thinking also of 1 Timothy and the hypocrite therein who *dispu-teth over words*.[2] He felt a terrible inner resistance but could not feel what it was that it resisted. This was the truth. All the different angles and ways they had come at the decision together did not ever include it—the word— for had he once said it, avowed that he did love her, loved Sheri Fisher, then it all would have been transformed. It would not be a different stance or angle, but a difference in the very thing they were praying and deciding on together. Sometimes they had prayed together over the phone, in a kind of half code in case anybody accidentally picked up the extension. She continued to sit as if thinking, in the pose of thinking, like that one statue. They were right up next to each other on the table. He was looking over past her at the tree in the water. But he could not say he did: it was not true.

But neither did he ever open up and tell her straight out he did not love her. This might be his *lie by omission*. This might be the frozen resistance— were he to look right at her and tell her he didn't, she would keep the appointment and go. He knew this. Something in him, though, some ter-rible weakness or lack of values, could not tell her. It felt like a muscle he did not have. He didn't know why; he just could not do it, or even pray to do it. She believed he was good, serious in his values. Part of him seemed willing to more or less just about lie to someone with that kind of faith and

2. See 1 Timothy 6.3–4: "If any man teach otherwise, and consent not to wholesome words, *even* the words of our Lord Jesus Christ, and to the doctrine which is according to godliness; He is proud, knowing nothing, but doting about questions and strifes of words, whereof cometh envy, strife, railings, evil surmisings."

trust, and what did that make him? How could such a type of individual even pray? What it really felt like was a taste of the reality of what might be meant by Hell. Lane Dean had never believed in Hell as a lake of fire or a loving God consigning folks to a burning lake of fire—he knew in his heart this was not true. What he believed in was a living God of compassion and love and the possibility of a personal relationship with Jesus Christ through whom this love was enacted in human time. But sitting here beside this girl as unknown to him now as outer space, waiting for whatever she might say to unfreeze him, now he felt like he could see the edge or outline of what a real vision of Hell might be. It was of two great and terrible armies within himself, opposed and facing each other, silent. There would be battle but no victor. Or never a battle—the armies would stay like that, motionless, looking across at each other, and seeing therein something so different and alien from themselves that they could not understand, could not hear each other's speech as even words or read anything from what their face looked like, frozen like that, opposed and uncomprehending, for all human time. Two-hearted, a hypocrite to yourself either way.

When he moved his head, a part of the lake further out flashed with sun—the water up close wasn't black now, and you could see into the shallows and see that all the water was moving but gently, this way and that—and in this same way he besought to return to himself as Sheri moved her leg and started to turn beside him. He could see the man in the suit and gray hat standing motionless now at the lake's rim, holding something under one arm and looking across at the opposite side where a row of little forms on camp chairs sat in a way that meant they had lines in the water for crappie—which mostly only your blacks from the East Side ever did—and the little white shape at the row's end a Styrofoam creel. In his moment or time at the lake now just to come, Lane Dean first felt he could take this all in whole: everything seemed distinctly lit, for the circle of the pin oak's shade had rotated off all the way, and they sat now in sun with their shadow a two-headed thing in the grass before them. He was looking or gazing again at where the downed tree's branches seemed to all bend so sharply just under the shallows' surface when he was given to know that through all this frozen silence he'd despised he had, in truth, been praying, or some little part of his heart he could not hear had, for he was answered now with a type of vision, what he would later call within his own mind a vision or *moment of grace*. He was not a hypocrite, just broken and split off like all men. Later on, he believed that what happened was he'd had a moment of almost seeing them both as Jesus saw them—as blind but groping, wanting to please God despite their inborn fallen nature. For in that same given moment he saw, quick as light, into

Sheri's heart, and was made to know what would occur here as she finished turning to him and the man in the hat watched the fishing and the downed elm shed cells into the water. This down-to-earth girl that smelled good and wanted to be a nurse would take and hold one of his hands in both of hers to unfreeze him and make him look at her, and she would say that she cannot do it. That she is sorry she did not know this sooner, that she hadn't meant to lie—she agreed because she'd wanted to believe that she could, but she cannot. That she will carry this and have it; she has to. With her gaze clear and steady. That all night last night she prayed and searched inside herself and decided this is what love commands of her. That Lane should please please sweetie let her finish. That listen—this is her own decision and obliges him to nothing. That she knows he does not love her, not that way, has known it all this time, and that it's all right. That it is as it is and it's all right. She will carry this, and have it, and love it and make no claim on Lane except his good wishes and respecting what she has to do. That she releases him, all claim, and hopes he finishes up at P.J.C. and does so good in his life and has all joy and good things. Her voice will be clear and steady, and she will be lying, for Lane has been given to read her heart. To see through her. One of the opposite side's blacks raises his arm in what may be greeting, or waving off a bee. There is a mower cutting grass someplace off behind them. It will be a terrible, last-ditch gamble born out of the desperation in Sheri Fisher's soul, the knowledge that she can neither do this thing today nor carry a child alone and shame her family. Her values blocked the way either way, Lane could see, and she has no other options or choice—this lie is not a sin. Galatians 4:16, *Have I then become your enemy?*[3] She is gambling that he is good. There on the table, neither frozen nor yet moving, Lane Dean, Jr., sees all this, and is moved with pity, and also with something more, something without any name he knows, that is given to him in the form of a question that never once in all the long week's thinking and division had even so much as occurred—why is he so sure he doesn't love her? Why is one kind of love any different? What if he has no earthly idea what love is? What would even Jesus do? For it was just now he felt her two small strong soft hands on his, to turn him. What if he was just afraid, if the truth was no more than this, and if what to pray for was not even love but simple courage, to meet both her eyes as she says it and trust his heart?

2007

---

3. "Am I therefore become your enemy, because I tell you the truth?" (Gal. 4.16). Earlier in this letter, Paul exhorts the Galatians to understand that when they "knew not God," they inevitably served "them which by nature are no gods," but now that they know God such "bondage" is instead a choice. At the same time, he reminds them that he is, like them, fallible, and that despite that "temptation which was in my flesh ye despised [me] not, nor rejected."

QUESTIONS

1. How would you summarize or characterize Lane Dean, Jr.'s conflicts, both internal and external? How does his faith intensify or even create those conflicts and help him resolve them?
2. How is your interpretation of Lane Dean, Jr.'s character and conflicts shaped by all that the story withholds from us, including dialogue; Sheri's point of view or thoughts; explicit information about the nature of Sheri's "appointment" or of the "it" he "wished [. . .] never happened" (par. 3); a description of what actually happens at the end rather than Lane Dean's "vision" of what would happen and/or his later "belie[f]" about what happened?
3. What different definitions of "good people" or of a "good person" are implied here, or how might Lane Dean, Jr.'s understanding of what it means to be "good people" change over the course of the story? What part does the idea of hypocrisy play in those definitions?

SUGGESTIONS FOR WRITING

1. Choose any story in this anthology in which a character changes because of the events that occur in the story. Write an essay exploring exactly how, when, and why the character changes.
2. Choose any story in this chapter and write an essay analyzing its handling of character and methods of characterization. Do the story's characters tend to be more flat or round, static or dynamic, highly individualized or nearly indistinguishable? Is indirect or direct characterization more important? How important is each type of evidence listed on the checklist that appears earlier in this chapter? Why and how is this treatment of character appropriate to the story?
3. Write an essay comparing how the adult lives and personalities of the two central characters in RECITATIF are shaped by their experience in the orphanage. Why and how is this experience so traumatic? How does each character understand and cope with this experience over time? In these terms, how are Twyla and Roberta both similar and different, and what role does Maggie play in their efforts to come to terms with their past?
4. Write an essay exploring how plotting—especially sequence and pace—and narration—including focus, voice, tense, and (biblical) allusion—contribute to the characterization of Lane Dean, Jr., in GOOD PEOPLE.

4

SETTING

If plot and action are the way fictional works answer the question *What happened?* and characters are the *who*, **setting** is the *where* and *when*. All action in fiction, as in the real world, takes place in a context or setting—a time and place and a social environment or milieu.

TEMPORAL AND PHYSICAL, GENERAL AND PARTICULAR SETTING

The **time**—a work's *temporal setting* or *plot time*—can be roughly the same as that in which the work was written (its *author time*); or it can be much later, as in most science fiction; or much earlier, as in most **historical fiction**. Especially in short stories, which tend not to cover as much time or space as novels do, time may be very restricted, involving only a few hours or even minutes. Yet even in short stories, the action may span years or even decades.

Similarly, the place—a work's *geographical* or *physical setting*—might be limited to a single locale, or it might encompass several disparate ones. Those places might be common and ordinary, unique and extraordinary, or fantastic and even impossible according to the laws of our world (as in modern **fantasy** or **magic realism**).

Even when a story's action takes place in multiple times and places, we still sometimes refer to its *setting* (singular). By this, we indicate what we might call the entire story's *general setting*—the year(s) and the region, country, or even world in which the story unfolds and which often provides a historical and cultural context for the action. The general setting of Margaret Mitchell's historical novel *Gone with the Wind* (1936), for instance, is the Civil War–era South. But this novel, like many, has numerous *particular settings*; it opens, for instance, on an April morning on the porch of a north Georgia mansion called Tara, where Scarlett O'Hara flirts with two beaus and ignores their talk of a possible war to come. To fully appreciate the nature and role of setting, we thus need to consider the specific time of day and year as well as the specific locales in which the action unfolds.

Some stories merely offer hints about setting; others describe setting in great sensory detail. Especially in the latter case, we might be tempted to skim through what seems like mere "scenery" or "background information" to find out what happens next or how things turn out. But in good fiction, setting always functions as an integral part of the whole.

FUNCTIONS OF SETTING

Fiction often relies on setting to establish mood, situation, and character. The first sentence of Edgar Allan Poe's short story "The Fall of the House of Usher" (1839), for example, quickly sets the tone:

> During the whole of a dull, dark, and soundless day in the autumn of the year, when the clouds hung oppressively low in the heavens, I had been passing alone, on horseback, through a singularly dreary tract of country; and at length found myself, as the shades of the evening drew on, within view of the melancholy House of Usher.

This sentence aims to instill in the reader the same fear, "melancholy," and "sense of insufferable gloom" the narrator feels. With it, Poe prepares the reader emotionally, as well as mentally, for the sad and eerie tale that is about to unfold. He also generates suspense and certain expectations about just what might happen, as well as empathy with the narrator-protagonist.

Here, as in other fiction, specific details prove crucial to setting's emotional effect and meaning precisely because, as Poe's narrator himself observes,

> there are combinations of very simple natural objects which have the power of thus affecting us [. . .]. It was possible, I reflected, that a mere different arrangement of the particulars of the scene, of the details of the picture, would be sufficient to modify [. . .] its [. . .] impression.

In addition to creating such emotional impressions, setting can reveal or even shape a character's personality, outlook, and values; it can occasionally be an actor in the plot; and it often prompts characters' actions. (Who might you become and what might you do if you lived in the isolated, gloomy House of Usher?) Descriptions of setting may even (as in the first boxed example below) suggest a key **conflict** or **theme**. To gloss over descriptions of setting would thus mean not only missing much of the pleasure fiction affords but also potentially misreading its meanings. Setting is one of the many ways we learn about characters and the chief means by which characters and plots take on a larger historical, social, or even universal significance.

VAGUE AND VIVID SETTINGS

Not all stories, of course, rely so heavily on setting as Poe's does. In some individual works and in some subgenres, the general time, place, or both may be so vague as to seem, at first glance, unimportant. Many folktales and fairy tales take place in **archetypal** settings: "A long time ago," in "the forest" or "a village" or "a cottage," "in a land far, far away." By offering little, if any, specific information about their settings—neither locating the "forest" or "village" or faraway land in a place we can find on a map or a time we can locate on a calendar or clock, nor describing it in any detail—these works implicitly urge us to see the conflicts and aspects of human experience they depict (death, grief, a mother's relationship to her child, the danger and incomprehensibility of the unknown) as timeless and universal. Here, the very lack of attention to setting paradoxically turns out to be all-important.

At the opposite extreme are works and subgenres of fiction in which setting generates the conflicts, defines the characters, and gives the story purpose and meaning—so much so that there would be little, if any, story left if all the details about setting were removed or the characters and plot were somehow transported to a different time, place, and social milieu. Without their settings, what would remain of historical novels like *Gone with the Wind* or Nathaniel Hawthorne's *The Scarlet Letter* (1850)? An even more extreme example is Italo Calvino's fantasy novel INVISIBLE CITIES, which consists almost entirely of a series of descriptions of impossible, yet often hauntingly beautiful places like the following one.

ITALO CALVINO
From *Invisible Cities*

W hat makes Argia different from other cities is that it has earth instead of air. The streets are completely filled with dirt, clay packs the rooms to the ceiling, on every stair another stairway is set in negative, over the roofs of the houses hang layers of rocky terrain like skies with clouds. We do not know if the inhabitants can move about the city, widening the worm tunnels and the crevices where roots twist: the dampness destroys people's bodies and they have scant strength; everyone is better off remaining still, prone; anyway, it is dark.

From up here, nothing of Argia can be seen; some say, "It's down below there," and we can only believe them. The place is deserted. At night, putting your ear to the ground, you can sometimes hear a door slam.

1972

◦ ◦ ◦

Most fiction, of course, occupies a middle ground between the extremes of Calvino's novel or historical fiction (with their highly particularized settings) versus folklore (with its generic, archetypal setting). Though all fiction may ultimately deal with some types of people, aspects of human experience, and conflicts that can crop up in some form or fashion anywhere or any time, much fiction also draws our attention to the way people, their experience, and their conflicts are twisted into a particular "form and fashion" by specific contexts.

Analyzing Descriptions of Setting: An Example and an Exercise

The novel *Gone with the Wind*, like the movie, opens on the front porch of Tara, where a carefree Scarlett O'Hara flirts with the Tarleton twins and studiously ignores the first rumors of war. Then the narrator pulls back to show us, with great detail, both the time of year and the landscape in which that porch is situated. After you read the following description, write a paragraph or two that draws on details from the passage to explain the feelings and impressions it conjures up, the functions it might serve at the beginning of the novel, and the way it achieves its effects. How, for example, might this description **foreshadow** and even help explain subsequent events? Why else might the novel need all this detail?

Spring had come early that year, with warm quick rains and sudden frothing of pink peach blossoms and dogwood dappling with white stars the dark river swamp and far-off hills. Already the plowing was nearly finished, and the bloody glory of the sunset colored the fresh-cut furrows of red Georgia clay to even redder hues. The moist hungry earth, waiting upturned for the cotton seeds, showed pinkish on the sandy tops of furrows, vermilion and scarlet and maroon where shadows lay along the sides of the trenches. The whitewashed brick plantation house seemed an island set in a wild red sea, a sea of spiraling, curving, crescent billows petrified suddenly at the moment when the pink-tipped waves were breaking into surf. For here were no long, straight furrows, such as could be seen in the yellow clay fields of the flat middle Georgia country or in the lush black earth of the coastal plantations. The rolling foothill country of north Georgia was plowed in a million curves to keep the rich earth from washing down into the river bottoms.

It was a savagely red land, blood-colored after rains, brick dust in droughts, the best cotton land in the world. It was a pleasant land of white houses, peaceful plowed fields and sluggish yellow rivers, but a land of contrasts, of bright sun glare and densest shade. The plantation clearings

(continued on next page)

(continued)

and miles of cotton fields smiled up to a warm sun, placid, complacent. At their edges rose the virgin forests, dark and cool even in the hottest noons, mysterious, a little sinister, the soughing pines seem to wait with an age-old patience, to threaten with soft sighs: "Be careful! Be careful! We had you once. We can take you back again."

TRADITIONAL EXPECTATIONS OF TIME AND PLACE

The effects and meanings evoked by setting depend on our traditional associations with, and often unconscious assumptions about, particular times, places, and even such factors as weather conditions—autumn, evening, a deserted country road, a house grand enough to have a name, a sky full of low and lowering clouds (to refer back to the Poe example).

Traditional associations derive, in part, from literature and myth, and some are culturally specific. (To someone unfamiliar with the Old Testament, an apple orchard would simply be an apple orchard, without any suggestion of evil or sin. Likewise, to someone who knows little about the U.S. Civil War, a big white house in the middle of a cotton field might seem like nothing more than a very beautiful place full of lucky, wealthy, happy people.) These associations also come from our learning, our experience, our own specific social and historical context, and even our primal instincts and physical condition as human beings. Almost all of us are more vulnerable in the dark and in inclement weather. And people do behave differently and expect different things to happen in different times and places—on a Saturday versus a Sunday versus a Monday, during spring break versus midsemester or midweek, at a posh beach resort we are just visiting versus the grocery store in our own neighborhood, and so on.

Often, however, authors draw on such associations precisely in order to reverse and question them. John Updike has said that he was initially inspired to write A & P because a suburban grocery store seemed just the sort of mundane place no reader would expect either heroism or a story to take place. ("Why don't you ever read a story set in an A & P?" he reportedly asked his wife.) By reversing expectations in this way, stories not only deepen their emotional effect but also encourage us to rethink our assumptions about particular times and places and the people who inhabit them.

This early scene from *Gone with the Wind* (1939) takes place on the porch of a mansion in Georgia, just before the start of the Civil War.

Connecting Setting, Point of View, and Character: An Example and an Exercise

For the purpose of analysis, we distinguish setting from other elements such as character, plot, point of view, and language. Perhaps paradoxically, we need to do so precisely in order to understand how these elements work together. The following passage from Alice Randall's controversial novel *The Wind Done Gone* (2002), for example, paints a dramatically different picture of the antebellum South than do earlier novels and films like *Gone with the Wind*, in part because it looks at that time and place from a very different point of view.

After you read the passage, write a paragraph or two about how its effect and meaning are shaped by point of view and **figurative language**

(continued on next page)

(continued)

or **imagery**. What might the passage tell us about Randall's narrator? How does the passage encourage us to rethink traditional views of the antebellum South?

Alternatively, compare this passage to the one from Mitchell's *Gone with the Wind* in this chapter's first "Example and Exercise," focusing on how each passage differently depicts the same time and place and how each passage's effect and meaning derive from its point of view and from its distinctive use of somewhat similar language and images.

Mammy worked from can't-see in the morning to can't-see at night, in that great whitewashed wide-columned house surrounded by curvy furrowed fields. The mud, the dirt, was so red, when you looked at the cotton blooming in a field it brought to mind a sleeping gown after childbirth—all soft white cotton and blood.

If it was mine to be able to paint pictures, if I possessed the gift of painting, I would paint a cotton gown balled up and thrown into a corner waiting to be washed, and I would call it "Georgia."

. . .

Setting is key to each of the stories gathered in this chapter. The settings in these stories range from the United States to Russia and China; from the late-nineteenth century to the late-twentieth; from coastal resorts to crowded, cosmopolitan cities. The stories take place in just about every season and all kinds of weather, but regardless of the specific setting each paints a revealing portrait of a time and place. Just as our own memories of important experiences include complex impressions of when and where they occurred—the weather, the shape of the room, the music that was playing, even the fashions or the events in the news back then—so stories rely on setting to evoke emotion and generate meaning.

Questions about Setting

General Setting

- What is the general temporal and geographical setting of this work of fiction? How do you know?
- How important does the general setting seem to be? In what ways is it important? What about the plot and characters would remain the same

if they were magically transported to a different setting? What wouldn't?
For example, how does the setting
  ◦ create or shape conflict?
  ◦ affect characters' personalities, outlooks, and actions?
  ◦ shape our impressions of who the characters are and what they
    represent?
  ◦ establish mood?

Particular Settings

• Does all the action occur in one time and place, or in more than one? If
  the latter, what are those times and places?
• What patterns do you notice regarding where and when things happen?
  Which characters are associated with each setting? How do different
  characters relate to the same setting? When, how, and why do characters move from one setting to another? Are there significant deviations
  from these patterns?
• Are particular settings described in detail, or merely sketched? If the
  former, what seems significant about the details? How might they establish mood, reveal character, and affect individual characters and their
  interactions with one another?

ANTON CHEKHOV
(1860–1904)
The Lady with the Dog[1]

The grandson of an emancipated serf, Anton
Chekhov was born in the Russian town of Tagan-
rog. In 1875, his father, a grocer facing bankruptcy
and imprisonment, fled to Moscow, and soon the
rest of the family lost their house to a former
friend and lodger, a situation that Chekhov would revisit in his play *The Cherry
Orchard* (1904). In 1884, Chekhov received his MD from the University of Moscow. He purchased an estate near Moscow in the early 1890s and became both
an industrious landowner and doctor to the local peasants. After contributing
stories to magazines and journals throughout the 1880s, he began writing for
the stage in 1887, the same year he published his first collection of fiction. Chekhov himself once declared that fiction is "a lawful wife, but the Stage is a noisy,
flashy, and insolent mistress." Forced by tuberculosis to winter on the coast

1. Translated by Constance Garnett.

after 1897, Chekhov married the actress Olga Knipper in 1901, but the couple had no children.

I

It was said that a new person had appeared on the sea-front: a lady with a little dog. Dmitri Dmitritch Gurov, who had by then been a fortnight at Yalta,[2] and so was fairly at home there, had begun to take an interest in new arrivals. Sitting in Verney's pavilion, he saw, walking on the sea-front, a fair-haired young lady of medium height, wearing a *béret*; a white Pomeranian dog was running behind her.

And afterwards he met her in the public gardens and in the square several times a day. She was walking alone, always wearing the same *béret*, and always with the same white dog; no one knew who she was, and every one called her simply "the lady with the dog."

"If she is here alone without a husband or friends, it wouldn't be amiss to make her acquaintance," Gurov reflected.

He was under forty, but he had a daughter already twelve years old, and two sons at school. He had been married young, when he was a student in his second year, and by now his wife seemed half as old again as he. She was a tall, erect woman with dark eyebrows, staid and dignified, and, as she said of herself, intellectual. She read a great deal, used phonetic spelling, called her husband, not Dmitri, but Dimitri, and he secretly considered her unintelligent, narrow, inelegant, was afraid of her, and did not like to be at home. He had begun being unfaithful to her long ago—had been unfaithful to her often, and, probably on that account, almost always spoke ill of women, and when they were talked about in his presence, used to call them "the lower race."

5   It seemed to him that he had been so schooled by bitter experience that he might call them what he liked, and yet he could not get on for two days together without "the lower race." In the society of men he was bored and not himself, with them he was cold and uncommunicative; but when he was in the company of women he felt free, and knew what to say to them and how to behave; and he was at ease with them even when he was silent. In his appearance, in his character, in his whole nature, there was something attractive and elusive which allured women and disposed them in his favour; he knew that, and some force seemed to draw him, too, to them.

2. Russian city on the Black Sea; a resort.

Experience often repeated, truly bitter experience, had taught him long ago that with decent people, especially Moscow people—always slow to move and irresolute—every intimacy, which at first so agreeably diversifies life and appears a light and charming adventure, inevitably grows into a regular problem of extreme intricacy, and in the long run the situation becomes unbearable. But at every fresh meeting with an interesting woman this experience seemed to slip out of his memory, and he was eager for life, and everything seemed simple and amusing.

One evening he was dining in the gardens, and the lady in the *béret* came up slowly to take the next table. Her expression, her gait, her dress, and the way she did her hair told him that she was a lady, that she was married, that she was in Yalta for the first time and alone, and that she was dull there. . . . The stories told of the immorality in such places as Yalta are to a great extent untrue; he despised them, and knew that such stories were for the most part made up by persons who would themselves have been glad to sin if they had been able; but when the lady sat down at the next table three paces from him, he remembered these tales of easy conquests, of trips to the mountains, and the tempting thought of a swift, fleeting love affair, a romance with an unknown woman, whose name he did not know, suddenly took possession of him.

He beckoned coaxingly to the Pomeranian, and when the dog came up to him he shook his finger at it. The Pomeranian growled: Gurov shook his finger at it again.

The lady looked at him and at once dropped her eyes.

"He doesn't bite," she said, and blushed. 10

"May I give him a bone?" he asked; and when she nodded he asked courteously, "Have you been long in Yalta?"

"Five days."

"And I have already dragged out a fortnight here."

There was a brief silence.

"Time goes fast, and yet it is so dull here!" she said, not looking at him. 15

"That's only the fashion to say it is dull here. A provincial will live in Belyov or Zhidra and not be dull, and when he comes here it's 'Oh, the dulness! Oh, the dust!' One would think he came from Grenada."[3]

She laughed. Then both continued eating in silence, like strangers, but after dinner they walked side by side; and there sprang up between them the light jesting conversation of people who are free and satisfied, to whom it does not matter where they go or what they talk about. They walked and talked of the strange light on the sea: the water was of a soft warm lilac hue, and there was a golden streak from the moon upon it. They talked of

3. Romantic city in southern Spain.

how sultry it was after a hot day. Gurov told her that he came from Moscow, that he had taken his degree in Arts, but had a post in a bank; that he had trained as an opera-singer, but had given it up, that he owned two houses in Moscow. . . . And from her he learnt that she had grown up in Petersburg, but had lived in S— since her marriage two years before, that she was staying another month in Yalta, and that her husband, who needed a holiday too, might perhaps come and fetch her. She was not sure whether her husband had a post in a Crown Department or under the Provincial Council[4]—and was amused by her own ignorance. And Gurov learnt, too, that she was called Anna Sergeyevna.

Afterwards he thought about her in his room at the hotel—thought she would certainly meet him next day; it would be sure to happen. As he got into bed he thought how lately she had been a girl at school, doing lessons like his own daughter; he recalled the diffidence, the angularity, that was still manifest in her laugh and her manner of talking with a stranger. This must have been the first time in her life she had been alone in surroundings in which she was followed, looked at, and spoken to merely from a secret motive which she could hardly fail to guess. He recalled her slender, delicate neck, her lovely grey eyes.

"There's something pathetic about her, anyway," he thought, and fell asleep.

II

20 A week had passed since they had made acquaintance. It was a holiday. It was sultry indoors, while in the street the wind whirled the dust round and round, and blew people's hats off. It was a thirsty day, and Gurov often went into the pavilion, and pressed Anna Sergeyevna to have syrup and water or an ice. One did not know what to do with oneself.

In the evening when the wind had dropped a little, they went out on the groyne to see the steamer come in. There were a great many people walking about the harbour; they had gathered to welcome some one, bringing bouquets. And two peculiarities of a well-dressed Yalta crowd were very conspicuous: the elderly ladies were dressed like young ones, and there were great numbers of generals.

Owing to the roughness of the sea, the steamer arrived late, after the sun had set, and it was a long time turning about before it reached the groyne. Anna Sergeyevna looked through her lorgnette at the steamer and the passengers as though looking for acquaintances, and when she turned to Gurov her eyes were shining. She talked a great deal and asked discon-

4. That is, a post in a national department, appointed by the czar, or a post in an elective local council.

nected questions, forgetting next moment what she had asked; then she dropped her lorgnette in the crush.

The festive crowd began to disperse; it was too dark to see people's faces. The wind had completely dropped, but Gurov and Anna Sergeyevna still stood as though waiting to see some one else come from the steamer. Anna Sergeyevna was silent now, and sniffed the flowers without looking at Gurov.

"The weather is better this evening," he said. "Where shall we go now? Shall we drive somewhere?"

She made no answer.   25

Then he looked at her intently, and all at once put his arm round her and kissed her on the lips, and breathed in the moisture and the fragrance of the flowers; and he immediately looked round him, anxiously wondering whether any one had seen them.

"Let us go to your hotel," he said softly. And both walked quickly.

The room was close and smelt of the scent she had bought at the Japanese shop. Gurov looked at her and thought: "What different people one meets in the world!" From the past he preserved memories of careless, good-natured women, who loved cheerfully and were grateful to him for the happiness he gave them, however brief it might be; and of women like his wife who loved without any genuine feeling, with superfluous phrases, affectedly, hysterically, with an expression that suggested that it was not love nor passion, but something more significant; and of two or three others, very beautiful, cold women, on whose faces he had caught a glimpse of a rapacious expression—an obstinate desire to snatch from life more than it could give, and these were capricious, unreflecting, domineering, unintelligent women not in their first youth, and when Gurov grew cold to them their beauty excited his hatred, and the lace on their linen seemed to him like scales.

But in this case there was still the diffidence, the angularity of inexperienced youth, an awkward feeling; and there was a sense of consternation as though some one had suddenly knocked at the door. The attitude of Anna Sergeyevna—"the lady with the dog"—to what had happened was somehow peculiar, very grave, as though it were her fall—so it seemed, and it was strange and inappropriate. Her face dropped and faded, and on both sides of it her long hair hung down mournfully; she mused in a dejected attitude like "the woman who was a sinner" in an old-fashioned picture.

"It's wrong," she said. "You will be the first to despise me now."   30

There was a water-melon on the table. Gurov cut himself a slice and began eating it without haste. There followed at least half an hour of silence.

Anna Sergeyevna was touching; there was about her the purity of a good, simple woman who had seen little of life. The solitary candle burning on the table threw a faint light on her face, yet it was clear that she was very unhappy.

"How could I despise you?" asked Gurov. "You don't know what you are saying."

"God forgive me," she said, and her eyes filled with tears. "It's awful."

35   "You seem to feel you need to be forgiven."

"Forgiven? No. I am a bad, low woman; I despise myself and don't attempt to justify myself. It's not my husband but myself I have deceived. And not only just now; I have been deceiving myself for a long time. My husband may be a good, honest man, but he is a flunkey! I don't know what he does there, what his work is, but I know he is a flunkey! I was twenty when I was married to him. I have been tormented by curiosity; I wanted something better. 'There must be a different sort of life,' I said to myself. I wanted to live! To live, to live! . . . I was fired by curiosity . . . you don't understand it, but, I swear to God, I could not control myself; something happened to me: I could not be restrained. I told my husband I was ill, and came here. . . . And here I have been walking about as though I were dazed, like a mad creature; . . . and now I have become a vulgar, contemptible woman whom any one may despise."

Gurov felt bored already, listening to her. He was irritated by the naïve tone, by this remorse, so unexpected and inopportune; but for the tears in her eyes, he might have thought she was jesting or playing a part.

"I don't understand," he said softly. "What is it you want?"

She hid her face on his breast and pressed close to him.

40   "Believe me, believe me, I beseech you . . ." she said. "I love a pure, honest life, and sin is loathsome to me. I don't know what I am doing. Simple people say: 'The Evil One has beguiled me.' And I may say of myself now that the Evil One has beguiled me."

"Hush, hush! . . ." he muttered.

He looked at her fixed, scared eyes, kissed her, talked softly and affectionately, and by degrees she was comforted, and her gaiety returned; they both began laughing.

Afterwards when they went out there was not a soul on the sea-front. The town with its cypresses had quite a deathlike air, but the sea still broke noisily on the shore; a single barge was rocking on the waves, and a lantern was blinking sleepily on it.

They found a cab and drove to Oreanda.

45   "I found out your surname in the hall just now: it was written on the board—Von Diderits," said Gurov. "Is your husband a German?"

"No; I believe his grandfather was a German, but he is an Orthodox Russian himself."

At Oreanda they sat on a seat not far from the church, looked down at the sea, and were silent. Yalta was hardly visible through the morning mist; white clouds stood motionless on the mountain-tops. The leaves did not stir on the trees, grasshoppers chirruped, and the monotonous hollow sound of the sea rising up from below, spoke of the peace, of the eternal sleep awaiting us. So it must have sounded when there was no Yalta, no Oreanda here; so it sounds now, and it will sound as indifferently and monotonously when we are all no more. And in this constancy, in this complete indifference to the life and death of each of us, there lies hid, perhaps, a pledge of our eternal salvation, of the unceasing movement of life upon earth, of unceasing progress towards perfection. Sitting beside a young woman who in the dawn seemed so lovely, soothed and spellbound in these magical surroundings—the sea, mountains, clouds, the open sky—Gurov thought how in reality everything is beautiful in this world when one reflects: everything except what we think or do ourselves when we forget our human dignity and the higher aims of our existence.

A man walked up to them—probably a keeper—looked at them and walked away. And this detail seemed mysterious and beautiful, too. They saw a steamer come from Theodosia, with its lights out in the glow of dawn.

"There is dew on the grass," said Anna Sergeyevna, after a silence.

"Yes. It's time to go home." 50

They went back to the town.

Then they met every day at twelve o'clock on the sea-front, lunched and dined together, went for walks, admired the sea. She complained that she slept badly, that her heart throbbed violently; asked the same questions, troubled now by jealousy and now by the fear that he did not respect her sufficiently. And often in the square or gardens, when there was no one near them, he suddenly drew her to him and kissed her passionately. Complete idleness, these kisses in broad daylight while he looked round in dread of some one's seeing them, the heat, the smell of the sea, and the continual passing to and fro before him of idle, well-dressed, well-fed people, made a new man of him; he told Anna Sergeyevna how beautiful she was, how fascinating. He was impatiently passionate, he would not move a step away from her, while she was often pensive and continually urged him to confess that he did not respect her, did not love her in the least, and thought of her as nothing but a common woman. Rather late almost every evening they drove somewhere out of town, to Oreanda or to the waterfall; and the expedition was always a success, the scenery invariably impressed them as grand and beautiful.

They were expecting her husband to come, but a letter came from him, saying that there was something wrong with his eyes, and he entreated his wife to come home as quickly as possible. Anna Sergeyevna made haste to go.

"It's a good thing I am going away," she said to Gurov. "It's the finger of destiny!"

55   She went by coach and he went with her. They were driving the whole day. When she had got into a compartment of the express, and when the second bell had rung, she said:

"Let me look at you once more . . . look at you once again. That's right."

She did not shed tears, but was so sad that she seemed ill, and her face was quivering.

"I shall remember you . . . think of you," she said. "God be with you; be happy. Don't remember evil against me. We are parting forever—it must be so, for we ought never to have met. Well, God be with you."

The train moved off rapidly, its lights soon vanished from sight, and a minute later there was no sound of it, as though everything had conspired together to end as quickly as possible that sweet delirium, that madness. Left alone on the platform, and gazing into the dark distance, Gurov listened to the chirrup of the grasshoppers and the hum of the telegraph wires, feeling as though he had only just waked up. And he thought, musing, that there had been another episode or adventure in his life, and it, too, was at an end, and nothing was left of it but a memory. . . . He was moved, sad, and conscious of a slight remorse. This young woman whom he would never meet again had not been happy with him; he was genuinely warm and affectionate with her, but yet in his manner, his tone, and his caresses there had been a shade of light irony, the coarse condescension of a happy man who was, besides, almost twice her age. All the time she had called him kind, exceptional, lofty; obviously he had seemed to her different from what he really was, so he had unintentionally deceived her. . . .

60   Here at the station was already a scent of autumn; it was a cold evening.

"It's time for me to go north," thought Gurov as he left the platform. "High time!"

III

At home in Moscow everything was in its winter routine; the stoves were heated, and in the morning it was still dark when the children were having breakfast and getting ready for school, and the nurse would light the lamp for a short time. The frosts had begun already. When the first snow has fallen, on the first day of sledge-driving it is pleasant to see the white earth, the white roofs, to draw soft, delicious breath, and the season brings back the days of one's youth. The old limes and birches, white with hoar-frost, have a good-natured expression; they are nearer to one's heart than cypresses and palms, and near them one doesn't want to be thinking of the sea and the mountains.

Gurov was Moscow born; he arrived in Moscow on a fine frosty day, and when he put on his fur coat and warm gloves, and walked along Petro-vka, and when on Saturday evening he heard the ringing of the bells, his recent trip and the places he had seen lost all charm for him. Little by little he became absorbed in Moscow life, greedily read three newspapers a day, and declared he did not read the Moscow papers on principle! He already felt a longing to go to restaurants, clubs, dinner-parties, anniversary celebrations, and he felt flattered at entertaining distinguished lawyers and artists, and at playing cards with a professor at the doctors' club. He could already eat a whole plateful of salt fish and cabbage. . . .

In another month, he fancied, the image of Anna Sergeyevna would be shrouded in a mist in his memory, and only from time to time would visit him in his dreams with a touching smile as others did. But more than a month passed, real winter had come, and everything was still clear in his memory as though he had parted with Anna Sergeyevna only the day before. And his memories glowed more and more vividly. When in the evening stillness he heard from his study the voices of his children, pre-paring their lessons, or when he listened to a song or the organ at the res-taurant, or the storm howled in the chimney, suddenly everything would rise up in his memory: what had happened on the groyne, and the early morning with the mist on the mountains, and the steamer coming from Theodosia, and the kisses. He would pace a long time about his room, remembering it all and smiling; then his memories passed into dreams, and in his fancy the past was mingled with what was to come. Anna Sergeyevna did not visit him in dreams, but followed him about everywhere like a shadow and haunted him. When he shut his eyes he saw her as though she were living before him, and she seemed to him lovelier, younger, ten-derer than she was; and he imagined himself finer than he had been in Yalta. In the evenings she peeped out at him from the bookcase, from the fireplace, from the corner—he heard her breathing, the caressing rustle of her dress. In the street he watched the women, looking for some one like her.

He was tormented by an intense desire to confide his memories to some one. But in his home it was impossible to talk of his love, and he had no one outside; he could not talk to his tenants nor to any one at the bank. And what had he to talk of? Had he been in love, then? Had there been anything beautiful, poetical, or edifying or simply interesting in his rela-tions with Anna Sergeyevna? And there was nothing for him but to talk vaguely of love, of woman, and no one guessed what it meant; only his wife twitched her black eyebrows, and said: "The part of a lady-killer does not suit you at all, Dimitri."

One evening, coming out of the doctors' club with an official with whom he had been playing cards, he could not resist saying:

"If only you knew what a fascinating woman I made the acquaintance of in Yalta!"

The official got into his sledge and was driving away, but turned suddenly and shouted:

"Dmitri Dmitritch!"

70   "What?"

"You were right this evening: the sturgeon was a bit too strong!"

These words, so ordinary, for some reason moved Gurov to indignation, and struck him as degrading and unclean. What savage manners, what people! What senseless nights, what uninteresting, uneventful days! The rage for card-playing, the gluttony, the drunkenness, the continual talk always about the same thing. Useless pursuits and conversations always about the same things absorb the better part of one's time, the better part of one's strength, and in the end there is left a life grovelling and curtailed, worthless and trivial, and there is no escaping or getting away from it—just as though one were in a madhouse or a prison.

Gurov did not sleep all night, and was filled with indignation. And he had a headache all next day. And the next night he slept badly; he sat up in bed, thinking, or paced up and down his room. He was sick of his children, sick of the bank; he had no desire to go anywhere or to talk of anything.

In the holidays in December he prepared for a journey, and told his wife he was going to Petersburg to do something in the interests of a young friend—and he set off for S——. What for? He did not very well know himself. He wanted to see Anna Sergeyevna and to talk with her—to arrange a meeting, if possible.

75   He reached S—— in the morning, and took the best room at the hotel, in which the floor was covered with grey army cloth, and on the table was an inkstand, grey with dust and adorned with a figure on horseback, with its hat in its hand and its head broken off. The hotel porter gave him the necessary information; Von Diderits lived in a house of his own in Old Gontcharny Street—it was not far from the hotel: he was rich and lived in good style, and had his own horses; every one in the town knew him. The porter pronounced the name "Dridirits."

Gurov went without haste to Old Gontcharny Street and found the house. Just opposite the house stretched a long grey fence adorned with nails.

"One would run away from a fence like that," thought Gurov, looking from the fence to the windows of the house and back again.

He considered: to-day was a holiday, and the husband would probably be at home. And in any case it would be tactless to go into the house and upset her. If he were to send her a note it might fall into her husband's hands, and then it might ruin everything. The best thing was to trust to chance. And he kept walking up and down the street by the fence, waiting for the chance. He saw a beggar go in at the gate and dogs fly at him; then an hour later he heard a piano, and the sounds were faint and indistinct. Probably it was Anna Sergeyevna playing. The front door suddenly opened, and an old woman came out, followed by the familiar white Pomeranian. Gurov was on the point of calling to the dog, but his heart began beating violently, and in his excitement he could not remember the dog's name.

He walked up and down, and loathed the grey fence more and more, and by now he thought irritably that Anna Sergeyevna had forgotten him, and was perhaps already amusing herself with some one else, and that that was very natural in a young woman who had nothing to look at from morning till night but that confounded fence. He went back to his hotel room and sat for a long while on the sofa, not knowing what to do, then he had dinner and a long nap.

"How stupid and worrying it is!" he thought when he woke and looked at the dark windows: it was already evening. "Here I've had a good sleep for some reason. What shall I do in the night?"

He sat on the bed, which was covered by a cheap grey blanket, such as one sees in hospitals, and he taunted himself in his vexation:

"So much for the lady with the dog . . . so much for the adventure. . . . You're in a nice fix. . . ."

That morning at the station a poster in large letters had caught his eye. "The Geisha"[5] was to be performed for the first time. He thought of this and went to the theatre.

"It's quite possible she may go to the first performance," he thought.

The theatre was full. As in all provincial theatres, there was a fog above the chandelier, the gallery was noisy and restless; in the front row the local dandies were standing up before the beginning of the performance, with their hands behind them; in the Governor's box the Governor's daughter, wearing a boa, was sitting in the front seat, while the Governor himself lurked modestly behind the curtain with only his hands visible; the orchestra was a long time tuning up; the stage curtain swayed. All the time the audience were coming in and taking their seats Gurov looked at them eagerly.

5. Operetta by Sidney Jones (1861–1946) that toured eastern Europe in 1898–99.

Anna Sergeyevna, too, came in. She sat down in the third row, and when Gurov looked at her his heart contracted, and he understood clearly that for him there was in the whole world no creature so near, so precious, and so important to him; she, this little woman, in no way remarkable, lost in a provincial crowd, with a vulgar lorgnette in her hand, filled his whole life now, was his sorrow and his joy, the one happiness that he now desired for himself, and to the sounds of the inferior orchestra, of the wretched provincial violins, he thought how lovely she was. He thought and dreamed.

A young man with small side-whiskers, tall and stooping, came in with Anna Sergeyevna and sat down beside her; he bent his head at every step and seemed to be continually bowing. Most likely this was the husband whom at Yalta, in a rush of bitter feeling, she had called a flunkey. And there really was in his long figure, his side-whiskers, and the small bald patch on his head, something of the flunkey's obsequiousness; his smile was sugary, and in his buttonhole there was some badge of distinction like the number on a waiter.

During the first interval the husband went away to smoke; she remained alone in her stall. Gurov, who was sitting in the stalls, too, went up to her and said in a trembling voice, with a forced smile:

"Good-evening."

90 She glanced at him and turned pale, then glanced again with horror, unable to believe her eyes, and tightly gripped the fan and the lorgnette in her hands, evidently struggling with herself not to faint. Both were silent. She was sitting, he was standing, frightened by her confusion and not venturing to sit down beside her. The violins and the flute began tuning up. He felt suddenly frightened; it seemed as though all the people in the boxes were looking at them. She got up and went quickly to the door; he followed her, and both walked senselessly along passages, and up and down stairs, and figures in legal, scholastic, and civil service uniforms, all wearing badges, flitted before their eyes. They caught glimpses of ladies, of fur coats hanging on pegs; the draughts blew on them, bringing a smell of stale tobacco. And Gurov, whose heart was beating violently, thought:

"Oh, heavens! Why are these people here and this orchestra! . . ."

And at that instant he recalled how when he had seen Anna Sergeyevna off at the station he had thought that everything was over and they would never meet again. But how far they were still from the end!

On the narrow, gloomy staircase over which was written "To the Amphi-theatre," she stopped.

"How you have frightened me!" she said, breathing hard, still pale and overwhelmed. "Oh, how you have frightened me! I am half dead. Why have you come? Why?"

"But do understand, Anna, do understand . . ." he said hastily in a low 95 voice. "I entreat you to understand. . . ."

She looked at him with dread, with entreaty, with love; she looked at him intently, to keep his features more distinctly in her memory.

"I am so unhappy," she went on, not heeding him. "I have thought of nothing but you all the time; I live only in the thought of you. And I wanted to forget, to forget you; but why, oh, why, have you come?"

On the landing above them two schoolboys were smoking and looking down, but that was nothing to Gurov; he drew Anna Sergeyevna to him, and began kissing her face, her cheeks, and her hands.

"What are you doing, what are you doing!" she cried in horror, pushing him away. "We are mad. Go away to-day; go away at once. . . . I beseech you by all that is sacred, I implore you. . . . There are people coming this way!"

Some one was coming up the stairs.   100

"You must go away," Anna Sergeyevna went on in a whisper. "Do you hear, Dmitri Dmitritch? I will come and see you in Moscow. I have never been happy; I am miserable now, and I never, never shall be happy, never! Don't make me suffer still more! I swear I'll come to Moscow. But now let us part. My precious, good, dear one, we must part!"

She pressed his hand and began rapidly going downstairs, looking round at him, and from her eyes he could see that she really was unhappy. Gurov stood for a little while, listened, then, when all sound had died away, he found his coat and left the theatre.

IV

And Anna Sergeyevna began coming to see him in Moscow. Once in two or three months she left S——, telling her husband that she was going to consult a doctor about an internal complaint—and her husband believed her, and did not believe her. In Moscow she stayed at the Slaviansky Bazaar hotel, and at once sent a man in a red cap to Gurov. Gurov went to see her, and no one in Moscow knew of it.

Once he was going to see her in this way on a winter morning (the messenger had come the evening before when he was out). With him walked his daughter, whom he wanted to take to school: it was on the way. Snow was falling in big wet flakes.

"It's three degrees above freezing-point, and yet it is snowing," said Gurov 105 to his daughter. "The thaw is only on the surface of the earth; there is quite a different temperature at a greater height in the atmosphere."

"And why are there no thunderstorms in the winter, father?"

He explained that, too. He talked, thinking all the while that he was going to see *her*, and no living soul knew of it, and probably never would know. He had two lives: one, open, seen and known by all who cared to know, full of relative truth and of relative falsehood, exactly like the lives of his friends and acquaintances; and another life running its course in secret. And through some strange, perhaps accidental, conjunction of circumstances, everything that was essential, of interest and of value to him, everything in which he was sincere and did not deceive himself, everything that made the kernel of his life, was hidden from other people; and all that was false in him, the sheath in which he hid himself to conceal the truth— such, for instance, as his work in the bank, his discussions at the club, his "lower race," his presence with his wife at anniversary festivities—all that was open. And he judged of others by himself, not believing in what he saw, and always believing that every man had his real, most interesting life under the cover of secrecy and under the cover of night. All personal life rested on secrecy, and possibly it was partly on that account that civilised man was so nervously anxious that personal privacy should be respected.

After leaving his daughter at school, Gurov went on to the Slaviansky Bazaar. He took off his fur coat below, went upstairs, and softly knocked at the door. Anna Sergeyevna, wearing his favourite grey dress, exhausted by the journey and the suspense, had been expecting him since the evening before. She was pale; she looked at him, and did not smile, and he had hardly come in when she fell on his breast. Their kiss was slow and prolonged, as though they had not met for two years.

"Well, how are you getting on there?" he asked. "What news?"

110 "Wait; I'll tell you directly. . . . I can't talk."

She could not speak; she was crying. She turned away from him, and pressed her handkerchief to her eyes.

"Let her have her cry out. I'll sit down and wait," he thought, and he sat down in an arm-chair.

Then he rang and asked for tea to be brought him, and while he drank his tea she remained standing at the window with her back to him. She was crying from emotion, from the miserable consciousness that their life was so hard for them; they could only meet in secret, hiding themselves from people, like thieves! Was not their life shattered?

"Come, do stop!" he said.

115 It was evident to him that this love of theirs would not soon be over, that he could not see the end of it. Anna Sergeyevna grew more and more attached to him. She adored him, and it was unthinkable to say to her that it was bound to have an end some day; besides, she would not have believed it!

He went up to her and took her by the shoulders to say something affectionate and cheering, and at that moment he saw himself in the looking-glass.

His hair was already beginning to turn grey. And it seemed strange to him that he had grown so much older, so much plainer during the last few years. The shoulders on which his hands rested were warm and quivering. He felt compassion for this life, still so warm and lovely, but probably already not far from beginning to fade and wither like his own. Why did she love him so much? He always seemed to women different from what he was, and they loved in him not himself, but the man created by their imagination, whom they had been eagerly seeking all their lives; and afterwards, when they noticed their mistake, they loved him all the same. And not one of them had been happy with him. Time passed, he had made their acquaintance, got on with them, parted, but he had never once loved; it was anything you like, but not love.

And only now when his head was grey he had fallen properly, really in love—for the first time in his life.

Anna Sergeyevna and he loved each other like people very close and akin, like husband and wife, like tender friends; it seemed to them that fate itself had meant them for one another, and they could not understand why he had a wife and she a husband; and it was as though they were a pair of birds of passage, caught and forced to live in different cages. They forgave each other for what they were ashamed of in their past, they forgave everything in the present, and felt that this love of theirs had changed them both.

In moments of depression in the past he had comforted himself with 120 any arguments that came into his mind, but now he no longer cared for arguments; he felt profound compassion, he wanted to be sincere and tender. . . .

"Don't cry, my darling," he said. "You've had your cry; that's enough. . . . Let us talk now, let us think of some plan."

Then they spent a long while taking counsel together, talked of how to avoid the necessity for secrecy, for deception, for living in different towns and not seeing each other for long at a time. How could they be free from this intolerable bondage?

"How? How?" he asked, clutching his head. "How?"

And it seemed as though in a little while the solution would be found, and then a new and splendid life would begin; and it was clear to both of them that they had still a long, long road before them, and that the most complicated and difficult part of it was only just beginning.

1899

QUESTIONS

1. When Gurov and Anna take their first walk together, they discuss "the strange light of the sea: the water was of a soft warm lilac hue, and there was a golden

streak from the moon upon it" (par. 17). Why do you think Chekhov waits until this moment to provide descriptive details of the story's setting in Yalta?

2. How do the weather and season described in each section relate to the action in that section?

3. What is Gurov's attitude toward his affair with Anna at the outset? What is Anna's attitude? What are some indications that both Gurov and Anna are unprepared for the relationship that develops between them?

AMY TAN
(b. 1952)
A Pair of Tickets

Amy Tan was born in Oakland, California, just two and a half years after her parents immigrated from China. She received her MA in linguistics from San Jose State University and has worked on programs for disabled children and as a freelance writer. In 1987, at age thirty-five, she visited China for the first time—"As soon as my feet touched China, I became Chinese"—and returned to write her first book, *The Joy Luck Club* (1989), a novel composed of stories told by four Chinese immigrant women and their American-born daughters. Tan has written more novels—including *The Kitchen God's Wife* (1991), *The Hundred Secret Senses* (1995), *The Bonesetter's Daughter* (2000), and *Saving Fish from Drowning* (2006)— and has coauthored two children's books. Her first book of nonfiction, *The Opposite of Fate: A Book of Musings* (2003), explores lucky accidents, choice, and memory. Tan is also a backup singer for Rock Bottom Remainders, a rock band made up of fellow writers, including Stephen King and Dave Barry; they make appearances at benefits that support literacy programs for children.

The minute our train leaves the Hong Kong border and enters Shenzhen, China, I feel different. I can feel the skin on my forehead tingling, my blood rushing through a new course, my bones aching with a familiar old pain. And I think, My mother was right. I am becoming Chinese.

"Cannot be helped," my mother said when I was fifteen and had vigorously denied that I had any Chinese whatsoever below my skin. I was a sophomore at Galileo High in San Francisco, and all my Caucasian friends agreed: I was about as Chinese as they were. But my mother had studied at a famous nursing school in Shanghai, and she said she knew all about genetics. So there was no doubt in her mind, whether I agreed or not: Once you are born Chinese, you cannot help but feel and think Chinese.

"Someday you will see," said my mother. "It's in your blood, waiting to be let go."

And when she said this, I saw myself transforming like a werewolf, a mutant tag of DNA suddenly triggered, replicating itself insidiously into a *syndrome*, a cluster of telltale Chinese behaviors, all those things my mother did to embarrass me—haggling with store owners, pecking her mouth with a toothpick in public, being color-blind to the fact that lemon yellow and pale pink are not good combinations for winter clothes.

But today I realize I've never really known what it means to be Chi- 5 nese. I am thirty-six years old. My mother is dead and I am on a train, carrying with me her dreams of coming home. I am going to China.

We are going to Guangzhou, my seventy-two-year-old father, Canning Woo, and I, where we will visit his aunt, whom he has not seen since he was ten years old. And I don't know whether it's the prospect of seeing his aunt or if it's because he's back in China, but now he looks like he's a young boy, so innocent and happy I want to button his sweater and pat his head. We are sitting across from each other, separated by a little table with two cold cups of tea. For the first time I can ever remember, my father has tears in his eyes, and all he is seeing out the train window is a sectioned field of yellow, green, and brown, a narrow canal flanking the tracks, low rising hills, and three people in blue jackets riding an ox-driven cart on this early October morning. And I can't help myself. I also have misty eyes, as if I had seen this a long, long time ago, and had almost forgotten.

In less than three hours, we will be in Guangzhou, which my guidebook tells me is how one properly refers to Canton these days. It seems all the cities I have heard of, except Shanghai, have changed their spellings. I think they are saying China has changed in other ways as well. Chungking is Chongqing. And Kweilin is Guilin. I have looked these names up, because after we see my father's aunt in Guangzhou, we will catch a plane to Shanghai, where I will meet my two half-sisters for the first time.

They are my mother's twin daughters from her first marriage, little babies she was forced to abandon on a road as she was fleeing Kweilin for Chungking in 1944. That was all my mother had told me about these daughters, so they had remained babies in my mind, all these years, sitting on the side of a road, listening to bombs whistling in the distance while sucking their patient red thumbs.

And it was only this year that someone found them and wrote with this joyful news. A letter came from Shanghai, addressed to my mother. When I first heard about this, that they were alive, I imagined my identical sisters transforming from little babies into six-year-old girls. In my mind, they were seated next to each other at a table, taking turns with the fountain pen. One would write a neat row of characters: *Dearest Mama. We are alive.* She would brush back her wispy bangs and hand the other sister the pen, and she would write: *Come get us. Please hurry.*

10   Of course they could not know that my mother had died three months before, suddenly, when a blood vessel in her brain burst. One minute she was talking to my father, complaining about the tenants upstairs, scheming how to evict them under the pretense that relatives from China were moving in. The next minute she was holding her head, her eyes squeezed shut, groping for the sofa, and then crumpling softly to the floor with fluttering hands.

So my father had been the first one to open the letter, a long letter it turned out. And they did call her Mama. They said they always revered her as their true mother. They kept a framed picture of her. They told her about their life, from the time my mother last saw them on the road leaving Kweilin to when they were finally found.

And the letter had broken my father's heart so much—these daughters calling my mother from another life he never knew—that he gave the letter to my mother's old friend Auntie Lindo and asked her to write back and tell my sisters, in the gentlest way possible, that my mother was dead.

But instead Auntie Lindo took the letter to the Joy Luck Club and discussed with Auntie Ying and Auntie An-mei what should be done, because they had known for many years about my mother's search for her twin daughters, her endless hope. Auntie Lindo and the others cried over this double tragedy, of losing my mother three months before, and now again. And so they couldn't help but think of some miracle, some possible way of reviving her from the dead, so my mother could fulfill her dream.

So this is what they wrote to my sisters in Shanghai: "Dearest Daughters, I too have never forgotten you in my memory or in my heart. I never gave up hope that we would see each other again in a joyous reunion. I am only sorry it has been too long. I want to tell you everything about my life since I last saw you. I want to tell you this when our family comes to see you in China. . . ." They signed it with my mother's name.

15   It wasn't until all this had been done that they first told me about my sisters, the letter they received, the one they wrote back.

"They'll think she's coming, then," I murmured. And I had imagined my sisters now being ten or eleven, jumping up and down, holding hands, their pigtails bouncing, excited that their mother—*their* mother—was coming, whereas my mother was dead.

"How can you say she is not coming in a letter?" said Auntie Lindo. "She is their mother. She is your mother. You must be the one to tell them. All these years, they have been dreaming of her." And I thought she was right.

But then I started dreaming, too, of my mother and my sisters and how it would be if I arrived in Shanghai. All these years, while they waited to be found, I had lived with my mother and then had lost her. I imagined seeing my sisters at the airport. They would be standing on their tiptoes, looking anxiously, scanning from one dark head to another as we got off the plane. And I would recognize them instantly, their faces with the identical worried look.

"*Jyejye, Jyejye*. Sister, Sister. We are here," I saw myself saying in my poor version of Chinese.

"Where is Mama?" they would say, and look around, still smiling, two 20 flushed and eager faces. "Is she hiding?" And this would have been like my mother, to stand behind just a bit, to tease a little and make people's patience pull a little on their hearts. I would shake my head and tell my sisters she was not hiding.

"Oh, that must be Mama, no?" one of my sisters would whisper excitedly, pointing to another small woman completely engulfed in a tower of presents. And that, too, would have been like my mother, to bring mountains of gifts, food, and toys for children—all bought on sale—shunning thanks, saying the gifts were nothing, and later turning the labels over to show my sisters, "Calvin Klein, 100% wool."

I imagined myself starting to say, "Sisters, I am sorry, I have come alone . . ." and before I could tell them—they could see it in my face— they were wailing, pulling their hair, their lips twisted in pain, as they ran away from me. And then I saw myself getting back on the plane and coming home.

After I had dreamed this scene many times—watching their despair turn from horror into anger—I begged Auntie Lindo to write another letter. And at first she refused.

"How can I say she is dead? I cannot write this," said Auntie Lindo with a stubborn look.

"But it's cruel to have them believe she's coming on the plane," I said. 25 "When they see it's just me, they'll hate me."

"Hate you? Cannot be." She was scowling. "You are their own sister, their only family."

"You don't understand," I protested.

"What I don't understand?" she said.

And I whispered, "They'll think I'm responsible, that she died because I didn't appreciate her."

And Auntie Lindo looked satisfied and sad at the same time, as if this 30 were true and I had finally realized it. She sat down for an hour, and when she stood up she handed me a two-page letter. She had tears in her eyes. I realized that the very thing I had feared, she had done. So even if she had written the news of my mother's death in English, I wouldn't have had the heart to read it.

"Thank you," I whispered.

The landscape has become gray, filled with low flat cement buildings, old factories, and then tracks and more tracks filled with trains like ours passing by in the opposite direction. I see platforms crowded with people wearing drab Western clothes, with spots of bright colors: little children wearing pink and yellow, red and peach. And there are soldiers in olive green and red, and old ladies in gray tops and pants that stop mid-calf. We are in Guangzhou.

Before the train even comes to a stop, people are bringing down their belongings from above their seats. For a moment there is a dangerous shower of heavy suitcases laden with gifts to relatives, half-broken boxes wrapped in miles of string to keep the contents from spilling out, plastic bags filled with yarn and vegetables and packages of dried mushrooms, and camera cases. And then we are caught in a stream of people rushing, shoving, pushing us along, until we find ourselves in one of a dozen lines waiting to go through customs. I feel as if I were getting on a number 30 Stockton bus in San Francisco. I am in China, I remind myself. And somehow the crowds don't bother me. It feels right. I start pushing too.

I take out the declaration forms and my passport. "Woo," it says at the top, and below that, "June May," who was born in "California, U.S.A.," in 1951. I wonder if the customs people will question whether I'm the same person as in the passport photo. In this picture, my chin-length hair is swept back and artfully styled. I am wearing false eyelashes, eye shadow, and lip liner. My cheeks are hollowed out by bronze blusher. But I had not expected the heat in October. And now my hair hangs limp with the humidity. I wear no makeup; in Hong Kong my mascara had melted into dark circles and everything else had felt like layers of grease. So today my face is plain, unadorned except for a thin mist of shiny sweat on my forehead and nose.

35   Even without makeup, I could never pass for true Chinese. I stand five-foot-six, and my head pokes above the crowd so that I am eye level only with other tourists. My mother once told me my height came from my grandfather, who was a northerner, and may have even had some Mongol blood. "This is what your grandmother once told me," explained my mother. "But now it is too late to ask her. They are all dead, your grandparents, your uncles, and their wives and children, all killed in the war, when a bomb fell on our house. So many generations in one instant."

She had said this so matter-of-factly that I thought she had long since gotten over any grief she had. And then I wondered how she knew they were all dead.

"Maybe they left the house before the bomb fell," I suggested.

"No," said my mother. "Our whole family is gone. It is just you and I."

"But how do you know? Some of them could have escaped."

"Cannot be," said my mother, this time almost angrily. And then her 40
frown was washed over by a puzzled blank look, and she began to talk as if
she were trying to remember where she had misplaced something. "I went
back to that house. I kept looking up to where the house used to be. And it
wasn't a house, just the sky. And below, underneath my feet, were four stories of burnt bricks and wood, all the life of our house. Then off to the side I
saw things blown into the yard, nothing valuable. There was a bed someone
used to sleep in, really just a metal frame twisted up at one corner. And a
book, I don't know what kind, because every page had turned black. And I
saw a teacup which was unbroken but filled with ashes. And then I found
my doll, with her hands and legs broken, her hair burned off. . . . When I
was a little girl, I had cried for that doll, seeing it all alone in the store window,
and my mother had bought it for me. It was an American doll with yellow hair.
It could turn its legs and arms. The eyes moved up and down. And when
I married and left my family home, I gave the doll to my youngest niece,
because she was like me. She cried if that doll was not with her always. Do
you see? If she was in the house with that doll, her parents were there, and
so everybody was there, waiting together, because that's how our family was."

The woman in the customs booth stares at my documents, then glances at
me briefly, and with two quick movements stamps everything and sternly
nods me along. And soon my father and I find ourselves in a large area filled
with thousands of people and suitcases. I feel lost and my father looks
helpless.

"Excuse me," I say to a man who looks like an American. "Can you tell
me where I can get a taxi?" He mumbles something that sounds Swedish
or Dutch.

"Syau Yen! Syau Yen!" I hear a piercing voice shout from behind me. An
old woman in a yellow knit beret is holding up a pink plastic bag filled with
wrapped trinkets. I guess she is trying to sell us something. But my father is
staring down at this tiny sparrow of a woman, squinting into her eyes. And
then his eyes widen, his face opens up and he smiles like a pleased little boy.

"Aiyi! Aiyi!"—Auntie Auntie!—he says softly.

"Syau Yen!" coos my great-aunt. I think it's funny she has just called my 45
father "Little Wild Goose." It must be his baby milk name, the name used
to discourage ghosts from stealing children.

They clasp each other's hands—they do not hug—and hold on like this,
taking turns saying, "Look at you! You are so old. Look how old you've
become!" They are both crying openly, laughing at the same time, and I

bite my lip, trying not to cry. I'm afraid to feel their joy. Because I am thinking how different our arrival in Shanghai will be tomorrow, how awkward it
will feel.

Now Aiyi beams and points to a Polaroid picture of my father. My father
had wisely sent pictures when he wrote and said we were coming. See
how smart she was, she seems to intone as she compares the picture to my
father. In the letter, my father had said we would call her from the hotel
once we arrived, so this is a surprise, that they've come to meet us. I wonder if my sisters will be at the airport.

It is only then that I remember the camera. I had meant to take a picture of my father and his aunt the moment they met. It's not too late.

"Here, stand together over here," I say, holding up the Polaroid. The
camera flashes and I hand them the snapshot. Aiyi and my father still
stand close together, each of them holding a corner of the picture, watching as their images begin to form. They are almost reverentially quiet. Aiyi is
only five years older than my father, which makes her around seventy-
seven. But she looks ancient, shrunken, a mummified relic. Her thin hair
is pure white, her teeth are brown with decay. So much for stories of Chinese women looking young forever, I think to myself.

50   Now Aiyi is crooning to me: *"Jandale."* So big already. She looks up at
me, at my full height, and then peers into her pink plastic bag—her gifts
to us, I have figured out—as if she is wondering what she will give to me,
now that I am so old and big. And then she grabs my elbow with her sharp
pincerlike grasp and turns me around. A man and a woman in their fifties
are shaking hands with my father, everybody smiling and saying, "Ah!
Ah!" They are Aiyi's oldest son and his wife, and standing next to them
are four other people, around my age, and a little girl who's around ten.
The introductions go by so fast, all I know is that one of them is Aiyi's
grandson, with his wife, and the other is her granddaughter, with her husband. And the little girl is Lili, Aiyi's great-granddaughter.

Aiyi and my father speak the Mandarin dialect from their childhood,
but the rest of the family speaks only the Cantonese of their village. I understand only Mandarin but can't speak it that well. So Aiyi and my father
gossip unrestrained in Mandarin, exchanging news about people from
their old village. And they stop only occasionally to talk to the rest of us,
sometimes in Cantonese, sometimes in English.

"Oh, it is as I suspected," says my father, turning to me. "He died last
summer." And I already understood this. I just don't know who this person, Li Gong, is. I feel as if I were in the United Nations and the transla-
tors had run amok.

"Hello," I say to the little girl. "My name is Jing-mei." But the little girl
squirms to look away, causing her parents to laugh with embarrassment. I try

to think of Cantonese words I can say to her, stuff I learned from friends in Chinatown, but all I can think of are swear words, terms for bodily functions, and short phrases like "tastes good," "tastes like garbage," and "she's really ugly." And then I have another plan: I hold up the Polaroid camera, beckoning Lili with my finger. She immediately jumps forward, places one hand on her hip in the manner of a fashion model, juts out her chest, and flashes me a toothy smile. As soon as I take the picture she is standing next to me, jumping and giggling every few seconds as she watches herself appear on the greenish film.

By the time we hail taxis for the ride to the hotel, Lili is holding tight onto my hand, pulling me along.

In the taxi, Aiyi talks nonstop, so I have no chance to ask her about the 55 different sights we are passing by.

"You wrote and said you would come only for one day," says Aiyi to my father in an agitated tone. "One day! How can you see your family in one day! Toishan is many hours' drive from Guangzhou. And this idea to call us when you arrive. This is nonsense. We have no telephone."

My heart races a little. I wonder if Auntie Lindo told my sisters we would call from the hotel in Shanghai?

Aiyi continues to scold my father. "I was so beside myself, ask my son, almost turned heaven and earth upside down trying to think of a way! So we decided the best was for us to take the bus from Toishan and come into Guangzhou—meet you right from the start."

And now I am holding my breath as the taxi driver dodges between trucks and buses, honking his horn constantly. We seem to be on some sort of long freeway overpass, like a bridge above the city. I can see row after row of apartments, each floor cluttered with laundry hanging out to dry on the balcony. We pass a public bus, with people jammed in so tight their faces are nearly wedged against the window. Then I see the skyline of what must be downtown Guangzhou. From a distance, it looks like a major American city, with highrises and construction going on everywhere. As we slow down in the more congested part of the city, I see scores of little shops, dark inside, lined with counters and shelves. And then there is a building, its front laced with scaffolding made of bamboo poles held together with plastic strips. Men and women are standing on narrow platforms, scraping the sides, working without safety straps or helmets. Oh, would OSHA[1] have a field day here, I think.

Aiyi's shrill voice rises up again: "So it is a shame you can't see our village, 60 our house. My sons have been quite successful, selling our vegetables in

1. The Occupational Safety and Health Administration, a division of the U.S. Department of Labor.

the free market. We had enough these last few years to build a big house, three stories, all of new brick, big enough for our whole family and then some. And every year, the money is even better. You Americans aren't the only ones who know how to get rich!"

The taxi stops and I assume we've arrived, but then I peer out at what looks like a grander version of the Hyatt Regency. "This is communist China?" I wonder out loud. And then I shake my head toward my father. "This must be the wrong hotel." I quickly pull out our itinerary, travel tickets, and reservations. I had explicitly instructed my travel agent to choose something inexpensive, in the thirty-to-forty-dollar range. I'm sure of this. And there it says on our itinerary: Garden Hotel, Huanshi Dong Lu. Well, our travel agent had better be prepared to eat the extra, that's all I have to say.

The hotel is magnificent. A bellboy complete with uniform and sharp-creased cap jumps forward and begins to carry our bags into the lobby. Inside, the hotel looks like an orgy of shopping arcades and restaurants all encased in granite and glass. And rather than be impressed, I am worried about the expense, as well as the appearance it must give Aiyi, that we rich Americans cannot be without our luxuries even for one night.

But when I step up to the reservation desk, ready to haggle over this booking mistake, it is confirmed. Our rooms are prepaid, thirty-four dollars each. I feel sheepish, and Aiyi and the others seem delighted by our temporary surroundings. Lili is looking wide-eyed at an arcade filled with video games.

Our whole family crowds into one elevator, and the bellboy waves, saying he will meet us on the eighteenth floor. As soon as the elevator door shuts, everybody becomes very quiet, and when the door finally opens again, everybody talks at once in what sounds like relieved voices. I have the feeling Aiyi and the others have never been on such a long elevator ride.

65   Our rooms are next to each other and are identical. The rugs, drapes, bedspreads are all in shades of taupe. There's a color television with remote-control panels built into the lamp table between the two twin beds. The bathroom has marble walls and floors. I find a built-in wet bar with a small refrigerator stocked with Heineken beer, Coke Classic, and Seven-Up, mini-bottles of Johnnie Walker Red, Bacardi rum, and Smirnoff vodka, and packets of M & M's, honey-roasted cashews, and Cadbury chocolate bars. And again I say out loud, "This is communist China?"

My father comes into my room. "They decided we should just stay here and visit," he says, shrugging his shoulders. "They say, Less trouble that way. More time to talk."

"What about dinner?" I ask. I have been envisioning my first real Chinese feast for many days already, a big banquet with one of those soups steaming out of a carved winter melon, chicken wrapped in clay, Peking duck, the works.

My father walks over and picks up a room service book next to a *Travel & Leisure* magazine. He flips through the pages quickly and then points to the menu. "This is what they want," says my father.

So it's decided. We are going to dine tonight in our rooms, with our family, sharing hamburgers, french fries, and apple pie à la mode.

Aiyi and her family are browsing the shops while we clean up. After a hot 70 ride on the train, I'm eager for a shower and cooler clothes.

The hotel has provided little packets of shampoo which, upon opening, I discover is the consistency and color of hoisin sauce.[2] This is more like it, I think. This is China. And I rub some in my damp hair.

Standing in the shower, I realize this is the first time I've been by myself in what seems like days. But instead of feeling relieved, I feel forlorn. I think about what my mother said, about activating my genes and becoming Chinese. And I wonder what she meant.

Right after my mother died, I asked myself a lot of things, things that couldn't be answered, to force myself to grieve more. It seemed as if I wanted to sustain my grief, to assure myself that I had cared deeply enough.

But now I ask the questions mostly because I want to know the answers. What was that pork stuff she used to make that had the texture of sawdust? What were the names of the uncles who died in Shanghai? What had she dreamt all these years about her other daughters? All the times when she got mad at me, was she really thinking about them? Did she wish I were they? Did she regret that I wasn't?

At one o'clock in the morning, I awake to tapping sounds on the window. 75 I must have dozed off and now I feel my body uncramping itself. I'm sitting on the floor, leaning against one of the twin beds. Lili is lying next to me. The others are asleep, too, sprawled out on the beds and floor. Aiyi is seated at a little table, looking very sleepy. And my father is staring out the window, tapping his fingers on the glass. The last time I listened my father was telling Aiyi about his life since he last saw her. How he had gone to Yenching University, later got a post with a newspaper in Chungking, met my mother there, a young widow. How they later fled together to Shanghai to try to find my mother's family house, but there was nothing there. And then they traveled eventually to Canton and then to Hong Kong, then Haiphong and finally to San Francisco. . . .

---

2. Sweet brownish-red sauce made from soybeans, sugar, water, spices, garlic, and chili.

"Suyuan didn't tell me she was trying all these years to find her daughters," he is now saying in a quiet voice. "Naturally, I did not discuss her daughters with her. I thought she was ashamed she had left them behind."

"Where did she leave them?" asks Aiyi. "How were they found?"

I am wide awake now. Although I have heard parts of this story from my mother's friends.

"It happened when the Japanese took over Kweilin," says my father.

80 "Japanese in Kweilin?" says Aiyi. "That was never the case. Couldn't be. The Japanese never came to Kweilin."

"Yes, that is what the newspapers reported. I know this because I was working for the news bureau at the time. The Kuomintang[3] often told us what we could say and could not say. But we knew the Japanese had come into Kwangsi Province. We had sources who told us how they had captured the Wuchang-Canton railway. How they were coming overland, making very fast progress, marching toward the provincial capital."

Aiyi looks astonished. "If people did not know this, how could Suyuan know the Japanese were coming?"

"An officer of the Kuomintang secretly warned her," explains my father. "Suyuan's husband also was an officer and everybody knew that officers and their families would be the first to be killed. So she gathered a few possessions and, in the middle of the night, she picked up her daughters and fled on foot. The babies were not even one year old."

"How could she give up those babies!" sighs Aiyi. "Twin girls. We have never had such luck in our family." And then she yawns again.

85 "What were they named?" she asks. I listen carefully. I had been planning on using just the familiar "Sister" to address them both. But now I want to know how to pronounce their names.

"They have their father's surname, Wang," says my father. "And their given names are Chwun Yu and Chwun Hwa."

"What do the names mean?" I ask.

"Ah." My father draws imaginary characters on the window. "One means 'Spring Rain,' the other 'Spring Flower,'" he explains in English, "because they born in the spring, and of course rain come before flower, same order these girls are born. Your mother like a poet, don't you think?"

I nod my head. I see Aiyi nod her head forward, too. But it falls forward and stays there. She is breathing deeply, noisily. She is asleep.

90 "And what does Ma's name mean?" I whisper.

---

3. National People's Party, led by Generalissimo Chiang Kai-shek (1887–1975), which fought successfully against the Japanese occupation before being defeated militarily in 1949 by the Chinese Communist Party, led by Mao Zedong (1893–1976).

"'Suyuan,'" he says, writing more invisible characters on the glass. "The way she write it in Chinese, it mean 'Long-Cherished Wish.' Quite a fancy name, not so ordinary like flower name. See this first character, it mean something like 'Forever Never Forgotten.' But there is another way to write 'Suyuan.' Sound exactly the same, but the meaning is opposite." His finger creates the brushstrokes of another character. "The first part look the same: 'Never Forgotten.' But the last part add to first part make the whole word mean 'Long-Held Grudge.' Your mother get angry with me, I tell her her name should be Grudge."

My father is looking at me, moist-eyed. "See, I pretty clever, too, hah?"

I nod, wishing I could find some way to comfort him. "And what about my name," I ask, "what does 'Jing-mei' mean?"

"Your name also special," he says. I wonder if any name in Chinese is not something special. "'Jing' like excellent *jing*. Not just good, it's something pure, essential, the best quality. *Jing* is good leftover stuff when you take impurities out of something like gold, or rice, or salt. So what is left— just pure essence. And 'Mei,' this is common *mei,* as in *meimei,* 'younger sister.'"

I think about this. My mother's long-cherished wish. Me, the younger 95 sister who was supposed to be the essence of the others. I feed myself with the old grief, wondering how disappointed my mother must have been. Tiny Aiyi stirs suddenly, her head rolls and then falls back, her mouth opens as if to answer my question. She grunts in her sleep, tucking her body more closely into the chair.

"So why did she abandon those babies on the road?" I need to know, because now I feel abandoned too.

"Long time I wondered this myself," says my father. "But then I read that letter from her daughters in Shanghai now, and I talk to Auntie Lindo, all the others. And then I knew. No shame in what she done. None."

"What happened?"

"Your mother running away—" begins my father.

"No, tell me in Chinese," I interrupt. "Really, I can understand." 100

He begins to talk, still standing at the window, looking into the night.

After fleeing Kweilin, your mother walked for several days trying to find a main road. Her thought was to catch a ride on a truck or wagon, to catch enough rides until she reached Chungking, where her husband was stationed.

She had sewn money and jewelry into the lining of her dress, enough, she thought, to barter rides all the way. If I am lucky, she thought, I will not have to trade the heavy gold bracelet and jade ring. These were things from her mother, your grandmother.

By the third day, she had traded nothing. The roads were filled with people, everybody running and begging for rides from passing trucks. The trucks rushed by, afraid to stop. So your mother found no rides, only the start of dysentery pains in her stomach.

105   Her shoulders ached from the two babies swinging from scarf slings. Blisters grew on the palms from holding two leather suitcases. And then the blisters burst and began to bleed. After a while, she left the suitcases behind, keeping only the food and a few clothes. And later she also dropped the bags of wheat flour and rice and kept walking like this for many miles, singing songs to her little girls, until she was delirious with pain and fever.

Finally, there was not one more step left in her body. She didn't have the strength to carry those babies any farther. She slumped to the ground. She knew she would die of her sickness, or perhaps from thirst, from starvation, or from the Japanese, who she was sure were marching right behind her.

She took the babies out of the slings and sat them on the side of the road, then lay down next to them. You babies are so good, she said, so quiet. They smiled back, reaching their chubby hands for her, wanting to be picked up again. And then she knew she could not bear to watch her babies die with her.

She saw a family with three young children in a cart going by. "Take my babies, I beg you," she cried to them. But they stared back with empty eyes and never stopped.

She saw another person pass and called out again. This time a man turned around, and he had such a terrible expression—your mother said it looked like death itself—she shivered and looked away.

110   When the road grew quiet, she tore open the lining of her dress, and stuffed jewelry under the shirt of one baby and money under the other. She reached into her pocket and drew out the photos of her family, the picture of her father and mother, the picture of herself and her husband on their wedding day. And she wrote on the back of each the names of the babies and this same message: "Please care for these babies with the money and valuables provided. When it is safe to come, if you bring them to Shanghai, 9 Weichang Lu, the Li family will be glad to give you a generous reward. Li Suyuan and Wang Fuchi."

And then she touched each baby's cheek and told her not to cry. She would go down the road to find them some food and would be back. And without looking back, she walked down the road, stumbling and crying, thinking only of this one last hope, that her daughters would be found by a kindhearted person who would care for them. She would not allow herself to imagine anything else.

She did not remember how far she walked, which direction she went, when she fainted, or how she was found. When she awoke, she was in the back of a bouncing truck with several other sick people, all moaning. And she began to scream, thinking she was now on a journey to Buddhist hell. But the face of an American missionary lady bent over her and smiled, talking to her in a soothing language she did not understand. And yet she could somehow understand. She had been saved for no good reason, and it was now too late to go back and save her babies.

When she arrived in Chungking, she learned her husband had died two weeks before. She told me later she laughed when the officers told her this news, she was so delirious with madness and disease. To come so far, to lose so much and to find nothing.

I met her in a hospital. She was lying on a cot, hardly able to move, her dysentery had drained her so thin. I had come in for my foot, my missing toe, which was cut off by a piece of falling rubble. She was talking to herself, mumbling.

"Look at these clothes," she said, and I saw she had on a rather unusual dress for wartime. It was silk satin, quite dirty, but there was no doubt it was a beautiful dress.

"Look at this face," she said, and I saw her dusty face and hollow cheeks, her eyes shining black. "Do you see my foolish hope?"

"I thought I had lost everything, except these two things," she murmured. "And I wondered which I would lose next. Clothes or hope? Hope or clothes?"

"But now, see here, look what is happening," she said, laughing, as if all her prayers had been answered. And she was pulling hair out of her head as easily as one lifts new wheat from wet soil.

It was an old peasant woman who found them. "How could I resist?" the peasant woman later told your sisters when they were older. They were still sitting obediently near where your mother had left them, looking like little fairy queens waiting for their sedan to arrive.

The woman, Mei Ching, and her husband, Mei Han, lived in a stone cave. There were thousands of hidden caves like that in and around Kweilin so secret that the people remained hidden even after the war ended. The Meis would come out of their cave every few days and forage for food supplies left on the road, and sometimes they would see something that they both agreed was a tragedy to leave behind. So one day they took back to their cave a delicately painted set of rice bowls, another day a little footstool with a velvet cushion and two new wedding blankets. And once, it was your sisters.

They were pious people, Muslims, who believed the twin babies were a sign of double luck, and they were sure of this when, later in the evening, they discovered how valuable the babies were. She and her husband had never seen rings and bracelets like those. And while they admired the pictures, knowing the babies came from a good family, neither of them could read or write. It was not until many months later that Mei Ching found someone who could read the writing on the back. By then, she loved these baby girls like her own.

In 1952 Mei Han, the husband, died. The twins were already eight years old, and Mei Ching now decided it was time to find your sisters' true family.

She showed the girls the picture of their mother and told them they had been born into a great family and she would take them back to see their true mother and grandparents. Mei Ching told them about the reward, but she swore she would refuse it. She loved these girls so much, she only wanted them to have what they were entitled to—a better life, a fine house, educated ways. Maybe the family would let her stay on as the girls' amah.[4] Yes, she was certain they would insist.

Of course, when she found the place at 9 Weichang Lu, in the old French Concession, it was something completely different. It was the site of a factory building, recently constructed, and none of the workers knew what had become of the family whose house had burned down on that spot.

125 Mei Ching could not have known, of course, that your mother and I, her new husband, had already returned to that same place in 1945 in hopes of finding both her family and her daughters.

Your mother and I stayed in China until 1947. We went to many different cities—back to Kweilin, to Changsha, as far south as Kunming. She was always looking out of one corner of her eye for twin babies, then little girls. Later we went to Hong Kong, and when we finally left in 1949 for the United States, I think she was even looking for them on the boat. But when we arrived, she no longer talked about them. I thought, At last, they have died in her heart.

When letters could be openly exchanged between China and the United States, she wrote immediately to old friends in Shanghai and Kweilin. I did not know she did this. Auntie Lindo told me. But of course, by then, all the street names had changed. Some people had died, others had moved away. So it took many years to find a contact. And when she did find an old schoolmate's address and wrote asking her to look for her daughters, her friend wrote back and said this was impossible, like looking for a needle on the bottom of the ocean. How did she know her daughters were in Shanghai and not somewhere else in China? The friend, of course, did not ask, How do you know your daughters are still alive?

4. Maidservant or nurse.

So her schoolmate did not look. Finding babies lost during the war was a matter of foolish imagination, and she had no time for that.

But every year, your mother wrote to different people. And this last year, I think she got a big idea in her head, to go to China and find them herself. I remember she told me, "Canning, we should go, before it is too late, before we are too old." And I told her we were already too old, it was already too late.

I just thought she wanted to be a tourist! I didn't know she wanted to go   130 and look for her daughters. So when I said it was too late, that must have put a terrible thought in her head that her daughters might be dead. And I think this possibility grew bigger and bigger in her head, until it killed her.

Maybe it was your mother's dead spirit who guided her Shanghai schoolmate to find her daughters. Because after your mother died, the schoolmate saw your sisters, by chance, while shopping for shoes at the Number One Department Store on Nanjing Dong Road. She said it was like a dream, seeing these two women who looked so much alike, moving down the stairs together. There was something about their facial expressions that reminded the schoolmate of your mother.

She quickly walked over to them and called their names, which of course, they did not recognize at first, because Mei Ching had changed their names. But your mother's friend was so sure, she persisted. "Are you not Wang Chwun Yu and Wang Chwun Hwa?" she asked them. And then these double-image women became very excited, because they remembered the names written on the back of an old photo, a photo of a young man and woman they still honored, as their much-loved first parents, who had died and become spirit ghosts still roaming the earth looking for them.

At the airport, I am exhausted. I could not sleep last night. Aiyi had followed me into my room at three in the morning, and she instantly fell asleep on one of the twin beds, snoring with the might of a lumberjack. I lay awake thinking about my mother's story, realizing how much I have never known about her, grieving that my sisters and I had both lost her.

And now at the airport, after shaking hands with everybody, waving goodbye, I think about all the different ways we leave people in this world. Cheerily waving good-bye to some at airports, knowing we'll never see each other again. Leaving others on the side of the road, hoping that we will. Finding my mother in my father's story and saying good-bye before I have a chance to know her better.

Aiyi smiles at me as we wait for our gate to be called. She is so old. I put   135 one arm around her and one arm around Lili. They are the same size, it seems. And then it's time. As we wave good-bye one more time and enter the waiting area, I get the sense I am going from one funeral to another. In my hand I'm clutching a pair of tickets to Shanghai. In two hours we'll be there.

The plane takes off. I close my eyes. How can I describe to them in my broken Chinese about our mother's life? Where should I begin?

"Wake up, we're here," says my father. And I awake with my heart pounding in my throat. I look out the window and we're already on the runway. It's gray outside.

And now I'm walking down the steps of the plane, onto the tarmac and toward the building. If only, I think, if only my mother had lived long enough to be the one walking toward them. I am so nervous I cannot even feel my feet. I am just moving somehow.

Somebody shouts, "She's arrived!" And then I see her. Her short hair. Her small body. And that same look on her face. She has the back of her hand pressed hard against her mouth. She is crying as though she had gone through a terrible ordeal and were happy it is over.

140 And I know it's not my mother, yet it is the same look she had when I was five and had disappeared all afternoon, for such a long time, that she was convinced I was dead. And when I miraculously appeared, sleepy-eyed, crawling from underneath my bed, she wept and laughed, biting the back of her hand to make sure it was true.

And now I see her again, two of her, waving, and in one hand there is a photo, the Polaroid I sent them. As soon as I get beyond the gate, we run toward each other, all three of us embracing, all hesitations and expectations forgotten.

"Mama, Mama," we all murmur, as if she is among us.

My sisters look at me, proudly. *"Meimei jandale,"* says one sister proudly to the other. "Little Sister has grown up." I look at their faces again and I see no trace of my mother in them. Yet they still look familiar. And now I also see what part of me is Chinese. It is so obvious. It is my family. It is in our blood. After all these years, it can finally be let go.

My sisters and I stand, arms around each other, laughing and wiping the tears from each other's eyes. The flash of the Polaroid goes off and my father hands me the snapshot. My sisters and I watch quietly together, eager to see what develops.

145 The gray-green surface changes to the bright colors of our three images, sharpening and deepening all at once. And although we don't speak, I know we all see it: Together we look like our mother. Her same eyes, her same mouth, open in surprise to see, at last, her long-cherished wish.

1989

QUESTIONS

1. Why is the opening scene of A PAIR OF TICKETS—the train journey from Hong Kong to Guangzhou—an appropriate setting for June May's remark that she is "becoming Chinese" (par. 1)?
2. When June May arrives in Guangzhou, what are some details that seem familiar to her, and what are some that seem exotic? Why is she so preoccupied with comparing China to America?
3. June May says that she "could never pass for true Chinese" (par. 35), yet by the end of the story she has discovered "what part of [her] is Chinese" (par. 143). How does the meaning of "Chinese" evolve throughout the story?

JUDITH ORTIZ COFER
(b. 1952)
Volar[1]

Born in Hormigueros, Puerto Rico, Judith Ortiz Cofer just two years later moved with her family, first to New Jersey and later to Georgia, experiences that would inspire much of her later fiction and poetry. "How can you inject passion and purpose into your work if it has no roots?" she asks, avowing that her own roots include a long line of women storytellers who "infected" her at a very early age with the desire to tell stories both on and off the page. After earning an MA at Florida Atlantic University (1977), Ortiz Cofer returned to Georgia, where she is an emeritus professor at the University of Georgia. Among her numerous publications are the novels *The Line of the Sun* (1989), in which a young girl relates the history of her ne'er-do-well uncle's emigration from Puerto Rico, *The Meaning of Consuelo* (2003), and *Call Me Maria* (2006); the poetry collection *A Love Story Beginning in Spanish* (2005); and *The Latin Deli* (1993) and *The Year of Our Revolution* (1998), two collections that seamlessly interweave fiction, nonfiction, and poetry, thereby demonstrating, in Ortiz Cofer's words, "the need to put things together in a holistic way."

A t twelve I was an avid consumer of comic books—*Supergirl* being my favorite. I spent my allowance of a quarter a day on two twelve-cent comic books or a double issue for twenty-five. I had a stack of *Legion*

1. To fly (Spanish).

of Super Heroes and *Supergirl* comic books in my bedroom closet that was as tall as I am. I had a recurring dream in those days: that I had long blond hair and could fly. In my dream I climbed the stairs to the top of our apartment building as myself, but as I went up each flight, changes would be taking place. Step by step I would fill out: My legs would grow long, my arms harden into steel, and my hair would magically go straight and turn a golden color. Of course I would add the bonus of breasts, but not too large; Supergirl had to be aerodynamic. Sleek and hard as a supersonic missile. Once on the roof, my parents safely asleep in their beds, I would get on tiptoe, arms outstretched in the position for flight, and jump out my fifty-story-high window into the black lake of the sky. From up there, over the rooftops, I could see everything, even beyond the few blocks of our barrio;[2] with my X-ray vision I could look inside the homes of people who interested me. Once I saw our landlord, whom I knew my parents feared, sitting in a treasure-room dressed in an ermine coat and a large gold crown. He sat on the floor counting his dollar bills. I played a trick on him. Going up to his building's chimney, I blew a little puff of my superbreath into his fireplace, scattering his stacks of money so that he had to start counting all over again. I could more or less program my Supergirl dreams in those days by focusing on the object of my current obsession. This way I "saw" into the private lives of my neighbors, my teachers, and in the last days of my childish fantasy and the beginning of adolescence, into the secret room of the boys I liked. In the mornings I'd wake up in my tiny bedroom with the incongruous—at least in our tiny apartment—white "princess" furniture my mother had chosen for me, and find myself back in my body: my tight curls still clinging to my head, skinny arms and legs and flat chest unchanged.

In the kitchen my mother and father would be talking softly over a café con leche.[3] She would come "wake me" exactly forty-five minutes after they had gotten up. It was their time together at the beginning of each day and even at an early age I could feel their disappointment if I interrupted them by getting up too early. So I would stay in my bed recalling my dreams of flight, perhaps planning my next flight. In the kitchen they would be discussing events in the barrio. Actually, he would be carrying that part of the conversation; when it was her turn to speak she would, more often than not, try shifting the topic toward her desire to see her *familia* on the Island: *How about a vacation in Puerto Rico together this year, Querido?*[4] *We could rent a car, go to the beach. We could . . .* And he would answer patiently,

2. Spanish-speaking neighborhood or district in the United States or any district in a Spanish-speaking country.
3. Coffee with milk (Spanish).
4. Beloved, dear (Spanish).

gently, *Mi amor,*[5] *do you know how much it would cost for all of us to fly there? It is not possible for me to take the time off* . . . *Mi vida,*[6] *please understand.* . . . And I knew that soon she would rise from the table. Not abruptly. She would light a cigarette and look out the kitchen window. The view was of a dismal alley that was littered with refuse thrown from windows. The space was too narrow for anyone larger than a skinny child to enter safely, so it was never cleaned. My mother would check the time on the clock over her sink, the one with a prayer for patience and grace written in Spanish. A birthday gift. She would see that it was time to wake me. She'd sigh deeply and say the same thing the view from her kitchen window always inspired her to say: *Ay, si yo pudiera volar.*[7]

1993

QUESTIONS

1. VOLAR seems simultaneously vague about its general setting and much more detailed about its particular setting, at least when it comes to place (versus time). How does this combination of vagueness and specificity shape your response to the story and your sense of whom and what it is about?
2. What does the story suggest about how the characters have been shaped by their environment? about how they feel about it, and why?
3. What is the effect of the way Spanish is used both in the title and throughout the story itself? What might these uses of Spanish add to our understanding of the setting, the characters, and their conflicts?

SUGGESTIONS FOR WRITING

1. Write an essay in which you compare the use of setting in any two stories in this book. You might compare the re-creation of two similar settings, such as landscapes far from home, foreign cities, or stifling suburbs; or you might contrast the treatment of different kinds of settings. Be sure to consider not only the authors' descriptive techniques but also the way the authors use setting to shape plot, point of view, and character.
2. In A PAIR OF TICKETS, Amy Tan provides detailed descriptions of June May's journeys to Guangzhou and Shanghai. In his account of his wife's escape from Kweilin, June May's father says little about the landscape. Write an essay in which you compare the two very different storytelling techniques used in this story.
3. In at least two of the stories in this chapter, a place encountered for the first time by a traveler is described with great vividness: the city of Guangzhou in A PAIR OF TICKETS and the city of Yalta in THE LADY WITH THE DOG. Citing examples

5. My love (Spanish).
6. My life (Spanish).
7. Oh, if only I could fly (Spanish).

from these stories, write an essay in which you discuss the effect of new surroundings on our perceptions, emotions, and memories.

4. Choose any story in this chapter and write an essay that explores how the story both draws on and also encourages us to rethink our ideas about a particular place and time and social milieu, perhaps (but not necessarily) by showing us characters who themselves either come to see a setting differently or refuse to do so.

5. Whereas THE LADY WITH THE DOG and A PAIR OF TICKETS each cover a relatively long period of time and take us to a variety of places, the much shorter VOLAR has a more circumscribed setting. Write a response paper or essay exploring how these factors enhance our sense of the characters' conflicts and even the story's theme.

6. Write a story in which a newcomer brings a fresh perspective to a familiar setting.

SAMPLE WRITING: ESSAY

In the following essay, student writer Steven Matview explores the role of setting in Anton Chekhov's THE LADY WITH THE DOG. Read the essay responsively and critically, taking time to consider the details Steven chooses to highlight and the way he interprets them. Does he manage to build a convincing and thorough argument about the role of setting in "The Lady with the Dog"? What other details from the story might deserve a place in this argument? In particular, notice how Steven concentrates on temporal setting (the seasons) while commenting only briefly on spatial setting and on the interconnections between time and space in the story. If Steven were your classmate, what three things would you suggest he most needs to do in order to improve the essay in revision? (For ease of reference, we have altered the citations in this paper to refer to paragraph numbers. Unless your instructor indicates otherwise, however, you should always follow convention by instead citing page numbers when writing about fiction.)

Matview 1

Steven Matview
Professor Anne Stevens
English 298
6 March 2017

How Setting Reflects Emotions in Anton Chekhov's
"The Lady with the Dog"

Setting is important to Chekhov's "The Lady with the Dog." But wait, isn't setting important to all stories? Not necessarily. In many stories, like Hemingway's "Hills Like White Elephants," the plot could be happening anywhere, and it would not matter. But in "The Lady with the Dog" the setting plays an important role in the story, in particular to Dmitri, who is the main character and who experiences the most growth throughout. He goes from being a man at 40 who is full of youthful energy and thinks he has been loved by many women to an old man who realizes that he is just experiencing love for the first time. During the course of the narrative, the setting Chekhov maps out shows the progression of Dmitri's affair with Anna Sergeyevna, Dmitri's state of mind, and the changes that Dmitri undergoes. The setting in this story is just as important as any character. In fact, I would argue that the setting is the single most important component of the story.

Dmitri's relationship with the lady with the dog has its ups and downs, which are reflected in the seasons and the descriptions of weather. He makes this apparent when he says, "The weather is better this evening" (par. 24). Their lives are better when they are together in the summer. This is the time Dmitri and Anna meet and start their courtship. Both are married, and both have spent so much time forcing themselves to love their partners that they do not recognize real love when they feel it. Dmitri initially only wants a fling and doesn't even learn or use Anna's name, referring to her only as "the lady with the dog." There isn't any stress yet, and the two can be just happy with things the way they are. They go on dates and spend time together in Anna's hotel room. Dmitri starts to think of her as "Anna Sergeyevna—'the lady with the dog'" (par. 29), showing a shift within the relationship. He shows he's started to think of this as more of a relationship by using her full name but doesn't completely switch, as he adds in that epithet "lady with the dog." He is trying to resist because he is still married. Dmitri feels young and alive and thinks back to all the women he has made happy in his life.

Another aspect of the setting are the places described in the story, which relate to things the characters feel or know on a subconscious level. At the start of the story, Dmitri is staying at a seaside resort in Yalta. We know that a resort is an impersonal place, where someone can reinvent themselves or get away from the things they don't like about home. Dmitri reinvents his idea about what love is while getting away from a wife he does not care for. Dmitri meets Anna for the first time "in the public gardens" (par. 2). A garden is a place of growth, reflecting the soon-to-be growth of their relationship, as well as the growth Dmitri will experience as a person. They then go on a date, and we become privy to a metaphor describing Dmitri's marriage and how things will go with Anna: "Owing to the roughness of the sea, the steamer arrived late, after the sun had set, and it was a long time turning about before it reached the groyne" (par. 22). The steamer is Dmitri, the sea is his life, and the groyne, a device designed to disrupt the flow of water, is Anna. It took Dmitri longer to find true love, and he has gone through a rough time in a boring marriage, and now there is someone to break that up. This is when Dmitri starts to feel love for Anna, though he does not realize it is love because it is so different from what he has known in the past.

Things change as soon as the next season approaches. The first challenges that arise in the courtship of Dmitri and Anna come when the season begins to change from summer to autumn. Dmitri mentions here that "it was a cold evening" (par. 60), the first time cold is mentioned in the present (before it was only used to describe the unhappy places Anna and Dmitri were escaping from) and a stark contrast to his comment about the weather earlier in the story. Things are starting to get worse for the relationship. Word gets to Anna that she must travel back to her home to be with her husband, who has fallen ill. Dmitri finds that he does not want to let Anna go, that the fling he wanted has turned into something much more. Dmitri thinks that he was "warm and affectionate with [Anna]" (par. 59), terms associated with summer weather. But, with autumn approaching, Dmitri decides that they were not really in love. This is because the feeling he has does not resemble the forced love he has always experienced with his wife and mistresses, but it is brought up as the object of his "warm feelings" leaves and is replaced with the "cold night."

Change of place goes hand in hand with a change of seasons and weather here. And we are told shortly before Anna leaves that "Yalta was hardly visible through the morning mist; white clouds stood motionless on the mountain-tops" (par. 47). The mist covering Yalta is like the uncertainty that lies in their future as the summer is winding down. Neither can see clearly what will come from their summer tryst when the time comes to separate. White is a color that is often associated with purity, and Dmitri is experiencing a pure, true kind of love for the first time, but he also has obstacles to overcome that are represented by the mountains.

Dmitri thinks he will get over Anna quickly now that she's gone, but winter brings him even more hardships. The most difficult time the couple face comes in the season of winter. Winter is a cold season often affiliated with sadness and the absence of hope. We find out that "[t]he frosts had begun already" (par. 62), meaning the bad times have already started, and we join Dmitri after he's already been back in Moscow for a short time. In Moscow Dmitri has not stopped thinking of Anna Sergeyevna, who is only referred to by her full name now. Referring to her as "Anna Sergeyevna" instead of "the lady with the dog" is a subtle way of letting us know that Dmitri is thinking of her as more than a fling that has gone by, as we saw earlier that he only called her "the lady with the dog" when he didn't have feelings for her. They are separated by cities and by circumstance, and it seems the relationship might be over. In winter all the plants die, and Dmitri and Anna, whose relationship first blossomed in a garden, seem to have a dead relationship. We find out that "more than a month passed" and that "real winter had come" (par. 64), real winter representing the increasing feelings of separation anxiety Dmitri is suffering from.

We get more visual descriptions in Moscow and Anna's unnamed city relating to the characters' thoughts. After Anna leaves and Dmitri returns to his home in Moscow, we find out that he wants to escape to "restaurants, clubs, dinner-parties, [and] anniversary celebrations" (par. 63), showing us that Dmitri is feeling repressed at home compared to the freedom he had at the resort. After confiding in a local his problems, Dmitri thinks, "there is no escaping or getting away from it—just as though one were in a madhouse or a prison" (par. 72). A madhouse and a prison are two places that no one wants to be. Both places are where you are kept from loved ones. But they are also places you are put in when you have done something wrong, a hint that Dmitri feels he's made mistakes in the past, done his time, and now wants to be free to be with Anna.

Dmitri then decides to go to Anna's city, which is left unnamed in the story. This reflects that it is really Dmitri's journey. Dmitri has a hard time reaching Anna at first, as she is tucked away in the house she shares with her husband. When Dmitri finally does confront Anna she does not initially seem happy to see him. Dmitri confronts Anna at a performance of the play *The Geisha*. The opera and the opera house it is performed in have many qualities that suggest Dmitri's emotional state. The opera house is described as having "a fog above the chandelier," and its "gallery was noisy and restless" (par. 85). Dmitri has lots of noisy thoughts in his head as he approaches Anna with uncertainty. As Dmitri approaches Anna the musicians begin tuning their instruments. They are getting ready for the big performance, as Dmitri is getting ready to renew his relationship with Anna. Anna at first appears to be unhappy and takes Dmitri down a path of winding corridors and then up and down a "narrow, gloomy staircase" (par. 93). The outlook seems gloomy for Dmitri, but she does agree to see him again and proceeds to profess her love for him.

At the end of winter, with spring fast approaching, things between Dmitri and Anna begin to show slight improvement over early winter. The weather is described as being "three degrees above freezing-point, and yet it is snowing" (par. 105). Things are getting better for Dmitri, who knows now that Anna loves him and wants to be with him, but it's not all great yet as both are still married and forced to keep their relationship a secret. The open-air setting of the gardens that their relationship started in is replaced by a hotel room, giving the final scene a claustrophobic feel as Anna wonders how they can be together. At the end of the story the couple is still trying to find a way to make their relationship work when we are told, "it seemed as though in a little while the solution would be found" (par. 124). Winter is ending, and spring, a season of growth, new beginnings, and love, is on the horizon. From this we might deduce that the couple will make it, at least into the spring.

But will they? The fact that the story ends with the couple in a "gray area" is fitting because gray, a color associated with ambiguity (shades of gray compared to a black-and-white situation; a "gray area"), in fact appears often in the story. Dmitri is in a situation that involves a lot of moral ambiguity. During the course of the narrative he ends up in love with a married woman while he himself is also married. They begin existing in this gray area where we as readers begin to wonder if what they are doing is really wrong, since they are committing adultery. Anna's eyes are gray, reminding us that Dmitri is entering into a moral gray area whenever he is engaging in this relationship. When Dmitri goes to find Anna and resume their relationship in her home town, he stays at a hotel room whose "floor was covered with grey army cloth" (par. 75) and where there is gray dust and a gray blanket. He enters another gray area when he wants to do what his heart says is right by reuniting with Anna, but doing so is committing more adultery.

But I feel that the recurring gray colors also imply something besides ambiguity—the sadness and lack of excitement that Dmitri has always had in his life thanks to his unhappy marriage and that he might, paradoxically, have come to expect or even need. We can see this when he refers to his hotel in Anna's city as "the best room at the hotel" (par. 75), but filled with items of gray, or when Anna is "wearing his favourite grey dress" (par. 108). The hotel room and Anna are both things that are great or that he adores, but they have that tinge of sadness, represented by the gray, that he needs.

Looking back over the story, we as readers can come to our own conclusions about whether or not Dmitri and Anna stay together. From looking at the progression of the weather we see that in the summer things are good, in fall bad situations arise, winter is the worst time, and the dawn of spring shows slight hope. Following this progression, I believe that when spring finally hits they will be able to come up with a plan to stay a couple. Dmitri and Anna would be happy. We would see Dmitri and Anna figuring out a way to make their relationship public and no longer to be confined to enclosed hiding places. The real question then would be whether the gray would fade out of Dmitri's life after he finds a happiness with Anna that will last past the following summer or whether the cycle is just doomed to repeat itself, as summer eventually turns into winter and the brightest of colors and emotions fade into gray.

Work Cited

Chekhov, Anton. "The Lady with the Dog." *The Norton Introduction to Literature*, edited by Kelly J. Mays, portable 12th ed., W. W. Norton, 2017, pp. 171-85.

5 SYMBOL AND FIGURATIVE LANGUAGE

A symbol is something that represents something else. Sometimes a symbol resembles or closely relates to what it represents, but often the association is arbitrary or subtle. Even so, through common usage, many symbols are instantly understood by almost everyone in a particular group. Although we rarely think of them as such, the letters of the English alphabet are themselves symbols, representing different sounds. We simply learn to recognize them, however, without thinking about whether there is any resemblance between what the symbols look like and what they represent. In other languages, one character may stand for an object or concept, such as the Chinese characters for "fire." Yet some symbols do help us by resembling what they stand for, such as the symbol for a fire alarm.

Similarly, abstractions may be represented by symbols that resemble things that are associated with them:

Although the smiley face can simply mean "Smile!" its meanings when used as an "emoticon" in e-mails and text messages range from "I like this" to "Just

213

joking." The skull and crossbones symbol is used on warning labels to indicate that the contents are poisonous, but it has also been associated with death, cemeteries, and pirates.

Other symbols are more arbitrary, having no literal connection with what they represent. Octagons and the color red have little to do with stopping a car, but most Americans, even if they are too young to drive, understand what a stop sign means. Such symbols, though not based on resemblances, elicit an unconscious and reflexive response from us. The meaning of a symbol is not always so concrete and practical, however. The U.S. national flag is an arbitrary symbol, having no direct resemblance to what it represents, but most people recognize its primary significance; the "stars and stripes" undoubtedly stands for the United States. Nevertheless, the flag differs from a traffic sign in that the flag evokes much more varied, complex, and even conflicting responses.

LITERARY SYMBOLISM

A **symbol** usually conveys an abstraction or cluster of abstractions, from the ideal to the imperceptible or the irrational, in a more concrete form. A symbol in a work of literature compares or puts together two things that are in some ways dissimilar. But literary symbolism rarely comes down to a simple equation of one thing to another. Unlike an arbitrary symbol such as a letter or traffic sign, a symbol in literature usually carries richer and more varied meanings, as does a flag or a religious image. And because of its significance, a symbol usually appears or is hinted at numerous times throughout the work. In reading literature, it may be challenging to recognize symbols, and readers may have good reasons to disagree about their interpretation, since literary works often incorporate symbolism for which there is no single "correct" interpretation. No one would say that reading a short story should be like a treasure hunt for some shiny symbol that clearly reveals all the hidden meanings; the complexity remains and requires further exploration even when we have recognized a symbol's significance at some level. A literary symbol may be understood as an extended figure of speech that rewards further interpretation.

Traditional Symbols and Archetypes

Some symbols have been in use by many people for a long time (in which case they are known as *traditional symbols*); a white dove, for example, is a traditional symbol of peace and love. A rose can be a symbol of godly love, of romantic desire, of female beauty, of mortality (because the flower wilts), or of hidden cruelty (because it has thorns). The snake has traditionally been a symbol of evil, but in Rudyard Kipling's *The Jungle Book* (1894), the python Ka, while frightening, is on the side of law and order. A few symbolic character types, plots, objects, or settings—for example, the trickster, the quest, the garden—have become so pervasive and have recurred in so many cultures that they are considered **archetypes** (literary elements that recur in the litera-ture and myths of multiple cultures). Fire, water, a flower, or a tree can all be considered archetypes because numerous cultures use them symbolically, often within their system of religion or myth. Literary symbolism frequently borrows from the symbols and archetypes associated with religion or myth.

Allegory and Myth

A common literary form, especially in works written by and for religious believers, is the **allegory**, which may be regarded as an "extended" symbol or series of symbols that encompasses a whole work. In an allegory, concrete things and abstract concepts may be associated with each other across a narrative that consistently maintains at least two distinct levels of meaning. Because allegories set up series of correspondences, they usually help the reader translate these correspondences through the use of names that readily function as labels, often with obvious moral implications. In *The Pilgrim's Progress* (1678), probably the most famous prose allegory in English, the cen-tral character is named Christian; he was born in the City of Destruction and sets out for the Celestial City, passes through the Slough of Despond and Vanity Fair, meets men named Pliable and Obstinate, and so on. The point of an allegory is not to make us hunt for disguised meanings, so it is no defect if an allegory's intended meaning is clear. Instead, the purpose is to let us enjoy an invented world where everything is especially meaningful and everything corresponds to something else according to a moral or other-wise "correct" plan.

When an entire story is allegorical or symbolic, it is sometimes called a **myth**. *Myth* originally referred to a story of communal origin that provided an explanation or religious interpretation of humanity, nature, the universe, or the relations among them. Sometimes we apply the term *myth* to stories associated with religions we do not believe in, and sometimes to literature that seeks to express experiences or truths that transcend any one location, culture, or time.

FIGURES OF SPEECH

Figures of speech, or **figurative language**, are similar to symbols in that they supplement or replace literal meaning, often by creating imaginative con-nections between our ideas and our senses. Sometimes referred to as *tropes* (literally, "turnings"), figures of speech could be described as *bending* the usual meaning of language and *shaping* our response to a work. Whether or not they have anything to do with spatial forms or "figures," or whether they rely on vision, such tropes contribute to what are called the **images** or **imagery** of a story. Many figures of speech are known by the Latin or Greek names used in classical Greek and Roman **rhetoric**, the art and science of speech and persuasion.

Just as you can enjoy gymnastics or diving events during the Olympics without knowing the names of the specific twists and turns, you can enjoy the figurative language in a story without identifying each figure of speech. Yet for the purposes of interpreting and writing about literature, it is important to learn some basic terms and distinctions so that you have access to a shared and economical language for describing your responses and the techniques that trigger them. The box below defines some of the most frequently encountered figures of speech.

Key Figures of Speech

allegory an extended association, often sustained in every element (character, plot, setting, etc.) and throughout an entire work, between two levels of meaning, usually literal and abstract. In *Animal Farm* (1945), for example, George Orwell uses an uprising of barnyard animals as an allegory for the Bolshevik revolution in Russia.

allusion a reference, usually brief, to another text or some person or entity external to the work. Examples may range from a direct quotation of the Bible to the mention of a famous name.

irony a meaning or outcome contrary to what is expected; in *verbal irony*, a speaker or narrator says one thing and means the reverse. When the intended meaning is harshly critical or mocking, it is called *sarcasm*. If a teenager says, "I just love it when my mom lectures me," she may well be using irony.

metaphor a representation of one thing as if it were something else, without a verbal signal such as *like* or *as*. When Scout, in *To Kill a Mockingbird* (1960), remarks that she "inched sluggishly along the treadmill of the Maycomb County school system," she doesn't indicate what literally happened at school. She figuratively suggests how it felt by implicitly comparing the experience to being on a treadmill.

metonymy using the name of one thing to refer to another thing associated with it. The common phrase *red tape* is a metonym for excessive paperwork and procedure that slows down an official transaction, based on the fact that papers used to be tied up with red tape.

oxymoron a combination of contradictory or opposite ideas, qualities, or entities, as in *wise fool*.

personification   sometimes called *anthropomorphism*, attributing human qualities to objects or animals. In THE OPEN BOAT, Stephen Crane personifies the birds who "sat comfortably in groups" and looked at the men with "unblinking scrutiny." He pushes personification to comic extreme in the shipwrecked men's thoughts: "If this old ninny-woman, Fate, cannot do better than this [. . . .] she is an old hen who knows not her intention." Here, "hen" is a metaphor for a silly woman, who in turn personifies the idea of destiny or fate.

simile   a representation of one thing as if it were something else, with an explicit verbal signal such as *like* or *as*. In *To Kill a Mockingbird*, Scout describes a teacher who "looked and smelled like a peppermint drop" and bored students "wriggling like a bucket of Catawba worms."

symbol   a person, place, object, or image that represents more than its literal meaning. A symbol is more than a passing comparison (such as a simile); instead, as in allegory, its meaning usually relates to most details and themes of the work. Unlike allegory, a symbol usually associates more than two entities or ideas and may be obscure or ambiguous in its meaning. Short stories (or poems) may refer to their central symbolic figure in the title, as in CATHEDRAL.

synecdoche   a form of metonymy (or name substitution) in which the part represents the whole (a *sail* refers to a ship).

INTERPRETING SYMBOLISM AND FIGURATIVE LANGUAGE

The context of an entire story or poem or play can guide you in deciding how far to push your own "translation" of a figure of speech or whether a metaphor has the deeper significance of a symbol. It is best to read the entire story and note all of the figures of speech or imagery before you examine one as a symbol. Often, a symbol is a focal point in a story, a single object or situation that draws the attention of one or more characters.

In F. Scott Fitzgerald's *The Great Gatsby* (1925), for example, a faded billboard featuring a pair of bespectacled eyes takes on a central and multilayered significance, though there is no longstanding tradition of symbolic meaning for billboards or spectacles. Although the billboard is a purely realistic detail of setting (one can easily imagine seeing something like it along any highway today), it comes to function as a symbol, too, only because of the number of times and specific ways it is discussed by the narrator and characters. When one character, George Wilson, looks up at the looming eyes and remarks, "God sees everything," it becomes pretty clear what the billboard symbolizes to him. Yet when another character immediately reminds Wilson that what he sees is only "an advertisement," we are forced to consider both what Wilson's interpretation might tell us about him and with what alternative or additional meanings the rest of the novel might invest this object. The symbol remains ambiguous and complex.

Effective symbols and figurative language cannot be extracted from the story they serve, but they can leave a lasting image of what the story is about. With guidance and practice, identifying and interpreting literary symbolism and other figurative language will begin to feel almost as familiar to you as reading the letter symbols on a page, though the meanings may be subtle, ambiguous, and far-reaching rather than straightforward.

Responding to Symbolism: Some Guidelines

- Read the story carefully, noting any details that seem to have exceptional significance, such as names, repeated actions or statements, recurring references to objects, peculiar places, allusions, or other figures of speech.
- Using your list of such possibly symbolic details, look back through the story to find the passages that feature these details. Are any of the passages connected to each other in a pattern? Do any of these interconnected details suggest themes?
- Note any symbols or images that you recognize from mythology, religion, or any other literature, art, or popular culture. Look again at the way the story presents such material. What are the signals that the fire is more than a fire, the tree is more than a tree, the ring is more than a ring? If the story invents its own symbol, find any words in the story that show how the characters see something meaningful in it.
- Once you have found a symbol—an aspect of the story that is a figure of speech, trope, image, or connection between literal and nonliteral; is extended beyond a few sentences; is more complicated than an allegory's one-to-one translation; and may be interpreted in multiple ways—review every aspect of the story, on the literal level, that relates to this symbol.
- As you write about the symbol or symbolism in a story, consider your claims about its meaning. Try not to narrow down the possible meanings of either the symbol or the story, but at the same time don't make overly grand claims for their ability to reveal the meaning of life. When in doubt, refer back to the story and its characterization, plot, and setting.
- Remember to cite specific passages that will help your reader understand the symbol's significance. Your reader may suspect that you are reading too much into it or miscasting its meanings, so this evidence is crucial to explaining your interpretation and persuading your reader that it is reasonable.

NATHANIEL HAWTHORNE
(1804–64)
The Birth-Mark

Nathaniel Hawthorne was born in Salem, Massachusetts, a descendant of Puritan immigrants. Educated at Bowdoin College, he was agonizingly slow in winning recognition for his work and supported himself from time to time in government service—working in the customhouses of Boston and Salem and serving as the U.S. consul in Liverpool. His early collections of stories, *Twice-Told Tales* (1837) and *Mosses from an Old Manse* (1846), did not sell well, and it was not until the publication of his most famous novel, *The Scarlet Letter* (1850), that his fame spread beyond a discerning few. His other novels include *The House of the Seven Gables* (1851) and *The Blithedale Romance* (1852). Burdened by a deep sense of guilt for his family's role in the notorious Salem witchcraft trials over a century before he was born (one ancestor had been a judge), Hawthorne used fiction as a means of exploring the moral dimensions of sin and the human soul.

In the latter part of the last century[1] there lived a man of science, an eminent proficient in every branch of natural philosophy,[2] who not long before our story opens had made experience of a spiritual affinity more attractive than any chemical one. He had left his laboratory to the care of an assistant, cleared his fine countenance from the furnace-smoke, washed the stain of acids from his fingers, and persuaded a beautiful woman to become his wife. In those days, when the comparatively recent discovery of electricity and other kindred mysteries of Nature seemed to open paths into the region of miracle, it was not unusual for the love of science to rival the love of woman in its depth and absorbing energy. The higher intellect, the imagination, the spirit, and even the heart might all find their congenial aliment in pursuits which, as some of their ardent votaries believed, would ascend from one step of powerful intelligence to another, until the philosopher should lay his hand on the secret of creative force and perhaps make new worlds for himself. We know not whether Aylmer possessed this degree of faith in man's ultimate control over nature. He had devoted himself, however, too unreservedly to scientific studies ever to be weakened

1. That is, the eighteenth century; this story was first published in 1843.
2. The body of knowledge we now call science.

from them by any second passion. His love for his young wife might prove the stronger of the two; but it could only be by intertwining itself with his love of science and uniting the strength of the latter to his own.

Such a union accordingly took place, and was attended with truly remarkable consequences and a deeply impressive moral. One day, very soon after their marriage, Aylmer sat gazing at his wife with a trouble in his countenance that grew stronger until he spoke.

"Georgiana," said he, "has it never occurred to you that the mark upon your cheek might be removed?"

"No, indeed," said she, smiling; but, perceiving the seriousness of his manner, she blushed deeply. "To tell you the truth, it has been so often called a charm, that I was simple enough to imagine it might be so."

5   "Ah, upon another face perhaps it might," replied her husband; "but never on yours. No, dearest Georgiana, you came so nearly perfect from the hand of Nature, that this slightest possible defect, which we hesitate whether to term a defect or a beauty, shocks me, as being the visible mark of earthly imperfection."

"Shocks you, my husband!" cried Georgiana, deeply hurt; at first reddening with momentary anger, but then bursting into tears. "Then why did you take me from my mother's side? You cannot love what shocks you!"

To explain this conversation, it must be mentioned that in the center of Georgiana's left cheek there was a singular mark, deeply interwoven, as it were, with the texture and substance of her face. In the usual state of her complexion—a healthy though delicate bloom—the mark wore a tint of deeper crimson, which imperfectly defined its shape amid the surrounding rosiness. When she blushed it gradually became more indistinct, and finally vanished amid the triumphant rush of blood that bathed the whole cheek with its brilliant glow. But if any shifting motion caused her to turn pale there was the mark again, a crimson stain upon the snow, in what Aylmer sometimes deemed an almost fearful distinctness. Its shape bore not a little similarity to the human hand, though of the smallest pygmy size. Georgiana's lovers were wont to say that some fairy at her birth-hour had laid her tiny hand upon the infant's cheek, and left this impress there in token of the magic endowments that were to give her such sway over all hearts. Many a desperate swain would have risked life for the privilege of pressing his lips to the mysterious hand. It must not be concealed, however, that the impression wrought by this fairy sign-manual varied exceedingly according to the difference of temperament in the beholders. Some fastidious persons—but they were exclusively of her own sex—affirmed that the bloody hand, as they chose to call it, quite destroyed the effect of Georgiana's beauty and rendered her countenance even hideous. But it would be as reasonable to say that one of those small blue stains which sometimes occur in the purest statuary marble would convert the Eve of Powers[3] to a monster. Masculine observers, if the birthmark did not heighten their admiration, contented themselves with wishing it away, that the world might possess one living specimen of ideal loveliness without the semblance of a flaw. After his marriage—for he thought little or nothing of the matter before—Aylmer discovered that this was the case with himself.

Had she been less beautiful—if Envy's self could have found aught else to sneer at—he might have felt his affection heightened by the prettiness of this mimic hand, now vaguely portrayed, now lost, now stealing forth again and glimmering to and fro with every pulse of emotion that throbbed within her heart; but, seeing her otherwise so perfect, he found this one defect grow more and more intolerable with every moment of their united lives. It was the fatal flaw of humanity which Nature, in one shape or another, stamps ineffaceably on all her productions, either to imply that they are temporary and finite, or that their perfection must be wrought by toil and pain. The crimson hand expressed the ineludible gripe in which mortality clutches the highest and purest of earthly mould, degrading them into kindred with the lowest, and even with the very brutes, like whom their visible frames return to dust. In this manner, selecting it as the symbol of his wife's liability to sin, sorrow, decay, and death, Aylmer's somber imagination was not long in rendering the birthmark a frightful object, causing him more trouble and horror than ever Georgiana's beauty, whether of soul or sense, had given him delight.

At all the seasons which should have been their happiest he invariably, and without intending it, nay, in spite of a purpose to the contrary, reverted to this one disastrous topic. Trifling as it at first appeared, it so connected itself with innumerable trains of thought and modes of feeling that it became the central point of all. With the morning twilight Aylmer opened his eyes upon his wife's face and recognized the symbol of imperfection; and when they sat together at the evening hearth his eyes wandered stealthily to her cheek, and beheld, flickering with the blaze of the wood-fire, the spectral hand that wrote mortality where he would fain[4] have worshipped. Georgiana soon learned to shudder at his gaze. It needed but a glance with the peculiar expression that his face often wore to change the roses of her cheek into a death-like paleness, amid which the crimson hand was brought strongly out, like a bas relief of ruby on the whitest marble.

3. Hiram Powers (1805–73), American sculptor and friend of Hawthorne, produced noted marble statues, including *Eve Tempted* and *Eve Disconsolate*.
4. Eagerly, preferably.

10   Late one night, when the lights were growing dim so as hardly to betray
the stain on the poor wife's cheek, she herself, for the first time, voluntarily
took up the subject.

"Do you remember, my dear Aylmer," said she, with a feeble attempt at
a smile, "have you any recollection, of a dream last night about this odious
hand?"

"None! none whatever!" replied Aylmer, starting; but then he added, in
a dry, cold tone, affected for the sake of concealing the real depth of his
emotion, "I might well dream of it; for, before I fell asleep, it had taken a
pretty firm hold of my fancy."

"And you did dream of it?" continued Georgiana, hastily; for she dreaded
lest a gush of tears should interrupt what she had to say. "A terrible dream!
I wonder that you can forget it. Is it possible to forget this one expression?—
'It is in her heart now; we must have it out!' Reflect, my husband; for by all
means I would have you recall that dream."

The mind is in a sad state when Sleep, the all-involving, cannot confine
her specters within the dim region of her sway, but suffers them to break
forth, affrighting this actual life with secrets that perchance belong to a
deeper one. Aylmer now remembered his dream. He had fancied himself
with his servant Aminadab attempting an operation for the removal of the
birth-mark; but the deeper went the knife, the deeper sank the hand, until
at length its tiny grasp appeared to have caught hold of Georgiana's heart;
whence, however, her husband was inexorably resolved to cut or wrench it
away.

15   When the dream had shaped itself perfectly in his memory, Aylmer sat
in his wife's presence with a guilty feeling. Truth often finds its way to the
mind close muffled in robes of sleep, and then speaks with uncompromising
directness of matters in regard to which we practice an unconscious self-
deception during our waking moments. Until now he had not been aware
of the tyrannizing influence acquired by one idea over his mind, and of
the lengths which he might find in his heart to go for the sake of giving
himself peace.

"Aylmer," resumed Georgiana, solemnly, "I know not what may be the
cost to both of us to rid me of this fatal birth-mark. Perhaps its removal
may cause cureless deformity; or it may be the stain goes as deep as life
itself. Again: do we know that there is a possibility, on any terms, of unclasp-
ing the firm gripe of this little hand which was laid upon me before I came
into the world?"

"Dearest Georgiana, I have spent much thought upon the subject,"
hastily interrupted Aylmer. "I am convinced of the perfect practicability of
its removal."

"If there be the remotest possibility of it," continued Georgiana, "let the attempt be made, at whatever risk. Danger is nothing to me; for life, while this hateful mark makes me the object of your horror and disgust—life is a burden which I would fling down with joy. Either remove this dreadful hand, or take my wretched life! You have deep science. All the world bears witness of it. You have achieved great wonders. Cannot you remove this little, little mark, which I cover with the tips of two small fingers? Is this beyond your power, for the sake of your own peace, and to save your poor wife from madness?"

"Noblest, dearest, tenderest wife," cried Aylmer, rapturously, "doubt not my power. I have already given this matter the deepest thought— thought which might almost have enlightened me to create a being less perfect than yourself. Georgiana, you have led me deeper than ever into the heart of science. I feel myself fully competent to render this dear cheek as faultless as its fellow; and then, most beloved, what will be my triumph when I shall have corrected what Nature left imperfect in her fairest work! Even Pygmalion,[5] when his sculptured woman assumed life, felt not greater ecstasy than mine will be."

"It is resolved, then," said Georgiana, faintly smiling. "And, Aylmer, 20 spare me not, though you should find the birth-mark take refuge in my heart at last."

Her husband tenderly kissed her cheek—her right cheek—not that which bore the impress of the crimson hand.

The next day Aylmer apprised his wife of a plan that he had formed whereby he might have opportunity for the intense thought and constant watchfulness which the proposed operation would require; while Georgiana, likewise, would enjoy the perfect repose essential to its success. They were to seclude themselves in the extensive apartments occupied by Aylmer as a laboratory, and where, during his toilsome youth, he had made discoveries in the elemental powers of Nature that had roused the admiration of all the learned societies in Europe. Seated calmly in this laboratory, the pale philosopher had investigated the secrets of the highest cloud-region and of the profoundest mines; he had satisfied himself of the causes that kindled and kept alive the fires of the volcano; and had explained the mystery of fountains, and how it is that they gush forth, some so bright and pure, and others with such rich medicinal virtues, from the dark bosom of the earth. Here, too, at an earlier period, he had studied the wonders of the human frame, and attempted to fathom the very process

5. Pygmalion was a legendary artist of Cyprus who fell in love with the statue he made of a beautiful woman; in Ovid's *Metamorphoses*, she comes to life.

by which Nature assimilates all her precious influences from earth and air, and from the spiritual world, to create and foster man, her masterpiece. The latter pursuit, however, Aylmer had long laid aside in unwilling recognition of the truth—against which all seekers sooner or later stumble—that our great creative Mother, while she amuses us with apparently working in the broadest sunshine, is yet severely careful to keep her own secrets, and, in spite of her pretended openness, shows us nothing but results. She permits us, indeed, to mar, but seldom to mend, and, like a jealous patentee, on no account to make. Now, however, Aylmer resumed these half-forgotten investigations; not, of course, with such hopes or wishes as first suggested them; but because they involved much physiological truth and lay in the path of his proposed scheme for the treatment of Georgiana.

As he led her over the threshold of the laboratory Georgiana was cold and tremulous. Aylmer looked cheerfully into her face, with intent to reassure her, but was so startled with the intense glow of the birth-mark upon the whiteness of her cheek that he could not restrain a strong convulsive shudder. His wife fainted.

"Aminadab! Aminadab!" shouted Aylmer, stamping violently on the floor.

25   Forthwith there issued from an inner apartment a man of low stature, but bulky frame, with shaggy hair hanging about his visage, which was grimed with the vapors of the furnace. This personage had been Aylmer's underworker during his whole scientific career, and was admirably fitted for that office by his great mechanical readiness, and the skill with which, while incapable of comprehending a single principle, he executed all the details of his master's experiments. With his vast strength, his shaggy hair, his smoky aspect, and the indescribable earthiness that incrusted him, he seemed to represent man's physical nature; while Aylmer's slender figure, and pale, intellectual face, were no less apt a type of the spiritual element.

"Throw open the door of the boudoir, Aminadab," said Aylmer, "and burn a pastil."[6]

"Yes, master," answered Aminadab, looking intently at the lifeless form of Georgiana; and then he muttered to himself. "If she were my wife, I'd never part with that birth-mark."

When Georgiana recovered consciousness she found herself breathing an atmosphere of penetrating fragrance, the gentle potency of which had recalled her from her death-like faintness. The scene around her looked like enchantment. Aylmer had converted those smoky, dingy, somber rooms, where he had spent his brightest years in recondite pursuits, into a series

6. Pastille, a lozenge or tablet of medicinal incense.

of beautiful apartments not unfit to be the secluded abode of a lovely woman. The walls were hung with gorgeous curtains, which imparted the combination of grandeur and grace that no other species of adornment can achieve; and, as they fell from the ceiling to the floor, their rich and ponderous folds, concealing all angles and straight lines, appeared to shut in the scene from infinite space. For aught Georgiana knew, it might be a pavilion among the clouds. And Aylmer, excluding the sunshine, which would have interfered with his chemical processes, had supplied its place with perfumed lamps, emitting flames of various hue, but all uniting in a soft, impurpled radiance. He now knelt by his wife's side, watching her earnestly, but without alarm; for he was confident in his science, and felt that he could draw a magic circle round her within which no evil might intrude.

"Where am I? Ah, I remember," said Georgiana, faintly; and she placed her hand over her cheek to hide the terrible mark from her husband's eyes.

"Fear not, dearest!" exclaimed he. "Do not shrink from me! Believe me,   30 Georgiana, I even rejoice in this single imperfection, since it will be such a rapture to remove it."

"O, spare me!" sadly replied his wife. "Pray do not look at it again. I never can forget that convulsive shudder."

In order to soothe Georgiana, and, as it were, to release her mind from the burden of actual things, Aylmer now put in practice some of the light and playful secrets which science had taught him among its profounder lore. Airy figures, absolutely bodiless ideas, and forms of unsubstantial beauty came and danced before her, imprinting their momentary footsteps on beams of light. Though she had some indistinct idea of the method of these optical phenomena, still the illusion was almost perfect enough to warrant the belief that her husband possessed say over the spiritual world. Then again, when she felt a wish to look forth from her seclusion, immediately, as if her thoughts were answered, the procession of external existence flitted across a screen. The scenery and the figures of actual life were perfectly represented but with that bewitching yet indescribable difference which always makes a picture, an image, or a shadow so much more attractive than the original. When wearied of this, Aylmer bade her cast her eyes upon a vessel containing a quantity of earth. She did so, with little interest at first; but was soon startled to perceive the germ of a plant shooting upward from the soil. Then came the slender stalk; the leaves gradually unfolded themselves; and amid them was a perfect and lovely flower.

"It is magical!" cried Georgiana. "I dare not touch it."

"Nay, pluck it," answered Aylmer—"pluck it, and inhale its brief perfume while you may. The flower will wither in a few moments and leave nothing save its brown seed vessels; but thence may be perpetuated a race as ephemeral as itself."

35   But Georgiana had no sooner touched the flower than the whole plant suffered a blight, its leaves turning coal-black as if by the agency of fire.

"There was too powerful a stimulus," said Aylmer, thoughtfully.

To make up for this abortive experiment, he proposed to take her portrait by a scientific process of his own invention. It was to be affected by rays of light striking upon a polished plate of metal. Georgiana assented; but, on looking at the result, was affrighted to find the features of the portrait blurred and indefinable; while the minute figure of a hand appeared where the cheek should have been. Aylmer snatched the metallic plate and threw it into a jar of corrosive acid.

Soon, however, he forgot these mortifying failures. In the intervals of study and chemical experiment he came to her flushed and exhausted, but seemed invigorated by her presence, and spoke in glowing language of the resources of his art. He gave a history of the long dynasty of the alchemists, who spent so many ages in quest of the universal solvent by which the golden principle might be elicited from all things vile and base.[7] Aylmer appeared to believe that, by the plainest scientific logic, it was altogether within the limits of possibility to discover this long-sought medium. "But," he added, "a philosopher who should go deep enough to acquire the power would attain too lofty a wisdom to stoop to the exercise of it." Not less singular were his opinions in regard to the elixir vitae.[8] He more than intimated that it was at his option to concoct a liquid that should prolong life for years, perhaps interminably; but that it would produce a discord in Nature which all the world, and chiefly the quaffer of the immortal nostrum, would find cause to curse.

"Aylmer, are you in earnest?" asked Georgiana, looking at him with amazement and fear. "It is terrible to possess such power, or even to dream of possessing it."

40   "O, do not tremble, my love," said her husband. "I would not wrong either you or myself by working such inharmonious effects upon our lives; but I would have you consider how trifling, in comparison, is the skill requisite to remove this little hand."

At the mention of the birth-mark, Georgiana, as usual, shrank as if a red-hot iron had touched her cheek.

Again Aylmer applied himself to his labors. She could hear his voice in the distant furnace-room giving directions to Aminadab, whose harsh,

---

7. Before the advent of modern chemistry, alchemists studied the properties of matter in a search for spiritual essences and the secret of transforming base metals into gold.
8. Literally, the drink or potion of life (Latin), imagined to give immortality.

uncouth, misshapen tones were audible in response, more like the grunt or growl of a brute than human speech. After hours of absence, Aylmer reappeared and proposed that she should now examine his cabinet of chemical products and natural treasures of the earth. Among the former he showed her a small vial, in which, he remarked, was contained a gentle yet most powerful fragrance, capable of impregnating all the breezes that blow across a kingdom. They were of inestimable value, the contents of that little vial; and, as he said so, he threw some of the perfume into the air and filled the room with piercing and invigorating delight.

"And what is this?" asked Georgiana, pointing to a small crystal globe containing a gold-colored liquid. "It is so beautiful to the eye that I could imagine it the elixir of life."

"In one sense it is," replied Aylmer; "or rather, the elixir of immortality. It is the most precious poison that ever was concocted in this world. By its aid I could apportion the lifetime of any mortal at whom you might point your finger. The strength of the dose would determine whether he were to linger out years, or drop dead in the midst of a breath. No king on his guarded throne could keep his life if I, in my private station, should deem that the welfare of millions justified me in depriving him of it."

"Why do you keep such a terrific drug?" inquired Georgiana, in horror. 45

"Do not mistrust me, dearest," said her husband, smiling; "its virtuous potency is yet greater than its harmful one. But see! here is a powerful cosmetic. With a few drops of this in a vase of water, freckles may be washed away as easily as the hands are cleansed. A stronger infusion would take the blood out of the cheek, and leave the rosiest beauty a pale ghost."

"Is it with this lotion that you intend to bathe my cheek?" asked Georgiana, anxiously.

"O no," hastily replied her husband; "this is merely superficial. Your case demands a remedy that shall go deeper."

In his interviews with Georgiana, Aylmer generally made minute inquiries as to her sensations, and whether the confinement of the rooms and the temperature of the atmosphere agreed with her. These questions had such a particular drift that Georgiana began to conjecture that she was already subjected to certain physical influences, either breathed in with the fragrant air or taken with her food. She fancied likewise, but it might be altogether fancy, that there was a stirring up of her system—a strange, indefinite sensation creeping through her veins, and tingling, half painfully, half pleasurably, at her heart. Still, whenever she dared to look into the mirror, there she beheld herself pale as a white rose and with the crimson birth-mark stamped upon her cheek. Not even Aylmer now hated it so much as she.

To dispel the tedium of the hours which her husband found it necessary to devote to the processes of combination and analysis, Georgiana 50 turned over the volumes of his scientific library. In many dark old tomes she met with chapters full of romance and poetry. They were the works of the philosophers of the Middle Ages, such as Albertus Magnus, Cornelius Agrippa, Paracelsus, and the famous friar who created the prophetic Brazen Head.[9] All these antique naturalists stood in advance of their centuries, yet were imbued with some of their credulity, and therefore were believed, and perhaps imagined themselves to have acquired from the investigation of Nature a power above Nature, and from physics a sway over the spiritual world. Hardly less curious and imaginative were the early volumes of the Transactions of the Royal Society,[1] in which the members, knowing little of the limits of natural possibility, were continually recording wonders or proposing methods whereby wonders might be wrought.

But, to Georgiana, the most engrossing volume was a large folio from her husband's own hand, in which he had recorded every experiment of his scientific career, its original aim, the methods adopted for its development, and its final success or failure, with the circumstances to which either event was attributable. The book, in truth, was both the history and emblem of his ardent, ambitious, imaginative, yet practical and laborious life. He handled physical details as if there were nothing beyond them; yet spiritualized them all, and redeemed himself from materialism by his strong and eager aspiration towards the infinite. In his grasp the veriest clod of earth assumed a soul. Georgiana, as she read, reverenced Aylmer and loved him more profoundly than ever, but with a less entire dependence on his judgment than heretofore. Much as he had accomplished, she could not but observe that his most splendid successes were almost invariably failures, if compared with the ideal at which he aimed. His brightest diamonds were the merest pebbles, and felt to be so by himself, in comparison with the inestimable gems which lay hidden beyond his reach. The volume, rich with achievements that had won renown for its author, was yet as melancholy a record as ever mortal hand had penned. It was the sad confession and continual exemplification of the shortcomings of the composite man, the spirit burdened with clay and working in matter, and of the despair that assails the higher nature at finding itself so miserably thwarted by the earthly part. Perhaps every man of genius, in whatever sphere, might recognize the image of his own experience in Aylmer's journal.

9. The Brazen Head, a brass bust of a man, was supposed to be able to answer any question; the "famous friar" is Roger Bacon (c. 1214–94), an English natural philosopher, as scientists were then called. Albertus Magnus (1193/1206–80), Agrippa (1496–1535), and Paracelsus (1493–1541) were all European experimenters reputed to have near-magical powers in alchemy or astrology.
1. *The Philosophical Transactions of the Royal Society* is the oldest scientific journal in English, published since 1665.

So deeply did these reflections affect Georgiana that she laid her face upon the open volume and burst into tears. In this situation she was found by her husband.

"It is dangerous to read in a sorcerer's books," said he with a smile, though his countenance was uneasy and displeased. "Georgiana, there are pages in that volume which I can scarcely glance over and keep my senses. Take heed lest it prove as detrimental to you."

"It has made me worship you more than ever," said she.

"Ah, wait for this one success," rejoined he, "then worship me if you 55 will. I shall deem myself hardly unworthy of it. But come, I have sought you for the luxury of your voice. Sing to me, dearest."

So she poured out the liquid music of her voice to quench the thirst of his spirit. He then took his leave with a boyish exuberance of gayety, assuring her that her seclusion would endure but a little longer, and that the result was already certain. Scarcely had he departed when Georgiana felt irresistibly impelled to follow him. She had forgotten to inform Aylmer of a symptom which for two or three hours past had begun to excite her attention. It was a sensation in the fatal birth-mark, not painful, but which induced a restlessness throughout her system. Hastening after her husband, she intruded for the first time into the laboratory.

The first thing that struck her eye was the furnace, that hot and feverish worker, with the intense glow of its fire, which by the quantities of soot clustered above it seemed to have been burning for ages. There was a distilling-apparatus in full operation. Around the room were retorts, tubes, cylinders, crucibles, and other apparatus of chemical research. An electrical machine stood ready for immediate use. The atmosphere felt oppressively close, and was tainted with gaseous odors which had been tormented forth by the processes of science. The severe and homely simplicity of the apartment, with its naked walls and brick pavement, looked strange, accustomed as Georgiana had become to the fantastic elegance of her boudoir. But what chiefly, indeed almost solely, drew her attention, was the aspect of Aylmer himself.

He was pale as death, anxious and absorbed, and hung over the furnace as if it depended upon his utmost watchfulness whether the liquid which it was distilling should be the draught of immortal happiness or misery. How different from the sanguine and joyous mien that he had assumed for Georgiana's encouragement!

"Carefully now, Aminadab; carefully, thou human machine; carefully, thou man of clay," muttered Aylmer, more to himself than his assistant. "Now, if there be a thought too much or too little, it is all over."

"Ho! ho!" mumbled Aminadab. "Look, master! look!" 60

Aylmer raised his eyes hastily, and at first reddened, then grew paler than ever, on beholding Georgiana. He rushed towards her and seized her arm with a gripe that left the print of his fingers upon it. "Why do you come hither? Have you no trust in your husband?" cried he, impetuously. "Would you throw the blight of that fatal birth-mark over my labors? It is not well done. Go, prying woman! go!"

"Nay, Aylmer," said Georgiana with the firmness of which she possessed no stinted endowment, "it is not you that have a right to complain. You mistrust your wife; you have concealed the anxiety with which you watch the development of this experiment. Think not so unworthily of me, my husband. Tell me all the risk we run, and fear not that I shall shrink; for my share in it is far less than your own."

"No, no, Georgiana!" said Aylmer, impatiently; "it must not be."

65 "I submit," replied she, calmly. "And, Aylmer, I shall quaff whatever draught you bring me; but it will be on the same principle that would induce me to take a dose of poison if offered by your hand."

"My noble wife," said Aylmer, deeply moved, "I knew not the height and depth of your nature until now. Nothing shall be concealed. Know, then, that this crimson hand, superficial as it seems, has clutched its grasp into your being with a strength of which I had no previous conception. I have already administered agents powerful enough to do aught except to change your entire physical system. Only one thing remains to be tried. If that fail us we are ruined."

"Why did you hesitate to tell me this?" asked she.

"Because, Georgiana," said Aylmer, in a low voice, "there is danger."

"Danger? There is but one danger—that this horrible stigma shall be left upon my cheek!" cried Georgiana. "Remove it, remove it, whatever be the cost, or we shall both go mad!"

70 "Heaven knows your words are too true," said Aylmer, sadly. "And now, dearest, return to your boudoir. In a little while all will be tested."

He conducted her back and took leave of her with a solemn tenderness which spoke far more than his words how much was now at stake. After his departure Georgiana became rapt in musings. She considered the character of Aylmer, and did it completer justice than at any previous moment. Her heart exulted, while it trembled, at his honorable love—so pure and lofty that it would accept nothing less than perfection, nor miserably make itself contented with an earthlier nature than he had dreamed of. She felt how much more precious was such a sentiment than that meaner kind which would have borne with the imperfection for her sake, and have been guilty of treason to holy love by degrading its perfect idea to the level of the actual; and with her whole spirit she prayed that, for a single moment, she might satisfy his highest and deepest conception. Longer than one moment she well knew it could not be; for his spirit was ever on the march, ever ascending, and each instant required something that was beyond the scope of the instant before.

The sound of her husband's footsteps aroused her. He bore a crystal goblet containing a liquor colorless as water, but bright enough to be the draught of immortality. Aylmer was pale; but it seemed rather the consequence of a highly wrought state of mind and tension of spirit than of fear or doubt.

"The concoction of the draught has been perfect," said he, in answer to Georgiana's look. "Unless all my science have deceived me, it cannot fail."

"Save on your account, my dearest Aylmer," observed his wife, "I might wish to put off this birth-mark of mortality by relinquishing mortality itself in preference to any other mode. Life is but a sad possession to those who have attained precisely the degree of moral advancement at which I stand. Were I weaker and blinder, it might be happiness. Were I stronger, it might be endured hopefully. But, being what I find myself, methinks I am of all mortals the most fit to die."

"You are fit for heaven without tasting death!" replied her husband. 75 "But why do we speak of dying? The draught cannot fail. Behold its effect upon this plant."

On the window-seat there stood a geranium diseased with yellow blotches, which had overspread all its leaves. Aylmer poured a small quantity of the liquid upon the soil in which it grew. In a little time, when the roots of the plant had taken up the moisture, the unsightly blotches began to be extinguished in a living verdure.

"There needed no proof," said Georgiana, quietly. "Give me the goblet. I joyfully stake all upon your word."

"Drink, then, thou lofty creature!" exclaimed Aylmer, with fervid admiration. "There is no taint of imperfection on thy spirit. Thy sensible frame, too, shall soon be all perfect."

She quaffed the liquid and returned the goblet to his hand.

"It is grateful," said she, with a placid smile. "Methinks it is like water 80 from a heavenly fountain; for it contains I know not what of unobtrusive fragrance and deliciousness. It allays a feverish thirst that had parched me for many days. Now, dearest, let me sleep. My earthly senses are closing over my spirit like the leaves around the heart of a rose at sunset."

She spoke the last words with a gentle reluctance, as if it required almost more energy than she could command to pronounce the faint and lingering syllables. Scarcely had they loitered through her lips ere she was lost in slumber. Aylmer sat by her side, watching her aspect with the emotions proper to a man, the whole value of whose existence was involved in the process now to be tested. Mingled with this mood, however, was the philosophic investigation characteristic of the man of science. Not the minutest symptom escaped him. A heightened flush of the cheek, a slight irregularity of breath, a quiver of the eyelid, a hardly perceptible tremor through the frame—such were the details which, as the moments passed, he wrote down in his folio volume. Intense thought had set its stamp upon every previous page of that volume; but the thoughts of years were all concentrated upon the last.

While thus employed, he failed not to gaze often at the fatal hand, and not without a shudder. Yet once, by a strange and unaccountable impulse, he pressed it with his lips. His spirit recoiled, however, in the very act; and Georgiana, out of the midst of her deep sleep, moved uneasily and murmured, as if in remonstrance. Again Aylmer resumed his watch. Nor was it without avail. The crimson hand, which at first had been strongly visible upon the marble paleness of Georgiana's cheek, now grew more faintly outlined. She remained not less pale than ever; but the birth-mark, with every breath that came and went, lost somewhat of its former distinctness. Its presence had been awful; its departure was more awful still. Watch the stain of the rainbow fading out of the sky, and you will know how that mysterious symbol passed away.

"By Heaven! it is wellnigh gone!" said Aylmer to himself, in almost irrepressible ecstasy. "I can scarcely trace it now. Success! success! And now it is like the faintest rose-color. The lightest flush of blood across her cheek would overcome it. But she is so pale!"

He drew aside the window-curtain and suffered the light of natural day to fall into the room and rest upon her cheek. At the same time he heard a gross, hoarse chuckle, which he had long known as his servant Aminadab's expression of delight.

85   "Ah, clod! ah, earthly mass!" cried Aylmer, laughing in a sort of frenzy, "you have served me well! Matter and spirit—earth and heaven—have both done their part in this! Laugh, thing of the senses! You have earned the right to laugh."

These exclamations broke Georgiana's sleep. She slowly unclosed her eyes and gazed into the mirror which her husband had arranged for that purpose. A faint smile flitted over her lips when she recognized how barely perceptible was now that crimson hand which had once blazed forth with such disastrous brilliancy as to scare away all their happiness. But then her eyes sought Aylmer's face with a trouble and anxiety that he could by no means account for.

"My poor Aylmer!" murmured she.

"Poor? Nay, richest, happiest, most favored!" exclaimed he. "My peerless bride, it is successful! You are perfect!"

"My poor Aylmer," she repeated, with a more than human tenderness, "you have aimed loftily; you have done nobly. Do not repent that, with so high and pure a feeling, you have rejected the best the earth could offer. Aylmer, dearest Aylmer, I am dying!"

Alas! it was too true! The fatal hand had grappled with the mystery 90 of life, and was the bond by which an angelic spirit kept itself in union with a mortal frame. As the last crimson tint of the birth-mark—that sole token of human imperfection—faded from her cheek, the parting breath of the now perfect woman passed into the atmosphere, and her soul, lingering a moment near her husband, took its heavenward flight. Then a hoarse, chuckling laugh was heard again! Thus ever does the gross fatality of earth exult in its invariable triumph over the immortal essence which, in this dim sphere of half-development, demands the completeness of a higher state. Yet, had Aylmer reached a profounder wisdom, he need not thus have flung away the happiness which would have woven his mortal life of the self-same texture with the celestial. The momentary circumstance was too strong for him; he failed to look beyond the shadowy scope of time, and, living once for all in eternity, to find the perfect future in the present.

1843

QUESTIONS

1. What difference would it make if the mark on Georgiana's cheek were shaped like a fish, a heart, or an irregular oval? Why (and when) does the mark appear redder or more visible or faint? If the birthmark is explicitly a "symbol of imperfection" (par. 9), what *kinds* of imperfection does it represent?
2. Aylmer says to his wife, "Even Pygmalion, when his sculptured woman assumed life, felt not greater ecstasy than mine will be" (par. 19). How does this literary allusion to the myth of Pygmalion enhance the meaning of THE BIRTH-MARK? Is this allusion ironic, given what happens to Alymer's project to make his wife perfect?
3. Look closely at the settings of the story, from the laboratory to the boudoir. Note the similes, metaphors, and other figures of speech that help characterize these places. How do these different patterns of imagery contribute to the symbolism of the story? to an allegorical reading of the story?

EDWIDGE DANTICAT
(b. 1969)

A Wall of Fire Rising

When she was twelve, Edwidge Danticat moved from Port-au-Prince, Haiti, to Brooklyn, New York, where her parents had relocated eight years before. Having grown up speaking only French and Creole, Danticat published her first writing in English at age fourteen, a newspaper article about her immigration to the United States that developed into her first novel, *Breath, Eyes, Memory* (1994). Danticat received a degree in French literature from Barnard College and an MFA from Brown University. *Krik? Krak!* (1991), a collection of short stories, was nominated for the National Book Award. Her second novel, *The Farming of Bones* (1998), is based on the 1937 massacre of Haitians at the border of the Dominican Republic. In 2002, Danticat published *After the Dance: A Walk through Carnival in Jacmel, Haiti*, an account of her travels. More recent publications include *The Dew Breaker* (2004), a collection of stories that examines the life of a Haitian torturer; *Brother, I'm Dying* (2007), winner of the National Book Critics Circle Award for Autobiography; the essay collection *Create Dangerously: The Immigrant Artist at Work* (2010); and the novel *Claire of the Sea Light* (2013).

"Listen to what happened today," Guy said as he barged through the rattling door of his tiny shack.

His wife, Lili, was squatting in the middle of their one-room home, spreading cornmeal mush on banana leaves for their supper.

"Listen to what happened to *me* today!" Guy's seven-year-old son— Little Guy—dashed from a corner and grabbed his father's hand. The boy dropped his composition notebook as he leaped to his father, nearly stepping into the corn mush and herring that his mother had set out in a trio of half gourds on the clay floor.

"Our boy is in a play." Lili quickly robbed Little Guy of the honor of telling his father the news.

5   "A play?" Guy affectionately stroked the boy's hair.

The boy had such tiny corkscrew curls that no amount of brushing could ever make them all look like a single entity. The other boys at the

Lycée Jean-Jacques[1] called him "pepper head" because each separate kinky strand was coiled into a tight tiny ball that looked like small peppercorns. "When is this play?" Guy asked both the boy and his wife. "Are we going to have to buy new clothes for this?"

Lili got up from the floor and inclined her face towards her husband's in order to receive her nightly peck on the cheek.

"What role do you have in the play?" Guy asked, slowly rubbing the tip of his nails across the boy's scalp. His fingers made a soft grating noise with each invisible circle drawn around the perimeters of the boy's head. Guy's fingers finally landed inside the boy's ears, forcing the boy to giggle until he almost gave himself the hiccups.

"Tell me, what is your part in the play?" Guy asked again, pulling his 10
fingers away from his son's ear.

"I am Boukman," the boy huffed out, as though there was some laughter caught in his throat.

"Show Papy your lines," Lili told the boy as she arranged the three open gourds on a piece of plywood raised like a table on two bricks, in the middle of the room. "My love, Boukman is the hero of the play."

The boy went back to the corner where he had been studying and pulled out a thick book carefully covered in brown paper.

"You're going to spend a lifetime learning those." Guy took the book from the boy's hand and flipped through the pages quickly. He had to strain his eyes to see the words by the light of an old kerosene lamp, which that night—like all others—flickered as though it was burning its very last wick.

"All these words seem so long and heavy," Guy said. "You think you can 15
do this, son?"

"He has one very good speech," Lili said. "Page forty, remember, son?"

The boy took back the book from his father. His face was crimped in an of-course-I-remember look as he searched for page forty.

"Bouk-man," Guy struggled with the letters of the slave revolutionary's name as he looked over his son's shoulders. "I see some very hard words here, son."

"He already knows his speech," Lili told her husband.

"Does he now?" asked Guy. 20

"We've been at it all afternoon," Lili said. "Why don't you go on and recite that speech for your father?"

The boy tipped his head towards the rusting tin on the roof as he prepared to recite his lines.

---

1. Haiti is French speaking; Little Guy attends a *lycée* (school) named after Jean-Jacques Dessalines (1758–1806), the founder of independent Haiti. A former slave, Dessalines was declared emperor Jacques I in 1804.

Lili wiped her hands on an old apron tied around her waist and stopped to listen.

"Remember what you are," Lili said, "a great rebel leader. Remember, it is the revolution."

25   "Do we want him to be all of that?" Guy asked.

"He is Boukman," Lili said. "What is the only thing on your mind now, Boukman?"

"Supper," Guy whispered, enviously eyeing the food cooling off in the middle of the room. He and the boy looked at each other and began to snicker.

"Tell us the other thing that is on your mind," Lili said, joining in their laughter.

"Freedom!" shouted the boy, as he quickly slipped into his role.

30   "Louder!" urged Lili.

"Freedom is on my mind!" yelled the boy.

"Why don't you start, son?" said Guy. "If you don't, we'll never get to that other thing that we have on our minds."

The boy closed his eyes and took a deep breath. At first, his lips parted but nothing came out. Lili pushed her head forward as though she were holding her breath. Then like the last burst of lightning out of clearing sky, the boy began.

"*A wall of fire is rising and in the ashes, I see the bones of my people. Not only those people whose dark hollow faces I see daily in the fields, but all those souls who have gone ahead to haunt my dreams. At night I relive once more the last caresses from the hand of a loving father, a valiant love, a beloved friend.*"[2]

35   It was obvious that this was a speech written by a European man, who gave to the slave revolutionary Boukman the kind of European phrasing that might have sent the real Boukman turning in his grave. However, the speech made Lili and Guy stand on the tips of their toes from great pride. As their applause thundered in the small space of their shack that night, they felt as though for a moment they had been given the rare pleasure of hearing the voice of one of the forefathers of Haitian independence in the forced baritone of their only child. The experience left them both with a strange feeling that they could not explain. It left the hair on the back of their necks standing on end. It left them feeling much more love than they ever knew that they could add to their feeling for their son.

2. On the night of August 22, 1791, slaves led by a slave foreman named Boukman (who was secretly a voodoo high priest) built a "wall of fire" that destroyed many plantations in the north of the French colony of Saint-Domingue, marking the beginning of a mass slave revolt that would lead, fourteen years later, to the establishment of independent Haiti.

"Bravo," Lili cheered, pressing her son into the folds of her apron. "Long live Boukman and long live my boy."

"Long live our supper," Guy said, quickly batting his eyelashes to keep tears from rolling down his face.

The boy kept his eyes on his book as they ate their supper that night. Usually Guy and Lili would not have allowed that, but this was a special occasion. They watched proudly as the boy muttered his lines between swallows of cornmeal.

The boy was still mumbling the same words as the three of them used the last of the rainwater trapped in old gasoline containers and sugarcane pulp from the nearby sugarcane mill to scrub the gourds that they had eaten from.

When things were really bad for the family, they boiled clean sugar- 40 cane pulp to make what Lili called her special sweet water tea. It was supposed to suppress gas and kill the vermin in the stomach that made poor children hungry. That and a pinch of salt under the tongue could usually quench hunger until Guy found a day's work or Lili could manage to buy spices on credit and then peddle them for a profit at the marketplace.

That night, anyway, things were good. Everyone had eaten enough to put all their hunger vermin to sleep.

The boy was sitting in front of the shack on an old plastic bucket turned upside down, straining his eyes to find the words on the page. Sometimes when there was no kerosene for the lamp, the boy would have to go sit by the side of the road and study under the street lamps with the rest of the neighborhood children. Tonight, at least, they had a bit of their own light.

Guy bent down by a small clump of old mushrooms near the boy's feet, trying to get a better look at the plant. He emptied the last drops of rainwater from a gasoline container on the mushroom, wetting the bulging toes sticking out of his sons' sandals, which were already coming apart around his endlessly growing feet.

Guy tried to pluck some of the mushrooms, which were being pushed into the dust as though they wanted to grow beneath the ground as roots. He took one of the mushrooms in his hand, running his smallest finger over the round bulb. He clipped the stem and buried the top in a thick strand of his wife's hair.

The mushroom looked like a dried insect in Lili's hair. 45

"It sure makes you look special," Guy said, teasing her.

"Thank you so much," Lili said, tapping her husband's arm. "It's nice to know that I deserve these much more than roses."

Taking his wife's hand, Guy said, "Let's go to the sugar mill."

"Can I study my lines there?" the boy asked.
50   "You know them well enough already," Guy said.
"I need many repetitions," the boy said.

Their feet sounded as though they were playing a wet wind instrument as they slipped in and out of the puddles between the shacks in the shanty-town. Near the sugar mill was a large television screen in an iron grill cage that the government had installed so that the shantytown dwellers could watch the state-sponsored news at eight o'clock every night. After the news, a gendarme[3] would come and turn off the television set, taking home the key. On most nights, the people stayed at the site long after this gen-darme had gone and told stories to one another beneath the big blank screen. They made bonfires with dried sticks, corn husks, and paper, cursing the authorities under their breath.

There was a crowd already gathering for the nightly news event. The sugar mill workers sat in the front row in chairs or on old buckets.

Lili and Guy passed the group, clinging to their son so that in his child-hood naïveté he wouldn't accidentally glance at the wrong person and be called an insolent child. They didn't like the ambiance of the nightly news watch. They spared themselves trouble by going instead to the sugar mill, where in the past year they had discovered their own wonder.

55   Everyone knew that the family who owned the sugar mill were eccen-tric "Arabs," Haitians of Lebanese or Palestinian descent whose family had been in the country for generations. The Assad family had a son who, it seems, was into all manner of odd things, the most recent of which was a hot-air balloon, which he had brought to Haiti from America and occa-sionally flew over the shantytown skies.

As they approached the fence surrounding the field where the large wicker basket and deflated balloon rested on the ground, Guy let go of the hands of both his wife and the boy.

Lili walked on slowly with her son. For the last few weeks, she had been feeling as though Guy was lost to her each time he reached this point, twelve feet away from the balloon. As Guy pushed his hand through the barbed wire, she could tell from the look on his face that he was thinking of sitting inside the square basket while the smooth rainbow surface of the balloon itself floated above his head. During the day, when the field was open, Guy would walk up to the basket, staring at it with the same kind of longing that most men display when they admire very pretty girls.

Lili and the boy stood watching from a distance as Guy tried to push his hand deeper, beyond the chain link fence that separated him from the

3. Policeman or guard (French).

balloon. He reached into his pants pocket and pulled out a small pocket-knife, sharpening the edges on the metal surface of the fence. When his wife and child moved closer, he put the knife back in his pocket, letting his fingers slide across his son's tightly coiled curls.

"I wager you I can make this thing fly," Guy said.

"Why do you think you can do that?" Lili asked.   60

"I know it," Guy replied.

He followed her as she circled the sugar mill, leading to their favorite spot under a watch light. Little Guy lagged faithfully behind them. From this distance, the hot-air balloon looked like an odd spaceship.

Lili stretched her body out in the knee-high grass in the field. Guy reached over and tried to touch her between her legs.

"You're not one to worry, Lili," he said. "You're not afraid of the frogs, lizards, or snakes that could be hiding in this grass?"

"I am here with my husband," she said. "You are here to protect me if   65 anything happens."

Guy reached into his shirt pocket and pulled out a lighter and a crumpled piece of paper. He lit the paper until it burned to an ashy film. The burning paper floated in the night breeze for a while, landing in fragments on the grass.

"Did you see that, Lili?" Guy asked with a flame in his eyes brighter than the lighter's. "Did you see how the paper floated when it was burned? This is how that balloon flies."

"What did you mean by saying that you could make it fly?" Lili asked.

"You already know all my secrets," Guy said as the boy came charging towards them.

"Papa, could you play *Lago* with me?" the boy asked.   70

Lili lay peacefully on the grass as her son and husband played hide-and-seek. Guy kept hiding and his son kept finding him as each time Guy made it easier for the boy.

"We rest now." Guy was becoming breathless.

The stars were circling the peaks of the mountains, dipping into the cane fields belonging to the sugar mill. As Guy caught his breath, the boy raced around the fence, running as fast as he could to purposely make himself dizzy.

"Listen to what happened today," Guy whispered softly in Lili's ear.

"I heard you say that when you walked in the house tonight," Lili said.   75

"With the boy's play, I forgot to ask you."

The boy sneaked up behind them, his face lit up, though his brain was spinning. He wrapped his arms around both their necks.

"We will go back home soon," Lili said.

"Can I recite my lines?" asked the boy.

"We have heard them," Guy said. "Don't tire your lips."

80   The boy mumbled something under his breath. Guy grabbed his ear and twirled it until it was a tiny ball in his hand. The boy's face contorted with agony as Guy made him kneel in the deep grass in punishment.

Lili looked tortured as she watched the boy squirming in the grass, obviously terrified of the crickets, lizards, and small snakes that might be there.

"Perhaps we should take him home to bed," she said.

"He will never learn," Guy said, "if I say one thing and you say another."

Guy got up and angrily started walking home. Lili walked over, took her son's hand, and raised him from his knees.

85   "You know you must not mumble," she said.

"I was saying my lines," the boy said.

"Next time say them loud," Lili said, "so he knows what is coming out of your mouth."

That night Lili could hear her son muttering his lines as he tucked himself in his corner of the room and drifted off to sleep. The boy still had the book with his monologue in it clasped under his arm as he slept.

Guy stayed outside in front of the shack as Lili undressed for bed. She loosened the ribbon that held the old light blue cotton skirt around her waist and let it drop past her knees. She grabbed half a lemon that she kept in the corner by the folded mat that she and Guy unrolled to sleep on every night. Lili let her blouse drop to the floor as she smoothed the lemon over her ashen legs.

90   Guy came in just at that moment and saw her bare chest by the light of the smaller castor oil lamp that they used for the later hours of the night. Her skin had coarsened a bit over the years, he thought. Her breasts now drooped from having nursed their son for two years after he was born. It was now easier for him to imagine their son's lips around those breasts than to imagine his anywhere near them.

He turned his face away as she fumbled for her nightgown. He helped her open the mat, tucking the blanket edges underneath.

Fully clothed, Guy dropped onto the mat next to her. He laid his head on her chest, rubbing the spiky edges of his hair against her nipples.

"What was it that happened today?" Lili asked, running her fingers along Guy's hairline, an angular hairline, almost like a triangle, in the middle of his forehead. She nearly didn't marry him because it was said that people with angular hairlines often have very troubled lives.

"I got a few hours' work for tomorrow at the sugar mill," Guy said. "That's what happened today."

95   "It was such a long time coming," Lili said.

It was almost six months since the last time Guy had gotten work there. The jobs at the sugar mill were few and far between. The people who had them never left, or when they did they would pass the job on to another family member who was already waiting on line.

Guy did not seem overjoyed about the one day's work.

"I wish I had paid more attention when you came in with the news," Lili said. "I was just so happy about the boy."

"I was born in the shadow of that sugar mill," Guy said. "Probably the first thing my mother gave me to drink as a baby was some sweet water tea from the pulp of the sugarcane. If anyone deserves to work there, I should."

"What will you be doing for your day's work?" 100

"Would you really like to know?"

"There is never any shame in honest work," she said.

"They want me to scrub the latrines."

"It's honest work," Lili said, trying to console him.

"I am still number seventy-eight on the permanent hire list," he said. "I 105 was thinking of putting the boy on the list now, so maybe by the time he becomes a man he can be up for a job."

Lili's body jerked forward, rising straight up in the air. Guy's head dropped with a loud thump onto the mat.

"I don't want him on that list," she said. "For a young boy to be on any list like that might influence his destiny. I don't want him on the list."

"Look at me," Guy said. "If my father had worked there, if he had me on the list, don't you think I would be working?"

"If you have any regard for me," she said, "you will not put him on the list."

She groped for her husband's chest in the dark and laid her head on it. 110 She could hear his heart beating loudly as though it were pumping double, triple its normal rate.

"You won't put the boy on any lists, will you?" she implored.

"Please, Lili, no more about the boy. He will not go on the list."

"Thank you."

"Tonight I was looking at that balloon in the yard behind the sugar mill," he said. "I have been watching it real close."

"I know." 115

"I have seen the man who owns it," he said. "I've seen him get in it and put it in the sky and go up there like it was some kind of kite and he was the kite master. I see the men who run after it trying to figure out where it will land. Once I was there and I was one of those men who were running and I actually guessed correctly. I picked a spot in the sugarcane fields. I picked the spot from a distance and it actually landed there."

"Let me say something to you, Guy—"

"Pretend that this is the time of miracles and we believed in them. I watched the owner for a long time, and I think I can fly that balloon. The first time I saw him do it, it looked like a miracle, but the more and more I saw it, the more ordinary it became."

"You're probably intelligent enough to do it," she said.

120   "I am intelligent enough to do it. You're right to say that I can."

"Don't you think about hurting yourself?"

"Think like this. Can't you see yourself up there? Up in the clouds somewhere like some kind of bird?"

"If God wanted people to fly, he would have given us wings on our backs."

"You're right, Lili, you're right. But look what he gave us instead. He gave us reasons to want to fly. He gave us the air, the birds, our son."

125   "I don't understand you," she said.

"Our son, your son, you do not want him cleaning latrines."

"He can do other things."

"Me too. I can do other things too."

A loud scream came from the corner where the boy was sleeping. Lili and Guy rushed to him and tried to wake him. The boy was trembling when he opened his eyes.

130   "What is the matter?" Guy asked.

"I cannot remember my lines," the boy said.

Lili tried to string together what she could remember of her son's lines. The words slowly came back to the boy. By the time he fell back to sleep, it was almost dawn.

The light was slowly coming up behind the trees. Lili could hear the whispers of the market women, their hisses and swearing as their sandals dug into the sharp-edged rocks on the road.

She turned her back to her husband as she slipped out of her nightgown, quickly putting on her day clothes.

135   "Imagine this," Guy said from the mat on the floor. "I have never really seen your entire body in broad daylight."

Lili shut the door behind her, making her way out to the yard. The empty gasoline containers rested easily on her head as she walked a few miles to the public water fountains. It was harder to keep them steady when the containers were full. The water splashed all over her blouse and rippled down her back.

The sky was blue as it was most mornings, a dark indigo-shaded turquoise that would get lighter when the sun was fully risen.

Guy and the boy were standing in the yard waiting for her when she got back.

"You did not get much sleep, my handsome boy," she said, running her wet fingers over the boy's face.

"He'll be late for school if we do not go right now," Guy said. "I want to drop him off before I start work." 140

"Do we remember our lines this morning?" Lili asked, tucking the boy's shirt down deep into his short pants.

"We just recited them," Guy said. "Even I know them now."

Lili watched them walk down the footpath, her eyes following them until they disappeared.

As soon as they were out of sight, she poured the water she had fetched into a large calabash, letting it stand beside the house.

She went back into the room and slipped into a dry blouse. It was never too early to start looking around, to scrape together that night's meal. 145

"Listen to what happened again today," Lili said when Guy walked through the door that afternoon.

Guy blotted his face with a dust rag as he prepared to hear the news. After the day he'd had at the factory, he wanted to sit under a tree and have a leisurely smoke, but he did not want to set a bad example for his son by indulging his very small pleasures.

"You tell him, son," Lili urged the boy, who was quietly sitting in a corner, reading.

"I've got more lines," the boy announced, springing up to his feet. "Papy, do you want to hear them?"

"They are giving him more things to say in the play," Lili explained, "because he did such a good job memorizing so fast." 150

"My compliments, son. Do you have your new lines memorized too?" Guy asked.

"Why don't you recite your new lines for your father?" Lili said.

The boy walked to the middle of the room and prepared to recite. He cleared his throat, raising his eyes towards the ceiling.

"*There is so much sadness in the faces of my people. I have called on their gods, now I call on our gods. I call on our young. I call on our old. I call on our mighty and the weak. I call on everyone and anyone so that we shall all let out one piercing cry that we may either live freely or we should die.*"

"I see your new lines have as much drama as the old ones," Guy said. 155 He wiped a tear away, walked over to the chair, and took the boy in his arms. He pressed the boy's body against his chest before lowering him to the ground.

"Your new lines are wonderful, son. They're every bit as affecting as the old." He tapped the boy's shoulder and walked out of the house.

"What's the matter with Papy?" the boy asked as the door slammed shut behind Guy.

"His heart hurts," Lili said.

After supper, Lili took her son to the field where she knew her husband would be. While the boy ran around, she found her husband sitting in his favorite spot behind the sugar mill.

160   "Nothing, Lili," he said. "Ask me nothing about this day that I have had."

She sat down on the grass next to him, for once feeling the sharp edges of the grass blades against her ankles.

"You're really good with that boy," he said, drawing circles with his smallest finger on her elbow. "You will make a performer of him. I know you will. You can see the best in that whole situation. It's because you have those stars in your eyes. That's the first thing I noticed about you when I met you. It was your eyes, Lili, so dark and deep. They drew me like danger draws a fool."

He turned over on the grass so that he was staring directly at the moon up in the sky. She could tell that he was also watching the hot-air balloon behind the sugar mill fence out of the corner of his eye.

"Sometimes I know you want to believe in me," he said. "I know you're wishing things for me. You want me to work at the mill. You want me to get a pretty house for us. I know you want these things too, but mostly you want me to feel like a man. That's why you're not one to worry about, Lili. I know you can take things as they come."

165   "I don't like it when you talk this way," she said.

"Listen to this, Lili. I want to tell you a secret. Sometimes, I just want to take that big balloon and ride it up in the air. I'd like to sail off somewhere and keep floating until I got to a really nice place with a nice plot of land where I could be something new. I'd build my own house, keep my own garden. Just *be* something new."

"I want you to stay away from there."

"I know you don't think I should take it. That can't keep me from wanting."

"You could be injured. Do you ever think about that?"

170   "Don't you ever want to be something new?"

"I don't like it," she said.

"Please don't get angry with me," he said, his voice straining almost like the boy's.

"If you were to take that balloon and fly away, would you take me and the boy?"

"First you don't want me to take it and now you want to go?"

"I just want to know that when you dream, me and the boy, we're always 175
in your dreams."

He leaned his head on her shoulders and drifted off to sleep. Her back ached as she sat there with his face pressed against her collar bone. He drooled and the saliva dripped down to her breasts, soaking her frayed polyester bra. She listened to the crickets while watching her son play, muttering his lines to himself as he went in a circle around the field. The moon was glowing above their heads. Winking at them, as Guy liked to say, on its way to brighter shores.

Opening his eyes, Guy asked her, "How do you think a man is judged after he's gone?"

How did he expect her to answer something like that?

"People don't eat riches," she said. "They eat what it can buy."

"What does that mean, Lili? Don't talk to me in parables. Talk to me 180 honestly."

"A man is judged by his deeds," she said. "The boy never goes to bed hungry. For as long as he's been with us, he's always been fed."

Just as if he had heard himself mentioned, the boy came dashing from the other side of the field, crashing in a heap on top of his parents.

"My new lines," he said. "I have forgotten my new lines."

"Is this how you will be the day of this play, son?" Guy asked. "When people give you big responsibilities, you have to try to live up to them."

The boy had relearned his new lines by the time they went to bed. 185

That night, Guy watched his wife very closely as she undressed for bed.

"I would like to be the one to rub that piece of lemon on your knees tonight," he said.

She handed him the half lemon, then raised her skirt above her knees. Her body began to tremble as he rubbed his fingers over her skin.

"You know that question I asked you before," he said, "how a man is 190 remembered after he's gone? I know the answer now. I know because I remember my father, who was a very poor struggling man all his life. I remember him as a man that I would never want to be."

Lili got up with the break of dawn the next day. The light came up quickly above the trees. Lili greeted some of the market women as they walked together to the public water fountain.

On her way back, the sun had already melted a few gray clouds. She found the boy standing alone in the yard with a terrified expression on his face, the old withered mushrooms uprooted at his feet. He ran up to meet her, nearly knocking her off balance.

"What happened?" she asked. "Have you forgotten your lines?"

The boy was breathing so heavily that his lips could not form a single word.

195 "What is it?" Lili asked, almost shaking him with anxiety.

"It's Papa," he said finally, raising a stiff finger in the air.

The boy covered his face as his mother looked up at the sky. A rainbow-colored balloon was floating aimlessly above their heads.

"It's Papa," the boy said. "He is in it."

She wanted to look down at her son and tell him that it wasn't his father, but she immediately recognized the spindly arms, in a bright flowered shirt that she had made, gripping the cables.

200 From the field behind the sugar mill a group of workers were watching the balloon floating in the air. Many were clapping and cheering, calling out Guy's name. A few of the women were waving their head rags at the sky, shouting, "Go! Beautiful, go!"

Lili edged her way to the front of the crowd. Everyone was waiting, watching the balloon drift higher up into the clouds.

"He seems to be right over our heads," said the factory foreman, a short slender mulatto with large buckteeth.

Just then, Lili noticed young Assad, his thick black hair sticking to the beads of sweat on his forehead. His face had the crumpled expression of disrupted sleep.

"He's further away than he seems," said young Assad. "I still don't understand. How did he get up there? You need a whole crew to fly these things."

205 "I don't know," the foreman said. "One of my workers just came in saying there was a man flying above the factory."

"But how the hell did he start it?" Young Assad was perplexed.

"He just did it," the foreman said.

"Look, he's trying to get out!" someone hollered.

A chorus of screams broke out among the workers.

210 The boy was looking up, trying to see if his father was really trying to jump out of the balloon. Guy was climbing over the side of the basket. Lili pressed her son's face into her skirt.

Within seconds, Guy was in the air hurtling down towards the crowd. Lili held her breath as she watched him fall. He crashed not far from where Lili and the boy were standing, his blood immediately soaking the landing spot.

The balloon kept floating free, drifting on its way to brighter shores. Young Assad rushed towards the body. He dropped to his knees and checked the wrist for a pulse, then dropped the arm back to the ground.

"It's over!" The foreman ordered the workers back to work.

Lili tried to keep her son's head pressed against her skirt as she moved closer to the body. The boy yanked himself away and raced to the edge of the field where his father's body was lying on the grass. He reached the body as young Assad still knelt examining the corpse. Lili rushed after him.

"He is mine," she said to young Assad. "He is my family. He belongs 215
to me."

Young Assad got up and raised his head to search the sky for his aimless balloon, trying to guess where it would land. He took one last glance at Guy's bloody corpse, then raced to his car and sped away.

The foreman and another worker carried a cot and blanket from the factory.

Little Guy was breathing quickly as he looked at his father's body on the ground. While the foreman draped a sheet over Guy's corpse, his son began to recite the lines from his play.

"A wall of fire is rising and in the ashes, I see the bones of my people. Not only those people whose dark hollow faces I see daily in the fields, but all those souls who have gone ahead to haunt my dreams. At night I relive once more the last caresses from the hand of a loving father, a valiant love, a beloved friend."

"Let me look at him one last time," Lili said, pulling back the sheet. 220

She leaned in very close to get a better look at Guy's face. There was little left of that countenance that she had loved so much. Those lips that curled when he was teasing her. That large flat nose that felt like a feather when rubbed against hers. And those eyes, those night-colored eyes. Though clouded with blood, Guy's eyes were still bulging open. Lili was searching for some kind of sign—a blink, a smile, a wink—something that would remind her of the man that she had married.

"His eyes aren't closed," the foreman said to Lili. "Do you want to close them, or should I?"

The boy continued reciting his lines, his voice rising to a man's grieving roar. He kept his eyes closed, his fists balled at his side as he continued with his newest lines.

"There is so much sadness in the faces of my people. I have called on their gods, now I call on our gods. I call on our young. I call on our old. I call on our mighty and the weak. I call on everyone and anyone so that we shall all let out one piercing cry that we may either live freely or we should die."

"Do you want to close the eyes?" the foreman repeated impatiently. 225

"No, leave them open," Lili said. "My husband, he likes to look at the sky."

1991

QUESTIONS

1. What do you think the hot-air balloon symbolizes to Assad, its owner? to Guy? to the implied author?
2. The title of the story alludes to a speech that Little Guy must memorize for a school play about Haiti's history. The lines of the speech are rich in figurative language, including metaphors: "*A wall of fire is rising and in the ashes, I see the bones of my people*" (par. 34). How do the title's allusion and other aspects of the story confirm that the speech's image of "a wall of fire" is symbolic?
3. What do you think happens at the end of A WALL OF FIRE RISING? Is Guy's plunge to the earth a deliberate suicide or an accident? What are some symbolic interpretations of both possibilities?

SUGGESTIONS FOR WRITING

1. Choose either story in this chapter, read it thoroughly, and follow the guidelines for responding to symbolism that appear earlier in this chapter. Write an essay in which you explore the various meanings of the story's major symbol and the way these emerge over the course of the story.
2. In THE BIRTH-MARK, Aylmer the scientist is portrayed as "spiritual" and "intellectual," in contrast with his crudely physical laboratory assistant, Aminadab (par. 25). Write an essay in which you argue that the allegory of Aylmer's terrible experiment on his wife refers not only to a man's desire for immortal beauty but also to his desire for control of everything physical, including the laborer.
3. Write an essay in which you compare the way symbolism works in THE BIRTH-MARK and A WALL OF FIRE RISING. For example, what is the effect and significance of both the magical atmosphere of Hawthorne's story and the way its characters explicitly refer to particular objects as symbols? How might symbolism work differently in Danticat's story because of its realistic, contemporary setting and plot and the fact that its characters don't explicitly refer to anything as a symbol?

6 THEME

At some point, a responsive reader of any story or novel will inevitably ask, *Why does it all matter? What does it all mean? What's the point?* When we ask what a text means, we are inquiring, at least in part, about its **theme**—a general idea or insight conveyed by the work in its entirety. Theme is certainly not the only way fiction matters nor the only thing we take away from our experience of reading it. Nor is theme fiction's *point* in the sense of its sole "objective" or "purpose." Yet theme is a fictional work's *point* in the sense of its "essential meaning" (or meanings). And our experience of any work isn't complete unless we grapple with the question of its theme.

On rare occasions, we might not have to grapple hard or look far: A very few texts, such as **fables** and certain fairy tales and folktales, explicitly state their themes. To succeed, however, even these works must ultimately "earn" their themes, bringing a raw statement to life through their characters, plot, setting, symbols, and narration. The following fable, by Aesop, succinctly makes its point through a brief dialogue.

AESOP
The Two Crabs

One fine day two crabs came out from their home to take a stroll on the sand. "Child," said the mother, "you are walking very ungracefully. You should accustom yourself to walking straight forward without twisting from side to side."

"Pray, mother," said the young one, "do but set the example yourself, and I will follow you."

"EXAMPLE IS THE BEST PRECEPT."

In most works, however, all the elements work together to imply an unstated theme that usually requires re-reading to decipher. Even the most careful and responsive readers will likely disagree about just what the theme is or how best to state it. And each statement of a given theme will imply a slightly different view of what matters most and why.

THEME(S): SINGULAR OR PLURAL?

In practice, readers disagree about the precise meaning of the term *theme*. One source of disagreement hinges on the question of whether any single work of fiction can convey more than one theme. On one side of the debate are those who use the word *theme* to refer only to the central or main idea of a work. On the other are those who use the term, as we generally do in this book, to refer to any idea a work conveys. While the former readers tend to talk about *the* theme, the latter instead refer to *a* theme in order to stress that each theme is only one of many. Regardless of whether we call all of the ideas expressed in a work *themes* or instead refer to some of them as *subthemes,* the essential points on which all agree are that a single literary work often expresses multiple ideas and that at least one of those ideas is likely to be more central or overarching and inclusive than others.

THE TWO CRABS demonstrates that even the most simple and straightforward of stories can convey more than one idea. This fable's stated theme, "Example is the best precept," emerges only because the little crab "back-talks" to its mother, implicitly suggesting another theme: that children are sometimes wiser than their parents or even that we sometimes learn by questioning, rather than blindly following, authority. The fact that crabs naturally "twist from side to side"—that no crab *can* walk straight—certainly adds **irony** to the fable, but might it also imply yet another theme?

BE SPECIFIC: THEME AS IDEA VERSUS TOPIC OR SUBJECT

Often, you will see the term *theme* used very loosely to refer to a topic or subject captured in a noun phrase—"the wisdom of youth," "loss of innocence," "the dangers of perfectionism"—or even a single noun—"loss," "youth," "grief," or "prejudice." Identifying such topics—especially those specific enough to require a noun phrase rather than a simple noun—can be a useful first step on the way to figuring out a particular story's themes and also to grouping stories together for the purpose of comparison.

For now, though, we urge you to consider this merely a first step on the path to interpreting a story. The truth is, we haven't yet said anything very insightful, revealing, or debatable about the meaning of an individual story until we articulate the idea it expresses *about* a topic such as love, prejudice, or grief. To state a theme in this much more restricted and helpful sense you will need at least one complete sentence. Note, however, that a complete sentence is still not necessarily a statement of theme. For example, an online student essay begins with the less than scintillating sentence, "In Nathaniel Hawthorne's 'The Birthmark' the reader finds several themes—guilt, evil, love and alienation." One reason this sentence is both unexciting and unhelpful is that—despite its specific list of topics—we could in fact substitute for THE BIRTH-MARK almost any other story in this book. (Try it yourself.) Notice how much more interesting things get, however, when we instead articulate the story's particular insight about just one of these very general topics: "Nathaniel Hawthorne's 'The Birth-Mark' shows us that we too often destroy the very thing we love by trying to turn the good into the perfect."

DON'T BE TOO SPECIFIC: THEME AS GENERAL IDEA

Though a theme is specific in the sense that it is a complete idea or statement rather than a topic, it is nonetheless a *general* idea rather than one that describes the characters, plot, or settings unique to one story. Theme is a general insight illustrated *through* these elements rather than an insight *about* any of them. Look again at the statement above—"Nathaniel Hawthorne's 'The Birth-Mark' shows us that we too often destroy the very thing we love by trying to turn the good into the perfect." Now compare this statement with one such as this: "In Nathaniel Hawthorne's 'The Birth-Mark,' the scientist Aylmer kills his wife because he can't tolerate imperfection." Though both statements are valid, only the first of them is truly a statement of theme—of what the story shows us about love through Aylmer rather than what it suggests about Aylmer himself.

THEME VERSUS MORAL

In some cases, a theme may take the form of a **moral**—a rule of conduct or maxim for living. But most themes are instead general observations and insights about how humans actually *do* behave, or about how life, the world, or some particular corner of it actually *is*, rather than moral imperatives about how people *should* behave or how life *should* ideally be. As one contemporary critic puts it, a responsive reader should thus "ask not *What does this story teach?* but *What does this story reveal?*" By the same token, we're usually on safer and more fertile ground if we phrase a theme as a statement rather than as a command. Hawthorne's "The Birth-Mark," for example, certainly demonstrates the dangers of arrogantly seeking a perfection that isn't natural or human. As a result, we might well be tempted to reduce its theme to a moral such as "Accept imperfection," "Avoid arrogance," or "Don't mess with Mother Nature." None of these statements is wholly inappropriate to the story. Yet each of them seems to underestimate the story's complexity and especially its implicit emphasis on all that humanity gains, as well as loses, in the search for perfection. As a result, a better statement of the story's theme might be "Paradoxically, both our drive for perfection and our inevitable imperfection together make us human."

As you decipher and discuss the themes of the stories that follow, keep in mind that to identify a theme is not to "close the case" but rather to begin a more searching investigation of the details that make each story vivid and unique. Theme is an abstraction from the story; the story and its details do not disappear or lose significance once distilled into theme, nor could you reconstruct a story merely from a statement of its theme. Indeed, theme and story are fused, inseparable. Or, as Flannery O'Connor puts it, "You tell a story because a statement [alone] would be inadequate." Often difficult to put into words, themes are nonetheless the essential common ground that helps you care about a story and relate it to your own life—even though it seems to be about lives and experiences very different from your own.

Tips for Identifying Themes

Because theme emerges from a work in its entirety and from all the other elements working together, there is no "one-size-fits-all" method for identifying theme. Here, however, are some things to look for and consider as you read and re-read the work.

TIP	EXAMPLE
1. Pay attention to the title. A title will seldom spell out in full a work's main theme, but some titles do suggest a central topic or topics or a clue to theme. Probe the rest of the story to see what, if any, insights about that topic it ultimately seems to offer.	What might Alice Munro's "Boys and Girls" suggest about how girls' initiation into adulthood differs from boys'?
2. List any recurring phrases and words, especially those for abstract concepts (e.g., love, honor). Certain concrete terms (especially if noted in the title) may likewise provide clues; objects of value or potency might attract significant attention in the text (an heirloom, a weapon, a	Versions of the word *blind* occur six times in the relatively short first paragraph of Raymond Carver's "Cathedral," and the word recurs throughout the story. What different kinds of blindness does the story depict? What truth or insight about blindness might it ultimately offer?

TIP	EXAMPLE
tree in a garden). Then probe the story to see how and where else it might implicitly deal with that concept or entity and what, if any, conclusions the story proposes.	
3. Identify any statements that the characters or narrator(s) make about a general concept, issue, or topic such as human nature, the natural world, and so on. Look, too, for statements that potentially have a general meaning or application beyond the story, even if they refer to a specific situation in it. Then consider whether and how the story as a whole corroborates, overturns, or complicates any one such view or statement.	In Nathaniel Hawthorne's "The Birth-Mark," the narrator suggests that "Nature . . . stamps ineffaceably on all her productions" some "flaw," either as a reminder "that they are temporary and finite, or that their perfection must be wrought by toil and pain" (par. 8). What does the narrator mean, and how might the story demonstrate or complicate this general statement?
4. If a character changes over the course of the story, articulate the truth or insight that he or she seems to discover. Then consider whether and how the story as a whole corroborates or complicates that insight.	By the end of John Updike's "A & P," its protagonist-narrator, Sammy, seems to realize that life is going to be harder for him than he previously realized. Does the story endorse his insight? If so, what might it suggest about why or for whom specifically life might be especially hard?
5. Identify a conflict depicted in the work and state it in general terms or turn it into a general question, leaving out any reference to specific characters, situations, and so on. Then think about the insight or theme that might be implied by the way the conflict is resolved.	Judith Ortiz Cofer's "Volar" seems to explore a conflict between dreams and wishes, on the one hand, and "reality," on the other. According to the story, what aspects of "reality" most interfere with the realization of our dreams?

STEPHEN CRANE
(1871–1900)
The Open Boat

One of fourteen children, Stephen Crane and his family moved frequently before settling, after his father's death in 1880, in Asbury Park, New Jersey. Crane sporadically attended various preparatory schools and colleges without excelling at much besides baseball. Determined to be a journalist, he left school for the last time in 1891 and began contributing pieces to New York newspapers. His city experiences led him to write *Maggie: A Girl of the Streets*, a realist social-reform novel published in 1893 at his own expense. His next novel, *The Red Badge of Courage* (1895), presented a stark picture of the Civil War and brought him widespread fame; many of his stories were published in the collections *The Open Boat and Other Tales of Adventure* (1898) and *The Monster and Other Stories* (1899). Crane served as a foreign correspondent, reporting on conflicts in Cuba and Greece, and lived his last years abroad, dying of tuberculosis at the age of twenty-eight.

A Tale Intended to Be after the Fact:[1] Being the Experience of Four Men from the Sunk Steamer Commodore

I

None of them knew the color of the sky. Their eyes glanced level and were fastened upon the waves that swept toward them. These waves were of the hue of slate, save for the tops, which were of foaming white, and all of the men knew the colors of the sea. The horizon narrowed and widened, and dipped and rose, and at all times its edge was jagged with waves that seemed thrust up in points like rocks.

Many a man ought to have a bathtub larger than the boat which here rode upon the sea. These waves were most wrongfully and barbarously abrupt and tall, and each froth-top was a problem in small-boat navigation.

The cook squatted in the bottom, and looked with both eyes at the six inches of gunwale which separated him from the ocean. His sleeves were rolled over his fat forearms, and the two flaps of his unbuttoned vest dan-

---

1. Crane had an experience very like the one here re-created in fiction. His autobiographical account of his adventure at sea was published in the *New York Press* on January 7, 1897.

gled as he bent to bail out the boat. Often he said, "Gawd! that was a narrow clip." As he remarked it he invariably gazed eastward over the broken sea.

The oiler, steering with one of the two oars in the boat, sometimes raised himself suddenly to keep clear of water that swirled in over the stern. It was a thin little oar, and it seemed often ready to snap.

The correspondent, pulling at the other oar, watched the waves and 5 wondered why he was there.

The injured captain, lying in the bow, was at this time buried in that profound dejection and indifference which comes, temporarily at least, to even the bravest and most enduring when, willy-nilly, the firm fails, the army loses, the ship goes down. The mind of the master of a vessel is rooted deep in the timbers of her, though he command for a day or a decade; and this captain had on him the stern impression of a scene in the grays of dawn of seven turned faces, and later a stump of a topmast with a white ball on it, that slashed to and fro at the waves, went low and lower, and down. Thereafter there was something strange in his voice. Although steady, it was deep with mourning, and of a quality beyond oration or tears.

"Keep'er a little more south, Billie," said he.

"A little more south, sir," said the oiler in the stern.

A seat in his boat was not unlike a seat upon a bucking broncho, and by the same token a broncho is not much smaller. The craft pranced and reared and plunged like an animal. As each wave came, and she rose for it, she seemed like a horse making at a fence outrageously high. The manner of her scramble over these walls of water is a mystic thing, and, moreover, at the top of them were ordinarily these problems in white water, the foam racing down from the summit of each wave requiring a new leap, and a leap from the air. Then, after scornfully bumping a crest, she would slide and race and splash down a long incline, and arrive bobbing and nodding in front of the next menace.

A singular disadvantage of the sea lies in the fact that after successfully 10 surmounting one wave you discover that there is another behind it just as important and just as nervously anxious to do something effective in the way of swamping boats. In a ten-foot dinghy one can get an idea of the resources of the sea in the line of waves that is not probable to the average experience, which is never at sea in a dinghy. As each slaty wall of water approached, it shut all else from the view of the men in the boat, and it was not difficult to imagine that this particular wave was the final outburst of the ocean, the last effort of the grim water. There was a terrible grace in the move of the waves, and they came in silence, save for the snarling of the crests.

In the wan light the faces of the men must have been gray. Their eyes must have glinted in strange ways as they gazed steadily astern. Viewed from a balcony, the whole thing would, doubtless, have been weirdly picturesque. But the men in the boat had no time to see it, and if they had had leisure, there were other things to occupy their minds. The sun swung steadily up the sky, and they knew it was broad day because the color of the sea changed from slate to emerald-green streaked with amber lights, and the foam was like tumbling snow. The process of the breaking day was unknown to them. They were aware only of this effect upon the color of the waves that rolled toward them.

In disjointed sentences the cook and the correspondent argued as to the difference between a life-saving station and a house of refuge. The cook had said: "There's a house of refuge just north of the Mosquito Inlet Light, and as soon as they see us they'll come off in their boat and pick us up."

"As soon as who see us?" said the correspondent.

"The crew," said the cook.

15   "Houses of refuge don't have crews," said the correspondent. "As I understand them, they are only places where clothes and grub are stored for the benefit of shipwrecked people. They don't carry crews."

"Oh, yes, they do," said the cook.

"No, they don't," said the correspondent.

"Well, we're not there yet, anyhow," said the oiler, in the stern.

"Well," said the cook, "perhaps it's not a house of refuge that I'm thinking of as being near Mosquito Inlet Light; perhaps it's a life-saving station."

20   "We're not there yet," said the oiler in the stern.

II

As the boat bounced from the top of each wave the wind tore through the hair of the hatless men, and as the craft plopped her stern down again the spray slashed past them. The crest of each of these waves was a hill, from the top of which the men surveyed for a moment a broad tumultuous expanse, shining and wind-riven. It was probably splendid, it was probably glorious, this play of the free sea, wild with lights of emerald and white and amber.

"Bully good thing it's an on-shore wind," said the cook. "If not, where would we be? Wouldn't have a show."

"That's right," said the correspondent.

The busy oiler nodded his assent.

25   Then the captain, in the bow, chuckled in a way that expressed humor, contempt, tragedy, all in one. "Do you think we've got much of a show now, boys?" said he.

Whereupon the three were silent, save for a trifle of hemming and hawing. To express any particular optimism at this time they felt to be childish and stupid, but they all doubtless possessed this sense of the situation in their minds. A young man thinks doggedly at such times. On the other

hand, the ethics of their condition was decidedly against any open suggestion of hopelessness. So they were silent.

"Oh, well," said the captain, soothing his children, "we'll get ashore all
right."

But there was that in his tone which made them think; so the oiler
quoth, "Yes! if this wind holds."

The cook was bailing. "Yes! if we don't catch hell in the surf."

Canton-flannel[2] gulls flew near and far. Sometimes they sat down on 30
the sea, near patches of brown seaweed that rolled over the waves with a
movement like carpets on a line in a gale. The birds sat comfortably in
groups, and they were envied by some in the dinghy, for the wrath of the
sea was no more to them than it was to a covey of prairie chickens a thousand miles inland. Often they came very close and stared at the men with
black bead-like eyes. At these times they were uncanny and sinister in
their unblinking scrutiny, and the men hooted angrily at them, telling them
to be gone. One came, and evidently decided to alight on the top of the
captain's head. The bird flew parallel to the boat and did not circle, but
made short sidelong jumps in the air in chicken fashion. His black eyes were
wistfully fixed upon the captain's head. "Ugly brute," said the oiler to the
bird. "You look as if you were made with a jackknife." The cook and the correspondent swore darkly at the creature. The captain naturally wished to
knock it away with the end of the heavy painter,[3] but he did not dare do it,
because anything resembling an emphatic gesture would have capsized
this freighted boat; and so, with his open hand, the captain gently and
carefully waved the gull away. After it had been discouraged from the
pursuit the captain breathed easier on account of his hair, and others
breathed easier because the bird struck their minds at this time as being
somehow gruesome and ominous.

In the meantime the oiler and the correspondent rowed; and also they
rowed. They sat together in the same seat, and each rowed an oar. Then
the oiler took both oars; then the correspondent took both oars, then the
oiler; then the correspondent. They rowed and they rowed. The very tick-
lish part of the business was when the time came for the reclining one in
the stern to take his turn at the oars. By the very last star of truth, it is easier
to steal eggs from under a hen than it was to change seats in the dinghy.
First the man in the stern slid his hand along the thwart and moved with
care, as if he were of Sèvres.[4] Then the man in the rowing-seat slid his hand
along the other thwart. It was all done with the most extraordinary care.

2. Plain-weave cotton fabric.
3. Mooring rope attached to the bow of a boat.
4. Type of fine china.

As the two sidled past each other, the whole party kept watchful eyes on the coming wave, and the captain cried: "Look out, now! Steady, there!"

The brown mats of seaweed that appeared from time to time were like islands, bits of earth. They were travelling, apparently, neither one way nor the other. They were, to all intents, stationary. They informed the men in the boat that it was making progress slowly toward the land.

The captain, rearing cautiously in the bow after the dinghy soared on a great swell, said that he had seen the lighthouse at Mosquito Inlet. Presently the cook remarked that he had seen it. The correspondent was at the oars then, and for some reason he too wished to look at the lighthouse; but his back was toward the far shore, and the waves were important, and for some time he could not seize an opportunity to turn his head. But at last there came a wave more gentle than the others, and when at the crest of it he swiftly scoured the western horizon.

"See it?" said the captain.

35   "No," said the correspondent, slowly; "I didn't see anything."

"Look again," said the captain. He pointed. "It's exactly in that direction."

At the top of another wave the correspondent did as he was bid, and this time his eyes chanced on a small, still thing on the edge of the swaying horizon. It was precisely like the point of a pin. It took an anxious eye to find a lighthouse so tiny.

"Think we'll make it, Captain?"

"If this wind holds and the boat don't swamp, we can't do much else," said the captain.

40   The little boat, lifted by each towering sea and splashed viciously by the crests, made progress that in the absence of seaweed was not apparent to those in her. She seemed just a wee thing wallowing, miraculously top up, at the mercy of five oceans. Occasionally a great spread of water, like white flames, swarmed into her.

"Bail her, cook," said the captain, serenely.

"All right, Captain," said the cheerful cook.

III

It would be difficult to describe the subtle brotherhood of men that was here established on the seas. No one said that it was so. No one mentioned it. But it dwelt in the boat, and each man felt it warm him. They were a captain, an oiler, a cook, and a correspondent, and they were friends—friends in a more curiously iron-bound degree than may be common. The hurt captain, lying against the water jar in the bow, spoke always in a low voice and calmly; but he could never command a more ready and swiftly obedient crew than the motley three of the dinghy. It was more than a mere recognition of what was best for the common safety. There was surely in it a quality that was personal and heart-felt. And after this devotion to the commander of the boat, there was this comradeship, that the correspondent, for instance, who had been taught to be cynical of men, knew even at the time was the best experience of his life. But no one said that it was so. No one mentioned it.

"I wish we had a sail," remarked the captain. "We might try my overcoat on the end of an oar, and give you two boys a chance to rest." So the cook and the correspondent held the mast and spread wide the overcoat; the oiler steered; and the little boat made good way with her new rig. Sometimes the oiler had to scull sharply to keep a sea from breaking into the boat, but otherwise sailing was a success.

Meanwhile the lighthouse had been growing slowly larger. It had now 45 almost assumed color, and appeared like a little gray shadow on the sky. The man at the oars could not be prevented from turning his head rather often to try for a glimpse of this little gray shadow.

At last, from the top of each wave, the men in the tossing boat could see land. Even as the lighthouse was an upright shadow on the sky, this land seemed but a long black shadow on the sea. It certainly was thinner than paper. "We must be about opposite New Smyrna,"[5] said the cook, who had coasted this shore often in schooners. "Captain, by the way, I believe they abandoned that life-saving station there about a year ago."

"Did they?" said the captain.

The wind slowly died away. The cook and the correspondent were not now obliged to slave in order to hold high the oar. But the waves continued their old impetuous swooping at the dinghy, and the little craft, no longer underway, struggled woundily over them. The oiler or the correspondent took the oars again.

Shipwrecks are *apropos* of nothing. If men could only train for them and have them occur when the men had reached pink condition, there would be less drowning at sea. Of the four in the dinghy none had slept any time worth mentioning for two days and two nights previous to embarking in the dinghy, and in the excitement of clambering about the deck of a foundering ship they had also forgotten to eat heartily.

For these reasons, and for others, neither the oiler nor the correspon- 50 dent was fond of rowing at this time. The correspondent wondered ingenuously how in the name of all that was sane could there be people who thought it amusing to row a boat. It was not an amusement; it was a diabolical punishment, and even a genius of mental aberrations could never conclude that it was anything but a horror to the muscles and a crime against the back. He mentioned to the boat in general how the amusement

5. Town on the Florida coast.

of rowing struck him, and the weary-faced oiler smiled in full sympathy. Previously to the foundering, by the way, the oiler had worked a double watch in the engine-room of the ship.

"Take her easy, now, boys," said the captain. "Don't spend yourselves. If we have to run a surf you'll need all your strength, because we'll sure have to swim for it. Take your time."

Slowly the land arose from the sea. From a black line it became a line of black and a line of white—trees and sand. Finally the captain said that he could make out a house on the shore. "That's the house of refuge, sure," said the cook. "They'll see us before long, and come out after us."

The distant lighthouse reared high. "The keeper ought to be able to make us out now, if he's looking through a glass," said the captain. "He'll notify the life-saving people."

"None of those other boats could have got ashore to give word of the wreck," said the oiler, in a low voice, "else the life-boat would be out hunting us."

55   Slowly and beautifully the land loomed out of the sea. The wind came again. It had veered from the northeast to the southeast. Finally a new sound struck the ears of the men in the boat. It was the low thunder of the surf on the shore. "We'll never be able to make the lighthouse now," said the captain. "Swing her head a little more north, Billie."

"A little more north, sir," said the oiler.

Whereupon the little boat turned her nose once more down the wind, and all but the oarsman watched the shore grow. Under the influence of this expansion doubt and direful apprehension were leaving the minds of the men. The management of the boat was still most absorbing, but it could not prevent a quiet cheerfulness. In an hour, perhaps, they would be ashore.

Their backbones had become thoroughly used to balancing in the boat, and they now rode this wild colt of a dinghy like circus men. The correspondent thought that he had been drenched to the skin, but happening to feel in the top pocket of his coat, he found therein eight cigars. Four of them were soaked with sea-water; four were perfectly scatheless. After a search, somebody produced three dry matches; and thereupon the four waifs rode impudently in their little boat and, with an assurance of an impending rescue shining in their eyes, puffed at the big cigars, and judged well and ill of all men. Everybody took a drink of water.

IV

"Cook," remarked the captain, "there don't seem to be any signs of life about your house of refuge."

60   "No," replied the cook. "Funny they don't see us!"

STEPHEN CRANE *The Open Boat* 261

A broad stretch of lowly coast lay before the eyes of the men. It was of low dunes topped with dark vegetation. The roar of the surf was plain, and sometimes they could see the white lip of a wave as it spun up the beach. A tiny house was blocked out black upon the sky. Southward, the slim lighthouse lifted its little gray length.

Tide, wind, and waves were swinging the dinghy northward. "Funny they don't see us," said the men.

The surf's roar was here dulled, but its tone was nevertheless thunderous and mighty. As the boat swam over the great rollers the men sat listening to this roar. "We'll swamp sure," said everybody.

It is fair to say here that there was not a life-saving station within twenty miles in either direction; but the men did not know this fact, and in consequence they made dark and opprobrious remarks concerning the eyesight of the nation's life-savers. Four scowling men sat in the dinghy and surpassed records in the invention of epithets.

"Funny they don't see us."   65

The light-heartedness of a former time had completely faded. To their sharpened minds it was easy to conjure pictures of all kinds of incompetency and blindness and, indeed, cowardice. There was the shore of the populous land, and it was bitter and bitter to them that from it came no sign.

"Well," said the captain, ultimately, "I suppose we'll have to make a try for ourselves. If we stay out here too long, we'll none of us have strength left to swim after the boat swamps."

And so the oiler, who was at the oars, turned the boat straight for the shore. There was a sudden tightening of muscles. There was some thinking.

"If we don't all get ashore," said the captain—"if we don't all get ashore, I suppose you fellows know where to send news of my finish?"

They then briefly exchanged some addresses and admonitions. As for   70
the reflections of the men, there was a great deal of rage in them. Perchance they might be formulated thus: "If I am going to be drowned—if I am going to be drowned—if I am going to be drowned, why, in the name of the seven mad gods who rule the sea, was I allowed to come thus far and contemplate sand and trees? Was I brought here merely to have my nose dragged away as I was about to nibble the sacred cheese of life? It is preposterous. If this old ninny-woman, Fate, cannot do better than this, she should be deprived of the management of men's fortunes. She is an old hen who knows not her intention. If she has decided to drown me, why did she not do it in the beginning and save me all this trouble? The whole affair is absurd. . . . But no; she cannot mean to drown me. She dare not drown me. She cannot drown me. Not after all this work." Afterward the man might have had an impulse to shake his fist at the clouds. "Just you drown me, now, and then hear what I call you!"

The billows that came at this time were more formidable. They seemed always just about to break and roll over the little boat in a turmoil of foam. There was a preparatory and long growl in the speech of them. No mind unused to the sea would have concluded that the dinghy could ascend these sheer heights in time. The shore was still afar. The oiler was a wily surf-man. "Boys," he said, swiftly, "she won't live three minutes more, and we're too far out to swim. Shall I take her to sea again, Captain?"

"Yes; go ahead!" said the captain.

This oiler, by a series of quick miracles and fast and steady oarsmanship, turned the boat in the middle of the surf and took her safely to sea again.

There was a considerable silence as the boat bumped over the furrowed sea to deeper water. Then somebody in gloom spoke: "Well, anyhow, they must have seen us from the shore by now."

75   The gulls went in slanting flight up the wind toward the gray, desolate east. A squall, marked by dingy clouds and clouds brick-red, like smoke from a burning building, appeared from the southeast.

"What do you think of those life-saving people? Ain't they peaches?"

"Funny they haven't seen us."

"Maybe they think we're out here for sport! Maybe they think we're fishin'. Maybe they think we're damned fools."

It was a long afternoon. A changed tide tried to force them southward, but wind and wave said northward. Far ahead, where coast-line, sea, and sky formed their mighty angle, there were little dots which seemed to indicate a city on the shore.

80   "St. Augustine."

The captain shook his head. "Too near Mosquito Inlet."

And the oiler rowed, and then the correspondent rowed; then the oiler moved. It was a weary business. The human back can become the seat of more aches and pains than are registered in books for the composite anatomy of a regiment. It is a limited area, but it can become the theatre of innumerable muscular conflicts, tangles, wrenches, knots, and other comforts.

"Did you ever like to row, Billie?" asked the correspondent.

"No," said the oiler. "Hang it."

85   When one exchanged the rowing-seat for a place in the bottom of the boat, he suffered a bodily depression that caused him to be careless of everything save an obligation to wiggle one finger. There was cold sea-water swashing to and fro in the boat, and he lay in it. His head, pillowed on a thwart, was within an inch of the swirl of a wave-crest, and sometimes a particularly obstreperous sea came inboard and drenched him once more. But these matters did not annoy him. It is almost certain that if the boat had capsized he would have tumbled comfortably out upon the ocean as if he felt sure that it was a great soft mattress.

"Look! There's a man on the shore!"

"There? See 'im? See 'im?"

"Yes, sure! He's walking along."

"Now he's stopped. Look! He's facing us!"

"He's waving at us!"   90

"So he is! By thunder!"

"Ah, now we're all right! Now we're all right! There'll be a boat out here for us in half an hour."

"He's going on. He's running. He's going up to that house there."

The remote beach seemed lower than the sea, and it required a searching glance to discern the little black figure. The captain saw a floating stick, and they rowed to it. A bath towel was by some weird chance in the boat, and, tying this on the stick, the captain waved it. The oarsman did not dare turn his head, so he was obliged to ask questions.

"What's he doing now?"   95

"He's standing still again. He's looking, I think. . . . There he goes again—toward the house. . . . Now he's stopped again."

"Is he waving at us?"

"No, not now; he was, though."

"Look! There comes another man!"

"He's running."   100

"Look at him go, would you!"

"Why, he's on a bicycle. Now he's met the other man. They're both waving at us. Look!"

"There comes something up the beach."

"What the devil is that thing?"

"Why, it looks like a boat."   105

"Why, certainly, it's a boat."

"No; it's on wheels."

"Yes, so it is. Well, that must be the life-boat. They drag them along shore on a wagon."

"That's the life-boat, sure."

"No, by God, it's—it's an omnibus."   110

"I tell you it's a life-boat."

"It is not! It's an omnibus. I can see it plain. See? One of these big hotel omnibuses."

"By thunder, you're right. It's an omnibus, sure as fate. What do you suppose they are doing with an omnibus? Maybe they are going around collecting the life-crew, hey?"

"That's it, likely. Look! There's a fellow waving a little black flag. He's standing on the steps of the omnibus. There comes those other two fellows. Now they're all talking together. Look at the fellow with the flag. Maybe he ain't waving it!"

115   "That ain't a flag, is it? That's his coat. Why, certainly, that's his coat."

"So it is: it's his coat. He's taken it off and is waving it around his head. But would you look at him swing it!"

"Oh, say, there isn't any life-saving station there. That's just a winter-resort."

"What's that idiot with the coat mean? What's he signaling, anyhow?"

"It looks as if he were trying to tell us to go north. There must be a life-saving station up there."

120   "No; he thinks we're fishing. Just giving us a merry hand. See? Ah, there, Willie!"

"Well, I wish I could make something out of those signals. What do you suppose he means?"

"He don't mean anything; he's just playing."

"Well, if he'd just signal us to try the surf again, or to go to sea and wait, or go north, or go south, or go to hell, there would be some reason in it. But look at him! He just stands there and keeps his coat revolving like a wheel. The ass!"

"There come more people."

125   "Now there's quite a mob. Look! Isn't that a boat?"

"Where? Oh, I see where you mean. No, that's no boat."

"That fellow is still waving his coat."

"He must think we like to see him to do that. Why don't he quit? It don't mean anything."

"I don't know. I think he is trying to make us go north. It must be that there's a life-saving station there somewhere."

130   "Say, he ain't tired yet. Look at 'im wave!"

"Wonder how long he can keep that up. He's been revolving his coat ever since he caught sight of us. He's an idiot. Why aren't they getting men to bring a boat out? A fishing boat—one of those big yawls—could come out here all right. Why don't he do something?"

"Oh, it's all right now."

"They'll have a boat out here for us in less than no time, now that they've seen us."

A faint yellow tone came into the sky over the low land. The shadows on the sea slowly deepened. The wind bore coldness with it, and the men began to shiver.

135   "Holy smoke!" said one, allowing his voice to express his impious mood, "if we keep on monkeying out here! If we've got to flounder out here all night!"

"Oh, we'll never have to stay here all night! Don't you worry. They've seen us now, and it won't be long before they'll come chasing out after us."

The shore grew dusky. The man waving a coat blended gradually into this gloom, and it swallowed in the same manner the omnibus and the group of people. The spray, when it dashed uproariously over the side, made the voyagers shrink and swear like men who were being branded.

"I'd like to catch the chump who waved the coat. I feel like socking him one, just for luck."

"Why? What did he do?"

"Oh, nothing, but then he seemed so damned cheerful." 140

In the meantime the oiler rowed, and then the correspondent rowed, and then the oiler rowed. Gray-faced and bowed forward, they mechanically, turn by turn, plied the leaden oars. The form of the lighthouse had vanished from the southern horizon, but finally a pale star appeared, just lifting from the sea. The streaked saffron in the west passed before the all-merging darkness, and the sea to the east was black. The land had vanished, and was expressed only by the low and drear thunder of the surf.

"If I am going to be drowned—if I am going to be drowned—if I am going to be drowned, why, in the name of the seven mad gods who rule the sea, was I allowed to come thus far and contemplate sand and trees? Was I brought here merely to have my nose dragged away as I was about to nibble the sacred cheese of life?"

The patient captain, drooped over the water-jar, was sometimes obliged to speak to the oarsman.

"Keep her head up! Keep her head up!"

"Keep her head up, sir." The voices were weary and low. 145

This was surely a quiet evening. All save the oarsman lay heavily and listlessly in the boat's bottom. As for him, his eyes were just capable of noting the tall black waves that swept forward in a most sinister silence, save for an occasional subdued growl of a crest.

The cook's head was on a thwart, and he looked without interest at the water under his nose. He was deep in other scenes. Finally he spoke. "Billie," he murmured, dreamfully, "what kind of pie do you like best?"

V

"Pie!" said the oiler and the correspondent, agitatedly. "Don't talk about those things, blast you!"

"Well," said the cook, "I was just thinking about ham sandwiches, and ——"

A night on the sea in an open boat is a long night. As darkness settled 150 finally, the shine of the light, lifting from the sea in the south, changed to full gold. On the northern horizon a new light appeared, a small bluish gleam on the edge of the waters. These two lights were the furniture of the world. Otherwise there was nothing but waves.

Two men huddled in the stern, and distances were so magnificent in the dinghy that the rower was enabled to keep his feet partly warm by thrusting them under his companions. Their legs indeed extended far under the rowing-seat until they touched the feet of the captain forward. Sometimes, despite the efforts of the tired oarsman, a wave came piling into the boat, an icy wave of the night, and the chilling water soaked them anew. They would twist their bodies for a moment and groan, and sleep the dead sleep once more, while the water in the boat gurgled about them as the craft rocked.

The plan of the oiler and the correspondent was for one to row until he lost the ability, and then arouse the other from his sea-water couch in the bottom of the boat.

The oiler plied the oars until his head drooped forward and the over-powering sleep blinded him; and he rowed yet afterward. Then he touched a man in the bottom of the boat, and called his name. "Will you spell me for a little while?" he said meekly.

"Sure, Billie," said the correspondent, awaking and dragging himself to a sitting position. They exchanged places carefully, and the oiler, cuddling down in the sea-water at the cook's side, seemed to go to sleep instantly.

155 The particular violence of the sea had ceased. The waves came without snarling. The obligation of the man at the oars was to keep the boat headed so that the tilt of the rollers would not capsize her, and to preserve her from filling when the crests rushed past. The black waves were silent and hard to be seen in the darkness. Often one was almost upon the boat before the oarsman was aware.

In a low voice the correspondent addressed the captain. He was not sure that the captain was awake, although this iron man seemed to be always awake. "Captain, shall I keep her making for that light north, sir?"

The same steady voice answered him. "Yes. Keep it about two points off the port bow."

The cook had tied a life-belt around himself in order to get even the warmth which this clumsy cork contrivance could donate, and he seemed almost stove-like when a rower, whose teeth invariably chattered wildly as soon as he ceased his labor, dropped down to sleep.

The correspondent, as he rowed, looked down at the two men sleeping underfoot. The cook's arm was around the oiler's shoulders, and, with their fragmentary clothing and haggard faces, they were the babes of the sea—a grotesque rendering of the old babes in the wood.

160 Later he must have grown stupid at his work, for suddenly there was a growling of water, and a crest came with a roar and a swash into the boat, and it was a wonder that it did not set the cook afloat in his life-belt. The

cook continued to sleep, but the oiler sat up, blinking his eyes and shaking with the new cold.

"Oh, I'm awful sorry, Billie," said the correspondent, contritely.

"That's all right, old boy," said the oiler, and lay down again and was asleep.

Presently it seemed that even the captain dozed, and the correspondent thought that he was the one man afloat on all the ocean. The wind had a voice as it came over the waves, and it was sadder than the end.

There was a long, loud swishing astern of the boat, and a gleaming trail of phosphorescence, like blue flame, was furrowed on the black waters. It might have been made by a monstrous knife.

Then there came a stillness, while the correspondent breathed with   165
open mouth and looked at the sea.

Suddenly there was another swish and another long flash of bluish light, and this time it was alongside the boat, and might almost have been reached with an oar. The correspondent saw an enormous fin speed like a shadow through the water, hurling the crystalline spray and leaving the long glowing trail.

The correspondent looked over his shoulder at the captain. His face was hidden, and he seemed to be asleep. He looked at the babes of the sea. They certainly were asleep. So, being bereft of sympathy, he leaned a little way to one side and swore softly into the sea.

But the thing did not then leave the vicinity of the boat. Ahead or astern, on one side or the other, at intervals long or short, fled the long sparkling streak, and there was to be heard the *whirroo* of the dark fin. The speed and power of the thing was greatly to be admired. It cut the water like a gigantic and keen projectile.

The presence of this biding thing did not affect the man with the same horror that it would if he had been a picnicker. He simply looked at the sea dully and swore in an undertone.

Nevertheless, it is true that he did not wish to be alone with the thing.   170
He wished one of his companions to awake by chance and keep him company with it. But the captain hung motionless over the water-jar and the oiler and the cook in the bottom of the boat were plunged in slumber.

VI

"If I am going to be drowned—if I am going to be drowned—if I am going to be drowned, why, in the name of the seven mad gods who rule the sea, was I allowed to come thus far and contemplate sand and trees?"

During this dismal night, it may be remarked that a man would conclude that it was really the intention of the seven mad gods to drown him, despite the abominable injustice of it. For it was certainly an abominable injustice to drown a man who had worked so hard, so hard. The man felt it would be a crime most unnatural. Other people had drowned at sea since galleys swarmed with painted sails, but still——

When it occurs to a man that nature does not regard him as important, and that she feels she would not maim the universe by disposing of him, he at first wishes to throw bricks at the temple, and he hates deeply the fact that there are no bricks and no temples. Any visible expression of nature would surely be pelleted with his jeers.

Then, if there be no tangible thing to hoot, he feels, perhaps, the desire to confront a personification and indulge in pleas, bowed to one knee, and with hands supplicant, saying, "Yes, but I love myself."

175 A high cold star on a winter's night is the word he feels that she says to him. Thereafter he knows the pathos of his situation.

The men in the dinghy had not discussed these matters, but each had, no doubt, reflected upon them in silence and according to his mind. There was seldom any expression upon their faces save the general one of complete weariness. Speech was devoted to the business of the boat.

To chime the notes of his emotions, a verse mysteriously entered the correspondent's head. He had even forgotten that he had forgotten this verse, but it suddenly was in his mind.

A soldier of the Legion lay dying in Algiers;
There was lack of woman's nursing, there was dearth of woman's tears;
But a comrade stood beside him, and he took the comrade's hand,
And he said, "I never more shall see my own, my native land."[6]

In his childhood the correspondent had been made acquainted with the fact that a soldier of the Legion lay dying in Algiers, but he had never regarded it as important. Myriads of his schoolfellows had informed him of the soldier's plight, but the dinning had naturally ended by making him perfectly indifferent. He had never considered it his affair that a soldier of the Legion lay dying in Algiers, nor had it appeared to him as a matter for sorrow. It was less to him than the breaking of a pencil's point.

Now, however, it quaintly came to him as a human, living thing. It was no longer merely a picture of a few throes in the breast of a poet, meanwhile drinking tea and warming his feet at the grate; it was an actuality—stern, mournful, and fine.

The correspondent plainly saw the soldier. He lay on the sand with his feet out straight and still. While his pale left hand was upon his chest in

6. From "Bingen on the Rhine," by Caroline Norton (1808–77).

an attempt to thwart the going of his life, the blood came between his fingers. In the far Algerian distance, a city of low square forms was set against a sky that was faint with the last sunset hues. The correspondent, plying the oars and dreaming of the slow and slower movements of the lips of the soldier, was moved by a profound and perfectly impersonal comprehension. He was sorry for the soldier of the Legion who lay dying in Algiers.

The thing which had followed the boat and waited had evidently grown 180 bored at the delay. There was no longer to be heard the slash of the cutwater, and there was no longer the flame of the long trail. The light in the north still glimmered, but it was apparently no nearer to the boat. Sometimes the boom of the surf rang in the correspondent's ears, and he turned the craft seaward then and rowed harder. Southward, some one had evidently built a watch-fire on the beach. It was too low and too far to be seen, but it made a shimmering, roseate reflection upon the bluff in back of it, and this could be discerned from the boat. The wind came stronger, and sometimes a wave suddenly raged out like a mountain-cat, and there was to be seen the sheen and sparkle of a broken crest.

The captain, in the bow, moved on his water-jar and sat erect. "Pretty long night," he observed to the correspondent. He looked at the shore. "Those life-saving people take their time."

"Did you see that shark playing around?"

"Yes, I saw him. He was a big fellow, all right."

"Wish I had known you were awake."

Later the correspondent spoke into the bottom of the boat. "Billie!" There 185 was a slow and gradual disentanglement. "Billie, will you spell me?"

"Sure," said the oiler.

As soon as the correspondent touched the cold, comfortable seawater in the bottom of the boat and had huddled close to the cook's life-belt he was deep in sleep, despite the fact that his teeth played all the popular airs. This sleep was so good to him that it was but a moment before he heard a voice call his name in a tone that demonstrated the last stages of exhaustion. "Will you spell me?"

"Sure, Billie."

The light in the north had mysteriously vanished, but the correspondent took his course from the wide-awake captain.

Later in the night they took the boat farther out to sea, and the captain 190 directed the cook to take one oar at the stern and keep the boat facing the seas. He was to call out if he should hear the thunder of the surf. This plan enabled the oiler and the correspondent to get respite together. "We'll give those boys a chance to get into shape again," said the captain. They curled down and, after a few preliminary chatterings and trembles, slept once more the dead sleep. Neither knew they had bequeathed to the cook the company of another shark, or perhaps the same shark.

As the boat caroused on the waves, spray occasionally bumped over the side and gave them a fresh soaking, but this had no power to break their repose. The ominous slash of the wind and the water affected them as it would have affected mummies.

"Boys," said the cook, with the notes of every reluctance in his voice, "she's drifted in pretty close. I guess one of you had better take her to sea again." The correspondent, aroused, heard the crash of the toppled crests.

As he was rowing, the captain gave him some whiskey-and-water, and this steadied the chills out of him. "If I ever get ashore and anybody shows me even a photograph of an oar——"

At last there was a short conversation.

195   "Billie! . . . Billie, will you spell me?"

"Sure," said the oiler.

VII

When the correspondent again opened his eyes, the sea and the sky were each of the gray hue of the dawning. Later, carmine and gold was painted upon the waters. The morning appeared finally, in its splendor, with a sky of pure blue, and the sunlight flamed on the tips of the waves.

On the distant dunes were set many little black cottages, and a tall white windmill reared above them. No man, nor dog, nor bicycle appeared on the beach. The cottages might have formed a deserted village.

The voyagers scanned the shore. A conference was held in the boat. "Well," said the captain, "if no help is coming, we might better try a run through the surf right away. If we stay out here much longer we will be too weak to do anything for ourselves at all." The others silently acquiesced in this reasoning. The boat was headed for the beach. The correspondent wondered if none ever ascended the tall wind-tower,[7] and if then they never looked seaward. This tower was a giant, standing with its back to the plight of the ants. It represented in a degree, to the correspondent, the serenity of nature amid the struggles of the individual—nature in the wind, and nature in the vision of men. She did not seem cruel to him then, nor beneficent, nor treacherous, nor wise. But she was indifferent, flatly indifferent. It is, perhaps, plausible that a man in this situation, impressed with the unconcern of the universe, should see the innumerable flaws of his life, and have them taste wickedly in his mind, and wish for another chance. A distinction between right and wrong seems absurdly clear to him, then, in this new ignorance of the grave-edge, and he understands that if he were

---

7. Watchtower for observing weather.

given another opportunity he would mend his conduct and his words, and be better and brighter during an introduction or at a tea.

"Now, boys," said the captain, "she is going to swamp sure. All we can 200 do is to work her in as far as possible, and then when she swamps, pile out and scramble for the beach. Keep cool now, and don't jump until she swamps sure."

The oiler took the oars. Over his shoulders he scanned the surf. "Captain," he said, "I think I'd better bring her about and keep her head-on to the seas and back her in."

"All right, Billie," said the captain. "Back her in." The oiler swung the boat then, and, seated in the stern, the cook and the correspondent were obliged to look over their shoulders to contemplate the lonely and indifferent shore.

The monstrous inshore rollers heaved the boat high until the men were again enabled to see the white sheets of water scudding up the slanted beach. "We won't get in very close," said the captain. Each time a man could wrest his attention from the rollers, he turned his glance toward the shore, and in the expression of the eyes during this contemplation there was a singular quality. The correspondent, observing the others, knew that they were not afraid, but the full meaning of their glances was shrouded.

As for himself, he was too tired to grapple fundamentally with the fact. He tried to coerce his mind into thinking of it, but the mind was dominated at this time by the muscles, and the muscles said they did not care. It merely occurred to him that if he should drown it would be a shame.

There were no hurried words, no pallor, no plain agitation. The men 205 simply looked at the shore. "Now, remember to get well clear of the boat when you jump," said the captain.

Seaward the crest of a roller suddenly fell with a thunderous crash, and the long white comber came roaring down upon the boat.

"Steady now," said the captain. The men were silent. They turned their eyes from the shore to the comber and waited. The boat slid up the incline, leaped at the furious top, bounced over it, and swung down the long back of the wave. Some water had been shipped, and the cook bailed it out.

But the next crest crashed also. The tumbling, boiling flood of white water caught the boat and whirled it almost perpendicular. Water swarmed in from all sides. The correspondent had his hands on the gunwale at this time, and when the water entered at that place he swiftly withdrew his fingers, as if he objected to wetting them.

The little boat, drunken with this weight of water, reeled and snuggled deeper into the sea.

"Bail her out, cook! Bail her out!" said the captain. 210

"All right, Captain," said the cook.

"Now, boys, the next one will do for us sure," said the oiler. "Mind to jump clear of the boat."

The third wave moved forward, huge, furious, implacable. It fairly swallowed the dinghy, and almost simultaneously the men tumbled into the sea. A piece of life-belt had lain in the bottom of the boat, and as the correspondent went overboard he held this to his chest with his left hand.

The January water was icy, and reflected immediately that it was colder than he had expected to find it off the coast of Florida. This appeared to his dazed mind as a fact important enough to be noted at the time. The coldness of the water was sad; it was tragic. This fact was somehow mixed and confused with his opinion of his own situation, so that it seemed almost a proper reason for tears. The water was cold.

215   When he came to the surface he was conscious of little but the noisy water. Afterward he saw his companions in the sea. The oiler was ahead in the race. He was swimming strongly and rapidly. Off to the correspondent's left, the cook's great white and corked back bulged out of the water, and in the rear the captain was hanging with his one good hand to the keel of the overturned dinghy.

There is a certain immovable quality to a shore, and the correspondent wondered at it amid the confusion of the sea.

It seemed also very attractive; but the correspondent knew that it was a long journey, and he paddled leisurely. The piece of life-preserver lay under him, and sometimes he whirled down the incline of a wave as if he were on a hand-sled.

But finally he arrived at a place in the sea where travel was beset with difficulty. He did not pause swimming to inquire what manner of current had caught him, but there his progress ceased. The shore was set before him like a bit of scenery on a stage, and he looked at it and understood with his eyes each detail of it.

As the cook passed, much farther to the left, the captain was calling to him, "Turn over on your back, cook! Turn over on your back and use the oar."

220   "All right, sir." The cook turned on his back, and, paddling with an oar, went ahead as if he were a canoe.

Presently the boat also passed to the left of the correspondent, with the captain clinging with one hand to the keel. He would have appeared like a man raising himself to look over a board fence if it were not for the extraordinary gymnastics of the boat. The correspondent marvelled that the captain could still hold to it.

They passed on nearer to shore—the oiler, the cook, the captain—and following them went the water-jar, bouncing gaily over the seas.

The correspondent remained in the grip of this strange new enemy, a current. The shore, with its white slope of sand and its green bluff topped with little silent cottages, was spread like a picture before him. It was very near to him then, but he was impressed as one who, in a gallery, looks at a scene from Brittany or Algiers.

He thought: "I am going to drown? Can it be possible? Can it be possible? Can it be possible?" Perhaps an individual must consider his own death to be the final phenomenon of nature.

But later a wave perhaps whirled him out of this small deadly current, 225 for he found suddenly that he could again make progress toward the shore. Later still he was aware that the captain, clinging with one hand to the keel of the dinghy, had his face turned away from the shore and toward him, and was calling his name. "Come to the boat! Come to the boat!"

In his struggle to reach the captain and the boat, he reflected that when one gets properly wearied drowning must really be a comfortable arrangement—a cessation of hostilities accompanied by a large degree of relief; and he was glad of it, for the main thing in his mind for some moments had been horror of the temporary agony; he did not wish to be hurt.

Presently he saw a man running along the shore. He was undressing with most remarkable speed. Coat, trousers, shirt, everything flew magically off him.

"Come to the boat!" called the captain.

"All right, Captain." As the correspondent paddled, he saw the captain let himself down to bottom and leave the boat. Then the correspondent performed his one little marvel of the voyage. A large wave caught him and flung him with ease and supreme speed completely over the boat and far beyond it. It struck him even then as an event in gymnastics and a true miracle of the sea. An overturned boat in the surf is not a plaything to a swimming man.

The correspondent arrived in water that reached only to his waist, but 230 his condition did not enable him to stand for more than a moment. Each wave knocked him into a heap, and the undertow pulled at him.

Then he saw the man who had been running and undressing, and undressing and running, come bounding into the water. He dragged ashore the cook, and then waded toward the captain; but the captain waved him away and sent him to the correspondent. He was naked—naked as a tree in winter; but a halo was about his head, and he shone like a saint. He gave a strong pull, and a long drag, and a bully heave at the correspondent's hand. The correspondent, schooled in the minor formulae, said, "Thanks, old man." But suddenly the man cried, "What's that?" He pointed a swift finger. The correspondent said, "Go."

In the shallows, face downward, lay the oiler. His forehead touched sand that was periodically, between each wave, clear of the sea.

The correspondent did not know all that transpired afterward. When he achieved safe ground he fell, striking the sand with each particular part of his body. It was as if he had dropped from a roof, but the thud was grateful to him.

It seems that instantly the beach was populated with men with blankets, clothes, and flasks, and women with coffee-pots and all the remedies sacred to their minds. The welcome of the land to the men from the sea was warm and generous; but a still and dripping shape was carried slowly up the beach, and the land's welcome for it could only be the different and sinister hospitality of the grave.

235   When it came night, the white waves paced to and fro in the moonlight, and the wind brought the sound of the great sea's voice to the men on the shore, and they felt that they could then be interpreters.

1898

QUESTIONS

1. When do you become aware that your view of events in THE OPEN BOAT is limited to things seen and heard by the four men in the boat? In what specific ways is that important to the story's effect? Where does the story's perspective "expand" to include larger reflections and generalizations? How are they justified by the narrative point of view?
2. Examine paragraphs 3–6; then differentiate the four men as fully as you can. What distinguishing features help you keep them straight as the narrative proceeds? What facts are provided later about each of the men? In which of the men do you become most interested as the story develops?
3. Which, if any, of the following seem like apt statements of the story's theme, and why? Which, if any, seems most central?

   a. All human beings are ultimately the same in that we are all equally powerless against nature.
   b. As the novelist George Eliot once said, "Character is destiny."
   c. In the face of disaster, people tend to become selfless, forgetting their differences and bonding together.
   d. Our individual fates are ultimately determined by forces beyond our control.
   e. We can never know the full truth; all we have is our own limited individual perspective.
   f. Pride is man's downfall.

YASUNARI KAWABATA
(1899–1972)
The Grasshopper and the Bell Cricket[1]

Born in Osaka, Japan, to a prosperous family, Yasunari Kawabata graduated from Tokyo Imperial
University in 1924 and had his first literary success with the semiautobiographical novella *The
Izu Dancer* (1926). He cofounded the journal *Contemporary Literature* in support
of the Neosensualist movement, which had much in common with the European
literary movements of Dadaism, Expressionism, and Cubism. His best-known
works include *Snow Country* (1937), *Thousand Cranes* (1952), *The Sound of the
Mountain* (1954), *The Lake* (1955), *The Sleeping Beauty* (1960), *The Old Capital*
(1962), and the collection *Palm-of-the-Hand Stories* (translated in 1988). Kawabata
was awarded the Nobel Prize for Literature in 1968. After long suffering from
poor health, he committed suicide in 1972.

Walking along the tile-roofed wall of the university, I turned aside
and approached the upper school. Behind the white board fence
of the school playground, from a dusky clump of bushes under the black
cherry trees, an insect's voice could be heard. Walking more slowly and
listening to that voice, and furthermore reluctant to part with it, I turned
right so as not to leave the playground behind. When I turned to the left,
the fence gave way to an embankment planted with orange trees. At the
corner, I exclaimed with surprise. My eyes gleaming at what they saw up
ahead, I hurried forward with short steps.

At the base of the embankment was a bobbing cluster of beautiful varicolored lanterns, such as one might see at a festival in a remote country
village. Without going any farther, I knew that it was a group of children
on an insect chase among the bushes of the embankment. There were
about twenty lanterns. Not only were there crimson, pink, indigo, green,
purple, and yellow lanterns, but one lantern glowed with five colors at
once. There were even some little red store-bought lanterns. But most of
the lanterns were beautiful square ones which the children had made
themselves with love and care. The bobbing lanterns, the coming together
of children on this lonely slope—surely it was a scene from a fairy tale?

1. Translated by Lane Dunlop.

One of the neighborhood children had heard an insect sing on this slope one night. Buying a red lantern, he had come back the next night to find the insect. The night after that, there was another child. This new child could not buy a lantern. Cutting out the back and front of a small carton and papering it, he placed a candle on the bottom and fastened a string to the top. The number of children grew to five, and then to seven. They learned how to color the paper that they stretched over the windows of the cutout cartons, and to draw pictures on it. Then these wise child-artists, cutting out round, three-cornered, and lozenge leaf shapes in the cartons, coloring each little window a different color, with circles and diamonds, red and green, made a single and whole decorative pattern. The child with the red lantern discarded it as a tasteless object that could be bought at a store. The child who had made his own lantern threw it away because the design was too simple. The pattern of light that one had had in hand the night before was unsatisfying the morning after. Each day, with cardboard, paper, brush, scissors, penknife, and glue, the children made new lanterns out of their hearts and minds. Look at my lantern! Be the most unusually beautiful! And each night, they had gone out on their insect hunts. These were the twenty children and their beautiful lanterns that I now saw before me.

Wide-eyed, I loitered near them. Not only did the square lanterns have old-fashioned patterns and flower shapes, but the names of the children who had made them were cut out in squared letters of the syllabary. Different from the painted-over red lanterns, others (made of thick cutout cardboard) had their designs drawn onto the paper windows, so that the candle's light seemed to emanate from the form and color of the design itself. The lanterns brought out the shadows of the bushes like dark light. The children crouched eagerly on the slope wherever they heard an insect's voice.

5   "Does anyone want a grasshopper?" A boy, who had been peering into a bush about thirty feet away from the other children, suddenly straightened up and shouted.

"Yes! Give it to me!" Six or seven children came running up. Crowding behind the boy who had found the grasshopper, they peered into the bush. Brushing away their outstretched hands and spreading out his arms, the boy stood as if guarding the bush where the insect was. Waving the lantern in his right hand, he called again to the other children.

"Does anyone want a grasshopper? A grasshopper!"

"I do! I do!" Four or five more children came running up. It seemed you could not catch a more precious insect than a grasshopper. The boy called out a third time.

"Doesn't anyone want a grasshopper?"

10   Two or three more children came over.

"Yes. I want it."

It was a girl, who just now had come up behind the boy who'd discovered the insect. Lightly turning his body, the boy gracefully bent forward. Shifting the lantern to his left hand, he reached his right hand into the bush.

"It's a grasshopper."

"Yes. I'd like to have it."

The boy quickly stood up. As if to say "Here!" he thrust out his fist that 15 held the insect at the girl. She, slipping her left wrist under the string of her lantern, enclosed the boy's fist with both hands. The boy quietly opened his fist. The insect was transferred to between the girl's thumb and index finger.

"Oh! It's not a grasshopper. It's a bell cricket." The girl's eyes shone as she looked at the small brown insect.

"It's a bell cricket! It's a bell cricket!" The children echoed in an envious chorus.

"It's a bell cricket. It's a bell cricket."

Glancing with her bright intelligent eyes at the boy who had given her the cricket, the girl opened the little insect cage hanging at her side and released the cricket in it.

"It's a bell cricket." 20

"Oh, it's a bell cricket," the boy who'd captured it muttered. Holding up the insect cage close to his eyes, he looked inside it. By the light of his beautiful many colored lantern, also held up at eye level, he glanced at the girl's face.

Oh, I thought. I felt slightly jealous of the boy, and sheepish. How silly of me not to have understood his actions until now! Then I caught my breath in surprise. Look! It was something on the girl's breast which neither the boy who had given her the cricket, nor she who had accepted it, nor the children who were looking at them noticed.

In the faint greenish light that fell on the girl's breast, wasn't the name "Fujio" clearly discernible? The boy's lantern, which he held up alongside the girl's insect cage, inscribed his name, cut out in the green papered aperture, onto her white cotton kimono. The girl's lantern, which dangled loosely from her wrist, did not project its pattern so clearly, but still one could make out, in a trembling patch of red on the boy's waist, the name "Kiyoko." This chance interplay of red and green—if it was chance or play—neither Fujio nor Kiyoko knew about.

Even if they remembered forever that Fujio had given her the cricket and that Kiyoko had accepted it, not even in dreams would Fujio ever know that his name had been written in green on Kiyoko's breast or that Kiyoko's name had been inscribed in red on his waist, nor would Kiyoko ever know that Fujio's name had been inscribed in green on her breast or that her own name had been written in red on Fujio's waist.

25   Fujio! Even when you have become a young man, laugh with pleasure at a girl's delight when, told that it's a grasshopper, she is given a bell cricket; laugh with affection at a girl's chagrin when, told that it's a bell cricket, she is given a grasshopper.

Even if you have the wit to look by yourself in a bush away from the other children, there are not many bell crickets in the world. Probably you will find a girl like a grasshopper whom you think is a bell cricket.

And finally, to your clouded, wounded heart, even a true bell cricket will seem like a grasshopper. Should that day come, when it seems to you that the world is only full of grasshoppers, I will think it a pity that you have no way to remember tonight's play of light, when your name was written in green by your beautiful lantern on a girl's breast.

1988

QUESTIONS

1. Who might the narrator of this story be? What clues are provided in the story?
2. What might the grasshopper and the bell cricket each come to symbolize in the story?
3. Might the final three paragraphs of this story come close to stating its theme(s)? How would you state the theme(s)?

SUGGESTIONS FOR WRITING

1. Choose any story in this chapter and write an essay exploring how character, point of view, setting, symbolism, or any recurring word or phrase contributes to the development of theme. Be sure to state that theme in a sentence.
2. Sometimes the theme in a work of literature can be expressed as a strong, clear statement: "A always follows from B," or "An X can never be a Y." More often, though, especially in modern literature, authors offer subtler, often ambiguous themes that deliberately undermine our faith in simple absolutes: "A doesn't necessarily always follow B," or "There are times when an X can be a Y." Write an essay in which you argue that one of the stories in this chapter has an "always" or "never" kind of theme, and contrast it to the more indeterminate theme of another story. Alternatively, use your essay to explain why we might be both tempted and wrong to see one of these stories as having an "always" or "never" theme. What is the overly simplistic version of the theme, and what is the more complex one?
3. Write an essay comparing the way Stephen Crane's THE OPEN BOAT and Nathaniel Hawthorne's THE BIRTH-MARK portray the relationship between human beings and nature. What is similar and different about the nature-related themes of the two stories?
4. Write your own fable, perhaps reworking or modernizing one by Aesop. Be sure both to state the theme and to make sure it is demonstrated in the fable itself.

READING MORE FICTION

TONI CADE BAMBARA
(1939–95)

The Lesson

Born in New York City, Toni Cade Bambara grew up in Harlem and Bedford-Stuyvesant, two of New York's poorest neighborhoods. She began writing as a child and took her last name from a signature on a sketchbook she found in a trunk belonging to her great-grandmother. (The Bambara are a people of northwest Africa.) After graduating from Queens College, she wrote fiction in "the predawn in-betweens" while studying for her MA at the City College of New York and working at a variety of jobs: dancer, social worker, recreation director, psychiatric counselor, college English teacher, literary critic, and film producer. Bambara began to publish her stories in 1962. Her fiction includes two collections of stories, *Gorilla, My Love* (1972) and *The Sea Birds Are Still Alive* (1977), as well as two novels, *The Salt Eaters* (1980) and *If Blessing Comes* (1987). Bambara also edited two anthologies, *The Black Woman* (1970) and *Stories for Black Folks* (1971).

B ack in the days when everyone was old and stupid or young and foolish and me and Sugar were the only ones just right, this lady moved on our block with nappy[1] hair and proper speech and no makeup. And quite naturally we laughed at her, laughed the way we did at the junk man who went about his business like he was some big-time president and his sorry-ass horse his secretary. And we kinda hated her too, hated the way we did the winos who cluttered up our parks and pissed on our handball walls and stank up our hallways and stairs so you couldn't halfway play hide-and-seek without a goddamn gas mask. Miss Moore was her name. The only woman on the block with no first name. And she was black as hell, cept for her feet, which were fish-white and spooky. And she was always planning these boring-ass things for us to do, us being my cousin, mostly, who lived on the block cause we all moved North the same time and to the same apartment then spread out gradual to breathe. And our parents would yank our heads into some kinda shape and crisp up our

1. Untreated and unstraightened, naturally curly or coiled.

clothes so we'd be presentable for travel with Miss Moore, who always looked like she was going to church, though she never did. Which is just one of the things the grown-ups talked about when they talked behind her back like a dog. But when she came calling with some sachet she'd sewed up or some gingerbread she'd made or some book, why then they'd all be too embarrassed to turn her down and we'd get handed over all spruced up. She'd been to college and said it was only right that she should take responsibility for the young ones' education, and she not even related by marriage or blood. So they'd go for it. Specially Aunt Gretchen. She was the main gofer in the family. You got some ole dumb shit foolishness you want somebody to go for, you send for Aunt Gretchen. She been screwed into the go-along for so long, it's a blood-deep natural thing with her. Which is how she got saddled with me and Sugar and Junior in the first place while our mothers were in a la-de-da apartment up the block having a good ole time.

So this one day Miss Moore rounds us all up at the mailbox and it's puredee hot and she's knockin herself out about arithmetic. And school suppose to let up in summer I heard, but she don't never let up. And the starch in my pinafore scratching the shit outta me and I'm really hating this nappy-head bitch and her goddamn college degree. I'd much rather go to the pool or to the show where it's cool. So me and Sugar leaning on the mailbox being surly, which is a Miss Moore word. And Flyboy checking out what everybody brought for lunch. And Fat Butt already wasting his peanut-butter-and-jelly sandwich like the pig he is. And Junebug punchin on Q.T.'s arm for potato chips. And Rosie Giraffe shifting from one hip to the other waiting for somebody to step on her foot or ask her if she from Georgia so she can kick ass, preferably Mercedes'. And Miss Moore asking us do we know what money is, like we a bunch of retards. I mean real money, she say, like it's only poker chips or monopoly papers we lay on the grocer. So right away I'm tired of this and say so. And would much rather snatch Sugar and go to the Sunset and terrorize the West Indian kids and take their hair ribbons and their money too. And Miss Moore files that remark away for next week's lesson on brotherhood, I can tell. And finally I say we oughta get to the subway cause it's cooler and besides we might meet some cute boys. Sugar done swiped her mama's lipstick, so we ready.

So we heading down the street and she's boring us silly about what things cost and what our parents make and how much goes for rent and how money ain't divided up right in this country. And then she gets to the part about we all poor and live in the slums, which I don't feature. And I'm ready to speak on that, but she steps out in the street and hails two cabs just like that. Then she hustles half the crew in with her and hands me a five-dollar bill and tells me to calculate 10 percent tip for the driver. And we're off. Me and Sugar and Junebug and Flyboy hangin out the window and hollering to everybody, putting lipstick on each other cause Flyboy a faggot anyway, and making farts with our sweaty armpits. But I'm mostly trying to figure how to spend this money. But they all fascinated with the meter ticking and Junebug starts laying bets as to how much it'll read when Flyboy can't hold his breath no more. Then Sugar lays bets as to how much it'll be when we get there. So I'm stuck. Don't nobody want to go for my plan, which is to jump out at the next light and run off to the first bar-b-que we can find. Then the driver tells us to get the hell out cause we there already. And the meter reads eighty-five cents. And I'm stalling to figure out the tip and Sugar say give him a dime. And I decide he don't need it bad as I do, so later for him. But then he tries to take off with Junebug foot still in the door so we talk about his mama something ferocious. Then we check out that we on Fifth Avenue[2] and everybody dressed up in stockings. One lady in a fur coat, hot as it is. White folks crazy.

"This is the place," Miss Moore say, presenting it to us in the voice she uses at the museum. "Let's look in the windows before we go in."

"Can we steal?" Sugar asks very serious like she's getting the ground rules 5 squared away before she plays. "I beg your pardon," say Miss Moore, and we fall out. So she leads us around the windows of the toy store and me and Sugar screamin, "This is mine, that's mine, I gotta have that, that was made for me, I was born for that," till Big Butt drowns us out.

"Hey, I'm goin to buy that there."

"That there? You don't even know what it is, stupid."

"I do so," he say punchin on Rosie Giraffe. "It's a microscope."

"Whatcha gonna do with a microscope, fool?"

"Look at things." 10

"Like what, Ronald?" ask Miss Moore. And Big Butt ain't got the first notion. So here go Miss Moore gabbing about the thousands of bacteria in a drop of water and the somethinorother in a speck of blood and the million and one living things in the air around us is invisible to the naked eye. And what she say that for? Junebug go to town on that "naked" and we rolling. Then Miss Moore ask what it cost. So we all jam into the window smudgin it up and the price tag say $300. So then she ask how long'd take for Big Butt and Junebug to save up their allowances. "Too long," I say. "Yeh," adds Sugar, "outgrown it by that time." And Miss Moore say no, you never outgrow learning instruments. "Why, even medical students and interns and," blah, blah, blah. And we ready to choke Big Butt for bringing it up in the first damn place.

"This here costs four hundred eighty dollars," say Rosie Giraffe. So we pile up all over her to see what she pointin out. My eyes tell me it's a chunk of

2. Major Manhattan street famous for its expensive, exclusive shops.

glass cracked with something heavy, and different-color inks dripped into the splits, then the whole thing put into a oven or something. But for $480 it don't make sense.

"That's a paperweight made of semi-precious stones fused together under tremendous pressure," she explains slowly, with her hands doing the mining and all the factory work.

"So what's a paperweight?" asks Rosie Giraffe.

15   "To weigh paper with, dumbbell," say Flyboy, the wise man from the East.[3]

"Not exactly," say Miss Moore, which is what she say when you warm or way off too. "It's to weigh paper down so it won't scatter and make your desk untidy." So right away me and Sugar curtsy to each other and then to Mercedes who is more the tidy type.

"We don't keep paper on top of the desk in my class," say Junebug, figuring Miss Moore crazy or lyin one.

"At home, then," she say. "Don't you have a calendar and a pencil case and a blotter[4] and a letter-opener on your desk at home where you do your homework?" And she know damn well what our homes look like cause she nosys around in them every chance she gets.

"I don't even have a desk," say Junebug. "Do we?"

20   "No. And I don't get no homework neither," say Big Butt.

"And I don't even have a home," say Flyboy like he do at school to keep the white folks off his back and sorry for him. Send this poor kid to camp posters, is his specialty.

"I do," says Mercedes. "I have a box of stationery on my desk and a picture of my cat. My godmother bought the stationery and the desk. There's a big rose on each sheet and the envelopes smell like roses."

"Who wants to know about your smelly-ass stationery," say Rosie Giraffe fore I can get my two cents in.

"It's important to have a work area all your own so that . . ."

25   "Will you look at this sailboat, please," say Flyboy, cuttin her off and pointin to the thing like it was his. So once again we tumble all over each other to gaze at this magnificent thing in the toy store which is just big enough to maybe sail two kittens across the pond if you strap them to the posts tight. We all start reciting the price tag like we in assembly. "Hand-crafted sailboat of fiberglass at one thousand one hundred ninety-five dollars."

---

3. Allusion to the biblical story of the three wise men who traveled from the East to visit the newborn Christ.

4. Framed sheet or pad of paper designed to protect a desktop from excess ink.

"Unbelievable," I hear myself say and am really stunned. I read it again for myself just in case the group recitation put me in a trance. Same thing. For some reason this pisses me off. We look at Miss Moore and she lookin at us, waiting for I dunno what.

"Who'd pay all that when you can buy a sailboat set for a quarter at Pop's, a tube of glue for a dime, and a ball of string for eight cents? "It must have a motor and a whole lot else besides," I say. "My sailboat cost me about fifty cents."

"But will it take water?" say Mercedes with her smart ass.

"Took mine to Alley Pond Park once," say Flyboy. "String broke, Lost it. Pity."

"Sailed mine in Central Park and it keeled over and sank. Had to ask   30 my father for another dollar."

"And you got the strap," laugh Big Butt. "The jerk didn't even have a string on it. My old man wailed on his behind."

Little Q.T. was staring hard at the sailboat and you could see he wanted it bad. But he too little and somebody'd just take it from him. So what the hell. "This boat for kids, Miss Moore?"

"Parents silly to buy something like that just to get all broke up," say Rosie Giraffe.

"That much money it should last forever," I figure.

"My father'd buy it for me if I wanted it."   35

"Your father, my ass," say Rosie Giraffe getting a chance to finally push Mercedes.

"Must be rich people shop here," say Q.T.

"You are a very bright boy," say Flyboy. "What was your first clue?" And he rap him on the head with the back of his knuckles, since Q.T. the only one he could get away with. Though Q.T. liable to come up behind you years later and get his licks in when you half expect it.

"What I want to know is," I says to Miss Moore though I never talk to her, I wouldn't give the bitch that satisfaction, "is how much a real boat costs? I figure a thousand'd get you a yacht any day."

"Why don't you check that out," she says, "and report back to the group?"   40 Which really pains my ass. If you gonna mess up a perfectly good swim day least you could do is have some answers. "Let's go in," she say like she got something up her sleeve. Only she don't lead the way. So me and Sugar turn the corner to where the entrance is, but when we get there I kinda hang back. Not that I'm scared, what's there to be afraid of, just a toy store. But I feel funny, shame. But what I got to be shamed about? Got as much right to go in as anybody. But somehow I can't seem to get hold of the door, so I step away for Sugar to lead. But she hangs back too. And I look at her and she looks at me and this is ridiculous. I mean, damn, I have never ever been shy about doing nothing or going nowhere. But then Mercedes steps up and then Rosie Giraffe and Big Butt crowd in behind and shove, and next thing we all stuffed into the doorway with only Mercedes squeezing past us, smoothing out her jumper and walking right down the aisle. Then the rest of us tumble in like a glued-together jigsaw done all wrong. And people lookin at us. And it's like the time me and Sugar crashed into the Catholic church on a dare. But once we got in there and everything so hushed and holy and the candles and the bowin and the handkerchiefs on all the drooping heads, I just couldn't go through with the plan. Which was for me to run up to the altar and do a tap dance while Sugar played the nose flute and messed around in the holy water. And Sugar kept givin me the elbow. Then later teased me so bad I tied her up in the shower and turned it on and locked her in. And she'd be there till this day if Aunt Gretchen hadn't finally figured I was lyin about the boarder[5] takin a shower.

Same thing in the store. We all walkin on tiptoe and hardly touchin the games and puzzles and things. And I watched Miss Moore who is steady watchin us like she waitin for a sign. Like Mama Drewery watches the sky and sniffs the air and takes note of just how much slant is in the bird formation. Then me and Sugar bump smack into each other, so busy gazing at the toys, 'specially the sailboat. But we don't laugh and go into our fat-lady bump-stomach routine. We just stare at that price tag. Then Sugar run a finger over the whole boat. And I'm jealous and want to hit her. Maybe not her, but I sure want to punch somebody in the mouth.

"Watcha bring us here for, Miss Moore?"

"You sound angry, Sylvia. Are you mad about something?" Givin me one of them grins like she tellin a grown-up joke that never turns out to be funny. And she's lookin very closely at me like maybe she plannin to do my portrait from memory. I'm mad, but I won't give her that satisfaction. So I slouch around the store bein very bored and say, "Let's go."

Me and Sugar at the back of the train watchin the tracks whizzin by large then small then gettin gobbled up in the dark. I'm thinkin about this tricky toy I saw in the store. A clown that somersaults on a bar then does chin-ups just cause you yank lightly at his leg. Cost $35. I could see me askin my mother for a $35 birthday clown. "You wanna who that costs what?" she'd say, cocking her head to the side to get a better view of the hole in my head. Thirty-five dollars could buy new bunk beds for Junior and Gretchen's boy. Thirty-five dollars and the whole household could go visit Granddaddy Nelson in the country. Thirty-five dollars would pay for the rent and the piano bill too. Who are these people that spend that

---

5. Tenant in another person's house.

much for performing clowns and $1,000 for toy sailboats? What kinda work they do and how they live and how come we ain't in on it? Where we are is who we are, Miss Moore always pointin out. But it don't necessarily have to be that way, she always adds then waits for somebody to say that poor people have to wake up and demand their share of the pie and don't none of us know what kind of pie she talkin about in the first damn place. But she ain't so smart cause I still got her four dollars from the taxi and she sure ain't gettin it. Messin up my day with this shit. Sugar nudges me in my pocket and winks.

Miss Moore lines us up in front of the mailbox where we started from, seem like years ago, and I got a headache for thinkin so hard. And we lean all over each other so we can hold up under the draggy-ass lecture she always finishes us off with at the end before we thank her for borin us to tears. But she just looks at us like she readin tea leaves. Finally she say, "Well, what did you think of F.A.O. Schwarz?"[6]

Rosie Giraffe mumbles, "White folks crazy."

"I'd like to go there again when I get my birthday money," says Mercedes, and we shove her out the pack so she has to lean on the mailbox by herself.

"I'd like a shower. Tiring day," say Flyboy.

Then Sugar surprises me by sayin, "You know, Miss Moore, I don't think all of us here put together eat in a year what that sailboat costs." And Miss Moore lights up like somebody goosed her. "And?" she say, urging Sugar on. Only I'm standin on her foot so she don't continue.

"Imagine for a minute what kind of society it is in which some people can spend on a toy what it would cost to feed a family of six or seven. What do you think?"

"I think," say Sugar pushing me off her feet like she never done before, cause I whip her ass in a minute, "that this is not much of a democracy if you ask me. Equal chance to pursue happiness means an equal crack at the dough, don't it?" Miss Moore is besides herself and I am disgusted with Sugar's treachery. So I stand on her foot one more time to see if she'll shove me. She shuts up, and Miss Moore looks at me, sorrowfully I'm thinkin. And somethin weird is goin on, I can feel it in my chest.

"Anybody else learn anything today?" lookin dead at me.

I walk away and Sugar has to run to catch up and don't even seem to notice when I shrug her arm off my shoulder.

"Well, we got four dollars anyway," she says.

"Uh hunh."

45

50

55

---

6. Manhattan toy store (1862–2015), once one of the world's largest, renowned for its expensive, one-of-a-kind offerings.

"We could go to Hascombs and get half a chocolate layer and then go to the Sunset and still have plenty money for potato chips and ice-cream sodas."

"Uh hunh."

"Race you to Hascombs," she say.

We start down the block and she gets ahead which is O.K. by me cause I'm goin to the West End and then over to the Drive to think this day through. She can run if she want to and even run faster. But ain't nobody gonna beat me at nuthin.

1972

AUTHORS ON THEIR WORK
TONI CADE BAMBARA (1939–95)

From "How She Came By Her Name" (1996)*

I went to the library and read a bunch of [short-story] collections and noticed that the voice was consistent, but it was a boring and monotonous voice. Oh, your voice is supposed to be consistent in a collection, I figured. Then I pulled out a lot of stories that had a young protagonist-narrator because that voice is kind of consistent—a young, tough, compassionate girl.

The book [Gorilla, My Love] came out, and I never dreamed that such a big fuss would be made. "Oh, Gorilla, My Love, what a radical use of dialect! What a bold, political angle on linguistics!" At first I felt like a fraud. It didn't have anything to do with a political stance. I just thought people lived and moved around in this particular language system. It is also the language system I tend to remember childhood in. This is the language many of us speak. It just seemed polite to handle the characters in this mode.

*"How She Came by Her Name: An Interview with Louis Massiah." *Deep Sightings and Rescue Missions: Fiction, Essays, and Conversations*, edited by Toni Morrison, Pantheon Books, 1996, pp. 201–45.

KATE CHOPIN
(1850–1904)
The Story of an Hour

Katherine O'Flaherty was born in St. Louis, Missouri, to a Creole-Irish family that enjoyed a high place in society. Her father died when she was four, and Kate was raised by her mother, grandmother, and great-grandmother. Very well read at a young age, she received her formal education at the St. Louis Academy of the Sacred Heart. In 1870, she married Oscar Chopin, a Louisiana businessman, and lived with him in Natchitoches Parish and New Orleans, where she became a close observer of Creole and Cajun life. Following her husband's sudden death in 1884, she returned to St. Louis, where she raised her six children and began her literary career. In slightly more than a decade she produced a substantial body of work, including the story collections *Bayou Folk* (1894) and *A Night in Acadie* (1897) and the classic novella *The Awakening* (1899), which was greeted with a storm of criticism for its frank treatment of female sexuality.

Knowing that Mrs. Mallard was afflicted with a heart trouble, great care was taken to break to her as gently as possible the news of her husband's death.

It was her sister Josephine who told her, in broken sentences; veiled hints that revealed in half concealing. Her husband's friend Richards was there, too, near her. It was he who had been in the newspaper office when intelligence of the railroad disaster was received, with Brently Mallard's name leading the list of "killed." He had only taken the time to assure himself of its truth by a second telegram, and had hastened to forestall any less careful, less tender friend in bearing the sad message.

She did not hear the story as many women have heard the same, with a paralyzed inability to accept its significance. She wept at once, with sudden, wild abandonment, in her sister's arms. When the storm of grief had spent itself she went away to her room alone. She would have no one follow her.

There stood, facing the open window, a comfortable, roomy armchair. Into this she sank, pressed down by a physical exhaustion that haunted her body and seemed to reach into her soul.

She could see in the open square before her house the tops of trees that ⁵ were all aquiver with the new spring life. The delicious breath of rain was in the air. In the street below a peddler was crying his wares. The notes of a distant song which some one was singing reached her faintly, and countless sparrows were twittering in the eaves.

There were patches of blue sky showing here and there through the clouds that had met and piled one above the other in the west facing her window.

She sat with her head thrown back upon the cushion of the chair, quite motionless, except when a sob came up into her throat and shook her, as a child who has cried itself to sleep continues to sob in its dreams.

She was young, with a fair, calm face, whose lines bespoke repression and even a certain strength. But now there was a dull stare in her eyes, whose gaze was fixed away off yonder on one of those patches of blue sky. It was not a glance of reflection, but rather indicated a suspension of intelligent thought.

There was something coming to her and she was waiting for it, fearfully. What was it? She did not know; it was too subtle and elusive to name. But she felt it, creeping out of the sky, reaching toward her through the sounds, the scents, the color that filled the air.

10   Now her bosom rose and fell tumultuously. She was beginning to recognize this thing that was approaching to possess her, and she was striving to beat it back with her will—as powerless as her two white slender hands would have been.

When she abandoned herself a little whispered word escaped her slightly parted lips. She said it over and over under her breath: "free, free, free!" The vacant stare and the look of terror that had followed it went from her eyes. They stayed keen and bright. Her pulses beat fast, and the coursing blood warmed and relaxed every inch of her body.

She did not stop to ask if it were or were not a monstrous joy that held her. A clear and exalted perception enabled her to dismiss the suggestion as trivial.

She knew that she would weep again when she saw the kind, tender hands folded in death; the face that had never looked save with love upon her, fixed and gray and dead. But she saw beyond that bitter moment a long procession of years to come that would belong to her absolutely. And she opened and spread her arms out to them in welcome.

There would be no one to live for her during those coming years; she would live for herself. There would be no powerful will bending hers in that blind persistence with which men and women believe they have a right to impose a private will upon a fellow-creature. A kind intention or a cruel intention made the act seem no less a crime as she looked upon it in that brief moment of illumination.

15   And yet she had loved him—sometimes. Often she had not. What did it matter! What could love, the unsolved mystery, count for in face of this

possession of self-assertion which she suddenly recognized as the strongest impulse of her being!

"Free! Body and soul free!" she kept whispering.

Josephine was kneeling before the closed door with her lips to the keyhold, imploring for admission. "Louise, open the door! I beg; open the door—you will make yourself ill. What are you doing, Louise? For heaven's sake open the door."

"Go away. I am not making myself ill." No; she was drinking in a very elixir of life through that open window.

Her fancy was running riot along those days ahead of her. Spring days, and summer days, and all sorts of days that would be her own. She breathed a quick prayer that life might be long. It was only yesterday she had thought with a shudder that life might be long.

She arose at length and opened the door to her sister's importunities. 20 There was a feverish triumph in her eyes, and she carried herself unwittingly like a goddess of Victory. She clasped her sister's waist, and together they descended the stairs. Richards stood waiting for them at the bottom.

Some one was opening the front door with a latchkey. It was Brently Mallard who entered, a little travel-stained, composedly carrying his gripsack and umbrella. He had been far from the scene of accident, and did not even know there had been one. He stood amazed at Josephine's piercing cry; at Richards' quick motion to screen him from the view of his wife.

But Richards was too late.

When the doctors came they said she had died of heart disease—of joy that kills.

1894

LOUISE ERDRICH
(b. 1954)

Love Medicine

Born in Minnesota of German American and French Chippewa descent, Louise Erdrich grew up in Wahpeton, North Dakota, as a member of the Turtle Mountain Band of Chippewa. She attended Dartmouth College and received an MFA in creative writing from Johns Hopkins University. Her first novel, *Love Medicine* (1984), a collection of linked stories, won the National Book Critics Circle Award. In her subsequent publications—*The Beet Queen* (1986), *Tracks* (1988), *The Bingo Palace* (1993), and *Tales of Burning Love* (1996)—she pursued her focus on the lives of Native Americans in contemporary North Dakota. In 1991 she jointly authored the best-selling novel *The Crown of Columbus* with her husband, Michael Dorris. Her recent works include the novels *The Last Report on the Miracles at Little No Horse* (2001), *The Plague of Doves* (2008), *The Round House* (2012), and *Books and Islands in Ojibwa County: Traveling through the Land of My Ancestors* (2014). She lives in Minnesota with her family and dogs.

I never really done much with my life, I suppose. I never had a television. Grandma Kashpaw had one inside her apartment at the Senior Citizens, so I used to go there and watch my favorite shows. For a while she used to call me the biggest waste on the reservation and hark back to how she saved me from my own mother, who wanted to tie me in a potato sack and throw me in a slough. Sure, I was grateful to Grandma Kashpaw for saving me like that, for raising me, but gratitude gets old. After a while, stale. I had to stop thanking her. One day I told her I had paid her back in full by staying at her beck and call. I'd do anything for Grandma. She knew that. Besides, I took care of Grandpa like nobody else could, on account of what a handful he'd gotten to be.

But that was nothing. I know the tricks of mind and body inside out without ever having trained for it, because I got the touch. It's a thing you got to be born with. I got secrets in my hands that nobody ever knew to ask. Take Grandma Kashpaw with her tired veins all knotted up in her legs like clumps of blue snails. I take my fingers and I snap them on the knots. The medicine flows out of me. The touch. I run my fingers up the maps of those rivers of veins or I knock very gentle above their hearts or I make a circling motion on their stomachs, and it helps them. They feel much better. Some women pay me five dollars.

I couldn't do the touch for Grandpa, though. He was a hard nut. You know, some people fall right through the hole in their lives. It's invisible, but they come to it after time, never knowing where. There is this woman here, Lulu Lamartine, who always had a thing for Grandpa. She loved him since she was a girl and always said he was a genius. Now she says that his mind got so full it exploded.

How can I doubt that? I know the feeling when your mental power builds up too far. I always used to say that's why the Indians got drunk. Even statistically we're the smartest people on the earth. Anyhow with Grandpa I couldn't hardly believe it, because all my youth he stood out as a hero to me. When he started getting toward second childhood he went through different moods. He would stand in the woods and cry at the top of his shirt. It scared me, scared everyone, Grandma worst of all.

Yet he was so smart—do you believe it?—that he *knew* he was getting 5
foolish.

He said so. He told me that December I failed school and come back
on the train to Hoopdance. I didn't have nowhere else to go. He picked me
up there and he said it straight out: "I'm getting into my second childhood." And then he said something else I still remember: "I been chosen
for it. I couldn't say no." So I figure that a man so smart all his life—tribal
chairman and the star of movies and even pictured in the statehouse and
on cans of snuff—would know what he's doing by saying yes. I think he
was called to second childhood like anybody else gets a call for the priest-
hood or the army or whatever. So I really did not listen too hard when the
doctor said this was some kind of disease old people got eating too much
sugar. You just can't tell me that a man who went to Washington and gave
them bureaucrats what for could lose his mind from eating too much
Milky Way. No, he put second childhood on himself.

Behind those songs he sings out in the middle of Mass, and back of
those stories that everybody knows by heart, Grandpa is thinking hard
about life. I know the feeling. Sometimes I'll throw up a smokescreen to
think behind. I'll hitch up to Winnipeg and play the Space Invaders[1] for
six hours, but all the time there and back I will be thinking some fairly
deep thoughts that surprise even me, and I'm used to it. As for him, if it
was just the thoughts there wouldn't be no problem. Smokescreen is what
irritates the social structure, see, and Grandpa has done things that just
distract people to the point they want to throw him in the cookie jar where
they keep the mentally insane. He's far from that, I know for sure, but
even Grandma had trouble keeping her patience once he started sneaking
off to Lamartine's place. He's not supposed to have his candy, and Lulu
feeds it to him. That's *one* of the reasons why he goes.

Grandma tried to get me to put the touch on Grandpa soon after he
began stepping out. I didn't want to, but before Grandma started telling
me again what a bad state my bare behind was in when she first took me
home, I thought I should at least pretend.

I put my hands on either side of Grandpa's head. You wouldn't look at
him and say he was crazy. He's a fine figure of a man, as Lamartine would
say, with all his hair and half his teeth, a beak like a hawk, and cheeks
like the blades of a hatchet. They put his picture on all the tourist guides
to North Dakota and even copied his face for artistic paintings. I guess
you could call him a monument all of himself. He started grinning when
I put my hands on his templates, and I knew right then he knew how
come I touched him. I knew the smokescreen was going to fall.

1. Extremely popular and influential 1980s arcade video game.

10   And I was right: just for a moment it fell.

"Let's pitch whoopee," he said across my shoulder to Grandma.

They don't use that expression much around here anymore, but for damn sure it must have meant something. It got her goat right quick.

She threw my hands off his head herself and stood in front of him, overmatching him pound for pound, and taller too, for she had a growth spurt in middle age while he had shrunk, so now the length and breadth of her surpassed him. She glared and spoke her piece into his face about how he was off at all hours tomcatting and chasing Lamartine again and making a damn old fool of himself.

"And you got no more whoopee to pitch anymore anyhow!" she yelled at last, surprising me so my jaw just dropped, for us kids all had pretended for so long that those rustling sounds we heard from their side of the room at night never happened. She sure had pretended it, up till now, anyway. I saw that tears were in her eyes. And that's when I saw how much grief and love she felt for him. And it gave me a real shock to the system. You see I thought love got easier over the years so it didn't hurt so bad when it hurt, or feel so good when it felt good. I thought it smoothed out and old people hardly noticed it. I thought it curled up and died, I guess. Now I saw it rear up like a whip and lash.

15   She loved him. She was jealous. She mourned him like the dead.

And he just smiled into the air, trapped in the seams of his mind.

So I didn't know what to do. I was in a laundry then. They was like parents to me, the way they had took me home and reared me. I could see her point for wanting to get him back the way he was so at least she could argue with him, sleep with him, not be shamed out by Lamartine. She'd always love him. That hit me like a ton of bricks. For one whole day I felt this odd feeling that cramped my hands. When you have the touch, that's where longing gets you. I never loved like that. It made me feel all inspired to see them fight, and I wanted to go out and find a woman who I would love until one of us died or went crazy. But I'm not like that really. From time to time I heal a person all up good inside, however when it comes to the long shot I doubt that I got staying power.

And you need that, staying power, going out to love somebody. I knew this quality was not going to jump on me with no effort. So I turned my thoughts back to Grandma and Grandpa. I felt her side of it with my hands and my tangled guts, and I felt his side of it within the stretch of my mentality. He had gone out to lunch one day and never came back. He was fishing in the middle of Matchimanito. And there was big thoughts on his line, and he kept throwing them back for even bigger ones that would explain to him, say, the meaning of how we got here and why we have to leave so soon. All in all, I could not see myself treating Grandpa with the touch, bringing him back, when the real part of him had chose to be off thinking somewhere. It was only the rest of him that stayed around causing trouble, after all, and we could handle most of it without any problem. Besides, it was hard to argue with his reasons for doing some things. Take Holy Mass. I used to go there just every so often, when I got frustrated mostly, because even though I know the Higher Power dwells everyplace, there's something very calming about the cool greenish inside of our mission. Or so I thought, anyway. Grandpa was the one who stripped off my delusions in this matter, for it was he who busted right through what Father calls the sacred serenity of the place.

We filed in that time. Me and Grandpa. We sat down in our pews. 20 Then the rosary got started up pre-Mass and that's when Grandpa filled up his chest and opened his mouth and belted out them words.

HAIL MARIE FULL OF GRACE.

He had a powerful set of lungs.

And he kept on like that. He did not let up. He hollered and he yelled them prayers, and I guess people was used to him by now, because they only muttered theirs and did not quit and gawk like I did. I was getting red-faced, I admit. I give him the elbow once or twice, but that wasn't nothing to him. He kept on. He shrieked to heaven and he pleaded like a movie actor and he pounded his chest like Tarzan in the Lord I Am Not Worthies. I thought he might hurt himself. Then after a while I guess I got used to it, and that's when I wondered: how come?

So afterwards I out and asked him. "How come? How come you yelled?"

"God don't hear me otherwise," said Grandpa Kashpaw. 25

I sweat. I broke right into a little cold sweat at my hairline because I knew this was perfectly right and for years not one damn other person had noticed it. God's been going deaf. Since the Old Testament, God's been deafening up on us. I read, see. Besides the dictionary, which I'm constantly in use of, I had this Bible once. I read it. I found there was discrepancies between then and now. It struck me. Here God used to raineth bread from clouds, smite the Phillipines, sling fire down on red-light districts where people got stabbed. He even appeared in person every once in a while. God used to pay attention, is what I'm saying.

Now there's your God in the Old Testament and there is Chippewa Gods as well. Indian Gods, good and bad, like tricky Nanabozho or the water monster, Missepeshu, who lives over in Matchimanito. That water monster was the last God I ever heard to appear. It had a weakness for young girls and grabbed one of the Pillagers off her rowboat. She got to shore all right, but only after this monster had its way with her. She's an old lady now. Old Lady Pillager. She still doesn't like to see her family fish that lake.

Our Gods aren't perfect, is what I'm saying, but at least they come around. They'll do a favor if you ask them right. You don't have to yell. But you do have to know, like I said, how to ask in the right way. That makes problems, because to ask proper was an art that was lost to the Chippewas once the Catholics gained ground. Even now, I have to wonder if Higher Power turned it back, if we got to yell, or if we just don't speak its language.

I looked around me. How else could I explain what all I had seen in my short life—King smashing his fist in things, Gordie drinking himself down to the Bismarck hospitals, or Aunt June left by a white man to wander off in the snow. How else to explain the times my touch don't work, and farther back, to the oldtime Indians who was swept away in the outright germ warfare and dirty-dog killing of the whites. In those times, us Indians was so much kindlier than now.

30   We took them in.

Oh yes, I'm bitter as an old cutworm just thinking of how they done to us and doing still.

So Grandpa Kashpaw just opened my eyes a little there. Was there any sense relying on a God whose ears was stopped? Just like the government? I says then, right off, maybe we got nothing but ourselves. And that's not much, just personally speaking. I know I don't got the cold hard potatoes it takes to understand everything. Still, there's things I'd like to do. For instance, I'd like to help some people like my Grandpa and Grandma Kashpaw get back some happiness within the tail ends of their lives.

I told you once before I couldn't see my way clear to putting the direct touch on Grandpa's mind, and I kept my moral there, but something soon happened to make me think a little bit of mental adjustment wouldn't do him and the rest of us no harm.

It was after we saw him one afternoon in the sunshine courtyard of the Senior Citizens with Lulu Lamartine. Grandpa used to like to dig there. He had his little dandelion fork out, and he was prying up them dandelions right and left while Lamartine watched him.

35   "He's scratching up the dirt, all right," said Grandma, watching Lamartine watch Grandpa out the window.

Now Lamartine was about half the considerable size of Grandma, but you would never think of sizes anyway. They were different in an even more noticeable way. It was the difference between a house fixed up with paint and picky fence, and a house left to weather away into the soft earth, is what I'm saying. Lamartine was jacked up, latticed, shuttered, and vinyl sided, while Grandma sagged and bulged on her slipped foundations and let her hair go the silver gray of rain-dried lumber. Right now, she eyed the Lamartine's pert flowery dress with such a look it despaired me. I knew what this could lead to with Grandma. Alternating tongue storms and rock-hard silences was hard on a man, even one who didn't notice, like Grandpa. So I went fetching him.

But he was gone when I popped through the little screen door that led out on the courtyard. There was nobody out there either, to point which way they went. Just the dandelion fork quibbling upright in the ground. That gave me an idea. I snookered over to the Lamartine's door and I listened in first, then knocked. But nobody. So I went walking through the lounges and around the card tables. Still nobody. Finally it was my touch that led me to the laundry room. I cracked the door. I went in. There they were. And he was really loving her up good, boy, and she was going hell for leather. Sheets was flapping on the lines above, and washcloths, pillowcases, shirts was also flying through the air, for they was trying to clear out a place for themselves in a high-heaped but shallow laundry cart. The washers and dryers was all on, chock-full of quarters, shaking and moaning. I couldn't hear what Grandpa and the Lamartine was billing and cooing, and they couldn't hear me.

I didn't know what to do, so I went inside and shut the door.

The Lamartine wore a big curly light-brown wig. Looked like one of them squeaky little white-people dogs. Poodles they call them. Anyway, that wig is what saved us from the worse. For I could hardly shout and tell them I was in there, no more could I try and grab him. I was trapped where I was. There was nothing I could really do but hold the door shut. I was scared of somebody else upsetting in and really getting an eyeful. Turned out though, in the heat of the clinch, as I was trying to avert my eyes you see, the Lamartine's curly wig jumped off her head. And if you ever been in the midst of something and had a big change like that occur in the someone, you can't help know how it devastates your basic urges. Not only that, but her wig was almost with a life of its own. Grandpa's eyes were bugging at the change already, and swear to God if the thing didn't rear up and pop him in the face like it was going to start something. He scrambled up, Grandpa did, and the Lamartine jumped up after him all addled looking. They just stared at each other, huffing and puffing, with quizzical expression. The surprise seemed to drive all sense completely out of Grandpa's mind.

"The letter was what started the fire," he said. "I never would have done it." 40

"What letter?" said the Lamartine. She was stiff-necked now, and elegant, even bald, like some alien queen. I gave her back the wig. The Lamartine replaced it on her head, and whenever I saw her after that, I couldn't help thinking of her bald, with special powers, as if from another planet.

"That was a close call," I said to Grandpa after she had left.

But I think he had already forgot the incident. He just stood there all quiet and thoughtful. You really wouldn't think he was crazy. He looked like he was just about to say something important, explaining himself. He said something, all right, but it didn't have nothing to do with anything that made sense.

He wondered where the heck he put his dandelion fork. That's when I decided about the mental adjustment.

45   Now what was mostly our problem was not so much that he was not all there, but that what was there of him often hankered after Lamartine. If we could put a stop to that, I thought, we might be getting someplace. But here, see, my touch was of no use. For what could I snap my fingers at to make him faithful to Grandma? Like the quality of staying power, this faithfulness was invisible. I know it's something that you got to acquire, but I never known where from. Maybe there's no rhyme or reason to it, like my getting the touch, and then again maybe it's a kind of magic.

It was Grandma Kashpaw who thought of it in the end. She knows things. Although she will not admit she has a scrap of Indian blood in her, there's no doubt in my mind she's got some Chippewa. How else would you explain the way she'll be sitting there, in front of her TV story, rocking in her armchair and suddenly she turns on me, her brown eyes hard as lake-bed flint.

"Lipsha Morrissey," she'll say, "you went out last night and got drunk." How did she know that? I'll hardly remember it myself. Then she'll say she just had a feeling or ache in the scar of her hand or a creak in her shoulder. She is constantly being told things by little aggravations in her joints or by her household appliances. One time she told Gordie never to ride with a crazy Lamartine boy. She had seen something in the polished-up tin of her bread toaster. So he didn't. Sure enough, the time came we heard how Lyman and Henry went out of control in their car, ending up in the river. Lyman swam to the top, but Henry never made it.

Thanks to Grandma's toaster, Gordie was probably spared.

50   Someplace in the blood Grandma Kashpaw knows things. She also remembers things, I found. She keeps things filed away. She's got a memory like them video games that don't forget your score. One reason she remembers so many details about the trouble I gave her in early life is so she can flash back her total when she needs to.

Like now. Take the love medicine. I don't know where she remembered that from. It came tumbling from her mind like an asteroid off the corner of the screen.[2]

---

2. Allusion to Asteroids, another popular 1980s video arcade game.

Of course she starts out by mentioning the time I had this accident in church and did she leave me there with wet overalls? No she didn't. And ain't I glad? Yes I am. Now what you want now, Grandma? But when she mentions them love medicines, I feel my back prickle at the danger. These love medicines is something of an old Chippewa specialty. No other tribe has got them down so well. But love medicines is not for the layman to handle. You don't just go out and get one without paying for it. Before you get one, even, you should go through one hell of a lot of mental condensation. You got to think it over. Choose the right one. You could really mess up your life grinding up the wrong little thing.

So anyhow, I said to Grandma I'd give this love medicine some thought. I knew the best thing was to go ask a specialist like Old Lady Pillager, who lives up in a tangle of bush and never shows herself. But the truth is I was afraid of her, like everyone else. She was known for putting the twisted mouth on people, seizing up their hearts. Old Lady Pillager was serious business, and I have always thought it best to steer clear of that whenever I could. That's why I took the powers in my own hands. That's why I did what I could.

I put my whole mentality to it, nothing held back. After a while I 55 started to remember things I'd heard gossiped over.

I heard of this person once who carried a charm of seeds that looked like baby pearls. They was attracted to a metal knife, which made them powerful. But I didn't know where them seeds grew. Another love charm I heard about I couldn't go along with, because how was I suppose to catch frogs in the act, which it required. Them little creatures is slippery and fast. And then the powerfullest of all, the most extreme, involved nail clips and such. I wasn't anywhere near asking Grandma to provide me all the little body bits that this last love recipe called for. I went walking around for days just trying to think up something that would work.

Well I got it. If it hadn't been the early fall of the year, I never would have got it. But I was sitting underneath a tree one day down near the school just watching people's feet go by when something tells me, look up! Look up! So I look up, and I see two honkers, Canada geese, the kind with little masks on their faces, a bird what mates for life. I see them flying right over my head naturally preparing to land in some slough on the reservation, which they certainly won't get off of alive.

It hits me, anyway. Them geese, they mate for life. And I think to myself, just what if I went out and got a pair? And just what if I fed some part—say the goose heart—of the female to Grandma and Grandpa ate the other heart? Wouldn't that work? Maybe it's all invisible, and then maybe again it's magic. Love is a stony road. We know that for sure. If it's true that the higher feelings of devotion get lodged in the heart like people say, then we'd be home free. If not, eating goose heart couldn't harm nobody anyway. I thought it was worth my effort, and Grandma Kashpaw thought so, too. She had always known a good idea when she heard one. She borrowed me Grandpa's gun.

So I went out to this particular slough, maybe the exact same slough I never got thrown in by my mother, thanks to Grandma Kashpaw, and I hunched down in a good comfortable pile of rushes. I got my gun loaded up. I ate a few of these soft baloney sandwiches Grandma made me for lunch. And then I waited. The cattails blown back and forth above my head. Them stringy blue herons was spearing up their prey. The thing I know how to do best in this world, the thing I been training for all my life, is to wait. Sitting there and sitting there was no hardship on me. I got to thinking about some funny things that happened. There was this one time that Lulu Lamartine's little blue tweety bird, a paraclete, I guess you'd call it, flown up inside her dress and got lost within there. I recalled her running out into the hallway trying to yell something, shaking. She was doing a right good jig there, cutting the rug for sure, and the thing is it *never* flown out. To this day people speculate where it went. They fear she might perhaps of crushed it in her corsets. It sure hasn't ever yet been seen alive. I thought of funny things for a while, but then I used them up, and strange things that happened started weaseling their way into my mind.

60   I got to thinking quite naturally of the Lamartine's cousin named Wristwatch. I never knew what his real name was. They called him Wristwatch because he got his father's broken wristwatch as a young boy when his father passed on. Never in his whole life did Wristwatch take his father's watch off. He didn't care if it worked, although after a while he got sensitive when people asked what time it was, teasing him. He often put it to his ear like he was listening to the tick. But it was broken for good and forever, people said so, at least that's what they thought.

Well I saw Wristwatch smoking in his pickup one afternoon and by nine that evening he was dead.

He died sitting at the Lamartine's table, too. As she told it, Wristwatch had just eaten himself a good-size dinner and she said would he take seconds on the hot dish when he fell over to the floor. They turnt him over. He was gone. But here's the strange thing: when the Senior Citizen's orderly took the pulse he noticed that the wristwatch Wristwatch wore was now working. The moment he died the wristwatch started keeping perfect time. They buried him with the watch still ticking on his arm.

I got to thinking. What if some gravediggers dug up Wristwatch's casket in two hundred years and that watch was still going? I thought what question they would ask and it was this: Whose hand wound it?

I started shaking like a piece of grass at just the thought.

Not to get off the subject or nothing. I was still hunkered in the slough. 65
It was passing late into the afternoon and still no honkers had touched
down. Now I don't need to tell you that the waiting did not get to me, it was
the chill. The rushes was very soft, but damp. I was getting cold and debating to leave, when they landed. Two geese swimming here and there as
big as life, looking deep into each other's little pinhole eyes. Just the ones
I was looking for. So I lifted Grandpa's gun to my shoulder and I aimed
perfectly, and *blam! Blam!* I delivered two accurate shots. But the thing is,
them shots missed. I couldn't hardly believe it. Whether it was that the stock
had warped or the barrel got bent someways, I don't quite know, but
anyway them geese flown off into the dim sky, and Lipsha Morrissey
was left there in the rushes with evening fallen and his two cold hands
empty. He had before him just the prospect of another day of bone-cracking
chill in them rushes, and the thought of it got him depressed.

Now it isn't my style, in no way, to get depressed.

So I said to myself, Lipsha Morrissey, you're a happy S.O.B. who could
be covered up with weeds by now down at the bottom of this slough, but
instead you're alive to tell the tale. You might have problems in life, but
you still got the touch. You got the power, Lipsha Morrissey. Can't argue
that. So put your mind to it and figure out how not to be depressed.

I took my advice. I put my mind to it. But I never saw at the time how
my thoughts led me astray toward a tragic outcome none could have known.
I ignored all the danger, all the limits, for I was tired of sitting in the slough
and my feet were numb. My face was aching. I was chilled, so I played with
fire. I told myself love medicine was simple. I told myself the old superstitions was just that—strange beliefs. I told myself to take the ten dollars
Mary MacDonald had paid me for putting the touch on her arthritis joint,
and the other five I hadn't spent yet from winning bingo last Thursday.
I told myself to go down to the Red Owl store.

And here is what I did that made the medicine backfire. I took an evil
shortcut. I looked at birds that was dead and froze.

All right. So now I guess you will say, "Slap a malpractice suit on Lipsha 70
Morrissey."

I heard of those suits. I used to think it was a color clothing quack doctors had to wear so you could tell them from the good ones. Now I know
better that it's law.

As I walked back from the Red Owl with the rock-hard, heavy turkeys,
I argued to myself about malpractice. I thought of faith. I thought to myself
that faith could be called belief against the odds and whether or not there's
any proof. How does that sound? I thought how we might have to yell to
be heard by Higher Power, but that's not saying it's not *there.* And that is

faith for you. It's belief even when the goods don't deliver. Higher Power makes promises we all know they can't back up, but anybody ever go and slap an old malpractice suit on God? Or the U.S. government? No they don't. Faith might be stupid, but it gets us through. So what I'm heading at is this. I finally convinced myself that the real actual power to the love medicine was not the goose heart itself but the faith in the cure.

I didn't believe it, I knew it was wrong, but by then I had waded so far into my lie I was stuck there. And then I went one step further.

The next day, I cleaned the hearts away from the paper packages of gizzards inside the turkeys. Then I wrapped them hearts with a clean hankie and brung them both to get blessed up at the mission. I wanted to get official blessings from the priest, but when Father answered the door to the rectory, wiping his hands on a little towel, I could tell he was a busy man.

75 "Booshoo,[3] Father," I said. "I got a slight request to make of you this afternoon."

"What is it?" he said.

"Would you bless this package?" I held out the hankie with the hearts tied inside it.

He looked at the package, questioning it.

"It's turkey hearts," I honestly had to reply.

80 A look of annoyance crossed his face.

"Why don't you bring this matter over to Sister Martin," he said. "I have duties."

And so, although the blessing wouldn't be as powerful, I went over to the Sisters with the package.

I rung the bell, and they brought Sister Martin to the door. I had her as a music teacher, but I was always so shy then. I never talked out loud. Now, I had grown taller than Sister Martin. Looking down, I saw that she was not feeling up to snuff. Brown circles hung under her eyes.

"What's the matter?" she said, not noticing who I was.

85 "Remember me, Sister?"

She squinted up at me.

"Oh yes," she said after a moment. "I'm sorry, you're the youngest of the Kashpaws. Gordie's brother."

Her face warmed up.

"Lipsha," I said, "that's my name."

90 "Well, Lipsha," she said, smiling broad at me now, "what can I do for you?"

They always said she was the kindest-hearted of the Sisters up the hill, and she was. She brought me back into their own kitchen and made me take a big yellow wedge of cake and a glass of milk.

---

3. That is, *Bonjour,* French for "good day" or "hello."

"Now tell me," she said, nodding at my package. "What have you got wrapped up so carefully in those handkerchiefs?"

Like before, I answered honestly.

"Ah," said Sister Martin. "Turkey hearts." She waited.

"I hoped you could bless them."   95

She waited some more, smiling with her eyes. Kindhearted though she was, I began to sweat. A person could not pull the wool down over Sister Martin. I stumbled through my mind for an explanation, quick, that wouldn't scare her off.

"They're a present," I said, "for Saint Kateri's[4] statue."

"She's not a saint yet."

"I know," I stuttered on. "In the hopes they will crown her."

"Lipsha," she said, "I never heard of such a thing."   100

So I told her. "Well the truth is," I said, "it's a kind of medicine."

"For what?"

"Love."

"Oh Lipsha," she said after a moment, "you don't need any medicine. I'm sure any girl would like you exactly the way you are."

I just sat there. I felt miserable, caught in my pack of lies.   105

"Tell you what," she said, seeing how bad I felt, "my blessing won't make any difference anyway. But there is something you can do."

I looked up at her, hopeless.

"Just be yourself."

I looked down at my plate. I knew I wasn't much to brag about right then, and I shortly became even less. For as I walked out the door I stuck my fingers in the cup of holy water that was sacred from their touches. I put my fingers in and blessed the hearts, quick, with my own hand.

I went back to Grandma and sat down in her little kitchen at the Senior   110
Citizens. I unwrapped them hearts on the table, and her hard agate eyes went soft. She said she wasn't even going to cook those hearts up but eat them raw so their power would go down strong as possible.

I couldn't hardly watch when she munched hers. Now that's true love. I was worried about how she would get Grandpa to eat his, but she told me she'd think of something and don't worry. So I did not. I was supposed to hide off in her bedroom while she put dinner on a plate for Grandpa and fixed up the heart so he'd eat it. I caught a glint of the plate she was

4. Kateri Kekakwitha (1656–80), "Lily of the Mohawk," born in what is now upstate New York to a Mohawk father and an Algonquin mother who was a devout Christian. Following the deaths of her parents, Kateri moved to a Jesuit mission near Montreal to spend the rest of her short life in prayer and chastity. Miracles were attributed to her after her death; she was beatified in 1980 and canonized in 1991.

making for him. She put that heart smack on a piece of lettuce like in a restaurant and then attached to it a little heap of boiled peas.

He sat down. I was listening in the next room.

She said, "Why don't you have some mash potato?" So he had some mash potato. Then she gave him a little piece of boiled meat. He ate that. Then she said, "Why you didn't never touch your salad yet. See that heart? I'm feeding you it because the doctor said your blood needs building up."

I couldn't help it, at that point I peeked through a crack in the door.

115   I saw Grandpa picking at that heart on his plate with a certain look. He didn't look appetized at all, is what I'm saying. I doubted our plan was going to work. Grandma was getting worried, too. She told him one more time, loudly, that he had to eat that heart.

"Swallow it down," she said. "You'll hardly notice it."

He just looked at her straight on. The way he looked at her made me think I was going to see the smokescreen drop a second time, and sure enough it happened.

"What you want me to eat this for so bad?" he asked her uncannily.

Now Grandma knew the jig was up. She knew that he knew she was working medicine. He put his fork down. He rolled the heart around his saucer plate.

120   "I don't want to eat this," he said to Grandma. "It don't look good."

"Why it's fresh grade-A," she told him. "One hundred percent."

He didn't ask percent what, but his eyes took on an even more warier look.

"Just go on and try it," she said, taking the salt shaker up in her hand. She was getting annoyed. "Not tasty enough? You want me to salt it for you?" She waved the shaker over his plate.

"All right, skinny white girl!" She had got Grandpa mad. Oopsy-daisy, he popped the heart into his mouth. I was about to yawn loudly and come out of the bedroom. I was about ready for this crash of wills to be over, when I saw he was still up to his old tricks. First he rolled it into one side of his cheek. "Mmmmm," he said. Then he rolled it into the other side of his cheek. "Mmmmmmm," again. Then he stuck his tongue out with the heart on it and put it back, and there was no time to react. He had pulled Grandma's leg once too far. Her goat was got. She was so mad she hopped up quick as a wink and slugged him between the shoulderblades to make him swallow.

125   Only thing is, he choked.

He choked real bad. A person can choke to death. You ever sit down at a restaurant table and up above you there is a list of instructions what to do if something slides down the wrong pipe? It sure makes you chew slow, that's for damn sure. When Grandpa fell off his chair better believe me that little graphic illustrated poster fled into my mind. I jumped out the bedroom. I done everything within my power that I could do to unlodge what was choking him. I squeezed underneath his rib cage. I socked him in the back. I was desperate. But here's the factor of decision: he wasn't choking on the heart alone. There was more to it than that. It was other things that choked him as well. It didn't seem like he wanted to struggle or fight. Death came and tapped his chest, so he went just like that. I'm sorry all through my body at what I done to him with that heart, and there's those who will say Lipsha Morrissey is just excusing himself off the hook by giving song and dance about how Grandpa gave up. Maybe I can't admit what I did. My touch had gone worthless, that is true. But here is what I seen while he lay in my arms.

You hear a person's life will flash before their eyes when they're in danger. It was him in danger, not me, but it was *his* life come over me. I saw him dying, and it was like someone pulled the shade down in a room. His eyes clouded over and squeezed shut, but just before that I looked in. He was still fishing in the middle of Matchimanito. Big thoughts was on his line and he had half a case of beer in the boat. He waved at me, grinned, and then the bobber went under.

Grandma had gone out of the room crying for help. I bunched my force up in my hands and I held him. I was so wound up I couldn't even breathe. All the moments he had spent with me, all the times he had hoisted me on his shoulders or pointed into the leaves was concentrated in that moment. Time was flashing back and forth like a pinball machine. Lights blinked and balls hopped and rubber bands chirped, until suddenly I realized the last ball had gone down the drain and there was nothing. I felt his force leaving him, flowing out of Grandpa never to return. I felt his mind weakening. The bobber going under in the lake. And I felt the touch retreat back into the darkness inside my body, from where it came.

One time, long ago, both of us were fishing together. We caught a big old snapper what started towing us around like it was a motor. "This here fishline is pretty damn good," Grandpa said. "Let's keep this turtle on and see where he takes us." So we rode along behind that turtle, watching as from time to time it surfaced. The thing was just about the size of a washtub. It took us all around the lake twice, and as it was traveling, Grandpa said something as a joke. "Lipsha," he said, "we are glad your mother didn't want you because we was always looking for a boy like you who would tow us around the lake."

"I ain't no snapper. Snappers is so stupid they stay alive when their head's chopped off," I said.

"That ain't stupidity," said Grandpa. "Their brain's just in their heart, like yours is."

When I looked up, I knew the fuse had blown between my heart and my mind and that a terrible understanding was to be given.

Grandma got back into the room and I saw her stumble. And then she went down too. It was like a house you can't hardly believe has stood so long, through years of record weather, suddenly goes down in the worst yet. It makes sense, is what I'm saying, but you still can't hardly believe it. You think a person you know has got through death and illness and being broke and living on commodity rice will get through anything. Then they fold and you see how fragile were the stones that underpinned them. You see how instantly the ground can shift you thought was solid. You see the stop signs and the yellow dividing markers of roads you traveled and all the instructions you had played according to vanish. You see how all the everyday things you counted on was just a dream you had been having by which you run your whole life. She had been over me, like a sheer overhang of rock dividing Lipsha Morrissey from outer space. And now she went underneath. It was as though the banks gave way on the shores of Matchimanito, and where Grandpa's passing was just the bobber swallowed under by his biggest thought, her fall was the house and the rock under it sliding after, sending half the lake splashing up to the clouds.

135   Where there was nothing.

You play them games never knowing what you see. When I fell into the dream alongside of both of them I saw that the dominions I had defended myself from anciently was but delusions of the screen. Blips of light. And I was scot-free now, whistling through space.

I don't know how I come back. I don't know from where. They was slapping my face when I arrived back at Senior Citizens and they was oxygenating her. I saw her chest move, almost unwilling. She sighed the way she would when somebody bothered her in the middle of a row of beads she was counting. I think it irritated her to no end that they brought her back. I knew from the way she looked after they took the mask off, she was not going to forgive them disturbing her restful peace. Nor was she forgiving Lipsha Morrissey. She had been stepping out onto the road of death, she told the children later at the funeral. I asked was there any stop signs or dividing markers on that road, but she clamped her lips in a vise the way she always done when she was mad.

Which didn't bother me. I knew when things had cleared out she wouldn't have no choice. I was not going to speculate where the blame was put for Grandpa's death. We was in it together. She had slugged him between the shoulders. My touch had failed him, never to return.

All the blood children and the took-ins, like me, came home from Minneapolis and Chicago, where they had relocated years ago. They stayed with friends on the reservation or with Aurelia or slept on Grandma's floor. They were struck down with grief and bereavement to be sure, every one of them. At the funeral I sat down in the back of the church with Albertine. She had gotten all skinny and ragged haired from cramming all her years of study into two or three. She had decided that to be a nurse was not enough for her so she was going to be a doctor. But the way she was straining her mind didn't look too hopeful. Her eyes were bloodshot from driving and crying. She took my hand. From the back we watched all the children and the mourners as they hunched over their prayers, their hands stuffed full of Kleenex. It was someplace in that long sad service that my vision shifted. I began to see things different, more clear. The family kneeling down turned to rocks in a field. It struck me how strong and reliable grief was, and death. Until the end of time, death would be our rock.

So I had perspective on it all, for death gives you that. All the Kashpaw 140 children had done various things to me in their lives—shared their folks with me, loaned me cash, beat me up in secret—and I decided, because of death, then and there I'd call it quits. If I ever saw King again, I'd shake his hand. Forgiving somebody else made the whole thing easier to bear.

Everybody saw Grandpa off into the next world. And then the Kashpaws had to get back to their jobs, which was numerous and impressive. I had a few beers with them and I went back to Grandma, who had sort of got lost in the shuffle of everybody being sad about Grandpa and glad to see one another.

Zelda had sat beside her the whole time and was sitting with her now. I wanted to talk to Grandma, say how sorry I was, that it wasn't her fault, but only mine. I would have, but Zelda gave me one of her looks of strict warning as if to say, "I'll take care of Grandma. Don't horn in on the women."

If only Zelda knew, I thought, the sad realities would change her. But of course I couldn't tell the dark truth.

It was evening, late. Grandma's light was on underneath a crack in the door. About a week had passed since we buried Grandpa. I knocked first but there wasn't no answer, so I went right in. The door was unlocked. She was there but she didn't notice me at first. Her hands were tied up in her rosary, and her gaze was fully absorbed in the easy chair opposite her, the one that had always been Grandpa's favorite. I stood there, staring with her, at the little green nubs in the cloth and plastic armrest covers and the sad little hair-tonic stain he had made on the white doily where he laid his head. For the life of me I couldn't figure what she was staring at. Thin space. Then she turned.

"He ain't gone yet," she said. 145

Remember that chill I luckily didn't get from waiting in the slough? I got it now. I felt it start from the very center of me, where fear hides, waiting to attack. It spiraled outward so that in minutes my fingers and teeth were shaking and clattering. I knew she told the truth. She seen Grandpa. Whether or not he had been there is not the point. She had *seen* him, and that meant anybody else could see him, too. Not only that but, as is usually the case with these here ghosts, he had a certain uneasy reason to come back. And of course Grandma Kashpaw had scanned it out.

I sat down. We sat together on the couch watching his chair out of the corner of our eyes. She had found him sitting in his chair when she walked in the door.

"It's the love medicine, my Lipsha," she said. "It was stronger than we thought. He came back even after death to claim me to his side."

I was afraid. "We shouldn't have tampered with it," I said. She agreed. For a while we sat still. I don't know what she thought, but my head felt screwed on backward. I couldn't accurately consider the situation, so I told Grandma to go to bed. I would sleep on the couch keeping my eye on Grandpa's chair. Maybe he would come back and maybe he wouldn't. I guess I feared the one as much as the other, but I got to thinking, see, as I lay there in darkness, that perhaps even through my terrible mistakes some good might come. If Grandpa did come back, I thought he'd return in his right mind. I could talk with him. I could tell him it was all my fault for playing with power I did not understand. Maybe he'd forgive me and rest in peace. I hoped this. I calmed myself and waited for him all night.

150   He fooled me though. He knew what I was waiting for, and it wasn't what he was looking to hear. Come dawn I heard a blood-splitting cry from the bedroom and I rushed in there. Grandma turnt the lights on. She was sitting on the edge of the bed and her face looked harsh, pinched-up, gray.

"He was here," she said. "He came and laid down next to me in bed. And he touched me."

Her heart broke down. She cried. His touch was so cold. She laid back in bed after a while, as it was morning, and I went to the couch. As I lay there, falling asleep, I suddenly felt Grandpa's presence and the barrier between us like a swollen river. I felt how I had wronged him. How awful was the place where I had sent him. Behind the wall of death, he'd watched the living eat and cry and get drunk. He was lonesome, but I understood he meant no harm.

"Go back," I said to the dark, afraid and yet full of pity. "You got to be with your own kind now," I said. I felt him retreating, like a sigh, growing less. I felt his spirit as it shrunk back through the walls, the blinds, the brick courtyard of Senior Citizens. "Look up Aunt June," I whispered as he left.

I slept late the next morning, a good hard sleep allowing the sun to rise and warm the earth. It was past noon when I awoke. There is nothing, to my mind, like a long sleep to make those hard decisions that you neglect under stress of wakefulness. Soon as I woke up that morning, I saw exactly what I'd say to Grandma. I had gotten humble in the past week, not just losing the touch but getting jolted into the understanding that would prey on me from here on out. Your life feels different on you, once you greet death and understand your heart's position. You wear your life like a garment from the mission bundle sale ever after—lightly because you realize you never paid nothing for it, cherishing because you know you won't ever come by such a bargain again. Also you have the feeling someone wore it before you and someone will after. I can't explain that, not yet, but I'm putting my mind to it.

"Grandma," I said, "I got to be honest about the love medicine." 155

She listened. I knew from then on she would be listening to me the way I had listened to her before. I told her about the turkey hearts and how I had them blessed. I told her what I used as love medicine was purely a fake, and then I said to her what my understanding brought me.

"Love medicine ain't what brings him back to you, Grandma. No, it's something else. He loved you over time and distance, but he went off so quick he never got the chance to tell you how he loves you, how he doesn't blame you, how he understands. It's true feeling, not no magic. No supermarket heart could have brung him back."

She looked at me. She was seeing the years and days I had no way of knowing, and she didn't believe me. I could tell this. Yet a look came on her face. It was like the look of mothers drinking sweetness from their children's eyes. It was tenderness.

"Lipsha," she said, "you was always my favorite."

She took the beads off the bedpost, where she kept them to say at 160 night, and she told me to put out my hand. When I did this, she shut the beads inside of my fist and held them there a long minute, tight, so my hand hurt. I almost cried when she did this. I don't really know why. Tears shot up behind my eyelids, and yet it was nothing. I didn't understand, except her hand was so strong, squeezing mine.

The earth was full of life and there were dandelions growing out the window, thick as thieves, already seeded, fat as big yellow plungers. She let my hand go. I got up. "I'll go out and dig a few dandelions," I told her.

Outside, the sun was hot and heavy as a hand on my back. I felt it flow down my arms, out my fingers, arrowing through the ends of the fork into the earth. With every root I prized up there was return, as if I was kin to its secret lesson. The touch got stronger as I worked through the grassy afternoon. Uncurling from me like a seed out of the blackness where I was lost, the touch spread. The spiked leaves full of bitter mother's milk.

A buried root. A nuisance people dig up and throw in the sun to wither.
A globe of frail seeds that's indestructible.

1982

WILLIAM FAULKNER
(1897–1962)
A Rose for Emily

A native of Oxford, Mississippi, William Faulkner
left high school without graduating, joined the
Royal Canadian Air Force in 1918, and in the mid-
1920s lived briefly in New Orleans, where he was
encouraged as a writer by Sherwood Anderson.
He then spent a few miserable months as a clerk
in a New York bookstore, published a collection of poems, *The Marble Faun*, in
1924, and took a long walking tour of Europe in 1925 before returning to Mississippi. With the publication of *Sartoris* in 1929, Faulkner began a cycle of works,
featuring recurrent characters and set in fictional Yoknapatawpha County,
including *The Sound and the Fury* (1929), *As I Lay Dying* (1930), *Light in August*
(1932), *Absalom, Absalom!* (1936), *The Hamlet* (1940), and *Go Down, Moses*
(1942). He spent time in Hollywood, writing screenplays for *The Big Sleep* and
other films, and lived his last years in Charlottesville, Virginia. Faulkner received
the Nobel Prize for Literature in 1950.

I

When Miss Emily Grierson died, our whole town went to her funeral: the
men through a sort of respectful affection for a fallen monument, the
women mostly out of curiosity to see the inside of her house, which no
one save an old man-servant—a combined gardener and cook—had seen
in at least ten years.

It was a big, squarish frame house that had once been white, decorated
with cupolas and spires and scrolled balconies in the heavily lightsome style
of the seventies,[1] set on what had once been our most select street. But
garages and cotton gins had encroached and obliterated even the august
names of that neighborhood; only Miss Emily's house was left, lifting its

---

1. The 1870s, the decade following the Civil War between the "Union and Confederate soldiers" mentioned at the end of the paragraph.

stubborn and coquettish decay above the cotton wagons and the gasoline pumps—an eyesore among eyesores. And now Miss Emily had gone to join the representatives of those august names where they lay in the cedar-bemused cemetery among the ranked and anonymous graves of Union and Confederate soldiers who fell at the battle of Jefferson.

Alive, Miss Emily had been a tradition, a duty, and a care; a sort of hereditary obligation upon the town, dating from that day in 1894 when Colonel Sartoris, the mayor—he who fathered the edict that no Negro woman should appear on the streets without an apron—remitted her taxes, the dispensation dating from the death of her father on into perpetuity. Not that Miss Emily would have accepted charity. Colonel Sartoris invented an involved tale to the effect that Miss Emily's father had loaned money to the town, which the town, as a matter of business, preferred this way of repaying. Only a man of Colonel Sartoris' generation and thought could have invented it, and only a woman could have believed it.

When the next generation, with its more modern ideas, became mayors and aldermen, this arrangement created some little dissatisfaction. On the first of the year they mailed her a tax notice. February came, and there was no reply. They wrote her a formal letter, asking her to call at the sheriff's office at her convenience. A week later the mayor wrote her himself, offering to call or to send his car for her, and received in reply a note on paper of an archaic shape, in a thin, flowing calligraphy in faded ink, to the effect that she no longer went out at all. The tax notice was also enclosed, without comment.

They called a special meeting of the Board of Aldermen. A deputation 5 waited upon her, knocked at the door through which no visitor had passed since she ceased giving china-painting lessons eight or ten years earlier. They were admitted by the old Negro into a dim hall from which a stairway mounted into still more shadow. It smelled of dust and disuse—a close, dank smell. The Negro led them into the parlor. It was furnished in heavy, leather-covered furniture. When the Negro opened the blinds of one window, a faint dust rose sluggishly about their thighs, spinning with slow motes in the single sun-ray. On a tarnished gilt easel before the fireplace stood a crayon portrait of Miss Emily's father.

They rose when she entered—a small, fat woman in black, with a thin gold chain descending to her waist and vanishing into her belt, leaning on an ebony cane with a tarnished gold head. Her skeleton was small and spare; perhaps that was why what would have been merely plumpness in another was obesity in her. She looked bloated, like a body long submerged in motionless water, and of that pallid hue. Her eyes, lost in the fatty ridges of her face, looked like two small pieces of coal pressed into a lump of dough as they moved from one face to another while the visitors stated their errand.

She did not ask them to sit. She just stood in the door and listened quietly until the spokesman came to a stumbling halt. Then they could hear the invisible watch ticking at the end of the gold chain.

Her voice was dry and cold. "I have no taxes in Jefferson. Colonel Sartoris explained it to me. Perhaps one of you can gain access to the city records and satisfy yourselves."

"But we have. We are the city authorities, Miss Emily. Didn't you get a notice from the sheriff, signed by him?"

"I received a paper, yes," Miss Emily said. "Perhaps he considers himself the sheriff. . . . I have no taxes in Jefferson."

"But there is nothing on the books to show that, you see. We must go by the—"

"See Colonel Sartoris. I have no taxes in Jefferson."

"But, Miss Emily—"

"See Colonel Sartoris." (Colonel Sartoris had been dead almost ten years.) "I have no taxes in Jefferson. Tobe!" The Negro appeared. "Show these gentlemen out."

II

So she vanquished them, horse and foot, just as she had vanquished their fathers thirty years before about the smell. That was two years after her father's death and a short time after her sweetheart—the one we believed would marry her—had deserted her. After her father's death she went out very little; after her sweetheart went away, people hardly saw her at all. A few of the ladies had the temerity to call, but were not received, and the only sign of life about the place was the Negro man—a young man then—going in and out with a market basket.

"Just as if a man—any man—could keep a kitchen properly," the ladies said; so they were not surprised when the smell developed. It was another link between the gross, teeming world and the high and mighty Griersons.

A neighbor, a woman, complained to the mayor, Judge Stevens, eighty years old.

"But what will you have me do about it, madam?" he said.

"Why, send her word to stop it," the woman said. "Isn't there a law?"

"I'm sure that won't be necessary," Judge Stevens said. "It's probably just a snake or a rat that nigger of hers killed in the yard. I'll speak to him about it."

The next day he received two more complaints, one from a man who came in diffident deprecation. "We really must do something about it, Judge. I'd be the last one in the world to bother Miss Emily, but we've got to do something." That night the Board of Aldermen met—three gray-beards and one younger man, a member of the rising generation.

"It's simple enough," he said. "Send her word to have her place cleaned up. Give her a certain time to do it in, and if she don't . . ."

"Dammit, sir," Judge Stevens said, "will you accuse a lady to her face of smelling bad?"

So the next night, after midnight, four men crossed Miss Emily's lawn and slunk about the house like burglars, sniffing along the base of the brickwork and at the cellar openings while one of them performed a regular sowing motion with his hand out of a sack slung from his shoulder. They broke open the cellar door and sprinkled lime there, and in all the outbuildings. As they recrossed the lawn, a window that had been dark was lighted and Miss Emily sat in it, the light behind her, and her upright torso motionless as that of an idol. They crept quietly across the lawn and into the shadow of the locusts that lined the street. After a week or two the smell went away.

That was when people had begun to feel really sorry for her. People in 25 our town, remembering how old lady Wyatt, her great-aunt, had gone completely crazy at last, believed that the Griersons held themselves a little too high for what they really were. None of the young men were quite good enough for Miss Emily and such. We had long thought of them as a tableau; Miss Emily a slender figure in white in the background, her father a spraddled silhouette in the foreground, his back to her and clutching a horsewhip, the two of them framed by the back-flung front door. So when she got to be thirty and was still single, we were not pleased exactly, but vindicated; even with insanity in the family she wouldn't have turned down all of her chances if they had really materialized.

When her father died, it got about that the house was all that was left to her; and in a way, people were glad. At last they could pity Miss Emily. Being left alone, and a pauper, she had become humanized. Now she too would know the old thrill and the old despair of a penny more or less.

The day after his death all the ladies prepared to call at the house and offer condolence and aid, as is our custom. Miss Emily met them at the door, dressed as usual and with no trace of grief on her face. She told them that her father was not dead. She did that for three days, with the ministers calling on her, and the doctors, trying to persuade her to let them dispose of the body. Just as they were about to resort to law and force, she broke down, and they buried her father quickly.

We did not say she was crazy then. We believed she had to do that. We remembered all the young men her father had driven away, and we knew that with nothing left, she would have to cling to that which had robbed her, as people will.

III

She was sick for a long time. When we saw her again, her hair was cut short, making her look like a girl, with a vague resemblance to those angels in colored church windows—sort of tragic and serene.

30 The town had just let the contracts for paving the sidewalks, and in the summer after her father's death they began to work. The construction company came with niggers and mules and machinery, and a foreman named Homer Barron, a Yankee—a big, dark, ready man, with a big voice and eyes lighter than his face. The little boys would follow in groups to hear him cuss the niggers, and the niggers singing in time to the rise and fall of picks. Pretty soon he knew everybody in town. Whenever you heard a lot of laughing anywhere about the square, Homer Barron would be in the center of the group. Presently we began to see him and Miss Emily on Sunday afternoons driving in the yellow-wheeled buggy and the matched team of bays from the livery stable.

At first we were glad that Miss Emily would have an interest, because the ladies all said, "Of course a Grierson would not think seriously of a Northerner, a day laborer." But there were still others, older people, who said that even grief could not cause a real lady to forget *noblesse oblige*—without calling it *noblesse oblige*.[2] They just said, "Poor Emily. Her kinsfolk should come to her." She had some kin in Alabama; but years ago her father had fallen out with them over the estate of old lady Wyatt, the crazy woman, and there was no communication between the two families. They had not even been represented at the funeral.

And as soon as the old people said, "Poor Emily," the whispering began. "Do you suppose it's really so?" they said to one another. "Of course it is. What else could . . ." This behind their hands; rustling of craned silk and satin behind jalousies[3] closed upon the sun of Sunday afternoon as the thin, swift clop-clop-clop of the matched team passed: "Poor Emily."

She carried her head high enough—even when we believed that she was fallen. It was as if she demanded more than ever the recognition of her dignity as the last Grierson; as if it had wanted that touch of earthiness to reaffirm her imperviousness. Like when she bought the rat poison, the arsenic. That was over a year after they had begun to say "Poor Emily," and while the two female cousins were visiting her.

"I want some poison," she said to the druggist. She was over thirty then, still a slight woman, though thinner than usual, with cold, haughty black eyes in a face the flesh of which was strained across the temples and

---

2. Obligation, coming with noble or upper-class birth, to behave with honor and generosity toward those less privileged.
3. Window blinds made of adjustable horizontal slats.

about the eyesockets as you imagine a lighthouse-keeper's face ought to look. "I want some poison," she said.

"Yes, Miss Emily. What kind? For rats and such? I'd recom—"   35
"I want the best you have. I don't care what kind."

The druggist named several. "They'll kill anything up to an elephant. But what you want is—"

"Arsenic," Miss Emily said. "Is that a good one?"

"Is . . . arsenic? Yes ma'am. But what you want—"

"I want arsenic."   40

The druggist looked down at her. She looked back at him, erect, her face like a strained flag. "Why, of course," the druggist said. "If that's what you want. But the law requires you to tell what you are going to use it for."

Miss Emily just stared at him, her head tilted back in order to look him eye for eye, until he looked away and went and got the arsenic and wrapped it up. The Negro delivery boy brought her the package; the druggist didn't come back. When she opened the package at home there was written on the box, under the skull and bones: "For rats."

IV

So the next day we all said, "She will kill herself"; and we said it would be the best thing. When she had first begun to be seen with Homer Barron, we had said, "She will marry him." Then we said, "She will persuade him yet," because Homer himself had remarked—he liked men, and it was known that he drank with the younger men in the Elk's Club—that he was not a marrying man. Later we said, "Poor Emily," behind the jalousies as they passed on Sunday afternoon in the glittering buggy, Miss Emily with her head high and Homer Barron with his hat cocked and a cigar in his teeth, reins and whip in a yellow glove.

Then some of the ladies began to say that it was a disgrace to the town and a bad example to the young people. The men did not want to interfere, but at last the ladies forced the Baptist minister—Miss Emily's people were Episcopal—to call upon her. He would never divulge what happened during that interview, but he refused to go back again. The next Sunday they again drove about the streets, and the following day the minister's wife wrote to Miss Emily's relations in Alabama.

So she had blood-kin under her roof again and we sat back to watch   45
developments. At first nothing happened. Then we were sure that they were to be married. We learned that Miss Emily had been to the jeweler's and ordered a man's toilet set in silver, with the letters H. B. on each piece. Two days later we learned that she had bought a complete outfit of men's clothing, including a nightshirt, and we said, "They are married." We were really

glad. We were glad because the two female cousins were even more Grierson than Miss Emily had ever been.

So we were not surprised when Homer Barron—the streets had been finished some time since—was gone. We were a little disappointed that there was not a public blowing-off, but we believed that he had gone on to prepare for Miss Emily's coming, or to give her a chance to get rid of the cousins. (By that time it was a cabal, and we were all Miss Emily's allies to help circumvent the cousins.) Sure enough, after another week they departed. And, as we had expected all along, within three days Homer Barron was back in town. A neighbor saw the Negro man admit him at the kitchen door at dusk one evening.

And that was the last we saw of Homer Barron. And of Miss Emily for some time. The Negro man went in and out with the market basket, but the front door remained closed. Now and then we would see her at a window for a moment, as the men did that night when they sprinkled the lime, but for almost six months she did not appear on the streets. Then we knew that this was to be expected too; as if that quality of her father which had thwarted her woman's life so many times had been too virulent and too furious to die.

When we next saw Miss Emily, she had grown fat and her hair was turning gray. During the next few years it grew grayer and grayer until it attained an even pepper-and-salt iron-gray, when it ceased turning. Up to the day of her death at seventy-four it was still that vigorous iron-gray, like the hair of an active man.

From that time on her front door remained closed, save for a period of six or seven years, when she was about forty, during which she gave lessons in china-painting. She fitted up a studio in one of the downstairs rooms, where the daughters and grand-daughters of Colonel Sartoris' contemporaries were sent to her with the same regularity and in the same spirit that they were sent on Sundays with a twenty-five cent piece for the collection plate. Meanwhile her taxes had been remitted.

50   Then the newer generation became the backbone and the spirit of the town, and the painting pupils grew up and fell away and did not send their children to her with boxes of color and tedious brushes and pictures cut from the ladies' magazines. The front door closed upon the last one and remained closed for good. When the town got free postal delivery Miss Emily alone refused to let them fasten the metal numbers above her door and attach a mailbox to it. She would not listen to them.

Daily, monthly, yearly we watched the Negro grow grayer and more stooped, going in and out with the market basket. Each December we sent her a tax notice, which would be returned by the post office a week later, unclaimed. Now and then we would see her in one of the downstairs windows—she had evidently shut up the top floor of the house—like the carven torso of an idol in a niche, looking or not looking at us, we could never tell which. Thus she passed from generation to generation—dear, inescapable, impervious, tranquil, and perverse.

And so she died. Fell ill in the house filled with dust and shadows, with only a doddering Negro man to wait on her. We did not even know she was sick; we had long since given up trying to get any information from the Negro. He talked to no one, probably not even to her, for his voice had grown harsh and rusty, as if from disuse.

She died in one of the downstairs rooms, in a heavy walnut bed with a curtain, her gray head propped on a pillow yellow and moldy with age and lack of sunlight.

V

The Negro met the first of the ladies at the front door and let them in, with their hushed, sibilant voices and their quick, curious glances, and then he disappeared. He walked right through the house and out the back and was not seen again.

The two female cousins came at once. They held the funeral on the 55 second day, with the town coming to look at Miss Emily beneath a mass of bought flowers, with the crayon face of her father musing profoundly above the bier and the ladies sibilant and macabre; and the very old men— some in their brushed Confederate uniforms—on the porch and the lawn, talking of Miss Emily as if she had been a contemporary of theirs, believing that they had danced with her and courted her perhaps, confusing time with its mathematical progression, as the old do, to whom all the past is not a diminishing road, but, instead, a huge meadow which no winter ever quite touches, divided from them now by the narrow bottleneck of the most recent decade of years.

Already we knew that there was one room in that region above stairs which no one had seen in forty years, and which would have to be forced. They waited until Miss Emily was decently in the ground before they opened it.

The violence of breaking down the door seemed to fill this room with pervading dust. A thin, acrid pall as of the tomb seemed to lie everywhere upon this room decked and furnished as for a bridal: upon the valance curtains of faded rose color, upon the rose-shaded lights, upon the dressing table, upon the delicate array of crystal and the man's toilet things backed with tarnished silver, silver so tarnished that the monogram was obscured. Among them lay a collar and tie, as if they had just been removed, which, lifted, left upon the surface a pale crescent in the dust. Upon a chair hung the suit, carefully folded; beneath it the two mute shoes and the discarded socks.

The man himself lay in the bed.

For a long while we just stood there, looking down at the profound and fleshless grin. The body had apparently once lain in the attitude of an embrace, but now the long sleep that outlasts love, that conquers even the grimace of love, had cuckolded him. What was left of him, rotted beneath what was left of the nightshirt, had become inextricable from the bed in which he lay; and upon him and upon the pillow beside him lay that even coating of the patient and biding dust.

60   Then we noticed that in the second pillow was the indentation of a head. One of us lifted something from it, and leaning forward, that faint and invisible dust dry and acrid in the nostrils, we saw a long strand of iron-gray hair.

1931

CHARLOTTE PERKINS GILMAN
(1860–1935)
The Yellow Wallpaper

Charlotte Anna Perkins was born in Hartford, Connecticut. After a painful, lonely childhood and several years of supporting herself as a governess, art teacher, and designer of greeting cards, Perkins married the artist Charles Stetson. Following her several extended periods of depression, Charles Stetson put his wife in the care of a doctor who, in her own words, "sent me home with the solemn advice to 'live as domestic a life as [. . .] possible,' to 'have but two hours' intellectual life a day,' and 'never to touch pen, brush, or pencil again' as long as I lived." Three months of this regimen brought her "near the borderline of utter mortal ruin" and inspired her masterpiece, "The Yellow Wallpaper." In 1900, she married George Houghton Gilman, having divorced Stetson in 1892. Her nonfiction works, springing from the early women's movement, include *Women and Economics* (1898) and *Man-Made World* (1911). She also wrote several utopian novels, including *Moving the Mountain* (1911) and *Herland* (1915).

I
t is very seldom that mere ordinary people like John and myself secure ancestral halls for the summer.

A colonial mansion, a hereditary estate, I would say a haunted house, and reach the height of romantic felicity—but that would be asking too much of fate!

Still I will proudly declare that there is something queer about it.

Else, why should it be let so cheaply? And why have stood so long untenanted?

John laughs at me, of course, but one expects that in marriage. 5

John is practical in the extreme. He has no patience with faith, an intense horror of superstition, and he scoffs openly at any talk of things not to be felt and seen and put down in figures.

John is a physician, and *perhaps*—(I would not say it to a living soul, of course, but this is dead paper and a great relief to my mind—) *perhaps* that is one reason I do not get well faster.

You see he does not believe I am sick!

And what can one do?

If a physician of high standing, and one's own husband, assures 10 friends and relatives that there is really nothing the matter with one but temporary nervous depression—a slight hysterical tendency—what is one to do?

My brother is also a physician, and also of high standing, and he says the same thing.

So I take phosphates or phosphites—whichever it is, and tonics, and journeys, and air, and exercise, and am absolutely forbidden to "work" until I am well again.

Personally, I disagree with their ideas.

Personally, I believe that congenial work, with excitement and change, would do me good.

But what is one to do? 15

I did write for a while in spite of them; but it *does* exhaust me a good deal—having to be so sly about it, or else meet with heavy opposition.

I sometimes fancy that in my condition if I had less opposition and more society and stimulus—but John says the very worst thing I can do is to think about my condition, and I confess it always makes me feel bad.

So I will let it alone and talk about the house.

The most beautiful place! It is quite alone, standing well back from the road, quite three miles from the village. It makes me think of English places that you read about, for there are hedges and walls and gates that lock, and lots of separate little houses for the gardeners and people.

There is a *delicious* garden! I never saw such a garden—large and shady, 20 full of box-bordered paths, and lined with long grape-covered arbors with seats under them.

There were greenhouses, too, but they are all broken now.

There was some legal trouble, I believe, something about the heirs and co-heirs; anyhow, the place has been empty for years.

That spoils my ghostliness, I am afraid, but I don't care—there is something strange about the house—I can feel it.

I even said so to John one moonlight evening, but he said what I felt was a *draught*, and shut the window.

25   I get unreasonably angry with John sometimes. I'm sure I never used to be so sensitive. I think it is due to this nervous condition.

But John says if I feel so, I shall neglect proper self-control; so I take pains to control myself—before him, at least, and that makes me very tired.

I don't like our room a bit. I wanted one downstairs that opened on the piazza and had roses all over the window, and such pretty old-fashioned chintz hangings! but John would not hear of it.

He said there was only one window and not room for two beds, and no near room for him if he took another.

He is very careful and loving, and hardly lets me stir without special direction.

30   I have a schedule prescription for each hour in the day; he takes all care from me, and so I feel basely ungrateful not to value it more.

He said we came here solely on my account, that I was to have perfect rest and all the air I could get. "Your exercise depends on your strength, my dear," said he, "and your food somewhat on your appetite; but air you can absorb all the time." So we took the nursery at the top of the house.

It is a big, airy room, the whole floor nearly, with windows that look all ways, and air and sunshine galore. It was nursery first and then playroom and gymnasium, I should judge; for the windows are barred for little children, and there are rings and things in the walls.

The paint and paper look as if a boys' school had used it. It is stripped off—the paper—in great patches all around the head of my bed, about as far as I can reach, and in a great place on the other side of the room low down. I never saw a worse paper in my life.

One of those sprawling flamboyant patterns committing every artistic sin.

35   It is dull enough to confuse the eye in following, pronounced enough to constantly irritate and provoke study, and when you follow the lame uncertain curves for a little distance they suddenly commit suicide—plunge off at outrageous angles, destroy themselves in unheard of contradictions.

The color is repellant, almost revolting; a smouldering unclean yellow, strangely faded by the slow-turning sunlight.

It is a dull yet lurid orange in some places, a sickly sulphur tint in others.

No wonder the children hated it! I should hate it myself if I had to live in this room long.

There comes John, and I must put this away,—he hates to have me write a word.

We have been here two weeks, and I haven't felt like writing before, since 40 that first day.

I am sitting by the window now, up in this atrocious nursery, and there is nothing to hinder my writing as much as I please, save lack of strength.

John is away all day, and even some nights when his cases are serious.

I am glad my case is not serious!

But these nervous troubles are dreadfully depressing.

John does not know how much I really suffer. He knows there is no 45 *reason* to suffer, and that satisfies him.

Of course it is only nervousness. It does weigh on me so not to do my duty in any way!

I mean to be such a help to John, such a real rest and comfort, and here I am a comparative burden already!

Nobody would believe what an effort it is to do what little I am able,—to dress and entertain, and order things.

It is fortunate Mary is so good with the baby. Such a dear baby!

And yet I *cannot* be with him, it makes me so nervous. 50

I suppose John never was nervous in his life. He laughs at me so about this wallpaper!

At first he meant to repaper the room, but afterwards he said that I was letting it get the better of me, and that nothing was worse for a nervous patient than to give way to such fancies.

He said that after the wallpaper was changed it would be the heavy bedstead, and then the barred windows, and then that gate at the head of the stairs, and so on.

"You know the place is doing you good," he said, "and really, dear, I don't care to renovate the house just for a three months' rental."

"Then do let us go downstairs," I said, "there are such pretty rooms 55 there."

Then he took me in his arms and called me a blessed little goose, and said he would go down cellar, if I wished, and have it whitewashed into the bargain.

But he is right enough about the beds and windows and things.

It is an airy and comfortable room as any one need wish, and, of course, I would not be so silly as to make him uncomfortable just for a whim.

I'm really getting quite fond of the big room, all but that horrid paper.

Out of one window I can see the garden, those mysterious deep-shaded 60 arbors, the riotous old-fashioned flowers, and bushes and gnarly trees.

Out of another I get a lovely view of the bay and a little private wharf belonging to the estate. There is a beautiful shaded lane that runs down there from the house. I always fancy I see people walking in these numerous paths and arbors, but John has cautioned me not to give way to fancy in the least. He says that with my imaginative power and habit of story-making, a nervous weakness like mine is sure to lead to all manner of excited fancies, and that I ought to use my will and good sense to check the tendency. So I try.

I think sometimes that if I were only well enough to write a little it would relieve the press of ideas and rest me.

But I find I get pretty tired when I try.

It is so discouraging not to have any advice and companionship about my work. When I get really well, John says we will ask Cousin Henry and Julia down for a long visit; but he says he would as soon put fireworks in my pillow-case as to let me have those stimulating people about now.

65   I wish I could get well faster.

But I must not think about that. This paper looks to me as if it *knew* what a vicious influence it had!

There is a recurrent spot where the pattern lolls like a broken neck and two bulbous eyes stare at you upside down.

I get positively angry with the impertinence of it and the everlastingness. Up and down and sideways they crawl, and those absurd, unblinking eyes are everywhere. There is one place where two breadths didn't match, and the eyes go all up and down the line, one a little higher than the other.

I never saw so much expression in an inanimate thing before, and we all know how much expression they have! I used to lie awake as a child and get more entertainment and terror out of blank walls and plain furniture than most children could find in a toy-store.

70   I remember what a kindly wink the knobs of our big, old bureau used to have, and there was one chair that always seemed like a strong friend.

I used to feel that if any of the other things looked too fierce I could always hop into that chair and be safe.

The furniture in this room is no worse than inharmonious, however, for we had to bring it all from downstairs. I suppose when this was used as a playroom they had to take the nursery things out, and no wonder! I never saw such ravages as the children have made here.

The wallpaper, as I said before, is torn off in spots, and it sticketh closer than a brother—they must have had perseverance as well as hatred.

Then the floor is scratched and gouged and splintered, the plaster itself is dug out here and there, and this great heavy bed which is all we found in the room, looks as if it had been through the wars.

But I don't mind it a bit—only the paper. 75

There comes John's sister. Such a dear girl as she is, and so careful of me! I must not let her find me writing.

She is a perfect and enthusiastic housekeeper, and hopes for no better profession. I verily believe she thinks it is the writing which made me sick!

But I can write when she is out, and see her a long way off from these windows.

There is one that commands the road, a lovely shaded winding road, and one that just looks off over the country. A lovely country, too, full of great elms and velvet meadows.

This wallpaper has a kind of sub-pattern in a different shade, a particu- 80 larly irritating one, for you can only see it in certain lights, and not clearly then.

But in the places where it isn't faded and where the sun is just so—I can see a strange, provoking, formless sort of figure, that seems to skulk about behind that silly and conspicuous front design.

There's sister on the stairs!

Well, the Fourth of July is over! The people are all gone and I am tired out. John thought it might do me good to see a little company, so we just had mother and Nellie and the children down for a week.

Of course I didn't do a thing. Jennie sees to everything now.

But it tired me all the same. 85

John says if I don't pick up faster he shall send me to Weir Mitchell[1] in the fall.

But I don't want to go there at all. I had a friend who was in his hands once, and she says he is just like John and my brother, only more so!

Besides, it is such an undertaking to go so far.

I don't feel as if it was worth while to turn my hand over for anything, and I'm getting dreadfully fretful and querulous.

I cry at nothing, and cry most of the time. 90

Of course I don't when John is here, or anybody else, but when I am alone.

And I am alone a good deal just now. John is kept in town very often by serious cases, and Jennie is good and lets me alone when I want her to.

So I walk a little in the garden or down that lovely lane, sit on the porch under the roses, and lie down up here a good deal.

I'm getting really fond of the room in spite of the wallpaper. Perhaps *because* of the wallpaper.

---

1. Silas Weir Mitchell (1829–1914), American physician, novelist, and specialist in nerve disorders, popularized the rest cure.

95   It dwells in my mind so!

I lie here on this great immovable bed—it is nailed down, I believe—and follow that pattern about by the hour. It is as good as gymnastics, I assure you. I start, we'll say, at the bottom, down in the corner over there where it has not been touched, and I determine for the thousandth time that I *will* follow that pointless pattern to some sort of conclusion.

I know a little of the principle of design, and I know this thing was not arranged on any laws of radiation, or alternation, or repetition, or symmetry, or anything else that I ever heard of.

It is repeated, of course, by the breadths, but not otherwise.

Looked at in one way each breadth stands alone, the bloated curves and flourishes—a kind of "debased Romanesque" with *delirium tremens*—go waddling up and down in isolated columns of fatuity.

100   But, on the other hand, they connect diagonally, and the sprawling outlines run off in great slanting waves of optic horror, like a lot of wallowing seaweeds in full chase.

The whole thing goes horizontally, too, at least it seems so, and I exhaust myself in trying to distinguish the order of its going in that direction.

They have used a horizontal breadth for a frieze, and that adds wonderfully to the confusion.

There is one end of the room where it is almost intact, and there, when the crosslights fade and the low sun shines directly upon it, I can almost fancy radiation after all,—the interminable grotesque seem to form around a common center and rush off in headlong plunges of equal distraction.

It makes me tired to follow it. I will take a nap I guess.

105 I don't know why I should write this.

I don't want to.

I don't feel able.

And I know John would think it absurd. But I *must* say what I feel and think in some way—it is such a relief!

But the effort is getting to be greater than the relief.

110   Half the time now I am awfully lazy, and lie down ever so much.

John says I mustn't lose my strength, and has me take cod liver oil and lots of tonics and things, to say nothing of ale and wine and rare meat.

Dear John! He loves me very dearly, and hates to have me sick. I tried to have a real earnest reasonable talk with him the other day, and tell him how I wish he would let me go and make a visit to Cousin Henry and Julia.

But he said I wasn't able to go, nor able to stand it after I got there; and I did not make out a very good case for myself, for I was crying before I had finished.

It is getting to be a great effort for me to think straight. Just this nervous weakness I suppose.

And dear John gathered me up in his arms, and just carried me upstairs 115 and laid me on the bed, and sat by me and read to me till it tired my head.

He said I was his darling and his comfort and all he had, and that I must take care of myself for his sake, and keep well.

He says no one but myself can help me out of it, that I must use my will and self-control and not let any silly fancies run away with me.

There's one comfort, the baby is well and happy, and does not have to occupy this nursery with the horrid wallpaper.

If we had not used it, that blessed child would have! What a fortunate escape! Why, I wouldn't have a child of mine, an impressionable little thing, live in such a room for worlds.

I never thought of it before, but it is lucky that John kept me here after 120 all, I can stand it so much easier than a baby, you see.

Of course I never mention it to them any more—I am too wise,—but I keep watch of it all the same.

There are things in that paper that nobody knows but me, or ever will.

Behind that outside pattern the dim shapes get clearer every day.

It is always the same shape, only very numerous.

And it is like a woman stooping down and creeping about behind that 125 pattern. I don't like it a bit. I wonder—I begin to think—I wish John would take me away from here!

It is so hard to talk with John about my case, because he is so wise, and because he loves me so.

But I tried it last night.

It was moonlight. The moon shines in all around just as the sun does.

I hate to see it sometimes, it creeps so slowly, and always comes in by one window or another.

John was asleep and I hated to waken him, so I kept still and watched 130 the moonlight on that undulating wallpaper till I felt creepy.

The faint figure behind seemed to shake the pattern, just as if she wanted to get out.

I got up softly and went to feel and see if the paper *did* move, and when I came back John was awake.

"What is it, little girl?" he said. "Don't go walking about like that— you'll get cold."

I thought it was a good time to talk, so I told him that I really was not gaining here, and that I wished he would take me away.

"Why, darling!" said he, "our lease will be up in three weeks, and I can't 135 see how to leave before.

"The repairs are not done at home, and I cannot possibly leave town just now. Of course if you were in any danger, I could and would, but you really are better, dear, whether you can see it or not. I am a doctor, dear, and I know. You are gaining flesh and color, your appetite is better, I feel really much easier about you."

"I don't weigh a bit more," said I, "nor as much; and my appetite may be better in the evening when you are here, but it is worse in the morning when you are away!"

"Bless her little heart!" said he with a big hug, "she shall be as sick as she pleases! But now let's improve the shining hours by going to sleep, and talk about it in the morning!"

"And you won't go away?" I asked gloomily.

140   "Why, how can I, dear? It is only three weeks more and then we will take a nice little trip of a few days while Jennie is getting the house ready. Really dear you are better!"

"Better in body perhaps—" I began, and stopped short, for he sat up straight and looked at me with such a stern, reproachful look that I could not say another word.

"My darling," said he, "I beg of you, for my sake and for our child's sake, as well as for your own, that you will never for one instant let that idea enter your mind! There is nothing so dangerous, so fascinating, to a temperament like yours. It is a false and foolish fancy. Can you not trust me as a physician when I tell you so?"

So of course I said no more on that score, and we went to sleep before long. He thought I was asleep first, but I wasn't, and lay there for hours trying to decide whether that front pattern and the back pattern really did move together or separately.

On a pattern like this, by daylight, there is a lack of sequence, a defiance of law, that is a constant irritant to a normal mind.

145   The color is hideous enough, and unreliable enough, and infuriating enough, but the pattern is torturing.

You think you have mastered it, but just as you get well underway in following, it turns a back-somersault and there you are. It slaps you in the face, knocks you down, and tramples upon you. It is like a bad dream.

The outside pattern is a florid arabesque, reminding one of a fungus. If you can imagine a toadstool in joints, an interminable string of toadstools, budding and sprouting in endless convolutions—why, that is something like it.

That is, sometimes!

There is one marked peculiarity about this paper, a thing nobody seems to notice but myself, and that is that it changes as the light changes.

150   When the sun shoots in through the east window—I always watch for that first long, straight ray—it changes so quickly that I never can quite believe it.

That is why I watch it always.

By moonlight—the moon shines in all night when there is a moon—I wouldn't know it was the same paper.

At night in any kind of light, in twilight, candlelight, lamplight, and worst of all by moonlight, it becomes bars! The outside pattern I mean, and the woman behind it is as plain as can be.

I didn't realize for a long time what the thing was that showed behind, that dim sub-pattern, but now I am quite sure it is a woman.

By daylight she is subdued, quiet. I fancy it is the pattern that keeps her so still. It is so puzzling. It keeps me quiet by the hour.

I lie down ever so much now. John says it is good for me, and to sleep all I can.

Indeed he started the habit by making me lie down for an hour after each meal.

It is a very bad habit I am convinced, for you see I don't sleep.

And that cultivates deceit, for I don't tell them I'm awake—O no!

The fact is I am getting a little afraid of John.

He seems very queer sometimes, and even Jennie has an inexplicable look.

It strikes me occasionally, just as a scientific hypothesis,—that perhaps it is the paper!

I have watched John when he did not know I was looking, and come into the room suddenly on the most innocent excuses, and I've caught him several times *looking at the paper!* And Jennie too. I caught Jennie with her hand on it once.

She didn't know I was in the room, and when I asked her in a quiet, a very quiet voice, with the most restrained manner possible, what she was doing with the paper—she turned around as if she had been caught stealing, and looked quite angry—asked me why I should frighten her so!

Then she said that the paper stained everything it touched, that she had found yellow smooches on all my clothes and John's, and she wished we would be more careful!

Did not that sound innocent? But I know she was studying that pattern, and I am determined that nobody shall find it out but myself!

Life is very much more exciting now than it used to be. You see I have something more to expect, to look forward to, to watch. I really do eat better, and am more quiet than I was.

John is so pleased to see me improve! He laughed a little the other day, and said I seemed to be flourishing in spite of my wallpaper.

I turned it off with a laugh. I had no intention of telling him it was *because* of the wallpaper—he would make fun of me. He might even want to take me away.

170   I don't want to leave now until I have found it out. There is a week more, and I think that will be enough.

I'm feeling ever so much better! I don't sleep much at night, for it is so interesting to watch developments; but I sleep a good deal in the daytime.

In the daytime it is tiresome and perplexing.

There are always new shoots on the fungus, and new shades of yellow all over it. I cannot keep count of them, though I have tried conscientiously.

It is the strangest yellow, that wallpaper! It makes me think of all the yellow things I ever saw—not beautiful ones like buttercups, but old foul, bad yellow things.

175   But there is something else about that paper—the smell! I noticed it the moment we came into the room, but with so much air and sun it was not bad. Now we have had a week of fog and rain, and whether the windows are open or not, the smell is here.

It creeps all over the house.

I find it hovering in the dining-room, skulking in the parlor, hiding in the hall, lying in wait for me on the stairs.

It gets into my hair.

Even when I go to ride, if I turn my head suddenly and surprise it— there is that smell!

180   Such a peculiar odor, too! I have spent hours in trying to analyze it, to find what it smelled like.

It is not bad—at first, and very gentle, but quite the subtlest, most enduring odor I ever met.

In this damp weather it is awful, I wake up in the night and find it hanging over me.

It used to disturb me at first. I thought seriously of burning the house—to reach the smell.

But now I am used to it. The only thing I can think of that it is like is the *color* of the paper! A yellow smell.

185   There is a very funny mark on this wall, low down, near the mopboard. A streak that runs round the room. It goes behind every piece of furniture, except the bed, a long, straight, even *smooch*, as if it had been rubbed over and over.

I wonder how it was done and who did it, and what they did it for. Round and round and round—round and round and round—it makes me dizzy!

I really have discovered something at last.

Through watching so much at night, when it changes so, I have finally found out.

The front pattern *does* move—and no wonder! The woman behind shakes it!

Sometimes I think there are a great many women behind, and sometimes only one, and she crawls around fast, and her crawling shakes it all over.

Then in the very bright spots she keeps still, and in the very shady spots she just takes hold of the bars and shakes them hard.

And she is all the time trying to climb through. But nobody could climb through that pattern—it strangles so; I think that is why it has so many heads.

They get through, and then the pattern strangles them off and turns them upside down, and makes their eyes white!

If those heads were covered or taken off it would not be half so bad.

I think that woman gets out in the daytime!

And I'll tell you why—privately—I've seen her!

I can see her out of every one of my windows!

It is the same woman, I know, for she is always creeping, and most women do not creep by daylight.

I see her in that long shaded lane, creeping up and down. I see her in those dark grape arbors, creeping all around the garden.

I see her on that long road under the trees, creeping along, and when a carriage comes she hides under the blackberry vines.

I don't blame her a bit. It must be very humiliating to be caught creeping by daylight!

I always lock the door when I creep by daylight. I can't do it at night, for I know John would suspect something at once.

And John is so queer now, that I don't want to irritate him. I wish he would take another room! Besides, I don't want anybody to get that woman out at night but myself.

I often wonder if I could see her out of all the windows at once.

But, turn as fast as I can, I can only see out of one at one time.

And though I always see her, she *may* be able to creep faster than I can turn!

I have watched her sometimes away off in the open country, creeping as fast as a cloud shadow in a high wind.

If only that top pattern could be gotten off from the under one! I mean to try it, little by little.

I have found out another funny thing, but I shan't tell it this time! It does not do to trust people too much.

There are only two more days to get this paper off, and I believe John is beginning to notice. I don't like the look in his eyes.

And I heard him ask Jennie a lot of professional questions about me. She had a very good report to give.

She said I slept a good deal in the daytime.

John knows I don't sleep very well at night, for all I'm so quiet!

He asked me all sorts of questions, too, and pretended to be very loving and kind.

215   As if I couldn't see through him!

Still, I don't wonder he acts so, sleeping under this paper for three months.

It only interests me, but I feel sure John and Jennie are secretly affected by it.

Hurrah! This is the last day, but it is enough. John is to stay in town over night, and won't be out until this evening.

Jennie wanted to sleep with me—the sly thing! but I told her I should undoubtedly rest better for a night all alone.

220   That was clever, for really I wasn't alone a bit! As soon as it was moonlight and that poor thing began to crawl and shake the pattern, I got up and ran to help her.

I pulled and she shook, I shook and she pulled, and before morning we had peeled off yards of that paper.

A strip about as high as my head and half around the room.

And then when the sun came and that awful pattern began to laugh at me, I declared I would finish it to-day!

We go away to-morrow, and they are moving all my furniture down again to leave things as they were before.

225   Jennie looked at the wall in amazement, but I told her merrily that I did it out of pure spite at the vicious thing.

She laughed and said she wouldn't mind doing it herself, but I must not get tired.

How she betrayed herself that time!

But I am here, and no person touches this paper but me,—not *alive!*

She tried to get me out of the room—it was too patent! But I said it was so quiet and empty and clean now that I believed I would lie down again and sleep all I could; and not to wake me even for dinner—I would call when I woke.

230   So now she is gone, and the servants are gone, and the things are gone, and there is nothing left but that great bedstead nailed down, with the canvas mattress we found on it.

We shall sleep downstairs to-night, and take the boat home to-morrow.

I quite enjoy the room, now it is bare again.

How those children did tear about here!

This bedstead is fairly gnawed!

But I must get to work. 235

I have locked the door and thrown the key down into the front path.

I don't want to go out, and I don't want to have anybody come in, till John comes.

I want to astonish him.

I've got a rope up here that even Jennie did not find. If that woman does get out, and tries to get away, I can tie her!

But I forgot I could not reach far without anything to stand on! 240

This bed will *not* move!

I tried to lift and push it until I was lame, and then I got so angry I bit off a little piece at one corner—but it hurt my teeth.

Then I peeled off all the paper I could reach standing on the floor. It sticks horribly and the pattern just enjoys it! All those strangled heads and bulbous eyes and waddling fungus growths just shriek with derision!

I am getting angry enough to do something desperate. To jump out of the window would be admirable exercise, but the bars are too strong even to try.

Besides I wouldn't do it. Of course not. I know well enough that a step 245 like that is improper and might be misconstrued.

I don't like to *look* out of the windows even—there are so many of those creeping women, and they creep so fast.

I wonder if they all come out of that wallpaper as I did?

But I am securely fastened now by my well-hidden rope—you don't get *me* out in the road there!

I suppose I shall have to get back behind the pattern when it comes night, and that is hard!

It is so pleasant to be out in this great room and creep around as I 250 please!

I don't want to go outside. I won't, even if Jennie asks me to.

For outside you have to creep on the ground, and everything is green instead of yellow.

But here I can creep smoothly on the floor, and my shoulder just fits in that long smooch around the wall, so I cannot lose my way.

Why there's John at the door!

It is no use, young man, you can't open it! 255

How he does call and pound!

Now he's crying for an axe.

It would be a shame to break down that beautiful door!

"John dear!" said I in the gentlest voice, "the key is down by the front steps, under a plantain leaf!"

That silenced him for a few moments. 260

Then he said—very quietly indeed, "Open the door, my darling!"

"I can't," said I. "The key is down by the front door under a plantain leaf!"

And then I said it again, several times, very gently and slowly, and said it so often that he had to go and see, and he got it of course, and came in. He stopped short by the door.

"What is the matter?" he cried. "For God's sake, what are you doing!"

265   I kept on creeping just the same, but I looked at him over my shoulder.

"I've got out at last," said I, "in spite of you and Jane. And I've pulled off most of the paper, so you can't put me back!"

Now why should that man have fainted? But he did, and right across my path by the wall, so that I had to creep over him every time!

1892

JAMES JOYCE
(1882–1941)
Araby

In 1902, after graduating from University College, Dublin, James Joyce left Ireland for Paris, returning a year later. In October 1904, he eloped with Nora Barnacle and settled in Trieste, where he taught English for the Berlitz school. Though he lived as an expatriate for the rest of his life, all of his fiction is set in his native Dublin. Joyce had more than his share of difficulties with publication and censorship. His volume of short stories, *Dubliners*, completed in 1905, was not published until 1914. His novel *Portrait of the Artist as a Young Man*, dated "Dublin 1904, Trieste 1914," appeared first in America, in 1916. His great novel *Ulysses* (1921) was banned for a dozen years in the United States and as long or longer elsewhere. In addition, Joyce published a play, *Exiles* (1918); two collections of poetry, *Chamber Music* (1907) and *Pomes Penyeach* (1927); and the monumental, experimental, and puzzling novel *Finnegans Wake* (1939).

North Richmond Street, being blind,[1] was a quiet street except at the hour when the Christian Brothers' School set the boys free. An uninhabited house of two storeys stood at the blind end, detached from its neighbours in a square ground. The other houses of the street, con-

---

1. That is, a dead-end street.

scious of decent lives within them, gazed at one another with brown imperturbable faces.

The former tenant of our house, a priest, had died in the back drawing-room. Air, musty from having been long enclosed, hung in all the rooms, and the waste room behind the kitchen was littered with old useless papers. Among these I found a few paper-covered books, the pages of which were curled and damp: *The Abbot*, by Walter Scott, *The Devout Communicant* and *The Memoirs of Vidocq*.[2] I liked the last best because its leaves were yellow. The wild garden behind the house contained a central apple-tree and a few straggling bushes under one of which I found the late tenant's rusty bicycle-pump. He had been a very charitable priest; in his will he had left all his money to institutions and the furniture of his house to his sister.

When the short days of winter came dusk fell before we had well eaten our dinners. When we met in the street the houses had grown sombre. The space of sky above us was the colour of ever-changing violet and towards it the lamps of the street lifted their feeble lanterns. The cold air stung us and we played till our bodies glowed. Our shouts echoed in the silent street. The career of our play brought us through the dark muddy lanes behind the houses where we ran the gantlet of the rough tribes from the cottages, to the back doors of the dark dripping gardens where odours arose from the ashpits,[3] to the dark odorous stables where a coachman smoothed and combed the horse or shook music from the buckled harness. When we returned to the street light from the kitchen windows had filled the areas. If my uncle was seen turning the corner we hid in the shadow until we had seen him safely housed. Or if Mangan's sister came out on the doorstep to call her brother in to his tea we watched her from our shadow peer up and down the street. We waited to see whether she would remain or go in and, if she remained, we left our shadow and walked up to Mangan's steps resignedly. She was waiting for us, her figure defined by the light from the half-opened door. Her brother always teased her before he obeyed and I stood by the railings looking at her. Her dress swung as she moved her body and the soft rope of her hair tossed from side to side.

Every morning I lay on the floor in the front parlour watching her door. The blind was pulled down to within an inch of the sash so that I could not

---

2. The "memoirs" were probably *not* written by François Vidocq (1775–1857), a French criminal who became chief of detectives and died poor and disgraced for his part in a crime that he solved. *The Abbot*: the 1820 novel by Sir Walter Scott (1771–1834) is a romance about the Catholic Mary, Queen of Scots (1542–87), who was beheaded. *The Devout Communicant: or Pious Meditations and Aspirations for the Three Days Before and Three Days after Receiving the Holy Eucharist* (1813) is a Catholic religious tract.
3. Where fireplace ashes and other household refuse were dumped.

be seen. When she came out on the doorstep my heart leaped. I ran to the hall, seized my books and followed her. I kept her brown figure always in my eye and, when we came near the point at which our ways diverged, I quickened my pace and passed her. This happened morning after morning. I had never spoken to her, except for a few casual words, and yet her name was like a summons to all my foolish blood.

5 Her image accompanied me even in places the most hostile to romance. On Saturday evenings when my aunt went marketing I had to go to carry some of the parcels. We walked through the flaring streets, jostled by drunken men and bargaining women,

Magnificent Representation
OF
AN ORIENTAL CITY.
CAIRO DONKEYS & DONKEY BOYS
AN ARAB ENCAMPMENT.
INTERNATIONAL TUG-OF-WAR
DANCES BY 250 TRAINED CHILDREN.
Eastern Magic from the Egyptian Hall, London.
CAFE CHANTANT WITH ALL THE LATEST PARISIAN SUCCESSES.
SKIRT DANCING up to Date.
TABLEAUX. THEATRICALS. CHRISTY MINSTRELS.
GRAND THEATRE OF VARIETIES.
"THE ALHAMBRA," An Orchestra of 50 Performers.
Switchback Railways and Roundabouts.
" MENOTTI," The King of the Air,
THE GREAT STOCKHOLM WONDER.
BICYCLE POLO. RIFLE & CLAY PIGEON SHOOTING.
DANCING.
THE EUTERPEAN LADIES' ORCHESTRA.
EIGHT MILITARY BANDS,
Magnificent Displays of Fireworks,
BY BROCK, OF THE CRYSTAL PALACE, LONDON.

ADMISSION • • ONE SHILLING

amid the curses of labourers, the shrill litanies of shop-boys who stood on guard by the barrels of pigs' cheeks, the nasal chanting of street-singers, who sang a *come-all-you* about O'Donovan Rossa,[4] or a ballad about the troubles in our native land. These noises converged in a single sensation of life for me: I imagined that I bore my chalice safely through a throng of foes. Her name sprang to my lips at moments in strange prayers and praises which I myself did not understand. My eyes were often full of tears (I could not tell why) and at times a flood from my heart seemed to pour itself out into my bosom. I thought little of the future. I did not know whether I would ever speak to her or not or, if I spoke to her, how I could tell her of my confused adoration. But my body was like a harp and her words and gestures were like fingers running upon the wires.

One evening I went into the back drawing-room in which the priest had died. It was a dark rainy evening and there was no sound in the house.

4. Jeremiah O'Donovan (1831–1915) was a militant Irish nationalist who fought on despite prison terms and banishment. *Come-all-you:* a song, of which there were many, that began "Come, all you Irishmen."

Through one of the broken panes I heard the rain impinge upon the earth, the fine incessant needles of water playing in the sodden beds. Some distant lamp or lighted window gleamed below me. I was thankful that I could see so little. All my senses seemed to desire to veil themselves and, feeling that I was about to slip from them, I pressed the palms of my hands together until they trembled, murmuring: *O love! O love!* many times.

At last she spoke to me. When she addressed the first words to me I was so confused that I did not know what to answer. She asked me was I going to *Araby*.[5] I forget whether I answered yes or no. It would be a splendid bazaar, she said; she would love to go.

—And why can't you? I asked.

While she spoke she turned a silver bracelet round and round her wrist. She could not go, she said, because there would be a retreat[6] that week in her convent. Her brother and two other boys were fighting for their caps and I was alone at the railings. She held one of the spikes, bowing her head towards me. The light from the lamp opposite our door caught the white curve of her neck, lit up her hair that rested there and, falling, lit up the hand upon the railing. It fell over one side of her dress and caught the white border of a petticoat, just visible as she stood at ease.

—It's well for you, she said.

—If I go, I said, I will bring you something.

What innumerable follies laid waste my waking and sleeping thoughts after that evening! I wished to annihilate the tedious intervening days. I chafed against the work of school. At night in my bedroom and by day in the classroom her image came between me and the page I strove to read. The syllables of the word *Araby* were called to me through the silence in which my soul luxuriated and cast an Eastern enchantment over me. I asked for leave to go to the bazaar on Saturday night. My aunt was surprised and hoped it was not some Freemason[7] affair. I answered few questions in class. I watched my master's face pass from amiability to sternness; he hoped I was not beginning to idle. I could not call my wandering thoughts together. I had hardly any patience with the serious work of life which, now that it stood between me and my desire, seemed to me child's play, ugly monotonous child's play.

On Saturday morning I reminded my uncle that I wished to go to the bazaar in the evening. He was fussing at the hall-stand, looking for the hat-brush, and answered me curtly:

—Yes, boy, I know.

10

5. Charity bazaar billed as a "Grand Oriental Fete," Dublin, May 1894.
6. Period of withdrawal dedicated to prayer and religious study.
7. Freemasons—members of an influential, secretive, and highly ritualistic fraternal organization—were considered enemies of Catholics.

15   As he was in the hall I could not go into the front parlour and lie at the window. I left the house in bad humour and walked slowly towards the school. The air was pitilessly raw and already my heart misgave me.

When I came home to dinner my uncle had not yet been home. Still it was early. I sat staring at the clock for some time and, when its ticking began to irritate me, I left the room. I mounted the staircase and gained the upper part of the house. The high cold empty gloomy rooms liberated me and I went from room to room singing. From the front window I saw my companions playing below in the street. Their cries reached me weakened and indistinct and, leaning my forehead against the cool glass, I looked over at the dark house where she lived. I may have stood there for an hour, seeing nothing but the brown-clad figure cast by my imagination, touched discreetly by the lamplight at the curved neck, at the hand upon the railings and at the border below the dress.

When I came downstairs again I found Mrs Mercer sitting at the fire. She was an old garrulous woman, a pawnbroker's widow, who collected used stamps for some pious purpose. I had to endure the gossip of the tea-table. The meal was prolonged beyond an hour and still my uncle did not come. Mrs Mercer stood up to go: she was sorry she couldn't wait any longer, but it was after eight o'clock and she did not like to be out late, as the night air was bad for her. When she had gone I began to walk up and down the room, clenching my fists. My aunt said:

—I'm afraid you may put off your bazaar for this night of Our Lord.

At nine o'clock I heard my uncle's latchkey in the halldoor. I heard him talking to himself and heard the hallstand rocking when it had received the weight of his overcoat. I could interpret these signs. When he was midway through his dinner I asked him to give me the money to go to the bazaar. He had forgotten.

20   —The people are in bed and after their first sleep now, he said.

I did not smile. My aunt said to him energetically:

—Can't you give him the money and let him go? You've kept him late enough as it is.

My uncle said he was very sorry he had forgotten. He said he believed in the old saying: *All work and no play makes Jack a dull boy.* He asked me where I was going and, when I had told him a second time he asked me did I know *The Arab's Farewell to his Steed.*[8] When I left the kitchen he was about to recite the opening lines of the piece to my aunt.

I held a florin[9] tightly in my hand as I strode down Buckingham Street towards the station. The sight of the streets thronged with buyers and

8. Or *The Arab's Farewell to His Horse*, a sentimental nineteenth-century poem by Caroline Norton. The speaker has sold the horse.
9. A two-shilling piece, thus four times the "sixpenny entrance" fee.

glaring with gas recalled to me the purpose of my journey. I took my seat in a third-class carriage of a deserted train. After an intolerable delay the train moved out of the station slowly. It crept onward among ruinous houses and over the twinkling river. At Westland Row Station a crowd of people pressed to the carriage doors; but the porters moved them back, saying that it was a special train for the bazaar. I remained alone in the bare carriage. In a few minutes the train drew up beside an improvised wooden platform. I passed out on to the road and saw by the lighted dial of a clock that it was ten minutes to ten. In front of me was a large building which displayed the magical name.

I could not find any sixpenny entrance and, fearing that the bazaar would be closed, I passed in quickly through a turnstile, handing a shilling to a weary-looking man. I found myself in a big hall girdled at half its height by a gallery. Nearly all the stalls were closed and the greater part of the hall was in darkness. I recognized a silence like that which pervades a church after a service. I walked into the centre of the bazaar timidly. A few people were gathered about the stalls which were still open. Before a curtain, over which the words *Café Chantant*[1] were written in coloured lamps, two men were counting money on a salver. I listened to the fall of the coins.

Remembering with difficulty why I had come I went over to one of the stalls and examined porcelain vases and flowered tea-sets. At the door of the stall a young lady was talking and laughing with two young gentlemen. I remarked their English accents and listened vaguely to their conversation.

—O, I never said such a thing!

—O, but you did!

—O, but I didn't!

—Didn't she say that?

—Yes. I heard her.

—O, there's a . . . fib!

Observing me the young lady came over and asked me did I wish to buy anything. The tone of her voice was not encouraging; she seemed to have spoken to me out of a sense of duty. I looked humbly at the great jars that stood like eastern guards at either side of the dark entrance to the stall and murmured:

—No, thank you.

The young lady changed the position of one of the vases and went back to the two young men. They began to talk of the same subject. Once or twice the young lady glanced at me over her shoulder.

1. Café with music (French).

I lingered before her stall, though I knew my stay was useless, to make my interest in her wares seem the more real. Then I turned away slowly and walked down the middle of the bazaar. I allowed the two pennies to fall against the sixpence in my pocket. I heard a voice call from one end of the gallery that the light was out. The upper part of the hall was now completely dark.

Gazing up into the darkness I saw myself as a creature driven and derided by vanity; and my eyes burned with anguish and anger.

1914

FRANZ KAFKA
(1883–1924)
A Hunger Artist[1]

Born into a middle-class Jewish family in Prague, Franz Kafka earned a doctorate in law from the German University in that city and held an inconspicuous position in the civil service for many years. Emotionally and physically ill for the last seven or eight years of his short life, he died of tuberculosis in Vienna, never having married (though he was twice engaged to the same woman and lived with an actress in Berlin for some time before he died) and not having published his three major novels, *The Trial* (1925), *The Castle* (1926), and *Amerika* (1927). Indeed, he ordered his friend Max Brod to destroy them and other works he had left in manuscript. Fortunately, Brod did not; and not long after Kafka's death, his sometimes-dreamlike, sometimes-nightmarish work became known and admired all over the world. His stories in English translation are collected in *The Great Wall of China* (1933), *The Penal Colony* (1948), and *The Complete Stories* (1976).

During these last decades the interest in professional fasting has markedly diminished. It used to pay very well to stage such great performances under one's own management, but today that is quite impossible. We live in a different world now. At one time the whole town took a lively interest in the hunger artist; from day to day of his fast the excitement mounted; everybody wanted to see him at least once a day; there were people who bought season tickets for the last few days and sat from morning till night

---

1. Translated by Edwin and Willa Muir.

in front of his small barred cage; even in the nighttime there were visiting hours, when the whole effect was heightened by torch flares; on fine days the cage was set out in the open air, and then it was the children's special treat to see the hunger artist; for their elders he was often just a joke that happened to be in fashion, but the children stood open-mouthed, holding each other's hands for greater security, marveling at him as he sat there pallid in black tights, with his ribs sticking out so prominently, not even on a seat but down among straw on the ground, sometimes giving a courteous nod, answering questions with a constrained smile, or perhaps stretching an arm through the bars so that one might feel how thin it was, and then again withdrawing deep into himself, paying no attention to anyone or anything, not even to the all-important striking of the clock that was the only piece of furniture in his cage, but merely staring into vacancy with half shut eyes, now and then taking a sip from a tiny glass of water to moisten his lips.

Besides casual onlookers there were also relays of permanent watchers selected by the public, usually butchers, strangely enough, and it was their task to watch the hunger artist day and night, three of them at a time, in case he should have some secret recourse to nourishment. This was nothing but a formality, instituted to reassure the masses, for the initiates knew well enough that during his fast the artist would never in any circumstances, not even under forcible compulsion, swallow the smallest morsel of food: the honor of his profession forbade it. Not every watcher, of course, was capable of understanding this, there were often groups of night watchers who were very lax in carrying out their duties and deliberately huddled together in a retired corner to play cards with great absorption, obviously intending to give the hunger artist the chance of a little refreshment, which they supposed he could draw from some private hoard. Nothing annoyed the artist more than such watchers; they made him miserable; they made his fast seem unendurable; sometimes he mastered his feebleness sufficiently to sing during their watch for as long as he could keep going, to show them how unjust their suspicions were. But that was of little use; they only wondered at his cleverness in being able to fill his mouth even while singing. Much more to his taste were the watchers who sat close up to the bars, who were not content with the dim night lighting of the hall but focused him in the full glare of the electric pocket torch[2] given them by the impresario. The harsh light did not trouble him at all, in any case he could never sleep properly, and he could always drowse a little, whatever the light, at any hour, even when the hall was thronged with noisy onlookers. He was quite happy at the prospect of spending a

2. Flashlight.

sleepless night with such watchers; he was ready to exchange jokes with them, to tell them stories out of his nomadic life, anything at all to keep them awake and demonstrate to them again that he had no eatables in his cage and that he was fasting as not one of them could fast. But his happiest moment was when the morning came and an enormous breakfast was brought them, at his expense, on which they flung themselves with the keen appetite of healthy men after a weary night of wakefulness. Of course there were people who argued that this breakfast was an unfair attempt to bribe the watchers, but that was going rather too far, and when they were invited to take on a night's vigil without a breakfast, merely for the sake of the cause, they made themselves scarce, although they stuck stubbornly to their suspicions.

Such suspicions, anyhow, were a necessary accompaniment to the profession of fasting. No one could possibly watch the hunger artist continuously, day and night, and so no one could produce first-hand evidence that the fast had really been rigorous and continuous; only the artist himself could know that, he was therefore bound to be the sole completely satisfied spectator of his own fast. Yet for other reasons he was never satisfied; it was not perhaps mere fasting that had brought him to such skeleton thinness that many people had regretfully to keep away from his exhibitions, because the sight of him was too much for them, perhaps it was dissatisfaction with himself that had worn him down. For he alone knew, what no other initiate knew, how easy it was to fast. It was the easiest thing in the world. He made no secret of this, yet people did not believe him, at the best they set him down as modest; most of them, however, thought he was out for publicity or else was some kind of cheat who found it easy to fast because he had discovered a way of making it easy, and then had the impudence to admit the fact, more or less. He had to put up with all that, and in the course of time had got used to it, but his inner dissatisfaction always rankled, and never yet, after any term of fasting—this must be granted to his credit—had he left the cage of his own free will. The longest period of fasting was fixed by his impresario at forty days,[3] beyond that term he was not allowed to go, not even in great cities, and there was good reason for it, too. Experience had proved that for about forty days the interest of the public could be stimulated by a steadily increasing pressure of advertisement, but after that the town began to lose interest, sympathetic support began notably to fall off; there were of course local variations as between one town and another or one country and another, but as a general rule forty days marked the limit. So on the fortieth

3. Common biblical length of time; in the New Testament, Jesus fasts for forty days in the desert and has visions of both God and the devil.

day the flower-bedecked cage was opened, enthusiastic spectators filled the hall, a military band played, two doctors entered the cage to measure the results of the fast, which were announced through a megaphone, and finally two young ladies appeared, blissful at having been selected for the honor, to help the hunger artist down the few steps leading to a small table on which was spread a carefully chosen invalid repast. And at this very moment the artist always turned stubborn. True, he would entrust his bony arms to the outstretched helping hands of the ladies bending over him, but stand up he would not. Why stop fasting at this particular moment, after forty days of it? He had held out for a long time, an illimitably long time; why stop now, when he was in his best fasting form, or rather, not yet quite in his best fasting form? Why should he be cheated of the fame he would get for fasting longer, for being not only the record hunger artist of all time, which presumably he was already, but for beating his own record by a performance beyond human imagination, since he felt that there were no limits to his capacity for fasting? His public pretended to admire him so much, why should it have so little patience with him; if he could endure fasting longer, why shouldn't the public endure it? Besides, he was tired, he was comfortable sitting in the straw, and now he was supposed to lift himself to his full height and go down to a meal the very thought of which gave him a nausea that only the presence of the ladies kept him from betraying, and even that with an effort. And he looked up into the eyes of the ladies who were apparently so friendly and in reality so cruel, and shook his head, which felt too heavy on its strengthless neck. But then there happened yet again what always happened. The impresario came forward, without a word—for the band made speech impossible—lifted his arms in the air above the artist, as if inviting Heaven to look down upon its creature here in the straw, this suffering martyr, which indeed he was, although in quite another sense; grasped him round the emaciated waist, with exaggerated caution, so that the frail condition he was in might be appreciated; and committed him to the care of the blenching ladies, not without secretly giving him a shaking so that his legs and body tottered and swayed. The artist now submitted completely; his head lolled on his breast as if it had landed there by chance; his body was hollowed out; his legs in a spasm of self-preservation clung close to each other at the knees, yet scraped on the ground as if it were not really solid ground, as if they were only trying to find solid ground; and the whole weight of his body, a feather-weight after all, relapsed onto one of the ladies, who, looking round for help and panting a little—this post of honor was not at all what she had expected it to be—first stretched her neck as far as she could to keep her face at least free from contact with the artist, when finding this impossible, and her more fortunate companion not coming to her aid but merely holding extended on her own trembling hand the little bunch of knucklebones that was the artist's, to the great delight of the spectators burst into tears and had to be replaced by an attendant who had long been stationed in readiness. Then came the food, a little of which the impresario managed to get between the artist's lips, while he sat in a kind of half-fainting trance, to the accompaniment of cheerful patter designed to distract the public's attention from the artist's condition; after that, a toast was drunk to the public, supposedly prompted by a whisper from the artist in the impresario's ear; the band confirmed it with a mighty flourish, the spectators melted away, and no one had any cause to be dissatisfied with the proceedings, no one except the hunger artist himself, he only, as always.

So he lived for many years, with small regular intervals of recuperation, in visible glory, honored by the world, yet in spite of that troubled in spirit, and all the more troubled because no one would take his trouble seriously. What comfort could he possibly need? What more could he possibly wish for? And if some good-natured person, feeling sorry for him, tried to console him by pointing out that his melancholy was probably caused by fasting, it could happen, especially when he had been fasting for some time, that he reacted with an outburst of fury and to the general alarm began to shake the bars of his cage like a wild animal. Yet the impresario had a way of punishing these outbreaks which he rather enjoyed putting into operation. He would apologize publicly for the artist's behavior, which was only to be excused, he admitted, because of the irritability caused by fasting, a condition hardly to be understood by well-fed people; then by natural transition he went on to mention the artist's equally incomprehensible boast that he could fast for much longer than he was doing; he praised the high ambition, the good will, the great self-denial undoubtedly implicit in such a statement; and then quite simply countered it by bringing out photographs, which were also on sale to the public, showing the artist on the fortieth day of a fast lying in bed almost dead from exhaustion. This perversion of the truth, familiar to the artist though it was, always unnerved him afresh and proved too much for him. What was a consequence of the premature ending of his fast was here presented as the cause of it! To fight against this lack of understanding, against a whole world of non-understanding, was impossible. Time and again in good faith he stood by the bars listening to the impresario, but as soon as the photographs appeared he always let go and sank with a groan back on to his straw, and the reassured public could once more come close and gaze at him.

5   A few years later when the witnesses of such scenes called them to mind, they often failed to understand themselves at all. For meanwhile the aforementioned change in public interest had set in; it seemed to happen

almost overnight; there may have been profound causes for it, but who was going to bother about that; at any rate the pampered hunger artist suddenly found himself deserted one fine day by the amusement seekers, who went streaming past him to other more favored attractions. For the last time the impresario hurried him over half Europe to discover whether the old interest might still survive here and there; all in vain; everywhere, as if by secret agreement, a positive revulsion from professional fasting was in evidence. Of course it could not really have sprung up so suddenly as all that, and many premonitory symptoms which had not been sufficiently remarked or suppressed during the rush and glitter of success now came retrospectively to mind, but it was now too late to take any countermeasures. Fasting would surely come into fashion again at some future date, yet that was no comfort for those living in the present. What, then, was the hunger artist to do? He had been applauded by thousands in his time and could hardly come down to showing himself in a street booth at village fairs, and as for adopting another profession, he was not only too old for that but too fanatically devoted to fasting. So he took leave of the impresario, his partner in an unparalleled career, and hired himself to a large circus; in order to spare his own feelings he avoided reading the conditions of his contract.

A large circus with its enormous traffic in replacing and recruiting men, animals and apparatus can always find a use for people at any time, even for a hunger artist, provided of course that he does not ask too much, and in this particular case anyhow it was not only the artist who was taken on but his famous and long-known name as well, indeed considering the peculiar nature of his performance, which was not impaired by advancing age, it could not be objected that here was an artist past his prime, no longer at the height of his professional skill, seeking a refuge in some quiet corner of a circus; on the contrary, the hunger artist averred that he could fast as well as ever, which was entirely credible, he even alleged that if he were allowed to fast as he liked, and this was at once promised him without more ado, he could astound the world by establishing a record never yet achieved, a statement which certainly provoked a smile among the other professionals, since it left out of account the change in public opinion, which the hunger artist in his zeal conveniently forgot.

He had not, however, actually lost his sense of the real situation and took it as a matter of course that he and his cage should be stationed, not in the middle of the ring as a main attraction, but outside, near the animal cages, on a site that was after all easily accessible. Large and gaily painted placards made a frame for the cage and announced what was to be seen inside it. When the public came thronging out in the intervals to see the animals, they could hardly avoid passing the hunger artist's cage and stopping there for a moment, perhaps they might even have stayed longer had not those pressing behind them in the narrow gangway, who did not understand why they should be held up on their way toward the excitements of the menagerie, made it impossible for anyone to stand gazing quietly for any length of time. And that was the reason why the hunger artist, who had of course been looking forward to these visiting hours as the main achievement of his life, began instead to shrink from them. At first he could hardly wait for the intervals; it was exhilarating to watch the crowds come streaming his way, until only too soon—not even the most obstinate self-deception, clung to almost consciously, could hold out against the fact—the conviction was borne in upon him that these people, most of them, to judge from their actions, again and again, without exception, were all on their way to the menagerie. And the first sight of them from the distance remained the best. For when they reached his cage he was at once deafened by the storm of shouting and abuse that arose from the two contending factions, which renewed themselves continuously, of those who wanted to stop and stare at him—he soon began to dislike them more than the others—not out of real interest but only out of obstinate self-assertiveness, and those who wanted to go straight on to the animals. When the first great rush was past, the stragglers came along, and these, whom nothing could have prevented from stopping to look at him as long as they had breath, raced past with long strides, hardly even glancing at him, in their haste to get to the menagerie in time. And all too rarely did it happen that he had a stroke of luck, when some father of a family fetched up before him with his children, pointed a finger at the hunger artist and explained at length what the phenomenon meant, telling stories of earlier years when he himself had watched similar but much more thrilling performances, and the children, still rather uncomprehending, since neither inside nor outside school had they been sufficiently prepared for this lesson—what did they care about fasting?—yet showed by the brightness of their intent eyes that new and better times might be coming. Perhaps, said the hunger artist to himself many a time, things would be a little better if his cage were set not quite so near the menagerie. That made it too easy for people to make their choice, to say nothing of what he suffered from the stench of the menagerie, the animals' restlessness by night, the carrying past of raw lumps of flesh for the beasts of prey, the roaring at feeding times, which depressed him continually. But he did not dare to lodge a complaint with the management; after all, he had the animals to thank for the troops of people who passed his cage, among whom there might always be one here and there to take an interest in him, and who could tell where they might seclude him if he called attention to his existence and thereby to the fact that, strictly speaking, he was only an impediment on the way to the menagerie.

A small impediment, to be sure, one that grew steadily less. People grew familiar with the strange idea that they could be expected, in times like these, to take an interest in a hunger artist, and with this familiarity the verdict went out against him. He might fast as much as he could, and he did so; but nothing could save him now, people passed him by. Just try to explain to anyone the art of fasting! Anyone who has no feeling for it cannot be made to understand it. The fine placards grew dirty and illegible, they were torn down; the little notice board telling the number of fast days achieved, which at first was changed carefully every day, had long stayed at the same figure, for after the first few weeks even this small task seemed pointless to the staff; and so the artist simply fasted on and on, as he had once dreamed of doing, and it was no trouble to him, just as he had always foretold, but no one counted the days, no one, not even the artist himself, knew what records he was already breaking, and his heart grew heavy. And when once in a time some leisurely passer-by stopped, made merry over the old figure on the board and spoke of swindling, that was in its way the stupidest lie ever invented by indifference and inborn malice, since it was not the hunger artist who was cheating; he was working honestly, but the world was cheating him of his reward.

Many more days went by, however, and that too came to an end. An overseer's eye fell on the cage one day and he asked the attendants why this perfectly good cage should be left standing there unused with dirty straw inside it; nobody knew, until one man, helped out by the notice board, remembered about the hunger artist. They poked into the straw with sticks and found him in it. "Are you still fasting?" asked the overseer. "When on earth do you mean to stop?" "Forgive me, everybody," whispered the hunger artist; only the overseer, who had his ear to the bars, understood him. "Of course," said the overseer, and tapped his forehead with a finger to let the attendants know what state the man was in, "we forgive you." "I always wanted you to admire my fasting," said the hunger artist. "We do admire it," said the overseer, affably. "But you shouldn't admire it," said the hunger artist. "Well, then we don't admire it," said the overseer, "but why shouldn't we admire it?" "Because I have to fast, I can't help it," said the hunger artist. "What a fellow you are," said the overseer, "and why can't you help it?" "Because," said the hunger artist, lifting his head a little and speaking, with his lips pursed, as if for a kiss, right into the overseer's ear, so that no syllable might be lost, "because I couldn't find the food I liked. If I had found it, believe me, I should have made no fuss and stuffed myself like you or anyone else." These were his last words, but in his dimming eyes remained the firm though no longer proud persuasion that he was still continuing to fast.

10   "Well, clear this out now!" said the overseer, and they buried the hunger artist, straw and all. Into the cage they put a young panther. Even the most insensitive felt it refreshing to see this wild creature leaping around the cage that had so long been dreary. The panther was all right. The food he liked was brought him without hesitation by the attendants; he seemed not even to miss his freedom; his noble body, furnished almost to the bursting point with all that it needed, seemed to carry freedom around with it too; somewhere in his jaws it seemed to lurk; and the joy of life streamed with such ardent passion from his throat that for the onlookers it was not easy to stand the shock of it. But they braced themselves, crowded round the cage, and did not want ever to move away.

1924

JHUMPA LAHIRI
(b. 1967)

Interpreter of Maladies

Born in London and raised in Rhode Island, Jhumpa Lahiri is the daughter of Bengali parents; much of her fiction addresses the difficulty of reconciling an Indian heritage with life in the United States. Lahiri earned a BA from Barnard College and several degrees from Boston University: an MA in English, an MFA in creative writing, an MA in comparative studies in literature and the arts, and a PhD in Renaissance studies. She has published many stories in well-known periodicals such as the *New Yorker* and won the 2000 Pulitzer Prize for her first collection, *Interpreter of Maladies* (1999), a best seller that has been translated into twenty-nine languages. Her second collection, *Unaccustomed Earth* (2008), debuted at the top of the *New York Times* best-seller list. Lahiri is also the author of two novels: *The Namesake* (2003) was made into a film in 2006; *The Lowland* (2013) was short-listed for both the Man Booker Prize and the National Book Award.

A t the tea stall Mr. and Mrs. Das bickered about who should take Tina to the toilet. Eventually Mrs. Das relented when Mr. Das pointed out that he had given the girl her bath the night before. In the rearview mirror Mr. Kapasi watched as Mrs. Das emerged slowly from his bulky white Ambassador, dragging her shaved, largely bare legs across the back seat. She did not hold the little girl's hand as they walked to the rest room.

They were on their way to see the Sun Temple at Konarak.[1] It was a dry, bright Saturday, the mid-July heat tempered by a steady ocean breeze, ideal weather for sightseeing. Ordinarily Mr. Kapasi would not have stopped so soon along the way, but less than five minutes after he'd picked up the family that morning in front of Hotel Sandy Villa, the little girl had complained. The first thing Mr. Kapasi had noticed when he saw Mr. and Mrs. Das, standing with their children under the portico of the hotel, was that they were very young, perhaps not even thirty. In addition to Tina they had two boys, Ronny and Bobby, who appeared very close in age and had teeth covered in a network of flashing silver wires. The family looked Indian but dressed as foreigners did, the children in stiff, brightly colored clothing and caps with translucent visors. Mr. Kapasi was accustomed to foreign tourists; he was assigned to them regularly because he could speak English. Yesterday he had driven an elderly couple from Scotland, both with spotted faces and fluffy white hair so thin it exposed their sunburnt scalps. In comparison, the tanned, youthful faces of Mr. and Mrs. Das were all the more striking. When he'd introduced himself, Mr. Kapasi had pressed his palms together in greeting, but Mr. Das squeezed hands like an American so that Mr. Kapasi felt it in his elbow. Mrs. Das, for her part, had flexed one side of her mouth, smiling dutifully at Mr. Kapasi, without displaying any interest in him.

As they waited at the tea stall, Ronny, who looked like the older of the two boys, clambered suddenly out of the back seat, intrigued by a goat tied to a stake in the ground.

"Don't touch it," Mr. Das said. He glanced up from his paperback tour book, which said "INDIA" in yellow letters and looked as if it had been published abroad. His voice, somehow tentative and a little shrill, sounded as though it had not yet settled into maturity.

"I want to give it a piece of gum," the boy called back as he trotted 5 ahead.

Mr. Das stepped out of the car and stretched his legs by squatting briefly to the ground. A clean-shaven man, he looked exactly like a magnified version of Ronny. He had a sapphire blue visor, and was dressed in shorts, sneakers, and a T-shirt. The camera slung around his neck, with an impressive telephoto lens and numerous buttons and markings, was the only complicated thing he wore. He frowned, watching as Ronny rushed toward the goat, but appeared to have no intention of intervening. "Bobby, make sure that your brother doesn't do anything stupid."

1. In paragraphs 91–98, the story provides an accurate history and description of the Sun Temple at Konarak (or Konarak), still a pilgrimage as well as tourist site near the east coast in the Orissa region of India. According to legend, the temple was built because Samba, son of Lord Krishna, was cured of leprosy by Surya, the sun god.

"I don't feel like it," Bobby said, not moving. He was sitting in the front seat beside Mr. Kapasi, studying a picture of the elephant god taped to the glove compartment.

"No need to worry," Mr. Kapasi said. "They are quite tame." Mr. Kapasi was forty-six years old, with receding hair that had gone completely silver, but his butterscotch complexion and his unlined brow, which he treated in spare moments to dabs of lotus-oil balm, made it easy to imagine what he must have looked like at an earlier age. He wore gray trousers and a matching jacket-style shirt, tapered at the waist, with short sleeves and a large pointed collar, made of a thin but durable synthetic material. He had specified both the cut and the fabric to his tailor—it was his preferred uniform for giving tours because it did not get crushed during his long hours behind the wheel. Through the windshield he watched as Ronny circled around the goat, touched it quickly on its side, then trotted back to the car.

"You left India as a child?" Mr. Kapasi asked when Mr. Das had settled once again into the passenger seat.

10 "Oh, Mina and I were both born in America," Mr. Das announced with an air of sudden confidence. "Born and raised. Our parents live here now, in Assansol.[2] They retired. We visit them every couple years." He turned to watch as the little girl ran toward the car, the wide purple bows of her sundress flopping on her narrow brown shoulders. She was holding to her chest a doll with yellow hair that looked as if it had been chopped, as a punitive measure, with a pair of dull scissors. "This is Tina's first trip to India, isn't it, Tina?"

"I don't have to go to the bathroom anymore," Tina announced.

"Where's Mina?" Mr. Das asked.

Mr. Kapasi found it strange that Mr. Das should refer to his wife by her first name when speaking to the little girl. Tina pointed to where Mrs. Das was purchasing something from one of the shirtless men who worked at the tea stall. Mr. Kapasi heard one of the shirtless men sing a phrase from a popular Hindi love song as Mrs. Das walked back to the car, but she did not appear to understand the words of the song, for she did not express irritation, or embarrassment, or react in any other way to the man's declarations.

He observed her. She wore a red-and-white-checkered skirt that stopped above her knees, slip-on shoes with a square wooden heel, and a close-fitting blouse styled like a man's undershirt. The blouse was decorated at chest-level with a calico appliqué in the shape of a strawberry. She was a short woman, with small hands like paws, her frosty pink fingernails painted

---

2. Or Asonsol, a city in northeastern India, not far from Calcutta and about three hundred miles from Puri, the coastal city in Orissa that the Das family is visiting. Puri is both a tourist resort and a Hindu holy city, said to be dominated by the forces of both the gods and humanity.

to match her lips, and was slightly plump in her figure. Her hair, shorn only a little longer than her husband's, was parted far to one side. She was wearing large dark brown sunglasses with a pinkish tint to them, and carried a big straw bag, almost as big as her torso, shaped like a bowl, with a water bottle poking out of it. She walked slowly, carrying some puffed rice tossed with peanuts and chili peppers in a large packet made from newspapers. Mr. Kapasi turned to Mr. Das.

"Where in America do you live?"   15

"New Brunswick, New Jersey."

"Next to New York?"

"Exactly. I teach middle school there."

"What subject?"

"Science. In fact, every year I take my students on a trip to the Museum   20 of Natural History in New York City. In a way we have a lot in common, you could say, you and I. How long have you been a tour guide, Mr. Kapasi?"

"Five years."

Mrs. Das reached the car. "How long's the trip?" she asked, shutting the door.

"About two and a half hours," Mr. Kapasi replied.

At this Mrs. Das gave an impatient sigh, as if she had been traveling her whole life without pause. She fanned herself with a folded Bombay film magazine written in English.

"I thought that the Sun Temple is only eighteen miles north of Puri,"   25 Mr. Das said, tapping on the tour book.

"The roads to Konarak are poor. Actually it is a distance of fifty-two miles," Mr. Kapasi explained.

Mr. Das nodded, readjusting the camera strap where it had begun to chafe the back of his neck.

Before starting the ignition, Mr. Kapasi reached back to make sure the cranklike locks on the inside of each of the back doors were secured. As soon as the car began to move the little girl began to play with the lock on her side, clicking it with some effort forward and backward, but Mrs. Das said nothing to stop her. She sat a bit slouched at one end of the back seat, not offering her puffed rice to anyone. Ronny and Tina sat on either side of her, both snapping bright green gum.

"Look," Bobby said as the car began to gather speed. He pointed with his finger to the tall trees that lined the road. "Look."

"Monkeys!" Ronny shrieked. "Wow!"   30

They were seated in groups along the branches, with shining black faces, silver bodies, horizontal eyebrows, and crested heads. Their long gray tails dangled like a series of ropes among the leaves. A few scratched themselves with black leathery hands, or swung their feet, staring as the car passed.

"We call them the hanuman," Mr. Kapasi said. "They are quite common in the area."

As soon as he spoke, one of the monkeys leaped into the middle of the road, causing Mr. Kapasi to brake suddenly. Another bounced onto the hood of the car, then sprang away. Mr. Kapasi beeped his horn. The children began to get excited, sucking in their breath and covering their faces partly with their hands. They had never seen monkeys outside of a zoo, Mr. Das explained. He asked Mr. Kapasi to stop the car so that he could take a picture.

While Mr. Das adjusted his telephoto lens, Mrs. Das reached into her straw bag and pulled out a bottle of colorless nail polish, which she proceeded to stroke on the tip of her index finger.

35   The little girl stuck out a hand. "Mine too. Mommy, do mine too."

"Leave me alone," Mrs. Das said, blowing on her nail and turning her body slightly. "You're making me mess up."

The little girl occupied herself by buttoning and unbuttoning a pinafore on the doll's plastic body.

"All set," Mr. Das said, replacing the lens cap.

The car rattled considerably as it raced along the dusty road, causing them all to pop up from their seats every now and then, but Mrs. Das continued to polish her nails. Mr. Kapasi eased up on the accelerator, hoping to produce a smoother ride. When he reached for the gearshift the boy in front accommodated him by swinging his hairless knees out of the way. Mr. Kapasi noted that this boy was slightly paler than the other children. "Daddy, why is the driver sitting on the wrong side in this car, too?" the boy asked.

40   "They all do that here, dummy," Ronny said.

"Don't call your brother a dummy," Mr. Das said. He turned to Mr. Kapasi. "In America, you know . . . it confuses them."

"Oh yes, I am well aware," Mr. Kapasi said. As delicately as he could, he shifted gears again, accelerating as they approached a hill in the road. "I see it on *Dallas*, the steering wheels are on the left-hand side."

"What's *Dallas*?" Tina asked, banging her now naked doll on the seat behind Mr. Kapasi.

"It went off the air," Mr. Das explained. "It's a television show."[3]

45   They were all like siblings, Mr. Kapasi thought as they passed a row of date trees. Mr. and Mrs. Das behaved like an older brother and sister, not parents. It seemed that they were in charge of the children only for the day; it was hard to believe they were regularly responsible for anything other than themselves. Mr. Das tapped on his lens cap, and his tour book, dragging his thumbnail occasionally across the pages so that they made a

3. Reruns of this American television show (1978–91) featuring the rich, dysfunctional Ewing family of Dallas continue worldwide.

scraping sound. Mrs. Das continued to polish her nails. She had still not removed her sunglasses. Every now and then Tina renewed her plea that she wanted her nails done, too, and so at one point Mrs. Das flicked a drop of polish on the little girl's finger before depositing the bottle back inside her straw bag.

"Isn't this an air-conditioned car?" she asked, still blowing on her hand. The window on Tina's side was broken and could not be rolled down.

"Quit complaining," Mr. Das said. "It isn't so hot."

"I told you to get a car with air-conditioning," Mrs. Das continued. "Why do you do this, Raj, just to save a few stupid rupees. What are you saving us, fifty cents?"

Their accents sounded just like the ones Mr. Kapasi heard on American television programs, though not like the ones on *Dallas.*

"Doesn't it get tiresome, Mr. Kapasi, showing people the same thing 50 every day?" Mr. Das asked, rolling down his own window all the way. "Hey, do you mind stopping the car. I just want to get a shot of this guy."

Mr. Kapasi pulled over to the side of the road as Mr. Das took a picture of a barefoot man, his head wrapped in a dirty turban, seated on top of a cart of grain sacks pulled by a pair of bullocks. Both the man and the bullocks were emaciated. In the back seat Mrs. Das gazed out another window, at the sky, where nearly transparent clouds passed quickly in front of one another.

"I look forward to it, actually," Mr. Kapasi said as they continued on their way. "The Sun Temple is one of my favorite places. In that way it is a reward for me. I give tours on Fridays and Saturdays only. I have another job during the week."

"Oh? Where?" Mr. Das asked.

"I work in a doctor's office."

"You're a doctor?" 55

"I am not a doctor. I work with one. As an interpreter."

"What does a doctor need an interpreter for?"

"He has a number of Gujarati patients. My father was Gujarati, but many people do not speak Gujarati in this area,[4] including the doctor. And so the doctor asked me to work in his office, interpreting what the patients say."

"Interesting. I've never heard of anything like that," Mr. Das said.

Mr. Kapasi shrugged. "It is a job like any other." 60

"But so romantic," Mrs. Das said dreamily, breaking her extended silence. She lifted her pinkish brown sunglasses and arranged them on top

4. Gujarat is a northwestern region of India, on the Arabian Sea. Mr. Kapasi speaks several of India's disparate regional languages—those of Bengal and Orissa, near where he lives, and Gujarati, from the opposite coast—along with the more widespread Hindi and English.

of her head like a tiara. For the first time, her eyes met Mr. Kapasi's in the rearview mirror: pale, a bit small, their gaze fixed but drowsy.

Mr. Das craned to look at her. "What's so romantic about it?"

"I don't know. Something." She shrugged, knitting her brows together for an instant. "Would you like a piece of gum, Mr. Kapasi?" she asked brightly. She reached into her straw bag and handed him a small square wrapped in green-and-white-striped paper. As soon as Mr. Kapasi put the gum in his mouth a thick sweet liquid burst onto his tongue.

"Tell us more about your job, Mr. Kapasi," Mrs. Das said.

65 "What would you like to know, madame?"

"I don't know," she shrugged, munching on some puffed rice and licking the mustard oil from the corners of her mouth. "Tell us a typical situation." She settled back in her seat, her head tilted in a patch of sun, and closed her eyes. "I want to picture what happens."

"Very well. The other day a man came in with a pain in his throat."

"Did he smoke cigarettes?"

"No. It was very curious. He complained that he felt as if there were long pieces of straw stuck in his throat. When I told the doctor he was able to prescribe the proper medication."

70 "That's so neat."

"Yes," Mr. Kapasi agreed after some hesitation.

"So these patients are totally dependent on you," Mrs. Das said. She spoke slowly, as if she were thinking aloud. "In a way, more dependent on you than the doctor."

"How do you mean? How could it be?"

"Well, for example, you could tell the doctor that the pain felt like a burning, not straw. The patient would never know what you had told the doctor, and the doctor wouldn't know that you had told the wrong thing. It's a big responsibility."

75 "Yes, a big responsibility you have there, Mr. Kapasi," Mr. Das agreed.

Mr. Kapasi had never thought of his job in such complimentary terms. To him it was a thankless occupation. He found nothing noble in interpreting people's maladies, assiduously translating the symptoms of so many swollen bones, countless cramps of bellies and bowels, spots on people's palms that changed color, shape, or size. The doctor, nearly half his age, had an affinity for bell-bottom trousers and made humorless jokes about the Congress party.[5] Together they worked in a stale little infirmary where

5. The Indian National Congress party, founded in 1885, led the movement for independence from Britain (gained in 1947) through the successive leadership of Mohandas Gandhi (1869–1948) and Jawaharlal Nehru (1889–1964). The party divided and subdivided, but a faction once led by Indira Gandhi (1917–84) dominated through the 1980s and much of the 1990s, despite being constantly accused of corruption and the use of violent tactics.

Mr. Kapasi's smartly tailored clothes clung to him in the heat, in spite of the blackened blades of a ceiling fan churning over their heads. The job was a sign of his failings. In his youth he'd been a devoted scholar of foreign languages, the owner of an impressive collection of dictionaries. He had dreamed of being an interpreter for diplomats and dignitaries, resolving conflicts between people and nations, settling disputes of which he alone could understand both sides. He was a self-educated man. In a series of notebooks, in the evenings before his parents settled his marriage, he had listed the common etymologies of words, and at one point in his life he was confident that he could converse, if given the opportunity, in English, French, Russian, Portuguese, and Italian, not to mention Hindi, Bengali, Orissi, and Gujarati. Now only a handful of European phrases remained in his memory, scattered words for things like saucers and chairs. English was the only non-Indian language he spoke fluently anymore. Mr. Kapasi knew it was not a remarkable talent. Sometimes he feared that his children knew better English than he did, just from watching television. Still, it came in handy for the tours.

He had taken the job as an interpreter after his first son, at the age of seven, contracted typhoid—that was how he had first made the acquaintance of the doctor. At the time Mr. Kapasi had been teaching English in a grammar school, and he bartered his skills as an interpreter to pay the increasingly exorbitant medical bills. In the end the boy had died one evening in his mother's arms, his limbs burning with fever, but then there was the funeral to pay for, and the other children who were born soon enough, and the newer, bigger house, and the good schools and tutors, and the fine shoes and the television, and the countless other ways he tried to console his wife and to keep her from crying in her sleep, and so when the doctor offered to pay him twice as much as he earned at the grammar school, he accepted. Mr. Kapasi knew that his wife had little regard for his career as an interpreter. He knew it reminded her of the son she'd lost, and that she resented the other lives he helped, in his own small way, to save. If ever she referred to his position, she used the phrase "doctor's assistant," as if the process of interpretation were equal to taking someone's temperature, or changing a bedpan. She never asked him about the patients who came to the doctor's office, or said that his job was a big responsibility.

For this reason it flattered Mr. Kapasi that Mrs. Das was so intrigued by his job. Unlike his wife, she had reminded him of its intellectual challenges. She had also used the word "romantic." She did not behave in a romantic way toward her husband, and yet she had used the word to describe him. He wondered if Mr. and Mrs. Das were a bad match, just as he and his wife were. Perhaps they, too, had little in common apart from three children and a decade of their lives. The signs he recognized from his own marriage were there—the bickering, the indifference, the protracted silences. Her sudden interest in him, an interest she did not express in either her husband or her children, was mildly intoxicating. When Mr. Kapasi thought once again about how she had said "romantic," the feeling of intoxication grew.

80   He began to check his reflection in the rearview mirror as he drove, feeling grateful that he had chosen the gray suit that morning and not the brown one, which tended to sag a little in the knees. From time to time he glanced through the mirror at Mrs. Das. In addition to glancing at her face he glanced at the strawberry between her breasts, and the golden brown hollow in her throat. He decided to tell Mrs. Das about another patient, and another: the young woman who had complained of a sensation of raindrops in her spine, the gentleman whose birthmark had begun to sprout hairs. Mrs. Das listened attentively, stroking her hair with a small plastic brush that resembled an oval bed of nails, asking more questions, for yet another example. The children were quiet, intent on spotting more monkeys in the trees, and Mr. Das was absorbed by his tour book, so it seemed like a private conversation between Mr. Kapasi and Mrs. Das. In this manner the next half hour passed, and when they stopped for lunch at a roadside restaurant that sold fritters and omelette sandwiches, usually something Mr. Kapasi looked forward to on his tours so that he could sit in peace and enjoy some hot tea, he was disappointed. As the Das family settled together under a magenta umbrella fringed with white and orange tassels, and placed their orders with one of the waiters who marched about in tricornered caps, Mr. Kapasi reluctantly headed toward a neighboring table.

"Mr. Kapasi, wait. There's room here," Mrs. Das called out. She gathered Tina onto her lap, insisting that he accompany them. And so, together, they had bottled mango juice and sandwiches and plates of onions and potatoes deep-fried in graham-flour batter. After finishing two omelette sandwiches Mr. Das took more pictures of the group as they ate.

"How much longer?" he asked Mr. Kapasi as he paused to load a new roll of film in the camera.

"About half an hour more."

By now the children had gotten up from the table to look at more monkeys perched in a nearby tree, so there was a considerable space between Mrs. Das and Mr. Kapasi. Mr. Das placed the camera to his face and squeezed one eye shut, his tongue exposed at one corner of his mouth. "This looks funny. Mina, you need to lean in closer to Mr. Kapasi."

85   She did. He could smell a scent on her skin, like a mixture of whiskey and rosewater. He worried suddenly that she could smell his perspiration, which he knew had collected beneath the synthetic material of his shirt.

He polished off his mango juice in one gulp and smoothed his silver hair with his hands. A bit of the juice dripped onto his chin. He wondered if Mrs. Das had noticed.

She had not. "What's your address, Mr. Kapasi?" she inquired, fishing for something inside her straw bag.

"You would like my address?"

"So we can send you copies," she said. "Of the pictures." She handed him a scrap of paper which she had hastily ripped from a page of her film magazine. The blank portion was limited, for the narrow strip was crowded by lines of text and a tiny picture of a hero and heroine embracing under a eucalyptus tree.

The paper curled as Mr. Kapasi wrote his address in clear, careful letters. She would write to him, asking about his days interpreting at the doctor's office, and he would respond eloquently, choosing only the most entertaining anecdotes, ones that would make her laugh out loud as she read them in her house in New Jersey. In time she would reveal the disappointment of her marriage, and he his. In this way their friendship would grow, and flourish. He would possess a picture of the two of them, eating fried onions under a magenta umbrella, which he would keep, he decided, safely tucked between the pages of his Russian grammar. As his mind raced, Mr. Kapasi experienced a mild and pleasant shock. It was similar to a feeling he used to experience long ago when, after months of translating with the aid of a dictionary, he would finally read a passage from a French novel, or an Italian sonnet, and understand the words, one after another, unencumbered by his own efforts. In those moments Mr. Kapasi used to believe that all was right with the world, that all struggles were rewarded, that all of life's mistakes made sense in the end. The promise that he would hear from Mrs. Das now filled him with the same belief.

When he finished writing his address Mr. Kapasi handed her the paper, 90 but as soon as he did so he worried that he had either misspelled his name, or accidentally reversed the numbers of his postal code. He dreaded the possibility of a lost letter, the photograph never reaching him, hovering somewhere in Orissa, close but ultimately unattainable. He thought of asking for the slip of paper again, just to make sure he had written his address accurately, but Mrs. Das had already dropped it into the jumble of her bag.

They reached Konarak at two-thirty. The temple, made of sandstone, was a massive pyramid-like structure in the shape of a chariot. It was dedicated to the great master of life, the sun, which struck three sides of the edifice as it made its journey each day across the sky. Twenty-four giant wheels were carved on the north and south sides of the plinth. The whole thing was drawn by a team of seven horses, speeding as if through the heavens. As they approached, Mr. Kapasi explained that the temple had been built between A.D. 1243 and 1255, with the efforts of twelve hundred artisans, by the great ruler of the Ganga dynasty, King Narasimhadeva the First, to commemorate his victory against the Muslim army.

"It says the temple occupies about a hundred and seventy acres of land," Mr. Das said, reading from his book.

"It's like a desert," Ronny said, his eyes wandering across the sand that stretched on all sides beyond the temple.

"The Chandrabhaga River once flowed one mile north of here. It is dry now," Mr. Kapasi said, turning off the engine.

95   They got out and walked toward the temple, posing first for pictures by the pair of lions that flanked the steps. Mr. Kapasi led them next to one of the wheels of the chariot, higher than any human being, nine feet in diameter.

"'The wheels are supposed to symbolize the wheel of life,'" Mr. Das read. "'They depict the cycle of creation, preservation, and achievement of realization.' Cool." He turned the page of his book. "'Each wheel is divided into eight thick and thin spokes, dividing the day into eight equal parts. The rims are carved with designs of birds and animals, whereas the medallions in the spokes are carved with women in luxurious poses, largely erotic in nature.'"

What he referred to were the countless friezes of entwined naked bodies, making love in various positions, women clinging to the necks of men, their knees wrapped eternally around their lovers' thighs. In addition to these were assorted scenes from daily life, of hunting and trading, of deer being killed with bows and arrows and marching warriors holding swords in their hands.

It was no longer possible to enter the temple, for it had filled with rubble years ago, but they admired the exterior, as did all the tourists Mr. Kapasi brought there, slowly strolling along each of its sides. Mr. Das trailed behind, taking pictures. The children ran ahead, pointing to figures of naked people, intrigued in particular by the Nagamithunas, the half-human, half-serpentine couples who were said, Mr. Kapasi told them, to live in the deepest waters of the sea. Mr. Kapasi was pleased that they liked the temple, pleased especially that it appealed to Mrs. Das. She stopped every three or four paces, staring silently at the carved lovers, and the processions of elephants, and the topless female musicians beating on two-sided drums.

Though Mr. Kapasi had been to the temple countless times, it occurred to him, as he, too, gazed at the topless women, that he had never seen his own wife fully naked. Even when they had made love she kept the panels of her blouse hooked together, the string of her petticoat knotted around her waist. He had never admired the backs of his wife's legs the way he now admired those of Mrs. Das, walking as if for his benefit alone. He had, of course, seen plenty of bare limbs before, belonging to the American and European ladies who took his tours. But Mrs. Das was different. Unlike the other women, who had an interest only in the temple, and kept their noses buried in a guidebook, or their eyes behind the lens of a camera, Mrs. Das had taken an interest in him.

Mr. Kapasi was anxious to be alone with her, to continue their private 100 conversation, yet he felt nervous to walk at her side. She was lost behind her sunglasses, ignoring her husband's requests that she pose for another picture, walking past her children as if they were strangers. Worried that he might disturb her, Mr. Kapasi walked ahead, to admire, as he always did, the three life-sized bronze avatars of Surya, the sun god, each emerging from its own niche on the temple facade to greet the sun at dawn, noon, and evening. They wore elaborate headdresses, their languid, elongated eyes closed, their bare chests draped with carved chains and amulets. Hibiscus petals, offerings from previous visitors, were strewn at their gray-green feet. The last statue, on the northern wall of the temple, was Mr. Kapasi's favorite. This Surya had a tired expression, weary after a hard day of work, sitting astride a horse with folded legs. Even his horse's eyes were drowsy. Around his body were smaller sculptures of women in pairs, their hips thrust to one side.

"Who's that?" Mrs. Das asked. He was startled to see that she was standing beside him.

"He is the Astachala-Surya," Mr. Kapasi said. "The setting sun."

"So in a couple of hours the sun will set right here?" She slipped a foot out of one of her square-heeled shoes, rubbed her toes on the back of her other leg.

"That is correct."

She raised her sunglasses for a moment, then put them back on again. 105 "Neat."

Mr. Kapasi was not certain exactly what the word suggested, but he had a feeling it was a favorable response. He hoped that Mrs. Das had understood Surya's beauty, his power. Perhaps they would discuss it further in their letters. He would explain things to her, things about India, and she would explain things to him about America. In its own way this correspondence would fulfill his dream, of serving as an interpreter between nations. He looked at her straw bag, delighted that his address lay nestled among its contents. When he pictured her so many thousands of miles away he plummeted, so much so that he had an overwhelming urge to wrap his arms around her, to freeze with her, even for an instant, in an embrace witnessed by his favorite Surya. But Mrs. Das had already started walking.

"When do you return to America?" he asked, trying to sound placid.

"In ten days."

He calculated: A week to settle in, a week to develop the pictures, a few days to compose her letter, two weeks to get to India by air. According to his schedule, allowing room for delays, he would hear from Mrs. Das in approximately six weeks' time.

110   The family was silent as Mr. Kapasi drove them back, a little past four-thirty, to Hotel Sandy Villa. The children had bought miniature granite versions of the chariot's wheels at a souvenir stand, and they turned them round in their hands. Mr. Das continued to read his book. Mrs. Das untangled Tina's hair with her brush and divided it into two little ponytails.

Mr. Kapasi was beginning to dread the thought of dropping them off. He was not prepared to begin his six-week wait to hear from Mrs. Das. As he stole glances at her in the rearview mirror, wrapping elastic bands around Tina's hair, he wondered how he might make the tour last a little longer. Ordinarily he sped back to Puri using a shortcut, eager to return home, scrub his feet and hands with sandalwood soap, and enjoy the evening newspaper and a cup of tea that his wife would serve him in silence. The thought of that silence, something to which he'd long been resigned, now oppressed him. It was then that he suggested visiting the hills at Udayagiri and Khandagiri, where a number of monastic dwellings were hewn out of the ground, facing one another across a defile. It was some miles away, but well worth seeing, Mr. Kapasi told them.

"Oh yeah, there's something mentioned about it in this book," Mr. Das said. "Built by a Jain king or something."[6]

"Shall we go then?" Mr. Kapasi asked. He paused at a turn in the road. "It's to the left."

Mr. Das turned to look at Mrs. Das. Both of them shrugged.

115   "Left, left," the children chanted.

Mr. Kapasi turned the wheel, almost delirious with relief. He did not know what he would do or say to Mrs. Das once they arrived at the hills. Perhaps he would tell her what a pleasing smile she had. Perhaps he would compliment her strawberry shirt, which he found irresistibly becoming. Perhaps, when Mr. Das was busy taking a picture, he would take her hand.

He did not have to worry. When they got to the hills, divided by a steep path thick with trees, Mrs. Das refused to get out of the car. All along the path, dozens of monkeys were seated on stones, as well as on the branches

6. This site is not a major tourist attraction; "giri" means mountain. Jainism, one of the several main religions of India, is an atheist sect that emerged from Hinduism around 580 BCE, at about the same time as Buddhism.

of the trees. Their hind legs were stretched out in front and raised to shoulder level, their arms resting on their knees.

"My legs are tired," she said, sinking low in her seat. "I'll stay here."

"Why did you have to wear those stupid shoes?" Mr. Das said. "You won't be in the pictures."

"Pretend I'm there."   120

"But we could use one of these pictures for our Christmas card this year. We didn't get one of all five of us at the Sun Temple. Mr. Kapasi could take it."

"I'm not coming. Anyway, those monkeys give me the creeps."

"But they're harmless," Mr. Das said. He turned to Mr. Kapasi. "Aren't they?"

"They are more hungry than dangerous," Mr. Kapasi said. "Do not provoke them with food, and they will not bother you."

Mr. Das headed up the defile with the children, the boys at his side,   125
the little girl on his shoulders. Mr. Kapasi watched as they crossed paths with a Japanese man and woman, the only other tourists there, who paused for a final photograph, then stepped into a nearby car and drove away. As the car disappeared out of view some of the monkeys called out, emitting soft whooping sounds, and then walked on their flat black hands and feet up the path. At one point a group of them formed a little ring around Mr. Das and the children. Tina screamed in delight. Ronny ran in circles around his father. Bobby bent down and picked up a fat stick on the ground. When he extended it, one of the monkeys approached him and snatched it, then briefly beat the ground.

"I'll join them," Mr. Kapasi said, unlocking the door on his side. "There is much to explain about the caves."

"No. Stay a minute," Mrs. Das said. She got out of the back seat and slipped in beside Mr. Kapasi. "Raj has his dumb book anyway." Together, through the windshield, Mrs. Das and Mr. Kapasi watched as Bobby and the monkey passed the stick back and forth between them.

"A brave little boy," Mr. Kapasi commented.

"It's not so surprising," Mrs. Das said.

"No?"   130

"He's not his."

"I beg your pardon?"

"Raj's. He's not Raj's son."

Mr. Kapasi felt a prickle on his skin. He reached into his shirt pocket for the small tin of lotus-oil balm he carried with him at all times, and applied it to three spots on his forehead. He knew that Mrs. Das was watching him, but he did not turn to face her. Instead he watched as the figures of Mr. Das and the children grew smaller, climbing up the steep path, pausing every now and then for a picture, surrounded by a growing number of monkeys.

135 "Are you surprised?" The way she put it made him choose his words with care.

"It's not the type of thing one assumes," Mr. Kapasi replied slowly. He put the tin of lotus-oil balm back in his pocket.

"No, of course not. And no one knows, of course. No one at all. I've kept it a secret for eight whole years." She looked at Mr. Kapasi, tilting her chin as if to gain a fresh perspective. "But now I've told you."

Mr. Kapasi nodded. He felt suddenly parched, and his forehead was warm and slightly numb from the balm. He considered asking Mrs. Das for a sip of water, then decided against it.

"We met when we were very young," she said. She reached into her straw bag in search of something, then pulled out a packet of puffed rice. "Want some?"

140 "No, thank you."

She put a fistful in her mouth, sank into the seat a little, and looked away from Mr. Kapasi, out the window on her side of the car. "We married when we were still in college. We were in high school when he proposed. We went to the same college, of course. Back then we couldn't stand the thought of being separated, not for a day, not for a minute. Our parents were best friends who lived in the same town. My entire life I saw him every weekend, either at our house or theirs. We were sent upstairs to play together while our parents joked about our marriage. Imagine! They never caught us at anything, though in a way I think it was all more or less a setup. The things we did those Friday and Saturday nights, while our parents sat downstairs drinking tea . . . I could tell you stories, Mr. Kapasi."

As a result of spending all her time in college with Raj, she continued, she did not make many close friends. There was no one to confide in about him at the end of a difficult day, or to share a passing thought or a worry. Her parents now lived on the other side of the world, but she had never been very close to them, anyway. After marrying so young she was overwhelmed by it all, having a child so quickly, and nursing, and warming up bottles of milk and testing their temperature against her wrist while Raj was at work, dressed in sweaters and corduroy pants, teaching his students about rocks and dinosaurs. Raj never looked cross or harried, or plump as she had become after the first baby.

Always tired, she declined invitations from her one or two college girlfriends, to have lunch or shop in Manhattan. Eventually the friends stopped calling her, so that she was left at home all day with the baby, surrounded by toys that made her trip when she walked or wince when she sat, always cross and tired. Only occasionally did they go out after Ronny was born, and even more rarely did they entertain. Raj didn't mind; he looked forward to coming home from teaching and watching television and bouncing Ronny on his knee. She had been outraged when Raj told her that a Punjabi friend,[7] someone whom she had once met but did not remember, would be staying with them for a week for some job interviews in the New Brunswick area.

Bobby was conceived in the afternoon, on a sofa littered with rubber teething toys, after the friend learned that a London pharmaceutical company had hired him, while Ronny cried to be freed from his playpen. She made no protest when the friend touched the small of her back as she was about to make a pot of coffee, then pulled her against his crisp navy suit. He made love to her swiftly, in silence, with an expertise she had never known, without the meaningful expressions and smiles Raj always insisted on afterward. The next day Raj drove the friend to JFK.[8] He was married now, to a Punjabi girl, and they lived in London still, and every year they exchanged Christmas cards with Raj and Mina, each couple tucking photos of their families into the envelopes. He did not know that he was Bobby's father. He never would.

"I beg your pardon, Mrs. Das, but why have you told me this information?" Mr. Kapasi asked when she had finally finished speaking, and had turned to face him once again.

"For God's sake, stop calling me Mrs. Das. I'm twenty-eight. You probably have children my age."

"Not quite." It disturbed Mr. Kapasi to learn that she thought of him as a parent. The feeling he had had toward her, that had made him check his reflection in the rearview mirror as they drove, evaporated a little.

"I told you because of your talents." She put the packet of puffed rice back into her bag without folding over the top.

"I don't understand," Mr. Kapasi said.

"Don't you see? For eight years I haven't been able to express this to anybody, not to friends, certainly not to Raj. He doesn't even suspect it. He thinks I'm still in love with him. Well, don't you have anything to say?"

"About what?"

"About what I've just told you. About my secret, and about how terrible it makes me feel. I feel terrible looking at my children, and at Raj, always terrible. I have terrible urges, Mr. Kapasi, to throw things away. One day I had the urge to throw everything I own out of the window, the television, the children, everything. Don't you think it's unhealthy?"

He was silent.

7. Person from the Punjab, a northern region of India, near Pakistan.
8 . John F. Kennedy International Airport, in New York City.

155 "Mr. Kapasi, don't you have anything to say? I thought that was your job."
"My job is to give tours, Mrs. Das."
"Not that. Your other job. As an interpreter."
"But we do not face a language barrier. What need is there for an interpreter?"
"That's not what I mean. I would never have told you otherwise. Don't you realize what it means for me to tell you?"
"What does it mean?"

160 "It means that I'm tired of feeling so terrible all the time. Eight years, Mr. Kapasi, I've been in pain eight years. I was hoping you could help me feel better, say the right thing. Suggest some kind of remedy."

He looked at her, in her red plaid skirt and strawberry T-shirt, a woman not yet thirty, who loved neither her husband nor her children, who had already fallen out of love with life. Her confession depressed him, depressed him all the more when he thought of Mr. Das at the top of the path, Tina clinging to his shoulders, taking pictures of ancient monastic cells cut into the hills to show his students in America, unsuspecting and unaware that one of his sons was not his own. Mr. Kapasi felt insulted that Mrs. Das should ask him to interpret her common, trivial little secret. She did not resemble the patients in the doctor's office, those who came glassy-eyed and desperate, unable to sleep or breathe or urinate with ease, unable, above all, to give words to their pains. Still, Mr. Kapasi believed it was his duty to assist Mrs. Das. Perhaps he ought to tell her to confess the truth to Mr. Das. He would explain that honesty was the best policy. Honesty, surely, would help her feel better, as she'd put it. Perhaps he would offer to preside over the discussion, as a mediator. He decided to begin with the most obvious question, to get to the heart of the matter, and so he asked, "Is it really pain you feel, Mrs. Das, or is it guilt?"

She turned to him and glared, mustard oil thick on her frosty pink lips. She opened her mouth to say something, but as she glared at Mr. Kapasi some certain knowledge seemed to pass before her eyes, and she stopped. It crushed him; he knew at that moment that he was not even important enough to be properly insulted. She opened the car door and began walking up the path, wobbling a little on her square wooden heels, reaching into her straw bag to eat handfuls of puffed rice. It fell through her fingers, leaving a zig-zagging trail, causing a monkey to leap down from a tree and devour the little white grains. In search of more, the monkey began to follow Mrs. Das. Others joined him, so that she was soon being followed by about half a dozen of them, their velvety tails dragging behind.

Mr. Kapasi stepped out of the car. He wanted to holler, to alert her in some way, but he worried that if she knew they were behind her, she would grow nervous. Perhaps she would lose her balance. Perhaps they would pull at her bag or her hair. He began to jog up the path, taking a fallen branch in his hand to scare away the monkeys. Mrs. Das continued walking, oblivious, trailing grains of puffed rice. Near the top of the incline, before a group of cells fronted by a row of squat stone pillars, Mr. Das was kneeling on the ground, focusing the lens of his camera. The children stood under the arcade, now hiding, now emerging from view.

"Wait for me," Mrs. Das called out. "I'm coming."

Tina jumped up and down. "Here comes Mommy!" 165

"Great," Mr. Das said without looking up. "Just in time. We'll get Mr. Kapasi to take a picture of the five of us."

Mr. Kapasi quickened his pace, waving his branch so that the monkeys scampered away, distracted, in another direction.

"Where's Bobby?" Mrs. Das asked when she stopped.

Mr. Das looked up from the camera. "I don't know. Ronny, where's Bobby?"

Ronny shrugged. "I thought he was right here." 170

"Where is he?" Mrs. Das repeated sharply. "What's wrong with all of you?"

They began calling his name, wandering up and down the path a bit. Because they were calling, they did not initially hear the boy's screams. When they found him, a little farther down the path under a tree, he was surrounded by a group of monkeys, over a dozen of them, pulling at his T-shirt with their long black fingers. The puffed rice Mrs. Das had spilled was scattered at his feet, raked over by the monkeys' hands. The boy was silent, his body frozen, swift tears running down his startled face. His bare legs were dusty and red with welts from where one of the monkeys struck him repeatedly with the stick he had given to it earlier.

"Daddy, the monkey's hurting Bobby," Tina said.

Mr. Das wiped his palms on the front of his shorts. In his nervousness he accidentally pressed the shutter on his camera; the whirring noise of the advancing film excited the monkeys, and the one with the stick began to beat Bobby more intently. "What are we supposed to do? What if they start attacking?"

"Mr. Kapasi," Mrs. Das shrieked, noticing him standing to one side. 175 "Do something, for God's sake, do something!"

Mr. Kapasi took his branch and shooed them away, hissing at the ones that remained, stomping his feet to scare them. The animals retreated slowly, with a measured gait, obedient but unintimidated. Mr. Kapasi gathered Bobby in his arms and brought him back to where his parents and siblings were standing. As he carried him he was tempted to whisper a secret into the boy's ear. But Bobby was stunned, and shivering with fright, his legs bleeding slightly where the stick had broken the skin. When Mr. Kapasi delivered him to his parents, Mr. Das brushed some dirt off the boy's T-shirt and put the visor on him the right way. Mrs. Das reached into her straw bag to find a bandage which she taped over the cut on his knee. Ronny offered his brother a fresh piece of gum. "He's fine. Just a little scared, right, Bobby?" Mr. Das said, patting the top of his head.

"God, let's get out of here," Mrs. Das said. She folded her arms across the strawberry on her chest. "This place gives me the creeps."

"Yeah. Back to the hotel, definitely," Mr. Das agreed.

"Poor Bobby," Mrs. Das said. "Come here a second. Let Mommy fix your hair." Again she reached into her straw bag, this time for her hairbrush, and began to run it around the edges of the translucent visor. When she whipped out the hairbrush, the slip of paper with Mr. Kapasi's address on it fluttered away in the wind. No one but Mr. Kapasi noticed. He watched as it rose, carried higher and higher by the breeze, into the trees where the monkeys now sat, solemnly observing the scene below. Mr. Kapasi observed it too, knowing that this was the picture of the Das family he would pre-serve forever in his mind.

1999

GABRIEL GARCÍA MÁRQUEZ
(1928–2014)
A Very Old Man with Enormous Wings: A Tale for Children[1]

Born in Aracataca, Colombia, a remote town near the Caribbean coast, Gabriel García Márquez studied law at the University of Bogotá and then worked as a journalist in Latin America, Europe, and the United States. In 1967, he took up permanent residence in Barcelona, Spain. His first published book, *Leaf Storm* (1955), set in the fictional small town of Macondo, is based on the myths and legends of his childhood home. His most famous novel, *One Hundred Years of Solitude* (1967), fuses magic, reality, fable, and fantasy to present six generations of one Macondo family, a microcosm of many of the social, political, and economic problems of Latin America. Among his many works are *The Autumn of the Patriarch* (1975), *Chronicle of a Death Foretold* (1981), *Love in the Time of Cholera* (1987), *Of Love and Other Demons* (1994), and *Living to Tell the Tale* (2003), a three-volume set of memoirs. Márquez won the Nobel Prize for Literature in 1982.

---

1. Translated by Gregory Rabassa.

On the third day of rain they had killed so many crabs inside the house that Pelayo had to cross his drenched courtyard and throw them into the sea, because the newborn child had a temperature all night and they thought it was due to the stench. The world had been sad since Tuesday. Sea and sky were a single ashgray thing and the sands of the beach, which on March nights glimmered like powdered light, had become a stew of mud and rotten shellfish. The light was so weak at noon that when Pelayo was coming back to the house after throwing away the crabs, it was hard for him to see what it was that was moving and groaning in the rear of the courtyard. He had to go very close to see that it was an old man, a very old man, lying face down in the mud, who, in spite of his tremendous efforts, couldn't get up, impeded by his enormous wings.

Frightened by that nightmare, Pelayo ran to get Elisenda, his wife, who was putting compresses on the sick child, and he took her to the rear of the courtyard. They both looked at the fallen body with mute stupor. He was dressed like a ragpicker.[2] There were only a few faded hairs left on his bald skull and very few teeth in his mouth, and his pitiful condition of a drenched great-grandfather had taken away any sense of grandeur he might have had. His huge buzzard wings, dirty and half-plucked, were forever entangled in the mud. They looked at him so long and so closely that Pelayo and Elisenda very soon overcame their surprise and in the end found him familiar. Then they dared speak to him, and he answered in an incomprehensible dialect with a strong sailor's voice. That was how they skipped over the inconvenience of the wings and quite intelligently concluded that he was a lonely castaway from some foreign ship wrecked by the storm. And yet, they called in a neighbor woman who knew everything about life and death to see him, and all she needed was one look to show them their mistake.

"He's an angel," she told them. "He must have been coming for the child, but the poor fellow is so old that the rain knocked him down."

On the following day everyone knew that a flesh-and-blood angel was held captive in Pelayo's house. Against the judgment of the wise neighbor woman, for whom angels in those times were the fugitive survivors of a celestial conspiracy, they did not have the heart to club him to death. Pelayo watched over him all afternoon from the kitchen, armed with his bailiff's[3] club, and before going to bed he dragged him out of the mud and locked him up with the hens in the wire chicken coop. In the middle of the night, when the rain stopped, Pelayo and Elisenda were still killing crabs. A short time afterward the child woke up without a fever and with a desire to eat.

---

2. Someone who earns a living by collecting rags and other refuse.
3. Local government official, usually one employed to make arrests and serve warrants.

Then they felt magnanimous and decided to put the angel on a raft with fresh water and provisions for three days and leave him to his fate on the high seas. But when they went out into the courtyard with the first light of dawn, they found the whole neighborhood in front of the chicken coop having fun with the angel, without the slightest reverence, tossing him things to eat through the openings in the wire as if he weren't a super-natural creature but a circus animal.

5   Father Gonzaga arrived before seven o'clock, alarmed at the strange news. By that time onlookers less frivolous than those at dawn had already arrived and they were making all kinds of conjectures concerning the captive's future. The simplest among them thought that he should be named mayor of the world. Others of sterner mind felt that he should be promoted to the rank of five-star general in order to win all wars. Some visionaries hoped that he could be put to stud in order to implant on earth a race of winged wise men who could take charge of the universe. But Father Gonzaga, before becoming a priest, had been a robust woodcutter. Standing by the wire, he reviewed his catechism in an instant and asked them to open the door so that he could take a close look at that pitiful man who looked more like a huge decrepit hen among the fascinated chickens. He was lying in a corner drying his open wings in the sunlight among the fruit peels and breakfast leftovers that the early risers had thrown him. Alien to the impertinences of the world, he only lifted his antiquarian eyes and murmured something in his dialect when Father Gonzaga went into the chicken coop and said good morning to him in Latin. The parish priest had his first suspicion of an imposter when he saw that he did not understand the language of God or know how to greet His ministers. Then he noticed that seen close up he was much too human: he had an unbearable smell of the outdoors, the back side of his wings was strewn with parasites and his main feathers had been mistreated by terrestrial winds, and nothing about him measured up to the proud dignity of angels. Then he came out of the chicken coop and in a brief sermon warned the curious against the risks of being ingenuous. He reminded them that the devil had the bad habit of making use of carnival tricks in order to confuse the unwary. He argued that if wings were not the essential element in determining the difference between a hawk and an airplane, they were even less so in the recognition of angels. Nevertheless, he promised to write a letter to his bishop so that the latter would write to his primate[4] so that the latter would write to the Supreme Pontiff in order to get the final verdict from the highest courts.

His prudence fell on sterile hearts. The news of the captive angel spread with such rapidity that after a few hours the courtyard had the bustle of a

4. Highest bishop of a given state.

marketplace and they had to call in troops with fixed bayonets to disperse the mob that was about to knock the house down. Elisenda, her spine all twisted from sweeping up so much marketplace trash, then got the idea of fencing in the yard and charging five cents admission to see the angel.

The curious came from far away. A traveling carnival arrived with a flying acrobat who buzzed over the crowd several times, but no one paid any attention to him because his wings were not those of an angel but, rather, those of a sidereal[5] bat. The most unfortunate invalids on earth came in search of health: a poor woman who since childhood had been counting her heartbeats and had run out of numbers; a Portuguese man who couldn't sleep because the noise of the stars disturbed him; a sleepwalker who got up at night to undo the things he had done while awake; and many others with less serious ailments. In the midst of that shipwreck disorder that made the earth tremble, Pelayo and Elisenda were happy with fatigue, for in less than a week they had crammed their rooms with money and the line of pilgrims waiting their turn to enter still reached beyond the horizon.

The angel was the only one who took no part in his own act. He spent his time trying to get comfortable in his borrowed nest, befuddled by the hellish heat of the oil lamps and sacramental candles that had been placed along the wire. At first they tried to make him eat some mothballs, which, according to the wisdom of the wise neighbor woman, were the food prescribed for angels. But he turned them down, just as he turned down the papal lunches[6] that the penitents brought him, and they never found out whether it was because he was an angel or because he was an old man that in the end he ate nothing but eggplant mush. His only supernatural virtue seemed to be patience. Especially during the first days, when the hens pecked at him, searching for the stellar parasites that proliferated in his wings, and the cripples pulled out feathers to touch their defective parts with, and even the most merciful threw stones at him, trying to get him to rise so they could see him standing. The only time they succeeded in arousing him was when they burned his side with an iron for branding steers, for he had been motionless for so many hours that they thought he was dead. He awoke with a start, ranting in his hermetic language and with tears in his eyes, and he flapped his wings a couple of times, which brought on a whirlwind of chicken dung and lunar dust and a gale of panic that did not seem to be of this world. Although many thought that his reaction had been one not of rage but of pain, from then on they were careful not to annoy him, because the majority understood that his passivity was not that of a hero taking his ease but that of a cataclysm in repose.

5. Of, or relating to, the stars.
6. Expensive, elaborately prepared meals.

Father Gonzaga held back the crowd's frivolity with formulas of maid-servant inspiration while awaiting the arrival of a final judgment on the nature of the captive. But the mail from Rome showed no sense of urgency. They spent their time finding out if the prisoner had a navel, if his dialect had any connection with Aramaic, how many times he could fit on the head of a pin, or whether he wasn't just a Norwegian with wings. Those meager letters might have come and gone until the end of time if a provi-dential event had not put an end to the priest's tribulations.

10   It so happened that during those days, among so many other carnival attractions, there arrived in town the traveling show of the woman who had been changed into a spider for having disobeyed her parents. The admission to see her was not only less than the admission to see the angel, but people were permitted to ask her all manner of questions about her absurd state and to examine her up and down so that no one would ever doubt the truth of her horror. She was a frightful tarantula the size of a ram and with the head of a sad maiden. What was most heart-rending, how-ever, was not her outlandish shape but the sincere affliction with which she recounted the details of her misfortune. While still practically a child she had sneaked out of her parents' house to go to a dance, and while she was coming back through the woods after having danced all night without permission, a fearful thunderclap rent the sky in two and through the crack came the lightning bolt of brimstone that changed her into a spider. Her only nourishment came from the meatballs that charitable souls chose to toss into her mouth. A spectacle like that, full of so much human truth and with such a fearful lesson, was bound to defeat without even trying that of a haughty angel who scarcely deigned to look at mortals. Besides, the few miracles attributed to the angel showed a certain mental disorder, like the blind man who didn't recover his sight but grew three new teeth, or the paralytic who didn't get to walk but almost won the lottery, and the leper whose sores sprouted sunflowers. Those consolation miracles, which were more like mocking fun, had already ruined the angel's reputation when the woman who had been changed into a spider finally crushed him completely. That was how Father Gonzaga was cured forever of his insom-nia and Pelayo's courtyard went back to being as empty as during the time it had rained for three days and crabs walked through the bedrooms.

The owners of the house had no reason to lament. With the money they saved they built a two-story mansion with balconies and gardens and high netting so that crabs wouldn't get in during the winter, and with iron bars on the windows so that angels wouldn't get in. Pelayo also set up a rabbit warren close to town and gave up his job as bailiff for good, and Elisenda bought some satin pumps with high heels and many dresses of iridescent silk, the kind worn on Sunday by the most desirable women in those times. The chicken coop was the only thing that didn't receive any attention. If they washed it down with creolin[7] and burned tears of myrrh inside it every so often, it was not in homage to the angel but to drive away the dungheap stench that still hung everywhere like a ghost and was turning the new house into an old one. At first, when the child learned to walk, they were careful that he not get too close to the chicken coop. But then they began to lose their fears and got used to the smell, and before the child got his second teeth he'd gone inside the chicken coop to play, where the wires were falling apart. The angel was no less standoffish with him than with other mortals, but he tolerated the most ingenious infamies with the patience of a dog who had no illusions. They both came down with chicken pox at the same time. The doctor who took care of the child couldn't resist the temptation to listen to the angel's heart, and he found so much whistling in the heart and so many sounds in his kidneys that it seemed impossible for him to be alive. What surprised him most, however, was the logic of his wings. They seemed so natural on that completely human organism that he couldn't understand why other men didn't have them too.

When the child began school it had been some time since the sun and rain had caused the collapse of the chicken coop. The angel went dragging himself about here and there like a stray dying man. They would drive him out of the bedroom with a broom and a moment later find him in the kitchen. He seemed to be in so many places at the same time that they grew to think that he'd been duplicated, that he was reproducing himself all through the house, and the exasperated and unhinged Elisenda shouted that it was awful living in that hell full of angels. He could scarcely eat and his antiquarian eyes had also become so foggy that he went about bumping into posts. All he had left were the bare cannulae of his last feathers. Pelayo threw a blanket over him and extended him the charity of letting him sleep in the shed, and only then did they notice that he had a temperature at night, and was delirious with the tongue twisters of an old Norwegian. That was one of the few times they became alarmed, for they thought he was going to die and not even the wise neighbor woman had been able to tell them what to do with dead angels.

And yet he not only survived his worst winter, but seemed improved with the first sunny days. He remained motionless for several days in the farthest corner of the courtyard, where no one would see him, and at the beginning of December some large, stiff feathers began to grow on his wings, the feathers of a scarecrow, which looked more like another misfortune of decrepitude. But he must have known the reason for those changes, for he was quite careful that no one should notice them, that no one should hear the sea chanteys that he sometimes sang under the stars. One morning Elisenda was cutting some bunches of onions for lunch

7. Disinfectant.

when a wind that seemed to come from the high seas blew into the kitchen. Then she went to the window and caught the angel in his first attempts at flight. They were so clumsy that his fingernails opened a furrow in the vegetable patch and he was on the point of knocking the shed down with the ungainly flapping that slipped on the light and couldn't get a grip on the air. But he did manage to gain altitude. Elisenda let out a sigh of relief, for herself and for him, when she saw him pass over the last houses, holding himself up in some way with the risky flapping of a senile vulture. She kept watching him even when she was through cutting the onions and she kept on watching until it was no longer possible for her to see him, because then he was no longer an annoyance in her life but an imaginary dot on the horizon of the sea.

1968

HERMAN MELVILLE
(1819–91)

Bartleby, the Scrivener:
A Story of Wall Street

When his father died in debt, twelve-year-old Herman Melville's life of privilege became one of struggle. At eighteen, he left his native New York to teach in a backwoods Massachusetts school, then trained as a surveyor; finding no work, he became a sailor in 1839. After five years in the South Seas, he wrote *Typee* (1846) and *Omoo* (1847), sensationalized and wildly popular accounts of his voyages. They proved the pinnacle of Melville's career in his lifetime, however; *Mardi* (1849) was judged too abstruse, the travel narratives *Redburn* (1849) and *White-Jacket* (1850) too listless. Melville's magnum opus, *Moby Dick* (1851), was alternately shunned and condemned. His later novels—*Pierre* (1852), *Israel Potter* (1853), and *The Confidence-Man* (1856)—as well as his poetry collection *Battle-Pieces* (1866) were all but ignored. Melville's reputation as one of the giants of American literature was established only after his death; the novella *Billy Budd, Sailor* (not published until 1924), like *Moby Dick*, is judged a masterpiece.

I am a rather elderly man. The nature of my avocations for the last thirty years has brought me into more than ordinary contact with what would seem an interesting and somewhat singular set of men, of whom as yet nothing that I know of has ever been written:—I mean the law-copyists or scriveners. I have known very many of them, professionally and privately, and if I pleased, could relate divers histories, at which good-natured gentlemen might smile, and sentimental souls might weep. But I waive the biographies of all other scriveners for a few passages in the life of Bartleby, who was a scrivener the strangest I ever saw or heard of. While of other law-copyists I might write the complete life, of Bartleby nothing of that sort can be done. I believe that no materials exist for a full and satisfactory biography of this man. It is an irreparable loss to literature. Bartleby was one of those beings of whom nothing is ascertainable, except from the original sources, and in his case those are very small. What my own astonished eyes saw of Bartleby, *that* is all I know of him, except, indeed, one vague report which will appear in the sequel.[1]

Ere introducing the scrivener, as he first appeared to me, it is fit I make some mention of myself, my *employées*, my business, my chambers, and general surroundings; because some such description is indispensable to an adequate understanding of the chief character about to be presented.

Imprimis:[2] I am a man who, from his youth upwards, has been filled with a profound conviction that the easiest way of life is the best. Hence, though I belong to a profession proverbially energetic and nervous, even to turbulence, at times, yet nothing of that sort have I ever suffered to invade my peace. I am one of those unambitious lawyers who never addresses a jury, or in any way draws down public applause; but in the cool tranquillity of a snug retreat, do a snug business among rich men's bonds and mortgages and title-deeds. All who know me, consider me an eminently *safe* man. The late John Jacob Astor,[3] a personage little given to poetic enthusiasm, had no hesitation in pronouncing my first grand point to be prudence; my next, method. I do not speak it in vanity, but simply record the fact, that I was not unemployed in my profession by the late John Jacob Astor; a name which, I admit, I love to repeat, for it hath a rounded and orbicular sound to it, and rings like unto bullion. I will freely add that I was not insensible to the late John Jacob Astor's good opinion.

Some time prior to the period at which this little history begins, my avocations had been largely increased. The good old office, now extinct in the State of New York, of a Master in Chancery[4] had been conferred upon me. It was not a very arduous office, but very pleasantly remunerative. I seldom lose my temper; much more seldom indulge in dangerous indignation at

1. That is, in the following story.
2. In the first place.
3. New York fur merchant and landowner (1763–1848) who died the richest man in the United States.
4 . A court of chancery can temper the law, applying "dictates of conscience" or "the principles of natural justice"; the office of Master was abolished in 1847.

wrongs and outrages; but I must be permitted to be rash here and declare, that I consider the sudden and violent abrogation of the office of Master in Chancery, by the new Constitution, as a—premature act; inasmuch as I had counted upon a life-lease of the profits, whereas I only received those of a few short years. But this is by the way.

5   My chambers were up stairs at No. —— Wall Street. At one end they looked upon the white wall of the interior of a spacious skylight shaft, penetrating the building from top to bottom. This view might have been considered rather tame than otherwise, deficient in what landscape painters call "life." But if so, the view from the other end of my chambers offered, at least, a contrast, if nothing more. In that direction my windows commanded an unobstructed view of a lofty brick wall, black by age and everlasting shade; which wall required no spyglass to bring out its lurking beauties, but for the benefit of all near-sighted spectators, was pushed up to within ten feet of my window panes. Owing to the great height of the surrounding buildings, and my chambers being on the second floor, the interval between this wall and mine not a little resembled a huge square cistern.

At the period just preceding the advent of Bartleby, I had two persons as copyists in my employment, and a promising lad as an office-boy. First, Turkey; second, Nippers, third, Ginger Nut. These may seem names the like of which are not usually found in the Directory.[5] In truth they were nicknames, mutually conferred upon each other by my three clerks, and were deemed expressive of their respective persons or characters. Turkey was a short, pursy[6] Englishman of about my own age, that is, somewhere not far from sixty. In the morning, one might say, his face was of a fine florid hue, but after twelve o'clock, meridian—his dinner hour—it blazed like a grate full of Christmas coals; and continued blazing—but, as it were, with a gradual wane—till 6 o'clock, P.M. or thereabouts, after which I saw no more of the proprietor of the face, which gaining its meridian with the sun, seemed to set with it, to rise, culminate, and decline the following day, with the like regularity and undiminished glory. There are many singular coincidences I have known in the course of my life, not the least among which was the fact, that exactly when Turkey displayed his fullest beams from his red and radiant countenance, just then, too, at that critical moment, began the daily period when I considered his business capacities as seriously disturbed for the remainder of the twenty-four hours. Not that he was absolutely idle, or averse to business then; far from it. The difficulty was, he was apt to be altogether too energetic. There was a strange, inflamed, flurried, flighty recklessness of activity about him. He

5. Post Office Directory.
6. Fat, short-winded.

would be incautious in dipping his pen into his inkstand. All his blots upon my documents were dropped there after twelve o'clock, meridian. Indeed, not only would he be reckless and sadly given to making blots in the afternoon, but some days he went further, and was rather noisy. At such times, too, his face flamed with augmented blazonry, as if cannel coal had been heaped on anthracite.[7] He made an unpleasant racket with his chair; spilled his sand-box; in mending his pens, impatiently split them all to pieces, and threw them on the floor in a sudden passion; stood up and leaned over his table, boxing his papers about in a most indecorous manner, very sad to behold in an elderly man like him. Nevertheless, as he was in many ways a most valuable person to me, and all the time before twelve o'clock, meridian, was the quickest, steadiest creature too, accomplishing a great deal of work in a style not easy to be matched—for these reasons, I was willing to overlook his eccentricities, though indeed, occasionally, I remonstrated with him. I did this very gently, however, because, though the civilest, nay, the blandest and most reverential of men in the morning, yet in the afternoon he was disposed, upon provocation, to be slightly rash with his tongue, in fact, insolent. Now, valuing his morning services as I did, and resolved not to lose them; yet, at the same time made uncomfortable by his inflamed ways after twelve o'clock; and being a man of peace, unwilling by my admonitions to call forth unseemly retorts from him; I took upon me, one Saturday noon (he was always worse on Saturdays), to hint to him, very kindly, that perhaps now that he was growing old, it might be well to abridge his labors; in short, he need not come to my chambers after twelve o'clock, but, dinner over, had best go home to his lodgings and rest himself till tea-time. But no; he insisted upon his afternoon devotions. His countenance became intolerably fervid, as he oratorically assured me—gesticulating with a long ruler at the other end of the room—that if his services in the morning were useful, how indispensable, then, in the afternoon?

"With submission, sir," said Turkey on this occasion, "I consider myself your right-hand man. In the morning I but marshal and deploy my columns; but in the afternoon I put myself at their head, and gallantly charge the foe, thus!"—and he made a violent thrust with the ruler.

"But the blots, Turkey," intimated I.

"True,—but, with submission, sir, behold these hairs! I am getting old. Surely, sir, a blot or two of a warm afternoon is not to be severely urged against gray hairs. Old age—even if it blot the page—is honorable. With submission, sir, we *both* are getting old."

This appeal to my fellow-feeling was hardly to be resisted. At all events, 10 I saw that go he would not. So I made up my mind to let him stay, resolving,

---

7. Fast, bright-burning coal heaped on slow-burning, barely glowing coal.

nevertheless, to see to it, that during the afternoon he had to do with my less important papers.

Nippers, the second on my list, was a whiskered, sallow, and, upon the whole, rather piratical-looking young man of about five and twenty. I always deemed him the victim of two evil powers—ambition and indigestion. The ambition was evinced by a certain impatience of the duties of a mere copyist, an unwarrantable usurpation of strictly professional affairs, such as the original drawing up of legal documents. The indigestion seemed betokened in an occasional nervous testiness and grinning irritability, causing the teeth to audibly grind together over mistakes committed in copying; unnecessary maledictions, hissed, rather than spoken, in the heat of business; and especially by a continual discontent with the height of the table where he worked. Though of a very ingenious mechanical turn, Nippers could never get this table to suit him. He put chips under it, blocks of various sorts, bits of pasteboard, and at last went so far as to attempt an exquisite adjustment by final pieces of folded blotting-paper. But no invention would answer. If, for the sake of easing his back, he brought the table lid at a sharp angle well up towards his chin, and wrote there like a man using the steep roof of a Dutch house for his desk:—then he declared that it stopped the circulation in his arms. If now he lowered the table to his waistbands, and stooped over it in writing, then there was a sore aching in his back. In short, the truth of the matter was, Nippers knew not what he wanted. Or, if he wanted any thing, it was to be rid of a scrivener's table altogether. Among the manifestations of his diseased ambition was a fondness he had for receiving visits from certain ambiguous-looking fellows in seedy coats, whom he called his clients. Indeed I was aware that not only was he, at times, considerable of a ward-politician, but he occasionally did a little business at the Justices' courts, and was not unknown on the steps of the Tombs.[8] I have good reason to believe, however, that one individual who called upon him at my chambers, and who, with a grand air, he insisted was his client, was no other than a dun,[9] and the alleged title-deed, a bill. But with all his failings, and the annoyances he caused me, Nippers, like his compatriot Turkey, was a very useful man to me; wrote a neat, swift hand; and, when he chose, was not deficient in a gentlemanly sort of deportment. Added to this, he always dressed in a gentlemanly sort of way: and so, incidentally, reflected credit upon my chambers. Whereas with respect to Turkey, I had much ado to keep him from being a reproach to me. His clothes were apt to look oily and smell of eating-houses. He wore his pantaloons very loose and baggy in summer. His coats were execrable;

8. Prison in New York City.
9. Bill collector.

his hat not to be handled. But while the hat was a thing of indifference to me, inasmuch as his natural civility and deference, as a dependent Englishman, always led him to doff it the moment he entered the room, yet his coat was another matter. Concerning his coats, I reasoned with him; but with no effect. The truth was, I suppose, that a man with so small an income, could not afford to sport such a lustrous face and a lustrous coat at one and the same time. As Nippers once observed, Turkey's money went chiefly for red ink. One winter day I presented Turkey with a highly-respectable looking coat of my own, a padded gray coat, of a most comfortable warmth, and which buttoned straight up from the knee to the neck. I thought Turkey would appreciate the favor, and abate his rashness and obstreperousness of afternoons. But no. I verily believe that buttoning himself up in so downy and blanket-like a coat had a pernicious effect upon him; upon the same principle that too much oats are bad for horses. In fact, precisely as a rash, restive horse is said to feel his oats, so Turkey felt his coat. It made him insolent. He was a man whom prosperity harmed.

Though concerning the self-indulgent habits of Turkey I had my own private surmises, yet touching Nippers I was well persuaded that whatever might be his faults in other respects, he was, at least, a temperate young man. But indeed, nature herself seemed to have been his vintner,[1] and at his birth charged him so thoroughly with an irritable, brandy-like disposition, that all subsequent potations were needless. When I consider how, amid the stillness of my chambers, Nippers would sometimes impatiently rise from his seat, and stooping over his table, spread his arms wide apart, seize the whole desk, and move it, and jerk it, with a grim, grinding motion on the floor, as if the table were a perverse voluntary agent, intent on thwarting and vexing him; I plainly perceive that for Nippers, brandy and water were altogether superfluous.

It was fortunate for me that, owing to its peculiar cause—indigestion—the irritability and consequent nervousness of Nippers, were mainly observable in the morning, while in the afternoon he was comparatively mild. So that Turkey's paroxysms only coming on about twelve o'clock, I never had to do with their eccentricities at one time. Their fits relieved each other like guards. When Nippers' was on, Turkey's was off; and *vice versa*. This was a good natural arrangement under the circumstances.

Ginger Nut, the third on my list, was a lad some twelve years old. His father was a carman,[2] ambitious of seeing his son on the bench instead of a cart, before he died. So he sent him to my office as student at law, errand boy, and cleaner and sweeper, at the rate of one dollar a week. He had a

---

1. Wine seller.
2. Driver of wagon or cart that hauls goods.

little desk to himself, but he did not use it much. Upon inspection, the drawer exhibited a great array of the shells of various sorts of nuts. Indeed, to this quick-witted youth the whole noble science of the law was contained in a nutshell. Not the least among the employments of Ginger Nut, as well as one which he discharged with the most alacrity, was his duty as cake and apple purveyor for Turkey and Nippers. Copying law papers being proverbially a dry, husky sort of business, my two scriveners were fain to moisten their mouths very often with Spitzenbergs[3] to be had at the numerous stalls nigh the Custom House and Post Office. Also, they sent Ginger Nut very frequently for that peculiar cake—small, flat, round, and very spicy—after which he had been named by them. Of a cold morning when business was but dull, Turkey would gobble up scores of these cakes, as if they were mere wafers—indeed they sell them at the rate of six or eight for a penny—the scrape of his pen blending with the crunching of the crisp particles in his mouth. Of all the fiery afternoon blunders and flurried rashnesses of Turkey, was his once moistening a ginger-cake between his lips, and clapping it on to a mortgage for a seal. I came within an ace of dismissing him then. But he mollified me by making an oriental bow, and saying—"With submission, sir, it was generous of me to find you in[4] stationery on my own account."

15   Now my original business—that of a conveyancer and title hunter,[5] and drawer-up of recondite documents of all sorts—was considerably increased by receiving the master's office. There was now great work for scriveners. Not only must I push the clerks already with me, but I must have additional help. In answer to my advertisement, a motionless young man one morning stood upon my office threshold, the door being open, for it was summer. I can see that figure now—pallidly neat, pitiably respectable, incurably forlorn! It was Bartleby.

After a few words touching his qualifications, I engaged him, glad to have among my corps of copyists a man of so singularly sedate an aspect, which I thought might operate beneficially upon the flighty temper of Turkey, and the fiery one of Nippers.

I should have stated before that ground glass folding-doors divided my premises into two parts, one of which was occupied by my scriveners, the other by myself. According to my humor I threw open these doors, or closed them. I resolved to assign Bartleby a corner by the folding-doors, but on my side of them, so as to have this quiet man within easy call, in case any trifling thing was to be done. I placed his desk close up to a small side-window

3. Red-and-yellow American apple.
4. Supply you with.
5. Lawyer who draws up deeds for transferring property, and one who searches out legal control of title deeds.

in that part of the room, a window which originally had afforded a lateral view of certain grimy backyards and bricks, but which, owing to subsequent erections, commanded at present no view at all, though it gave some light. Within three feet of the panes was a wall, and the light came down from far above, between two lofty buildings, as from a very small opening in a dome. Still further to a satisfactory arrangement, I procured a high green folding screen, which might entirely isolate Bartleby from my sight, though not remove him from my voice. And thus, in a manner, privacy and society were conjoined.

At first Bartleby did an extraordinary quantity of writing. As if long famishing for something to copy, he seemed to gorge himself on my documents. There was no pause for digestion. He ran a day and night line, copying by sunlight and by candlelight. I should have been quite delighted with his application, had he been cheerfully industrious. But he wrote on silently, palely, mechanically.

It is, of course, an indispensable part of a scrivener's business to verify the accuracy of his copy, word by word. Where there are two or more scriveners in an office, they assist each other in this examination, one reading from the copy, the other holding the original. It is a very dull, wearisome, and lethargic affair. I can readily imagine that to some sanguine temperaments it would be altogether intolerable. For example, I cannot credit that the mettlesome poet Byron would have contentedly sat down with Bartleby to examine a law document of, say, five hundred pages, closely written in a crimpy hand.

Now and then, in the haste of business, it had been my habit to assist in comparing some brief document myself, calling Turkey or Nippers for this purpose. One object I had in placing Bartleby so handy to me behind the screen, was to avail myself of his services on such trivial occasions. It was on the third day, I think, of his being with me, and before any necessity had arisen for having his own writing examined, that, being much hurried to complete a small affair I had in hand, I abruptly called to Bartleby. In my haste and natural expectancy of instant compliance, I sat with my head bent over the original on my desk, and my right hand sideways, and somewhat nervously extended with the copy, so that immediately upon emerging from his retreat, Bartleby might snatch it and proceed to business without the least delay. 20

In this very attitude did I sit when I called to him, rapidly stating what it was I wanted him to do—namely, to examine a small paper with me. Imagine my surprise, nay, my consternation, when without moving from his privacy, Bartleby, in a singularly mild, firm voice, replied, "I would prefer not to."

I sat awhile in perfect silence, rallying my stunned faculties. Immediately it occurred to me that my ears had deceived me, or Bartleby had entirely misunderstood my meaning. I repeated my request in the clearest tone I could assume. But in quite as clear a one came the previous reply, "I would prefer not to."

"Prefer not to," echoed I, rising in high excitement, and crossing the room with a stride. "What do you mean? Are you moon-struck?[6] I want you to help me compare this sheet here—take it," and I thrust it towards him.

"I would prefer not to," said he.

25   I looked at him steadfastly. His face was leanly composed; his gray eye dimly calm. Not a wrinkle of agitation rippled him. Had there been the least uneasiness, anger, impatience or impertinence in his manner; in other words, had there been anything ordinarily human about him, doubtless I should have violently dismissed him from the premises. But as it was, I should have as soon thought of turning my pale plaster-of-paris bust of Cicero[7] out-of-doors. I stood gazing at him awhile, as he went on with his own writing, and then reseated myself at my desk. This is very strange, thought I. What had one best do? But my business hurried me. I concluded to forget the matter for the present, reserving it for my future leisure. So calling Nippers from the other room, the paper was speedily examined.

A few days after this, Bartleby concluded four lengthy documents, being quadruplicates of a week's testimony taken before me in my High Court of Chancery. It became necessary to examine them. It was an important suit, and great accuracy was imperative. Having all things arranged I called Turkey, Nippers and Ginger Nut from the next room, meaning to place the four copies in the hands of my four clerks, while I should read from the original. Accordingly Turkey, Nippers and Ginger Nut had taken their seats in a row, each with his document in hand, when I called to Bartleby to join this interesting group.

"Bartleby! quick, I am waiting."

I heard a slow scrape of his chair legs on the uncarpeted floor, and soon he appeared standing at the entrance of his hermitage.

"What is wanted?" said he mildly.

30   "The copies, the copies," said I hurriedly. "We are going to examine them. There"—and I held towards him the fourth quadruplicate.

"I would prefer not to," he said, and gently disappeared behind the screen.

For a few moments I was turned into a pillar of salt,[8] standing at the head of my seated column of clerks. Recovering myself, I advanced towards the screen, and demanded the reason for such extraordinary conduct.

6. Crazy.
7. Marcus Tullius Cicero (106–43 BCE), pro-republican Roman statesman, barrister, writer, and orator.
8. Struck dumb; in Genesis 19.26, Lot's wife, defying God's command, "looked back from behind him, and she became a pillar of salt."

"*Why* do you refuse?"

"I would prefer not to."

With any other man I should have flown outright into a dreadful pas- 35
sion, scorned all further words, and thrust him ignominiously from my
presence. But there was something about Bartleby that not only strangely
disarmed me, but in a wonderful manner touched and disconcerted me. I
began to reason with him.

"These are your own copies we are about to examine. It is labor saving to
you, because one examination will answer for your four papers. It is common
usage. Every copyist is bound to help examine his copy. Is it not so? Will you
not speak? Answer!"

"I prefer not to," he replied in a flute-like tone. It seemed to me that while
I had been addressing him, he carefully revolved every statement that I
made; fully comprehended the meaning; could not gainsay the irresistible
conclusion; but, at the same time, some paramount consideration prevailed with him to reply as he did.

"You are decided, then, not to comply with my request—a request
made according to common usage and common sense?"

He briefly gave me to understand that on that point my judgment was
sound. Yes: his decision was irreversible.

It is not seldom the case that when a man is browbeaten in some unpre- 40
cedented and violently unreasonable way, he begins to stagger in his own
plainest faith. He begins, as it were, vaguely to surmise that, wonderful as
it may be, all the justice and all the reason is on the other side. Accordingly, if any disinterested persons are present, he turns to them for some
reinforcement for his own faltering mind.

"Turkey," said I, "what do you think of this? Am I not right?"

"With submission, sir," said Turkey, with his blandest tone, "I think
that you are."

"Nippers," said I, "what do *you* think of it?"

"I think I should kick him out of the office."

(The reader of nice perceptions will here perceive that, it being morn- 45
ing, Turkey's answer is couched in polite and tranquil terms, but Nippers
replies in ill-tempered ones. Or, to repeat a previous sentence, Nippers's
ugly mood was on duty, and Turkey's off.)

"Ginger Nut," said I, willing to enlist the smallest suffrage[9] in my behalf,
"what do *you* think of it?"

"I think, sir, he's a little *luny*," replied Ginger Nut, with a grin.

"You hear what they say," said I, turning towards the screen, "come forth
and do your duty."

9. Favorable vote.

But he vouchsafed no reply. I pondered a moment in sore perplexity. But once more business hurried me. I determined again to postpone the consideration of this dilemma to my future leisure. With a little trouble we made out to examine the papers without Bartleby, though at every page or two, Turkey deferentially dropped his opinion that this proceeding was quite out of the common; while Nippers, twitching in his chair with a dyspeptic nervousness, ground out between his set teeth occasional hissing maledictions against the stubborn oaf behind the screen. And for his (Nippers's) part, this was the first and the last time he would do another man's business without pay.

50   Meanwhile Bartleby sat in his hermitage, oblivious to everything but his own peculiar business there.

Some days passed, the scrivener being employed upon another lengthy work. His late remarkable conduct led me to regard his ways narrowly. I observed that he never went to dinner; indeed that he never went anywhere. As yet I had never of my personal knowledge known him to be outside of my office. He was a perpetual sentry in the corner. At about eleven o'clock though, in the morning, I noticed that Ginger Nut would advance toward the opening in Bartleby's screen, as if silently beckoned thither by a gesture invisible to me where I sat. The boy would then leave the office jingling a few pence, and reappear with a handful of ginger-nuts which he delivered in the hermitage, receiving two of the cakes for his trouble.

He lives, then, on ginger-nuts, thought I; never eats a dinner, properly speaking; he must be a vegetarian then; but no; he never eats even vegetables, he eats nothing but ginger-nuts. My mind then ran on in reveries concerning the probable effects upon the human constitution of living entirely on ginger-nuts. Ginger-nuts are so called because they contain ginger as one of their peculiar constituents, and the final flavoring one. Now what was ginger? A hot, spicy thing. Was Bartleby hot and spicy? Not at all. Ginger, then, had no effect upon Bartleby. Probably he preferred it should have none.

Nothing so aggravates an earnest person as a passive resistance. If the individual so resisted be of a not inhumane temper, and the resisting one perfectly harmless in his passivity; then, in the better moods of the former, he will endeavor charitably to construe to his imagination what proves impossible to be solved by his judgment. Even so, for the most part, I regarded Bartleby and his ways. Poor fellow! thought I, he means no mischief; it is plain he intends no insolence; his aspect sufficiently evinces that his eccentricities are involuntary. He is useful to me. I can get along with him. If I turn him away, the chances are he will fall in with some less indulgent employer, and then he will be rudely treated, and perhaps driven forth miserably to starve. Yes. Here I can cheaply purchase a delicious self-approval. To befriend Bartleby; to humor him in his strange wilfulness, will cost me little or nothing, while I lay up in my soul what will eventually prove a sweet morsel for my conscience. But this mood was not invariable with me. The passiveness of Bartleby sometimes irritated me. I felt strangely goaded on to encounter him in new opposition, to elicit some angry spark from him answerable to my own. But indeed I might as well have essayed to strike fire with my knuckles against a bit of Windsor soap.[1] But one afternoon the evil impulse in me mastered me, and the following little scene ensued:

"Bartleby," said I, "when those papers are all copied, I will compare them with you."

"I would prefer not to."   55

"How? Surely you do not mean to persist in that mulish vagary?"

No answer.

I threw open the folding-doors near by, and turning upon Turkey and Nippers, exclaimed in an excited manner—

"He says, a second time, he won't examine his papers. What do you think of it, Turkey?"

It was afternoon, be it remembered. Turkey sat glowing like a brass   60
boiler, his bald head steaming, his hands reeling among his blotted papers.

"Think of it?" roared Turkey; "I think I'll just step behind his screen, and black his eyes for him!"

So saying, Turkey rose to his feet and threw his arms into a pugilistic position. He was hurrying away to make good his promise, when I detained him, alarmed at the effect of incautiously rousing Turkey's combativeness after dinner.

"Sit down, Turkey," said I, "and hear what Nippers has to say. What do you think of it, Nippers? Would I not be justified in immediately dismissing Bartleby?"

"Excuse me, that is for you to decide, sir. I think his conduct quite unusual, and indeed unjust, as regards Turkey and myself. But it may only be a passing whim."

"Ah," exclaimed I, "you have strangely changed your mind then—you   65
speak very gently of him now."

"All beer," cried Turkey; "gentleness is effects of beer—Nippers and I dined together today. You see how gentle *I* am, sir. Shall I go and black his eyes?"

"You refer to Bartleby, I suppose. No, not today, Turkey," I replied; "pray, put up your fists."

I closed the doors, and again advanced towards Bartleby. I felt additional incentives tempting me to my fate. I burned to be rebelled against again. I remembered that Bartleby never left the office.

---

1. Scented soap, usually brown.

"Bartleby," said I, "Ginger Nut is away; just step round to the Post Office, won't you? (it was but a three minutes' walk,) and see if there is anything for me."

70   "I would prefer not to."

"You *will* not?"

"I *prefer* not."

I staggered to my desk, and sat there in a deep study. My blind inveteracy returned. Was there any other thing in which I could procure myself to be ignominiously repulsed by this lean, penniless wight?—my hired clerk? What added thing is there, perfectly reasonable, that he will be sure to refuse to do?

"Bartleby!"

75   No answer.

"Bartleby," in a louder tone.

No answer.

"Bartleby," I roared.

Like a very ghost, agreeably to the laws of magical invocation, at the third summons, he appeared at the entrance of his hermitage.

80   "Go to the next room, and tell Nippers to come to me."

"I prefer not to," he respectfully and slowly said, and mildly disappeared.

"Very good, Bartleby," said I, in a quiet sort of serenely severe self-possessed tone, intimating the unalterable purpose of some terrible retribution very close at hand. At the moment I half intended something of the kind. But upon the whole, as it was drawing towards my dinner-hour, I thought it best to put on my hat and walk home for the day, suffering much from perplexity and distress of mind.

Shall I acknowledge it? The conclusion of this whole business was, that it soon became a fixed fact of my chambers, that a pale young scrivener, by the name of Bartleby, had a desk there; that he copied for me at the usual rate of four cents a folio (one hundred words); but he was permanently exempt from examining the work done by him, that duty being transferred to Turkey and Nippers, one of compliment doubtless to their superior acuteness; moreover, said Bartleby was never on any account to be dispatched on the most trivial errand of any sort; and that even if entreated to take upon him such a matter, it was generally understood that he would prefer not to—in other words, that he would refuse point-blank.

As days passed on, I became considerably reconciled to Bartleby. His steadiness, his freedom from all dissipation, his incessant industry (except when he chose to throw himself into a standing revery behind his screen), his great stillness, his unalterableness of demeanor under all circumstances, made him a valuable acquisition. One prime thing was this,—*he was always there*;—first in the morning, continually through the day, and the last at night. I had a singular confidence in his honesty. I felt my most precious papers perfectly safe in his hands. Sometimes to be sure I could not, for the very soul of me, avoid falling into sudden spasmodic passions with him. For it was exceeding difficult to bear in mind all the time those strange peculiarities, privileges, and unheard of exemptions, forming the tacit stipulations on Bartleby's part under which he remained in my office. Now and then, in the eagerness of dispatching pressing business, I would inadvertently summon Bartleby, in a short, rapid tone, to put his finger, say, on the incipient tie of a bit of red tape with which I was about compressing some papers. Of course, from behind the screen the usual answer, "I prefer not to," was sure to come; and then, how could a human creature with the common infirmities of our nature, refrain from bitterly exclaiming upon such perverseness—such unreasonableness? However, every added repulse of this sort which I received only tended to lessen the probability of my repeating the inadvertence.

Here it must be said, that according to the custom of most legal gentle- 85 men occupying chambers in densely-populated law buildings, there were several keys to my door. One was kept by a woman residing in the attic, which person weekly scrubbed and daily swept and dusted my apartments. Another was kept by Turkey for convenience sake. The third I sometimes carried in my own pocket. The fourth I knew not who had.

Now, one Sunday morning I happened to go to Trinity Church, to hear a celebrated preacher, and finding myself rather early on the ground, I thought I would walk round to my chambers for a while. Luckily I had my key with me; but upon applying it to the lock, I found it resisted by something inserted from the inside. Quite surprised, I called out; when to my consternation a key was turned from within; and thrusting his lean visage at me, and holding the door ajar, the apparition of Bartleby appeared, in his shirt sleeves, and otherwise in a strangely tattered dishabille, saying quietly that he was sorry, but he was deeply engaged just then, and— preferred not admitting me at present. In a brief word or two, he moreover added, that perhaps I had better walk round the block two or three times, and by that time he would probably have concluded his affairs.

Now, the utterly unsurmised appearance of Bartleby, tenanting my law-chambers of a Sunday morning, with his cadaverously gentlemanly *nonchalance*, yet withal firm and self-possessed, had such a strange effect upon me, that incontinently I slunk away from my own door, and did as desired. But not without sundry twinges of impotent rebellion against the mild effrontery of this unaccountable scrivener. Indeed, it was his wonderful mildness, chiefly, which not only disarmed me, but unmanned me, as it were. For I consider that one, for the time, is sort of unmanned when he tranquilly permits his hired clerk to dictate to him, and order him away from his own premises. Furthermore, I was full of uneasiness as to what Bartleby could possibly be doing in my office in his shirt sleeves, and in an otherwise dismantled condition of a Sunday morning. Was anything amiss going on? Nay, that was out of the question. It was not to be thought of for a moment that Bartleby was an immoral person. But what could he be doing there?—copying? Nay again, whatever might be his eccentricities, Bartleby was an eminently decorous person. He would be the last man to sit down to his desk in any state approaching to nudity. Besides, it was Sunday; and there was something about Bartleby that forbade the supposition that he would by any secular occupation violate the proprieties of the day.

Nevertheless, my mind was not pacified; and full of a restless curiosity, at last I returned to the door. Without hindrance I inserted my key, opened it, and entered. Bartleby was not to be seen. I looked round anxiously, peeped behind his screen; but it was very plain that he was gone. Upon more closely examining the place, I surmised that for an indefinite period Bartleby must have ate, dressed, and slept in my office, and that too without plate, mirror, or bed. The cushioned seat of a ricketty old sofa in one corner bore the faint impress of a lean, reclining form. Rolled away under his desk, I found a blanket under the empty grate, a blacking box[2] and brush; on a chair, a tin basin, with soap and a ragged towel; in a newspaper a few crumbs of ginger-nuts and a morsel of cheese. Yes, thought I, it is evident enough that Bartleby has been making his home here, keeping bachelor's hall all by himself. Immediately then the thought came sweeping across me, What miserable friendlessness and loneliness are here revealed! His poverty is great; but his solitude, how horrible! Think of it. Of a Sunday, Wall Street is deserted as Petra;[3] and every night of every day it is an emptiness. This building too, which of weekdays hums with industry and life, at nightfall echoes with sheer vacancy, and all through Sunday is forlorn. And here Bartleby makes his home; sole spectator of a solitude which he has seen all populous—a sort of innocent and transformed Marius brooding among the ruins of Carthage![4]

For the first time in my life a feeling of overpowering stinging melancholy seized me. Before, I had never experienced aught but a not-unpleasing

2. Box of black shoe polish.
3. Once a flourishing Middle Eastern trade center, long in ruins.
4. Gaius (or Caius) Marius (157–86 BCE), Roman consul and general, expelled from Rome in 88 BCE by Sulla; when an officer of Sextilius, the governor, forbade him to land in Africa, Marius replied, "Go tell him that you have seen Caius Marius sitting in exile among the ruins of Carthage," applying the example of the fortune of that city to the change of his own condition. The image was so common that a few years after "Bartleby," Dickens apologizes for using it: "like that lumbering Marius among the ruins of Carthage, who has sat heavy on a thousand millions of similes" ("The Calais Night-Mail," in *The Uncommercial Traveler*).

sadness. The bond of a common humanity now drew me irresistibly to gloom. A fraternal melancholy! For both I and Bartleby were sons of Adam. I remembered the bright silks and sparkling faces I had seen that day, in gala trim, swan-like sailing down the Mississippi of Broadway; and I contrasted them with the pallid copyist, and thought to myself, Ah, happiness courts the light, so we deem the world is gay; but misery hides aloof, so we deem that misery there is none. These sad fancyings—chimeras, doubtless, of a sick and silly brain—led on to other and more special thoughts, concerning the eccentricities of Bartleby. Presentiments of strange discoveries hovered round me. The scrivener's pale form appeared to me laid out, among uncaring strangers, in its shivering winding sheet.

Suddenly I was attracted by Bartleby's closed desk, the key in open 90 sight left in the lock.

I mean no mischief, seek the gratification of no heartless curiosity, thought I; besides, the desk is mine, and its contents too, so I will make bold to look within. Everything was methodically arranged, the papers smoothly placed. The pigeonholes were deep, and removing the files of documents, I groped into their recesses. Presently I felt something there, and dragged it out. It was an old bandanna handkerchief, heavy and knotted. I opened it, and saw it was a savings' bank.

I now recalled all the quiet mysteries which I had noted in the man. I remembered that he never spoke but to answer; that though at intervals he had considerable time to himself, yet I had never seen him reading—no, not even a newspaper; that for long periods he would stand looking out, at his pale window behind the screen, upon the dead brick wall; I was quite sure he never visited any refectory or eating house; while his pale face clearly indicated that he never drank beer like Turkey, or tea and coffee even, like other men; that he never went anywhere in particular that I could learn; never went out for a walk, unless indeed that was the case at present; that he had declined telling who he was, or whence he came, or whether he had any relatives in the world; that though so thin and pale, he never complained of ill health. And more than all, I remembered a certain unconscious air of pallid—how shall I call it?—of pallid haughtiness, say, or rather an austere reserve about him, which had positively awed me into my tame compliance with his eccentricities, when I had feared to ask him to do the slightest incidental thing for me, even though I might know, from his long-continued motionlessness, that behind his screen he must be standing in one of those dead-wall reveries of his.

Revolving all these things, and coupling them with the recently discovered fact that he made my office his constant abiding place and home, and not forgetful of his morbid moodiness; revolving all these things, a prudential feeling began to steal over me. My first emotions had been those of pure melancholy and sincerest pity; but just in proportion as the forlorn-ness of Bartleby grew and grew to my imagination, did that same melan-choly merge into fear, that pity into repulsion. So true it is, and so terrible too, that up to a certain point the thought or sight of misery enlists our best affections; but, in certain special cases, beyond that point it does not. They err who would assert that invariably this is owing to the inherent selfish-ness of the human heart. It rather proceeds from a certain hopelessness of remedying excessive and organic ill. To a sensitive being, pity is not seldom pain. And when at last it is perceived that such pity cannot lead to effec-tual succor, common sense bids the soul be rid of it. What I saw that morn-ing persuaded me that the scrivener was the victim of innate and incurable disorder. I might give alms to his body; but his body did not pain him; it was his soul that suffered, and his soul I could not reach.

I did not accomplish the purpose of going to Trinity Church that morn-ing. Somehow, the things I had seen disqualified me for the time from churchgoing. I walked homeward, thinking what I would do with Bartleby. Finally, I resolved upon this;—I would put certain calm questions to him the next morning, touching his history, &c., and if he declined to answer them openly and unreservedly (and I supposed he would prefer not), then to give him a twenty-dollar bill over and above whatever I might owe him, and tell him his services were no longer required; but that if in any other way I could assist him, I would be happy to do so, especially if he desired to return to his native place, wherever that might be, I would willingly help to defray the expenses. Moreover, if, after reaching home, he found himself at any time in want of aid, a letter from him would be sure of a reply.

95   The next morning came.

"Bartleby," said I, gently calling to him behind his screen.

No reply.

"Bartleby," said I, in a still gentler tone, "come here; I am not going to ask you to do anything you would prefer not to do—I simply wish to speak to you."

Upon this he noiselessly slid into view.

100   "Will you tell me, Bartleby, where you were born?"

"I would prefer not to."

"Will you tell me *anything* about yourself?"

"I would prefer not to."

"But what reasonable objection can you have to speak to me? I feel friendly towards you."

105   He did not look at me while I spoke, but kept his glance fixed upon my bust of Cicero, which as I then sat, was directly behind me, some six inches above my head.

"What is your answer, Bartleby?" said I, after waiting a considerable time for a reply, during which his countenance remained immovable, only there was the faintest conceivable tremor of the white attenuated mouth.

"At present I prefer to give no answer," he said, and retired into his hermitage.

It was rather weak in me I confess, but his manner on this occasion nettled me. Not only did there seem to lurk in it a certain calm disdain, but his perverseness seemed ungrateful, considering the undeniable good usage and indulgence he had received from me.

Again I sat ruminating what I should do. Mortified as I was at his behavior, and resolved as I had been to dismiss him when I entered my office, nevertheless I strangely felt something superstitious knocking at my heart, and forbidding me to carry out my purpose, and denouncing me for a villain if I dared to breathe one bitter word against this forlornest of mankind. At last, familiarly drawing my chair behind his screen, I sat down and said: "Bartleby, never mind then about revealing your history; but let me entreat you, as a friend, to comply as far as may be with the usages of this office. Say now you will help to examine papers tomorrow or next day: in short, say now that in a day or two you will begin to be a little reasonable:—say so, Bartleby."

"At present I would prefer not to be a little reasonable," was his mildly 110 cadaverous reply.

Just then the folding-doors opened, and Nippers approached. He seemed suffering from an unusually bad night's rest, induced by severer indigestion than common. He overheard those final words of Bartleby.

"*Prefer not*, eh?" gritted Nippers—"I'd *prefer* him, if I were you, sir," addressing me—"I'd *prefer* him; I'd give him preferences, the stubborn mule! What is it, sir, pray, that he *prefers* not to do now?"

Bartleby moved not a limb.

"Mr. Nippers," said I, "I'd prefer that you would withdraw for the present."

Somehow, of late I had got into the way of involuntarily using this word 115 "prefer" upon all sorts of not exactly suitable occasions. And I trembled to think that my contact with the scrivener had already and seriously affected me in a mental way. And what further and deeper aberration might it not yet produce? This apprehension had not been without efficacy in determining me to summary means.

As Nippers, looking very sour and sulky, was departing, Turkey blandly and deferentially approached.

"With submission, sir," said he, "yesterday I was thinking about Bartleby here, and I think that if he would but prefer to take a quart of good ale every day, it would do much towards mending him and enabling him to assist in examining his papers."

"So you have got the word too," said I, slightly excited.

"With submission, what word, sir?" asked Turkey, respectfully crowding himself into the contracted space behind the screen, and by so doing making me jostle the scrivener. "What word, sir?"

120 "I would prefer to be left alone here," said Bartleby, as if offended at being mobbed in his privacy.

"*That's* the word, Turkey," said I—"*that's* it."

"Oh, *prefer?* oh yes—queer word. I never use it myself. But, sir, as I was saying, if he would but prefer—"

"Turkey," interrupted I, "you will please withdraw."

"Oh certainly, sir, if you prefer that I should."

125 As he opened the folding-door to retire, Nippers at his desk caught a glimpse of me, and asked whether I would prefer to have a certain paper copied on blue paper or white. He did not in the least roguishly accent the word *prefer.* It was plain that it involuntarily rolled from his tongue. I thought to myself, surely I must get rid of a demented man, who already has in some degree turned the tongues, if not the heads of myself and clerks. But I thought it prudent not to break the dismission at once.

The next day I noticed that Bartleby did nothing but stand at his window in his dead-wall revery. Upon asking him why he did not write, he said that he had decided upon doing no more writing.

"Why, how now? what next?" exclaimed I, "do no more writing?"

"No more."

"And what is the reason?"

130 "Do you not see the reason for yourself," he indifferently replied.

I looked steadfastly at him, and perceived that his eyes looked dull and glazed. Instantly it occurred to me, that his unexampled diligence in copying by his dim window for the first few weeks of his stay with me might have temporarily impaired his vision.

I was touched. I said something in condolence with him. I hinted that of course he did wisely in abstaining from writing for a while; and urged him to embrace that opportunity of taking wholesome exercise in the open air. This, however, he did not do. A few days after this, my other clerks being absent, and being in a great hurry to dispatch certain letters by the mail, I thought that, having nothing else earthly to do, Bartleby would surely be less inflexible than usual, and carry these letters to the post office. But he blankly declined. So, much to my inconvenience, I went myself.

Still added days went by. Whether Bartleby's eyes improved or not, I could not say. To all appearance, I thought they did. But when I asked him if they did, he vouchsafed no answer. At all events, he would do no copying. At last, in reply to my urgings, he informed me that he had permanently given up copying.

"What!" exclaimed I; "suppose your eyes should get entirely well—better than ever before—would you not copy then?"

"I have given up copying," he answered, and slid aside.   135

He remained, as ever, a fixture in my chamber. Nay—if that were possible—he became still more of a fixture than before. What was to be done? He would do nothing in the office: why should he stay there? In plain fact, he had now become a millstone[5] to me, not only useless as a necklace, but afflictive to bear. Yet I was sorry for him. I speak less than truth when I say that, on his own account, he occasioned me uneasiness. If he would but have named a single relative or friend, I would instantly have written, and urged their taking the poor fellow away to some convenient retreat. But he seemed alone, absolutely alone in the universe. A bit of wreck in the mid-Atlantic. At length, necessities connected with my business tyrannized over all other considerations. Decently as I could, I told Bartleby that in six days' time he must unconditionally leave the office. I warned him to take measures, in the interval, for procuring some other abode. I offered to assist him in this endeavor, if he himself would but take the first step towards a removal. "And when you finally quit me, Bartleby," added I, "I shall see that you go not away entirely unprovided. Six days from this hour, remember."

At the expiration of that period, I peeped behind the screen, and lo! Bartleby was there.

I buttoned up my coat, balanced myself; advanced slowly towards him, touched his shoulder, and said, "The time has come; you must quit this place; I am sorry for you; here is money; but you must go."

"I would prefer not," he replied, with his back still towards me.

"You *must*."   140

He remained silent.

Now I had an unbounded confidence in this man's common honesty. He had frequently restored to me sixpences and shillings[6] carelessly dropped upon the floor, for I am apt to be very reckless in such shirt-button affairs. The proceeding then which followed will not be deemed extraordinary.

"Bartleby," said I, "I owe you twelve dollars on account; here are thirty-two; the odd twenty are yours.—Will you take it?" and I handed the bills towards him.

But he made no motion.

5. Heavy stone for grinding grain. See Matthew 18.6: "But whoso shall offend one of these little ones which believe in me, it were better for him that a millstone were hanged about his neck, and that he were drowned in the depth of the sea."
6. Coins.

145   "I will leave them here then," putting them under a weight on the table.
Then taking my hat and cane and going to the door I tranquilly turned
and added—"After you have removed your things from these offices,
Bartleby, you will of course lock the door—since everyone is now gone
for the day but you—and if you please, slip your key underneath the mat,
so that I may have it in the morning. I shall not see you again; so good-bye
to you. If hereafter in your new place of abode I can be of any service
to you, do not fail to advise me by letter. Good-bye, Bartleby, and fare
you well."

But he answered not a word; like the last column of some ruined temple, he remained standing mute and solitary in the middle of the otherwise deserted room.

As I walked home in a pensive mood, my vanity got the better of my
pity. I could not but highly plume myself on my masterly management in
getting rid of Bartleby. Masterly I call it, and such it must appear to any
dispassionate thinker. The beauty of my procedure seemed to consist in
its perfect quietness. There was no vulgar bullying, no bravado of any sort,
no choleric hectoring, and striding to and fro across the apartment, jerking out vehement commands for Bartleby to bundle himself off with his
beggarly traps.[7] Nothing of the kind. Without loudly bidding Bartleby
depart—as an inferior genius might have done—I *assumed* the ground
that depart he must; and upon that assumption built all I had to say. The
more I thought over my procedure, the more I was charmed with it.
Nevertheless, next morning, upon awakening, I had my doubts,—I had
somehow slept off the fumes of vanity. One of the coolest and wisest
hours a man has is just after he awakes in the morning. My procedure
seemed as sagacious as ever,—but only in theory. How it would prove in
practice—there was the rub. It was truly a beautiful thought to have
assumed Bartleby's departure; but, after all, that assumption was simply
my own, and none of Bartleby's. The great point was, not whether I had
assumed that he would quit me, but whether he would prefer so to do. He
was more a man of preferences than assumptions.

After breakfast, I walked downtown, arguing the probabilities *pro* and
con. One moment I thought it would prove a miserable failure, and Bartleby
would be found all alive at my office as usual; the next moment it seemed
certain that I should see his chair empty. And so I kept veering about. At
the corner of Broadway and Canal Street, I saw quite an excited group of
people standing in earnest conversation.

"I'll take odds he doesn't," said a voice as I passed.

150   "Doesn't go?—done!" said I, "put up your money."

7. Personal belongings, luggage.

I was instinctively putting my hand in my pocket to produce my own, when I remembered that this was an election day. The words I had overheard bore no reference to Bartleby, but to the success or non-success of some candidate for the mayoralty. In my intent frame of mind, I had, as it were, imagined that all Broadway shared in my excitement, and were debating the same question with me. I passed on, very thankful that the uproar of the street screened my momentary absent-mindedness.

As I had intended, I was earlier than usual at my office door. I stood listening for a moment. All was still. He must be gone. I tried the knob. The door was locked. Yes, my procedure had worked to a charm; he indeed must be vanished. Yet a certain melancholy mixed with this: I was almost sorry for my brilliant success. I was fumbling under the door mat for the key, which Bartleby was to have left there for me, when accidentally my knee knocked against a panel, producing a summoning sound, and in response a voice came to me from within—"Not yet; I am occupied."

It was Bartleby.

I was thunderstruck. For an instant I stood like the man who, pipe in mouth, was killed one cloudless afternoon long ago in Virginia, by summer lightning; at his own warm open window he was killed, and remained leaning out there upon the dreamy afternoon, till some one touched him, when he fell.

"Not gone!" I murmured at last. But again obeying that wondrous ascendancy which the inscrutable scrivener had over me, and from which ascendency, for all my chafing, I could not completely escape, I slowly went downstairs and out into the street, and while walking round the block, considered what I should next do in this unheard-of perplexity. Turn the man out by an actual thrusting I could not; to drive him away by calling him hard names would not do; calling in the police was an unpleasant idea; and yet, permit him to enjoy his cadaverous triumph over me,—this too I could not think of. What was to be done? or, if nothing could be done, was there anything further that I could *assume* in the matter? Yes, as before I had prospectively assumed that Bartleby would depart, so now I might retrospectively assume that departed he was. In the legitimate carrying out of this assumption, I might enter my office in a great hurry, and pretending not to see Bartleby at all, walk straight against him as if he were air. Such a proceeding would in a singular degree have the appearance of a home-thrust.[8] It was hardly possible that Bartleby could withstand such an application of the doctrine of assumptions. But upon second thoughts the success of the plan seemed rather dubious. I resolved to argue the matter over with him again.

155

---

8. In fencing, a successful thrust to the opponent's body.

"Bartleby," said I, entering the office, with a quietly severe expression, "I am seriously displeased. I am pained, Bartleby. I had thought better of you. I had imagined you of such a gentlemanly organization, that in any delicate dilemma a slight hint would suffice—in short, an assumption. But it appears I am deceived. Why," I added, unaffectedly starting, "you have not even touched that money yet," pointing to it, just where I had left it the evening previous.

He answered nothing.

"Will you, or will you not, quit me?" I now demanded in a sudden passion, advancing close to him.

"I would prefer *not* to quit you," he replied, gently emphasizing the *not*.

160 "What earthly right have you to stay here? Do you pay any rent? Do you pay my taxes? Or is this property yours?"

He answered nothing.

"Are you ready to go on and write now? Are your eyes recovered? Could you copy a small paper for me this morning? or help examine a few lines? or step round to the post office? In a word, will you do anything at all, to give a coloring to your refusal to depart the premises?"

He silently retired into his hermitage.

I was now in such a state of nervous resentment that I thought it but prudent to check myself at present from further demonstrations. Bartleby and I were alone. I remembered the tragedy of the unfortunate Adams and the still more unfortunate Colt in the solitary office of the latter;[9] and how poor Colt, being dreadfully incensed by Adams, and imprudently permitting himself to get wildly excited, was at unawares hurried into his fatal act—an act which certainly no man could possibly deplore more than the actor himself. Often it had occurred to me in my ponderings upon the subject, that had that altercation taken place in the public street, or at a private residence, it would not have terminated as it did. It was the circumstance of being alone in a solitary office, up stairs, of a building entirely unhallowed by humanizing domestic associations—an uncarpeted office, doubtless, of a dusty, haggard sort of appearance;—this it must have been, which greatly helped to enhance the irritable desperation of the hapless Colt.

165 But when this old Adam[1] of resentment rose in me and tempted me concerning Bartleby, I grappled him and threw him. How? Why, simply by recalling the divine injunction: "A new commandment[2] give I unto you, that

9. In 1841, John C. Colt, brother of the famous gunmaker, unintentionally killed Samuel Adams, a printer, when he hit him on the head during a fight.
1. Sinful element in human nature; see, e.g., "Invocation of Blessing on the Child" in the Book of Common Prayer: "Grant that the old Adam in this child may be so buried, that the new man may be raised up in him." Christ is sometimes called the "new Adam."
2. In John 13.34, where, however, the phrasing is "I give unto . . ."

ye love one another." Yes, this it was that saved me. Aside from higher considerations, charity often operates as a vastly wise and prudent principle—a great safeguard to its possessor. Men have committed murder for jealousy's sake, and anger's sake, and hatred's sake, and selfishness' sake, and spiritual pride's sake; but no man that ever I heard of, ever committed a diabolical murder for sweet charity's sake. Mere self-interest, then, if no better motive can be enlisted, should, especially with high-tempered men, prompt all beings to charity and philanthropy. At any rate, upon the occasion in question, I strove to drown my exasperated feelings towards the scrivener by benevolently construing his conduct. Poor fellow, poor fellow! thought I, he don't mean anything; and besides, he has seen hard times, and ought to be indulged.

I endeavored also immediately to occupy myself, and at the same time to comfort my despondency. I tried to fancy that in the course of the morning, at such time as might prove agreeable to him, Bartleby, of his own free accord, would emerge from his hermitage, and take up some decided line of march in the direction of the door. But no. Half-past twelve o'clock came; Turkey began to glow in the face, overturn his inkstand, and become generally obstreperous; Nippers abated down into quietude and courtesy; Ginger Nut munched his noon apple; and Bartleby remained standing at his window in one of his profoundest dead-wall reveries. Will it be credited? Ought I to acknowledge it? That afternoon I left the office without saying one further word to him.

Some days now passed, during which, at leisure intervals I looked a little into "Edwards on the Will," and "Priestley on Necessity."[3] Under the circumstances, those books induced a salutary feeling. Gradually I slid into the persuasion that these troubles of mine touching the scrivener, had been all predestinated from eternity, and Bartleby was billeted upon me for some mysterious purpose of an all-wise Providence, which it was not for a mere mortal like me to fathom. Yes, Bartleby, stay there behind your screen, thought I; I shall persecute you no more; you are harmless and noiseless as any of these old chairs; in short, I never feel so private as when I know you are here. At least I see it, I feel it; I penetrate to the predestinated purpose of my life. I am content. Others may have loftier parts to enact; but my mission in this world, Bartleby, is to furnish you with office-room for such period as you may see fit to remain.

3. Jonathan Edwards (1703–58), New England Calvinist theologian and revivalist, in *The Freedom of the Will* (1754), argued that human beings are not in fact free, for though they choose according to the way they see things, that way is predestinated (by biography, environment, and character), and they act out of personality rather than by will. Joseph Priestley (1733–1804), dissenting preacher, scientist, grammarian, and philosopher, argued in *The Doctrine of Philosophical Necessity* (1777) that free will is theologically objectionable, metaphysically incomprehensible, and morally undesirable.

I believe that this wise and blessed frame of mind would have continued with me, had it not been for the unsolicited and uncharitable remarks obtruded upon me by my professional friends who visited the rooms. But thus it often is, that the constant friction of illiberal minds wears out at last the best resolves of the more generous. Though to be sure, when I reflected upon it, it was not strange that people entering my office should be struck by the peculiar aspect of the unaccountable Bartleby, and so be tempted to throw out some sinister observations concerning him. Sometimes an attorney having business with me, and calling at my office, and finding no one but the scrivener there, would undertake to obtain some sort of precise information from him touching my whereabouts; but without heeding his idle talk, Bartleby would remain standing immovable in the middle of the room. So after contemplating him in that position for a time, the attorney would depart, no wiser than he came.

Also, when a Reference[4] was going on, and the room full of lawyers and witnesses and business was driving fast; some deeply occupied legal gentleman present, seeing Bartleby wholly unemployed, would request him to run round to his (the legal gentleman's) office and fetch some papers for him. Thereupon, Bartleby would tranquilly decline, and yet remain idle as before. Then the lawyer would give a great stare, and turn to me. And what could I say? At last I was made aware that all through the circle of my professional acquaintance, a whisper of wonder was running round, having reference to the strange creature I kept at my office. This worried me very much. And as the idea came upon me of his possibly turning out a long-lived man, and keep occupying my chambers, and denying my authority; and perplexing my visitors; and scandalizing my professional reputation; and casting a general gloom over the premises; keeping soul and body together to the last upon his savings (for doubtless he spent but half a dime a day), and in the end perhaps outlive me, and claim possession of my office by right of his perpetual occupancy: as all these dark anticipations crowded upon me more and more, and my friends continually intruded their relentless remarks upon the apparition in my room; a great change was wrought in me. I resolved to gather all my faculties together, and forever rid me of this intolerable incubus.[5]

170   Ere revolving any complicated project, however, adapted to this end, I first simply suggested to Bartleby the propriety of his permanent departure. In a calm and serious tone, I commended the idea to his careful and mature consideration. But having taken three days to meditate upon it, he apprised me that his original determination remained the same; in short, that he still preferred to abide with me.

4. Consultation or committee meeting.
5. Evil spirit.

What shall I do? I now said to myself, buttoning up my coat to the last button. What shall I do? what ought I to do? what does conscience say I *should* do with this man, or rather ghost. Rid myself of him, I must; go, he shall. But how? You will not thrust him, the poor, pale, passive mortal,— you will not thrust such a helpless creature out of your door? you will not dishonor yourself by such cruelty? No, I will not, I cannot do that. Rather would I let him live and die here, and then mason up his remains in the wall. What then will you do? For all your coaxing, he will not budge. Bribes he leaves under your own paperweight on your table; in short, it is quite plain that he prefers to cling to you.

Then something severe, something unusual must be done. What! surely you will not have him collared by a constable, and commit his inno- cent pallor to the common jail? And upon what ground could you procure such a thing to be done?—a vagrant, is he? What! he a vagrant, a wan- derer, who refuses to budge? It is because he will *not* be a vagrant, then, that you seek to count him *as* a vagrant. That is too absurd. No visible means of support: there I have him. Wrong again: for indubitably he *does* support himself, and that is the only unanswerable proof that any man can show of his possessing the means so to do. No more then. Since he will not quit me, I must quit him. I will change my offices; I will move elsewhere; and give him fair notice, that if I find him on my new premises I will then proceed against him as a common trespasser.

Acting accordingly, next day I thus addressed him: "I find these cham- bers too far from the City Hall; the air is unwholesome. In a word, I pro- pose to remove my offices next week, and shall no longer require your services. I tell you this now, in order that you may seek another place."

He made no reply, and nothing more was said.

On the appointed day I engaged carts and men, proceeded to my cham- bers, and having but little furniture, everything was removed in a few hours. Throughout, the scrivener remained standing behind the screen, which I directed to be removed the last thing. It was withdrawn; and being folded up like a huge folio, left him the motionless occupant of a naked room. I stood in the entry watching him a moment, while something from within me upbraided me.

I re-entered, with my hand in my pocket—and—and my heart in my mouth.

"Good-bye, Bartleby; I am going—good-bye, and God some way bless you; and take that," slipping something in his hand. But it dropped upon the floor, and then,—strange to say—I tore myself from him whom I had so longed to be rid of.

Established in my new quarters, for a day or two I kept the door locked, and started at every footfall in the passages. When I returned to my rooms after any little absence, I would pause at the threshold for an instant, and attentively listen, ere applying my key. But these fears were needless. Bartleby never came nigh me.

I thought all was going well, when a perturbed-looking stranger visited me, inquiring whether I was the person who had recently occupied rooms at No. —— Wall Street.

180   Full of forebodings, I replied that I was.

"Then sir," said the stranger, who proved a lawyer, "you are responsible for the man you left there. He refuses to do any copying; he refuses to do anything; he says he prefers not to; and he refuses to quit the premises."

"I am very sorry, sir," said I, with assumed tranquillity, but an inward tremor, "but, really, the man you allude to is nothing to me—he is no relation or apprentice of mine, that you should hold me responsible for him."

"In mercy's name, who is he?"

"I certainly cannot inform you. I know nothing about him. Formerly I employed him as a copyist; but he has done nothing for me now for some time past."

185   "I shall settle him then,—good morning, sir."

Several days passed, and I heard nothing more; and though I often felt a charitable prompting to call at the place and see poor Bartleby, yet a certain squeamishness of I know not what withheld me.

All is over with him, by this time, thought I at last, when through another week no further intelligence reached me. But coming to my room the day after, I found several persons waiting at my door in a high state of nervous excitement.

"That's the man—here he comes," cried the foremost one, whom I recognized as the lawyer who had previously called upon me alone.

"You must take him away, sir, at once," cried a portly person among them, advancing upon me, and whom I knew to be the landlord of No. —— Wall Street. "These gentlemen, my tenants, cannot stand it any longer; Mr. B——" pointing to the lawyer, "has turned him out of his room, and he now persists in haunting the building generally, sitting upon the banisters of the stairs by day, and sleeping in the entry by night. Everybody is concerned; clients are leaving the offices; some fears are entertained of a mob; something you must do, and that without delay."

190   Aghast at this torrent, I fell back before it, and would fain have locked myself in my new quarters. In vain I persisted that Bartleby was nothing to me—no more than to anyone else. In vain:—I was the last person known to have anything to do with him, and they held me to the terrible account. Fearful then of being exposed in the papers (as one person present obscurely threatened) I considered the matter, and at length said, that if the lawyer would give me a confidential interview with the scrivener, in his (the law-

yer's) own room, I would that afternoon strive my best to rid them of the nuisance they complained of.

Going upstairs to my old haunt, there was Bartleby silently sitting upon the banister at the landing.

"What are you doing here, Bartleby?" said I.

"Sitting upon the banister," he mildly replied.

I motioned him into the lawyer's room, who then left us.

"Bartleby," said I, "are you aware that you are the cause of great tribula- 195 tion to me, by persisting in occupying the entry after being dismissed from the office?"

No answer.

"Now one of two things must take place. Either you must do something, or something must be done to you. Now what sort of business would you like to engage in? Would you like to re-engage in copying for someone?"

"No; I would prefer not to make any change."

"Would you like a clerkship in a drygoods store?"

"There is too much confinement about that. No, I would not like a 200 clerkship; but I am not particular."

"Too much confinement," I cried, "why you keep yourself confined all the time!"

"I would prefer not to take a clerkship," he rejoined, as if to settle that little item at once.

"How would a bartender's business suit you? There is no trying of the eyesight in that."

"I would not like it at all; though, as I said before, I am not particular."

His unwonted wordiness inspirited me. I returned to the charge. 205

"Well then, would you like to travel through the country collecting bills for the merchants? That would improve your health."

"No, I would prefer to be doing something else."

"How then would going as a companion to Europe, to entertain some young gentleman with your conversation,—how would that suit you?"

"Not at all. It does not strike me that there is anything definite about that. I like to be stationary. But I am not particular."

"Stationary you shall be then," I cried, now losing all patience, and for 210 the first time in all my exasperating connection with him fairly flying into a passion. "If you do not go away from these premises before night, I shall feel bound—indeed I *am* bound—to—to—to quit the premises myself!" I rather absurdly concluded, knowing not with what possible threat to try to frighten his immobility into compliance. Despairing of all further efforts, I was precipitately leaving him, when a final thought occurred to me— one which had not been wholly unindulged before.

"Bartleby," said I, in the kindest tone I could assume under such exciting circumstances, "will you go home with me now—not to my office, but my dwelling—and remain there till we can conclude upon some convenient arrangement for you at our leisure? Come, let us start now, right away."

"No: at present I would prefer not to make any change at all."

I answered nothing; but effectually dodging everyone by the suddenness and rapidity of my flight, rushed from the building, ran up Wall Street toward Broadway, and jumping into the first omnibus was soon removed from pursuit. As soon as tranquillity returned I distinctly perceived that I had now done all that I possibly could, both in respect to the demands of the landlord and his tenants, and with regard to my own desire and sense of duty, to benefit Bartleby, and shield him from rude persecution. I now strove to be entirely carefree and quiescent; and my conscience justified me in the attempt; though indeed it was not so successful as I could have wished. So fearful was I of being again hunted out by the incensed landlord and his exasperated tenants, that, surrendering my business to Nippers, for a few days I drove about the upper part of the town and through the suburbs, in my rockaway;[6] crossed over to Jersey City and Hoboken, and paid fugitive visits to Manhattanville and Astoria. In fact I almost lived in my rockaway for the time.

When again I entered my office, lo, a note from the landlord lay upon the desk. I opened it with trembling hands. It informed me that the writer had sent to the police, and had Bartleby removed to the Tombs as a vagrant. Moreover, since I knew more about him than anyone else, he wished me to appear at that place, and make a suitable statement of the facts. These tidings had a conflicting effect upon me. At first I was indignant; but at last almost approved. The landlord's energetic, summary disposition had led him to adopt a procedure which I do not think I would have decided upon myself; and yet as a last resort, under such peculiar circumstances, it seemed the only plan.

215   As I afterwards learned, the poor scrivener, when told that he must be conducted to the Tombs, offered not the slightest obstacle, but in his pale unmoving way, silently acquiesced.

Some of the compassionate and curious bystanders joined the party; and headed by one of the constables arm in arm with Bartleby, the silent procession filed its way through all the noise, and heat, and joy of the roaring thoroughfares at noon.

The same day I received the note I went to the Tombs, or to speak more properly, the Halls of Justice. Seeking the right officer, I stated the pur-

6. Light, four-wheeled carriage.

pose of my call, and was informed that the individual I described was indeed within. I then assured the functionary that Bartleby was a perfectly honest man, and greatly to be compassionated, however unaccountably eccentric. I narrated all I knew, and closed by suggesting the idea of letting him remain in as indulgent confinement as possible till something less harsh might be done—though indeed I hardly knew what. At all events, if nothing else could be decided upon, the alms-house must receive him. I then begged to have an interview.

Being under no disgraceful charge, and quite serene and harmless in all his ways, they had permitted him freely to wander about the prison, and especially in the inclosed grass-platted yards thereof. And so I found him there, standing all alone in the quietest of the yards, his face towards a high wall, while all around, from the narrow slits of the jail windows, I thought I saw peering out upon him the eyes of murderers and thieves.

"Bartleby!"

"I know you," he said, without looking round,—"and I want nothing to 220
say to you."

"It was not I that brought you here, Bartleby," said I, keenly pained at his implied suspicion. "And to you, this should not be so vile a place. Nothing reproachful attaches to you by being here. And see, it is not so sad a place as one might think. Look, there is the sky, and here is the grass."

"I know where I am," he replied, but would say nothing more, and so I left him.

As I entered the corridor again, a broad meat-like man, in an apron, accosted me, and jerking his thumb over his shoulder said—"Is that your friend?"

"Yes."

"Does he want to starve? If he does, let him live on the prison fare, 225
that's all."

"Who are you?" asked I, not knowing what to make of such an unofficially-speaking person in such a place.

"I am the grub-man. Such gentlemen as have friends here, hire me to provide them with something good to eat."

"Is this so?" said I, turning to the turnkey.

He said it was.

"Well then," said I, slipping some silver into the grub-man's hands (for 230
so they called him). "I want you to give particular attention to my friend there; let him have the best dinner you can get. And you must be as polite to him as possible."

"Introduce me, will you?" said the grub-man, looking at me with an expression which seemed to say he was all impatience for an opportunity to give a specimen of his breeding.

Thinking it would prove of benefit to the scrivener, I acquiesced; and asking the grub-man his name, went up with him to Bartleby.

"Bartleby, this is Mr. Cutlets; you will find him very useful to you."

"Your sarvant, sir, your sarvant," said the grub-man, making a low salutation behind his apron. "Hope you find it pleasant here, sir;—spacious grounds—cool apartments, sir—hope you'll stay with us some time—try to make it agreeable. May Mrs. Cutlets and I have the pleasure of your company to dinner, sir, in Mrs. Cutlets' private room?"

235   "I prefer not to dine today," said Bartleby, turning away. "It would disagree with me; I am unused to dinners." So saying he slowly moved to the other side of the inclosure, and took up a position fronting the dead-wall.

"How's this?" said the grub-man, addressing me with a stare of astonishment. "He's odd, ain't he?"

"I think he is a little deranged," said I, sadly.

"Deranged? deranged is it? Well now, upon my word, I thought that friend of yourn was a gentleman forger; they are always pale and genteel-like, them forgers. I can't help pity 'em—can't help it, sir. Did you know Monroe Edwards?"[7] he added touchingly, and paused. Then laying his hand pityingly on my shoulder, sighed, "he died of consumption at Sing Sing. So you weren't acquainted with Monroe?"

"No, I was never socially acquainted with any forgers. But I cannot stop longer. Look to my friend yonder. You will not lose by it. I will see you again."

240   Some few days after this, I again obtained admission to the Tombs, and went through the corridors in quest of Bartleby; but without finding him.

"I saw him coming from his cell not long ago," said a turnkey, "may be he's gone to loiter in the yards."

So I went in that direction.

"Are you looking for the silent man?" said another turnkey passing me. "Yonder he lies—sleeping in the yard there. 'Tis not twenty minutes since I saw him lie down."

The yard was entirely quiet. It was not accessible to the common prisoners. The surrounding walls, of amazing thickness, kept off all sounds behind them. The Egyptian character of the masonry weighed upon me with its gloom. But a soft imprisoned turf grew under foot. The heart of the eternal pyramids, it seemed, wherein, by some strange magic, through the clefts, grass seed, dropped by birds, had sprung.

245   Strangely huddled at the base of the wall, his knees drawn up, and lying on his side, his head touching the cold stones, I saw the wasted Bar-

---

7. Famously flamboyant swindler and forger (1808–47) who died in Sing Sing prison, north of New York City.

tleby. But nothing stirred. I paused; then went close up to him; stooped over, and saw that his dim eyes were open; otherwise he seemed profoundly sleeping. Something prompted me to touch him. I felt his hand, when a tingling shiver ran up my arm and down my spine to my feet.

The round face of the grub-man peered upon me now. "His dinner is ready. Won't he dine today, either? Or does he live without dining?"

"Lives without dining," said I, and closed the eyes.

"Eh!—He's asleep, ain't he?"

"With kings and counsellors,"[8] murmured I.

There would seem little need for proceeding further in this history. 250 Imagination will readily supply the meager recital of poor Bartleby's interment. But ere parting with the reader, let me say, that if this little narrative has sufficiently interested him, to awaken curiosity as to who Bartleby was, and what manner of life he led prior to the present narrator's making his acquaintance, I can only reply, that in such curiosity I fully share, but am wholly unable to gratify it. Yet here I hardly know whether I should divulge one little item of rumor, which came to my ear a few months after the scrivener's decease. Upon what basis it rested, I could never ascertain; and hence, how true it is I cannot now tell. But inasmuch as this vague report has not been without a certain strange suggestive interest to me, however sad, it may prove the same with some others; and so I will briefly mention it. The report was this: that Bartleby had been a subordinate clerk in the Dead Letter Office at Washington, from which he had been suddenly removed by a change in the administration. When I think over this rumor, I cannot adequately express the emotions which seize me. Dead letters! does it not sound like dead men? Conceive a man by nature and misfortune prone to a pallid hopelessness, can any business seem more fitted to heighten it than that of continually handling these dead letters, and assorting them for the flames? For by the cartload they are annually burned. Sometimes from out the folded paper the pale clerk takes a ring:—the finger it was meant for, perhaps, molders in the grave; a banknote sent in swiftest charity:—he whom it would relieve, nor eats nor hungers any more; pardon for those who died despairing; hope for those who died unhoping; good tidings for those who died stifled by unrelieved calamities. On errands of life, these letters speed to death.

Ah Bartleby! Ah humanity!

1853

---

8. That is, dead. See Job 3.13–14: "[T]hen had I been at rest, With kings and counsellors of the earth, which built desolate places for themselves."

ALICE MUNRO
(b. 1931)
Boys and Girls

Described by novelist Jonathan Franzen as having "a strong claim to being the best fiction writer now working in North America" and by the committee that awarded her the 2013 Nobel Prize for Literature as a "master of the contemporary short story," Alice Munro today enjoys an enviably high reputation. That was long in coming and unexpected for a girl raised during the Great Depression and World War II, on a farm in southwestern Ontario—that unglamorous terrain she has since so vividly memorialized in her fiction. She began publishing stories while attending the University of Western Ontario. But when her two-year scholarship ran out, she left the university, married James Munro, and moved first to Vancouver and then to Victoria, where the couple raised three daughters. Though her stories appeared sporadically during the 1950s, it was not until 1968 that then-thirty-eight-year-old Munro published her first book and with it won the first of multiple Governor General's Awards, Canada's highest literary prize. Divorced and remarried, Munro returned to Ontario and began regularly publishing collections including *Something I've Been Meaning to Tell You* (1974), *The Progress of Love* (1986), *Open Secrets* (1994), the Booker Prize–winning *View from Castle Rock* (2006), and *Dear Life* (2012). One reason Munro has not achieved the wide fame many believe she merits is her focus on short fiction: The one work she published as a novel, *Lives of Girls and Women* (1971), is in fact a series of interlinked stories.

M y father was a fox farmer. That is, he raised silver foxes, in pens; and in the fall and early winter, when their fur was prime, he killed them and skinned them and sold their pelts to the Hudson's Bay Company or the Montreal Fur Traders. These companies supplied us with heroic calendars to hang, one on each side of the kitchen door. Against a background of cold blue sky and black pine forests and treacherous northern rivers, plumed adventurers planted the flags of England or of France; magnificent savages bent their backs to the portage.

For several weeks before Christmas, my father worked after supper in the cellar of our house. The cellar was white-washed, and lit by a hundred-watt bulb over the worktable. My brother Laird and I sat on the top step and watched. My father removed the pelt inside-out from the body of the fox, which looked surprisingly small, mean and rat-like, deprived of its arrogant weight of fur. The naked, slippery bodies were collected in a sack and buried at the dump. One time the hired man, Henry Bailey, had taken a swipe at me with this sack, saying, "Christmas present!" My mother thought that was not funny. In fact she disliked the whole pelting operation—that was what the killing, skinning, and preparation of the furs was called—and wished it did not have to take place in the house. There was the smell. After the pelt had been stretched inside-out on a long board my father scraped away delicately, removing the little clotted webs of blood vessels, the bubbles of fat; the smell of blood and animal fat, with the strong primitive odour of the fox itself, penetrated all parts of the house. I found it reassuringly seasonal, like the smell of oranges and pine needles.

Henry Bailey suffered from bronchial troubles. He would cough and cough until his narrow face turned scarlet, and his light blue, derisive eyes filled up with tears; then he took the lid off the stove, and, standing well back, shot out a great clot of phlegm—hsss—straight into the heart of the flames. We admired him for this performance and for his ability to make his stomach growl at will, and for his laughter, which was full of high whistlings and gurglings and involved the whole faulty machinery of his chest. It was sometimes hard to tell what he was laughing at, and always possible that it might be us.

After we had been sent to bed we could still smell fox and still hear Henry's laugh, but these things, reminders of the warm, safe, brightly lit downstairs world, seemed lost and diminished, floating on the stale cold air upstairs. We were afraid at night in the winter. We were not afraid of *outside* though this was the time of year when snowdrifts curled around our house like sleeping whales and the wind harassed us all night, coming up from the buried fields, the frozen swamp, with its old bugbear chorus of threats and misery. We were afraid of *inside*, the room where we slept. At this time the upstairs of our house was not finished. A brick chimney went up one wall. In the middle of the floor was a square hole, with a wooden railing around it; that was where the stairs came up. On the other side of the stairwell were the things that nobody had any use for any more—a soldiery roll of linoleum, standing on end, a wicker baby carriage, a fern basket, china jugs and basins with cracks in them, a picture of the Battle of Balaclava,[1] very sad to look at. I had told Laird, as soon as he was old enough to understand such things, that bats and skeletons lived over there; whenever a man escaped from the county jail, twenty miles away, I imagined that he had somehow let himself in the window and was hiding behind the linoleum. But we had rules to keep us safe. When the light was

1. Indecisive Crimean War battle fought on October 25, 1854, famous for the Charge of the Light Brigade.

on, we were safe as long as we did not step off the square of worn carpet which defined our bedroom-space; when the light was off no place was safe but the beds themselves. I had to turn out the light kneeling on the end of my bed, and stretching as far as I could to reach the cord.

5   In the dark we lay on our beds, our narrow life rafts, and fixed our eyes on the faint light coming up the stairwell, and sang songs. Laird sang "Jingle Bells," which he would sing any time, whether it was Christmas or not, and I sang "Danny Boy." I loved the sound of my own voice, frail and supplicating, rising in the dark. We could make out the tall frosted shapes of the windows now, gloomy and white. When I came to the part, *When I am dead, as dead I well may be*—a fit of shivering caused not by the cold sheets but by pleasurable emotion almost silenced me. *You'll kneel and say, an Ave there above me*—What was an Ave? Every day I forgot to find out.

Laird went straight from singing to sleep. I could hear his long, satisfied, bubbly breaths. Now for the time that remained to me, the most perfectly private and perhaps the best time of the whole day, I arranged myself tightly under the covers and went on with one of the stories I was telling myself from night to night. These stories were about myself, when I had grown a little older; they took place in a world that was recognizably mine, yet one that presented opportunities for courage, boldness and self-sacrifice, as mine never did. I rescued people from a bombed building (it discouraged me that the real war[2] had gone on so far away from Jubilee). I shot two rabid wolves who were menacing the schoolyard (the teachers cowered terrified at my back). I rode a fine horse spiritedly down the main street of Jubilee, acknowledging the townspeople's gratitude for some yet-to-be-worked-out piece of heroism (nobody ever rode a horse there, except King Billy in the Orangemen's Day[3] parade). There was always riding and shooting in these stories, though I had only been on a horse twice—bareback because we did not own a saddle—and the second time I had slid right around and dropped under the horse's feet; it had stepped placidly over me. I really was learning to shoot, but I could not hit anything yet, not even tin cans on fence posts.

Alive, the foxes inhabited a world my father made for them. It was surrounded by a high guard fence, like a medieval town, with a gate that was padlocked at night. Along the streets of this town were ranged large, sturdy pens. Each of them had a real door that a man could go through, a wooden ramp along the wire, for the foxes to run up and down on, and a

2. World War II (1939–45).

3. The Orange Society is an Irish Protestant group named after William of Orange, who, as King William III of England, defeated the Catholic James II. The society sponsors an annual procession on July 12 to commemorate the victory of William III at the Battle of the Boyne (1690).

kennel—something like a clothes chest with airholes—where they slept and stayed in winter and had their young. There were feeding and watering dishes attached to the wire in such a way that they could be emptied and cleaned from the outside. The dishes were made of old tin cans, and the ramps and kennels of odds and ends of old lumber. Everything was tidy and ingenious; my father was tirelessly inventive and his favourite book in the world was *Robinson Crusoe*.[4] He had fitted a tin drum on a wheelbarrow, for bringing water down to the pens. This was my job in summer, when the foxes had to have water twice a day. Between nine and ten o'clock in the morning, and again after supper, I filled the drum at the pump and trundled it down through the barnyard to the pens, where I parked it, and filled my watering can and went along the streets. Laird came too, with his little cream and green gardening can, filled too full and knocking against his legs and slopping water on his canvas shoes. I had the real watering can, my father's, though I could only carry it three-quarters full.

The foxes all had names, which were printed on a tin plate and hung beside their doors. They were not named when they were born, but when they survived the first year's pelting and were added to the breeding stock. Those my father had named were called names like Prince, Bob, Wally and Betty. Those I had named were called Star or Turk, or Maureen or Diana. Laird named one Maud after a hired girl we had when he was little, one Harold after a boy at school, and one Mexico, he did not say why.

Naming them did not make pets out of them, or anything like it. Nobody but my father ever went into the pens, and he had twice had blood-poisoning from bites. When I was bringing them their water they prowled up and down on the paths they had made inside their pens, barking seldom—they saved that for nighttime, when they might get up a chorus of community frenzy—but always watching me, their eyes burning, clear gold, in their pointed, malevolent faces. They were beautiful for their delicate legs and heavy, aristocratic tails and the bright fur sprinkled on dark down their backs—which gave them their name—but especially for their faces, drawn exquisitely sharp in pure hostility, and their golden eyes.

Besides carrying water I helped my father when he cut the long grass, and the lamb's quarter and flowering money-musk, that grew between the pens. He cut with the scythe and I raked into piles. Then he took a pitchfork and threw freshcut grass all over the top of the pens, to keep the foxes cooler and shade their coats, which were browned by too much sun. My father did not talk to me unless it was about the job we were doing. In this he was quite different from my mother, who, if she was feeling cheerful,

4. Novel (1719) by Daniel Defoe about a man shipwrecked on a desert island; it goes into great detail about the ingenious contraptions he fashions from simple materials.

would tell me all sorts of things—the name of a dog she had had when she was a little girl, the names of boys she had gone out with later on when she was grown up, and what certain dresses of hers had looked like—she could not imagine now what had become of them. Whatever thoughts and stories my father had were private, and I was shy of him and would never ask him questions. Nevertheless I worked willingly under his eyes, and with a feeling of pride. One time a feed salesman came down into the pens to talk to him and my father said, "Like to have you meet my new hired man." I turned away and raked furiously, red in the face with pleasure.

"Could of fooled me," said the salesman. "I thought it was only a girl."

After the grass was cut, it seemed suddenly much later in the year. I walked on stubble in the earlier evening, aware of the reddening skies, the entering silences, of fall. When I wheeled the tank out of the gate and put the padlock on, it was almost dark. One night at this time I saw my mother and father standing talking on the little rise of ground we called the gang-way, in front of the barn. My father had just come from the meathouse; he had his stiff bloody apron on, and a pail of cut-up meat in his hand.

It was an odd thing to see my mother down at the barn. She did not often come out of the house unless it was to do something—hang out the wash or dig potatoes in the garden. She looked out of place, with her bare lumpy legs, not touched by the sun, her apron still on and damp across the stomach from the supper dishes. Her hair was tied up in a kerchief, wisps of it falling out. She would tie her hair up like this in the morning, saying she did not have time to do it properly, and it would stay tied up all day. It was true, too; she really did not have time. These days our back porch was piled with baskets of peaches and grapes and pears, bought in town, and onions and tomatoes and cucumbers grown at home, all waiting to be made into jelly and jam and preserves, pickles and chili sauce. In the kitchen there was a fire in the stove all day, jars clinked in boiling water, sometimes a cheese-cloth bag was strung on a pole between two chairs, straining blue-black grape pulp for jelly. I was given jobs to do and I would sit at the table peeling peaches that had been soaked in the hot water, or cutting up onions, my eyes smarting and streaming. As soon as I was done I ran out of the house, trying to get out of earshot before my mother thought of what she wanted me to do next. I hated the hot dark kitchen in summer, the green blinds and the flypapers, the same old oilcloth table and wavy mirror and bumpy lino-leum. My mother was too tired and preoccupied to talk to me, she had no heart to tell about the Normal School Graduation Dance; sweat trickled over her face and she was always counting under her breath, pointing at jars, dumping cups of sugar. It seemed to me that work in the house was endless, dreary and peculiarly depressing; work done out of doors, and in my father's service, was ritualistically important.

I wheeled the tank up to the barn, where it was kept, and I heard my mother saying, "Wait till Laird gets a little bigger, then you'll have a real help."

What my father said I did not hear. I was pleased by the way he stood 15 listening, politely as he would to a salesman or a stranger, but with an air of wanting to get on with his real work. I felt my mother had no business down here and I wanted him to feel the same way. What did she mean about Laird? He was no help to anybody. Where was he now? Swinging himself sick on the swing, going around in circles, or trying to catch caterpillars. He never once stayed with me till I was finished.

"And then I can use her more in the house," I heard my mother say. She had a dead-quiet, regretful way of talking about me that always made me uneasy. "I just get my back turned and she runs off. It's not like I had a girl in the family at all."

I went and sat on a feed bag in the corner of the barn, not wanting to appear when this conversation was going on. My mother, I felt, was not to be trusted. She was kinder than my father and more easily fooled, but you could not depend on her, and the real reasons for the things she said and did were not to be known. She loved me, and she sat up late at night making a dress of the difficult style I wanted, for me to wear when school started, but she was also my enemy. She was always plotting. She was plotting now to get me to stay in the house more, although she knew I hated it (*because* she knew I hated it) and keep me from working for my father. It seemed to me she would do this simply out of perversity, and to try her power. It did not occur to me that she could be lonely, or jealous. No grown-up could be; they were too fortunate. I sat and kicked my heels monotonously against a feed bag, raising dust, and did not come out till she was gone.

At any rate, I did not expect my father to pay any attention to what she said. Who could imagine Laird doing my work—Laird remembering the padlock and cleaning out the watering-dishes with a leaf on the end of a stick, or even wheeling the tank without it tumbling over? It showed how little my mother knew about the way things really were.

I have forgotten to say what the foxes were fed. My father's bloody apron reminded me. They were fed horsemeat. At this time most farmers still kept horses, and when a horse got too old to work, or broke a leg or got down and would not get up, as they sometimes did, the owner would call my father, and he and Henry went out to the farm in the truck. Usually they shot and butchered the horse there, paying the farmer from five to twelve dollars. If they had already too much meat on hand, they would bring the horse back alive, and keep it for a few days or weeks in our stable, until the meat was needed. After the war the farmers were buying tractors and gradually getting rid of horses altogether, so it sometimes happened that we got a good healthy horse, that there was just no use for any more. If this happened in the winter we might keep the horse in our stable till spring, for we had plenty of hay and if there was a lot of snow—and the plow did not always get our road cleared—it was convenient to be able to go to town with a horse and cutter.[5]

20   The winter I was eleven years old we had two horses in the stable. We did not know what names they had had before, so we called them Mack and Flora. Mack was an old black workhorse, sooty and indifferent. Flora was a sorrel mare, a driver. We took them both out in the cutter. Mack was slow and easy to handle. Flora was given to fits of violent alarm, veering at cars and even at other horses, but we loved her speed and high-stepping, her general air of gallantry and abandon. On Saturdays we went down to the stable and as soon as we opened the door on its cosy, animal-smelling darkness Flora threw up her head, rolled her eyes, whinnied despairingly and pulled herself through a crisis of nerves on the spot. It was not safe to go into her stall; she would kick.

This winter also I began to hear a great deal more on the theme my mother had sounded when she had been talking in front of the barn. I no longer felt safe. It seemed that in the minds of the people around me there was a steady undercurrent of thought, not to be deflected, on this one subject. The word *girl* had formerly seemed to me innocent and unburdened, like the world *child*; now it appeared that it was no such thing. A girl was not, as I had supposed, simply what I was; it was what I had to become. It was a definition, always touched with emphasis, with reproach and disappointment. Also it was a joke on me. Once Laird and I were fighting, and for the first time ever I had to use all my strength against him; even so, he caught and pinned my arm for a moment, really hurting me. Henry saw this, and laughed, saying, "Oh, that there Laird's gonna show you, one of these days!" Laird was getting a lot bigger. But I was getting bigger too.

My grandmother came to stay with us for a few weeks and I heard other things. "Girls don't slam doors like that." "Girls keep their knees together when they sit down." And worse still, when I asked some questions, "That's none of girls' business." I continued to slam the doors and sit as awkwardly as possible, thinking that by such measures I kept myself free.

When spring came, the horses were let out in the barnyard. Mack stood against the barn wall trying to scratch his neck and haunches, but Flora trotted up and down and reared at the fences, clattering her hooves against the rails. Snow drifts dwindled quickly, revealing the hard grey and brown

5. Small, light sleigh.

earth, the familiar rise and fall of the ground, plain and bare after the fantastic landscape of winter. There was a great feeling of opening-out, of release. We just wore rubbers now, over our shoes; our feet felt ridiculously light. One Saturday we went out to the stable and found all the doors open, letting in the unaccustomed sunlight and fresh air. Henry was there, just idling around looking at his collection of calendars which were tacked up behind the stalls in a part of the stable my mother had probably never seen. "Come to say goodbye to your old friend Mack?" Henry said. "Here, you give him a taste of oats." He poured some oats into Laird's cupped hands and Laird went to feed Mack. Mack's teeth were in bad shape. He ate very slowly, patiently shifting the oats around in his mouth, trying to find a stump of a molar to grind it on. "Poor old Mack," said Henry mournfully. "When a horse's teeth's gone, he's gone. That's about the way."

"Are you going to shoot him today?" I said. Mack and Flora had been in the stable so long I had almost forgotten they were going to be shot.

Henry didn't answer me. Instead he started to sing in a high, trembly, mocking-sorrowful voice, *Oh, there's no more work, for poor Uncle Ned, he's gone where the good darkies go.*[6] Mack's thick, blackish tongue worked diligently at Laird's hand. I went out before the song was ended and sat down on the gangway.

I had never seen them shoot a horse, but I knew where it was done. Last summer Laird and I had come upon a horse's entrails before they were buried. We had thought it was a big black snake, coiled up in the sun. That was around in the field that ran up beside the barn. I thought that if we went inside the barn, and found a wide crack or knothole to look through we would be able to see them do it. It was not something I wanted to see; just the same, if a thing really happened, it was better to see it, and know.

My father came down from the house, carrying the gun.

"What are you doing here?" he said.

"Nothing."

"Go on up and play around the house."

He sent Laird out of the stable. I said to Laird, "Do you want to see them shoot Mack?" and without waiting for an answer led him around to the front door of the barn, opened it carefully, and went in. "Be quiet or they'll hear us," I said. We could hear Henry and my father talking in the stable, then the heavy, shuffling steps of Mack being backed out of his stall.

In the loft it was cold and dark. Thin, crisscrossed beams of sunlight fell through the cracks. The hay was low. It was a rolling country, hills and hollows, slipping under our feet. About four feet up was a beam going around the walls. We piled hay up in one corner and I boosted Laird up

25

30

---

6. Lines from the Stephen Foster (1826–64) song "Old Uncle Ned."

and hoisted myself. The beam was not very wide; we crept along it with our hands flat on the barn walls. There were plenty of knotholes, and I found one that gave me the view I wanted—a corner of the barnyard, the gate, part of the field. Laird did not have a knothole and began to complain. I showed him a widened crack between two boards. "Be quiet and wait. If they hear you you'll get us in trouble."

35 My father came in sight carrying the gun. Henry was leading Mack by the halter. He dropped it and took out his cigarette papers and tobacco; he rolled cigarettes for my father and himself. While this was going on Mack nosed around in the old, dead grass along the fence. Then my father opened the gate and they took Mack through. Henry led Mack way from the path to a patch of ground and they talked together, not loud enough for us to hear. Mack again began searching for a mouthful of fresh grass, which was not to be found. My father walked away in a straight line, and stopped short at a distance which seemed to suit him. Henry was walking away from Mack too, but sideways, still negligently holding on to the halter. My father raised the gun and Mack looked up as if he had noticed something and my father shot him.

Mack did not collapse at once but swayed, lurched sideways and fell, first on his side; then he rolled over on his back and, amazingly, kicked his legs for a few seconds in the air. At this Henry laughed, as if Mack had done a trick for him. Laird, who had drawn a long, groaning breath of surprise when the shot was fired, said out loud, "He's not dead." And it seemed to me it might be true. But his legs stopped, he rolled on his side again, his muscles quivered and sank. The two men walked over and looked at him in a businesslike way; they bent down and examined his forehead where the bullet had gone in, and now I saw his blood on the brown grass.

"Now they just skin him and cut him up," I said. "Let's go." My legs were a little shaky and I jumped gratefully down into the hay. "Now you've seen how they shoot a horse," I said in a congratulatory way, as if I had seen it many times before. "Let's see if any barn cat's had kittens in the hay." Laird jumped. He seemed young and obedient again. Suddenly I remembered how, when he was little, I had brought him into the barn and told him to climb the ladder to the top beam. That was in the spring, too, when the hay was low. I had done it out of a need for excitement, a desire for something to happen so that I could tell about it. He was wearing a little bulky brown and white checked coat, made down from one of mine. He went all the way up, just as I told him, and sat down on the top beam with the hay far below him on one side, and the barn floor and some old machinery on the other. Then I ran screaming to my father, "Laird's up on the top beam!" My father came, my mother came, my father went up the ladder talking very quietly and brought Laird down under his arm, at which my mother leaned against the ladder and began to cry. They said to me, "Why weren't you watching him?" but nobody ever knew the truth. Laird did not know enough to tell. But whenever I saw the brown and white checked coat hanging in the closet, or at the bottom of the rag bag, which was where it ended up, I felt a weight in my stomach, the sadness of unexorcized guilt.

I looked at Laird who did not even remember this, and I did not like the look on this thin, winter-pale face. His expression was not frightened or upset, but remote, concentrating. "Listen," I said, in an unusually bright and friendly voice, "you aren't going to tell, are you?"

"No," he said absently.

"Promise."

"Promise," he said. I grabbed the hand behind his back to make sure he was not crossing his fingers. Even so, he might have a nightmare; it might come out that way. I decided I had better work hard to get all thoughts of what he had seen out of his mind—which, it seemed to me, could not hold very many things at a time. I got some money I had saved and that afternoon we went into Jubilee and saw a show, with Judy Canova,[7] at which we both laughed a great deal. After that I thought it would be all right.

Two weeks later I knew they were going to shoot Flora. I knew from the night before, when I heard my mother ask if the hay was holding out all right, and my father said, "Well, after to-morrow there'll just be the cow, and we should be able to put her out to grass in another week." So I knew it was Flora's turn in the morning.

This time I didn't think of watching it. That was something to see just one time. I had not thought about it very often since, but sometimes when I was busy, working at school, or standing in front of the mirror combing my hair and wondering if I would be pretty when I grew up, the whole scene would flash into my mind: I would see the easy, practised way my father raised the gun, and hear Henry laughing when Mack kicked his legs in the air. I did not have any great feeling of horror and opposition, such as a city child might have had; I was too used to seeing the death of animals as a necessity by which we lived. Yet I felt a little ashamed, and there was a new wariness, a sense of holding-off, in my attitude to my father and his work.

It was a fine day, and we were going around the yard picking up tree branches that had been torn off in winter storms. This was something we had been told to do, and also we wanted to use them to make a teepee. We heard Flora whinny, and then my father's voice and Henry's shouting, and we ran down to the barnyard to see what was going on.

---

7. American comedian (1913–83) best known for her yodeling in hillbilly movies of the 1940s.

45   The stable door was open. Henry had just brought Flora out, and she had broken away from him. She was running free in the barnyard, from one end to the other. We climbed up on the fence. It was exciting to see her running, whinnying, going up on her hind legs, prancing and threatening like a horse in a Western movie, an unbroken ranch horse, though she was just an old driver, an old sorrel mare. My father and Henry ran after her and tried to grab the dangling halter. They tried to work her into a corner, and they had almost succeeded when she made a run between them, wild-eyed, and disappeared around the corner of the barn. We heard the rails clatter down as she got over the fence, and Henry yelled, "She's into the field now!"

That meant she was in the long L-shaped field that ran up by the house. If she got around the center, heading towards the lane, the gate was open; the truck had been driven into the field this morning. My father shouted to me, because I was on the other side of the fence, nearest the lane, "Go shut the gate!"

I could run very fast. I ran across the garden, past the tree where our swing was hung, and jumped across a ditch into the lane. There was the open gate. She had not got out, I could not see her up on the road; she must have run to the other end of the field. The gate was heavy. I lifted it out of the gravel and carried it across the roadway. I had it half-way across when she came in sight, galloping straight towards me. There was just time to get the chain on. Laird came scrambling through the ditch to help me.

Instead of shutting the gate, I opened it as wide as I could. I did not make any decision to do this, it was just what I did. Flora never slowed down; she galloped straight past me, and Laird jumped up and down, yelling, "Shut it, shut it!" even after it was too late. My father and Henry appeared in the field a moment too late to see what I had done. They only saw Flora heading for the township road. They would think I had not got there in time.

They did not waste any time asking about it. They went back to the barn and got the gun and the knives they used, and put these in the truck; then they turned the truck around and came bouncing up the field toward us. Laird called to them, "Let me go too, let me go too!" and Henry stopped the truck and they took him in. I shut the gate after they were all gone.

50   I supposed Laird would tell. I wondered what would happen to me. I had never disobeyed my father before, and I could not understand why I had done it. Flora would not really get away. They would catch up with her in the truck. Or if they did not catch her this morning somebody would see her and telephone us this afternoon or tomorrow. There was no wild country here for her to run to, only farms. What was more, my father had paid for her, we needed the meat to feed the foxes, we needed the foxes to make our living. All I had done was make more work for my father

who worked hard enough already. And when my father found out about it he was not going to trust me any more, he would know that I was not entirely on his side. I was on Flora's side, and that made me no use to anybody, not even to her. Just the same, I did not regret it; when she came running at me and I held the gate open, that was the only thing I could do.

I went back to the house, and my mother said, "What's all the commotion?" I told her that Flora had kicked down the fence and got away. "Your poor father," she said, "now he'll have to go chasing over the countryside. Well, there isn't any use planning dinner before one." She put up the ironing board. I wanted to tell her, but thought better of it and went upstairs and sat on my bed.

Lately I had been trying to make my part of the room fancy, spreading the bed with old lace curtains, and fixing myself a dressing-table with some leftovers of cretonne for a skirt. I planned to put up some kind of barricade between my bed and Laird's, to keep my section separate from his. In the sunlight, the lace curtains were just dusty rags. We did not sing at night any more. One night when I was singing Laird said, "You sound silly," and I went right on but the next night I did not start. There was not so much need to anyway, we were no longer afraid. We knew it was just old furniture over there, old jumble and confusion. We did not keep to the rules. I still stayed awake after Laird was asleep and told myself stories, but even in these stories something different was happening, mysterious alterations took place. A story might start off in the old way, with a spectacular danger, a fire or wild animals, and for a while I might rescue people; then things would change around, and instead, somebody would be rescuing me. It might be a boy from our class at school, or even Mr. Campbell, our teacher, who tickled girls under the arms. And at this point the story concerned itself at great length with what I looked like—how long my hair was, and what kind of dress I had on; by the time I had these details worked out the real excitement of the story was lost.

It was later than one o'clock when the truck came back. The tarpaulin was over the back, which meant there was meat in it. My mother had to heat dinner up all over again. Henry and my father had changed from their bloody overalls into ordinary working overalls in the barn, and they washed their arms and necks and faces at the sink, and splashed water on their hair and combed it. Laird lifted his arm to show off a streak of blood. "We shot old Flora," he said, "and cut her up in fifty pieces."

"Well I don't want to hear about it," my mother said. "And don't come to my table like that."

My father made him go and wash the blood off.

We sat down and my father said grace and Henry pasted his chewing-gum on the end of his fork, the way he always did; when he took it off he

55

would have us admire the pattern. We began to pass the bowls of steaming, overcooked vegetables. Laird looked across the table at me and said proudly, distinctly, "Anyway it was her fault Flora got away."

"What?" my father said.

"She could of shut the gate and she didn't. She just open' it up and Flora run out."

"Is that right?" my father said.

60   Everybody at the table was looking at me. I nodded, swallowing food with great difficulty. To my shame, tears flooded my eyes.

My father made a curt sound of disgust. "What did you do that for?"

I did not answer. I put down my fork and waited to be sent from the table, still not looking up.

But this did not happen. For some time nobody said anything, then Laird said matter-of-factly, "She's crying."

"Never mind," my father said. He spoke with resignation, even good humour, the words which absolved and dismissed me for good. "She's only a girl," he said.

65   I didn't protest that, even in my heart. Maybe it was true.

1968

FLANNERY O'CONNOR
(1925–1964)

A Good Man Is Hard to Find

Mary Flannery O'Connor was born in Savannah, Georgia, studied at the Georgia State College for Women, and won a fellowship to the Writers' Workshop of the University of Iowa, from which she received her MFA. In 1950, she was first diagnosed with lupus, an autoimmune disorder that also afflicted her father and would trouble her for the rest of her brief life. Her first novel, *Wise Blood*, was published in 1952, and her first collection of stories, *A Good Man Is Hard to Find*, in 1955. She was able to complete only one more novel, *The Violent Bear It Away* (1960), and a second collection of stories, *Everything That Rises Must Converge* (1965), before her death. Her posthumously published *Complete Stories* won the National Book Award in 1972. A collection of letters, edited by Sally Fitzgerald under the title *The Habit of Being*, appeared in 1979.

The grandmother didn't want to go to Florida. She wanted to visit some of her connections in east Tennessee and she was seizing at every chance to change Bailey's mind. Bailey was the son she lived with, her only boy. He was sitting on the edge of his chair at the table, bent over the orange sports section of the *Journal*. "Now look here, Bailey," she said, "see here, read this," and she stood with one hand on her thin hip and the other rattling the newspaper at his bald head. "Here this fellow that calls himself The Misfit is aloose from the Federal Pen and headed toward Florida and you read here what it says he did to these people. Just you read it. I wouldn't take my children in any direction with a criminal like that aloose in it. I couldn't answer to my conscience if I did."

Bailey didn't look up from his reading so she wheeled around then and faced the children's mother, a young woman in slacks, whose face was as broad and innocent as a cabbage and was tied around with a green head-kerchief that had two points on the top like a rabbit's ears. She was sitting on the sofa, feeding the baby his apricots out of a jar. "The children have been to Florida before," the old lady said. "You all ought to take them somewhere else for a change so they would see different parts of the world and be broad. They never have been to east Tennessee."

The children's mother didn't seem to hear her but the eight-year-old boy, John Wesley, a stocky child with glasses, said, "If you don't want to go to Florida, why dontcha stay at home?" He and the little girl, June Star, were reading the funny papers on the floor.

"She wouldn't stay at home to be queen for a day," June Star said without raising her yellow head.

"Yes and what would you do if this fellow, The Misfit, caught you?" the grandmother asked.

"I'd smack his face," John Wesley said.

"She wouldn't stay at home for a million bucks," June Star said. "Afraid she'd miss something. She has to go everywhere we go."

"All right, Miss," the grandmother said. "Just remember that the next time you want me to curl your hair."

June Star said her hair was naturally curly.

The next morning the grandmother was the first one in the car, ready to go. She had her big black valise that looked like the head of a hippopotamus in one corner, and underneath it she was hiding a basket with Pitty Sing,[1] the cat, in it. She didn't intend for the cat to be left alone in the house for three days because he would miss her too much and she was afraid he

5

10

1. Named after Pitti-Sing, one of the "three little maids from school" in Gilbert and Sullivan's operetta *The Mikado* (1885).

might brush against one of the gas burners and accidentally asphyxiate himself. Her son, Bailey, didn't like to arrive at a motel with a cat.

She sat in the middle of the back seat with John Wesley and June Star on either side of her. Bailey and the children's mother and the baby sat in front and they left Atlanta at eight forty-five with the mileage on the car at 55890. The grandmother wrote this down because she thought it would be interesting to say how many miles they had been when they got back. It took them twenty minutes to reach the outskirts of the city.

The old lady settled herself comfortably, removing her white cotton gloves and putting them up with her purse on the shelf in front of the back window. The children's mother still had on slacks and still had her head tied up in a green kerchief, but the grandmother had on a navy blue straw sailor hat with a bunch of white violets on the brim and a navy blue dress with a small white dot in the print. Her collars and cuffs were white organdy trimmed with lace and at her neckline she had pinned a purple spray of cloth violets containing a sachet. In case of an accident, anyone seeing her dead on the highway would know at once that she was a lady.

She said she thought it was going to be a good day for driving, neither too hot nor too cold, and she cautioned Bailey that the speed limit was fifty-five miles an hour and that the patrolmen hid themselves behind billboards and small clumps of trees and sped out after you before you had a chance to slow down. She pointed out interesting details of the scenery: Stone Mountain; the blue granite that in some places came up to both sides of the highway; the brilliant red clay banks slightly streaked with purple; and the various crops that made rows of green lace-work on the ground. The trees were full of silver-white sunlight and the meanest of them sparkled. The children were reading comic magazines and their mother had gone back to sleep.

"Let's go through Georgia fast so we won't have to look at it much," John Wesley said.

15   "If I were a little boy," said the grandmother, "I wouldn't talk about my native state that way. Tennessee has the mountains and Georgia has the hills."

"Tennessee is just a hillbilly dumping ground," John Wesley said, "and Georgia is a lousy state too."

"You said it," June Star said.

"In my time," said the grandmother, folding her thin veined fingers, "children were more respectful of their native states and their parents and everything else. People did right then. Oh look at the cute little pickaninny!" she said and pointed to a Negro child standing in the door of a shack. "Wouldn't that make a picture, now?" she asked and they all turned and looked at the little Negro out of the back window. He waved.

"He didn't have any britches on," June Star said.

"He probably didn't have any," the grandmother explained. "Little nig- 20
gers in the country don't have things like we do. If I could paint, I'd paint
that picture," she said.

The children exchanged comic books.

The grandmother offered to hold the baby and the children's mother
passed him over the front seat to her. She set him on her knee and
bounced him and told him about the things they were passing. She rolled
her eyes and screwed up her mouth and stuck her leathery thin face into
his smooth bland one. Occasionally he gave her a faraway smile. They
passed a large cotton field with five or six graves fenced in the middle of it,
like a small island. "Look at the graveyard!" the grandmother said, pointing it out. "That was the old family burying ground. That belonged to the
plantation."

"Where's the plantation?" John Wesley asked.

"Gone with the Wind,"[2] said the grandmother. "Ha. Ha."

When the children finished all the comic books they had brought, they 25
opened the lunch and ate it. The grandmother ate a peanut butter sandwich
and an olive and would not let the children throw the box and the paper
napkins out the window. When there was nothing else to do they played a
game by choosing a cloud and making the other two guess what shape it
suggested. John Wesley took one the shape of a cow and June Star guessed
a cow and John Wesley said, no, an automobile, and June Star said he didn't
play fair, and they began to slap each other over the grandmother.

The grandmother said she would tell them a story if they would keep
quiet. When she told a story, she rolled her eyes and waved her head and
was very dramatic. She said once when she was a maiden lady she had been
courted by a Mr. Edgar Atkins Teagarden from Jasper, Georgia. She said he
was a very good-looking man and a gentleman and that he brought her a
watermelon every Saturday afternoon with his initials cut in it, E. A. T.
Well, one Saturday, she said, Mr. Teagarden brought the watermelon and
there was nobody at home and he left it on the front porch and returned in
his buggy to Jasper, but she never got the watermelon, she said, because a
nigger boy ate it when he saw the initials, E. A. T.! This story tickled John
Wesley's funny bone and he giggled and giggled but June Star didn't think
it was any good. She said she wouldn't marry a man that just brought her a
watermelon on Saturday. The grandmother said she would have done
well to marry Mr. Teagarden because he was a gentleman and had bought

2. Title of an immensely popular novel, published in 1936, by Margaret Mitchell (1900–49); the
novel depicts a large, prosperous Southern plantation, Tara, that is destroyed by Northern
troops in the American Civil War.

Coca-Cola stock when it first came out and that he had died only a few years ago, a very wealthy man.

They stopped at The Tower for barbecued sandwiches. The Tower was a part stucco and part wood filling station and dance hall set in a clearing outside of Timothy. A fat man named Red Sammy Butts ran it and there were signs stuck here and there on the building and for miles up and down the highway saying, TRY RED SAMMY'S FAMOUS BARBECUE. NONE LIKE FAMOUS RED SAMMY'S! RED SAM! THE FAT BOY WITH THE HAPPY LAUGH! A VETERAN! RED SAMMY'S YOUR MAN!

Red Sammy was lying on the bare ground outside The Tower with his head under a truck while a gray monkey about a foot high, chained to a small chinaberry tree, chattered nearby. The monkey sprang back into the tree and got on the highest limb as soon as he saw the children jump out of the car and run toward him.

Inside, The Tower was a long dark room with a counter at one end and tables at the other and dancing space in the middle. They all sat down at a board table next to the nickelodeon[3] and Red Sam's wife, a tall burnt-brown woman with hair and eyes lighter than her skin, came and took their order. The children's mother put a dime in the machine and played "The Tennessee Waltz," and the grandmother said that tune always made her want to dance. She asked Bailey if he would like to dance but he only glared at her. He didn't have a naturally sunny disposition like she did and trips made him nervous. The grandmother's brown eyes were very bright. She swayed her head from side to side and pretended she was dancing in her chair. June Star said play something she could tap to so the children's mother put in another dime and played a fast number and June Star stepped out onto the dance floor and did her tap routine.

30   "Ain't she cute?" Red Sam's wife said, leaning over the counter. "Would you like to come be my little girl?"

"No I certainly wouldn't," June Star said. "I wouldn't live in a broken-down place like this for a million bucks!" and she ran back to the table.

"Ain't she cute?" the woman repeated, stretching her mouth politely.

"Aren't you ashamed?" hissed the grandmother.

Red Sam came in and told his wife to quit lounging on the counter and hurry up with these people's order. His khaki trousers reached just to his hip bones and his stomach hung over them like a sack of meal swaying under his shirt. He came over and sat down at a table nearby and let out a combination sigh and yodel. "You can't win," he said. "You can't win," and he wiped his sweating red face off with a gray handkerchief. "These days you don't know who to trust," he said. "Ain't that the truth?"

---

3. Jukebox.

"People are certainly not nice like they used to be," said the 35 grandmother.

"Two fellers come in here last week," Red Sammy said, "driving a Chrysler. It was a old beat-up car but it was a good one and these boys looked all right to me. Said they worked at the mill and you know I let them fellers charge the gas they bought? Now why did I do that?"

"Because you're a good man!" the grandmother said at once.

"Yes'm, I suppose so," Red Sam said as if he were struck with this answer.

His wife brought the orders, carrying the five plates all at once without a tray, two in each hand and one balanced on her arm. "It isn't a soul in this green world of God's that you can trust," she said. "And I don't count nobody out of that, not nobody," she repeated, looking at Red Sammy.

"Did you read about that criminal, The Misfit, that's escaped?" asked 40 the grandmother.

"I wouldn't be a bit surprised if he didn't attact this place right here," said the woman. "If he hears about it being here, I wouldn't be none surprised to see him. If he hears it's two cent in the cash register, I wouldn't be a tall surprised if he . . ."

"That'll do," Red Sam said. "Go bring these people their Co'-Colas," and the woman went off to get the rest of the order.

"A good man is hard to find," Red Sammy said. "Everything is getting terrible. I remember the day you could go off and leave your screen door unlatched. Not no more."

He and the grandmother discussed better times. The old lady said that in her opinion Europe was entirely to blame for the way things were now. She said the way Europe acted you would think we were made of money and Red Sam said it was no use talking about it, she was exactly right. The children ran outside into the white sunlight and looked at the monkey in the lacy chinaberry tree. He was busy catching fleas on himself and biting each one carefully between his teeth as if it were a delicacy.

They drove off again into the hot afternoon. The grandmother took cat 45 naps and woke up every few minutes with her own snoring. Outside of Toombsboro she woke up and recalled an old plantation that she had visited in this neighborhood once when she was a young lady. She said the house had six white columns across the front and that there was an avenue of oaks leading up to it and two little wooden trellis arbors on either side in front where you sat down with your suitor after a stroll in the garden. She recalled exactly which road to turn off to get to it. She knew that Bailey would not be willing to lose any time looking at an old house, but the more she talked about it, the more she wanted to see it once again and find out if the little twin arbors were still standing. "There was a secret panel in this house," she said craftily, not telling the truth but wishing that she were, "and the story went that all the family silver was hidden in it when Sherman came through but it was never found . . ."

"Hey!" John Wesley said. "Let's go see it! We'll find it! We'll poke all the woodwork and find it! Who lives there? Where do you turn off at? Hey Pop, can't we turn off there?"

"We never have seen a house with a secret panel!" June Star shrieked. "Let's go to the house with the secret panel! Hey Pop, can't we go see the house with the secret panel!"

"It's not far from here, I know," the grandmother said. "It wouldn't take over twenty minutes."

Bailey was looking straight ahead. His jaw was as rigid as a horseshoe. "No," he said.

50   The children began to yell and scream that they wanted to see the house with the secret panel. John Wesley kicked the back of the front seat and June Star hung over her mother's shoulder and whined desperately into her ear that they never had any fun even on their vacation, that they could never do what THEY wanted to do. The baby began to scream and John Wesley kicked the back of the seat so hard that his father could feel the blows in his kidney.

"All right!" he shouted and drew the car to a stop at the side of the road. "Will you all shut up? Will you all just shut up for one second? If you don't shut up, we won't go anywhere."

"It would be very educational for them," the grandmother murmured.

"All right," Bailey said, "but get this: this is the only time we're going to stop for anything like this. This is the one and only time."

"The dirt road that you have to turn down is about a mile back," the grandmother directed. "I marked it when we passed."

55   "A dirt road," Bailey groaned.

After they had turned around and were headed toward the dirt road, the grandmother recalled other points about the house, the beautiful glass over the front doorway and the candle-lamp in the hall. John Wesley said that the secret panel was probably in the fireplace.

"You can't go inside this house," Bailey said. "You don't know who lives there."

"While you all talk to the people in front, I'll run around behind and get in a window," John Wesley suggested.

"We'll all stay in the car," his mother said.

60   They turned onto the dirt road and the car raced roughly along in a swirl of pink dust. The grandmother recalled the times when there were no paved roads and thirty miles was a day's journey. The dirt road

was hilly and there were sudden washes in it and sharp curves on dangerous embankments. All at once they would be on a hill, looking down over the blue tops of trees for miles around, then the next minute, they would be in a red depression with the dust-coated trees looking down on them.

"This place had better turn up in a minute," Bailey said, "or I'm going to turn around."

The road looked as if no one had traveled on it in months.

"It's not much farther," the grandmother said and just as she said it, a horrible thought came to her. The thought was so embarrassing that she turned red in the face and her eyes dilated and her feet jumped up, upsetting her valise in the corner. The instant the valise moved, the newspaper top she had over the basket under it rose with a snarl and Pitty Sing, the cat, sprang onto Bailey's shoulder.

The children were thrown to the floor and their mother, clutching the baby, out the door onto the ground; the old lady was thrown into the front seat. The car turned over once and landed right-side-up in a gulch off the side of the road. Bailey remained in the driver's seat with the cat—gray-striped with a broad white face and an orange nose—clinging to his neck like a caterpillar.

As soon as the children saw they could move their arms and legs, they 65 scrambled out of the car, shouting, "We've had an ACCIDENT!" The grandmother was curled up under the dashboard, hoping she was injured so that Bailey's wrath would not come down on her all at once. The horrible thought she had had before the accident was that the house she had remembered so vividly was not in Georgia but in Tennessee.

Bailey removed the cat from his neck with both hands and flung it out the window against the side of a pine tree. Then he got out of the car and started looking for the children's mother. She was sitting against the side of the red gutted ditch, holding the screaming baby, but she only had a cut down her face and a broken shoulder. "We've had an ACCIDENT!" the children screamed in a frenzy of delight.

"But nobody's killed," June Star said with disappointment as the grandmother limped out of the car, her hat still pinned to her head but the broken front brim standing up at a jaunty angle and the violet spray hanging off the side. They all sat down in the ditch, except the children, to recover from the shock. They were all shaking.

"Maybe a car will come along," said the children's mother hoarsely.

"I believe I have injured an organ," said the grandmother, pressing her side, but no one answered her. Bailey's teeth were clattering. He had on a yellow sport shirt with bright blue parrots designed in it and his face was

as yellow as the shirt. The grandmother decided that she would not mention that the house was in Tennessee.

70   The road was about ten feet above and they could see only the tops of
the trees on the other side of it. Behind the ditch they were sitting in there
were more woods, tall and dark and deep. In a few minutes they saw a car
some distance away on top of a hill, coming slowly as if the occupants
were watching them. The grandmother stood up and waved both arms
dramatically to attract their attention. The car continued to come on
slowly, disappeared around a bend and appeared again, moving even
slower, on top of the hill they had gone over. It was a big black battered
hearselike automobile. There were three men in it.

It came to a stop just over them and for some minutes, the driver looked
down with a steady expressionless gaze to where they were sitting, and
didn't speak. Then he turned his head and muttered something to the
other two and they got out. One was a fat boy in black trousers and a red
sweat shirt with a silver stallion embossed on the front of it. He moved
around on the right side of them and stood staring, his mouth partly open
in a kind of loose grin. The other had on khaki pants and a blue striped
coat and a gray hat pulled down very low, hiding most of his face. He
came around slowly on the left side. Neither spoke.

The driver got out of the car and stood by the side of it, looking down at
them. He was an older man than the other two. His hair was just beginning
to gray and he wore silver-rimmed spectacles that gave him a scholarly
look. He had a long creased face and didn't have on any shirt or undershirt.
He had on blue jeans that were too tight for him and was holding a black
hat and a gun. The two boys also had guns.

"We've had an ACCIDENT!" the children screamed.

The grandmother had the peculiar feeling that the bespectacled man
was someone she knew. His face was as familiar to her as if she had known
him all her life but she could not recall who he was. He moved away from
the car and began to come down the embankment, placing his feet carefully so that he wouldn't slip. He had on tan and white shoes and no
socks, and his ankles were red and thin. "Good afternoon," he said. "I see
you all had you a little spill."

75   "We turned over twice!" said the grandmother.

"Oncet," he corrected. "We seen it happen. Try their car and see will it
run, Hiram," he said quietly to the boy with the gray hat.

"What you got that gun for?" John Wesley asked. "Whatcha gonna do
with that gun?"

"Lady," the man said to the children's mother, "would you mind calling
them children to sit down by you? Children make me nervous. I want all
you all to sit down right together there where you're at."

"What are you telling US what to do for?" June Star asked.

Behind them the line of woods gaped like a dark open mouth. "Come 80 here," said their mother.

"Look here now," Bailey began suddenly, "we're in a predicament! We're in . . ."

The grandmother shrieked. She scrambled to her feet and stood staring. "You're The Misfit!" she said. "I recognized you at once!"

"Yes'm," the man said, smiling slightly as if he were pleased in spite of himself to be known, "but it would have been better for all of you, lady, if you hadn't of reckernized me."

Bailey turned his head sharply and said something to his mother that shocked even the children. The old lady began to cry and The Misfit reddened.

"Lady," he said, "don't you get upset. Sometimes a man says things he 85 don't mean. I don't reckon he meant to talk to you thataway."

"You wouldn't shoot a lady, would you?" the grandmother said and removed a clean handkerchief from her cuff and began to slap at her eyes with it.

The Misfit pointed the toe of his shoe into the ground and made a little hole and then covered it up again. "I would hate to have to," he said.

"Listen," the grandmother almost screamed, "I know you're a good man. You don't look a bit like you have common blood. I know you must come from nice people!"

"Yes mam," he said, "finest people in the world." When he smiled he showed a row of strong white teeth. "God never made a finer woman than my mother and my daddy's heart was pure gold," he said. The boy with the red sweat shirt had come around behind them and was standing with his gun at his hip. The Misfit squatted down on the ground. "Watch them children, Bobby Lee," he said. "You know they make me nervous." He looked at the six of them huddled together in front of him and he seemed to be embarrassed as if he couldn't think of anything to say. "Ain't a cloud in the sky," he remarked, looking up at it. "Don't see no sun but don't see no cloud neither."

"Yes, it's a beautiful day," said the grandmother. "Listen," she said, "you 90 shouldn't call yourself The Misfit because I know you're a good man at heart. I can just look at you and tell."

"Hush!" Bailey yelled. "Hush! Everybody shut up and let me handle this!" He was squatting in the position of a runner about to sprint forward but he didn't move.

"I pre-chate that, lady," The Misfit said and drew a little circle in the ground with the butt of his gun.

"It'll take a half a hour to fix this here car," Hiram called, looking over the raised hood of it.

"Well, first you and Bobby Lee get him and that little boy to step over yonder with you," The Misfit said, pointing to Bailey and John Wesley. "The boys want to ast you something," he said to Bailey. "Would you mind stepping back in them woods there with them?"

95   "Listen," Bailey began, "we're in a terrible predicament! Nobody realizes what this is," and his voice cracked. His eyes were as blue and intense as the parrots in his shirt and he remained perfectly still.

The grandmother reached up to adjust her hat brim as if she were going to the woods with him but it came off in her hand. She stood staring at it and after a second she let it fall on the ground. Hiram pulled Bailey up by the arm as if he were assisting an old man. John Wesley caught hold of his father's hand and Bobby Lee followed. They went off toward the woods and just as they reached the dark edge, Bailey turned and supporting himself against a gray naked pine trunk, he shouted, "I'll be back in a minute, Mamma, wait on me!"

"Come back this instant!" his mother shrilled but they all disappeared into the woods.

"Bailey Boy!" the grandmother called in a tragic voice but she found she was looking at The Misfit squatting on the ground in front of her. "I just know you're a good man," she said desperately. "You're not a bit common!"

"Nome, I ain't a good man," The Misfit said after a second as if he had considered her statement carefully, "but I ain't the worst in the world neither. My daddy said I was a different breed of dog from my brothers and sisters. 'You know,' Daddy said, 'it's some that can live their whole life out without asking about it and it's others has to know why it is, and this boy is one of the latters. He's going to be into everything!'" He put on his black hat and looked up suddenly and then away deep into the woods as if he were embarrassed again. "I'm sorry I don't have on a shirt before you ladies," he said, hunching his shoulders slightly. "We buried our clothes that we had on when we escaped and we're just making do until we can get better. We borrowed these from some folks we met," he explained.

100   "That's perfectly all right," the grandmother said. "Maybe Bailey has an extra shirt in his suitcase."

"I'll look and see terrectly," The Misfit said.

"Where are they taking him?" the children's mother screamed.

"Daddy was a card himself," The Misfit said. "You couldn't put anything over on him. He never got in trouble with the Authorities though. Just had the knack of handling them."

"You could be honest too if you'd only try," said the grandmother. "Think how wonderful it would be to settle down and live a comfortable life and not have to think about somebody chasing you all the time."

The Misfit kept scratching in the ground with the butt of his gun as   105
if he were thinking about it. "Yes'm, somebody is always after you," he
murmured.

The grandmother noticed how thin his shoulder blades were just
behind his hat because she was standing up looking down on him. "Do
you ever pray?" she asked.

He shook his head. All she saw was the black hat wiggle between his
shoulder blades. "Nome," he said.

There was a pistol shot from the woods, followed closely by another.
Then silence. The old lady's head jerked around. She could hear the wind
move through the tree tops like a long satisfied insuck of breath. "Bailey
Boy!" she called.

"I was a gospel singer for a while," The Misfit said. "I been most everything. Been in the arm service, both land and sea, at home and abroad,
been twict married, been an undertaker, been with the railroads, plowed
Mother Earth, been in a tornado, seen a man burnt alive oncet," and
looked up at the children's mother and the little girl who were sitting close
together, their faces white and their eyes glassy; "I even seen a woman
flogged," he said.

"Pray, pray," the grandmother began, "pray, pray. . . ."   110

"I never was a bad boy that I remember of," The Misfit said in an almost
dreamy voice, "but somewheres along the line I done something wrong
and got sent to the penitentiary. I was buried alive," and he looked up and
held her attention to him by a steady stare.

"That's when you should have started to pray," she said. "What did you
do to get sent to the penitentiary that first time?"

"Turn to the right, it was a wall," The Misfit said, looking up again at the
cloudless sky. "Turn to the left, it was a wall. Look up it was a ceiling, look
down it was a floor. I forgot what I done, lady. I set there and set there, trying to remember what it was I done and I ain't recalled it to this day. Oncet
in a while, I would think it was coming to me, but it never come."

"Maybe they put you in by mistake," the old lady said vaguely.

"Nome," he said. "It wasn't no mistake. They had the papers on me."   115

"You must have stolen something," she said.

The Misfit sneered slightly. "Nobody had nothing I wanted," he said. "It
was a head-doctor at the penitentiary said what I had done was kill my
daddy but I known that for a lie. My daddy died in nineteen ought nineteen of the epidemic flu and I never had a thing to do with it. He was
buried in the Mount Hopewell Baptist churchyard and you can go there
and see for yourself."

"If you would pray," the old lady said, "Jesus would help you."

"That's right," The Misfit said.

120   "Well then, why don't you pray?" she asked trembling with delight suddenly.

"I don't want no hep," he said. "I'm doing all right by myself."

Bobby Lee and Hiram came ambling back from the woods. Bobby Lee was dragging a yellow shirt with bright blue parrots in it.

"Thow me that shirt, Bobby Lee," The Misfit said. The shirt came flying at him and landed on his shoulder and he put it on. The grandmother couldn't name what the shirt reminded her of. "No, lady," The Misfit said while he was buttoning it up, "I found out the crime don't matter. You can do one thing or you can do another, kill a man or take a tire off his car, because sooner or later you're going to forget what it was you done and just be punished for it."

The children's mother had begun to make heaving noises as if she couldn't get her breath. "Lady," he asked, "would you and that little girl like to step off yonder with Bobby Lee and Hiram and join your husband?"

125   "Yes, thank you," the mother said faintly. Her left arm dangled helplessly and she was holding the baby, who had gone to sleep, in the other. "Hep that lady up, Hiram," The Misfit said as she struggled to climb out of the ditch, "and Bobby Lee, you hold onto that little girl's hand."

"I don't want to hold hands with him," June Star said. "He reminds me of a pig."

The fat boy blushed and laughed and caught her by the arm and pulled her off into the woods after Hiram and her mother.

Alone with The Misfit, the grandmother found that she had lost her voice. There was not a cloud in the sky nor any sun. There was nothing around her but woods. She wanted to tell him that he must pray. She opened and closed her mouth several times before anything came out. Finally she found herself saying, "Jesus, Jesus," meaning, Jesus will help you, but the way she was saying it, it sounded as if she might be cursing.

"Yes'm," The Misfit said as if he agreed. "Jesus thown everything off balance. It was the same case with Him as with me except He hadn't committed any crime and they could prove I had committed one because they had the papers on me. Of course," he said, "they never shown me my papers. That's why I sign myself now. I said long ago, you get you a signature and sign everything you do and keep a copy of it. Then you'll know what you done and you can hold up the crime to the punishment and see do they match and in the end you'll have something to prove you ain't been treated right. I call myself The Misfit," he said, "because I can't make what all I done wrong fit what all I gone through in punishment."

130   There was a piercing scream from the woods, followed closely by a pistol report. "Does it seem right to you, lady, that one is punished a heap and another ain't punished at all?"

"Jesus!" the old lady cried. "You've got good blood! I know you wouldn't shoot a lady! I know you come from nice people! Pray! Jesus, you ought not to shoot a lady. I'll give you all the money I've got!"

"Lady," The Misfit said, looking beyond her far into the woods, "there never was a body that give the undertaker a tip."

There were two more pistol reports and the grandmother raised her head like a parched old turkey hen crying for water and called, "Bailey Boy, Bailey Boy!" as if her heart would break.

"Jesus was the only One that ever raised the dead." The Misfit continued, "and He shouldn't have done it. He thown everything off balance. If He did what He said, then it's nothing for you to do but thow away everything and follow Him, and if He didn't, then it's nothing for you to do but enjoy the few minutes you got left the best way you can—by killing somebody or burning down his house or doing some other meanness to him. No pleasure but meanness," he said and his voice had become almost a snarl.

"Maybe He didn't raise the dead," the old lady mumbled, not knowing 135 what she was saying and feeling so dizzy that she sank down in the ditch with her legs twisted under her.

"I wasn't there so I can't say He didn't," The Misfit said. "I wisht I had of been there," he said, hitting the ground with his fist. "It ain't right I wasn't there because if I had of been there I would of known. Listen lady," he said in a high voice, "if I had of been there I would of known and I wouldn't be like I am now." His voice seemed about to crack and the grandmother's head cleared for an instant. She saw the man's face twisted close to her own as if he were going to cry and she murmured, "Why you're one of my babies. You're one of my own children!" She reached out and touched him on the shoulder. The Misfit sprang back as if a snake had bitten him and shot her three times through the chest. Then he put his gun down on the ground and took off his glasses and began to clean them.

Hiram and Bobby Lee returned from the woods and stood over the ditch, looking down at the grandmother who half sat and half lay in a puddle of blood with her legs crossed under her like a child's and her face smiling up at the cloudless sky.

Without his glasses, The Misfit's eyes were red-rimmed and pale and defenseless-looking. "Take her off and thow her where you thown the others," he said, picking up the cat that was rubbing itself against his leg.

"She was a talker, wasn't she?" Bobby Lee said, sliding down the ditch with a yodel.

"She would of been a good woman," The Misfit said, "if it had been 140 somebody there to shoot her every minute of her life."

"Some fun!" Bobby Lee said.

"Shut up, Bobby Lee," The Misfit said. "It's no real pleasure in life."

1953

TILLIE OLSEN
(1912–2007)
I Stand Here Ironing

As Margaret Atwood has remarked of Tillie Olsen, "Few writers have gained such wide respect," even "reverence," "based on such a small body of published work"—only one unfinished novel, a short-story collection, and a book of nonfiction. Born in 1912 to poor Jewish *émigrés* from Russia, Tillie Lerner came of age at the start of the Great Depression, leaving high school without graduating to work at various low-paying jobs and launch a lifelong career as an unpaid (and twice-jailed) activist. After giving birth to a daughter, Olsen moved to San Francisco in 1933, eventually marrying—and having three more daughters with—union organizer Jack Olsen. Raising four children while working at various paid and unpaid jobs, Olsen later remarked, "It is no accident that the first work I considered publishable began: 'I stand here ironing. . . .'" Appearing in *The Best American Short Stories of 1957*, the story became the cornerstone of her first book, the award-winning 1961 collection *Tell Me a Riddle*. Thanks to the numerous prestigious prizes and teaching jobs that followed, Olsen published yet another "Best American Short Story" ("Requa") in 1970, and, in 1974, a revised but still incomplete version of the novel she had begun four decades earlier. A collection of essays and speeches, *Silences* (1978), movingly details the silencing effects of poverty and prejudice, social forces that Olsen tirelessly fought through her activism, her writing, and her mentorship of other would-be writers.

I stand here ironing, and what you asked me moves tormented back and forth with the iron.

"I wish you would manage the time to come in and talk with me about your daughter. I'm sure you can help me understand her. She's a youngster who needs help and whom I'm deeply interested in helping."

"Who needs help." . . . Even if I came, what good would it do? You think because I am her mother I have a key, or that in some way you could use me as a key? She has lived for nineteen years. There is all that life that has happened outside of me, beyond me.

And when is there time to remember, to sift, to weigh, to estimate, to total? I will start and there will be an interruption and I will have to gather it all together again. Or I will become engulfed with all I did or did not do, with what should have been and what cannot be helped.

She was a beautiful baby. The first and only one of our five that was 5 beautiful at birth. You do not guess how new and uneasy her tenancy in her now-loveliness. You did not know her all those years she was thought homely, or see her poring over her baby pictures, making me tell her over and over how beautiful she had been—and would be, I would tell her—and was now, to the seeing eye. But the seeing eyes were few or non-existent. Including mine.

I nursed her. They feel that's important nowadays. I nursed all the children, but with her, with all the fierce rigidity of first motherhood, I did like the books then said. Though her cries battered me to trembling and my breasts ached with swollenness, I waited till the clock decreed.

Why do I put that first? I do not even know if it matters, or if it explains anything.

She was a beautiful baby. She blew shining bubbles of sound. She loved motion, loved light, loved color and music and textures. She would lie on the floor in her blue overalls patting the surface so hard in ecstasy her hands and feet would blur. She was a miracle to me, but when she was eight months old I had to leave her daytimes with the woman downstairs to whom she was no miracle at all, for I worked or looked for work and for Emily's father, who "could no longer endure" (he wrote in his good-bye note) "sharing want with us."

I was nineteen. It was the pre-relief, pre-WPA[1] world of the depression. I would start running as soon as I got off the streetcar, running up the stairs, the place smelling sour, and awake or asleep to startle awake, when she saw me she would break into a clogged weeping that could not be comforted, a weeping I can hear yet.

After a while I found a job hashing[2] at night so I could be with her 10 days, and it was better. But it came to where I had to bring her to his family and leave her.

It took a long time to raise the money for her fare back. Then she got chicken pox and I had to wait longer. When she finally came, I hardly knew her, walking quick and nervous like her father, looking like her father, thin, and dressed in a shoddy red that yellowed her skin and glared at the pockmarks. All the baby loveliness gone.

She was two. Old enough for nursery school they said, and I did not know then what I know now—the fatigue of the long day, and the lacerations of group life in the kinds of nurseries that are only parking places for children.

1. Works Progress Administration; between 1935 and 1943 this federal agency, part of the Roosevelt administration's New Deal, employed 8.5 million people thrown out of work by the Great Depression. *Pre-relief*: that is, before the government assistance programs initiated during the Great Depression.
2. Waitressing, usually at a diner or other inexpensive restaurant.

Except that it would have made no difference if I had known. It was the only place there was. It was the only way we could be together, the only way I could hold a job.

And even without knowing, I knew. I knew that the teacher was evil because all these years it has curdled into my memory, the little boy hunched in the corner, her rasp, "why aren't you outside, because Alvin hits you? that's no reason, go out, scaredy." I knew Emily hated it even if she did not clutch and implore "don't go Mommy" like the other children, mornings.

15 She always had a reason why we should stay home. Momma, you look sick. Momma, I feel sick. Momma, the teachers aren't there today, they're sick. Momma, we can't go, there was a fire there last night. Momma, it's a holiday today, no school, they told me.

But never a direct protest, never rebellion. I think of our others in their three-, four-year-oldness—the explosions, the tempers, the denunciations, the demands—and I feel suddenly ill. I put the iron down. What in me demanded that goodness in her? And what was the cost, the cost to her of such goodness?

The old man living in the back once said in his gentle way: "You should smile at Emily more when you look at her." What *was* in my face when I looked at her? I loved her. There were all the acts of love.

It was only with the others I remembered what he said, and it was the face of joy, and not of care or tightness or worry I turned to them—too late for Emily. She does not smile easily, let alone almost always as her brothers and sisters do. Her face is closed and sombre, but when she wants, how fluid. You must have seen it in her pantomimes, you spoke of her rare gift for comedy on the stage that rouses a laughter out of the audience so dear they applaud and applaud and do not want to let her go.

Where does it come from, that comedy? There was none of it in her when she came back to me that second time, after I had had to send her away again. She had a new daddy now to learn to love, and I think perhaps it was a better time.

20 Except when we left her alone nights, telling ourselves she was old enough.

"Can't you go some other time, Mommy, like tomorrow?" she would ask. "Will it be just a little while you'll be gone? Do you promise?"

The time we came back, the front door open, the clock on the floor in the hall. She rigid awake. "It wasn't just a little while. I didn't cry. Three times I called you, just three times, and then I ran downstairs to open the door so you could come faster. The clock talked loud. I threw it away, it scared me what it talked."

She said the clock talked loud again that night I went to the hospital to have Susan. She was delirious with the fever that comes before red measles, but she was fully conscious all the week I was gone and the week after we were home when she could not come near the new baby or me.

She did not get well. She stayed skeleton thin, not wanting to eat, and night after night she had nightmares. She would call for me, and I would rouse from exhaustion to sleepily call back: "You're all right, darling, go to sleep, it's just a dream," and if she still called, in a sterner voice, "now go to sleep, Emily, there's nothing to hurt you." Twice, only twice, when I had to get up for Susan anyhow, I went in to sit with her.

Now when it is too late (as if she would let me hold and comfort her like I do the others) I get up and go to her at once at her moan or restless stirring. "Are you awake, Emily? Can I get you something?" And the answer is always the same: "No, I'm all right, go back to sleep, Mother." 25

They persuaded me at the clinic to send her away to a convalescent home in the country where "she can have the kind of food and care you can't manage for her, and you'll be free to concentrate on the new baby." They still send children to that place. I see pictures on the society page of sleek young women planning affairs to raise money for it, or dancing at the affairs, or decorating Easter eggs or filling Christmas stockings for the children.

They never have a picture of the children so I do not know if the girls still wear those gigantic red bows and the ravaged looks on the every other Sunday when parents can come to visit "unless otherwise notified"—as we were notified the first six weeks.

Oh it is a handsome place, green lawns and tall trees and fluted flower beds. High up on the balconies of each cottage the children stand, the girls in their red bows and white dresses, the boys in white suits and giant red ties. The parents stand below shrieking up to be heard and the children shriek down to be heard, and between them the invisible wall "Not To Be Contaminated by Parental Germs or Physical Affection."

There was a tiny girl who always stood hand in hand with Emily. Her parents never came. One visit she was gone. "They moved her to Rose Cottage" Emily shouted in explanation. "They don't like you to love anybody here."

She wrote once a week, the labored writing of a seven-year-old. "I am fine. How is the baby. If I write my leter nicly I will have a star. Love." There never was a star. We wrote every other day, letters she could never hold or keep but only hear read—once. "We simply do not have room for children to keep any personal possessions," they patiently explained when we pieced one Sunday's shrieking together to plead how much it would mean to Emily, who loved so to keep things, to be allowed to keep her letters and cards. 30

Each visit she looked frailer. "She isn't eating," they told us.

(They had runny eggs for breakfast or mush with lumps, Emily said later, I'd hold it in my mouth and not swallow. Nothing ever tasted good, just when they had chicken.)

It took us eight months to get her released home, and only the fact that she gained back so little of her seven lost pounds convinced the social worker.

I used to try to hold and love her after she came back, but her body would stay stiff, and after a while she'd push away. She ate little. Food sickened her, and I think much of life too. Oh she had physical lightness and brightness, twinkling by on skates, bouncing like a ball up and down up and down over the jump rope, skimming over the hill; but these were momentary.

35   She fretted about her appearance, thin and dark and foreign-looking at a time when every little girl was supposed to look or thought she should look a chubby blonde replica of Shirley Temple.[3] The doorbell sometimes rang for her, but no one seemed to come and play in the house or be a best friend. Maybe because we moved so much.

There was a boy she loved painfully through two school semesters. Months later she told me how she had taken pennies from my purse to buy him candy. "Licorice was his favorite and I brought him some every day, but he still liked Jennifer better'n me. Why, Mommy?" The kind of question for which there is no answer.

School was a worry to her. She was not glib or quick in a world where glibness and quickness were easily confused with ability to learn. To her overworked and exasperated teachers she was an overconscientious "slow learner" who kept trying to catch up and was absent entirely too often.

I let her be absent, though sometimes the illness was imaginary. How different from my now-strictness about attendance with the others. I wasn't working. We had a new baby, I was home anyhow. Sometimes, after Susan grew old enough, I would keep her home from school, too, to have them all together.

Mostly Emily had asthma, and her breathing, harsh and labored, would fill the house with a curiously tranquil sound. I would bring the two old dresser mirrors and her boxes of collections to her bed. She would select beads and single earrings, bottle tops and shells, dried flowers and pebbles, old postcards and scraps, all sorts of oddments; then she and Susan would play Kingdom, setting up landscapes and furniture, peopling them with action.

40   Those were the only times of peaceful companionship between her and Susan. I have edged away from it, that poisonous feeling between them,

---

3. Famously curly-haired and dimpled child actress, singer, and dancer (1928–2014) who starred in such films as *Baby Take a Bow* (1934) and *Heidi* (1937).

that terrible balancing of hurts and needs I had to do between the two, and did so badly, those earlier years.

Oh there are conflicts between the others too, each one human, needing, demanding, hurting, taking—but only between Emily and Susan, no, Emily toward Susan that corroding resentment. It seems so obvious on the surface, yet it is not obvious. Susan, the second child, Susan, golden- and curly-haired and chubby, quick and articulate and assured, everything in appearance and manner Emily was not; Susan, not able to resist Emily's precious things, losing or sometimes clumsily breaking them; Susan telling jokes and riddles to company for applause while Emily sat silent (to say to me later: that was *my* riddle, Mother, I told it to Susan); Susan, who for all the five years' difference in age was just a year behind Emily in developing physically.

I am glad for that slow physical development that widened the difference between her and her contemporaries, though she suffered over it. She was too vulnerable for that terrible world of youthful competition, of preening and parading, of constant measuring of yourself against every other, of envy, "If I had that copper hair," "If I had that skin. . . ." She tormented herself enough about not looking like the others, there was enough of the unsureness, the having to be conscious of words before you speak, the constant caring—what are they thinking of me? without having it all magnified by the merciless physical drives.

Ronnie is calling. He is wet and I change him. It is rare there is such a cry now. That time of motherhood is almost behind me when the ear is not one's own but must always be racked and listening for the child cry, the child call. We sit for a while and I hold him, looking out over the city spread in charcoal with its soft aisles of light. "*Shoogily*," he breathes and curls closer. I carry him back to bed, asleep. *Shoogily*. A funny word, a family word, inherited from Emily, invented by her to say: *comfort*.

In this and other ways she leaves her seal, I say aloud. And startle at my saying it. What do I mean? What did I start to gather together, to try and make coherent? I was at the terrible, growing years. War years.[4] I do not remember them well. I was working, there were four smaller ones now, there was not time for her. She had to help be a mother, and housekeeper, and shopper. She had to set her seal. Mornings of crisis and near hysteria trying to get lunches packed, hair combed, coats and shoes found, everyone to school or Child Care on time, the baby ready for transportation. And always the paper scribbled on by a smaller one, the book looked at by Susan then mislaid, the homework not done. Running out to that huge school where she was one, she was lost, she was a drop; suffering over her unpreparedness, stammering and unsure in her classes.

4. World War II (1939–1945); America's direct involvement began in 1941.

45   There was so little time left at night after the kids were bedded down. She
would struggle over books, always eating (it was in those years she developed her enormous appetite that is legendary in our family) and I would be
ironing, or preparing food for the next day, or writing V-mail[5] to Bill, or
tending the baby. Sometimes, to make me laugh, or out of her despair, she
would imitate happenings or types at school.

I think I said once: "Why don't you do something like this in the school
amateur show?" One morning she phoned me at work, hardly understandable through the weeping: "Mother, I did it. I won, I won; they gave me first
prize; they clapped and clapped and wouldn't let me go."

Now suddenly she was Somebody, and as imprisoned in her difference
as she had been in her anonymity.

She began to be asked to perform at other high schools, even in colleges, then at city and statewide affairs. The first one we went to, I only
recognized her that first moment when thin, shy, she almost drowned
herself into the curtains. Then: Was this Emily? The control, the command, the convulsing and deadly clowning, the spell, then the roaring,
stamping audience, unwilling to let this rare and precious laughter out of
their lives.

Afterwards: You ought to do something about her with a gift like that—
but without money or knowing how, what does one do? We have left it
all to her, and the gift has as often eddied inside, clogged and clotted, as
been used and growing.

50   She is coming. She runs up the stairs two at a time with her light grace-
ful step, and I know she is happy tonight. Whatever it was that occasioned
your call did not happen today.

"Aren't you ever going to finish the ironing, Mother? Whistler painted
his mother in a rocker.[6] I'd have to paint mine standing over an ironing
board." This is one of her communicative nights and she tells me everything and nothing as she fixes herself a plate of food out of the icebox.

She is so lovely. Why did you want me to come in at all? Why were you
concerned? She will find her way.

She starts up the stairs to bed. "Don't get *me* up with the rest in the
morning." "But I thought you were having midterms." "Oh, those," she comes
back in, kisses me, and says quite lightly, "in a couple of years when we'll
all be atom-dead[7] they won't matter a bit."

5. Victory Mail: mail system for communicating with soldiers during World War II.
6. Allusion to the painting popularly known as *Whistler's Mother* (1871), by American artist
James Abbot McNeil Whistler (1834–1903).
7. That is, killed by an atomic bomb. U.S. forces dropped atomic bombs on Japan at the end of
World War II, and within a few years the Soviet Union developed an atomic bomb of its own;
the ensuing decades of tense nuclear standoff became known as the Cold War.

She has said it before. She *believes* it. But because I have been dredging the past, and all that compounds a human being is so heavy and meaningful in me, I cannot endure it tonight.

I will never total it all. I will never come in to say: She was a child seldom 55 smiled at. Her father left me before she was a year old. I had to work away from her her first six years when there was work, or I sent her home and to his relatives. There were years she had care she hated. She was dark and thin and foreign-looking in a world where the prestige went to blondeness and curly hair and dimples, she was slow where glibness was prized. She was a child of anxious, not proud, love. We were poor and could not afford for her the soil of easy growth. I was a young mother, I was a distracted mother. There were the other children pushing up, demanding. Her younger sister seemed all that she was not. There were years she did not let me touch her. She kept too much in herself, her life was such she had to keep too much in herself. My wisdom came too late. She has much to her and probably little will come of it. She is a child of her age, of depression, of war, of fear.

Let her be. So all that is in her will not bloom—but in how many does it? There is still enough left to live by. Only help her to know—help make it so there is cause for her to know—that she is more than this dress on the ironing board, helpless before the iron.

1953–54

DAVID SEDARIS
(b. 1956)
Jesus Shaves

Dubbed by some "the funniest writer alive," David Sedaris uses his own life and the absurdities of the everyday as fodder for stories that often blur the line between fiction and nonfiction. Juxtaposing the highbrow with the lowbrow, they treat everything from his fleeting interests in crystal meth and bee-sized suits of armor to his brother's basement barbecue-sauce business. Sedaris was raised in the suburbs of Raleigh, North Carolina, after his Greek American family moved there from New York. Openly gay, Sedaris points to his inability to play jazz guitar as the source of his father's disappointment—"Fortunately there were six of us [. . .] it was easy to get lost in the crowd." After graduating from the School of the Art Institute of Chicago, he worked a series of now-well-documented menial jobs in New York City and Chicago before radio host Ira Glass discovered him at a Chicago nightclub, reading from his diary. "Santaland Diaries," which recounts his adventures as a department-store elf, was later featured on National Public Radio, making Sedaris an overnight sensation. Author of multiple *New York Times* best sellers, including *Me Talk Pretty One Day* (2000), *Dress Your Family in Corduroy and Denim* (2004), *When You Are Engulfed in Flames* (2008), and *Let's Explore Diabetes with Owls* (2013), as well as *Squirrel Seeks Chipmunk* (2010), "a collection of fables without morals," Sedaris has also collaborated with his sister, actress-comedian Amy Sedaris, on a number of plays, including *Incident at Cobbler's Knob* (1997) and *The Book of Liz* (2002). As renowned for his voice and comic timing as for his writing, Sedaris draws sellout crowds on his worldwide reading tours.

"And what does one do on the fourteenth of July? Does one celebrate Bastille Day?"

It was my second month of French class, and the teacher was leading us in an exercise designed to promote the use of *one*, our latest personal pronoun.

"Might one sing on Bastille Day?" she asked. "Might one dance in the street? Somebody give me an answer."

Printed in our textbooks was a list of major holidays alongside a scattered arrangement of photos depicting French people in the act of celebration. The object was to match the holiday with the corresponding picture. It was simple enough but seemed an exercise better suited to the use of the word *they*. I didn't know about the rest of the class, but when Bastille Day eventually rolled around, I planned to stay home and clean my oven.

5   Normally, when working from the book, it was my habit to tune out my fellow students and scout ahead, concentrating on the question I'd calculated might fall to me, but this afternoon, we were veering from the usual format. Questions were answered on a volunteer basis, and I was able to sit back, confident that the same few students would do the talking. Today's discussion was dominated by an Italian nanny, two chatty Poles, and a pouty, plump Moroccan woman who had grown up speaking French and had enrolled in the class to improve her spelling.[1] She'd covered these lessons back in the third grade and took every opportunity to demonstrate her superiority. A question would be asked and she'd give the answer, behaving as though this were a game show and, if quick enough, she might go home with a tropical vacation or a side-by-side refrigerator-freezer. By the end of her first day, she'd raised her hand so many times, her shoulder had given out. Now she just leaned back in her seat and shouted the

---

1. France controlled most of Morocco between 1912 and 1956; as a result, though Arabic is now the country's official language, French is still widely taught and serves as the primary language of business and government.

answers, her bronzed arms folded across her chest like some great grammar genie.

We finished discussing Bastille Day, and the teacher moved on to Easter, which was represented in our textbook by a black-and-white photograph of a chocolate bell lying upon a bed of palm fronds.

"And what does one do on Easter? Would anyone like to tell us?"

The Italian nanny was attempting to answer the question when the Moroccan student interrupted, shouting, "Excuse me, but what's an Easter?"

Despite her having grown up in a Muslim country, it seemed she might have heard it mentioned once or twice, but no. "I mean it," she said. "I have no idea what you people are talking about."

The teacher then called upon the rest of us to explain.   10

The Poles led the charge to the best of their ability. "It is," said one, "a party for the little boy of God who call his self Jesus and . . . oh, shit."

She faltered, and her fellow countryman came to her aid. "He call his self Jesus, and then he be die one day on two . . . morsels of . . . lumber."

The rest of the class jumped in, offering bits of information that would have given the pope an aneurysm.

"He die one day, and then he go above of my head to live with your   15 father."

"He weared the long hair, and after he died, the first day he come back here for to say hello to the peoples."

"He nice, the Jesus."

"He make the good things, and on the Easter we be sad because somebody makes him dead today."

Part of the problem had to do with grammar. Simple nouns such as *cross* and *resurrection* were beyond our grasp, let alone such complicated reflexive phrases as "To give of yourself your only begotten son." Faced with the challenge of explaining the cornerstone of Christianity, we did what any self-respecting group of people might do. We talked about food instead.

"Easter is a party for to eat of the lamb," the Italian nanny explained.   20 "One, too, may eat of the chocolate."

"And who brings the chocolate?" the teacher asked.

I knew the word, and so I raised my hand, saying, "The Rabbit of Easter. He bring of the chocolate."

My classmates reacted as though I'd attributed the delivery to the Antichrist. They were mortified.

"A rabbit?" The teacher, assuming I'd used the wrong word, positioned her index fingers on top of her head, wiggling them as though they were ears. "You mean one of these? A rabbit rabbit?"

25   "Well, sure," I said. "He come in the night when one sleep on a bed. With a hand he have the basket and foods."

The teacher sadly shook her head, as if this explained everything that was wrong with my country. "No, no," she said. "Here in France the chocolate is brought by the big bell that flies in from Rome."[2]

I called for a time-out. "But how do the bell know where you live?"

"Well," she said, "how does a rabbit?"

It was a decent point, but at least a rabbit has eyes. That's a start. Rabbits move from place to place, while most bells can only go back and forth—and they can't even do that on their own power. On top of that, the Easter Bunny has character; he's someone you'd like to meet and shake hands with. A bell has all the personality of a cast-iron skillet. It's like saying that come Christmas, a magic dustpan flies in from the North Pole, led by eight flying cinder blocks. Who wants to stay up all night so they can see a bell? And why fly one in from Rome when they've got more bells than they know what to do with right here in Paris? That's the most implausible aspect of the whole story, as there's no way the bells of France would allow a foreign worker to fly in and take their jobs. That Roman bell would be lucky to get work cleaning up after a French bell's dog—and even then he'd need papers. It just didn't add up.

30   Nothing we said was of any help to the Moroccan student. A dead man with long hair supposedly living with her father, a leg of lamb served with palm fronds and chocolate. Confused and disgusted, she shrugged her massive shoulders and turned her attention back to the comic book she kept hidden beneath her binder. I wondered then if, without the language barrier, my classmates and I could have done a better job making sense of Christianity, an idea that sounds pretty far-fetched to begin with.

In communicating any religious belief, the operative word is *faith*, a concept illustrated by our very presence in that classroom. Why bother struggling with the grammar lessons of a six-year-old if each of us didn't believe that, against all reason, we might eventually improve? If I could hope to one day carry on a fluent conversation, it was a relatively short leap to believing that a rabbit might visit my home in the middle of the night, leaving behind a handful of chocolate kisses and a carton of menthol cigarettes. So why stop there? If I could believe in myself, why not give other improbabilities the benefit of the doubt? I accepted the idea that an omniscient God had cast me in his own image and that he watched

2. In remembrance of Jesus's death, bells across France are customarily silenced from the Thursday before Good Friday until Easter morning; children are encouraged to believe that the bells fly to Rome to visit the pope, returning with gifts.

over me and guided me from one place to the next. The virgin birth, the resurrection, and the countless miracles—my heart expanded to encompass all the wonders and possibilities of the universe.

A bell, though, that's fucked up.

2000

JOHN UPDIKE
(1932–2009)
A & P[1]

The man *The Oxford Encyclopedia of American Literature* dubs "perhaps America's most versatile, prolific, and distinguished man of letters of the second half of the twentieth century" spent the early years of his life in Reading and rural Shilling-ton, Pennsylvania. John Updike went on to study English literature at Harvard, where he also contributed cartoons and articles to the famous *Lampoon*. Marrying a Radcliffe fine-arts student in 1953, Updike the next year graduated summa cum laude and sold both his first poem and his first story to the *New Yorker*, whose staff he joined in 1955. Though he would continue to contribute essays, poems, and fiction to the *New Yorker* for the rest of his life, in 1957 Updike moved with his young family from Manhattan to rural Massachusetts. In the two years following the move, he published both his first book, a collection of poems (1958), and his first novel (1959). Updike went on to publish some twenty-one novels, thirteen short-story collections, seven volumes of poetry (including *Collected Poems, 1953–1993* [1993]), as well as seven collections of essays, a play, and a memoir. He is best known for the tetralogy tracing the life of high-school basketball star turned car salesman Harry C. Rabbit Angstrom. Begun with *Rabbit, Run* in 1960, the series of novels includes *Rabbit Is Rich* (1981) and *Rabbit at Rest* (1990), both of which were awarded Pulitzer Prizes.

In walks these three girls in nothing but bathing suits. I'm in the third checkout slot, with my back to the door, so I don't see them until they're over by the bread. The one that caught my eye first was the one in the plaid green two-piece. She was a chunky kid, with a good tan and a sweet broad soft-looking can with those two crescents of white just under

---

1. Supermarket, part of a chain, originally known as the Great Atlantic and Pacific Tea Company, in business from 1859 to 2015.

it, where the sun never seems to hit, at the top of the backs of her legs. I
stood there with my hand on a box of HiHo crackers trying to remember
if I rang it up or not. I ring it up again and the customer starts giving me
hell. She's one of these cash-register-watchers, a witch about fifty with
rouge on her cheekbones and no eyebrows, and I know it made her day to
trip me up. She'd been watching cash registers for fifty years and probably never seen a mistake before.

By the time I got her feathers smoothed and her goodies into a bag—
she gives me a little snort in passing, if she'd been born at the right time
they would have burned her over in Salem[2]—by the time I get her on her
way the girls had circled around the bread and were coming back, without
a pushcart, back my way along the counters, in the aisle between the check-
outs and the Special bins. They didn't even have shoes on. There was this
chunky one, with the two-piece—it was bright green and the seams on
the bra were still sharp and her belly was still pretty pale so I guessed she
just got it (the suit)—there was this one, with one of those chubby berry-
faces, the lips all bunched together under her nose, this one, and a tall
one, with black hair that hadn't quite frizzed right, and one of these sun-
bur̲̲   ̲as too long—you
kno   *Prima-donna ?*   g" and "attractive"
but   h is why they like
her   e so tall. She was
the   ↘ around and making   his queen, she just
walked straight on slowly, on these long white prima-donna legs. She came
down a little hard on her heels, as if she didn't walk in her bare feet that
much, putting down her heels and then letting the weight move along to
her toes as if she was testing the floor with every step, putting a little deliberate extra action into it. You never know for sure how girls' minds work (do
you really think it's a mind in there or just a little buzz like a bee in a glass
jar?) but you got the idea she had talked the other two into coming in here
with her, and now she was showing them how to do it, walk slow and hold
yourself straight.

She had on a kind of dirty-pink—beige maybe, I don't know—bathing
suit with a little nubble all over it and, what got me, the straps were down.
They were off her shoulders looped loose around the cool tops of her arms,
and I guess as a result the suit had slipped a little on her, so all around the
top of the cloth there was this shining rim. If it hadn't been there you
wouldn't have known there could have been anything whiter than those

2. The store is located not far from Salem, Massachusetts, where in 1692 nineteen women and
men were hanged after being convicted of witchcraft.

shoulders. With the straps pushed off, there was nothing between the top of the suit and the top of her head except just *her*, this clean bare plane of the top of her chest down from the shoulder bones like a dented sheet of metal tilted in the light. I mean, it was more than pretty.

She had sort of oaky hair that the sun and salt had bleached, done up in a bun that was unravelling, and a kind of prim face. Walking into the A & P with your straps down, I suppose it's the only kind of face you *can* have. She held her head so high her neck, coming up out of those white shoulders, looked kind of stretched, but I didn't mind. The longer her neck was, the more of her there was.

She must have felt in the corner of her eye me and over my shoulder 5 Stokesie in the second slot watching, but she didn't tip. Not this queen. She kept her eyes moving across the racks, and stopped, and turned so slow it made my stomach rub the inside of my apron, and buzzed to the other two, who kind of huddled against her for relief, and then they all three of them went up the cat-and-dog-food-breakfast-cereal-macaroni-rice-raisins-seasonings-spreads-spaghetti-soft-drinks-crackers-and-cookies aisle. From the third slot I look straight up this aisle to the meat counter, and I watched them all the way. The fat one with the tan sort of fumbled with the cookies, but on second thought she put the package back. The sheep pushing their carts down the aisle—the girls were walking against the usual traffic (not that we have one-way signs or anything)—were pretty hilarious. You could see them, when Queenie's white shoulders dawned on them, kind of jerk, or hop, or hiccup, but their eyes snapped back to their own baskets and on they pushed. I bet you could set off dynamite in an A & P and the people would by and large keep reaching and checking oatmeal off their lists and muttering "Let me see, there was a third thing, began with A, asparagus, no, ah, yes, applesauce!" or whatever it is they do mutter. But there was no doubt, this jiggled them. A few houseslaves in pin curlers even looked around after pushing their carts past to make sure what they had seen was correct.

You know, it's one thing to have a girl in a bathing suit down on the beach, where what with the glare nobody can look at each other much anyway, and another thing in the cool of the A & P, under the fluorescent lights, against all those stacked packages, with her feet paddling along naked over our checkerboard green-and-cream rubber-tile floor.

"Oh Daddy," Stokesie said beside me. "I feel so faint."

"Darling," I said. "Hold me tight." Stokesie's married, with two babies chalked up on his fuselage already, but as far as I can tell that's the only difference. He's twenty-two, and I was nineteen this April.

"Is it done?" he asks, the responsible married man finding his voice. I forgot to say he thinks he's going to be manager some sunny day, maybe in

1990 when it's called the Great Alexandrov and Petrooshki Tea Company or something.

10 What he meant was, our town is five miles from a beach, with a big summer colony out on the Point, but we're right in the middle of town, and the women generally put on a shirt or shorts or something before they get out of the car into the street. And anyway these are usually women with six children and varicose veins mapping their legs and nobody, including them, could care less. As I say, we're right in the middle of town, and if you stand at our front doors you can see two banks and the Congregational church and the newspaper store and three real-estate offices and about twenty-seven old freeloaders tearing up Central Street because the sewer broke again. It's not as if we're on the Cape; we're north of Boston and there's people in this town haven't seen the ocean for twenty years.

The girls had reached the meat counter and were asking McMahon something. He pointed, they pointed, and they shuffled out of sight behind a pyramid of Diet Delight peaches. All that was left for us to see was old McMahon patting his mouth and looking after them sizing up their joints. Poor kids, I began to feel sorry for them, they couldn't help it.

Now here comes the sad part of the story, at least my family says it's sad, but I don't think it's so sad myself. The store's pretty empty, it being Thursday afternoon, so there was nothing much to do except lean on the register and wait for the girls to show up again. The whole store was like a pinball machine and I didn't know which tunnel they'd come out of. After a while they come around out of the far aisle, around the light bulbs, records at discount of the Caribbean Six or Tony Martin Sings[3] or some such gunk you wonder they waste the wax on, sixpacks of candy bars, and plastic toys done up in cellophane that fall apart when a kid looks at them anyway. Around they come, Queenie still leading the way, and holding a little gray jar in her hand. Slots Three through Seven are unmanned and I could see her wondering between Stokes and me, but Stokesie with his usual luck draws an old party in baggy gray pants who stumbles up with four giant cans of pineapple juice (what do these bums *do* with all that pineapple juice? I've often asked myself) so the girls come to me. Queenie puts down the jar and I take it into my fingers icy cold. Kingfish Fancy Herring Snacks in Pure Sour Cream: 49¢. Now her hands are empty, not a ring or a brace-let, bare as God made them, and I wonder where the money's coming from.

---

3. Typical titles of record albums at the time of the story (1962). Tony Martin (1913–2012), a popular singer and actor, was featured on radio and television in the 1940s and 1950s.

Still with that prim look she lifts a folded dollar bill out of the hollow at the center of her nubbled pink top. The jar went heavy in my hand. Really, I thought that was so cute.

Then everybody's luck begins to run out. Lengel comes in from haggling with a truck full of cabbages on the lot and is about to scuttle into that door marked MANAGER behind which he hides all day when the girls touch his eye. Lengel's pretty dreary, teaches Sunday school and the rest, but he doesn't miss that much. He comes over and says, "Girls, this isn't the beach."

Queenie blushes, though maybe it's just a brush of sunburn I was noticing for the first time, now that she was so close. "My mother asked me to pick up a jar of herring snacks." Her voice kind of startled me, the way voices do when you see the people first, coming out so flat and dumb yet kind of tony, too, the way it ticked over "pick up" and "snacks." All of a sudden I slid right down her voice into her living room. Her father and the other men were standing around in ice-cream coats and bow ties and the women were in sandals picking up herring snacks on toothpicks off a big glass plate and they were all holding drinks the color of water with olives and sprigs of mint in them. When my parents have somebody over they get lemonade and if it's a real racy affair Schlitz in tall glasses with "They'll Do It Every Time" cartoons stencilled on.[4]

"That's all right," Lengel said. "But this isn't the beach." His repeating 15 this struck me as funny, as if it had just occurred to him, and he had been thinking all these years the A & P was a great big dune and he was the head lifeguard. He didn't like my smiling—as I say he doesn't miss much—but he concentrates on giving the girls that sad Sunday-school-superintendent stare.

Queenie's blush is no sunburn now, and the plump one in plaid, that I liked better from the back—a really sweet can—pipes up, "We weren't doing any shopping. We just came in for the one thing."

"That makes no difference," Lengel tells her, and I could see from the way his eyes went that he hadn't noticed she was wearing a two-piece before. "We want you decently dressed when you come in here."

"We *are* decent," Queenie says suddenly, her lower lip pushing, getting sore now that she remembers her place, a place from which the crowd that runs the A & P must look pretty crummy. Fancy Herring Snacks flashed in her very blue eyes.

"Girls, I don't want to argue with you. After this come in here with your shoulders covered. It's our policy." He turns his back. That's policy for you.

---

4. Schlitz is an inexpensive brand of beer. The cheap glasses are decorated with a popular saying derived from a syndicated series of single-panel cartoons printed between 1929 and 2008.

Policy is what the kingpins want. What the others want is juvenile delinquency.

20   All this while, the customers had been showing up with their carts but, you know, sheep, seeing a scene, they had all bunched up on Stokesie, who shook open a paper bag as gently as peeling a peach, not wanting to miss a word. I could feel in the silence everybody getting nervous, most of all Lengel, who asks me, "Sammy, have you rung up their purchase?"

I thought and said "No" but it wasn't about that I was thinking. I go through the punches, 4, 9, GROC, TOT—it's more complicated than you think, and after you do it often enough, it begins to make a little song, that you hear words to, in my case "Hello (*bing*) there, you (*gung*) hap-py pee-pul (*splat*)!"—the *splat* being the drawer flying out. I uncrease the bill, tenderly as you may imagine, it just having come from between the two smoothest scoops of vanilla I had ever known were there, and pass a half and a penny into her narrow pink palm, and nestle the herrings in a bag and twist its neck and hand it over, all the time thinking.

The girls, and who'd blame them, are in a hurry to get out, so I say "I quit" to Lengel quick enough for them to hear, hoping they'll stop and watch me, their unsuspected hero. They keep right on going, into the electric eye; the door flies open and they flicker across the lot to their car, Queenie and Plaid and Big Tall Goony-Goony (not that as raw material she was so bad), leaving me with Lengel and a kink in his eyebrow.

"Did you say something, Sammy?"

"I said I quit."

25   "I thought you did."

"You didn't have to embarrass them."

"It was they who were embarrassing us."

I started to say something that came out "Fiddle-de-doo." It's a saying of my grandmother's, and I know she would have been pleased.

"I don't think you know what you're saying," Lengel said.

30   "I know you don't," I said. "But I do." I pull the bow at the back of my apron and start shrugging it off my shoulders. A couple customers that had been heading for my slot begin to knock against each other, like scared pigs in a chute.

Lengel sighs and begins to look very patient and old and gray. He's been a friend of my parents for years. "Sammy, you don't want to do this to your Mom and Dad," he tells me. It's true, I don't. But it seems to me that once you begin a gesture it's fatal not to go through with it. I fold the apron, "Sammy" stitched in red on the pocket, and put it on the counter, and drop the bow tie on top of it. The bow tie is theirs, if you've ever wondered. "You'll feel this for the rest of your life," Lengel says, and I know that's true, too, but remembering how he made that pretty girl blush makes me so scrunchy inside I punch the No Sale tab and the machine whirs "pee-pul" and the drawer splats out. One advantage to this scene taking place in summer, I can follow this up with a clean exit, there's no fumbling around getting your coat and galoshes, I just saunter into the electric eye in my white shirt that my mother ironed the night before, and the door heaves itself open, and outside the sunshine is skating around on the asphalt.

I look around for my girls, but they're gone, of course. There wasn't anybody but some young married screaming with her children about some candy they didn't get by the door of a powder-blue Falcon station wagon. Looking back in the big windows, over the bags of peat moss and alumi-num lawn furniture stacked on the pavement, I could see Lengel in my place in the slot, checking the sheep through. His face was dark gray and his back stiff, as if he'd just had an injection of iron, and my stomach kind of fell as I felt how hard the world was going to be to me hereafter.

1962

AUTHORS ON THEIR WORK
JOHN UPDIKE (1932–2009)

From "An Interview with John Updike" (1995)*

There is always some ambiguity or some room for various responses to a story. But I certainly see him [Sammy] as a typical, well-intentioned Amer-ican male trying to find his way in the society and full of good impulses. I think that he quit his job on a good impulse. [. . .] A kind of feminist protest, in a way, is what he does here. Who knows what his adult life will bring, but I think for the moment he's a boy who's tried to reach out of his immediate environment toward something bigger and better.

*"An Interview with John Updike." Interview by Donald M. Murray, directed by Bruce Schwartz (1995), posted by Murray. *Spike*, 2001.

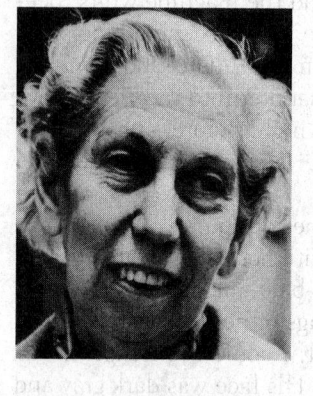

EUDORA WELTY
(1909–2001)
Why I Live at the P.O.

Known as the "First Lady of Southern Literature," Eudora Welty was born and raised in Jackson, Mississippi, attended Mississippi State College for Women, and earned a BA from the University of Wisconsin. Among the countless awards she received were two Guggenheim Fellowships, six O. Henry Awards, a Pulitzer Prize, the French Legion of Honor, the National Medal for Literature, and the Presidential Medal of Freedom. Although she wrote five novels, including *The Robber Bridegroom* (1942), *Ponder Heart* (1954), and *The Optimist's Daughter* (1972), Welty is best known for her short stories, many of which appear in *The Collected Stories of Eudora Welty* (1980). Among her nonfiction works are *One Writer's Beginnings* (1984), *A Writer's Eye: Collected Book Reviews* (1994), and five collections of her photographs, including *One Place, One Time* (1978) and *Photographs* (1989). In 1998 the Library of America published a two-volume edition of her selected works, making her the first living author they had published.

I was getting along fine with Mama, Papa-Daddy, and Uncle Rondo until my sister Stella-Rondo just separated from her husband and came back home again. Mr. Whitaker! Of course I went with Mr. Whitaker first, when he first appeared here in China Grove, taking "Pose Yourself" photos, and Stella-Rondo broke us up. Told him I was one-sided. Bigger on one side than the other, which is a deliberate, calculated falsehood: I'm the same. Stella-Rondo is exactly twelve months to the day younger than I am and for that reason she's spoiled.

She's always had anything in the world she wanted and then she'd throw it away. Papa-Daddy give her this gorgeous Add-a-Pearl necklace when she was eight years old and she threw it away playing baseball when she was nine, with only two pearls.

So as soon as she got married and moved away from home the first thing she did was separate! From Mr. Whitaker! This photographer with the popeyes she said she trusted. Came home from one of those towns up in Illinois and to our complete surprise brought this child of two.

Mama said she like to make her drop dead for a second. "Here you had this marvelous blonde child and never so much as wrote your mother a word about it," says Mama. "I'm thoroughly ashamed of you." But of course she wasn't.

Stella-Rondo just calmly takes off this *hat,* I wish you could see it. She 5 says, "Why, Mama, Shirley-T.'s adopted, I can prove it."

"How?" says Mama, but all I says was, "H'm!" There I was over the hot stove, trying to stretch two chickens over five people and a completely unexpected child into the bargain without one moment's notice.

"What do you mean—'H'm'?" says Stella-Rondo, and Mama says, "I heard that, Sister."

I said that oh, I didn't mean a thing, only that whoever Shirley-T. was, she was the spit-image of Papa-Daddy if he'd cut off his beard, which of course he'd never do in the world. Papa-Daddy's Mama's papa and sulks.

Stella-Rondo got furious! She said, "Sister, I don't need to tell you you got a lot of nerve and always did have and I'll thank you to make no future reference to my adopted child whatsoever."

"Very well," I said. "Very well, very well. Of course I noticed at once she 10 looks like Mr. Whitaker's side too. That frown. She looks like a cross between Mr. Whitaker and Papa-Daddy."

"Well, all I can say is she isn't."

"She looks exactly like Shirley Temple to me," says Mama, but Shirley-T. just ran away from her.

So the first thing Stella-Rondo did at the table was turn Papa-Daddy against me.

"Papa-Daddy," she says. He was trying to cut up his meat. "Papa-Daddy!" I was taken completely by surprise. Papa-Daddy is about a million years old and's got this long-long beard. "Papa-Daddy, Sister says she fails to understand why you don't cut off your beard."

So Papa-Daddy l-a-y-s down his knife and fork! He's real rich. Mama 15 says he is, he says he isn't. So he says, "Have I heard correctly? You don't understand why I don't cut off my beard?"

"Why," I says, "Papa-Daddy, of course I understand, I did not say any such a thing, the idea!"

He says, "Hussy!"

I says, "Papa-Daddy, you know I wouldn't any more want you to cut off your beard than the man in the moon. It was the farthest thing from my mind! Stella-Rondo sat there and made that up while she was eating breast of chicken."

But he says, "So the postmistress fails to understand why I don't cut off my beard. Which job I got you through my influence with the government. 'Bird's nest'—is that what you call it?"

Not that it isn't the next to smallest P.O. in the entire state of 20 Mississippi.

I says, "Oh, Papa-Daddy," I says, "I didn't say any such a thing, I never dreamed it was a bird's nest, I have always been grateful though this is the next to smallest P.O. in the state of Mississippi, and I do not enjoy being referred to as a hussy by my own grandfather."

But Stella-Rondo says, "Yes, you did say it too. Anybody in the world could of heard you, that had ears."

"Stop right there," says Mama, looking at *me*.

So I pulled my napkin straight back through the napkin ring and left the table.

25 As soon as I was out of the room Mama says, "Call her back, or she'll starve to death," but Papa-Daddy says, "This is the beard I started growing on the Coast when I was fifteen years old." He would of gone on till nightfall if Shirley-T. hadn't lost the Milky Way she ate in Cairo.

So Papa-Daddy says, "I am going out and lie in the hammock, and you can all sit here and remember my words: I'll never cut off my beard as long as I live, even one inch, and I don't appreciate it in you at all." Passed right by me in the hall and went straight out and got in the hammock.

It would be a holiday. It wasn't five minutes before Uncle Rondo suddenly appeared in the hall in one of Stella-Rondo's flesh-colored kimonos, all cut on the bias, like something Mr. Whitaker probably thought was gorgeous.

"Uncle Rondo!" I says. "I didn't know who that was! Where are you going?"

"Sister," he says, "get out of my way, I'm poisoned."

30 "If you're poisoned stay away from Papa-Daddy," I says. "Keep out of the hammock. Papa-Daddy will certainly beat you on the head if you come within forty miles of him. He thinks I deliberately said he ought to cut off his beard after he got me the P.O., and I've told him and told him and told him, and he acts like he just don't hear me. Papa-Daddy must of gone stone deaf."

"He picked a fine day to do it then," says Uncle Rondo, and before you could say "Jack Robinson" flew out in the yard.

What he'd really done, he'd drunk another bottle of that prescription. He does it every single Fourth of July as sure as shooting, and it's horribly expensive. Then he falls over in the hammock and snores. So he insisted on zigzagging right on out to the hammock, looking like a half-wit.

Papa-Daddy woke with this horrible yell and right there without moving an inch he tried to turn Uncle Rondo against me. I heard every word he said. Oh, he told Uncle Rondo I didn't learn to read till I was eight years old and he didn't see how in the world I ever got the mail put up at the P.O., much less read it all, and he said if Uncle Rondo could only fathom the lengths he had gone to get me that job! And he said on the other hand he thought Stella-Rondo had a brilliant mind and deserved credit for getting out of town. All the time he was just lying there swinging as pretty as you please and looping out his beard, and poor Uncle Rondo was *pleading* with him to slow down the hammock, it was making him as dizzy as a witch to watch it. But that's what Papa-Daddy likes about a hammock. So Uncle Rondo was too dizzy to get turned against me for the time being. He's Mama's only brother and is a good case of a one-track mind. Ask anybody. A certified pharmacist.

Just then I heard Stella-Rondo raising the upstairs window. While she was married she got this peculiar idea that it's cooler with the windows shut and locked. So she has to raise the window before she can make a soul hear her outdoors.

So she raises the window and says, "*Oh!*" You would have thought she was mortally wounded. 35

Uncle Rondo and Papa-Daddy didn't even look up, but kept right on with what they were doing. I had to laugh.

I flew up the stairs and threw the door open! I says, "What in the wide world's the matter, Stella-Rondo? You mortally wounded?"

"No," she says, "I am not mortally wounded but I wish you would do me the favor of looking out that window there and telling me what you see."

So I shade my eyes and look out the window.

"I see the front yard," I says. 40

"Don't you see any human beings?"

"I see Uncle Rondo trying to run Papa-Daddy out of the hammock," I says. "Nothing more. Naturally, it's so suffocating-hot in the house, with all the windows shut and locked, everybody who cares to stay in their right mind will have to go out and get in the hammock before the Fourth of July is over."

"Don't you notice anything different about Uncle Rondo?" asks Stella-Rondo.

"Why, no, except he's got on some terrible-looking flesh-colored contraption I wouldn't be found dead in, is all I can see," I says.

"Never mind, you won't be found dead in it, because it happens to be 45 part of my trousseau, and Mr. Whitaker took several dozen photographs of me in it," says Stella-Rondo. "What on earth could Uncle Rondo *mean* by wearing part of my trousseau out in the broad open daylight without saying so much as 'Kiss my foot,' *knowing* I only got home this morning after my separation and hung my negligee up on the bathroom door, just as nervous as I could be?"

"I'm sure I don't know, and what do you expect me to do about it?" I says. "Jump out the window?"

"No, I expect nothing of the kind. I simply declare that Uncle Rondo looks like a fool in it, that's all," she says. "It makes me sick to my stomach."

"Well, he looks as good as he can," I says. "As good as anybody in reason could." I stood up for Uncle Rondo, please remember. And I said to Stella-Rondo, "I think I would do well not to criticize so freely if I were you and came home with a two-year-old child I had never said a word about, and no explanation whatever about my separation."

"I asked you the instant I entered this house not to refer one more time to my adopted child, and you gave me your word of honor you would not," was all Stella-Rondo would say, and started pulling out every one of her eyebrows with some cheap Kress tweezers.

50   So I merely slammed the door behind me and went down and made some green-tomato pickle. Somebody had to do it. Of course Mama had turned both the Negroes loose; she always said no earthly power could hold one anyway on the Fourth of July, so she wouldn't even try. It turned out that Jaypan fell in the lake and came within a very narrow limit of drowning.

So Mama trots in. Lifts up the lid and says, "H'm! Not very good for your Uncle Rondo in his precarious condition, I must say. Or poor little adopted Shirley-T. Shame on you!"

That made me tired. I says, "Well, Stella-Rondo had better thank her lucky stars it was her instead of me came trotting in with that very peculiar-looking child. Now if it had been me that trotted in from Illinois and brought a peculiar-looking child or two, I shudder to think of the reception I'd of got, much less controlled the diet of an entire family."

"But you must remember, Sister, that you were never married to Mr. Whitaker in the first place and didn't go up to Illinois to live," says Mama, shaking a spoon in my face. "If you had I would of been just as overjoyed to see you and your little adopted girl as I was to see Stella-Rondo, when you wound up with your separation and came on back home."

"You would not," I says.

55   "Don't contradict me, I would," says Mama.

But I said she couldn't convince me though she talked till she was blue in the face. Then I said, "Besides, you know as well as I do that that child is not adopted."

"She most certainly is adopted," says Mama, stiff as a poker.

I says, "Why, Mama, Stella-Rondo had her just as sure as anything in this world, and just too stuck up to admit it."

"Why, Sister," said Mama. "Here I thought we were going to have a pleasant Fourth of July, and you start right out not believing a word your own baby sister tells you!"

"Just like Cousin Annie Flo. Went to her grave denying the facts of 60
life," I reminded Mama.

"I told you if you ever mentioned Annie Flo's name I'd slap your face,"
says Mama, and slaps my face.

"All right, you wait and see," I says.

"I," says Mama, "*I* prefer to take my children's word for anything when
it's humanly possible." You ought to see Mama, she weighs two hundred
pounds and has real tiny feet.

Just then something perfectly horrible occurred to me.

"Mama," I says, "can that child talk?" I simply had to whisper! "Mama, 65
I wonder if that child can be—you know—in any way? Do you realize?" I
says, "that she hasn't spoke one single, solitary word to a human being up
to this minute? This is the way she looks," I says, and I looked like this.

Well, Mama and I just stood there and stared at each other. It was
horrible!

"I remember well that Joe Whitaker frequently drank like a fish," says
Mama. "I believed to my soul he drank *chemicals*." And without another
word she marches to the foot of the stairs and calls Stella-Rondo.

"Stella-Rondo? O-o-o-o-o! Stella-Rondo!"

"What?" says Stella-Rondo from upstairs. Not even the grace to get up
off the bed.

"Can that child of yours talk?" asks Mama. 70

Stella-Rondo says, "Can she what?"

"Talk! Talk!" says Mama. "Burdyburdyburdyburdy!"

So Stella-Rondo yells back, "Who says she can't talk?"

"Sister says so," says Mama.

"You didn't have to tell me, I know whose word of honor don't mean a 75
thing in this house," says Stella-Rondo.

And in a minute the loudest Yankee voice I ever heard in my life yells
out, "OE'm Pop-OE the Sailor-r-r-r Ma-a-an!" and then somebody
jumps up and down in the upstairs hall. In another second the house
would of fallen down.

"Not only talks, she can tap-dance!" calls Stella-Rondo. "Which is more
than some people I won't name can do."

"Why, the little precious darling thing!" Mama says, so surprised. "Just
as smart as she can be!" Starts talking baby talk right there. Then she
turns on me. "Sister, you ought to be thoroughly ashamed! Run upstairs
this instant and apologize to Stella-Rondo and Shirley-T."

"Apologize for what?" I says. "I merely wondered if the child was normal,
that's all. Now that she's proved she is, why, I have nothing further to say."

But Mama just turned on her heel and flew out, furious. She ran right 80
upstairs and hugged the baby. She believed it was adopted. Stella-Rondo

hadn't done a thing but turn her against me from upstairs while I stood there helpless over the hot stove. So that made Mama, Papa-Daddy, and the baby all on Stella-Rondo's side.

Next, Uncle Rondo.

I must say that Uncle Rondo has been marvelous to me at various times in the past and I was completely unprepared to be made to jump out of my skin, the way it turned out. Once Stella-Rondo did something perfectly horrible to him—broke a chain letter from Flanders Field—and he took the radio back he had given her and gave it to me. Stella-Rondo was furious! For six months we all had to call her Stella instead of Stella-Rondo, or she wouldn't answer. I always thought Uncle Rondo had all the brains of the entire family. Another time he sent me to Mammoth Cave with all expenses paid.

But this would be the day he was drinking that prescription, the Fourth of July.

So at supper Stella-Rondo speaks up and says she thinks Uncle Rondo ought to try to eat a little something. So finally Uncle Rondo said he would try a little cold biscuits and ketchup, but that was all. So *she* brought it to him.

85   "Do you think it wise to disport with ketchup in Stella-Rondo's flesh-colored kimono?" I says. Trying to be considerate! If Stella-Rondo couldn't watch out for her trousseau, somebody had to.

"Any objections?" asks Uncle Rondo, just about to pour out all of the ketchup.

"Don't mind what she says, Uncle Rondo," says Stella-Rondo. "Sister has been devoting this solid afternoon to sneering out my bedroom window at the way you look."

"What's that?" says Uncle Rondo. Uncle Rondo has got the most terrible temper in the world. Anything is liable to make him tear the house down if it comes at the wrong time.

So Stella-Rondo says, "Sister says, 'Uncle Rondo certainly does look like a fool in that pink kimono!'"

90   Do you remember who it was really said that?

Uncle Rondo spills out all the ketchup and jumps out of his chair and tears off the kimono and throws it down on the dirty floor and puts his foot on it. It had to be sent all the way to Jackson to the cleaners and re-pleated.

"So that's your opinion of your Uncle Rondo, is it?" he says. "I look like a fool, do I? Well, that's the last straw. A whole day in this house with nothing to do, and then to hear you come out with a remark like that behind my back!"

"I didn't say any such of a thing, Uncle Rondo," I says, "and I'm not saying who did, either. Why, I think you look all right. Just try to take care of yourself and not talk and eat at the same time," I says. "I think you better go lie down."

"Lie down my foot," says Uncle Rondo. I ought to of known by that he was fixing to do something perfectly horrible.

So he didn't do anything that night in the precarious state he was in— 95 just played Casino with Mama and Stella-Rondo and Shirley-T. and gave Shirley-T. a nickel with a head on both sides. It tickled her nearly to death, and she called him "Papa." But at 6:30 A.M. the next morning, he threw a whole five-cent package of some unsold one-inch firecrackers from the store as hard as he could into my bedroom and they every one went off. Not one bad one in the string. Anybody else, there'd be one that wouldn't go off.

Well, I'm just terribly susceptible to noise of any kind, the doctor has always told me I was the most sensitive person he had ever seen in his whole life, and I was simply prostrated. I couldn't eat! People tell me they heard it as far as the cemetery, and old Aunt Jep Patterson, that had been holding her own so good, thought it was Judgment Day and she was going to meet her whole family. It's usually so quiet here.

And I'll tell you it didn't take me any longer than a minute to make up my mind what to do. There I was with the whole entire house on Stella-Rondo's side and turned against me. If I have anything at all I have pride.

So I just decided I'd go straight down to the P.O. There's plenty of room there in the back, I says to myself.

Well! I made no bones about letting the family catch on to what I was up to. I didn't try to conceal it.

The first thing they knew, I marched in where they were all playing 100 Old Maid and pulled the electric oscillating fan out by the plug, and everything got real hot. Next I snatched the pillow I'd done the needle-point on right off the davenport from behind Papa-Daddy. He went "Ugh!" I beat Stella-Rondo up the stairs and finally found my charm bracelet in her bureau drawer under a picture of Nelson Eddy.[1]

"So that's the way the land lies," says Uncle Rondo. There he was, piecing on the ham. "Well, Sister, I'll be glad to donate my army cot if you got any place to set it up, providing you'll leave right this minute and let me get some peace." Uncle Rondo was in France.

"Thank you kindly for the cot and 'peace' is hardly the word I would select if I had to resort to firecrackers at 6:30 A.M. in a young girl's bedroom," I says to him. "And as to where I intend to go, you seem to forget

---

1. Opera singer (1901–67) who enjoyed phenomenal popularity in the 1930s and 1940s when he costarred in numerous film musicals with Jeanette MacDonald. The two were known as "America's Singing Sweethearts."

my position as postmistress of China Grove, Mississippi," I says. "I've always got the P.O."

Well, that made them all sit up and take notice.

I went out front and started digging up some four-o'clocks to plant around the P.O.

105   "Ah-ah-ah!" says Mama, raising the window. "Those happen to be my four-o'clocks. Everything planted in that star is mine. I've never known you to make anything grow in your life."

"Very well," I says. "But I take the fern. Even you, Mama, can't stand there and deny that I'm the one watered that fern. And I happen to know where I can send in a box top and get a packet of one thousand mixed seeds, no two the same kind, free."

"Oh, where?" Mama wants to know.

But I says, "Too late. You 'tend to your house, and I'll 'tend to mine. You hear things like that all the time if you know how to listen to the radio. Perfectly marvelous offers. Get anything you want free."

So I hope to tell you I marched in and got that radio, and they could of all bit a nail in two, especially Stella-Rondo, that it used to belong to, and she well knew she couldn't get it back, I'd sue for it like a shot. And I very politely took the sewing-machine motor I helped pay the most on to give Mama for Christmas back in 1929, and a good big calendar, with the first-aid remedies on it. The thermometer and the Hawaiian ukulele certainly were rightfully mine, and I stood on the step-ladder and got all my watermelon-rind preserves and every fruit and vegetable I'd put up, every jar. Then I began to pull the tacks out of the bluebird wall vases on the archway to the dining room.

110   "Who told you you could have those, Miss Priss?" says Mama, fanning as hard as she could.

"I bought 'em and I'll keep track of 'em," I says. "I'll tack 'em up one on each side of the post-office window, and you can see 'em when you come to ask me for your mail, if you're so dead to see 'em."

"Not I! I'll never darken the door to that post office again if I live to be a hundred," Mama says. "Ungrateful child! After all the money we spent on you at the Normal."[2]

"Me either," says Stella-Rondo. "You can just let my mail lie there and *rot*, for all I care. I'll never come and relieve you of a single, solitary piece."

"I should worry," I says. "And who you think's going to sit down and write you all those big fat letters and postcards, by the way? Mr. Whitaker? Just because he was the only man ever dropped down in China Grove and

2. That is, normal school (teachers' college).

you got him—unfairly—is he going to sit down and write you a lengthy correspondence after you come home giving no rhyme nor reason whatsoever for your separation and no explanation for the presence of that child? I may not have your brilliant mind, but I fail to see it."

So Mama says, "Sister, I've told you a thousand times that Stella-Rondo 115 simply got homesick, and this child is far too big to be hers," and she says, "Now, why don't you just sit down and play Casino?"

Then Shirley-T. sticks out her tongue at me in this perfectly horrible way. She has no more manners than the man in the moon. I told her she was going to cross her eyes like that some day and they'd stick.

"It's too late to stop me now," I says. "You should have tried that yesterday. I'm going to the P.O. and the only way you can possibly see me is to visit me there."

So Papa-Daddy says, "You'll never catch me setting foot in that post office, even if I should take a notion into my head to write a letter some place." He says, "I won't have you reachin' out of that little old window with a pair of shears and cuttin' off any beard of mine. I'm too smart for you!"

"We all are," says Stella-Rondo.

But I said, "If you're so smart, where's Mr. Whitaker?" 120

So then Uncle Rondo says, "I'll thank you from now on to stop reading all the orders I get on postcards and telling everybody in China Grove what you think is the matter with them," but I says, "I draw my own conclusions and will continue in the future to draw them." I says, "If people want to write their innermost secrets on penny postcards, there's nothing in the wide world you can do about it, Uncle Rondo."

"And if you think we'll ever *write* another postcard you're sadly mistaken," says Mama.

"Cutting off your nose to spite your face then," I says. "But if you're all determined to have no more to do with the U.S. mail, think of this: What will Stella-Rondo do now, if she wants to tell Mr. Whitaker to come after her?"

"Wah!" says Stella-Rondo. I knew she'd cry. She had a conniption fit right there in the kitchen.

"It will be interesting to see how long she holds out," I says. "And now— 125 I am leaving."

"Good-bye," says Uncle Rondo.

"Oh, I declare," says Mama, "to think that a family of mine should quarrel on the Fourth of July, or the day after, over Stella-Rondo leaving old Mr. Whitaker and having the sweetest little adopted child! It looks like we'd all be glad!"

"Wah!" says Stella-Rondo, and has a fresh conniption fit.

"He left *her*—you mark my words," I says. "That's Mr. Whitaker. I know Mr. Whitaker. After all, I knew him first. I said from the beginning he'd up and leave her. I foretold every single thing that's happened."

130 "Where did he go?" asks Mama.

"Probably to the North Pole, if he knows what's good for him," I says.

But Stella-Rondo just bawled and wouldn't say another word. She flew to her room and slammed the door.

"Now look what you've gone and done, Sister," says Mama. "You go apologize."

"I haven't the time, I'm leaving," I says.

135 "Well, what are you waiting around for?" asks Uncle Rondo.

So I just picked up the kitchen clock and marched off, without saying, "Kiss my foot," or anything, and never did tell Stella-Rondo good-bye.

There was a girl going along on a little wagon right in front.

"Nigger girl," I says, "come help me haul these things down the hill, I'm going to live in the post office."

Took her nine trips in her express wagon. Uncle Rondo came out on the porch and threw her a nickel.

140 And that's the last I've laid eyes on any of my family or my family laid eyes on me for five solid days and nights. Stella-Rondo may be telling the most horrible tales in the world about Mr. Whitaker, but I haven't heard them. As I tell everybody, I draw my own conclusions.

But oh, I like it here. It's ideal, as I've been saying. You see, I've got everything cater-cornered, the way I like it. Hear the radio? All the war news. Radio, sewing machine, book ends, ironing board and that great big piano lamp—peace, that's what I like. Butter-bean vines planted all along the front where the strings are.

Of course, there's not much mail. My family are naturally the main people in China Grove, and if they prefer to vanish from the face of the earth, for all the mail they get or the mail they write, why, I'm not going to open my mouth. Some of the folks here in town are taking up for me and some turned against me. I know which is which. There are always people who will quit buying stamps just to get on the right side of Papa-Daddy.

But here I am, and here I'll stay. I want the world to know I'm happy.

And if Stella-Rondo should come to me this minute, on bended knees, and *attempt* to explain the incidents of her life with Mr. Whitaker, I'd simply put my fingers in both my ears and refuse to listen.

1941

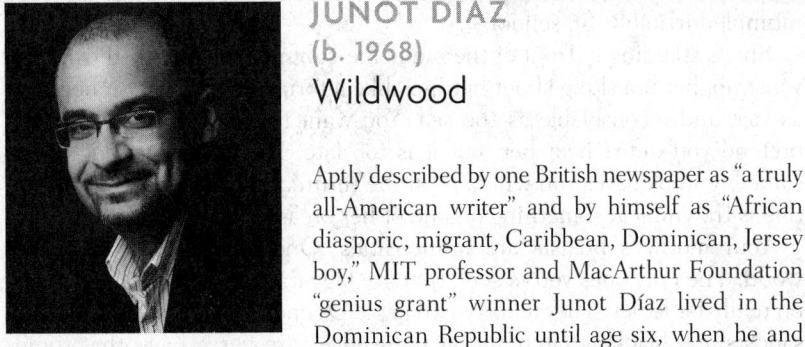

JUNOT DÍAZ
(b. 1968)
Wildwood

Aptly described by one British newspaper as "a truly all-American writer" and by himself as "African diasporic, migrant, Caribbean, Dominican, Jersey boy," MIT professor and MacArthur Foundation "genius grant" winner Junot Díaz lived in the Dominican Republic until age six, when he and the rest of his family joined his father in the United States. While his mother worked on a factory assembly line and his father, a former military policeman, drove a forklift, Díaz and his four siblings navigated life in what he calls a "very black, very Puerto Rican and very poor" New Jersey neighborhood. Díaz supported himself through college, earning a BA in English from Rutgers and a Cornell MFA. A year after graduating, Díaz published *Drown* (1996), a collection of interrelated short stories. A decade later, his novel, *The Brief Wondrous Life of Oscar Wao* (2007), won numerous prizes, including both a National Book Critics Circle Award and a Pulitzer. *Oscar Wao* is a tale of a lovelorn and utterly lovable "ghetto nerd," who dreams of becoming the next J. R. R. Tolkien and three generations of his Dominican American family. Díaz published a second short-story collection, *This Is How you Lose Her* (2012), and cofounded the pioneering Voices of Our Nations Arts Foundation to nurture the work of writers of color. "Wildwood," published almost simultaneously as both a short story and a chapter of *Oscar Wao*, is something of a departure for Díaz thanks to its female narrator-protagonist. But it is characteristic in its creation of an entirely new fictional language to capture the unique voices, experiences, and outlooks of its funny, complicated, thoroughly all-American cast of characters.

t's never the changes we want that change everything.

This is how it all starts: with your mother calling you into the bathroom. You will remember what you were doing at that precise moment for the rest of your life: you were reading "Watership Down"[1] and the bucks and their does were making the dash for the raft and you didn't want to stop reading, the book had to go back to your brother tomorrow, but then

1. Richard Adams's classic novel (1972) about the adventures of a community of English rabbits who, inspired by the prophetic vision of one of their youngest and smallest members, must flee their doomed warren and create a new home.

she called you again, louder, her I'm-not-fucking-around voice, and you mumbled irritably, Sí, señora.

She is standing in front of the medicine-cabinet mirror, naked from the waist up, her bra slung about her hips like a torn sail, the scar on her back as vast and inconsolable as the sea. You want to return to your book, to pretend you didn't hear her, but it is too late. Her eyes meet yours, the same big smoky eyes you will have in the future. Ven acá,[2] she commands. She is frowning at something on one of her breasts.

Your mother's breasts are immensities. One of the wonders of the world. The only ones you've seen that are bigger are in nudie magazines or on really fat ladies. They're forty-two triple Ds and the aureoles are as big as saucers and black as pitch and at their edges are fierce hairs that sometimes she plucks and sometimes she doesn't. These breasts have always embarrassed you and when you walk in public with her you are conscious of them. After her face and her hair, her tetas are what she is most proud of. Your father could never get enough of them, she always brags. But given the fact that he ran off on her after their third year of marriage it seemed in the end that he could.

5   You dread conversations with your mother. These one-sided dressing-downs. You figure that she has called you in to give you another earful about your diet. Your mom's convinced that if you only eat more plátanos you will suddenly acquire her extraordinary train-wrecking secondary sex characteristics. Even at that age you are nothing if not your mother's daughter. You are twelve years old and already as tall as her, a long slender-necked ibis of a girl. You have her straight hair, which makes you look more Hindu than Dominican, and a behind that the boys haven't been able to stop talking about since the fifth grade and whose appeal you do not yet understand. You have her complexion, too, which means you are dark as night. But for all your similarities the tides of inheritance have yet to reach your chest. You have only the slightest hint of breasts: from most angles you're flat as a board and you're thinking she's going to order you to stop wearing bras again because they're suffocating your potential breasts, discouraging them from popping out. You're ready to argue with her to the death, because you're as possessive of your bras as you are of the pads you now buy yourself.

But no, she doesn't say a word about eating more plátanos. Instead, she takes your right hand and guides you. Your mom is rough in all things, but this time she is gentle. You did not think her capable of it.

Do you feel that? she asks in her too familiar raspy voice.

2. Come here (Spanish).

At first all you feel is the density of the tissue and the heat of her, like a bread that never stopped rising. She kneads your fingers into her. You're as close as you've ever been and your breathing is what you hear. Don't you feel that? She turns toward you. Coño, muchacha,[3] stop looking at me and feel. 10

So you close your eyes and your fingers are pushing down and you're thinking of Helen Keller[4] and how when you were little you wanted to be her except more nunnish and then suddenly you do feel something. A knot just beneath her skin, tight and secretive as a plot. And at that moment, for reasons you will never quite understand, you are overcome by the feeling, the premonition, that something in your life is about to change. You become light-headed and you can feel a throbbing in your blood, a rhythm, a drum. Bright lights zoom through you like photon torpedoes, like comets. You don't know how or why you know this thing, but that you know it cannot be doubted. It is exhilarating. For as long as you've been alive you've had bruja[5] ways; even your mother will not begrudge you that much. Hija de Liborio, she called you after you picked your tía's[6] winning numbers for her and when you guessed correctly how old to the day she'd been when she left home for the U.S. (a fact she'd never told anyone). You assumed Liborio was a relative. That was before Santo Domingo, before you knew about the Great Power of God.

I feel it, you say, too loudly. Lo siento.[7]

And like that, everything changes. Before the winter is out the doctors remove that breast you were kneading and its partner, along with the auxiliary lymph nodes. Because of the operations, your mother will have trouble lifting her arms over her head for the rest of her life. Her hair begins to fall out and one day she pulls it all out herself and puts it in a plastic bag. You change, too. Not right away, but it happens. And it's in that bathroom that it all begins. That you begin.

A punk chick. That's what I became. A Siouxsie and the Banshees-loving[8] punk chick. The Puerto Rican kids on the block couldn't stop laughing

---

3. Damn, girl (Dominican Spanish).

4. Famously blind and deaf American author, activist, and lecturer (1880–1968).

5. Witch (Spanish).

6. Aunt's (Spanish). *Hija de Liborio*: literally, child of Liborio (Spanish), an allusion to Olivorio Liborio Mateo (1876–1922), a peasant farmer turned messianic faith healer regarded by his followers as an incarnation of Christ; remnants of his once-powerful Liborista movement still survive.

7. I feel it (Spanish).

8. English rock band (1976–96) created and fronted by Siouxsie Sioux, hailed by the London *Times* as inventing "a form of post-punk discord [. . .] as influential as it was underrated."

when they saw my hair; they called me Blacula. And the morenos,[9] they didn't know what to say; they just called me devil-bitch. Yo, devil-bitch, yo, yo! My tía Rubelka thought it was some kind of mental illness. Hija, she said while frying pastelitos, maybe you need *help*. But my mother was the worst. It's the last straw, she screamed. The. Last. Straw. But it always was with her. Mornings when I came downstairs she'd be in the kitchen making her coffee in la greca and listening to Radio WADO[1] and when she saw me and my hair she'd get mad all over again, as if during the night she'd forgotten who I was.

15   My mother was one of the tallest women in Paterson[2] and her anger was just as tall. It pincered you in its long arms, and if you showed any weakness you were finished. Que muchacha tan fea,[3] she said in disgust, splashing the rest of her coffee in the sink. Fea had become my name. It was nothing new, to tell the truth. She'd been saying stuff like that all our lives. My mother would never win any awards, believe me. You could call her an absentee parent: if she wasn't at work she was sleeping and when she wasn't sleeping all she did was scream and hit. As kids, me and Oscar were more scared of our mother than we were of the dark or el cuco.[4] She would hit us anywhere, in front of anyone, always free with the chanclas and the correa,[5] but now with her cancer there wasn't much she could do anymore. The last time she tried to whale on me it was because of my hair, but instead of cringing or running I punched her hand. It was a reflex more than anything, but once it happened I knew I couldn't take it back, not ever, and so I just kept my fist clenched, waiting for whatever came next, for her to attack me with her teeth like she had this one lady in the Pathmark.[6] But she just stood there shaking, in her stupid wig and her stupid bata,[7] with two huge foam prostheses in her bra, the smell of burning wig all around us. I almost felt sorry for her. This is how you treat your mother? she cried. And if I could I would have broken the entire length of my life across her face, but instead I screamed back, And this is how you treat your daughter?

Things had been bad between us all year. How could they not have been? She was my Old World Dominican mother who had come alone to

9. Literally, browns (Spanish), a term for people with dark skin.
1. Spanish-language news and talk station owned by Univision. *La greca*: Italian-style aluminum stovetop espresso pot (Spanish).
2. New Jersey city in the New York Metropolitan area, home to many Hispanic and Middle Eastern immigrants.
3. What an ugly girl (Spanish).
4. Mythical ghost-monster, a sort of Spanish-language "boogie-man."
5. Belt (Spanish). *Chanclas*: flip-flops (Spanish).
6. Grocery store, part of a chain owned (as A&P is) by the Great Atlantic and Pacific Tea Company.
7. Bathrobe (Spanish).

the United States and I was her only daughter, the one she had raised up herself with the help of nobody, which meant it was her duty to keep me crushed under her heel. I was fourteen and desperate for my own patch of world that had nothing to do with her. I wanted the life that I used to see when I watched "Big Blue Marble"[8] as a kid, the life that drove me to make pen pals and to borrow atlases from school. The life that existed beyond Paterson, beyond my family, beyond Spanish. And as soon as she became sick I saw my chance and I'm not going to pretend or apologize; I saw my chance and eventually I took it.

If you didn't grow up like I did then you don't know and if you don't know it's probably better you don't judge. You don't know the hold our mothers have on us, even the ones that are never around—*especially* the ones that are never around. What it's like to be the perfect Dominican daughter, which is just a nice way of saying a perfect Dominican slave. You don't know what it's like to grow up with a mother who never said anything that wasn't negative, who was always suspicious, always tearing you down and splitting your dreams straight down the seams. On TV and in books mothers talk to daughters, about life, about themselves, but on Main Street in Paterson mothers say not a word unless it's to hurt you. When my first pen pal, Tomoko, stopped writing me after three letters my mother was the one who said, You think someone's going to lose life writing to you? Of course I cried; I was eight and I had already planned that Tomoko and her family would adopt me. My mother, of course, saw clean into the marrow of those dreams and laughed. I wouldn't write to you, either, she said.

She was that kind of mother: who makes you doubt yourself, who would wipe you out if you let her. But I'm not going to pretend, either. For a long time I let her say what she wanted about me and, what was worse, for a long time I believed her. I was a fea, I was a worthless, I was an idiota. From ages two to thirteen I believed her and because I believed her I was the perfect hija. I was the one cooking, cleaning, doing the wash, buying groceries, writing letters to the bank to explain why a house payment was going to be late, translating. I had the best grades in my class. I never caused trouble, even when the morenas used to come after me with scissors because of my straight straight hair. I stayed at home and made sure my little brother Oscar was fed and everything ran right while she was at work. I raised him and I raised me. I was the one. You're my hija, she said, that's what you're supposed to be doing. When that thing happened to me when I was eight and I finally told her what our neighbor had done she told me to shut my mouth and stop crying and I did exactly that, I shut my

---

8. American television series for children (1974–83); featuring stories about children around the world, the show sponsored an international pen-pal club.

mouth and clenched my legs and my mind and within a year I couldn't have told you what he looked like or even his name. All you do is complain, she said to me, but you have no idea what life really is. Sí, señora.

When she told me that I could go on my sixth-grade sleepaway to Bear Mountain[9] and I bought a backpack with my own paper-route money and wrote Bobby Santos notes because he was promising to break into my cabin and kiss me in front of everyone I believed her and when on the morning of the trip she announced that I wasn't going and I said, But you promised, and she said, Muchacha del diablo,[1] I promised you nothing, I didn't throw my backpack at her or pull out my hair, and when it was Laura Saenz who ended up kissing Bobby Santos, not me, I didn't say anything, either. I just lay in my room with stupid Bear-Bear and sang under my breath, imagining where I would run away to when I grew up. To Japan maybe, where I would track down Tomoko, or to Austria, where my singing would inspire a remake of "The Sound of Music."

20   All my favorite books from that period were about runaways—"Watership Down," "The Incredible Journey," "My Side of the Mountain"[2]—and when Bon Jovi's "Runaway"[3] came out I imagined it was me they were singing about. No one had any idea. I was the tallest, dorkiest girl in school, the one who dressed up as Wonder Woman[4] every Halloween, the one who never said a word. People saw me in my glasses and my hand-me-down clothes and could not have imagined what I was capable of. And then when I was twelve I got that feeling, the scary witchy one, and before I knew it my mother was sick and the wildness that had been in me all along, that I had tried to tamp down with chores and with homework and with promises that once I reached college I would be able to do whatever I pleased, burst out. I couldn't help it. I tried to keep it down, but it just flooded through all my quiet spaces. It was a message more than a feeling, a message that tolled like a bell: Change, change, change.

It didn't happen overnight. Yes the wildness was in me, yes it kept my heart beating fast all the long day, yes it danced around me while I walked down the street, yes it let me look boys straight in the face when they stared at me, yes it turned my laugh from a cough into a wild fever, but I was still scared. How could I not be? I was my mother's daughter. Her hold

9. New York state park, located in the mountains along the Hudson River.
1. Devil girl (Spanish).
2. 1959 novel about the adventures of a twelve-year-old boy who flees his family's cramped New York City apartment and learns to survive on his own in the Catskill Mountains. The Incredible Journey: novel (1961) and, later, a Disney movie (1963) about a bull terrier, a Siamese cat, and a Labrador retriever who trek through the Canadian wilderness in search of their human masters.
3. Earliest hit record by the rock band formed in New Jersey in 1983.
4. Fictional superhero featured in DC Comics since the 1940s and in an American television series (1975–79).

on me was stronger than love. And then one day I was walking home with Karen Cepeda, who at that time was my friend. Karen did the goth thing really well; she had spiky Robert Smith[5] hair and wore all black and had the skin color of a ghost. Walking with her in Paterson was like walking with the bearded lady. Everybody would stare and it was the scariest thing and that was, I guess, why I did it.

We were walking down Main and being glared at by everybody and out of nowhere I said, Karen, I want you to cut my hair. As soon as I said it I knew. The feeling in my blood, the rattle, came over me again. Karen raised her eyebrow: What about your mother? You see, it wasn't just me—everybody was scared of Belicia de León.

Fuck her, I said.

Karen looked at me like I was being stupid—I never cursed, but that was something else that was about to change. The next day we locked ourselves in her bathroom while downstairs her father and uncles were bellowing at some soccer game. Well, how do you want it? she asked. I looked at the girl in the mirror for a long time. All I knew was that I didn't want to see her ever again. I put the clippers in Karen's hand, turned them on, and guided her hand until it was all gone.

So now you're punk? Karen asked uncertainly.   25

Yes, I said.

The next day my mother threw the wig at me. You're going to wear this. You're going to wear it every day. And if I see you without it on I'm going to kill you!

I didn't say a word. I held the wig over the burner.

Don't do it, she said as the burner clicked. Don't you dare—

It went up in a flash, like gasoline, like a stupid hope, and if I hadn't   30
thrown it in the sink it would have taken my hand. The smell was horrible, like all the chemicals from all the factories in Elizabeth.[6]

That was when she slapped at me, when I struck her hand and she snatched it back, like I was the fire.

Of course everyone thought I was the worst daughter ever. My tía and our neighbors kept saying, Hija, she's your mother, she's dying, but I wouldn't listen. When I hit her hand, a door opened. And I wasn't about to turn my back on it.

But God how we fought! Sick or not, dying or not, my mother wasn't going to go down easy. She wasn't una pendeja.[7] I'd seen her slap grown men, push

---

5. Former Siouxsie and the Banshees guitarist (b. 1959) and (since 1976) lead singer-songwriter of the English rock band the Cure.
6. Elizabeth, New Jersey is home to a major oil refinery consistently ranked as among the nation's worst polluters.
7. Dumbass, fool, pushover, or coward (Spanish).

white police officers onto their asses, curse a whole group of bochincheras.[8] She had raised me and my brother by herself, she had worked three jobs until she could buy this house we lived in, she had survived being abandoned by my father, she had come from Santo Domingo all by herself, and as a young girl she'd been beaten, set on fire, left for dead. (This last part she didn't tell me, my tía Rubelka did, in a whisper, Your mother almost died, she almost died, and when I asked my mother about it at dinner she took my dinner and gave it to my brother.) That was my mother and there was no way she was going to let me go without killing me first. Figurín de mierda, she called me. You think you're someone, but you ain't nada.[9]

She dug hard, looking for my seams, wanting me to tear like always, but I didn't, I wasn't going to. It was that feeling I had that my life was waiting for me on the other side that made me fearless. When she threw away my Smiths and Sisters of Mercy posters—aquí yo no quiero maricones[1]—I bought replacements. When she threatened to rip up my new clothes I started keeping them in my locker and at Karen's house. When she told me that I had to quit my job at the Greek diner I explained to my boss that my mother was starting to lose it because of her chemo, and when she called to say I couldn't work there anymore he just handed me the phone and stared out at his customers in embarrassment. When she changed the locks on me—I had started staying out late, going to the Limelight because even though I was fourteen I looked twenty-five—I would knock on Oscar's window and he would let me in, scared because the next day my mother would run around the house screaming, Who the hell let that hija de la gran puta[2] in the house? Who? Who? And Oscar would be at the breakfast table stammering, I don't know, Mami, I don't.

35   Her rage filled the house, like flat stale smoke. It got into everything, into our hair and our food, like the fallout they told us about in school that would one day drift down soft as snow. My brother didn't know what to do. He stayed in his room, though sometimes he would lamely try to ask me what was going on. Nothing. You can tell me, Lola, he said, and I could only laugh. You need to lose weight, I told him.

In those final weeks I knew better than to go near my mother. Most of the time she just looked at me with the stink eye, but sometimes without warning she would grab me by my throat and hang on until I pried her

---

8. Gossips (Spanish).
9. Nothing (Spanish). *Figurín de mierda*: literally, perhaps something like figure made of crap; figuratively, a phony, something that only looks refined (Spanish).
1. I don't want to have those fags here (Spanish). *Smiths and Sisters of Mercy*: influential British alternative rock bands of the 1980s, fronted by highly literary singer-songwriter Morrissey (who once described himself as "humasexual") and Andrew Eldritch.
2. Daughter of a bitch (Spanish).

fingers off. She didn't bother talking to me unless it was to make death threats: When you grow up you'll meet me in a dark alley when you least expect it and then I'll kill you and nobody will know I did it! Gloating as she said this.

You're crazy, I told her.

You don't call me crazy, she said, and then she sat down panting.

It was bad, but no one expected what came next. So obvious when you think about it.

All my life I'd been swearing that one day I would just disappear.   40
And one day I did.

I ran off, dique,[3] because of a boy.

What can I really tell you about him? He was like all boys: beautiful and callow and, like an insect, he couldn't sit still. Un blanquito[4] with long hairy legs who I met one night at the Limelight.

His name was Aldo.

He was nineteen and lived down at the Jersey Shore with his seventy-   45
four-year-old father. In the back of his Oldsmobile on University I pulled my leather skirt up and my fishnet stockings down and the smell of me was everywhere. I didn't let him go all the way, but still. The spring of my sophomore year we wrote and called each other at least once a day. I even drove down with Karen to visit him in Wildwood[5] (she had a license, I didn't). He lived and worked near the boardwalk, one of three guys who operated the bumper cars, the only one without tattoos. You should stay, he told me that night while Karen walked ahead of us on the beach. Where would I live? I asked, and he smiled. With me. Don't lie, I said, but he looked out at the surf. I want you to come, he said seriously.

He asked me three times. I counted, I know.

That summer my brother announced that he was going to dedicate his life to designing role-playing games, and my mother was trying to keep a second job for the first time since her operation. It wasn't working out. She was coming home exhausted, and since I wasn't helping, nothing around the house was getting done. Some weekends my tía Rubelka would help out with the cooking and cleaning and would lecture us both, but she had her own family to look after, so most of the time we were on our own. Come, he said on the phone. And then in August Karen left for Slippery Rock.[6] She had graduated from high school a year early. If I don't see

---

3. Supposedly or so they say (Dominican Spanish).
4. Little white boy (Spanish).
5. Beachfront community on the Jersey shore; the town's population surges from around 5,000 in the off-season to over 200,000 in season.
6. University in Pennsylvania about fifty miles north of Pittsburgh.

Paterson again it will be too soon, she said before she left. Five days later, school started. I cut class six times in the first two weeks. I just couldn't do school anymore. Something inside wouldn't let me. It didn't help that I was reading "The Fountainhead" and had decided that I was Dominique and Aldo was Roark.[7] And finally what we'd all been waiting for happened. My mother announced at dinner, quietly, I want you both to listen to me: the doctor is running more tests on me.

Oscar looked like he was going to cry. He put his head down. And my reaction? I looked at her and said, Could you please pass the salt?

These days I don't blame her for smacking me across my face, but right then it was all I needed. We jumped on each other and the table fell and the sancocho[8] spilled all over the floor and Oscar just stood in the corner bellowing, Stop it, stop it, stop it!

Hija de tu maldita madre![9] she shrieked. And I said, This time I hope you die from it.

For a couple of days the house was a war zone, and then on Friday she let me out of my room and I was allowed to sit next to her on the sofa and watch novelas with her. She was waiting for her blood work to come back, but you would never have known her life was in the balance. She watched the TV like it was the only thing that mattered, and whenever one of the characters did something underhanded she would start waving her arms: Someone has to stop her! Can't they see what that puta[1] is up to?

I hate you, I said very quietly, but she didn't hear.

Go get me some water, she said. Put an ice cube in it.

That was the last thing I did for her. The next morning I was on the bus bound for the shore. One bag, two hundred dollars in tips, Tío[2] Rudolfo's old knife, and the only picture my mother had of my father, which she had hidden under her bed (she was in the picture, too, but I pretended not to notice). I was so scared. I couldn't stop shaking. The whole ride down I was expecting the sky to split open and my mother to reach down and shake me. But it didn't happen. Nobody but the man across the aisle noticed me. You're really beautiful, he said. Like a girl I once knew.

I didn't write them a note. That's how much I hated them. Her.

That night while Aldo and I lay in his sweltering kitty-litter-infested room I told him: I want you to do it to me.

---

7. Influential and controversial best seller (1943) by Ayn Rand; a celebration of individualism, it chronicles young architect Howard Roark's struggles to achieve success without compromising, even with the equally headstrong architect's daughter (Dominique Francon) with whom he eventually falls in love.
8. Thick soup or stew common in South America and the Caribbean.
9. Child of a motherfucker, considered one of the worst possible insults in Dominican Spanish.
1. Whore (Spanish).
2. Uncle (Spanish).

He started unbuttoning my pants. Are you sure?
Definitely, I said grimly.

He had a long thin dick that hurt like hell, but the whole time I just said, Oh yes, Aldo, yes, because that was what I imagined you were supposed to say while you were losing your virginity to some boy you thought you loved.

It was like the stupidest thing I ever did. I was miserable. And so bored. 60 But of course I wouldn't admit it. I had run away, so I was happy! Happy!

Aldo had neglected to mention, all those times he asked me to live with him, that his father hated him like I hated my mother. Aldo, Sr., had been in the Second World War and he'd never forgiven the "Japs" for all the friends he had lost. My dad's so full of shit, Aldo said. He never left Fort Dix.[3] I don't think his father said nine words to me the whole time I lived with them. He was one mean vicjito[4] and even had a padlock on the refrigerator. Stay the hell out of it, he told me. We couldn't even get ice cubes out.

Aldo and his dad lived in one of the cheapest little bungalows on New Jersey Avenue, and me and Aldo slept in a room where his father kept the litter box for his two cats, and at night we would move it out into the hallway, but he always woke up before us and put it back in the room: I told you to leave my crap alone! Which is funny when you think about it. But it wasn't funny then. I got a job selling French fries on the boardwalk and between the hot oil and the cat piss I couldn't smell anything else. On my days off I would drink with Aldo or I would sit in the sand dressed in all black and try to write in my journal, which I was sure would form the foundation for a utopian society after we blew ourselves into radioactive kibble. Sometimes boys would walk up to me and throw lines at me like, Who fuckin' died? They would sit down next to me in the sand. You a good-looking girl, you should be in a bikini. Why, so you can rape me? Jesus Christ, one of them said, jumping to his feet. What the hell is wrong with you?

To this day I don't know how I lasted. At the beginning of October I was laid off from the French-fry palace; by then most of the boardwalk was closed up and I had nothing to do except hang out at the public library, which was even smaller than my high-school one. Aldo had moved on to working with his dad at his garage, which only made them more pissed off at each other and by extension more pissed off at me. When they got home they would drink Schlitz[5] and complain about the Phillies. I guess I should count myself lucky that they didn't decide to bury the

---

3. U.S. military post just south of Trenton, New Jersey.
4. Old man (Spanish).
5. Notoriously cheap American beer.

hatchet by gangbanging me. I stayed out as much as I could and waited for the feeling to come back to me, to tell me what I should do next, but I was bone dry, bereft, no visions whatsoever. I started to think that maybe it was like in the books: as soon as I lost my virginity I lost my power. I got really mad at Aldo after that. You're a drunk, I told him. And an idiot. So what, he shot back. Your pussy smells. Then stay out of it! I will!

But of course I was happy! Happy! I kept waiting to run into my family posting flyers of me on the boardwalk—my mom, the tallest blackest chestiest thing in sight, Oscar looking like the Brown Blob, my tía Rubelka, maybe even my tío if they could get him off the heroin long enough—but the closest I came to any of that was some flyers someone had put up for a lost cat. That's white people for you. They lose a cat and it's an all-points bulletin, but we Dominicans lose a daughter and we might not even cancel our appointment at the salon.

65   By November I was so finished. I would sit there with Aldo and his putrid father and the old shows would come on the TV, the ones me and my brother used to watch when we were kids, "Three's Company," "What's Happening!!," "The Jeffersons,"[6] and my disappointment would grind against some organ that was very soft and tender. It was starting to get cold, too, and wind just walked right into the bungalow and got under your blankets or jumped in the shower with you. It was awful. I kept having these stupid visions of my brother trying to cook for himself. Don't ask me why. I was the one who cooked for us. The only thing Oscar knew how to make was grilled cheese. I imagined him thin as a reed, wandering around the kitchen, opening cabinets forlornly. I even started dreaming about my mother, except in my dreams she was young, my age, and it was because of those dreams that I realized something obvious: she had run away, too, and that was why we were all in the United States.

I put away the photo of her and my father, but the dreams didn't stop. I guess when a person is with you they're only with you when they're with you, but when they're gone, when they're really gone, they're with you forever.

And then at the end of November Aldo, my wonderful boyfriend, decided to be cute. I knew he was getting unhappy with us, but I didn't know exactly how bad it was until one night he had his friends over. His

---

6. Like *Three's Company* (1977–84) and *What's Happening!!* (1976–79), a popular American sitcom (1975–85). Where *What's Happening!!* focuses on three working-class African American teens in Los Angeles, both *The Jeffersons* and *Three's Company* focus partly on the conflicts and humor arising from particular living arrangements: the former features a newly affluent African American family who have moved from working-class Queens into a luxurious Manhattan high-rise; in the latter, which has an all-Caucasian cast, two young women can maintain their apartment only by convincing their landlord that their male roommate is gay.

father had gone to Atlantic City[7] and they were all drinking and smoking and telling dumb jokes and suddenly Aldo says, Do you know what Pontiac stands for? Poor Old Nigger Thinks It's A Cadillac. Who was he looking at when he told his punch line? He was looking straight at me.

That night he wanted me but I pushed his hand away. Don't touch me. Don't get sore, he said, putting my hand on his cock. It wasn't nothing. And then he laughed.

So what did I do a couple days later—a really dumb thing. I called home. The first time no one answered. The second time it was Oscar. The de León residence, how may I direct your call? That was my brother for you. This is why everybody in the world hated his guts.

It's me, dumb-ass.

Lola. He was so quiet and then I realized he was crying. Where *are* you?

You don't want to know. I switched ears, trying to keep my voice casual. How is everybody?

Lola, Mami's going to *kill* you.

Dumb-ass, could you keep your voice down. Mami isn't home, is she? She's working.

What a surprise, I said. Mami working. On the last minute of the last hour of the last day my mother would be at work. She would be at work when the missiles were in the air.

I guess I must have missed him real bad or I just wanted to see somebody who knew anything about me, or the cat piss had damaged my common sense, because I gave him the address of a coffee shop on the boardwalk and told him to bring my clothes and some of my books.

Bring me money, too.

He paused. I don't know where Mami keeps it.

You know, Mister. Just bring it.

How much? he asked timidly.

All of it.

That's a lot of money, Lola.

Just bring me the money, Oscar.

O.K., O.K. He inhaled deeply. Will you at least tell me if you're O.K. or not?

I'm O.K., I said, and that was the only point in the conversation where I almost cried. I kept quiet until I could speak again and then I asked him how he was going to get down here without our mother finding out.

You know me, he said weakly. I might be a dork, but I'm a resourceful dork.

7. Somewhat rundown New Jersey beach town renowned for its casinos.

90   I should have known not to trust anybody whose favorite books as a
child were Encyclopedia Brown.[8] But I wasn't really thinking; I was so
looking forward to seeing him.
       By then I had this plan. I was going to convince my brother to run away
with me. My plan was that we would go to Dublin. I had met a bunch of
Irish guys on the boardwalk and they had sold me on their country. I would
become a backup singer for U2[9] and both Bono and the drummer would
fall in love with me, and Oscar could become the Dominican James Joyce.[1]
I really believed it would happen, too. That's how deluded I was by then.
       The next day I walked into the coffee shop, looking brand-new, and he
was there, with the bag. Oscar, I said, laughing. You're so fat!
       I know, he said, ashamed. I was worried about you.
       We embraced for like an hour and then he started crying. Lola, I'm sorry.
95   It's O.K., I said, and that's when I looked up and saw my mother and
my tía Rubelka and my tío Rudolfo boiling out of the kitchen.
       Oscar! I screamed, but it was too late. My mother already had me in
her hands. She looked so thin and worn, almost like a hag, but she was
holding on to me like I was her last nickel, and underneath her red wig her
green eyes were *furious*. I noticed, absently, that she had dressed up for
the occasion. That was typical. Muchacha del diablo, she shrieked. I managed to haul her out of the coffee shop and when she pulled back her hand
to smack me I broke free. I ran for it. Behind me I could feel her sprawling, hitting the curb hard with a crack, but I wasn't looking back. No—I
was running. In elementary school, whenever we had field day I was
always the fastest girl in my grade, took home all the ribbons; they said it
wasn't fair, because I was so big, but I didn't care. I could even have beaten
the boys if I'd wanted to, so there was no way my sick mother, my messed-
up tíos, and my fat brother were going to catch me. I was going to run as
fast as my long legs could carry me. I was going to run down the boardwalk, past Aldo's miserable house, out of Wildwood, out of New Jersey,
and I wasn't going to stop. I was going to *fly*.

       Anyway, that's how it *should* have worked out. But I looked back. I couldn't
help it. It's not like I didn't know my Bible, all the pillars-of-salt stuff,[2] but

8. Fictional series (1963–2012) about the adventures of bookish boy detective Leroy ("Encyclopedia") Brown.
9. Wildly successful Irish rock band formed in Dublin in 1976 by, among others, frontman
Bono, guitarist The Edge, and drummer Larry Mullen, Jr.
1. Celebrated Dublin-born author (1882–1941) of books including the short-story collection
Dubliners (1914).
2. In the book of Genesis, Lot and his wife flee the iniquitous Sodom at the behest of angels
who warn them not to look back lest they share in that city's well-earned destruction; when
Lot's wife ignores the warning, she turns into a pillar of salt.

when you're someone's daughter that she raised by herself with no help from nobody habits die hard. I just wanted to make sure my mom hadn't broken her arm or smashed open her skull. I mean, really, who the hell wants to kill her own mother by accident? That's the only reason I glanced back. She was sprawled on the ground, her wig had fallen out of reach, her poor bald head out in the day like something private and shameful, and she was bawling like a lost calf, Hija, hija! And there I was wanting to run off into my future. It was right then that I needed that feeling to guide me, but it wasn't anywhere in sight. Only me. In the end I didn't have the ovaries. She was on the ground, bald as a baby, crying, probably a month away from dying, and here I was, her one and only daughter. And there was nothing I could do about it. So I walked back and when I reached down to help her she clamped on to me with both hands. That was when I realized she hadn't been crying at all. She'd been faking! Her smile was like a lion's.

Ya te tengo,[3] she said, jumping triumphantly to her feet. Te tengo.

And that is how I ended up in Santo Domingo.[4] I guess my mother thought it would be harder for me to run away from an island where I knew no one, and in a way she was right. I'm into my sixth month here and these days I'm just trying to be philosophical about the whole thing. I wasn't like that at first, but in the end I had to let it go. It was like the fight between the egg and the rock, my abuela[5] said. No winning.

I'm actually going to school, not that it's going to count when I return to 100 Paterson, but it keeps me busy and out of trouble and around people my own age. You don't need to be around us viejos all day, Abuela says. I have mixed feelings about the school. For one thing, it's improved my Spanish a lot. It's a private school, a Carol Morgan[6] wanna-be filled with people my tío Carlos Moya calls los hijos de mami y papi.[7] And then there's me. If you think it was tough being a goth in Paterson, try being a Dominican york in one of those private schools back in D.R. You will never meet bitchier girls in your whole life. They whisper about me to death. Someone else would have had a nervous breakdown, but after Wildwood I'm not so brittle. I don't let it get to me.

And the irony of all ironies? I'm on our school's track team. I joined because my friend Rosio, the scholarship girl from Los Mina,[8] told me I

---

3. Now I've got you (Spanish).
4. Capital city (founded 1496) of the Dominican Republic, which, along with the Republic of Haiti, occupies Hispaniola Island.
5. Grandmother (Spanish).
6. Prestigious English-language school in Santo Domingo, founded in 1933 by U.S. missionaries Carol and Barney Morgan.
7. Spoiled kids, something like "Daddy's girls" and "Mommy's boys" (Spanish).
8. Neighborhood in Santo Domingo.

could win a spot on the team on the length of my legs alone. Those are the pins of a winner, she prophesied. Well, she must have known something I didn't, because I'm now our school's top runner in the four hundred metres and under. That I have talent at this simple thing never ceases to amaze me. Karen would pass out if she could see me running sprints out behind my school while Coach Cortés screams at us, first in Spanish and then in Catalán. Breathe, breathe, *breathe!* I've got like no fat left on me and the musculature of my legs impresses everyone, even me. I can't wear shorts anymore without causing traffic jams, and the other day when my abuela accidentally locked us out of the house she turned to me in frustration and said, Hija, just kick the door open. That pushed a laugh out of both of us.

So much has changed these last months, in my head, my heart. Rosio has me dressing up like a real Dominican girl. She's the one who fixes my hair and helps me with my makeup, and sometimes when I see myself in mirrors I don't even know who I am anymore. Not that I'm unhappy or anything. Even if I found a hot-air balloon that would whisk me straight to U2's house I'm not sure I would take it. (I'm still not talking to my traitor brother, though.) The truth is I'm even thinking of staying one more year. Abuela doesn't want me ever to leave—I'll miss you, she says so simply it can't be anything but true—and my mom has told me I can stay if I want to but that I would be welcome at home, too. Tía Rubelka tells me she's hanging tough, my mother, that she's back to two jobs. They sent me a picture of the whole family and Abuela framed it and I can't look at it without misting up. My mother's not wearing her fakies in it; she looks so thin I don't even recognize her.

Just know that I would die for you, she told me the last time we talked. And before I could say anything she hung up.

But that's not what I wanted to tell you. It's about that crazy feeling that started this whole mess, the bruja feeling that comes singing out of my bones, that takes hold of me the way blood seizes cotton. The feeling that tells me that everything in my life is about to change. It's come back. Just the other day I woke up from all these dreams and it was there, pulsing inside of me. I imagine this is what it feels like to have a child in you. At first I was scared, because I thought it was telling me to run away again, but every time I looked around our house, every time I saw my abuela the feeling got stronger, so I knew this was something different.

105   I was dating a boy by then, a sweet morenito[9] by the name of Max Sánchez, who I had met in Los Mina while visiting Rosio. He's short, but his smile and his snappy dressing make up for a lot. Because I'm from

9. Literally, *moreno* (brown) plus *-ito* (a diminutive suffix) equals "little brown" (Spanish), that is, a little brown-skinned boy.

Nueba Yol[1] he talks about how rich he's going to become and I try to explain to him that I don't care about that, but he looks at me like I'm crazy. I'm going to get a white Mercedes-Benz, he says. Tú verás.[2] But it's the job he has that I love best, that got me and him started. In Santo Domingo two or three theatres often share the same set of reels for a movie, so when the first theatre finishes with the first reel they put it in Max's hands and he rides his motorcycle like crazy to make it to the second theatre and then he drives back, waits, picks up the second reel, and so on. If he's held up or gets into an accident the first reel will end and there will be no second reel and the people in the audience will throw bottles. So far he's been blessed, he tells me while kissing his San Miguel[3] medal. Because of me, he brags, one movie becomes three. I'm the man who puts together the pictures. Max is not from la clase alta,[4] as my abuela would describe it, and if any of the stuck-up bitches in school saw us they would just about die, but I'm fond of him. He holds open doors, he calls me his morena; when he's feeling brave he touches my arm gently and then pulls back.

Anyway I thought maybe the feeling was about Max, and so one day I let him take me to one of the love motels. He was so excited he almost fell off the bed, and the first thing he wanted was to look at my ass. I never knew my big ass could be such a star attraction, but he kissed it, four, five times, gave me goose bumps with his breath, and pronounced it a tesoro. When we were done and he was in the bathroom washing himself I stood in front of the mirror naked and looked at my culo for the first time. A tesoro,[5] I repeated. A treasure.

Well? Rosio asked at school. And I nodded once, quickly, and she grabbed me and laughed and all the girls I hated turned to look, but what could they do? Happiness, when it comes, is stronger than all the jerk girls in Santo Domingo combined.

But I was still confused. Because the feeling, it just kept getting stronger and stronger, wouldn't let me sleep, wouldn't give me any peace. I started losing races, which was something I never did.

You ain't so great, are you, gringa,[6] the girls on the other teams hissed at me, and I could only hang my head. Coach Cortés was so unhappy he just locked himself in his car and wouldn't say anything to any of us.

---

1. New York City (Spanish).
2. You'll see (Spanish).
3. St. Michael (Spanish), leader of God's army and angel of death, who ensures the redeemed soul's safe passage to heaven.
4. The upper class (Spanish).
5. Treasure (Spanish). *Culo*: ass (Spanish).
6. English-speaking foreigner (Spanish).

110   The whole thing was driving me crazy, and then one night I came home from being out with Max. He had taken me for a walk along the Malecón[7]— he never had money for anything else—and we had watched the bats zig-zagging over the palms and an old ship head into the distance. While I stretched my hamstrings, he talked quietly about moving to the U.S. My abuela was waiting for me at the living-room table. Even though she still wears black to mourn the husband she lost when she was young she's one of the most handsome women I've ever known. We have the same jagged lightning-bolt part, and when I saw her at the airport, the first time in ten years, I didn't want to admit it but I knew that things were going to be O.K. between us. She stood like she was her own best thing[8] and when she saw me she said, Hija, I have waited for you since the day you left. And then she hugged me and kissed me and said, I'm your abuela, but you can call me La Inca.[9]

Standing over her that night, her part like a crack in her hair, I felt a surge of tenderness. I put my arms around her and that was when I noticed that she was looking at photos. Old photos, the kind I'd never seen in my house. Photos of my mother when she was young, before she had her breasts. She was even skinnier than me! I picked the smallest photo up. Mami was standing in front of a bakery. Even with an apron on she looked potent, like someone who was going to be someone.

She was very guapa, I said casually.

Abuela snorted. Guapa soy yo. Your mother was a diosa. But so cabeza dura. When she was your age we never got along. She was cabeza dura and I was . . . exigente.[1] You and her are more alike than you think.

I know she ran away. From you. From Santo Domingo.

115   La Inca stared at me, incredulous. Your mother didn't run away. We had to *send* her away. To keep her from being murdered. To keep us all from being murdered. She didn't listen and she fell in love with the wrong man. She didn't listen. Jesu Cristo, hija—

She was about to say something more and then she stopped.

---

7. Santo Domingo's world-famous oceanfront promenade.
8. Perhaps an allusion to Toni Morrison's novel *Beloved* (1987), in which a man works to convince his lover, a mother grieving for her children, that she, not they, is her "own best thing." In interviews, Díaz has referred to his "relationship with" Morrison's work as "the most sustained love of mine, the one that's carried me through all these years."
9. The Incan (Spanish), a noble, member, or follower of the Indian peoples who established, in what is now Peru, pre-Columbia America's largest empire (c. thirteenth century through 1572).
1. Demanding. *Guapa soy yo*: I am pretty or attractive. *Diosa*: goddess. *Cabeza dura*: hard-headed (all Spanish).

And that's when it hit with the force of a hurricane. The *feeling*. My abuela was sitting there, forlorn, trying to cobble together the right words, and I could not move or breathe. I felt like I always did in the last seconds of a race, when I was sure that I was going to explode. She was about to say something and I was waiting for whatever she was going to give me. I was waiting to begin.

2007

POETRY

Edna St. Vincent Millay

POETRY
Reading, Responding, Writing

Ways of reading poetry and reasons for doing so differ almost as widely as poems themselves, and in ways we can perhaps best appreciate by considering poetry's functions in other times and places. Though you might be aware, for example, that medieval noblemen paid courtly "bards" to commemorate their achievements and thereby help them to maintain their own prestige and power, you might be surprised to learn that since 2007 millions of people across the Middle East have tuned in to watch *Prince of Poets*, a reality show in which poets rather than pop singers compete for audience votes.

Such phenomena might come as a surprise to us simply because today, at least in the West, we don't tend to think of poetry as having great popular appeal or political potency. Millions of us may be moved by the way hip-hop artists use rhyme and rhythm to boast about, or "celebrate and sing," themselves; to show us the danger and excitement of life on the streets; or even to get out the vote. Yet "poetry" seems to many of us a thing apart, something either to suffer, to cherish, or to simply be baffled and intimidated by precisely because it seems so arcane, so different and difficult, so essentially irrelevant to the rest of our lives. Though one rarely hears anyone say of all fiction either "I hate it" or "I love it" or "I just don't get it," if you're like most people, you've probably said, thought, or heard someone else say at least one of these things about poetry.

This chapter and the ones that follow welcome poetry-lovers. But they neither require you to be one nor aim to convert you. They do, we hope, demonstrate a few key points:

- Poetry itself isn't all one thing: *Poems differ as much as the people who write and read them, or as much as music and movies do.* They can be by turns goofy, sad, or angry; they can tell a story, comment on current events, or simply describe the look of a certain time of day. Deciding that you "love," "hate," "get," or "don't get" all poetry based on your experience of one poem or of one kind of poetry is a little like either deciding you love all music because Mozart moves you or giving up on music entirely because Lady Gaga leaves you cold.
- *A good poem is not a secret message one needs a special decoder ring or an advanced degree to decipher.* Any thoughtful person who's willing to try can make sense of it, though some poems certainly do

invite us to rethink our idea of what "making sense" might mean. Poetry has spoken to millions of ordinary people across the centuries and around the world, so at least some poems can speak to us, too, if we give both them and ourselves a chance. By the same token, even the most devoted, experienced poetry lovers among us can become better, more responsive, more thoughtful readers by simply reading more and different kinds of poetry and by exploring, as the following chapters do, the various elements and techniques with which poetry is made.

- People around the world have often turned to poetry to express their feelings and longings precisely because *poetry is, in certain vital ways, distinct from other forms of writing.* Each genre plays by its own rules and has its own history and traditions, so reading poetry effectively, like succeeding in a video game, does involve learning and playing by certain rules. Any one poem may open itself to multiple responses and interpretations, just as a game may allow you many ways of advancing to the next level. But in both cases there are limits. Neither is a free-for-all in which "anything goes." (In both cases, too, some difficulty can be essential to the fun.) *A poem wouldn't mean anything if it could mean everything.*

- *Yet the questions we ask of a poem and the techniques we use to understand it are simply variations of the same ones we use in reading fiction or drama.* Indeed, some poems narrate action just as a short story does; others work much like plays.

- Finally, *poems aren't nearly as fragile as we take them to be when we worry about "over-reading" or "analyzing them to death."* You can't kill a poem. But a poem does experience a sort of living death if it's not read, re-read, and pondered over. Poems need you. Not only can they bear the weight of your careful attention, but they also deserve it: the best of them are, after all, the result of someone else's. William Wordsworth may have done much to shape our contemporary ideas about poetry when he famously described it as "the spontaneous overflow of powerful feelings," but his own poems were, like most great poems, the result of weeks, even years, of writing and revision.

DEFINING POETRY

But what, after all, is poetry? Trying to define poetry is a bit like trying to catch a snowflake; you can do it, but at the very same moment, the snowflake begins to melt and disappear. With poems, as with fiction, one can always come up with particular examples that don't do what the definition insists they must, as well as numerous writers and readers who will disagree. Yet to claim that poetry eludes all definition is merely to reinforce the idea that it is simply too mysterious for ordinary mortals. Without being all-sufficient or entirely

satisfying, a dictionary definition can at least give us a starting point. Here
are two such definitions of poetry:

1. Writing that formulates a *concentrated* imaginative awareness of experience in language chosen and *arranged* to create a specific *emotional
   response* through meaning, sound, and *rhythm.* (*Merriam-Webster*)
2. Composition in verse or some comparable *patterned arrangement* of
   language in which the expression of *feelings* and ideas is given *intensity* by the use of distinctive style and *rhythm*[. . .] . Traditionally associated with explicit formal departure from the *patterns* of ordinary
   speech or prose, e.g., in the use of elevated diction, figurative language, and syntactical reordering. (*The Oxford English Dictionary*)

Different as they are, both of these definitions stress four elements: 1) the "patterned arrangement of language" to 2) generate "rhythm" and thereby both
3) express and evoke specific "emotion[s]" or "feelings" in 4) a "concentrated"
way, or with "intensity."

But what does all that really mean? To test drive this definition, let's look at
an example. And let's pick a tough one: HEAD, HEART, taken from *The Collected Stories of Lydia Davis*, is usually classified as a work of fiction, and it
certainly does have the elements of one, including **characters** and some **action**
arranged into a **plot** brought to us by a **narrator.** Yet one reviewer of Davis's
Collected Stories tellingly describes this one as "a poem of a story." What specific features of the following story might make it work like a poem? Which, if
any, of the features essential to poetry might it lack?

LYDIA DAVIS
Head, Heart

Heart weeps.
Head tries to help heart.
Head tells heart how it is, again:
You will lose the ones you love. They will all go. But even the earth
    will go, someday.
5 Heart feels better, then.
But the words of head do not remain long in the ears of heart.
Heart is so new to this.
I want them back, says heart.
Head is all heart has.
10 Help, head. Help heart.

2007

If difficulty were essential to poetry, "Head, Heart" would not seem to qualify. It's hard to imagine less formal, even less elementary, **diction** or **syntax.**

And the whole seems relatively easy to paraphrase (often a helpful thing to do when first encountering a poem): When we're sad about losing someone we love, we reason with ourselves that loss is inevitable because everything earthly, even the earth itself, can't last forever. Such rational explanations give us comfort, but that comfort is itself temporary; we still miss those we've lost and have to keep calling on our heads to help our hearts cope.

We do have emotion here, then, as well as a **conflict** between emotion and reason—and even when they lack plots, most poems do explore conflicts, just as stories and plays do. But do we have a poem? Does it matter that "Head, Heart" depends entirely on two **figures of speech**—**metonymy**, the use of the name of one thing for another closely associated thing (here, "head" for "reason," and "heart" for "emotion"), as well as **personification**, the representation of an object or an abstraction (here, "head" and "heart") as a person (capable of weeping and talking, for example)? Though fiction and drama both use figurative language, we often describe such language as "poetic," even when it occurs in a story or play, because poems do tend to depend much more on it (as we discuss further in ch. 11).

Does it matter that "Head, Heart" is short—just seventy-one words? Though poems come in every size, many poems are short or at least shorter than the typical work of fiction. Brevity is one way that *some* poems achieve the "concentration" and "intensity" the dictionaries take to be essential. Such concentration invites, even requires, ours. As poet Billy Collins puts it, "Poetry offers us the possibility of modulating our pace." The very brevity of a poem can teach us simply to slow down for a moment and pay attention—not only to the details within the poem, but also, through them, to whatever in the world or in ourselves the poem attends to. Sometimes that's all a poem does—simply invites us to pay attention to something we wouldn't notice otherwise.

Regardless of their overall length, moreover, almost all poems concentrate our attention and modulate our pace by doling out words a few at a time, arranging them not just into sentences (as in prose), but into discreet **lines**. One result is much more blank space and thus more silences and pauses than in prose. For this reason alone, "Head, Heart" looks and works like a poem. And the deliberateness with which it does so is signaled by the fact that one of its sentences is divided so as to span multiple lines. (Line 3 ends with a colon, not a period.) By arranging words into lines and, often, into **stanzas**, the poet, not a typesetter or printer, determines where words fall on the page. And that perhaps is the most important aspect of that arrangement of language that has differentiated poetry from prose since poetry became a written, as well as spoken, art (an issue discussed further in ch. 15). All printings of a poem, if accurate, reproduce exactly the same breaks and space the words precisely the same way on the page.

AUTHORS ON THEIR CRAFT
BILLY COLLINS ON THE POET AS "LINE-MAKER"

From "A Brisk Walk: An Interview with Billy Collins" (2006)*

I'm a line-maker. I think that's what makes poets different from prose-writers. [. . .] We think not just in sentences the way prose writers do but also in lines. [. . .] When I'm constructing a poem, I'm trying to write one good line after another. [. . .] I'm not thinking of just writing a paragraph and then chopping it up. I'm very conscious of the fact that every line should have a cadence to it. It should contribute to the progress of the poem. And that the ending of the line is a way of turning the reader's attention back into the interior of the poem.

*"A Brisk Walk: An Interview with Billy Collins." Interview by Joel Whitney. *Guernica*, 14 June 2006, www.guernicamag.com/interviews/a_brisk_walk/.

One result is that line endings and beginnings inevitably get more of our attention, bear more oomph and meaning. Notice how many of the lines of "Head, Heart" begin with *head* and *heart* and how these words repeat in a pattern (*Heart, Head, Head, Heart, Heart, Head*—and then *Help*), as if the line-beginnings themselves enact the same interplay between "head" and "heart" that the sentences describe. Conversely, certain end-words reverberate: *again*, for example, suggests the repetitive familiarity of this conflict, one that paradoxically seems all the more difficult or poignant because it's both repetitive (each person goes through this again and again) and familiar (all of us go through this); *then* alerts us to the temporariness of the comfort head offers heart, preparing us for the *But* in the next line.

Again and *then* also reverberate in us and with each other because they **rhyme**, just as *head, heart,* and *help* **alliterate**. These words share a special aural, as well as spatial and visual, relationship to each other. Though prose writers certainly make their appeal to us in part through sound, poetry remains, as it has been for thousands of years, a more insistently aural form—one that appeals through aural patterning to what Davis here humorously, but not wrongly, calls "the ears of heart" (line 6). As poet Mary Oliver puts it, "To make a poem, we must make sounds. Not random sounds, but chosen sounds."

But are there qualities essential to poetry that "Head, Heart" lacks? Is it, for example, sufficiently aural in its appeal? Does it have genuine rhythm? Perhaps so, perhaps not. As you work your way through the rest of the chapters in this section and read more poems, we encourage you to keep thinking critically about our definitions in order to hone your own sense of just what poetry is, how it works, and what it does.

POETIC SUBGENRES AND KINDS

All poems share some common elements, use some of the same techniques, and thus require us to ask some of the same questions. Later in this chapter, we'll outline some of the steps you can follow and some of the questions you can pose as you read, respond to, and write about any poem. But different sorts of poems also work by slightly different rules and thus invite somewhat different responses and questions.

Poems may be classified into subgenres based on various characteristics, including their length, appearance, and formal features (patterns of rhyme and rhythm, for example); their subject; or even the type of **situation** and **setting** (time and place) they depict. (A **sonnet**, for example, has fourteen lines. Defined broadly, an **elegy** is simply any poem about death.) A single poem might well represent multiple subgenres or at least might contain elements of more than one. (One could write an elegy that is also a sonnet, for instance.)

Since Aristotle's time, however, readers and writers have also often divided poems into three broad categories or subgenres—**narrative, dramatic**, or **lyric**—based upon their mode of presentation. Put simply, poems that have a plot are either narrative poems (if they feature a narrator) or dramatic poems (if they don't), and many poems that lack a plot are lyrics. The rest of this section describes each of these subgenres in more detail, starting with the one that most resembles fiction and ending with the dramatic monologue, a sort of hybrid that combines features of both dramatic and lyric poetry.

As the dramatic monologue demonstrates, the borders between narrative, dramatic, and lyric poetry are fuzzy, contestable, and shifting. Some poems will cross those borders; others will resist these categories altogether. And the very definition of lyric poetry has not only changed over time, but also remains contested today. The ultimate goal isn't to definitively pigeonhole every poem but rather to develop a language through which to recognize, describe, and explore different poetic modes. Knowing which mode dominates in a particular poem can help ensure that we privilege the right questions as we read and write about it. Learning the conventions of particular subgenres and kinds allows us to better adjust to individual poems, to compare them to each other, and to appreciate how each creatively uses and reworks generic conventions.

Narrative Poetry

Like a work of prose fiction, a narrative poem tells a story; in other words, it has a plot related by a narrator, though its plot might be based on actual rather than made-up events. Comprising the same elements discussed in the Fiction section of this book, a narrative poem encourages us to ask the same questions—about character, plot, narration, and so on—that we do when reading a short story or novel. (See "Questions about the Elements of Fiction" in "Fiction: Reading, Responding, Writing.")

In centuries past, narrative poetry was a—even *the*—dominant subgenre of poetry. As a result, there are many different kinds of narrative poems, including book-length **epics** like Homer's *Iliad*; chivalric **romances** like Thomas Malory's *Le Morte d'Arthur*; grisly murder **ballads**, often rooted in actual events; and a range of harder-to-classify works of varying lengths such as the relatively short example below.

EDWIN ARLINGTON ROBINSON
Richard Cory

Whenever Richard Cory went down town,
We people on the pavement looked at him:
He was a gentleman from sole to crown,
Clean favored, and imperially slim.

5 And he was always quietly arrayed,
And he was always human when he talked;
But still he fluttered pulses when he said,
"Good-morning," and he glittered when he walked.

And he was rich—yes, richer than a king—
10 And admirably schooled in every grace:
In fine,[1] we thought that he was everything
To make us wish that we were in his place.

So on we worked, and waited for the light,
And went without the meat, and cursed the bread;
15 And Richard Cory, one calm summer night,
Went home and put a bullet through his head.

                                    1897

- How does the poem characterize Richard Cory? What is the effect of the first-personal plural narration?
- What details in the poem's first three stanzas might make its final stanza simultaneously surprising, ironic, and predictable?

1. In conclusion, in sum.

Dramatic Poetry

For centuries, plays were written exclusively or mainly in verse; as a result, drama itself was understood not as a genre in its own right (as we think of it today) but rather as a subgenre of poetry. "Dramatic poetry" thus meant and still can mean actual plays in verse (or *verse drama*). But any poem that consists wholly of dialogue among characters, unmediated by a narrator, counts as a dramatic poem. And we might even apply that label to poems like the following in which narration is kept to the barest minimum. Indeed, this narrator's only words are "said she," and since every other word in the poem is spoken by one female character to another, the poem essentially reads like a scene from a play. Notice, though, that the poem also depends on techniques of formal organization and patterning unique to poetry: In each of the poem's six stanzas, for example, one woman speaks the first lines, while her companion gets the last line (or two).

THOMAS HARDY
The Ruined Maid

"O 'Melia,[2] my dear, this does everything crown!
Who could have supposed I should meet you in Town?
And whence such fair garments, such prosperi-ty?"—
"O didn't you know I'd been ruined?" said she.

5 —"You left us in tatters, without shoes or socks,
Tired of digging potatoes, and spudding up docks;[3]
And now you've gay bracelets and bright feathers three!"—
"Yes: that's how we dress when we're ruined," said she.

—"At home in the barton[4] you said 'thee' and 'thou,'
10 And 'thik oon,' and 'theäs oon,' and 't'other'; but now
Your talking quite fits 'ee for high compa-ny!"—
"Some polish is gained with one's ruin," said she.

—"Your hands were like paws then, your face blue and bleak
But now I'm bewitched by your delicate cheek,
15 And your little gloves fit as on any la-dy!"—
"We never do work when we're ruined," said she.

—"You used to call home-life a hag-ridden dream,
And you'd sigh, and you'd sock;[5] but at present you seem
To know not of megrims[6] or melancho-ly!"—
20 "True. One's pretty lively when ruined," said she.

2. Short for Amelia.   3. Spading up weeds.   4. Farmyard.   5. Sigh (English dialect).
6. Migraine headaches.

—"I wish I had feathers, a fine sweeping gown,
And a delicate face, and could strut about Town!"—
"My dear—a raw country girl, such as you be,
Cannot quite expect that. You ain't ruined," said she.

1866

When we read and write about dramatic poems, we can usefully bring to
bear the same questions we do in reading drama. (See "Questions to Ask When
Reading a Play" in "Drama: Reading, Responding, Writing.") But when it
comes to short poems like THE RUINED MAID, questions about sets, staging,
and even plot will usually be much less relevant than those related to character and conflict, as well as setting, tone, language, symbol, and theme. In
Hardy's poem, for example, how are each of the two speakers characterized by
how they speak, as well as *what* they say? How is our view of them, and especially of 'Melia, "the ruined maid," affected by the formal pattern mentioned
earlier, which ensures (among other things) that she gets the last line? How
might this pattern, along with rhythm and rhyme, also add **irony** to the poem?

Lyric Poetry

For good historical reasons, lyric poems probably best fulfill your expectations of what poetry should be like. Yet lyric poetry has been and still is
defined in myriad ways. The word *lyric* derives from the ancient Greeks, for
whom it designated a short poem chanted or sung by a single singer to the
accompaniment of a stringed instrument called a lyre (hence, the word *lyric*
and the fact that we today also use the word *lyrics* to denote the words of
any song). Scholars believe that the earliest "lyrics" in the Greek sense were
likely associated with religious occasions and feelings, especially those
related to celebration, praise, and mourning. Ever since, the lyric has been
associated with brevity, musicality, a single speaker, and the expression of
intense feeling. Not surprisingly, at least a few specific kinds of lyric, including the **ode** and the **elegy**, originated in the ancient world.

Over the centuries, the lyric's boundaries have expanded and become
less clear. Few lyrics are intended to be sung at all, much less to a lyre. But
everyone agrees that relatively short poems that focus primarily on the
feelings, impressions, and thoughts—that is, on the subjective, inward
experience—of a single first-person speaker are lyrics.

Below are two examples very different from each other in subject matter
and tone. Yet with these, as with all lyrics, our initial questions in both reading and writing will likely focus on each speaker's situation and inward
experience of it. What is each speaker experiencing, feeling, and thinking,
and how exactly does the poem make that state of mood and mind at once
vivid and relevant to us?

WILLIAM WORDSWORTH
[I wandered lonely as a cloud]

I wandered lonely as a cloud
That floats on high o'er vales and hills,
When all at once I saw a crowd,
A host, of golden daffodils;
5 Beside the lake, beneath the trees,
Fluttering and dancing in the breeze.

Continuous as the stars that shine
And twinkle on the milky way,
They stretched in never-ending line
10 Along the margin of a bay:
Ten thousand saw I at a glance,
Tossing their heads in sprightly dance.

The waves beside them danced; but they
Out-did the sparkling waves in glee:
15 A poet could not but be gay,
In such a jocund company:
I gazed—and gazed—but little thought
What wealth the show to me had brought:

For oft, when on my couch I lie
20 In vacant or in pensive mood,
They flash upon that inward eye
Which is the bliss of solitude;
And then my heart with pleasure fills,
And dances with the daffodils.

1807

• According to the speaker, what is "the bliss of solitude" (line 22)?
  Why and how does "solitude" become less "lonely" for him (line 1)?
• What about the relationship between human beings and nature might
  be implied by the speaker's description of his particular experience?

FRANK O'HARA
Poem

Lana Turner[7] has collapsed!
I was trotting along and suddenly
it started raining and snowing
and you said it was hailing
5 but hailing hits you on the head
hard so it was really snowing and
raining and I was in such a hurry
to meet you but the traffic
was acting exactly like the sky
10 and suddenly I see a headline
LANA TURNER HAS COLLAPSED!
there is no snow in Hollywood
there is no rain in California
I have been to lots of parties
15 and acted perfectly disgraceful
but I never actually collapsed
oh Lana Turner we love you get up
                                        1962

- What or whom exactly does this poem seem to make fun of? Does the poem also convey more serious sentiments?
- What current celebrity seems to you like the best potential substitute for Lana Turner? What about both this celebrity's public persona and the poem itself make your choice seem especially appropriate?

What makes these lyrics different from narrative and dramatic poems? Though both include action ("wander[ing]," "trotting," and so on), that action doesn't quite add up to a plot; what we have might be better described as a situation, scene, or incident. Similarly, though the poems vividly describe external things, from "golden daffodils" to "traffic," greater emphasis ultimately falls on how the "I" experiences and feels about them—the internal, subjective experience or state of mind and mood that those outward things inspire or reflect. Both poems thus encourage us to focus almost exclusively on the complex emotional experience and thoughts of a particular speaker in a specific situation, but ones that we can, if the poem is effective, ultimately understand as having a much wider, sometimes even universal, resonance and relevance.

7. American actress (1921–95); in 1958, Turner's lover was stabbed to death by her daughter, who was determined to have acted in self-defense.

Most lyrics require us to infer a general theme from a specific experience, but some offer more explicit reflection, commentary, even argument. As you read the following example, notice what happens in line 5 (exactly halfway through the poem), as the speaker turns from personal statements to more impersonal, argumentative ones. How does personal reflection relate to, even enable, argument here?

PHILLIS WHEATLEY
On Being Brought from Africa to America

'Twas mercy brought me from my Pagan land,
Taught my benighted soul to understand
That there's a God, that there's a Saviour too:
Once I redemption neither sought nor knew.
5 Some view our sable race with scornful eye,
"Their colour is a diabolic die."
Remember, Christians, Negroes, black as Cain,[8]
May be refin'd, and join th' angelic train.

1773

- What do the poem's first four lines imply about how the speaker feels about "being brought from Africa to America" and about what motivates these feelings?
- What two "view[s]" of Africans are contrasted in the last four lines (line 5)? According to the entire poem, which is the right view, and why and how so?

Descriptive or Observational Lyrics

As Wheatley's poem demonstrates, lyrics come in many varieties. Quite a few are more exclusively descriptive or observational than the examples above, insofar as they describe something or someone to us without bringing much attention to the speaker's personal state of mind or feelings. As we've noted, after all, some poems simply give us the opportunity to look more closely and carefully at something in the world around us. Nineteenth-century poet Percy Bysshe Shelley suggested, in fact, that all poetry's major purpose is just that—helping us see in a new way. Poetry, he said, "strips the veil of familiarity from the world, and lays bare [its] naked and sleeping beauty" and "wonder." Over a century later, American poet James Dickey expressed a similar idea somewhat differently when he defined a poet as "someone who notices and is enormously taken by things that somebody else would walk by."

8. One of Adam's sons, who killed his brother Abel. (See Gen. 4.)

Obviously, any descriptive poem inevitably reflects its speaker's point of view. Yet lyrics of this type invite us to focus more on what they describe than on the subjective, internal experience or feelings of the speaker doing the describing. As a result, our focus in reading and writing will probably be how the poem characterizes, and encourages us to see, think, and feel about, whatever it describes—whether a moment, a person, an object, or a phenomenon. What is described in each of the poems that follow? What figures of speech are used, and with what implications and effects?

EMILY DICKINSON
[The Sky is low—the Clouds are mean]

The Sky is low—the Clouds are mean.
A Travelling Flake of Snow
Across a Barn or through a Rut
Debates if it will go—
5 A Narrow Wind complains all Day
How some one treated him
Nature, like Us, is sometimes caught
Without her Diadem—

1866

• Whom does the speaker seem to mean by "Us," and what might this poem imply about the similarity between "Nature" and "Us" (line 7)?

BILLY COLLINS
Divorce

Once, two spoons in bed,
now tined forks

across a granite table
and the knives they have hired.

2008

• This poem consists almost entirely of **metaphor** (implied comparison). What is compared to what here? How would you describe the poem's **tone**? (Is it funny, sad, bitter, or some combination of these?) Why and how so?

The Dramatic Monologue

Finally, we come to the **dramatic monologue**, a subgenre of poem that—by residing somewhere in between lyric and dramatic poetry—can teach us more about both. Robert Browning, the nineteenth-century British poet often credited with inventing this kind of poem, tellingly labeled his own works "dramatic lyrics," describing them as "dramatic in principle," "lyric in expression." On the one hand, the dramatic monologue is "lyric in expression" or like a lyric poem because it features a single speaker who discusses him- or herself. On the other hand, it is "dramatic in principle" or resembles a scene from a play for at least two reasons. First, the poem's primary focus is characterization, an obviously fictional or historical speaker's often unintentional revelation of his or her personality, outlook, and values. Such poems tend to offer us a window into an entire, complex psychology and even life history rather than simply one experience or feeling of a speaker we otherwise discover little about (as in lyrics). Often, too, dramatic monologues invite us to see their speakers and situations somewhat differently than the speakers themselves do, much as does fiction narrated by *unreliable narrators*. Second, the speaker of a dramatic monologue often addresses one or more silent **auditors** whose identity we can only infer from the speaker's words *to* them. The questions we pose in reading and writing about such poems thus often center on character and characterization and on the gap between our perception of the speaker and his or her situation, on the one hand, and the speaker's own self-representation, on the other.

Invented in the nineteenth century, this subgenre remains as popular with contemporary songwriters as with contemporary poets. Bruce Springsteen's albums *Nebraska* (1982) and *The Rising* (2002), for instance, consist mainly of dramatic monologues. Below, you will find the lyrics to one of these, followed by a poem that takes the form of an imaginary letter, thus putting an interesting twist on the conventions regarding "speakers" and "auditors."

BRUCE SPRINGSTEEN
Nebraska

I saw her standin' on her front lawn
    just twirlin' her baton
Me and her went for a ride, sir, and ten
    innocent people died

5 From the town of Lincoln, Nebraska,
    with a sawed-off .410 on my lap
Through the badlands of Wyoming I
    killed everything in my path

I can't say that I'm sorry for the things
10 that we done
At least for a little while, sir, me and
her we had us some fun

The jury brought in a guilty verdict and
the judge he sentenced me to death
15 Midnight in a prison storeroom with
leather straps across my chest

Sheriff, when the man pulls that
switch, sir, and snaps my poor head back
You make sure my pretty baby is sittin'
20   right there on my lap

They declared me unfit to live, said into
that great void my soul'd be hurled
They wanted to know why I did what I did
Well, sir, I guess there's just a meanness in this world[9]

1982

- What different motives and explanations for the speaker's actions might NEBRASKA provide by means of what he says, how he speaks, and how his speech is rendered on the page? Might the song as a whole offer explanations that the speaker doesn't offer, at least consciously or directly?

ROBERT HAYDEN
A Letter from Phillis Wheatley

(London, 1773)

Dear Obour[1]
        Our crossing was without
event. I could not help, at times,
reflecting on that first—my Destined—
5 voyage long ago (I yet
have some remembrance of its Horrors)[2]

---

9. Allusion to words spoken by a murderer in Flannery O'Connor's "A Good Man Is Hard to Find" (par. 134).

1. Obour Tanner, a Rhode Island slave and Wheatley's intimate friend and frequent correspondent.

2. Born in Africa c. 1753–54, Wheatley was taken at around age eight on the slave ship *Phillis* to America, where she was purchased by Boston merchant John Wheatley. In 1773, John Wheatley sent her to London with his son, Nathaniel, a visit at least partly motivated by concerns about her health.

and marvelling at God's Ways.
Last evening, her Ladyship³ presented me
to her illustrious Friends.
10 I scarce could tell them anything
of Africa, though much of Boston
and my hope of Heaven. I read
my latest Elegies to them.
"O Sable Muse!" the Countess cried,
15 embracing me, when I had done.
I held back tears, as is my wont,
and there were tears in Dear
Nathaniel's eyes.
    At supper—I dined apart
20 like captive Royalty—
the Countess and her Guests promised
signatures affirming me
True Poetess, albeit once a slave.⁴
Indeed, they were most kind, and spoke,
25 moreover, of presenting me
at Court (I thought of Pocahontas)⁵—
an Honor, to be sure, but one,
I should, no doubt, as Patriot decline.
    My health is much improved;
30 I feel I may, if God so Wills,
entirely recover here.
Idyllic England! Alas, there is
no Eden without its Serpent. Beneath
chiming Complaisance I hear him hiss;
35 I see his flickering tongue
when foppish would-be Wits
murmur of the Yankee Pedlar
and his Cannibal Mockingbird.
    Sister, forgive th'intrusion of
40 my Sombreness—Nocturnal Mood
I would not share with any save
your trusted Self. Let me disperse,

---

3. Selina Hastings, Countess of Huntingdon (1707–91), helped arrange publication of Wheatley's first book of poems, which appeared in London just months after the poet's return to the United States.
4. Wheatley's *Poems on Various Subjects, Religious and Moral* (1773) was prefaced by a letter, signed by seventeen eminent Bostonians, attesting to the poems' authenticity.
5. Daughter of an Algonquian Indian chief (c. 1595–1617), Pocahontas famously befriended Virginia's first English colonists, led by Captain John Smith; she died while visiting England, where she had been presented at the court of King James I.

in closing, such unseemly Gloom
by mention of an Incident
45 you may, as I, consider Droll:
Today, a little Chimney Sweep,
his face and hands with soot quite Black,
staring hard at me, politely asked:
"Does you, M'lady, sweep chimneys too?"
50 I was amused, but Dear Nathaniel
(ever Solicitous) was not.
   I pray the Blessings of Our Lord
   and Saviour Jesus Christ
   will Abundantly be yours.
55   Phillis
                 1977

- What internal and external conflicts seem to be revealed here? What conflict does Wheatley herself seem aware of? Why might Hayden have chosen both this particular moment in Wheatley's life and this particular addressee (Obour Tanner)?
- How does Hayden's portrayal of both Wheatley's feelings and others' views of her compare to Wheatley's own characterization of these in ON BEING BROUGHT FROM AFRICA TO AMERICA?

RESPONDING TO POETRY

Not all poems are as readily accessible as those in this chapter, and even those that are take on additional meanings if we approach them systematically, bringing to bear specific reading habits and skills and some knowledge of poetic genres and traditions. Experience will give you a sense of what to expect, but knowing what to expect isn't everything. As a reader of poetry, you should always be open—to new experiences, new feelings, new ideas, new forms of expression. Every poem is a potential new experience, and you will often discover something new with every re-reading.

Steps to Follow, Questions to Ask, and Sample Reading Notes

No one can give you a method that will offer you total experience of all poems. But because individual poems share characteristics with other poems, taking certain steps can prompt you both to ask the right questions and to devise compelling answers. If you are relatively new to poetry, encounter a poem that seems especially difficult, or plan to write about a poem, you may need to tackle these steps one at a time, pausing to write even as you read and respond. With further experience, you will often find that you can skip steps or run through them quickly and almost automatically, though your experience and understanding of any poem will be enriched if you slow down and take your time.

Try the first step on your own, then we will both detail and demonstrate the others.

1. **Listen to a poem first.** When you encounter a new poem, try reading it through once without thinking too much about what it means. Try to simply listen to the poem, even if you read silently, and much as you might a song on the radio. Or better yet, read it aloud. Doing so will help you hear the poem's sound qualities, get a clearer impression of its **tone**, and start making sense of its **syntax**, the way words combine into sentences.

APHRA BEHN
On Her Loving Two Equally

I

How strongly does my passion flow,
Divided equally twixt[6] two?
Damon had ne'er subdued my heart
Had not Alexis took his part;
5 Nor could Alexis powerful prove,
Without my Damon's aid, to gain my love.

II

When my Alexis present is,
Then I for Damon sigh and mourn;
But when Alexis I do miss,
10 Damon gains nothing but my scorn.
But if it chance they both are by,
For both alike I languish, sigh, and die.

III

Cure then, thou mighty wingèd god,[7]
This restless fever in my blood:
15 One golden-pointed dart take back:
But which, O Cupid, wilt thou take?
If Damon's, all my hopes are crossed;
Or that of my Alexis, I am lost.

1684

6. Between.
7. Cupid, who, according to myth, shot darts of lead and of gold at the hearts of lovers, corresponding to false love and true love, respectively.

Now that you've read Behn's poem, read through the remaining steps and see how one reader used them as a guide for responding. Later, return to these steps as you read and respond to other poems.

2. **Articulate your expectations, starting with the title.** Poets often try to surprise readers, but you can appreciate such surprises only if you first define your expectations. As you read a poem, take note of what you expect and where, when, and how the poem fulfills, or perhaps frustrates, your expectations.

> The title of Aphra Behn's "On Her Loving Two Equally" makes me think the poem will be about a woman. But can someone really "love two equally"? Maybe this is the question the poem will ask. If so, I expect its answer to be "no" because I don't think this is possible. If so, maybe the title is a sort of pun—"On Her Loving *Too* Equally."

3. **Read the syntax literally.** What the sentences literally say is only a starting point, but it is vital. You cannot begin to explore what a poem means unless you first know what it says. Though poets arrange words into lines and stanzas, they usually write in complete sentences, just as writers in other genres do. At the same time and partly in order to create the sort of aural and visual patterns discussed earlier in this chapter, poets make much more frequent use of **inversion** (a change in normal word order or syntax). To ensure you don't misread, first "translate" the poem rather than fixing on certain words and free-associating or leaping to conclusions. To translate accurately, especially with poems written before the twentieth century, you may need to break this step down into the following smaller steps:

a. *Identify sentences.* For now, ignore the line breaks and look for sentences or independent clauses (word groups that can function as complete sentences). These will typically be preceded and followed by a period (.), a semicolon (;), a colon (:), or a dash (—).

> The eighteen lines of Behn's poem can be broken down into nine sentences.
> 1. How strongly does my passion flow, Divided equally twixt two?
> 2. Damon had ne'er subdued my heart, Had not Alexis took his part;
> 3. Nor could Alexis powerful prove, Without my Damon's aid, to gain my love.
> 4. When my Alexis present is, Then I for Damon sigh and mourn;
> 5. But when Alexis I do miss, Damon gains nothing but my scorn.
> 6. But if it chance they both are by, For both alike I languish, sigh, and die.

7. Cure then, thou mighty wingèd god, This restless fever in my blood;

8. One golden-pointed dart take back: But which, O Cupid, wilt thou take?

9. If Damon's, all my hopes are crossed; Or that of my Alexis, I am lost.

b. *Reorder sentences.* Identify the main elements—subject(s), verb(s), object(s)—of each sentence or independent clause, and if necessary rearrange them in normative word order. (In English, this order tends to be subject-verb-object except in the case of a question; in either case, dependent clauses come at the beginning or end of the main clause and next to whatever element they modify.)

c. *Replace each pronoun with the antecedent noun it replaces;* if the antecedent is ambiguous, indicate all the possibilities.

In the following sentences, the reordered words appear in italics, nouns substituted for pronouns appear in parentheses:

1. How strong does my passion flow, Divided equally twixt two?

2. Damon had ne'er subdued my heart Had not Alexis took (Alexis's or Damon's) part;

3. Nor could Alexis prove powerful *to gain my love Without my Damon's aid.*

4. When my Alexis *is* present, Then I *sigh and mourn* for Damon;

5. But when I do *miss* Alexis, Damon gains nothing but my scorn.

6. But if it chance both (Damon and Alexis) are by, *I languish, sigh, and die* For both (Damon and Alexis) alike.

7. *thou mighty wingèd god,* Cure then This restless fever in my blood;

8. *take back* One golden-pointed dart: But which wilt thou take, *O Cupid?*

9. *If Damon's,* all my hopes are crossed; Or that (dart) of my Alexis, I am lost.

d. *Translate sentences into modern prose.* Use a dictionary to define unfamiliar or ambiguous words or words that seem to be used in an unfamiliar or unexpected way. Add any implied words necessary to link the parts of a sentence to each other and one sentence logically to the next. At this stage, don't move to outright paraphrase; instead, stick closely to the original.

Below, added words appear in brackets, substituted definitions in parentheses:

1. How strongly does my passion flow [when it is] divided equally between two [people]?

2. Damon would never have (*conquered* or *tamed*) my heart if Alexis had not taken (Damon or Alexis's) (*portion*) [of my heart].
3. Nor could Alexis [have] prove[n] powerful [enough] to gain my love without my Damon's aid.
4. When my Alexis is present, then I sigh and mourn for Damon;
5. But when I miss Alexis, Damon doesn't gain anything (except) my scorn.
6. But if it (*so happens*) that both (Damon and Alexis) are [near]by [me], I languish, sigh, and die for both (Damon and Alexis) alike.
7. [Cupid], (you) mighty god (*with wings*), cure then this restless fever in my blood;
8. Take back one [of your two] darts [with] pointed gold [tips]: But which [of these darts] will you take, O Cupid?
9. If [on the one hand, you take away] Damon's [dart], all my hopes are (*opposed, invalidated, spoiled*); Or [if, on the other hand, you take away] Alexis's [arrow], I am (*desperate, ruined, destroyed; no longer claimed or possessed by anyone; helpless or unable to find my way*).

e. *Note any ambiguities in the original language that you might have ignored in your translation.* For example, look for modifiers that might modify more than one thing; verbs that might have multiple subjects or objects; words that have multiple relevant meanings.

In the second sentence, "his" could refer either to Damon or Alexis since both names appear in the first part of this sentence; in other words, this could say either "Alexis took Damon's part" or "Alexis took his own part." But what about the word *part*? I translated this as *portion*, and I assumed it referred back to "heart," partly because the two words come at the ends of lines 3 ("heart") and 4 ("part") and also rhyme. But two other definitions of *part* might make sense here: "the role of a character in a play" or "one's . . . allotted task (as in an action)," and "one of the opposing sides in a conflict or dispute," which in this case could be the "conflict" over the speaker's love. On the one hand, then, I could translate this either "Alexis took his own portion of my heart"; "Alexis played his own role in my life or in this three-way courtship drama"; or "Alexis defended his own side in the battle for my love." On the other hand, I could translate it as "Alexis took Damon's part of my heart"; "Alexis played Damon's role"; or even "Alexis defended Damon's side in the battle for my love."

4. **Consult reference works.** In addition to using a dictionary to define unfamiliar or ambiguous words, look up anything else to which the poem refers that you either don't understand or that you suspect

might be ambiguous: a place, a person, a myth, a quotation, an idea, etc.

According to *Britannica.com*, Cupid was the "ancient Roman god of love" and "often appeared as a winged infant carrying a bow and a quiver of arrows whose wounds inspired love or passion in his every victim." It makes sense, then, that the speaker of this poem would think that she might stop loving one of these men if Cupid took back the arrow that made her love him. But the poem wasn't written in ancient Rome (it's dated 1684), so is the speaker just kidding or being deliberately "poetic" when she calls on Cupid? And what about the names "Damon" and "Alexis"? Were those common in the seventeenth century? Maybe so, if a poet could be named "Aphra Behn."

5. **Figure out who, where, when, and what happens.** Once you have gotten a sense of the literal meaning of each sentence, ask the following very general factual questions about the whole poem. Remember that not all of the questions will suit every poem. (Which questions apply will depend in part on whether the poem is narrative, dramatic, or lyric.) At this point, stick to the facts. What do you know for sure?

Who?
• Who is, or who are, the poem's **speaker(s)**?
• Who is, or who are, the **auditor(s)**, if any?
• Who are the other **characters**, if any, that appear in the poem?

The title suggests that the speaker is a woman who loves two people. In the poem, she identifies these as two men—Damon and Alexis. The speaker doesn't seem to address anyone in particular (certainly not the two men she talks about) except in the third stanza, when she addresses Cupid—first through the **epithet** "mighty wingèd god" (line 13) and then by name (line 16). (Because Cupid isn't present, this is an **apostrophe**.)

Where? When?
• Where is the speaker?
• Where and when do any actions described in the poem take place? That is, what is the poem's **setting**?

No place or time is specified in Behn's poem. The poem is dated 1684, and the antiquated diction ("twixt," line 2; "wilt," line 16) seems appropriate to that time. But nothing in the poem makes the situation or feelings it describes specific to a time or place. The speaker doesn't say things like "Last Thursday, when Damon and I were hanging out in the

garden . . . ," for example. She seems to describe situations that keep
happening repeatedly rather than specific incidents.

What?
- What is the **situation** described in the poem?
- What, if anything, literally happens over the course of it, or what
  action, if any, does it describe?
- Or, if the poem doesn't have a **plot**, then how would you describe
  its internal structure? Even when a poem seems less interested
  in telling a story than in simply capturing a feeling or describing
  something or someone, you can still usually read in it some kind of
  progression or development or even an argument. When and how
  does the subject matter or focus or address shift over the course of
  the poem?

The basic situation is that the speaker loves two men equally. In the
second stanza she describes recurring situations—being with one of
the men and not the other or being with both of them at once—and the
feelings that result. Then, in the third stanza, she imagines what would
happen if she stopped loving one of them. The topic or subject essentially remains the same throughout, but there are two subtle shifts. First
is the shift from addressing anyone in stanzas one and two to addressing Cupid in stanza three. Second, there are shifts in verb tense and
time: The first stanza floats among various tenses ("does," line 1; "took,"
line 4), the second sticks to the present tense ("is," "sigh," "mourn," etc.),
and the third shifts to future ("wilt," line 16). As a result, I would say that
the poem has two parts: in one, the speaker characterizes her situation
in the present and recent past; in the other she explores a possible
alternative future (that she ends up not liking any better).

6. **Formulate tentative answers to the questions, *Why does it matter? What does it all mean?***

   - Why should the poem matter to anyone other than the poet, or
     what might the poem show and say to readers?
   - What problems, issues, questions, or **conflicts** does the poem
     explore that might be relevant to people other than the speaker(s)
     or the poet—to humanity in general, to the poet's contempo-
     raries, to people of a certain type or in a certain situation, and so
     forth?
   - How is each problem or conflict developed and resolved over the
     course of the poem, or how is each question answered? What con-
     clusions does the poem seem to reach about these, or what are its
     themes?

The title and first two lines pose a question: How strong is our love if we love two people instead of one? We tend to assume that anything that is "divided" is less strong than something unified. The use of the word *flow* in the first line reinforces that assumption because it implicitly compares love to something that flows: A river, for example, "flows," and when a river divides into two streams, each is smaller and its flow less strong than the river's. So the way the speaker articulates the question implies an answer: Love, like a river, isn't strong and sure when divided.

But the rest of the poem undermines that answer. In the first stanza, the speaker points out that each lover and his love has "aided" and added to the "power" of the other: Neither man would have "gain[ed her] love" if the other hadn't. The second stanza gives a more concrete sense of why: Since we tend to yearn for what we don't have at the moment, being with one of these men makes her miss the other one. But if both men are present, she feels the same about both and perhaps even feels *more* complete and satisfied.

As if realizing she can't solve the problem herself, she turns in the third stanza to Cupid and asks him to help by taking away her love for either Damon or Alexis. As soon as she asks for this, though, she indicates that the result would be unhappiness. In the end, the poem seems to say (or its theme is) that love *doesn't* flow or work like a river because love can actually be stronger when we love more than one person, as if it's multiplied instead of lessened by division.

Clearly, this is the opposite of what I expected, which was that the poem would ask whether it was possible to love two people and conclude it wasn't. The conflict is also different than I expected—though there's an external conflict between the two men (maybe), the focus is on the speaker's internal conflict, but that conflict isn't over which guy to choose but about how this is actually working (*I love both of them equally; each love reinforces the other*) versus how she thinks things *should* work (*I'm not supposed to love two equally*).

7. **Consider how the poem's form contributes to its effect and meaning.**

- How is the poem organized on the page, into lines and/or stanzas, for example? (What are the lines and stanzas like in terms of length, shape, and so on? Are they all alike, or do they vary? Are lines **enjambed** or **end-stopped**?)
- What are the poem's other formal features? (Is there **rhyme** or another form of aural patterning such as **alliteration**? What is the poem's base **meter**, and are there interesting variations? If not, how else might you describe the poem's rhythm?)

• How do the poem's overall form and its various formal features contribute to its meaning and effect? In other words, what gets lost when you translate the poem into modern prose?

The stanza organization underscores shifts in the speaker's approach to her situation. But organization reinforces meaning in other ways as well. On the one hand, the division into three stanzas and the choice to number them, plus the fact that each stanza has three sentences, mirror the three-way struggle or "love triangle" described in the poem. On the other hand because the poem has 18 *lines* and 9 *sentences*, every sentence is "divided equally twixt two" *lines*. Sound and especially rhyme reinforce this pattern since the two lines that make up one sentence usually rhyme with each other (to form a **couplet**). The only lines that aren't couplets are those that begin the second stanza, where we instead have alternating rhyme—*is* (line 7) rhymes with *miss* (line 9), *mourn* (line 8) rhymes with *scorn* (line 10). But these lines describe how the speaker "miss[es]" one man when the other is "by," a sensation she arguably reproduces in readers by ensuring that we twice "miss" the rhyme that the rest of the poem leads us to expect.

8. **Investigate and consider the ways the poem both uses and departs from poetic conventions, especially those related to form and subgenre.** Does the poem use a traditional verse form (such as **blank verse**) or a traditional stanza form (such as **ballad stanza**)? Is it a specific subgenre or kind of poem—a **sonnet**, an **ode**, a **ballad**, for example? If so, how does that affect its meaning? Over time, stanza and verse forms have been used in certain ways and to certain ends, and particular subgenres have observed certain conventions. As a result, they generate particular expectations for readers familiar with such traditions, and poems gain additional meaning by both fulfilling and defying those expectations. For example, **anapestic** meter (two unstressed syllables followed by a stressed one, as in *Tennessee*) is usually used for comic poems, so when poets use it in a serious poem they are probably making a point.

9. **Argue.** Discussion with others—both out loud and in writing—usually results in clarification and keeps you from being too dependent on personal biases and preoccupations that sometimes mislead even the best readers. Discussing a poem with someone else (especially someone who thinks very differently) or sharing what you've written about the poem can expand your perspective and enrich your experience.

WRITING ABOUT POETRY

If you follow the steps outlined above and keep notes on your personal responses to the poems you read, you will have already begun writing informally. You have also generated ideas and material you can use in more formal writing. To demonstrate how, we conclude this chapter with two examples of such writing. Both grow out of the notes earlier in this chapter. Yet each is quite different in form and content. The first example is a relatively informal response paper that investigates the allusions in Aphra Behn's ON HER LOVING TWO EQUALLY, following up on the discoveries and questions generated by consulting reference works (as in step 4 above). The second example is an essay on the poem that defends and develops as a thesis one answer to the questions, Why does it matter? What does it all mean? (as in step 6 above) by drawing on discoveries made in earlier and later steps.

As these examples illustrate, there are many different ways to write about poems, just as there are many different things to say about any one. But all such writing begins with a clear sense of the poem itself and your responses to it. Effective writing also depends on a willingness to listen carefully to the poem and to ask genuine questions about how it works, what it says and means, and how it both fulfills and challenges your expectations about life, as well as poetry.

From bardic chronicles to imaginary letters, brief introspective lyrics to action-packed epics, "poetry" comes in many sizes, shapes, and varieties; serves myriad purposes for many diverse audiences; and offers pleasures and rewards both like and unlike those we get from fiction, drama, music, or any other art form. In part, though, that's because poetry is something of a trickster and a trespasser, crossing in and out of those other generic domains and trying on their clothes, even as it inhabits and wears very special ones all its own. Poetry speaks to head, as well as heart; ears, as well as eyes. If you keep yours open, it just might speak to you in ways you never expected.

SAMPLE WRITING: RESPONSE PAPER

The following response paper investigates the allusions in Aphra Behn's ON HER LOVING TWO EQUALLY by drawing upon information from reference works. Not all response papers involve research, but we have included one that does in order to demonstrate both how you can use information from credible secondary sources to test and deepen your personal response to a poem and how you can develop reading notes into a thoughtful informal response paper.

Names in "On Her Loving Two Equally"

Aphra Behn's "On Her Loving Two Equally" is dated 1684, but refers to an ancient, pagan god. That seems weird and made me curious about what he was doing in the poem. According to the *Encyclopedia Britannica Online*, Cupid was the "ancient Roman god of love," "often appeared as a winged infant carrying a bow and a quiver of arrows whose wounds inspired love or passion in his every victim," and "was sometimes portrayed wearing armour like that of Mars, the God of war, perhaps to suggest ironic parallels between warfare and romance" ("Cupid"). It makes sense, then, that the speaker of this poem would think that she might stop loving one of these guys if Cupid took back the arrow that made her love him. And the reference to Cupid also reinforces the association in the poem between "warfare" or at least conflict "and romance." (The speaker is internally conflicted, and there is also an external conflict between the two male lovers.)

I'm still not sure whether the speaker is kidding or being deliberately "poetic" by talking to an ancient Roman god. But either way, this reinforces the idea I had when I was reading, that the poem isn't very specific about time or place. The poem makes the speaker's situation seem like something that has happened or could happen anytime, anywhere.

But what about the names Damon and Alexis? Were these real names in seventeenth-century England, which is apparently where Behn was

---

from? According to the Oxford *Dictionary of First Names*, "Damon" is "a classical Greek name" that was

made famous in antiquity by the story of Damon and Pythias. In the early 4th century BC Pythias was condemned to death by Dionysius, ruler of Syracuse. His friend Damon offered to stand surety for him, and took his place in the condemned cell while Pythias put his affairs in order. When Pythias duly returned to be executed rather than absconding and leaving his friend to his fate, Dionysius was so impressed by the trust and friendship of the two young men that he pardoned both of them. ("Damon")

This doesn't tell me for sure whether there were really men named "Damon" in seventeenth-century England, but it's now clear that using the name "Damon" is another way of alluding to "antiquity" and maybe making this situation and poem seem "antique." But the story of Damon and Pythias seems even more relevant. When I was translating this poem, I noticed that it could imply that Damon and Alexis were actually helping each other, not just fighting over the speaker (especially because "his," in line 4, could refer to either man). Does the fact that the most famous Damon was willing to sit in prison and even be executed to help his best friend give me more evidence that I'm right? On the other hand, does it matter that the name comes from a word meaning " 'to tame, subdue' (often a euphemism for 'kill')" ("Damon")?

I couldn't find anything nearly this interesting about "Alexis," except that it is a Latin form of a Greek name that originally came from a word that means "to defend" ("Alexis").

To sum up, I think two things are important: (1) by referring to Cupid and naming her boyfriends Damon and Alexis, Behn makes her poem and her speaker's situation seem "antique," even for the seventeenth century, and implies her situation could happen anytime anywhere; and (2) the fact that the men's names mean "to tame, subdue," even "kill," and "to defend" makes the conflict in the poem more intense, but the fact that the world's most famous Damon sacrificed himself for his friend might add fuel to the idea that these rivals are also friends who are helping each other. Maybe there's even more "loving two equally" going on here than I thought at first? If the speaker loves each of these guys more because she loves the other one, is that true of them, too? This poem is crazy!

Works Cited

"Alexis." *A Dictionary of First Names*, edited by Patrick Hanks, et al.,
    2nd ed., Oxford UP, 2006. *Oxford Reference Online*, doi:10.1093/acref
    /9780198610601.001.0001.

Behn, Aphra. "On Her Loving Two Equally." *The Norton Introduction to
    Literature*, edited by Kelly J. Mays, portable 12th ed., W. W. Norton,
    2017, p. 493.

"Cupid." *Encyclopaedia Britannica Online*, 5 May 2015, www.britannica
    .com/topic/Cupid.

"Damon." *A Dictionary of First Names*, edited by Patrick Hanks, et al.,
    2nd ed., Oxford UP, 2006. *Oxford Reference Online*, doi:10.1093/acref
    /9780198610601.001.0001.

SAMPLE WRITING: ESSAY

The following sample essay develops the observations about Aphra Behn's
ON HER LOVING TWO EQUALLY in this chapter, demonstrating how you can
turn notes about a poem into a coherent, well-structured essay. As this
essay also shows, however, you will often discover new ways of looking at a
poem (or any literary text) in the very process of writing about it. (For
guidelines on correctly quoting and citing poetry, see "Writing about Literature," chapter 21.)

The writer begins by considering why she is drawn to the poem, even
though it does not express her ideal of love. She then uses her personal
response to the poem as a starting point for analyzing it in greater depth.

Multiplying by Dividing in Aphra Behn's
"On Her Loving Two Equally"

My favorite poem in "Reading, Responding, Writing" is Aphra Behn's
"On Her Loving Two Equally"—not because it expresses my ideal of love,
but because it challenges conventional ideals. The main ideal or assumption explored in the poem is that true love is exclusive and monogamous,
as the very titles of poems like "How Do *I* [singular] Love *Thee* [singular]?"
or "To *My* Dear and Loving [and One and Only] Husband" insist (emphasis
added). The mere title of Behn's poem upsets that idea by insisting that at
least one woman is capable of "Loving Two Equally." In fact, one thing that
is immediately interesting about Behn's poem is that, though it poses and
explores a question, its question is not "Can a woman love two equally?"
The title and the poem take it for granted that she can. Instead, the poem
asks whether equally loving two people lessens the power or quality of
love—or, as the speaker puts it in the first two lines, "How strongly does
my passion flow, / Divided equally twixt two?" Every aspect of this poem
suggests that when it comes to love, as opposed to math, division leads
to multiplication.

This answer grabs attention because it is so counterintuitive and unconventional. Forget love for just a minute: It's common sense that anything that is divided is smaller and weaker than something unified. In math, for example, division is the opposite of multiplication; if we divide one number by another, we get a number smaller than the first number, if not the second. Although Behn's use of the word *flow* to frame her question compares love to a river instead of a number, the implication is the same: When a river divides into two streams, each of them is smaller than the river, and its flow less strong; as a result, each stream is more easily dammed up or diverted than the undivided river. So the way the speaker initially poses her question seems to support the conventional view: Love is stronger when it "flows" toward one person, weaker when divided between two.

However conventional and comforting that implied answer, however, it's one the poem immediately rejects. In the remaining lines of the first stanza, the speaker insists that each of her two lovers and the love she feels for him has *not* lessened the strength of her feelings for the other, but the reverse. Each lover and each love has "aid[ed]" (line 6) the other, making him and it more "powerful" (5). Indeed, she says, neither man would have "subdued [her] heart" (3) or "gain[ed her] love" (6) at all if the other hadn't done so as well.

In the second stanza, the speaker gives us a somewhat more concrete sense of why this might be the case. On the one hand, being with either one of these men ("When Alexis present is," 7) actually makes her both "scorn" him (10) and "miss" (9) the man who's not there ("I for Damon sigh and mourn," 8). This isn't really a paradox; we often yearn more for the person or thing we don't have (the grass is always greener on the *other* side of the fence), and we often lose our appreciation for nearby, familiar things and people. What is far away and inaccessible is often dearer to us because its absence either makes us aware of what it means to us or allows us to forget its flaws and idealize it.

Perhaps because all of this makes the speaker feel that she can't possibly solve the problem by herself, the speaker turns in the third stanza to Cupid—the deity who is supposed to control these things by shooting a "golden-pointed dart" (15) into the heart of each lover. She asks him to solve her dilemma for her by "tak[ing] back" her love for either Damon or Alexis (15). As with her question in the first stanza, however, this plea is taken back as soon as it's formulated, for if she loses Damon, "all [her] hopes are crossed"; if she loses Alexis, she is "lost" (17-18).

Here and throughout the poem, the speaker's main preoccupation seems to be what *she* feels and what this situation is like for *her*—"*my* passion" (1), "*my* heart" (3), "*my* Damon's aid, . . . *my* love" (6), "*my* Alexis" (7), "*I* . . . sigh and mourn" (8), "*I* do miss" (9), "*my* scorn" (10), "*I* languish, sigh, and die" (12), "This restless fever in *my* blood" (14), "*my* hopes" (17), "*my* Alexis" and "*I* am lost" (18). Yet the poem implies that the payoff here is not hers alone and that her feelings are not purely selfish. Both times the word *gain* appears in the poem, for example, her lovers' gains and feelings are the focus—the fact that Alexis is able "to gain [her] love" thanks to "Damon's aid" (6) and that "Damon gains nothing but my scorn" when she is missing Alexis (10). Moreover, ambiguous wording in the first stanza suggests that the men here may be actively, intentionally helping to create this situation and even acting in contradictory, selfish and unselfish, ways. When the speaker says that "Damon had ne'er subdued my heart / Had not Alexis took his part" (3-4), *his* could refer to Alexis or Damon and *part* could mean "a portion" (of her "heart," presumably), "a role" (in her life or in this courtship drama), or a "side in a dispute or conflict" (over her love). Thus, she could be saying that Alexis (unselfishly) defended Damon's suit; (selfishly) fought against Damon or took a share or role that properly belonged to Damon; and/or (neutrally) took his (Alexis's) own share or role or defended his (Alexis's) own cause. Perhaps all of this *has* been the case at various times; people do behave in contradictory ways when they are in love, especially when they perceive that they have a rival. It's also true that men and women alike often more highly prize something or someone that someone else prizes, too. So perhaps each lover's "passion" for her also "flow[s]" more strongly than it would otherwise precisely because he has a rival.

In the end, the poem thus seems to say that love *doesn't* flow or work like a river because love isn't a tangible or quantifiable thing. As a result, love is also different from the sort of battle implied by the martial language of the first stanza in which someone wins only if someone else loses. The poem attributes this to the perversity of the human heart—especially our tendency to yearn for what we can't have and what we think other people want, too.

Through its form, the poem demonstrates that division can increase instead of lessen meaning, as well as love. On the one hand, just as the poem's content stresses the power of the love among *three people*, so the poem's form also stresses "threeness" as well as "twoness." It is after all divided into *three* distinctly numbered stanzas, and each stanza consists of *three* sentences. On the other hand, every *sentence* is "divided equally twixt two" *lines*, just as the speaker's "passion" is divided equally between two men. Formally, then, the poem mirrors the kinds of division it describes. Sound and especially rhyme reinforce this pattern since the two lines that make up one sentence usually rhyme with each other to form a couplet. The only lines that don't conform to this pattern come at the beginning of the second stanza where we instead have alternating rhyme—*is* (7) rhymes with *miss* (9), *mourn* (8) rhymes with *scorn* (10). But here, again, form reinforces content since these lines describe how the speaker "miss[es]" one man when the other is "by," a sensation that she arguably reproduces in us as we read by ensuring we twice "miss" the rhyme that the rest of the poem leads us to expect.

Because of the way it challenges our expectations and our conventional ideas about romantic love, the poem might well make us uncomfortable, perhaps all the more so because the speaker and poet here are female. For though we tend to think all true lovers should be loyal and monogamous, this has been expected even more of women than of men. What the poem says about love might make more sense and seem less strange and even objectionable, however, if we think of other, nonromantic kinds of love: After all, do we really think that our mother and father love us less if their love is "divided equally twixt" ourselves and our siblings, or do we love each of our parents less because there are two of *them*? If we think of these familial kinds of love, it becomes much easier to accept Behn's suggestion that love multiplies when we spread it around.

Work Cited

Behn, Aphra. "On Her Loving Two Equally." *The Norton Introduction to Literature*, edited by Kelly J. Mays, portable 12th ed., W. W. Norton, 2017, p. 493.

Understanding the Text

7. SPEAKER: WHOSE VOICE DO WE HEAR?

Poems are personal. The thoughts and feelings they express belong to a specific person, and however general or universal their sentiments seem to be, poems come to us as the expression of an individual human voice. That voice is often a voice of the poet, but not always. Poets sometimes create characters just as writers of fiction or drama do. And the **speaker** of a poem may express ideas or feelings very different from the poet's own.

Usually there is much more to a poem than the characterization of the speaker, but often it is necessary first to identify the speaker and determine his or her character before we can appreciate what else goes on in the poem. And sometimes, in looking for the speaker of the poem we discover the gist of the entire poem.

NARRATIVE POEMS AND THEIR SPEAKERS

In the following narrative poem, the poet has created two speakers, each of whom has a distinctive voice. The first speaker here acts as a **narrator**, setting the scene and introducing the second speaker. As you read the poem, notice how your impressions of "the lady in skunk" (line 2) are shaped by both her words and the narrator's.

X. J. KENNEDY
In a Prominent Bar in Secaucus One Day

*To the tune of "The Old Orange Flute" or the tune of
"Sweet Betsy from Pike"*

In a prominent bar in Secaucus[1] one day
Rose a lady in skunk with a topheavy sway,
Raised a knobby red finger—all turned from their beer—
While with eyes bright as snowcrust she sang high and clear:

---

1. Small town on the Hackensack River in New Jersey, a few miles west of Manhattan.

5 "Now who of you'd think from an eyeload of me
That I once was a lady as proud as could be?
Oh I'd never sit down by a tumbledown drunk
If it wasn't, my dears, for the high cost of junk.

"All the gents used to swear that the white of my calf
10 Beat the down of a swan by a length and a half.
In the kerchief of linen I caught to my nose
Ah, there never fell snot, but a little gold rose.

"I had seven gold teeth and a toothpick of gold.
My Virginia cheroot was a leaf of it rolled
15 And I'd light it each time with a thousand in cash—
Why the bums used to fight if I flicked them an ash.

"Once the toast of the Biltmore,[2] the belle of the Taft,
I would drink bottle beer at the Drake, never draft,
And dine at the Astor on Salisbury steak
20 With a clean tablecloth for each bite I did take.

"In a car like the Roxy[3] I'd roll to the track,
A steel-guitar trio, a bar in the back,
And the wheels made no noise, they turned over so fast,
Still it took you ten minutes to see me go past.

25 "When the horses bowed down to me that I might choose,
I bet on them all, for I hated to lose.
Now I'm saddled each night for my butter and eggs
And the broken threads race down the backs of my legs.

"Let you hold in mind, girls, that your beauty must pass
30 Like a lovely white clover that rusts with its grass.
Keep your bottoms off barstools and marry you young
Or be left—an old barrel with many a bung.

"For when time takes you out for a spin in his car
You'll be hard-pressed to stop him from going too far
35 And be left by the roadside, for all your good deeds,
Two toadstools for tits and a face full of weeds."

All the house raised a cheer, but the man at the bar
Made a phonecall and up pulled a red patrol car
And she blew us a kiss as they copped her away
40 From that prominent bar in Secaucus, N.J.

1961

2. Like the Taft, Drake, and Astor, a once-fashionable New York hotel.
3. Luxurious old New York theater and movie house, the site of many "world premieres" in the
heyday of Hollywood.

We learn about the singer in this poem primarily through her own words, although we may not believe everything she tells us about her past. From her introduction in the first stanza we get some general notion of her appearance and condition, but it is she who tells us that she is a junkie (line 8) and a prostitute (lines 27, 32) and that her face and figure have seen better days (lines 32, 36). That information could make her a sad case, and the poem might lament her state or encourage us to lament it, but instead she presents herself in a light, friendly, and theatrical way. The comedy is bittersweet, perhaps, but she is allowed to present herself, through her own words and attitudes, as a likable character—someone who has survived life's disappointments and retained her dignity. The self-portrait accumulates almost completely through how she talks about herself, and the poet develops our attitude toward her by allowing her to recount her story herself, in her own words—or rather in words he has chosen for her.

SPEAKERS IN THE DRAMATIC MONOLOGUE

Like all **dramatic monologues**, the following poem has no narrator at all. Rather, it consists entirely of the words of a single, fictional speaker in a specific time, place, and dramatic situation, very like a character in a play.

ROBERT BROWNING
Soliloquy of the Spanish Cloister

Gr-r-r—there go, my heart's abhorrence!
   Water your damned flower-pots, do!
If hate killed men, Brother Lawrence,
   God's blood, would not mine kill you!
5 What? your myrtle-bush wants trimming?
   Oh, that rose has prior claims—
Needs its leaden vase filled brimming?
   Hell dry you up with its flames!

At the meal we sit together:
10   *Salve tibi!*[4] I must hear
Wise talk of the kind of weather,
   Sort of season, time of year:
Not a plenteous cork-crop: scarcely
   Dare we hope oak-galls,[5] *I doubt:*

---

4. Hail to thee (Latin). Italics usually indicate the words of Brother Lawrence here mockingly reproduced by the speaker.   5. Abnormal growth on oak trees, used for tanning.

15 *What's the Latin name for "parsley"?*
    What's the Greek name for Swine's Snout?

    Whew! We'll have our platter burnished,
       Laid with care on our own shelf!
    With a fire-new spoon we're furnished,
20   And a goblet for ourself,
    Rinsed like something sacrificial
       Ere 'tis fit to touch our chaps[6]—
    Marked with L. for our initial!
       (He-he! There his lily snaps!)

25 *Saint*, forsooth! While brown Dolores
       —Squats outside the Convent bank
    With Sanchicha, telling stories,
       Steeping tresses in the tank,
    Blue-black, lustrous, thick like horsehairs,
30   —Can't I see his dead eye glow,
    Bright as 'twere a Barbary corsair's?[7]
       (That is, if he'd let it show!)

    When he finishes refection,
       Knife and fork he never lays
35 Cross-wise, to my recollection,
       As do I, in Jesu's praise.
    I the Trinity illustrate,
       Drinking watered orange-pulp—
    In three sips the Arian[8] frustrate;
40   —While he drains his at one gulp.

    Oh, those melons? If he's able
       We're to have a feast! so nice!
    One goes to the Abbot's table,
       All of us get each a slice.
45 How go on your flowers? None double?
       Not one fruit-sort can you spy?
    Strange!—And I, too, at such trouble,
       —Keep them close-nipped on the sly!

    There's a great text in Galatians,
50   Once you trip on it, entails
    Twenty-nine distinct damnations,[9]
       One sure, if another fails:

---

6. Jaws.   7. African pirate's.   8. Heretical sect that denied the Trinity.
9. Galatians 5.15–23 provides a long list of possible offenses, though they do not add up to twenty-nine.

If I trip him just a-dying,
   Sure of heaven as sure can be,
55 Spin him round and send him flying
   Off to hell, a Manichee?[1]

Or, my scrofulous French novel
   On gray paper with blunt type!
Simply glance at it, you grovel
60 Hand and foot in Belial's gripe.[2]
If I double down its pages
   At the woeful sixteenth print,
When he gathers his greengages,
   Ope a sieve and slip it in't?

65 Or, there's Satan!—one might venture
   Pledge one's soul to him, yet leave
Such a flaw in the indenture
   —As he'd miss till, past retrieve,
Blasted lay that rose-acacia
70 We're so proud of! *Hy, Zy, Hine* . . .[3]
'St, there's Vespers! *Plena gratiâ*
   Ave, Virgo.[4] Gr-r-r—you swine!

1842

Not many poems begin with a growl, and this harsh sound turns out to be fair warning that we are about to meet a real beast, even though he is in the clothing of a religious man. In line 1 he shows himself to hold a most uncharitable attitude toward his fellow monk, Brother Lawrence, and by line 4 he has uttered two profanities and admitted his intense feelings of hatred and vengefulness. His ranting and roaring is full of exclamation points (four in the first stanza!), and he reveals his own personality and character when he imagines curses and unflattering nicknames for Brother Lawrence or plots malicious jokes on him. By the end, we have accumulated no knowledge of Brother Lawrence that makes him seem a fit target for such rage (except that he is pious, dutiful, and pleasant—perhaps enough to make this sort of speaker despise him), but we should have discovered much about the speaker's character and habits.

The speaker characterizes himself; the details accumulate into a fairly full portrait, even though here we do not have either a narrator's description (as in Kennedy's IN A PROMINENT BAR) or another speaker to give us perspective.

1. Heretic. According to the Manichean heresy, the world was divided into the forces of good and evil, each equally powerful.   2. That is, in the devil's clutches.
3. Possibly the beginning of an incantation or curse.
4. Opening words of the *Ave Maria*, here reversed: "Full of grace, Hail, Virgin" (Latin).

Except for the moments when the speaker mimics or parodies Brother Law-rence (usually in italic type), we have only the speaker's own words and thoughts. But that is enough; the poet has controlled them so carefully that we know what he thinks of the speaker. The whole poem has been about the speaker and his attitudes; the point has been to characterize the speaker and develop in us a dislike of him and what he stands for.

In reading a poem like this aloud, we would want our voice to suggest all the speaker's unlikable features. We would also need to suggest, through tone of voice, the author's contemptuous mocking of them, and we would want, like an actor, to create strong disapproval in the hearer. The poem's words (the ones the author has given to the speaker) clearly imply those attitudes, and we would want our voice to express them.

THE LYRIC AND ITS SPEAKER

With narrative poems and dramatic monologues, we are usually in no dan-ger of mistaking the speaker for the poet. Lyrics may present more of a challenge. When there is a pointed discrepancy between the speaker of a **lyric** and what we know of the poet—when the speaker is a woman, for example, and the poet is a man—we know we have a fictional speaker to contend with and that the point (or at least *one* point) of the poem is to observe the characterization carefully.

Sometimes even in lyrics poets "borrow" a character from history and ask readers to factor in historical facts and contexts. In the following poem, for example, the Canadian poet Margaret Atwood draws heavily on facts and traditions about a nineteenth-century émigré from Scotland to Canada. The poem is a lyric spoken in the first person, but its speaker is a fictional character based on a real woman.

The poem comes from a volume called *The Journals of Susanna Moodie: Poems by Margaret Atwood* (1970). A frontier pioneer, Moodie (1803–84) her-self wrote two books about Canada, *Roughing It in the Bush* and *Life in the Clearings,* and Atwood found their observations rather stark and disorga-nized. She wrote her Susanna Moodie poems to refocus the "character" and to reconstruct Moodie's actual geographical exploration and self-discovery. To fully understand these thoughts and meditations, then, we need to know something of the history behind them. Yet even without such knowledge, we can appreciate the poem's powerful evocation of the speaker's situation and feelings.

MARGARET ATWOOD
Death of a Young Son by Drowning

He, who navigated with success
the dangerous river of his own birth
once more set forth

on a voyage of discovery
5   into the land I floated on
but could not touch to claim.

His feet slid on the bank,
the currents took him;
he swirled with ice and trees in the swollen water

10   and plunged into distant regions,
his head a bathysphere;[5]
through his eyes' thin glass bubbles

he looked out, reckless adventurer
on a landscape stranger than Uranus
15   we have all been to and some remember.

There was an accident; the air locked,
he was hung in the river like a heart.
They retrieved the swamped body,

cairn of my plans and future charts,
20   with poles and hooks
from among the nudging logs.

It was spring, the sun kept shining, the new grass
leapt to solidity;
my hands glistened with details.

25   After the long trip I was tired of waves.
My foot hit rock. The dreamed sails
collapsed, ragged.

I planted him in this country
like a flag.

1970

Even when poets present themselves as if they were speaking directly to
us in their own voices, their poems present only a partial portrait, something
considerably less than the full personality and character of the poet. Though

---

5. Manned spherical chamber for deep-sea observation.

there is not an obviously created character—someone with distinct characteristics that are different from those of the poet—strategies of characterization are used to present the person speaking in one way and not another. As a result, you should still differentiate between the speaker and the poet.

AUTHORS ON THEIR CRAFT
BILLY COLLINS AND SHARON OLDS ON "FINDING YOUR OWN VOICE"

From "A Brisk Walk: An Interview with Billy Collins" (2006)*

[. . . T]here's this pet phrase about writing that is bandied around [. . .] "finding your own voice as a poet," which I suppose means that you come out from under the direct influence of other poets and have perhaps found a way to combine those influences so that it appears to be your own voice. But I think you could also put it a different way. You, quote, find your voice, unquote, when you are able to invent this one character who resembles you, obviously, and probably is more like you than anyone else on earth, but is not the equivalent to you.

It is like a fictional character in that it has a very distinctive voice, a voice that seems to be able to accommodate and express an attitude that you are comfortable staying with but an attitude that is flexible enough to cover a number of situations.

. . .

From "Olds' Worlds" (2008)**

[. . . O]nce a poem is written, and [. . .] it's rewritten, and maybe published, and I'm in front of people, reading it aloud—I'm not too embarrassed by that [. . .] It doesn't feel personal. It feels like art—a made thing—the "I" in it not myself anymore, but, I'd hope, some pronoun that a reader or hearer could slip into. But how much can a poem reflect or embody a life anyhow? You can want to come close, but it's so profoundly different—the actual body, the flesh, the mortal life.

*"A Brisk Walk: An Interview with Billy Collins." Interview by Joel Whitney. *Guernica*, 14 June 2006, www.guernicamag.com/interviews/a_brisk_walk/.
**"Olds' Worlds." Interview by Marianne Macdonald. *The Guardian*, 26 July 2008, www.theguardian.com/books/2008/jul/26/poetry.

Although the poet is probably writing about a personal, actual experience in the following poem, he is also making a character of himself—that is, characterizing himself in a certain way, emphasizing some parts of himself and not others. We can call this character a **persona**.

WILLIAM WORDSWORTH
She Dwelt among the Untrodden Ways

She dwelt among the untrodden ways
 Beside the springs of Dove,[6]
A Maid whom there were none to praise
 And very few to love:

5 A violet by a mossy stone
 Half hidden from the eye!
—Fair as a star, when only one
 Is shining in the sky.

She lived unknown, and few could know
10 When Lucy ceased to be;
But she is in her grave, and, oh,
 The difference to me!

1800

Did Lucy actually live? Was she a friend of the poet? We don't know; the poem doesn't tell us, and even biographers of Wordsworth are unsure. What we do know is that Wordsworth was able to represent grief very powerfully. Whether the speaker is the historical Wordsworth or not, that speaker is a major focus of the poem, and it is his feelings that the poem isolates and expresses. We need to recognize some characteristics of the speaker and be sensitive to his feelings for the poem to work.

Analyzing Speakers: An Exercise

In the following poem, we do not get a full sense of the speaker until well into the poem. As you read, try to imagine the tone of voice you think this person would use. Exactly when do you begin to know what she sounds like?

---

6. Small stream in the Lake District in northern England, near where Wordsworth lived.

DOROTHY PARKER
A Certain Lady

Oh, I can smile for you, and tilt my head,
    And drink your rushing words with eager lips,
And paint my mouth for you a fragrant red,
    And trace your brows with tutored finger-tips.
5 When you rehearse your list of loves to me,
    Oh, I can laugh and marvel, rapturous-eyed.
And you laugh back, nor can you ever see
    The thousand little deaths my heart has died.
And you believe, so well I know my part,
10   That I am gay as morning, light as snow,
And all the straining things within my heart
    You'll never know.
Oh, I can laugh and listen, when we meet,
    And you bring tales of fresh adventurings—
15 Of ladies delicately indiscreet,
    Of lingering hands, and gently whispered things.
And you are pleased with me, and strive anew
    To sing me sagas of your late delights.
Thus do you want me—marveling, gay, and true—
20   Nor do you see my staring eyes of nights.
And when, in search of novelty, you stray,
    Oh, I can kiss you blithely as you go . . .
And what goes on, my love, while you're away,
    You'll never know.

1937

To whom does the speaker seem to be talking? What sort of person is he? How do you feel about him? Which habits and attitudes of his do you like least? How soon can you tell that the speaker is not altogether happy about his conversation and conduct? In what tone of voice would you read the first twenty-two lines aloud? What attitude would you try to express toward the person spoken to? What tone would you use for the last two lines? How would you describe the speaker's personality? What aspects of her behavior are most crucial to the poem's effect?

The poems we have looked at in this chapter—and those that follow—all suggest the value of beginning the reading of any poem with three simple questions: Who is speaking? What do we know about him or her? What kind of person is she or he? Putting together the evidence that the poem presents in answer to such questions can often take us a long way into the poem. For some poems, such questions won't help a great deal because the speaking voice is too indistinct or the character too scantily presented. But starting with such questions will often lead you toward the central experience the poem offers.

POEMS FOR FURTHER STUDY

WALT WHITMAN
[I celebrate myself, and sing myself]

I celebrate myself, and sing myself,
And what I assume you shall assume,
For every atom belonging to me as good belongs to you.
I loafe and invite my soul,
5   I lean and loafe at my ease observing a spear of summer grass.

My tongue, every atom of my blood, form'd from this soil, this air,
Born here of parents born here from parents the same, and their
    parents the same,
I, now thirty-seven years old in perfect health begin,
Hoping to cease not till death.
10   Creeds and schools in abeyance,
Retiring back a while sufficed at what they are, but never forgotten,
I harbor for good or bad, I permit to speak at every hazard,
Nature without check with original energy.

                                                        1855, 1881

• What is characteristically American about the speaker of this poem?

LANGSTON HUGHES
Ballad of the Landlord

Landlord, landlord,
My roof has sprung a leak.
Don't you 'member I told you about it
Way last week?

5   Landlord, landlord,
These steps is broken down.

When you come up yourself
It's a wonder you don't fall down.

Ten Bucks you say I owe you?
10 Ten Bucks you say is due?
Well, that's Ten Bucks more'n I'll pay you
Till you fix this house up new.

What? You gonna get eviction orders?
You gonna cut off my heat?
15 You gonna take my furniture and
Throw it in the street?

Um-huh! You talking high and mighty.
Talk on—till you get through.
You ain't gonna be able to say a word
20 If I land my fist on you.

Police! Police!
Come and get this man!
He's trying to ruin the government
And overturn the land!

25 Copper's whistle!
Patrol bell!
Arrest.

Precinct Station.
Iron cell.
30 Headlines in press:

MAN THREATENS LANDLORD
TENANT HELD NO BAIL
JUDGE GIVES NEGRO 90 DAYS IN COUNTY JAIL.
                                                    1940

- **Who are the various speakers in this poem? What is the effect of
  Hughes's choice not to give us all the words of all the speakers?**

E. E. CUMMINGS
[next to of course god america i]

"next to of course god america i
love you land of the pilgrims' and so forth oh
say can you see by the dawn's early my
country 'tis of centuries come and go
5 and are no more what of it we should worry

in every language even deafanddumb
thy sons acclaim your glorious name by gorry
by jingo by gee by gosh by gum
why talk of beauty what could be more beaut-
10 iful than these heroic happy dead
who rushed like lions to the roaring slaughter
they did not stop to think they died instead
then shall the voice of liberty be mute?"

He spoke. And drank rapidly a glass of water
1926

• Except for the last line, this poem works much like a dramatic monologue. What can you discern about the situation in which the quoted
words are spoken? about the speaker and his or her audience? about
the poem's attitude toward the speaker?

GWENDOLYN BROOKS
We Real Cool

The Pool Players,
Seven at the Golden Shovel.

We real cool. We
Left school. We

5 Lurk late. We
Strike straight. We

Sing sin. We
Thin gin. We

Jazz June. We
10 Die soon.
1950

• Who are "we" in this poem? Do you think that the speaker and the poet
share the same idea of what is "cool"?

LUCILLE CLIFTON
cream of wheat

sometimes at night
we stroll the market aisles
ben and jemima and me   they

```
      walk in front    remembering this and that
  5   i lag behind
      trying to remove my chefs cap
      wondering about what ever pictured me
      then left me personless
      Rastus
 10   i read in an old paper
      i was called rastus
      but no mother ever
      gave that to her son    toward dawn
      we return to our shelves
 15   our boxes    ben and jemima and me
      we pose and smile   i simmer   what
      is my name
```

                                                    2008

- At what point and how did you begin to figure out just who the
  speaker of this poem is? What is the effect of the shifts between plural
  and singular, "we" and "I"?

ELIZABETH BISHOP
Exchanging Hats

Unfunny uncles who insist
in trying on a lady's hat,
—oh, even if the joke falls flat,
we share your slight transvestite twist

5 in spite of our embarrassment.
Costume and custom are complex.
The headgear of the other sex
inspires us to experiment.

Anandrous[7] aunts, who, at the beach
10 with paper plates upon your laps,
keep putting on the yachtsmen's caps
with exhibitionistic screech,

the visors hanging o'er the ear
so that the golden anchors drag,
15 —the tides of fashion never lag.
Such caps may not be worn next year.

---

7. Literally, "husbandless."

Or you who don the paper plate
itself, and put some grapes upon it,
or sport the Indian's feather bonnet,
20 —perversities may aggravate

the natural madness of the hatter.
And if the opera hats collapse
and crowns grow drafty, then, perhaps,
he thinks what might a miter matter?

25 Unfunny uncle, you who wore a
hat too big, or one too many,
tell us, can't you, are there any
stars inside your black fedora?

Aunt exemplary and slim,
30 with avernal[8] eyes, we wonder
what slow changes they see under
their vast, shady, turned-down brim.

1956

- The speaker in this poem uses the first-person plural ("we," line 4; "our,"
line 5; "us," line 8). Who might "we" be? How might your response to
the poem change if the speaker instead used the first-person singular
("I") or the third-person plural ("they")?

SUGGESTIONS FOR WRITING

1. Several of the poems in this chapter create characters and imply situations,
as in drama. Write an essay in which you describe and analyze the main
speaker of any poem in this chapter.
2. Write an essay in which you compare the speakers in any two poems in this
chapter. What kinds of self-image do they have? In each poem, what is the
implied distance between the speaker and the poet?
3. Choose any of the poems in this or the previous chapter and write an essay
about the way a poet can create irony and humor through the use of a speaker
who is clearly distinct from the poet himself or herself.
4. Write a poem, short story, or personal essay in which the speaker or narrator
is a character mentioned by a speaker in any of the poems in this chapter—
for example, someone who hears the song sung in X. J. Kennedy's IN A PROM-
INENT BAR IN SECAUCUS ONE DAY, the lover in Dorothy Parker's A CERTAIN
LADY, or Ben and Jemima in CREAM OF WHEAT. How might the same situation, as well as the main speaker of these poems, look and sound different
when viewed from another speaker's point of view and described in another
speaker's voice?

8. Infernal.

8 SITUATION AND SETTING: WHAT HAPPENS? WHERE? WHEN?

Questions about the **speaker** in a poem (*Who?* questions) lead to questions about *What?* and *Why?* as well as *Where?* and *When?* First you identify the imagined **situation** in the poem: To whom is the speaker speaking? Is there an **auditor** in the poem? Is anyone else present or referred to in the poem? What is happening? Why is this event or communication occurring, and why is it significant? As soon as you zoom in on answers to such questions about persons and actions, you also encounter questions about place and time. (Where and when does the action or communication take place?) In other words, situation entails **setting**.

The place involved in a poem is its *spatial setting*, and the time is its *temporal setting*. The temporal setting may be a specific date or an era, a season of the year or a time of day. Temporal or spatial setting often influences our expectations, although a poet may surprise us by making something very different from what we had thought was familiar. We tend, for example, to think of spring as a time of discovery and growth, and poems set in spring are likely to make use of that association. Similarly, morning usually suggests discovery—beginnings, vitality, the world fresh and new.

Not all poems have an identifiable situation or setting, just as not all poems have a speaker who is easily distinguishable from the author. Poems that simply present a series of thoughts and feelings directly, in a reflective way, may not present anything resembling a scene with action, dialogue, or description. But many poems depend crucially on a sense of place, a sense of time, and scenes that resemble those in plays or films. And questions about these matters will often lead you to define not only the "facts" but also the feelings central to the design a poem has on its readers.

To understand the dialogue in Thomas Hardy's THE RUINED MAID, for example, we need to recognize that the two women are meeting after an extended period of separation (the situation) and that they meet in a town rather than the rural area in which they grew up together (the setting). We infer (from the opening lines) that the meeting is accidental and that no other friends are present for the conversation. The poem's whole "story" depends on their situation: After leading separate lives for a while, they have some catching up to do. We don't know what specific town they are in or what year, season, or time of day it is—and those details are not important to the poem's effect.

More specific settings matter in other poems. In Robert Browning's SOLIL-OQUY OF THE SPANISH CLOISTER, the setting, a monastery, adds to the irony because of the gross inappropriateness of the speaker's sentiments and attitudes in a supposedly holy place.

Situation and setting may be treated in various ways in a poem, ranging from silence to the barest hints of description to full photographic detail. Often it is relatively easy to identify the situation at the beginning of a poem, but the implications of setting, and what happens as the poem unfolds, may be subtler. Poets often rely on readers to fill in the gaps, drawing on their knowledge of circumstances and familiar experiences in the present or in the past. The poem may specify only a few aspects of a *kind* of setting, such as a motel room in the afternoon.

SITUATION

Both of the poems below involve motherhood, but each portrays an entirely different situation. How would you summarize each?

RITA DOVE
Daystar

> She wanted a little room for thinking:
> but she saw diapers steaming on the line,
> a doll slumped behind the door.
> So she lugged a chair behind the garage
> 5 to sit out the children's naps.
>
> Sometimes there were things to watch—
> the pinched armor of a vanished cricket,
> a floating maple leaf. Other days
> she stared until she was assured
> 10 when she closed her eyes
> she'd see only her own vivid blood.
>
> She had an hour, at best, before Liza appeared
> pouting from the top of the stairs.
> And just *what* was mother doing
> 15 out back with the field mice? Why,
> building a palace. Later
> that night when Thomas rolled over and
> lurched into her, she would open her eyes
> and think of the place that was hers

20 for an hour—where
   she was nothing,
   pure nothing, in the middle of the day.
                                    1986

LINDA PASTAN
To a Daughter Leaving Home

When I taught you
at eight to ride
a bicycle, loping along
beside you
5 as you wobbled away
on two round wheels,
my own mouth rounding
in surprise when you pulled
ahead down the curved
10 path of the park,
I kept waiting
for the thud
of your crash as I
sprinted to catch up,
15 while you grew
smaller, more breakable
with distance,
pumping, pumping
for your life, screaming
20 with laughter,
the hair flapping
behind you like a
handkerchief waving
goodbye.
                    1988

   The mother in Dove's DAYSTAR, overwhelmed by the demands of young children, needs a room of her own. All she can manage, however, is a brief hour of respite. The situation is virtually the whole story here. Nothing really happens except that daily events (washing diapers, picking up toys, looking at crickets and leaves, explaining the world to children, having sex) surround her brief private hour and make it precious. Being "nothing" (lines 21 and 22) takes on great value in these circumstances.

   The particulars of time and place in Pastan's To A DAUGHTER LEAVING HOME are even less specific; the incident the poem describes happened a long time ago, and its vividness is a function of memory. The speaker here thinks back nostalgically to a moment when her daughter made an earlier (but briefer) departure. Though we learn very little about the speaker, at least directly, we may infer quite a bit about her—her affection for her daughter, the kind of mother she has been, her anxiety at the new departure that seems to resemble the earlier wobbly ride into the distance. The daughter is now, the poem implies, old enough to "leave home" in a full sense, but we do not know the specific reason or what the present circumstances are. Only the title tells us the situation, and (like "Daystar") the poem is all situation.

THE CARPE DIEM POEM

The following two poems from the 1600s represent similar situations: In each, a male speaker addresses a female auditor whom he desires. The poems belong to the tradition of **carpe diem** (Latin for "seize the day") because the speaker is urging his auditor, his lover, to enjoy pleasures now, before they die. The woman is resisting because of her concern for chastity or social rules. The action of these poems is implied in the shifts in what the speaker is saying. What does the woman do in THE FLEA? Can you imagine the woman's response in TO HIS COY MISTRESS?

JOHN DONNE
The Flea

Mark but this flea, and mark in this,[1]
How little that which thou deny'st me is;
It sucked me first, and now sucks thee,
And in this flea our two bloods mingled be;
5 Thou know'st that this cannot be said
A sin, nor shame, nor loss of maidenhead.
    Yet this enjoys before it woo,
    And pampered[2] swells with one blood made of two,
    And this, alas, is more than we would do.[3]

10 Oh stay,[4] three lives in one flea spare,
Where we almost, yea more than, married are.
This flea is you and I, and this
Our marriage bed, and marriage temple is;

---

1. Medieval preachers and rhetoricians asked their hearers to "mark" (look at) an object that illustrated a moral or philosophical lesson they wished to emphasize.
2. Fed luxuriously.
3. According to the medical theory of Donne's era, conception involved the literal mingling of the lovers' blood. 4. Desist.

Though parents grudge, and you, we're met
15   And cloistered in these living walls of jet.
Though use[5] make you apt to kill me,
Let not to that, self-murder added be,
And sacrilege, three sins in killing three.

Cruel and sudden, hast thou since
20   Purpled thy nail in blood of innocence?
Wherein could this flea guilty be,
Except in that drop which it sucked from thee?
Yet thou triumph'st, and say'st that thou
Find'st not thyself, nor me, the weaker now;
25   'Tis true; then learn how false fears be;
Just so much honor, when thou yield'st to me,
Will waste, as this flea's death took life from thee.

                                                                      1633

• What lines help you imagine what the speaker is doing as he speaks?
  what the auditor does or says?

ANDREW MARVELL
To His Coy Mistress

Had we but world enough, and time,
This coyness,[6] lady, were no crime.
We would sit down, and think which way
To walk, and pass our long love's day.
5   Thou by the Indian Ganges' side
Shouldst rubies[7] find: I by the tide
Of Humber would complain.[8] I would
Love you ten years before the Flood,
And you should if you please refuse
10   Till the conversion of the Jews.[9]
My vegetable love[1] should grow
Vaster than empires, and more slow;
An hundred years should go to praise

---

5. Habit.   6. Hesitancy, modesty (not necessarily suggesting calculation).
7. Talismans that are supposed to preserve virginity.
8. Write love complaints, conventional songs lamenting the cruelty of love. *Humber*: a river and
estuary in Marvell's hometown of Hull.
9. Which, according to popular Christian belief, will occur just before the end of the world.
1. Which is capable only of passive growth, not of consciousness. The "vegetable soul" is lower
than the other two divisions of the soul, "animal" and "rational."

Thine eyes, and on thy forehead gaze;
15 Two hundred to adore each breast,
But thirty thousand to the rest.
An age at least to every part,
And the last age should show your heart.
For, lady, you deserve this state;[2]
20 Nor would I love at lower rate.
    But at my back I always hear
Time's wingèd chariot hurrying near;
And yonder all before us lie
Deserts of vast eternity.
25 Thy beauty shall no more be found,
Nor, in thy marble vault, shall sound
My echoing song; then worms shall try
That long preserved virginity,
And your quaint honor turn to dust,
30 And into ashes all my lust:
The grave's a fine and private place,
But none, I think, do there embrace.
    Now therefore, while the youthful hue
Sits on thy skin like morning dew,[3]
35 And while thy willing soul transpires[4]
At every pore with instant fires,
Now let us sport us while we may,
And now, like am'rous birds of prey,
Rather at once our time devour
40 Than languish in his slow-chapped[5] pow'r.
Let us roll all our strength and all
Our sweetness up into one ball,
And tear our pleasures with rough strife
Thorough[6] the iron gates of life.
45 Thus, though we cannot make our sun
Stand still,[7] yet we will make him run.[8]

1681

• How does each stanza develop the speaker's argument? Is it persuasive?

---

2. Dignity.   3. The text reads "glew." "Lew" (warmth) has also been suggested as an emendation.
4. Breathes forth.
5. Slow-jawed. Chronos (Time), ruler of the world in early Greek myth, devoured all of his children except Zeus, who was hidden. Later, Zeus seized power (see line 46 and note).
6. Through.   7. To lengthen his night of love with Alcmene, Zeus made the sun stand still.
8. Each sex act was believed to shorten life by one day.

SETTING

Frequently a poem's setting draws on common notions of a particular time or place. Setting a poem in a garden, for example, or writing about apples almost inevitably reminds readers of the Garden of Eden because it is an important and widely recognized part of the Western heritage. Even people who don't read at all or who lack Judeo-Christian religious commitments are likely to know about Eden, and poets writing in Western cultures can count on that knowledge. A reference to something outside the poem that carries a history of meaning and strong emotional associations is called an **allusion**. For example, gardens may carry suggestions of innocence and order, or temptation and the Fall, or both, depending on how the poem handles the allusion.

Specific, well-known places may similarly be associated with particular ideas, values, ways of life, or natural phenomena. The titles of many poems refer, like the following one, directly to specific places or times.

MATTHEW ARNOLD
Dover Beach[9]

The sea is calm tonight.
The tide is full, the moon lies fair
Upon the straits; on the French coast the light
Gleams and is gone; the cliffs of England stand,
5 Glimmering and vast, out in the tranquil bay.
Come to the window, sweet is the night-air!
Only, from the long line of spray
Where the sea meets the moon-blanched land,
Listen! you hear the grating roar
10 Of pebbles which the waves draw back, and fling,
At their return, up the high strand,
Begin, and cease, and then again begin,
With tremulous cadence slow, and bring
The eternal note of sadness in.

15 Sophocles long ago
Heard it on the Aegean, and it brought
Into his mind the turbid ebb and flow
Of human misery,[1] we

---

9. At the narrowest point on the English Channel. The light on the French coast (lines 3–4) would be about twenty miles away.

1. In Sophocles's *Antigone*, lines 637–46, the chorus compares the fate of the house of Oedipus to the waves of the sea.

Find also in the sound a thought,
20 Hearing it by this distant northern sea.

The Sea of Faith
Was once, too, at the full, and round earth's shore
Lay like the folds of a bright girdle furled.
But now I only hear
25 Its melancholy, long, withdrawing roar,
Retreating, to the breath
Of the night-wind, down the vast edges drear
And naked shingles² of the world.

Ah, love, let us be true
30 To one another! for the world, which seems
To lie before us like a land of dreams,
So various, so beautiful, so new,
Hath really neither joy, nor love, nor light,
Nor certitude, nor peace, nor help for pain;
35 And we are here as on a darkling plain
Swept with confused alarms of struggle and flight,
Where ignorant armies clash by night.

c. 1851

The situation and setting of DOVER BEACH are concrete and specific. It is night by the seashore, and the speaker is gazing at the view from a room with someone he invites to "come to the window" (line 6) and "listen" (line 9); later he says to this person, "Ah, love, let us be true / To one another!" (lines 29–30). Most readers have assumed that the speaker and his companion are about to travel from Dover across the sea to France and that the situation is a honeymoon, or at least that the couple is young and married; after all the "world [. . .] seems / To lie before us [. . .] / so new" (lines 30–32). Although this poem is not a prayer, it is a kind of plea for hope despite the modern loss of faith. The tide is now full, but the poet hears a destructive repetition of rising and falling waves (the pebbles will be worn down eventually), and he dwells on the "withdrawing" side of this pattern. For centuries, Christian belief, "the Sea of Faith" (line 21), was at high tide, but now the speaker can only "hear" it "[r]etreating" (lines 24, 26). On the one hand, then, the specifics of setting—the fact that it is night, that the speaker looks out on a stony beach lined with cliffs, and so on—seem to evoke the sense of danger, isolation, and uncertainty the speaker feels as a result of the loss of faith. On the other hand, however, might details of setting introduce hope into the poem, especially when we combine them with our knowledge of how tides ebb and flow and how the dark of night gives way to the light of morning?

2. Pebble-strewn beaches.

THE OCCASIONAL POEM

While much of the poetry in this anthology expresses personal feelings, and while some of it is tied to the poet's autobiographical circumstances, a great deal of poetry written over the centuries has focused not on individuals but on political or historical topics and themes. The setting of **epic** poetry may be as broad as a nation or even the cosmos. Poems have been written to instruct readers about religion, science, philosophy, and the art of poetry, among many other topics, with an appropriate range of settings and situations. The poet may wish to influence readers' sympathies or loyalties toward different sides in a conflict, or to record and honor a specific event such as an inauguration. A poem written about or for a specific occasion is called an **occasional poem**, and such a poem is *referential*; that is, it *refers* to a certain historical time or event.

Sometimes it is hard to place ourselves fully in another time or place in order to imagine sympathetically what a particular historical moment would have been like, and even the best poetic efforts, by themselves, do not necessarily transport us there. For such poems we need, at the least, specific historical information—plus a willingness to be transported by a name, a date, or a dramatic situation.

Here, however, is a relatively recent example: an occasional poem that works to capture the significance of a recent, public event by considering it in the historical perspective inspired by a very specific setting.

MARTÍN ESPADA
Litany at the Tomb of Frederick Douglass[3]

Mount Hope Cemetery, Rochester, New York
November 7, 2008

This is the longitude and latitude of the impossible;
this is the epicenter of the unthinkable;
this is the crossroads of the unimaginable:
the tomb of Frederick Douglass, three days after the election.

5 This is a world spinning away from the gravity of centuries,
where the grave of a fugitive slave has become an altar.
This is the tomb of a man born as chattel, who taught himself to
     read in secret,
scraping the letters in his name with chalk on wood; now on the
     anvil-flat stone

---

3. Escaped slave (1817–95) who was involved in the Underground Railroad and became a major spokesman for abolition, especially through his autobiography (1845) and his Rochester-based newspaper, the *North Star*.

a campaign button fills the O in *Douglass*. The button says: *Obama*.
10 This is the tomb of a man in chains, who left his fingerprints
   on the slavebreaker's throat so the whip would never carve his
      back again;
   now a labor union T-shirt drapes itself across the stone, offered up
   by a nurse, a janitor, a bus driver. A sticker on the sleeve says: *I Voted
      Today*.
   This is the tomb of a man who rolled his call to arms off the press,
15 peering through spectacles at the abolitionist headline; now a
      newspaper
   spreads above his dates of birth and death. The headline says: *Obama
      Wins*.
   This is the stillness at the heart of the storm that began in the body
   of the first slave, dragged aboard the first ship to America. Yellow
      leaves
   descend in waves, and the newspaper flutters on the tomb, like
      the sails
20 Douglass saw in the bay, like the eyes of a slave closing to watch
      himself
   escape with the tide. Believers in spirits would see the pages
      trembling
   on the stone and say: *look how the slave boy teaches himself to read*.
   I say a prayer, the first in years: that here we bury what we call
   the impossible, the unthinkable, the unimaginable, now and
      forever. *Amen*.

                                                                    2008

AUTHORS ON THEIR WORK
MARTÍN ESPADA (b. 1957)

From "Poetry Month: Martín Espada" (2011)*

While we all have our criticisms of President Obama, we must not forget the history he made in 2008, and the history we all made by voting for him and the feeling behind the making of that history. [. . .] Right after the election, I found myself in Rochester, New York. And it so happens that's where Frederick Douglass is buried, and so this is the poem that came out of it.

First, it's not an Obama poem; it's a Frederick Douglass poem. Second, it's a poem about the making of history; it's about how we felt at the moment that history was made. [. . .] We can't lose that feeling, even as we become frustrated or disillusioned. [. . .] We can't lose the way we felt at that moment [. . .].

*"Poetry Month: Martín Espada." Interview by Brian Lehrer. *The Brian Lehrer Show*, WNYC, 14 Apr. 2011, www.wnyc.org/story/124060-poetry-month-martin-espada/.

ONE POEM, MULTIPLE SITUATIONS AND SETTINGS

Though many poems depict a single situation and setting, a single poem will sometimes juxtapose multiple "scenes." In such cases, we need both to determine the situation and setting particular to each scene and to consider how the poem interrelates its various scenes to create a singular effect and meaning.

The following poem describes several different scenes. Some seem to have actually occurred at particular places and times (when the main speaker was "In sixth grade," for example [line 1]). Others seem hypothetical, abstract, or generic—events that might or often do happen almost anywhere to almost anybody (like "choos[ing] / persimmons," lines 6–7). Still others seem indeterminate as to time and/or place (Did "Donna undres[s]" only once [line 18]? When?). How many different scenes of each type can you discern? What connects them to each other? For example, how might at least some of these scenes demonstrate or discuss various kinds of "precision" (lines 5, 82)? How so, and what kinds?

LI-YOUNG LEE
Persimmons

In sixth grade Mrs. Walker
slapped the back of my head
and made me stand in the corner
for not knowing the difference
5 between *persimmon* and *precision*.
How to choose
persimmons. This is precision.
Ripe ones are soft and brown-spotted.
Sniff the bottoms. The sweet one
10 will be fragrant. How to eat:
put the knife away, lay down newspaper.
Peel the skin tenderly, not to tear the meat.

Chew the skin, suck it,
and swallow. Now, eat
15 the meat of the fruit,
so sweet,
all of it, to the heart.

Donna undresses, her stomach is white.
In the yard, dewy and shivering
20 with crickets, we lie naked,
face-up, face-down.
I teach her Chinese.
Crickets: *chiu chiu.* Dew: I've forgotten.
Naked: I've forgotten.
25 *Ni, wo:* you and me.
I part her legs,
remember to tell her
she is beautiful as the moon.

Other words
30 that got me into trouble were
fight and *fright, wren* and *yarn.*
Fight was what I did when I was frightened,
fright was what I felt when I was fighting.
Wrens are small, plain birds,
35 yarn is what one knits with.
Wrens are soft as yarn.
My mother made birds out of yarn.
I loved to watch her tie the stuff;
a bird, a rabbit, a wee man.

40 Mrs. Walker brought a persimmon to class
and cut it up
so everyone could taste
a *Chinese apple.* Knowing
it wasn't ripe or sweet, I didn't eat
45 but watched the other faces.

My mother said every persimmon has a sun
inside, something golden, glowing,
warm as my face.

Once, in the cellar, I found two wrapped in newspaper,
50 forgotten and not yet ripe.
I took them and set both on my bedroom windowsill,
where each morning a cardinal
sang, *The sun, the sun.*

Finally understanding
55 he was going blind,
my father sat up all one night
waiting for a song, a ghost.
I gave him the persimmons,
swelled, heavy as sadness,
60 and sweet as love.

This year, in the muddy lighting
of my parents' cellar, I rummage, looking
for something I lost.
My father sits on the tired, wooden stairs,
65 black cane between his knees,
hand over hand, gripping the handle.

He's so happy that I've come home.
I ask how his eyes are, a stupid question.
All gone, he answers.

70 Under some blankets, I find a box.
Inside the box I find three scrolls.
I sit beside him and untie
three paintings by my father:
Hibiscus leaf and a white flower.
75 Two cats preening.
Two persimmons, so full they want to drop from the cloth.

He raises both hands to touch the cloth,
asks, *Which is this?*

This is persimmons, Father.

80 *Oh, the feel of the wolftail on the silk,*
the strength, the tense
precision in the wrist.
I painted them hundreds of times
eyes closed. These I painted blind.
85 *Some things never leave a person:*
scent of the hair of one you love,
the texture of persimmons,
in your palm, the ripe weight.

1986

ONE SITUATION AND SETTING, MULTIPLE POEMS

Careful attention to situation and setting can be helpful not only in understanding how any one poem works or means but also in appreciating the differences among poems. We can usefully compare *any* two or more poems that focus on a similar situation or setting. But some poems deliberately invite such comparison by revisiting precisely the same situation and setting depicted in other, earlier poems.

The following two poems, by Christopher Marlowe and Sir Walter Raleigh, provide a famous example of this sort of response. Like all **pastoral** poems, these are both set in a rural landscape and concerned with the simple life of country folk, usually (as here) shepherds, who live an outdoor life and tend to basic human needs. Yet Marlowe's is the more conventional of the two insofar as it presents that landscape and that life in stylized, idealized terms—as a simple, timeless world of beauty, music, and love that implicitly operates as a kind of counter to, and interlude from, the more urbane, adult, complicated, time-bound "real world." Raleigh's poem is only one of many replies to Marlowe's, which itself indirectly alludes and responds to countless, even earlier works in the pastoral tradition.

CHRISTOPHER MARLOWE
The Passionate Shepherd to His Love

Come live with me and be my love,
And we will all the pleasures prove[4]
That valleys, groves, hills, and fields,
Woods, or steepy mountain yields.

5   And we will sit upon the rocks,
Seeing the shepherds feed their flocks,
By shallow rivers to whose falls
Melodious birds sing madrigals.

And I will make thee beds of roses
10   And a thousand fragrant posies,
A cap of flowers, and a kirtle[5]
Embroidered all with leaves of myrtle;

A gown made of the finest wool
Which from our pretty lambs we pull;
15   Fair linèd slippers for the cold,
With buckles of the purest gold;

4. Experience.   5. Gown.

A belt of straw and ivy buds,
With coral clasps and amber studs:
And if these pleasures may thee move,
20 Come live with me, and be my love.

The shepherd swains[6] shall dance and sing
For thy delight each May morning:
If these delights thy mind may move,
Then live with me and be my love.

                                        1600

SIR WALTER RALEIGH
The Nymph's Reply to the Shepherd

If all the world and love were young,
And truth in every shepherd's tongue,
These pretty pleasures might me move
To live with thee and be thy love.

5 Time drives the flocks from field to fold,
When rivers rage, and rocks grow cold,
And Philomel[7] becometh dumb;
The rest complain of cares to come.

The flowers do fade, and wanton fields
10 To wayward winter reckoning yields:
A honey tongue, a heart of gall,
Is fancy's spring, but sorrow's fall.

Thy gowns, thy shoes, thy beds of roses,
Thy cap, thy kirtle, and thy posies
15 Soon break, soon wither, soon forgotten;
In folly ripe, in reason rotten.

Thy belt of straw and ivy buds,
Thy coral clasps and amber studs,
All these in me no means can move
20 To come to thee and be thy love.

But could youth last, and love still breed,
Had joys no date,[8] nor age no need,
Then these delights my mind might move
To live with thee and be thy love.

                                        1600

6. Youths.   7. The nightingale.   8. End.

Raleigh's poem replies to Marlowe's by giving us the same situation and setting as perceived and described by a different speaker—the nymph rather than the shepherd. The following, much more recent poem takes a somewhat different tack, offering us not one but two different perspectives on the situation and setting depicted in Matthew Arnold's "Dover Beach"—that of the original poem's silent female **auditor** as related to us by another (presumably male) speaker.

ANTHONY HECHT
The Dover Bitch

A Criticism of Life[9]

> *for Andrews Wanning*[1]

So there stood Matthew Arnold and this girl
With the cliffs of England crumbling away behind them,
And he said to her, "Try to be true to me,
And I'll do the same for you, for things are bad
5 All over, etc., etc."
Well now, I knew this girl. It's true she had read
Sophocles in a fairly good translation
And caught that bitter allusion to the sea,[2]
But all the time he was talking she had in mind
10 The notion of what his whiskers would feel like
On the back of her neck. She told me later on
That after a while she got to looking out
At the lights across the channel, and really felt sad,
Thinking of all the wine and enormous beds
15 And blandishments in French and the perfumes.
And then she got really angry. To have been brought
All the way down from London, and then be addressed
As a sort of mournful cosmic last resort
Is really tough on a girl, and she was pretty.
20 Anyway, she watched him pace the room
And finger his watch-chain and seem to sweat a bit,
And then she said one or two unprintable things.
But you mustn't judge her by that. What I mean to say is,
She's really all right. I still see her once in a while
25 And she always treats me right. We have a drink

9. Matthew Arnold, critic as well as poet, famously wrote that poetry should be "a criticism of life."
1. Professor of literature at Bard College.
2. See "Dover Beach," lines 9–18.

And I give her a good time, and perhaps it's a year
Before I see her again, but there she is,
Running to fat, but dependable as they come.
And sometimes I bring her a bottle of *Nuit d'Amour*.[3]

                                                          1968

POEMS FOR FURTHER STUDY

Consider the *Who? What? Why? Where?* and *When?* questions as you read
the following poems.

NATASHA TRETHEWEY
Pilgrimage

Vicksburg, Mississippi[4]

Here, the Mississippi carved
        its mud-dark path, a graveyard

for skeletons of sunken riverboats.
        Here, the river changed its course,

5   turning away from the city
        as one turns, forgetting, from the past—

the abandoned bluffs, land sloping up
        above the river's bend—where now

the Yazoo fills the Mississippi's empty bed.
10   Here, the dead stand up in stone, white

marble, on Confederate Avenue. I stand
        on ground once hollowed by a web of caves;

they must have seemed like catacombs,
        in 1863, to the woman sitting in her parlor,

15   candlelit, underground. I can see her
        listening to shells explode, writing herself

into history, asking *what is to become
of all the living things in this place?*

3. French for "Night of Love," presumably a bottle of perfume.
4. On July 4, 1863, the city surrendered to Union forces under Ulysses S. Grant after a forty-day
siege; coming just a day after the Confederate defeat at Gettysburg, Vicksburg's surrender is
often regarded as a major turning point in the Civil War.

This whole city is a grave. Every spring—
20   *Pilgrimage*—the living come to mingle

with the dead, brush against their cold shoulders
    in the long hallways, listen all night

to their silence and indifference, relive
    their dying on the green battlefield.

25 At the museum, we marvel at their clothes—
    preserved under glass—so much smaller

than our own, as if those who wore them
    were only children. We sleep in their beds,

the old mansions hunkered on the bluffs, draped
30   in flowers—funereal—a blur

of petals against the river's gray.
    The brochure in my room calls this

living history. The brass plate on the door reads
    Prissy's[5] *Room.* A window frames

35 the river's crawl toward the Gulf. In my dream,
    the ghost of history lies down beside me,

rolls over, pins me beneath a heavy arm.

                                        2006

• What different historical times and situations meet in a single place
   in this poem? Why and how so?

KELLY CHERRY
Alzheimer's

He stands at the door, a crazy old man
Back from the hospital, his mind rattling
Like the suitcase, swinging from his hand,
That contains shaving cream, a piggy bank,
5 A book he sometimes pretends to read,
His clothes. On the brick wall beside him
Roses and columbine slug it out for space, claw the mortar.
The sun is shining, as it does late in the afternoon
In England, after rain.
10 Sun hardens the house, reifies it,

5. Scarlett O'Hara's maid in Margaret Mitchell's novel *Gone with the Wind* (1936).

Strikes the iron grillwork like a smithy
And sparks fly off, burning in the bushes—
The rosebushes—
While the white wood trim defines solidity in space.
15 This is his house. He remembers it as his,
Remembers the walkway he built between the front room
And the garage, the rhododendron he planted in back,
The car he used to drive. He remembers himself,
A younger man, in a tweed hat, a man who loved
20 Music. There is no time for that now. No time for music,
The peculiar screeching of strings, the luxurious
Fiddling with emotion.
Other things have become more urgent.
Other matters are now of greater import, have more
25 Consequence, must be attended to. The first
Thing he must do, now that he is home, is decide who
This woman is, this old, white-haired woman
Standing here in the doorway,
Welcoming him in.

                                                1997

- How do phrases like "a crazy old man" and "a book he sometimes pretends to read" indicate the speaker's feelings toward the man she
  describes (lines 1, 5)? Does the tone shift at some point? Where? What
  might the poem encourage you to speculate about the speaker's relationship to the people described? about their relationship to each other?

JUDITH ORTIZ COFER
The Latin Deli: An Ars Poetica[6]

Presiding over a formica counter,
plastic Mother and Child magnetized
to the top of an ancient register,
the heady mix of smells from the open bins
5 of dried codfish, the green plantains
hanging in stalks like votive offerings,
she is the Patroness of Exiles,
a woman of no-age who was never pretty,
who spends her days selling canned memories
10 while listening to the Puerto Ricans complain
that it would be cheaper to fly to San Juan
than to buy a pound of Bustelo coffee here,
and to Cubans perfecting their speech

---

6. Art of Poetry (Latin), after the title of a treatise by the Roman Poet Horace (65–8 BCE).

of a "glorious return" to Havana—where no one
15 has been allowed to die and nothing to change until then;
to Mexicans who pass through, talking lyrically
of *dólares* to be made in El Norte[7]—
                    all wanting the comfort
of spoken Spanish, to gaze upon the family portrait
of her plain wide face, her ample bosom
20 resting on her plump arms, her look of maternal interest
as they speak to her and each other
of their dreams and their disillusions—
how she smiles understanding,
when they walk down the narrow aisles of her store
25 reading the labels of packages aloud, as if
they were the names of lost lovers: *Suspiros,*[8]
Merengues, the stale candy of everyone's childhood.
                      She spends her days
slicing *jamón y queso*[9] and wrapping it in wax paper
tied with string: plain ham and cheese
30 that would cost less at the A&P,[1] but it would not satisfy
the hunger of the fragile old man lost in the folds
of his winter coat, who brings her lists of items
that he reads to her like poetry, or the others,
whose needs she must divine, conjuring up products
35 from places that now exist only in their hearts—
closed ports she must trade with.

                                   1993

- What keeps people shopping at the Latin Deli (versus a chain store)?
  How is this poem an "ars poetica," or what might it say about "the art
  of poetry" as practiced by a Mexican American poet like Ortiz Cofer?

ADRIENNE SU
Escape from the Old Country

I never had to make one,
no sickening weeks by ocean,

no waiting for the aerogrammes[2]
that gradually ceased to come.

7. The North (referring to the United States). *Dólares*: Dollars (Spanish).
8. Sighs (Spanish); like *Merengues*, a type of candy.
9. Ham and cheese (Spanish).
1. Supermarket, part of a chain, originally known as the Great Atlantic and Pacific Tea Company, in business from 1859 to 2015.
2. Airmail letter, especially one on specially designed stationery.

5   Spent the babysitting money
    on novels, shoes, and movies,

    yet the neighborhood stayed empty.
    It had nothing to do with a journey

    not undertaken, nor with dialect,
10 nor with a land that waited

    to be rediscovered, then rejected.
    As acid rain collected

    above the suburban hills, I tried
    to imagine being nothing, tried

15 to be able to claim, "I have
    no culture," and be believed.

    Yet the land occupies the person
    even as the semblance of freedom

    invites a kind of recklessness.
20 Tradition, unobserved, unasked,

    hangs on tight; ancestors roam
    into reverie, interfering at the most

    awkward moments, first flirtations,
    in doorways and dressing rooms—

25 But of course. Here in America,
    no one escapes. In the end, each traveler

    returns to the town where, everyone
    knew, she hadn't even been born.

                                        2006

- In the context of the rest of the poem, what are the various possible
  meanings of the sentence "Here in America, / no one escapes" (lines
  25–26)?

SUGGESTIONS FOR WRITING

1. Matthew Arnold's DOVER BEACH and Natasha Trethewey's PILGRIMAGE are
   meditations on history and human destiny derived from the poets' close
   observation of particular places and times. Write an essay in which you examine one poem's descriptive language and the way it creates a suitable setting
   for the speaker's philosophical musings.
2. Write an essay comparing the two carpe diem poems in this chapter. Concentrate on how each poem differently handles the same basic situation: How
   does each speaker go about convincing his auditor to "seize the day"? In what

ways are the two poems alike, and what difference do their different situations make?

3. Martín Espada claims that his occasional poem is about Frederick Douglass rather than President Obama. Write an essay exploring whether and why that seems to be the case. Why, according to the poem, was the election of Obama both an especially good occasion for remembering Douglass and itself an occasion worth commemorating in a poem? What and whom exactly are commemorated here? Alternatively, compare Espada's poem to Natasha Trethewey's. What might each poem suggest about history and memory, time and place?

4. Kelly Cherry's ALZHEIMER'S uses contrasts—especially before and after—to characterize the ravages of Alzheimer's disease. What evidence does the poem provide about what the man used to be like? What specific changes have come about? How does the setting of the poem suggest some of those changes? In what ways do the stabilities of house, landscape, and other people clarify what has happened? Write an essay about the function of the poem's setting.

5. Choose any poem in this anthology in which you think setting is especially key to the poem's effect and meaning or in which you think the meaningfulness of setting depends on the associations of particular times and/or places. Write an essay explaining why and how so.

9

THEME AND TONE

Poetry is full of surprises. Poems express anger or outrage just as effectively as love or sadness, and good poems can be written about going to a rock concert or having lunch or mowing the lawn, as well as about making love or smelling flowers or listening to Beethoven. Even poems on "predictable" subjects can surprise us with unpredicted attitudes or sudden twists. Knowing that a poem is about some particular subject or topic—love, for example, or death—may give us a general idea of what to expect, but it never tells us altogether what we will find in a particular poem. Labeling a poem a "love poem" or a "death poem" is a convenient way to speak of its topic. But poems that may be loosely called "love poems" or "death poems" may have little else in common, may express utterly different attitudes or ideas, and may concentrate on very different aspects of the subject. Letting a poem speak to us means more than merely figuring out its topic; it means listening to *how* the poem says what it says. *What* a poem says involves its **theme**. *How* a poem makes that statement involves its **tone**—the poem's attitude or feelings toward its topic. No two poems on the same subject affect us in exactly the same way; their themes and tones vary, and even similar themes may be expressed in various ways, creating different tones and effects.

TONE

Tone, a term borrowed from acoustics and music, refers to the qualities of the language a speaker uses in social situations or in a poem, and it also refers to a speaker's intended effect. Tone is closely related to style and diction; it is an effect of the speaker's expressions, *as if* showing a real person's feelings, manner, and attitude or relationship to a listener and to the particular subject or situation. Thus, the speaker may use angry or mocking words, may address the listener intimately or distantly, may sincerely confess or coolly observe, may paint a grand picture or narrate a legend.

The following poem describes a romantic encounter of sorts, but its tone may surprise you. As you read the poem, work first to identify its **speaker**, **situation**, and **setting**. Then try both to capture its tone in a single word or two and to figure out which features of the poem help to create that tone.

W. D. SNODGRASS
Leaving the Motel

Outside, the last kids holler
Near the pool: they'll stay the night.
Pick up the towels; fold your collar
Out of sight.

5 Check: is the second bed
Unrumpled, as agreed?
Landlords have to think ahead
In case of need,

Too. Keep things straight: don't take
10 The matches, the wrong keyrings—
We've nowhere we could keep a keepsake—
Ashtrays, combs, things

That sooner or later others
Would accidentally find.
15 Check: take nothing of one another's
And leave behind

Your license number only,
Which they won't care to trace;
We've paid. Still, should such things get lonely,
20 Leave in their vase

An aspirin to preserve
Our lilacs, the wayside flowers
We've gathered and must leave to serve
A few more hours;

25 That's all. We can't tell when
We'll come back, can't press claims,
We would no doubt have other rooms then,
Or other names.

                                    1968

    The title and details of LEAVING THE MOTEL indicate the situation and setting: Two secret lovers are at the end of an afternoon sexual encounter in a motel room (perhaps one is speaking for both of them), reminding themselves not to leave or take with them any clues for "others" (line 13)—their spouses?—to find.

    Whereas many poems on the topic of love confirm an enduring attachment or express desire or suggest erotic experience, this poem focuses on the effort to erase a stolen encounter. The two lovers have no names; indeed, they have registered under false names. They have already paid for this temporary shelter, can't stay the night like other guests or build a home with children of their own, and are running through a checklist of their agreements and duties ("Check," "Keep things straight," "Check" [lines 5, 9, 15]). Other than the "wayside" lilacs (line 22), the objects mentioned are trivial, from matches and keyrings to license numbers. The matter-of-fact but hurried tone suggests that they wish to hide any deep feelings (hinted at in the last two stanzas in the wish to make "claims" or preserve flowers [line 26]). The failure to express love—or guilt—enhances the effect when the tone shifts, at the word "still" (line 19), to the second thoughts about leaving something behind. The poem's short rhyming lines, sounding brisk and somewhat impersonal, contrast with the situation and add to the tone of subdued regret that nothing lasts.

THEME

Our response to the tone of a poem, however it surprises or jars or stirs us, guides us to understand its theme (or themes): what the poem expresses about its topic. A theme is not simply a work's subject or its topic; it is a statement *about* that topic. Although we can usually agree on what a poem is about without much difficulty, it is harder to determine how to state a poem's theme. Not only may a theme be expressed in several different ways, but a single poem may also have more than one theme. Sometimes the poet explicitly states a poem's theme, and such a statement may clarify why the author chose a particular mode of presentation and how the poem fits into the author's own patterns of thinking and growing. However, the author's words may give a misleading view of how most people read the poem, just as a person's self-assessment may not be all we need in order to understand his or her character. Further study of the poem is necessary to understand how it fulfills—or fails to fulfill—the author's intentions. Despite the difficulty of identifying and expressing themes, doing so is an important step in understanding and writing about poetry.

Topic Versus Tone and Theme: A Comparative Exercise

Reading two or more poems with similar topics side by side may suggest how each is distinctive in what it has to say and how it does so—its theme and tone. The following two poems are about animals, although both of them place their final emphasis on human beings: The animal in each case is only the means to the end of exploring human nature. The poems share the assumption that animal behavior may appear to reflect human habits and conduct, and that it may reveal much about us; in each case the character central to the poem is revealed to be surprisingly unlike the way she thinks of herself. But the poems differ in their tones, in the specific relationship between the woman and the animals, and in their themes.

How would you describe the tone of the following poem? its topic and theme?

MAXINE KUMIN
Woodchucks

Gassing the woodchucks didn't turn out right.
The knockout bomb from the Feed and Grain Exchange
was featured as merciful, quick at the bone
and the case we had against them was airtight,
5 both exits shoehorned shut with puddingstone,[1]
but they had a sub-sub-basement out of range.

Next morning they turned up again, no worse
for the cyanide than we for our cigarettes
and state-store Scotch, all of us up to scratch.
10 They brought down the marigolds as a matter of course
and then took over the vegetable patch
nipping the broccoli shoots, beheading the carrots.

The food from our mouths, I said, righteously thrilling
to the feel of the .22, the bullets' neat noses.
15 I, a lapsed pacifist fallen from grace
puffed with Darwinian pieties for killing,
now drew a bead on the littlest woodchuck's face.
He died down in the everbearing roses.

Ten minutes later I dropped the mother. She
20 flipflopped in the air and fell, her needle teeth
still hooked in a leaf of early Swiss chard.
Another baby next. O one-two-three
the murderer inside me rose up hard,
the hawkeye killer came on stage forthwith.

25 There's one chuck left. Old wily fellow, he keeps
me cocked and ready day after day after day.

1. Mixture of cement, pebbles, and gravel.

All night I hunt his humped-up form. I dream
I sight along the barrel in my sleep.
If only they'd all consented to die unseen
30 gassed underground the quiet Nazi way.

1972

As you read WOODCHUCKS aloud, how does your tone of voice change
from beginning to end? What tone do you use to read the ending? How
does the hunter feel about her increasing attraction to violence? Why
does the poem begin by calling the gassing of the woodchucks "merciful" (line 3) and end by describing it as "the quiet Nazi way" (line 30)?
What names does the hunter call herself? How does the name-calling
affect your feelings about her? Exactly when does the hunter begin to
enjoy the feel of the gun and the idea of killing? How does the poet make
that clear?

ADRIENNE RICH
Aunt Jennifer's Tigers

Aunt Jennifer's tigers prance across a screen,
Bright topaz denizens of a world of green.
They do not fear the men beneath the tree;
They pace in sleek chivalric certainty.

5 Aunt Jennifer's fingers fluttering through her wool
Find even the ivory needle hard to pull.
The massive weight of Uncle's wedding band
Sits heavily upon Aunt Jennifer's hand.

When Aunt is dead, her terrified hands will lie
10 Still ringed with ordeals she was mastered by.
The tigers in the panel that she made
Will go on prancing, proud and unafraid.

1951

In this poem, why are tigers a particularly appropriate contrast to the
woman embroidering or cross-stitching a hunting scene? What words
describing the tigers seem particularly significant? Why are Aunt Jennifer's
hands described as "terrified" (line 9)? What clues does the poem give
about why Aunt Jennifer is so afraid? How does the poem make you feel
about Aunt Jennifer's life and death? How would you describe the tone
of the poem? Why does the poem begin and end with the tigers?

AUTHORS ON THEIR WORK
ADRIENNE RICH (1929–2012)

From "When We Dead Awaken: Writing as Re-Vision" (1971)*

In writing this poem, composed and apparently cool as it is, I thought I was creating a portrait of an imaginary woman. But this woman suffers from the opposition of her imagination, worked out in tapestry, and her lifestyle, "ringed with ordeals she was mastered by." It was important to me that Aunt Jennifer was a person as distinct from myself as possible—distanced by the formalism of the poem, by its objective, observant tone—even by putting the woman in a different generation.

*"When We Dead Awaken: Writing as Re-Vision." Women's Forum of the MLA, Dec. 1971, Chicago. Address.

Questions for Comparing Poems

Here are some questions and steps for identifying, interpreting, and comparing the topic, theme, and tone of more than one poem. Some of these steps will be familiar to you already, and you may discover other ways to illuminate poetic themes and tones in addition to the guidelines offered here. As you respond to these questions or prompts, be sure to note line numbers to cite your evidence, according to this format: "puddingstone" (line 5) or "her terrified hands will lie / Still ringed with ordeals" (lines 9–10).

1. Read each poem through slowly and carefully.
2. Compare the titles. How do the titles point to the topics and possible themes, and are these similar or different? Take Woodchucks and Aunt Jennifer's Tigers, for example. What different qualities do we associate with woodchucks or tigers, animals rarely kept as pets?
3. What is the situation and setting in each poem? Make a list of the words in each poem that name objects or indicate actions. Which things or scenes are most significant, and how would you visualize or imagine them? Compare your notes on situation, setting, objects, and actions in both poems.
4. Who are the speakers? Are there other people in the poems? Is anyone identified as a listener or auditor? Are any things or beings (such

(continued on next page)

(continued)

as animals) personified or given human traits? Compare the speakers and other personalities in the poems.

5. What happens in each poem? Look closely at each stanza. Could the stanzas or lines be rearranged without making a difference? Does one poem tell of a single event or short passage of time, whereas another describes repeated actions or longer periods? Is one poem more eventful than the other?

6. Write down four or five words that describe the tone of each poem. Do these words also describe the language or style of each poem? Can you use all or some of the same words for both poems?

7. What is different about the two styles and forms, including length? Notice the rhythms and sounds, any regular or irregular patterns of **meter** or **rhyme**, and the shape of the stanzas.

8. Re-read the poems and try to express their themes in complete sentences. Then try to combine the two themes in a single statement that notes similarities and differences between them. Does your statement comparing the themes resemble your comparison of the tone and style of the two poems? Do the themes relate to similar or different historical, political, and social issues or contexts featured in the poems? Do the poems develop their themes with comparable **allusions** to myth, religion, literature, art, or other familiar or traditional ideas or associations?

9. Drawing on your notes and responses to the other questions, outline and write an essay comparing the two poems.

THEME AND CONFLICT

Since a theme is an idea implied by all of the elements of the poem working together, identifying theme—as opposed to topic and tone—can sometimes be a tough and tricky business. In reading and writing about poetry, then, it often helps to focus first—and most—on conflict. Though we usually think of conflict as an aspect of plot, even perfectly plotless poems are almost always organized around and devoted to exploring conflicts and tensions. To begin to identify these, look for contrasts and think about the conflict they imply.

Take, for example, AUNT JENNIFER's TIGERS. Though it might be hard to say at first just what the theme of Rich's poem might be, it's hard to miss the contrast that it builds and is built around. Where the tigers Aunt Jennifer embroiders "prance" and "pace" freely, "proud and unafraid" through a world as colorful and as lasting as they are (lines 1, 4, 12), Aunt Jennifer and her world seem just the opposite: Nothing but her fingers and hands move at all in the poem, and even they are "terrified" and tentative, "fluttering through her wool," "weight[ed]" down by a heavy "wedding band" in life and stilled permanently by death (lines 9, 5, 7). We have, then, not just a contrast but a multifaceted conflict—between imaginary and real worlds, between individual vision and social obligation. What the poem concludes about this conflict is its theme, but starting with questions about conflict often provides not only an easier way into the poem but also a much richer, more textured experience and understanding of it.

The following poem is in fact all about just this issue—the role of conflict in poetry. As you read the poem, try to identify the contrasts it sets up, the underlying conflict those contrasts point to, and the theme that ultimately emerges. Then test your own interpretation of the poem against the author's comments about how the poem came to be and what, for her, it's all about.

ADRIENNE SU
On Writing

A love poem risks becoming a ruin,
public, irretrievable, a form of tattooing,

while loss, being permanent,
can sustain a thousand documents.

5 Loss predominates in history,
smorgasbord of death, betrayal, heresy,

crime, contagion, deployment, divorce.
A writer could remain aboard

the ship of grief and thrive, never
10 approaching the shores of rapture.

What can be said about elation
that the elated, seeking consolation

from their joy, will go to books for?
It's wiser and quicker to look for

15 a poem in the dentist's chair
than in the luxury suite where

eternal love, declared, turns out
to be eternal. Who cares about

a stranger's bliss? Thus the juncture
20 where I'm stalled, unaccustomed

to integrity, despite your presence,
our tranquility, and every confidence.

2012

AUTHORS ON THEIR WORK
ADRIENNE SU (b. 1967)

From *The Best American Poetry 2013* (2013)*

When I started assembling my newest manuscript, *The House Unburned*, I found it to be suffering from structural gaps and an excess of grief and regret. [. . .]

To round it out, I needed to come up with some poems of happiness, or at least the absence of unhappiness. This presented a problem, since, as I'm always telling students, successful poems are born of uncertainty, interior conflict, the modes of struggle that lack clear solutions. I went back and forth between two selves: the editor, whose vision for the collection required some happier poems, and the poet, who raged against the affront of an assignment so lacking in ambiguity. How, argued the poet, can happiness, gratification, or success be complex enough to give life to a poem?

Eventually, the answer came with a shift in setting. If the poem could be about writing, conflict would be inherent in the question. So I gave myself permission to write about writing. Now that I had a conflict, the road to the poem appeared. (198)

**The Best American Poetry 2013.* Edited by Denise Duhamel and David Lehman, Scribner Poetry, 2013.

POEMS FOR FURTHER STUDY

WILLIAM BLAKE
London

I wander through each chartered street,
Near where the chartered Thames does flow,
And mark in every face I meet
Marks of weakness, marks of woe.

5 In every cry of every man,
In every Infant's cry of fear,
In every voice, in every ban,
The mind-forged manacles I hear.

How the Chimney-sweeper's cry
10 Every black'ning Church appalls;

And the hapless Soldier's sigh
Runs in blood down Palace walls.

But most through midnight streets I hear
How the youthful Harlot's curse
15 Blasts the new-born Infant's tear,
And blights with plagues the Marriage hearse.

1794

• Does the tone of this poem seem sad, angry, or both? Why and how
so? How might the repeated word "chartered" (lines 1 and 2) suggest
a theme?

PAUL LAURENCE DUNBAR
Sympathy

I know what the caged bird feels, alas!
    When the sun is bright on the upland slopes;
When the wind stirs soft through the springing grass,
    And the river flows like a stream of glass;
5   When the first bird sings and the first bud opens,
And the faint perfume from its chalice steals—
I know what the caged bird feels!

I know why the caged bird beats his wing
    Till its blood is red on the cruel bars;
10 For he must fly back to his perch and cling
When he fain[2] would be on the bough a-swing;
    And a pain still throbs in the old, old scars
And they pulse again with a keener sting—
I know why he beats his wing!

15 I know why the caged bird sings, ah me,
    When his wing is bruised and his bosom sore,—
When he beats his bars and he would be free;
It is not a carol of joy or glee,
    But a prayer that he sends from his heart's deep core,
20 But a plea, that upward to Heaven he flings—
I know why the caged bird sings!

1893

• How might your interpretation of this poem's theme change depending on whether or not you consider the date of its publication and/or
the fact that its author was African American?

2. Gladly.

W. H. AUDEN
[Stop all the clocks, cut off the telephone]

Stop all the clocks, cut off the telephone,
Prevent the dog from barking with a juicy bone,
Silence the pianos and with muffled drum
Bring out the coffin, let the mourners come.

5   Let aeroplanes circle moaning overhead
Scribbling on the sky the message He Is Dead,
Put crêpe bows round the white necks of the public doves,
Let the traffic policemen wear black cotton gloves.

He was my North, my South, my East and West,
10   My working week and my Sunday rest,
My noon, my midnight, my talk, my song;
I thought that love would last for ever: I was wrong.

The stars are not wanted now: put out every one;
Pack up the moon and dismantle the sun;
15   Pour away the ocean and sweep up the wood;
For nothing now can ever come to any good.

c. 1936

• In what tone of voice would you read line 12? How might you turn
this line into a statement of the poem's theme?

SHARON OLDS
Last Night

The next day, I am almost afraid.
Love? It was more like dragonflies
in the sun, 100 degrees at noon,
the ends of their abdomens stuck together, I
5   close my eyes when I remember. I hardly
knew myself, like something twisting and
twisting out of a chrysalis,
enormous, without language, all
head, all shut eyes, and the humming
10   like madness, the way they writhe away,
and do not leave, back, back,
away, back. Did I know you? No kiss,
no tenderness—more like killing, death-grip

holding to life, genitals
15 like violent hands clasped tight
barely moving, more like being closed
in a great jaw and eaten, and the screaming
I groan to remember it, and when we started
to die, then I refuse to remember,
20 the way a drunkard forgets. After,
you held my hands extremely hard as my
body moved in shudders like the ferry when its
axle is loosed past engagement, you kept me
sealed exactly against you, our hairlines
25 wet as the arc of a gateway after
a cloudburst, you secured me in your arms till I slept—
that was love, and we woke in the morning
clasped, fragrant, buoyant, that was
the morning after love.

1996

• What comparison is the speaker of this poem making between "drag-onflies / in the sun" and a night of love-making (lines 2–3)? What other comparisons are made in the poem? How do they work together and contribute to tone and theme?

KAY RYAN
Repulsive Theory

Little has been made
of the soft, skirting action
of magnets reversed,
while much has been
5 made of attraction.
But is it not this pillowy
principle of repulsion
that produces the
doily edges of oceans
10 or the arabesques of thought?
And do these cutout coasts
and incurved rhetorical beaches
not baffle the onslaught
of the sea or objectionable people
15 and give private life
what small protection it's got?
Praise then the oiled motions

of avoidance, the pearly
convolutions of all that
20 slides off or takes a
wide berth; praise every
eddying vacancy of Earth,
all the dimpled depths
of pooling space, the whole
25 swirl set up by fending-off—
extending far beyond the personal,
I'm convinced—
immense and good
in a cosmological sense:
30 unpressing us against
each other, lending
the necessary never
to never-ending.

2003

• What is the "theory" articulated in this poem? Might that theory be
the poem's theme?

SIMON J. ORTIZ
My Father's Song

Wanting to say things,
I miss my father tonight.
His voice, the slight catch,
the depth from his thin chest,
5 the tremble of emotion
in something he has just said
to his son, his song:

We planted corn one Spring at Acu[3]—
we planted several times
10 but this one particular time
I remember the soft damp sand
in my hand.

My father had stopped at one point
to show me an overturned furrow;

---

3. Alternative name for Acoma village and/or pueblo, about sixty miles west of Albuquerque,
New Mexico. Sometimes translated as "the place that always was," it is the oldest continuously inhabited community in the United States.

15 the plowshare had unearthed
the burrow nest of a mouse
in the soft moist sand.

Very gently, he scooped tiny pink animals
into the palm of his hand
20 and told me to touch them.
We took them to the edge
of the field and put them in the shade
of a sand moist clod.

I remember the very softness
25 of cool and warm sand and tiny alive mice
and my father saying things.

1976

• What are the "things" that the speaker wants to say (line 1)? Are they
the same "things" he remembers his father saying (line 26)? Does the
poem itself say these things?

ROBERT HAYDEN
Those Winter Sundays

Sundays too my father got up early
and put his clothes on in the blueblack cold,
then with cracked hands that ached
from labor in the weekday weather made
5 banked fires blaze. No one ever thanked him.

I'd wake and hear the cold splintering, breaking.
When the rooms were warm, he'd call,
and slowly I would rise and dress,
fearing the chronic angers of that house,

10 Speaking indifferently to him,
who had driven out the cold
and polished my good shoes as well.
What did I know, what did I know
of love's austere and lonely offices?

1966

• Why does the poem begin with the words "Sundays too" (rather than,
say, "On Sundays")? What are the "austere and lonely offices" to which
the poem's final line refers?

MARTÍN ESPADA
Of the Threads That Connect the Stars

Did you ever see stars? asked my father with a cackle. He was not
speaking of the heavens, but the white flash in his head when a
  fist burst
between his eyes. In Brooklyn, this would cause men and boys
  to slap
the table with glee; this might be the only heavenly light we'd
  ever see.

5 I never saw stars. The sky in Brooklyn was a tide of smoke rolling
  over us
from the factory across the avenue, the mattresses burning in the
  junkyard,
the ruins where squatters would sleep, the riots of 1966[4] that
  kept me
locked in my room like a suspect. My father talked truce on the
  streets.

My son can see the stars through the tall barrel of a telescope.
10 He names the galaxies with the numbers and letters of
  astronomy.
I cannot see what he sees in the telescope, no matter how many
  eyes I shut.
I understand a smoking mattress better than the language of
  galaxies.

My father saw stars. My son sees stars. The earth rolls beneath
our feet. We lurch ahead, and one day we have walked this far.

2013

• How does the poem differentiate and connect three generations of one
family by describing the stars each did or didn't, do or don't, see?

SUGGESTIONS FOR WRITING

1. Choose any two poems in this chapter that express positive and negative feelings about their topics. How do the tones of the poems combine or contrast
the feelings? Is there a shift in tone in each poem? If so, where? How is the
shift revealed through language? Write an essay in which you compare the
way each poet accomplishes this shifting of tone.

4. In July 1966, violent conflict repeatedly erupted between blacks and Puerto Ricans in Brooklyn's troubled Bedford-Stuyvesant neighborhood.

2. Write an essay in which you consider the use of language to create tone in any two or more poems on the same subject. How do the tones suit the themes of these poems?

3. Write an essay on Maxine Kumin's Woodchucks in which you show that the speaker's conflict between sympathy and murderous instinct is reflected in the mixed tone and varied vocabulary. Focus on formal and informal tone, noting phrases from law or religion—"the case we had against them"; "fallen from grace" (lines 4, 15)—or from everyday speech—"up to scratch," "food from our mouths" (lines 9, 13). How does the diction, or word choice, of the poem affect its tone?

4. Reimagine W. D. Snodgrass's Leaving the Motel as a poem in which the speaker and lover are happy and delighted with each other and certain that the relationship will last forever. What details and phrases would need to be changed for the poem to express a positive feeling about the relationship? Write an essay in which you relate the tone of the poem to the subject of secret and short-lived sexual relationships.

SAMPLE WRITING: RESPONSE PAPER

In the response paper that follows, Stephen Bordland works through Auden's poem STOP ALL THE CLOCKS, CUT OFF THE TELEPHONE more or less line by line, writing down whatever ideas come to him. The form of this paper is less important than the process of thinking carefully about the poem's music, emotions, and meanings. As you can see, by the time Stephen reaches the end of his response, he has decided on a topic for the more formal essay that he will write later.

Bordland 1

Stephen Bordland
Professor O'Connor
English 157
1 January 2017

Response Paper on W. H. Auden's "Stop all the clocks,
cut off the telephone"

    I first heard this poem read aloud when I saw the movie *Four Weddings and a Funeral* on cable. The character who read the poem was reading it at the funeral of his lover. It was perfectly suited to the story and was very moving. I was struck by the actor's reading because the poem seemed to have a steady rhythm for several lines and then suddenly hit what sounded like a dead end—"I thought that love would last forever: I was wrong" (line 12). Hearing the actor's reading of this poem made me want to read it myself, to see if the poem would still affect me if I read/heard it outside of the context of an emotional scene in a movie. It did, and I think that the "I was wrong" line is the key—a turning point, I guess.

    In the anthology, the poem seems to have no actual title (at least that's how I interpret the fact that the first line is in brackets where the

---

Bordland 2

title usually goes), but I did some searching on the Internet and found that this poem was once called "Funeral Blues." If I were reading the poem for the first time under that title, I would at least know that the poem has something to do with death right from the start. But this title makes the poem sound irreverent rather than sincerely painful. I wonder if that would have been true in the 1930s, when Auden wrote the poem. There were lots of blues and jazz songs of that era whose titles ended in "Blues" (like Robert Johnson's "Kindhearted Woman Blues"), so maybe the title wasn't meant to be read the way that I'm reading it. Anyway, I don't know if Auden himself changed the title, or if there's another story there, but I think it's a better poem without the title.

The poem starts with a request to an unknown person (everyone?) to make some common aspects of daily life go away: "Stop all the clocks" (1) presumably because time seems to be standing still; "cut off the telephone" (1) presumably because the speaker wants to be alone and undisturbed, cut off from human contact. I'm not sure what's implied by "Prevent the dog from barking with a juicy bone" (2) mainly because I'm confused about the literal meaning: Are we supposed to prevent the dog from barking by giving him a juicy bone (one way to interpret "with a juicy bone"), or are we supposed to prevent the dog with a juicy bone in his mouth (another way of interpreting "with a juicy bone") from barking at all? I don't think I really have a handle on what this line means in relation to the other ones, but I'll leave it for now. In the next line, "Silence the pianos" (3) clearly means that the speaker wants no music now that his lover is dead, except for the "muffled drum" (3) that will accompany the coffin and mourners in the fourth line. It's interesting that all of these things so far are sounds—the tick-tock of the clock, the ring of the telephone, a barking dog, music. They all seem to stand in for something, too—for the passing of time, contact with other people (and with pets?), joy as expressed by music.

The image of "aeroplanes" (5) circling overhead (and "moaning" [5]—that's a really good choice of words) writing "He is Dead" (6) is very strong and would have been a very modern reference at the time of this poem (c. 1936). A *Christian Science Monitor* article about a "skywriting" pilot says that "[s]kywriting's heyday was from the 1930s to the early 1950s when Pepsi Cola used skywriting as its main way of advertising" (Hartill), so the reference here is to a commercial medium being used to make as many people as possible aware of the speaker's loss. If a poet tried to make a

Bordland 3

reference to something equivalent today, it would have to be a television advertisement or a blog, maybe. I wonder if a modern poet could really pull off a reference to a TV ad and still make it sound sincerely sad.

I'm not sure what the "crêpe bows round the white necks of the public doves" (7) means. Would the bows even be visible? Does "crêpe" imply a color, or is it just a type of fabric? And what is a public dove? I'm not sure I like the repetition in this line of three adjective/noun pairs: "crepe bows," "white necks," "public doves." It seems too precious or "poetic." The "traffic policemen" (8) that I've seen all wear white gloves so that their hand movements can be seen clearly. The speaker wants them all to wear "black cotton gloves," the appropriate color for mourning, but that would probably create real problems for the drivers trying to see what the policemen are directing them to do. So, I wonder if the bows on doves and black gloves on cops are both there to show us that the speaker is feeling not just the sort of grief that moves him to write poetry, but also the sort of intense pain that makes him want to throw the rest of the world into the same confusion and chaos he's experiencing. Or at least, he's not only asking to be alone, but also wanting the rest of the world to share his grief.

In the next four lines, the speaker turns to himself and his lover: "He was my North, my South, my East and West / My working week and my Sunday rest" (9-12).

These lines flow so smoothly, with a soothing, regular rhythm; they're almost sing-songy. But they don't seem sappy or wrong in this poem; they seem painfully sincere. The author uses place (as described by the compass) and time (the whole week, the reference to noon and midnight) to make very clear, in case we hadn't figured it out from the preceding lines, that his lover was everything to him. In the fourth line of this section, this regular rhythm is interrupted, or even stopped dead: "I thought that love would last for ever: I was wrong" (12). This is a very true and moving conclusion to reach, but it also seems ironic, once we read to the end of the poem. If the speaker was wrong to believe (before the death of his lover) that love would last forever, isn't it possible that he's wrong about the conclusion "nothing now can ever come to any good" (16)—that grief will last forever?

I think that Auden probably intended us to be aware of this irony. It seems to me that the poem is broken into three major parts. First, we sympathize with the speaker's grief and sense of loss. Then we're supposed to stop at the point where the speaker makes a judgment about his

Bordland 4

understanding of the world prior to that loss ("I thought that love would last for ever: I was wrong" [12]) and to spend a moment absorbing the meaning of that judgment. Finally, as we read the most extreme expression of the speaker's loss ("Pack up the moon and dismantle the sun" [14]), we can see that although we sympathize and understand, we also know something that the speaker doesn't know at the moment. Just as his love apparently blinded the speaker to love's inevitable end, so his profound grief is probably blinding him to grief's inevitable end. Also, it may just be me, but it seems that this last part is almost too dramatic or theatrical, as if maybe the speaker has made some sort of transition from being unself-consciously mournful to being self-consciously aware that the way he's expressing himself is poetic.

Back to the idea about the irony: The poem itself seems to be arguing against the notion that love cannot last forever (or, okay, a very long time). After all, people are still reading this poem, and I bet people will continue to read it for as long as people read poetry. That's about as close to forever as we get on this earth, so even though the lovers of this poem are long dead, their love lives on, in a way. Auden must have been aware of this when he was writing the poem. I wonder if he ever said anything in letters, essays, or speeches about art and immortality? If so, I think I'll write a paper on that topic as addressed in this poem.

Bordland 5

Works Cited

Auden, W. H. "Stop all the clocks, cut off the telephone." *The Norton Introduction to Literature*, edited by Kelly J. Mays, portable 12th ed., W. W. Norton, 2017, p. 556.

Hartill, Lane. "Sky Writer." *Christian Science Monitor*, 25 Jan. 2000, www.csmonitor.com/2000/0125/p22s1.html.

# LANGUAGE: WORD CHOICE
AND ORDER

Fiction and drama depend on language just as poetry does, but in a poem almost everything comes down to the particular meanings and implications, as well as sound and shape, of individual words. When we read stories and plays, we generally focus our attention on character and plot, and although words determine how we imagine those characters and how we respond to what happens to them, we are not as likely to pause over any one word as we may need to when reading a poem. Because poems are often short, much depends on every word in them. Sometimes, as though they were distilled prose, poems contain only the essential words. They say just barely enough to communicate in the most basic way, using elemental signs—each of which is chosen for exactly the right shade of meaning or feeling or both. But elemental does not necessarily mean simple, and these signs may be very rich in their meanings and complex in their effects. The poet's word choice—the **diction** of a poem—determines not only meaning but also just about every effect the poem produces.

PRECISION AND AMBIGUITY

Let's look first at poems that create some of their effects by examining—or playing with—a single word. Here, multiple meanings or the shiftiness, ambiguity, and uncertainty of a word are at issue. The following short poem, for example, depends almost entirely on the ways we use the word *play*.

SARAH CLEGHORN
[The golf links lie so near the mill]

The golf links lie so near the mill
That almost every day
The laboring children can look out
And see the men at play.

1915

While traveling in the American South, Cleghorn had seen, right next to a golf course, a textile mill that employed quite young children. Her poem doesn't *say* that we expect men to work and children to play; it just assumes our expectation and builds an effect of *dramatic irony*—an incongruity between what we expect and what actually occurs—out of the observation. The poem saves almost all of its devastating effect for the final word, after the situation has been carefully described and the irony set up.

In the following poem, a word used over and over acquires multiple meanings and refuses to be limited to a single one. Here, the importance of a word involves its ambiguity (that is, its having more than one possible meaning) rather than its precision or exactness. How many different meanings of the words *lie* and *lay* can you distinguish in the poem?

MARTHA COLLINS

Lies

Anyone can get it wrong, laying low
when she ought to lie, but is it a lie
for her to say she laid him when we know
he wouldn't lie still long enough to let
5 her do it? A good lay is not a song,
not anymore; a good lie is something
else: lyrics, lines, what if you say *dear sister*
when you have no sister, what if you say *guns*
when you saw no guns, though you know
10 they're there? *She laid down her arms; she lay
down, her arms by her sides.* If we don't know,
do we lie if we say? If we don't say, do we lie
down on the job? To arms! in any case
dear friends. If we must lie, let's not lie around.

1999

DENOTATION AND CONNOTATION

Although the unambiguous or "dictionary" meaning of words—that is, their **denotation**—is certainly important, words are more than hard blocks of meaning on whose sense everyone agrees. They also carry emotional force and shades of suggestion. The words we use indicate not only what we mean but how we feel about it and want to encourage others to feel. A person who holds office is, quite literally (and unemotionally), an *officeholder*—the word denotes what he or she does. But if we want to imply that a particular officeholder is wise, trustworthy, and deserving of political support, we may call that person a *civil servant*, a *political leader*, or an *elected official*, whereas if we want to promote distrust or contempt of that same officeholder we might say *politician* or *bureaucrat* or *political hack*. These terms have clear **connotations**—suggestions of emotional coloration that imply our attitude and invite a similar one from our hearers. In poems, as in life, what words connote can be just as important as what they denote; some poems work primarily through denotation and some more through connotation.

The following **epitaph**, for example, which describes one person's mixed feelings about another, depends heavily on the connotations of fairly common words.

WALTER DE LA MARE
Slim Cunning Hands

Slim cunning hands at rest, and cozening eyes—
Under this stone one loved too wildly lies;
How false she was, no granite could declare;
    Nor all earth's flowers, how fair.

1950

What the speaker in SLIM CUNNING HANDS remembers about the dead woman—her hands, her eyes—tells part of the story; her physical presence was clearly important to him. The poem's other nouns—*stone, granite, flowers*—all remind us of her death and its finality. All these words denote objects having to do with the rituals that memorialize a departed life. Granite and stone connote finality as well, and flowers connote fragility and suggest the brevity of life (which is why they have become the symbolic language of funerals). The way the speaker talks about the woman expresses, in just a few words, the complexity of his love for her. She was loved, he says, too "wildly"—by him perhaps, and apparently by others. The excitement she offered is suggested by the word, as is the lack of control. The words *cunning* and *cozening* imply both her falsity and, perhaps, her wildness; they suggest her calculation, cleverness, and untrustworthiness as well as her skill, persuasiveness, and ability to please. Moreover, coming at the end of the second line, the word *lies* has more than one meaning. The body "lies" under the stone, but the woman's falsity has by now become too prominent to ignore as a second meaning. And the word *fair*, a simple yet very inclusive word, suggests how totally attractive the speaker finds her: Her beauty can no more be expressed by flowers than her fickleness can be expressed by something as permanent as words in stone. But the word *fair*, in the emphatic position as the final word, also implies two other meanings that seem to resonate, ironically, with what

we have already learned about her from the speaker: "impartial" and "just."
"Impartial" she may be in her preferences (as the word *false* suggests), but to
the speaker she is hardly "just," and the final defining word speaks both to her
appearance and (ironically) to her character. Simple words here tell us perhaps all we need to know of a long story—or at least the speaker's version of it.
Words like *fair* and *cozening* are clearly loaded. They imply more emotionally than they mean literally. They have strong, clear connotations; they
tell us what to think, what evaluation to make; and they suggest the basis
for the evaluation.

Sometimes word choice in poems is less dramatic and less obviously significant but equally important. Often, in fact, simple appropriateness makes
the words in a poem work, and words that do not call special attention to
themselves can be the most effective. Precision of denotation may be just as
impressive and productive of specific effects as the resonance or ambiguous
suggestiveness of connotation. Often poems achieve their power by a combination of verbal effects, setting off elaborate **figures of speech** or other
complicated strategies with simple words chosen to indicate exact actions,
moments, or states of mind.

Words are the starting point for all poetry, of course, and almost every
word is likely to be significant, either denotatively or connotatively or both.
Poets who know their craft pick each word with care to express exactly what
needs to be expressed and to suggest every emotional shade that the poem is
calculated to evoke in us.

Word Choice: An Example and an Exercise

Before you read the following poem, notice the three words in the
title. What do they lead you to expect? What questions do they raise?
Jot down your thoughts on a piece of paper. Then, as you read the
poem, take note of key words and try to be conscious of the emotional
effects and impressions they create.

THEODORE ROETHKE
My Papa's Waltz

The whiskey on your breath
Could make a small boy dizzy;
But I hung on like death:
Such waltzing was not easy.

5 We romped until the pans
   Slid from the kitchen shelf;
   My mother's countenance
   Could not unfrown itself.

   The hand that held my wrist
10 Was battered on one knuckle;
   At every step you missed
   My right ear scraped a buckle.

   You beat time on my head
   With a palm caked hard by dirt,
15 Then waltzed me off to bed
   Still clinging to your shirt.
                              1948

Exactly how does the situation in MY PAPA'S WALTZ and the poem itself
fulfill or defy your expectations? How does it answer your questions?
How does it characterize the waltz and the speaker's feelings about it?
Which words are most suggestive in these terms? What clues are there
in the word choice that an adult is remembering a childhood experience? How scared was the boy at the time? How does the grown adult
now evaluate the emotions he felt when he was a boy?

WORD ORDER AND PLACEMENT

Individual words qualify and amplify one another—suggestions clarify other
suggestions, and meanings grow upon meanings—and thus how words are
put together and where individual words are located matters. Notice, for
example, that in "Slim Cunning Hands" the final emphasis is on how *fair* in
appearance the woman was; the speaker's last word describes the quality he
can't forget despite her lack of a different kind of fairness and his distrust
of her. Even though it doesn't justify everything else, her beauty mitigates
all the disappointment and hurt. Putting the word *fair* at the end of the line
and of the poem gives it special emphasis and meaning.

That one word, *fair*, does not stand all by itself, however, any more than any
other word in a poem can be considered all alone. Every word exists within
larger units of meaning—sentences, patterns of comparison and contrast, the
whole poem—and where the word is and how it is used are often important.
The final word or words may be especially emphatic (as in "Slim Cunning
Hands"), and words that are repeated take on a special intensity, as *lie* does in

Lies. Certain words may stand out because they are unusual or used in an unusual way (like *unfrown* or *waltzing* in "My Papa's Waltz") or because they are given an artificial prominence—through unusual sentence structure, for example, or because the title calls special attention to them. In a poem, as opposed to a prose work, moreover, the number and placement of words in a line and the spacing of the words and lines stays the same in every printed version. Where words come—in a line, in a stanza—and how they are spatially and visually related to other words also helps determine their force and meaning.

The subtlety and force of word choice are sometimes strongly affected by **syntax**—the way the sentences are put together. When you find unusual syntax or spacing, you can be pretty sure that something there merits special attention. Notice the odd sentence constructions in the second and third stanzas of "My Papa's Waltz"—the way the speaker talks about the abrasion of buckle on ear in line 12, for example. He does not say that the buckle scraped his ear, but rather "My right ear scraped a buckle." Reversing the more common expression makes a big difference in the effect created; the speaker avoids placing blame and refuses to specify any unpleasant effect. Had he said that the buckle scraped his ear, we would have to worry about the fragile ear. The syntax channels our feeling and helps control what we think of the "waltz."

In the most curious part of the poem, the second stanza, the silent mother appears, and the syntax on both sides of the semicolon is peculiar. In lines 5–6, the connection between the romping and the pans falling is stated oddly: "We romped *until* the pans / Slid from the kitchen shelf" (emphasis added). The speaker does not say that they knocked down the pans or imply awkwardness, but he does suggest energetic activity and duration. He implies intensity, almost intention—as though the romping would not be complete until the pans fell. And the clause about the mother—odd but effective—makes her position clear. A silent bystander in this male ritual, she doesn't seem frightened or angry. She seems to be holding a frown, or to have it molded on her face, as though it were part of her own ritual, and perhaps a facet of her stern character as well. The syntax implies that she *has to* maintain the frown, and the falling of the pans almost seems to be for her benefit. She disapproves, but she remains their audience.

Sometimes poems create, as well, a powerful sense of the way minds and emotions work by varying normal syntactical order in special ways. Listen for and watch, for example, what happens a few lines into the following poem. What does it suggest about what is happening inside the speaker?

SHARON OLDS
Sex without Love

How do they do it, the ones who make love
without love? Beautiful as dancers,
gliding over each other like ice-skaters
over the ice, fingers hooked
5 inside each other's bodies, faces
red as steak, wine, wet as the
children at birth whose mothers are going to
give them away. How do they come to the
come to the   come to the   God   come to the
10 still waters, and not love
the one who came there with them, light
rising slowly as steam off their joined
skin? These are the true religious,
the purists, the pros, the ones who will not
15 accept a false Messiah, love the
priest instead of the God. They do not
mistake the lover for their own pleasure,
they are like great runners: they know they are alone
with the road surface, the cold, the wind,
20 the fit of their shoes, their over-all cardio-
vascular health—just factors, like the partner
in the bed, and not the truth, which is the
single body alone in the universe
against its own best time.

1984

The poem starts calmly enough, with a simple rhetorical question
implying that the speaker just cannot understand sex without love. Lines
2–4 carefully compare such sexual activity with two other artful activities,
and the speaker—although plainly disapproving—seems coolly in control
of the analysis and evaluation. But by the end of the fourth line, something begins to seem odd: "[H]ooked" seems too ugly and extreme a way to
characterize the lovers' fingers, however much the speaker may disapprove,
and by line 6 the syntax seems to break down. How does "wine" fit the
syntax of the line? Is it parallel with "steak," another example of redness?
Or is it somehow related to the last part of the sentence, parallel with
"faces"? Neither of these possibilities quite works. At best, the punctuation is inadequate; at worst, the speaker's mind is working too fast for
the language it generates, scrambling its images. We can't yet be sure what
is going on, but by the ninth line the lack of control is manifest with

the compulsive repeating (three times) of "come to the" and the interjected "God."

Such verbal behavior—here concretized by the way the poem orders its words and spaces them on the page—invites us to reevaluate the speaker's moralizing relative to her emotional involvement with the issues and with her representation of sexuality itself. The speaker's own values, as well as those who have sex without love, become a subject for evaluation.

. . .

Words, the basic materials of poetry, come in many varieties and can be used in many different ways and in different—sometimes surprising—combinations. They are seldom simple or transparent, even when we know their meanings and recognize their syntactical combinations as ordinary and conventional. Carefully examining them, individually and collectively, is a crucial part of reading poems, and being able to ask good questions about the words that poems use and the way they use them is one of the most basic—and rewarding—skills a reader of poetry can develop.

POEMS FOR FURTHER STUDY

GERARD MANLEY HOPKINS
Pied Beauty[1]

Glory be to God for dappled things—
    For skies of couple-color as a brinded[2] cow;
      For rose-moles all in stipple[3] upon trout that swim;
Fresh-firecoal chestnut-falls;[4] finches' wings;
5   Landscape plotted and pieced—fold, fallow, and plow;
      And all trades, their gear and tackle and trim.
All things counter, original, spare, strange;
    Whatever is fickle, freckled (who knows how?)
      With swift, slow; sweet, sour; adazzle, dim;
10 He fathers-forth whose beauty is past change;
      Praise him.

1887

- How many ways of expressing mixed color can you find in this poem?
How does Hopkins expand the meaning of "pied beauty"?

1. Particolored beauty: having patches or sections of more than one color.
2. Streaked or spotted. 3. Rose-colored dots or flecks.
4. Fallen chestnuts as red as burning coals.

WILLIAM CARLOS WILLIAMS
The Red Wheelbarrow

so much depends
upon

a red wheel
barrow

5 glazed with rain
water

beside the white
chickens.
                    1923

• How does setting the words "barrow", "water", and "chickens" on lines
of their own help to substantiate the poem's first line?

This Is Just to Say

I have eaten
the plums
that were in
the icebox

5 and which
you were probably
saving
for breakfast

Forgive me
10 they were delicious
so sweet
and so cold
            1934

• What is meant by "This" in the poem's title? What is the apparent
occasion for this poem?

KAY RYAN
Blandeur

If it please God,
let less happen.

Even out Earth's
rondure, flatten
5 Eiger,[5] blanden
the Grand Canyon.
Make valleys
slightly higher,
widen fissures
10 to arable land,
remand your
terrible glaciers
and silence
their calving,
15 halving or doubling
all geographical features
toward the mean.
Unlean against our hearts.
Withdraw your grandeur
20 from these parts.

2000

- How does the poem define the made-up words (or neologisms)
blandeur and *blanden*? How does it play on the word *grandeur* and
its connotations?

A. E. STALLINGS
Shoulda, Woulda, Coulda

The mood made him tense—
How she sharpened conditional[6] futures
On strops[7] of might-have-beens,
The butchered present in sutures.

5 He cursed in the fricative,[8]
The way she could not act,
Or live in the indicative,[9]
Only contrary to fact.

5. Mountain in the Swiss Alps.
6. In grammar, verb mood or tense used in expressing what might happen given the right conditions, as in "she *would eat* if he made her a sandwich."
7. Leather strap or similar device used to sharpen a razor.
8. In phonetics, consonant sound, such as the English *f* or *v*.
9. In grammar, mood of verbs expressing a simple statement of fact.

> Tomorrow should have been vast,
> 10 Bud-packed, grenade-gravid,[1]
> Not just a die miscast.
>
> It made him sad, it made him livid:
> How she construed from the imperfect[2] past
> A future less vivid.

2013

- How does this poem end up playing on the various meanings of the words "mood" and "tense" (line 1)? What exactly about the attitude of the woman described in the poem makes her male counterpart first "tense," then "sad" and "livid" (lines 1, 12)?

SUGGESTIONS FOR WRITING

1. Choose one poem in this book in which a single word seems crucial to that poem's total effect and theme. Write an essay in which you work out carefully why and how that's the case.
2. Choose one poem in this book in which syntax (the order of words in sentences) or the placement of words on the page seems especially key to the poem's overall effect and meaning. Write an essay explaining how and why considering word order, in either or both of these senses, might change or deepen a reader's understanding of the poem.
3. Language is a topic of (as well as tool used in) Martha Collins's LIES, A. E. Stallings's SHOULDA, WOULDA, COULDA, and even Kay Ryan's BLANDEUR. Write an essay exploring what any of these poems has to say about poetry or language and how word choice, order, and placement help the poem express or illustrate it.

---

1. Pregnant, distended with or full of.
2. In grammar, of or relating to a verb tense used to designate a continuing state or incomplete action, especially in the past, as in "We used to speak regularly" and "I was eating."

11 PICTURING: VISUAL IMAGERY AND FIGURES OF SPEECH

The language of poetry is often visual and pictorial. Rather than depending primarily on abstract ideas and elaborate reasoning, poems depend more on concrete and specific words that create images in our minds. Poems thus help us see things afresh or feel them suggestively through our other physical senses, such as hearing or touch. Sound is, as we will see, a vital aspect of poetry. But most poems use the sense of sight to help us form, in our minds, visual impressions, images that communicate more directly than concepts. We "see" yellow leaves on a branch, a father and son waltzing precariously, or two lovers sitting together on the bank of a stream, so that our response begins from a vivid visual impression of exactly what is happening. Some people think that those media and arts that challenge the imagination of a hearer or reader—radio drama, for example, or poetry—allow us to respond more fully than those (such as television or theater) that actually show things more fully to our physical senses. Certainly these media leave more to our imagination, to our mind's eye.

Poems are sometimes quite abstract—they can even be *about* abstractions like grandeur or history. But usually they are quite concrete in what they ask us to see. One reason is that they often begin in a poet's mind with a picture or an image: of a person, a place, an event, or an object of observation. That image may be based on something the poet has actually seen but it may also be totally imaginary and only based on the "real world" in the sense that it draws on the poet's sense of what the world is like. Even when a poet begins with an idea that draws on visual experience, however, the reader still has to *imagine* (through the poem's words) an image, some person or thing or action that the poem describes. The poet must rely on words to help the reader to flesh out that mental image. In a sense, then, the reader becomes a visual artist, but the poet directs the visualization by evoking specific responses through words. *How* that happens can involve quite complicated verbal strategies—or even *visual* ones that draw on the possibilities of print (see ch. 15).

The languages of description are quite varied. The visual qualities of poetry result partly from the two aspects of poetic language described in chapter 10: on the one hand, the precision of individual words, and, on the other hand, precision's opposite—the reach, richness, and ambiguity of suggestion that

577

words sometimes accrue. Visualization can also derive from sophisticated rhetorical and literary devices (**figures of speech**, for example, as we will see later in this chapter). But often description begins simply with naming—providing the word (noun, verb, adjective, or adverb) that will trigger images familiar from a reader's own experience. A reader can readily imagine a *dog* or *cat* or *house* or *flower* when each word is named, but not all readers will envision the same kind of dog or flower until the word is qualified in some way. So the poet may specify that the dog is a greyhound or poodle, or that the flower is a daffodil or a lilac or Queen Anne's lace; or the poet may indicate colors, sizes, specific movements, or particular identifying features. Such description can involve either narrowing by category or expanding through detail, and often comparisons are either explicitly or implicitly involved. Notice how this works in the two following poems. In the first, Richard Wilbur's THE BEAUTI-FUL CHANGES, for example, the comparison between wading through flowers in a meadow and wading among waves in the sea both suggests how the first experience feels and etches it visually in our minds. More than just a matter of naming, using precise words, and providing basic information, description involves qualification and comparison. Sometimes, as in the second poem below, the poet needs to tell us what *not* to picture, dissociating what the poem describes from other possible images we may have in mind. Different features in the language of description add up to something that describes a whole—a picture or scene—as well as a series of individualized objects.

Seeing in the mind's eye—the re-creation of visual experience—requires different skills from poets and readers. Poets use all the linguistic strategies they can think of to re-create for us something they have already "seen." Poets depend on our having had a rich variety of visual experiences and try to draw on those experiences by using common, evocative words and then refining the process through more elaborate verbal devices. We as readers inhabit the process the other way around, trying to draw on our previous knowledge so that we can "see" by following verbal clues. In the poems that follow, notice the ways that description inspires specific images, and pay attention to how shape, color, relationship, and perspective become clear, not only through individual words but also through combinations of words and phrases that suggest appearance and motion.

RICHARD WILBUR
The Beautiful Changes

One wading a Fall meadow finds on all sides
The Queen Anne's Lace[1] lying like lilies

---

1. Plant sometimes called "wild carrot," with delicate, fingerlike leaves and flat clusters of small white flowers.

On water; it glides
So from the walker, it turns
5 Dry grass to a lake, as the slightest shade of you
Valleys my mind in fabulous blue Lucernes.[2]

The beautiful changes as a forest is changed
By a chameleon's tuning his skin to it;
As a mantis, arranged
10 On a green leaf, grows
Into it, makes the leaf leafier, and proves
Any greenness is deeper than anyone knows.

Your hands hold roses always in a way that says
They are not only yours; the beautiful changes
15 In such kind ways,
Wishing ever to sunder
Things and things' selves for a second finding, to lose
For a moment all that it touches back to wonder.

1947

• What part of speech is "Beautiful" in the poem's title and lines 7
and 14? What part of speech is "Changes"? What is meant by "the
beautiful changes / In such kind ways" (lines 14–15)?

LYNN POWELL
Kind of Blue

Not Delft or
delphinium, not Wedgewood[3]
among the knickknacks, not wide-eyed chicory
evangelizing in the devil strip—

5 But way on down in the moonless
octave below midnight, honey,
way down where you can't tell cerulean from teal.

Not Mason jars of moonshine, not
waverings of silk, not the long-legged hunger
10 of a heron or the peacock's
iridescent id—

2. Alfalfa, a plant resembling clover, with small purple flowers. Lake Lucerne is famed for its
deep blue color and picturesque Swiss setting amid limestone mountains.
3. Wedgwood pottery, often of a distinctive blue, manufactured by a company founded in England.
Delft: city in southern Holland renowned for the manufacture of ceramics.

But Delilahs[4] of darkness, darling,
and the muscle of the mind
giving in.

15 Not sullen snow slumped
against the garden, not the first instinct of flame,
not small, stoic ponds, or the cold derangement
of a jealous sea—

But bluer than the lips of Lazarus, baby,
20 before Sweet Jesus himself could figure out
what else in the world to do but weep.

2004

• How does this poem help us envision a certain "kind of blue" by creating images of what it isn't? How do the images develop over the course
of the poem?

METAPHOR

Being visual does not just mean describing; telling us facts; indicating shapes,
colors, and specific details. Often the vividness of the picture in our minds
depends on comparisons made through figures of speech. What we are trying to imagine is pictured in terms of something else familiar to us, and we
are asked to think of one thing as if it were something else. Many such comparisons, in which something is pictured or figured forth in terms of something already familiar to us, are taken for granted in daily life. Things we
can't see or that aren't familiar to us are imaged as things we already know;
for example, God is said to be like a father; Italy is said to be shaped like a
boot; life is compared to a forest, a journey, or a sea. When the comparison
is implicit, describing something as if it were something else, it is called a
metaphor.

In the poem that follows, the poet helps us visualize old age and approaching death by making comparisons with familiar things—the coming of winter,
the approach of sunset, and the dying embers of a fire.

WILLIAM SHAKESPEARE
[That time of year thou mayst in me behold]

That time of year thou mayst in me behold
When yellow leaves, or none, or few, do hang

4. Perhaps an allusion to the biblical Delilah, who conspired with the rulers of Philistine to
destroy Samson's strength by seducing him and cutting off his hair.

Upon those boughs which shake against the cold,
Bare ruined choirs, where late the sweet birds sang.
5 In me thou see'st the twilight of such day
As after sunset fadeth in the west;
Which by and by[5] black night doth take away,
Death's second self,[6] that seals up all in rest.
In me thou see'st the glowing of such fire,
10 That on the ashes of his youth doth lie,
As the deathbed whereon it must expire,
Consumed with that which it was nourished by.
This thou perceiv'st, which makes thy love more strong,
To love that well which thou must leave ere long.

                                                    1609

The first four lines of THAT TIME OF YEAR evoke images of the late autumn, but notice that the poet does not have the speaker say directly that his physical condition and age make him resemble autumn. He draws the comparison without stating it as a comparison: You can see my own state, he says, in the coming of winter, when almost all the leaves have fallen from the trees. The speaker portrays himself *indirectly* by talking about the passing of the year. The poem uses metaphor; that is, one thing is pictured *as if* it were something else. "That time of year" goes on to another metaphor in lines 5–8 and still another in lines 9–12, and each metaphor contributes to our understanding of the speaker's sense of his old age and approaching death. More important, however, is the way the metaphors give us feelings, an emotional sense of the speaker's age and of his own attitude toward aging. Through the metaphors we come to understand, appreciate, and to some extent share the increasing sense of urgency that the poem expresses. Our emotional sense of the poem depends largely on the way each metaphor is developed and by the way each metaphor leads, with its own kind of internal logic, to another, even as later metaphors build on earlier ones. Look back at the poem. What does each metaphor contribute?

"That time of year" represents an unusually intricate use of images to organize a poem and focus its emotional impact. Not all poems depend on such a full and varied use of metaphor. Sometimes rather than accumulating metaphors, a poet presents a single metaphor that extends over a section of a poem (in which case it is called an *extended metaphor*) or even over the whole poem (in which case it is called a *controlling metaphor*). The following poem depends from the beginning—even from its title—on a single controlling metaphor.

5. Shortly.   6. Sleep.

LINDA PASTAN
Marks

My husband gives me an A
for last night's supper,
an incomplete for my ironing,
a B plus in bed.
5 My son says I am average,
an average mother, but if
.I put my mind to it
I could improve.
My daughter believes
10 in Pass/Fail and tells me
I pass. Wait 'til they learn
I'm dropping out.

1978

The speaker in MARKS is obviously less than pleased with the idea of continually being judged, and the metaphor of marks (or grades) as a way of talking about her performance of family duties suggests her irritation. The list of the roles implies the many things expected of her, and the three different systems of marking (letter grades, categories to be checked off on a chart, and pass/fail) detail the difficulties of multiple standards. The poem retains the language of schooldays all the way to the end ("learn," line 11; "dropping out," line 12), and the major effect of the poem depends on the irony of the speaker's surrendering to the metaphor the family has thrust upon her; if she is to be judged as if she were a student, she retains the right to leave the system. Ironically, she joins the system (adopts the metaphor for herself) in order to defeat it.

PERSONIFICATION

Another figure of speech, **personification**, involves treating an abstraction, such as death or justice or beauty, as if it were a person. When "That time of year" talks about the coming of night and of sleep, for example, Sleep is personified as the "second self" of Death (that is, as a kind of "double" for death [line 8]). If personification in this poem is a brief gesture, it proves much more obvious and central in the following poem, though in this case, too, it is death that the poet personifies. How so, and with what implications and effects?

EMILY DICKINSON
[Because I could not stop for Death—]

Because I could not stop for Death—
He kindly stopped for me—
The Carriage held but just Ourselves—
And Immortality.

5　We slowly drove—He knew no haste
And I had put away
My labor and my leisure too,
For His Civility—

We passed the School, where Children strove
10　At Recess—in the Ring—
We passed the Fields of Gazing Grain—
We passed the Setting Sun—

Or rather—He passed Us—
The Dews drew quivering and chill—
15　For only Gossamer,[7] my Gown—
My Tippet—only Tulle[8]—

We paused before a House that seemed
A Swelling of the Ground—
The Roof was scarcely visible—
20　The Cornice—in the Ground—

Since then—'tis Centuries—and yet
Feels shorter than the Day
I first surmised the Horses' Heads
Were toward Eternity—

c. 1863

- What vision of death and the afterlife is implied by the way death is personified and characterized in the poem? by the details the speaker offers about the carriage ride she takes with him?

SIMILE AND ANALOGY

Sometimes, in poetry as in prose, comparisons are made explicitly, as in the following poem.

---

7. Soft, sheer fabric.　8. Fine net fabric. *Tippet*: shawl.

ROBERT BURNS
A Red, Red Rose

O, my luve's like a red, red rose
That's newly sprung in June.
O, my luve is like the melodie
That's sweetly played in tune.

5 As fair art thou, my bonnie lass,
So deep in luve am I;
And I will luve thee still, my dear,
Till a' the seas gang[9] dry.

Till a' the seas gang dry, my dear,
10 And the rocks melt wi' the sun;
And I will luve thee still, my dear,
While the sands o' life shall run.

And fare thee weel, my only luve,
And fare thee weel a while!
15 And I will come again, my luve,
Though it were ten thousand mile.

1796

The first four lines make two explicit comparisons: The speaker says that his love is "like a [. . .] rose" (line 1) and "like [a] melodie" (line 3). Such *explicit* comparisons are called **similes**, and usually (as here) the comparison involves the word *like* or the word *as*. Similes work much as do metaphors, except that usually they are used more passingly, more incidentally; they make a quick comparison and usually do not elaborate. The two similes in A RED, RED ROSE assume that we already have a favorable opinion of roses and of melodies. Here the poet does not develop the comparison or even remind us of attractive details about roses or tunes. He pays the quick compliment and moves on.

Similes sometimes develop more elaborate comparisons than this and occasionally, as in the poem below, even govern a poem (in which case they are called *analogies*).

9. Go.

TODD BOSS
My Love for You Is So Embarrassingly

grand . . . would you mind terribly, my groundling,[1]
   if I compared it to the *Hindenburg*[2] (I mean,
   before it burned)—that vulnerable, elephantine

   dream of transport, a fabric *Titanic*[3] on an ocean
5   of air? There: with binoculars, dear, you can
   just make me out, in a gondola window, wildly

      flapping both arms as the ship's shadow
      moves like a vagrant country across the
      country where you live in relative safety. I pull

10   that oblong shadow along behind me wherever
   I go. It is so big, and goes so slowly, it alters
   ground temperatures noticeably, makes

      housewives part kitchen curtains, wrings
      whimpers from German shepherds. Aren't I
15   ridiculous? Isn't it anachronistic, this

   dirigible devotion, this Zeppelin affection, a moon
   that touches, with a kiss of wheels, the ground
   you take for granted beneath your heels?—

                                 2011

ALLUSION

Like many poems, Todd Boss's humorous MY LOVE FOR YOU IS SO EMBAR-
RASSINGLY depends on multiple figures of speech: by comparing his love to the
Hindenburg and, in turn, the *Hindenburg* (line 2) to the *Titanic* (line 4), the
speaker makes use not only of analogy and metaphor but also of **allusion**, a
brief reference to a fictitious or actual person, place, or thing and, usually, to
the stories or **myth** surrounding it. Like metaphor and simile, allusion allows
poets to economically suggest a wealth of sometimes complex images, feelings,
and ideas by relying on widely shared literary and cultural knowledge. In this

1. Literally, someone on the ground; figuratively, a person of unsophisticated taste, like a spectator who stood in the pit of an Elizabethan theater
2. German airship famously destroyed by fire during a failed docking attempt over New Jersey,
May 6, 1937.
3. British passenger liner sunk on April 15, 1912, after colliding with an iceberg on its maiden
voyage.

particular case, knowing something about both what happened to the *Hindenburg* and the *Titanic* and what "dream[s]" of human ingenuity and power were destroyed along with them gives us a much more specific, vivid picture of how something might be simultaneously "vulnerable" and "elephantine," exhilarating and terrifying, transcendent and potentially disastrous (lines 4, 3).

Sometimes "getting" an allusion or even recognizing one requires us to learn something new. Many of the footnotes in this book and others like it aim to help you with that. But whenever you come across a name or other reference in a poem that you don't understand or a phrase that seems oddly familiar, it's well worth your while to consult a reference book or the Internet. Allusions are one of the ways poems engage with the larger world, participating in a vast conversation they invite and even expect you, too, to be a part of.

Below are two poems that rely on an array of allusions—to everything from historical events, myths, and poems to rock stars. As you read the poems, try not only to spot all the allusions but also to tease out what specifically each contributes to the poem in which it appears.

AMIT MAJMUDAR
Dothead

Well yes, I said, my mother wears a dot.
I know they said "third eye" in class, but it's not
an *eye* eye, not like that. It's not some freak
third eye that opens on your forehead like
5 on some Chernobyl baby.[4] What it means
is, what it's *showing* is, there's this unseen
eye, on the inside. And she's marking it.
It's how the X that says where treasure's at
is not the treasure, but as good as treasure.—
10 All right. What I said wasn't half so measured.
In fact, I didn't say a thing. Their laughter
had made my mouth go dry. Lunch was after
World History; that week was India—myths,
caste system, suttee,[5] all the Greatest Hits.
15 The white kids I was sitting with were friends,
at least as I defined a friend back then.
So wait, said Nick, does *your* mom wear a dot?
I nodded, and I caught a smirk on Todd—
She wear it to the shower? And to bed?—
20 while Jesse sucked his chocolate milk and Brad

---

4. That is, a baby born with birth defects as a result of the explosion that occurred in April 1986 at the Chernobyl Nuclear Power Plant in Ukraine.
5. Custom of a Hindu widow voluntarily being cremated on her husband's funeral pyre.

was getting ready for another stab.
I said, Hand me that ketchup packet there.
And Nick said, What? I snatched it, twitched the tear,
and squeezed a dollop on my thumb and worked
25 circles till the red planet entered the house of war
and on my forehead for the world to see
my third eye burned those schoolboys in their seats,
their flesh in little puddles underneath,
pale pools where Nataraja[6] cooled his feet.

2011

PATRICIA LOCKWOOD
What Is the Zoo for What

The word "zoo" is a zoo for the zoo.

A fountain is a zoo for water, the song
is a zoo for sound, the harmonica
is a zoo for the hot breath of Neil Young,[7]
            vagina is a zoo for baby.

5 Baby, girl baby, is a zoo for vagina.

The rose is a zoo for the smell of the rose,
the smell of the rose rattles its cage,
the zookeeper throws something bleeding
to it, the something bleeding is not enough,
10 a toddler fell into the cage of the rose,
the toddler was entirely eaten. His name
was Rilke,[8] it was in all the papers.
A Little Pine Box is a zoo for him now,
            it said in all the papers.

Then all the kids started doing it. Falling
15 into the violet's cage, approaching the cave

6. The Lord of Dancers, an avatar of the Hindu god Shiva, whose ecstatic twirling expresses the cyclic energy of the universe.
7. Influential Canadian singer-songwriter, musician, and activist (b. 1945); though he is primarily known as a guitarist, Young's only number-one hit, "Heart of Gold" (1972), features one of rock's best-known harmonica solos.
8. Rainer Maria Rilke (1875–1926), one of history's most famous and influential German-language poets, known especially for lyrics relying on intensely physical imagery and symbolism. According to one biographer (E. M. Butler), "There is no doubt that roses," in particular, "cast a spell upon Rilke," whose "roses were always explicitly in enclosed spaces: in death-bed chambers, in his study at night, in rose-bowls, bringing summer into a room."

where the smell of violets slept, getting
their whole head clawed off by it.
Neil Young did it to a buttercup
and his face got absolutely mauled.

20 The music that was piped into the zoo
let all the longing escape from it
and it ran riot over the earth, full
of the sight of the smell of a buttercup
rearranging the face of Neil Young,
25 attacking pets at random, attacking
me in my bed as I slept, attacking
the happy wagging ends of my poems.

Can I put Neil Young in a poem.
Will he get trapped in there forever.

30 My voice is a zoo right now for this,
and this paces very much inside it,
it would like very much to escape
and eat hot blood again and go home,
and right down to the restless way
35 I walk I am an argument against zoos.

Zoo is very cruel. Let everything out
and live in the wild. Let it hunt for itself
again. Get the stink of human hand off it.

But the hand is a zoo for hold.

2013

*   *   *

All figurative language involves an attempt to clarify something *and* to
prompt readers to feel a certain way about it. Saying that one's love is like
a rose implies a delicate and fragile beauty and invites our senses into play
so that we can share sensuously a response to appealing fragrance and soft
touch, just as the shivering boughs and dying embers in "That time of year"
suggest separation and loss at the same time that they invite us to share both
the cold sense of loneliness and the warmth of old friendship.

Once you start looking for them, you will find figures of speech in poem
after poem; they are among the most common devices through which poets
share their visions with us.

POEMS FOR FURTHER STUDY

WILLIAM SHAKESPEARE
[Shall I compare thee to a summer's day?]

Shall I compare thee to a summer's day?
Thou art more lovely and more temperate.
Rough winds do shake the darling buds of May,
And summer's lease hath all too short a date.
5 Sometime too hot the eye of heaven shines,
And often is his gold complexion dimmed;
And every fair from fair sometime declines,
By chance or nature's changing course untrimmed.
But thy eternal summer shall not fade,
10 Nor lose possession of that fair thou ow'st,
Nor shall Death brag thou wand'rest in his shade,
When in eternal lines to time thou grow'st.
    So long as men can breathe or eyes can see,
    So long lives this,[9] and this gives life to thee.

                      1609

• What sort of promise does the speaker make with this poem? Why can he boast that "thy eternal summer shall not fade" (line 9)?

ANONYMOUS[1]
The Twenty-Third Psalm

The Lord is my shepherd; I shall not want.
He maketh me to lie down in green pastures: he leadeth me beside
    the still waters.
He restoreth my soul: he leadeth me in the paths of righteousness
    for his name's sake.
Yea, though I walk through the valley of the shadow of death,
    I will fear no evil: for thou art with me;
    thy rod and thy staff they comfort me.
5 Thou preparest a table before me in the presence of mine enemies:
    thou anointest my head with oil; my cup runneth over.
Surely goodness and mercy shall follow me all the days of my life:
    and I will dwell in the house of the Lord for ever.

9. This poem.
1. Traditionally attributed to King David. This English translation is from the King James Version of the Bible (1611).

• What is the controlling metaphor in this poem? At what point in the psalm does the controlling metaphor shift?

JOHN DONNE
[Batter my heart, three-personed God][2]

Batter my heart, three-personed God; for You
As yet but knock, breathe, shine, and seek to mend;
That I may rise and stand, o'erthrow me, and bend
Your force, to break, blow, burn, and make me new.
5 I, like an usurped town, to another due,
Labor to admit You, but Oh, to no end!
Reason, Your viceroy[3] in me, me should defend,
But is captived, and proves weak or untrue.
Yet dearly I love You, and would be loved fain,[4]
10 But am betrothed unto Your enemy:
Divorce me, untie or break that knot again,
Take me to You, imprison me, for I,
Except You enthrall me, never shall be free,
Nor ever chaste, except You ravish me.

1633

• In the poem's controlling metaphor, who is the speaker? Who, or what, is God? To whom is the speaker "betrothed" (line 10)?

RANDALL JARRELL
The Death of the Ball Turret Gunner[5]

From my mother's sleep I fell into the State,
And I hunched in its belly till my wet fur froze.
Six miles from earth, loosed from its dream of life,
I woke to black flak and the nightmare fighters.
5 When I died they washed me out of the turret with a hose.

1945

2. From the sequence *Holy Sonnets*.
3. One who rules as the representative of someone of higher rank.   4. Gladly.
5. A ball turret was a Plexiglas sphere set into the belly of a B-17 or B-24 [airplane] and inhabited by two .50 caliber machine-guns and one man, a short small man. When this gunner tracked with his machine-guns a fighter attacking his bomber from below, he revolved with the turret; hunched upside-down in his little sphere, he looked like the foetus in the womb. The fighters which attacked him were armed with cannon firing explosive shells. The hose was a steam hose [Jarrell's note].

• What is meant by "I fell into the State (line 1)"? What do the words "sleep," "dream," and "nightmare" (lines 1, 3, 4) suggest about the situation?

SUGGESTIONS FOR WRITING

1. Choose any poem in this chapter and explore the meaning and effect of its metaphor(s). Does the poem make use of an extended or controlling metaphor or of multiple metaphors? If the latter, how do the metaphors relate to and build on each other?
2. Choose any poem in this book that uses personification and write an essay exploring how this figure of speech contributes both to the emotional effect of the poem and its theme(s). (In addition to the Emily Dickinson poem in this chapter, other good options include John Keats's To Autumn, and John Donne's Death, Be Not Proud.)
3. Research the design of World War II bombers like the B-17 and the B-24. Try to find a picture of the gunner in the ball turret of such an airplane, and note carefully his body position. Write an essay in which you explain how Randall Jarrell's The Death of the Ball Turret Gunner uses visual details to create its fetal and birth metaphors.
4. Look online for the lyrics to some of your favorite songs and identify the figures of speech used in each. Write an essay explaining which of these figures seem the most creative and effective, and why.
5. Choose any poem in this book that relies on at least one allusion to something or someone initially unfamiliar to you. After researching whatever the poem alludes to, write an informal response paper or essay exploring how the poem works and means differently to an informed reader.

12

SYMBOL

Properly used, the term *symbol* suggests one of the most basic things about poems—their ability to get beyond what words signify and to make larger claims about meanings in the verbal world. All words go beyond themselves. They are not simply a collection of sounds: They signify something beyond their sounds, often things or actions or ideas. Words describe not only a verbal universe but also a world in which actions occur, acts have implications, and events have meaning. Sometimes words signify something beyond themselves, say, *rock* or *tree* or *cloud*, and symbolize something as well, such as solidity or life or dreams. Words can—when their implications are agreed on by tradition, convention, or habit—stand for things beyond their most immediate meanings or significations and become symbols, and even simple words that have accumulated no special power from previous use may be given special significance in special circumstances—in poetry as in life itself.

A **symbol** is, put simply, something that stands for something else. The everyday world is full of common examples; a flag, a logo, a trademark, or a skull and crossbones all suggest things beyond themselves, and everyone likely understands what their display indicates, whether or not each viewer shares a commitment to what is thus represented. In common usage a prison symbolizes confinement, constriction, and loss of freedom, and in specialized traditional usage a cross may symbolize oppression, cruelty, suffering, death, resurrection, triumph, or an intersection of some kind (as in *crossroads* and *crosscurrents*). The specific symbolic significance depends on the context; for example, a reader might determine significance by looking at contiguous details in a poem and by examining the poem's attitude toward a particular tradition or body of beliefs. A star means one thing to a Jewish poet and something else to a Christian poet, still something else to a sailor or an actor. In a very literal sense, words themselves are all symbols (they stand for objects, actions, or qualities, not just for letters or sounds), but symbols in poetry are those words and phrases that have a range of reference beyond their literal signification or **denotation**.

THE INVENTED SYMBOL

Poems sometimes create a symbol out of a thing, action, or event that has no previously agreed-upon symbolic significance. Such a symbol is sometimes called an *invented symbol*. The following poem, for example, gives an action symbolic significance.

JAMES DICKEY
The Leap

The only thing I have of Jane MacNaughton
Is one instant of a dancing-class dance.
She was the fastest runner in the seventh grade,
My scrapbook says, even when boys were beginning
5 To be as big as the girls,
But I do not have her running in my mind,
Though Frances Lane is there, Agnes Fraser,
Fat Betty Lou Black in the boys-against-girls
Relays we ran at recess: she must have run

10 Like the other girls, with her skirts tucked up
So they would be like bloomers,
But I cannot tell; that part of her is gone.
What I do have is when she came,
With the hem of her skirt where it should be
15 For a young lady, into the annual dance
Of the dancing class we all hated, and with a light
Grave leap, jumped up and touched the end
Of one of the paper-ring decorations

To see if she could reach it. She could,
20 And reached me now as well, hanging in my mind
From a brown chain of brittle paper, thin
And muscular, wide-mouthed, eager to prove
Whatever it proves when you leap
In a new dress, a new womanhood, among the boys
25 Whom you easily left in the dust
Of the passionless playground. If I said I saw
In the paper where Jane MacNaughton Hill,

Mother of four, leapt to her death from a window
Of a downtown hotel, and that her body crushed-in
30 The top of a parked taxi, and that I held
Without trembling a picture of her lying cradled
In that papery steel as though lying in the grass,

One shoe idly off, arms folded across her breast,
I would not believe myself. I would say
35 The convenient thing, that it was a bad dream
Of maturity, to see that eternal process

Most obsessively wrong with the world
Come out of her light, earth-spurning feet
Grown heavy: would say that in the dusty heels
40 Of the playground some boy who did not depend
On speed of foot, caught and betrayed her.
Jane, stay where you are in my first mind:
It was odd in that school, at that dance.
I and the other slow-footed yokels sat in corners
45 Cutting rings out of drawing paper

Before you leapt in your new dress
And touched the end of something I began,
Above the couples struggling on the floor,
New men and women clutching at each other
50 And prancing foolishly as bears: hold on
To that ring I made for you, Jane—
My feet are nailed to the ground
By dust I swallowed thirty years ago—
While I examine my hands.

1967

Memory is crucial to THE LEAP. The fact that Jane MacNaughton's grace-ful leap in dancing class has stuck in the speaker's mind all these years means that this leap was important to him, meant something to him, stood for some-thing in his mind. For the speaker, the leap is an "instant" and the "only thing" he has of Jane (lines 2, 1). He remembers its grace and ease, and he struggles at several points to articulate its meaning (lines 16–26, 44–50), but even without articulation or explanation it remains in his head as a visual memory, a symbol of something beyond himself, something he cannot do, something he wanted to be. What that leap stood for, or symbolized, was boldness, confi-dence, accomplishment, maturity, Jane's ability to go beyond her fellow stu-dents in dancing class—the transcending of childhood by someone entering adulthood. Her feet now seem "earth-spurning" (line 38) in that original leap, and they separate her from everyone else. Jane MacNaughton was beyond the speaker's abilities and any attempt he could make to articulate his hopes, but she was not beyond his dreams. And even before he could say so, she symbol-ized a dream.

The leap to her death seems cruelly wrong and ironic after the grace of her earlier leap. In memory she is suspended in air, as if there were no gravity, no coming back to earth, as if life could exist as dream. And so the photograph, re-created in precise detail, is a cruel dashing of the speaker's dream—a detailed record of the ending of a leap, a denial of the suspension in which his memory had held her. His dream is grounded; her mortality is insistent. But the speaker still wants to hang on to that symbolic moment (line 42), which he confronts in a more mature context but will never altogether replace or surrender.

The leap is ultimately symbolic in the *poem*, too, not just in the speaker's mind. In the poem (and for us as readers) its symbolism is double: The first leap symbolizes aspiration, and the second symbolizes the frustration and grounding of high hopes; the two are complementary, one impossible to imagine without the other. The poem is horrifying in some ways, a dramatic reminder that human beings don't ultimately transcend their mortality, their limits, no matter how heroic or unencumbered by gravity they may once have seemed. But the poem is not altogether sad and despairing, partly because it still affirms the validity of the original leap and partly because it creates and elaborates another symbol: the paper chain.

The chain connects Jane to the speaker both literally and figuratively. It is, in part, *his* paper chain that she had leaped to touch in dancing class (lines 18–19), and he thinks of her first leap as "touch[ing] the end of something I began" (line 47). He and the other earthbound, "slow-footed yokels" (line 44) made the chain, and it connects them to her original leap, just as a photograph glimpsed in the newspaper connects the speaker to her second leap. And so the paper chain becomes the poem's symbol of linkage, connecting lower accomplishment to higher possibility, the artisan to the artist, material substance to the act of imagination. At the end the speaker examines the hands that made the chain because those hands certify his connection to her and to the imaginative leap she had made for him. The chain thus symbolizes not only the lower capabilities of those who cannot leap like the budding Jane could, but also (later) the connection with her leap as both transcendence and mortality.

Like the leap, the chain is elevated to special meaning, given symbolic significance, only by the poet's treatment of it. A leap and a chain have no necessary significance in themselves to most of us—at least no significance that we have all agreed upon—but they may take on significance in specific circumstances or a specific text.

THE TRADITIONAL SYMBOL

Other objects and acts have a built-in significance because of past usage in literature, or tradition, or the stories a culture develops to explain itself and its beliefs. Such things have acquired an agreed-upon significance, an accepted value in our minds. They already stand for something before the poet cites them; they are *traditional symbols*. Poets assume that their readers will recognize the traditional meanings of these symbols, and the poem does not have to propose or argue a particular symbolic value. Birds, for example, traditionally symbolize flight, freedom from confinement, detachment from earthbound limits, the ability to soar beyond rationality and transcend mortal limits. Traditionally, birds have also been linked with imagination, especially poetic imagination, and poets often identify with them as pure and ideal singers of songs.

One traditional symbol, the rose, may be a simple and fairly plentiful flower in its season, but it has so long stood for particular qualities that merely to name it creates predictable expectations. Its beauty, delicacy, fragrance, shortness of life, and depth of color have made it a symbol of the transitoriness of beauty, and countless poets have counted on its accepted symbolism— sometimes to compliment a friend (as Robert Burns does in A RED, RED ROSE) or sometimes to make a point about the nature of symbolism. The following poem draws, in quite a traditional way, on the traditional meanings.

EDMUND WALLER
Song

>   Go, lovely rose!
> Tell her that wastes her time and me
>   That now she knows,
> When I resemble[1] her to thee,
> 5 How sweet and fair she seems to be.
>
>   Tell her that's young,
> And shuns to have her graces spied,
>   That hadst thou sprung
> In deserts, where no men abide,
> 10 Thou must have uncommended died.
>
>   Small is the worth
> Of beauty from the light retired;
>   Bid her come forth,
> Suffer herself to be desired,
> 15 And not blush so to be admired.
>
>   Then die! that she
> The common fate of all things rare
>   May read in thee;
> How small a part of time they share
> 20 That are so wondrous sweet and fair!
>   1645

---

1. Compare.

The speaker in Song sends the rose to his love in order to have it speak its traditional meanings of beauty and transitoriness. He counts on accepted symbolism to make his point and hurry her into accepting his advances. Likewise, the poet does not elaborate or argue these things because he does not need to; he counts on the familiarity of the tradition (though, of course, readers unfamiliar with the tradition will not respond in the same way— that is one reason it is difficult to fully appreciate texts from another linguistic or cultural tradition).

Poets may use traditional symbols to invoke predictable responses—in effect using shortcuts to meaning by repeating acts of signification sanctioned by time and cultural habit. But often poets examine the tradition even as they employ it, and sometimes they revise or reverse meanings built into the tradition. Symbols do not necessarily stay the same over time, and poets often turn even the most traditional symbols to their own original uses. Knowing the traditions of poetry—reading a lot of poems and observing how they tend to use certain words, metaphors, and symbols—can be very useful in reading new poems, but traditions evolve, and individual poems do highly individual things. Knowing the past never means being able to interpret new texts with certainty. Symbolism makes things happen, but individual poets and texts determine what will happen and how. How does the following poem both draw and comment on the traditional symbolism of roses?

DOROTHY PARKER
One Perfect Rose

A single flow'r he sent me, since we met.
    All tenderly his messenger he chose;
Deep-hearted, pure, with scented dew still wet—
    One perfect rose.

5 I knew the language of the floweret;
    "My fragile leaves," it said, "his heart enclose."
Love long has taken for his amulet
    One perfect rose.

Why is it no one ever sent me yet
10   One perfect limousine, do you suppose?
Ah no, it's always just my luck to get
    One perfect rose.

           1937

THE SYMBOLIC POEM

Sometimes symbols—traditional or not—become so insistent in the world of a poem that the larger referential world is left almost totally behind. In such cases the symbol is everything, and the poem does not just *use* symbols but becomes a symbolic poem, usually a highly individualized one dependent on an internal system introduced by the individual poet.

Here is one such poem.

WILLIAM BLAKE
The Sick Rose[2]

O rose, thou art sick.
The invisible worm
That flies in the night
In the howling storm

5   Has found out thy bed
Of crimson joy,
And his dark secret love
Does thy life destroy.

1794

The poem does not seem to be about or refer to a real rose. Rather the poem is about what the rose represents—not in this case something altogether understandable through the traditional meanings of *rose*.

We usually associate the rose with beauty and love, often with sex; and here several key terms have sexual connotations: "worm," "bed," and "crimson joy" (lines 2, 5, 6). The violation of the rose by the worm is the poem's main concern; the violation seems to have involved secrecy, deceit, and "dark" motives (line 7), and the result is sickness rather than the joy of love. The poem is sad; it involves a sense of hurt and tragedy, nearly of despair. The poem cries out against the misuse of the rose, against its desecration, implying that instead of a healthy joy in sensuality and sexuality, there has been in this case destruction and hurt, perhaps because of misunderstanding and repression and lack of sensitivity.

But to say so much about this poem we have to extrapolate from other poems by Blake, and we have to introduce information from outside the poem. Fully symbolic poems often require that we thus go beyond the formal procedures of reading that we have discussed so far. As presented in this poem, the rose is not part of the normal world that we ordinarily see, and it is symbolic

2. In Renaissance emblem books, the scarab beetle, worm, and rose are closely associated: The beetle feeds on dung, and the smell of the rose is fatal to it.

in a special sense. The poet does not simply take an object from our everyday world and give it special significance, making it a symbol in the same way that James Dickey does with the leap. In Blake's poem the rose seems to belong to its own world, a world made entirely inside the poem or the poet's head. The rose is not referential, or not primarily so. The whole poem is symbolic; it lives in its own world. But what is the rose here a symbol of? In general terms, we can say from what the poem tells us; but we may not be as confident as we can be in the more nearly recognizable world of THE LEAP or ONE PERFECT ROSE. In THE SICK ROSE, it seems inappropriate to ask the standard questions: What rose? Where? Which worm? What are the particulars here? In the world of this poem worms can fly and may be invisible. We are altogether in a world of meanings that have been formulated according to a special system of knowledge and code of belief. We will feel comfortable and confident in that world only if we read many poems written by the poet (in this case, William Blake) within the same symbolic system.

Negotiation of meanings in symbolic poems can be very difficult indeed. Reading symbolic poems is an advanced skill that depends on knowledge of context, especially the lives and work of authors and the special literary and cultural traditions they work from. But usually the symbols you will find in poems *are* referential of meanings we all share, and you can readily discover these meanings by carefully studying the poems themselves.

POEMS FOR FURTHER STUDY

JOHN KEATS
Ode to a Nightingale

I

My heart aches, and a drowsy numbness pains
    My sense, as though of hemlock I had drunk,
Or emptied some dull opiate to the drains
    One minute past, and Lethe-wards[3] had sunk:
5 'Tis not through envy of thy happy lot,
    But being too happy in thine happiness,
        That thou, light-wingèd Dryad[4] of the trees,
            In some melodious plot
Of beechen green, and shadows numberless,
10   Singest of summer in full-throated ease.

II

O, for a draught of vintage! that hath been
    Cooled a long age in the deep-delvèd earth,

3. Toward the river of forgetfulness (Lethe) in Hades.   4. Wood nymph.

Tasting of Flora[5] and the country green,
Dance, and Provençal song,[6] and sunburnt mirth!
15 O for a beaker full of the warm South,
Full of the true, the blushful Hippocrene,[7]
With beaded bubbles winking at the brim,
And purple-stainèd mouth;
That I might drink, and leave the world unseen,
20 And with thee fade away into the forest dim:

III
Fade far away, dissolve, and quite forget
What thou among the leaves hast never known,
The weariness, the fever, and the fret
Here, where men sit and hear each other groan;
25 Where palsy shakes a few, sad, last gray hairs,
Where youth grows pale, and specter-thin, and dies;
Where but to think is to be full of sorrow
And leaden-eyed despairs,
Where Beauty cannot keep her lustrous eyes,
30 Or new Love pine at them beyond tomorrow.

IV
Away! away! for I will fly to thee,
Not charioted by Bacchus and his pards,[8]
But on the viewless[9] wings of Poesy,
Though the dull brain perplexes and retards:
35 Already with thee! tender is the night,
And haply the Queen-Moon is on her throne,
Clustered around by all her starry Fays;[1]
But here there is no light,
Save what from heaven is with the breezes blown
40 Through verdurous glooms and winding mossy ways.

V
I cannot see what flowers are at my feet,
Nor what soft incense hangs upon the boughs,
But, in embalmèd[2] darkness, guess each sweet
Wherewith the seasonable month endows

---

5. Roman goddess of flowers.
6. The medieval troubadours of Provence were famous for their love songs.
7. Fountain of the Muses on Mt. Helicon, whose waters bring poetic inspiration.
8. The Roman god of wine was sometimes portrayed in a chariot drawn by leopards.
9. Invisible. 1. Fairies. 2. Fragrant, aromatic.

45 The grass, the thicket, and the fruit-tree wild;
  White hawthorn, and the pastoral eglantine;[3]
  Fast fading violets covered up in leaves;
  And mid-May's eldest child,
  The coming musk-rose, full of dewy wine,
50 The murmurous haunt of flies on summer eves.

VI

Darkling[4] I listen; and, for many a time
  I have been half in love with easeful Death,
  Called him soft names in many a musèd rhyme,
  To take into the air my quiet breath;
55 Now more than ever seems it rich to die,
  To cease upon the midnight with no pain,
  While thou art pouring forth thy soul abroad
  In such an ecstasy!
  Still wouldst thou sing, and I have ears in vain—
60 To thy high requiem become a sod.

VII

Thou wast not born for death, immortal Bird!
  No hungry generations tread thee down;
  The voice I hear this passing night was heard
  In ancient days by emperor and clown:
65 Perhaps the selfsame song that found a path
  Through the sad heart of Ruth,[5] when, sick for home,
  She stood in tears amid the alien corn;
  The same that ofttimes hath
  Charmed magic casements, opening on the foam
70 Of perilous seas, in faery lands forlorn.

VIII

Forlorn! the very word is like a bell
  To toll me back from thee to my sole self!
  Adieu! the fancy cannot cheat so well
  As she is famed to do, deceiving elf.
75 Adieu! adieu! thy plaintive anthem fades
  Past the near meadows, over the still stream,
  Up the hillside; and now 'tis buried deep

---

3. Sweetbriar or honeysuckle. 4. In the dark.
5. Virtuous Moabite widow who, according to the Old Testament book of Ruth, left her own country to accompany her mother-in-law, Naomi, back to Naomi's native land. She supported herself as a gleaner.

In the next valley-glades:
Was it a vision, or a waking dream?
80   Fled is that music:—Do I wake or sleep?

                                        May 1819

• Since birds obviously die, just as humans do, what might the speaker
  mean when he declares, "Thou wast not born for death, immortal
  Bird!" (line 61)? That is, how, according to the poem, is the bird
  "immortal" in a way the speaker isn't? How might this help you begin
  to understand what the bird comes to symbolize in the poem?

ROBERT FROST
The Road Not Taken

Two roads diverged in a yellow wood,
And sorry I could not travel both
And be one traveler, long I stood
And looked down one as far as I could
5 To where it bent in the undergrowth;

Then took the other, as just as fair,
And having perhaps the better claim,
Because it was grassy and wanted wear;
Though as for that the passing there
10 Had worn them really about the same,

And both that morning equally lay
In leaves no step had trodden black.
Oh, I kept the first for another day!
Yet knowing how way leads on to way,
15 I doubted if I should ever come back.

I shall be telling this with a sigh
Somewhere ages and ages hence:
Two roads diverged in a wood, and I—
I took the one less traveled by,
20 And that has made all the difference.

                                        1916

• What sort of choices might the fork in the road represent? In these
  terms, what seems most important about the description of the roads?
  Why and how might it matter that the poem's famous last lines (about
  the great "difference" [line 20] it made to take the road "less traveled
  by" [line 19]) are framed as something the speaker imagines saying
  "with a sigh" at some point in the distant future (line 16)?

HOWARD NEMEROV
The Vacuum

The house is so quiet now
The vacuum cleaner sulks in the corner closet,
Its bag limp as a stopped lung, its mouth
Grinning into the floor, maybe at my
5 Slovenly life, my dog-dead youth.

I've lived this way long enough,
But when my old woman died her soul
Went into that vacuum cleaner, and I can't bear
To see the bag swell like a belly, eating the dust
10 And the woolen mice, and begin to howl

Because there is old filth everywhere
She used to crawl, in the corner and under the stair.
I know now how life is cheap as dirt,
And still the hungry, angry heart
15 Hangs on and howls, biting at air.

1955

• What does the vacuum come to symbolize? How might the poem play
on the various meanings of the word *vacuum*?

ADRIENNE RICH
Diving into the Wreck

First having read the book of myths,
and loaded the camera,
and checked the edge of the knife-blade,
I put on
5 the body-armor of black rubber
the absurd flippers
the grave and awkward mask.
I am having to do this
not like Cousteau[6] with his
10 assiduous team
aboard the sun-flooded schooner
but here alone.

---

6. Jacques-Yves Cousteau (1910–97), French writer and underwater explorer.

There is a ladder.
The ladder is always there
15 hanging innocently
close to the side of the schooner.
We know what it is for,
we who have used it.
Otherwise
20 it's a piece of maritime floss
some sundry equipment.

I go down.
Rung after rung and still
the oxygen immerses me
25 the blue light
the clear atoms
of our human air.
I go down.
My flippers cripple me,
30 I crawl like an insect down the ladder
and there is no one
to tell me when the ocean
will begin.

First the air is blue and then
35 it is bluer and then green and then
black I am blacking out and yet
my mask is powerful
it pumps my blood with power
the sea is another story
40 the sea is not a question of power
I have to learn alone
to turn my body without force
in the deep element.

And now: it is easy to forget
45 what I came for
among so many who have always
lived here
swaying their crenellated fans
between the reefs
50 and besides
you breathe differently down here.

I came to explore the wreck.
The words are purposes.
The words are maps.

55 I came to see the damage that was done
    and the treasures that prevail.
    I stroke the beam of my lamp
    slowly along the flank
    of something more permanent
60 than fish or weed

    the thing I came for:
    the wreck and not the story of the wreck
    the thing itself and not the myth
    the drowned face always staring
65 toward the sun
    the evidence of damage
    worn by salt and sway into this threadbare beauty
    the ribs of the disaster
    curving their assertion
70 among the tentative haunters.

    This is the place.
    And I am here, the mermaid whose dark hair
    streams black, the merman in his armored body
    We circle silently
75 about the wreck
    we dive into the hold.
    I am she: I am he

    whose drowned face sleeps with open eyes
    whose breasts still bear the stress
80 whose silver, copper, vermeil cargo lies
    obscurely inside barrels
    half-wedged and left to rot
    we are the half-destroyed instruments
    that once held to a course
85 the water-eaten log
    the fouled compass

    We are, I am, you are
    by cowardice or courage
    the one who find our way
90 back to this scene
    carrying a knife, a camera
    a book of myths
    in which
    our names do not appear.

1972   1973

• What word or phrase first signals that DIVING INTO THE WRECK is to be understood symbolically, not literally? What are some possible symbolic interpretations of the wreck and the dive?

ROO BORSON
After a Death

Seeing that there's no other way,
I turn his absence into a chair.
I can sit in it,
gaze out through the window.
5 I can do what I do best
and then go out into the world.
And I can return then with my useless love,
to rest,
because the chair is there.

                                          1989

• Why do you think the speaker chooses to symbolize her absent loved one with a chair?

BRIAN TURNER
Jundee Ameriki[7]

Many the healers of the body.
Where the healers of the soul?
      —AHMAD SHAUQI

At the VA hospital in Long Beach, California,
Dr. Sushruta scores open a thin layer of skin
to reveal an object traveling up through muscle.
It is a kind of weeping the body does, expelling
5 foreign material, sometimes years after injury.
Dr. Sushruta lifts slivers of shrapnel, bits
of coarse gravel, road debris, diamond
points of glass—the minutiae of the story
reconstructing a cold afternoon in Baghdad,
10 November of 2005. The body offers aged cloth
from an *abaya*[8] dyed in blood, shards of bone.
And if he were to listen intently, he might hear
the roughened larynx of this woman calling up

---

7. American soldier (Arabic).   8. Loose, long robe worn by some Muslim women.

through the long corridors of flesh, saying
15   *Allah al Akbar*,[9] before releasing
her body's weapon, her dark and lasting gift
for this *jundee Ameriki*, who carries fragments
of the war inscribed in scar tissue,
a deep, intractable pain, the dull grief of it
20   the body must learn to absorb.

2009

• What objects or actions in this poem operate as symbols, and for what?

BRIAN TURNER (b. 1967)

From "War and Peace: An Interview with Poet Brian Turner" (2009)*

[. . .] Iraq will never be finished in our lifetimes—for the veterans who have come back home, for many of them, and then also for the Iraqis, who we can easily forget because we don't have to deal with them. We don't see them, we don't meet them, we don't have to go visit them or help them with anything. They're clear across the horizon in some foreign country. But we are intimately connected.

•   •   •

I think people still very much want to talk about these things, but they don't have that avenue. And I do think poetry and art can offer some avenues in, towards the emotional content, not so much the geopolitical possibilities and discussions, but the human content. . . . It offers people a way into a moment, and into a world that maybe they've never been a part of or seen and that they can experience a small portion of it and then be reconnected or reengaged to a discussion. I definitely think it's useful.

*"War and Peace: An Interview with Poet Brian Turner." Interview by Stefene Russell. *St. Louis*, 1 Apr. 2009, www.stlmag.com/War-and-Peace-An-Interview-With-Poet-Brian-Turner/.

---

9. Common misrendering of "Allahu akbar," meaning "God is great" or "greatest."

SUGGESTIONS FOR WRITING

1. Consider the poems about roses in this chapter, and write a paragraph about each poem showing how it establishes specific symbolism for the rose. What generalizations can you draw about the rose's traditional meanings in poetry? If you can, find other poems about roses outside of this anthology to determine if your generalizations still apply.

2. Is there a "correct" interpretation of Adrienne Rich's DIVING INTO THE WRECK or of Brian Turner's JUNDEE AMERIKI? If one interpretation seems to fit all the particulars of the poem, does that mean it's better than other possible interpretations? Write an essay in which you explore the poem's symbolism and argue for or against the idea that there is a single best way to understand this poem. Can ambiguity serve a poet's purpose, or does it ultimately undercut a poem's meaning and significance?

3. Choose any poem in this book in which an object or action seems to function as a symbol. Write an essay exploring that symbol's various possible meanings.

THE SOUNDS OF POETRY

Much of what happens in a poem happens in your mind's eye, but some of it happens in your "mind's ear" and in your voice. Poems are full of meaningful sounds and silences as well as words and sentences. Besides choosing words for their meanings, poets choose words because they have certain sounds, and poems use sound effects to create a mood or establish a tone, just as films do.

Historically, poetry began as an oral phenomenon. Early bards in many cultures chanted or recited their verses, often accompanied by a musical instrument of some kind, and poetry remains a vocal art, dependent on the human voice. Often poems that seem very difficult when looked at silently come alive when turned into sound. The music and rhythms become clearer, and saying the words aloud or hearing them spoken is very good practice for learning to hear in your mind's ear when you read silently.

RHYME

Rhyme—repetition or correspondence of the terminal sounds of words—is perhaps the single most familiar of sound devices poets use, though of course not all poems use it. Early English poetry, in fact, used **alliteration**, instead of rhyming words at the end of the poetic lines, to balance the first and second half of each line, and much, if not most, modern poetry is written in **free verse**—that is, without rhyme or regular **meter**. From the later Middle Ages until the twentieth century, however, the music of rhyme was central to both the sound and the formal conception of most poems in the Western world. Because poetry was originally an oral art (many poems were only later written down, if at all), various kinds of memory devices (sometimes called *mnemonic devices*) were built into poems to help reciters remember them. Rhyme was one such device, and most people still find it easier to memorize poetry that rhymes. The simple pleasure of hearing familiar sounds repeated at regular intervals may help account for the traditional popularity of rhyme. Rhyme also gives poetry a special aural quality that distinguishes it from prose. According to the established taste in eras before our own, there was a decorum or proper behavior in poetry as in other things: A poem should not in any way be mistaken for prose, which was thought to be artistically inferior to poetry and primarily utilitarian.

Some English poets (especially in the Renaissance) did experiment—often very successfully—with unrhymed verse, but the cultural pressure for rhyme was almost constant. Why? Custom, combined with the sense of proper decorum, accounted in part for the assumption that rhyme was necessary to poetry, but there was probably more to it than that. Rather, the poets' sense that poetry was an imitation of larger relationships in the universe made it seem natural to use rhyme to represent or re-create a sense of pattern, harmony, correspondence, symmetry, and order. The sounds of poetry were thus, poets reasoned, reminders of cosmic harmony, of the music of the spheres that animated all creation. In a modern world increasingly perceived as fragmented and chaotic, there may be less of a tendency to assume or assert a sense of harmony and symmetry. It would be too simple to say that rhyme in a poem necessarily means that the poet has a firm sense of cosmic order, or that an unrhymed poem testifies to chaos. But the cultural assumptions of different times have influenced the expectations and practices of both poets and readers.

Rhyme also provides a kind of discipline for the poet, a way of harnessing poetic talents and keeping a rein on the imagination. Robert Frost said that writing free verse was pointless, like playing tennis without a net. Frost speaks for many traditional poets in suggesting that writing good poetry requires discipline and great care with formal elements such as rhyme or rhythm. More recent poets have often chosen to play by new rules or to invent their own as they go along, preferring the sparer tones that unrhymed poetry provides. Contemporary poets of course still care about the sounds of their poetry, but they may replace rhyme with other aural devices or mix regular rhyme and meter with more flexible lines, paying tribute to tradition as well as the unexpectedness of experience.

End Rhyme and Rhyme Scheme

When we think of rhyme in poetry, what we likely think of first is the most common type—*end rhyme*, which occurs when the last words in two or more lines of a poem rhyme with each other. When we speak of a poem's *rhyme scheme*, we refer to its particular pattern of end rhymes. To indicate rhyme scheme, we conventionally assign a different letter of the alphabet to each rhyme sound, reusing the same letter every time the same terminal sound repeats in later lines. Here, for example, are the first two stanzas of Thomas Hardy's THE RUINED MAID, which have a rhyme scheme of *aabb, ccbb* thanks to the way each stanza ends with the very same (long *e*) sound:

"O 'Melia, my dear, this does everything crown!   *a*
Who could have supposed I should meet you in Town?   *a*

And whence such fair garments, such prosperi-ty?"—   b
"O didn't you know I'd been ruined?" said she.   b

—"You left us in tatters, without shoes or socks,   c
Tired of digging potatoes, and spudding up docks;   c
And now you've gay bracelets and bright feathers three!"—   b
"Yes: that's how we dress when we're ruined," said she.   b

Since any two adjacent lines that rhyme form a **couplet**, we could also or instead describe "The Ruined Maid" as a poem comprised entirely of rhyming couplets.

Internal, Slant, and Eye Rhyme

Though end rhyme alone determines the rhyme scheme of a poem, it isn't the only kind: *Internal rhyme* occurs when a word within (and thus *internal to*) a line rhymes with another word in the same or adjacent lines, as in the following lines from Samuel Taylor Coleridge's "The Rime of the Ancient Mariner" (internal rhyming words appear in italics):

> In mist or *cloud*, on mast or *shroud*,
> It perched for vespers nine;
> Whiles all the *night*, through fog-smoke *white*,
> Glimmered the *white* moonshine.

Whether end or internal, rhymes differ, too, in type. Technically, rhyme (or what is sometimes called *perfect*, *true*, or *full rhyme*) requires that words share consonants and vowel sounds, as do "cloud" and "shroud," "night" and "white." When words share one but not the other, we have a version of what's variously called *off*, *half*, *near*, or *slant rhyme*—that is, a rhyme slightly "off" or only approximate. (The words *all* and *bowl*, for example, share consonant sounds, but their vowel sounds differ, and the opposite is true of *dark* and *heart*.) Another device more common in poetry written since the later nineteenth century, and (like internal rhyme) ubiquitous in hip-hop lyrics, slant rhyme can produce a variety of effects, all deriving from the poem's failure to provide the sounds our ears expect, whether our brains know it or not. Much the same in reverse is true of *eye rhyme*: As much a visual as an aural device, it occurs, as its name suggests, when words *look* like they should rhyme, but don't, as with *bear* and *ear*, *Yeats* and *Keats*.

ONOMATOPOEIA, ALLITERATION, ASSONANCE, AND CONSONANCE

Sometimes the sounds in poems just provide special effects, rather like a musical score behind a film, setting the mood and getting us into an appropriate frame of mind. But often sound and meaning go hand in hand, and the poet finds words whose sounds echo the action or make a point by stressing the relationship among words and the things they signify.

A single word that captures or approximates the sound of what it describes, such as *splash* or *squish* or *murmur*, is an *onomatopoeic* word, and the device itself is **onomatopoeia**.

But poets can also turn sound into sense by choosing and ordering words so as to create distinctive, meaningful aural patterns. Rhyme is one such device, but three other important ones are

- **alliteration**—the repetition of usually initial consonant sounds through a sequence of words, as in "The Wicked Witch of the West";
- **consonance**—the repetition of consonant sounds, especially at the end of words or syllables, without the correspondence of vowel sounds necessary to create rhyme, as in "abstruser musings" (from Coleridge's FROST AT MIDNIGHT) or "That was a stroke of luck"; and
- **assonance**—the repetition of vowel sounds in a sequence of words with different endings, as in "The death of the poet was kept from his poems" (from W. H. Auden's IN MEMORY OF W. B. YEATS).

Used effectively, such devices can be powerful tools, generating meaning, as well as creating mood or simply providing emphasis. A case in point is the following excerpt from the world's most famous *mock epic*, which describes a scene that may seem at once foreign and familiar to you: A young woman (or "nymph") sits at a mirrored dressing table (or "toilet"), littered with cosmetics and other accouterments, and, with the help of her lady's maid, prepares herself for the day ahead—fixing her hair, applying makeup, and so on. Given the way these activities are characterized as a distinctly twisted religious ritual (in lines 123–30), what is the effect and significance of alliteration, particularly in line 140 (which here appears in bold)?

ALEXANDER POPE
From *The Rape of the Lock*

> And now, unveil'd, the toilet stands displayed,
> Each silver vase in mystic order laid.
> 125 First, rob'd in white, the nymph intent adores
> With head uncover'd, the cosmetic pow'rs.
> A heav'nly image in the glass appears,
> To that she bends, to that her eyes she rears;
> Th' inferior priestess,[1] at her altar's side,
> 130 Trembling, begins the sacred rites of pride.

---

1. That is, the lady's maid.

Unnumber'd treasures ope at once, and here
The various off'rings of the world appear;
From each she nicely culls with curious[2] toil,
And decks the goddess with the glitt'ring spoil.
135 This casket India's glowing gems unlocks,
And all Arabia breathes from yonder box.
The tortoise here and elephant unite,
Transform'd to combs, the speckled and the white.[3]
Here files of pins extend their shining rows,
140 **Puffs, powders, patches, bibles, billet-doux.**[4]
Now awful[5] beauty puts on all its arms;
The fair each moment rises in her charms,
Repairs her smiles, awakens ev'ry grace,
And calls forth all the wonders of her face
                                          1712, 1714

SOUND POEMS

The following poems place especially heavy emphasis on sound and aural patterning. As you read them, try to identify which sound devices they use and with what effects.

HELEN CHASIN
The Word *Plum*

The word *plum* is delicious

pout and push, luxury of
self-love, and savoring murmur

full in the mouth and falling
5 like fruit

taut skin
pierced, bitten, provoked into
juice, and tart flesh

---

2. Strange, unusual.
3. The hair combs, in other words, are made from tortoiseshell (which is "speckled") and ivory from an elephant's tusk (which is "white").
4. Love letter (French). *Patches*: tiny pieces of silk or plaster worn to hide a blemish or heighten one's beauty.   5. Awe-inspiring.

question
10 and reply, lip and tongue
of pleasure.

1968

KENNETH FEARING
Dirge

1-2-3 was the number he played but today the number came 3-2-1;
Bought his Carbide at 30, and it went to 29; had the favorite at
Bowie[6] but the track was slow—

O executive type, would you like to drive a floating-power, knee-
action, silk-upholstered six? Wed a Hollywood star? Shoot the
course in 58? Draw to the ace, king, jack?
O fellow with a will who won't take no, watch out for three cigarettes on the same, single match; O democratic voter born in
August under Mars, beware of liquidated rails—

5 Denouement to denouement, he took a personal pride in the
certain, certain way he lived his own, private life,
But nevertheless, they shut off his gas; nevertheless, the bank
foreclosed; nevertheless, the landlord called; nevertheless, the
radio broke,

And twelve o'clock arrived just once too often,
Just the same he wore one gray tweed suit, bought one straw hat,
drank one straight Scotch, walked one short step, took one long
look, drew one deep breath,
Just one too many,

10 And wow he died as wow he lived,
Going whop to the office and blooie home to sleep and biff got
married and bam had children and oof got fired,
Zowie did he live and zowie did he die,

With who the hell are you at the corner of his casket, and where
the hell're we going on the right-hand silver knob, and who the
hell cares walking second from the end with an American
Beauty[7] wreath from why the hell not,

6. Racetrack in Maryland. *Carbide*: stock in the Union Carbide Corporation.
7. A variety of rose.

Very much missed by the circulation staff of the New York Evening
Post; deeply, deeply mourned by the B.M.T.[8]

15 Wham, Mr. Roosevelt; pow, Sears Roebuck; awk, big dipper; bop,
summer rain;

Bong, Mr., bong, Mr., bong, Mr., bong.

1935

ALEXANDER POPE
Sound and Sense[9]

337 But most by numbers[1] judge a poet's song,
And smooth or rough, with them, is right or wrong;
In the bright muse though thousand charms conspire,[2]
340 Her voice is all these tuneful fools admire,
Who haunt Parnassus[3] but to please their ear,
Not mend their minds; as some to church repair,
Not for the doctrine, but the music there.
These, equal syllables[4] alone require,
345 Though oft the ear the open vowels tire,
While expletives[5] their feeble aid do join,
And ten low words oft creep in one dull line,
While they ring round the same unvaried chimes,
With sure returns of still expected rhymes.
350 Where'er you find "the cooling western breeze,"
In the next line, it "whispers through the trees";
If crystal streams "with pleasing murmurs creep,"
The reader's threatened (not in vain) with "sleep."
Then, at the last and only couplet fraught
355 With some unmeaning thing they call a thought,
A needless Alexandrine[6] ends the song,
That, like a wounded snake, drags its slow length along.

---

8. New York City subway line.
9. From *An Essay on Criticism*, Pope's poem on the art of poetry and the problems of literary
criticism. The passage excerpted here follows a discussion of several common weaknesses of
critics—failure to regard an author's intention, for example, or overemphasis on clever metaphors and ornate style.
1. Meter, rhythm, sound.   2. Unite.
3. Mountain in Greece, traditionally associated with the Muses and considered the seat of
poetry and music.   4. Regular accents.   5. Filler words, such as "do."
6. Line of six metrical feet, sometimes used in pentameter poems to vary the pace mechanically. Line 357 is an alexandrine.

> Leave such to tune their own dull rhymes, and know
> What's roundly smooth, or languishingly slow;
> 360 And praise the easy vigor of a line,
> Where Denham's strength and Waller's[7] sweetness join.
> True ease in writing comes from art, not chance,
> As those move easiest who have learned to dance.
> 'Tis not enough no harshness gives offense,
> 365 The sound must seem an echo to the sense:
> Soft is the strain when Zephyr[8] gently blows,
> And the smooth stream in smoother numbers flows;
> But when loud surges lash the sounding shore,
> The hoarse, rough verse should like the torrent roar.
> 370 When Ajax[9] strives, some rock's vast weight to throw,
> The line too labors, and the words move slow;
> Not so, when swift Camilla[1] scours the plain,
> Flies o'er th' unbending corn, and skims along the main.
> Hear how Timotheus'[2] varied lays surprise,
> 375 And bid alternate passions fall and rise!
> While, at each change, the son of Libyan Jove[3]
> Now burns with glory, and then melts with love;
> Now his fierce eyes with sparkling fury glow,
> Now sighs steal out, and tears begin to flow:
> 380 Persians and Greeks like turns of nature[4] found,
> And the world's victor stood subdued by sound!
> The pow'r of music all our hearts allow,
> And what Timotheus was, is DRYDEN now.

1711

Helen Chasin's poem THE WORD *PLUM* savors the sounds of the word as well as the taste and feel of the fruit itself. It is almost as if the poem is tasting the sounds and rolling them slowly on the tongue. The alliterative second and third lines even replicate the *p*, *l*, *uh*, and *m* sounds of the word while imitating the squishy sounds of eating the fruit. Words like "delicious" and "luxury" sound juicy, and other words, such as "murmur," imitate sounds of satisfaction and pleasure. Even the process of eating is in part re-created

---

7. Sir John Denham and Edmund Waller, seventeenth-century poets credited with perfecting the heroic couplet.   8. The west wind.
9. A Greek hero of the Trojan War, noted for his strength.
1. A woman warrior in Virgil's *Aeneid*.
2. Court musician of Alexander the Great, celebrated in a famous poem by John Dryden (see line 383) for the power of his music over Alexander's emotions.
3. In Greek tradition, the chief god of any people was often given the name Zeus (Jove), and the chief god of Libya (the Greek name for all of Africa) was called Zeus Ammon. Alexander visited his oracle and was proclaimed son of the god.   4. Similar alternations of emotion.

aurally. The tight, clipped sounds of "taut skin / pierced" (lines 6–7) suggest the way teeth sharply break the skin and slice quickly into the soft flesh of a plum, and the words describing the tartness ("provoked," "question," lines 7, 9) force the lips to pucker and the tongue and palate to meet and hold, as if the mouth were savoring a tart fruit. The poet is having fun here refashioning the sensual appeal of a plum, teasing the sounds and meanings out of available words. The words must mean something appropriate and describe something accurately first of all, of course, but when they also imitate the sounds and feel of the process they describe, they do double duty.

As its title implies, Kenneth Fearing's DIRGE is a musical lament, in this case for a businessman who took many chances and saw his investments and life go down the drain in the Great Depression of the early 1930s. The expressive cartoon words here like "oof" and "blooie" (line 11) echo the action. Reading aloud, you will notice that the poem employs rhythms much as a song would and that it frequently shifts its pace and mood. Notice how carefully the first two lines are balanced, and then how quickly the rhythm shifts as the "executive type" is addressed directly in line 3. (Especially long lines, like line 2, and irregular line lengths here create some of the poem's special sound effects.) In the direct address, the poem first picks up the rapid lingo of advertising. In stanza 3, the rhythm shifts again, but the poem gives us helpful clues about how to read. Line 5 sounds like prose and is long, drawn out, and rather dull (like its subject), but line 6 sets up a regular (and monotonous) rhythm with its repeated "nevertheless," which punctuates the rhythm like a drumbeat: "But nevertheless, *tuh-tuh-tuh-tuh-tuh*; nevertheless, *tuh-tuh-tuh-tuh*; nevertheless, *tuh-tuh-tuh-tuh*; nevertheless, *tuh-tuh-tuh-tuh-tuh*." In the next stanza comes more repetitive phrasing, this time guided by the word "one" in conjunction with other one-syllable words: "wore *one* gray tweed suit, bought *one* straw hat, *tuh* one *tuh-tuh*, *tuh* one *tuh-tuh*, *tuh* one *tuh-tuh*, *tuh* one *tuh-tuh*." And then a new rhythm and a new technique begin in stanza 5, which again imitates the language of comic books. You have to say words like "whop" and "zowie" aloud and in the rhythm of the whole sentence to get the full effect of how boring his life is, no matter how he tries to jazz it up. And so it goes—the repeating rhythms of routine—until the final bell ("Bong . . . bong . . . bong . . . bong") tolls rhythmically for the dead man in the final clanging line.

Written in a very different era and style, Pope's SOUND AND SENSE uses a number of echoic or onomatopoeic words. In some lines pleasant and unpleasant consonant sounds underline a particular point or emphasize a mood. When the poet talks about a particular weakness in poetry, he illustrates it at the same time—by using open vowels (line 345), expletives (line 346), monosyllabic words (line 347), predictable rhymes (lines 350–53), or long, slow lines (line 357). He similarly illustrates the good qualities of poetry as well (line 360, for example). But the main effects of the passage come from an interaction of several ingenious strategies at once. In lines 339 and

340, for example, Pope produces complex sound effects in addition to the harmony of a rhyming **couplet** ("conspire," "admire"). Assonance echoes in the *oo* vowel sounds in "muse," "tuneful," and "fools"; alliteration repeats consonants in "*r*ight or *wr*ong" and "tune*f*ul *f*ools." Ironically, the *muse*-ical voice here is a bit out of tune to those who have good poetic taste: Pope intends the *r* and *f* sounds to feel both cute and awkward, as a comment on people who only want easy listening and miss poetry's other "charms," including its meaning (compared to the "doctrine" that is the real purpose of a church service, in line 343).

With a similar technique of demonstrating principles of poetic style and taste, the pace of lines 347, 357, and 359 is controlled by clashing consonant sounds as well as long vowels. Line 347 seems much longer than it is because almost every one-syllable word ends in a consonant that refuses to blend with the beginning of the next word, making the words hard to say without distinct, awkward pauses between them. In lines 357 and 359, long vowels such as those in "wounded," "snake," "slow," "along," "roundly," and "smooth" slow down the pace, and awkward, hard-to-pronounce consonants are again juxtaposed. The commas also provide nearly full stops in the middle of these lines to slow us down still more. Similarly, the harsh lashing of the shore in lines 368–69 is accomplished partly by onomatopoeia and partly by the dominance of rough consonants in line 369. (In Pope's time, the English *r* was still trilled gruffly so that it could be made to sound extremely *rrr*ough and ha*rrr*sh.) Almost every line in this passage demonstrates how to make sound echo sense.

POETIC METER

In the Western world, we can thank the ancient Greeks for systematizing an understanding of meter and providing a vocabulary (including the words *rhythm* and *meter*) that enables us to discuss the art of poetry. *Meter* comes from a Greek word meaning "measure": What we measure in the English language are the patterns of stressed (or accented) syllables that occur naturally when we speak, and, just as when we measure length, the unit we use in measuring poetry is the **foot**. Most traditional poetry in English uses the accentual-syllabic form of meter—meaning that its rhythmic pattern is based on both a set number of syllables per line and a regular pattern of accents in each line. Not all poems have a regular metrical pattern, and not all metered poems follow only one pattern throughout. But like everyday speech, the language of poetry always has *some* accents (as in this italic emphasis on "some"), and poets arrange that rhythm for effect. Thus in nonmetrical as well as metrical poetry, a reader should "listen" for patterns of stress.

The Basic Metrical Feet of Poetry in English

iamb: an unstressed or unaccented syllable followed by a stressed or accented one ("she wént," "belíeve"). This meter is called *iambic*.

trochee: a stressed syllable followed by an unstressed one ("méter," "Hómer"). This meter is called *trochaic*.

anapest: two unstressed syllables followed by a stressed one ("comprehénd," "after yóu"). This meter is called *anapestic*.

dactyl: a stressed syllable followed by two unstressed ones ("róundabout," "dínnertime"). This meter is called *dactylic*.

rising or falling: the above feet either begin or end with the stressed syllable, as if they lose or gain momentum or "height." Hence iambic and anapestic are called rising meters, and trochaic and dactylic are called falling meters.

Other Kinds of Feet

spondee: two stressed syllables. Spondaic feet vary or interrupt the prevailing rhythm, emphasizing a syllable that we would expect to be unstressed ("Lást cáll," "Dón't gó").

pyrrhic: two unstressed syllables. Pyrrhic feet similarly interrupt the expected rising or falling beats, placing an unstressed syllable where we expect an emphasis ("ŭntŏ," "ĭs ă").

Spondees and pyrrhic feet depend on prevailing meter and usually appear singly or only a few times in a row. It is difficult to imagine (or to write or speak) a line or sentence that either has no unstressed syllables— a constant strong beat (spondaic)—or lacks stressed syllables—a rippling monotone (pyrrhic).

Because the concept of meter derives from poetic traditions in Greek and Latin that counted syllables rather than accents, other possible combinations of syllables acquired names, for instance, *amphibrach* (unstressed, stressed, unstressed—noted by Coleridge in his demonstration of meter, METRICAL FEET, below). But since most meter in poetry in English depends on accents rather than the number of syllables, the terms above cover most of the variations that you will encounter.

Counting Feet, or Meter

A line of poetry is subdivided into feet in order to "measure" its meter. The terms are easy enough to understand if you recall geometry or other numeric terminology. Remember that this is a count *not* of the

(*continued on next page*)

(*continued*)

number of syllables but of stresses; thus, for example, monometer could have two or three syllables per line.

monometer:	one foot
dimeter:	two feet
trimeter:	three feet
tetrameter:	four feet
pentameter:	five feet
hexameter:	six feet
heptameter:	seven feet
octameter:	eight feet

Counting the number of feet—that is, the number of accents, stresses, or strong beats per line—helps you identify the *kind* of feet in the line. Thus the terms are combined: *Iambic pentameter* has five iambs per line; *trochaic tetrameter* has four trochees per line, and so on.

Scansion

Scansion is the technique of listening to and marking stressed and unstressed syllables, counting the syllables and feet. Often, you will need to scan several lines before you can be sure of the "controlling" metrical pattern or "base meter" of a poem.

In the following poem, Samuel Taylor Coleridge playfully names and illustrates many types of meter. By marking syllables himself as stressed or unstressed, he also illustrates how scansion works.

SAMUEL TAYLOR COLERIDGE
Metrical Feet

Lesson for a Boy[5]

Trōchĕe trīps frŏm lōng tŏ shŏrt;[6]
From long to long in solemn sort
Slōw Spōndēe stālks; strōng fŏŏt! yet ill able
Ēvĕr tŏ cōme ŭp wĭth Dācty̆l trĭsy̆llăblĕ.
5 Ĭāmbĭcs mārch frŏm shŏrt tŏ lōng—
    Wĭth ă lēāp ănd ă bōūnd thĕ swĭft Ānăpĕsts thrōng;

5. Written originally for Coleridge's son Hartley, the poem was later adapted for his younger son, Derwent.
6. Long and short marks over syllables are Coleridge's.

One syllable long, with one short at each side,
Ămphībrăchy̆s hāstes wĭth ă stātely̆ stride—
Fīrst ănd lāst bēĭng lōng, mīddlĕ shŏrt, Ămphĭmācer
10 Strīkes hĭs thūndērĭng hōōfs līke ă prōūd hīgh-brĕd Rācer.
If Derwent be innocent, steady, and wise,
And delight in the things of earth, water, and skies;
Tender warmth at his heart, with these meters to show it,
With sound sense in his brains, may make Derwent a poet—
15 May crown him with fame, and must win him the love
Of his father on earth and his Father above.
My dear, dear child!
Could you stand upon Skiddaw,[7] you would not from its whole ridge
See a man who so loves you as your fond s. t. coleridge.

1806

Hearing a poem properly involves practice—listening to others read poetry
and especially to yourself as you read poems aloud. Your dictionary will show
you the stresses for every word of more than one syllable, and the governing
stress of individual words will largely control the patterns in a line: If you read
a line for its sense (almost as if it were prose), you will usually see the line's
basic pattern. But single-syllable words can be a challenge because they may
or may not be stressed, depending on their syntactic function and the full
meaning of the sentence. Normally, important functional words, such as one-
syllable nouns and verbs, are stressed (as in normal conversation or in prose),
while conjunctions (such as *and* or *but*), prepositions (such as *on* or *with*), and
articles (such as *an* or *the*) are unstressed.

Here are the first two lines of Alexander Pope's "Sound and Sense,"
marked to show the stressed syllables:

But móst | by núm- | bers júdge | a pó- | et's sóng,
And smóoth | or róugh, | with thém, | is ríght | or wróng.

These lines, like so many in English literature, provide an example of *iambic
pentameter*—that is, each line consists of five iambic feet. Notice that there
is nothing forced or artificial in the sound of these lines; the words flow easily.
In fact, linguists contend that English is naturally iambic, and even the most
ordinary, "unpoetic" utterances often fall into this pattern: "Please tell me if
you've heard this one before." "They said she had a certain way with words."
"The baseball game was televised at nine."
Here are a few more examples of various meters.

iambic pentameter: "In sé- | quent tóil | all fór- | wards dó | conténd" (Wil-
liam Shakespeare, "Like as the waves . . .")

7. Mountain in the lake country of northern England (where Coleridge lived in his early years),
near the town of Derwent.

trochaic octameter: "Ónce u- | pón a | mídnight | dréary, | whíle I | póndered, | wéak and | wéary" (Edgar Allan Poe, "The Raven")
anapestic tetrameter: "There are mán- | y who sáy | that a dóg | has his dáy" (Dylan Thomas)

Although scanning lines of poetry by reading them aloud, marking syllables as unstressed or stressed, and adding up feet may seem like a counting game that has little to do with the meaning of poetry, it is an important way to understand the sound effects of a poem. Like different styles of music, different meters tend to express different moods or to suit different themes. When you know the basic meter of a poem, you are more alert to subtle variations in the pattern. Poets avoid the predictable or the lulling by using certain "change-ups" in the dominant meter or line length, such as substitution of a different foot (e.g., a trochee or spondee instead of an iamb); **caesura**, a short pause within a line often signaled by punctuation; or **enjambment**, extending the end of the grammatical sentence beyond the end of the poetic line.

Notice that the following example is perfectly regular dactylic hexameter until the final foot, a trochee. Also notice that Longfellow has placed a caesura within a long line.

"Thís is the | fórest pri- | méval. The | múrmuring | pínes and the | hémlocks"
(Henry Wadsworth Longfellow, *Evangeline*)

Substitution of one metrical foot for another—to accommodate idioms and conversational habits or to create a special effect or emphasis—is quite common, especially in the first foot of a line. Shakespeare often begins an iambic line with a trochee:

Líke as | the wáves | make towárds | the péb- | bled shóre

Or consider this line from John Milton's *Paradise Lost*, a poem written mainly in iambic pentameter:

Rócks, cáves, | lákes, féns, | bógs, déns, | and Shádes | of Déath

Here Milton substitutes three spondees for the first three iambs in a pentameter line. John Dryden's "To the Memory of Mr. Oldham" arguably begins with two spondees, a pyrrhic, and an iamb before settling into a regular iambic pentameter:

Fárewéll, | tóo lít | tle, and | tóo láte | ly knówn,

As Dryden's poem shows, meter does leave room for discussion; some readers might read the line above as iambic throughout, and others might read the last three feet as iambic: The natural emphasis on the first word after the caesura, "and," could make the predictable word "too" unstressed. The way you actually read a line, once you have "heard" the basic rhythm, is influenced by two factors: normal pronunciation and prose sense (on the one hand) and the predominant pattern of the poem (on the other). Since these two forces are constantly in tension and are sometimes contradictory, you can almost never fully predict the actual reading of a line, and good reading aloud (like every other art) depends less on formula than on subtlety and flexibility. And, again, very good readers sometimes disagree about whether or not to stress certain syllables. We have noted the use of substitution, and many poems since around 1900 have taken liberties with meter and rhyme. Some poets (such as Marianne Moore) have favored counting syllables rather than accents. Even more widespread is free verse, which does without any governing pattern of stresses or line lengths.

Scansion: An Exercise

Each of the following poems is written in a different meter. Using the terms defined in "Poetic Meter" (on pp. 619–20), as well as in Coleridge's poem "Metrical Feet," pair the following poems with their corresponding meters. (The answers are on p. 632.)

1. ANONYMOUS
[There was a young girl from St. Paul]

There was a young girl from St. Paul,
Wore a newspaper-dress to a ball.
  The dress caught on fire
  And burned her entire
Front page, sporting section and all.

(Note that this poem is a **limerick** and uses a meter common to this subgenre.)

2. ALFRED, LORD TENNYSON
From The Charge of the Light Brigade[8]

    1.

Half a league, half a league,
  Half a league onward,
All in the valley of Death
  Rode the six hundred.

8. On October 25, 1854—during the Crimean war—miscommunication among commanders led a British cavalry troop to charge directly into a Russian artillery assault, leading to heavy casualties and an ignominious defeat.

(*continued on next page*)

(*continued*)

5 "Forward, the Light Brigade!
"Charge for the guns!" he said:
Into the valley of Death
Rode the six hundred.

2.

"Forward, the Light Brigade!"
10 Was there a man dismay'd?
Not tho' the soldier knew
    Someone had blunder'd:
Theirs not to make reply,
Theirs not to reason why,
15 Theirs but to do and die:
Into the valley of Death
    Rode the six hundred.

1854

3. JANE TAYLOR
The Star

'Twinkle, twinkle, little star,
How I wonder what you are!
Up above the world so high,
Like a diamond in the sky.

5 When the blazing sun is gone,
When he nothing shines upon,
Then you show your little light,
Twinkle, twinkle, all the night.

Then the trav'ller in the dark,
10 Thanks you for your tiny spark;
He could not see which way to go,
If you did not twinkle so.

In the dark blue sky you keep,
And often through my curtains peep,
15 For you never shut your eye
Till the sun is in the sky.

As your bright and tiny spark
Lights the trav'ller in the dark,

20 Though I know not what you are,
Twinkle, twinkle, little star.

1806

4. ANNE BRADSTREET
To My Dear and Loving Husband

If ever two were one, then surely we.
If ever man were loved by wife, then thee;
If ever wife was happy in a man,
Compare with me ye women if you can.
5 I prize thy love more than whole mines of gold,
Or all the riches that the East doth hold.
My love is such that rivers cannot quench,
Nor aught but love from thee give recompense.
Thy love is such I can no way repay;
10 The heavens reward thee manifold, I pray.
Then while we live, in love let's so persever,
That when we live no more we may live ever.

1678

Sound and Sense: A Comparative Exercise

To get a vivid sense of the difference sound can make to the tone and meaning of a poem—and just how you can *use* what you've learned about meter, rhyme, and other sound devices—try comparing the two following poems, both inspired by World War I (1914–18). The first is the most famous of several poems originally published in the British newspaper the *Daily Mail* by Jessie Pope (1868–1941), an English journalist famous, before the war, as a writer of light verse. The second poem is the work of Wilfred Owen (1893–1918), an aspiring English poet who voluntarily enlisted in 1915 (the same year Pope's poem appeared) and, from January 1917, served as an officer on the French front. Begun some nine months later, during Owen's hospitalization for shell shock, and originally entitled "To Jessie Pope," his poem is in some ways as much about traditional poetic representations of war as it is about war itself.

(*continued on next page*)

(*continued*)

As you read the two poems, pay careful attention to how each uses all of the various sound devices discussed in this chapter, particularly meter and rhyme. How precisely do such sound effects contribute to the poems' very different tones and themes and their very different views of war?

JESSIE POPE
The Call

Who's for the trench—
    Are you, my laddie?
Who'll follow French[9]—
    Will you, my laddie?
5 Who's fretting to begin,
Who's going out to win?
And who wants to save his skin—
    Do you, my laddie?

Who's for the khaki suit—
10   Are you, my laddie?
Who longs to charge and shoot—
    Do you, my laddie?
Who's keen on getting fit,
Who means to show his grit,
15 And who'd rather wait a bit—
    Would you, my laddie?

Who'll earn the Empire's[1] thanks—
    Will you, my laddie?
Who'll swell the victor's ranks—
20   Will you, my laddie?
When that procession comes,
Banners and rolling drums—
Who'll stand and bite his thumbs—
    Will you, my laddie?

                  1915

9. Field-Marshall John French (1852–1925), commander in chief of the British Expeditionary Force for the first two years of World War I (1914–16).
1. At the start of World War I, the British Empire was the largest in human history, covering over eleven million square miles of the earth's surface; the desire to maintain or expand empire was one major cause of the war.

WILFRED OWEN
Dulce et Decorum Est[2]

Bent double, like old beggars under sacks,
Knock-kneed, coughing like hags, we cursed through sludge,
Till on the haunting flares we turned our backs
And towards our distant rest began to trudge.
5 Men marched asleep. Many had lost their boots
But limped on, blood-shod. All went lame; all blind;
Drunk with fatigue; deaf even to the hoots
Of disappointed shells that dropped behind.

Gas! Gas! Quick, boys!—An ecstasy of fumbling,
10 Fitting the clumsy helmets just in time;
But someone still was yelling out and stumbling
And floundering like a man in fire or lime.—
Dim, through the misty panes and thick green light
As under a green sea, I saw him drowning.

15 In all my dreams, before my helpless sight,
He plunges at me, guttering, choking, drowning.

If in some smothering dreams you too could pace
Behind the wagon that we flung him in,
And watch the white eyes writhing in his face,
20 His hanging face, like a devil's sick of sin;
If you could hear, at every jolt, the blood
Come gargling from the froth-corrupted lungs,
Obscene as cancer, bitter as the cud
Of vile, incurable sores on innocent tongues,—
25 My friend, you would not tell with such high zest
To children ardent for some desperate glory,
The old Lie: Dulce et decorum est
Pro patria mori.

1917

---

2. Part of a phrase from Horace (Roman poet and satirist, 65–68 BCE), quoted in full in the last lines of Owen's poem: "It is sweet and proper to die for one's country" (Latin).

POEMS FOR FURTHER STUDY

WILLIAM SHAKESPEARE
[Like as the waves make towards the pebbled shore]

Like as the waves make towards the pebbled shore,
So do our minutes hasten to their end,
Each changing place with that which goes before,
In sequent toil all forwards do contend.[3]
5 Nativity, once in the main[4] of light,
Crawls to maturity, wherewith being crowned,
Crooked[5] eclipses 'gainst his glory fight,
And Time that gave doth now his gift confound.[6]
Time doth transfix[7] the flourish set on youth
10 And delves the parallels[8] in beauty's brow,
Feeds on the rarities of nature's truth,
And nothing stands but for his scythe to mow.
And yet to times in hope[9] my verse shall stand,
Praising thy worth, despite his cruel hand.

1609

• Which lines in this poem vary the basic iambic meter? What is the effect of these variations?

GERARD MANLEY HOPKINS
Spring and Fall

to a young child

Márgarét áre you gríeving[1]
Over Goldengrove unleaving?
Leáves, like the things of man, you
With your fresh thoughts care for, can you?
5 Áh! ás the heart grows older
It will come to such sights colder
By and by, nor spare a sigh
Though worlds of wanwood leafmeal[2] lie;

---

3. Struggle. *Sequent:* successive.   4. High seas. *Nativity:* newborn life.   5. Perverse.
6. Bring to nothing.   7. Pierce.   8. Lines, wrinkles.   9. In the future.
1. Hopkins's own accent markings.
2. Broken up, leaf by leaf (analogous to "piecemeal"). *Wanwood:* pale, gloomy woods.

And yet you will weep and know why.
10 Now no matter, child, the name:
Sórrow's spríngs áre the same.
Nor mouth had, no nor mind, expressed
What heart heard of, ghost[3] guessed:
It ís the blight man was born for,
15 It is Margaret you mourn for.

                                    1880

• How does this poem's heavy use of alliteration serve its exploration
  of youth and age, life and death?

WALT WHITMAN
Beat! Beat! Drums!

1

Beat! beat! drums!—Blow! bugles! blow!
Through the windows—through doors—burst like a
    force of armed men,
Into the solemn church, and scatter the congregation;
Into the school where the scholar is studying:
5 Leave not the bridegroom quiet—no happiness must he have now
    with his bride;
Nor the peaceful farmer any peace plowing his field or gathering
    his grain;
So fierce you whirr and pound, you drums—so shrill you bugles
    blow.

2

Beat! beat! drums!—Blow! bugles! blow!
Over the traffic of cities—over the rumble of wheels in the
    streets:
10 Are beds prepared for sleepers at night in the houses? No sleepers
    must sleep in those beds;
No bargainers' bargains by day—no brokers or speculators—Would
    they continue?
Would the talkers be talking? would the singer attempt to sing?
Would the lawyer rise in the court to state his case before the
    judge?
Then rattle quicker, heavier drums—you bugles wilder blow.

3. Soul.

3

15 Beat! beat! drums!—Blow! bugles! blow!
Make no parley—stop for no expostulation;
Mind not the timid—mind not the weeper or prayer;
Mind not the old man beseeching the young man;
Let not the child's voice be heard, nor the mother's entreaties;
    Recruit! Recruit!
20 Make the very trestles to shake under the dead, where they lie in
    their shrouds awaiting the hearses.
So strong you thump, O terrible drums—so loud you bugles blow.

                                                        1861

> • How does Whitman use various sound devices to mimic both the sound
> he asks the drums and bugles to make and the effects he imagines those
> sounds having? How might the poem's date affect your sense of the
> poem, particularly its final stanza?

KEVIN YOUNG
Ode to Pork

I wouldn't be here
without you. Without you
I'd be umpteen
pounds lighter & a lot
5   less alive. You stuck
round my ribs even
when I treated you like a dog
dirty, I dare not eat.
I know you're the blues
10 because loving you
may kill me—but still you
rock me down slow
as hamhocks on the stove.
Anyway you come
15 fried, cured, burnt
to within one inch
of your life I love. Babe,
I revere your every
nickname—bacon, chitlin,
20 cracklin, sin.
Some call you murder,
shame's stepsister—

then dress you up
& declare you white
25 & healthy, but you always
come back, sauced, to me.
Adam himself gave up
a rib to see yours
piled pink beside him.
30 Your heaven is the only one
worth wanting—
you keep me all night
cursing your four-
letter name, the next
35 begging for you again.

2007

- How do sound effects contribute to the tone of ODE TO PORK? to the poem's characterization of the speaker's relationship to pork? How might they make the poem sound like a blues song?

SUGGESTIONS FOR WRITING

1. Read Pope's SOUND AND SENSE carefully twice—once silently and once aloud—and then mark the stressed and unstressed syllables. Single out all the lines that have major variations from the basic iambic pentameter pattern. Pick out six lines with variations that seem to you worthy of comment, and write a paragraph on each in which you show how the variation contributes to the specific effects achieved in that line and the corresponding point Pope conveys about poetic style.

2. Try your hand at writing limericks in imitation of THERE WAS A YOUNG GIRL FROM ST. PAUL; study the rhythmic patterns and line lengths carefully, and imitate them exactly in your poem. Begin your limerick with "There once was a _____ from_____" (using a place for which you think you can find a comic rhyme).

3. Write an essay exploring how Wilfred Owen uses meter (including substitutions) and rhyme, as well as other sound devices, in DULCE ET DECORUM EST both to capture the experience of war and its effects and to respond critically to traditional war poetry, perhaps by comparing this poem to Jessie Pope's THE CALL. If you choose to draw on Pope's poem, however, you might also want to consider how the poem works and means differently when titled "Dulce et Decorum Est" rather than (as it originally was) "To Jessie Pope."

4. Pope's SOUND AND SENSE contains this advice for poets: "But when loud surges lash the sounding shore, / The hoarse, rough verse should like the torrent roar" (lines 368–69). In other words, he counsels that the sound of the poet's description should match the sense of what the poem is describing. Write an essay in which you examine the sound and sense in Shakespeare's

LIKE AS THE WAVES MAKE TOWARDS THE PEBBLED SHORE. How does the poem achieve a harmony of meaning and sound?

5. Write an essay in which you discuss any poem in this book in which sound seems a more important element than anything else, even the meaning of words. What is the point of writing and reading this kind of poetry? Can it achieve its effects through silent reading, or must it be experienced aloud?

ANSWERS TO SCANSION EXERCISE: 1. anapestic,   2. dactylic,   3. trochaic,   4. iambic.

INTERNAL STRUCTURE

"Proper words in proper places": That is how one great writer of English prose, Jonathan Swift, described good writing. A good poet finds appropriate words, and already we have looked at some implications for readers of the verbal choices a poet makes. But the poet must also decide where to put those words—how to arrange them for maximum semantic, as well as visual and aural, effect—because individual words, figures of speech, symbols, and sounds exist not only within phrases and sentences and rhythmic patterns, but also within the larger whole of the poem. How should the words be arranged and the poem organized? What comes first and what last? What principle or idea of organization will inform the poem? How do the parts combine into a whole? And what is the effect of that arrangement? Considering these questions from the poet's point of view (What is my plan? Where shall I begin? Where do I want to go?) can help us notice the effects of structural choices.

DIVIDING POEMS INTO "PARTS"

It's useful to think of most poems—whether narrative, dramatic, or **lyric**—as informally divisible into parts, distinguished from each other by shifts in subject matter or topic, in **tone**, in address, in tense, or in mode (from narration to reflection or description, for example), and so on. As you read a new poem, look out for such shifts, however subtle, to determine how many parts you think the poem has and how each part relates to, and builds on, the one before. The following lyric, for example, seems to have two parts. How does each part relate to the other? What differentiates and connects them?

PAT MORA
Sonrisas

I live in a doorway
between two rooms, I hear
quiet clicks, cups of black
coffee, *click, click* like facts

5   budgets, tenure, curriculum,
from careful women in crisp beige
suits, quick beige smiles
that seldom sneak into their eyes.

I peek
10   in the other room señoras
in faded dresses stir sweet
milk coffee, laughter whirls
with steam from fresh *tamales*
    sh, sh, mucho ruido,[1]
15   they scold one another,
press their lips, trap smiles
in their dark, Mexican eyes.

                    1986

This poem's two parts closely resemble each other in that each describes
the women who inhabit one of the "two rooms" the speaker "live[s]" "between."
Both descriptions include sights ("crisp beige / suits," "faded dresses"), sounds
("quiet clicks," "laughter"), and even the suggestion of tastes ("black / coffee,"
"sweet / milk coffee"). Yet the relation between the two parts and the two
rooms is clearly one of contrast ("crisp / [. . .] suits" *versus* "faded dresses,"
"quiet clicks" *versus* "laughter," etc.). Here different languages, habits, sights,
sounds, and values characterize the worlds symbolized by the two rooms, and
the poem is organized around the contrast between them. The meaning of the
poem (the difference between the two worlds and the experience of living
between them) is very nearly the same as the structure.

    To fully understand that meaning and the poem, we would need to tease
out all those contrasts and their implications. We would also need to consider the significance of the author's choice not only to make the two parts
essentially equal in length, but also to order them as she does. How would
the poem and our sense of the speaker's feelings about the two rooms be different if we simply rearranged its lines, as follows?

                I live in a doorway
                between two rooms, I hear señoras
                in faded dresses stir sweet
                milk coffee, laughter whirls
                with steam from fresh *tamales*
                    sh, sh, mucho ruido,
                they scold one another,
                press their lips, trap smiles
                in their dark, Mexican eyes.

1. A lot of noise.

> I peek
> in the other room, I hear
> quiet clicks, cups of black
> coffee, *click, click* like facts
>   budgets, tenure, curriculum,
> from careful women in crisp beige
> suits, quick beige smiles
> that seldom sneak into their eyes.

INTERNAL VERSUS EXTERNAL OR FORMAL "PARTS"

In SONRISAS, the internal division created by the speaker's shift in focus (from one room and world to another) corresponds to the poem's formal or "external" division into two **stanzas** and two sentences. Internal and external or formal divisions need not always coincide with each other, however. Major shifts in a poem can and do occur in the middle of a stanza, a line, even a sentence. Take the following poem. Only one sentence and one stanza long, it has no formal divisions at all. Yet it, too, arguably divides into two parts. As you read the poem, consider whether you agree and, if so, where you think the shift occurs.

GALWAY KINNELL
Blackberry Eating

> I love to go out in late September
> among the fat, overripe, icy, black blackberries
> to eat blackberries for breakfast,
> the stalks very prickly, a penalty
> 5 they earn for knowing the black art
> of blackberry-making; and as I stand among them
> lifting the stalks to my mouth, the ripest berries
> fall almost unbidden to my tongue,
> as words sometimes do, certain peculiar words
> 10 like *strengths* or *squinched*,
> many-lettered, one-syllabled lumps,
> which I squeeze, squinch open, and splurge well
> in the silent, startled, icy, black language
> of blackberry-eating in late September.
>   1980

The poem's first eight lines relate the speaker's experience of just what the title leads us to expect—blackberry eating. But notice what happens in line 9: The speaker's focus shifts from the topic of blackberries to the topic of words, with the word "as" signaling that we're entering the second phase of an **analogy** (or extended **simile**) comparing the experience we've just read about (eating blackberries) to the one we now begin to read about (forming words), with both berries and words "fall[ing] almost unbidden to [the] tongue" (line 8). Here, then, the relation between the poem's two parts and the two objects and experiences they describe is one of likeness rather than contrast. Fittingly enough for a poem about connection and comparison, as well as vaguely round "lumps" of things (line 11), the poem's final line ends with the same words as its first ("late September"). In a sense, then, the poem might be described as having a circular, as well as two-part (or "bipartite"), structure.

LYRICS AS INTERNAL DRAMAS

Obviously, not all poems consist of only two parts, as do those above. The following poem, for example, arguably divides into three parts. Just as important, in this poem the relationship between the parts seems to be one of development, tracing a change of outlook or attitude *within* the speaker.

SEAMUS HEANEY
Punishment[2]

> I can feel the tug
> of the halter at the nape
> of her neck, the wind
> on her naked front.
>
> 5 It blows her nipples
> to amber beads,
> it shakes the frail rigging
> of her ribs.
>
> I can see her drowned
> 10 body in the bog,
> the weighing stone,
> the floating rods and boughs.
>
> Under which at first
> she was a barked sapling

---

2. According to the Roman historian Tacitus (c. 56–c. 120 CE), Germanic peoples punished adulterous women by first shaving their heads and then banishing or killing them. In 1951, in Windeby, Germany, the naked body of a young girl from the first century CE was pulled from the bog where she had been murdered. In contemporary Ireland, "betraying sisters" (line 38) have sometimes been punished by the Irish Republican Army for associating with British soldiers.

15 that is dug up
oak-bone, brain-firkin:

her shaved head
like a stubble of black corn,
her blindfold a soiled bandage,
20 her noose a ring

to store
the memories of love.
Little adulteress,
before they punished you

25 you were flaxen-haired,
undernourished, and your
tar-black face was beautiful.
My poor scapegoat,

I almost love you
30 but would have cast, I know,
the stones of silence.
I am the artful voyeur

of your brain's exposed
and darkened combs,
35 your muscles' webbing
and all your numbered bones:

I who have stood dumb
when your betraying sisters,
cauled[3] in tar,
40 wept by the railings,

who would connive
in civilized outrage
yet understand the exact
and tribal, intimate revenge.
                1975

    Here, the first shift seems to come in line 23 (again, in the middle of a stanza rather than its beginning): Up to this point, the speaker has described the long-dead girl in the third person (e.g., "*her* neck," "*her* nipples," lines 3, 5; emphasis added). And despite his twice-repeated emphasis on his own perceptions and responses ("*I* can feel," "*I* can see," lines 1, 9; emphasis added), the girl herself gets most of the attention. Starting in line 23, however,

3. Wrapped or enclosed as if in a caul (the inner fetal membrane of higher vertebrates that sometimes covers the head at birth).

the speaker begins to speak to the girl directly, addressing her in the second person ("you") and through **epithets** ("Little adulteress," "poor scapegoat," lines 23, 28). Verb tense shifts, too ("were," line 25), as the speaker begins to imagine the girl's life "before they punished" her (line 24). In at least two ways, then, the speaker seems to be coming closer to the girl, now seeing and addressing her as a human being with a history rather than as a thing to be looked at and talked *about*. At the same time, the speaker focuses more on himself as well, expressing his emotions ("I almost love you," line 29) and reflecting somewhat critically on the way he looked at the girl's body—and allowed us to—earlier in the poem ("I am the artful voyeur," line 32).

Subject matter and tense shift again, however, in line 37: The poem's final two stanzas consider the speaker's behavior toward the "betraying sisters" (line 38) in an indeterminate past ("I [. . .] have," line 37), as if here he describes not one specific experience, but rather a composite of many. Aside from the "your," in line 38, the girl herself seems to have disappeared from the poem (so much so that even that "your" now seems potentially ambiguous: Might it now also refer to someone else?). Though in this poem, unlike BLACKBERRY EATING, we don't have the word *as* to signal an analogy, it seems clear that Heaney's speaker has, over the course of the poem, come to see a similarity between his own complex attitude toward the long-dead girl and the "betraying sisters," the behavior of those responsible for these women's various punishments, and even between writing a poem about such women and punishing them. How and why so?

Though PUNISHMENT is by no means a dramatic poem in the literal sense, it does—like some other lyrics—relate an internal drama of sorts, tracing the process through which its speaker comes to see or accept, as well as share with us, some truth about or insight into the world or himself that he didn't see or accept previously, somewhat as a fictional character might in a dramatic or narrative poem or in a short story. In reading and writing about such poems, a good topic to explore might well be just what insight the speaker comes to over the course of the poem, and when and why so.

Analyzing Internal Structure: An Exercise

Like "Punishment," both of the following poems arguably trace a development in their speakers' perceptions of themselves or the world around them, even if the realization to which the speakers come and the process by which they get there differ. As you read each poem, think about where and why the shifts come both in the poem and in the speaker's outlook. In which poem does the change within the speaker seem to happen *during* the poem itself (as in "Punishment"), and which poem might instead depict the change as one that happened at some earlier, unspecified point in time?

SAMUEL TAYLOR COLERIDGE
Frost at Midnight

The frost performs its secret ministry,
Unhelped by any wind. The owlet's cry
Came loud—and hark, again! loud as before.
The inmates of my cottage, all at rest,
5 Have left me to that solitude, which suits
Abstruser musings: save that at my side
My cradled infant slumbers peacefully.
'Tis calm indeed! so calm, that it disturbs
And vexes meditation with its strange
10 And extreme silentness. Sea, hill, and wood,
This populous village! Sea, and hill, and wood,
With all the numberless goings on of life,
Inaudible as dreams! the thin blue flame
Lies on my low burnt fire, and quivers not;
15 Only that film,[4] which fluttered on the grate,
Still flutters there, the sole unquiet thing.
Methinks, its motion in this hush of nature
Gives it dim sympathies with me who live,
Making it a companionable form,
20 Whose puny flaps and freaks the idling Spirit
By its own moods interprets, every where
Echo or mirror seeking of itself,
And makes a toy of Thought.

　　　　　　　　　But O! how oft,
How oft, at school, with most believing mind,
25 Presageful, have I gazed upon the bars,
To watch that fluttering stranger! and as oft
With unclosed lids, already had I dreamt
Of my sweet birth-place, and the old church-tower,
Whose bells, the poor man's only music, rang

(continued on next page)

4. In all parts of the kingdom these films are called *strangers* and supposed to portend the arrival of some absent friend [Coleridge's note]. The "film" is a piece of soot fluttering on the bar of the grate.

(continued)

30 From morn to evening, all the hot Fair-day,
    So sweetly, that they stirred and haunted me
    With a wild pleasure, falling on mine ear
    Most like articulate sounds of things to come!
    So gazed I, till the soothing things I dreamt
35 Lulled me to sleep, and sleep prolonged my dreams!
    And so I brooded all the following morn,
    Awed by the stern preceptor's face, mine eye
    Fixed with mock study on my swimming book:
    Save if the door half opened, and I snatched
40 A hasty glance, and still my heart leaped up,
    For still I hoped to see the stranger's face,
    Townsman, or aunt, or sister more beloved,
    My play-mate when we both were clothed alike![5]

    Dear Babe, that sleepest cradled by my side,
45 Whose gentle breathings, heard in this deep calm,
    Fill up the interspersed vacancies
    And momentary pauses of the thought!
    My babe so beautiful! it thrills my heart
    With tender gladness, thus to look at thee,
50 And think that thou shalt learn far other lore
    And in far other scenes! For I was reared
    In the great city, pent 'mid cloisters dim,
    And saw nought lovely but the sky and stars.
    But thou, my babe! shalt wander like a breeze
55 By lakes and sandy shores, beneath the crags
    Of ancient mountain, and beneath the clouds,
    Which image in their bulk both lakes and shores
    And mountain crags: so shalt thou see and hear
    The lovely shapes and sounds intelligible
60 Of that eternal language, which thy God
    Utters, who from eternity doth teach
    Himself in all, and all things in himself.
    Great universal Teacher! he shall mould
    Thy spirit, and by giving make it ask.

65   Therefore all seasons shall be sweet to thee,
    Whether the summer clothe the general earth
    With greenness, or the redbreast sit and sing

5. Late eighteenth-century custom called for all infants to wear dresses, regardless of
gender.

Betwixt the tufts of snow on the bare branch
Of mossy apple-tree, while the nigh thatch
70 Smokes in the sun-thaw; whether the eave-drops fall
Heard only in the trances of the blast,
Or if the secret ministry of frost
Shall hang them up in silent icicles,
Quietly shining to the quiet Moon.

1798

• Coleridge described some of his poems, including FROST AT
MIDNIGHT, as having a circular structure. How and why might
this poem seem circular, or in what way does its end resemble
its beginning? In what way are the two different? How might
the resemblance and difference help us recognize the change
in the speaker's outlook?

SHARON OLDS
The Victims

When Mother divorced you, we were glad. She took it and
took it, in silence, all those years and then
kicked you out, suddenly, and her
kids loved it. Then you were fired, and we
5 grinned inside, the way people grinned when
Nixon's helicopter lifted off the South
Lawn for the last time.[6] We were tickled
to think of your office taken away,
your secretaries taken away,
10 your lunches with three double bourbons,
your pencils, your reams of paper. Would they take your
suits back, too, those dark
carcasses hung in your closet, and the black
noses of your shoes with their large pores?
15 She had taught us to take it, to hate you and take it
until we pricked with her for your
annihilation, Father. Now I
pass the bums in doorways, the white
slugs of their bodies gleaming through slits in their
20 suits of compressed silt, the stained

(*continued on next page*)

6. When Richard Nixon resigned the U.S. presidency on August 8, 1974, his exit from
the White House (by helicopter from the lawn) was televised live.

(*continued*)

> flippers of their hands, the underwater
> fire of their eyes, ships gone down with the
> lanterns lit, and I wonder who took it and
> took it from them in silence until they had
> 25 given it all away and had nothing
> left but this.

1984

> • How are the speakers' shifting attitudes toward her father (and
> the poem's parts) both related and differentiated by repetition
> of the word *took?*

MAKING ARGUMENTS ABOUT STRUCTURE

Dividing a poem into parts and analyzing its internal structure as we have here isn't an exact science: Different readers might well come to slightly different conclusions about the nature, timing, and significance of key shifts and thus about just how many parts a poem might be said to have, how one part relates to another, and what sort of whole those parts create. It seems quite possible, for example, to argue that THE VICTIMS has either two parts or three, depending on what you make of lines 15–17 (up to the word "Now"), or that FROST AT MIDNIGHT has three, four, even five parts. In these cases, as in many others, there is no single correct answer. Indeed, ample room for disagreement is in a way precisely the point: Formulating your own ideas about just where important shifts come in a poem and just why they're important, identifying good evidence to support your conclusions, and considering alternative ways of understanding the poem's structure may take you far down the path to developing your own particular argument about how the poem as a whole works and means.

POEMS WITHOUT "PARTS"

As we've seen, too, dividing a poem into parts is simply a useful way to *begin* to explore and analyze its structure rather than the entire point or end of such analysis. And this is all the more obviously the case with those poems that contain no major shifts and thus no distinct "parts" at all. Such poems nonetheless have a distinct structure; their authors, too, must figure out how to organize their material so as to create something like a beginning, middle, and end. And here, too, such structural choices determine how the poem moves and means. The following poem is a case in point: One sentence and one stanza long, with no major shifts, how does it nonetheless manage both to cohere and develop? What picture of America results both from its particular details and the way they are organized?

WALT WHITMAN
I Hear America Singing

I hear America singing, the varied carols I hear,
Those of mechanics, each one singing his as it should be blithe and
    strong,
The carpenter singing his as he measures his plank or beam,
The mason singing his as he makes ready for work, or leaves off work,
5 The boatman singing what belongs to him in his boat, the deckhand
    singing on the steamboat deck,
The shoemaker singing as he sits on his bench, the hatter singing
    as he stands,
The wood-cutter's song, the ploughboy's on his way in the morning,
    or at noon intermission or at sundown,
The delicious singing of the mother, or of the young wife at work,
    or of the girl sewing or washing,
Each singing what belongs to him or her and to none else,
10 The day what belongs to the day—at night the party of young fellows,
    robust, friendly,
Singing with open mouths their strong melodious songs.

1860

By limiting himself to a single sentence and a single stanza, which none-theless refers to a multitude of people and "songs," Whitman produces a poem that structurally embodies the motto on the U.S. seal—*e pluribus unum*, "Out of many, one." The "many ones" with whom the poem begins are all ordinary men who work with their hands: From "mechanics" (line 2) to a "boatman" (line 5) and "ploughboy" (line 7), they work on land and shore, in city and country. Though line 8 doesn't constitute a major shift, it does subtly broaden and further develop the poem's picture of America: Women enter the poem; and though they, too, are depicted "at work," the fact that they are identified specifically as a "mother," "young wife," and "girl" introduces, too, the idea both of generations and of family, two important social groups that intervene between many individuals, on the one hand, and an entire country, on the other. Finally, at poem's end, we move from "day" to "night" and from labor to leisure, in a way that makes clear that these oppositions and time itself have also been structuring principles all along: Line 4, after all, describes the mason as singing "as he makes ready for [. . .] or leaves off work," line 7 the ploughboy and wood-cutter each making "his way in the morning, or at noon intermission or at sundown." By its close, then, the poem has shown us a full day of life in Whitman's version of America and in the lives of those whose various, unique "carols" (line 1) combine to create a single American song.

POEMS FOR FURTHER STUDY

As you read each of the following poems, consider the following questions: Does the poem seem to divide into internal "parts"? If so, where and why? What are the major shifts? How does each part build on the last? How do the parts combine into a meaningful whole? If the poem doesn't seem divisible into parts, what are its organizing principles? How does the poem build and develop, and what overall picture or even **theme** results?

WILLIAM SHAKESPEARE
[Th' expense of spirit in a waste of shame]

Th' expense of spirit in a waste[7] of shame
Is lust in action; and, till action, lust
Is perjured, murderous, bloody, full of blame,
Savage, extreme, rude, cruel, not to trust;
5 Enjoyed no sooner but despisèd straight:
Past reason hunted; and no sooner had,
Past reason hated, as a swallowed bait,
On purpose laid to make the taker mad:
Mad in pursuit, and in possession so;
10 Had, having, and in quest to have, extreme;
A bliss in proof,[8] and proved, a very woe;
Before, a joy proposed; behind, a dream.
All this the world well knows; yet none knows well
To shun the heaven that leads men to this hell.

1609

• Paraphrase this poem. What emotional stages accompany the carrying out of a violent or lustful act? Is Shakespeare an insightful psychologist? What is his major insight about how lust works?

7. Using up; also, desert. *Expense*: expending.   8. In the act.

PERCY BYSSHE SHELLEY
Ode to the West Wind

I

O wild West Wind, thou breath of Autumn's being,
Thou, from whose unseen presence the leaves dead
Are driven, like ghosts from an enchanter fleeing,

Yellow, and black, and pale, and hectic red,
5 Pestilence-stricken multitudes: O thou,
Who chariotest to their dark wintry bed

The wingèd seeds, where they lie cold and low,
Each like a corpse within its grave, until
Thine azure sister of the Spring shall blow

10 Her clarion[9] o'er the dreaming earth, and fill
(Driving sweet buds like flocks to feed in air)
With living hues and odors plain and hill:

Wild Spirit, which art moving everywhere;
Destroyer and preserver; hear, oh, hear!

II

15 Thou on whose stream, mid the steep sky's commotion,
Loose clouds like earth's decaying leaves are shed,
Shook from the tangled boughs of Heaven and Ocean,

Angels[1] of rain and lightning: there are spread
On the blue surface of thine aëry surge,
20 Like the bright hair uplifted from the head

Of some fierce Maenad,[2] even from the dim verge
Of the horizon to the zenith's height,
The locks of the approaching storm. Thou dirge

Of the dying year, to which this closing night
25 Will be the dome of a vast sepulcher,
Vaulted with all thy congregated might

Of vapors, from whose solid atmosphere
Black rain, and fire, and hail will burst: oh, hear!

9. Trumpet call. 1. Messengers.
2. Frenzied female votary of Dionysus, the Greek god of vegetation and fertility who was supposed to die in the fall and rise again each spring.

III

Thou who didst waken from his summer dreams
30 The blue Mediterranean, where he lay,
   Lulled by the coil of his crystàlline streams,

Beside a pumice isle in Baiae's bay,[3]
And saw in sleep old palaces and towers
Quivering within the wave's intenser day,

35 All overgrown with azure moss and flowers
   So sweet, the sense faints picturing them! Thou
   For whose path the Atlantic's level powers

Cleave themselves into chasms, while far below
The sea-blooms and the oozy woods which wear
40 The sapless foliage of the ocean, know

Thy voice, and suddenly grow gray with fear,
And tremble and despoil themselves:[4] oh, hear!

IV

If I were a dead leaf thou mightest bear;
If I were a swift cloud to fly with thee;
45 A wave to pant beneath thy power, and share

The impulse of thy strength, only less free
Than thou, O uncontrollable! If even
I were as in my boyhood, and could be

The comrade of thy wanderings over Heaven,
50 As then, when to outstrip thy skyey speed
   Scarce seemed a vision; I would ne'er have striven

As thus with thee in prayer in my sore need.
Oh, lift me as a wave, a leaf, a cloud!
I fall upon the thorns of life! I bleed!

55 A heavy weight of hours has chained and bowed
   One too like thee: tameless, and swift, and proud.

V

Make me thy lyre, even as the forest is:
What if my leaves are falling like its own!
The tumult of thy mighty harmonies

3. Where Roman emperors had erected villas, west of Naples.
4. The vegetation at the bottom of the sea . . . sympathizes with that of the land in the change
of seasons [Shelley's note].

60 Will take from both a deep, autumnal tone,
Sweet though in sadness. Be thou, Spirit fierce,
My spirit! Be thou me, impetuous one!

Drive my dead thoughts over the universe
Like withered leaves to quicken a new birth!
65 And, by the incantation of this verse,

Scatter, as from an unextinguished hearth
Ashes and sparks, my words among mankind!
Be through my lips to unawakened earth

The trumpet of a prophecy! O Wind,
70 If Winter comes, can Spring be far behind?

                                                    1820

• What attributes of the West Wind does the speaker want his poetry
to embody? In what ways is this poem like the wind it describes? What
is the effect of its structure?

PHILIP LARKIN
Church Going

Once I am sure there's nothing going on
I step inside, letting the door thud shut.
Another church: matting, seats, and stone,
And little books; sprawlings of flowers, cut
5 For Sunday, brownish now; some brass and stuff
Up at the holy end; the small neat organ;
And a tense, musty, unignorable silence,
Brewed God knows how long. Hatless, I take off
My cycle-clips in awkward reverence,

10 Move forward, run my hand around the font.
From where I stand, the roof looks almost new—
Cleaned, or restored? Someone would know: I don't.
Mounting the lectern, I peruse a few
Hectoring large-scale verses, and pronounce
15 "Here endeth" much more loudly than I'd meant.
The echoes snigger briefly. Back at the door
I sign the book, donate an Irish sixpence,
Reflect the place was not worth stopping for.

Yet stop I did: in fact I often do,
20 And always end much at a loss like this,
Wondering what to look for; wondering, too,

When churches fall completely out of use
What we shall turn them into, if we shall keep
A few cathedrals chronically on show,
25 Their parchment, plate and pyx in locked cases,
And let the rest rent-free to rain and sheep.
Shall we avoid them as unlucky places?

Or, after dark, will dubious women come
To make their children touch a particular stone;
30 Pick simples⁵ for a cancer; or on some
Advised night see walking a dead one?
Power of some sort or other will go on
In games, in riddles, seemingly at random;
But superstition, like belief, must die,
35 And what remains when disbelief has gone?
Grass, weedy pavement, brambles, buttress, sky,

A shape less recognizable each week,
A purpose more obscure. I wonder who
Will be the last, the very last, to seek
40 This place for what it was; one of the crew
That tap and jot and know what rood-lofts⁶ were?
Some ruin-bibber,⁷ randy for antique,
Or Christmas-addict, counting on a whiff
Of gown-and-bands and organ-pipes and myrrh?
45 Or will he be my representative,

Bored, uninformed, knowing the ghostly silt
Dispersed, yet tending to this cross of ground
Through suburb scrub because it held unspilt
So long and equably what since is found
50 Only in separation—marriage, and birth,
And death, and thoughts of these—for whom was built
This special shell? For, though I've no idea
What this accoutered frowsty barn is worth,
It pleases me to stand in silence here;

55 A serious house on serious earth it is,
In whose blent⁸ air all our compulsions meet,
Are recognized, and robed as destinies.
And that much never can be obsolete,
Since someone will forever be surprising

---

5. Medicinal herbs.
6. Galleries atop the screens (on which crosses are mounted) that divide the naves or main bodies of churches from the choirs or chancels.
7. Literally, ruin-drinker: someone extremely attracted to antiquarian objects.   8. Blended.

60 A hunger in himself to be more serious,
    And gravitating with it to this ground,
    Which, he once heard, was proper to grow wise in,
    If only that so many dead lie round.

                                                  1955

   • Describe the parts of this poem. How do the first two stanzas differ
     from the rest of the poem? Where and how does the poem shift from
     the personal to the general?

AUTHORS ON THEIR WORK
PHILIP LARKIN (1922–85)

From "A Conversation with Ian Hamilton" (1964)*

It ["Church Going"] is of course an entirely secular poem. I was a bit irritated by an American who insisted to me it was a religious poem. It isn't
religious at all. Religion surely means that the affairs of this world are
under divine surveillance, and so on, and I go to some pains to point out
that I don't bother about that kind of thing. [. . .]
      [. . .] the poem is about going to church, not religion—I tried to suggest
this by the title—and the union of the important stages of human life—
birth, marriage and death—that going to church represents; and my own
feeling that when they are dispersed into the registry office and the cre-
matorium chapel life will become thinner in consequence. (22)

                              •   •   •

From "An Interview with John Haffenden" (1981)**

It ["Church Going"] came from the first time I saw a ruined church in
Northern Ireland, and I'd never seen a ruined church before—discarded.
It shocked me. Now of course it's commonplace: churches are not so
much ruined as turned into bingo-halls, warehouses for refrigerators or
split-level houses for architects.

It's not clear in the poem that you began with a ruined church.
No, it wasn't in the poem, but when you go into a church there's a feeling
of something . . . well . . . over, derelict.

*Some critics have discerned in it a yearning for a latter-day Christian or
religious sanction. Is that so?*
I suppose so. I'm not someone who's lost faith: I never had it. I was bap-
tized [. . .] but not confirmed. Aren't religions shaped in terms of what

people want? No one could help hoping Christianity was true, or at least the happy ending—rising from the dead and our sins forgiven. One longs for these miracles, and so in a sense one longs for religion. But "Church Going" isn't that kind of poem: it's a humanist poem, a celebration of the dignity of . . . well, you know what it says. (56–57)

*"A Conversation with Ian Hamilton." *Further Requirements: Interviews, Broadcasts, Statements and Book Reviews,* edited by Anthony Thwaite, Faber and Faber, 2001, pp. 19–26. Originally published in *London Magazine,* Nov. 1946.
**"An Interview with John Haffenden." *Further Requirements: Interviews, Broadcasts, Statements and Book Reviews,* edited by Anthony Thwaite, Faber and Faber, 2001, pp. 47–62. Originally published in *Viewpoints: Poets in Conversation with John Haffenden,* 1981.

SUGGESTIONS FOR WRITING

1. What words and patterns are repeated in the different stanzas of Shelley's ODE TO THE WEST WIND? What differences are there from stanza to stanza? What "progress" does the poem make? Write an essay in which you discuss the ways that meaning and structure are intertwined in Shelley's poem.
2. Write an essay that explores the use of contrast in Pat Mora's SONRISAS. How is each of the two rooms in the poem characterized by way of contrast with the other? What do they individually and jointly symbolize? What does the poem show through this contrast?
3. Pick out any poem you have read in this book that seems particularly effective in the way it is put together. Write an essay in which you consider how the poem is organized—that is, what structural principles it employs. What do the choices of speaker, situation, and setting have to do with the poem's structure? What other artistic decisions contribute to its structure?

SAMPLE WRITING: ESSAY-IN-PROGRESS

The following piece of writing by student Lindsay Gibson was originally just one section of a longer essay on multiple poems by Philip Larkin. Though the beginning and middle of the piece work fine out of that context, you'll notice that we haven't supplied either the complete title or the real conclusion that the piece needs to have in order to be an entire, effective essay. What should the piece be titled? How might it be brought to a more satisfying conclusion?

You will notice, too, that the essay focuses only in part and somewhat unevenly on issues related to internal structure. How might the essay make more of the poem's structure? More generally, what are the weakest and strongest moments and aspects of the essay? How might its argument be improved or expanded? Answering such questions for yourself or discussing them with your classmates might be a useful way to better understand the qualities of a good argument, a good title, and a good conclusion.

Lindsay Gibson
Dr. Nick Lolordo
Modern British Poetry
27 January 2017

Philip Larkin's "Church Going"

Philip Larkin is one of the semester's most fascinating poets. His use of colloquial language, regular meter, and rhyme sets him slightly apart from other poets of his day, many of whom write in varying forms of verse, use nearly indecipherable language, and rarely, if ever, make use of rhyme at all. Many of his poems are fraught with existential crises, the nature of which only someone living in the postmodern world could understand; consequently, his poems contain a lot of meaning for the contemporary reader.

Larkin's most fascinating poem, "Church Going," embodies many of his best attributes as a poet: it uses everyday, standard English and is therefore easy to read and understand, yet its stanzas contain a real search for meaning that its simple language might not immediately invite the reader to ponder. The poem also addresses one of Larkin's main preoccupations: religion, and specifically the role of religion in a postmodern world. Even with all of this, the most engaging aspect of the poem is the duality reflected in its structure: at first and on the one hand, the speaker makes quiet fun of religion; later and on the other hand, he reveals to us his own search for meaning and the answers that he realizes religion may or may not be able to give him.

The first two stanzas of "Church Going" contain a narrative of a seemingly secular man entering a church he has passed along his way. The speaker observes the layout of the building, the various accoutrements common to a church, and views it all with a mild sense of sarcasm or awkward reverence. His language almost insists on his self-proclaimed ignorance: "Someone would know; I don't" (line 12). And he foreshadows the rest of the poem when appraising the roof of the church as one would an antique: "Cleaned, or restored?" (12). At the end of the second stanza, the speaker reflects that "the place was not worth stopping for" (18). Yet stop he did, and that tells us volumes about what the rest of the poem is about.

In the third stanza, the poem's tone and the speaker's attitude shift as the speaker begins to ponder big questions about religion in today's world: does it have any meaning left? Should it? The speaker reveals to us that he often stops at churches like these, searching for meaning, yet "Wondering what to look for" (21), not even knowing what the questions are that he wants answered. His use of words like "parchment, plate and pyx" (25) reveals to us that he is not as ignorant about religious liturgy as he would have us believe—which, in turn, is further evidence of the dual nature of the poem: The speaker wants us to believe he doesn't know or care about anything to do with religion, yet he has been on his quest for meaning long enough to know the names of things he claims he does not. The last line of the third stanza poses another compelling question, this time about the future: after churches fall out of use, "Shall we avoid them as unlucky places?" (27). The question of whether, when faith is finally dead, people will still cling to superstitions such as luck and supernatural powers of whatever nature is a fascinating one.

The speaker goes on to explore this question in the next few stanzas by imagining some specific ways in which superstition might persist after religion is gone: women might take their children to "touch a particular stone" (29) or pick herbs around the church to use for medicinal purposes. But in all these imagined examples, no one actually goes to the church to worship anymore. In stanza 4, the speaker presents various tableaus of people using the church for more and more mundane uses, such as a student of architecture, someone else who only likes to see the ruins of old buildings simply because they're old, and finally, and somewhat paradoxically, a "Christmas-addict" (43) who (presumably) wants to see the last religious remnants of his beloved, commoditized, and commercialized holiday. The last person who might visit the church in this post-religion world might even be a doppelganger of the speaker himself, who, though claiming to be "bored" and "uninformed" (46), visits the church because "it held unspilt / So long and equably what since is found / Only in separation—marriage, and birth, / And death, and thoughts of these" (48-51). Once again the speaker insists that he is ignorant and careless of religion, but goes on to betray the fact that even if he does not believe in the religion itself, he is fascinated by the idea that it held "unspilt" what people now only find in marriages, births, and deaths: meaning. It is at this point that the reader can truly appreciate the point and purpose of this whole poem: meaning, and the search for it. It seems poignant that the speaker realizes there is more *meaning* in the church itself than any other place, whether actual belief in religion is there or not.

The last stanza seems to be an attempt on the speaker's part to reconcile the opposing forces of the poem—the speaker's insistence that he cares nothing for religion and that religion is meaningless anyway versus his existential need to find some kind of meaning that will justify his existence and maybe even the beliefs of others. The speaker finally respects what the church does for people, including himself: one's "compulsions meet, / Are recognised, and robed as destinies" (56-57). When one wonders if compulsions are merely that, one can go to church and be told that he or she is part of a larger whole—one's destiny. And if compulsions can be transformed into destinies, at least in the mind of the wonderer, then there will always be value in such a service: "that much never can be obsolete" (58), according to the speaker of the poem.

The last stanzas of the poem are devoted to a man who gravitates to the church because he "once heard [it] was proper to grow wise in, / If only that so many dead lie round" (62-63). Once again, the speaker shows us that even

Gibson 4

when belief in the religion associated with the church is completely gone, a sense of reverence, if only for the dead, will remain. The belief may be gone, but the sense of a community among people searching for, and perhaps finding, meaning will remain, and people will always be drawn to that, no matter what their belief system (or lack thereof).

The poem itself has another overarching concern that merits discussion: death. There are many images of or mentions of death throughout the poem: There are "flowers, cut / For Sunday, brownish now" (4-5), the words "Here endeth" (15) echoing through the small church, the possibility of someone seeing a "walking dead one" (31), the assertion that "superstition, like belief, must die" (34), talk of the "ghostly silt / Dispersed" (46-47), thoughts of "marriage, and birth, / And death" (50-51). And finally, the last image in the poem is the abandoned church's graveyard in which "so many dead lie round" (62). Throughout the poem there is death: death of people, death of ideas, death of faith. Death's pervasiveness is one more way the poem struggles with its dual nature: the poem narrates a serious search for meaning, yet the very definition of death is that there *is* no meaning. Death is the end, there is nothing more. Any search for meaning is rendered meaningless anyway upon one's death. The speaker implies that there is even an end to the search for meaning itself. The speaker asks in line 35, perhaps the most powerful line of the whole poem, "And what remains when disbelief has gone?" What is left over when even "disbelief" has died? Is it the beginning of another cycle in the search for meaning, or has even the "faith" that there is nothing out there died as well?

The poem "Church Going" is a very layered, intensive look at all the things that matter to us as human beings: meaning, death, hope, hopelessness, and the way all of these things blend together in the perpetual existential crisis that is man's very existence.

Gibson 5

Work Cited

Larkin, Philip. "Church Going." *The Norton Introduction to Literature*, edited by Kelly J. Mays, portable 12th ed., W. W. Norton, 2017, pp. 647-49.

EXTERNAL FORM

The previous chapters have discussed many of the *internal* features of a poem that make it unique: the **tone** and characteristics of its **speaker**; its **situation** and **setting** and its **themes**; its **diction**, **imagery**, and sounds. This chapter ventures into the *external* form of a poem, including its arrangement on the page and into both visual and verbal units. These formal aspects are external in being recognizable; like the fashion and fabric of clothing that expresses the personality of an individual, the external form is an appropriate garb or guise for the unique internal action and meaning of the poem. When reading a poem, you might immediately notice its stanza breaks. Or you might quickly recognize that the poem takes a traditional form such as the **sonnet**, or that it simply looks odd. These formal features guide readers as well as the poet. They help readers feel and appreciate repetitions and connections, changes and gaps, in the language as well as the meaning of the poem.

STANZAS

Most poems of more than a few lines are divided into **stanzas**—groups of lines divided from other groups by white space on the page. Putting some space between groupings of lines has the effect of sectioning a poem, giving its physical appearance a series of divisions that sometimes correspond to turns of thought, changes of scene or image, or other shifts in structure or direction of the kind examined in the last chapter. In John Donne's The Flea, for example, the stanza divisions mark distinct stages in the action: Between the first and second stanzas, the speaker stops his companion from killing the flea; between the second and third stanzas, the companion follows through on her intention and kills the flea. Any formal division of a poem into stanzas is important to consider; what appear to be gaps or silences may be structural markers.

Historically, stanzas have most often been organized by patterns of **rhyme**, and often of **meter**, too; thus stanza divisions have traditionally been a visual indicator of patterns in sound. In most traditional stanza forms, the pattern of rhyme is repeated in stanza after stanza throughout the poem, until voice and ear become familiar with the pattern and come to expect it. The repetition of pattern allows us to hear deviations from the pattern as well, just as we do in music.

TRADITIONAL STANZA FORMS

As the poems in this anthology demonstrate, the forms that stanzas can take are limitless. Over time, however, certain stanza forms have become traditional, or "fixed." In using traditional stanza forms, poets thus often implicitly or explicitly allude and even respond to previous poets and poems that have used the same form. Like musicians, they also generate new effects, meanings, and music through meaningful variations on traditional forms.

Terza Rima

In Shelley's ODE TO THE WEST WIND, the first and third lines in each stanza rhyme, and the middle line then rhymes with the first and third lines of the next stanza.

O wild West Wind, thou breath of Autumn's being,	*a*
Thou, from whose unseen presence the leaves dead	*b*
Are driven, like ghosts from an enchanter fleeing,	*a*
Yellow, and black, and pale, and hectic red,	*b*
Pestilence-stricken multitudes: O thou,	*c*
Who chariotest to their dark wintry bed	*b*
The wingèd seeds, where they lie cold and low,	*c*
Each like a corpse within its grave, until	*d*
Thine azure sister of the Spring shall blow	*c*

In this stanza form, known as **terza rima**, the stanzas are linked to each other by a common sound: one rhyme sound from each stanza is picked up in the next stanza, and so on to the end of the poem (though sometimes poems in this form have sections that use varied rhyme schemes). Most traditional stanza forms involve a metrical pattern as well as a rhyme scheme. Terza rima, like most English fixed stanza and verse forms, involves **iambic** meter (unstressed and stressed syllables alternating regularly), and each line has five beats (**pentameter**).

As the title of the following poem announces, it, too, is written—at least mostly—in terza rima. And it depends, for its full effect, on our knowing not only that this stanza form was used by Dante in *The Divine Comedy*, written in Italian in the early 1300s, but also that this three-book epic depicts the poet's journey through Hell (or the inferno) and Purgatory to Paradise.

RICHARD WILBUR

Terza Rima

In this great form, as Dante proved in Hell,
There is no dreadful thing that can't be said
In passing. Here, for instance, one could tell

How our jeep skidded sideways toward the dead
5 Enemy soldier with the staring eyes,
Bumping a little as it struck his head,

And then flew on, as if toward Paradise[1]

2008

- What might this poem communicate—about, for example, war, poetry, and/or death—by starting out, but not ending, in terza rima?

Terza rima requires many rhymes, and thus many different rhyme words, and therefore it is not very common in English, a language not as rich in rhyme possibilities as Italian or French. English is derived from so many different language families that it has fewer similar word endings than languages that mainly derive from a single language family.

Spenserian Stanza

Named for Edmund Spenser, who used it to great effect in his long poem *The Faerie Queene*, the **Spenserian stanza** is even more rhyme-rich than terza rima, using only three rhyme sounds in nine rhymed lines, as in John Keats's *The Eve of St. Agnes*:

Her falt'ring hand upon the balustrade,	*a*
Old Angela was feeling for the stair,	*b*
When Madeline, St. Agnes' charmèd maid,	*a*
Rose, like a missioned spirit, unaware:	*b*
With silver taper's light, and pious care,	*b*
She turned, and down the agèd gossip led	*c*
To a safe level matting. Now prepare,	*b*
Young Porphyro, for gazing on that bed;	*c*
She comes, she comes again, like ring dove frayed and fled	*c*

Notice that while the first eight lines of a Spenserian stanza are in iambic pentameter, the ninth has one extra foot, making it iambic **hexameter**.

---

1. Perhaps an allusion, too, to Emily Dickinson's "[Because I could not stop for Death—]," which ends with a horse-drawn carriage driven by Death carrying the speaker "toward Eternity—" (line 24).

Ballad Stanza

The much more common **ballad stanza** has only one set of rhymes in four lines; lines 1 and 3 in each stanza do not rhyme at all. And while those lines are in iambic **tetrameter** (4 beats/feet), lines 2 and 4 are rhymed iambic **trimeter** (3 beats/feet).

The king sits in Dumferling toune,	*a*
Drinking the blude-reid wine:	*b*
"O whar will I get guid sailor,	*c*
To sail this ship of mine?"	*b*

TRADITIONAL VERSE FORMS

Though ballad stanza takes its name from the fact that it is often used in the particular subgenre of poem known as the **ballad**, stanza forms are not themselves subgenres of poetry, but rather a form that can be used for various kinds of poems. The same is true of other traditional verse forms—set patterns of rhythm and rhyme that govern whole poems or parts of them rather than individual stanzas. Three especially useful verse forms to know are the couplet, blank verse, and free verse.

Any pair of consecutive lines that share *end rhymes* is called a *rhyming couplet*, regardless of their meter. Andrew Marvell's To His Coy Mistress, for example, consists entirely of iambic tetrameter couplets, beginning with these two:

Had we but world enough, and time,	*a*
This coyness, Lady, were no crime.	*a*
We would sit down and think which way	*b*
To walk and pass our long love's day.	*b*

A *heroic couplet*, however, requires iambic pentameter, as in Alexander Pope's Sound and Sense:

But most by numbers judge a poet's song,	*a*
And smooth or rough, with them, is right or wrong;	*a*
In the bright muse though thousand charms conspire,	*b*
Her voice is all these tuneful fools admire	*b*

Near the other end of the spectrum from the heroic couplet sits **blank verse**, which consists of lines with regular meter, usually iambic pentameter, but no discernible rhyme scheme, as in these lines, which Adam speaks to Eve in John Milton's epic *Paradise Lost:*

Well hast thou motioned, well thy thoughts employed,
How we might best fulfil the work which here
God hath assigned us; nor of me shalt pass

Unpraised: for nothing lovelier can be found
In woman, than to study household good,
And good works in her husband to promote.

Though here used by Milton to describe lofty events of cosmic significance, blank verse was among the least formal and most natural of traditional verse forms until the explosion of **free verse** in the twentieth century. Now perhaps the most common of verse forms, free verse is "free" precisely because it's defined wholly by what it lacks—both regular meter and rhyme. The wildly different lengths of the following lines from THE WORD *PLUM* make its use of free verse especially obvious:

> taut skin
> pierced, bitten, provoked into
> juice, and tart flesh

FIXED FORMS OR FORM-BASED SUBGENRES

Again, all these stanza and verse forms can be used in many different kinds of poems. But some kinds or subgenres of poetry are defined wholly by their use of very particular formal patterns. Perhaps the most famous of these are the sonnet and the **haiku**, to which we devote the albums that follow this chapter. Others include the **limerick** (see, for example, THERE WAS A YOUNG GIRL FROM ST. PAUL), the **villanelle** (DO NOT GO GENTLE INTO THAT GOOD NIGHT, below), the **palindrome** (MYTH, below), and the **sestina** (see below). Though relatively rare for much of the twentieth century, such traditional fixed forms have in recent years become increasingly popular once again. *McSweeney's Internet Tendency*, the online version of the famously eccentric literary magazine edited by novelist Dave Eggers, included no new poetry except sestinas between 2003 and 2006, and you can still find hundreds of examples on its Web site.

You can probably deduce the principles involved in each of these fixed forms by looking carefully at an example; if you have trouble, look at the definitions in the glossary.

TRADITIONAL FORMS: POEMS FOR FURTHER STUDY

DYLAN THOMAS
Do Not Go Gentle into That Good Night[2]

Do not go gentle into that good night,
Old age should burn and rave at close of day;
Rage, rage against the dying of the light.

2. Written during the final illness of the poet's father.

Though wise men at their end know dark is right,
5 Because their words had forked no lightning they
Do not go gentle into that good night.

Good men, the last wave by, crying how bright
Their frail deeds might have danced in a green bay,
Rage, rage against the dying of the light.

10 Wild men who caught and sang the sun in flight,
And learn, too late, they grieved it on its way,
Do not go gentle into that good night.

Grave men, near death, who see with blinding sight
Blind eyes could blaze like meteors and be gay,
15 Rage, rage against the dying of the light.

And you, my father, there on the sad height,
Curse, bless, me now with your fierce tears, I pray.
Do not go gentle into that good night.
Rage, rage against the dying of the light.

1952

• What do the wise, good, wild, and grave men have in common with the
speaker's father? Why do you think Thomas chose such a strict form,
the villanelle, for such an emotionally charged subject?

NATASHA TRETHEWEY
Myth

I was asleep while you were dying.
It's as if you slipped through some rift, a hollow
I make between my slumber and my waking,

the Erebus[3] I keep you in, still trying
5 not to let go. You'll be dead again tomorrow,
but in dreams you live. So I try taking

you back into morning. Sleep-heavy, turning,
my eyes open, I find you do not follow.
Again and again, this constant forsaking.

10 Again and again, this constant forsaking:
my eyes open, I find you do not follow.
You back into morning, sleep-heavy, turning.

---

3. In Greek mythology, the dark region of the underworld through which the dead pass en route
to Hades.

But in dreams you live. So I try taking,
not to let go. You'll be dead again tomorrow.
15 The Erebus I keep you in—still, trying—

I make between my slumber and my waking.
It's as if you slipped through some rift, a hollow.
I was asleep while you were dying.

2007

• How does Trethewey's use of a palindromic structure contribute to the
poem's evocation of grief? Why do you think the poem is called MYTH?

ELIZABETH BISHOP
Sestina

September rain falls on the house.
In the failing light, the old grandmother
sits in the kitchen with the child
beside the Little Marvel Stove,
5 reading the jokes from the almanac,
laughing and talking to hide her tears.

She thinks that her equinoctial tears
and the rain that beats on the roof of the house
were both foretold by the almanac,
10 but only known to a grandmother.
The iron kettle sings on the stove.
She cuts some bread and says to the child,

It's time for tea now; but the child
is watching the teakettle's small hard tears
15 dance like mad on the hot black stove,
the way the rain must dance on the house.
Tidying up, the old grandmother
hangs up the clever almanac

on its string. Birdlike, the almanac
20 hovers half open above the child,
hovers above the old grandmother
and her teacup full of dark brown tears.
She shivers and says she thinks the house
feels chilly, and puts more wood in the stove.

25 *It was to be,* says the Marvel Stove.
I know what I know, says the almanac.
With crayons the child draws a rigid house
and a winding pathway. Then the child

puts in a man with buttons like tears
30　and shows it proudly to the grandmother.

But secretly, while the grandmother
busies herself about the stove,
the little moons fall down like tears
from between the pages of the almanac
35　into the flower bed the child
has carefully placed in the front of the house.

Time to plant tears, says the almanac.
The grandmother sings to the marvellous stove
and the child draws another inscrutable house.

1965

• Try to derive from SESTINA the "rules" that govern the sestina form.
Why do you think Bishop chose this form for her poem?

CIARA SHUTTLEWORTH
Sestina

You
used
to
love
5　me
well.

Well,
you—
me—
10　used
love
to . . .

to . . .
well . . .
15　love.
You
used
me.

Me,
20　too,

used . . .
well . . .
you.
Love,

25　love
me.
You,
too
well
30　used,

used
love
well.
Me,
35　too.
You!

You used
to love
me well.

2010

• How does Shuttleworth use punctuation to produce meaning in this especially economical sestina?

THE WAY A POEM LOOKS

Like stanza breaks, other arrangements of print and space help guide the voice and the mind to a clearer sense of sound and meaning. But sometimes poems are written to be seen rather than heard, and their appearance on the page is crucial to their effect. E. E. Cummings's poem l(a, for example, tries to visualize typographically what the poet asks you to see in your mind's eye.

E. E. CUMMINGS
[l(a]

l(a
le
af
fa
ll
s)
one
l
iness
           1958

The unusual spacing of words in the following poem, with some run together and others widely separated, provides a guide to reading, regulating both speed and sense, so that the poem can capture aloud some of the boy's wide-eyed enthusiasm, remembered now from a later perspective. (Notice how the word "defunct" helps establish the time and point of view.)

E. E. CUMMINGS
[Buffalo Bill's][4]

Buffalo Bill's
defunct
          who used to
          ride a watersmooth-silver
5   stallion
and break onetwothreefourfive pigeonsjustlikethat
                                              Jesus
he was a handsome man
                    and what i want to know is

4. From Cummings's *Portraits* XXI.

how do you like your blueeyed boy
10 Mister Death

1923

CONCRETE POETRY

Occasionally, poems are composed in a specific shape so that they look like physical objects. The idea that poems can be related to the visual arts is an old one. Theodoric in ancient Greece is credited with inventing *technopaegnia*— that is, the construction of poems with visual appeal. Once, the shaping of words to resemble an object was thought to have mystical power, but more recent attempts at **concrete poetry**, or shaped verse, are usually playful exercises that attempt to supplement (or replace) verbal meanings with devices from painting and sculpture. Here are two examples.

GEORGE HERBERT
Easter Wings

Lord, who createdst man in wealth and store,[5]
Though foolishly he lost the same,
Decaying more and more
Till he became
Most poor:
With thee
O let me rise
As larks,[6] harmoniously,
And sing this day thy victories:
Then shall the fall further the flight in me.

My tender age in sorrow did begin;
And still with sicknesses and shame
Thou didst so punish sin,
That I became
Most thin.
With thee
Let me combine,
And feel this day thy victory;
For, if I imp[7] my wing on thine,
Affliction shall advance the flight in me.

1633

5. In plenty.   6. Which herald the morning.
7. Engraft. In falconry, to engraft feathers in a damaged wing, so as to restore the powers of flight (*OED*).

• How do this poem's decreasing and increasing line lengths correspond to the meaning of the words? Why do you think Herbert has
chosen to present the poem sideways?

SUGGESTIONS FOR WRITING

1. Trace the variations in imagery of light and darkness in Thomas's Do Not Go
Gentle into That Good Night. How do we know that light represents life
and darkness death (rather than, say, sight and blindness)? How does the poet
use the strict formal requirements of the villanelle to emphasize this interplay
of light and darkness? Write an essay in which you discuss the interaction of
form and content in Do Not Go Gentle into That Good Night.
2. Which of the poems either mentioned or reproduced in this chapter do you
think makes the most effective use of any traditional stanza or verse form?
Why and how so? Write a response paper in which you explore your response
to the poem and how it is shaped by the poet's choice of a traditional form.
3. Every poem has a particular form, whether or not it adheres to a traditional
stanza or verse form or to conventional ideas about line, rhythm, or spacing.
Examine closely the form of any poem in this book, including its arrangement
on the page and division into lines and stanzas. How does the poet use form
to shape sound, emotion, and meaning? Write an essay examining the relationship between the poem's theme and its external form.

From *Black, Grey and White: A Book of Visual Sonnets* by David Miller.

The Sonnet

The **sonnet**, one of the most persistent and familiar fixed forms, originated in the Middle Ages in Italian and French poetry. It dominated English poetry in the late sixteenth and early seventeenth centuries and then was revived several times from the early nineteenth century onward. Except for some early experiments with length, the sonnet has always been fourteen lines long, and it usually is written in **iambic pentameter**. It is most often printed as if it were a single stanza, although it actually has formal divisions defined by its various rhyme schemes. For more than four centuries, the sonnet has been surprisingly resilient, and it continues to attract a variety of poets. As a verse form, the sonnet is contained, compact, demanding; whatever it does, it must do concisely. It is best suited to intensity of feeling and concentration of figurative language and expression.

Most sonnets are structured according to one of two principles of division. The *English*, or *Shakespearean, sonnet* is divided into three units of four lines each (quatrains) and a final unit of two lines (couplet), and sometimes the line spacing reflects this division. Ordinarily its rhyme scheme reflects the structure: The scheme of *abab cdcd efef gg* is the classic one, but many variations from that pattern still reflect the basic 4-4-4-2 division. In the *Italian*, or *Petrarchan, sonnet* (the Italian poet Petrarch was an early master of this form), the fundamental break is between the first eight lines (called an octave) and the last six (called a sestet). Its "typical" rhyme scheme is *abbaabba cdecde*, although it, too, produces many variations that still reflect the basic division into two parts, an octave and a sestet.

The two kinds of sonnet structures are useful for different sorts of argument. The 4-4-4-2 structure works very well for constructing a poem that makes a three-step argument (with either a quick summary or a dramatic turn at the end) or for setting up brief, cumulative images. Shakespeare's THAT TIME OF YEAR THOU MAYST IN ME BEHOLD, for example, uses the 4-4-4-2 structure to mark the progressive steps toward death and the parting of lovers by using three distinct images and then summarizing. In the two-part structure of the Italian sonnet, the octave states a proposition or generalization, and the sestet provides a particular example, consequence, or application of it; alternatively, the second part may turn away from the first to present a new position or response. The final lines may, for example, reverse the first eight and achieve a paradox or irony in the poem, or the poem may nearly balance two comparable arguments. Basically, the 8-6 structure lends itself to poems with two points to make, or to those that make one point and then illustrate or complicate it.

During the Renaissance, poets regularly employed the sonnet for love poems; many modern sonnets continue to be about love or private life, and many poets continue to use a personal, apparently open and sincere **tone** in their sonnets. But poets often find the sonnet's compact form and rigid demands equally useful for a variety of subjects and tones. Sonnets may be about subjects other than love: politics, philosophy, discovery. And their tones vary widely, too, from the anger and remorse of TH' EXPENSE OF SPIRIT IN A WASTE OF SHAME to the tender awe of HOW DO I LOVE THEE? (below). Many poets seem to take the kind of comfort in the careful limits of the form that William Wordsworth describes in NUNS FRET NOT (below), finding in its two basic variations, the English sonnet and the Italian sonnet, a wealth of ways to organize their materials into coherent structures.

Sometimes a neat and precise structure is altered as particular needs or effects may demand. And the two basic structures, Shakespearean and Petrarchan, certainly do not define all the structural possibilities within a fourteen-line poem, even if they are the most traditional ways of taking advantage of the sonnet's compact and contained form.

Which of the following sonnets follow the Italian model? the English? In each case, how do form, structure, and content work together? How does each poet adapt the traditional form to his or her particular purpose? Aside from particular patterns of rhyme and meter, what other conventions of the sonnet can you identify? How do individual poems use, rework, even comment on those conventions? (To see how one student answered some of these questions by comparing sonnets by two different writers, see the essay by Melissa Makolin that follows ch. 15.)

HENRY CONSTABLE
[My lady's presence makes the roses red]

My lady's presence makes the roses red,
Because to see her lips they blush for shame.
The lily's leaves, for envy, pale became,
And her white hands in them this envy bred.
5   The marigold the leaves abroad doth spread,
Because the sun's and her power is the same.
The violet of purple colour came,
Dyed in the blood she made my heart to shed.
In brief: all flowers from her their virtue take;
10   From her sweet breath their sweet smells do proceed;
The living heat which her eyebeams doth make
Warmeth the ground and quickeneth the seed.
The rain, wherewith she watereth the flowers,
Falls from mine eyes, which she dissolves in showers.

1594

• Which type of sonnet is this? How do external form and internal structure here work together?

WILLIAM SHAKESPEARE
[My mistress' eyes are nothing like the sun]

My mistress' eyes are nothing like the sun;
Coral is far more red than her lips' red;
If snow be white, why then her breasts are dun,[1]
If hairs be wires, black wires grow on her head.
5 I have seen roses damasked[2] red and white,
But no such roses see I in her cheeks;
And in some perfumes is there more delight
Than in the breath that from my mistress reeks.
I love to hear her speak, yet well I know
10 That music hath a far more pleasing sound;
I grant I never saw a goddess go;[3]
My mistress, when she walks, treads on the ground.
And yet, by heaven, I think my love as rare
As any she belied with false compare.

1609

• How might this poem respond to sonnets like Constable's MY LADY'S PRESENCE . . .?

[Not marble, nor the gilded monuments]

Not marble, nor the gilded monuments
Of princes, shall outlive this powerful rhyme;
But you shall shine more bright in these contènts
Than unswept stone, besmeared with sluttish time.
5 When wasteful war shall statues overturn,
And broils[4] root out the work of masonry,
Nor Mars his[5] sword nor war's quick fire shall burn
The living record of your memory.
'Gainst death and all-oblivious enmity
10 Shall you pace forth; your praise shall still find room
Even in the eyes of all posterity

---

1. Mouse-colored.   2. Variegated.   3. Walk.   4. Roots of plants.
5. Mars his: Mars's. *Nor*: neither.

That wear this world out to the ending doom.[6]
So, till the judgment that yourself arise,
You live in this, and dwell in lovers' eyes.

                                                    1609

• How does each quatrain build on the last?

[Let me not to the marriage of true minds]

Let me not to the marriage of true minds
Admit impediments.[7] Love is not love
Which alters when it alteration finds,
Or bends with the remover to remove:
5 Oh, no! it is an ever-fixèd mark,
That looks on tempests and is never shaken;
It is the star to every wandering bark,
Whose worth's unknown, although his height be taken.[8]
Love's not Time's fool, though rosy lips and cheeks
10 Within his bending sickle's compass come;
Love alters not with his brief hours and weeks,
But bears it out even to the edge of doom.
If this be error and upon me proved,
I never writ, nor no man ever loved.

                                                    1609

• What might the speaker mean when he says that love doesn't "ben[d]"
  with the remover to remove" (line 4)? How might the rest of the poem
  explain and develop this statement?

JOHN MILTON
[When I consider how my light is spent]

When I consider how my light is spent,
    Ere half my days, in this dark world and wide,
    And that one talent which is death to hide[9]

6. Judgment Day.
7. The Church of England's marriage service contains this address to the witnesses: "If any of
you know cause or just impediments why these persons should not be joined together [. . .]"
8. That is, measuring the altitude of stars (for purposes of navigation) is not a way to measure
value.
9. In the parable of the talents (Matt. 25), the servants who earned interest on their master's
money (his talents) while he was away were called "good and faithful"; the one who simply hid
the money and then returned it was condemned and sent away.

Lodged with me useless, though my soul more bent
5 To serve therewith my Maker, and present
My true account, lest he returning chide;
"Doth God exact day-labor, light denied?"
I fondly ask; but Patience to prevent[1]
That murmur, soon replies, "God doth not need
10 Either man's work or his own gifts; who best
Bear his mild yoke, they serve him best. His state
Is kingly. Thousands at his bidding speed
And post o'er land and ocean without rest:
They also serve who only stand and wait."

c. 1652

• How might the timing of the poem's shift to Patience (in the middle
of line 8) be meaningful? Paraphrase the speaker's question and
Patience's reply.

WILLIAM WORDSWORTH
Nuns Fret Not

Nuns fret not at their convent's narrow room;
And hermits are contented with their cells;
And students with their pensive citadels;
Maids at the wheel, the weaver at his loom,
5 Sit blithe and happy; bees that soar for bloom,
High as the highest Peak of Furness-fells,[2]
Will murmur by the hour in foxglove bells:
In truth the prison, unto which we doom
Ourselves, no prison is: and hence for me,
10 In sundry moods, 'twas pastime to be bound
Within the sonnet's scanty plot of ground;
Pleased if some souls (for such there needs must be)
Who have felt the weight of too much liberty,
Should find brief solace there, as I have found.

1807

• What does this poem imply about the sonnet's appeal?

1. Forestall. *Fondly*: foolishly.
2. Mountains in England's Lake District, where Wordsworth lived.

ELIZABETH BARRETT BROWNING
How Do I Love Thee?

How do I love thee? Let me count the ways.
I love thee to the depth and breadth and height
My soul can reach, when feeling out of sight
For the ends of Being and ideal Grace.
5 I love thee to the level of every day's
Most quiet need, by sun and candlelight.
I love thee freely, as men strive for Right;
I love thee purely, as they turn from Praise;
I love thee with the passion put to use
10 In my old griefs, and with my childhood's faith.
I love thee with a love I seemed to lose
With my lost saints—I love thee with the breath,
Smiles, tears of all my life!—and, if God choose,
I shall but love thee better after death.

1850

• How many "ways" of loving does the speaker "count" in the poem
(line 1)? How do these ways relate to and build on each other?

CHRISTINA ROSSETTI
In an Artist's Studio

One face looks out from all his canvases,
    One selfsame figure sits or walks or leans;
    We found her hidden just behind those screens,
That mirror gave back all her loveliness.
5 A queen in opal or in ruby dress,
    A nameless girl in freshest summer-greens,
    A saint, an angel—every canvas means
The same one meaning, neither more nor less.
He feeds upon her face by day and night,
10   And she with true kind eyes looks back on him
Fair as the moon and joyful as the light:
    Not wan with waiting, not with sorrow dim;
Not as she is, but was when hope shone bright;
    Not as she is, but as she fills his dream.

1856

• What might this poem suggest about the relationship between painter
and subject? How might the poem's form encourage us to compare
painting to poetry?

EDNA ST. VINCENT MILLAY
[What lips my lips have kissed, and where, and why]

What lips my lips have kissed, and where, and why,
I have forgotten, and what arms have lain
Under my head till morning; but the rain
Is full of ghosts tonight, that tap and sigh
5 Upon the glass and listen for reply,
And in my heart there stirs a quiet pain
For unremembered lads that not again
Will turn to me at midnight with a cry.
Thus in the winter stands the lonely tree,
10 Nor knows what birds have vanished one by one,
Yet knows its boughs more silent than before:
I cannot say what loves have come and gone;
I only know that summer sang in me
A little while, that in me sings no more.

1923

• **What are the poem's principal parts? Why does the Italian/Petrarchan
model suit this sonnet?**

[Women have loved before as I love now]

Women have loved before as I love now;
At least, in lively chronicles of the past—
Of Irish waters by a Cornish prow
Or Trojan waters by a Spartan mast
5 Much to their cost invaded—here and there,
Hunting the amorous line, skimming the rest,
I find some woman bearing as I bear
Love like a burning city in the breast.
I think however that of all alive
10 I only in such utter, ancient way
Do suffer love; in me alone survive
The unregenerate passions of a day
When treacherous queens, with death upon the tread,
Heedless and wilful, took their knights to bed.

1931

• **What does this poem imply about the difference between ancient and
modern ways of loving?**

[I, being born a woman and distressed]

I, being born a woman and distressed
By all the needs and notions of my kind,
Am urged by your propinquity to find
Your person fair, and feel a certain zest
5 To bear your body's weight upon my breast:
So subtly is the fume of life designed,
To clarify the pulse and cloud the mind,
And leave me once again undone, possessed.
Think not for this, however, the poor treason
10 Of my stout blood against my staggering brain,
I shall remember you with love, or season
My scorn with pity,—let me make it plain:
I find this frenzy insufficient reason
For conversation when we meet again.

1923

• What feelings are expressed here? What does the poem imply about
the source or cause of these feelings?

[I will put Chaos into fourteen lines]

I will put Chaos into fourteen lines
And keep him there; and let him thence escape
If he be lucky; let him twist, and ape
Flood, fire, and demon—his adroit designs
5 Will strain to nothing in the strict confines
Of this sweet Order, where, in pious rape,
I hold his essence and amorphous shape,
Till he with Order mingles and combines.
Past are the hours, the years, of our duress,
10 His arrogance, our awful servitude:
I have him. He is nothing more nor less
Than something simple not yet understood;
I shall not even force him to confess;
Or answer. I will only make him good.

1923

• What might this sonnet suggest about the value or appeal of the
sonnet form?

ROBERT FROST
Range-Finding

The battle rent a cobweb diamond-strung
And cut a flower beside a groundbird's nest
Before it stained a single human breast.
The stricken flower bent double and so hung.
5 And still the bird revisited her young.
A butterfly its fall had dispossessed,
A moment sought in air his flower of rest,
Then slightly stooped to it and fluttering clung.
On the bare upland pasture there had spread
10 O'ernight 'twixt mullein stalks a wheel of thread
And straining cables wet with silver dew.
A sudden passing bullet shook it dry.
The indwelling spider ran to greet the fly,
But finding nothing, sullenly withdrew.

1916

• What is the "battle" of line 1? What is the poem's actual subject?

Design

I found a dimpled spider, fat and white,
On a white heal-all,[3] holding up a moth
Like a white piece of rigid satin cloth—
Assorted characters of death and blight
5 Mixed ready to begin the morning right,
Like the ingredients of a witches' broth—
A snow-drop spider, a flower like a froth,
And dead wings carried like a paper kite.

What had that flower to do with being white,
10 The wayside blue and innocent heal-all?
What brought the kindred spider to that height,
Then steered the white moth thither in the night?
What but design of darkness to appall?—
If design govern in a thing so small.

1936

• How does this poem confound our usual preconceptions about "light"
and "darkness"? How does its elaborate form complement its theme?

3. Plant, also called the "all-heal" and "self-heal," with tightly clustered violet-blue flowers.

GWENDOLYN BROOKS
First Fight. Then Fiddle.

First fight. Then fiddle. Ply the slipping string
With feathery sorcery; muzzle the note
With hurting love; the music that they wrote
Bewitch, bewilder. Qualify to sing
5 Threadwise. Devise no salt, no hempen thing
For the dear instrument to bear. Devote
The bow to silks and honey. Be remote
A while from malice and from murdering.
But first to arms, to armor. Carry hate
10 In front of you and harmony behind.
Be deaf to music and to beauty blind.
Win war. Rise bloody, maybe not too late
For having first to civilize a space
Wherein to play your violin with grace.

1949

• After advising "First fight. Then fiddle," the speaker discusses first
music, then conflict. Why do you think the poet has arranged her
material this way? Why a sonnet?

GWEN HARWOOD
In the Park

She sits in the park. Her clothes are out of date.
Two children whine and bicker, tug her skirt.
A third draws aimless patterns in the dirt.
Someone she loved once passes by—too late

5 to feign indifference to that casual nod.
"How nice," et cetera. "Time holds great surprises."
From his neat head unquestionably rises
a small balloon . . . "but for the grace of God . . ."

They stand a while in flickering light, rehearsing
10 the children's names and birthdays. "It's so sweet
to hear their chatter, watch them grow and thrive,"
she says to his departing smile. Then, nursing
the youngest child, sits staring at her feet.
To the Wind she says, "They have eaten me alive."

1963

• What is the implication of the "small balloon" (line 8) that rises from the head of the man who passes by?

BILLY COLLINS
Sonnet

All we need is fourteen lines, well, thirteen now,
and after this one just a dozen
to launch a little ship on love's storm-tossed seas,
then only ten more left like rows of beans.
5 How easily it goes unless you get Elizabethan
and insist the iambic bongos must be played
and rhymes positioned at the ends of lines,
one for every station of the cross.
But hang on here while we make the turn
10 into the final six where all will be resolved,
where longing and heartache will find an end,
where Laura will tell Petrarch[4] to put down his pen,
take off those crazy medieval tights,
blow out the lights, and come at last to bed.

1999

• In what respects is Collins's poem a traditional sonnet? In what respects is it not? What might it suggest about the relationship between love and poetry, especially as portrayed in traditional sonnets?

HARRYETTE MULLEN
Dim Lady[5]

My honeybunch's peepers are nothing like neon. Today's special at Red Lobster is redder than her kisser. If Liquid Paper is white, her racks are institutional beige. If her mop were Slinkys, dishwater Slinkys would grow on her noggin. I have
5 seen tablecloths in Shakey's Pizza Parlors, red and white, but no such picnic colors do I see in her mug. And in some minty-fresh mouthwashes there is more sweetness than in the garlic breeze my main squeeze wheezes. I love to hear her rap, yet I'm aware that Muzak has a hipper beat. I don't know any
10 Marilyn Monroes. My ball and chain is plain from head to toe.

4. Italian poet Francesco Petrarch (1304–74), regarded as a father of the sonnet form. Many of his love poems were inspired by Laura, who may have been the wife of a local nobleman.
5. Shakespeare's sonnets frequently address or refer to the so-called Dark Lady.

And yet, by gosh, my scrumptious Twinkie has as much sex
appeal for me as any lanky model or platinum movie idol
who's hyped beyond belief.

2002

• How might Mullen's poem essentially "do unto" Shakespeare's MY MIS-
TRESS' EYES ARE NOTHING LIKE THE SUN much as Shakespeare's poem
itself does to earlier, especially Petrarchan sonnets? What is the effect
of Mullen's diction? her use of brand names? Is DIM LADY a sonnet?

SUGGESTIONS FOR WRITING

1. Consider carefully the structure of, and sequencing in, Brooks's FIRST FIGHT.
THEN FIDDLE. How do various uses of sound in the poem (rhyme, onomatopoeia, and alliteration, for example) reinforce its themes and tones? Write an
essay in which you explore the relationship between "sound and sense" in the
poem.
2. Some of the sonnets in this book, such as those by Shakespeare, adhere closely
to the classic English model; others, such as Milton's WHEN I CONSIDER HOW
MY LIGHT IS SPENT, follow the Italian model; and some, such as those by Billy
Collins and Gwen Harwood, bear only slight resemblance to either of the traditional sonnet models. Take any four sonnets in this book as the basis for an
essay in which you compare the various ways poets have used the sonnet form
to achieve their unique artistic purposes.
3. Several poems in this album are not only sonnets but also commentaries on
the sonnet or on certain conventions associated with it such as Petrarchan
"conceits" (Shakespeare's MY MISTRESS' EYES . . .) or the relation between
(male) speaker and (female) subject or love object. Write an essay comparing
at least two of these poems. What does each ultimately suggest about the sonnet through both its form and its content?

SAMPLE WRITING: COMPARATIVE ESSAY

The student essay below was written in response to the following assignment:

> Your second essay for the course should be 6–9 pages long and should analyze two or more poems included in *The Norton Introduction to Literature*. The poems must be by the same author.
>
> You are *strongly* encouraged to pay attention to how the poems' meaning and effect are shaped by some aspect or aspects of their form. Those aspects might include specific formal features such as rhyme, meter, alliteration, or assonance, and/or external form or subgenre—the fact that a poem is a Shakespearean or Petrarchan sonnet, a haiku, or a dramatic monologue, for example. (In terms of the latter, you might consider how the poem's effect and meaning are shaped by the very fact that it takes a particular form.)

In her essay, student writer Melissa Makolin draws on three sonnets by William Shakespeare to argue for the distinctiveness and radicalism of the views expressed in two sonnets by another author, Edna St. Vincent Millay. In a sense, then, Makolin's essay focuses simultaneously on external form (ch. 15) and the author's work, even as it explores gender and engages in a kind of feminist criticism (see "Critical Approaches"). That's a lot to tackle in a relatively short essay, and you will no doubt find things both to admire and to criticize about Makolin's argument. At what points do you find yourself agreeing with her interpretation? disagreeing? wanting more evidence or more analysis of the evidence provided? more contextual information—about literary tradition, the author, or historical and cultural context? Where and how might the essay's logic seem faulty or its claims contradictory? In the end, what might you take away from this sample essay about how to craft an effective, persuasive argument about an author's work?

Melissa Makolin
Dr. Mays
English 298X
15 February 2017

Out-Sonneting Shakespeare: An Examination of
Edna St. Vincent Millay's Use of the Sonnet Form

Edna St. Vincent Millay is known not only for her poetry, but also for the feminist ideals she represents therein. She was an extremely talented poet who turned the sonnet form on its head, using the traditionally restrictive form previously used almost exclusively by male poets to express feminist ideas that were radical for her time. Sonnets, especially as written by Shakespeare and Petrarch, are often about the physical beauty of an idealized but also objectified woman, and they implicitly emphasize the man's dominance over her. Millay uses the sonnet form to assert a much different view of femininity, sexuality, and biological dominance. She uses a form known for its poetic limitations to reject social limitations. She uses a form previously used to objectify women to portray them as sexual beings with power and control over their own bodies and lives. The paradox of Millay's poetry is that she uses a poetically binding, male-dominated form to show that she will not be bound either by literary tradition or societal mores regarding inter-gender relations.

The idea of a woman seeking physical pleasure in defiance of societal constraints is one that was revolutionary when "Women have loved before as I love now" and "I, being born a woman and distressed" were published, in 1931 and 1923 respectively. They are poems about a woman's lust leading her to select a sexual partner based on her physical needs rather than on the desire for love. This is a concept that Shakespeare would have found very contentious for three reasons. First, Shakespeare did not agree with acting on lust of any kind; in fact, this is the topic of his sonnet "Th' expense of spirit in a waste of shame." It is a fourteen-line treatise on the evils that result from acting on lustful urges in which Shakespeare declares,

Th'expense of spirit in a waste of shame
Is lust in action; and, till action, lust
Is perjured, murderous, bloody, full of blame,
Savage, extreme, rude, cruel, not to trust. (lines 1-4)

Makolin 2

Lust, sexual or otherwise, is a pathway to a hell both religious and secular. Seventeenth-century society dramatically constricted the liberties of women in particular and didn't encourage sexual freedom for either gender.

Second, the majority of Shakespeare's sonnets simultaneously idealize and trivialize the two things they celebrate: women and love. In poems such as "My mistress' eyes are nothing like the sun," he treats women either as objects of an ordered, almost courtly love or as objects of mild ridicule. In this poem's first twelve lines, he mocks his mistress by describing her halitosis (7-8), referring to her breasts as "dun" (3) and her hair as "black wires" (4), references to all the contemporary conventions of beauty to which she does not conform. He not only tells her what the ideal of feminine beauty is, but also makes light of the various ways in which she does not live up to it. He justifies these hurtful insults by reassuring the poor woman that she is "as rare / As any she belied with false compare" (13-14). He mocks her appearance by telling her that she is special and beautiful in her own way only because he loves her. Insulting someone, breaking down her self-esteem, and convincing her that she could be loved by no one else are tactics used in abusive relationships to subjugate one's partner. This is not love, and the role of women in the traditional Shakespeare sonnet is far from empowered.

Third and finally, in addition to idealizing while simultaneously trivializing women, Shakespeare's sonnets also demean the concept of love. To Shakespeare, a woman is worthy of love either because she is an ideal of physical beauty or because he is noble enough to love her despite her flaws (as in "My mistress' eyes are nothing like the sun"). He takes this warped concept one step further, though, by creating an ideal of love that is egotistical and unhealthy for both parties. In "Shall I compare thee to a summer's day?," he spends the first twelve lines describing the ways in which this particular woman fulfills the contemporary ideals of beauty. It is clear that he ardently reveres her physical appearance, and the poem ends with the kind of declaration of personal devotion consistent with love. The turn, however, exhibits a malignant narcissism when it reassures the beloved that "So long as men can breathe or eyes can see, / So long lives this, and this gives life to thee" (13-14). The object of the speaker's affection is just that, an object that only exists as an appendage to him. Shakespeare makes it clear that it is only because of his poetic greatness that their love will persist through the ages. He uses the poetic form to relegate women to the position of objects.

Makolin 3

The sonnets of Edna St. Vincent Millay use Shakespearean and Petrarchan forms to offer quite a different view of the role of women. She sees herself as a liberated woman, and she is not afraid to defy social conventions by taking lovers and discarding them when necessary. In writing sonnets about actively satisfying her lust, she also defies literary conventions, completely changing the male-female power dynamic of past sonnets by male writers. In "Women have loved before as I love now," Millay discusses how women throughout history have felt the same lust that she feels, but unlike other more timid and traditional women, she is willing to join the ranks of the brave women of antiquity and to satisfy her passions despite the potential cost. This poem celebrates the women who choose to act against the standards set for them. Describing them as "treacherous queens, with death upon the tread, / Heedless and wilful, [who] took their knights to bed" makes them sound heroic, and it shifts control in the sexual relationship from the man to the woman (13-14). In Millay's version, the women sexually dominate the men and temporarily free themselves from the constraints of an oppressive society. Further, by alluding to the famous females of the "lively chronicles of the past" (2), she shows not only that this behavior is natural and heroic, but also that it is historically valid. The specific women she alludes to when referring to "Irish waters by a Cornish prow" (3) and "Trojan waters by a Spartan mast" (4) are respectively Iseult, the adulteress of the classic work of medieval passion *The Romance of Tristan and Iseult*, and Helen of Troy (or any of the other libidinous women) of the Homeric epics.

The fact that Millay uses the sonnet form to illustrate sexual liberation is significant for several reasons. First, it shows that she understands the restrictions placed upon her, both as a poet and as a woman. Second, using the sonnet shows that she can hold her own against the great male poets and write within the boundaries that they have erected; the subject matter of her poetry shows that she chooses not to. Lastly, it is significant because, in using the sonnet form for her own feminist purposes, she directly confronts Shakespeare's one-dimensional portrayal of women by proposing her own view of ideal femininity.

The second of Edna St. Vincent Millay's sonnets that defies the ideals set forth by Shakespeare is "I, being born a woman and distressed." It is a poem about impermanent lust, not eternal love. The speaker tells her lover that her feelings are purely physical ("a certain zest / To bear your body's weight upon breast," 4-5) and simply arise out of human biology ("the needs and notions of my kind," 2) and close quarters ("propinquity," 3). Emotional and physical needs are two things which need not be dependent on each other, and temporary desire does not have to lead to anything lasting. Consummation of a relationship was never discussed in the time of Shakespeare as a tenet of courtly love because women were supposed to be angelic ideals rather than real people with carnal desires. Millay's speaker defies these unrealistic and unattainable ideals of eternal adoration by warning her lover not to "'Think" that "I shall remember you with love" (9, 11), illustrating that desire is impermanent. In fact, it is just a temporary "frenzy" and "insufficient reason" even to have a "conversation when we meet again" (13-14). Lust in Millay's world is fleeting, whereas the love of Shakespeare's world is final and complete once the man conquers all and the woman takes her place on his arm. Millay's poem might seem cynical, but it represents a more realistic view of female and male interactions; life and love are transitory and to be enjoyed in the moment because sexual urges can be sated, are biologically determined, and essential to survival, while emotional ones are (relatively) inconsequential and satisfied in other ways.

Millay draws on Shakespeare as a kind of foil by using the form so associated with his name as a vehicle for her very different views on the same topics. Millay brings sexual relationships to a far more terrestrial level with her assertions that women have primal urges that must be satisfied and that submission to ascribed gender roles is not necessary in order to obtain this satisfaction. She presents a radically modern view of relationships. She lambastes the Shakespearean paradigm of the idealized woman, a traditionally beautiful possession of the egotistical man. By using the Shakespearean sonnet form to propose her own revamped, modern vision of woman, a self-aware person who fearlessly relishes the idea of her own emotional and sexual independence, Millay redefines both "woman" and "love."

Makolin 5

Works Cited

Mays, Kelly J., editor. *The Norton Introduction to Literature*. Portable 12th
     ed., W. W. Norton, 2017.
Millay, Edna St. Vincent. "I, being born a woman and distressed." Mays,
     p. 674.
---. "Women have loved before as I love now." Mays, p. 673.
Shakespeare, William. "Th' expense of spirit in a waste of shame." Mays,
     p. 644.
---. "My mistress' eyes are nothing like the sun." Mays, p. 669.
---. "Shall I compare thee to a summer's day?" Mays, p. 589.

Reading More Poetry

JULIA ALVAREZ
"Poetry Makes Nothing Happen"?

—W. H. AUDEN[1]

Listening to a poem on the radio,
Mike Holmquist stayed awake on his drive home
from Laramie[2] on Interstate 80,
tapping his hand to the beat of some lines
5   by Longfellow;[3] while overcome by grief
one lonesome night when the bathroom cabinet
still held her husband's meds, May Quinn reached out
for a book by Yeats instead and fell asleep
cradling "When You Are Old," not the poet's best,
10 but still . . . poetry made nothing happen,

which was good, given what May had in mind.
Writing a paper on a Bishop poem,[4]
Jenny Klein missed her ride but arrived home
to the cancer news in a better frame of mind.
15 While troops dropped down into Afghanistan
in the living room, Naomi Stella clapped
to the nursery rhyme her father had turned on,
All the king's horses and all the king's men . . .
If only poetry had made nothing happen!
20 If only the president had listened to Auden!

Faith Chaney, Lulú Pérez, Sunghee Chen—
there's a list as long as an epic poem
of folks who'll swear a poem has never done
a thing for them . . . except . . . perhaps adjust

---

1. See "In Memory of W. B. Yeats," line 36.
2. In Wyoming.
3. American poet Henry Wadsworth Longfellow (1807–82).
4. Elizabeth Bishop (1911–79).

25 the sunset view one cloudy afternoon,
    which made them see themselves or see the world
    in a different light—degrees of change so small
    only a poem registers them at all.
    That's why they can be trusted, why poems might
30 still save us from what happens in the world.

                                                  2003

ANONYMOUS
Sir Patrick Spens

The king sits in Dumferling toune,[5]
    Drinking the blude-reid[6] wine:
"O whar will I get guid sailor,
    To sail this ship of mine?"

5 Up and spake an eldern knicht,
    Sat at the king's richt knee:
"Sir Patrick Spens is the best sailor
    That sails upon the sea."

The king has written a braid[7] letter
10   And signed it wi' his hand,
And sent it to Sir Patrick Spens,
    Was walking on the sand.

The first line that Sir Patrick read,
    A loud lauch[8] lauched he;
15 The next line that Sir Patrick read,
    The tear blinded his ee.[9]

"O wha is this has done this deed,
    This il deed done to me,
To send me out this time o' the year,
20   To sail upon the sea?

"Make haste, make haste, my merry men all,
    Our guid ship sails the morn."
"O say na sae,[1] my master dear,
    For I fear a deadly storm.

25 "Late, late yestre'en I saw the new moon
    Wi' the auld moon in her arm,

---

5. Town.   6. Bloodred.   7. Broad: explicit.   8. Laugh.   9. Eye.   1. Not so.

And I fear, I fear, my dear mastér,
    That we will come to harm."

O our Scots nobles were richt laith[2]
30   To weet their cork-heeled shoon,[3]
But lang owre a[4] the play were played
    Their hats they swam aboon.[5]

O lang, lang, may their ladies sit,
    Wi' their fans into their hand,
35 Or ere they see Sir Patrick Spens
    Come sailing to the land.

O lang, lang, may the ladies stand
    Wi' their gold kems[6] in their hair,
Waiting for their ain[7] dear lords,
40   For they'll see them na mair.

Half o'er, half o'er to Aberdour
    It's fifty fadom deep,
And there lies guid Sir Patrick Spens
    Wi' the Scots lords at his feet.

                c. 13th century

W. H. AUDEN
In Memory of W. B. Yeats

    (*d. January, 1939*)

I

He disappeared in the dead of winter:
The brooks were frozen, the airports almost deserted,
And snow disfigured the public statues;
The mercury sank in the mouth of the dying day.
5 What instruments we have agree
The day of his death was a dark cold day.

Far from his illness
The wolves ran on through the evergreen forests,
The peasant river was untempted by the fashionable quays;

---

2. Right loath: very reluctant.
3. To wet their cork-heeled shoes. Cork was expensive, and thus such shoes were a mark of wealth and status.   4. Before all.   5. Above.   6. Combs.   7. Own

10   By mourning tongues
    The death of the poet was kept from his poems.

    But for him it was his last afternoon as himself,
    An afternoon of nurses and rumors;
    The provinces of his body revolted,
15   The squares of his mind were empty,
    Silence invaded the suburbs,
    The current of his feeling failed; he became his admirers.

    Now he is scattered among a hundred cities
    And wholly given over to unfamiliar affections,
20   To find his happiness in another kind of wood
    And be punished under a foreign code of conscience.
    The words of a dead man
    Are modified in the guts of the living.

    But in the importance and noise of tomorrow
25   When the brokers are roaring like beasts on the floor of the
        Bourse,[8]
    And the poor have the sufferings to which they are fairly
        accustomed,
    And each in the cell of himself is almost convinced of his freedom,
    A few thousand will think of this day
    As one thinks of a day when one did something slightly unusual.
30   What instruments we have agree
    The day of his death was a dark cold day.

II

    You were silly like us; your gift survived it all:
    The parish of rich women, physical decay,
    Yourself. Mad Ireland hurt you into poetry.
35   Now Ireland has her madness and her weather still,
    For poetry makes nothing happen: it survives
    In the valley of its making where executives
    Would never want to tamper, flows on south
    From ranches of isolation and the busy griefs,
40   Raw towns that we believe and die in; it survives,
    A way of happening, a mouth.

III

    Earth, receive an honored guest:
    William Yeats is laid to rest.

8. Paris stock exchange.

Let the Irish vessel lie
45 Emptied of its poetry.

In the nightmare of the dark
All the dogs of Europe bark,
And the living nations wait,
Each sequestered in its hate;

50 Intellectual disgrace
Stares from every human face,
And the seas of pity lie
Locked and frozen in each eye.

Follow, poet, follow right
55 To the bottom of the night,
With your unconstraining voice
Still persuade us to rejoice;

With the farming of a verse
Make a vineyard of the curse,
60 Sing of human unsuccess
In a rapture of distress;

In the deserts of the heart
Let the healing fountain start,
In the prison of his days
65 Teach the free man how to praise.

1939

Musée des Beaux Arts[9]

About suffering they were never wrong,
The Old Masters: how well they understood
Its human position; how it takes place
While someone else is eating or opening a window or just walking
dully along;
5 How, when the aged are reverently, passionately waiting
For the miraculous birth, there always must be
Children who did not specially want it to happen, skating
On a pond at the edge of the wood:
They never forgot
10 That even the dreadful martyrdom must run its course
Anyhow in a corner, some untidy spot

9. The Museum of the Fine Arts, in Brussels, Belgium.

Where the dogs go on with their doggy life and the torturer's horse
Scratches its innocent behind on a tree.

In Brueghel's *Icarus*,[1] for instance: how everything turns away
15 Quite leisurely from the disaster; the plowman may
Have heard the splash, the forsaken cry,
But for him it was not an important failure; the sun shone
As it had to on the white legs disappearing into the green
Water; and the expensive delicate ship that must have seen
20 Something amazing, a boy falling out of the sky,
Had somewhere to get to and sailed calmly on.

1938

BASHŌ[2]
[A village without bells—]

A village without bells—
    how do they live?
        spring dusk.

[This road—]

    This road—
no one goes down it,
    autumn evening.

WILLIAM BLAKE
The Lamb

    Little Lamb, who made thee?
    Dost thou know who made thee?
Gave thee life, and bid thee feed
By the stream and o'er the mead;

---

1. *Landscape with the Fall of Icarus*, by Pieter Bruegel the Elder (1525?–69), located in the Brussels museum. According to Greek myth, Daedalus and his son, Icarus, escaped from imprisonment by using homemade wings of feathers and wax; but Icarus flew too near the sun, the wax melted, and he fell into the sea and drowned. In the Bruegel painting the central figure is a peasant plowing, and several other figures are more immediately noticeable than Icarus, who, disappearing into the sea, is easy to miss in the lower right-hand corner.
2. Matsuo Bashō (1644–94) is usually considered the first great master poet of haiku. Translations by Robert Hass.

5 Gave thee clothing of delight,
   Softest clothing woolly bright;
   Gave thee such a tender voice,
   Making all the vales rejoice?
      Little Lamb, who made thee?
10   Dost thou know who made thee?

      Little Lamb, I'll tell thee!
      Little Lamb, I'll tell thee:
   He is calléd by thy name,
   For he calls himself a Lamb,
15 He is meek and he is mild;
   He became a little child.
   I a child and thou a lamb,
   We are callèd by his name.
      Little Lamb, God bless thee!
20   Little Lamb, God bless thee!
                              1789

The Tyger

   Tyger! Tyger! burning bright
   In the forests of the night,
   What immortal hand or eye
   Could frame thy fearful symmetry?

5 In what distant deeps or skies
   Burnt the fire of thine eyes?
   On what wings dare he aspire?
   What the hand dare seize the fire?

   And what shoulder, & what art,
10 Could twist the sinews of thy heart?
   And when thy heart began to beat,
   What dread hand? & what dread feet?

   What the hammer? what the chain?
   In what furnace was thy brain?
15 What the anvil? what dread grasp
   Dare its deadly terrors clasp?

   When the stars threw down their spears
   And water'd heaven with their tears,
   Did he smile his work to see?
20 Did he who made the Lamb make thee?

Tyger! Tyger! burning bright
In the forests of the night,
What immortal hand or eye
Dare frame thy fearful symmetry?

1794

The Chimney Sweeper

A little black thing among the snow:
Crying weep, weep, in notes of woe!
Where are thy father & mother? say?
They are both gone up to the church to pray.

5   Because I was happy upon the heath,
And smil'd among the winters snow:
They clothed me in the clothes of death,
And taught me to sing the notes of woe.

And because I am happy, & dance & sing,
10 They think they have done me no injury:
And are gone to praise God & his Priest & King
Who make up a heaven of our misery.

1794

ROBERT BROWNING
My Last Duchess

Ferrara[3]

That's my last Duchess painted on the wall,
Looking as if she were alive. I call
That piece a wonder, now: Frà Pandolf's hands[4]
Worked busily a day, and there she stands.
5   Will't please you sit and look at her? I said
"Frà Pandolf" by design, for never read
Strangers like you that pictured countenance,
The depth and passion of its earnest glance,

3. Alfonso II, Duke of Ferrara in Italy in the mid-sixteenth century, is the presumed speaker of this dramatic monologue, which is loosely based on historical events. The duke's first wife—whom he had married when she was fourteen—died under suspicious circumstances at seventeen, and he then negotiated through an agent (this poem's auditor) for the hand of the niece of the count of Tyrol in Austria.
4. Frà Pandolf is, like Claus (line 56), fictitious.

But to myself they turned (since none puts by
10 The curtain I have drawn for you, but I)
And seemed as they would ask me, if they durst,
How such a glance came there; so, not the first
Are you to turn and ask thus. Sir, 'twas not
Her husband's presence only, called that spot
15 Of joy into the Duchess' cheek: perhaps
Frà Pandolf chanced to say "Her mantle laps
Over my lady's wrist too much," or "Paint
Must never hope to reproduce the faint
Half-flush that dies along her throat": such stuff
20 Was courtesy, she thought, and cause enough
For calling up that spot of joy. She had
A heart—how shall I say?—too soon made glad,
Too easily impressed; she liked whate'er
She looked on, and her looks went everywhere.
25 Sir, 'twas all one! My favor at her breast,
The dropping of the daylight in the West,
The bough of cherries some officious fool
Broke in the orchard for her, the white mule
She rode with round the terrace—all and each
30 Would draw from her alike the approving speech,
Or blush, at least. She thanked men,—good! but thanked
Somehow—I know not how—as if she ranked
My gift of a nine-hundred-years-old name
With anybody's gift. Who'd stoop to blame
35 This sort of trifling? Even had you skill
In speech—which I have not—to make your will
Quite clear to such an one, and say, "Just this
Or that in you disgusts me; here you miss,
Or there exceed the mark"—and if she let
40 Herself be lessoned so, nor plainly set
Her wits to yours, forsooth, and made excuse,
—E'en then would be some stooping; and I choose
Never to stoop. Oh sir, she smiled, no doubt,
Whene'er I passed her; but who passed without
45 Much the same smile? This grew; I gave commands;
Then all smiles stopped together. There she stands
As if alive. Will 't please you rise? We'll meet
The company below, then. I repeat,
The Count your master's known munificence
50 Is ample warrant that no just pretense
Of mine for dowry will be disallowed;
Though his fair daughter's self, as I avowed

At starting, is my object. Nay, we'll go
Together down, sir. Notice Neptune, though,
55 Taming a sea-horse, thought a rarity,
Which Claus of Innsbruck cast in bronze for me!

1842

SAMUEL TAYLOR COLERIDGE
Kubla Khan

Or, a Vision in a Dream[5]

In Xanadu did Kubla Khan
A stately pleasure-dome decree:
Where Alph, the sacred river, ran
Through caverns measureless to man
5   Down to a sunless sea.
So twice five miles of fertile ground
With walls and towers were girdled round:
And here were gardens bright with sinuous rills
Where blossomed many an incense-bearing tree;
10 And here were forests ancient as the hills,
Enfolding sunny spots of greenery.
But oh! that deep romantic chasm which slanted
Down the green hill athwart a cedarn cover![6]
A savage place! as holy and enchanted
15 As e'er beneath a waning moon was haunted
By woman wailing for her demon-lover![7]
And from this chasm, with ceaseless turmoil seething,
As if this earth in fast thick pants were breathing,
A mighty fountain momently[8] was forced,
20 Amid whose swift half-intermitted burst
Huge fragments vaulted like rebounding hail,
Or chaffy grain beneath the thresher's flail:
And 'mid these dancing rocks at once and ever
It flung up momently the sacred river.
25 Five miles meandering with a mazy motion

5. Coleridge said that he wrote this fragment immediately after waking from an opium dream and that after he was interrupted by a caller he was unable to finish the poem.
6. That is, from side to side beneath a cover of cedar trees.
7. In a famous and often-imitated German ballad, the lady Lenore is carried off on horseback by the specter of her lover and married to him at his grave.
8. Suddenly.

Through wood and dale the sacred river ran,
Then reached the caverns measureless to man,
And sank in tumult to a lifeless ocean:
And 'mid this tumult Kubla heard from far
30 Ancestral voices prophesying war!

The shadow of the dome of pleasure
Floated midway on the waves;
Where was heard the mingled measure
From the fountain and the caves.
35 It was a miracle of rare device,
A sunny pleasure-dome with caves of ice!

A damsel with a dulcimer
In a vision once I saw:
It was an Abyssinian maid,
40 And on her dulcimer she played,
Singing of Mount Abora.
Could I revive within me
Her symphony and song,
To such a deep delight 'twould win me,
45 That with music loud and long,
I would build that dome in air,
That sunny dome! those caves of ice!
And all who heard should see them there,
And all should cry, Beware! Beware!
50 His flashing eyes, his floating hair!
Weave a circle round him thrice,
And close your eyes with holy dread,
For he on honey-dew hath fed,
And drunk the milk of Paradise.

1798

BILLY COLLINS
Introduction to Poetry

I ask them to take a poem
and hold it up to the light
like a color slide

or press an ear against its hive.

5 I say drop a mouse into a poem
and watch him probe his way out,

or walk inside the poem's room
and feel the walls for a light switch.

I want them to water-ski
10 across the surface of a poem
waving at the author's name on the shore.

But all they want to do
is tie the poem to a chair with rope
and torture a confession out of it.

15 They begin beating it with a hose
to find out what it really means.

1988

COUNTEE CULLEN
Yet Do I Marvel

I doubt not God is good, well-meaning, kind,
And did He stoop to quibble could tell why
The little buried mole continues blind,
Why flesh that mirrors Him must some day die,
5 Make plain the reason tortured Tantalus[9]
Is baited by the fickle fruit, declare
If merely brute caprice dooms Sisyphus[1]
To struggle up a never-ending stair.
Inscrutable His ways are, and immune
10 To catechism by a mind too strewn
With petty cares to slightly understand
What awful brain compels His awful hand.
Yet do I marvel at this curious thing:
To make a poet black, and bid him sing!

1925

E. E. CUMMINGS
[in Just-][2]

in Just-
spring   when the world is mud-

---

9. Figure in Greek myth condemned, for ambiguous reasons, to stand up to his neck in water he couldn't drink and to be within sight of fruit he couldn't reach to eat.
1. King of Corinth who, in Greek myth, was condemned eternally to roll a huge stone uphill.
2. First poem in the series *Chansons innocentes* (French for "Songs of Innocence").

luscious the little
lame balloonman

5 whistles   far   and wee

and eddieandbill come
running from marbles and
piracies and it's
spring

10 when the world is puddle-wonderful

the queer
old balloonman whistles
far   and   wee
and bettyandisbel come dancing

15 from hop-scotch and jump-rope and

it's
spring
and
    the
20   goat-footed

balloonMan[3] whistles
far
and
wee

             1923

EMILY DICKINSON
[I dwell in Possibility—]

I dwell in Possibility—
A fairer House than Prose—
More numerous of Windows—
Superior—for Doors—

5 Of Chambers as the Cedars—
Impregnable of Eye—
And for an Everlasting Roof
The Gambrels[4] of the Sky—

3. Pan, whose Greek name means "everything," is traditionally represented with a syrinx (or the pipes of Pan). The upper half of his body is human, the lower half goat; as the father of Silenus he is associated with the spring rites of Dionysus.
4. Roofs with double slopes.

Of Visitors—the fairest—
10 For Occupation—This—
The spreading wide my narrow Hands
To gather Paradise—

c. 1862

[I stepped from Plank to Plank]

I stepped from Plank to Plank
A slow and cautious way
The Stars about my Head I felt
About my Feet the Sea.

5   I knew not but the next
Would be my final inch—
This gave me that precarious Gait
Some call Experience.

c. 1864

[My Life had stood—a Loaded Gun—]

My Life had stood—a Loaded Gun—
In Corners—till a Day
The Owner passed—identified—
And carried Me away—

5   And now We roam in Sovereign Woods—
And now We hunt the Doe—
And every time I speak for Him—
The Mountains straight reply—

And do I smile, such cordial light
10 Upon the Valley glow—
It is as a Vesuvian face
Had let its pleasure through—

And when at Night—Our good Day done—
I guard My Master's Head—
15 'Tis better than the Eider-Duck's
Deep Pillow—to have shared—

To foe of His—I'm deadly foe—
None stir the second time—
On whom I lay a Yellow Eye—
20 Or an emphatic Thumb—

Though I than He—may longer live
He longer must—than I—
For I have but the power to kill,
Without—the power to die—

c. 1863

[A narrow Fellow in the Grass]

A narrow Fellow in the Grass
Occasionally rides—
You may have met Him—did you not
His notice sudden is—

5 The Grass divides as with a Comb—
A spotted shaft is seen—
And then it closes at your feet
And opens further on—

He likes a Boggy Acre
10 A Floor too cool for Corn—
Yet when a Boy, and Barefoot—
I more than once at Noon

Have passed, I thought, a Whip lash
Unbraiding in the Sun
15 When stooping to secure it
It wrinkled, and was gone—

Several of Nature's People
I know, and they know me—
I feel for them a transport
20 Of cordiality—

But never met this Fellow
Attended, or alone
Without a tighter breathing
And Zero at the Bone—

1866

[Tell all the truth but tell it slant—]

Tell all the truth but tell it slant—
Success in Circuit lies
Too bright for our infirm Delight
The Truth's superb surprise

5 As Lightning to the Children eased
With explanation kind
The Truth must dazzle gradually
Or every man be blind—

                          1872

[Wild Nights—Wild Nights!]

Wild Nights—Wild Nights!
Were I with thee
Wild Nights should be
Our luxury!

5 Futile—the Winds—
To a Heart in port—
Done with the Compass—
Done with the Chart!

Rowing in Eden—
10 Ah, the Sea!
Might I but moor—Tonight—
In Thee!

                          c. 1861

JOHN DONNE
The Canonization

For God's sake hold your tongue and let me love!
   Or[5] chide my palsy or my gout,
My five gray hairs or ruined fortune flout;
With wealth your state, your mind with arts improve,
5   Take you a course, get you a place,
      Observe his Honor or his Grace,
Or the king's real or his stampèd face[6]
      Contemplate; what you will, approve,
         So you will let me love.

10 Alas, alas, who's injured by my love?
      What merchant's ships have my sighs drowned?
Who says my tears have overflowed his ground?

---

5. Either.   6. On coins.

When did my colds a forward spring remove?
    When did the heats which my veins fill
15   Add one man to the plaguy bill?[7]
Soldiers find wars, and lawyers find out still
    Litigious men which quarrels move,
        Though she and I do love.

Call us what you will, we are made such by love.
20   Call her one, me another fly,
    We're tapers too, and at our own cost die;[8]
And we in us find th' eagle and the dove.[9]
    The phoenix riddle hath more wit[1]
    By us; we two, being one, are it.
25 So to one neutral thing both sexes fit,
    We die and rise the same, and prove
        Mysterious by this love.

We can die by it, if not live by love;
    And if unfit for tombs and hearse
30 Our legend be, it will be fit for verse,[2]
    And if no piece of chronicle we prove,
    We'll build in sonnets pretty rooms[3]
(As well a well-wrought urn becomes[4]
The greatest ashes, as half-acre tombs),
35   And by these hymns all shall approve
        Us canonized for love.

And thus invoke us: "You whom reverent love
    Made one another's hermitage,
You to whom love was peace, that now is rage,
40 Who did the whole world's soul extract, and drove[5]
    Into the glasses of your eyes
    (So made such mirrors and such spies
That they did all to you epitomize)

7. List of plague victims.
8. Tapers (candles) consume themselves. To "die" is Renaissance slang for consummating the sexual act, which was popularly believed to shorten life by one day. *Fly*: a traditional symbol of transitory life.
9. Traditional symbols of strength and purity.
1. Meaning. According to tradition, only one phoenix existed at a time, dying in a funeral pyre of its own making and being reborn from its own ashes. The bird's existence was thus a riddle akin to a religious mystery (line 27), and a symbol sometimes fused with Christian representations of immortality.
2. That is, if we don't turn out to be an authenticated piece of historical narrative.
3. In Italian, *stanza* means "room."   4. Befits.   5. Compressed.

Countries, towns, courts; beg from above
45   A pattern of your love!"

1633

[Death, be not proud]

Death be not proud, though some have callèd thee
Mighty and dreadful, for thou art not so;
For those whom thou think'st thou dost overthrow
Die not, poor Death, nor yet canst thou kill me.
5 From rest and sleep, which but thy pictures[6] be,
    Much pleasure; then from thee much more must flow,
    And soonest[7] our best men with thee do go,
    Rest of their bones, and soul's delivery.[8]
Thou art slave to Fate, Chance, kings, and desperate men,
10 And dost with Poison, War, and Sickness dwell;
    And poppy or charms can make us sleep as well,
    And better than thy stroke; why swell'st[9] thou then?
One short sleep past, we wake eternally
And death shall be no more; Death, thou shalt die.

1633

Song

Go, and catch a falling star,
    Get with child a mandrake root,[1]
Tell me, where all past years are,
    Or who cleft the devil's foot,
5 Teach me to hear mermaids singing
    Or to keep off envy's stinging,
            And find
            What wind
Serves to advance an honest mind.

10 If thou beest born to strange sights,[2]
        Things invisible to see,
    Ride ten thousand days and nights,
        Till age snow white hairs on thee;
    Thou, when thou return'st, wilt tell me
15 All strange wonders that befell thee,

---

6. Likenesses.   7. Most willingly.   8. Deliverance.   9. Puff with pride.
1. The forked mandrake root looks vaguely like a pair of human legs.
2. That is, if you have supernatural powers.

And swear
No where
Lives a woman true, and fair.

If thou find'st one, let me know:
20   Such a pilgrimage were sweet.
Yet do not, I would not go,
Though at next door we might meet:
Though she were true when you met her,
And last till you write your letter,
25   Yet she
Will be
False, ere I come, to two, or three.

1633

A Valediction: Forbidding Mourning

As virtuous men pass mildly away,
    And whisper to their souls to go,
Whilst some of their sad friends do say,
    "The breath goes now," and some say, "No,"

5 So let us melt, and make no noise,
    No tear-floods, nor sigh-tempests move;
'Twere profanation of our joys
    To tell the laity our love.

Moving of the earth[3] brings harms and fears,
10   Men reckon what it did and meant;
But trepidation of the spheres,[4]
    Though greater far, is innocent.

Dull sublunary[5] lovers' love
    (Whose soul is sense) cannot admit
15 Absence, because it doth remove
    Those things which elemented[6] it.

But we, by a love so much refined
    That our selves know not what it is,

---

3. Earthquakes.
4. Renaissance theory that the celestial spheres trembled and thus caused unexpected variations in their orbits. Such movements are "innocent" because earthlings do not observe or fret
about them.
5. Below the moon—that is, changeable. According to the traditional cosmology that Donne
invokes here, the moon is the dividing line between the immutable celestial world and the muta-
ble earthly one.   6. Comprised.

Inter-assured of the mind,
20   Care less, eyes, lips, and hands to miss.

Our two souls therefore, which are one,
   Though I must go, endure not yet
A breach, but an expansion,
   Like gold to airy thinness beat.

25 If they be two, they are two so
   As stiff twin compasses are two:
Thy soul, the fixed foot, makes no show
   To move, but doth, if the other do;

And though it in the center sit,
30   Yet when the other far doth roam,
It leans, and hearkens after it,
   And grows erect, as that comes home.

Such wilt thou be to me, who must,
   Like the other foot, obliquely run;
35 Thy firmness makes my circle[7] just,
   And makes me end where I begun.

                 1611?

PAUL LAURENCE DUNBAR
We Wear the Mask

We wear the mask that grins and lies,
It hides our cheeks and shades our eyes,—
This debt we pay to human guile;
With torn and bleeding hearts we smile,
5 And mouth with myriad subtleties.

Why should the world be over-wise,
In counting all our tears and sighs?
Nay, let them only see us, while
   We wear the mask.

10 We smile, but, O great Christ, our cries
To thee from tortured souls arise.
We sing, but oh the clay is vile
Beneath our feet, and long the mile;

---

7. Traditional symbol of perfection.

But let the world dream otherwise,
15   We wear the mask!

                          1895

T. S. ELIOT
The Love Song of J. Alfred Prufrock

S'io credesse che mia risposta fosse
a persona che mai tornasse al mondo,
questa fiamma staria senza più scosse.
Ma per ciò che giammai di questo fondo
non tornò vivo alcun, s'i'odo il vero,
senza tema d'infamia ti rispondo.[8]

Let us go then, you and I,
When the evening is spread out against the sky
Like a patient etherised upon a table;
Let us go, through certain half-deserted streets,
5 The muttering retreats
Of restless nights in one-night cheap hotels
And sawdust restaurants with oyster-shells:
Streets that follow like a tedious argument
Of insidious intent
10 To lead you to an overwhelming question . . .
Oh, do not ask, 'What is it?'
Let us go and make our visit.

In the room the women come and go
Talking of Michelangelo.[9]

15 The yellow fog that rubs its back upon the window-panes,
The yellow smoke that rubs its muzzle on the window-panes,
Licked its tongue into the corners of the evening,
Lingered upon the pools that stand in drains,
Let fall upon its back the soot that falls from chimneys,
20 Slipped by the terrace, made a sudden leap,

---

8. From Dante, *Inferno* (27.61–66): "If I thought that my reply would be / to one who would ever return to the world, / this flame would stay without further movement; // but since none has ever returned alive from this depth, / if what I hear is true, / I answer you without fear of infamy." The words are spoken by the character Guido da Montefeltro—imprisoned in flame in the depths of hell as a punishment for giving false counsel—to Dante, whom da Montefeltro believes will never return from his journey into the inferno.
9. Italian artist Michelangelo Buonarroti (1475–1564).

And seeing that it was a soft October night,
Curled once about the house, and fell asleep.

And indeed there will be time[1]
For the yellow smoke that slides along the street
25 Rubbing its back upon the window-panes;
There will be time, there will be time
To prepare a face to meet the faces that you meet;
There will be time to murder and create,
And time for all the works and days[2] of hands
30 That lift and drop a question on your plate;
Time for you and time for me,
And time yet for a hundred indecisions,
And for a hundred visions and revisions,
Before the taking of a toast and tea.

35 In the room the women come and go
Talking of Michelangelo.

And indeed there will be time
To wonder, 'Do I dare?' and, 'Do I dare?'
Time to turn back and descend the stair,
40 With a bald spot in the middle of my hair—
(They will say: 'How his hair is growing thin!')
My morning coat, my collar mounting firmly to the chin,
My necktie rich and modest, but asserted by a simple pin—
(They will say: 'But how his arms and legs are thin!')
45 Do I dare
Disturb the universe?
In a minute there is time
For decisions and revisions which a minute will reverse.

For I have known them all already, known them all—
50 Have known the evenings, mornings, afternoons,
I have measured out my life with coffee spoons;
I know the voices dying with a dying fall
Beneath the music from a farther room.
    So how should I presume?

55 And I have known the eyes already, known them all—
The eyes that fix you in a formulated phrase,

1. Echo of Andrew Marvell's "To His Coy Mistress" (1681), which famously begins, "Had we but world enough, and time / This coyness, lady, were no crime."
2. *Works and Days* is a poem composed about 700 BCE by the Greek writer Hesiod; lamenting the moral decay of the present, it celebrates simple life and hard work, especially agricultural labor.

And when I am formulated, sprawling on a pin,
When I am pinned and wriggling on the wall,
Then how should I begin
60 To spit out all the butt-ends of my days and ways?
　　And how should I presume?

And I have known the arms already, known them all—
Arms that are braceleted and white and bare
(But in the lamplight, downed with light brown hair!)
65 Is it perfume from a dress
That makes me so digress?
Arms that lie along a table, or wrap about a shawl.
　　And should I then presume?
　　And how should I begin?

　　　　　. . . . . .

70 Shall I say, I have gone at dusk through narrow streets
And watched the smoke that rises from the pipes
Of lonely men in shirt-sleeves, leaning out of windows? . . .
I should have been a pair of ragged claws
Scuttling across the floors of silent seas.

　　　　　. . . . . .

75 And the afternoon, the evening, sleeps so peacefully!
Smoothed by long fingers,
Asleep . . . tired . . . or it malingers,
Stretched on the floor, here beside you and me.
Should I, after tea and cakes and ices,
80 Have the strength to force the moment to its crisis?
But though I have wept and fasted, wept and prayed,
Though I have seen my head (grown slightly bald) brought in
　　upon a platter,[3]
I am no prophet—and here's no great matter;
I have seen the moment of my greatness flicker,
85 And I have seen the eternal Footman hold my coat, and snicker,
And in short, I was afraid.

And would it have been worth it, after all,
After the cups, the marmalade, the tea,
Among the porcelain, among some talk of you and me,
90 Would it have been worth while,

3. Like John the Baptist; at a banquet, King Herod has the prophet's head delivered on a plate
to Salome, the woman who requested his execution (Mark 6.17–28; Matt. 14.3–11).

To have bitten off the matter with a smile,
To have squeezed the universe into a ball[4]
To roll it towards some overwhelming question,
To say: 'I am Lazarus, come from the dead,[5]
95 Come back to tell you all, I shall tell you all'—
If one, settling a pillow by her head,
    Should say: 'That is not what I meant at all.
    That is not it, at all.'

And would it have been worth it, after all,
100 Would it have been worth while,
After the sunsets and the dooryards and the sprinkled streets,
After the novels, after the teacups, after the skirts that trail along
    the floor—
And this, and so much more?—
It is impossible to say just what I mean!
105 But as if a magic lantern threw the nerves in patterns on a
    screen:
Would it have been worth while
If one, settling a pillow or throwing off a shawl,
And turning toward the window, should say:
    'That is not it at all,
110   That is not what I meant, at all.'

          * * * * *

No! I am not Prince Hamlet,[6] nor was meant to be;
Am an attendant lord, one that will do
To swell a progress,[7] start a scene or two,
Advise the prince; no doubt, an easy tool,
115 Deferential, glad to be of use,
Politic, cautious, and meticulous;
Full of high sentence,[8] but a bit obtuse;
At times, indeed, almost ridiculous—
Almost, at times, the Fool.

---

4. Another echo of "To His Coy Mistress": "Let us roll all our strength and all / Our sweetness up into one ball, / And tear our pleasures with rough strife / Through the iron gates of life" (lines 41–44).

5. The New Testament relates the story of Jesus raising Lazarus from the dead in John 11.1–44.

6. Protagonist of Shakespeare's tragedy *Hamlet*, who is indecisive for much of the play.

7. Journey of a royal or noble person, or the representation of such a journey onstage as part of a play (as was common in Shakespeare's age).

8. Sententious; that is, he tends to speak in a pompous, formal manner.

120 I grow old . . . I grow old . . .
   I shall wear the bottoms of my trousers rolled.

Shall I part my hair behind? Do I dare to eat a peach?
I shall wear white flannel trousers, and walk upon the beach.
I have heard the mermaids singing, each to each.

125 I do not think that they will sing to me.

I have seen them riding seaward on the waves
Combing the white hair of the waves blown back
When the wind blows the water white and black.

We have lingered in the chambers of the sea
130 By sea-girls wreathed with seaweed red and brown
Till human voices wake us, and we drown.

                                1915

ROBERT FROST
Home Burial

He saw her from the bottom of the stairs
Before she saw him. She was starting down,
Looking back over her shoulder at some fear.
She took a doubtful step and then undid it
5 To raise herself and look again. He spoke
Advancing toward her: "What is it you see
From up there always?—for I want to know."
She turned and sank upon her skirts at that,
And her face changed from terrified to dull.
10 He said to gain time: "What is it you see?"
Mounting until she cowered under him.
"I will find out now—you must tell me, dear."
She, in her place, refused him any help,
With the least stiffening of her neck and silence.
15 She let him look, sure that he wouldn't see,
Blind creature; and awhile he didn't see.
But at last he murmured, "Oh," and again, "Oh."

"What is it—what?" she said.
                        "Just that I see."

"You don't," she challenged. "Tell me what it is."

20 "The wonder is I didn't see at once.
I never noticed it from here before.

I must be wonted[9] to it—that's the reason.
The little graveyard where my people are!
So small the window frames the whole of it.
25 Not so much larger than a bedroom, is it?
There are three stones of slate and one of marble,
Broad-shouldered little slabs there in the sunlight
On the sidehill. We haven't to mind *those*.
But I understand: it is not the stones,
30 But the child's mound—"

                              "Don't, don't, don't,

      don't," she cried.

She withdrew, shrinking from beneath his arm
That rested on the banister, and slid downstairs;
And turned on him with such a daunting look,
He said twice over before he knew himself:
35 "Can't a man speak of his own child he's lost?"

"Not you!—Oh, where's my hat? Oh, I don't need it!
I must get out of here. I must get air.—
I don't know rightly whether any man can."

"Amy! Don't go to someone else this time.
40 Listen to me. I won't come down the stairs."
He sat and fixed his chin between his fists.
"There's something I should like to ask you, dear."

"You don't know how to ask it."

                              "Help me, then."

Her fingers moved the latch for all reply.

45 "My words are nearly always an offense.
I don't know how to speak of anything
So as to please you. But I might be taught,
I should suppose. I can't say I see how.
A man must partly give up being a man
50 With womenfolk. We could have some arrangement
By which I'd bind myself to keep hands off
Anything special you're a-mind to name.
Though I don't like such things 'twixt those that love.
Two that don't love can't live together without them.
55 But two that do can't live together with them."

9. Habituated, accustomed.

She moved the latch a little. "Don't—don't go.
Don't carry it to someone else this time.
Tell me about it if it's something human.
Let me into your grief. I'm not so much
60 Unlike other folks as your standing there
Apart would make me out. Give me my chance.
I do think, though, you overdo it a little.
What was it brought you up to think it the thing
To take your mother-loss of a first child
65 So inconsolably—in the face of love.
You'd think his memory might be satisfied—"

"There you go sneering now!"

              "I'm not, I'm not!
You make me angry. I'll come down to you.
God, what a woman! And it's come to this,
70 A man can't speak of his own child that's dead."

"You can't because you don't know how to speak.
If you had any feelings, you that dug
With your own hand—how could you?—his little grave;
I saw you from that very window there,
75 Making the gravel leap and leap in air,
Leap up, like that, like that, and land so lightly
And roll back down the mound beside the hole.
I thought, Who is that man? I didn't know you.
And I crept down the stairs and up the stairs
80 To look again, and still your spade kept lifting.
Then you came in. I heard your rumbling voice
Out in the kitchen, and I don't know why,
But I went near to see with my own eyes.
You could sit there with the stains on your shoes
85 Of the fresh earth from your own baby's grave
And talk about your everyday concerns.
You had stood the spade up against the wall
Outside there in the entry, for I saw it."

"I shall laugh the worst laugh I ever laughed.
90 I'm cursed. God, if I don't believe I'm cursed."

"I can repeat the very words you were saying:
'Three foggy mornings and one rainy day
Will rot the best birch fence a man can build.'
Think of it, talk like that at such a time!

95 What had how long it takes a birch to rot
To do with what was in the darkened parlor?
You *couldn't* care! The nearest friends can go
With anyone to death, comes so far short
They might as well not try to go at all.
100 No, from the time when one is sick to death,
One is alone, and he dies more alone.
Friends make pretense of following to the grave,
But before one is in it, their minds are turned
And making the best of their way back to life
105 And living people, and things they understand.
But the world's evil. I won't have grief so
If I can change it. Oh, I won't, I won't!"

"There, you have said it all and you feel better.
You won't go now. You're crying. Close the door.
110 The heart's gone out of it: why keep it up?
Amy! There's someone coming down the road!"

"*You*—oh, you think the talk is all. I must go—
Somewhere out of this house. How can I make you—"

"If—you—do!" She was opening the door wider.
115 "Where do you mean to go? First tell me that.
I'll follow and bring you back by force. I *will!*—"

1915

Stopping by Woods on a Snowy Evening

Whose woods these are I think I know.
His house is in the village, though;
He will not see me stopping here
To watch his woods fill up with snow.

5 My little horse must think it queer
To stop without a farmhouse near
Between the woods and frozen lake
The darkest evening of the year.

He gives his harness bells a shake
10 To ask if there is some mistake.
The only other sound's the sweep
Of easy wind and downy flake.

The woods are lovely, dark, and deep,
But I have promises to keep,

15 And miles to go before I sleep,
And miles to go before I sleep.
                                    1923

ANGELINA GRIMKÉ
Tenebris[1]

There is a tree, by day,
That, at night,
Has a shadow,
A hand huge and black,
5 With fingers long and black.
    All through the dark,
Against the white man's house,
    In the little wind,
The black hand plucks and plucks
10   At the bricks.
The bricks are the color of blood and very small.
    Is it a black hand,
    Or is it a shadow?
                                    1927

SEAMUS HEANEY
Digging

Between my finger and my thumb
The squat pen rests; snug as a gun.

Under my window, a clean rasping sound
When the spade sinks into gravelly ground:
5 My father, digging. I look down

Till his straining rump among the flowerbeds
Bends low, comes up twenty years away
Stooping in rhythm through potato drills[2]
Where he was digging.

10 The coarse boot nestled on the lug, the shaft
Against the inside knee was levered firmly.

1. In darkness (Latin).
2. Small furrows in which seeds are sown.

He rooted out tall tops, buried the bright edge deep
To scatter new potatoes that we picked
Loving their cool hardness in our hands.

15   By God, the old man could handle a spade.
Just like his old man.

My grandfather cut more turf[3] in a day
Than any other man on Toner's bog.
Once I carried him milk in a bottle
20   Corked sloppily with paper. He straightened up
To drink it, then fell to right away
Nicking and slicing neatly, heaving sods
Over his shoulder, going down and down
For the good turf. Digging.

25   The cold smell of potato mould, the squelch and slap
Of soggy peat, the curt cuts of an edge
Through living roots awaken in my head.
But I've no spade to follow men like them.

Between my finger and my thumb
30   The squat pen rests.
I'll dig with it.

                                                    1966

GERARD MANLEY HOPKINS
God's Grandeur

The world is charged with the grandeur of God.
    It will flame out, like shining from shook foil;[4]
    It gathers to a greatness, like the ooze of oil
Crushed. Why do men then now not reck his rod?[5]
5   Generations have trod, have trod, have trod;
    And all is seared with trade; bleared, smeared with toil;
    And wears man's smudge and shares man's smell: the soil
Is bare now, nor can foot feel, being shod.

And for all this, nature is never spent;
10   There lives the dearest freshness deep down things;

---

3. Peat cut into slabs and dried to be used as fuel in stoves and furnaces.
4. "I mean foil in its sense of leaf or tinsel [. . .] . Shaken goldfoil gives off broad glares like
sheet lightning and also, and this is true of nothing else, owing to its zig-zag dints and creasings
and network of small many cornered facets, a sort of fork lightning too" (*Letters of Gerard Manley
Hopkins to Robert Bridges*, edited by C. C. Abbott, 1955, p. 169).   5. Heed his authority.

And though the last lights off the black West went
Oh, morning, at the brown brink eastward, springs—
Because the Holy Ghost over the bent
World broods with warm breast and with ah! bright wings.

c. 1877

The Windhover[6]

To Christ our Lord

I caught this morning morning's minion,[7] king-
   dom of daylight's dauphin,[8] dapple-dawn-drawn Falcon, in his
   riding
Of the rolling level underneath him steady air, and striding
High there, how he rung upon the rein of a wimpling[9] wing
5 In his ecstasy! then off, off forth on swing,
   As a skate's heel sweeps smooth on a bow-bend: the hurl and
   gliding
Rebuffed the big wind. My heart in hiding
Stirred for a bird,—the achieve of, the mastery of the thing!

Brute beauty and valor and act, oh, air, pride, plume, here
10   Buckle![1] AND the fire that breaks from thee then, a billion
Times told lovelier, more dangerous, O my chevalier![2]

   No wonder of it: shéer plód makes plow down sillion[3]
Shine, and blue-bleak embers, ah my dear,
   Fall, gall themselves, and gash gold-vermilion.

1877

Harlem

What happens to a dream deferred?

   Does it dry up
   Like a raisin in the sun?
   Or fester like a sore—
5   And then run?
   Does it stink like rotten meat?

---

6. Small hawk, the kestrel, which habitually hovers in the air, headed into the wind.
7. Favorite, beloved. 8. Heir to regal splendor. 9. Rippling.
1. Several meanings may apply: to join closely, to prepare for battle, to grapple with, to collapse.
2. Horseman, knight.
3. Narrow strip of land between furrows in an open field divided for separate cultivation.

Or crust and sugar over—
Like a syrupy sweet?
Maybe it just sags
10   Like a heavy load.

Or does it explode?

          1951

I, Too

I, too, sing America.

I am the darker brother.
They send me to eat in the kitchen
When company comes,
5 But I laugh,
And eat well,
And grow strong.

Tomorrow,
I'll sit at the table.
10 When company comes
Nobody'll dare
Say to me,
"Eat in the kitchen,"
Then.

15 Besides,
They'll see how beautiful I am
And be ashamed—

I, too, am America.

          1932

BEN JONSON
On My First Son

Farewell, thou child of my right hand,[4] and joy;
My sin was too much hope of thee, loved boy:
Seven years thou wert lent to me, and I thee pay,
Exacted by thy fate, on the just[5] day.
5 O could I lose all father now! for why
Will man lament the state he should envy,

---

4. Literal translation of the son's name, Benjamin.
5. Exact; the son died on his seventh birthday, in 1603.

To have so soon 'scaped world's and flesh's rage,
And, if no other misery, yet age?
Rest in soft peace, and asked, say, "Here doth lie
10 Ben Jonson his[6] best piece of poetry."
For whose sake henceforth all his vows be such
As what he loves may never like too much.

1616

JOHN KEATS
Ode on a Grecian Urn

I

Thou still unravished bride of quietness,
    Thou foster-child of silence and slow time,
Sylvan historian, who canst thus express
    A flowery tale more sweetly than our rhyme:
5 What leaf-fringed legend haunts about thy shape
    Of deities or mortals, or of both,
        In Tempe or the dales of Arcady?[7]
What men or gods are these? What maidens loath?
    What mad pursuit? What struggle to escape?
10   What pipes and timbrels? What wild ecstasy?

II

Heard melodies are sweet, but those unheard
    Are sweeter; therefore, ye soft pipes, play on;
Not to the sensual[8] ear, but, more endeared,
    Pipe to the spirit ditties of no tone:
15 Fair youth, beneath the trees, thou canst not leave
    Thy song, nor ever can those trees be bare;
        Bold Lover, never, never canst thou kiss,
Though winning near the goal—yet, do not grieve;
    She cannot fade, though thou hast not thy bliss,
20   For ever wilt thou love, and she be fair!

III

Ah, happy, happy boughs! that cannot shed
    Your leaves, nor ever bid the Spring adieu;

---

6. That is, Ben Jonson's (this was a common Renaissance form of the possessive).
7. Arcadia. Tempe is a beautiful valley near Mt. Olympus in Greece, and the valleys ("dales") of Arcadia are a picturesque section of the Peloponnesus; both came to be associated with the pastoral ideal.
8. Of the senses, as distinguished from the "ear" of the spirit or imagination.

And, happy melodist, unwearièd,
    For ever piping songs for ever new;
25 More happy love! more happy, happy love!
    For ever warm and still to be enjoyed,
      For ever panting, and for ever young;
All breathing human passion far above,
    That leaves a heart high-sorrowful and cloyed,
30   A burning forehead, and a parching tongue.

IV

Who are these coming to the sacrifice?
    To what green altar, O mysterious priest,
Lead'st thou that heifer lowing at the skies,
    And all her silken flanks with garlands dressed?
35 What little town by river or sea shore,
    Or mountain-built with peaceful citadel,
      Is emptied of its folk, this pious morn?
And, little town, thy streets for evermore
    Will silent be; and not a soul to tell
40   Why thou art desolate, can e'er return.

V

O Attic shape! Fair attitude! with brede[9]
Of marble men and maidens overwrought,[1]
    With forest branches and the trodden weed;
    Thou, silent form, dost tease us out of thought
45 As doth eternity: Cold Pastoral!
    When old age shall this generation waste,
      Thou shalt remain, in midst of other woe
Than ours, a friend to man, to whom thou say'st,
    Beauty is truth, truth beauty[2]—that is all
50   Ye know on earth, and all ye need to know.
May 1819   1820

To Autumn

I

Season of mists and mellow fruitfulness,
    Close bosom-friend of the maturing sun;

9. Woven pattern. *Attic*: Attica was the district of ancient Greece surrounding Athens.
1. Ornamented all over.
2. In some texts of the poem, "Beauty is truth, truth beauty" is in quotation marks, and in some texts it is not, leading to critical disagreements about whether the last line and a half are also inscribed on the urn or spoken by the poem's speaker.

Conspiring with him how to load and bless
    With fruit the vines that round the thatch-eves run;
5 To bend with apples the mossed cottage-trees,
    And fill all fruit with ripeness to the core;
        To swell the gourd, and plump the hazel shells
    With a sweet kernel; to set budding more,
    And still more, later flowers for the bees,
10   Until they think warm days will never cease,
        For Summer has o'er-brimmed their clammy cells.

                    II
Who hath not seen thee oft amid thy store?
    Sometimes whoever seeks abroad may find
    Thee sitting careless on a granary floor,
15   Thy hair soft-lifted by the winnowing wind,[3]
    Or on a half-reaped furrow sound asleep,
        Drowsed with the fume of poppies, while thy hook[4]
        Spares the next swath and all its twinèd flowers:
    And sometimes like a gleaner thou dost keep
20   Steady thy laden head across a brook;
    Or by a cider-press, with patient look,
        Thou watchest the last oozings hours by hours.

                    III
Where are the songs of Spring? Ay, where are they?
    Think not of them, thou hast thy music too—
25 While barrèd clouds bloom the soft-dying day,
    And touch the stubble-plains with rosy hue;
    Then in a wailful choir the small gnats mourn
        Among the river sallows,[5] borne aloft
            Or sinking as the light wind lives or dies;
30 And full-grown lambs loud bleat from hilly bourn;[6]
    Hedge-crickets sing; and now with treble soft
    The red-breast whistles from a garden-croft;[7]
        And gathering swallows twitter in the skies.
September 19, 1819   1820

---

3. Which sifts the grain from the chaff.   4. Scythe or sickle.   5. Shallows.   6. Domain.
7. Enclosed garden near a house.

ETHERIDGE KNIGHT
[Eastern guard tower]

Eastern guard tower
glints in sunset; convicts rest
like lizards on rocks.

[The falling snow flakes]

The falling snow flakes
Cannot blunt the hard aches nor
Match the steel stillness.

[Making jazz swing in]

Making jazz swing in
Seventeen syllables AIN'T
No square poet's job.

1960

Hard Rock Returns to Prison from the Hospital for the Criminal Insane

Hard Rock was "known not to take no shit
From nobody," and he had the scars to prove it:
Split purple lips, lumped ears, welts above
His yellow eyes, and one long scar that cut
5   Across his temple and plowed through a thick
Canopy of kinky hair.

The WORD was that Hard Rock wasn't a mean nigger
Anymore, that the doctors had bored a hole in his head,
Cut out part of his brain, and shot electricity
10 Through the rest. When they brought Hard Rock back,
Handcuffed and chained, he was turned loose,
Like a freshly gelded stallion, to try his new status.
And we all waited and watched, like indians at a corral,
To see if the WORD was true.

15 As we waited we wrapped ourselves in the cloak
Of his exploits: "Man, the last time, it took eight
Screws to put him in the Hole."[8] "Yeah, remember when he

---

8. Solitary confinement. *Screws:* guards.

Smacked the captain with his dinner tray?" "He set
The record for time in the Hole—67 straight days!"
20 "Ol Hard Rock! man, that's one crazy nigger."
And then the jewel of a myth that Hard Rock had once bit
A screw on the thumb and poisoned him with syphilitic spit.

The testing came, to see if Hard Rock was really tame.
A hillbilly called him a black son of a bitch
25 And didn't lose his teeth, a screw who knew Hard Rock
From before shook him down and barked in his face.
And Hard Rock did *nothing*. Just grinned and looked silly,
His eyes empty like knot holes in a fence.

And even after we discovered that it took Hard Rock
30 Exactly 3 minutes to tell you his first name,
We told ourselves that he had just wised up,
Was being cool; but we could not fool ourselves for long,
And we turned away, our eyes on the ground. Crushed.
He had been our Destroyer, the doer of things
35 We dreamed of doing but could not bring ourselves to do,
The fears of years, like a biting whip,
Had cut grooves too deeply across our backs.

1968

CLAUDE MCKAY
The Harlem Dancer

Applauding youths laughed with young prostitutes
And watched her perfect, half-clothed body sway;
Her voice was like the sound of blended flutes
Blown by black players upon a picnic day.
5 She sang and danced on gracefully and calm,
The light gauze hanging loose about her form;
To me she seemed a proudly-swaying palm
Grown lovelier for passing through a storm.
Upon her swarthy neck black shiny curls
10 Luxuriant fell; and tossing coins in praise,
The wine-flushed, bold-eyed boys, and even the girls,
Devoured her shape with eager, passionate gaze;
But looking at her falsely-smiling face,
I knew her self was not in that strange place.

1922

The White House

Your door is shut against my tightened face,
And I am sharp as steel with discontent;
But I possess the courage and the grace
To bear my anger proudly and unbent.
5 The pavement slabs burn loose beneath my feet,
And passion rends my vitals as I pass,
A chafing savage, down the decent street,
Where boldly shines your shuttered door of glass.
Oh, I must search for wisdom every hour,
10 Deep in my wrathful bosom sore and raw,
And find in it the superhuman power
To hold me to the letter of your law!
Oh, I must keep my heart inviolate
Against the poison of your deadly hate.

1937

PAT MORA
Elena

My Spanish isn't enough.
I remember how I'd smile
listening to my little ones,
understanding every word they'd say,
5 their jokes, their songs, their plots.
    Vamos a pedirle dulces a mamá. Vamos.[9]
But that was in Mexico.
Now my children go to American high schools.
They speak English. At night they sit around
10 the kitchen table, laugh with one another.
I stand by the stove and feel dumb, alone.
I bought a book to learn English.
My husband frowned, drank more beer.
My oldest said, "*Mamá*, he doesn't want you
15 to be smarter than he is." I'm forty,
embarrassed at mispronouncing words,
embarrassed at the laughter of my children,
the grocer, the mailman. Sometimes I take
my English book and lock myself in the bathroom,
20 say the thick words softly,

9. Let's go ask mama for sweets. Let's go (Spanish).

for if I stop trying, I will be deaf
when my children need my help.

1985

Gentle Communion

Even the long-dead are willing to move.
Without a word, she came with me from the desert.
Mornings she wanders through my rooms
making beds, folding socks.

5 Since she can't hear me anymore,
Mamande[1] ignores the questions I never knew
to ask, about her younger days, her red
hair, the time she fell and broke her nose
in the snow. I will never know.

10 When I try to make her laugh,
to disprove her sad album face, she leaves
the room, resists me as she resisted
grinning for cameras, make-up, English.

While I write, she sits and prays,
15 feet apart, legs never crossed,
the blue housecoat buttoned high
as her hair dries white, girlish
around her head and shoulders.

She closes her eyes, bows her head,
20 and like a child presses her hands together,
her patient flesh steeple, the skin
worn, like the pages of her prayer book.

Sometimes I sit in her wide-armed
chair as I once sat in her lap.
25 Alone, we played a quiet I Spy.
She peeled grapes I still taste.

She removes the thin skin, places
the luminous coolness on my tongue.
I know not to bite or chew. I wait
30 for the thick melt,
our private green honey.

1991

---

1. Child's conflation *of mama grande* (Spanish for "grandmother").

LINDA PASTAN
love poem

I want to write you
a love poem as headlong
as our creek
after thaw
5 when we stand
on its dangerous
banks and watch it carry
with it every twig
every dry leaf and branch
10 in its path
every scruple
when we see it
so swollen
with runoff
15 that even as we watch
we must grab
each other
and step back
we must grab each
20 other or
get our shoes
soaked we must
grab each other

                        1988

MARGE PIERCY
Barbie Doll

This girlchild was born as usual
and presented dolls that did pee-pee
and miniature GE stoves and irons
and wee lipsticks the color of cherry candy.
5 Then in the magic of puberty, a classmate said:
You have a great big nose and fat legs.

She was healthy, tested intelligent,
possessed strong arms and back,
abundant sexual drive and manual dexterity.
10 She went to and fro apologizing.
Everyone saw a fat nose on thick legs.

She was advised to play coy,
exhorted to come on hearty,
exercise, diet, smile and wheedle.
15 Her good nature wore out
like a fan belt.
So she cut off her nose and her legs
and offered them up.

In the casket displayed on satin she lay
20 with the undertaker's cosmetics painted on,
a turned-up putty nose,
dressed in a pink and white nightie.
Doesn't she look pretty? everyone said.
Consummation at last.
25 To every woman a happy ending.

1973

SYLVIA PLATH
Daddy

You do not do, you do not do
Any more, black shoe
In which I have lived like a foot
For thirty years, poor and white,
5 Barely daring to breathe or Achoo.

Daddy, I have had to kill you.
You died before I had time—
Marble-heavy, a bag full of God,
Ghastly statue with one gray toe[2]
10 Big as a Frisco seal

And a head in the freakish Atlantic
Where it pours bean green over blue
In the waters off beautiful Nauset.[3]
I used to pray to recover you.
15 Ach, du.[4]

In the German tongue, in the Polish town[5]
Scraped flat by the roller
Of wars, wars, wars.

2. Otto Plath, Sylvia's father, lost a toe to gangrene that resulted from diabetes.
3. Inlet on Cape Cod, Massachusetts. 4. Oh, you (German).
5. Otto Plath, an ethnic German, was born in Grabow, Poland.

But the name of the town is common.
20 My Polack friend

Says there are a dozen or two.
So I never could tell where you
Put your foot, your root,
I never could talk to you.
25 The tongue stuck in my jaw.

It stuck in a barb wire snare.
Ich,[6] ich, ich, ich,
I could hardly speak.
I thought every German was you.
30 And the language obscene

An engine, an engine
Chuffing me off like a Jew.
A Jew to Dachau, Auschwitz, Belsen.[7]
I began to talk like a Jew.
35 I think I may well be a Jew.

The snows of the Tyrol, the clear beer of Vienna[8]
Are not very pure or true.
With my gypsy-ancestress and my weird luck
And my Taroc[9] pack and my Taroc pack
40 I may be a bit of a Jew.

I have always been scared of *you*,
With your Luftwaffe,[1] your gobbledygoo.
And your neat moustache
And your Aryan[2] eye, bright blue.
45 Panzer[3]-man, panzer-man, O You—

Not God but a swastika
So black no sky could squeak through.
Every woman adores a Fascist,
The boot in the face, the brute
50 Brute heart of a brute like you.

You stand at the blackboard, daddy,
In the picture I have of you,
A cleft in your chin instead of your foot

6. German for "I."   7. Sites of World War II Nazi death camps.
8. The snow in the Tyrol (an Alpine region in Austria and northern Italy) is, legendarily, as pure
as the beer is clear in Vienna.   9. Tarot, playing cards used mainly for fortune-telling.
1. German air force.   2. People of Germanic lineage, often blond-haired and blue-eyed.
3. Literally "panther" (German), the Nazi tank corps' term for an armored vehicle.

But no less a devil for that, no not
55 Any less the black man who

Bit my pretty red heart in two.
I was ten when they buried you.
At twenty I tried to die
And get back, back, back to you.
60 I thought even the bones would do

But they pulled me out of the sack,
And they stuck me together with glue.[4]
And then I knew what to do.
I made a model of you,
65 A man in black with a Meinkampf[5] look

And a love of the rack and the screw.
And I said I do, I do.
So daddy, I'm finally through.
The black telephone's off at the root,
70 The voices just can't worm through.

If I've killed one man, I've killed two—
The vampire who said he was you
And drank my blood for a year,
Seven years, if you want to know.
75 Daddy, you can lie back now.

There's a stake in your fat black heart
And the villagers never liked you.
They are dancing and stamping on you.
They always *knew* it was you.
80 Daddy, daddy, you bastard, I'm through.
1962   1965

Lady Lazarus

I have done it again.
One year in every ten
I manage it—

A sort of walking miracle, my skin
5 Bright as a Nazi lampshade,
My right foot

---

4. Perhaps an allusion to Plath's recovery from her first suicide attempt.
5. Title of Adolf Hitler's autobiography and manifesto (1925–27); German for "my struggle."

A paperweight,
My face a featureless, fine
Jew linen.[6]

10   Peel off the napkin
O my enemy.
Do I terrify?—

The nose, the eye pits, the full set of teeth?
The sour breath
15   Will vanish in a day.

Soon, soon the flesh
The grave cave ate will be
At home on me

And I a smiling woman.
20   I am only thirty.
And like the cat I have nine times to die.

This is Number Three.
What a trash
To annihilate each decade.

25   What a million filaments.
The peanut-crunching crowd
Shoves in to see

Them unwrap me hand and foot—
The big strip tease.
30   Gentlemen, ladies

These are my hands
My knees.
I may be skin and bone,

Nevertheless, I am the same, identical woman.
35   The first time it happened I was ten.
It was an accident.

The second time I meant
To last it out and not come back at all.
I rocked shut

40   As a seashell.
They had to call and call
And pick the worms off me like sticky pearls.

6. During World War II, prisoners in some Nazi camps were gassed to death and their body
parts then turned into objects such as lampshades and paperweights.

Dying
Is an art, like everything else.
45 I do it exceptionally well.

I do it so it feels like hell.
I do it so it feels real.
I guess you could say I've a call.

It's easy enough to do it in a cell.
50 It's easy enough to do it and stay put.
It's the theatrical

Comeback in broad day
To the same place, the same face, the same brute
Amused shout:

55 "A miracle!"
That knocks me out.
There is a charge

For the eyeing of my scars, there is a charge
For the hearing of my heart—
60 It really goes.

And there is a charge, a very large charge
For a word or a touch
Or a bit of blood

Or a piece of my hair or my clothes.
65 So, so Herr Doktor.
So, Herr Enemy.

I am your opus,
I am your valuable,
The pure gold baby

70 That melts to a shriek.
I turn and burn.
Do not think I underestimate your great concern

Ash, ash—
You poke and stir.
75 Flesh, bone, there is nothing there—

A cake of soap,
A wedding ring,
A gold filling.

Herr God, Herr Lucifer
80 Beware
Beware.

Out of the ash
I rise with my red hair
And I eat men like air.

1965

EDGAR ALLAN POE
The Raven

Once upon a midnight dreary, while I pondered, weak and weary,
Over many a quaint and curious volume of forgotten lore,
While I nodded, nearly napping, suddenly there came a tapping,
As of some one gently rapping, rapping at my chamber door.
5 "'Tis some visitor," I muttered, "tapping at my chamber door—
         Only this, and nothing more."

Ah, distinctly I remember it was in the bleak December,
And each separate dying ember wrought its ghost upon the floor.
Eagerly I wished the morrow;—vainly I had sought to borrow
10 From my books surcease of sorrow—sorrow for the lost Lenore—
For the rare and radiant maiden whom the angels name Lenore—
         Nameless here for evermore.

And the silken sad uncertain rustling of each purple curtain
Thrilled me—filled me with fantastic terrors never felt before;
15 So that now, to still the beating of my heart, I stood repeating
 "'Tis some visitor entreating entrance at my chamber door;—
Some late visitor entreating entrance at my chamber door;—
         This it is, and nothing more."

Presently my soul grew stronger; hesitating then no longer,
20 "Sir," said I, "or Madam, truly your forgiveness I implore;
But the fact is I was napping, and so gently you came rapping,
And so faintly you came tapping, tapping at my chamber door,
That I scarce was sure I heard you"—here I opened wide the door;—
         Darkness there, and nothing more.

25 Deep into that darkness peering, long I stood there wondering,
   fearing,
Doubting, dreaming dreams no mortal ever dared to dream before;
But the silence was unbroken, and the darkness gave no token,
And the only word there spoken was the whispered word, "Lenore!"

This I whispered, and an echo murmured back the word, "Lenore!"—
30   Merely this, and nothing more.

Back into the chamber turning, all my soul within me burning,
Soon I heard again a tapping somewhat louder than before.
"Surely," said I, "surely that is something at my window lattice;
Let me see, then, what thereat is, and this mystery explore—
35 Let my heart be still a moment and this mystery explore;—
                    'Tis the wind and nothing more!"

Open here I flung the shutter, when, with many a flirt and flutter,
In there stepped a stately raven of the saintly days of yore;
Not the least obeisance made he; not an instant stopped or stayed
    he;
40 But, with mien of lord or lady, perched above my chamber door—
Perched upon a bust of Pallas[7] just above my chamber door—
                    Perched, and sat, and nothing more.

Then this ebony bird beguiling my sad fancy into smiling,
By the grave and stern decorum of the countenance it wore,
45 "Though thy crest be shorn and shaven, thou," I said, "art sure no
    craven,
Ghastly grim and ancient raven wandering from the Nightly shore—
Tell me what thy lordly name is on the Night's Plutonian[8] shore!"
                    Quoth the raven, "Nevermore."

Much I marvelled this ungainly fowl to hear discourse so plainly,
50 Though its answer little meaning—little relevancy bore,
For we cannot help agreeing that no living human being
Ever yet was blessed with seeing bird above his chamber door—
Bird or beast upon the sculptured bust above his chamber door,
                    With such name as "Nevermore."

55 But the raven, sitting lonely on the placid bust, spoke only
That one word, as if his soul in that one word he did outpour.
Nothing farther then he uttered—not a feather then he fluttered—
Till I scarcely more than muttered "Other friends have flown before—
On the morrow *he* will leave me, as my hopes have flown before."
60   Then the bird said "Nevermore."

Startled at the stillness broken by reply so aptly spoken,
"Doubtless," said I, "what it utters is its only stock and store
Caught from some unhappy master whom unmerciful Disaster
Followed fast and followed faster till his songs one burden bore—

7. Athena, the Greek goddess of wisdom. 8. Dark; Pluto was the ancient Greek god of the
underworld.

65 Till the dirges of his Hope that melancholy burden bore
            Of 'Never—nevermore.'"

But the raven still beguiling all my sad soul into smiling,
Straight I wheeled a cushioned seat in front of bird and bust and
      door;
Then, upon the velvet sinking, I betook myself to linking
70 Fancy unto fancy, thinking what this ominous bird of yore—
What this grim, ungainly, ghastly, gaunt, and ominous bird of yore
            Meant in croaking "Nevermore."

This I sat engaged in guessing, but no syllable expressing
To the fowl whose fiery eyes now burned into my bosom's core;
75 This and more I sat divining, with my head at ease reclining
On the cushion's velvet lining that the lamplight gloated o'er,
But whose velvet violet lining with the lamplight gloating o'er,
            She shall press, ah, nevermore!

Then, methought, the air grew denser, perfumed from an unseen
      censer
80 Swung by angels whose faint foot-falls tinkled on the tufted floor.
"Wretch," I cried, "thy God hath lent thee—by these angels he hath
      sent thee
Respite—respite and nepenthe⁹ from thy memories of Lenore!
Quaff, oh quaff this kind nepenthe and forget this lost Lenore!"
            Quoth the raven, "Nevermore."

85 "Prophet!" said I, "thing of evil!—prophet still, if bird or devil!—
Whether Tempter sent, or whether tempest tossed thee here ashore,
Desolate, yet all undaunted, on this desert land enchanted—
On this home by Horror haunted—tell me truly, I implore—
Is there—*is* there balm in Gilead?¹—tell me—tell me, I implore!"
90   Quoth the raven, "Nevermore."

"Prophet!" said I, "thing of evil—prophet still, if bird or devil!
By that Heaven that bends above us—by that God we both adore—
Tell this soul with sorrow laden if, within the distant Aidenn,²
It shall clasp a sainted maiden whom the angels name Lenore—
95 Clasp a rare and radiant maiden whom the angels name Lenore."
            Quoth the raven, "Nevermore."

"Be that word our sign of parting, bird or fiend!" I shrieked upstarting—
"Get thee back into the tempest and the Night's Plutonian shore!
Leave no black plume as a token of that lie thy soul hath spoken!

9. Drug reputed by the Greeks to cause forgetfulness or sorrow (pronounced "ne-PEN-thee").
1. See Jeremiah 8.22.   2. Eden.

100 Leave my loneliness unbroken!—quit the bust above my door!
Take thy beak from out my heart, and take thy form from off my
     door!"
                    Quoth the raven, "Nevermore."

And the raven, never flitting, still is sitting, still is sitting
On the pallid bust of Pallas just above my chamber door;
105 And his eyes have all the seeming of a demon's that is dreaming,
And the lamp-light o'er him streaming throws his shadow on the
     floor;
And my soul from out that shadow that lies floating on the floor
                    Shall be lifted—nevermore!

                                                    1844

EZRA POUND
In a Station of the Metro[3]

The apparition of these faces in the crowd;
Petals on a wet, black bough.

                    1913

The River-Merchant's Wife: A Letter

(after Rihaku)[4]

While my hair was still cut straight across my forehead
I played about the front gate, pulling flowers.
You came by on bamboo stilts, playing horse,
You walked about my seat, playing with blue plums.
5 And we went on living in the village of Chokan:
Two small people, without dislike or suspicion.

At fourteen I married My Lord you.
I never laughed, being bashful.
Lowering my head, I looked at the wall.
10 Called to, a thousand times, I never looked back.

At fifteen I stopped scowling,
I desired my dust to be mingled with yours
For ever and for ever and for ever.
Why should I climb the look out?

3. Paris subway.
4. Japanese name for Li Po, an eighth-century Chinese poet. Pound's poem is based on one by
Li Po, which Pound read in translation.

15 At sixteen you departed,
You went into far Ku-to-yen, by the river of swirling eddies,
And you have been gone five months.
The monkeys make sorrowful noise overhead.

You dragged your feet when you went out.
20 By the gate now, the moss is grown, the different mosses,
Too deep to clear them away!

The leaves fall early this autumn, in wind.
The paired butterflies are already yellow with August
Over the grass in the West garden;
25 They hurt me. I grow older.
If you are coming down through the narrows of the river Kiang,
Please let me know beforehand,
And I will come out to meet you
      As far as Cho-fu-Sa.

1915

DUDLEY RANDALL
Ballad of Birmingham

(On the bombing of a church in Birmingham, Alabama, 1963)[5]

"Mother dear, may I go downtown
Instead of out to play,
And march the streets of Birmingham
In a Freedom March today?"

5 "No, baby, no, you may not go,
For the dogs are fierce and wild,
And clubs and hoses, guns and jails
Aren't good for a little child."

"But, mother, I won't be alone.
10 Other children will go with me,
And march the streets of Birmingham
To make our country free."

"No, baby, no, you may not go,
For I fear those guns will fire.

---

5. Just before Sunday services on September 15, 1963, a bomb exploded in Birmingham's 16th Street Baptist Church, killing four girls, aged eleven to fourteen, and injuring at least twenty-one other members of the predominantly African American congregation.

15 But you may go to church instead
And sing in the children's choir."

She has combed and brushed her night-dark hair,
And bathed rose petal sweet,
And drawn white gloves on her small brown hands,
20 And white shoes on her feet.

The mother smiled to know her child
Was in the sacred place,
But that smile was the last smile
To come upon her face.

25 For when she heard the explosion,
Her eyes grew wet and wild.
She raced through the streets of Birmingham
Calling for her child.

She clawed through bits of glass and brick,
30 Then lifted out a shoe.
"Oh, here's the shoe my baby wore,
But, baby, where are you?"

                                    1969

ADRIENNE RICH
At a Bach Concert

Coming by evening through the wintry city
We said that art is out of love with life.
Here we approach a love that is not pity.

This antique discipline, tenderly severe,
5 Renews belief in love yet masters feeling,
Asking of us a grace in what we bear.

Form is the ultimate gift that love can offer—
The vital union of necessity
With all that we desire, all that we suffer.

10 A too-compassionate art is half an art.
Only such proud restraining purity
Restores the else-betrayed, too-human heart.

                                    1951

History[6]

Should I simplify my life for you?
Don't ask how I began to love men.
Don't ask how I began to love women.
Remember the forties songs, the slowdance numbers
5 the small sex-filled gas-rationed Chevrolet?
Remember walking in the snow and who was gay?
Cigarette smoke of the movies, silver-and-gray
profiles, dreaming the dreams of he-and-she
breathing the dissolution of the wisping silver plume?
10 Dreaming that dream we leaned applying lipstick
by the gravestone's mirror when we found ourselves
playing in the cemetery. In Current Events she said
the war in Europe is over, the Allies
and she wore no lipstick have won the war[7]
15 and we raced screaming out of Sixth Period.

Dreaming that dream
we had to maze our ways through a wood
where lips were knives breasts razors and I hid
in the cage of my mind scribbling
20 *this map stops where it all begins*
into a red-and-black notebook.
Remember after the war when peace came down
as plenty for some and they said we were saved
in an eternal present and we knew the world could end?
25 —Remember after the war when peace rained down
on the winds from Hiroshima Nagasaki Utah Nevada?[8]
and the socialist queer Christian teacher jumps from the hotel
window?[9]
and L.G. saying *I want to sleep with you but not for sex*
and the red-and-black enamelled coffee-pot dripped slow through
the dark grounds
30 —appetite terror power tenderness
the long kiss in the stairwell the switch thrown

---

6. Poem 4 in Rich's sequence "Inscriptions."
7. World War II (1939–45), fought between the Allies or Allied powers (including France, Great Britain, the United States, and the Soviet Union) and the Axis powers (Germany, Japan, Italy).
8. Sites of atomic bomb explosions, the first two in Japan near the end of World War II, the last two at test sites in the American desert.
9. Allusion to the critic Francis Otto Matthiessen (1902–50), who taught at Harvard while Rich was an undergraduate there.

on two Jewish Communists[1] married to each other
the definitive crunch of glass at the end of the wedding?[2]
(When shall we learn, what should be clear as day,
35 *We cannot choose what we are free to love?)*[3]

1995

PERCY BYSSHE SHELLEY
Ozymandias[4]

I met a traveler from an antique land,
Who said—"Two vast and trunkless[5] legs of stone
Stand in the desert. . . . Near them, on the sand,
Half sunk a shattered visage lies, whose frown,
5 And wrinkled lip, and sneer of cold command,
Tell that its sculptor well those passions read
Which yet survive, stamped on these lifeless things,
The hand that mocked them, and the heart that fed;[6]
And on the pedestal, these words appear:
10 My name is Ozymandias, King of Kings,
Look on my Works, ye Mighty, and despair!
Nothing beside remains. Round the decay
Of that colossal Wreck, boundless and bare
The lone and level sands stretch far away."

1817   1818

WALLACE STEVENS
Anecdote of the Jar

I placed a jar in Tennessee,
And round it was, upon a hill.

1. Julius and Ethel Rosenberg, executed as spies by the United States in 1953.
2. At Jewish weddings the groom breaks a glass to commemorate the loss of Jerusalem and the Temple.
3. Opening lines of W. H. Auden's poem "Canzone" (1942).
4. Ancient Greek name for Egyptian pharaoh Ramses II (13th century BCE); according to one early Greek historian, Egypt's largest statue bore the inscription "I am Ozymandias king of kings; if anyone wishes to know what I am and where I lie, let him surpass me in some of my exploits."
5. Without a torso.
6. That is, because they are "stamped on" the statue's features, the king's passions outlive ("survive") both his "heart," which "fed" them, and the sculptor's "hand that mocked them," with *mock* meaning both imitated and satirized.

It made the slovenly wilderness
Surround that hill.

5 The wilderness rose up to it,
And sprawled around, no longer wild.
The jar was round upon the ground
And tall and of a port in air.

It took dominion everywhere.
10 The jar was gray and bare.
It did not give of bird or bush,
Like nothing else in Tennessee.

1923

The Emperor of Ice-Cream

Call the roller of big cigars,
The muscular one, and bid him whip
In kitchen cups concupiscent curds.[7]
Let the wenches dawdle in such dress
5 As they are used to wear, and let the boys
Bring flowers in last month's newspapers.
Let be be finale of seem.[8]
The only emperor is the emperor of ice-cream.

Take from the dresser of deal,
10 Lacking the three glass knobs, that sheet
On which she embroidered fantails[9] once
And spread it so as to cover her face.
If her horny feet protrude, they come
To show how cold she is, and dumb.
15 Let the lamp affix its beam.
The only emperor is the emperor of ice-cream.

1923

---

7. "The words 'concupiscent curds' have no genealogy; they are merely expressive: at least, I hope they are expressive. They express the concupiscence of life, but, by contrast with the things in relation to them in the poem, they express or accentuate life's destitution, and it is this that gives them something more than a cheap lustre" (Wallace Stevens, *Letters*. Edited by Holly Stevens, U of California P, 1996, p. 500).
8. "The true sense of Let be be the finale of seem is let being become the conclusion or denouement of appearing to be: in short, icecream is an absolute good. The poem is obviously not about icecream, but about being as distinguished from seeming to be" (*Letters* 341).
9. Fantail pigeons.

ALFRED, LORD TENNYSON
Tears, Idle Tears[1]

Tears, idle tears, I know not what they mean,
Tears from the depth of some divine despair
Rise in the heart, and gather to the eyes,
In looking on the happy autumn-fields,
5 And thinking of the days that are no more.

Fresh as the first beam glittering on a sail,
That brings our friends up from the underworld,
Sad as the last which reddens over one
That sinks with all we love below the verge;
10 So sad, so fresh, the days that are no more.

Ah, sad and strange as in dark summer dawns
The earliest pipe of half-awakened birds
To dying ears, when unto dying eyes
The casement slowly grows a glimmering square;
15 So sad, so strange, the days that are no more.

Dear as remembered kisses after death,
And sweet as those by hopeless fancy feigned
On lips that are for others; deep as love,
Deep as first love, and wild with all regret;
20 O Death in Life, the days that are no more!

1847

Ulysses[2]

It little profits that an idle king,
By this still hearth, among these barren crags,
Matched with an agèd wife,[3] mete and dole
Unequal laws unto a savage race,
5 That hoard, and sleep, and feed, and know not me.

I cannot rest from travel; I will drink
Life to the lees.[4] All times I have enjoyed
Greatly, have suffered greatly, both with those

1. One of the songs from Tennyson's book-length narrative poem *The Princess.*
2. After the Trojan War ended, Ulysses (or Odysseus), king of Ithaca and one of the war's Greek heroes, returned to his island home (line 34). Homer's account of the situation is in book 11 of *The Odyssey,* but Dante's account of Ulysses in canto 26 of the *Inferno* is the more immediate background of Tennyson's poem.   3. Penelope.
4. That is, all the way down to the bottom of the cup.

That loved me, and alone; on shore, and when
10 Through scudding drifts the rainy Hyades[5]
Vexed the dim sea. I am become a name;
For always roaming with a hungry heart
Much have I seen and known—cities of men
And manners, climates, councils, governments,
15 Myself not least, but honored of them all—
And drunk delight of battle with my peers,
Far on the ringing plains of windy Troy.
I am a part of all that I have met;
Yet all experience is an arch wherethrough
20 Gleams that untraveled world, whose margin fades
For ever and for ever when I move.
How dull it is to pause, to make an end,
To rust unburnished, not to shine in use!
As though to breathe were life. Life piled on life
25 Were all too little, and of one to me
Little remains; but every hour is saved
From that eternal silence, something more,
A bringer of new things; and vile it were
For some three suns to store and hoard myself,
30 And this gray spirit yearning in desire
To follow knowledge like a sinking star,
Beyond the utmost bound of human thought.

This is my son, mine own Telemachus,
To whom I leave the scepter and the isle—
35 Well-loved of me, discerning to fulfill
This labor, by slow prudence to make mild
A rugged people, and through soft degrees
Subdue them to the useful and the good.
Most blameless is he, centered in the sphere
40 Of common duties, decent not to fail
In offices of tenderness, and pay
Meet adoration to my household gods,
When I am gone. He works his work, I mine.

There lies the port; the vessel puffs her sail:
45 There gloom the dark, broad seas. My mariners,
Souls that have toiled, and wrought, and thought with me—
That ever with a frolic welcome took
The thunder and the sunshine, and opposed
Free hearts, free foreheads—you and I are old;

---

5. Group of stars believed to predict the rain when they rose at the same time as the sun.

50 Old age hath yet his honor and his toil.
Death closes all; but something ere the end,
Some work of noble note, may yet be done,
Not unbecoming men that strove with Gods.
The lights begin to twinkle from the rocks;
55 The long day wanes; the slow moon climbs; the deep
Moans round with many voices. Come, my friends,
'Tis not too late to seek a newer world.
Push off, and sitting well in order smite
The sounding furrows; for my purpose holds
60 To sail beyond the sunset, and the baths
Of all the western stars, until I die.
It may be that the gulfs will wash us down;[6]
It may be we shall touch the Happy Isles,[7]
And see the great Achilles, whom we knew.
65 Though much is taken, much abides; and though
We are not now that strength which in old days
Moved earth and heaven, that which we are, we are:
One equal temper of heroic hearts,
Made weak by time and fate, but strong in will
70 To strive, to seek, to find, and not to yield.

                                                    1833

DEREK WALCOTT
A Far Cry from Africa

A wind is ruffling the tawny pelt
Of Africa. Kikuyu,[8] quick as flies,
Batten upon the bloodstreams of the veldt.[9]
Corpses are scattered through a paradise.
5 Only the worm, colonel of carrion, cries:
"Waste no compassion on these separate dead!"
Statistics justify and scholars seize
The salients of colonial policy.
What is that to the white child hacked in bed?
10 To savages, expendable as Jews?

---

6. Beyond the Gulf of Gibraltar was supposed to lie a chasm that led to Hades, the underworld.
7. Elysium, the Islands of the Blessed, where heroes like Achilles (line 64) go after death.
8. East African tribe whose members, as Mau Mau fighters, conducted an eight-year insurrection against British colonial settlers in Kenya.
9. Open plains, neither cultivated nor thickly forested (Afrikaans).

Threshed out by beaters,[1] the long rushes break
In a white dust of ibises whose cries
Have wheeled since civilization's dawn
From the parched river or beast-teeming plain.
15 The violence of beast on beast is read
As natural law, but upright man
Seeks his divinity by inflicting pain.
Delirious as these worried beasts, his wars
Dance to the tightened carcass of a drum,
20 While he calls courage still that native dread
Of the white peace contracted by the dead.

Again brutish necessity wipes its hands
Upon the napkin of a dirty cause, again
A waste of our compassion, as with Spain,[2]
25 The gorilla wrestles with the superman.
I who am poisoned with the blood of both,
Where shall I turn, divided to the vein?
I who have cursed
The drunken officer of British rule, how choose
30 Between this Africa and the English tongue I love?
Betray them both, or give back what they give?
How can I face such slaughter and be cool?
How can I turn from Africa and live?

                                                1962

WALT WHITMAN
Facing West from California's Shores

Facing west, from California's shores,
Inquiring, tireless, seeking what is yet unfound,
I, a child, very old, over waves, towards the house of maternity,[3] the
    land of migrations, look afar,
Look off the shores of my Western sea, the circle almost circled:
5 For starting westward from Hindustan, from the vales of
        Kashmere,
From Asia, from the north, from the God, the sage, and the hero,

---

1. In big-game hunting, natives are hired to beat the brush, driving birds—such as ibises—and other animals into the open.
2. Spanish Civil War (1936–39), in which the Republican loyalists were supported politically by liberals in the West and militarily by Soviet Communists, and the Nationalist rebels by Nazi Germany and Fascist Italy.
3. Asia, as the supposed birthplace of the human race.

From the south, from the flowery peninsulas and the spice islands,
Long having wandered since, round the earth having wandered,
Now I face home again, very pleased and joyous;
10 (But where is what I started for, so long ago?
And why is it yet unfound?)

1860

A Noiseless Patient Spider

A noiseless patient spider,
I marked where on a little promontory it stood isolated,
Marked how to explore the vacant vast surrounding,
It launched forth filament, filament, filament, out of itself,
5 Ever unreeling them, ever tirelessly speeding them.

And you O my soul where you stand,
Surrounded, detached, in measureless oceans of space,
Ceaselessly musing, venturing, throwing, seeking the spheres to
      connect them,
Till the bridge you will need be formed, till the ductile anchor hold,
10 Till the gossamer thread you fling catch somewhere, O my soul.

1881

RICHARD WILBUR
Love Calls Us to the Things of This World

   The eyes open to a cry of pulleys,
And spirited from sleep, the astounded soul
Hangs for a moment bodiless and simple
As false dawn.
5   Outside the open window
The morning air is all awash with angels.

   Some are in bed-sheets, some are in blouses,
Some are in smocks: but truly there they are.
Now they are rising together in calm swells
10 Of halcyon[4] feeling, filling whatever they wear
With the deep joy of their impersonal breathing;
      Now they are flying in place, conveying
The terrible speed of their omnipresence, moving
And staying like white water; and now of a sudden
15 They swoon down into so rapt a quiet

---

4. Serene.

That nobody seems to be there.
                    The soul shrinks

    From all that it is about to remember,
    From the punctual rape of every blessed day,
20 And cries,
              "Oh, let there be nothing on earth but laundry,
    Nothing but rosy hands in the rising steam
    And clear dances done in the sight of heaven."

    Yet, as the sun acknowledges
25 With a warm look the world's hunks and colors,
    The soul descends once more in bitter love
    To accept the waking body, saying now
    In a changed voice as the man yawns and rises,
       "Bring them down from their ruddy gallows;
30 Let there be clean linen for the backs of thieves;
    Let lovers go fresh and sweet to be undone,
    And the heaviest nuns walk in a pure floating
    Of dark habits,
                keeping their difficult balance."

                                        1956

WILLIAM CARLOS WILLIAMS
The Dance

    In Brueghel's great picture, The Kermess,[5]
    the dancers go round, they go round and
    around, the squeal and the blare and the
    tweedle of bagpipes, a bugle and fiddles
5 tipping their bellies (round as the thick-
    sided glasses whose wash they impound)
    their hips and their bellies off balance
    to turn them. Kicking and rolling about
    the Fair Grounds, swinging their butts, those
10 shanks must be sound to bear up under such
    rollicking measures, prance as they dance
    in Brueghel's great picture, The Kermess.

                                        1944

5. A painting by Pieter Brueghel the Elder (1525?–69).

WILLIAM WORDSWORTH
[The world is too much with us]

The world is too much with us; late and soon,
Getting and spending, we lay waste our powers:
Little we see in Nature that is ours;
We have given our hearts away, a sordid boon![6]
5 This Sea that bares her bosom to the moon;
The winds that will be howling at all hours,
And are up-gathered now like sleeping flowers;
For this, for every thing, we are out of tune;
It moves us not.—Great God! I'd rather be
10 A Pagan suckled in a creed outworn;
So might I, standing on this pleasant lea,
Have glimpses that would make me less forlorn;
Have sight of Proteus rising from the sea;
Or hear old Triton[7] blow his wreathèd horn.

1807

[A slumber did my spirit seal][8]

A slumber did my spirit seal;
I had no human fears:
She seemed a thing that could not feel
The touch of earthly years.

5 No motion has she now, no force;
She neither hears nor sees;
Rolled round in earth's diurnal[9] course,
With rocks, and stones, and trees.

1799   1800

W. B. YEATS
All Things Can Tempt Me

All things can tempt me from this craft of verse:
One time it was a woman's face, or worse—

6. Gift. It is the act of giving the heart away that is sordid.
7. Sea deity, usually represented as blowing on a conch shell. *Proteus*: an old man of the sea who
(in *The Odyssey*) can assume a variety of shapes.
8. This poem is part of the same sequence of so-called Lucy poems that includes "She Dwelt
among the Untrodden Ways." 9. Daily.

The seeming needs of my fool-driven land;
Now nothing but comes readier to the hand
5 Than this accustomed toil. When I was young,
I had not given a penny for a song
Did not the poet sing it with such airs
That one believed he had a sword upstairs;
Yet would be now, could I but have my wish,
10 Colder and dumber and deafer than a fish.

                                                    1910

Easter 1916[1]

I have met them at close of day
Coming with vivid faces
From counter or desk among gray
Eighteenth-century houses.
5 I have passed with a nod of the head
Or polite meaningless words,
Or have lingered awhile and said
Polite meaningless words,
And thought before I had done
10 Of a mocking tale or a gibe
To please a companion
Around the fire at the club,
Being certain that they and I
But lived where motley is worn:
15 All changed, changed utterly:
A terrible beauty is born.

That woman's[2] days were spent
In ignorant good-will,
Her nights in argument
20 Until her voice grew shrill.
What voice more sweet than hers
When, young and beautiful,
She rode to harriers?

1. On Easter Monday, 1916, nationalist leaders proclaimed an Irish Republic. After a week of
street fighting, the British government put down the Easter Rebellion and executed a number
of prominent nationalists, including the four mentioned in lines 75–76, all of whom Yeats knew
personally.
2. Countess Constance Georgina Markiewicz (1868–1927), a beautiful and well-born young
woman from County Sligo who became a vigorous nationalist. At first she was condemned to
death, but her sentence was later commuted to life imprisonment, and she was granted amnesty
in 1917.

This man[3] had kept a school
25 And rode our wingèd horse,[4]
This other[5] his helper and friend
Was coming into his force;
He might have won fame in the end,
So sensitive his nature seemed,
30 So daring and sweet his thought.
This other man[6] I had dreamed
A drunken, vainglorious lout.
He had done most bitter wrong
To some who are near my heart,
35 Yet I number him in the song;
He, too, has resigned his part
In the casual comedy;
He, too, has been changed in his turn,
Transformed utterly:
40 A terrible beauty is born.

Hearts with one purpose alone
Through summer and winter seem
Enchanted to a stone
To trouble the living stream.
45 The horse that comes from the road,
The rider, the birds that range
From cloud to tumbling cloud,
Minute by minute they change;
A shadow of cloud on the stream
50 Changes minute by minute;
A horse-hoof slides on the brim,
And a horse plashes within it;
The long-legged moor-hens dive,
And hens to moor-cocks call;
55 Minute by minute they live:
The stone's in the midst of all.

Too long a sacrifice
Can make a stone of the heart.
O when may it suffice?

3. Patrick Pearse (1879–1916), who led the assault on the Dublin Post Office, from which the proclamation of a republic was issued. A schoolmaster by profession, he had championed the restoration of the Gaelic language in Ireland and was an active political writer and poet.
4. The mythological Pegasus, a traditional symbol of poetic inspiration.
5. Thomas MacDonagh (1878–1916), also a writer and teacher.
6. Major John MacBride (1868–1916), who had married Yeats's beloved Maud Gonne in 1903 but separated from her two years later.

60 That is Heaven's part, our part
    To murmur name upon name,
    As a mother names her child
    When sleep at last has come
    On limbs that had run wild.
65 What is it but nightfall?
    No, no, not night but death;
    Was it needless death after all?
    For England may keep faith[7]
    For all that is done and said.
70 We know their dream; enough
    To know they dreamed and are dead;
    And what if excess of love
    Bewildered them till they died?
    I write it out in a verse—
75 MacDonagh and MacBride
    And Connolly[8] and Pearse
    Now and in time to be,
    Wherever green is worn,
    Are changed, changed utterly;
80 A terrible beauty is born.

                                    1916

The Lake Isle of Innisfree[9]

I will arise and go now, and go to Innisfree,
And a small cabin build there, of clay and wattles made,
Nine bean-rows will I have there, a hive for the honey-bee,
And live alone in the bee-loud glade.

5 And I shall have some peace there, for peace comes dropping slow,
Dropping from the veils of the morning to where the cricket sings;
There midnight's all a glimmer, and noon a purple glow,
And evening full of the linnet's wings.

I will arise and go now, for always night and day
10 I hear lake water lapping with low sounds by the shore;
While I stand on the roadway, or on the pavements grey,
I hear it in the deep heart's core.

                                    1890

7. Before the uprising, the English had promised eventual home rule to Ireland.
8. James Connolly (1868–1916), the leader of the Easter uprising.
9. Island in Lough Gill, County Sligo, Ireland.

Leda and the Swan[1]

A sudden blow: the great wings beating still
Above the staggering girl, her thighs caressed
By the dark webs, her nape caught in his bill,
He holds her helpless breast upon his breast.

5 How can those terrified vague fingers push
The feathered glory from her loosening thighs?
And how can body, laid in that white rush,
But feel the strange heart beating where it lies?

A shudder in the loins engenders there
10 The broken wall, the burning roof and tower
And Agamemnon dead.
           Being so caught up,
So mastered by the brute blood of the air,
Did she put on his knowledge with his power
Before the indifferent beak could let her drop?

                    1923

The Second Coming[2]

Turning and turning in the widening gyre[3]
The falcon cannot hear the falconer;
Things fall apart; the center cannot hold;
Mere anarchy is loosed upon the world,
5 The blood-dimmed tide is loosed, and everywhere
The ceremony of innocence is drowned;
The best lack all conviction, while the worst
Are full of passionate intensity.

---

1. According to Greek myth, Zeus took the form of a swan to rape Leda, who became the mother of Helen of Troy; of Castor; and also of Clytemnestra, Agamemnon's wife and murderer. Helen's abduction from her husband, Menelaus, brother of Agamemnon, began the Trojan War (line 10). Yeats described the visit of Zeus to Leda as an annunciation like that to Mary (see Luke 1.26–38); "I imagine the annunciation that founded Greece as made to Leda" (*A Vision*).
2. The Second Coming of Christ, according to Matthew 24.29–44, will follow a time of "tribulation." In *A Vision* (1937), Yeats describes his view of history as dependent on cycles of about two thousand years: The birth of Christ had ended the cycle of Greco-Roman civilization, and now the Christian cycle seemed near an end, to be followed by an antithetical cycle, ominous in its portents.
3. Literally, the widening spiral of a falcon's flight. "Gyre" is Yeats's term for a cycle of history, which he diagrammed as a series of interpenetrating cones.

Surely some revelation is at hand;
10 Surely the Second Coming is at hand.
The Second Coming! Hardly are those words out
When a vast image out of *Spiritus Mundi*[4]
Troubles my sight: somewhere in sands of the desert
A shape with lion body and the head of a man,
15 A gaze blank and pitiless as the sun,
Is moving its slow thighs, while all about it
Reel shadows of the indignant desert birds.[5]
The darkness drops again; but now I know
That twenty centuries of stony sleep
20 Were vexed to nightmare by a rocking cradle,
And what rough beast, its hour come round at last,
Slouches towards Bethlehem to be born?

                                          January 1919

---

4. Or *Anima Mundi* (Latin), the spirit or soul of the world. Yeats considered this universal consciousness or memory a fund from which poets drew their images and symbols.
5. Yeats later wrote of the "brazen winged beast [. . .] described in my poem *The Second Coming*" as "associated with laughing, ecstatic destruction."

Biographical Sketches: Poets

Sketches are included for select poets.

W. H. AUDEN (1907–73)

Wystan Hugh Auden was born in York, England, to a medical officer and a nurse. Intending at first to become a scientist, Auden studied at Oxford, where he became the center of the "Oxford Group" of poets and leftist intellectuals. His travels during the 1930s led him to Germany, Iceland, China, Spain (where he was an ambulance driver in the civil war), and the United States (where he taught at various universities and, in 1946, became a naturalized citizen). A prolific writer of poems, plays, essays, and criticism, Auden won the Pulitzer Prize in 1948 for his collection of poems *The Age of Anxiety*, set in a New York City bar. Late in life he returned to Christ Church College, Oxford, where he was writer in residence. He is regarded as a masterly poet of political and intellectual conscience as well as one of the twentieth century's greatest lyric craftsmen.

BASHŌ (1644–94)

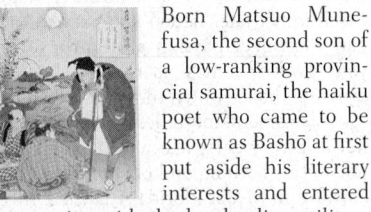

Born Matsuo Munefusa, the second son of a low-ranking provincial samurai, the haiku poet who came to be known as Bashō at first put aside his literary interests and entered into service with the local ruling military house. In 1666, following the feudal lord's death, Bashō left for Edo (now Tokyo), the military capital of the shogun's new government, to pursue a career as a professional poet. He supported himself as a teacher and editor of other people's poetry but ultimately developed a following and a sizable group of students. A seasoned traveler, Bashō maintained an austere existence on the road and at home, casting himself in travel narratives such as *Oku no hosomichi* (*The Narrow Road to the Interior*, 1694) as a pilgrim devoted to nature and Zen.

ELIZABETH BISHOP (1911–79)

Born in Worcester, Massachusetts, Elizabeth Bishop endured the death of her father before she was a year old and the institutionalization of her mother four years later. Bishop was raised first by her maternal grandmother in Nova Scotia, then by her paternal grandparents back in Worcester. At Vassar College she met the poet Marianne Moore, who encouraged her to give up plans for medical school and pursue a career in poetry. Bishop traveled through Canada, Europe, and South America, finally settling in Rio de Janeiro, where she lived for nearly twenty years. Her four volumes of poetry are *North and South* (1946); *A Cold Spring* (1955), which won the Pulitzer Prize; *Questions of Travel* (1965); and *Geography III* (1976), which won the National Book Critics' Circle Award.

WILLIAM BLAKE (1757–1828)

The son of a London haberdasher and his wife, William Blake studied drawing at ten and at fourteen was apprenticed to an engraver for seven years. After a first book of poems, *Poetical Sketches* (1783), he began experimenting with what he called "illuminated printing"—the words and pictures of each page were engraved in relief on copper, which was used to print sheets that were then partly colored by hand—a laborious and time-consuming process that resulted in books of singular beauty, no two of which are exactly alike. His great *Songs of Innocence and of Experience* (1794) were produced in this manner, as were his increasingly mythic and prophetic books, including *The Marriage of Heaven and Hell* (1793), *The Four Zoas* (1803), *Milton* (1804), and *Jerusalem* (1809). Blake devoted his later life to pictorial art, illustrating *The Canterbury Tales*, the Book of Job, and *The Divine Comedy*, on which he was hard at work when he died.

GWENDOLYN BROOKS (1917–2000)

Gwendolyn Brooks was born in Topeka, Kansas, and raised in Chicago, where she began writing poetry at the age of seven, and where she graduated from Wilson Junior College in 1936. Shortly after beginning her formal study of modern poetry at Chicago's Southside Community Art Center, Brooks produced her first book of poems, *A Street in Bronzeville* (1945). With her second volume, *Annie Allen* (1949), she became the first African American to win the Pulitzer Prize. Though her early work focused on what Langston Hughes called the "ordinary aspects of black life," during the mid-1960s she devoted her poetry to raising African American consciousness and to social activism. In 1968, she was named the Poet Laureate of Illinois; from 1985 to 1986, she became the first black woman ever to serve as poetry consultant to the Library of Congress.

ROBERT BROWNING (1812–89)

Born in London, Robert Browning attended London University but was largely self-educated, learning Latin, Greek, French, and Italian by the time he was fourteen. He was an accomplished but little-known poet and playwright when he began courting the already famous poet Elizabeth Barrett. After they eloped to Italy in 1846, the Brownings enjoyed a period of happiness during which they produced most of their best-known work. Following Elizabeth's death in 1861, Robert returned to England with their son and for the rest of his life enjoyed great literary and social success. His major collections are *Men and Women* (1855), dedicated to his wife, and *Dramatis Personae* (1864), which contains some of his finest dramatic monologues. Lionized as one of England's greatest poets by the time of his death, Browning is buried in Poets' Corner at London's Westminster Abbey.

JUDITH ORTIZ COFER (b. 1952)

Born in Hormigueros, Puerto Rico, Judith Ortiz Cofer just two years later moved with her family, first to New Jersey and later to Georgia, experiences that would inspire much of her later fiction and poetry. "How can you inject passion and purpose into your work if it has no roots?" she asks, avowing that her own roots include a long line of women storytellers who "infected" her at a very early age with the desire to tell stories both on and off the page. After earning an MA at Florida Atlantic University (1977), Ortiz Cofer returned to Georgia, where she currently serves as professor emerita at the University of Georgia.

Among her numerous publications are *The Line of the Sun* (1989), a novel in which a young girl relates the history of her ne'er-do-well uncle's emigration from Puerto Rico; the poetry collection *A Love Story Beginning in Spanish* (2005); *The Latin Deli: Prose and Poetry* (1993); and *In the Cruel Country: Notes for an Elegy* (2015).

SAMUEL TAYLOR COLERIDGE (1772–1834)

Born in the small town of Ottery St. Mary in rural Devonshire, England, Samuel Taylor Coleridge is among the greatest and most original of the nineteenth-century Romantic poets. He wrote three of the most haunting and powerful poems in English—*The Rime of the Ancient Mariner* (1798), *Christabel* (1816), and "Kubla Khan" (1816)—as well as immensely influential literary criticism and a treatise on biology. In 1795, in the midst of a failed experiment to establish a "Pantisocracy" (his form of ideal community), he met William Wordsworth, and in 1798 they jointly published their enormously influential *Lyrical Ballads*. Coleridge's physical ailments, addiction to opium, and profound sense of despair made his life difficult and tumultuous and certainly affected his work. Still, he remains a central figure in English literature.

BILLY COLLINS (b. 1941)

Sometimes described as "the most popular poet in America," Billy Collins enjoys the sort of celebrity status usually reserved for Hollywood actors like his friend Bill Murray, reportedly signing six-figure contracts for books-in-progress. As U.S. Poet Laureate (2001–03), however, Collins both refused to publish and hence profit from his poem "The Names," written in honor of the victims of the 9/11 attacks, and initiated philanthropic projects like *Poetry 180*, which aims at exciting high-schoolers' interest in poetry. Born in New York City, Collins credits his mother with awakening his love of poetry and teaching him the importance of "reading poetry as poetry [. . .] as a set of sounds set to rhythm"—lessons reinforced by his studies at the College of Holy Cross and the University of California–Riverside. Though Collins began publishing his work in the 1980s, it wasn't until 1991 that his book *Questions About Angels* thrust him into the spotlight. Since that time, he has published numerous collections, including *The Art of Drowning* (1995), *Taking off Emily Dickinson's Clothes* (2000), *Ballistics* (2008), and *Aimless Love* (2013). By his own account "unashamedly" "suburban," "domestic," and "middle class," Collins's deceptively simple poetry uses the material of the everyday to, as one reader put it, "help us feel the mystery of being alive."

MARTHA COLLINS (b. 1940)

Nebraska-born poet, teacher, translator, and editor Martha Collins grew up in Des Moines, Iowa, the late and only child of a pharmacist who wanted her to be a doctor and a pianist who fostered the love of music that still, she says, ensures "I usually hear the music of a poem before I begin to understand it." In the process of earning three degrees in English literature—a Stanford BA (1962) and an MA and PhD from the University of Iowa (1965, 1971)—Collins discovered, in her words, "that I didn't want to write about writers—I wanted to be one." Citing as inspirations poets as diverse as Wallace Stevens, Gwendolyn Brooks, John Ashbery, and Emily Dickinson—whom, she says, "taught me to care about everything I see," as well as "every word I write"—Collins published her first poetry collection, *The Catastrophe of Rainbows*, in 1985. In addition to later collections such as *The Arrangement of Space* (1991), *Some Things Words Can Do* (1998), *White Papers* (2012), and *Day unto Day* (2014), Collins's award-winning body of work includes both three books of poetry translated from the Vietnamese and *Blue Front* (2006), a book-length poem inspired by a lynching her father witnessed in Cairo, Illinois when he was only five. After over thirty years at the University of Massachusetts–Boston, where she founded and codirected the Creative Writing program, Collins returned to the Midwest in 1997, serving until 2007 as Pauline Delaney Professor of Creative Writing at Oberlin College in Ohio, where she still lives.

COUNTEE CULLEN (1903–46)

During his own lifetime, Countee Cullen was the most celebrated and honored poet of the Harlem Renaissance, and he claimed New York City as his birthplace. In fact, he may have been born in Louisville, Kentucky, and the circumstances of his childhood adoption by the Reverend Frederick Cullen remain obscure. It is certain, though, that the poet received a good education at New York's DeWitt Clinton High School and then New York University. After receiving his MA at Harvard, Cullen returned to New York in 1926 and soon established himself as the leading figure in the Harlem literary world, winning numerous awards for his poetry and editing the influential monthly column "The Dark Tower" for *Opportunity: Journal of Negro Life*. A playwright, novelist, translator, and anthologist, Cullen is best remembered as a poet; his work has been collected in the volume *My Soul's High Song: The Collected Writings of Countee Cullen, Voice of the Harlem Renaissance* (1991).

E. E. CUMMINGS (1894–1962)

Born in Cambridge, Massachusetts, the son of a Congregationalist minister, Edward Estlin Cummings attended Harvard University, where he wrote poetry in the Pre-Raphaelite and Metaphysical traditions. He joined the ambulance corps in France the day after the United States entered World War I but was imprisoned by the French due to his outspoken opposition to the war; he transmuted the experience into his first literary success, the novel *The Enormous Room* (1922). After the war, Cummings established himself as a poet and artist in New York City's Greenwich Village, made frequent trips to France and New Hampshire, and showed little interest in wealth or his growing celebrity. His variety of Modernism was distinguished by its playfulness, its formal experimentation, its lyrical directness, and above all its celebration of the individual.

EMILY DICKINSON (1830–86)

From childhood on, Emily Dickinson led a sequestered and obscure life. Yet her verse has traveled far beyond the cultured yet relatively circumscribed environment in which she lived: her room, her father's house, her family, a few close friends, and the small town of Amherst, Massachusetts. Indeed, along with Walt Whitman, her far more public contemporary, she all but invented American poetry. Born in Amherst, the daughter of a respected lawyer whom she revered ("His heart was pure and terrible," she once wrote), Dickinson studied for less than a year at the Mount Holyoke Female Seminary, returning permanently to her family home. She became more and more reclusive, dressing only in white, seeing no visitors, yet working ceaselessly at her poems—nearly eighteen hundred in all, only a few of which were published during her lifetime. After her death, her sister Lavinia discovered the rest in a trunk, neatly bound into packets with blue ribbons—among the most important bodies of work in all of American literature.

JOHN DONNE (1572–1631)

The first and greatest of the English writers who came to be known as the Metaphysical poets, John Donne wrote in a revolutionary style that combined highly intellectual conceits with complex, compressed phrasing. Born into an old Roman Catholic family at a time when Catholics were subject to constant harassment, Donne quietly abandoned his religion and had a promising legal career until a politically disastrous marriage ruined his worldly hopes. He struggled for years to support a large family; impoverished and despairing, he even wrote a treatise (*Biathanatos*) on the lawfulness of suicide. King James (who had ambitions for him as a preacher) eventually pressured Donne to take Anglican orders in 1615, and Donne became one of the great sermonizers of his day, rising to the position of dean of St. Paul's Cathedral in 1621. Donne's private devotions ("Meditations") were published in 1624, and he continued to write poetry until a few years before his death.

PAUL LAURENCE DUNBAR (1872–1906)

The son of former slaves, Paul Laurence Dunbar was born in Dayton, Ohio. He attended a white high school, where he showed an early talent for writing and was elected class president. Unable to afford further education, he then worked as an elevator operator, writing poems and newspaper articles in his spare time. Dunbar took out a loan to subsidize the printing of his first book, *Oak and Ivy* (1893), but with the publication of *Majors and Minors* (1895) and *Lyrics of Lowly Life* (1896), his growing reputation enabled him to support himself by writing and lecturing. Though acclaimed during his lifetime for his lyrical use of rural black dialect in volumes such as *Candle-Lightin'*

Time (1902), Dunbar was later criticized for adopting "white" literary conventions and accused of pandering to racist images of slaves and ex-slaves. He wrote novels and short stories in addition to poetry and dealt frankly with racial injustice in works such as *The Sport of the Gods* (1903) and *The Fourth of July and Race Outrages* (1903).

MARTÍN ESPADA (b. 1957)

At the age of thirteen, Martín Espada moved with his family to a Long Island neighborhood where they were the only Puerto Ricans, an experience he describes as "more traumatic than anything that ever happened to me on the so-called mean streets" of the racially diverse Brooklyn neighborhood he previously called home. By working everywhere from a bar and a ballpark to a primate lab and a transient hotel, Espada put himself through college, graduating from the University of Wisconsin–Madison with a BA in history, with a focus on Latin America. After earning a law degree at Northeastern University, in Boston, he went to work as a lawyer, specializing first in bilingual education, later in housing law. From age twenty, however, Espada was also writing poetry, inspired initially by a family friend's gift of both an anthology of Latin American revolutionary poetry and the prediction that "Tri tambien seras poeta" ("You will also become a poet"). Featuring barrio photos taken by his father, a community activist, Espada's first collection, *The Immigrant Iceboy's Bolero*, appeared in 1982. But it was his third, prize-winning book, *Rebellion Is the Circle of a Lover's Hand* (1990), that led the *New York Times* to predict he would be "the Latino poet of his generation." In the years since, Espada has done much to earn that title, securing a professorship at the University of Massachusetts–Amherst (in 1993) and publishing not only poetry collections ranging from *City of Coughing and Dead Radiators* (1993) to *The Republic of Poetry* (2006, a finalist for the Pulitzer) but also books of essays including *Zapata's Disciple* (1998), anthologies of Latino and Chicano poetry, and translations. What drives all that work, says Espada, is the same commitment he had as a lawyer: "to speak on behalf of" all those who lack not the ability but the "opportunity" to "speak for themselves."

ROBERT FROST (1874–1963)

Though his poetry identifies Frost with rural New England, he was born and lived to the age of eleven in San Francisco. Moving to New England after his father's death, Frost studied classics in high school, entered and dropped out of both Dartmouth and Harvard, and spent difficult years as an unrecognized poet before his first book, *A Boy's Will* (1913), was accepted and published in England. Frost's character was full of contradiction—he held "that we get forward as much by hating as by loving"—yet by the end of his long life he was one of the most honored poets of his time, as well as the most widely read. In 1961, two years before his death, he was invited to read a poem at John F. Kennedy's presidential inauguration ceremony. Frost's poems—masterfully crafted, sometimes deceptively simple—are collected in *The Poetry of Robert Frost* (1969).

ANGELINA GRIMKÉ (1880–1958)

Born in Boston, Angelina Grimké was the descendent of black slaves, white slaveholders, free blacks, and prominent white abolitionists, including her namesake, Angelina Weld Grimké. As a child, Angelina was abandoned by her white mother, whose middle-class family disapproved of her marriage to Archibald Grimké, a biracial lawyer and author who eventually became vice president of the NAACP. Grimké graduated from the Boston Normal School of Gymnastics in 1902 and then moved with her father to Washington, D.C., where she worked as a teacher and began to write poetry, essays, short stories, and plays. By the 1920s, she was publishing her work in the leading journals and anthologies of the Harlem Renaissance—*The Crisis, Opportunity,* Alain Locke's *The New Negro* (1925), Countee Cullen's *Caroling Dusk* (1927), and Robert Kerlin's *Negro Poets and Their Poems* (1928). Much of her finest writing can be found in *Selected Works of Angelina Weld Grimké* (1991).

ROBERT HAYDEN (1913–80)

Born in a Detroit ghetto, Asa Sheffey became "Robert Hayden" at eighteen months, when he was unofficially adopted by the neighbors who would raise him and whom he would remember in poems such as "Those Winter Sundays." Inspired by the Harlem Renaissance writers he discovered as a teenager, Hayden published his first poem in 1931. Severely nearsighted, he attended Detroit City College (1932–36), thanks only to state rehabilitation grants, and worked for the Federal Writers Project (1936–39), before studying with W. H. Auden at the University of Michigan (MA, 1944). Becoming "a poet who teaches [. . .] so that he can write a poem or two now and then," Hayden held professorships at historically black Fisk University (1946–69) and at the University of Michigan (1969–80). International acclaim came late: In 1966, Langston Hughes and seven other judges unanimously awarded Hayden the Grand Prize for Poetry at the First World Festival of Negro Arts in Senegal, and in 1976 he became the first African American appointed to the post now known as U.S. Poet Laureate. Like his masterpiece "Middle Passage" (1962), much of Hayden's poetry aims, he said, to "correct the distortions of Afro-American history." Yet he passionately insisted that he was not a "black artist" but an American one. Today he is widely and rightly regarded as among the very best of both.

SEAMUS HEANEY (1939–2013)

Considered "the most important Irish poet since Yeats," 1995 Nobel Prize–winner Seamus Heaney grew up with his eight siblings on Mossbawm Farm in rural County Derry, Northern Ireland. At twelve, however, scholarships took Heaney first to St. Columb's College and then Queen's University, Belfast, where he studied Irish, Latin, and Old English. Here, too, he discovered the poetry of authors such as Ted Hughes, Patrick Kavanagh, and Robert Frost, which, he said, first taught him to "trust" in the value of that "local" childhood experience that he once "considered archaic and irrelevant to 'the modern world.'" Rural life and labor, as well as the relationship between past and present, the "archaic" and the "modern," loom large from his earliest collection, *Death of a Naturalist* (1966), to much later ones such as *District and Circle* (2006). Most famous, perhaps, is *North* (1975), especially its sequence of poems inspired by both the ancient, yet somehow ageless, corpses discovered in Irish and Scandinavian bogs, and also by the increasingly violent conflict between Protestants and Catholics in Northern Ireland. Having earned virtually all of the highest honors that a contemporary poet could, Heaney also won acclaim both as a versatile and creative translator, most famously of *Beowulf* (2000) and *Antigone* (*The Burial at Thebes*, 2004), and as an essayist; his *Finders Keepers: Selected Prose, 1971–2001* (2002) won the Truman Capote Award for Literary Criticism, the largest annual prize of its kind. After teaching at Harvard from 1985 until 2006, Heaney lived in Dublin until his death.

GERARD MANLEY HOPKINS (1844–89)

Born the eldest of eight children of a marine-insurance adjuster and his wife, Gerard Manley Hopkins attended Oxford, where his ambition was to become a painter—until, at the age of twenty-two, he converted to Roman Catholicism and burned all his early poetry as too worldly. Not until after his seminary training and ordination as a Jesuit priest, in 1877, did he resume writing poetry, though he made few attempts to publish his verse, which many of his contemporaries found nearly incomprehensible. Near the end of his life, Hopkins was appointed professor of Greek at University College, Dublin, where—out of place, deeply depressed, and all but unknown—he died of typhoid. His poetry, collected and published by his friends, has been championed by modern poets, who admire its controlled tension, strong rhythm, and sheer exuberance.

LANGSTON HUGHES (1902–67)

Born in Joplin, Missouri, Langston Hughes was raised mainly by his maternal grandmother, though he lived intermittently with each of his parents. He studied at Columbia University but left to travel and work at a variety of jobs. Having already published poems in periodicals, anthologies, and his own first collection, *The Weary Blues* (1926), he graduated from Lincoln University; published a successful novel, *Not without Laughter* (1930); and became a major writer in the Harlem Renaissance. During the 1930s, he became involved in radical politics and traveled the world as a correspondent and columnist; during the 1950s, though, the FBI classified him as a security risk and limited his ability to travel. In addition to poems and novels, he wrote essays, plays, screenplays, and an autobiography; he also edited anthologies of literature and folklore.

JOHN KEATS (1795–1821)

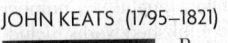

Because John Keats was the son of a London livery stable owner and his wife, reviewers would later disparage him as a working-class "Cockney poet." At fifteen he was apprenticed to a surgeon, and at twenty-one he became a licensed pharmacist—in the same year that his first two published poems, including the sonnet "On First Looking into Chapman's Homer," appeared in *The Examiner*, a journal edited by the critic and poet Leigh Hunt. Hunt introduced Keats to such literary figures as the poet Percy Bysshe Shelley and helped him publish his *Poems by John Keats* (1817). When his second book, the long poem *Endymion* (1818), was fiercely attacked by critics, Keats, suffering from a steadily worsening case of tuberculosis, knew that he would not live to realize his poetic promise. In July 1820, he published *Lamia, Isabella, The Eve of St. Agnes; and Other Poems*, which contained the poignant "To Autumn" and three other great odes: "Ode on a Grecian Urn," "Ode on Melancholy," and "Ode to a Nightingale"; early the next year, he died in Rome. In the years after Keats's death, his letters became almost as famous as his poetry.

ETHERIDGE KNIGHT (1931–91)

A native of Corinth, Mississippi, Etheridge Knight spent much of his adolescence carousing in pool halls, bars, and juke joints, developing a skillful oratorical style in an environment that prized verbal agility. During this time, he also became addicted to narcotics. He served in the U.S. Army from 1947 to 1951; in 1960 he was sentenced to eight years in prison for robbery. At the Indiana State Prison in Michigan City, he began to write poetry and in 1968 published his first collection, *Poems from Prison*. After his release, Knight joined the Black Arts movement, taught at a number of universities, and published works including *Black Voices from Prison* (1970), *Belly Song and Other Poems* (1973), and *Born of a Woman* (1980).

PHILIP LARKIN (1922–85)

Postwar England's most widely known and popular poet, so-called laureate of the common man Philip Larkin endured what he later described as a boring childhood as the second, belated, rather shy—because also nearsighted and stuttering—child of Coventry's city treasurer. Exempted from service in World War II because of his eyesight, Larkin graduated from Oxford in 1943 and became a librarian, mainly at Hull, where he headed the university library for thirty years (1955–85). Larkin credited his rediscovery of Thomas Hardy's poetry with "cur[ing]" him of the Yeatsian "Celtic fever" of his first collection, *The North Ship* (1945), and helping him to develop the mature style debuted in his second, *The Less Deceived* (1955). This critically acclaimed book made Larkin the undisputed leading light of "the Movement," a group of young poets who rejected the enigmatic, allusive, and—in their eyes—elitist modernism of T. S. Eliot and Ezra Pound in favor of a more straightforward and robust, if also skeptical and ironic, style. Notoriously publicity-averse, Larkin declined the position of Poet Laureate of the United Kingdom just a year before his death. In his lifetime, he published only two other volumes of verse, *The Whitsun Weddings* (1964) and *High Windows* (1974); two novels, *Jill* (1946) and *A Girl in Winter* (1947); *All What Jazz* (1970), a collection of jazz reviews originally written for the *Daily Telegraph*; and the best-selling *Required Writing: Miscellaneous Pieces 1955–1982* (1983). Since his death, Larkin has become a more controversial figure, thanks less to the previously unpublished work included in *Collected Poems* (1988) than to the publication of both his *Selected Letters* (1992) and Andrew Motion's revealing biography, *Philip Larkin: A Writer's Life* (1993).

CLAUDE MCKAY (1889–1948)

Festus Claudius McKay was born and raised in Sunny Ville, Clarendon Parish, Jamaica, the youngest of eleven children. He worked as a wheelwright and cabinetmaker, then briefly as a police constable, before writing and publishing two books of poetry in Jamaican dialect. In 1912, he emigrated to the United States, where he attended Booker T. Washington's Tuskegee Institute in Alabama and studied agricultural science at Kansas State College before moving to New York City. McKay supported himself through various jobs while becoming a prominent literary and political figure. The oldest Harlem Renaissance writer, McKay was also the first to publish, with the poetry collection *Harlem Shadows* (1922). His other works include the novels *Home to Harlem* (1928) and *Banana Bottom* (1933) and his autobiography, *A Long Way from Home* (1937).

EDNA ST. VINCENT MILLAY (1892–1950)

Born in Rockland, Maine, Edna St. Vincent Millay published her first poem at twenty, her first poetry collection at twenty-five. After graduating from Vassar College, she moved to New York City's Greenwich Village, where she both gained a reputation as a brilliant poet and became notorious for her bohemian life and her association with prominent artists, writers, and radicals. In 1923, she won the Pulitzer Prize for her collection *The Ballad of the Harp-Weaver*; in 1925, growing weary of fame, she and her husband moved to Austerlitz, New York, where she lived for the rest of her life. Although her work fell out of favor with mid-twentieth-century Modernists, who rejected her formalism as old-fashioned, her poetry—witty, acerbic, and superbly crafted—has found many new admirers today.

PAT MORA (b. 1942)

Born to Mexican American parents in El Paso, Texas, Pat Mora earned a BA and an MA from the University of Texas at El Paso. She has been a consultant on U.S.-Mexico youth exchanges; a museum director and administrator at her alma mater; and a teacher of English at all levels. Her poetry—collected in *Chants* (1985), *Borders* (1986), *Communion* (1991), *Agua Santa* (1995), *Aunt Carmen's Book of Practical Saints* (1997), and *Adobe Odes* (2006)—reflects and addresses her Chicana and southwestern background. Mora's other publications include *Nepantla: Essays from the Land in the Middle* (1993); a family memoir, *House of Houses* (1997); and many works for children and young adults.

SHARON OLDS (b. 1942)

Born in San Francisco; raised in Berkeley by fiercely religious, yet troubled parents; and educated at Stanford (BA, 1964) and Columbia (PhD, 1972) universities (where she wrote a dissertation on Ralph Waldo Emerson), poet Sharon Olds was thirty-seven when she published her first book of poetry, *Satan Says*, in 1981. Since then, she has come to rank as one of America's most important living poets, garnering National Book Critics' Circle Awards both for her 1984 collection *The Dead and the Living* and for *Strike Spark: Selected Poems* (2002). In 2013, she became the first woman to win the T.S. Eliot Prize for Poetry, for *Stag's Leap*, a collection that also earned a Pulitzer. Like the work of two writers to whom Olds is often compared, Walt Whitman and Sylvia Plath, however, hers has consistently provoked controversy, thanks mainly to its unflinching attention to, and distinctly female perspective on, the pleasures and pains of both the human body and the family, as well as emotional and literal violence. *The Dead and the Living* is divided between

"Poems for the Living," about the poet's experience as daughter and mother, and "Poems for the Dead," about the victims of international conflicts; *The Father* (1992) chronicles her father's death (from cancer), *One Secret Thing* (2008), her mother's. *Stag's Leap* (2013) deals with the disintegration of her 32-year marriage. As famous for her reticence off the page as for her candor on it, Olds teaches creative writing both at New York University and in a program for the severely disabled that she founded at NYU's Goldwater Hospital.

WILFRED OWEN (1893–1918)

Born in Oswestry, Shropshire, England, Wilfred Owen left school in 1911, having failed to win a scholarship to London University. He served as assistant to a vicar in Oxfordshire until 1913, when he left to teach English at a Berlitz school in Bordeaux. In 1915, Owen returned to England to enlist in the army and was sent to the front lines in France. Suffering from shell shock two years later, he was evacuated to Craiglockhart War Hospital, where he met the poets Siegfried Sassoon and Robert Graves. Five of Owen's poems were published in 1918, the year he returned to combat; he was killed one week before the signing of the armistice. His poems, which portray the horror of trench warfare and satirize the unthinking patriotism of those who cheered the war from their armchairs, are collected in the two-volume *Complete Poems and Fragments* (1983).

DOROTHY PARKER (1893–1967)

Born in West End, New Jersey, Dorothy Rothschild worked for both *Vogue* and *Vanity Fair* magazines before becoming a freelance writer. In 1917, she married Edwin Pond Parker II, whom she divorced in 1928. Her first book of verse, *Enough Rope* (1926), was a best-seller and was followed by *Sunset Gun* (1928), *Death and Taxes* (1931), and *Collected Poems: Not So Deep as a Well* (1936). In 1927, Parker became a book reviewer for the *New Yorker*, to which she contributed for most of her career. In 1933, Parker and her second husband, Alan Campbell, moved to Hollywood, where they collaborated as film writers. In addition, Parker wrote criticism, two plays, short stories, and news reports from the Spanish Civil War. She is probably best remembered, though, as the reigning wit at the "Round Table" at Manhattan's Algonquin Hotel, where, in the 1920s and '30s, she traded barbs with other prominent writers and humorists.

LINDA PASTAN (b. 1932)

Linda Pastan was born in New York City and raised in nearby Westchester County. After graduating from Radcliffe College, she received an MA in literature from Brandeis University. Although her first published poems appeared in *Mademoiselle* in 1955, Pastan spent many years concentrating on her husband and three children—indeed, much of her poetry deals with her own family life. Her many collections include *A Perfect Circle of Sun* (1971), *The Five Stages of Grief* (1978), American Book Award nominee *PM/AM: New and Selected Poems* (1982), *Carnival Evening: New and Selected Poems 1968–1998* (1998), *Queen of a Rainy Country* (2006), and *Traveling Light* (2011). She lives in Potomac, Maryland.

SYLVIA PLATH (1932–63)

Sylvia Plath was born in Boston; her father, a Polish immigrant, died when she was eight. After graduating from Smith College, Plath attended Cambridge University on a Fulbright scholarship, and there she met and married the poet Ted Hughes, with whom she had two children. As she documented in her novel *The Bell Jar* (1963), in 1953—between her junior and senior years of college—Plath became seriously depressed, attempted suicide, and was hospitalized. In 1963, the breakup of her marriage led to another suicide attempt, this time successful. Plath has attained cult status as much for her poems as for her "martyrdom" to art and life. In addition to her first volume of poetry, *The Colossus* (1960), Plath's work has been collected in *Ariel* (1966), *Crossing the Water* (1971), and *Winter Trees* (1972). Her selected letters were published in 1975; her expurgated journals in 1983; and her unabridged journals in 2000.

ALEXANDER POPE (1688–1744)

Son of a wealthy merchant, London-born Alexander Pope managed to become the greatest poet of his age, one of the most accomplished versifiers and satirists in English literary history, and the first British writer to make his living entirely by his pen despite—or, rather, thanks to—two obvious handicaps. One, tuberculosis of the spine, contracted in infancy, ensured that Pope was, in the words of his contemporaries, only "about four feet six high; very humpbacked and deformed," plagued with "the headache four days in a week, and [. . .] sick [. . .] the other three." Two, as a Roman Catholic, Pope was legally debarred from voting or holding public office, inheriting or purchasing land, living within ten miles of London, or attending any of England's so-called public schools or universities. Largely self-taught and unable to rely on patronage, the pugnacious, politically conservative Pope launched his career with poems celebrating natural beauty and love (*Pastorals* [1709] and *Windsor Forest* [1713]) but leapt to fame with two book-length poems in a very different spirit—the didactic *An Essay on Criticism*

(1711) and the brilliant mock epic *The Rape of the Lock* (1712, 1714). Made wealthy by his monumental translations of Homer's *Iliad* (1720) and *Odyssey* (1726), Pope retired to a five-acre villa in Twickenham, outside London. By the time of his death at age fifty-six, he had produced an unrivalled body of work that includes at least two other masterpieces, the merciless satire *The Dunciad* (1728) and the philosophical verse-treatise *An Essay on Man* (1734).

EZRA POUND (1885–1972)

Born in Hailey, Idaho, Ezra Pound studied at the University of Pennsylvania and Hamilton College before traveling to Europe in 1908. He remained there, living in Ireland, England, France, and Italy, for much of his life. Pound's tremendous ambition—to succeed in his own work and to influence the development of poetry and Western culture in general—led him to found the Imagist school of poetry, to advise and assist many great writers (Eliot, Joyce, Williams, Frost, and Hemingway, to name a few), and to write a number of highly influential critical works. His increasingly fiery and erratic behavior led to a charge of treason (he served as a propagandist for Italian Fascist Beni Mussolini during World War II), a diagnosis of insanity, and twelve years at St. Elizabeth's, an institution for the criminally insane.

ADRIENNE RICH (1929–2012)

Easily one of the foremost poets and public intellectuals of her time, Adrienne Rich was born in Baltimore, Maryland, daughter of a former concert pianist and of a renowned Johns Hopkins University pathologist. Rich's career as a poet began in 1951, when the Radcliffe College senior's first volume, *A Change of World* (1951), was selected by W. H. Auden for the prestigious Yale Younger Poets Award. Two years later, Rich married Harvard economist Alfred Conrad, with whom she had three children. As the 1950s gave way to the 1960s and '70s, Rich's life and work changed profoundly. Beginning with her 1963 collection, *Snapshots of a Daughter-in-Law*, her poetry became ever less tightly controlled and formal, as it became ever more politically and personally charged, reflecting her deep engagement with the feminist, antiwar, and civil rights movements. After her recently estranged husband's suicide (1970) and publication of the National Book Award–winning *Diving into the Wreck* (1974), Rich began a lifelong partnership with Jamaica-born novelist and editor Michelle Cliff and published her two most influential prose works, *Of Woman Born: Motherhood as Experience and Institution* (1976) and *On Lies, Secrets and Silence* (1979), which includes her landmark essay "Compulsory Heterosexuality and Lesbian Existence." In the decades that followed, Rich never rested on her countless laurels, fiercely pursuing both her craft and her campaign for social justice. Her thirtieth and last volume of verse, *Tonight No Poetry Will Serve*, came out in 2010, just two years before her death, at age eighty-two, from the rheumatoid arthritis she had battled for decades. In its obituary, the *New York Times* aptly dubbed her "a poet of towering reputation," whose work is "distinguished by an unswerving progressive vision and a dazzling, empathetic ferocity."

KAY RYAN (b. 1945)

Described by fellow poet J. D. McClatchy as "compact, exhilarating, strange affairs" full of sly wordplay and wit, Kay Ryan's poems are often compared to Emily Dickinson's. Like Dickinson, says Jack Foley, "Ryan can certainly be funny, but it is rarely without a sting." Typically less than 20 lines long and with lines often containing six syllables or less, Ryan's poems tend to have what she

calls "the most dangerous shape," one in which "nearly every word is on one edge or the other" and "you can't hide anything" because "Any crap is going to show." U.S. Poet Laureate from 2008 to 2010 and winner of the 2011 Pulitzer Prize for Poetry, Ryan earned such accolades the hard way. Raised in California's Mojave Desert and San Joaquin Valley by her oil-well-driller father and once rejected from the poetry club at UCLA, where she earned both BA (1967) and MA (1968) degrees in English, Ryan began teaching remedial English at the College of Marin in 1971, receiving widespread recognition for her poetry only some twenty years later. "All of us want instant success," she has said, "I'm glad I was on a sort of slow drip." This "drip" has produced over seven volumes, including *Say Uncle* (2000) and *The Best of It: New and Selected Poems* (2010). In 2009 Ryan was widowed by the death of Carol Adair, her partner of over thirty years. Although she is sometimes accused of being too apolitical by members of the gay community, Ryan's 30-plus years at Marin have made her a strong and vocal advocate of what she describes as America's "much underpraised and underfunded community colleges."

WILLIAM SHAKESPEARE (1554–1616)

Considering the great fame of his work, surprisingly little is known of William Shakespeare's life. Between 1585 and 1592, he left his birthplace of Stratford-upon-Avon for London to begin a career as playwright and actor. No dates of his professional career are recorded, however, nor can the order in which he composed his plays and poems be determined with any certainty. By 1594, he had established himself as a poet with two long works—*Venus and Adonis* and *The Rape of Lucrece*—and his more than 150 sonnets are supreme expressions of the form. His reputation, though, rests on the works he wrote for the theater. Shakespeare produced perhaps thirty-five plays in twenty-five years, proving himself a master of every dramatic genre: tragedy (in works such as *Macbeth, Hamlet, King Lear,* and *Othello*); historical drama (for example, *Richard III* and *Henry IV*); comedy (*Twelfth Night, As You Like It,* and many more); and romance (in plays such as *The Tempest* and *Cymbaline*). Without question, Shakespeare is the most quoted, discussed, and beloved English writer.

WALLACE STEVENS (1879–1955)

Born and raised in Reading, Pennsylvania, Wallace Stevens attended Harvard University and New York Law School. In New York City, he worked for a number of law firms, published poems in magazines, and befriended such literary figures as William Carlos Williams and Marianne Moore. In 1916, Stevens moved to Connecticut and began working for the Hartford Accident and Indemnity Company, where he became a vice president in 1934 and where he worked for the rest of his life, writing poetry at night and during vacations. He published his first collection, *Harmonium,* in 1923 and followed it with a series of volumes from 1935 until 1950, establishing himself as one of the twentieth century's most important poets. His lectures were collected in *The Necessary Angel: Essays on Reality and Imagination* (1951); his *Collected Poems* appeared in 1954.

ADRIENNE SU (b. 1967)

Adrienne Su grew up in Atlanta, Georgia, unaware, she says, of the ironies involved in being "viewed as Chinese," while "I knew no Chinese and thrived on the study of Latin." A graduate of Harvard and the University of Virginia, where she studied with Rita Dove, Gregory Orr, and Charles Wright, Su, by her own account, "started writing as soon as I could form a sentence on paper" and "started sending out work" while still in high school. Having worked as a freelance editor and writer, Su is today an associate professor of English and Poet-in-Residence at Pennsylvania's Dickinson College; a wife and mother; and the author of three poetry collections, *Middle Kingdom* (1997), *Sanctuary* (2006), and *Having None of It* (2009). Crediting her high-school Latin teacher and the ancient Roman poet Virgil with first teaching her the art of meter, and her early involvement in poetry slams with bolstering her commitment to writing "poems that on some levels can be read by anyone," Su also, in her words, "prefer[s] the daily to the exotic as subject matter," seeing writing as best when "it's woven into every life, as a ritual that fits somewhere between making pancakes for my kids and preparing a class for college students."

ALFRED, LORD TENNYSON (1809–92)

Certainly the most popular and perhaps the most important of the Victorian poets, Alfred, Lord Tennyson demonstrated his talents at an early age; he published his first volume in 1827. Encouraged to devote his life to poetry by a group of undergraduates at Cambridge University known as the "Apostles," Tennyson was particularly close to Arthur Hallam, whose sudden death in 1833 inspired the long elegy *In Memoriam* (1850). With that poem he achieved lasting fame and recognition; he was appointed Poet Laureate the year of its publication, succeeding Wordsworth. Despite the great popularity of his "journalistic" poems— "The Charge of the Light Brigade" (1854) is perhaps the best known—Tennyson's great theme was the past, both personal (*In the Valley of Cauteretz,* 1864) and national (*Idylls of the King,* 1869). Tennyson was made a baron in 1884; when he died, eight years later, he was buried in Poets' Corner in London's Westminster Abbey.

NATASHA TRETHEWEY (b. 1966)

Daughter of a social worker and a Canadian poet who met at a Kentucky college, but had to marry in Ohio because of laws banning interracial unions, Natasha Trethewey was born in her mother's hometown of Gulfport, Mississippi. After her parents' divorce, she lived with her mother in Atlanta, summering on the Gulf Coast with both her father and her mother's family. In 1985, Trethewey was just beginning her studies at the University of Georgia when her stepfather murdered her mother. Turning to poetry to deal with her grief, Trethewey earned her BA in 1989; an MA from Virginia's Hollins College, where her father was a professor (1991); and an MFA from the University of Massachusetts at Amherst (1995). After a short stint teaching at Auburn University, Trethewey moved to Emory and, in 2007, became only the fourth African American poet ever to win the Pulitzer Prize, for *Native Guard*. Her third collection, it explores the problem of individual and collective historical amnesia through elegies to her mother and a ten-sonnet sequence written from the perspective of a soldier in the first all-black regiment to fight on the Union side in the Civil War. The years 2007–08, however, also brought Trethewey loss and hardship when her brother was imprisoned on drug-related charges and her beloved grandmother died. Interweaving poetry, essays, and letters, her memoir *Beyond Katrina: A Meditation on the Mississippi Gulf Coast* (2010) reflects on both the region and her family's efforts to remember and rebuild.

WALT WHITMAN (1819–92)

Walt Whitman was born on a farm in West Hills, Long Island, to a British father and a Dutch mother. After working as a journalist throughout New York for many years, he taught for a time and founded his own newspaper, *The Long Islander*, in 1838; he then left journalism to work on *Leaves of Grass*, originally intended as a poetic treatise on American democratic idealism. Published privately in multiple editions from 1855 to 1874, the book of poems at first failed to reach a mass audience. In 1881, Boston's Osgood and Company published another edition of *Leaves of Grass*, which sold well until the district attorney called it "obscene literature" and stipulated that Whitman remove certain poems and phrases. He refused, and it was many years before his works were again published, this time in Philadelphia. By the time Whitman died, his work was revered, as it still is today, for its greatness of spirit and its exuberant American voice.

RICHARD WILBUR (b. 1921)

The son of a painter and a newspaperman's daughter, former U.S. Poet Laureate Richard Wilbur was raised in rural New Jersey, a background that may help to explain his precise imagery and keen interest in nature. Graduating from Amherst College into a world at war, Wilbur in 1942 married the woman who would remain his wife for over sixty years, joined the army, and, by his own account, began to "versify in earnest" because "One does not use poetry [. . .] as a means to organize oneself and the world, until one's world somehow gets out of hand." The many collections Wilbur published between his first, *The Beautiful Changes and Other Poems* (1947), and *Anterooms: New Poems and Translations* (2010) include two Pulitzer Prize winners: *Things of This World* (1956) and *New and Collected Poems* (1988). In recent decades Wilbur's poems have been increasingly lauded for the very qualities that drew criticism in the 30 years between his two Pulitzer Prizes: As critic Gerry Cunningham wittily puts it, "They never raise their voices, put knives to their throats, drink too much, tell dirty jokes, or take their clothes off in public." Using traditional patterns of rhyme and meter, they "acknowledge horror," but remain largely "untouched by it."

WILLIAM CARLOS WILLIAMS (1883–1963)

Born in Rutherford, New Jersey, William Carlos Williams attended school in Switzerland and New York and studied medicine at the University of Pennsylvania and the University of Leipzig in Germany. He spent most of his life in Rutherford, practicing medicine and gradually establishing himself as one of the great figures in American poetry. Early in his writing career he left the European-inspired Imagist movement in favor of a more uniquely American poetic style comprised of vital, local language, and "no ideas but in things." His shorter poems have been published in numerous collected editions, including the Pulitzer Prize–winning *Brueghel, and Other Poems* (1963); his five-volume philosophical poem, *Paterson*, was published in 1963. Among his other works are plays such as *A Dream of Love* (1948) and *Many Loves* (1950); a trilogy of novels—*White Mules* (1937), *In the Money* (1940), and *The Build-Up* (1952); his *Autobiography* (1951); his *Selected Essays* (1954); and his *Selected Letters* (1957).

WILLIAM WORDSWORTH (1770–1850)

Regarded by many as the greatest of the Romantic poets, William Wordsworth was born in Cockermouth in the English Lake District, a beautiful, mountainous region that his poetry helped make a popular tourist destination even in his own lifetime. He studied at Cambridge and then spent a year in France, hoping to witness the French Revolution firsthand; as the

Revolution's "glorious renovation" dissolved into anarchy and then tyranny, Wordsworth was forced to return to England. Remarkably, he managed to establish "a saving intercourse with my true self" and to write some of his finest poetry, including the early version of his autobiographical masterpiece, *The Prelude*, which first appeared in 1805 and then again, much altered, in 1850. In 1798, Wordsworth and his friend Samuel Taylor Coleridge published *Lyrical Ballads*, which contained many of their greatest poems and can be considered the founding document of English Romanticism. Revered by the reading public, Wordsworth served as Poet Laureate from 1843 until his death in 1850.

WILLIAM BUTLER YEATS (1865–1939)

William Butler Yeats was born in Dublin, Ireland, and, though he spent most of his youth in London, became the preeminent Irish poet of the twentieth century. Immersed in Irish history, folklore, and politics, as well as spiritualism and the occult, he attended art school for a time but left to devote himself to poetry that was, early in his career, self-consciously dreamy and ethereal. Yeats's poems became tighter and more passionate with his reading of philosophers such as Nietzsche, his involvement (mainly through theater) with the Irish nationalist cause, and his desperate love for the actress and nationalist Maud Gonne. He was briefly a senator in the newly independent Irish government before withdrawing from active public life to Thoor Ballylee, a crumbling Norman tower that Yeats and his wife fashioned into a home. There he developed an elaborate mythology (published as *A Vision* in 1925) and wrote poems that explored fundamental questions of history and identity. He was awarded the Nobel Prize for Literature in 1923.

KEVIN YOUNG (b. 1970)

Poet Kevin Young was born in Lincoln, Nebraska and grew up mainly in the Midwest, before heading east to Harvard. There, he took courses with Seamus Heaney, participated—alongside Natasha Trethewey—in the influential Dark Room Collective, and wrote many of the poems that would eventually make up his first, award-winning collection (*Most Way Home*, 1995) on the way to earning a BA in English and American literature (1992). Shuttling between coasts, Young spent two years at Stanford University, in Northern California, before completing his MFA at Brown, in Rhode Island. As poems like "Ode to Pork" attest, however, Young also has deep southern roots. Both his mother—among the first black women to earn a PhD (in Chemistry) from the University of Nebraska—and his father—an ophthalmologist who was also an avid hunter and cook—grew up in rural Louisiana, where much of Young's extended family still lives. Since 2005, when he married editor Kate Tuttle, Young has lived mainly in Atlanta, Georgia, where he currently serves as both Atticus Haygood Professor of English and Creative Writing and Curator of the Raymond Danowski Poetry Library at Emory University. Young's astonishingly diverse collections of verse include *Black Maria* (2005), about fictional private eye A. K. A. Jones; *Ardency* (2011), about the real-life Africans who managed to wrest control of the slave ship *Amistad* in 1839; and *Book of Hours* (2014), which moves from poems grappling with his father's 2004 death, in a hunting accident, to those inspired by the birth of Young's first son some two years later.

DRAMA

Arthur Miller

DRAMA
Reading, Responding, Writing

s noted in the introduction, many cultures have had oral literatures: histories, romances, poems to be recited or sung. Our own era has its share of oral art forms, of course, but "literary" fiction and poetry are now most often read privately, silently, from the printed page. Most contemporary fiction writers and poets write with an understanding that their work will be experienced and enjoyed this way.

In contrast, **drama** is written primarily to be performed—by actors, on a stage, for an audience. Playwrights work with an understanding that the words on the page are just the first step—a map of sorts—toward the ultimate goal: a collaborative, publicly performed work of art. They create plays fully aware of the possibilities that go beyond printed words and extend to physical actions, stage devices, and other theatrical techniques for creating effects and modifying audience responses. Although the script of a play may be the most essential piece in the puzzle that makes up the final work of art, the play text is not the final, complete work.

To attend a play—that is, to be part of an audience—represents a very different kind of experience from the usually solitary act of reading. On the stage, real human beings, standing for imaginary characters, deliver lines and perform actions for you to see and hear. In turn, the actors adapt in subtle ways to the reactions of the people who attend the performance and whose responses are no longer wholly private but have become, in part, communal.

When you attend the performance of a play, then, you become a collaborator in the creation of a unique work of art: not the play *text* but instead a specific *interpretation* of that text. No two performances of a play can ever be identical, just as no two interpretations of a play can be exactly the same.

READING DRAMA

In many respects, of course, reading drama is similar to reading fiction. In both cases we anticipate what will happen next; we imagine the characters, settings, and actions; we respond to the symbolic suggestiveness of images; and we notice thematic patterns that are likely to matter in the end. But because most plays are written to be performed, reading plays is also somewhat different from reading fiction or poetry. In fiction, for example, there is a mediator or **narrator**, someone standing between us and the events. In contrast, drama rarely has such an interpreter or mediator to tell us what is happening or to shape our responses. Play texts instead rely on **stage directions** (the italicized descriptions of the set, characters, and actions), while **exposition** (the explanation of the past and current situation) emerges only here and there through dialogue.

For this reason, reading drama may place a greater demand on the imagination than reading fiction does: The reader must be his or her own narrator and interpreter. Such exercise for the imagination can prove rewarding, however, for it has much in common with the imaginative work that a director, actors, and other artists involved in a staged production do. In re-creating a play as we read it, we are essentially imagining the play as if it were being performed by live actors in real time. We "cast" the characters, we design the set with its furniture and props, and we choreograph or "block" the physical action, according to the cues in the text.

In reading drama even more than in reading fiction, we construct our ideas of character and personality from what characters say. In some plays, especially those with a modernist or experimental bent, certain lines of dialogue can be mystifying; other characters, as well as the audience or readers, can be left wondering what a speech means. On the one hand, such puzzling lines can become clearer in performance when we see and hear actors deliver them. On the other hand, plays that call for several characters to speak at once or to talk at cross purposes can be much easier to understand from the printed script than in performance. In interpreting dialogue, you will naturally draw on your own experiences of comparable situations or similar personalities, as well as your familiarity with other plays or stories.

Questions to Ask When Reading a Play

In reading drama as in reading fiction, you can begin to understand a text by asking some basic questions about the elements of drama.

- **Expectations:** What do you expect
  - from the title? from the first sentence, paragraph, or speech?
  - after the first events or interactions of characters? as the **conflict** is resolved?
- **Characterization:** Who are the characters? Is there a list of characters printed after the title of the play? What do you notice about their names or any identification of their roles, character types, or relationships?
  - Who is/are the **protagonist**(s)?
  - Who is/are the **antagonist**(s) (villain, opponent, obstacle)?
  - Who are the other characters?

(continued on next page)

(*continued*)

- ○ What does each character know at any moment in the **action**? What does each character expect at any point? What does the audience know or expect that is different from what the characters know or expect?
- • **Plot**: What happens in the play?
  - ○ Do the characters or situations change during the play?
  - ○ What are the differences between the beginning, middle, and end of the play? Is it divided into acts? Would there be an intermission in a performance?
  - ○ Can you summarize the plot? Is it a recognizable kind or genre such as **tragedy, comedy, farce,** or mystery?
- • **Setting**: What is the setting of the play?
  - ○ *When* does the action occur? Is it contemporary or set in the past? Do the stage directions specify a day of the week, a season, a time of day?
  - ○ Are there any time changes during the play? Are the scenes in chronological order, or are there any scenes that are supposed to take place earlier or simultaneously? Does the passage of time in the lives of the characters correspond with the passage of time onstage? Or do we understand that time has passed and events have occurred offstage and between scenes?
  - ○ *Where* does it take place? Is it in the United States or another country, or in a specific town or region? Do the stage directions describe the scene that an audience would see on stage, and does this remain the same or does it change during the play? How many scene changes are there?
- • **Style**: What do you notice about how the play is written?
  - ○ What is the style of the dialogue? Are the sentences and speeches short or long? Is the vocabulary simple or complex? Do characters ever speak at the same time, or do they always take turns? Does the play instruct actors to be silent for periods of time? Which characters speak most often?
  - ○ Are there any **images** or figures of speech?
  - ○ What is the **tone** or mood? Does the play make the reader or audience feel sad, amused, worried, curious?
- • **Theme**: What does the play mean? Can you express its theme or themes?
  - ○ Answers to these big questions may be found in many instances by returning to your answers to the questions above. The play's meaning or theme depends on all its features.

THINKING THEATRICALLY

As you read a play, you should not only make mental or written notes but also raise some of the questions an actor might ask in preparing a role, or that a director might ask before choosing a cast: How should this line be spoken? What kind of person is this character, and what are his or her motives in each scene? What does the play suggest about what made the character this way—family, environment, experience? Which characters are present or absent (onstage or off) in which scenes, and how do the characters onstage or off influence one another? Would you, as "director" of an imaginary performance, tell the actors to move in certain directions, together or apart; to express certain emotions and intentions; to speak in quiet, angry, sarcastic, or agonized tones?

Besides trying to understand the characters, you should consider ways that the play could be produced, designed, and staged. How might a set designer create a kitchen, drawing room, garden, woods, or other space for the actors to move in, and how many set changes are there in the play? What would the audience see through any windows or doors in an imaginary building? How would lighting give an impression of the time of day or season? Would sound effects or music be necessary (such as a gunshot, radio, or telephone)? What sort of costumes are specified in the stage directions, and how would costumes help express character types and their relationships, as well as the historical time period? What essential props must be provided for the actors to use, and what other props are optional?

As you read Susan Glaspell's TRIFLES, keep these kinds of questions in mind. Try to create a mental image of the settings and of each character, and think about different ways the lines might be delivered and their effect on an audience's response.

SUSAN GLASPELL
(1876–1948)
Trifles

Though today remembered almost exclusively for her masterful *Trifles* (1916), Susan Glaspell wrote over a dozen plays, fifty short stories, nine novels, and a memoir, in addition to playing a key role in the development of twentieth-century American theater. Born in Davenport, Iowa, she graduated from Drake University in 1899 and spent two years at the *Des Moines Daily News*, where she covered the trial of a fifty-seven-year-old woman accused of murdering her sleeping husband with an axe. When Glaspell's short stories began appearing in magazines, she returned to Davenport. There, she became involved with George Cram Cook, a former English professor, socialist, and married father of two. The two wed in 1913 and moved east, eventually settling in New York's Greenwich Village and Cape Cod, Massachusetts, where they founded the Provincetown Playhouse (later the Playwright's Theater), an extraordinary gathering of freethinking, Left-leaning actors, directors, and playwrights that included Edna St. Vincent Millay and a then-unknown Eugene O'Neill. Between 1916 and 1922, this pioneering group reportedly staged more plays by women than any other contemporary theater; among them were eleven by Glaspell, ranging from realistic dramas such as *Trifles* and satirical comedies like *Woman's Honor* (1918) to her expressionistic *The Verge* (1921). Widowed in 1924, Glaspell ended a brief second marriage in 1931, the same year that her last play, *Alison's House*, won the Pulitzer Prize for Drama. Having published her first novel in 1909 and multiple best sellers in the 1920s and 1930s, Glaspell spent the last years of her life writing fiction in Provincetown.

CHARACTERS

SHERIFF   MRS. PETERS, *Sheriff's wife*
COUNTY ATTORNEY   MRS. HALE
HALE

SCENE: *The kitchen in the now abandoned farmhouse of* JOHN WRIGHT, *a gloomy kitchen, and left without having been put in order—unwashed pans under the sink, a loaf of bread outside the bread-box, a dish-towel on the table—other signs of incompleted work. At the rear the outer door opens and the* SHERIFF *comes in followed by the* COUNTY ATTORNEY *and* HALE. *The* SHERIFF *and* HALE *are men in middle life, the* COUNTY ATTORNEY *is a young man; all are much bundled up and go at once to the stove. They are followed by the two women—the* SHERIFF's *wife first; she is a slight wiry woman, a thin nervous face.* MRS. HALE *is larger and would ordinarily be called more comfortable looking, but she is disturbed now and looks fearfully about as she enters. The women have come in slowly, and stand close together near the door.*

COUNTY ATTORNEY: [*Rubbing his hands.*] This feels good. Come up to the fire, ladies.

MRS. PETERS: [*After taking a step forward.*] I'm not—cold.

SHERIFF: [*Unbuttoning his overcoat and stepping away from the stove as if to mark the beginning of official business.*] Now, Mr. Hale, before we move things about, you explain to Mr. Henderson just what you saw when you came here yesterday morning.

COUNTY ATTORNEY: By the way, has anything been moved? Are things just as you left them yesterday?

SHERIFF: [*Looking about.*] It's just the same. When it dropped below zero last night I thought I'd better send Frank out this morning to make a fire for us—no use getting pneumonia with a big case on, but I told him not to touch anything except the stove—and you know Frank.

COUNTY ATTORNEY: Somebody should have been left here yesterday.

SHERIFF: Oh—yesterday. When I had to send Frank to Morris Center for that man who went crazy—I want you to know I had my hands full yesterday. I knew you could get back from Omaha by today and as long as I went over everything here myself—

COUNTY ATTORNEY: Well, Mr. Hale, tell just what happened when you came here yesterday morning.

HALE: Harry and I had started to town with a load of potatoes. We came along the road from my place and as I got here I said, "I'm going to see if I can't get John Wright to go in with me on a party telephone."[1] I spoke to Wright about it once before and he put me off, saying folks talked too much anyway, and all he asked was peace and quiet—I guess you know about how much he talked himself; but I thought maybe if I went to the house and talked about it before his wife, though I said to Harry that I didn't know as what his wife wanted made much difference to John—

COUNTY ATTORNEY: Let's talk about that later, Mr. Hale. I do want to talk about that, but tell now just what happened when you got to the house.

HALE: I didn't hear or see anything; I knocked at the door, and still it was all quiet inside. I knew they must be up, it was past eight o'clock. So I knocked again, and I thought I heard somebody say, "Come in." I wasn't sure, I'm not sure yet, but I opened the door—this door [*Indicating the door by which the two women are still standing.*] and there in that rocker—[*Pointing to it.*] sat Mrs. Wright.

[*They all look at the rocker.*]

COUNTY ATTORNEY: What—was she doing?

HALE: She was rockin' back and forth. She had her apron in her hand and was kind of—pleating it.

COUNTY ATTORNEY: And how did she—look?

HALE: Well, she looked queer.

COUNTY ATTORNEY: How do you mean—queer?

HALE: Well, as if she didn't know what she was going to do next. And kind of done up.

---

1. That is, a party line in which a number of households each have extensions of a single line, a common arrangement in the early twentieth century, especially in rural areas.

COUNTY ATTORNEY: How did she seem to feel about your coming?

HALE: Why, I don't think she minded—one way or other. She didn't pay much attention. I said, "How do, Mrs. Wright, it's cold, ain't it?" And she said, "Is it?"—and went on kind of pleating at her apron. Well, I was surprised; she didn't ask me to come up to the stove, or to set down, but just sat there, not even looking at me, so I said, "I want to see John." And then she—laughed. I guess you would call it a laugh. I thought of Harry and the team outside, so I said a little sharp: "Can't I see John?" "No," she says, kind o' dull like. "Ain't he home?" says I. "Yes," says she, "he's home." "Then why can't I see him?" I asked her, out of patience. "'Cause he's dead," says she. *"Dead?"* says I. She just nodded her head, not getting a bit excited, but rockin' back and forth. "Why—where is he?" says I, not knowing what to say. She just pointed upstairs—like that. [*Himself pointing to the room above.*] I got up, with the idea of going up there. I walked from there to here—then I says, "Why, what did he die of?" "He died of a rope round his neck," says she, and just went on pleatin' at her apron. Well, I went out and called Harry. I thought I might—need help. We went upstairs and there he was lyin'—

COUNTY ATTORNEY: I think I'd rather have you go into that upstairs, where you can point it all out. Just go on now with the rest of the story.

HALE: Well, my first thought was to get that rope off. It looked . . . [*Stops, his face twitches.*] . . . but Harry, he went up to him, and he said, "No, he's dead all right, and we'd better not touch anything." So we went back downstairs. She was still sitting that same way. "Has anybody been notified?" I asked. "No," says she, unconcerned. "Who did this, Mrs. Wright?" said Harry. He said it business-like—and she stopped pleatin' of her apron. "I don't know," she says. "You don't *know?*" says Harry. "No," says she. "Weren't you sleepin' in the bed with him?" says Harry. "Yes," says she, "but I was on the inside." "Somebody slipped a rope round his neck and strangled him and you didn't wake up?" says Harry. "I didn't wake up," she said after him. We must 'a looked as if we didn't see how that could be, for after a minute she said, "I sleep sound." Harry was going to ask her more questions but I said maybe we ought to let her tell her story first to the coroner, or the sheriff, so Harry went fast as he could to Rivers' place, where there's a telephone.

COUNTY ATTORNEY: And what did Mrs. Wright do when she knew that you had gone for the coroner?

HALE: She moved from that chair to this one over here [*Pointing to a small chair in the corner.*] and just sat there with her hands held together and looking down. I got a feeling that I ought to make some conversation, so I said I had come in to see if John wanted to put in a telephone, and at that she started to laugh, and then she stopped and looked at me—

scared. [*The* COUNTY ATTORNEY, *who has had his notebook out, makes a note.*] I dunno, maybe it wasn't scared. I wouldn't like to say it was. Soon Harry got back, and then Dr. Lloyd came, and you, Mr. Peters, and so I guess that's all I know that you don't.

COUNTY ATTORNEY: [*Looking around.*] I guess we'll go upstairs first—and then out to the barn and around there. [*To the* SHERIFF.] You're convinced that there was nothing important here—nothing that would point to any motive?

SHERIFF: Nothing here but kitchen things.

[*The* COUNTY ATTORNEY, *after again looking around the kitchen, opens the door of a cupboard closet. He gets up on a chair and looks on a shelf. Pulls his hand away, sticky.*]

COUNTY ATTORNEY: Here's a nice mess.

[*The women draw nearer.*]

MRS. PETERS: [*To the other woman.*] Oh, her fruit; it did freeze. [*To the* LAWYER.] She worried about that when it turned so cold. She said the fire'd go out and her jars would break.

SHERIFF: Well, can you beat the women! Held for murder and worryin' about her preserves.

COUNTY ATTORNEY: I guess before we're through she may have something more serious than preserves to worry about.

HALE: Well, women are used to worrying over trifles.

[*The two women move a little closer together.*]

COUNTY ATTORNEY: [*With the gallantry of a young politician.*] And yet, for all their worries, what would we do without the ladies? [*The women do not unbend. He goes to the sink, takes a dipperful of water from the pail and pouring it into a basin, washes his hands. Starts to wipe them on the roller towel, turns it for a cleaner place.*] Dirty towels! [*Kicks his foot against the pans under the sink.*] Not much of a housekeeper, would you say, ladies?

MRS. HALE: [*Stiffly.*] There's a great deal of work to be done on a farm.

COUNTY ATTORNEY: To be sure. And yet [*With a little bow to her.*] I know there are some Dickson county farmhouses which do not have such roller towels. [*He gives it a pull to expose its length again.*]

MRS. HALE: Those towels get dirty awful quick. Men's hands aren't always as clean as they might be.

COUNTY ATTORNEY: Ah, loyal to your sex, I see. But you and Mrs. Wright were neighbors. I suppose you were friends, too.

MRS. HALE: [*Shaking her head.*] I've not seen much of her of late years. I've not been in this house—it's more than a year.

COUNTY ATTORNEY: And why was that? You didn't like her?

MRS. HALE: I liked her all well enough. Farmers' wives have their hands full, Mr. Henderson. And then—

COUNTY ATTORNEY: Yes—?

MRS. HALE: [*Looking about.*] It never seemed a very cheerful place.

COUNTY ATTORNEY: No—it's not cheerful. I shouldn't say she had the homemaking instinct.

MRS. HALE: Well, I don't know as Wright had, either.

COUNTY ATTORNEY: You mean that they didn't get on very well?

MRS. HALE: No, I don't mean anything. But I don't think a place'd be any cheerfuller for John Wright's being in it.

COUNTY ATTORNEY: I'd like to talk more of that a little later. I want to get the lay of things upstairs now. [*He goes to the left, where three steps lead to a stair door.*]

SHERIFF: I suppose anything Mrs. Peters does'll be all right. She was to take in some clothes for her, you know, and a few little things. We left in such a hurry yesterday.

COUNTY ATTORNEY: Yes, but I would like to see what you take, Mrs. Peters, and keep an eye out for anything that might be of use to us.

MRS. PETERS: Yes, Mr. Henderson. [*The women listen to the men's steps on the stairs, then look about the kitchen.*]

MRS. HALE: I'd hate to have men coming into my kitchen, snooping around and criticizing. [*She arranges the pans under the sink which the* LAWYER *had shoved out of place.*]

MRS. PETERS: Of course it's no more than their duty.

MRS. HALE: Duty's all right, but I guess that deputy sheriff that came out to make the fire might have got a little of this on. [*Gives the roller towel a pull.*] Wish I'd thought of that sooner. Seems mean to talk about her for not having things slicked up when she had to come away in such a hurry.

MRS. PETERS: [*Who has gone to a small table in the left rear corner of the room, and lifted one end of a towel that covers a pan.*] She had bread set. [*Stands still.*]

MRS. HALE: [*Eyes fixed on a loaf of bread beside the bread box, which is on a low shelf at the other side of the room. Moves slowly toward it.*] She was going to put this in there. [*Picks up loaf, then abruptly drops it. In a manner of returning to familiar things.*] It's a shame about her fruit. I wonder if it's all gone. [*Gets up on the chair and looks.*] I think there's some here that's all right, Mrs. Peters. Yes—here; [*Holding it toward the window.*] this is cherries, too. [*Looking again.*] I declare I believe that's the only one. [*Gets down, bottle in her hand. Goes to the sink and wipes it off on the outside.*] She'll feel awful bad after all her hard work in the hot weather. I remember the afternoon I put up my cherries last summer. [*She puts the bottle on the big kitchen table, center of the room. With a sigh, is about to sit down in the rocking-chair. Before she is seated realizes what chair it is; with a slow look at it, steps back. The chair, which she has touched, rocks back and forth.*]

MRS. PETERS: Well, I must get those things from the front room closet. [*She goes to the door at the right, but after looking into the other room, steps back.*] You coming with me, Mrs. Hale? You could help me carry them. [*They go in the other room; reappear,* MRS. PETERS *carrying a dress and skirt,* MRS. HALE *following with a pair of shoes.*] My, it's cold in there. [*She puts the clothes on the big table, and hurries to the stove.*]

MRS. HALE: [*Examining the skirt.*] Wright was close. I think maybe that's why she kept so much to herself. She didn't even belong to the Ladies Aid. I suppose she felt she couldn't do her part, and then you don't enjoy things when you feel shabby. She used to wear pretty clothes and be lively, when she was Minnie Foster, one of the town girls singing in the choir. But that—oh, that was thirty years ago. This all you was to take in?

MRS. PETERS: She said she wanted an apron. Funny thing to want, for there isn't much to get you dirty in jail, goodness knows. But I suppose just to make her feel more natural. She said they was in the top drawer in this cupboard. Yes, here. And then her little shawl that always hung behind the door. [*Opens stair door and looks.*] Yes, here it is. [*Quickly shuts door leading upstairs.*]

MRS. HALE: [*Abruptly moving toward her.*] Mrs. Peters?

MRS. PETERS: Yes, Mrs. Hale?

MRS. HALE: Do you think she did it?

MRS. PETERS: [*In a frightened voice.*] Oh, I don't know.

MRS. HALE: Well, I don't think she did. Asking for an apron and her little shawl. Worrying about her fruit.

MRS. PETERS: [*Starts to speak, glances up, where footsteps are heard in the room above. In a low voice.*] Mr. Peters says it looks bad for her. Mr. Henderson is awful sarcastic in a speech and he'll make fun of her sayin' she didn't wake up.

MRS. HALE: Well, I guess John Wright didn't wake when they was slipping that rope under his neck.

MRS. PETERS: No, it's strange. It must have been done awful crafty and still. They say it was such a—funny way to kill a man, rigging it all up like that.

MRS. HALE: That's just what Mr. Hale said. There was a gun in the house. He says that's what he can't understand.

MRS. PETERS: Mr. Henderson said coming out that what was needed for the case was a motive; something to show anger, or—sudden feeling.

MRS. HALE: [*Who is standing by the table.*] Well, I don't see any signs of anger around here. [*She puts her hand on the dish towel which lies on the table, stands looking down at table, one half of which is clean, the other half messy.*] It's wiped to here. [*Makes a move as if to finish work, then turns and looks at loaf of bread outside the bread box. Drops towel. In that voice of coming back to familiar things.*] Wonder how they are finding things upstairs. I hope she had it a little more red-up[2] up there. You know, it seems kind of *sneaking.* Locking her up in town and then coming out here and trying to get her own house to turn against her!

MRS. PETERS: But Mrs. Hale, the law is the law.

MRS. HALE: I s'pose 'tis. [*Unbuttoning her coat.*] Better loosen up your things, Mrs. Peters. You won't feel them when you go out.

[MRS. PETERS *takes off her fur tippet, goes to hang it on hook at back of room, stands looking at the under part of the small corner table.*]

MRS. PETERS: She was piecing a quilt. [*She brings the large sewing basket and they look at the bright pieces.*]

MRS. HALE: It's log cabin pattern. Pretty, isn't it? I wonder if she was goin' to quilt it or just knot it?

[*Footsteps have been heard coming down the stairs. The* SHERIFF *enters followed by* HALE *and the* COUNTY ATTORNEY.]

SHERIFF: They wonder if she was going to quilt it or just knot it!

[*The men laugh, the women look abashed.*]

COUNTY ATTORNEY: [*Rubbing his hands over the stove.*] Frank's fire didn't do much up there, did it? Well, let's go out to the barn and get that cleared up.

[*The men go outside.*]

MRS. HALE: [*Resentfully.*] I don't know as there's anything so strange, our takin' up our time with little things while we're waiting for them to get the evidence. [*She sits down at the big table smoothing out a block with decision.*] I don't see as it's anything to laugh about.

MRS. PETERS: [*Apologetically.*] Of course they've got awful important things on their minds. [*Pulls up a chair and joins* MRS. HALE *at the table.*]

MRS. HALE: [*Examining another block.*] Mrs. Peters, look at this one. Here, this is the one she was working on, and look at the sewing! All the rest of it has been so nice and even. And look at this! It's all over the place!

2. Tidied up.

Why, it looks as if she didn't know what she was about! [*After she has said this they look at each other, then start to glance back at the door. After an instant* MRS. HALE *has pulled at a knot and ripped the sewing.*]

MRS. PETERS: Oh, what are you doing, Mrs. Hale?

MRS. HALE: [*Mildly.*] Just pulling out a stitch or two that's not sewed very good. [*Threading the needle.*] Bad sewing always made me fidgety.

MRS. PETERS: [*Nervously.*] I don't think we ought to touch things.

MRS. HALE: I'll just finish up this end. [*Suddenly stopping and leaning forward.*] Mrs. Peters?

MRS. PETERS: Yes, Mrs. Hale?

MRS. HALE: What do you suppose she was so nervous about?

MRS. PETERS: Oh—I don't know. I don't know as she was nervous. I sometimes sew awful queer when I'm just tired. [MRS. HALE *starts to say something, looks at* MRS. PETERS, *then goes on sewing.*] Well, I must get these things wrapped up. They may be through sooner than we think. [*Putting apron and other things together.*] I wonder where I can find a piece of paper, and string.

MRS. HALE: In that cupboard, maybe.

MRS. PETERS: [*Looking in cupboard.*] Why, here's a bird-cage. [*Holds it up.*] Did she have a bird, Mrs. Hale?

MRS. HALE: Why, I don't know whether she did or not—I've not been here for so long. There was a man around last year selling canaries cheap, but I don't know as she took one; maybe she did. She used to sing real pretty herself.

MRS. PETERS: [*Glancing around.*] Seems funny to think of a bird here. But she must have had one, or why would she have a cage? I wonder what happened to it.

MRS. HALE: I s'pose maybe the cat got it.

MRS. PETERS: No, she didn't have a cat. She's got that feeling some people have about cats—being afraid of them. My cat got in her room and she was real upset and asked me to take it out.

MRS. HALE: My sister Bessie was like that. Queer, ain't it?

MRS. PETERS: [*Examining the cage.*] Why, look at this door. It's broke. One hinge is pulled apart.

MRS. HALE: [*Looking too.*] Looks as if someone must have been rough with it.

MRS. PETERS: Why, yes. [*She brings the cage forward and puts it on the table.*]

MRS. HALE: I wish if they're going to find any evidence they'd be about it. I don't like this place.

MRS. PETERS: But I'm awful glad you came with me, Mrs. Hale. It would be lonesome for me sitting here alone.

MRS. HALE: It would, wouldn't it? [*Dropping her sewing.*] But I tell you what I do wish, Mrs. Peters. I wish I had come over sometimes when *she* was here. I—[*Looking around the room.*]—wish I had.

MRS. PETERS: But of course you were awful busy, Mrs. Hale—your house and your children.

MRS. HALE: I could've come. I stayed away because it weren't cheerful—and that's why I ought to have come. I—I've never liked this place. Maybe because it's down in a hollow and you don't see the road. I dunno what it is, but it's a lonesome place and always was. I wish I had come over to see Minnie Foster sometimes. I can see now—[*Shakes her head.*]

MRS. PETERS: Well, you mustn't reproach yourself, Mrs. Hale. Somehow we just don't see how it is with other folks until—something comes up.

MRS. HALE: Not having children makes less work—but it makes a quiet house, and Wright out to work all day, and no company when he did come in. Did you know John Wright, Mrs. Peters?

MRS. PETERS: Not to know him; I've seen him in town. They say he was a good man.

MRS. HALE: Yes—good; he didn't drink, and kept his word as well as most, I guess, and paid his debts. But he was a hard man, Mrs. Peters. Just to pass the time of day with him—[*Shivers.*] Like a raw wind that gets to the bone. [*Pauses, her eye falling on the cage.*] I should think she would 'a wanted a bird. But what do you suppose went with it?

MRS. PETERS: I don't know, unless it got sick and died. [*She reaches over and swings the broken door, swings it again, both women watch it.*]

MRS. HALE: You weren't raised round here, were you? [MRS. PETERS *shakes her head.*] You didn't know—her?

MRS. PETERS: Not till they brought her yesterday.

MRS. HALE: She—come to think of it, she was kind of like a bird herself— real sweet and pretty, but kind of timid and—fluttery. How—she— did—change. [*Silence; then as if struck by a happy thought and relieved to get back to everyday things.*] Tell you what, Mrs. Peters, why don't you take the quilt in with you? It might take up her mind.

MRS. PETERS: Why, I think that's a real nice idea, Mrs. Hale. There couldn't possibly be any objection to it, could there? Now, just what would I take? I wonder if her patches are in here—and her things. [*They look in the sewing basket.*]

MRS. HALE: Here's some red. I expect this has got sewing things in it. [*Brings out a fancy box.*] What a pretty box. Looks like something somebody would give you. Maybe her scissors are in here. [*Opens box. Suddenly puts her hand to her nose.*] Why—[MRS. PETERS *bends nearer, then turns her face away.*] There's something wrapped up in this piece of silk.

MRS. PETERS: Why, this isn't her scissors.

MRS. HALE: [*Lifting the silk.*] Oh, Mrs. Peters—it's—

[MRS. PETERS *bends closer.*]

MRS. PETERS: It's the bird.

MRS. HALE: [*Jumping up.*] But, Mrs. Peters—look at it! Its neck! Look at its neck! It's all—other side *to.*

MRS. PETERS: Somebody—wrung—its—neck.

[*Their eyes meet. A look of growing comprehension, of horror. Steps are heard outside.* MRS. HALE *slips box under quilt pieces, and sinks into her chair. Enter* SHERIFF *and* COUNTY ATTORNEY. MRS. PETERS *rises.*]

COUNTY ATTORNEY: [*As one turning from serious things to little pleasantries.*] Well ladies, have you decided whether she was going to quilt it or knot it?

MRS. PETERS: We think she was going to—knot it.

COUNTY ATTORNEY: Well, that's interesting, I'm sure. [*Seeing the bird-cage.*] Has the bird flown?

MRS. HALE: [*Putting more quilt pieces over the box.*] We think the—cat got it.

COUNTY ATTORNEY: [*Preoccupied.*] Is there a cat?

[MRS. HALE *glances in a quick covert way at* MRS. PETERS.]

MRS. PETERS: Well, not *now.* They're superstitious, you know. They leave.

COUNTY ATTORNEY: [*To* SHERIFF PETERS, *continuing an interrupted conversation.*] No sign at all of anyone having come from the outside. Their own rope. Now let's go up again and go over it piece by piece. [*They start upstairs.*] It would have to have been someone who knew just the—

[MRS. PETERS *sits down. The two women sit there not looking at one another, but as if peering into something and at the same time holding back. When they talk now it is in the manner of feeling their way over strange ground, as if afraid of what they are saying, but as if they cannot help saying it.*]

MRS. HALE: She liked the bird. She was going to bury it in that pretty box.

MRS. PETERS: [*In a whisper.*] When I was a girl—my kitten—there was a boy took a hatchet, and before my eyes—and before I could get there— [*Covers her face an instant.*] If they hadn't held me back I would have— [*Catches herself, looks upstairs where steps are heard, falters weakly.*]—hurt him.

MRS. HALE: [*With a slow look around her.*] I wonder how it would seem never to have had any children around. [*Pause.*] No, Wright wouldn't like the bird—a thing that sang. She used to sing. He killed that, too.

MRS. PETERS: [*Moving uneasily.*] We don't know who killed the bird.

MRS. HALE: I knew John Wright.

MRS. PETERS: It was an awful thing was done in this house that night, Mrs. Hale. Killing a man while he slept, slipping a rope around his neck that choked the life out of him.

MRS. HALE: His neck. Choked the life out of him. [*Her hand goes out and rests on the bird-cage.*]

MRS. PETERS: [*With rising voice.*] We don't know who killed him. We don't know.

MRS. HALE: [*Her own feeling not interrupted.*] If there's been years and years of nothing, then a bird to sing to you, it would be awful—still, after the bird was still.

MRS. PETERS: [*Something within her speaking.*] I know what stillness is. When we homesteaded in Dakota, and my first baby died—after he was two years old, and me with no other then—

MRS. HALE: [*Moving.*] How soon do you suppose they'll be through, looking for the evidence?

MRS. PETERS: I know what stillness is. [*Pulling herself back.*] The law has got to punish crime, Mrs. Hale.

MRS. HALE: [*Not as if answering that.*] I wish you'd seen Minnie Foster when she wore a white dress with blue ribbons and stood up there in the choir and sang. [*A look around the room.*] Oh, I wish I'd come over here once in a while! That was a crime! That was a crime! Who's going to punish that?

MRS. PETERS: [*Looking upstairs.*] We mustn't—take on.

MRS. HALE: I might have known she needed help! I know how things can be—for women. I tell you, it's queer, Mrs. Peters. We live close together and we live far apart. We all go through the same things—it's all just a different kind of the same thing. [*Brushes her eyes, noticing the bottle of fruit, reaches out for it.*] If I was you, I wouldn't tell her her fruit was gone. Tell her it ain't. Tell her it's all right. Take this in to prove it to her. She—she may never know whether it was broke or not.

MRS. PETERS: [*Takes the bottle, looks about for something to wrap it in; takes petticoat from the clothes brought from the other room, very nervously begins winding this around the bottle. In a false voice.*] My, it's a good thing the men couldn't hear us. Wouldn't they just laugh! Getting all stirred up over a little thing like a—dead canary. As if that could have anything to do with—with—wouldn't they *laugh*!

[*The men are heard coming down stairs.*]

MRS. HALE: [*Under her breath.*] Maybe they would—maybe they wouldn't.

COUNTY ATTORNEY: No, Peters, it's all perfectly clear except a reason for doing it. But you know juries when it comes to women. If there was some definite thing. Something to show—something to make a story about—a thing that would connect up with this strange way of doing it—

[*The women's eyes meet for an instant. Enter* HALE *from outer door.*]

HALE: Well, I've got the team around. Pretty cold out there.

COUNTY ATTORNEY: I'm going to stay here a while by myself. [*To the* SHERIFF.] You can send Frank out for me, can't you? I want to go over everything. I'm not satisfied that we can't do better.

SHERIFF: Do you want to see what Mrs. Peters is going to take in?

[*The* LAWYER *goes to the table, picks up the apron, laughs.*]

COUNTY ATTORNEY: Oh, I guess they're not very dangerous things the ladies have picked out. [*Moves a few things about, disturbing the quilt pieces which cover the box. Steps back.*] No, Mrs. Peters doesn't need supervising. For that matter, a sheriff's wife is married to the law. Ever think of it that way, Mrs. Peters?

MRS. PETERS: Not—just that way.

SHERIFF: [*Chuckling.*] Married to the law. [*Moves toward the other room.*] I just want you to come in here a minute, George. We ought to take a look at these windows.

COUNTY ATTORNEY: [*Scoffingly.*] Oh, windows!

SHERIFF: We'll be right out, Mr. Hale.

[HALE *goes outside. The* SHERIFF *follows the* COUNTY ATTORNEY *into the other room. Then* MRS. HALE *rises, hands tight together, looking intensely at* MRS. PETERS, *whose eyes make a slow turn, finally meeting* MRS. HALE's. *A moment* MRS. HALE *holds her, then her own eyes point the way to where the box is concealed. Suddenly* MRS. PETERS *throws back quilt pieces and tries to put the box in the bag she is wearing. It is too big. She opens box, starts to take bird out, cannot touch it, goes to pieces, stands there helpless. Sound of a knob turning in the other room.* MRS. HALE *snatches the box and puts it in the pocket of her big coat. Enter* COUNTY ATTORNEY *and* SHERIFF.]

COUNTY ATTORNEY: [*Facetiously.*] Well, Henry, at least we found out that she was not going to quilt it. She was going to—what is it you call it, ladies?

MRS. HALE: [*Her hand against her pocket.*] We call it—knot it, Mr. Henderson.

CURTAIN

1916

QUESTIONS

1. If we were watching a production of TRIFLES and had no cast list, how would we gradually piece together the fact that Mrs. Peters is the sheriff's wife? What are the earliest lines of dialogue that allow an audience to infer this fact?
2. What lines in the play characterize Mrs. Hale's reaction to the men's behavior and attitudes? What lines characterize Mrs. Peters's reaction to the men early in the play, and what lines show her feelings changing later in the play? What might account for the two women's initial differences and their evolving solidarity with Mrs. Wright?
3. What are the "trifles" that the men ignore and the two women notice? Why do the men dismiss them, and why do the women see these things as significant clues? What is the thematic importance of these "trifles"?
4. How would you stage the key moment of the play, Mrs. Hale's discovery of the bird in the sewing basket? What facial expression would she have? What body language? Where would you place Mrs. Peters, and what would she be doing? How would you use lighting to heighten the effectiveness of the scene?
5. If a twenty-first-century playwright were to write an updated version of TRIFLES, what details of plot, character, and setting would be different from those in Glaspell's play? What would be the same? What are some possible "trifles" that might serve the same dramatic functions as those in Glaspell's play?

RESPONDING TO DRAMA

When reading a play in order to write about it, you will need to keep a record of how you respond and what you observe as the action unfolds. Recording your thoughts as you read will help you clarify your expectations and attend to the way the play elicits and manages them. Below you will find examples of two ways of responding to a play. The first shows how you might jot down your initial impressions and questions in the margins as you read. The second shows how one reader used the questions on pages 769–70 to take more comprehensive, methodical notes on the same play. Each of these methods of note-taking has certain advantages, and you may well find that a combination of the two works best.

SAMPLE WRITING: ANNOTATION OF *TRIFLES*

Though the passage chosen for annotation here is the play's opening, any passage in a play—including stage directions, as well as dialogue—will reward close analysis.

Trifles

CHARACTERS

SHERIFF	MRS. PETERS, *Sheriff's wife*
COUNTY ATTORNEY	MRS. HALE
HALE	

SCENE: *The kitchen in the now abandoned farmhouse of* JOHN WRIGHT, *a gloomy kitchen, and left without having been put in order—unwashed pans under the sink, a loaf of bread outside the bread-box, a dish-towel on the table—other signs of incompleted work. At the rear the outer door opens and the* SHERIFF *comes in followed by the* COUNTY ATTORNEY *and* HALE. *The* SHERIFF *and* HALE *are men in middle life, the* COUNTY ATTORNEY *is a young man; all are much bundled up and go at once to the stove. They are followed by the two women—the* SHERIFF's *wife first; she is a slight wiry woman, a thin nervous face.* MRS. HALE *is larger and would ordinarily be called more comfortable looking, but she is disturbed now and looks fearfully about as she enters. The women have come in slowly, and stand close together near the door.*

COUNTY ATTORNEY: [*Rubbing his hands.*] This feels good. Come up to the fire, ladies.

MRS. PETERS: [*After taking a step forward.*] I'm not—cold.

SHERIFF: [*Unbuttoning his overcoat and stepping away from the stove as if to mark the beginning of official business.*] Now, Mr. Hale, before we move things about, you explain to Mr. Henderson just what you saw when you came here yesterday morning.

COUNTY ATTORNEY: By the way, has anything been moved? Are things just as you left them yesterday?

A "trifle" is something unimportant and also a kind of dessert. So is the play going to be about unimportant things? Is it a comedy?

Only character *not* identified either by job or relationship to somebody else. (Why not "Mr. Hale"?)

Why "now abandoned"? Who's John Wright? "Gloomy" doesn't sound like a comedy.

Is this a crime scene? Why refer to "work" (not "eating" or something)?

Women described more than men. They look different, but even the "comfortable looking" one (funny expression) isn't comfortable. They stick together.

Why hesitate?

Now attorney gets a name. Sounds like they are in court.

Second mention of things being moved: they're worried about evidence.

So this *is* "a big case." Is John Wright the criminal or victim?

Everyone knows everyone else. It's very cold, a harsh environment outside this kitchen. And it takes work to make it warm (lighting a fire).

It's a small town (in Nebraska?), but a lot of bad stuff is happening! Sheriff is defensive with attorney—source of conflict?

Again, everybody knows about everybody else.

Hale assumes most husbands would act differently around their wives, care about what they want—but maybe not Wright.

Attorney is worried about being "official," sticking to facts, actions, "business," and "that" (Wright's personality or feelings?) doesn't count.

Everyone gets up early—because of all the work they have to do?

SHERIFF: [*Looking about.*] It's just the same. When it dropped below zero last night I thought I'd better send Frank out this morning to make a fire for us—no use getting pneumonia with a big case on, but I told him not to touch anything except the stove—and you know Frank.

COUNTY ATTORNEY: Somebody should have been left here yesterday.

SHERIFF: Oh—yesterday. When I had to send Frank to Morris Center for that man who went crazy—I want you to know I had my hands full yesterday. I knew you could get back from Omaha by today and as long as I went over everything here myself—

COUNTY ATTORNEY: Well, Mr. Hale, tell just what happened when you came here yesterday morning.

HALE: Harry and I had started to town with a load of potatoes. We came along the road from my place and as I got here I said, "I'm going to see if I can't get John Wright to go in with me on a party telephone." I spoke to Wright about it once before and he put me off, saying folks talked too much anyway, and all he asked was peace and quiet—I guess you know about how much he talked himself; but I thought maybe if I went to the house and talked about it before his wife, though I said to Harry that I didn't know as what his wife wanted made much difference to John—

COUNTY ATTORNEY: Let's talk about that later, Mr. Hale. I do want to talk about that, but tell now just what happened when you got to the house.

HALE: I didn't hear or see anything; I knocked at the door, and still it was all quiet inside. I knew they must be up, it was past eight o'clock. So I knocked again, and I thought I heard

Really ordinary things now seem very creepy. Why are the women still standing by the door—because they are afraid? because they aren't part of "official business"? Are they witnesses, too? Why are they here?

She's not listed as character either. What happened?

somebody say, "Come in." I wasn't sure, I'm not sure yet, but I opened the door—this door [*Indicating the door by which the two women are still standing.*] and there in that rocker— [*Pointing to it.*] sat Mrs. Wright.

SAMPLE WRITING: READING NOTES

Below are examples of the questions an experienced reader might ask when reading the play TRIFLES for the first time, as well as responses to those questions. (See pp. 771–83.) Any of these notes might inspire ideas for essay topics on *Trifles*. This is just a selection of the many details that could be observed about this lasting play, in which details certainly matter.

Expectations

Does the title suggest anything? "Trifles" sounds like a comedy (a trifle is something trivial), but it might be ironic. But why does Hale say that "women are used to worrying over trifles"? I expect to find out that the title is significant in some way.

Characterization

Who are the characters? What are they like? Three men and two women in the cast of characters. After I read the stage directions and part of the dialogue, I check the list again to keep straight who is who. What kind of situation would bring together a sheriff, a county attorney, a farmer, and two wives? No actors are needed to play either Mr. Wright or Mrs. Wright. Some men who help Mr. Hale (Harry) and Mr. Peters (deputy Frank) are mentioned as coming and going but are never on stage.

The "county attorney" acts like a detective; he seems businesslike and thinks he's smarter than farmers and women. The stage directions specify that he speaks "With the gallantry of a young politician," but his flattery toward the women doesn't work. We find out his name is Mr. Henderson.

According to the stage directions, Mrs. Peters, the sheriff's wife, is "a slight wiry woman, a thin nervous face"; Mrs. Hale, the farmer's wife, is "larger and would ordinarily be called more comfortable looking." The casting of the two women would be important for contrast; a wider range of physical types would be suitable for the men. Everyone is cold, but only the men take comfort by the fire in the kitchen; the women are upset.

Is there a protagonist, an antagonist, or other types? There isn't a young hero or heroine of this play, and I wouldn't call anyone the villain unless it's the dead man.

Are the characters' names significant? There's nothing especially meaningful or unusual about the names, although "Hale" means healthy (as in "hale and hearty"), and "Wright" sounds just like "right," though obviously something's wrong in this house.

Plot

What happens? The big event has already happened; this is the scene of the crime. The men are looking for clues and leave the women in the kitchen, where they discover possible causes or motives for the crime. The women decide not to tell the men about either the evidence they find or their interpretation of it.

Are there scene changes? The whole scene is a fairly short uninterrupted period in one part of a farmhouse. Characters go offstage to other rooms or outdoors to the barn.

How is exposition handled? The county attorney asks Hale to "tell just what happened"; Hale explains what happened before the play started, describing how Mrs. Wright behaved. It comes as a shock to learn that Mrs. Wright told Hale he couldn't see John Wright " 'Cause [he was] dead." Shouldn't she have run to tell someone about the murder or have told Hale as soon as he arrived? When Hale reports that Mrs. Wright said her husband "died of a rope around his neck," it sounds suspicious. Could she have slept so soundly that she didn't realize someone had strangled Mr. Wright?

What events mark the rising action? When the men go upstairs and Mrs. Hale says, "I'd hate to have men coming into my kitchen, and snooping and criticizing," the women have a chance to notice more in the kitchen. Mrs. Hale recalls her relationship to Mrs. Wright, and the women discuss whether the wife really murdered her husband.

The men return to the kitchen on their way out to the barn just after the women discover the quilt pieces with the bad stitching. The next dialogue between the women is more open and brings out Mrs. Hale's regret for not having visited and supported Mrs. Wright in her unhappy marriage. They notice the empty birdcage.

What is the climax? Mrs. Hale finds the dead bird in the pretty box, and the two women understand what it means just before the men return to the kitchen briefly. From then on the women utter small lies to the men. Mrs. Peters for the first time reveals personal memories that suggest she can imagine Mrs. Wright's motives.

What is the resolution? As everyone prepares to leave, Mrs. Peters pretends the bird is insignificant, joining Mrs. Hale in protecting Mrs. Wright and playing along with the men's idea that there's nothing to notice in the kitchen. The women collaborate in hiding the bird.

What kind of play or plot is it? Like some detective stories, the play doesn't ask "whodunnit?" but why the murder was committed. Its mode of representation is a familiar type—domestic realism—in which the places, people, things, and even events are more or less ordinary. (Unfortunately, domestic violence is quite common.)

Setting
When does the action occur? The play appears to be contemporary with 1916 (a stove heater, party-line telephones, a horse-drawn wagon). It is a winter morning, and the scene takes perhaps an hour.

Where does the action occur? It is obviously farm country, perhaps in the Midwest, where farms are very far apart.

What is the atmosphere? The freezing weather reflects the feeling of the play and gives the characters a motive for gathering in the kitchen. John Wright is described as a chilly wind. The frozen house has ruined Mrs. Wright's preserves of summer fruit. The mess in the kitchen, especially the sticky spill of red fruit in the cupboard, seems related to the unhappiness and horror of the marriage and the crime.

Are there scene changes? Instead of several scenes over a longer time, showing the deteriorating marriage, the crisis over the bird, the murder itself, Mrs. Wright's sleepless night, and Mr. Hale's visit, the story unfolds in a single scene, in one room, on the second morning after the murder, between the entrance and exit of Mrs. Hale and Mrs. Peters. It is essential that the play focus on "kitchen things" and what the women visitors notice and think.

Style, Tone, Imagery
What is the style of the dialogue? The dialogue seems similar to everyday speech. There are some differences in speaking style that show the Hales are more rustic than the Peters and the county attorney. Hale has a relaxed way of telling a story: "then I says," etc. Mrs. Hale: "Those towels

get dirty awful quick" and "If I was you, I wouldn't tell her the fruit was gone. Tell her it *ain't.*"

How do nonverbal gestures and actions convey meaning? Many specific actions indicated in the stage directions are crucial to the play: everyone looking at the rocking chair, pointing to the room upstairs, looking at the loaf of bread that should have been put back in the bread box, etc.

Do any of the props seem to have symbolic meaning? Some objects in the play are so important they seem symbolic, though the play tries not to be too heavily poetic. All kinds of "trifles" are clues. For instance, the women get Mrs. Wright's clothes to bring to her in jail. "MRS. HALE: [*Examining the skirt.*] Wright was close," meaning stingy. Mrs. Hale's words convey a quick impression: The skirt looks "shabby" because John Wright didn't give his wife any money for clothes (he was "good" but stingy and cold).

There would be some colorful props on stage—the jar of cherries, the red cloth and other quilt material, the pretty box—all of them signs of what has gone wrong. The room itself is "gloomy" and has some dirty and messy things in plain sight; other things in the cupboards are eventually revealed. These props would add to the uncomfortable feeling of the play.

The closest thing to a symbol is the caged songbird. Even the men notice the broken door and missing bird. Mrs. Hale underlines the comparison to Mrs. Wright twice: "she was kind of like a bird," and later, "No, Wright wouldn't like the bird—a thing that sang. She used to sing. He killed that, too."

Theme
What is the theme of the play? The title calls attention to what the play is about. Glaspell didn't call it *The Caged Songbird* or *Murder in the Midwest* or something heavy-handed. The main action is a search for a motive to confirm what everyone believes, that Minnie Wright must have strangled her husband while he was sleeping in bed. But the underlying theme of the play seems to be about men's and women's different perspectives. How can women's everyday things be important? Why would anyone charged with murder worry about preserves? Even the women hope that Mrs. Wright's worry about having her apron and shawl in jail means she didn't commit the crime. The kitchen things—the trifles in her own house—"turn against her," but the women are able to hide evidence that the men consider insignificant.

WRITING ABOUT DRAMA

Writing an essay about drama, like writing about fiction or poetry, can sharpen your responses and focus your reading; at the same time, it can illuminate aspects of the work that other readers may have missed. When you write about drama, in a very real sense you perform the role that directors and actors take on in a stage performance: You offer your "reading" of the text, interpreting it in order to guide other readers' responses. But you also shape and refine your own response by attempting to express it clearly.

Using the notes you have taken while reading a play, try to locate the specific lines that have contributed to your expectations or your discoveries. Are these lines at the beginning, the middle, or the end of the play? Who gives most of the hints or misleading information? If there is one character who is especially unseeing, especially devious, or especially insightful, you might decide to write an essay describing the function of that character in the play. A good way to undertake such a study of a character in drama (as in fiction) is to imagine the work without that character. Mrs. Hale in *Trifles* is certainly the cleverest "detective," so why do we need Mrs. Peters as well? One obvious answer is that plays need dialogue, and we would find it artificial if Mrs. Hale talked mainly to herself. But a more interesting answer is that in a play the audience learns by witnessing characters with different temperaments responding to the same situation. As these remarks suggest, you can also develop essays that compare characters.

In addition to character studies, essays on drama can focus on the kinds of observations made above: expectations and plot structure; the presence and absence of characters or actions onstage; the different degrees of awareness of characters and audience at various points in the action; titles, stage directions, and other stylistic details, including **metaphors** or other imagery; and, of course, themes. As you write, you will probably discover that you can imagine directing or acting in a performance of the play, and you'll realize that interpreting a play is a crucial step in bringing it to life.

SUGGESTIONS FOR WRITING

1. The action in Glaspell's play unfolds continuously, without interruption, in a single, relatively small room (the kitchen of a farmhouse), with the two female characters never leaving the stage. Write a response paper or essay discussing how these three factors affect your responses to the play, to the crime being investigated, and to the various characters.
2. How do your sympathies for Mrs. Peters change over the course of TRIFLES? What might Mrs. Peters be said to represent in the clash of attitudes at the heart of the play? Write an essay in which you examine both Mrs. Peters's evolving character as it is revealed in TRIFLES and her significance to the play's theme.
3. How would you characterize Susan Glaspell's feminism as revealed in TRIFLES—does it seem radical or moderate? How does it compare to feminist

political and social ideas of our own time? (Consult three or more educational or library Web sites for biographical background on Glaspell; there are several sites offering teaching materials on TRIFLES as well. If time allows, you might also pursue sources that provide an overview of women's movements in the United States in the twentieth century.) Write an essay in which you explore the political leanings apparent in TRIFLES, both in the context of Glaspell's play (published in 1916) and in the broader historical context of the struggle for women's rights over the past century.

4. Write an essay in which you propose a production of TRIFLES, complete with details of how you would handle the casting, costumes, set design, lighting, and direction of the actors. What would be your overall controlling vision for the production? Would you attempt to reproduce faithfully the look and feel of the play as it might have been in 1916, or would you introduce innovations? How would you justify your choices in terms of dramatic effectiveness?

SAMPLE WRITING: RESPONSE PAPER

Response papers are a great way to begin moving from informal notes to a more formal essay. Though many response-paper assignments invite you to respond to any aspect or element of a literary text that grabs your attention, the following example was written in response to a more targeted assignment, one that asked students to "explore something specific about the way TRIFLES handles plot. For example, what are the major internal and/or external conflicts? Or what would you argue is the play's turning point, and why?" Student-writer Jessica Zezulka explored the last question. Marginal comments below are the instructor's. But what do you think of her answer? How might she strengthen and develop the argument she begins to make here about the play's turning point? What alternative answers or arguments occur to you?

Zezulka 1

Jessica Zezulka
Professor Mays
English 298
10 January 2017

Trifles Plot Response Paper

While the men dillydally over the facts, the so-called "evidence," the women in *Trifles* discover the missing piece: a motive for murder. The moment Mrs. Hale and Mrs. Peters find the dead canary in the hidden box is the turning point in the play. Up until that instant, their conversation seems trivial, to both a reader and the men involved. Upon discussing the little trifles, the quilt and the sewing, these two women have inadvertently stumbled across what the men are so desperate to find. This turning point changes the way the play is read, as well as the way you view the wife of the dead man.

> Might it be possible to read their conversation as less trivial (even up to this point) than the male characters do?

Zezulka 2

Mrs. Wright, accused of murdering her husband, appears almost crazy for just up and killing her spouse. The reader is as confused as the men at first, wondering why on earth would she do it? When you realize, along with the two women, that her motive was his brutal killing of the canary, you suddenly become privy to a secret that the men seemingly never learn. The play uses dramatic irony, where the reader knows the truth but the characters in the play are oblivious. Susan Glaspell timed this moment perfectly, giving the reader time to be both confused and then suddenly enlightened.

This turning point breeds sympathy for the accused murderess. Mrs. Wright is no longer just a good-wife-gone-bad. You as the reader follow the emotions of the two women in the empty house and can feel their almost immediate comprehension and understanding of both the situation and the woman involved. The wife becomes someone we can relate to, almost having a just cause for murdering her husband. As I said, Glaspell builds the tension to that point perfectly; the reader is all for the law being upheld until you know what led up to the murder. If you asked me, I'd say he deserved it. The women's discussion of *Trifles* led to the heart of the matter, a turning point that all but justifies John Wright's death.

Again, though, don't we have relevant evidence before that about the possible state (and effects) of this marriage, which might be just as relevant to motive? If so, what *really* makes this moment stand out?

|

Interesting! Irony certainly is key to the play, but not all the characters are equally "oblivious," right?

|

So might the play also turn on the conflict — or at least the contrast — between two possible ways of defining "innocence" or even two kinds of "law"?

Zezulka 3

Work Cited

Glaspell, Susan. *Trifles. The Norton Introduction to Literature*, edited by Kelly J. Mays, portable 12th ed., W. W. Norton, 2017, pp. 771-83.

SAMPLE WRITING: ESSAY

The following sample of student writing demonstrates how you might develop
an early response to a play into a more formal and thorough argument about
it. In her essay on Susan Glaspell's TRIFLES, Stephanie Ortega explores the
relationship among the female characters in order to offer her own answers
to more than one of the questions posed in the previous chapter's "Suggestions for Writing": How does Mrs. Peters's character evolve over the course of
Trifles? How is that evolution significant to the play's theme, or how might it
help to define the play's particular version of feminism?

As always, we encourage you to read the sample with a critical eye, identifying
what works and what doesn't so as to discover specific ways to improve your own
writing and reading. At what moments in the essay do you find yourself strongly
agreeing? discovering something new about or in Glaspell's play? At what
moments might you instead find yourself disagreeing or feeling either confused
or simply dissatisfied, wanting more? What exactly makes each of these moments
especially satisfying, interesting, persuasive, enlightening—or the reverse? If
Stephanie Ortega were your classmate, what three specific things would you
suggest she do in order to improve the essay in revision? Alternatively, what
three qualities of this essay might you want to emulate in your own work?

Ortega 1

Stephanie Ortega
Professor Mays
English 298
23 January 2017

A Journey of Sisterhood

Trifles begins at the start of a murder investigation. Mrs. Wright has
allegedly murdered her harsh husband, John Wright; and the Sheriff and

his wife, Mrs. Peters; the County Attorney; and the neighbors, Mr. and
Mrs. Hale, all come to the Wright house to investigate. Throughout the
entire play the women are always on stage, whereas the men enter and
exit, so the women are the play's focus. But Glaspell's *Trifles* is a feminist
play not only because of that, but also because of how it shows two or
even three very different women coming together in sisterhood.

  Mrs. Peters and Mrs. Hale are first introduced as they stand together by
the door of the house where the murder took place, yet though the women
stand together, their behavior and views initially seem wide apart. Whereas
Mrs. Hale stands up for her counterparts, Mrs. Peters and Mrs. Wright, from
the beginning, Mrs. Peters at first tends to stick up more for the men. When
the County Attorney makes a remark about Mrs. Wright not having been
much of a homemaker and having a dirty home, we see that Mrs. Hale
doesn't like men poking in Mrs. Wright's business and having input in the
doings of a house. Putting herself in Mrs. Wright's shoes, Mrs. Hale says,
"I'd hate to have men coming into *my* kitchen, snooping around and
criticizing" (776, emphasis added). But Mrs. Peters states that since it is
an investigation, "it's no more than th[e men's] duty" to poke around (776).
Later, when Mrs. Hale actually interferes with the investigation by trying
to tidy up the place and re-sew the badly stitched quilt they discover, Mrs.
Peters steps in, "*[n]ervously*" saying, "I don't think we ought to touch
things" (779). Mrs. Peters's only view is that of her husband; she knows and
seems to care very little about Mrs. Wright or her life before marriage as
Minnie Foster. As far as Mrs. Peters is concerned, "the law is the law" (778),
and she is "married to" it, as the County Attorney will say at the end of the
play (783); therefore she must abide by it.

  Mrs. Hale's identification with Minnie Foster only intensifies as the
play progresses. She remembers Minnie Foster as a carefree woman full
of energy and life, bright and cheery like a canary, implying that marriage
to John Wright "change[d]" all that (780). Mrs. Hale starts feeling guilty
for not visiting Mrs. Wright, telling Mrs. Peters multiple times that she
"wish[es she] had come over sometimes when *she* was here," and
eventually even suggesting that not coming to see Mrs. Wright was
"a crime" (780, 782).

  In part because of the way Mrs. Hale talks about her, Minnie Foster's
figurative presence becomes ever stronger, bringing Mrs. Hale and Mrs.
Peters together as they put themselves into her place, speculating about
her feelings and responses to the conditions of her life. When the women

come upon a box containing a bird that had its neck wrung, Mrs. Hale associates Mr. Wright's presumed killing of the songbird with his destruction of part of Mrs. Wright, speculating about her feelings: "No, Wright wouldn't like the bird—a thing that sang. She used to sing. He killed that, too" (781). Thus, Mr. Wright's killing of the bird is a symbolic killing of Minnie Foster's spirit. At this point, the women come to understand that Mrs. Wright was indeed the one who killed her husband because when the women realize that Mr. Wright wrung the bird's neck, the women finally know the reason for Mrs. Wright's "funny way" of killing him (777). (It's now that *Their eyes meet* with "*[a] look of growing comprehension, of horror*" [781].)

More importantly, here is where we really start to see a change in Mrs. Peters. For the first time she, too, interferes with the investigators, even though she doesn't actually destroy evidence or lie, when she responds to a question about the cat by simply saying that there is not one "*now*" (781). She expresses sympathy for Minnie Foster and identifies with her, based on her own memories of the way she felt both when her kitten was killed with a hatchet and, much later, when her first baby died, leaving her and her husband alone in the "stillness" of their isolated house (782). Mrs. Peters also states that had she gotten hold of the boy who killed her kitten long ago she would have gotten revenge just as Mrs. Peters and Mrs. Hale now speculate that Minnie Foster Wright did. The women each sympathize with Minnie Foster and the distant person she has become, Mrs. Wright.

By sympathizing with Mrs. Wright and paying attention to the "little things" the men don't consider solid "evidence" (778), the women have single-handedly sorted out a plausible sequence of events and, more importantly, a reason why Mrs. Wright killed her husband the way she did. Yet rather than reveal what they've learned, they slowly, in the silence of mutual sympathy, work together to cover Mrs. Wright's tracks and to protect her. Mrs. Peters is defying the actual law and starting to protect the law of women and sisterhood instead. Mrs. Hale, Mrs. Peters, and Mrs. Wright become one unit, opposing their intuitive feminine selves to the logical and analytical men.

Although Mrs. Wright never once appears on stage, her presence is what brings all three women closer. They are able to attain information that the men simply overlook. And it is this which brings the women forth in the union of sisterhood at the end of the play as they realize that "We [women] all go through the same things—it's all just a different kind of the same thing" (782).

Ortega 4

Work Cited

Glaspell, Susan. *Trifles*. *The Norton Introduction to Literature*, edited by
Kelly J. Mays, portable 12th ed., W. W. Norton, 2017, pp. 771-83.

Understanding the Text

16 ELEMENTS OF DRAMA

Most of us read more fiction than drama and are likely to encounter drama by watching filmed versions of it. Nonetheless, the skills you have developed in reading stories and poems come in handy when you read plays. And just as with fiction and poetry, you will understand and appreciate drama more fully by becoming familiar with the various elements of the **genre**.

CHARACTER

Character is possibly the most familiar and accessible of the elements; both fiction and drama feature one or more imaginary persons who take part in the action. The word *character* refers not only to a person represented in an imagined plot, whether narrated or acted out, but also to the unique qualities that make up a personality. From one point of view, "character" as a part in a plot and "character" as a kind of personality are both predictions: This sort of person is likely to see things from a certain angle and behave in certain ways. Notice that the idea of character includes both the individual differences among people and the classification of similar people into types. Whereas much realistic fiction emphasizes unique individuals rather than general character types, drama often compresses and simplifies personalities—a play has only about two hours at the most (sometimes much less) in which to show situations, appearances, and behaviors, without description or background other than **exposition** provided in the dialogue. The advantage of portraying character in broader strokes is that it heightens the contrasts between character types, adding to the drama: Differences provoke stronger reactions.

Plays are especially concerned with character because of the concrete manner in which they portray people on the stage. With a few exceptions (such as experiments in multimedia performance), the only words in the performance of a play are spoken by actors, and usually these actors are *in character*—that is, speaking as though they really were the people they play in the drama. (Rarely, plays have a **narrator** who observes and comments on the action from the sidelines, and in some plays a character may address the audience directly, but even when the actors apparently step outside of the imaginary frame, they are still part of the play and are still playing characters.) In fiction, the narrator's description and commentary can guide a reader's judgment about characters. Reading a play, you will have no such guide because drama relies almost exclusively on *indirect characterization* (see ch. 3). Apart from some clues about characters in the **stage directions**, you will need to imagine the appearance, manners, and movement of someone speaking the lines assigned to any one character. You can do this even as you read through a play for the first time, discovering the characters' attitudes and motivations as the scenes unfold. This ability to predict character and then to revise expectations as situations change is based not only on our experiences of people in real life but also on our familiarity with types of characters or roles that occur in many dramatic forms.

Consider the patterns of characters in many stories that are narrated or acted out, whether in novels, comic books, television series, Hollywood films, or even video games. In many of these forms, there is a leading role, a main character: the **protagonist**. The titles of plays such as HAMLET, ANTIGONE, or, a little less obviously, DEATH OF A SALESMAN imply that the play will be about a central character, the chief object of the playwright's and the reader's or audience's concern. Understanding the character of the protagonist—sometimes in contrast with an **antagonist**, the opponent of the main character—becomes the consuming interest of such a play. Especially in more traditional or popular genres, the protagonist may be called a **hero** or **heroine**, and the antagonist may be called the **villain**. Most characterization in professional theater, however, avoids depicting pure good and pure evil in a fight to the death. Most characters possess both negative and redeeming qualities.

As in other genres that represent people in action, in drama there are *minor characters* or supporting roles. At least since ancient Rome, romantic comedies have been structured around a leading man and woman, along with a comparable pair (often the "buddies" of the leads) whose problems may be less serious, whose characters may be less complex, or who in other ways support or complicate rather than dominate the action. Sometimes a minor character can be said to be a **foil**, a character designed to bring out qualities in another character by contrast. The main point to remember is that all the characters in a drama are interdependent and help characterize each other. Through dialogue and behavior, each brings out what is characteristic in the others.

Like movies, plays must respect certain limitations: the time an audience can be expected to sit and watch, the attention and sympathy an audience is likely to give to various characters, the amount of exposition that can be shown rather than spoken aloud. Because of these constraints, playwrights, screenwriters, casting directors, and actors must rely on shortcuts to convey character. Everyone involved, including the audience, consciously or unconsciously relies on stereotypes of various social roles to flesh out the dramatic action. Even a play that seeks to undermine stereotypes must still invoke them. In the United States today, casting—or typecasting—usually relies on an actor's social identity, from gender and race to occupation, region, and age. However, plays that rely too much on stereotypes, positive or negative, may leave everyone disappointed (or offended); a role that defies stereotypes can be more interesting to perform and to watch. Alternatively, a character can be so exceptional and unfamiliar that audiences will fail to recognize any connection to people they might meet, and their responses will fall flat. All dramatic roles, then, must have some connection to types of personality, and good roles modify such types just enough to make the character interesting. Playwrights often overturn or modify expectations of character in order to surprise an audience. So, too, do the actors who play those parts.

Every performance of a given character, like every production of a play, is an interpretation. Not just "adaptations"—Greek or Elizabethan plays set in modern times and performed in modern dress, for example—but even productions that seek to adhere faithfully to the written play are interpretations of what is vital or essential in it. John Malkovich, in the 1983–84 production of *Death of a Salesman*, did not portray Biff Loman as an outgoing, successful, hail-fellow-well-met jock, though that is apparently how the playwright originally envisioned the part. Malkovich saw Biff as only pretending to be a jock. Big-time athletes, he insisted, don't glad-hand people; they wait for people to come to them. The actor did not change the author's words, but by intonation, body language, and "stage business" (wordless gestures and actions) he suggested his own view of the character. In other words, he broke with the expectations associated with the character's type. As you read and develop your own interpretation of a play, try imagining various interpretations of its characters in order to reveal different possible meanings in the drama.

Questions about Character

- Who is the protagonist? Why and how so? Which other characters, if any, are main or major characters? Which are minor characters?
- What are the protagonist's most distinctive traits, and what is most distinctive about his or her outlook and values? What motivates the character? What is it about the character that creates internal and/or external conflict? Which lines or stage directions reveal most about the character?
- What are the roles of other characters? Which, if any, functions as an antagonist? Which, if any, serves as a foil? Does any character function as a narrator or **chorus**, providing background information and commentary? Why and how so?
- To what extent are any of the characters in the play "types"? How might this affect an audience's experience of the play? In what ways

might a director or actor choose to go against the expected types, and how would this complicate the play's overall effect and meaning?
- Which of the characters, or which aspects of the characters, does the play encourage us to sympathize with or to admire? to view negatively? Why and how so? Are there characters who might be more or less sympathetic, depending on how the role is cast and interpreted?
- If you were directing a production of this play, whom among your friends and acquaintances would you cast in each role, and why? If you were directing a movie version, what professional actors would you cast?

PLOT AND STRUCTURE

An important part of any storyteller's task, whether in narrative or dramatic genres, is the invention, selection, and arrangement of some **action**. Even carefully structured action cannot properly be called a full-scale **plot** without some unifying sense of purpose. That is, what happens should seem to happen for meaningful reasons. This does not mean, of course, that characters or the audience must be satisfied in their hopes or expectations, or that effective plays need to wrap up every loose end. It does mean that a reader or theatergoer should feel that the playwright has completed *this* play—that nothing essential is missing—though the play's outcome or overall effect may be difficult to sum up.

Conflict is the engine that drives plot, and the presentation of conflict shapes the dramatic structure of a play. A conflict whose outcome is never in doubt may have other kinds of interest, but it is not truly dramatic. In a dramatic conflict, each of the opposing forces must at some point seem likely to triumph or worthy of such triumph—whether conflict is *external* (one character versus another, or one group of characters versus another group, each of whom may represent a different worldview) or *internal* (within a single character torn between competing views, duties, needs, or desires), or even one idea or ideology versus another one. In *Hamlet*, for example, our interest in the struggle between Hamlet and Claudius depends on their being evenly matched. Claudius has possession of the throne and the queen, but Hamlet's role as the heir to the late king and his popularity with the people offset his opponent's strength.

The typical plot in drama, as in fiction, involves five stages: exposition, rising action, climax, falling action, and conclusion. **Exposition**, the first phase of plot, provides essential background information about the characters and situation as they exist at the beginning of a play and perhaps also about the events that got the characters to this point—as when, early in TRIFLES, Mr. Hale describes what happened before the play opens. The second phase,

rising action, begins when an **inciting incident** leads to conflict—as when, in *Trifles*, the men leave the women alone with what the latter soon discover to be crucial evidence. The moment when the conflict reaches its greatest pitch of intensity and its outcome is decided is the plot's third phase, its **climax** or **turning point**—in *Trifles*, perhaps the discovery of the dead bird and the act of covering up the evidence. The fourth stage, **falling action**, brings a release of emotional tension and moves the characters toward the **resolution** of their conflict and the plot itself toward its fifth and final stage, the **conclusion**. In *Trifles*, the men's return to the kitchen because, they believe, no evidence has been found can be called the falling action. The women's apparent decision to remain mute about what they have discovered can be called the resolution. The play concludes as the characters leave the Wrights' house. Unlike *Trifles*, some lengthy plays feature more than one plot. In such cases, the plot to which less time and attention is devoted is called the **subplot**.

Many older plays in the Western tradition, such as Shakespeare's, have five acts, each act roughly corresponding to—and thus emphasizing—a particular phase of plot. Acts are often further subdivided into scenes, each of which usually takes place in a somewhat different time and place and features a somewhat different combination of characters. Ancient Greek plays such as *Oedipus the King* are structured differently, such that individual scenes or *episodes* are separated by choral songs—that is, odes spoken or sung by the group of characters known as the chorus. Modern plays tend to have fewer acts and scenes than those of earlier eras, and plays such as *Trifles*—in which the action unfolds continuously and, usually, in a single time and place— have become so common that they have their own name: the *one-act play*.

In the performance of a play longer than one act, it has become customary to have at least one intermission, in part for the practical reason that the audience may need restrooms or refreshments. Breaks may be signaled by turning down stage lights, turning up the house lights, and lowering the curtain (if there is one).

On rare occasions, very long plays (such as Tony Kushner's *Angels in America* [1992–93]) are performed over more than one evening, with the obvious challenge of finding an audience willing and able to afford tickets and time for more than one performance; those who read such play "cycles" or **sequences** at their own pace at home have a certain advantage.

The key point is that the form of a play and the breaks between scenes or acts result from the nature of the play. Breaks can create suspense—a curtain comes down after an unexplained gunshot—or they can provide relief from tension or an emotional crisis.

Questions about Plot

- Read the first scene or the first few pages and then stop. What potential for conflict do you see here? What do you expect to happen in the rest of the play?
- How is the play divided into acts, scenes, or episodes, if at all? What is the effect of this structure? Does the division of the play correspond, more or less, to the five stages of plot development—exposition, rising action, climax, resolution, conclusion?
- Does the play show a relatively clear progression through the traditional stages of plot development, or does it seem to defy such conventions? If so, how, and what might the playwright achieve through these departures from tradition?
- What is the inciting incident or destabilizing event? How and why does this event destabilize the initial situation? How would you describe the conflict that develops? To what extent is it external, internal, or both?
- What is the climax, or turning point? Why and how so? How is the conflict resolved? How and why might this resolution fulfill or defy your expectations?

STAGES, SETS, AND SETTING

Most of us have been to a theater at one time or another, and we know what a conventional modern stage (the **proscenium stage**) looks like: a room with the wall missing between us and it (the so-called *fourth wall*). So when we read a modern play—that is, one written during the past two or three hundred years—and imagine it taking place before us, we think of it as happening on this kind of stage. Though there are also other modern types of stages—the **thrust stage**, where the audience sits around three sides of the major acting area, and the **arena stage**, where the audience sits all the way around the acting area and players make their entrances and their exits through the auditorium—most plays today are performed on a proscenium stage. Most of the plays in this book can be readily imagined as taking place on such a stage.

Ancient Greek plays and the plays of Shakespeare were originally staged quite differently from most modern plays, however, and although they may be played today on a proscenium stage, we might be confused as we read if we are unaware of the layout of the theaters for which they were first written. In the Greek theater, the audience sat on a raised semicircle of seats (**amphitheater**) halfway around a circular area (**orchestra**) used primarily for dancing by the chorus. At the back of the orchestra was the **skene**, or stage house, representing the palace or temple before which the action took place.

Shakespeare's stage, in contrast, basically involved a rectangular area built inside one end of a large enclosure like a circular walled-in yard; the audience stood on the ground or sat in stacked balconies around three sides of the principal acting area (rather like a thrust stage). There were additional acting areas on either side of this stage, as well as a recessed area at its back (which could represent Gertrude's chamber in *Hamlet*, for example) and an upper acting area (which could serve as Juliet's balcony). A trap door in the stage floor was used for occasional effects; the ghost of Hamlet's father probably entered and exited this way. Until three centuries ago—and certainly in Shakespeare's time—plays for large paying audiences were performed outdoors in daylight because of the difficulty and expense of lighting. If you are curious about Shakespeare's stage, you can visit a reconstruction of his Globe Theatre in Southwark, London, England, either in person or online at www.shakespearesglobe.org. Every summer, plays by Shakespeare are performed there for large international audiences willing to sit on hard benches around the arena or to stand as "groundlings" (a lucky few of whom can lean on the stage near the feet of the actors). The walls in the background of the stage are beautifully carved and painted, but there is no painted scenery, minimal furniture, few costume changes, no lighting, and no curtain around the stage (a cloth hanging usually covers the recessed area at the back of the stage). Three or four musicians may play period instruments on the balcony.

As the design of the Globe suggests, the conventions of dramatic writing and stage production have changed considerably over the centuries. Certainly this is true of the way playwrights convey a sense of place—one of the two key ingredients that make up a play's **setting**. Usually the audience is asked to imagine that the featured section of the auditorium is actually a particular place somewhere else. The audience of course knows it is a stage, more or less bare or elaborately disguised, but they accept it as a kitchen, a public square, a wooded park, an open road, or a room in a castle or a hut. *Oedipus the King* takes place entirely before the palace at Thebes. Following the general convention of ancient Greek drama, the play's setting never changes. When the action demands the presence of Teiresias, for example, the scene does not shift to him; instead, escorts bring him to the front of the palace. Similarly, important events that take place elsewhere are described by witnesses who arrive on the scene.

In Shakespeare's theater the conventions of place are quite different: The acting arena does not represent a single specific place but assumes a temporary identity according to the characters who inhabit it, their costumes, and their speeches. At the opening of *Hamlet* we know we are at a sentry station because a man dressed as a soldier challenges two others. By line 15, we know that we are in Denmark because the actors profess to be "liegemen to the Dane." At the end of the scene the actors leave the stage and in a sense take the sentry station with them. Shortly thereafter, a group of people dressed in court costumes and a man and a woman wearing crowns appear. As a theater audience, we must surmise from the costumes and dialogue that the acting area has now become a royal court; when we read the play, the stage directions give us a cue that the place has changed.

In a modern play, there are likely to be several changes of scene, each marked by the lowering of the curtain or the darkening of the stage while different sets and props are arranged. **Sets** (the design, decoration, and scenery) and **props** (articles or objects used on stage) vary greatly in modern productions of plays written in any period. Sometimes space is merely suggested—a circle of sand at one end of the stage, a blank wall behind—to emphasize universal themes or to stimulate the audience's imagination. More typically, a set uses realistic aids to the imagination. The set of *Trifles*, for example, must include at least a sink, a cupboard, a stove, a small table, a large kitchen table, and a rocking chair, as well as certain props: a bird cage, quilting pieces, and an ornamental box.

Time is the second key ingredient of setting, and conventions for representing time have also altered across the centuries. Three or four centuries ago, European dramatists and critics admired the conventions of classical Greek drama which, they believed, dictated that the action of a play should represent a very short time—sometimes as short as the actual performance time (two or three hours), and certainly no longer than a single day. This unity of time, one of the three so-called **classical unities**, impels a dramatist to select the moment when a stable situation should change and to fill in the necessary prior details by exposition. (These same critics maintained that a play should be unified in place and action as well; the kind of leaping from Denmark to England, or from court to forest, that happens in Shakespeare's plays, as well as subplots, were off-limits according to such standards. In *Trifles*, which observes the three unities, all the action before the investigators' visit to the farmhouse is summarized by characters during their brief visit, and the kitchen is the only part of the house seen by the audience.)

When there are gaps and shifts in time, they are often indicated between scenes with the help of scenery, sound effects, stage directions, or notes in the program. An actor must assist in conveying the idea of time if his or her character appears at different ages. Various conventions of classical or Elizabethan drama have also worked effectively to communicate to the audience the idea of the passage of time, from the choral odes in *Oedipus the King* to the breaks between scenes in Shakespeare plays.

Action within a play thus can take place in a wide range of locations and over many years rather than in the one place and the twenty-four-hour period demanded by critics who believed in the classical unities. And we can learn much about how a particular play works and what it means by paying attention to the way it handles setting and sets.

TONE, LANGUAGE, AND SYMBOL

In plays, as in other literary genres, **tone** is difficult to specify or explain. Perhaps tone is more important in drama than in other genres because it is, in performance, a spoken form, and vocal tone always affects the meaning of spoken words to some extent, in any culture or language. The actor—and any reader who wishes to imagine a play as spoken aloud—must infer from the written language just how to read a line, what tone of voice to use. The choice of tone must be a negotiation between the words of the playwright and the interpretation and skill of the actor or reader. At times stage directions will specify the tone of a line of dialogue, though even that must be only a hint, since there are many ways of speaking "intensely" or "angrily." Find a line in one of the plays printed here that has a stage direction telling the actor how to deliver it, and with one or two other people take turns saying it that way. If nothing else, such an experiment may help you appreciate the talent of good actors who can put on a certain tone of voice and make it seem natural and convincing. But it will also show you the many options for interpreting tone.

Dramatic *irony*, in which a character's perception is contradicted by what the audience knows, and even *situational irony*, in which a character's (and the audience's) expectations about what will happen are contradicted by what actually does happen, are relatively easy to detect. But *verbal irony*, in which a statement implies a meaning quite different from its obvious, literal meaning, can be fairly subtle and easy to miss. In the absence of clear stage directions, verbal irony—like other aspects of tone—can also be a matter of interpretation. That is, directors and actors, as well as readers and audiences, will often have to decide which lines in a play should be interpreted ironically. All three types of irony are nonetheless crucial to drama. As the very term *dramatic irony* suggests, drama—even more than fiction—depends for its effects on gaps between what the various characters and the audience know. And situational irony—the gap between expectations and outcomes and even between what characters seem to deserve and what they get—is an especially key component of **tragedy**.

Never hesitate to apply the skills you have developed in interpreting poetry to drama; after all, most early plays were written in some form of verse. Aspects of poetry often emerge in modern plays; for example, **monologues** or extended speeches by one character, while they rarely rhyme or have regular **meter**, may allow greater eloquence than is usual in everyday speech and may include revealing imagery and **figures of speech**. A character in Lorraine Hansberry's A RAISIN IN THE SUN, for example, uses **metaphor** and **personification**, as well as **alliteration**, to great effect when she remarks (in act 3) that "death done come in this here house [. . .] Done come walking in my house."

Simple actions or objects, too, often have metaphorical significance or turn into **symbols**. Effective plays often use props in this way, as *Trifles* does with the bird and its cage. And some plays, like some poems, may even be organized around *controlling metaphors*. As you read, pay close attention to metaphors or images, whether in language or more concrete form.

Allusions, references to other works of literature or art or something else external to the play, can enrich the text in similar ways. The title of Tom Stoppard's uproarious comedy *The Real Inspector Hound* (1968), for example, seems to be an allusion to Sir Arthur Conan Doyle's novel *The Hound of the Baskervilles* (1901–02), featuring Sherlock Holmes. Doyle's novel is a classic in the detective fiction genre, which Stoppard's *Inspector Hound* parodies. In a more serious vein, though New Orleans, where Tennessee Williams's *A Streetcar Named Desire* takes place, actually does contain a street called Elysian Fields, the play gets a good deal of symbolic mileage out of using this as a setting for the play thanks to the allusion to Greek mythology (in which the Elysian Fields were the final resting place of heroic and virtuous souls). Awareness of all the stylistic choices in the work can help you reach a clearer interpretation of the whole play.

Questions about Tone, Language, and Symbol

- Which lines in the play strike you as most ambiguous when it comes to the tone in which they should be spoken? Why and how so? What is the effect of that ambiguity, or how might an actor's or reader's decision about tone here affect the play as a whole?
- How would you describe the overall tone of the whole play? Do any moments or entire scenes or acts in the play seem interestingly different in terms of their tone?
- How do the play's characters differ from one another in terms of their tone? Does any character's tone change over the course of the play?
- Are any details—such as names; actions or statements; references to objects, props, or other details of setting; or allusions, metaphors, or other figures of speech—repeated throughout the play? Do any of these repeated details seem to have special significance? If so, what might that significance be?
- What types of irony, if any, are at work in the play? What is the effect of the irony?

THEME

Theme—a statement a work seems to make about a given issue or subject—is by its very nature the most comprehensive of the elements, embracing the impact of the entire work. Indeed, theme is not part of the work but is abstracted from it by the reader or audience. Since we, as interpreters, infer the theme and put it in our own words, we understandably often disagree about it. To arrive at your own statement of a theme, you need to consider all the elements of a play together: character, structure, setting (including time and place), tone, and other aspects of the style or the potential staging that create the entire effect.

Tips for Identifying Theme

Because theme emerges from a work in its entirety and from all the other elements working together, there's no one-size-fits-all method for discovering theme. Here, however, are some things to look for and consider as you read and re-read a play.

- Pay attention to the title. A title will seldom indicate a play's theme directly, but some titles do suggest a central topic or a key question.

Probe the rest of the play to see what insights, if any, about that topic or answers to that question it ultimately seems to offer.

- Identify any statements that the characters make about a general concept, issue, or topic such as human nature, the natural world, and so on, particularly in monologues or in debates between major characters. Look, too, for statements that potentially have a general meaning or application beyond the play, even if they refer to a specific situation. Then consider whether and how the play as a whole corroborates, overturns, or complicates any one such view or statement.

- If a character changes over the course of the play, try to articulate the truth or insight that he or she seems to discover. Then consider whether and how the play as a whole corroborates or complicates that insight.

- Identify a conflict depicted in the play and state it in general terms or turn it into a general question, leaving out any reference to specific characters, setting, and so on. Then think about the insight or theme that might be implied by the way the conflict is resolved.

. . .

Above all, try to understand a play on its own terms and to separate interpretation from evaluation. You may dislike symbolic or unrealistic drama until you get more used to it; if a play is not supposed to represent what real people would do in everyday life in that place and time, then it should not be criticized for failing to do so. Or you may find realistic plays about ordinary adults in middle America in the mid-twentieth century to be lacking in excitement or appeal. Yet if you read carefully, you may discover vigorous, moving portrayals of people trapped in situations all too familiar to them, if alien to you. Tastes may vary as widely as tones of speech, but if you are familiar with the elements of drama and the ways dramatic **conventions** vary over time and across cultures, you can become a good judge of theatrical literature, and you will notice more and more of the fine effects it can achieve. Nothing replaces the exhilaration and immediacy of a live theater performance, but reading and re-reading plays can yield a rich and rewarding appreciation of the dramatic art.

HENRIK IBSEN
(1828–1906)
A Doll House[1]

Born in Skien, Norway, Henrik Ibsen was apprenticed to an apothecary until 1850, when he left for
Oslo and published his first play, *Catilina*, a verse
tragedy. By 1857 Ibsen was director of Oslo's Norwegian Theater, but his early plays, such as *Love's
Comedy* (1862), were poorly received. Disgusted with what he saw as Norway's
backwardness, Ibsen left in 1864 for Rome, where he wrote two more verse plays,
Brand (1866) and *Peer Gynt* (1867), before turning to the realistic style and harsh
criticism of traditional social mores for which he is best known. *The League of
Youth* (1869), *Pillars of Society* (1877), *A Doll House* (1879), *Ghosts* (1881), *An
Enemy of the People* (1882), *The Wild Duck* (1884), and *Hedda Gabler* (1890) won
him a reputation throughout Europe as a controversial and outspoken advocate
of moral and social reform. Near the end of his life, Ibsen explored the human condition in the explicitly symbolic terms of *The Master Builder* (1892) and *When
We Dead Awaken* (1899). Ibsen's works had enormous influence on twentieth-
century drama.

CHARACTERS

TORVALD HELMER, *a lawyer*
NORA, *his wife*
DR. RANK
MRS. LINDE
NILS KROGSTAD, *a bank clerk*

THE HELMERS' THREE SMALL CHILDREN
ANNE-MARIE, *their nurse*
HELENE, *a maid*
A DELIVERY BOY

The action takes place in HELMER'S *residence.*

ACT I

A comfortable room, tastefully but not expensively furnished. A door to
the right in the back wall leads to the entryway; another to the left leads to
HELMER'S study. Between these doors, a piano. Midway in the left-hand
wall a door, and further back a window. Near the window a round table

1. Translated by Rolf Fjelde.

*with an armchair and a small sofa. In the right-hand wall, toward the rear,
a door, and nearer the foreground a porcelain stove with two armchairs and
a rocking chair beside it. Between the stove and the side door, a small table.
Engravings on the walls. An etagère with china figures and other small art
objects; a small bookcase with richly bound books; the floor carpeted; a fire
burning in the stove. It is a winter day.*

A bell rings in the entryway; shortly after we hear the door being unlocked.
NORA *comes into the room, humming happily to herself; she is wearing
street clothes and carries an armload of packages, which she puts down on
the table to the right. She has left the hall door open; and through it a*
DELIVERY BOY *is seen, holding a Christmas tree and a basket, which he gives
to the* MAID *who let them in.*

NORA: Hide the tree well, Helene. The children mustn't get a glimpse of it
till this evening, after it's trimmed. [*To the* DELIVERY BOY, *taking out her
purse.*] How much?
DELIVERY BOY: Fifty, ma'am.
NORA: There's a crown. No, keep the change. [*The* BOY *thanks her and leaves.*
NORA *shuts the door. She laughs softly to herself while taking off her street
things. Drawing a bag of macaroons from her pocket, she eats a couple, then
steals over and listens at her husband's study door.*] Yes, he's home. [*Hums
again as she moves to the table right.*]
HELMER: [*From the study.*] Is that my little lark twittering out there?
NORA: [*Busy opening some packages.*] Yes, it is.
HELMER: Is that my squirrel rummaging around?
NORA: Yes!
HELMER: When did my squirrel get in?
NORA: Just now. [*Putting the macaroon bag in her pocket and wiping her
mouth.*] Do come in, Torvald, and see what I've bought.
HELMER: Can't be disturbed. [*After a moment he opens the door and peers
in, pen in hand.*] Bought, you say? All that there? Has the little spend-
thrift been out throwing money around again?
NORA: Oh, but Torvald, this year we really should let ourselves go a bit. It's
the first Christmas we haven't had to economize.
HELMER: But you know we can't go squandering.
NORA: Oh yes, Torvald, we can squander a little now. Can't we? Just a tiny,
wee bit. Now that you've got a big salary and are going to make piles and
piles of money.
HELMER: Yes—starting New Year's. But then it's a full three months till
the raise comes through.
NORA: Pooh! We can borrow that long.

HELMER: Nora! [*Goes over and playfully takes her by the ear.*] Are your scatterbrains off again? What if today I borrowed a thousand crowns, and you squandered them over Christmas week, and then on New Year's Eve a roof tile fell on my head, and I lay there—

NORA: [*Putting her hand on his mouth.*] Oh! Don't say such things!

HELMER: Yes, but what if it happened—then what?

NORA: If anything so awful happened, then it just wouldn't matter if I had debts or not.

HELMER: Well, but the people I'd borrowed from?

NORA: Them? Who cares about them! They're strangers.

HELMER: Nora, Nora, how like a woman! No, but seriously, Nora, you know what I think about that. No debts! Never borrow! Something of freedom's lost—and something of beauty, too—from a home that's founded on borrowing and debt. We've made a brave stand up to now, the two of us; and we'll go right on like that the little while we have to.

NORA: [*Going toward the stove.*] Yes, whatever you say, Torvald.

HELMER: [*Following her.*] Now, now, the little lark's wings mustn't droop. Come on, don't be a sulky squirrel. [*Taking out his wallet.*] Nora, guess what I have here.

NORA: [*Turning quickly.*] Money!

HELMER: There, see. [*Hands her some notes.*] Good grief, I know how costs go up in a house at Christmastime.

NORA: Ten—twenty—thirty—forty. Oh, thank you, Torvald; I can manage no end on this.

HELMER: You really will have to.

NORA: Oh yes, I promise I will. But come here so I can show you everything I bought. And so cheap! Look, new clothes for Ivar here—and a sword. Here a horse and a trumpet for Bob. And a doll and a doll's bed here for Emmy; they're nothing much, but she'll tear them to bits in no time anyway. And here I have dress material and handkerchiefs for the maids. Old Anne-Marie really deserves something more.

HELMER: And what's in that package there?

NORA: [*With a cry.*] Torvald, no! You can't see that till tonight!

HELMER: I see. But tell me now, you little prodigal, what have you thought of for yourself?

NORA: For myself? Oh, I don't want anything at all.

HELMER: Of course you do. Tell me just what—within reason—you'd most like to have.

NORA: I honestly don't know. Oh, listen, Torvald—

HELMER: Well?

NORA: [*Fumbling at his coat buttons, without looking at him.*] If you want to give me something, then maybe you could—you could—

HELMER: Come, on, out with it.

NORA: [*Hurriedly.*] You could give me money, Torvald. No more than you think you can spare; then one of these days I'll buy something with it.

HELMER: But Nora—

NORA: Oh, please, Torvald darling, do that! I beg you, please. Then I could hang the bills in pretty gilt paper on the Christmas tree. Wouldn't that be fun?

HELMER: What are those little birds called that always fly through their fortunes?

NORA: Oh yes, spendthrifts; I know all that. But let's do as I say, Torvald; then I'll have time to decide what I really need most. That's very sensible, isn't it?

HELMER: [*Smiling.*] Yes, very—that is, if you actually hung onto the money I give you, and you actually used it to buy yourself something. But it goes for the house and for all sorts of foolish things, and then I only have to lay out some more.

NORA: Oh, but Torvald—

HELMER: Don't deny it, my dear little Nora. [*Putting his arm around her waist.*] Spendthrifts are sweet, but they use up a frightful amount of money. It's incredible what it costs a man to feed such birds.

NORA: Oh, how can you say that! Really, I save everything I can.

HELMER: [*Laughing.*] Yes, that's the truth. Everything you can. But that's nothing at all.

NORA: [*Humming, with a smile of quiet satisfaction.*] Hm, if you only knew what expenses we larks and squirrels have, Torvald.

HELMER: You're an odd little one. Exactly the way your father was. You're never at a loss for scaring up money; but the moment you have it, it runs right out through your fingers; you never know what you've done with it. Well, one takes you as you are. It's deep in your blood. Yes, these things are hereditary, Nora.

NORA: Ah, I could wish I'd inherited many of Papa's qualities.

HELMER: And I couldn't wish you anything but just what you are, my sweet little lark. But wait; it seems to me you have a very—what should I call it?—a very suspicious look today—

NORA: I do?

HELMER: You certainly do. Look me straight in the eye.

NORA: [*Looking at him.*] Well?

HELMER: [*Shaking an admonitory finger.*] Surely my sweet tooth hasn't been running riot in town today, has she?

NORA: No. Why do you imagine that?

HELMER: My sweet tooth really didn't make a little detour through the confectioner's?

NORA: No, I assure you, Torvald—

HELMER: Hasn't nibbled some pastry?

NORA: No, not at all.

HELMER: Not even munched a macaroon or two?

NORA: No, Torvald, I assure you, really—

HELMER: There, there now. Of course I'm only joking.

NORA: [*Going to the table, right.*] You know I could never think of going against you.

HELMER: No, I understand that; and you *have* given me your word. [*Going over to her.*] Well, you keep your little Christmas secrets to yourself, Nora darling. I expect they'll come to light this evening, when the tree is lit.

NORA: Did you remember to ask Dr. Rank?

HELMER: No. But there's no need for that; it's assumed he'll be dining with us. All the same, I'll ask him when he stops by here this morning. I've ordered some fine wine. Nora, you can't imagine how I'm looking forward to this evening.

NORA: So am I. And what fun for the children, Torvald!

HELMER: Ah, it's so gratifying to know that one's gotten a safe, secure job, and with a comfortable salary. It's a great satisfaction, isn't it?

NORA: Oh, it's wonderful!

HELMER: Remember last Christmas? Three whole weeks before, you shut yourself in every evening till long after midnight, making flowers for the Christmas tree, and all the other decorations to surprise us. Ugh, that was the dullest time I've ever lived through.

NORA: It wasn't at all dull for me.

HELMER: [*Smiling.*] But the outcome *was* pretty sorry, Nora.

NORA: Oh, don't tease me with that again. How could I help it that the cat came in and tore everything to shreds.

HELMER: No, poor thing, you certainly couldn't. You wanted so much to please us all, and that's what counts. But it's just as well that the hard times are past.

NORA: Yes, it's really wonderful.

HELMER: Now I don't have to sit here alone, boring myself, and you don't have to tire your precious eyes and your fair little delicate hands—

NORA: [*Clapping her hands.*] No, is it really true, Torvald, I don't have to? Oh, how wonderfully lovely to hear! [*Taking his arm.*] Now I'll tell you just how I've thought we should plan things. Right after Christmas— [*The doorbell rings.*] Oh, the bell. [*Straightening the room up a bit.*] Somebody would have to come. What a bore!

HELMER: I'm not at home to visitors, don't forget.

MAID: [*From the hall doorway.*] Ma'am, a lady to see you—

NORA: All right, let her come in.

MAID: [*To* HELMER.] And the doctor's just come too.

HELMER: Did he go right to my study?

MAID: Yes, he did.

[HELMER *goes into his room. The* MAID *shows in* MRS. LINDE, *dressed in traveling clothes, and shuts the door after her.*]

MRS. LINDE: [*In a dispirited and somewhat hesitant voice.*] Hello, Nora.

NORA: [*Uncertain.*] Hello—

MRS. LINDE: You don't recognize me.

NORA: No, I don't know—but wait, I think—[*Exclaiming.*] What! Kristine! Is it really you?

MRS. LINDE: Yes, it's me.

NORA: Kristine! To think I didn't recognize you. But then, how could I? [*More quietly.*] How you've changed, Kristine!

MRS. LINDE: Yes, no doubt I have. In nine—ten long years.

NORA: Is it so long since we met! Yes, it's all of that. Oh, these last eight years have been a happy time, believe me. And so now you've come in to town, too. Made the long trip in the winter. That took courage.

MRS. LINDE: I just got here by ship this morning.

NORA: To enjoy yourself over Christmas, of course. Oh, how lovely! Yes, enjoy ourselves, we'll do that. But take your coat off. You're not still cold? [*Helping her.*] There now, let's get cozy here by the stove. No, the easy chair there! I'll take the rocker here. [*Seizing her hands.*] Yes, now you have your old look again; it was only in that first moment. You're a bit more pale, Kristine—and maybe a bit thinner.

MRS. LINDE: And much, much older, Nora.

NORA: Yes, perhaps a bit older; a tiny, tiny bit; not much at all. [*Stopping short; suddenly serious.*] Oh, but thoughtless me, to sit here, chattering away. Sweet, good Kristine, can you forgive me?

MRS. LINDE: What do you mean, Nora?

NORA: [*Softly.*] Poor Kristine, you've become a widow.

MRS. LINDE: Yes, three years ago.

NORA: Oh, I knew it, of course; I read it in the papers. Oh, Kristine, you must believe me; I often thought of writing you then, but I kept postponing it, and something always interfered.

MRS. LINDE: Nora dear, I understand completely.

NORA: No, it was awful of me, Kristine. You poor thing, how much you must have gone through. And he left you nothing?

MRS. LINDE: No.

NORA: And no children?

MRS. LINDE: No.

NORA: Nothing at all, then?

MRS. LINDE: Not even a sense of loss to feed on.

NORA: [*Looking incredulously at her.*] But Kristine, how could that be?

MRS. LINDE: [*Smiling wearily and smoothing her hair.*] Oh, sometimes it happens, Nora.

NORA: So completely alone. How terribly hard that must be for you. I have three lovely children. You can't see them now; they're out with the maid. But now you must tell me everything—

MRS. LINDE: No, no, no, tell me about yourself.

NORA: No, you begin. Today I don't want to be selfish. I want to think only of you today. But there *is* something I must tell you. Did you hear of the wonderful luck we had recently?

MRS. LINDE: No, what's that?

NORA: My husband's been made manager in the bank, just think!

MRS. LINDE: Your husband? How marvelous!

NORA: Isn't it? Being a lawyer is such an uncertain living, you know, especially if one won't touch any cases that aren't clean and decent. And of course Torvald would never do that, and I'm with him completely there. Oh, we're simply delighted, believe me! He'll join the bank right after New Year's and start getting a huge salary and lots of commissions. From now on we can live quite differently—just as we want. Oh, Kristine, I feel so light and happy! Won't it be lovely to have stacks of money and not a care in the world?

MRS. LINDE: Well, anyway, it would be lovely to have enough for necessities.

NORA: No, not just for necessities, but stacks and stacks of money!

MRS. LINDE: [*Smiling.*] Nora, Nora, aren't you sensible yet? Back in school you were such a free spender.

NORA: [*With a quiet laugh.*] Yes, that's what Torvald still says. [*Shaking her finger.*] But "Nora, Nora" isn't as silly as you all think. Really, we've been in no position for me to go squandering. We've had to work, both of us.

MRS. LINDE: You too?

NORA: Yes, at odd jobs—needlework, crocheting, embroidery, and such— [*Casually.*] and other things too. You remember that Torvald left the department when we were married? There was no chance of promotion in his office, and of course he needed to earn more money. But that first year he drove himself terribly. He took on all kinds of extra work that kept him going morning and night. It wore him down, and then he fell deathly ill. The doctors said it was essential for him to travel south.

MRS. LINDE: Yes, didn't you spend a whole year in Italy?

NORA: That's right. It wasn't easy to get away, you know. Ivar had just been born. But of course we had to go. Oh, that was a beautiful trip, and it saved Torvald's life. But it cost a frightful sum, Kristine.

MRS. LINDE: I can well imagine.

NORA: Four thousand, eight hundred crowns it cost. That's really a lot of money.

MRS. LINDE: But it's lucky you had it when you needed it.

NORA: Well, as it was, we got it from Papa.

MRS. LINDE: I see. It was just about the time your father died.

NORA: Yes, just about then. And, you know, I couldn't make that trip out to nurse him. I had to stay here, expecting Ivar any moment, and with my poor sick Torvald to care for. Dearest Papa, I never saw him again, Kristine. Oh, that was the worst time I've known in all my marriage.

MRS. LINDE: I know how you loved him. And then you went off to Italy?

NORA: Yes. We had the means now, and the doctors urged us. So we left a month after.

MRS. LINDE: And your husband came back completely cured?

NORA: Sound as a drum!

MRS. LINDE: But—the doctor?

NORA: Who?

MRS. LINDE: I thought the maid said he was a doctor, the man who came in with me.

NORA: Yes, that was Dr. Rank—but he's not making a sick call. He's our closest friend, and he stops by at least once a day. No, Torvald hasn't had a sick moment since, and the children are fit and strong, and I am, too. [*Jumping up and clapping her hands.*] Oh, dear God, Kristine, what a lovely thing to live and be happy! But how disgusting of me—I'm talking of nothing but my own affairs. [*Sits on a stool close by* KRISTINE, *arms resting across her knees.*] Oh, don't be angry with me! Tell me, is it really true that you weren't in love with your husband? Why did you marry him, then?

MRS. LINDE: My mother was still alive, but bedridden and helpless—and I had my two younger brothers to look after. In all conscience, I didn't think I could turn him down.

NORA: No, you were right there. But was he rich at the time?

MRS. LINDE: He was very well off, I'd say. But the business was shaky, Nora. When he died, it all fell apart, and nothing was left.

NORA: And then—?

MRS. LINDE: Yes, so I had to scrape up a living with a little shop and a little teaching and whatever else I could find. The last three years have been like one endless workday without a rest for me. Now it's over, Nora. My poor mother doesn't need me, for she's passed on. Nor the boys, either; they're working now and can take care of themselves.

NORA: How free you must feel—

MRS. LINDE: No—only unspeakably empty. Nothing to live for now. [*Standing up anxiously.*] That's why I couldn't take it any longer out in that desolate hole. Maybe here it'll be easier to find something to do and keep my mind occupied. If I could only be lucky enough to get a steady job, some office work—

NORA: Oh, but Kristine, that's so dreadfully tiring, and you already look so tired. It would be much better for you if you could go off to a bathing resort.

MRS. LINDE: [*Going toward the window.*] I have no father to give me travel money, Nora.

NORA: [*Rising.*] Oh, don't be angry with me.

MRS. LINDE: [*Going to her.*] Nora dear, don't you be angry with me. The worst of my kind of situation is all the bitterness that's stored away. No one to work for, and yet you're always having to snap up your opportunities. You have to live; and so you grow selfish. When you told me the happy change in your lot, do you know I was delighted less for your sakes than for mine?

NORA: How so? Oh, I see. You think maybe Torvald could do something for you.

MRS. LINDE: Yes, that's what I thought.

NORA: And he will, Kristine! Just leave it to me; I'll bring it up so delicately— find something attractive to humor him with. Oh, I'm so eager to help you.

MRS. LINDE: How very kind of you, Nora, to be so concerned over me— doubly kind, considering you really know so little of life's burdens yourself.

NORA: I—? I know so little—?

MRS. LINDE: [*Smiling.*] Well, my heavens—a little needlework and such— Nora, you're just a child.

NORA: [*Tossing her head and pacing the floor.*] You don't have to act so superior.

MRS. LINDE: Oh?

NORA: You're just like the others. You all think I'm incapable of anything serious—

MRS. LINDE: Come now—

NORA: That I've never had to face the raw world.

MRS. LINDE: Nora dear, you've just been telling me all your troubles.

NORA: Hm! Trivia! [*Quietly.*] I haven't told you the big thing.

MRS. LINDE: Big thing? What do you mean?

NORA: You look down on me so, Kristine, but you shouldn't. You're proud that you worked so long and hard for your mother.

MRS. LINDE: I don't look down on a soul. But it *is* true: I'm proud—and happy, too—to think it was given to me to make my mother's last days almost free of care.

NORA: And you're also proud thinking of what you've done for your brothers.

MRS. LINDE: I feel I've a right to be.

NORA: I agree. But listen to this, Kristine—I've also got something to be proud and happy for.

MRS. LINDE: I don't doubt it. But whatever do you mean?

NORA: Not so loud. What if Torvald heard! He mustn't, not for anything in the world. Nobody must know, Kristine. No one but you.

MRS. LINDE: But what is it, then?

NORA: Come here. [*Drawing her down beside her on the sofa.*] It's true— I've also got something to be proud and happy for. I'm the one who saved Torvald's life.

MRS. LINDE: Saved—? Saved how?

NORA: I told you about the trip to Italy. Torvald never would have lived if he hadn't gone south—

MRS. LINDE: Of course; your father gave you the means—

NORA: [*Smiling.*] That's what Torvald and all the rest think, but—

MRS. LINDE: But—?

NORA: Papa didn't give us a pin. I was the one who raised the money.

MRS. LINDE: You? That whole amount?

NORA: Four thousand, eight hundred crowns. What do you say to that?

MRS. LINDE: But Nora, how was it possible? Did you win the lottery?

NORA: [*Disdainfully.*] The lottery? Pooh! No art to that.

MRS. LINDE: But where did you get it from then?

NORA: [*Humming, with a mysterious smile.*] Hmm, tra-la-la-la.

MRS. LINDE: Because you couldn't have borrowed it.

NORA: No? Why not?

MRS. LINDE: A wife can't borrow without her husband's consent.

NORA: [*Tossing her head.*] Oh, but a wife with a little business sense, a wife who knows how to manage—

MRS. LINDE: Nora, I simply don't understand—

NORA: You don't have to. Whoever said I *borrowed* the money? I could have gotten it other ways. [*Throwing herself back on the sofa.*] I could have gotten it from some admirer or other. After all, a girl with my ravishing appeal—

MRS. LINDE: You lunatic.

NORA: I'll bet you're eaten up with curiosity, Kristine.

MRS. LINDE: Now listen here, Nora—you haven't done something indiscreet?

NORA: [*Sitting up again.*] Is it indiscreet to save your husband's life?

MRS. LINDE: I think it's indiscreet that without his knowledge you—

NORA: But that's the point: he mustn't know! My Lord, can't you understand? He mustn't ever know the close call he had. It was to *me* the doctors came to say his life was in danger—that nothing could save him but
a stay in the south. Didn't I try strategy then! I began talking about how
lovely it would be for me to travel abroad like other young wives; I begged
and I cried; I told him please to remember my condition, to be kind and
indulge me; and then I dropped a hint that he could easily take out a
loan. But at that, Kristine, he nearly exploded. He said I was frivolous,
and it was his duty as man of the house not to indulge me in whims and
fancies—as I think he called them. Aha, I thought, now you'll just have
to be saved—and that's when I saw my chance.

MRS. LINDE: And your father never told Torvald the money wasn't from
him?

NORA: No, never. Papa died right about then. I'd considered bringing him
into my secret and begging him never to tell. But he was too sick at the
time—and then, sadly, it didn't matter.

MRS. LINDE: And you've never confided in your husband since?

NORA: For heaven's sake, no! Are you serious? He's so strict on that subject. Besides—Torvald, with all his masculine pride—how painfully
humiliating for him if he ever found out he was in debt to me. That
would just ruin our relationship. Our beautiful, happy home would
never be the same.

MRS. LINDE: Won't you ever tell him?

NORA: [*Thoughtfully.*] Yes—maybe sometime years from now, when I'm no
longer so attractive. Don't laugh! I only mean when Torvald loves me less
than now, when he stops enjoying my dancing and dressing up and reciting for him. Then it might be wise to have something in reserve—[*Breaking off.*] How ridiculous! That'll never happen—Well, Kristine, what do
you think of my big secret? I'm capable of something too, hm? You can
imagine, of course, how this thing hangs over me. It really hasn't been
easy meeting the payments on time. In the business world there's what
they call quarterly interest and what they call amortization, and these are
always so terribly hard to manage. I've had to skimp a little here and
there, wherever I could, you know. I could hardly spare anything from
my house allowance, because Torvald has to live well. I couldn't let the
children go poorly dressed; whatever I got for them, I felt I had to use up
completely—the darlings!

MRS. LINDE: Poor Nora, so it had to come out of your own budget, then?

NORA: Yes, of course. But I was the one most responsible, too. Every time
Torvald gave me money for new clothes and such, I never used more than
half; always bought the simplest, cheapest outfits. It was a godsend that
everything looks so well on me that Torvald never noticed. But it did

weigh me down at times, Kristine. It *is* such a joy to wear fine things. You understand.

MRS. LINDE: Oh, of course.

NORA: And then I found other ways of making money. Last winter I was lucky enough to get a lot of copying to do. I locked myself in and sat writing every evening till late in the night. Ah, I was tired so often, dead tired. But still it was wonderful fun, sitting and working like that, earning money. It was almost like being a man.

MRS. LINDE: But how much have you paid off this way so far?

NORA: That's hard to say, exactly. These accounts, you know, aren't easy to figure. I only know that I've paid out all I could scrape together. Time and again I haven't known where to turn. [*Smiling.*] Then I'd sit here dreaming of a rich old gentleman who had fallen in love with me—

MRS. LINDE: What! Who is he?

NORA: Oh, really! And that he'd died, and when his will was opened, there in big letters it said, "All my fortune shall be paid over in cash, immediately, to that enchanting Mrs. Nora Helmer."

MRS. LINDE: But Nora dear—who *was* this gentleman?

NORA: Good grief, can't you understand? The old man never existed; that was only something I'd dream up time and again whenever I was at my wits' end for money. But it makes no difference now; the old fossil can go where he pleases for all I care; I don't need him or his will— because now I'm free. [*Jumping up.*] Oh, how lovely to think of that, Kristine! Carefree! To know you're carefree, utterly carefree; to be able to romp and play with the children, and to keep up a beautiful, charming home—everything just the way Torvald likes it! And think, spring is coming, with big blue skies. Maybe we can travel a little then. Maybe I'll see the ocean again. Oh yes, it *is* so marvelous to live and be happy!

[*The front doorbell rings.*]

MRS. LINDE: [*Rising.*] There's the bell. It's probably best that I go.

NORA: No, stay. No one's expected. It must be for Torvald.

MAID: [*From the hall doorway.*] Excuse me, ma'am—there's a gentleman here to see Mr. Helmer, but I didn't know—since the doctor's with him—

NORA: Who is the gentleman?

KROGSTAD: [*From the doorway.*] It's me, Mrs. Helmer.

[MRS. LINDE *starts and turns away toward the window.*]

NORA: [*Stepping toward him, tense, her voice a whisper.*] You? What is it? Why do you want to speak to my husband?

KROGSTAD: Bank business—after a fashion. I have a small job in the invest-ment bank, and I hear now your husband is going to be our chief—

NORA: In other words, it's—

KROGSTAD: Just dry business, Mrs. Helmer. Nothing but that.

NORA: Yes, then please be good enough to step into the study. [*She nods indifferently as she sees him out by the hall door, then returns and begins stirring up the stove.*]

MRS. LINDE: Nora—who was that man?

NORA: That was a Mr. Krogstad—a lawyer.

MRS. LINDE: Then it really was him.

NORA: Do you know that person?

MRS. LINDE: I did once—many years ago. For a time he was a law clerk in our town.

NORA: Yes, he's been that.

MRS. LINDE: How he's changed.

NORA: I understand he had a very unhappy marriage.

MRS. LINDE: He's a widower now.

NORA: With a number of children. There now, it's burning. [*She closes the stove door and moves the rocker a bit to one side.*]

MRS. LINDE: They say he has a hand in all kinds of business.

NORA: Oh? That may be true; I wouldn't know. But let's not think about business. It's so dull.

[DR. RANK *enters from* HELMER's *study.*]

RANK: [*Still in the doorway.*] No, no, really—I don't want to intrude, I'd just as soon talk a little while with your wife. [*Shuts the door, then notices* MRS. LINDE.] Oh, beg pardon. I'm intruding here too.

NORA: No, not at all. [*Introducing him.*] Dr. Rank, Mrs. Linde.

RANK: Well now, that's a name much heard in this house. I believe I passed the lady on the stairs as I came.

MRS. LINDE: Yes, I take the stairs very slowly. They're rather hard on me.

RANK: Uh-hm, some touch of internal weakness?

MRS. LINDE: More overexertion, I'd say.

RANK: Nothing else? Then you're probably here in town to rest up in a round of parties?

MRS. LINDE: I'm here to look for work.

RANK: Is that the best cure for overexertion?

MRS. LINDE: One has to live, Doctor.

RANK: Yes, there's a common prejudice to that effect.

NORA: Oh, come on, Dr. Rank—you really do want to live yourself.

RANK: Yes, I really do. Wretched as I am, I'll gladly prolong my torment indefinitely. All my patients feel like that. And it's quite the same, too, with the morally sick. Right at this moment there's one of those moral invalids in there with Helmer—

MRS. LINDE: [*Softly.*] Ah!

NORA: Who do you mean?

RANK: Oh, it's a lawyer, Krogstad, a type you wouldn't know. His character is rotten to the root—but even he began chattering all-importantly about how he had to *live.*

NORA: Oh? What did he want to talk to Torvald about?

RANK: I really don't know. I only heard something about the bank.

NORA: I didn't know that Krog—that this man Krogstad had anything to do with the bank.

RANK: Yes, he's gotten some kind of berth down there. [*To* MRS. LINDE.] I don't know if you also have, in your neck of the woods, a type of person who scuttles about breathlessly, sniffing out hints of moral corruption, and then maneuvers his victim into some sort of key position where he can keep an eye on him. It's the healthy these days that are out in the cold.

MRS. LINDE: All the same, it's the sick who most need to be taken in.

RANK: [*With a shrug.*] Yes, there we have it. That's the concept that's turning society into a sanatorium.

[NORA, *lost in her thoughts, breaks out into quiet laughter and claps her hands.*]

RANK: Why do you laugh at that? Do you have any real idea of what society is?

NORA: What do I care about dreary old society? I was laughing at something quite different—something terribly funny. Tell me, Doctor—is everyone who works in the bank dependent now on Torvald?

RANK: Is that what you find so terribly funny?

NORA: [*Smiling and humming.*] Never mind, never mind [*Pacing the floor.*] Yes, that's really immensely amusing: that we—that Torvald has so much power now over all those people. [*Taking the bag out of her pocket.*] Dr. Rank, a little macaroon on that?

RANK: See here, macaroons! I thought they were contraband here.

NORA: Yes, but these are some that Kristine gave me.

MRS. LINDE: What? I—?

NORA: Now, now, don't be afraid. You couldn't possibly know that Torvald had forbidden them. You see, he's worried they'll ruin my teeth. But hmp! Just this once! Isn't that so, Dr. Rank? Help yourself! [*Puts a macaroon in his mouth.*] And you too, Kristine. And I'll also have one, only a little one—or two, at the most. [*Walking about again.*] Now I'm really tremendously happy. Now there's just one last thing in the world that I have an enormous desire to do.

RANK: Well! And what's that?

NORA: It's something I have such a consuming desire to say so Torvald could hear.

RANK: And why can't you say it?

NORA: I don't dare. It's quite shocking.

MRS. LINDE: Shocking?

RANK: Well, then it isn't advisable. But in front of us you certainly can. What do you have such a desire to say so Torvald could hear?

NORA: I have such a huge desire to say—to hell and be damned!

RANK: Are you crazy?

MRS. LINDE: My goodness, Nora!

RANK: Go on, say it. Here he is.

NORA: [*Hiding the macaroon bag.*] Shh, shh, shh!

[HELMER *comes in from his study, hat in hand, overcoat over his arm.*]

NORA: [*Going toward him.*] Well, Torvald dear, are you through with him?

HELMER: Yes, he just left.

NORA: Let me introduce you—this is Kristine, who's arrived here in town.

HELMER: Kristine—? I'm sorry, but I don't know—

NORA: Mrs. Linde, Torvald dear. Mrs. Kristine Linde.

HELMER: Of course. A childhood friend of my wife's, no doubt?

MRS. LINDE: Yes, we knew each other in those days.

NORA: And just think, she made the long trip down here in order to talk with you.

HELMER: What's this?

MRS. LINDE: Well, not exactly—

NORA: You see, Kristine is remarkably clever in office work, and so she's terribly eager to come under a capable man's supervision and add more to what she already knows—

HELMER: Very wise, Mrs. Linde.

NORA: And then when she heard that you'd become a bank manager—the story was wired out to the papers—then she came in as fast as she could and—Really, Torvald, for my sake you can do a little something for Kristine, can't you?

HELMER: Yes, it's not at all impossible. Mrs. Linde, I suppose you're a widow?

MRS. LINDE: Yes.

HELMER: Any experience in office work?

MRS. LINDE: Yes, a good deal.

HELMER: Well, it's quite likely that I can make an opening for you—

NORA: [*Clapping her hands.*] You see, you see!

HELMER: You've come at a lucky moment, Mrs. Linde.

MRS. LINDE: Oh, how can I thank you?

HELMER: Not necessary. [*Putting his overcoat on.*] But today you'll have to excuse me—

RANK: Wait, I'll go with you. [*He fetches his coat from the hall and warms it at the stove.*]

NORA: Don't stay out long, dear.

HELMER: An hour; no more.

NORA: Are you going too, Kristine?

MRS. LINDE: [*Putting on her winter garments.*] Yes, I have to see about a room now.

HELMER: Then perhaps we can all walk together.

NORA: [*Helping her.*] What a shame we're so cramped here, but it's quite impossible for us to—

MRS. LINDE: Oh, don't even think of it! Good-bye, Nora dear, and thanks for everything.

NORA: Good-bye for now. Of course you'll be back this evening. And you too, Dr. Rank. What? If you're well enough? Oh, you've got to be! Wrap up tight now.

[*In a ripple of small talk the company moves out into the hall; children's voices are heard outside on the steps.*]

NORA: There they are! There they are! [*She runs to open the door. The children come in with their nurse,* ANNE-MARIE.] Come in, come in! [*Bends down and kisses them.*] Oh, you darlings—! Look at them, Kristine. Aren't they lovely!

RANK: No loitering in the draft here.

HELMER: Come, Mrs. Linde—this place is unbearable now for anyone but mothers.

[DR. RANK, HELMER, *and* MRS. LINDE *go down the stairs.* ANNE-MARIE *goes into the living room with the children.* NORA *follows, after closing the hall door.*]

NORA: How fresh and strong you look. Oh, such red cheeks you have! Like apples and roses. [*The children interrupt her throughout the following.*] And it was so much fun? That's wonderful. Really? You pulled both Emmy and Bob on the sled? Imagine, all together! Yes, you're a clever boy, Ivar. Oh, let me hold her a bit, Anne-Marie. My sweet little doll baby! [*Takes the smallest from the nurse and dances with her.*] Yes, yes, Mama will dance with Bob as well. What? Did you throw snowballs? Oh, if I'd only been there! No, don't bother, Anne-Marie—I'll undress them myself. Oh yes, let me. It's such fun. Go in and rest; you look half frozen. There's hot coffee waiting for you on the stove. [*The nurse goes into the room to the left.* NORA *takes the children's winter things off, throwing them about, while the children talk to her all at once.*] Is that so? A big dog chased you? But it didn't bite? No, dogs never bite little, lovely doll babies. Don't peek in the packages, Ivar! What is it? Yes, wouldn't you like to know. No, no, it's an ugly something. Well? Shall we play? What shall we play? Hide-and-seek? Yes, let's play hide-and-seek. Bob must hide first. I must? Yes, let me hide first. [*Laughing and shouting, she and the children play in and out of the living room and the adjoining room to the right. At last* NORA *hides under the table. The children come storming in, search, but cannot find her, then hear her muffled laughter, dash over to the table, lift the cloth up and find her. Wild shouting. She creeps forward as if to scare them. More shouts. Meanwhile, a knock at the hall door; no one has noticed it. Now the door half opens, and* KROGSTAD *appears. He waits a moment; the game goes on.*]

KROGSTAD: Beg pardon, Mrs. Helmer—

NORA: [*With a strangled cry, turning and scrambling to her knees.*] Oh! What do you want?

KROGSTAD: Excuse me. The outer door was ajar; it must be someone forgot to shut it—

NORA: [*Rising.*] My husband isn't home, Mr. Krogstad.

KROGSTAD: I know that.

NORA: Yes—then what do you want here?

KROGSTAD: A word with you.

NORA: With—? [*To the children, quietly.*] Go in to Anne-Marie. What? No, the strange man won't hurt Mama. When he's gone, we'll play some more. [*She leads the children into the room to the left and shuts the door after them. Then, tense and nervous:*] You want to speak to me?

KROGSTAD: Yes, I want to.

NORA: Today? But it's not yet the first of the month—

KROGSTAD: No, it's Christmas Eve. It's going to be up to you how merry a Christmas you have.

NORA: What is it you want? Today I absolutely can't—

KROGSTAD: We won't talk about that till later. This is something else. You do have a moment to spare, I suppose?

NORA: Oh yes, of course—I do, except—

KROGSTAD: Good. I was sitting over at Olsen's Restaurant when I saw your husband go down the street—

NORA: Yes?

KROGSTAD: With a lady.

NORA: Yes. So?

KROGSTAD: If you'll pardon my asking: wasn't that lady a Mrs. Linde?

NORA: Yes.

KROGSTAD: Just now come into town?

NORA: Yes, today.

KROGSTAD: She's a good friend of yours?

NORA: Yes, she is. But I don't see—

KROGSTAD: I also knew her once.

NORA: I'm aware of that.

KROGSTAD: Oh? You know all about it. I thought so. Well, then let me ask you short and sweet: is Mrs. Linde getting a job in the bank?

NORA: What makes you think you can cross-examine me, Mr. Krogstad— you, one of my husband's employees? But since you ask, you might as well know—yes, Mrs. Linde's going to be taken on at the bank. And I'm the one who spoke for her, Mr. Krogstad. Now you know.

KROGSTAD: So I guessed right.

NORA: [*Pacing up and down.*] Oh, one does have a tiny bit of influence, I should hope. Just because I am a woman, don't think it means that— When one has a subordinate position, Mr. Krogstad, one really ought to be careful about pushing somebody who—hm—

KROGSTAD: Who has influence?

NORA: That's right.

KROGSTAD: [*In a different tone.*] Mrs. Helmer, would you be good enough to use your influence on my behalf?

NORA: What? What do you mean?

KROGSTAD: Would you please make sure that I keep my subordinate position in the bank?

NORA: What does that mean? Who's thinking of taking away your position?

KROGSTAD: Oh, don't play the innocent with me. I'm quite aware that your friend would hardly relish the chance of running into me again; and I'm also aware now whom I can thank for being turned out.

NORA: But I promise you—

KROGSTAD: Yes, yes, yes, to the point: there's still time, and I'm advising you to use your influence to prevent it.

NORA: But Mr. Krogstad, I have absolutely no influence.

KROGSTAD: You haven't? I thought you were just saying—

NORA: You shouldn't take me so literally. I! How can you believe that I have any such influence over my husband?

KROGSTAD: Oh, I've known your husband from our student days. I don't think the great bank manager's more steadfast than any other married man.

NORA: You speak insolently about my husband, and I'll show you the door.

KROGSTAD: The lady has spirit.

NORA: I'm not afraid of you any longer. After New Year's, I'll soon be done with the whole business.

KROGSTAD: [*Restraining himself.*] Now listen to me, Mrs. Helmer. If necessary, I'll fight for my little job in the bank as if it were life itself.

NORA: Yes, so it seems.

KROGSTAD: It's not just a matter of income; that's the least of it. It's something else—All right, out with it! Look, this is the thing. You know, just like all the others, of course, that once, a good many years ago, I did something rather rash.

NORA: I've heard rumors to that effect.

KROGSTAD: The case never got into court; but all the same, every door was closed in my face from then on. So I took up those various activities you know about. I had to grab hold somewhere; and I dare say I haven't been among the worst. But now I want to drop all that. My boys are growing up. For their sakes, I'll have to win back as much respect as possible here in town. That job in the bank was like the first rung in my ladder. And now your husband wants to kick me right back down in the mud again.

NORA: But for heaven's sake, Mr. Krogstad, it's simply not in my power to help you.

KROGSTAD: That's because you haven't the will to—but I have the means to make you.

NORA: You certainly won't tell my husband that I owe you money?

KROGSTAD: Hm—what if I told him that?

NORA: That would be shameful of you. [*Nearly in tears.*] This secret—my joy and my pride—that he should learn it in such a crude and disgusting way—learn it from you. You'd expose me to the most horrible unpleasantness—

KROGSTAD: Only unpleasantness?

NORA: [*Vehemently.*] But go on and try. It'll turn out the worse for you, because then my husband will really see what a crook you are, and then you'll *never* be able to hold your job.

KROGSTAD: I asked if it was just domestic unpleasantness you were afraid of?

NORA: If my husband finds out, then of course he'll pay what I owe at once, and then we'd be through with you for good.

KROGSTAD: [*A step closer.*] Listen, Mrs. Helmer—you've either got a very bad memory, or else no head at all for business. I'd better put you a little more in touch with the facts.

NORA: What do you mean?

KROGSTAD: When your husband was sick, you came to me for a loan of four thousand, eight hundred crowns.

NORA: Where else could I go?

KROGSTAD: I promised to get you that sum—

NORA: And you got it.

KROGSTAD: I promised to get you that sum, on certain conditions. You were so involved in your husband's illness, and so eager to finance your trip, that I guess you didn't think out all the details. It might just be a good idea to remind you. I promised you the money on the strength of a note I drew up.

NORA: Yes, and that I signed.

KROGSTAD: Right. But at the bottom I added some lines for your father to guarantee the loan. He was supposed to sign down there.

NORA: Supposed to? He did sign.

KROGSTAD: I left the date blank. In other words, your father would have dated his signature himself. Do you remember that?

NORA: Yes, I think—

KROGSTAD: Then I gave you the note for you to mail to your father. Isn't that so?

NORA: Yes.

KROGSTAD: And naturally you sent it at once—because only some five, six days later you brought me the note, properly signed. And with that, the money was yours.

NORA: Well, then; I've made my payments regularly, haven't I?

KROGSTAD: More or less. But—getting back to the point—those were hard times for you then, Mrs. Helmer.

NORA: Yes, they were.

KROGSTAD: Your father was very ill, I believe.

NORA: He was near the end.

KROGSTAD: He died soon after?

NORA: Yes.

KROGSTAD: Tell me, Mrs. Helmer, do you happen to recall the date of your father's death? The day of the month, I mean.

NORA: Papa died the twenty-ninth of September.

KROGSTAD: That's quite correct; I've already looked into that. And now we come to a curious thing—[*Taking out a paper.*] which I simply cannot comprehend.

NORA: Curious thing? I don't know—

KROGSTAD: This is the curious thing: that your father co-signed the note for your loan three days after his death.

NORA: How—? I don't understand.

KROGSTAD: Your father died the twenty-ninth of September. But look. Here your father dated his signature October second. Isn't that curious, Mrs. Helmer? [NORA *is silent.*] Can you explain it to me? [NORA *remains silent.*] It's also remarkable that the words "October second" and the year aren't written in your father's hand, but rather in one that I think I know. Well, it's easy to understand. Your father forgot perhaps to date his signature, and then someone or other added it, a bit sloppily, before anyone knew of his death. There's nothing wrong in that. It all comes down to the signature. And there's no question about *that*, Mrs. Helmer. It really *was* your father who signed his own name here, wasn't it?

NORA: [*After a short silence, throwing her head back and looking squarely at him.*] No, it wasn't. *I* signed papa's name.

KROGSTAD: Wait, now—are you fully aware that this is a dangerous confession?

NORA: Why? You'll soon get your money.

KROGSTAD: Let me ask you a question—why didn't you send the paper to your father?

NORA: That was impossible. Papa was so sick. If I'd asked him for his signature, I also would have had to tell him what the money was for. But I couldn't tell him, sick as he was, that my husband's life was in danger. That was just impossible.

KROGSTAD: Then it would have been better if you'd given up the trip abroad.

NORA: I couldn't possibly. The trip was to save my husband's life. I couldn't give that up.

KROGSTAD: But didn't you ever consider that this was a fraud against me?

NORA: I couldn't let myself be bothered by that. You weren't any concern of mine. I couldn't stand you, with all those cold complications you made, even though you knew how badly off my husband was.

KROGSTAD: Mrs. Helmer, obviously you haven't the vaguest idea of what you've involved yourself in. But I can tell you this: it was nothing more and nothing worse that I once did—and it wrecked my whole reputation.

NORA: You? Do you expect me to believe that you ever acted bravely to save your wife's life?

KROGSTAD: Laws don't inquire into motives.

NORA: Then they must be very poor laws.

KROGSTAD: Poor or not—if I introduce this paper in court, you'll be judged according to law.

NORA: This I refuse to believe. A daughter hasn't a right to protect her dying father from anxiety and care? A wife hasn't a right to save her husband's life? I don't know much about laws, but I'm sure that somewhere in the books these things are allowed. And you don't know anything about it—you who practice the law? You must be an awful lawyer, Mr. Krogstad.

KROGSTAD: Could be. But business—the kind of business we two are mixed up in—don't you think I know about that? All right. Do what you want now. But I'm telling you *this*: if I get shoved down a second time, you're going to keep me company. [*He bows and goes out through the hall.*]

NORA: [*Pensive for a moment, then tossing her head.*] Oh, really! Trying to frighten me! I'm not so silly as all that. [*Begins gathering up the children's clothes, but soon stops.*] But—? No, but that's impossible! I did it out of love.

THE CHILDREN: [*In the doorway, left.*] Mama, that strange man's gone out the door.

NORA: Yes, yes, I know it. But don't tell anyone about the strange man. Do you hear? Not even Papa!

THE CHILDREN: No, Mama. But now will you play again?

NORA: No, not now.

THE CHILDREN: Oh, but Mama, you promised.

NORA: Yes, but I can't now. Go inside; I have too much to do. Go in, go in, my sweet darlings. [*She herds them gently back in the room and shuts the door after them. Settling on the sofa, she takes up a piece of embroidery and makes some stitches, but soon stops abruptly.*] No! [*Throws the work aside, rises, goes to the hall door and calls out.*] Helene! Let me have the tree in here. [*Goes to the table, left, opens the table drawer, and stops again.*] No, but that's utterly impossible!

MAID: [*With the Christmas tree.*] Where should I put it, ma'am?

NORA: There. The middle of the floor.

MAID: Should I bring anything else?

NORA: No, thanks. I have what I need.

[*The* MAID, *who has set the tree down, goes out.*]

NORA: [*Absorbed in trimming the tree.*] Candles here—and flowers here. That terrible creature! Talk, talk, talk! There's nothing to it at all. The tree's going to be lovely. I'll do anything to please you, Torvald. I'll sing for you, dance for you—

[HELMER *comes in from the hall, with a sheaf of papers under his arm.*]

NORA: Oh! You're back so soon?

HELMER: Yes. Has anyone been here?

NORA: Here? No.

HELMER: That's odd. I saw Krogstad leaving the front door.

NORA: So? Oh yes, that's true. Krogstad was here a moment.

HELMER: Nora, I can see by your face that he's been here, begging you to put in a good word for him.

NORA: Yes.

HELMER: And it was supposed to seem like your own idea? You were to hide it from me that he'd been here. He asked you that, too, didn't he?

NORA: Yes, Torvald, but—

HELMER: Nora, Nora, and you could fall for that? Talk with that sort of person and promise him anything? And then in the bargain, tell me an untruth.

NORA: An untruth—?

HELMER: Didn't you say that no one had been here? [*Wagging his finger.*] My little songbird must never do that again. A songbird needs a clean beak to warble with. No false notes. [*Putting his arm about her waist.*] That's the way it should be, isn't it? Yes, I'm sure of it. [*Releasing her.*] And so, enough of that. [*Sitting by the stove.*] Ah, how snug and cozy it is here. [*Leafing among his papers.*]

NORA: [*Busy with the tree, after a short pause.*] Torvald!

HELMER: Yes.

NORA: I'm so much looking forward to the Stenborgs' costume party, day after tomorrow.

HELMER: And I can't wait to see what you'll surprise me with.

NORA: Oh, that stupid business!

HELMER: What?

NORA: I can't find anything that's right. Everything seems so ridiculous, so inane.

HELMER: So my little Nora's come to *that* recognition?

NORA: [*Going behind his chair, her arms resting on its back.*] Are you very busy, Torvald?

HELMER: Oh—

NORA: What papers are those?

HELMER: Bank matters.

NORA: Already?

HELMER: I've gotten full authority from the retiring management to make all necessary changes in personnel and procedure. I'll need Christmas week for that. I want to have everything in order by New Year's.

NORA: So that was the reason this poor Krogstad—

HELMER: Hm.

NORA: [*Still leaning on the chair and slowly stroking the nape of his neck.*] If you weren't so very busy, I would have asked you an enormous favor, Torvald.

HELMER: Let's hear. What is it?

NORA: You know, there isn't anyone who has your good taste—and I want so much to look well at the costume party. Torvald, couldn't you take over and decide what I should be and plan my costume?

HELMER: Ah, is my stubborn little creature calling for a lifeguard?

NORA: Yes, Torvald, I can't get anywhere without your help.

HELMER: All right—I'll think it over. We'll hit on something.

NORA: Oh, how sweet of you. [*Goes to the tree again. Pause.*] Aren't the red flowers pretty—? But tell me, was it really such a crime that this Krogstad committed?

HELMER: Forgery. Do you have any idea what that means?

NORA: Couldn't he have done it out of need?

HELMER: Yes, or thoughtlessness, like so many others. I'm not so heartless that I'd condemn a man categorically for just one mistake.

NORA: No, of course not, Torvald!

HELMER: Plenty of men have redeemed themselves by openly confessing their crimes and taking their punishment.

NORA: Punishment—?

HELMER: But now Krogstad didn't go that way. He got himself out by sharp practices, and that's the real cause of his moral breakdown.

NORA: Do you really think that would—?

HELMER: Just imagine how a man with that sort of guilt in him has to lie and cheat and deceive on all sides, has to wear a mask even with the nearest and dearest he has, even with his own wife and children. And with the children, Nora—that's where it's most horrible.

NORA: Why?

HELMER: Because that kind of atmosphere of lies infects the whole life of a home. Every breath the children take in is filled with the germs of something degenerate.

NORA: [*Coming closer behind him.*] Are you sure of that?

HELMER: Oh, I've seen it often enough as a lawyer. Almost everyone who goes bad early in life has a mother who's a chronic liar.

NORA: Why just—the mother?

HELMER: It's usually the mother's influence that's dominant, but the father's works in the same way, of course. Every lawyer is quite familiar with it. And still this Krogstad's been going home year in, year out, poisoning his own children with lies and pretense; that's why I call him morally lost. [*Reaching his hands out toward her.*] So my sweet little Nora must promise me never to plead his cause. Your hand on it. Come, come, what's this? Give me your hand. There, now. All settled. I can tell you it'd be impossible for me to work alongside of him. I literally feel physically revolted when I'm anywhere near such a person.

NORA: [*Withdraws her hand and goes to the other side of the Christmas tree.*] How hot it is here! And I've got so much to do.

HELMER: [*Getting up and gathering his papers.*] Yes, and I have to think about getting some of these read through before dinner. I'll think about your costume, too. And something to hang on the tree in gilt paper, I may even see about that. [*Putting his hand on her head.*] Oh you, my darling little songbird. [*He goes into his study and closes the door after him.*]

NORA: [*Softly, after a silence.*] Oh, really! it isn't so. It's impossible. It must
be impossible.

ANNE-MARIE: [*In the doorway, left.*] The children are begging so hard to
come in to Mama.

NORA: No, no, no, don't let them in to me! You stay with them, Anne-Marie.

ANNE-MARIE: Of course, ma'am. [*Closes the door.*]

NORA: [*Pale with terror*]. Hurt my children—! Poison my home? [*A
moment's pause; then she tosses her head.*] That's not true. Never. Never
in all the world.

ACT II

Same room. Beside the piano the Christmas tree now stands stripped of
ornament, burned-down candle stubs on its ragged branches. NORA's street
clothes lie on the sofa. NORA, alone in the room, moves restlessly about; at
last she stops at the sofa and picks up her coat.

NORA: [*Dropping the coat again.*] Someone's coming! [*Goes toward the door,
listens.*] No—there's no one. Of course—nobody's coming today, Christmas Day—or tomorrow, either. But maybe—[*Opens the door and looks
out.*] No, nothing in the mailbox. Quite empty. [*Coming forward.*] What
nonsense! He won't do anything serious. Nothing terrible could happen.
It's impossible. Why, I have three small children.

[ANNE-MARIE, *with a large carton, comes in from the room to the left.*]

ANNE-MARIE: Well, at last I found the box with the masquerade clothes.

NORA: Thanks. Put it on the table.

ANNE-MARIE: [*Does so.*] But they're all pretty much of a mess.

NORA: Ahh! I'd love to rip them in a million pieces!

ANNE-MARIE: Oh, mercy, they can be fixed right up. Just a little patience.

NORA: Yes, I'll go get Mrs. Linde to help me.

ANNE-MARIE: Out again now? In this nasty weather? Miss Nora will catch
cold—get sick.

NORA: Oh, worse things could happen—How are the children?

ANNE-MARIE: The poor mites are playing with their Christmas presents,
but—

NORA: Do they ask for me much?

ANNE-MARIE: They're so used to having Mama around, you know.

NORA: Yes, but Anne-Marie, I *can't* be together with them as much as I was.

ANNE-MARIE: Well, small children get used to anything.

NORA: You think so? Do you think they'd forget their mother if she was
gone for good?

ANNE-MARIE: Oh, mercy—gone for good!

NORA: Wait, tell me, Anne-Marie—I've wondered so often—how could you ever have the heart to give your child over to strangers?

ANNE-MARIE: But I had to, you know, to become little Nora's nurse.

NORA: Yes, but how could you *do* it?

ANNE-MARIE: When I could get such a good place? A girl who's poor and who's gotten in trouble is glad enough for that. Because that slippery fish, he didn't do a thing for me, you know.

NORA: But your daughter's surely forgotten you.

ANNE-MARIE: Oh, she certainly has not. She's written to me, both when she was confirmed and when she was married.

NORA: [*Clasping her about the neck.*] You old Anne-Marie, you were a good mother for me when I was little.

ANNE-MARIE: Poor little Nora, with no other mother but me.

NORA: And if the babies didn't have one, then I know that you'd—What silly talk! [*Opening the carton.*] Go in to them. Now I'll have to—Tomorrow you can see how lovely I'll look.

ANNE-MARIE: Oh, there won't be anyone at the party as lovely as Miss Nora. [*She goes off into the room, left.*]

NORA: [*Begins unpacking the box, but soon throws it aside.*] Oh, if I dared to go out. If only nobody would come. If only nothing would happen here while I'm out. What craziness—nobody's coming. Just don't think. This muff—needs a brushing. Beautiful gloves, beautiful gloves. Let it go. Let it go! One, two, three, four, five, six—[*With a cry.*] Oh, there they are! [*Poises to move toward the door, but remains irresolutely standing.* MRS. LINDE *enters from the hall, where she has removed her street clothes.*]

NORA: Oh, it's you, Kristine. There's no one else out there? How good that you've come.

MRS. LINDE: I hear you were up asking for me.

NORA: Yes, I just stopped by. There's something you really can help me with. Let's get settled on the sofa. Look, there's going to be a costume party tomorrow evening at the Stenborgs' right above us, and now Torvald wants me to go as a Neapolitan peasant girl and dance the tarantella[2] that I learned in Capri.

MRS. LINDE: Really, are you giving a whole performance?

NORA: Torvald says yes, I should. See, here's the dress. Torvald had it made for me down there; but now it's all so tattered that I just don't know—

MRS. LINDE: Oh, we'll fix that up in no time. It's nothing more than the trimmings—they're a bit loose here and there. Needle and thread? Good, now we have what we need.

2. Lively folk dance of southern Italy, thought to cure the bite of the tarantula.

NORA: Oh, how sweet of you!

MRS. LINDE: [*Sewing.*] So you'll be in disguise tomorrow, Nora. You know what? I'll stop by then for a moment and have a look at you all dressed up. But listen, I've absolutely forgotten to thank you for that pleasant evening yesterday.

NORA: [*Getting up and walking about.*] I don't think it was as pleasant as usual yesterday. You should have come to town a bit sooner, Kristine— Yes, Torvald really knows how to give a home elegance and charm.

MRS. LINDE: And you do, too, if you ask me. You're not your father's daughter for nothing. But tell me, is Dr. Rank always so down in the mouth as yesterday?

NORA: No, that was quite an exception. But he goes around critically ill all the time—tuberculosis of the spine, poor man. You know, his father was a disgusting thing who kept mistresses and so on—and that's why the son's been sickly from birth.

MRS. LINDE: [*Lets her sewing fall to her lap.*] But my dearest Nora, how do you know about such things?

NORA: [*Walking more jauntily.*] Hmp! When you've had three children, then you've had a few visits from—from women who know something of medicine, and they tell you this and that.

MRS. LINDE: [*Resumes sewing; a short pause.*] Does Dr. Rank come here every day?

NORA: Every blessed day. He's Torvald's best friend from childhood, and *my* good friend, too. Dr. Rank almost belongs to this house.

MRS. LINDE: But tell me—is he quite sincere? I mean, doesn't he rather enjoy flattering people?

NORA: Just the opposite. Why do you think that?

MRS. LINDE: When you introduced us yesterday, he was proclaiming that he'd often heard my name in this house; but later I noticed that your husband hadn't the slightest idea who I really was. So how could Dr. Rank—?

NORA: But it's all true, Kristine. You see, Torvald loves me beyond words, and, as he puts it, he'd like to keep me all to himself. For a long time he'd almost be jealous if I even mentioned any of my old friends back home. So of course I dropped that. But with Dr. Rank I talk a lot about such things, because he likes hearing about them.

MRS. LINDE: Now listen, Nora; in many ways you're still like a child. I'm a good deal older than you, with a little more experience. I'll tell you something: you ought to put an end to all this with Dr. Rank.

NORA: What should I put an end to?

MRS. LINDE: Both parts of it, I think. Yesterday you said something about a rich admirer who'd provide you with money—

NORA: Yes, one who doesn't exist—worse luck. So?

MRS. LINDE: Is Dr. Rank well off?

NORA: Yes, he is.

MRS. LINDE: With no dependents?

NORA: No, no one. But—

MRS. LINDE: And he's over here every day?

NORA: Yes, I told you that.

MRS. LINDE: How can a man of such refinement be so grasping?

NORA: I don't follow you at all.

MRS. LINDE: Now don't try to hide it, Nora. You think I can't guess who loaned you the forty-eight hundred crowns?

NORA: Are you out of your mind? How could you think such a thing! A friend of ours, who comes here every single day. What an intolerable situation that would have been!

MRS. LINDE: Then it really wasn't him.

NORA: No, absolutely not. It never even crossed my mind for a moment— And he had nothing to lend in those days; his inheritance came later.

MRS. LINDE: Well, I think that was a stroke of luck for you, Nora dear.

NORA: No, it never would have occurred to me to ask Dr. Rank—Still, I'm quite sure that if I had asked him—

MRS. LINDE: Which you won't, of course.

NORA: No, of course not. I can't see that I'd ever need to. But I'm quite positive that if I talked to Dr. Rank—

MRS. LINDE: Behind your husband's back?

NORA: I've got to clear up this other thing; *that's* also behind his back. I've *got* to clear it all up.

MRS. LINDE: Yes, I was saying that yesterday, but—

NORA: [*Pacing up and down.*] A man handles these problems so much better than a woman—

MRS. LINDE: One's husband does, yes.

NORA: Nonsense. [*Stopping.*] When you pay everything you owe, then you get your note back, right?

MRS. LINDE: Yes, naturally.

NORA: And can rip it into a million pieces and burn it up—that filthy scrap of paper!

MRS. LINDE: [*Looking hard at her, laying her sewing aside, and rising slowly.*] Nora, you're hiding something from me.

NORA: You can see it in my face?

MRS. LINDE: Something's happened to you since yesterday morning. Nora, what is it?

NORA: [*Hurrying toward her.*] Kristine! [*Listening.*] Shh! Torvald's home. Look, go in with the children a while. Torvald can't bear all this snipping and stitching. Let Anne-Marie help you.

MRS. LINDE: [*Gathering up some of the things.*] All right, but I'm not leaving here until we've talked this out. [*She disappears into the room, left, as* TORVALD *enters from the hall.*]

NORA: Oh, how I've been waiting for you, Torvald dear.

HELMER: Was that the dressmaker?

NORA: No, that was Kristine. She's helping me fix up my costume. You know, it's going to be quite attractive.

HELMER: Yes, wasn't that a bright idea I had?

NORA: Brilliant! But then wasn't I good as well to give in to you?

HELMER: Good—because you give in to your husband's judgment? All right, you little goose, I know you didn't mean it like that. But I won't disturb you. You'll want to have a fitting, I suppose.

NORA: And you'll be working?

HELMER: Yes. [*Indicating a bundle of papers.*] See. I've been down to the bank. [*Starts toward his study.*]

NORA: Torvald.

HELMER: [*Stops.*] Yes.

NORA: If your little squirrel begged you, with all her heart and soul, for something—?

HELMER: What's that?

NORA: Then would you do it?

HELMER: First, naturally, I'd have to know what it was.

NORA: Your squirrel would scamper about and do tricks, if you'd only be sweet and give in.

HELMER: Out with it.

NORA: Your lark would be singing high and low in every room—

HELMER: Come on, she does that anyway.

NORA: I'd be a wood nymph and dance for you in the moonlight.

HELMER: Nora—don't tell me it's that same business from this morning?

NORA: [*Coming closer.*] Yes, Torvald, I beg you, please!

HELMER: And you actually have the nerve to drag that up again?

NORA: Yes, yes, you've got to give in to me; you *have* to let Krogstad keep his job in the bank.

HELMER: My dear Nora, I've slated his job for Mrs. Linde.

NORA: That's awfully kind of you. But you could just fire another clerk instead of Krogstad.

HELMER: This is the most incredible stubbornness! Because you go and give an impulsive promise to speak up for him, I'm expected to—

NORA: That's not the reason, Torvald. It's for your own sake. That man does writing for the worst papers; you said it yourself. He could do you any amount of harm. I'm scared to death of him—

HELMER: Ah, I understand. It's the old memories haunting you.

NORA: What do you mean by that?

HELMER: Of course, you're thinking about your father.

NORA: Yes, all right. Just remember how those nasty gossips wrote in the papers about Papa and slandered him so cruelly. I think they'd have had him dismissed if the department hadn't sent you up to investigate, and if you hadn't been so kind and open-minded toward him.

HELMER: My dear Nora, there's a notable difference between your father and me. Your father's official career was hardly above reproach. But mine is; and I hope it'll stay that way as long as I hold my position.

NORA: Oh, who can ever tell what vicious minds can invent? We could be so snug and happy now in our quiet, carefree home—you and I and the children, Torvald! That's why I'm pleading with you so—

HELMER: And just by pleading for him you make it impossible for me to keep him on. It's already known at the bank that I'm firing Krogstad. What if it's rumored around now that the new bank manager was vetoed by his wife—

NORA: Yes, what then—?

HELMER: Oh yes—as long as our little bundle of stubbornness gets her way—! I should go and make myself ridiculous in front of the whole office—give people the idea I can be swayed by all kinds of outside pressure. Oh, you can bet I'd feel the effects of that soon enough! Besides— there's something that rules Krogstad right out at the bank as long as I'm the manager.

NORA: What's that?

HELMER: His moral failings I could maybe overlook if I had to—

NORA: Yes, Torvald, why not?

HELMER: And I hear he's quite efficient on the job. But he was a crony of mine back in my teens—one of those rash friendships that crop up again and again to embarrass you later in life. Well, I might as well say it straight out: we're on a first-name basis. And that tactless fool makes no effort at all to hide it in front of others. Quite the contrary—he thinks that entitles him to take a familiar air around me, and so every other second he comes booming out with his "Yes, Torvald!" and "Sure thing, Torvald!" I tell you, it's been excruciating for me. He's out to make my place in the bank unbearable.

NORA: Torvald, you can't be serious about all this.

HELMER: Oh no? Why not?

NORA: Because these are such petty considerations.

HELMER: What are you saying? Petty? You think I'm petty!

NORA: No, just the opposite, Torvald dear. That's exactly why—

HELMER: Never mind. You call my motives petty; then I might as well be just that. Petty! All right! We'll put a stop to this for good. [*Goes to the hall door and calls.*] Helene!

NORA: What do you want?

HELMER: [*Searching among his papers.*] A decision. [*The* MAID *comes in.*] Look here; take this letter; go out with it at once. Get hold of a messenger and have him deliver it. Quick now. It's already addressed. Wait, here's some money.

MAID: Yes, sir. [*She leaves with the letter.*]

HELMER: [*Straightening his papers.*] There, now, little Miss Willful.

NORA: [*Breathlessly.*] Torvald, what was that letter?

HELMER: Krogstad's notice.

NORA: Call it back, Torvald! There's still time. Oh, Torvald, call it back! Do it for my sake—for your sake, for the children's sake! Do you hear, Torvald; do it! You don't know how this can harm us.

HELMER: Too late.

NORA: Yes, too late.

HELMER: Nora dear, I can forgive you this panic, even though basically you're insulting me. Yes, you are! Or isn't it an insult to think that *I* should be afraid of a courtroom hack's revenge? But I forgive you anyway, because this shows so beautifully how much you love me. [*Takes her in his arms.*] This is the way it should be, my darling Nora. Whatever comes, you'll see: when it really counts, I have strength and courage enough as a man to take on the whole weight myself.

NORA: [*Terrified.*] What do you mean by that?

HELMER: The whole weight, I said.

NORA: [*Resolutely.*] No, never in all the world.

HELMER: Good. So we'll share it, Nora, as man and wife. That's as it should be. [*Fondling her.*] Are you happy now? There, there, there—not these frightened dove's eyes. It's nothing at all but empty fantasies—Now you should run through your tarantella and practice your tambourine. I'll go to the inner office and shut both doors, so I won't hear a thing; you can make all the noise you like. [*Turning in the doorway.*] And when Rank comes, just tell him where he can find me. [*He nods to her and goes with his papers into the study, closing the door.*]

NORA: [*Standing as though rooted, dazed with fright, in a whisper.*] He really could do it. He will do it. He'll do it in spite of everything. No, not that, never, never! Anything but that! Escape! A way out—[*The doorbell rings.*] Dr. Rank! Anything but that! *Anything*, whatever it is! [*Her hands pass over her face, smoothing it; she pulls herself together, goes over and opens the hall door.* DR. RANK *stands outside, hanging his fur coat up. During the following scene, it begins getting dark.*]

NORA: Hello, Dr. Rank. I recognized your ring. But you mustn't go in to Torvald yet; I believe he's working.

RANK: And you?

NORA: For you, I always have an hour to spare—you know that. [*He has entered, and she shuts the door after him.*]

RANK: Many thanks. I'll make use of these hours while I can.

NORA: What do you mean by that? While you can?

RANK: Does that disturb you?

NORA: Well, it's such an odd phrase. Is anything going to happen?

RANK: What's going to happen is what I've been expecting so long—but I honestly didn't think it would come so soon.

NORA: [*Gripping his arm.*] What is it you've found out? Dr. Rank, you have to tell me!

RANK: [*Sitting by the stove.*] It's all over with me. There's nothing to be done about it.

NORA: [*Breathing easier.*] Is it you—then—?

RANK: Who else? There's no point in lying to one's self. I'm the most miserable of all my patients, Mrs. Helmer. These past few days I've been auditing my internal accounts. Bankrupt! Within a month I'll probably be laid out and rotting in the churchyard.

NORA: Oh, what a horrible thing to say.

RANK: The thing itself is horrible. But the worst of it is all the other horror before it's over. There's only one final examination left; when I'm finished with that, I'll know about when my disintegration will begin. There's something I want to say. Helmer with his sensitivity has such a sharp distaste for anything ugly. I don't want him near my sickroom.

NORA: Oh, but Dr. Rank—

RANK: I won't have him in there. Under no condition. I'll lock my door to him—As soon as I'm completely sure of the worst, I'll send you my calling card marked with a black cross, and you'll know then the wreck has started to come apart.

NORA: No, today you're completely unreasonable. And I wanted you so much to be in a really good humor.

RANK: With death up my sleeve? And then to suffer this way for somebody else's sins. Is there any justice in that? And in every single family, in some way or another, this inevitable retribution of nature goes on—

NORA: [*Her hands pressed over her ears.*] Oh, stuff! Cheer up! Please—be gay!

RANK: Yes, I'd just as soon laugh at it all. My poor, innocent spine, serving time for my father's gay army days.

NORA: [*By the table, left.*] He was so infatuated with asparagus tips and *pâté de foie gras*, wasn't that it?

RANK: Yes—and with truffles.

NORA: Truffles, yes. And then with oysters, I suppose?

RANK: Yes, tons of oysters, naturally.

NORA: And then the port and champagne to go with it. It's so sad that all these delectable things have to strike at our bones.

RANK: Especially when they strike at the unhappy bones that never shared in the fun.

NORA: Ah, that's the saddest of all.

RANK: [Looks searchingly at her.] Hm.

NORA: [After a moment.] Why did you smile?

RANK: No, it was you who laughed.

NORA: No, it was you who smiled, Dr. Rank!

RANK: [Getting up.] You're even a bigger tease than I'd thought.

NORA: I'm full of wild ideas today.

RANK: That's obvious.

NORA: [Putting both hands on his shoulders.] Dear, dear Dr. Rank, you'll never die for Torvald and me.

RANK: Oh, that loss you'll easily get over. Those who go away are soon forgotten.

NORA: [Looks fearfully at him.] You believe that?

RANK: One makes new connections, and then—

NORA: Who makes new connections?

RANK: Both you and Torvald will when I'm gone. I'd say you're well under way already. What was that Mrs. Linde doing here last evening?

NORA: Oh, come—you can't be jealous of poor Kristine?

RANK: Oh yes, I am. She'll be my successor here in the house. When I'm down under, that woman will probably—

NORA: Shh! Not so loud. She's right in there.

RANK: Today as well. So you see.

NORA: Only to sew on my dress. Good gracious, how unreasonable you are. [Sitting on the sofa.] Be nice now, Dr. Rank. Tomorrow you'll see how beautifully I'll dance; and you can imagine then that I'm dancing only for you—yes, and of course for Torvald, too—that's understood. [Takes various items out of the carton.] Dr. Rank, sit over here and I'll show you something.

RANK: [Sitting.] What's that?

NORA: Look here. Look.

RANK: Silk stockings.

NORA: Flesh-colored. Aren't they lovely? Now it's so dark here, but tomorrow—No, no, no, just look at the feet. Oh well, you might as well look at the rest.

RANK: Hm—

NORA: Why do you look so critical? Don't you believe they'll fit?

RANK: I've never had any chance to form an opinion on that.

NORA: [*Glancing at him a moment.*] Shame on you. [*Hits him lightly on the ear with the stockings.*] That's for you. [*Puts them away again.*]

RANK: And what other splendors am I going to see now?

NORA: Not the least bit more, because you've been naughty. [*She hums a little and rummages among her things.*]

RANK: [*After a short silence.*] When I sit here together with you like this, completely easy and open, then I don't know—I simply can't imagine—whatever would have become of me if I'd never come into this house.

NORA: [*Smiling.*] Yes, I really think you feel completely at ease with us.

RANK: [*More quietly, staring straight ahead.*] And then to have to go away from it all—

NORA: Nonsense, you're not going away.

RANK: [*His voice unchanged.*]—and not even be able to leave some poor show of gratitude behind, scarcely a fleeting regret—no more than a vacant place that anyone can fill.

NORA: And if I asked you now for—? No—

RANK: For what?

NORA: For a great proof of your friendship—

RANK: Yes, yes?

NORA: No, I mean—for an exceptionally big favor—

RANK: Would you really, for once, make me so happy?

NORA: Oh, you haven't the vaguest idea what it is.

RANK: All right, then tell me.

NORA: No, but I can't, Dr. Rank—it's all out of reason. It's advice and help, too—and a favor—

RANK: So much the better. I can't fathom what you're hinting at. Just speak out. Don't you trust me?

NORA: Of course. More than anyone else. You're my best and truest friend, I'm sure. That's why I want to talk to you. All right, then, Dr. Rank: there's something you can help me prevent. You know how deeply, how inexpressibly dearly Torvald loves me; he'd never hesitate a second to give up his life for me.

RANK: [*Leaning close to her.*] Nora—do you think he's the only one—

NORA: [*With a slight start.*] Who—?

RANK: Who'd gladly give up his life for you.

NORA: [*Heavily.*] I see.

RANK: I swore to myself you should know this before I'm gone. I'll never find a better chance. Yes, Nora, now you know. And also you know now that you can trust me beyond anyone else.

NORA: [*Rising, natural and calm.*] Let me by.

RANK: [*Making room for her, but still sitting.*] Nora—

NORA: [*In the hall doorway.*] Helene, bring the lamp in. [*Goes over to the stove.*] Ah, dear Dr. Rank, that was really mean of you.

RANK: [*Getting up.*] That I've loved you just as deeply as somebody else? Was *that* mean?

NORA: No, but that you came out and told me. That was quite unnecessary—

RANK: What do you mean? Have you known—?

[*The* MAID *comes in with the lamp, sets it on the table, and goes out again.*]

RANK: Nora—Mrs. Helmer—I'm asking you: have you known about it?

NORA: Oh, how can I tell what I know or don't know? Really, I don't know what to say—Why did you have to be so clumsy, Dr. Rank! Everything was so good.

RANK: Well, in any case, you now have the knowledge that my body and soul are at your command. So won't you speak out?

NORA: [*Looking at him.*] After that?

RANK: Please, just let me know what it is.

NORA: You can't know anything now.

RANK: I have to. You mustn't punish me like this. Give me the chance to do whatever is humanly possible for you.

NORA: Now there's nothing you can do for me. Besides, actually, I don't need any help. You'll see—it's only my fantasies. That's what it is. Of course! [*Sits in the rocker, looks at him, and smiles.*] What a nice one you are, Dr. Rank. Aren't you a little bit ashamed, now that the lamp is here?

RANK: No, not exactly. But perhaps I'd better go—for good?

NORA: No, you certainly can't do that. You must come here just as you always have. You know Torvald can't do without you.

RANK: Yes, but *you?*

NORA: You know how much I enjoy it when you're here.

RANK: That's precisely what threw me off. You're a mystery to me. So many times I've felt you'd almost rather be with me than with Helmer.

NORA: Yes—you see, there are some people that one loves most and other people that one would almost prefer being with.

RANK: Yes, there's something to that.

NORA: When I was back home, of course I loved Papa most. But I always thought it was so much fun when I could sneak down to the maids' quarters, because they never tried to improve me, and it was always so amusing, the way they talked to each other.

RANK: Aha, so it's *their* place that I've filled.

NORA: [*Jumping up and going to him.*] Oh, dear, sweet Dr. Rank, that's not what I meant at all. But you can understand that with Torvald it's just the same as with Papa—

[*The* MAID *enters from the hall.*]

MAID: Ma'am—please! [*She whispers to* NORA *and hands her a calling card.*]

NORA: [*Glancing at the card.*] Ah! [*Slips it into her pocket.*]

RANK: Anything wrong?

NORA: No, no, not at all. It's only some—it's my new dress—

RANK: Really? But—there's your dress.

NORA: Oh, that. But this is another one—I ordered it—Torvald mustn't know—

RANK: Ah, now we have the big secret.

NORA: That's right. Just go in with him—he's back in the inner study. Keep him there as long as—

RANK: Don't worry. He won't get away. [*Goes into the study.*]

NORA: [*To the* MAID.] And he's standing waiting in the kitchen?

MAID: Yes, he came up by the back stairs.

NORA: But didn't you tell him somebody was here?

MAID: Yes, but that didn't do any good.

NORA: He won't leave?

MAID: No, he won't go till he's talked with you, ma'am.

NORA: Let him come in, then—but quietly. Helene, don't breathe a word about this. It's a surprise for my husband.

MAID: Yes, yes, I understand—[*Goes out.*]

NORA: This horror—it's going to happen. No, no, no, it can't happen, it mustn't.

[*She goes and bolts* HELMER's *door. The* MAID *opens the hall door for* KROGSTAD *and shuts it behind him. He is dressed for travel in a fur coat, boots, and a fur cap.*]

NORA: [*Going toward him.*] Talk softly. My husband's home.

KROGSTAD: Well, good for him.

NORA: What do you want?

KROGSTAD: Some information.

NORA: Hurry up, then. What is it?

KROGSTAD: You know, of course, that I got my notice.

NORA: I couldn't prevent it, Mr. Krogstad. I fought for you to the bitter end, but nothing worked.

KROGSTAD: Does your husband's love for you run so thin? He knows everything I can expose you to, and all the same he dares to—

NORA: How can you imagine he knows anything about this?

KROGSTAD: Ah, no—I can't imagine it either, now. It's not at all like my fine Torvald Helmer to have so much guts—

NORA: Mr. Krogstad, I demand respect for my husband!

KROGSTAD: Why, of course—all due respect. But since the lady's keeping it so carefully hidden, may I presume to ask if you're also a bit better informed than yesterday about what you've actually done?

NORA: More than you ever could teach me.

KROGSTAD: Yes, I *am* such an awful lawyer.

NORA: What is it you want from me?

KROGSTAD: Just a glimpse of how you are, Mrs. Helmer. I've been thinking about you all day long. A cashier, a night-court scribbler, a—well, a type like me also has a little of what they call a heart, you know.

NORA: Then show it. Think of my children.

KROGSTAD: Did you or your husband ever think of mine? But never mind. I simply wanted to tell you that you don't need to take this thing too seriously. For the present, I'm not proceeding with any action.

NORA: Oh no, really! Well—I knew that.

KROGSTAD: Everything can be settled in a friendly spirit. It doesn't have to get around town at all; it can stay just among us three.

NORA: My husband must never know anything of this.

KROGSTAD: How can you manage that? Perhaps you can pay me the balance?

NORA: No, not right now.

KROGSTAD: Or you know some way of raising the money in a day or two?

NORA: No way that I'm willing to use.

KROGSTAD: Well, it wouldn't have done you any good, anyway. If you stood in front of me with a fistful of bills, you still couldn't buy your signature back.

NORA: Then tell me what you're going to do with it.

KROGSTAD: I'll just hold onto it—keep it on file. There's no outsider who'll even get wind of it. So if you've been thinking of taking some desperate step—

NORA: I have.

KROGSTAD: Been thinking of running away from home—

NORA: I have!

KROGSTAD: Or even of something worse—

NORA: How could you guess that?

KROGSTAD: You can drop those thoughts.

NORA: How could you guess I was thinking of *that*?

KROGSTAD: Most of us think about *that* at first. I thought about it too, but I discovered I hadn't the courage—

NORA: [*Lifelessly.*] I don't either.

KROGSTAD: [*Relieved.*] That's true, you haven't the courage? You too?

NORA: I don't have it—I don't have it.

KROGSTAD: It would be terribly stupid, anyway. After that first storm at home blows out, why, then—I have here in my pocket a letter for your husband—

NORA: Telling everything?

KROGSTAD: As charitably as possible.

NORA: [*Quickly.*] He mustn't ever get that letter. Tear it up. I'll find some way to get money.

KROGSTAD: Beg pardon, Mrs. Helmer, but I think I just told you—

NORA: Oh, I don't mean the money I owe you. Let me know how much you want from my husband, and I'll manage it.

KROGSTAD: I don't want any money from your husband.

NORA: What do you want, then?

KROGSTAD: I'll tell you what. I want to recoup, Mrs. Helmer; I want to get on in the world—and there's where your husband can help me. For a year and a half I've kept myself clean of anything disreputable—all that time struggling with the worst conditions; but I was satisfied, working my way up step by step. Now I've been written right off, and I'm just not in the mood to come crawling back. I tell you, I want to move on. I want to get back in the bank—in a better position. Your husband can set up a job for me—

NORA: He'll never do that!

KROGSTAD: He'll do it. I know him. He won't dare breathe a word of protest. And once I'm in there together with him, you just wait and see! Inside of a year, I'll be the manager's right-hand man. It'll be Nils Krogstad, not Torvald Helmer, who runs the bank.

NORA: You'll never see the day!

KROGSTAD: Maybe you think you can—

NORA: I have the courage now—for *that.*

KROGSTAD: Oh, you don't scare me. A smart, spoiled lady like you—

NORA: You'll see; you'll see!

KROGSTAD: Under the ice, maybe? Down in the freezing, coal-black water? There, till you float up in the spring, ugly, unrecognizable, with your hair falling out—

NORA: You don't frighten me.

KROGSTAD: Nor do you frighten me. One doesn't do these things, Mrs. Helmer. Besides, what good would it be? I'd still have him safe in my pocket.

NORA: Afterwards? When I'm no longer—?

KROGSTAD: Are you forgetting that *I'll* be in control then over your final reputation? [NORA *stands speechless, staring at him.*] Good; now I've warned you. Don't do anything stupid. When Helmer's read my letter, I'll be waiting for his reply. And bear in mind that it's your husband himself who's forced me back to my old ways. I'll never forgive him for that. Goodbye, Mrs. Helmer. [*He goes out through the hall.*]

NORA: [*Goes to the hall door, opens it a crack, and listens.*] He's gone. Didn't leave the letter. Oh no, no, that's impossible too! [*Opening the door more and more.*] What's that? He's standing outside—not going downstairs. He's thinking it over? Maybe he'll—? [*A letter falls in the mailbox; then* KROGSTAD's *footsteps are heard, dying away down a flight of stairs.* NORA *gives a muffled cry and runs over toward the sofa table. A short pause.*] In the mailbox. [*Slips warily over to the hall door.*] It's lying there. Torvald, Torvald—now we're lost!

MRS. LINDE: [*Entering with the costume from the room, left.*] There now, I can't see anything else to mend. Perhaps you'd like to try—

NORA: [*In a hoarse whisper.*] Kristine, come here.

MRS. LINDE: [*Tossing the dress on the sofa.*] What's wrong? You look upset.

NORA: Come here. See that letter? *There!* Look—through the glass in the mailbox.

MRS. LINDE: Yes, yes, I see it.

NORA: That letter's from Krogstad—

MRS. LINDE: Nora—it's Krogstad who loaned you the money!

NORA: Yes, and now Torvald will find out everything.

MRS. LINDE: Believe me, Nora, it's best for both of you.

NORA: There's more you don't know. I forged a name.

MRS. LINDE: But for heaven's sake—?

NORA: I only want to tell you that, Kristine, so that you can be my witness.

MRS. LINDE: Witness? Why should I—?

NORA: If I should go out of my mind—it could easily happen—

MRS. LINDE: Nora!

NORA: Or anything else occurred—so I couldn't be present here—

MRS. LINDE: Nora, Nora, you aren't yourself at all!

NORA: And someone should try to take on the whole weight, all of the guilt, you follow me—

MRS. LINDE: Yes, of course, but why do you think—?

NORA: Then you're the witness that it isn't true, Kristine. I'm very much myself; my mind right now is perfectly clear; and I'm telling you: nobody else has known about this; I alone did everything. Remember that.

MRS. LINDE: I will. But I don't understand all this.

NORA: Oh, how could you ever understand it? It's the miracle now that's going to take place.

MRS. LINDE: The miracle?

NORA: Yes, the miracle. But it's so awful, Kristine. It mustn't take place, not for anything in the world.

MRS. LINDE: I'm going right over and talk with Krogstad.

NORA: Don't go near him; he'll do you some terrible harm!

MRS. LINDE: There was a time once when he'd gladly have done anything for me.

NORA: He?

MRS. LINDE: Where does he live?

NORA: Oh, how do I know? Yes. [*Searches in her pocket.*] Here's his card. But the letter, the letter—!

HELMER: [*From the study, knocking on the door.*] Nora!

NORA: [*With a cry of fear.*] Oh! What is it? What do you want?

HELMER: Now, now, don't be so frightened. We're not coming in. You locked the door—are you trying on the dress?

NORA: Yes, I'm trying it. I'll look just beautiful, Torvald.

MRS. LINDE: [*Who has read the card.*] He's living right around the corner.

NORA: Yes, but what's the use? We're lost. The letter's in the box.

MRS. LINDE: And your husband has the key?

NORA: Yes, always.

MRS. LINDE: Krogstad can ask for his letter back unread; he can find some excuse—

NORA: But it's just this time that Torvald usually—

MRS. LINDE: Stall him. Keep him in there. I'll be back as quick as I can. [*She hurries out through the hall entrance.*]

NORA: [*Goes to* HELMER's *door, opens it, and peers in.*] Torvald!

HELMER: [*From the inner study.*] Well—does one dare set foot in one's own living room at last? Come on, Rank, now we'll get a look—[*In the doorway.*] But what's this?

NORA: What, Torvald dear?

HELMER: Rank had me expecting some grand masquerade.

RANK: [*In the doorway.*] That was my impression, but I must have been wrong.

NORA: No one can admire me in my splendor—not till tomorrow.

HELMER: But Nora dear, you look so exhausted. Have you practiced too hard?

NORA: No, I haven't practiced at all yet.

HELMER: You know, it's necessary—

NORA: Oh, it's absolutely necessary, Torvald. But I can't get anywhere without your help. I've forgotten the whole thing completely.

HELMER: Ah, we'll soon take care of that.

NORA: Yes, take care of me, Torvald, please! Promise me that? Oh, I'm so nervous. That big party—You must give up everything this evening for me. No business—don't even touch your pen. Yes? Dear Torvald, promise?

HELMER: It's a promise. Tonight I'm totally at your service—you little helpless thing. Hm—but first there's one thing I want to—[*Goes toward the hall door.*]

NORA: What are you looking for?

HELMER: Just to see if there's any mail.

NORA: No, no, don't do that, Torvald!

HELMER: Now what?

NORA: Torvald, please. There isn't any.

HELMER: Let me look, though. [*Starts out.* NORA, *at the piano, strikes the first notes of the tarantella.* HELMER, *at the door, stops.*] Aha!

NORA: I can't dance tomorrow if I don't practice with you.

HELMER: [*Going over to her.*] Nora dear, are you really so frightened?

NORA: Yes, so terribly frightened. Let me practice right now; there's still time before dinner. Oh, sit down and play for me, Torvald. Direct me. Teach me, the way you always have.

HELMER: Gladly, if it's what you want. [*Sits at the piano.*]

NORA: [*Snatches the tambourine up from the box, then a long, varicolored shawl, which she throws around herself, whereupon she springs forward and cries out:*] Play for me now! Now I'll dance!

[HELMER *plays and* NORA *dances.* RANK *stands behind* HELMER *at the piano and looks on.*]

HELMER: [*As he plays.*] Slower. Slow down.

NORA: Can't change it.

HELMER: Not so violent, Nora!

NORA: Has to be just like this.

HELMER: [*Stopping.*] No, no, that won't do at all.

NORA: [*Laughing and swinging her tambourine.*] Isn't that what I told you?

RANK: Let me play for her.

HELMER: [*Getting up.*] Yes, go on. I can teach her more easily then.

[RANK *sits at the piano and plays;* NORA *dances more and more wildly.* HELMER *has stationed himself by the stove and repeatedly gives her directions; she seems not to hear them; her hair loosens and falls over her shoulders; she does not notice, but goes on dancing.* MRS. LINDE *enters.*]

MRS. LINDE: [*Standing dumbfounded at the door.*] Ah—!

NORA: [*Still dancing.*] See what fun, Kristine!

HELMER: But Nora darling, you dance as if your life were at stake.

NORA: And it is.

HELMER: Rank, stop! This is pure madness. Stop it, I say!

[RANK *breaks off playing, and* NORA *halts abruptly.*]

HELMER: [*Going over to her.*] I never would have believed it. You've forgotten everything I taught you.

NORA: [*Throwing away the tambourine.*] You see for yourself.

HELMER: Well, there's certainly room for instruction here.

NORA: Yes, you see how important it is. You've got to teach me to the very last minute. Promise me that, Torvald?

HELMER: You can bet on it.

NORA: You mustn't, either today or tomorrow, think about anything else but me; you mustn't open any letters—or the mailbox—

HELMER: Ah, it's still the fear of that man—

NORA: Oh yes, yes, that too.

HELMER: Nora, it's written all over you—there's already a letter from him out there.

NORA: I don't know. I guess so. But you mustn't read such things now; there mustn't be anything ugly between us before it's all over.

RANK: [*Quietly to* HELMER.] You shouldn't deny her.

HELMER: [*Putting his arm around her.*] The child can have her way. But tomorrow night, after you've danced—

NORA: Then you'll be free.

MAID: [*In the doorway, right.*] Ma'am, dinner is served.

NORA: We'll be wanting champagne, Helene.

MAID: Very good, ma'am. [*Goes out.*]

HELMER: So—a regular banquet, hm?

NORA: Yes, a banquet—champagne till daybreak! [*Calling out.*] And some macaroons, Helene. Heaps of them—just this once.

HELMER: [*Taking her hands.*] Now, now, now—no hysterics. Be my own little lark again.

NORA: Oh, I will soon enough. But go on in—and you, Dr. Rank. Kristine, help me put up my hair.

RANK: [*Whispering, as they go.*] There's nothing wrong—really wrong, is there?

HELMER: Oh, of course not. It's nothing more than this childish anxiety I was telling you about. [*They go out, right.*]

NORA: Well?

MRS. LINDE: Left town.

NORA: I could see by your face.

MRS. LINDE: He'll be home tomorrow evening. I wrote him a note.

NORA: You shouldn't have. Don't try to stop anything now. After all, it's a wonderful joy, this waiting here for the miracle.

MRS. LINDE: What is it you're waiting for?

NORA: Oh, you can't understand that. Go in to them; I'll be along in a moment.

[MRS. LINDE *goes into the dining room.* NORA *stands a short while as if composing herself; then she looks at her watch.*]

NORA: Five. Seven hours to midnight. Twenty-four hours to the midnight after, and then the tarantella's done. Seven and twenty-four? Thirty-one hours to live.

HELMER: [*In the doorway, right.*] What's become of the little lark?

NORA: [*Going toward him with open arms.*] Here's your lark!

ACT III

Same scene. The table, with chairs around it, has been moved to the center of the room. A lamp on the table is lit. The hall door stands open. Dance music drifts down from the floor above. MRS. LINDE *sits at the table, absently paging through a book, trying to read, but apparently unable to focus her thoughts. Once or twice she pauses, tensely listening for a sound at the outer entrance.*

MRS. LINDE: [*Glancing at her watch.*] Not yet—and there's hardly any time left. If only he's not—[*Listening again.*] Ah, there he is. [*She goes out in the hall and cautiously opens the outer door. Quiet footsteps are heard on the stairs. She whispers:*] Come in. Nobody's here.

KROGSTAD: [*In the doorway.*] I found a note from you at home. What's back of all this?

MRS. LINDE: I just *had* to talk to you.

KROGSTAD: Oh? And it just *had* to be here in this house?

MRS. LINDE: At my place it was impossible; my room hasn't a private entrance. Come in; we're all alone. The maid's asleep, and the Helmers are at the dance upstairs.

KROGSTAD: [*Entering the room.*] Well, well, the Helmers are dancing tonight? Really?

MRS. LINDE: Yes, why not?

KROGSTAD: How true—why not?

MRS. LINDE: All right, Krogstad, let's talk.

KROGSTAD: Do we two have anything more to talk about?

MRS. LINDE: We have a great deal to talk about.

KROGSTAD: I wouldn't have thought so.

MRS. LINDE: No, because you've never understood me, really.

KROGSTAD: Was there anything more to understand—except what's all too common in life? A calculating woman throws over a man the moment a better catch comes by.

MRS. LINDE: You think I'm so thoroughly calculating? You think I broke it off lightly?

KROGSTAD: Didn't you?

MRS. LINDE: Nils—is that what you really thought?

KROGSTAD: If you cared, then why did you write me the way you did?

MRS. LINDE: What else could I do? If I had to break off with you, then it was my job as well to root out everything you felt for me.

KROGSTAD: [*Wringing his hands.*] So that was it. And this—all this, simply for money!

MRS. LINDE: Don't forget I had a helpless mother and two small brothers. We couldn't wait for you, Nils; you had such a long road ahead of you then.

KROGSTAD: That may be; but you still hadn't the right to abandon me for somebody else's sake.

MRS. LINDE: Yes—I don't know. So many, many times I've asked myself if I did have that right.

KROGSTAD: [*More softly.*] When I lost you, it was as if all the solid ground dissolved from under my feet. Look at me; I'm a half-drowned man now, hanging onto a wreck.

MRS. LINDE: Help may be near.

KROGSTAD: It was near—but then you came and blocked it off.

MRS. LINDE: Without my knowing it, Nils. Today for the first time I learned that it's you I'm replacing at the bank.

KROGSTAD: All right—I believe you. But now that you know, will you step aside?

MRS. LINDE: No, because that wouldn't benefit you in the slightest.

KROGSTAD: Not "benefit" me, hm! I'd step aside anyway.

MRS. LINDE: I've learned to be realistic. Life and hard, bitter necessity have taught me that.

KROGSTAD: And life's taught me never to trust fine phrases.

MRS. LINDE: Then life's taught you a very sound thing. But you do have to trust in actions, don't you?

KROGSTAD: What does that mean?

MRS. LINDE: You said you were hanging on like a half-drowned man to a wreck.

KROGSTAD: I've good reason to say that.

MRS. LINDE: I'm also like a half-drowned woman on a wreck. No one to suffer with; no one to care for.

KROGSTAD: You made your choice.

MRS. LINDE: There wasn't any choice then.

KROGSTAD: So—what of it?

MRS. LINDE: Nils, if only we two shipwrecked people could reach across to each other.

KROGSTAD: What are you saying?

MRS. LINDE: Two on one wreck are at least better off than each on his own.

KROGSTAD: Kristine!

MRS. LINDE: Why do you think I came into town?

KROGSTAD: Did you really have some thought of me?

MRS. LINDE: I have to work to go on living. All my born days, as long as I can remember, I've worked, and it's been my best and my only joy. But now I'm completely alone in the world; it frightens me to be so empty and lost. To work for yourself—there's no joy in that. Nils, give me something—someone to work for.

KROGSTAD: I don't believe all this. It's just some hysterical feminine urge to go out and make a noble sacrifice.

MRS. LINDE: Have you ever found me to be hysterical?

KROGSTAD: Can you honestly mean this? Tell me—do you know everything about my past?

MRS. LINDE: Yes.

KROGSTAD: And you know what they think I'm worth around here.

MRS. LINDE: From what you were saying before, it would seem that with me you could have been another person.

KROGSTAD: I'm positive of that.

MRS. LINDE: Couldn't it happen still?

KROGSTAD: Kristine—you're saying this in all seriousness? Yes, you are! I can see it in you. And do you really have the courage, then—?

MRS. LINDE: I need to have someone to care for; and your children need a mother. We both need each other. Nils, I have faith that you're good at heart—I'll risk everything together with you.

KROGSTAD: [Gripping her hands.] Kristine, thank you, thank you—Now I know I can win back a place in their eyes. Yes—but I forgot—

MRS. LINDE: [Listening.] Shh! The tarantella. Go now! Go on!

KROGSTAD: Why? What is it?

MRS. LINDE: Hear the dance up there? When that's over, they'll be coming down.

KROGSTAD: Oh, then I'll go. But—it's all pointless. Of course, you don't know the move I made against the Helmers.

MRS. LINDE: Yes, Nils, I know.

KROGSTAD: And all the same, you have the courage to—?

MRS. LINDE: I know how far despair can drive a man like you.

KROGSTAD: Oh, if I only could take it all back.

MRS. LINDE: You easily could—your letter's still lying in the mailbox.

KROGSTAD: Are you sure of that?

MRS. LINDE: Positive. But—

KROGSTAD: [Looks at her searchingly.] Is that the meaning of it, then? You'll save your friend at any price. Tell me straight out. Is that it?

MRS. LINDE: Nils—anyone who's sold herself for somebody else once isn't going to do it again.

KROGSTAD: I'll demand my letter back.

MRS. LINDE: No, no.

KROGSTAD: Yes, of course. I'll stay here till Helmer comes down; I'll tell him to give me my letter again—that it only involves my dismissal—that he shouldn't read it—

MRS. LINDE: No, Nils, don't call the letter back.

KROGSTAD: But wasn't that exactly why you wrote me to come here?

MRS. LINDE: Yes, in that first panic. But it's been a whole day and night since then, and in that time I've seen such incredible things in this house. Helmer's got to learn everything; this dreadful secret has to be aired; those two have to come to a full understanding; all these lies and evasions can't go on.

KROGSTAD: Well, then, if you want to chance it. But at least there's one thing I can do, and do right away—

MRS. LINDE: [*Listening.*] Go now, go, quick! The dance is over. We're not safe another second.

KROGSTAD: I'll wait for you downstairs.

MRS. LINDE: Yes, please do; take me home.

KROGSTAD: I can't believe it; I've never been so happy. [*He leaves by way of the outer door; the door between the room and the hall stays open.*]

MRS. LINDE: [*Straightening up a bit and getting together her street clothes.*] How different now! How different! Someone to work for, to live for—a home to build. Well, it is worth the try! Oh, if they'd only come! [*Listening.*] Ah, there they are. Bundle up. [*She picks up her hat and coat.* NORA'S *and* HELMER'S *voices can be heard outside; a key turns in the lock, and* HELMER *brings* NORA *into the hall almost by force. She is wearing the Italian costume with a large black shawl about her; he has on evening dress, with a black domino[3] open over it.*]

NORA: [*Struggling in the doorway.*] No, no, no, not inside! I'm going up again. I don't want to leave so soon.

HELMER: But Nora dear—

NORA: Oh, I beg you, please, Torvald. From the bottom of my heart, *please*—only an hour more!

HELMER: Not a single minute, Nora darling. You know our agreement. Come on, in we go; you'll catch cold out here. [*In spite of her resistance, he gently draws her into the room.*]

MRS. LINDE: Good evening.

NORA: Kristine!

---

3. Hood worn by members of some religious orders.

HELMER: Why, Mrs. Linde—are you here so late?

MRS. LINDE: Yes, I'm sorry, but I did want to see Nora in costume.

NORA: Have you been sitting here, waiting for me?

MRS. LINDE: Yes. I didn't come early enough; you were all upstairs; and then I thought I really couldn't leave without seeing you.

HELMER: [*Removing* NORA's *shawl.*] Yes, take a good look. She's worth looking at, I can tell you that, Mrs. Linde. Isn't she lovely?

MRS. LINDE: Yes, I should say—

HELMER: A dream of loveliness, isn't she? That's what everyone thought at the party, too. But she's horribly stubborn—this sweet little thing. What's to be done with her? Can you imagine, I almost had to use force to pry her away.

NORA: Oh, Torvald, you're going to regret you didn't indulge me, even for just a half hour more.

HELMER: There, you see. She danced her tarantella and got a tumultuous hand—which was well earned, although the performance may have been a bit too naturalistic—I mean it rather overstepped the proprieties of art. But never mind—what's important is, she made a success, an overwhelming success. You think I could let her stay on after that and spoil the effect? Oh no; I took my lovely little Capri girl—my capricious little Capri girl, I should say—took her under my arm; one quick tour of the ballroom, a curtsy to every side, and then—as they say in novels—the beautiful vision disappeared. An exit should always be effective, Mrs. Linde, but that's what I can't get Nora to grasp. Phew, it's hot in here. [*Flings the domino on a chair and opens the door to his room.*] Why's it dark in here? Oh yes, of course. Excuse me. [*He goes in and lights a couple of candles.*]

NORA: [*In a sharp, breathless whisper.*] So?

MRS. LINDE: [*Quietly.*] I talked with him.

NORA: And—?

MRS. LINDE: Nora—you must tell your husband everything.

NORA: [*Dully.*] I knew it.

MRS. LINDE: You've got nothing to fear from Krogstad, but you have to speak out.

NORA: I won't tell.

MRS. LINDE: Then the letter will.

NORA: Thanks, Kristine. I know now what's to be done. Shh!

HELMER: [*Reentering.*] Well, then, Mrs. Linde—have you admired her?

MRS. LINDE: Yes, and now I'll say good night.

HELMER: Oh, come, so soon? Is this yours, this knitting?

MRS. LINDE: Yes, thanks. I nearly forgot it.

HELMER: Do you knit, then?

MRS. LINDE: Oh yes.

HELMER: You know what? You should embroider instead.

MRS. LINDE: Really? Why?

HELMER: Yes, because it's a lot prettier. See here, one holds the embroidery so, in the left hand, and then one guides the needle with the right—so— in an easy, sweeping curve—right?

MRS. LINDE: Yes, I guess that's—

HELMER: But, on the other hand, knitting—it can never be anything but ugly. Look, see here, the arms tucked in, the knitting needles going up and down—there's something Chinese about it. Ah, that was really a glorious champagne they served.

MRS. LINDE: Yes, good night, Nora, and don't be stubborn anymore.

HELMER: Well put, Mrs. Linde!

MRS. LINDE: Good night, Mr. Helmer.

HELMER: [*Accompanying her to the door.*] Good night, good night. I hope you get home all right. I'd be very happy to—but you don't have far to go. Good night, good night. [*She leaves. He shuts the door after her and returns.*] There, now, at last we got her out the door. She's a deadly bore, that creature.

NORA: Aren't you pretty tired, Torvald?

HELMER: No, not a bit.

NORA: You're not sleepy?

HELMER: Not at all. On the contrary, I'm feeling quite exhilarated. But you? Yes, you really look tired and sleepy.

NORA: Yes, I'm very tired. Soon now I'll sleep.

HELMER: See! You see! I was right all along that we shouldn't stay longer.

NORA: Whatever you do is always right.

HELMER: [*Kissing her brow.*] Now my little lark talks sense. Say, did you notice what a time Rank was having tonight?

NORA: Oh, was he? I didn't get to speak with him.

HELMER: I scarcely did either, but it's a long time since I've seen him in such high spirits. [*Gazes at her a moment, then comes nearer her.*] Hm— it's marvelous, though, to be back home again—to be completely alone with you. Oh, you bewitchingly lovely young woman!

NORA: Torvald, don't look at me like that!

HELMER: Can't I look at my richest treasure? At all that beauty that's mine, mine alone—completely and utterly.

NORA: [*Moving around to the other side of the table.*] You mustn't talk to me that way tonight.

HELMER: [*Following her.*] The tarantella is still in your blood, I can see—and it makes you even more enticing. Listen. The guests are beginning to go. [*Dropping his voice.*] Nora—it'll soon be quiet through this whole house.

NORA: Yes, I hope so.

HELMER: You do, don't you, my love? Do you realize—when I'm out at a party like this with you—do you know why I talk to you so little, and keep such a distance away; just send you a stolen look now and then— you know why I do it? It's because I'm imagining then that you're my secret darling, my secret young bride-to-be, and that no one suspects there's anything between us.

NORA: Yes, yes; oh, yes, I know you're always thinking of me.

HELMER: And then when we leave and I place the shawl over those fine young rounded shoulders—over that wonderful curving neck—then I pretend that you're my young bride, that we're just coming from the wedding, that for the first time I'm bringing you into my house—that for the first time I'm alone with you—completely alone with you, your trembling young beauty! All this evening I've longed for nothing but you. When I saw you turn and sway in the tarantella—my blood was pounding till I couldn't stand it—that's why I brought you down here so early—

NORA: Go away, Torvald! Leave me alone. I don't want all this.

HELMER: What do you mean? Nora, you're teasing me. You will, won't you? Aren't I your husband—?

[A knock at the outside door.]

NORA: [Startled.] What's that?

HELMER: [Going toward the hall.] Who is it?

RANK: [Outside.] It's me. May I come in a moment?

HELMER: [With quiet irritation.] Oh, what does he want now? [Aloud.] Hold on. [Goes and opens the door.] Oh, how nice that you didn't just pass us by!

RANK: I thought I heard your voice, and then I wanted so badly to have a look in. [Lightly glancing about.] Ah, me, these old familiar haunts. You have it snug and cozy in here, you two.

HELMER: You seemed to be having it pretty cozy upstairs, too.

RANK: Absolutely. Why shouldn't I? Why not take in everything in life? As much as you can, anyway, and as long as you can. The wine was superb—

HELMER: The champagne especially.

RANK: You noticed that too? It's amazing how much I could guzzle down.

NORA: Torvald also drank a lot of champagne this evening.

RANK: Oh?

NORA: Yes, and that always makes him so entertaining.

RANK: Well, why shouldn't one have a pleasant evening after a well-spent day?

HELMER: Well spent? I'm afraid I can't claim that.

RANK: [Slapping him on the back.] But I can, you see!

NORA: Dr. Rank, you must have done some scientific research today.

RANK: Quite so.

HELMER: Come now—little Nora talking about scientific research!

NORA: And can I congratulate you on the results?

RANK: Indeed you may.

NORA: Then they were good?

RANK: The best possible for both doctor and patient—certainty.

NORA: [*Quickly and searchingly.*] Certainty?

RANK: Complete certainty. So don't I owe myself a gay evening afterwards?

NORA: Yes, you're right, Dr. Rank.

HELMER: I'm with you—just so long as you don't have to suffer for it in the morning.

RANK: Well, one never gets something for nothing in life.

NORA: Dr. Rank—are you very fond of masquerade parties?

RANK: Yes, if there's a good array of odd disguises—

NORA: Tell me, what should we two go as at the next masquerade?

HELMER: You little featherhead—already thinking of the next!

RANK: We two? I'll tell you what: you must go as Charmed Life—

HELMER: Yes, but find a costume for *that!*

RANK: Your wife can appear just as she looks every day.

HELMER: That was nicely put. But don't you know what you're going to be?

RANK: Yes, Helmer, I've made up my mind.

HELMER: Well?

RANK: At the next masquerade I'm going to be invisible.

HELMER: That's a funny idea.

RANK: They say there's a hat—black, huge—have you never heard of the hat that makes you invisible? You put it on, and then no one on earth can see you.

HELMER: [*Suppressing a smile.*] Ah, of course.

RANK: But I'm quite forgetting what I came for. Helmer, give me a cigar, one of the dark Havanas.

HELMER: With the greatest pleasure. [*Holds out his case.*]

RANK: Thanks. [*Takes one and cuts off the tip.*]

NORA: [*Striking a match*] Let me give you a light.

RANK: Thank you. [*She holds the match for him; he lights the cigar.*] And now good-bye.

HELMER: Good-bye, good-bye, old friend.

NORA: Sleep well, Doctor.

RANK: Thanks for that wish.

NORA: Wish me the same.

RANK: You? All right, if you like—Sleep well. And thanks for the light. [*He nods to them both and leaves.*]

HELMER: [*His voice subdued.*] He's been drinking heavily.

NORA: [*Absently.*] Could be. [HELMER *takes his keys from his pocket and goes out in the hall.*] Torvald—what are you after?

HELMER: Got to empty the mailbox; it's nearly full. There won't be room for the morning papers.

NORA: Are you working tonight?

HELMER: You know I'm not. Why—what's this? Someone's been at the lock.

NORA: At the lock—?

HELMER: Yes, I'm positive. What do you suppose—? I can't imagine one of the maids—? Here's a broken hairpin. Nora, it's yours—

NORA: [*Quickly.*] Then it must be the children—

HELMER: You'd better break them of that. Hm, hm—well, opened it after all. [*Takes the contents out and calls into the kitchen.*] Helene! Helene, would you put out the lamp in the hall. [*He returns to the room, shutting the hall door, then displays the handful of mail.*] Look how it's piled up. [*Sorting through them.*] Now what's this?

NORA: [*At the window.*] The letter! Oh, Torvald, no!

HELMER: Two calling cards—from Rank.

NORA: From Dr. Rank?

HELMER: [*Examining them.*] "Dr. Rank, Consulting Physician." They were on top. He must have dropped them in as he left.

NORA: Is there anything on them?

HELMER: There's a black cross over the name. See? That's a gruesome notion. He could almost be announcing his own death.

NORA: That's just what he's doing.

HELMER: What! You've heard something? Something he's told you?

NORA: Yes. That when those cards came, he'd be taking his leave of us. He'll shut himself in now and die.

HELMER: Ah, my poor friend! Of course I knew he wouldn't be here much longer. But so soon—And then to hide himself away like a wounded animal.

NORA: If it has to happen, then it's best it happens in silence—don't you think so, Torvald?

HELMER: [*Pacing up and down.*] He'd grown right into our lives. I simply can't imagine him gone. He with his suffering and loneliness—like a dark cloud setting off our sunlit happiness. Well, maybe it's best this way. For him, at least. [*Standing still.*] And maybe for us too, Nora. Now we're thrown back on each other, completely. [*Embracing her.*] Oh you, my darling wife, how can I hold you close enough? You know what, Nora— time and again I've wished you were in some terrible danger, just so I could stake my life and soul and everything, for your sake.

NORA: [*Tearing herself away, her voice firm and decisive.*] Now you must read your mail, Torvald.

HELMER: No, no, not tonight. I want to stay with you, dearest.

NORA: With a dying friend on your mind?

HELMER: You're right. We've both had a shock. There's ugliness between us—these thoughts of death and corruption. We'll have to get free of them first. Until then—we'll stay apart.

NORA: [*Clinging about his neck.*] Torvald—good night! Good night!

HELMER: [*Kissing her on the cheek.*] Good night, little songbird. Sleep well, Nora. I'll be reading my mail now. [*He takes the letters into his room and shuts the door after him.*]

NORA: [*With bewildered glances, groping about, seizing* HELMER'S *domino, throwing it around her, and speaking in short, hoarse, broken whispers.*] Never see him again. Never, never. [*Putting her shawl over her head.*] Never see the children either—them, too. Never, never. Oh, the freezing black water! The depths—down—Oh, I wish it were over—He has it now; he's reading it—now. Oh no, no, not yet. Torvald, good-bye, you and the children—[*She starts for the hall; as she does,* HELMER *throws open his door and stands with an open letter in his hand.*]

HELMER: Nora!

NORA: [*Screams.*] Oh—!

HELMER: What is this? You know what's in this letter?

NORA: Yes, I know. Let me go! Let me out!

HELMER: [*Holding her back.*] Where are you going?

NORA: [*Struggling to break loose.*] You can't save me, Torvald!

HELMER: [*Slumping back.*] True! Then it's true what he writes? How horrible! No, no, it's impossible—it can't be true.

NORA: It *is* true. I've loved you more than all this world.

HELMER: Ah, none of your slippery tricks.

NORA: [*Taking one step toward him.*] Torvald—!

HELMER: What *is* this you've blundered into!

NORA: Just let me loose. You're not going to suffer for my sake. You're not going to take on my guilt.

HELMER: No more playacting. [*Locks the hall door.*] You stay right here and give me a reckoning. You understand what you've done? Answer! You understand?

NORA: [*Looking squarely at him, her face hardening.*] Yes. I'm beginning to understand everything now.

HELMER: [*Striding about.*] Oh, what an awful awakening! In all these eight years—she who was my pride and joy—a hypocrite, a liar—worse, worse—a criminal! How infinitely disgusting it all is! The shame! [NORA *says nothing and goes on looking straight at him. He stops in front of her.*] I should have suspected something of the kind. I should have known. All your father's flimsy values—Be still! All your father's flimsy values have come out in you. No religion, no morals, no sense of duty—Oh, how I'm punished for letting him off! I did it for your sake, and you repay me like this.

NORA: Yes, like this.

HELMER: Now you've wrecked all my happiness—ruined my whole future. Oh, it's awful to think of. I'm in a cheap little grafter's hands; he can do anything he wants with me, ask for anything, play with me like a puppet—and I can't breathe a word. I'll be swept down miserably into the depths on account of a featherbrained woman.

NORA: When I'm gone from this world, you'll be free.

HELMER: Oh, quit posing. Your father had a mess of those speeches too. What good would that ever do me if you were gone from this world, as you say? Not the slightest. He can still make the whole thing known; and if he does, I could be falsely suspected as your accomplice. They might even think that I was behind it—that I put you up to it. And all that I can thank you for—you that I've coddled the whole of our marriage. Can you see now what you've done to me?

NORA: [Icily calm.] Yes.

HELMER: It's so incredible, I just can't grasp it. But we'll have to patch up whatever we can. Take off the shawl. I said, take it off! I've got to appease him somehow or other. The thing has to be hushed up at any cost. And as for you and me, it's got to seem like everything between us is just as it was—to the outside world, that is. You'll go right on living in this house, of course. But you can't be allowed to bring up the children; I don't dare trust you with them—Oh, to have to say this to someone I've loved so much, and that I still—! Well, that's done with. From now on happiness doesn't matter; all that matters is saving the bits and pieces, the appearance— [The doorbell rings. HELMER starts.] What's that? And so late. Maybe the worst—? You think he'd—? Hide, Nora! Say you're sick. [NORA remains standing motionless. HELMER goes and opens the door.]

MAID: [Half dressed, in the hall.] A letter for Mrs. Helmer.

HELMER: I'll take it. [Snatches the letter and shuts the door.] Yes, it's from him. You don't get it; I'm reading it myself.

NORA: Then read it.

HELMER: [By the lamp.] I hardly dare. We may be ruined, you and I. But— I've got to know. [Rips open the letter, skims through a few lines, glances at an enclosure, then cries out joyfully.] Nora! [NORA looks inquiringly at him.] Nora! Wait—better check it again—Yes, yes, it's true. I'm saved. Nora, I'm saved!

NORA: And I?

HELMER: You too, of course. We're both saved, both of us. Look. He's sent back your note. He says he's sorry and ashamed—that a happy development in his life—oh, who cares what he says! Nora, we're saved! No one can hurt you. Oh, Nora, Nora—but first, this ugliness all has to go. Let me see—[*Takes a look at the note.*] No, I don't want to see it; I want the whole thing to fade like a dream. [*Tears the note and both letters to pieces, throws them into the stove and watches them burn.*] There—now there's nothing left—He wrote that since Christmas Eve you—Oh, they must have been three terrible days for you, Nora.

NORA: I fought a hard fight.

HELMER: And suffered pain and saw no escape but—No, we're not going to dwell on anything unpleasant. We'll just be grateful and keep on repeating: it's over now, it's over! You hear me, Nora? You don't seem to realize—it's over. What's it mean—that frozen look? Oh, poor little Nora, I understand. You can't believe I've forgiven you. But I have, Nora; I swear I have. I know that what you did, you did out of love for me.

NORA: That's true.

HELMER: You loved me the way a wife ought to love her husband. It's simply the means that you couldn't judge. But you think I love you any the less for not knowing how to handle your affairs? No, no—just lean on me; I'll guide you and teach you. I wouldn't be a man if this feminine helplessness didn't make you twice as attractive to me. You mustn't mind those sharp words I said—that was all in the first confusion of thinking my world had collapsed. I've forgiven you, Nora; I swear I've forgiven you.

NORA: My thanks for your forgiveness. [*She goes out through the door, right.*]

HELMER: No, wait—[*Peers in.*] What are you doing in there?

NORA: [*Inside.*] Getting out of my costume.

HELMER: [*By the open door.*] Yes, do that. Try to calm yourself and collect your thoughts again, my frightened little songbird. You can rest easy now; I've got wide wings to shelter you with. [*Walking about close by the door.*] How snug and nice our home is, Nora. You're safe here; I'll keep you like a hunted dove I've rescued out of a hawk's claws. I'll bring peace to your poor, shuddering heart. Gradually it'll happen, Nora; you'll see. Tomorrow all this will look different to you; then everything will be as it was. I won't have to go on repeating I forgive you; you'll feel it for yourself. How can you imagine I'd ever conceivably want to disown you—or even blame you in any way? Ah, you don't know a man's heart, Nora. For a man there's something indescribably sweet and satisfying in knowing he's forgiven his wife—and forgiven her out of a full and open heart. It's as if she belongs to him in two ways now: in a sense he's given her fresh into the world again, and she's become his wife and his child as well. From now on that's what you'll be to me—you little, bewildered, helpless thing. Don't be afraid of anything, Nora; just open your heart to me, and I'll be conscience and will to you both—[NORA *enters in her regular clothes.*] What's this? Not in bed? You've changed your dress?

NORA: Yes, Torvald, I've changed my dress.

HELMER: But why now, so late?

NORA: Tonight I'm not sleeping.

HELMER: But Nora dear—

NORA: [*Looking at her watch.*] It's still not so very late. Sit down, Torvald; we have a lot to talk over. [*She sits at one side of the table.*]

HELMER: Nora—what is this? That hard expression—

NORA: Sit down. This'll take some time. I have a lot to say.

HELMER: [*Sitting at the table directly opposite her.*] You worry me, Nora. And I don't understand you.

NORA: No, that's exactly it. You don't understand me. And I've never understood you either—until tonight. No, don't interrupt. You can just listen to what I say. We're closing out accounts, Torvald.

HELMER: How do you mean that?

NORA: [*After a short pause.*] Doesn't anything strike you about our sitting here like this?

HELMER: What's that?

NORA: We've been married now eight years. Doesn't it occur to you that this is the first time we two, you and I, man and wife, have ever talked seriously together?

HELMER: What do you mean—seriously?

NORA: In eight whole years—longer even—right from our first acquaintance, we've never exchanged a serious word on any serious thing.

HELMER: You mean I should constantly go and involve you in problems you couldn't possibly help me with?

NORA: I'm not talking of problems. I'm saying that we've never sat down seriously together and tried to get to the bottom of anything.

HELMER: But dearest, what good would that ever do you?

NORA: That's the point right there: you've never understood me. I've been wronged greatly, Torvald—first by Papa, and then by you.

HELMER: What! By us—the two people who've loved you more than anyone else?

NORA: [*Shaking her head.*] You never loved me. You've thought it fun to be in love with me, that's all.

HELMER: Nora, what a thing to say!

NORA: Yes, it's true now, Torvald. When I lived at home with Papa, he told me all his opinions, so I had the same ones too; or if they were different I hid them, since he wouldn't have cared for that. He used to call me his

doll-child, and he played with me the way I played with my dolls. Then
I came into your house—

HELMER: How can you speak of our marriage like that?

NORA: [*Unperturbed.*] I mean, then I went from Papa's hands into yours.
You arranged everything to your own taste, and so I got the same taste
as you—or I pretended to; I can't remember. I guess a little of both, first
one, then the other. Now when I look back, it seems as if I'd lived here
like a beggar—just from hand to mouth. I've lived by doing tricks for
you, Torvald. But that's the way you wanted it. It's a great sin what you
and Papa did to me. You're to blame that nothing's become of me.

HELMER: Nora, how unfair and ungrateful you are! Haven't you been
happy here?

NORA: No, never. I thought so—but I never have.

HELMER: Not—not happy!

NORA: No, only lighthearted. And you've always been so kind to me. But our
home's been nothing but a playpen. I've been your doll-wife here, just as at
home I was Papa's doll-child. And in turn the children have been my
dolls. I thought it was fun when you played with me, just as they thought
it fun when I played with them. That's been our marriage, Torvald.

HELMER: There's some truth in what you're saying—under all the raving
exaggeration. But it'll all be different after this. Playtime's over; now for
the schooling.

NORA: Whose schooling—mine or the children's?

HELMER: Both yours and the children's, dearest.

NORA: Oh, Torvald, you're not the man to teach me to be a good wife to
you.

HELMER: And you can say that?

NORA: And I—how am I equipped to bring up children?

HELMER: Nora!

NORA: Didn't you say a moment ago that that was no job to trust me with?

HELMER: In a flare of temper! Why fasten on that?

NORA: Yes, but you were so very right. I'm not up to the job. There's another
job I have to do first. I have to try to educate myself. You can't help me
with that. I've got to do it alone. And that's why I'm leaving you now.

HELMER: [*Jumping up.*] What's that?

NORA: I have to stand completely alone, if I'm ever going to discover myself
and the world out there. So I can't go on living with you.

HELMER: Nora, Nora!

NORA: I want to leave right away. Kristine should put me up for the night—

HELMER: You're insane! You've no right! I forbid you!

NORA: From here on, there's no use forbidding me anything. I'll take with
me whatever is mine. I don't want a thing from you, either now or later.

HELMER: What kind of madness is this!

NORA: Tomorrow I'm going home—I mean, home where I came from. It'll be easier up there to find something to do.

HELMER: Oh, you blind, incompetent child!

NORA: I must learn to be competent, Torvald.

HELMER: Abandon your home, your husband, your children! And you're not even thinking what people will say.

NORA: I can't be concerned about that. I only know how essential this is.

HELMER: Oh, it's outrageous. So you'll run out like this on your most sacred vows.

NORA: What do you think are my most sacred vows?

HELMER: And I have to tell you that! Aren't they your duties to your husband and children?

NORA: I have other duties equally sacred.

HELMER: That isn't true. What duties are they?

NORA: Duties to myself.

HELMER: Before all else, you're a wife and a mother.

NORA: I don't believe in that anymore. I believe that, before all else, I'm a human being, no less than you—or anyway, I ought to try to become one. I know the majority thinks you're right, Torvald, and plenty of books agree with you, too. But I can't go on believing what the majority says, or what's written in books. I have to think over these things myself and try to understand them.

HELMER: Why can't you understand your place in your own home? On a point like that, isn't there one everlasting guide you can turn to? Where's your religion?

NORA: Oh, Torvald, I'm really not sure what religion is.

HELMER: What—?

NORA: I only know what the minister said when I was confirmed. He told me religion was this thing and that. When I get clear and away by myself, I'll go into that problem too. I'll see if what the minister said was right, or, in any case, if it's right for me.

HELMER: A young woman your age shouldn't talk like that. If religion can't move you, I can try to rouse your conscience. You do have some moral feeling? Or, tell me—has that gone too?

NORA: It's not easy to answer that, Torvald. I simply don't know. I'm all confused about these things. I just know I see them so differently from you. I find out, for one thing, that the law's not at all what I'd thought—but I can't get it through my head that the law is fair. A woman hasn't a right to protect her dying father or save her husband's life! I can't believe that.

HELMER: You talk like a child. You don't know anything of the world you live in.

NORA: No, I don't. But now I'll begin to learn for myself. I'll try to discover who's right, the world or I.

HELMER: Nora, you're sick; you've got a fever. I almost think you're out of your head.

NORA: I've never felt more clearheaded and sure in my life.

HELMER: And—clearheaded and sure—you're leaving your husband and children?

NORA: Yes.

HELMER: Then there's only one possible reason.

NORA: What?

HELMER: You no longer love me.

NORA: No. That's exactly it.

HELMER: Nora! You can't be serious!

NORA: Oh, this is so hard, Torvald—you've been so kind to me always. But I can't help it. I don't love you anymore.

HELMER: [*Struggling for composure.*] Are you also clearheaded and sure about that?

NORA: Yes, completely. That's why I can't go on staying here.

HELMER: Can you tell me what I did to lose your love?

NORA: Yes, I can tell you. It was this evening when the miraculous thing didn't come—then I knew you weren't the man I'd imagined.

HELMER: Be more explicit; I don't follow you.

NORA: I've waited now so patiently eight long years—for, my Lord, I know miracles don't come every day. Then this crisis broke over me, and such a certainty filled me: *now* the miraculous event would occur. While Krogstad's letter was lying out there, I never for an instant dreamed that you could give in to his terms. I was so utterly sure you'd say to him: go on, tell your tale to the whole wide world. And when he'd done that—

HELMER: Yes, what then? When I'd delivered my own wife into shame and disgrace—!

NORA: When he'd done that, I was so utterly sure that you'd step forward, take the blame on yourself and say: I am the guilty one.

HELMER: Nora—!

NORA: You're thinking I'd never accept such a sacrifice from you? No, of course not. But what good would my protests be against you? That was the miracle I was waiting for, in terror and hope. And to stave that off, I would have taken my life.

HELMER: I'd gladly work for you day and night, Nora—and take on pain and deprivation. But there's no one who gives up honor for love.

NORA: Millions of women have done just that.

HELMER: Oh, you think and talk like a silly child.

NORA: Perhaps. But you neither think nor talk like the man I could join myself to. When your big fright was over—and it wasn't from any threat against me, only for what might damage you—when all the danger was past, for you it was just as if nothing had happened. I was exactly the same, your little lark, your doll, that you'd have to handle with double care now that I'd turned out so brittle and frail. [*Gets up.*] Torvald—in that instant it dawned on me that for eight years I've been living here with a stranger, and that I'd even conceived three children—oh, I can't stand the thought of it! I could tear myself to bits.

HELMER: [*Heavily.*] I see. There's a gulf that's opened between us—that's clear. Oh, but Nora, can't we bridge it somehow?

NORA: The way I am now, I'm no wife for you.

HELMER: I have the strength to make myself over.

NORA: Maybe—if your doll gets taken away.

HELMER: But to part! To part from you! No, Nora, no—I can't imagine it.

NORA: [*Going out, right.*] All the more reason why it has to be. [*She reenters with her coat and a small overnight bag, which she puts on a chair by the table.*]

HELMER: Nora, Nora, not now! Wait till tomorrow.

NORA: I can't spend the night in a strange man's room.

HELMER: But couldn't we live here like brother and sister—

NORA: You know very well how long that would last. [*Throws her shawl about her.*] Good-bye, Torvald. I won't look in on the children. I know they're in better hands than mine. The way I am now, I'm no use to them.

HELMER: But someday, Nora—someday—?

NORA: How can I tell? I haven't the least idea what'll become of me.

HELMER: But you're my wife, now and wherever you go.

NORA: Listen, Torvald—I've heard that when a wife deserts her husband's house just as I'm doing, then the law frees him from all responsibility. In any case, I'm freeing you from being responsible. Don't feel yourself bound, any more than I will. There has to be absolute freedom for us both. Here, take your ring back. Give me mine.

HELMER: That too?

NORA: That too.

HELMER: There it is.

NORA: Good. Well, now it's all over. I'm putting the keys here. The maids know all about keeping up the house—better than I do. Tomorrow, after I've left town, Kristine will stop by to pack up everything that's mine from home. I'd like those things shipped up to me.

HELMER: Over! All over! Nora, won't you ever think about me?

NORA: I'm sure I'll think of you often, and about the children and the house here.

HELMER: May I write you?

NORA: No—never. You're not to do that.

HELMER: Oh, but let me send you—

NORA: Nothing. Nothing.

HELMER: Or help you if you need it.

NORA: No. I accept nothing from strangers.

HELMER: Nora—can I never be more than a stranger to you?

NORA: [*Picking up the overnight bag.*] Ah, Torvald—it would take the greatest miracle of all—

HELMER: Tell me the greatest miracle!

NORA: You and I both would have to transform ourselves to the point that—Oh, Torvald, I've stopped believing in miracles.

HELMER: But I'll believe. Tell me! Transform ourselves to the point that—?

NORA: That our living together could be a true marriage. [*She goes out down the hall.*]

HELMER: [*Sinks down on a chair by the door, face buried in his hands.*] Nora! Nora! [*Looking about and rising.*] Empty. She's gone. [*A sudden hope leaps in him.*] The greatest miracle—?

[*From below, the sound of a door slamming shut.*]

1879

QUESTIONS

1. Though the three acts of A DOLL HOUSE are not formally divided into scenes, each does unfold as a series of relatively discreet, though continuous, episodes. In the first act, for example, the initial encounter between Nora and Helmer is followed by Nora's conversation with Mrs. Linde; a conversation among Mrs. Linde, Dr. Rank, and Nora, and then Torvald as well; a brief interlude in which Nora plays with her children; and, finally, her conversations first with Krogstad and then with her husband. What might the episodic structure itself tell us about Nora's character and situation? How is each of these episodes both similar to and different from the others, especially in terms of justifying or complicating Nora's assertion that everyone sees her the same way? What does each episode contribute to your impression of Nora's character and situation? to your degree of sympathy with her? Why and how does the order of the episodes matter? For example, what is the effect of Ibsen's choice to delay exposition regarding past events until the second episode (the conversation between Nora and Mrs. Linde)? By the end of this act, what do you see as the play's central conflict or conflicts?

2. How, if at all, has Nora or Torvald, or your impression of their characters and their marriage, changed by the beginning of act II? by its end? How has your interpretation of the conflict changed by this point? In these terms, what is the effect of the way this act is plotted and structured? Why does Nora decide not to confide everything to Dr. Rank and seek his help? What can you surmise at

this stage about Nora's plans and expectations for the immediate future? For what "miracle" is she "waiting"?

3. Act III begins with the first and only episode in which Nora does not appear. What is the effect of her absence? of the scene itself? How might this scene compare to the later one between Nora and Torvald? More generally, how does the relationship between Mrs. Linde and Krogstad compare to, and comment on, that between Nora and Torvald?

4. At the end of the play, Nora declares, "It's a great sin what you and Papa did to me. You're to blame that nothing's become of me." How does the play as a whole both endorse and complicate Nora's assessment?

5. To what extent might the play suggest that Nora is right or wrong—or both— to leave her family at the play's end? Why is or isn't this an appropriate or satisfying resolution of the conflict?

6. In what various ways might one interpret the very end of the play? That is, what "sudden hope leaps in" Helmer? What might he mean when he says, "The greatest miracle—"? What is the significance of the fact that we then hear "the sound of a door slamming shut"? Based on evidence from the rest of the play, what interpretation seems most valid to you? How does your inter-pretation of these words and actions affect your interpretation of the play's theme(s)?

7. In what way does A DOLL HOUSE make use of dramatic or situational irony? By the end of the play, what statements in earlier acts might seem like instances of verbal irony?

8. In act III, Mrs. Linde tells Krogstad that she believes he "could have been another person" had he married her, implying that it is, at least in part, forces outside ourselves that shape who we are and how we behave, regardless of our gender. Does the play as a whole seem to endorse that view? If so, what are the most important forces? What role, for example, do different characters— and the play as a whole—assign to heredity or parentage, to parenting, and to economics? In terms of the latter, why might it matter that characters in the play tend to use economic language and metaphors?

9. What is the significance of Ibsen's choice to have all the action in A DOLL HOUSE take place in one location? to make that location the interior of the Helmer home? to describe this interior as he does in the stage directions that begin each act? What is the effect of the fact that the play opens on Christmas Eve? that each act takes place on a different day? that the play ends forty-eight hours after it began? What other aspects of setting seem especially effective or important?

10. In terms of the play's conflict, theme(s), and characterization of Nora, Torvald, and their marriage, what role is played by each of the minor characters— Dr. Rank, Anne-Marie, and the Helmer children?

SUGGESTIONS FOR WRITING

1. Do any characters besides Nora change over the course of the play, or is it merely our perception of them that changes? Write an essay that answers this question with regard to Torvald, Mrs. Linde, or Krogstad, making sure to explain precisely when, how, and why either the character or your perception of

the character changes and how that change affects how the play as a whole works and what it means.

2. Write an essay exploring the symbolic or metaphorical significance of the masquerade or tarantella.

3. In a brief essay, explore the validity and significance of Nora's claim in act II that Dr. Rank is her "best and truest friend."

4. Write an essay that draws on evidence from Ibsen's play to make an argument about what most likely happens after the play ends, either to Mrs. Linde and Mr. Krogstad or to Nora and/or Torvald. What reasons, if any, for example, might the play give you for believing that Mrs. Linde and Krogstad will enjoy what Nora in the last act calls "a true marriage," or that "Those who go away are soon forgotten" and, perhaps, replaced (act II)?

5. A DOLL HOUSE was first performed in 1879, and its portrait of women's roles as daughters, wives, and mothers is in certain ways specific to the late nineteenth century, when—for example—a woman couldn't legally borrow money without her father's or husband's consent and seldom got custody of her children in cases of separation or divorce. Write an essay in which you analyze both how the play characterizes the role nineteenth-century women were expected to play as daughters, wives, *or* mothers, and why and how that characterization is and/or isn't relevant or accurate today.

6. Religion is explicitly discussed only at the very end of the play, when Torvald asks, "Where's your religion?" and Nora answers him. Yet the play takes place during a Christian holiday, and there is frequent talk of "miracles." Write an essay exploring what the play as a whole ultimately seems to suggest about Christianity, its status in the social world depicted in the play, and its role in generating conflict.

AUGUST WILSON
(1945–2005)
Fences

August Wilson died of liver cancer when he was only sixty. One of the most important dramatists in American theater history, he had come a long way, the hard way. Frederick August Kittel, Jr. (who would later take his mother's maiden name), was the son of a white, German-born baker and his wife, a black cleaning woman who singlehandedly raised their six children in Pittsburgh's down-at-heel Hill District. In 1957, when Wilson was twelve, his mother remarried. Her new husband was an African American sewer-department worker who, as Wilson learned only after his stepfather's death, had been both a high-school football star unable to secure a college scholarship and an ex-convict. After a series of bad experiences, Wilson left school at fifteen. Armed with a tenth-grade education, he took on a series of menial jobs, read his way through the public library, and served briefly in the Army. In 1968, he returned to the Hill, cofounding the Black Horizon Theater and debuting his first play. Fourteen years later, Wilson struck artistic gold with *Ma Rainey's Black Bottom* (1982), his first Broadway play and the second in what would become a ten-play cycle. Set mostly in the Hill and chronicling African American life in every decade of the twentieth century, the series earned Wilson two Pulitzers (for *Fences*, 1987, and *The Piano Lesson*, 1990); a Tony (for *Fences*); a Grammy (for the *Ma Rainey's* cast album); an Emmy (for his adaption of *Piano Lesson*); and eight Drama Critics Circle awards. Wilson often described *Fences* as his least representative, most conventional play, thanks to the way it revolves around a single "big character." Yet this, his best-known work, is also arguably among his most personal, set in the period of his youth and aimed, he said, at "uncover[ing] the nobility and the dignity" of the adults he grew up around—"that generation, which shielded its children from all of the indignities they went through."

For Lloyd Richards,[1]
who adds to whatever he touches

CHARACTERS

TROY MAXSON
JIM BONO, *Troy's friend*
ROSE, *Troy's wife*
LYONS, *Troy's oldest son by a previous marriage*

GABRIEL, *Troy's brother*
CORY, *Troy and Rose's son*
RAYNELL, *Troy's daughter*

SETTING: *The setting is the yard which fronts the only entrance to the Maxson household, an ancient two-story brick house set back off a small alley in a big-city neighborhood. The entrance to the house is gained by two or three steps leading to a wooden porch badly in need of paint.*

A relatively recent addition to the house and running its full width, the porch lacks congruence. It is a sturdy porch with a flat roof. One or two chairs of dubious value sit at one end where the kitchen window opens onto the porch. An old-fashioned icebox stands silent guard at the opposite end.

The yard is a small dirt yard, partially fenced (except during the last scene), with a wooden sawhorse, a pile of lumber, and other fence-building

---

1. Influential Canadian-American director-actor (1919–2006) whom August Wilson called his "guide, mentor, and provocateur"; the first black director of a Broadway play (Lorraine Hansberry's *A Raisin in the Sun*, 1959), artistic director of the Eugene O'Neill Theater Center and the Yale Repertory Theatre, and dean of the Yale School of Drama, Richards oversaw the first productions of all of Wilson's plays, beginning with *Ma Rainey's Black Bottom* (1982).

equipment off to the side. Opposite is a tree from which hangs a ball made of rags. A baseball bat leans against the tree. Two oil drums serve as garbage receptacles and sit near the house at right to complete the setting.

THE PLAY: *Near the turn of the century, the destitute of Europe sprang on the city with tenacious claws and an honest and solid dream. The city devoured them. They swelled its belly until it burst into a thousand furnaces and sewing machines, a thousand butcher shops and bakers' ovens, a thousand churches and hospitals and funeral parlors and moneylenders. The city grew. It nourished itself and offered each man a partnership limited only by his talent, his guile and his willingness and capacity for hard work. For the immigrants of Europe, a dream dared and won true.*

The descendants of African slaves were offered no such welcome or participation. They came from places called the Carolinas and the Virginias, Georgia, Alabama, Mississippi and Tennessee. They came strong, eager, searching. The city rejected them and they fled and settled along the riverbanks and under bridges in shallow, ramshackle houses made of sticks and tar paper. They collected rags and wood. They sold the use of their muscles and their bodies. They cleaned houses and washed clothes, they shined shoes, and in quiet desperation and vengeful pride, they stole, and lived in pursuit of their own dream. That they could breathe free, finally, and stand to meet life with the force of dignity and whatever eloquence the heart could call upon.

By 1957, the hard-won victories of the European immigrants had solidified the industrial might of America. War had been confronted and won with new energies that used loyalty and patriotism as its fuel. Life was rich, full and flourishing. The Milwaukee Braves won the World Series, and the hot winds of change that would make the sixties a turbulent, racing, dangerous and provocative decade had not yet begun to blow full.

> When the sins of our fathers visit us
> We do not have to play host.
> We can banish them with forgiveness
> As God, in His Largeness and Laws.
>
> —AUGUST WILSON

ACT ONE

Scene 1

It is 1957. Troy and Bono enter the yard, engaged in conversation. Troy is fifty-three years old, a large man with thick, heavy hands; it is this largeness that he strives to fill out and make an accommodation with. Together with his blackness, his largeness informs his sensibilities and the choices he has made in his life.

Of the two men, Bono is obviously the follower. His commitment to their friendship of thirty-odd years is rooted in his admiration of Troy's honesty, capacity for hard work, and his strength, which Bono seeks to emulate.

It is Friday night, payday, and the one night of the week the two men engage in a ritual of talk and drink. Troy is usually the most talkative and at times he can be crude and almost vulgar, though he is capable of rising to profound heights of expression. The men carry lunch buckets and wear or carry burlap aprons and are dressed in clothes suitable to their jobs as garbage collectors.

BONO: Troy, you ought to stop that lying!

TROY: I ain't lying! The nigger had a watermelon this big. (*Indicates with his hands*) Talking about . . . "What watermelon, Mr. Rand?" I like to fell out! "What watermelon, Mr. Rand?". . . . And it sitting there big as life.

BONO: What did Mr. Rand say?

TROY: Ain't said nothing. Figure if the nigger too dumb to know he carrying a watermelon, he wasn't gonna get much sense out of him. Trying to hide that great big old watermelon under his coat. Afraid to let the white man see him carry it home.

BONO: I'm like you . . . I ain't got no time for them kind of people.

TROY: Now what he look like getting mad 'cause he see the man from the union talking to Mr. Rand?

BONO: He come talking to me about . . . "Maxson gonna get us fired." I told him to get away from me with that. He walked away from me calling you a troublemaker. What Mr. Rand say?

TROY: Ain't said nothing. He told me to go down the commissioner's office next Friday. They called me down there to see them.

BONO: Well, as long as you got your complaint filed, they can't fire you. That's what one of them white fellows tell me.

TROY: I ain't worried about them firing me. They gonna fire me 'cause I asked a question? That's all I did. I went to Mr. Rand and asked him, "Why? Why you got the white mens driving and the colored lifting?" Told him, "What's the matter, don't I count? You think only white fellows got sense enough to drive a truck. That ain't no paper job! Hell, anybody can drive a truck. How come you got all whites driving and the colored lifting?" He told me, "Take it to the union." Well, hell, that's what I done! Now they wanna come up with this pack of lies.

BONO: I told Brownie if the man come and ask him any questions . . . just tell the truth! It ain't nothing but something they done trumped up on you 'cause you filed a complaint on them.

TROY: Brownie don't understand nothing. All I want them to do is change the job description. Give everybody a chance to drive the truck. Brownie can't see that. He ain't got that much sense.

BONO: How you figure he be making out with that gal be up at Taylors' all the time . . . that Alberta gal?

TROY: Same as you and me. Getting as much as we is. Which is to say nothing.

BONO: It is, huh? I figure you doing a little better than me . . . and I ain't saying what I'm doing.

TROY: Aw, nigger, look here . . . I know you. If you had got anywhere near that gal, twenty minutes later you be looking to tell somebody. And the first one you gonna tell . . . that you gonna want to brag to . . . is gonna be me.

BONO: I ain't saying that. I see where you be eyeing her.

TROY: I eye all the women. I don't miss nothing. Don't never let nobody tell you Troy Maxson don't eye the women.

BONO: You been doing more than eyeing her. You done bought her a drink or two.

TROY: Hell yeah, I bought her a drink! What that mean? I bought you one, too. What that mean 'cause I buy her a drink? I'm just being polite.

BONO: It's all right to buy her one drink. That's what you call being polite. But when you wanna be buying two or three . . . that's what you call eyeing her.

TROY: Look here, as long as you known me . . . you ever known me to chase after women?

BONO: Hell yeah! Long as I done known you. You forgetting I knew you when.

TROY: Naw, I'm talking about since I been married to Rose?

BONO: Oh, not since you been married to Rose. Now, that's the truth, there. I can say that.

TROY: All right then! Case closed.

BONO: I see you be walking up around Alberta's house. You supposed to be at Taylors' and you be walking up around there.

TROY: What you watching where I'm walking for? I ain't watching after you.

BONO: I seen you walking around there more than once.

TROY: Hell, you liable to see me walking anywhere! That don't mean nothing 'cause you see me walking around there.

BONO: Where she come from anyway? She just kinda showed up one day.

TROY: Tallahassee. You can look at her and tell she one of them Florida gals. They got some big healthy women down there. Grow them right up out the ground. Got a little bit of Indian in her. Most of them niggers down in Florida got some Indian in them.

BONO: I don't know about that Indian part. But she damn sure big and healthy. Woman wear some big stockings. Got them great big old legs and hips as wide as the Mississippi River.

TROY: Legs don't mean nothing. You don't do nothing but push them out of the way. But them hips cushion the ride!

BONO: Troy, you ain't got no sense.

TROY: It's the truth! Like you riding on Goodyears!

(Rose enters from the house. She is ten years younger than Troy. Her devotion to him stems from her recognition of the possibilities of her life without him: a succession of abusive men and their babies, a life of partying and running the streets, the church, or aloneness with its attendant pain and frustration. She recognizes Troy's spirit as a fine and illuminating one and she either ignores or forgives his faults, only some of which she recognizes. Though she doesn't drink, her presence is an integral part of the Friday night rituals. She alternates between the porch and the kitchen, where supper preparations are under way.)

ROSE: What you all out here getting into?

TROY: What you worried about what we getting into for? This is men talk, woman.

ROSE: What I care what you talking about? Bono, you gonna stay for supper?

BONO: No, I thank you, Rose. But Lucille say she cooking up a pot of pigfeet.

TROY: Pigfeet! Hell, I'm going home with you! Might even stay the night if you got some pigfeet. You got something in there to top them pigfeet, Rose?

ROSE: I'm cooking up some chicken. I got some chicken and collard greens.

TROY: Well, go on back in the house and let me and Bono finish what we was talking about. This is men talk. I got some talk for you later. You know what kind of talk I mean. You go on and powder it up.

ROSE: Troy Maxson, don't you start that now!

TROY *(Puts his arm around her)*: Aw, woman . . . come here. Look here, Bono . . . when I met this woman . . . I got out that place, say, "Hitch up my pony, saddle up my mare . . . there's a woman out there for me somewhere. I looked here. Looked there. Saw Rose and latched on to her." I latched on to her and told her—I'm gonna tell you the truth—I told her, "Baby, I don't wanna marry, I just wanna be your man." Rose told me . . . tell him what you told me, Rose.

ROSE: I told him if he wasn't the marrying kind, then move out the way so the marrying kind could find me.

TROY: That's what she told me. "Nigger, you in my way. You blocking the view! Move out the way so I can find me a husband." I thought it over two or three days. Come back—

ROSE: Ain't no two or three days nothing. You was back the same night.

TROY: Come back, told her . . . "Okay, baby . . . but I'm gonna buy me a banty rooster and put him out there in the backyard . . . and when he see a stranger come, he'll flap his wings and crow . . ." Look here, Bono, I could watch the front door by myself . . . it was that back door I was worried about.

ROSE: Troy, you ought not talk like that. Troy ain't doing nothing but telling a lie.

TROY: Only thing is . . . when we first got married . . . forget the rooster . . . we ain't had no yard!

BONO: I hear you tell it. Me and Lucille was staying down there on Logan Street. Had two rooms with the outhouse in the back. I ain't mind the outhouse none. But when that goddamn wind blow through there in the winter . . . that's what I'm talking about! To this day I wonder why in the hell I ever stayed down there for six long years. But see, I didn't know I could do no better. I thought only white folks had inside toilets and things.

ROSE: There's a lot of people don't know they can do no better than they doing now. That's just something you got to learn. A lot of folks still shop at Bella's.

TROY: Ain't nothing wrong with shopping at Bella's. She got fresh food.

ROSE: I ain't said nothing about if she got fresh food. I'm talking about what she charge. She charge ten cents more than the A&P.[2]

TROY: The A&P ain't never done nothing for me. I spends my money where I'm treated right. I go down to Bella, say, "I need a loaf of bread, I'll pay you Friday." She give it to me. What sense that make when I got money to go and spend it somewhere else and ignore the person who done right by me? That ain't in the Bible.

ROSE: We ain't talking about what's in the Bible. What sense it make to shop there when she overcharge?

TROY: You shop where you want to. I'll do my shopping where the people been good to me.

---

2. By the 1930s, the Great Atlantic and Pacific Tea Company, so named in 1859, was the leading supermarket chain in the United States.

ROSE: Well, I don't think it's right for her to overcharge. That's all I was saying.

BONO: Look here . . . I got to get on. Lucille be raising all kind of hell.

TROY: Where you going, nigger? We ain't finished this pint. Come here, finish this pint.

BONO: Well, hell, I am . . . if you ever turn the bottle loose.

TROY (*Hands him the bottle*): The only thing I say about the A&P is I'm glad Cory got that job down there. Help him take care of his school clothes and things. Gabe done moved out and things getting tight around here. He got that job . . . He can start to look out for himself.

ROSE: Cory done went and got recruited by a college football team.

TROY: I told that boy about that football stuff. The white man ain't gonna let him get nowhere with that football. I told him when he first come to me with it. Now you come telling me he done went and got more tied up in it. He ought to go and get recruited in how to fix cars or something where he can make a living.

ROSE: He ain't talking about making no living playing football. It's just something the boys in school do. They gonna send a recruiter by to talk to you. He'll tell you he ain't talking about making no living playing football. It's a honor to be recruited.

TROY: It ain't gonna get him nowhere. Bono'll tell you that.

BONO: If he be like you in the sports . . . he's gonna be all right. Ain't but two men ever played baseball as good as you. That's Babe Ruth and Josh Gibson.[3] Them's the only two men ever hit more home runs than you.

TROY: What it ever get me? Ain't got a pot to piss in or a window to throw it out of.

ROSE: Times have changed since you was playing baseball, Troy. That was before the war.[4] Times have changed a lot since then.

TROY: How in hell they done changed?

ROSE: They got lots of colored boys playing ball now. Baseball and football.

BONO: You right about that, Rose. Times have changed, Troy. You just come along too early.

TROY: There ought not never have been no time called too early! Now you take that fellow . . . what's that fellow they had playing right field for

3. Georgia-born catcher (1911–47) often called "the black Babe Ruth"; hailed by the Baseball Hall of Fame as "the greatest power hitter in black baseball," he died three months before integration of the major leagues. *Babe Ruth*: legendary outfielder, pitcher, and power hitter (1895–1948) for the Boston Red Sox and New York Yankees.
4. World War II (1939–45).

the Yankees back then? You know who I'm talking about, Bono. Used
to play right field for the Yankees.

ROSE: Selkirk?[5]

TROY: Selkirk! That's it! Man batting .269, understand? .269. What kind of
sense that make? I was hitting .432 with thirty-seven home runs! Man
batting .269 and playing right field for the Yankees! I saw Josh Gibson's
daughter yesterday. She walking around with raggedy shoes on her feet.
Now I bet you Selkirk's daughter ain't walking around with raggedy
shoes on her feet! I bet you that!

ROSE: They got a lot of colored baseball players now. Jackie Robinson[6] was
the first. Folks had to wait for Jackie Robinson.

TROY: I done seen a hundred niggers play baseball better than Jackie Robinson. Hell, I know some teams Jackie Robinson couldn't even make!
What you talking about Jackie Robinson. Jackie Robinson wasn't nobody.
I'm talking about if you could play ball then they ought to have let you
play. Don't care what color you were. Come telling me I come along too
early. If you could play . . . then they ought to have let you play.

(*Troy takes a long drink from the bottle.*)

ROSE: You gonna drink yourself to death. You don't need to be drinking
like that.

TROY: Death ain't nothing. I done seen him. Done wrassled with him. You
can't tell me nothing about death. Death ain't nothing but a fastball
on the outside corner. And you know what I'll do to that! Lookee here,
Bono . . . am I lying? You get one of them fastballs, about waist high,
over the outside corner of the plate where you can get the meat of the
bat on it . . . and good God! You can kiss it good-bye. Now, am I lying?

BONO: Naw, you telling the truth there. I seen you do it.

TROY: If I'm lying . . . that 450 feet worth of lying! (*Pause*) That's all death
is to me. A fastball on the outside corner.

ROSE: I don't know why you want to get on talking about death.

TROY: Ain't nothing wrong with talking about death. That's part of life.
Everybody gonna die. You gonna die, I'm gonna die. Bono's gonna die.
Hell, we all gonna die.

ROSE: But you ain't got to talk about it. I don't like to talk about it.

TROY: You the one brought it up. Me and Bono was talking about baseball . . . you tell me I'm gonna drink myself to death. Ain't that right,
Bono? You know I don't drink this but one night out of the week. That's

5. George Selkirk (1908–87), Canadian-born player who succeeded Babe Ruth as the New York
Yankees right fielder.
6. Brooklyn Dodgers first baseman (1919–72) who, in 1947, became the first black player in the
major leagues and, in 1949, the first black winner of the National League MVP Award.

Friday night. I'm gonna drink just enough to where I can handle it. Then I cuts it loose. I leave it alone. So don't you worry about me drinking myself to death. 'Cause I ain't worried about Death. I done seen him. I done wrestled with him.

Look here, Bono . . . I looked up one day and Death was marching straight at me. Like Soldiers on Parade! The Army of Death was marching straight at me. The middle of July, 1941. It got real cold just like it be winter. It seem like Death himself reached out and touched me on the shoulder. He touch me just like I touch you. I got cold as ice and Death standing there grinning at me.

ROSE: Troy, why don't you hush that talk.

TROY: I say . . . What you want, Mr. Death? You be wanting me? You done brought your army to be getting me? I looked him dead in the eye. I wasn't fearing nothing. I was ready to tangle. Just like I'm ready to tangle now. The Bible say be ever vigilant. That's why I don't get but so drunk. I got to keep watch.

ROSE: Troy was right down there in Mercy Hospital. You remember he had pneumonia? Laying there with a fever talking plumb out of his head.

TROY: Death standing there staring at me . . . carrying that sickle in his hand. Finally he say, "You want bound over for another year?" See, just like that . . . "You want bound over for another year?" I told him, "Bound over hell! Let's settle this now!"

It seem like he kinda fell back when I said that, and all the cold went out of me. I reached down and grabbed that sickle and threw it just as far as I could throw it . . . and me and him commenced to wrestling.

We wrestled for three days and three nights. I can't say where I found the strength from. Every time it seemed like he was gonna get the best of me, I'd reach way down deep inside myself and find the strength to do him one better.

ROSE: Every time Troy tell that story he find different ways to tell it. Different things to make up about it.

TROY: I ain't making up nothing. I'm telling you the facts of what happened. I wrestled with Death for three days and three nights and I'm standing here to tell you about it. (*Pause*) All right. At the end of the third night we done weakened each other to where we can't hardly move. Death stood up, throwed on his robe . . . had him a white robe with a hood on it. He throwed on that robe and went off to look for his sickle. Say, "I'll be back." Just like that. "I'll be back." I told him say, "Yeah, but . . . you gonna have to find me!" I wasn't no fool. I wasn't going looking for him. Death ain't nothing to play with. And I know he's gonna get me. I know I got to join his army . . . his camp followers. But as long as I keep my strength and see him coming . . . as long as I keep up my vigilance . . . he's gonna have to fight to get me. I ain't going easy.

BONO: Well, look here, since you got to keep up your vigilance . . . let me have the bottle.

TROY: Aw hell, I shouldn't have told you that part. I should have left out that part.

ROSE: Troy be talking that stuff and half the time don't even know what he be talking about.

TROY: Bono know me better than that.

BONO: That's right. I know you. I know you got some Uncle Remus[7] in your blood. You got more stories than the devil got sinners.

TROY: Aw hell, I done seen him too! Done talked with the devil.

ROSE: Troy, don't nobody want to be hearing all that stuff.

(Lyons enters the yard from the street. Thirty-four years old, Troy's son from a previous marriage, he sports a neatly trimmed goatee, sport coat and white shirt, tieless and buttoned at the collar. Though he fancies himself a musician, he is more caught up in the rituals and "idea" of being a musician than in the actual practice of the music. He has come to borrow money from Troy and, while he knows he will be successful, he is uncertain as to what extent his lifestyle will be held up to scrutiny and ridicule.)

LYONS: Hey, Pop.

TROY: What you come "Hey, Popping" me for?

LYONS: How you doing, Rose? *(Kisses her)* Mr. Bono. How you doing?

BONO: Hey, Lyons . . . how you been?

TROY: He must have been doing all right. I ain't seen him around here last week.

ROSE: Troy, leave your boy alone. He come by to see you and you wanna start all that nonsense.

TROY: I ain't bothering Lyons. *(Offers him the bottle)* Here, get you a drink. We got an understanding. I know why he come by to see me and he know I know.

LYONS: Come on, Pop . . . I just stopped by to say hi . . . see how you was doing.

TROY: You ain't stopped by yesterday.

ROSE: You gonna stay for supper, Lyons? I got some chicken cooking in the oven.

7. African American narrator of the folktales, adapted from African American originals, published by white Georgia journalist Joel Chandler Harris beginning in 1879, and featuring Br'er Rabbit.

LYONS: No, Rose . . . thanks. I was just in the neighborhood and thought I'd stop by for a minute.

TROY: You was in the neighborhood all right, nigger. You telling the truth there. You was in the neighborhood 'cause it's my payday.

LYONS: Well, hell, since you mentioned it . . . let me have ten dollars.

TROY: I'll be damned! I'll die and go to hell and play blackjack with the devil before I give you ten dollars.

BONO: That's what I want to know about . . . that devil you done seen.

LYONS: What . . . Pop done seen the devil? You too much, Pops.

TROY: Yeah, I done seen him. Talked to him too!

ROSE: You ain't seen no devil. I done told you that man ain't had nothing to do with the devil. Anything you can't understand, you want to call it the devil.

TROY: Look here, Bono . . . I went down to see Hertzberger about some furniture. Got three rooms for two-ninety-eight. That what it say on the radio. "Three rooms . . . two-ninety-eight." Even made up a little song about it. Go down there . . . man tell me I can't get no credit. I'm working every day and can't get no credit. What to do? I got an empty house with some raggedy furniture in it. Cory ain't got no bed. He's sleeping on a pile of rags on the floor. Working every day and can't get no credit. Come back here—Rose'll tell you—madder than hell. Sit down . . . try to figure what I'm gonna do. Come a knock on the door. Ain't been living here but three days. Who know I'm here? Open the door . . . devil standing there bigger than life. White fellow . . . got on good clothes and everything. Standing there with a clipboard in his hand. I ain't had to say nothing. First words come out of his mouth was . . . "I understand you need some furniture and can't get no credit." I liked to fell over. He say, "I'll give you all the credit you want, but you got to pay the interest on it." I told him, "Give me three rooms' worth and charge whatever you want." Next day a truck pulled up here and two men unloaded them three rooms. Man what drove the truck give me a book. Say send ten dollars, first of every month to the address in the book and everything will be all right. Say if I miss a payment the devil was coming back and it'll be hell to pay. That was fifteen years ago. To this day . . . the first of the month I send my ten dollars, Rose'll tell you.

ROSE: Troy lying.

TROY: I ain't never seen that man since. Now you tell me who else that could have been but the devil? I ain't sold my soul or nothing like that, you understand. Naw, I wouldn't have truck with the devil about nothing like that. I got my furniture and pays my ten dollars the first of the month just like clockwork.

BONO: How long you say you been paying this ten dollars a month?

TROY: Fifteen years!

BONO: Hell, ain't you finished paying for it yet? How much the man done charged you.

TROY: Aw hell, I done paid for it. I done paid for it ten times over! The fact is I'm scared to stop paying it.

ROSE: Troy lying. We got that furniture from Mr. Glickman, He ain't paying no ten dollars a month to nobody.

TROY: Aw hell, woman. Bono know I ain't that big a fool.

LYONS: I was just getting ready to say . . . I know where there's a bridge for sale.

TROY: Look here, I'll tell you this . . . it don't matter to me if he was the devil. It don't matter if the devil give credit. Somebody has got to give it.

ROSE: It ought to matter. You going around talking about having truck with the devil . . . God's the one you gonna have to answer to. He's the one gonna be at the Judgment.

LYONS: Yeah, well, look here, Pop . . . let me have that ten dollars. I'll give it back to you. Bonnie got a job working at the hospital.

TROY: What I tell you, Bono? The only time I see this nigger is when he wants something. That's the only time I see him.

LYONS: Come on, Pop, Mr. Bono don't want to hear all that. Let me have the ten dollars. I told you Bonnie working.

TROY: What that mean to me? "Bonnie working." I don't care if she working. Go ask her for the ten dollars if she working. Talking about "Bonnie working." Why ain't you working?

LYONS: Aw, Pop, you know I can't find no decent job. Where am I gonna get a job at? You know I can't get no job.

TROY: I told you I know some people down there. I can get you on the rubbish if you want to work. I told you that the last time you came by here asking me for something.

LYONS: Naw, Pop . . . thanks. That ain't for me. I don't wanna be carrying nobody's rubbish. I don't wanna be punching nobody's time clock.

TROY: What's the matter, you too good to carry people's rubbish? Where you think that ten dollars you talking about come from? I'm just supposed to haul people's rubbish and give my money to you 'cause you too lazy to work. You too lazy to work and wanna know why you ain't got what I got.

ROSE: What hospital Bonnie working at? Mercy?

LYONS: She's down at Passavant working in the laundry.

TROY: I ain't got nothing as it is. I give you that ten dollars and I got to eat beans the rest of the week. Naw . . . you ain't getting no ten dollars here.

LYONS: You ain't got to be eating no beans. I don't know why you wanna say that.

TROY: I ain't got no extra money. Gabe done moved over to Miss Pearl's paying her the rent and things done got tight around here. I can't afford to be giving you every payday.

LYONS: I ain't asked you to give me nothing. I asked you to loan me ten dollars. I know you got ten dollars.

TROY: Yeah, I got it. You know why I got it? 'Cause I don't throw my money away out there in the streets. You living the fast life . . . wanna be a musician . . . running around in them clubs and things . . . then, you learn to take care of yourself. You ain't gonna find me going and asking nobody for nothing. I done spent too many years without.

LYONS: You and me is two different people, Pop.

TROY: I done learned my mistake and learned to do what's right by it. You still trying to get something for nothing. Life don't owe you nothing. You owe it to yourself. Ask Bono. He'll tell you I'm right.

LYONS: You got your way of dealing with the world . . . I got mine. The only thing that matters to me is the music.

TROY: Yeah, I can see that! It don't matter how you gonna eat . . . where your next dollar is coming from. You telling the truth there.

LYONS: I know I got to eat. But I got to live too. I need something that gonna help me to get out of the bed in the morning. Make me feel like I belong in the world. I don't bother nobody. I just stay with my music 'cause that's the only way I can find to live in the world. Otherwise there ain't no telling what I might do. Now I don't come criticizing you and how you live. I just come by to ask you for ten dollars. I don't wanna hear all that about how I live.

TROY: Boy, your mama did a hell of a job raising you.

LYONS: You can't change me, Pop. I'm thirty-four years old. If you wanted to change me, you should have been there when I was growing up. I come by to see you . . . ask for ten dollars and you want to talk about how I was raised. You don't know nothing about how I was raised.

ROSE: Let the boy have ten dollars, Troy.

TROY *(To Lyons)*: What the hell you looking at me for? I ain't got no ten dollars. You know what I do with my money. *(To Rose)* Give him ten dollars if you want him to have it.

ROSE: I will. Just as soon as you turn it loose.

TROY *(Handing Rose the money)*: There it is. Seventy-six dollars and forty-two cents. You see this, Bono? Now, I ain't gonna get but six of that back.

ROSE: You ought to stop telling that lie. Here, Lyons. *(Hands him the money)*

LYONS: Thanks, Rose. Look . . . I got to run . . . I'll see you later.

TROY: Wait a minute. You gonna say, "Thanks, Rose," and ain't gonna look to see where she got that ten dollars from? See how they do me, Bono?

LYONS: I know she got it from you, Pop. Thanks. I'll give it back to you.

TROY: There he go telling another lie. Time I see that ten dollars . . . he'll be owing me thirty more.

LYONS: See you, Mr. Bono.

BONO: Take care, Lyons!

LYONS: Thanks, Pop. I'll see you again.

(*Lyons exits the yard.*)

TROY: I don't know why he don't go and get him a decent job and take care of that woman he got.

BONO: He'll be all right, Troy. The boy is still young.

TROY: The *boy* is thirty-four years old.

ROSE: Let's not get off into all that.

BONO: Look here . . . I got to be going. I got to be getting on. Lucille gonna be waiting.

TROY (*Puts his arm around Rose*): See this woman, Bono? I love this woman. I love this woman so much it hurts. I love her so much . . . I done run out of ways of loving her. So I got to go back to basics. Don't you come by my house Monday morning talking about time to go to work . . .'cause I'm still gonna be stroking!

ROSE: Troy! Stop it now!

BONO: I ain't paying him no mind, Rose. That ain't nothing but gin-talk. Go on, Troy. I'll see you Monday.

TROY: Don't you come by my house, nigger! I done told you what I'm gonna be doing.

(*The lights fade to black.*)

Scene 2

The lights come up on Rose hanging up clothes. She hums and sings softly to herself. It is the following morning.

ROSE (*Singing*):
 Jesus, be a fence all around me every day
 Jesus, I want you to protect me as I travel on my way.
 Jesus, be a fence all around me every day.

(*Troy enters from the house.*)

 Jesus, I want you to protect me
 As I travel on my way.

(To Troy) 'Morning. You ready for breakfast? I can fix it soon as I finish hanging up these clothes?

TROY: I got the coffee on. That'll be all right. I'll just drink some of that this morning.

ROSE: That 651 hit yesterday. That's the second time this month. Miss Pearl hit for a dollar . . . seem like those that need the least always get lucky. Poor folks can't get nothing.

TROY: Them numbers don't know nobody. I don't know why you fool with them. You and Lyons both.

ROSE: It's something to do.

TROY: You ain't doing nothing but throwing your money away.

ROSE: Troy, you know I don't play foolishly. I just play a nickel here and a nickel there.

TROY: That's two nickels you done thrown away.

ROSE: Now I hit sometimes . . . that makes up for it. It always comes in handy when I do hit. I don't hear you complaining then.

TROY: I ain't complaining now. I just say it's foolish. Trying to guess out of six hundred ways which way the number gonna come. If I had all the money niggers, these Negroes, throw away on numbers for one week— just one week—I'd be a rich man.

ROSE: Well, you wishing and calling it foolish ain't gonna stop folks from playing numbers. That's one thing for sure. Besides . . . some good things come from playing numbers. Look where Pope done bought him that restaurant off of numbers.

TROY: I can't stand niggers like that. Man ain't had two dimes to rub together. He walking around with his shoes all run over bumming money for cigarettes. All right. Got lucky there and hit the numbers . . .

ROSE: Troy, I know all about it.

TROY: Had good sense, I'll say that for him. He ain't throwed his money away. I seen niggers hit the numbers and go through two thousand dollars in four days. Man bought him that restaurant down there . . . fixed it up real nice . . . and then didn't want nobody to come in it! A Negro go in there and can't get no kind of service. I seen a white fellow come in there and order a bowl of stew. Pope picked all the meat out the pot for him. Man ain't had nothing but a bowl of meat! Negro come behind him and ain't got nothing but the potatoes and carrots. Talking about what numbers do for people, you picked a wrong example. Ain't done nothing but make a worser fool out of him than he was before.

ROSE: Troy, you ought to stop worrying about what happened at work yesterday.

TROY: I ain't worried. Just told me to be down there at the commissioner's office on Friday. Everybody think they gonna fire me. I ain't worried

about them firing me. You ain't got to worry about that. *(Pause)* Where's
Cory? Cory in the house? *(Calls)* Cory?

ROSE: He gone out.

TROY: Out, huh? He gone out 'cause he know I want him to help me with
this fence. I know how he is. That boy scared of work.

> *(Gabriel enters. He comes halfway down the alley and, hearing Troy's
> voice, stops.)*

He ain't done a lick of work in his life.

ROSE: He had to go to football practice. Coach wanted them to get in a little
extra practice before the season start.

TROY: I got his practice . . . running out of here before he get his chores done.

ROSE: Troy, what is wrong with you this morning? Don't nothing set right
with you. Go on back in there and go to bed . . . get up on the other side.

TROY: Why something got to be wrong with me? I ain't said nothing wrong
with me.

ROSE: You got something to say about everything. First it's the numbers . . . then it's the way the man runs his restaurant . . . then you done
got on Cory. What's it gonna be next? Take a look up there and see if
the weather suits you . . . or is it gonna be how you gonna put up the
fence with the clothes hanging in the yard.

TROY: You hit the nail on the head then.

ROSE: I know you like I know the back of my hand. Go on in there and get
you some coffee . . . see if that straighten you up. 'Cause you ain't right
this morning.

> *(Troy starts into the house and sees Gabriel. Gabriel starts singing.
> Troy's brother, he is seven years younger than Troy. Injured in World
> War II, he has a metal plate in his head. He carries an old trumpet tied
> around his waist and believes with every fiber of his being that he is the
> archangel Gabriel.[8] He carries a chipped basket with an assortment of
> discarded fruits and vegetables he has picked up in the strip district[9]
> and which he attempts to sell.)*

GABRIEL *(Singing)*:

> Yes, ma'am, I got plums
> You ask me how I sell them

---

8. Divine messenger in Jewish, Christian, and Islamic traditions. In the Bible, he appears to
Daniel (to explain his visions), to Zacharias (to prophesy John the Baptist's birth), and to Mary
(to announce that she will bear Jesus). He is also said to be the angelic trumpeter who will
announce the arrival of the Last Judgment and Christ's second coming.

9. Market district located on a narrow strip of land northeast of downtown Pittsburgh.

Oh ten cents apiece
Three for a quarter
Come and buy now
'Cause I'm here today
And tomorrow I'll be gone.

(Rose enters.)

Hey, Rose!

ROSE: How you doing, Gabe?

GABRIEL: There's Troy . . . Hey, Troy!

TROY: Hey, Gabe.

(Troy exits into the kitchen.)

ROSE *(To Gabriel)*: What you got there?

GABRIEL: You know what I got, Rose. I got fruits and vegetables.

ROSE *(Looking in the basket)*: Where's all these plums you talking about?

GABRIEL: I ain't got no plums today, Rose. I was just singing that. Have
some tomorrow. Put me in a big order for plums. Have enough plums
tomorrow for Saint Peter[1] and everybody.

(Troy reenters from the kitchen and crosses to the steps.)

(To Rose) Troy's mad at me.

TROY: I ain't mad at you. What I got to be mad at you about? You ain't done
nothing to me.

GABRIEL: I just moved over to Miss Pearl's to keep out from in your way.
I ain't mean no harm by it.

TROY: Who said anything about that? I ain't said anything about that.

GABRIEL: You ain't mad at me, is you?

TROY: Naw . . . I ain't mad at you, Gabe. If I was mad at you I'd tell you
about it.

GABRIEL: Got me two rooms. In the basement. Got my own door too.
Wanna see my key? *(Holds up a key)* That's my own key! Ain't nobody
else got a key like that. That's my key! My two rooms!

TROY: Well, that's good, Gabe. You got your own key . . . that's good.

ROSE: You hungry, Gabe? I was just fixing to cook Troy his breakfast.

GABRIEL: I'll take some biscuits. You got some biscuits? Did you know
when I was in Heaven . . . every morning me and Saint Peter would sit
down by the Gate and eat some big fat biscuits? Oh, yeah! We had us a

---

1. Apostle traditionally represented as guardian of heaven's gates because, in Matthew 16.19,
Jesus tells him, "I will give unto thee the keys of the kingdom of heaven [. . .]."

good time. We'd sit there and eat us them biscuits and then Saint Peter would go off to sleep and tell me to wake him up when it's time to open the Gates for the Judgment.

ROSE: Well, come on . . . I'll make up a batch of biscuits.

(Rose exits into the house.)

GABRIEL: Troy . . . Saint Peter got your name in the book. I seen it. It say . . . Troy Maxson. I say . . . I know him! He got the same name like what I got. That's my brother!

TROY: How many times you gonna tell me that, Gabe?

GABRIEL: Ain't got my name in the book. Don't have to have my name. I done died and went to Heaven. He got your name though. One morning Saint Peter was looking at his book . . . marking it up for the Judgment . . . and he let me see your name. Got it in there under M. Got Rose's name . . . I ain't seen it like I seen yours . . . but I know it's in there. He got a great big book. Got everybody's name what was ever been born. That's what he told me. But I seen your name. Seen it with my own eyes.

TROY: Go on in the house there. Rose going to fix you something to eat.

GABRIEL: Oh, I ain't hungry. I done had breakfast with Aunt Jemima. She come by and cooked me up a whole mess of flapjacks. Remember how we used to eat them flapjacks?

TROY: Go on in the house and get you something to eat now.

GABRIEL: I got to go sell my plums. I done sold some tomatoes. Got me two quarters. Wanna see? *(Shows Troy his quarters)* I'm gonna save them and buy me a new horn so Saint Peter can hear me when it's time to open the Gates. *(Stops suddenly. Listens)* Hear that? That's the hellhounds. I got to chase them out of here. Go on get out of here! Get out!

(Exits singing:)

Better get ready for the Judgment
Better get ready for the Judgment
My Lord is coming down.

(Rose enters from the house.)

TROY: He gone off somewhere.

GABRIEL *(Offstage)*:

Better get ready for the Judgment
Better get ready for the Judgment morning
Better get ready for the Judgment
My God is coming down.

ROSE: He ain't eating right. Miss Pearl say she can't get him to eat nothing.

TROY: What you want me to do about it, Rose? I done did everything I can for the man. I can't make him get well. Man got half his head blown away . . . what you expect?

ROSE: Seem like something ought to be done to help him.

TROY: Man don't bother nobody. He just mixed up from that metal plate he got in his head. Ain't no sense for him to go back into the hospital.

ROSE: Least he be eating right. They can help him take care of himself.

TROY: Don't nobody wanna be locked up, Rose. What you wanna lock him up for? Man go over there and fight the war . . . messin' around with them Japs, get half his head blown off . . . and they give him a lousy three thousand dollars. And I had to swoop down on that.

ROSE: Is you fixing to go into that again?

TROY: That's the only way I got a roof over my head . . . 'cause of that metal plate.

ROSE: Ain't no sense you blaming yourself for nothing. Gabe wasn't in no condition to manage that money. You done what was right by him. Can't nobody say you ain't done what was right by him. Look how long you took care of him . . . till he wanted to have his own place and moved over there with Miss Pearl.

TROY: That ain't what I'm saying, woman! I'm just stating the facts. If my brother didn't have that metal plate in his head . . . I wouldn't have a pot to piss in or a window to throw it out of. And I'm fifty-three years old. Now see if you can understand that!

(*He gets up from the porch and starts to exit the yard.*)

ROSE: Where you going off to? You been running out of here every Saturday for weeks. I thought you was gonna work on this fence?

TROY: I'm gonna walk down to Taylors'. Listen to the ball game. I'll be back in a bit. I'll work on it when I get back.

(*He exits the yard. The lights fade to black.*)

Scene 3

The lights come up on the yard. It is four hours later. Rose is taking down the clothes from the line. Cory enters carrying his football equipment.

ROSE: Your daddy like to had a fit with you running out of here this morning without doing your chores.

CORY: I told you I had to go to practice.

ROSE: He say you were supposed to help him with this fence.

CORY: He been saying that the last four or five Saturdays, and then he don't never do nothing, but go down to Taylors'. Did you tell him about the recruiter?

ROSE: Yeah, I told him.

CORY: What he say?

ROSE: He ain't said nothing too much. You get in there and get started on your chores before he gets back. Go on and scrub down them steps before he gets back here hollering and carrying on.

CORY: I'm hungry. What you got to eat, Mama?

ROSE: Go on and get started on your chores. I got some meat loaf in there. Go on and make you a sandwich . . . and don't leave no mess in there.

(Cory exits into the house. Rose continues to take down the clothes. Troy enters the yard and sneaks up and grabs her from behind.)

Troy! Go on, now. You liked to scared me to death. What was the score of the game? Lucille had me on the phone and I couldn't keep up with it.

TROY: What I care about the game? Come here, woman. *(Tries to kiss her)*

ROSE: I thought you went down Taylors' to listen to the game. Go on, Troy! You supposed to be putting up this fence.

TROY *(Attempting to kiss her again)*: I'll put it up when I finish with what is at hand.

ROSE: Go on, Troy. I ain't studying you.

TROY *(Chasing after her)*: I'm studying you . . . fixing to do my homework!

ROSE: Troy, you better leave me alone.

TROY: Where's Cory? That boy brought his butt home yet?

ROSE: He's in the house doing his chores.

TROY *(Calling)*: Cory! Get your butt out here, boy!

(Rose exits into the house with the laundry. Troy goes over to the pile of wood, picks up a board, and starts sawing. Cory enters from the house.)

You just now coming in here from leaving this morning?

CORY: Yeah, I had to go to football practice.

TROY: Yeah, what?

CORY: Yessir.

TROY: I ain't but two seconds off you noway. The garbage sitting in there overflowing . . . you ain't done none of your chores . . . and you come in here talking about, "Yeah."

CORY: I was just getting ready to do my chores now, Pop . . .

TROY: Your first chore is to help me with this fence on Saturday. Everything else come after that. Now get that saw and cut them boards.

(Cory takes the saw and begins cutting the boards. Troy continues working. There is a long pause.)

CORY: Hey, Pop . . . why don't you buy a TV?

TROY: What I want with a TV? What I want one of them for?

CORY: Everybody got one. Earl, Ba Bra . . . Jesse!

TROY: I ain't asked you who had one. I say what I want with one?

CORY: So you can watch it. They got lots of things on TV. Baseball games and everything. We could watch the World Series.

TROY: Yeah . . . and how much this TV cost?

CORY: I don't know. They got them on sale for around two hundred dollars.

TROY: Two hundred dollars, huh?

CORY: That ain't that much, Pop.

TROY: Naw, it's just two hundred dollars. See that roof you got over your head at night? Let me tell you something about that roof. It's been over ten years since that roof was last tarred. See now . . . the snow come this winter and sit up there on that roof like it is . . . and it's gonna seep inside. It's just gonna be a little bit . . . ain't gonna hardly notice it. Then the next thing you know, it's gonna be leaking all over the house. Then the wood rot from all that water and you gonna need a whole new roof. Now, how much you think it cost to get that roof tarred?

CORY: I don't know.

TROY: Two hundred and sixty-four dollars . . . cash money. While you thinking about a TV, I got to be thinking about the roof . . . and whatever else go wrong around here. Now if you had two hundred dollars, what would you do . . . fix the roof or buy a TV?

CORY: I'd buy a TV. Then when the roof started to leak . . . when it needed fixing . . . I'd fix it.

TROY: Where are you gonna get the money from? You done spent it for a TV. You gonna sit up and watch the water run all over your brand-new TV.

CORY: Aw, Pop. You got money. I know you do.

TROY: Where I got it at, huh?

CORY: You got it in the bank.

TROY: You wanna see my bankbook? You wanna see that seventy-three dollars and twenty-two cents I got sitting up in there.

CORY: You ain't got to pay for it all at one time. You can put a down payment on it and carry it home with you.

TROY: Not me. I ain't gonna owe nobody nothing if I can help it. Miss a payment and they come and snatch it right out your house. Then what you got? Now, soon as I get two hundred dollars clear, then I'll buy a TV. Right now, as soon as I get two hundred and sixty-four dollars, I'm gonna have this roof tarred.

CORY: Aw . . . Pop!

TROY: You go on and get you two hundred dollars and buy one if ya want it. I got better things to do with my money.

CORY: I can't get no two hundred dollars. I ain't never seen two hundred dollars.

TROY: I'll tell you what . . . you get you a hundred dollars and I'll put the other hundred with it.

CORY: All right, I'm gonna show you.

TROY: You gonna show me how you can cut them boards right now.

(Cory begins to cut the boards. There is a long pause.)

CORY: The Pirates won today. That makes five in a row.

TROY: I ain't thinking about the Pirates. Got an all-white team. Got that boy . . . that Puerto Rican boy . . . Clemente.[2] Don't even half-play him. That boy could be something if they give him a chance. Play him one day and sit him on the bench the next.

CORY: He gets a lot of chances to play.

TROY: I'm talking about playing regular. Playing every day so you can get your timing. That's what I'm talking about.

CORY: They got some white guys on the team that don't play every day. You can't play everybody at the same time.

TROY: If they got a white fellow sitting on the bench . . . you can bet your last dollar he can't play! The colored guy got to be twice as good before he get on the team. That's why I don't want you to get all tied up in them sports. Man on the team and what it get him? They got colored on the team and don't use them. Same as not having them. All them teams the same.

CORY: The Braves got Hank Aaron and Wes Covington.[3] Hank Aaron hit two home runs today. That makes forty-three.

TROY: Hank Aaron ain't nobody. That's what you supposed to do. That's how you supposed to play the game. Ain't nothing to it. It's just a matter of timing . . . getting the right follow-through. Hell, I can hit forty-three home runs right now!

CORY: Not off no major-league pitching, you couldn't.

TROY: We had better pitching in the Negro leagues. I hit seven home runs off of Satchel Paige.[4] You can't get no better than that!

---

2. Roberto Clemente (1934–72), Pittsburgh Pirates right fielder (1955–72), four-time National League batting champion, and winner of twelve Gold Gloves.

3. African American fielder (1932–2011) who played for the Milwaukee Braves from 1956 to 1961. *Hank Aaron*: legendary African American batsman (b. 1934) who played twenty-one seasons with the Milwaukee, later Atlanta, Braves (1954–74) and, in 1974–75, broke Babe Ruth's records for most home runs and runs batted in (RBIs).

4. Pitcher (1906–82); arguably the Negro Leagues' most famous player (1926–47), he pitched in the newly integrated major leagues from age forty-two to sixty (1948–66).

CORY: Sandy Koufax.[5] He's leading the league in strikeouts.

TROY: I ain't thinking of no Sandy Koufax.

CORY: You got Warren Spahn and Lew Burdette.[6] I bet you couldn't hit no home runs off of Warren Spahn.

TROY: I'm through with it now. You go on and cut them boards. (*Pause*) Your mama tell me you done got recruited by a college football team? Is that right?

CORY: Yeah. Coach Zellman say the recruiter gonna be coming by to talk to you. Get you to sign the permission papers.

TROY: I thought you supposed to be working down there at the A&P. Ain't you supposed to be working down there after school?

CORY: Mr. Stawicki say he gonna hold my job for me until after the football season. Say starting next week I can work weekends.

TROY: I thought we had an understanding about this football stuff? You suppose to keep up with your chores and hold that job down at the A&P. Ain't been around here all day on a Saturday. Ain't none of your chores done . . . and now you telling me you done quit your job.

CORY: I'm gonna be working weekends.

TROY: You damn right you are! And ain't no need for nobody coming around here to talk to me about signing nothing.

CORY: Hey, Pop . . . you can't do that. He's coming all the way from North Carolina.

TROY: I don't care where he coming from. The white man ain't gonna let you get nowhere with that football noway. You go on and get your book-learning so you can work yourself up in that A&P or learn how to fix cars or build houses or something, get you a trade. That way you have something can't nobody take away from you. You go on and learn how to put your hands to some good use. Besides hauling people's garbage.

CORY: I get good grades, Pop. That's why the recruiter wants to talk with you. You got to keep up your grades to get recruited. This way I'll be going to college. I'll get a chance . . .

TROY: First you gonna get your butt down there to the A&P and get your job back.

CORY: Mr. Stawicki done already hired somebody else 'cause I told him I was playing football.

TROY: You a bigger fool than I thought . . . to let somebody take away your job so you can play some football. Where you gonna get your money to

5. Brooklyn, later Los Angeles, Dodgers pitcher (b. 1935), the first player ever to win three Cy Young Awards, and the youngest ever elected to Baseball's Hall of Fame.

6. Like 1957 Cy Young Award winner Warren Spahn (1921–2003), a pitcher for the Boston, later Milwaukee, Braves (1926–2007), MVP of the 1957 World Series, the only World Series the Milwaukee Braves ever won and the first, since 1948, won by any non–New York team.

take out your girlfriend and whatnot? What kind of foolishness is that
to let somebody take away your job?

CORY: I'm still gonna be working weekends.

TROY: Naw . . . naw. You getting your butt out of here and finding you
another job.

CORY: Come on, Pop! I got to practice. I can't work after school and play
football too. The team needs me. That's what Coach Zellman say . . .

TROY: I don't care what nobody else say. I'm the boss . . . you understand?
I'm the boss around here. I do the only saying what counts.

CORY: Come on, Pop!

TROY: I asked you . . . did you understand?

CORY: Yeah . . .

TROY: What!?!

CORY: Yessir.

TROY: You go on down there to that A&P and see if you can get your job
back. If you can't do both . . . then you quit the football team. You've
got to take the crookeds with the straights.

CORY: Yessir. *(Pause)* Can I ask you a question?

TROY: What the hell you wanna ask me? Mr. Stawicki the one you got the
questions for.

CORY: How come you ain't never liked me?

TROY: Liked you? Who the hell say I got to like you? What law is there say
I got to like you? Wanna stand up in my face and ask a damn fool-ass
question like that. Talking about liking somebody. Come here, boy, when
I talk to you.

> *(Cory comes over to where Troy is working. He stands slouched over
> and Troy shoves him on his shoulder.)*

Straighten up, goddamn it! I asked you a question . . . what law is there
say I got to like you?

CORY: None.

TROY: Well, all right then! Don't you eat every day? *(Pause)* Answer me
when I talk to you! Don't you eat every day?

CORY: Yeah.

TROY: Nigger, as long as you in my house, you put that sir on the end of it
when you talk to me!

CORY: Yes . . . sir.

TROY: You eat every day.

CORY: Yessir!

TROY: Got a roof over your head.

CORY: Yessir!

TROY: Got clothes on your back.

CORY: Yessir.

TROY: Why you think that is?

CORY: 'Cause of you.

TROY: Aw, hell, I know its 'cause of me . . . but why do you think that is?

CORY (*Hesitant*): 'Cause you like me.

TROY: Like you? I go out of here every morning . . . bust my butt . . . putting up with them crackers every day . . . 'cause I like you? You about the biggest fool I ever saw. (*Pause*) It's my job. It's my responsibility! You understand that? A man got to take care of his family. You live in my house . . . sleep you behind on my bedclothes . . . fill you belly up with my food . . . 'cause you my son. You my flesh and blood. Not 'cause I like you! 'Cause it's my duty to take care of you. I owe a responsibility to you!

Let's get this straight right here . . . before it go along any further . . . I ain't got to like you. Mr. Rand don't give me my money come payday 'cause he likes me. He gives me 'cause he owe me. I done give you everything I had to give you. I gave you your life! Me and your mama worked that out between us. And liking your black ass wasn't part of the bargain. Don't you try and go through life worrying about if somebody like you or not. You best be making sure they doing right by you. You understand what I'm saying, boy?

CORY: Yessir.

TROY: Then get the hell out of my face, and get on down to that A&P.

(*Rose has been standing behind the screen door for much of the scene. She enters as Cory exits.*)

ROSE: Why don't you let the boy go ahead and play football, Troy? Ain't no harm in that. He's just trying to be like you with the sports.

TROY: I don't want him to be like me! I want him to move as far away from my life as he can get. You the only decent thing that ever happened to me. I wish him that. But I don't wish him a thing else from my life. I decided seventeen years ago that boy wasn't getting involved in no sports. Not after what they did to me in the sports.

ROSE: Troy, why don't you admit you was too old to play in the major leagues? For once . . . why don't you admit that?

TROY: What do you mean too old? Don't come telling me I was too old. I just wasn't the right color. Hell, I'm fifty-three years old and can do better than Selkirk's .269 right now!

ROSE: How's was you gonna play ball when you were over forty? Sometimes I can't get no sense out of you.

TROY: I got good sense, woman. I got sense enough not to let my boy get hurt over playing no sports. You been mothering that boy too much. Worried about if people like him.

ROSE: Everything that boy do . . . he do for you. He wants you to say, "Good job, son." That's all.

TROY: Rose, I ain't got time for that. He's alive. He's healthy. He's got to make his own way. I made mine. Ain't nobody gonna hold his hand when he get out there in that world.

ROSE: Times have changed from when you was young, Troy. People change. The world's changing around you and you can't even see it.

TROY (*Slow, methodical*): Woman . . . I do the best I can do. I come in here every Friday. I carry a sack of potatoes and a bucket of lard. You all line up at the door with your hands out. I give you the lint from my pockets. I give you my sweat and my blood. I ain't got no tears. I done spent them. We go upstairs in that room at night . . . and I fall down on you and try to blast a hole into forever. I get up Monday morning . . . find my lunch on the table. I go out. Make my way. Find my strength to carry me through to the next Friday. (*Pause*) That's all I got, Rose. That's all I got to give. I can't give nothing else.

(*Troy exits into the house. The lights fade to black.*)

Scene 4

It is Friday. Two weeks later. Cory starts out of the house with his football equipment. The phone rings.

CORY (*Calling*): I got it! (*Answers the phone, stands in the screen door talking*) Hello? Hey, Jesse. Naw . . . I was just getting ready to leave now.

ROSE (*Calling*): Cory!

CORY: I told you, man, them spikes is all tore up. You can use them if you want, but they ain't no good. Earl got some spikes.

ROSE (*Calling*): Cory!

CORY (*Calling to Rose*): Mam? I'm talking to Jesse. (*Into phone*) When she say that? (*Pause*) Aw, you lying, man. I'm gonna tell her you said that.

ROSE (*Calling*): Cory, don't you go nowhere!

CORY: I got to go to the game, Ma! (*Into the phone*) Yeah, hey, look, I'll talk to you later. Yeah, I'll meet you over Earl's house. Later. Bye, Ma.

(*Cory exits the house and starts out the yard.*)

ROSE: Cory, where you going off to? You got that stuff all pulled out and thrown all over your room.

CORY (*In the yard*): I was looking for my spikes. Jesse wanted to borrow my spikes.

ROSE: Get up there and get that cleaned up before your daddy get back in here.

CORY: I got to go to the game! I'll clean it up *when I get back.*

(*He exits.*)

ROSE: That's all he need to do is see that room all messed up.

(*Rose exits into the house. Troy and Bono enter the yard with a bottle. Troy is dressed in clothes other than his work clothes.*)

BONO: He told him the same thing he told you. Take it to the union.

TROY: Brownie ain't got that much sense. Man wasn't thinking about nothing. He wait until I confront them on it . . . then he wanna come crying seniority. (*Calls*) Hey, Rose!

BONO: I wish I could have seen Mr. Rand's face when he told you.

TROY: He couldn't get it out of his mouth! Liked to bit his tongue! When they called me down there to the commissioner's office . . . he thought they was gonna fire me. Like everybody else.

BONO: I didn't think they was gonna fire you. I thought they was gonna put you on the warning paper.

TROY: Hey, Rose! (*To Bono*) Yeah, Mr. Rand like to bit his tongue.

(*Troy breaks the seal on the bottle, takes a drink, and hands it to Bono.*)

BONO: I see you run right down to Taylors' and told that Alberta gal.

TROY (*Calling*): Hey, Rose! (*To Bono*) I told everybody. Hey, Rose! I went down there to cash my check.

ROSE (*Entering from the house*): Hush all that hollering, man! I know you out here. What they say down there at the commissioner's office?

TROY: You supposed to come when I call you, woman. Bono'll tell you that. (*To Bono*) Don't Lucille come when you call her?

ROSE: Man, hush your mouth. I ain't no dog . . . talk about "come when you call me."

TROY (*Puts his arm around Rose*): You hear this, Bono? I had me an old dog used to get uppity like that. You say, "C'mere, Blue!" . . . and he just lay there and look at you. End up getting a stick and chasing him away trying to make him come.

ROSE: I ain't studying you and your dog. I remember you used to sing that old song.

TROY (*Singing*):
Hear it ring! Hear it ring!
I had a dog his name was Blue.

ROSE: Don't nobody wanna hear you sing that old song.

TROY (*Singing*):
You know Blue was mighty true.

ROSE: Used to have Cory running around here singing that song.

BONO: Hell, I remember that song myself.

TROY (*Singing*):
> You know Blue was a good old dog.
> Blue treed a possum in a hollow log.

That was my daddy's song. My daddy made up that song.

ROSE: I don't care who made it up. Don't nobody wanna hear you sing it.

TROY (*Makes a song like calling a dog*): Come here, woman.

ROSE: You come in here carrying on, I reckon they ain't fired you. What they say down there at the commissioner's office?

TROY: Look here, Rose . . . Mr. Rand called me into his office today when I got back from talking to them people down there . . . it come from up top . . . he called me in and told me they was making me a driver.

ROSE: Troy, you kidding!

TROY: No I ain't. Ask Bono.

ROSE: Well, that's great, Troy. Now you don't have to hassle them people no more.

(*Lyons enters from the street.*)

TROY: Aw hell, I wasn't looking to see you today. I thought you was in jail. Got it all over the front page of the *Courier* about them raiding Seefus' place . . . where you be hanging out with all them thugs.

LYONS: Hey, Pop . . . that ain't got nothing to do with me. I don't go down there gambling. I go down there to sit in with the band. I ain't got nothing to do with the gambling part. They got some good music down there.

TROY: They got some rogues . . . is what they got.

LYONS: How you been, Mr. Bono? Hi, Rose.

BONO: I see where you playing down at the Crawford Grill tonight.

ROSE: How come you ain't brought Bonnie like I told you. You should have brought Bonnie with you, she ain't been over in a month of Sundays.

LYONS: I was just in the neighborhood . . . thought I'd stop by.

TROY: Here he come . . .

BONO: Your daddy got a promotion on the rubbish. He's gonna be the first colored driver. Ain't got to do nothing but sit up there and read the paper like them white fellows.

LYONS: Hey, Pop . . . if you knew how to read you'd be all right.

BONO: Naw . . . naw . . . you mean if the nigger knew how to *drive* he'd be all right. Been fighting with them people about driving and ain't even got a license. Mr. Rand know you ain't got no driver's license?

TROY: Driving ain't nothing. All you do is point the truck where you want it to go. Driving ain't nothing.

BONO: Do Mr. Rand know you ain't got no driver's license? That's what I'm talking about. I ain't asked if driving was easy. I asked if Mr. Rand know you ain't got no driver's license.

TROY: He ain't got to know. The man ain't got to know my business. Time he find out, I have two or three driver's licenses.

LYONS (*Going into his pocket*): Say, look here, Pop . . .

TROY: I knew it was coming. Didn't I tell you, Bono? I know what kind of "look here, Pop" that was. The nigger fixing to ask me for some money. It's Friday night. It's my payday. All them rogues down there on the avenue . . . the ones that ain't in jail . . . and Lyons is hopping in his shoes to get down there with them.

LYONS: See, Pop . . . if you'd give somebody else a chance to talk sometime, you'd see that I was fixing to pay you back your ten dollars like I told you. Here . . . I told you I'd pay you when Bonnie got paid.

TROY: Naw . . . you go ahead and keep that ten dollars. Put it in the bank. The next time you feel like you wanna come by here and ask me for something . . . you go on down there and get that.

LYONS: Here's your ten dollars, Pop. I told you I don't want you to give me nothing. I just wanted to borrow ten dollars.

TROY: Naw . . . you go on and keep that for the next time you want to ask me.

LYONS: Come on, Pop . . . here go your ten dollars.

ROSE: Why don't you go on and let the boy pay you back, Troy?

LYONS: Here you go, Rose. If you don't take it I'm gonna have to hear about it for the next six months. (*Hands her the money*)

ROSE: You can hand yours over here too, Troy.

TROY: You see this, Bono. You see how they do me.

BONO: Yeah, Lucille do me the same way.

(*Gabriel is heard singing offstage. He enters.*)

GABRIEL: Better get ready for the Judgment! Better get ready for . . . Hey! . . . Hey! There's Troy's boy!

LYONS: How you doing, Uncle Gabe?

GABRIEL: Lyons . . . The King of the Jungle! Rose . . . hey, Rose. Got a flower for you. (*Takes a rose from his pocket*) Picked it myself. That's the same rose like you is!

ROSE: That's right nice of you, Gabe.

LYONS: What you been doing, Uncle Gabe?

GABRIEL: Oh, I been chasing hellhounds and waiting on the time to tell Saint Peter to open the Gates.

LYONS: You been chasing hellhounds, huh? Well . . . you doing the right thing, Uncle Gabe. Somebody got to chase them.

GABRIEL: Oh, yeah . . . I know it. The devil's strong. The devil ain't no pushover. Hellhounds snipping at everybody's heels. But I got my trumpet
waiting on the Judgment time.

LYONS: Waiting on the Battle of Armageddon,[7] huh?

GABRIEL: Ain't gonna be too much of a battle when God get to waving that
Judgment sword. But the people's gonna have a hell of a time trying to
get into Heaven if them Gates ain't open.

LYONS *(Putting his arm around Gabriel)*: You hear this, Pop. Uncle Gabe,
you all right!

GABRIEL *(Laughing with Lyons)*: Lyons! King of the Jungle.

ROSE: You gonna stay for supper, Gabe. Want me to fix you a plate?

GABRIEL: I'll just take a sandwich, Rose. Don't want no plate. Just wanna
eat with my hands. I'll take a sandwich.

ROSE: How about you, Lyons? You staying? Got some short ribs cooking.

LYONS: Naw, I won't eat nothing till after we finished playing. *(Pause)* You
ought to come down and listen to me play, Pop.

TROY: I don't like that Chinese music. All that noise.

ROSE: Go on in the house and wash up, Gabe . . . I'll fix you a sandwich.

GABRIEL *(As he exits, to Lyons)*: Troy's mad at me.

LYONS: What you mad at Uncle Gabe for, Pop.

ROSE: He thinks Troy's mad at him 'cause he moved over to Miss Pearl's.

TROY: I ain't mad at the man. He can live where he want to live at.

LYONS: What he move over there for? Miss Pearl don't like nobody.

ROSE: She don't mind him none. She treats him real nice. She just don't
allow all that singing.

TROY: She don't mind that rent he be paying . . . that's what she don't mind.

ROSE: Troy, I ain't going through that with you no more. He's over there
'cause he want to have his own place. He can come and go as he please.

TROY: Hell, he could come and go as he please here. I wasn't stopping him.
I ain't put no rules on him.

ROSE: It ain't the same thing, Troy. And you know it.

   (Gabriel comes to the screen door.)

Now, that's the last I wanna hear about that. I don't wanna hear nothing else about Gabe and Miss Pearl. And next week . . .

GABRIEL: I'm ready for my sandwich, Rose.

ROSE: And next week . . . when that recruiter come from that school . . . I
want you to sign that paper and go on and let Cory play football. Then
that'll be the last I have to hear about that.

---

7. According to Christian tradition, the final, history-ending battle between the armies of good
and evil.

TROY (*To Rose as she exits into the house*): I ain't thinking about Cory nothing.

LYONS: What . . . Cory got recruited? What school he going to?

TROY: That boy walking around here smelling his piss . . . thinking he's grown. Thinking he's gonna do what he want, irrespective of what I say. Look here, Bono . . . I left the commissioner's office and went down to the A&P . . . that boy ain't working down there. He lying to me. Telling me he got his job back . . . telling me he working weekends . . . telling me he working after school . . . Mr. Stawicki tell me he ain't working down there at all!

LYONS: Cory just growing up. He's just busting at the seams trying to fill out your shoes.

TROY: I don't care what he's doing. When he get to the point where he wanna disobey me . . . then it's time for him to move on. Bono'll tell you that I bet he ain't never disobeyed his daddy without paying the consequences.

BONO: I ain't never had a chance. My daddy came on through . . . but I ain't never knew him to see him . . . or what he had on his mind or where he went. Just moving on through. Searching out the New Land. That's what the old folks used to call it. See a fellow moving around from place to place . . . woman to woman . . . called it Searching out the New Land. I can't say if he ever found it. I come along, didn't want no kids. Didn't know if I was gonna be in one place long enough to fix on them right as their daddy. I figured I was going searching too. As it turned out I been hooked up with Lucille near about as long as your daddy been with Rose. Going on sixteen years.

TROY: Sometimes I wish I hadn't known my daddy. He ain't cared nothing about no kids. A kid to him wasn't nothing. All he wanted was for you to learn how to walk so he could start you to working. When it come time for eating . . . he ate first. If there was anything left over, that's what you got. Man would sit down and eat two chickens and give you the wing.

LYONS: You ought to stop that, Pop. Everybody feed their kids. No matter how hard times is . . . everybody care about their kids. Make sure they have something to eat.

TROY: The only thing my daddy cared about was getting them bales of cotton in to Mr. Lubin. That's the only thing that mattered to him. Sometimes I used to wonder why he was living. Wonder why the devil hadn't come and got him. "Get them bales of cotton in to Mr. Lubin" and find out he owe him money . . .

LYONS: He should have just went on and left when he saw he couldn't get nowhere. That's what I would have done.

TROY: How he gonna leave with eleven kids? And where he gonna go? He ain't knew how to do nothing but farm. No, he was trapped and I think he knew it. But I'll say this for him . . . he felt a responsibility toward us. Maybe he ain't treated us the way I felt he should have . . . but without that responsibility he could have walked off and left us . . . made his own way.

BONO: A lot of them did. Back in those days what you talking about . . . they walk out their front door and just take on down one road or another and keep on walking.

LYONS: There you go! That's what I'm talking about.

BONO: Just keep on walking till you come to something else. Ain't you never heard of nobody having the walking blues? Well, that's what you call it when you just take off like that.

TROY: My daddy ain't had them walking blues! What you talking about? He stayed right there with his family. But he was just as evil as he could be. My mama couldn't stand him. Couldn't stand that evilness. She run off when I was about eight. She sneaked off one night after he had gone to sleep. Told me she was coming back for me. I ain't never seen her no more. All his women run off and left him. He wasn't good for nobody.

When my turn come to head out, I was fourteen and got to sniffing around Joe Canewell's daughter. Had us an old mule we called Greyboy. My daddy sent me out to do some plowing and I tied up Greyboy and went to fooling around with Joe Canewell's daughter. We done found us a nice spot, got real cozy with each other. She about thirteen and we done figured we was grown anyway . . . so we down there enjoying ourselves . . . ain't thinking about nothing. We didn't know Greyboy had got loose and wandered back to the house and my daddy was looking for me. We down there by the creek enjoying ourselves when my daddy come up on us. Surprised us. He had them leather straps off the mule and commenced to whupping me like there was no tomorrow. I jumped up, mad and embarrassed. I was scared of my daddy. When he commenced to whupping on me . . . . quite naturally I run to get out of the way. *(Pause)* Now I thought he was mad 'cause I ain't done my work. But I see where he was chasing me off so he could have the gal for himself. When I see what the matter of it was, I lost all fear of my daddy. Right there is where I become a man . . . at fourteen years of age. *(Pause)* Now it was my turn to run him off. I picked up them same reins that he had used on me. I picked up them reins and commenced to whupping on him. The gal jumped up and run off . . . and when my daddy turned to face me, I could see why the devil had never come to get him . . . 'cause he was the devil himself. I don't know what happened. When I woke up, I was laying right there by the creek, and

Blue . . . this old dog we had . . . was licking my face. I thought I was blind. I couldn't see nothing. Both my eyes were swollen shut. I laid there and cried. I didn't know what I was gonna do. The only thing I knew was the time had come for me to leave my daddy's house. And right there the world suddenly got big. And it was a long time before I could cut it down to where I could handle it.

Part of that cutting down was when I got to the place where I could feel him kicking in my blood and knew that the only thing that separated us was the matter of a few years.

(Gabriel enters from the house with a sandwich.)

LYONS: What you got there, Uncle Gabe?

GABRIEL: Got me a ham sandwich. Rose gave me a ham sandwich.

TROY: I don't know what happened to him. I done lost touch with everybody except Gabriel. But I hope he's dead. I hope he found some peace.

LYONS: That's a heavy story, Pop. I didn't know you left home when you was fourteen.

TROY: And didn't know nothing. The only part of the world I knew was the forty-two acres of Mr. Lubin's land. That's all I knew about life.

LYONS: Fourteen's kinda young to be out on your own. *(Phone rings)* I don't even think I was ready to be out on my own at fourteen. I don't know what I would have done.

TROY: I got up from the creek and walked on down to Mobile.[8] I was through with farming. Figured I could do better in the city. So I walked the two hundred miles to Mobile.

LYONS: Wait a minute . . . you ain't walked no two hundred miles, Pop. Ain't nobody gonna walk no two hundred miles. You talking about some walking there.

BONO: That's the only way you got anywhere back in them days.

LYONS: Shhh. Damn if I wouldn't have hitched a ride with somebody!

TROY: Who you gonna hitch it with? They ain't had no cars and things like they got now. We talking about 1918.

ROSE *(Entering)*: What you all out here getting into?

TROY *(To Rose)*: I'm telling Lyons how good he got it. He don't know nothing about this I'm talking.

ROSE: Lyons, that was Bonnie on the phone. She say you supposed to pick her up.

LYONS: Yeah, okay, Rose.

TROY: I walked on down to Mobile and hitched up with some of them fellows that was heading this way. Got up here and found out . . . not only

8. City in southwest Alabama, on the Gulf Coast near the Florida state line.

couldn't you get a job . . . you couldn't find no place to live. I thought I was in freedom. Shhh. Colored folks living down there on the riverbanks in whatever kind of shelter they could find for themselves. Right down there under the Brady Street Bridge. Living in shacks made of sticks and tarpaper. Messed around there and went from bad to worse. Started stealing. First it was food. Then I figured, hell, if I steal money I can buy me some food. Buy me some shoes too! One thing led to another. Met your mama. I was young and anxious to be a man. Met your mama and had you. What I do that for? Now I got to worry about feeding you and her. Got to steal three times as much. Went out one day looking for somebody to rob . . . that's what I was, a robber. I'll tell you the truth. I'm ashamed of it today. But it's the truth. Went to rob this fellow . . . pulled out my knife . . . and he pulled out a gun. Shot me in the chest. It felt just like somebody had taken a hot branding iron and laid it on me. When he shot me I jumped at him with my knife. They told me I killed him and they put me in the penitentiary and locked me up for fifteen years. That's where I met Bono. That's where I learned how to play baseball. Got out that place and your mama had taken you and went on to make life without me. Fifteen years was a long time for her to wait. But that fifteen years cured me of that robbing stuff. Rose'll tell you. She asked me when I met her if I had gotten all that foolishness out of my system. And I told her, "Baby, it's you and baseball all what count with me." You hear me, Bono? I meant it too. She say, "Which one comes first?" I told her, "Baby, ain't no doubt it's baseball . . . but you stick and get old with me and we'll both outlive this baseball." Am I right, Rose? And it's true.

ROSE: Man, hush your mouth. You ain't said no such thing. Talking about, "Baby, you know you'll always be number one with me." That's what you was talking.

TROY: You hear that, Bono. That's why I love her.

BONO: Rose'll keep you straight. You get off the track, she'll straighten you up.

ROSE: Lyons, you better get on up and get Bonnie. She waiting on you.

LYONS *(Gets up to go)*: Hey, Pop, why don't you come on down to the Grill and hear me play?

TROY: I ain't going down there. I'm too old to be sitting around in them clubs.

BONO: You got to be good to play down at the Grill.

LYONS: Come on, Pop . . .

TROY: I got to get up in the morning.

LYONS: You ain't got to stay long.

TROY: Naw, I'm gonna get my supper and go on to bed.

LYONS: Well, I got to go. I'll see you again.

TROY: Don't you come around my house on my payday.

ROSE: Pick up the phone and let somebody know you coming. And bring Bonnie with you. You know I'm always glad to see her.

LYONS: Yeah, I'll do that, Rose. You take care now. See you, Pop. See you, Mr. Bono. See you, Uncle Gabe.

GABRIEL: Lyons! King of the Jungle!

(Lyons exits.)

TROY: Is supper ready, woman? Me and you got some business to take care of. I'm gonna tear it up too.

ROSE: Troy, I done told you now!

TROY *(Puts his arm around Bono)*: Aw hell, woman . . . this is Bono. Bono like family. I done known this nigger since . . . how long I done know you?

BONO: It's been a long time.

TROY: I done known this nigger since Skippy was a pup. Me and him done been through some times.

BONO: You sure right about that.

TROY: Hell, I done know him longer than I known you. And we still standing shoulder to shoulder. Hey, look here, Bono . . . a man can't ask for no more than that. *(Drinks to him)* I love you, nigger.

BONO: Hell, I love you too . . . but I got to get home see my woman. You got yours in hand. I got to go get mine.

(Bono starts to exit as Cory enters the yard, dressed in his football uniform. He gives Troy a hard, uncompromising look.)

CORY: What you do that for, Pop? *(Throws his helmet down in the direction of Troy)*

ROSE: What's the matter? Cory . . . what's the matter?

CORY: Papa done went up to the school and told Coach Zellman I can't play football no more. Wouldn't even let me play the game. Told him to tell the recruiter not to come.

ROSE: Troy . . .

TROY: What you Troying me for. Yeah, I did it. And the boy know why I did it.

CORY: Why you wanna do that to me? That was the one chance I had.

ROSE: Ain't nothing wrong with Cory playing football, Troy.

TROY: The boy lied to me. I told the nigger if he wanna play football . . . to keep up his chores and hold down that job at the A&P. That was the conditions. Stopped down there to see Mr. Stawicki . . .

CORY: I can't work after school during the football season, Pop! I tried to tell you that Mr. Stawicki's holding my job for me. You don't never want to listen to nobody. And then you wanna go and do this to me!

TROY: I ain't done nothing to you. You done it to yourself.

CORY: Just 'cause you didn't have a chance! You just scared I'm gonna be better than you, that's all.

TROY: Come here.

ROSE: Troy . . .

(*Cory reluctantly crosses over to Troy.*)

TROY: All right! See. You done made a mistake.

CORY: I didn't even do nothing!

TROY: I'm gonna tell you what your mistake was. See . . . you swung at the ball and didn't hit it. That's strike one. See, you in the batter's box now. You swung and you missed. That's strike one. Don't you strike out!

(*The lights go down on the scene.*)

ACT TWO

Scene 1

The following morning. Cory is at the tree hitting the ball with the bat. He tries to mimic Troy, but his swing is awkward, less sure. Rose enters from the house.

ROSE: Cory, I want you to help me with this cupboard.

CORY: I ain't quitting the team. I don't care what Poppa say.

ROSE: I'll talk to him when he gets back. He had to go see about your Uncle Gabe. The police done arrested him. Say he was disturbing the peace. He'll be back directly. Come on in here and help me clean out the top of this cupboard.

(*Cory exits into the house. Rose sees Troy and Bono coming down the alley.*)

Troy . . . what they say down there?

TROY: Ain't said nothing. I give them fifty dollars and they let him go. I'll talk to you about it. Where's Cory?

ROSE: He's in there helping me clean out these cupboards.

TROY: Tell him to get his butt out here.

(*Troy and Bono go over to the pile of wood. Bono picks up the saw and begins sawing.*)

(*To Bono*) All they want is the money. That makes six or seven times I done went down there and got him. See me coming they stick out their hands.

BONO: Yeah, I know what you mean. That's all they care about . . . that money. They don't care about what's right. (*Pause*) Nigger, why you got to go and get some hard wood? You ain't doing nothing but building a little old fence. Get you some soft pine wood. That's all you need.

TROY: I know what I'm doing. This is outside wood. You put pine wood inside the house. Pine wood is inside wood. This here is outside wood. Now you tell me where the fence is gonna be?

BONO: You don't need this wood. You can put it up with pine wood and it'll stand as long as you gonna be here looking at it.

TROY: How you know how long I'm gonna be here, nigger? Hell, I might just live forever. Live longer than old man Horsely.

BONO: That's what Magee used to say.

TROY: Magee's a damn fool. Now you tell me who you ever heard of gonna pull their own teeth with a pair of rusty pliers.

BONO: The old folks . . . my granddaddy used to pull his teeth with pliers. They ain't had no dentists for the colored folks back then.

TROY: Get clean pliers! You understand? Clean pliers! Sterilize them! Besides we ain't living back then. All Magee had to do was walk over to Doc Goldblum's.

BONO: I see where you and that Tallahassee gal . . . that Alberta . . . I see where you all done got tight.

TROY: What you mean "got tight"?

BONO: I see where you be laughing and joking with her all the time.

TROY: I laughs and jokes with all of them, Bono. You know me.

BONO: That ain't the kind of laughing and joking I'm talking about.

(*Cory enters from the house.*)

CORY: How you doing, Mr. Bono?

TROY: Cory? Get that saw from Bono and cut some wood. He talking about the wood's too hard to cut. Stand back there, Jim, and let that young boy show you how it's done.

BONO: He's sure welcome to it.

(*Cory takes the saw and begins to cut the wood.*)

Whew-e-e! Look at that. Big old strong boy. Look like Joe Louis.[9] Hell, must be getting old the way I'm watching that boy whip through that wood.

CORY: I don't see why Mama want a fence around the yard noways.

---

9. Alabama-born boxer (1914–81) known as the "Brown Bomber," world heavyweight champion from 1937 to 1949.

TROY: Damn if I know either. What the hell she keeping out with it? She ain't got nothing nobody want.

BONO: Some people build fences to keep people out . . . and other people build fences to keep people in. Rose wants to hold on to you all. She loves you.

TROY: Hell, nigger, I don't need nobody to tell me my wife loves me, Cory . . . go on in the house and see if you can find that other saw.

CORY: Where's it at?

TROY: I said find it! Look for it till you find it!

(*Cory exits into the house.*)

What's that supposed to mean? Wanna keep us in?

BONO: Troy . . . I done known you seem like damn near my whole life. You and Rose both. I done know both of you all for a long time. I remember when you met Rose. When you was hitting them baseball out the park. A lot of them old gals was after you then. You had the pick of the litter. When you picked Rose, I was happy for you. That was the first time I knew you had any sense. I said . . . My man Troy knows what he's doing . . . I'm gonna follow this nigger . . . he might take me somewhere. I been following you too. I done learned a whole heap of things about life watching you. I done learned how to tell where the shit lies. How to tell it from the alfalfa. You done learned me a lot of things. You showed me how to not make the same mistakes . . . to take life as it comes along and keep putting one foot in front of the other. (*Pause*) Rose a good woman, Troy.

TROY: Hell, nigger, I know she a good woman. I been married to her for eighteen years. What you got on your mind, Bono?

BONO: I just say she a good woman. Just like I say anything. I ain't got to have nothing on my mind.

TROY: You just gonna say she a good woman and leave it hanging out there like that? Why you telling me she a good woman?

BONO: She loves you, Troy. Rose loves you.

TROY: You saying I don't measure up. That's what you trying to say. I don't measure up 'cause I'm seeing this other gal. I know what you trying to say.

BONO: I know what Rose means to you, Troy. I'm just trying to say I don't want to see you mess up.

TROY: Yeah, I appreciate that, Bono. If you was messing around on Lucille I'd be telling you the same thing.

BONO: Well, that's all I got to say. I just say that because I love you both.

TROY: Hell, you know me . . . I wasn't out there looking for nothing. You can't find a better woman than Rose. I know that. But seems like this woman just stuck on to me where I can't shake her loose. I done wrestled with it, tried to throw her off me . . . but she just stuck on tighter. Now she's stuck on for good.

BONO: You's in control . . . that's what you tell me all the time. You responsible for what you do.

TROY: I ain't ducking the responsibility of it. As long as it sets right in my heart . . . then I'm okay. 'Cause that's all I listen to. It'll tell me right from wrong every time. And I ain't talking about doing Rose no bad turn. I love Rose. She done carried me a long ways and I love and respect her for that.

BONO: I know you do. That's why I don't want to see you hurt her. But what you gonna do when she find out? What you got then? If you try and juggle both of them . . . sooner or later you gonna drop one of them. That's common sense.

TROY: Yeah, I hear what you saying, Bono. I been trying to figure a way to work it out.

BONO: Work it out right, Troy. I don't want to be getting all up between you and Rose's business . . . but work it so it come out right.

TROY: Aw hell, I get all up between you and Lucille's business. When you gonna get that woman that refrigerator she been wanting? Don't tell me you ain't got no money now. I know who your banker is. Mellon don't need that money bad as Lucille want that refrigerator. I'll tell you that.

BONO: Tell you what I'll do . . . when you finish building this fence for Rose . . . I'll buy Lucille that refrigerator.

TROY: You done stuck your foot in your mouth now!

(Troy grabs up a board and begins to saw. Bono starts to walk out the yard.)

Hey, nigger . . . where you going?

BONO: I'm going home. I know you don't expect me to help you now. I'm protecting my money. I wanna see you put up that fence by yourself. That's what I want to see. You'll be here another six months without me.

TROY: Nigger, you ain't right.

BONO: When it comes to my money . . . I'm as right as fireworks on the Fourth of July.

TROY: All right, we gonna see now. You better get out your bankbook.

(Bono exits, and Troy continues to work. Rose enters from the house.)

ROSE: What they say down there? What's happening with Gabe?

TROY: I went down there and got him out. Cost me fifty dollars. Say he was disturbing the peace. Judge set up a hearing for him in three weeks. Say to show cause why he shouldn't be recommitted.

ROSE: What was he doing that cause them to arrest him?

TROY: Some kids was teasing him and he run them off home. Say he was howling and carrying on. Some folks seen him and called the police. That's all it was.

ROSE: Well, what's you say? What'd you tell the judge?

TROY: Told him I'd look after him. It didn't make no sense to recommit the man. He stuck out his big greasy palm and told me to give him fifty dollars and take him on home.

ROSE: Where's he at now? Where'd he go off to?

TROY: He's gone on about his business. He don't need nobody to hold his hand.

ROSE: Well, I don't know. Seem like that would be the best place for him if they did put him into the hospital. I know what you're gonna say. But that's what I think would be best.

TROY: The man done had his life ruined fighting for what? And they wanna take and lock him up. Let him be free. He don't bother nobody.

ROSE: Well, everybody got their own way of looking at it I guess. Come on and get your lunch. I got a bowl of lima beans and some cornbread in the oven. Come on get something to eat. Ain't no sense you fretting over Gabe. (*Turns to go in the house*)

TROY: Rose . . . got something to tell you.

ROSE: Well, come on . . . wait till I get this food on the table.

TROY: Rose!

(*She stops and turns around.*)

I don't know how to say this. (*Pause*) I can't explain it none. It just sort of grows on you till it gets out of hand. It starts out like a little bush . . . and the next thing you know it's a whole forest.

ROSE: Troy . . . what is you talking about?

TROY: I'm talking, woman, let me talk. I'm trying to find a way to tell you . . . I'm gonna be a daddy. I'm gonna be somebody's daddy.

ROSE: Troy . . . you're not telling me this? You're gonna be . . . what?

TROY: Rose . . . now . . . see . . .

ROSE: You telling me you gonna be somebody's daddy? You telling your *wife* this?

(*Gabriel enters from the street. He carries a rose in his hand.*)

GABRIEL: Hey, Troy! Hey, Rose!

ROSE: I have to wait eighteen years to hear something like this.

GABRIEL: Hey, Rose . . . I got a flower for you. (*Hands it to her*) That's a rose. Same rose like you is.

ROSE: Thanks, Gabe.

GABRIEL: Troy, you ain't mad at me is you? Them bad mens come and put me away. You ain't mad at me is you?

TROY: Naw, Gabe, I ain't mad at you.

ROSE: Eighteen years and you wanna come with this.

GABRIEL *(Takes a quarter out of his pocket)*: See what I got? Got a brand-new quarter.

TROY: Rose . . . it's just . . .

ROSE: Ain't nothing you can say, Troy. Ain't no way of explaining that.

GABRIEL: Fellow that give me this quarter had a whole mess of them. I'm gonna keep this quarter till it stop shining.

ROSE: Gabe, go on in the house there. I got some watermelon in the frigidaire. Go on and get you a piece.

GABRIEL: Say, Rose . . . you know I was chasing hellhounds and them bad mens come and get me and take me away. Troy helped me. He come down there and told them they better let me go before he beat them up. Yeah, he did!

ROSE: You go on and get you a piece of watermelon, Gabe. Them bad mens is gone now.

GABRIEL: Okay, Rose . . . gonna get me some watermelon. The kind with the stripes on it.

(Gabriel exits into the house.)

ROSE: Why, Troy? Why? After all these years to come dragging this in to me now. It don't make no sense at your age. I could have expected this ten or fifteen years ago, but not now.

TROY: Age ain't got nothing to do with it, Rose.

ROSE: I done tried to be everything a wife should be. Everything a wife could be. Been married eighteen years and I got to live to see the day you tell me you been seeing another woman and done fathered a child by her. And you know I ain't never wanted no half nothing in my family. My whole family is half. Everybody got different fathers and mothers . . . my two sisters and my brother. Can't hardly tell who's who. Can't never sit down and talk about Papa and Mama. It's your papa and your mama and my papa and my mama . . .

TROY: Rose . . . stop it now.

ROSE: I ain't never wanted that for none of my children. And now you wanna drag your behind in here and tell me something like this.

TROY: You ought to know. It's time for you to know.

ROSE: Well, I don't want to know, goddamn it!

TROY: I can't just make it go away. It's done now. I can't wish the circumstance of the thing away.

ROSE: And you don't want to either. Maybe you want to wish me and my
boy away. Maybe that's what you want? Well, you can't wish us away.
I've got eighteen years of my life invested in you. You ought to have
stayed upstairs in my bed where you belong.

TROY: Rose . . . now listen to me . . . we can get a handle on this thing. We
can talk this out . . . come to an understanding.

ROSE: All of a sudden it's "we." Where was "we" at when you was down
there rolling around with some godforsaken woman? "We" should have
come to an understanding before you started making a damn fool of
yourself. You're a day late and a dollar short when it comes to an understanding with me.

TROY: It's just . . . She gives me a different idea . . . a different understanding about myself. I can step out of this house and get away from
the pressures and problems . . . be a different man. I ain't got to wonder
how I'm gonna pay the bills or get the roof fixed. I can just be a part of
myself that I ain't never been.

ROSE: What I want to know . . . is do you plan to continue seeing her.
That's all you can say to me.

TROY: I can sit up in her house and laugh. Do you understand what I'm
saying. I can laugh out loud . . . and it feels good. It reaches all the way
down to the bottom of my shoes. *(Pause)* Rose, I can't give that up.

ROSE: Maybe you ought to go on and stay down there with her . . . if she a
better woman than me.

TROY: It ain't about nobody being a better woman or nothing. Rose, you ain't
to blame. A man couldn't ask for no woman to be a better wife than
you've been. I'm responsible for it. I done locked myself into a pattern
trying to take care of you all that I forgot about myself.

ROSE: What the hell was I there for? That was my job, not somebody else's.

TROY: Rose, I done tried all my life to live decent . . . to live a
clean . . . hard . . . useful life. I tried to be a good husband to you. In every
way I knew how. Maybe I come into the world backwards, I don't know.
But . . . you born with two strikes on you before you come to the plate.
You got to guard it closely . . . always looking for the curveball on the
inside corner. You can't afford to let none get past you. You can't afford a
call strike. If you going down . . . you going down swinging. Everything
lined up against you. What you gonna do. I fooled them, Rose. I bunted.
When I found you and Cory and a halfway decent job . . . I was safe.
Couldn't nothing touch me. I wasn't gonna strike out no more. I wasn't
going back to the penitentiary, I wasn't gonna lay in the streets with a
bottle of wine. I was safe. I had me a family. A job. I wasn't gonna get
that last strike. I was on first looking for one of them boys to knock me
in. To get me home.

ROSE: You should have stayed in my bed, Troy.

TROY: Then when I saw that girl . . . she firmed up my backbone. And I got to thinking that if I tried . . . I just might be able to steal second. Do you understand, after eighteen years I wanted to steal second.

ROSE: You should have held me tight. You should have grabbed me and held on.

TROY: I stood on first base for eighteen years and I thought . . . well, god-damn it . . . go on for it!

ROSE: We're not talking about baseball! We're talking about you going off to lay in bed with another woman . . . and then bring it home to me. That's what we're talking about. We ain't talking about no baseball.

TROY: Rose, you're not listening to me. I'm trying the best I can to explain it to you. It's not easy for me to admit that I been standing in the same place for eighteen years.

ROSE: I been standing with you! I been right here with you, Troy. I got a life too. I gave eighteen years of my life to stand in the same spot with you. Don't you think I ever wanted other things? Don't you think I had dreams and hopes? What about my life? What about me? Don't you think it ever crossed my mind to want to know other men? That I wanted to lay up somewhere and forget about my responsibilities? That I wanted someone to make me laugh so I could feel good? You not the only one who's got wants and needs. But I held on to you, Troy. I took all my feelings, my wants and needs, my dreams . . . and I buried them inside you. I planted a seed and watched and prayed over it. I planted myself inside you and waited to bloom. And it didn't take me no eighteen years to find out the soil was hard and rocky and it wasn't never gonna bloom.

But I held on to you, Troy. I held you tighter. You was my husband. I owed you everything I had. Every part of me I could find to give you. And upstairs in that room . . . with the darkness falling in on me . . . I gave everything I had to try and erase the doubt that you wasn't the finest man in the world. And wherever you was going . . . I wanted to be there with you. 'Cause you was my husband. 'Cause that's the only way I was gonna survive as your wife. You always talking about what you give . . . and what you don't have to give. But you take too. You take . . . and don't even know nobody's giving!

(Rose turns to exit into the house; Troy grabs her arm.)

TROY: You say I take and don't give!

ROSE: Troy! You're hurting me.

TROY: You say I take and don't give.

ROSE: Troy . . . you're hurting my arm! Let go!

TROY: I done give you everything I got. Don't you tell that lie on me.

ROSE: Troy!

TROY: Don't you tell that lie on me!

(*Cory enters from the house.*)

CORY: Mama!

ROSE: Troy, you're hurting me.

TROY: Don't you tell me about no taking and giving.

(*Cory comes up behind Troy and grabs him. Troy, surprised, is thrown off balance just as Cory throws a glancing blow that catches him on the chest and knocks him down. Troy is stunned, as is Cory.*)

ROSE: Troy. Troy. No!

(*Troy gets to his feet and starts at Cory.*)

Troy . . . no. Please! Troy!

(*Rose pulls on Troy to hold him back. Troy stops himself.*)

TROY (*To Cory*): All right. That's strike two. You stay away from around me, boy. Don't you strike out. You living with a full count. Don't you strike out.

(*Troy exits out the yard as the lights go down on the scene.*)

Scene 2

It is six months later, early afternoon. Troy enters from the house and starts to exit the yard. Rose enters from the house.

ROSE: Troy, I want to talk to you.

TROY: All of a sudden, after all this time, you want to talk to me, huh? You ain't wanted to talk to me for months. You ain't wanted to talk to me last night. You ain't wanted no part of me then. What you wanna talk to me about now?

ROSE: Tomorrow's Friday.

TROY: I know what day tomorrow is. You think I don't know tomorrow's Friday? My whole life I ain't done nothing but look to see Friday coming and you got to tell me it's Friday.

ROSE: I want to know if you're coming home.

TROY: I always come home, Rose. You know that. There ain't never been a night I ain't come home.

ROSE: That ain't what I mean . . . and you know it. I want to know if you're coming straight home after work.

TROY: I figured I'd cash my check . . . hang out at Taylors' with the boys . . . maybe play a game of checkers . . .

ROSE: Troy, I can't live like this. I won't live like this. You livin' on borrowed time with me. It's been going on six months now you ain't been coming home.

TROY: I be here every night. Every night of the year. That's three hundred sixty-five days.

ROSE: I want you to come home tomorrow after work.

TROY: Rose . . . I don't mess up my pay. You know that now. I take my pay and I give it to you. I don't have no money but what you give me back. I just want to have a little time to myself . . . a little time to enjoy life.

ROSE: What about me? When's my time to enjoy life?

TROY: I don't know what to tell you, Rose. I'm doing the best I can.

ROSE: You ain't come home from work but time enough to change your clothes and run out . . . and you wanna call that the best you can do?

TROY: I'm going over to the hospital to see Alberta. She went into the hospital this afternoon. Look like she might have the baby early. I won't be gone long.

ROSE: Well, you ought to know. They went over to Miss Pearl's and got Gabe today. She said you told them to go ahead and lock him up.

TROY: I ain't said no such thing. Whoever told you that is telling a lie. Pearl ain't doing nothing but telling a big fat lie.

ROSE: She ain't had to tell me. I read it on the papers.

TROY: I ain't told them nothing of the kind.

ROSE: I saw it right there on the papers.

TROY: What it say, huh?

ROSE: It said you told them to take him.

TROY: Then they screwed that up, just the way they screw up everything. I ain't worried about what they got on the paper.

ROSE: Say the government send part of his check to the hospital and the other part to you.

TROY: I ain't got nothing to do with that if that's the way it works. I ain't made up the rules about how it work.

ROSE: You did Gabe just like you did Cory. You wouldn't sign the paper for Cory . . . but you signed for Gabe. You signed that paper.

(The phone is heard ringing inside the house.)

TROY: I told you I ain't signed nothing, woman! The only thing I signed was the release form. Hell, I can't read, I don't know what they had on that paper! I ain't signed nothing about sending Gabe away.

ROSE: I said send him to the hospital . . . you said let him be free . . . now you done went down there and signed him to the hospital for half his money. You went back on yourself, Troy. You gonna have to answer for that.

TROY: See now . . . you been over there talking to Miss Pearl. She done got mad 'cause she ain't getting Gabe's rent money. That's all it is. She's liable to say anything.

ROSE: Troy, I seen where you signed the paper.

TROY: You ain't seen nothing I signed. What she doing got papers on my brother anyway? Miss Pearl telling a big fat lie. And I'm gonna tell her about it too! You ain't seen nothing I signed. Say . . . you ain't seen nothing I signed.

(*Rose exits into the house to answer the phone. She returns.*)

ROSE: Troy . . . that was the hospital. Alberta had the baby.

TROY: What she have? What is it?

ROSE: It's a girl.

TROY: I better get on down to the hospital to see her.

ROSE: Troy . . .

TROY: Rose . . . I got to go see her now. That's only right . . . what's the matter . . . the baby's all right, ain't it?

ROSE: Alberta died having the baby.

TROY: Died . . . you say she's dead? Alberta's dead?

ROSE: They said they done all they could. They couldn't do nothing for her.

TROY: The baby? How's the baby?

ROSE: They say it's healthy. I wonder who's gonna bury her.

TROY: She had family, Rose. She wasn't living in the world by herself.

ROSE: I know she wasn't living in the world by herself.

TROY: Next thing you gonna want to know if she had any insurance.

ROSE: Troy, you ain't got to talk like that.

TROY: That's the first thing that jumped out your mouth. "Who's gonna bury her?" Like I'm fixing to take on that task for myself.

ROSE: I am your wife. Don't push me away.

TROY: I ain't pushing nobody away. Just give me some space. That's all. Just give me some room to breathe.

(*Rose exits into the house. Troy walks about the yard.*)

(*With a quiet rage that threatens to consume him*) All right . . . Mr. Death. See now . . . I'm gonna tell you what I'm gonna do. I'm gonna take and build me a fence around this yard. See? I'm gonna build me a fence around what belongs to me. And then I want you to stay on the other side. See? You stay over there until you're ready for me. Then you come on. Bring your army. Bring your sickle. Bring your wrestling clothes. I ain't gonna fall down on my vigilance this time. You ain't gonna sneak up on me no more. When you ready for me . . . when the top of your list say

"Troy Maxson" . . . that's when you come around here. You come up and knock on the front door. Ain't nobody else got nothing to do with this. This is between you and me. Man to man. You stay on the other side of that fence until you ready for me. Then you come up and knock on the front door. Anytime you want. I'll be ready for you.

(The lights fade to black.)

Scene 3

The lights come up on the porch. It is late evening three days later. Rose sits listening to the ball game, waiting for Troy. The final out of the game is made and Rose switches off the radio. Troy enters the yard carrying an infant wrapped in blankets. He stands back from the house and calls.

Rose enters and stands on the porch. There is a long, awkward silence, the weight of which grows heavier with each passing second.

TROY: Rose . . . I'm standing here with my daughter in my arms. She ain't but a wee bitty little old thing. She don't know nothing about grownups' business. She innocent . . . and she ain't got no mama.

ROSE: What you telling me for, Troy?

(She turns and exits into the house.)

TROY: Well . . . I guess we'll just sit out here on the porch.

(He sits down on the porch. There is an awkward indelicateness about the way he handles the baby. His largeness engulfs and seems to swallow her. He speaks loud enough for Rose to hear:)

A man's got to do what's right for him. I ain't sorry for nothing I done. It felt right in my heart. *(To the baby)* What you smiling at? Your daddy's a big man. Got these great big old hands. But sometimes he's scared. And right now your daddy's scared 'cause we sitting out here and ain't got no home. Oh, I been homeless before. I ain't had no little baby with me. But I been homeless. You just be out on the road by your lonesome and you see one of them trains coming and you just kinda go like this . . . *(Singing, as a lullaby:)*

Please, Mr. Engineer, let a man ride the line
Please, Mr. Engineer, let a man ride the line
I ain't got no ticket please let me ride the blinds.[1]

---

1. That is, hitch a free ride on the platform outside a rail car with no door at one end (hence, "blind").

(Rose enters from the house. Troy hearing her steps behind him, stands and faces her.)

She's my daughter, Rose. My own flesh and blood. I can't deny her no more than I can deny them boys. *(Pause)* You and them boys is my family. You and them and this child is all I got in the world. So I guess what I'm saying is . . . I'd appreciate it if you'd help me take care of her.

ROSE: Okay, Troy . . . you're right. I'll take care of your baby for you . . . 'cause . . . like you say . . . she's innocent . . . and you can't visit the sins of the father upon the child. A motherless child has got a hard time. *(Takes the baby from him)* From right now . . . this child got a mother. But you a womanless man.

(Rose turns and exits into the house with the baby. The lights fade to black.)

Scene 4

It is two months later. Lyons enters from the street. He knocks on the door and calls.

LYONS: Hey, Rose! *(Pause)* Rose!

ROSE *(From inside the house)*: Stop that yelling. You gonna wake up Raynell. I just got her to sleep.

LYONS: I just stopped by to pay Papa this twenty dollars I owe him. Where's Papa at?

ROSE: He should be here in a minute. I'm getting ready to go down to the church. Sit down and wait on him.

LYONS: I got to go pick up Bonnie over her mother's house.

ROSE: Well, sit it down there on the table. He'll get it.

LYONS: *(Enters the house and sets the money on the table)*: Tell Papa I said thanks. I'll see you again.

ROSE: All right, Lyons. We'll see you.

(Lyons starts to exit as Cory enters.)

CORY: Hey, Lyons.

LYONS: What's happening, Cory. Say man, I'm sorry I missed your graduation. You know I had a gig and couldn't get away. Otherwise, I would have been there, man. So what you doing?

CORY: I'm trying to find a job.

LYONS: Yeah, I know how that go, man. It's rough out here. Jobs are scarce.

CORY: Yeah, I know.

LYONS: Look here, I got to run. Talk to Papa . . . he know some people. He'll be able to help get you a job. Talk to him . . . see what he say.

CORY: Yeah . . . all right, Lyons.

LYONS: You take care. I'll talk to you soon. We'll find some time to talk.

(Lyons exits the yard. Cory wanders over to the tree, picks up the bat and assumes a batting stance. He studies an imaginary pitcher and swings. Dissatisfied with the result, he tries again. Troy enters. They eye each other for a beat. Cory puts the bat down and exits the yard. Troy starts into the house as Rose exits with Raynell. She is carrying a cake.)

TROY: I'm coming in and everybody's going out.

ROSE: I'm taking this cake down to the church for the bake sale. Lyons was by to see you. He stopped by to pay you your twenty dollars. It's laying in there on the table.

TROY *(Going into his pocket)*: Well . . . here go this money.

ROSE: Put it in there on the table, Troy. I'll get it.

TROY: What time you coming back?

ROSE: Ain't no use in you studying me. It don't matter what time I come back.

TROY: I just asked you a question, woman. What's the matter . . . can't I ask you a question?

ROSE: Troy, I don't want to go into it. Your dinner's in there on the stove. All you got to do is heat it up. And don't you be eating the rest of them cakes in there. I'm coming back for them. We having a bake sale at the church tomorrow.

(Rose exits the yard. Troy sits down on the steps, takes a pint bottle from his pocket, opens it and drinks. He begins to sing:)

TROY:

Hear it ring! Hear it ring!
Had an old dog his name was Blue
You know Blue was mighty true
You know Blue was a good old dog
Blue treed a possum in a hollow log
You know from that he was a good old dog.

(Bono enters the yard.)

BONO: Hey, Troy.

TROY: Hey, what's happening, Bono?

BONO: I just thought I'd stop by to see you.

TROY: What you stop by and see me for? You ain't stopped by in a month of Sundays. Hell, I must owe you money or something.

BONO: Since you got your promotion I can't keep up with you. Used to see you every day. Now I don't even know what route you working.

TROY: They keep switching me around. Got me out in Greentree now . . . hauling white folks' garbage.

BONO: Greentree, huh? You lucky, at least you ain't got to be lifting them barrels. Damn if they ain't getting heavier. I'm gonna put in my two years and call it quits.

TROY: I'm thinking about retiring myself.

BONO: You got it easy. You can *drive* for another five years.

TROY: It ain't the same, Bono. It ain't like working the back of the truck. Ain't got nobody to talk to . . . feel like you working by yourself. Naw, I'm thinking about retiring. How's Lucille?

BONO: She all right. Her arthritis get to acting up on her sometime. Saw Rose on my way in. She going down to the church, huh?

TROY: Yeah, she took up going down there. All them preachers looking for somebody to fatten their pockets. *(Pause)* Got some gin here.

BONO: Naw, thanks. I just stopped by to say hello.

TROY: Hell, nigger . . . you can take a drink. I ain't never known you to say no to a drink. You ain't got to work tomorrow.

BONO: I just stopped by. I'm fixing to go over to Skinner's. We got us a domino game going over his house every Friday.

TROY: Nigger, you can't play no dominoes. I used to whup you four games out of five.

BONO: Well, that learned me. I'm getting better.

TROY: Yeah? Well, that's all right.

BONO: Look here . . . I got to be getting on. Stop by sometime, huh?

TROY: Yeah, I'll do that, Bono. Lucille told Rose you bought her a new refrigerator.

BONO: Yeah, Rose told Lucille you had finally built your fence . . . so I figured we'd call it even.

TROY: I knew you would.

BONO: Yeah . . . okay. I'll be talking to you.

TROY: Yeah, take care, Bono. Good to see you. I'm gonna stop over.

BONO: Yeah. Okay, Troy.

(Bono exits. Troy drinks from the bottle.)

TROY:
Old Blue died and I dug his grave
Let him down with a golden chain
Every night when I hear old Blue bark
I know Blue treed a possum in Noah's Ark.
Hear it ring! Hear it ring!

(Cory enters the yard. Cory and Troy eye each other for a beat. Cory walks over to Troy, who sits in the middle of the steps.)

CORY: I got to get by.

TROY: Say what? What's you say?

CORY: You in my way. I got to get by.

TROY: You got to get by where? This is my house. Bought and paid for. In full. Took me fifteen years. And if you wanna go in my house and I'm sitting on the steps . . . you say excuse me. Like your mama taught you.

CORY: Come on, Pop . . . I got to get by.

(*Cory starts to maneuver his way past Troy. Troy grabs his leg and shoves him back.*)

TROY: You just gonna walk over top of me?

CORY: I live here too!

TROY (*Advancing on him*): You just gonna walk over top of me in my own house?

CORY: I ain't scared of you.

TROY: I ain't asked if you was scared of me. I asked you if you was fixing to walk over top of me in my own house? That's the question. You ain't gonna say excuse me? You just gonna walk over top of me?

CORY: If you wanna put it like that.

TROY: How else am I gonna put it?

CORY: I was walking by you to go into the house 'cause you sitting on the steps drunk, singing to yourself. You can put it like that.

TROY: Without saying excuse me??? (*Cory doesn't respond*) I asked you a question. Without saying excuse me???

CORY: I ain't got to say excuse me to you. You don't count around here no more.

TROY: Oh, I see . . . I don't count around here no more. You ain't got to say excuse me to your daddy. All of a sudden you done got so grown that your daddy don't count around here no more . . . Around here in his own house and yard that he done paid for with the sweat of his brow. You done got so grown to where you gonna take over. You gonna take over my house. Is that right? You gonna wear my pants. You gonna go in there and stretch out on my bed. You ain't got to say excuse me 'cause I don't count around here no more. Is that right?

CORY: That's right. You always talking this dumb stuff. Now, why don't you just get out my way.

TROY: I guess you got someplace to sleep and something to put in your belly. You got that, huh? You got that? That's what you need. You got that, huh?

CORY: You don't know what I got. You ain't got to worry about what I got.

TROY: You right! You one hundred percent right! I done spent the last seventeen years worrying about what you got. Now it's your turn, see? I'll tell you what to do. You grown . . . we done established that. You a man. Now, let's see you act like one. Turn your behind around and walk out this yard. And when you get out there in the alley . . . you can forget about this house. See? 'Cause this is my house. You go on and be a man and get your own house. You can forget about this. 'Cause this is mine. You go on and get yours 'cause I'm through with doing for you.

CORY: You talking about what you did for me . . . what'd you ever give me?

TROY: Them feet and bones! That pumping heart, nigger! I give you more than anybody else is ever gonna give you.

CORY: You ain't never gave me nothing! You ain't never done nothing but hold me back. Afraid I was gonna be better than you. All you ever did was try and make me scared of you. I used to tremble every time you called my name. Every time I heard your footsteps in the house. Wondering all the time . . . what's Papa gonna say if I do this? . . . What's he gonna say if I do that? . . . What's Papa gonna say if I turn on the radio? And Mama, too . . . she tries . . . but she's scared of you.

TROY: You leave your mama out of this. She ain't got nothing to do with this.

CORY: I don't know how she stand you . . . after what you did to her.

TROY: I told you to leave your mama out of this! (*Advances on Cory*)

CORY: What you gonna do . . . give me a whupping? You can't whup me no more. You're too old. You just an old man.

TROY (*Shoves him on his shoulder*): Nigger! That's what you are! You just another nigger on the street to me!

CORY: You crazy! You know that?

TROY: Go on now! You got the devil in you. Get on away from me!

CORY: You just a crazy old man . . . talking about I got the devil in me.

TROY: Yeah, I'm crazy! If you don't get on the other side of that yard . . . I'm gonna show you how crazy I am! Go on . . . get the hell out of my yard.

CORY: It ain't your yard. You took Uncle Gabe's money he got from the Army to buy this house and then you put him out.

TROY (*Advances on Cory*): Get your black ass out of my yard!

(*Troy's advance backs Cory up against the tree. Cory grabs the bat.*)

CORY: I ain't going nowhere! Come on . . . put me out! I ain't scared of you.

TROY: That's my bat!

CORY: Come on!

TROY: Put my bat down!

CORY: Come on, put me out.

(*Cory swings at Troy, who backs across the yard.*)

What's the matter? You so bad . . . put me out!

(Troy advances on Cory, who backs up.)

Come on! Come on!

TROY: You're gonna have to use it! You wanna draw that bat back on me . . . you're gonna have to use it.

CORY: Come on! . . . Come on!

(Cory swings the bat at Troy a second time. He misses. Troy continues to advance on him.)

TROY: You're gonna have to kill me! You wanna draw that bat back on me. You're gonna have to kill me.

(Cory, backed up against the tree, can go no farther. Troy taunts him. He sticks out his head and offers him a target.)

Come on! Come on!

(Cory is unable to swing the bat. Troy grabs it.)

Then I'll show you.

(Cory and Troy struggle over the bat. The struggle is fierce and fully engaged. Troy ultimately is the stronger, and takes the bat from Cory and stands over him ready to swing. He stops himself.)

Go on and get away from around my house.

(Cory, stung by his defeat, picks himself up, walks slowly out of the yard and up the alley.)

CORY: Tell Mama I'll be back for my things. *(Exits)*

TROY: They'll be on the other side of that fence.

I can't taste nothing. Hallelujah! I can't taste nothing no more. *(Assumes a batting posture and begins to taunt Death, the fastball in the outside corner)* Come on! It's between you and me now! Come on! Anytime you want! Come on! I be ready for you . . . but I ain't gonna be easy.

(The lights go down on the scene.)

Scene 5

The time is 1965. The lights come up in the yard. It is the morning of Troy's funeral. A funeral plaque with a light hangs beside the door. There is a small garden plot off to the side. There is noise and activity in the house as Rose, Gabriel, Lyons and Bono have gathered. The door opens and Raynell, seven years old, enters dressed in a flannel nightgown. She crosses to the garden and pokes around with a stick. Rose calls from the house.

ROSE: Raynell!
RAYNELL: Mam?
ROSE: What you doing out there?
RAYNELL: Nothing.

(Rose comes to the screen door.)

ROSE: Girl, get in here and get dressed. What you doing?
RAYNELL: Seeing if my garden growed.
ROSE: I told you it ain't gonna grow overnight. You got to wait.
RAYNELL: It don't look like it never gonna grow. Dag!
ROSE: I told you a watched pot never boils. Get in here and get dressed.
RAYNELL: This ain't even no pot, Mama.
ROSE: You just have to give it a chance. It'll grow. Now you come on and do what I told you. We got to be getting ready. This ain't no morning to be playing around. You hear me?
RAYNELL: Yes, Mam.

(Rose exits into the house. Raynell continues to poke at her garden with a stick. Cory enters. He is dressed in a Marine corporal's uniform, and carries a duffel bag. His posture is that of a military man, and his speech has a clipped sternness.)

CORY *(To Raynell)*: Hi. *(Pause)* I bet your name is Raynell.
RAYNELL: Uh-huh.
CORY: Is your mama home?

(Raynell runs up on the porch and calls through the screen door:)

RAYNELL: Mama . . . there's some man out here. Mama?

(Rose comes to the screen door.)

ROSE: Cory? Lord have mercy! Look here, you all!

(Rose and Cory embrace in a tearful reunion as Bono and Lyons enter from the house dressed in funeral clothes.)

BONO: Aw, looka here . . .
ROSE: Done got all grown up!
CORY: Don't cry, Mama. What you crying about?
ROSE: I'm just so glad you made it.
CORY: Hey, Lyons. How you doing, Mr. Bono.

(Lyons goes to embrace Cory.)

LYONS: Look at you, man. Look at you. Don't he look good, Rose. Got them corporal stripes.

ROSE: What took you so long.

CORY: You know how the Marines are, Mama. They got to get all their paperwork straight before they let you do anything.

ROSE: Well, I'm sure glad you made it. They let Lyons come. Your Uncle Gabe's still in the hospital. They don't know if they gonna let him out or not. I just talked to them a little while ago.

LYONS: A corporal in the United States Marines.

BONO: Your daddy knew you had it in you. He used to tell me all the time.

LYONS: Don't he look good, Mr. Bono?

BONO: Yeah, he remind me of Troy when I first met him. *(Pause)* Say, Rose, Lucille's down at the church with the choir. I'm gonna go down and get the pallbearers lined up. I'll be back to get you all.

ROSE: Thanks, Jim.

CORY: See you, Mr. Bono.

(Bono exits.)

LYONS *(With his arm around Raynell)*: Cory . . . look at Raynell. Ain't she precious? She gonna break a whole lot of hearts.

ROSE: Raynell, come and say hello to your brother. This is your brother, Cory. You remember Cory.

RAYNELL: No, Mam.

CORY: She don't remember me, Mama.

ROSE: Well, we talk about you. She heard us talk about you. *(To Raynell)* This is your brother Cory. Come on and say hello.

RAYNELL: Hi.

CORY: Hi. So you're Raynell. Mama told me a lot about you.

ROSE: You all come on into the house and let me fix you some breakfast. Keep up your strength.

CORY: I ain't hungry, Mama.

LYONS: You can fix me something, Rose. I'll be in there in a minute.

ROSE: Cory, you sure you don't want nothing. I know they ain't feeding you right.

CORY: No, Mama . . . thanks. I don't feel like eating. I'll get something later.

ROSE: Raynell . . . get on upstairs and get that dress on like I told you.

(Rose and Raynell exit into the house.)

LYONS: So . . . I hear you thinking about getting married.

CORY: Yeah, I done found the right one, Lyons. It's about time.

LYONS: Me and Bonnie been split up about four years now. About the time Papa retired. I guess she just got tired of all them changes I was putting her through. *(Pause)* I always knew you was gonna make something out yourself. Your head was always in the right direction. So . . . you gonna stay in . . . make it a career . . . put in your twenty years?

CORY: I don't know. I got six already, I think that's enough.

LYONS: Stick with Uncle Sam and retire early. Ain't nothing out here. I guess Rose told you what happened with me. They got me down the workhouse. I thought I was being slick cashing other people's checks.

CORY: How much time you doing?

LYONS: They give me three years. I got that beat now. I ain't got but nine more months. It ain't so bad. You learn to deal with it like anything else. You got to take the crookeds with the straights. That's what Papa used to say. He used to say that when he struck out. I seen him strike out three times in a row . . . and the next time up he hit the ball over the grandstand. Right out there in Homestead Field.[2] He wasn't satisfied hitting in the seats . . . he wanted to hit it over everything! After the game he had two hundred people standing around waiting to shake his hand. You got to take the crookeds with the straights. Yeah, Papa was something else.

CORY: You still playing?

LYONS: Cory . . . you know I'm gonna do that. There's some fellows down there we got us a band . . . we gonna try and stay together when we get out . . . but yeah, I'm still playing. It still helps me to get out of bed in the morning. As long as it do that I'm gonna be right there playing and trying to make some sense out of it.

ROSE (*Calling*): Lyons, I got these eggs in the pan.

LYONS: Let me go on and get these eggs, man. Get ready to go bury Papa. (*Pause*) How you doing? You doing all right?

(*Cory nods. Lyons touches him on the shoulder and they share a moment of silent grief. Lyons exits into the house. Cory wanders about the yard. Raynell enters.*)

RAYNELL: Hi.

CORY: Hi.

RAYNELL: Did you used to sleep in my room?

CORY: Yeah . . . that used to be my room.

RAYNELL: That's what Papa call it. "Cory's room." It got your football in the closet.

(*Rose comes to the screen door.*)

ROSE: Raynell, get in there and get them good shoes on.

RAYNELL: Mama, can't I wear these? Them other one hurt my feet.

2. Among the most renowned teams in the Negro League, the Homestead Grays originated in Homestead, Pennsylvania, just south of Pittsburgh, but moved to Pittsburgh's Forbes Field in the late 1930s.

ROSE: Well, they just gonna have to hurt your feet for a while. You ain't said they hurt your feet when you went down to the store and got them.

RAYNELL: They didn't hurt then. My feet done got bigger.

ROSE: Don't you give me no backtalk now. You get in there and get them shoes on.

(Raynell exits into the house.)

Ain't too much changed. He still got that piece of rag tied to that tree. He was out here swinging that bat. I was just ready to go back in the house. He swung that bat and then he just fell over. Seem like he swung it and stood there with this grin on his face . . . and then he just fell over. They carried him on down to the hospital, but I knew there wasn't no need . . . Why don't you come on in the house?

CORY: Mama . . . I got something to tell you. I don't know how to tell you this . . . but I've got to tell you . . . I'm not going to Papa's funeral.

ROSE: Boy, hush your mouth. That's your daddy you talking about. I don't want hear that kind of talk this morning. I done raised you to come to this? You standing there all healthy and grown talking about you ain't going to your daddy's funeral?

CORY: Mama . . . listen . . .

ROSE: I don't want to hear it, Cory. You just get that thought out of your head.

CORY: I can't drag Papa with me everywhere I go. I've got to say no to him. One time in my life I've got to say no.

ROSE: Don't nobody have to listen to nothing like that. I know you and your daddy ain't seen eye to eye, but I ain't got to listen to that kind of talk this morning. Whatever was between you and your daddy . . . the time has come to put it aside. Just take it and set it over there on the shelf and forget about it. Disrespecting your daddy ain't gonna make you a man, Cory. You got to find a way to come to that on your own. Not going to your daddy's funeral ain't gonna make you a man.

CORY: The whole time I was growing up . . . living in his house . . . Papa was like a shadow that followed you everywhere. It weighed on you and sunk into your flesh. It would wrap around you and lay there until you couldn't tell which one was you anymore. That shadow digging in your flesh. Trying to crawl in. Trying to live through you. Everywhere I looked, Troy Maxson was staring back at me . . . hiding under the bed . . . in the closet. I'm just saying I've got to find a way to get rid of that shadow, Mama.

ROSE: You just like him. You got him in you good.

CORY: Don't you tell me that, Mama.

ROSE: You Troy Maxson all over again.

CORY: I don't want to be Troy Maxson. I want to be me.

ROSE: You can't be nobody but who you are, Cory. That shadow wasn't
nothing but you growing into yourself. You either got to grow into it or
cut it down to fit you. But that's all you got to make life with. That's all
you got to measure yourself against that world out there. Your daddy
wanted you to be everything he wasn't . . . and at the same time he tried
to make you into everything he was. I don't know if he was right or
wrong . . . but I do know he meant to do more good than he meant to do
harm. He wasn't always right. Sometimes when he touched he bruised.
And sometimes when he took me in his arms he cut.

When I first met your daddy I thought, "Here is a man I can lay
down with and make a baby." That's the first thing I thought when I
seen him. I was thirty years old and had done seen my share of men.
But when he walked up to me and said, "I can dance a waltz that'll
make you dizzy," I thought, "Rose Lee, here is a man that you can open
yourself up to and be filled to bursting. Here is a man that can fill all
them empty spaces you been tipping around the edges of." One of them
empty spaces was being somebody's mother.

I married your daddy and settle down to cooking his supper and
keeping clean sheets on the bed. When your daddy walked through the
house he was so big he filled it up. That was my first mistake. Not to
make him leave some room for me. For my part in the matter. But at that
time I wanted that. I wanted a house that I could sing in. And that's
what your daddy gave me. I didn't know to keep up his strength I had to
give up little pieces of mine. I did that. I took on his life as mine and
mixed up the pieces so that you couldn't hardly tell which was which
anymore. It was my choice. It was my life and I didn't have to live it
like that. But that's what life offered me in the way of being a woman
and I took it. I grabbed hold of it with both hands.

By the time Raynell came into the house, me and your daddy had
done lost touch with one another. I didn't want to make my blessing
off of nobody's misfortune . . . but I took on to Raynell like she was all
them babies I had wanted and never had. *(The phone rings)* Like I'd
been blessed to relive a part of my life. And if the Lord see fit to keep
up my strength . . . I'm gonna do her just like your daddy did you . . . I'm
gonna give her the best of what's in me.

RAYNELL *(Entering, still with her old shoes)*: Mama . . . Reverend Tolliver
on the phone.

(Rose exits into the house.)

Hi.

CORY: Hi.

RAYNELL: You in the Army or the Marines?

CORY: Marines.

RAYNELL: Papa said it was the Army. Did you know Blue?

CORY: Blue? Who's Blue?

RAYNELL: Papa's dog what he sing about all the time.

CORY (*Singing*):

> Hear it ring! Hear it ring!
> I had a dog his name was Blue
> You know Blue was mighty true
> You know Blue was a good old dog
> Blue treed a possum in a hollow log
> You know from that he was a good old dog.
> Hear it ring! Hear it ring!

(*Raynell joins in singing.*)

CORY AND RAYNELL:

> Blue treed a possum out on a limb
> Blue looked at me and I looked at him
> Grabbed that possum and put him in a sack
> Blue stayed there till I came back
> Old Blue's feets was big and round
> Never allowed a possum to touch the ground.

> Old Blue died and I dug his grave
> I dug his grave with a silver spade
> Let him down with a golden chain
> And every night I call his name
> Go on Blue, you good dog you
> Go on Blue, you good dog you

RAYNELL:

> Blue laid down and died like a man
> Blue laid down and died . . .

CORY AND RAYNELL:

> Blue laid down and died like a man
> Now he's treeing possums in the Promised Land
> I'm gonna tell you this to let you know
> Blue's gone where the good dogs go
> When I hear Old Blue bark
> When I hear Old Blue bark
> Blue treed a possum in Noah's Ark
> Blue treed a possum in Noah's Ark.

(Rose comes to the screen door.)

ROSE: Cory, we gonna be ready to go in a minute.

CORY *(To Raynell)*: You go on in the house and change them shoes like Mama told you so we can go to Papa's funeral.

RAYNELL: Okay, I'll be back.

(Raynell exits into the house. Cory gets up and crosses over to the tree. Rose stands at the screen door watching him. Gabriel enters from the alley.)

GABRIEL *(Calling)*: Hey, Rose!

ROSE: Gabe?

GABRIEL: I'm here, Rose. Hey, Rose, I'm here!

(Rose enters from the house.)

ROSE: Lord . . . Look here, Lyons!

LYONS *(Enters from the house)*: See, I told you, Rose . . . I told you they'd let him come.

CORY: How you doing, Uncle Gabe?

LYONS: How you doing, Uncle Gabe?

GABRIEL: Hey, Rose. It's time. It's time to tell Saint Peter to open the Gates. Troy, you ready? You ready, Troy. I'm gonna tell Saint Peter to open the Gates. You get ready now.

(Gabriel, with great fanfare, braces himself to blow. The trumpet is without a mouthpiece. He puts the end of it into his mouth and blows with great force, like a man who has been waiting some twenty-odd years for this single moment. No sound comes out of the trumpet. He braces himself and blows again with the same result. A third time he blows. There is a weight of impossible description that falls away and leaves him bare and exposed to a frightful realization. It is a trauma that a sane and normal mind would be unable to withstand. He begins to dance. A slow, strange dance, eerie and life-giving. A dance of atavistic[3] signature and ritual. Lyons attempts to embrace him. Gabriel pushes Lyons away. Gabriel begins to howl in what is an attempt at song, or perhaps a song turning back into itself in an attempt at speech. He finishes his dance and the Gates of Heaven stand open as wide as God's closet.)

That's the way that go!

(Blackout.)

1987

---

3. Characterized by a reversion to an ancient or ancestral form.

QUESTIONS

1. In interviews, August Wilson describes FENCES as revolving so completely around its central character that it might "almost" be called "*The Life of Troy Maxson* or just *Troy Maxson*." To what extent does and doesn't that seem true?

2. Wilson also describes the play as "examin[ing] Troy's life layer by layer" to find out why he made the choices he made" (see "Authors on Their Work" below). How do you think the play ultimately answers that question? What does it seem to present as the key to Troy's character or the thing he values most?

3. According to the play, how have circumstances helped to make Troy the man he is? How might he and his life have been different had he turned fifty-three in either 1947 or 1967? had he been white?

4. Does Troy's character develop over the course of the play or only the way others see him? Why and how so?

5. What is the effect and significance of the fact that the play ends after Troy's death? How would the play work and mean differently if its final scene were omitted? if Troy died onstage?

6. What might the fence come to stand for or symbolize in the play? Why might *Fences*, plural, be a more apt title than *The Fence*?

7. How are father-son relationships depicted in the play? How does Troy's relationship with his father compare to and shape his relationship with his sons? Why do you think the play includes Lyons, as well as Cory?

8. How might Rose or your impression of her evolve over the course of the play? Why does she adopt Raynell, and what effect does this choice seem to have? Why might she begin to go to church?

9. What is the significance and effect of Wilson's choice to set the play in the Maxson's front yard? to punctuate the play with scenes that take place on Friday nights? not to show us Troy at work, Cory playing football, and so on?

SUGGESTIONS FOR WRITING

1. Why is Troy Maxson so insistent that his son quit the football team? What about your own cultural and historical context might make his attitude seem surprising? Write a response paper or essay exploring these questions.

2. Write an essay exploring Gabriel's role in the play. What is significant about his injuries and their cause, for example? about his fixation with Judgment Day? about his actions in the play's final scene? What might his final, "*frightful realization*" (933) be, and why, according to Wilson's stage directions, might "*the Gates of Heaven stand open as wide as God's closet*" only after that realization and the "*atavistic*" dance that follows it?

3. Write an essay exploring Wilson's characterization of Rose. What might the play suggest, through her, about the options available to, or conflicts faced by, women in general or African American women in particular in the 1950s? To what extent might Wilson's play reproduce or challenge our preconceptions about such women? Alternatively, consider how FENCES might reproduce or challenge stereotypical views of black men.

4. Write an epilogue to FENCES, a scene depicting Rose, Lyons, Cory, or Raynell in 1975. What do you imagine has happened to this character, and why and how

so? If Cory had a child, for example, what would his relationship with that child be like? What might he say to his child about his father, his mother, and his own childhood?

5. Research theories of tragedy and the tragic hero. Drawing on both these and evidence from Wilson's play, explain whether and how FENCES might be considered a tragedy or Troy Maxson a tragic hero.

6. Write an essay comparing Troy Maxson to Willie Lohman, in Arthur Miller's DEATH OF A SALESMAN. How might Wilson's character and play respond to Miller's?

AUTHORS ON THEIR WORK
AUGUST WILSON (1945–2005)

From Dennis Watlington, "Hurdling Fences" (1989)*

[. . .] I wanted to explore our commonalities of culture. What you have in *Fences* is a very specific situation, a black family which the forces of racism have molded and shaped, but you also have a husband-wife, father-son. White America looks at black America in this glancing manner. They pass right by the Troy Maxsons of the world and never stop to look at them. They talk about niggers as lazy and shiftless. Well, here's a man with responsibilities as prime to his life. I wanted to examine Troy's life layer by layer and find out why he made the choices he made. (109)

* * *

From "Men, Women, and Culture: A Conversation with August Wilson" (1993)**

[INTERVIEWER]: What makes Troy heroic? He's an ex-con, ex-baseball player, now a garbage collector; he exploits his brother and cheats on his wife— what is redeeming about him as an African American man?

WILSON: I think that, for me, this may be nothing more than his willingness to wrestle with his life, his willingness to engage no matter what the circumstances of his life. He hasn't given up despite the twists and turns it's given him. I find that both noble and heroic. (172)

*"Hurdling Fences." Interview by Dennis Watlington. *Vanity Fair*, no. 52, Apr. 1989, pp. 102–13.
**"Men, Women, and Culture: A Conversation with August Wilson." Interview by Nathan L. Grant. *American Drama*, vol. 5, no. 2, Spring 1996, pp. 100–22.

Reading More Drama

LORRAINE HANSBERRY
(1930–1965)
A Raisin in the Sun

The first African American woman to have a play produced on Broadway, Lorraine Hansberry was born in Chicago to a prominent family and even at a young age showed an interest in writing. She attended the University of Wisconsin, the Art Institute of Chicago, and Roosevelt University, then moved to New York City in order to concentrate on writing for the stage. After extensive fund-raising, Hansberry's play *A Raisin in the Sun* (loosely based on events involving her own family) opened in 1959 at the Ethel Barrymore Theatre on Broadway, received critical acclaim, and won the New York Drama Critics' Circle Award for Best Play. Hansberry's second production, *The Sign in Sidney Brustein's Window,* had a short run on Broadway in 1964. Shortly after, Hansberry died of cancer. *To Be Young, Gifted, and Black,* adapted from her writing, was produced off-Broadway in 1969 and published the next year, when her drama *Les Blancs* was also produced.

What happens to a dream deferred?

Does it dry up
Like a raisin in the sun?
Or fester like a sore—
And then run?
Does it stink like rotten meat?
Or crust and sugar over—
Like a syrupy sweet?
Maybe it just sags
Like a heavy load.

Or does it explode?

—LANGSTON HUGHES[1]

1. Hughes's poem, published in 1951, is titled "Harlem (A Dream Deferred)."

CAST OF CHARACTERS

RUTH YOUNGER

TRAVIS YOUNGER

WALTER LEE YOUNGER (BROTHER)

BENEATHA YOUNGER

LENA YOUNGER (MAMA)

JOSEPH ASAGAI

GEORGE MURCHISON

KARL LINDNER

BOBO

MOVING MEN

The action of the play is set in Chicago's Southside, sometime between World War II and the present.

ACT I

Scene One

The Younger living room would be a comfortable and well-ordered room if it were not for a number of indestructible contradictions to this state of being. Its furnishings are typical and undistinguished and their primary feature now is that they have clearly had to accommodate the living of too many people for too many years—and they are tired. Still, we can see that at some time, a time probably no longer remembered by the family (except perhaps for MAMA), *the furnishings of this room were actually selected with care and love and even hope—and brought to this apartment and arranged with taste and pride.*

That was a long time ago. Now the once loved pattern of the couch upholstery has to fight to show itself from under acres of crocheted doilies and couch covers which have themselves finally come to be more important than the upholstery. And here a table or a chair has been moved to disguise the worn places in the carpet; but the carpet has fought back by showing its weariness, with depressing uniformity, elsewhere on its surface.

Weariness has, in fact, won in this room. Everything has been polished, washed, sat on, used, scrubbed too often. All pretenses but living itself have long since vanished from the very atmosphere of this room.

Moreover, a section of this room, for it is not really a room unto itself, though the landlord's lease would make it seem so, slopes backward to provide a small kitchen area, where the family prepares the meals that are eaten in the living room proper, which must also serve as dining room. The single window that has been provided for these "two" rooms is located in this kitchen area. The sole natural light the family may enjoy in the course of a day is only that which fights its way through this little window.

At left, a door leads to a bedroom which is shared by MAMA *and her daughter,* BENEATHA. *At right, opposite, is a second room (which in the beginning of the life of this apartment was probably a breakfast room) which serves as a bedroom for* WALTER *and his wife,* RUTH.

Ruby Dee as Ruth, Sidney Poitier as Walter Lee Younger, and Diana Sands as Beneatha in the original 1959 Broadway production of *A Raisin in the Sun*

Time: Sometime between World War II and the present.
Place: Chicago's Southside.
At Rise: It is morning dark in the living room. TRAVIS *is asleep on the make-down bed at center. An alarm clock sounds from within the bedroom at right, and presently* RUTH *enters from that room and closes the door behind her. She crosses sleepily toward the window. As she passes her sleeping son she reaches down and shakes him a little. At the window she raises the shade and a dusky Southside morning light comes in feebly. She fills a pot with water and puts it on to boil. She calls to the boy, between yawns, in a slightly muffled voice.*

RUTH is about thirty. We can see that she was a pretty girl, even exceptionally so, but now it is apparent that life has been little that she expected, and disappointment has already begun to hang in her face. In a few years, before thirty-five even, she will be known among her people as a "settled woman."

She crosses to her son and gives him a good, final, rousing shake.

RUTH: Come on now, boy, it's seven thirty! [*Her son sits up at last, in a stupor of sleepiness.*] I say hurry up, Travis! You ain't the only person in the world got to use a bathroom! [*The child, a sturdy, handsome little boy of ten or eleven, drags himself out of the bed and almost blindly takes his towels and "today's clothes" from drawers and a closet and goes out to the bathroom, which is in an outside hall and which is shared by another family or families on the same floor. RUTH crosses to the bedroom door at right and opens it and calls in to her husband.*] Walter Lee! . . . It's after seven thirty! Lemme see you do some waking up in there now! [*She waits.*] You better get up from there, man! It's after seven thirty I tell you. [*She waits again.*] All right, you just go ahead and lay there and next thing you know Travis be finished and Mr. Johnson'll be in there and you'll be fussing and cussing round here like a mad man! And be late too! [*She waits, at the end of patience.*] Walter Lee—it's time for you to get up!

[*She waits another second and then starts to go into the bedroom, but is apparently satisfied that her husband has begun to get up. She stops, pulls the door to, and returns to the kitchen area. She wipes her face with a moist cloth and runs her fingers through her sleep-disheveled hair in a vain effort and ties an apron around her housecoat. The bedroom door at right opens and her husband stands in the doorway in his pajamas, which are rumpled and mismated. He is a lean, intense young man in his middle thirties, inclined to quick nervous movements and erratic speech habits—and always in his voice there is a quality of indictment.*]

WALTER: Is he out yet?

RUTH: What you mean *out*? He ain't hardly got in there good yet.

WALTER: [*Wandering in, still more oriented to sleep than to a new day.*] Well, what was you doing all that yelling for if I can't even get in there yet? [*Stopping and thinking.*] Check coming today?

RUTH: They *said* Saturday and this is just Friday and I hopes to God you ain't going to get up here first thing this morning and start talking to me 'bout no money—'cause I 'bout don't want to hear it.

WALTER: Something the matter with you this morning?

RUTH: No—I'm just sleepy as the devil. What kind of eggs you want?

WALTER: Not scrambled. [RUTH *starts to scramble eggs.*] Paper come? [RUTH *points impatiently to the rolled up* Tribune *on the table, and he gets it and spreads it out and vaguely reads the front page.*] Set off another bomb yesterday.

RUTH: [*Maximum indifference.*] Did they?

WALTER: [*Looking up.*] What's the matter with you?

RUTH: Ain't nothing the matter with me. And don't keep asking me that this morning.

WALTER: Ain't nobody bothering you. [*Reading the news of the day absently again.*] Say Colonel McCormick[2] is sick.

RUTH: [*Affecting tea-party interest.*] Is he now? Poor thing.

WALTER: [*Sighing and looking at his watch.*] Oh, me. [*He waits.*] Now what is that boy doing in that bathroom all this time? He just going to have to start getting up earlier. I can't be late to work on account of him fooling around in there.

RUTH: [*Turning on him.*] Oh, no he ain't going to be getting up no earlier no such thing! It ain't his fault that he can't get to bed no earlier nights 'cause he got a bunch of crazy good-for-nothing clowns sitting up running their mouths in what is supposed to be his bedroom after ten o'clock at night . . .

WALTER: That's what you mad about, ain't it? The things I want to talk about with my friends just couldn't be important in your mind, could they?

[*He rises and finds a cigarette in her handbag on the table and crosses to the little window and looks out, smoking and deeply enjoying this first one.*]

RUTH: [*Almost matter of factly, a complaint too automatic to deserve emphasis.*] Why you always got to smoke before you eat in the morning?

WALTER: [*At the window.*] Just look at 'em down there . . . Running and racing to work . . . [*He turns and faces his wife and watches her a moment at the stove, and then, suddenly.*] You look young this morning, baby.

RUTH: [*Indifferently.*] Yeah?

WALTER: Just for a second—stirring them eggs. It's gone now—just for a second it was—you looked real young again. [*Then, drily.*] It's gone now—you look like yourself again.

RUTH: Man, if you don't shut up and leave me alone.

WALTER: [*Looking out to the street again.*] First thing a man ought to learn in life is not to make love to no colored woman first thing in the morning. You all some evil people at eight o'clock in the morning.

---

2. Robert Rutherford McCormick (1880–1955), owner-publisher of the *Chicago Tribune*.

[TRAVIS *appears in the hall doorway, almost fully dressed and quite wide awake now, his towels and pajamas across his shoulders. He opens the door and signals for his father to make the bathroom in a hurry.*]

TRAVIS: [*Watching the bathroom.*] Daddy, come on!

[WALTER *gets his bathroom utensils and flies out to the bathroom.*]

RUTH: Sit down and have your breakfast, Travis.

TRAVIS: Mama, this is Friday. [*Gleefully.*] Check coming tomorrow, huh?

RUTH: You get your mind off money and eat your breakfast.

TRAVIS: [*Eating.*] This is the morning we supposed to bring the fifty cents to school.

RUTH: Well, I ain't got no fifty cents this morning.

TRAVIS: Teacher say we have to.

RUTH: I don't care what teacher say. I ain't got it. Eat your breakfast, Travis.

TRAVIS: I *am* eating.

RUTH: Hush up now and just eat!

[*The boy gives her an exasperated look for her lack of understanding, and eats grudgingly.*]

TRAVIS: You think Grandmama would have it?

RUTH: No! And I want you to stop asking your grandmother for money, you hear me?

TRAVIS: [*Outraged.*] Gaaaleee! I don't ask her, she just gimme it sometimes!

RUTH: Travis Willard Younger—I got too much on me this morning to be—

TRAVIS: Maybe Daddy—

RUTH: *Travis!*

[*The boy hushes abruptly. They are both quiet and tense for several seconds.*]

TRAVIS: [*Presently.*] Could I maybe go carry some groceries in front of the supermarket for a little while after school then?

RUTH: Just hush, I said. [TRAVIS *jabs his spoon into his cereal bowl viciously, and rests his head in anger upon his fists.*] If you through eating, you can get over there and make up your bed.

[*The boy obeys stiffly and crosses the room, almost mechanically, to the bed and more or less carefully folds the covering. He carries the bedding into his mother's room and returns with his books and cap.*]

TRAVIS: [*Sulking and standing apart from her unnaturally.*] I'm gone.

RUTH: [*Looking up from the stove to inspect him automatically.*] Come here. [*He crosses to her and she studies his head.*] If you don't take this comb and fix this here head, you better! [TRAVIS *puts down his books with a great sigh of oppression, and crosses to the mirror. His mother mutters under her breath about his "slubbornness."*] 'Bout to march out of here with that head looking just like chickens slept in it! I just don't know where you get your slubborn ways . . . And get your jacket, too. Looks chilly out this morning.

TRAVIS: [*With conspicuously brushed hair and jacket.*] I'm gone.

RUTH: Get carfare and milk money—[*Waving one finger.*]—and not a single penny for no caps, you hear me?

TRAVIS: [*With sullen politeness.*] Yes'm.

> [*He turns in outrage to leave. His mother watches after him as in his frustration he approaches the door almost comically. When she speaks to him, her voice has become a very gentle tease.*]

RUTH: [*Mocking; as she thinks he would say it.*] Oh, Mama makes me so mad sometimes, I don't know what to do! [*She waits and continues to his back as he stands stock-still in front of the door.*] I wouldn't kiss that woman good-bye for nothing in this world this morning! [*The boy finally turns around and rolls his eyes at her, knowing the mood has changed and he is vindicated; he does not, however, move toward her yet.*] Not for nothing in this world! [*She finally laughs aloud at him and holds out her arms to him and we see that it is a way between them, very old and practiced. He crosses to her and allows her to embrace him warmly but keeps his face fixed with masculine rigidity. She holds him back from her presently and looks at him and runs her fingers over the features of his face. With utter gentleness—*] Now—whose little old angry man are you?

TRAVIS: [*The masculinity and gruffness start to fade at last.*] Aw gaalee— Mama . . .

RUTH: [*Mimicking.*] Aw—gaaaaalleeeee, Mama! [*She pushes him, with rough playfulness and finality, toward the door.*] Get on out of here or you going to be late.

TRAVIS: [*In the face of love, new aggressiveness.*] Mama, could I *please* go carry groceries?

RUTH: Honey, it's starting to get so cold evenings.

WALTER: [*Coming in from the bathroom and drawing a make-believe gun from a make-believe holster and shooting at his son.*] What is it he wants to do?

RUTH: Go carry groceries after school at the supermarket.

WALTER: Well, let him go . . .

TRAVIS: [*Quickly, to the ally.*] I *have* to—she won't gimme the fifty cents . . .

WALTER: [*To his wife only.*] Why not?

RUTH: [*Simply, and with flavor.*] 'Cause we don't have it.

WALTER: [*To* RUTH *only.*] What you tell the boy things like that for? [*Reaching down into his pants with a rather important gesture.*] Here, son—

[*He hands the boy the coin, but his eyes are directed to his wife's.* TRAVIS *takes the money happily.*]

TRAVIS: Thanks, Daddy.

[*He starts out.* RUTH *watches both of them with murder in her eyes.* WALTER *stands and stares back at her with defiance, and suddenly reaches into his pocket again on an afterthought.*]

WALTER: [*Without even looking at his son, still staring hard at his wife.*] In fact, here's another fifty cents . . . Buy yourself some fruit today—or take a taxicab to school or something!

TRAVIS: Whoopee—

[*He leaps up and clasps his father around the middle with his legs, and they face each other in mutual appreciation; slowly* WALTER LEE *peeks around the boy to catch the violent rays from his wife's eyes and draws his head back as if shot.*]

WALTER: You better get down now—and get to school, man.

TRAVIS: [*At the door.*] O.K. Good-bye.

[*He exits.*]

WALTER: [*After him, pointing with pride.*] That's *my* boy. [*She looks at him in disgust and turns back to her work.*] You know what I was thinking 'bout in the bathroom this morning?

RUTH: No.

WALTER: How come you always try to be so pleasant!

RUTH: What is there to be pleasant 'bout!

WALTER: You want to know what I was thinking 'bout in the bathroom or not!

RUTH: I know what you thinking 'bout.

WALTER: [*Ignoring her.*] 'Bout what me and Willy Harris was talking about last night.

RUTH: [*Immediately—a refrain.*] Willy Harris is a good-for-nothing loud mouth.

WALTER: Anybody who talks to me has got to be a good-for-nothing loud mouth, ain't he? And what you know about who is just a good-for-nothing loud mouth? Charlie Atkins was just a "good-for-nothing loud mouth" too, wasn't he! When he wanted me to go in the dry-cleaning business with him. And now—he's grossing a hundred thousand a year. A hundred thousand dollars a year! You still call *him* a loud mouth!

RUTH: [*Bitterly.*] Oh, Walter Lee . . .

[*She folds her head on her arms over the table.*]

WALTER: [*Rising and coming to her and standing over her.*] You tired, ain't you? Tired of everything. Me, the boy, the way we live—this beat-up hole— everything. Ain't you? [*She doesn't look up, doesn't answer.*] So tired— moaning and groaning all the time, but you wouldn't do nothing to help, would you? You couldn't be on my side that long for nothing, could you?

RUTH: Walter, please leave me alone.

WALTER: A man needs for a woman to back him up . . .

RUTH: Walter—

WALTER: Mama would listen to you. You know she listen to you more than she do me and Bennie. She think more of you. All you have to do is just sit down with her when you drinking your coffee one morning and talking 'bout things like you do and— [*He sits down beside her and demonstrates graphically what he thinks her methods and tone should be.*] —you just sip your coffee, see, and say easy like that you been thinking 'bout that deal Walter Lee is so interested in, 'bout the store and all, and sip some more coffee, like what you saying ain't really that important to you—And the next thing you know, she be listening good and asking you questions and when I come home—I can tell her the details. This ain't no fly-by-night proposition, baby. I mean we figured it out, me and Willy and Bobo.

RUTH: [*With a frown.*] Bobo?

WALTER: Yeah. You see, this little liquor store we got in mind cost seventy-five thousand and we figured the initial investment on the place be 'bout thirty thousand, see. That be ten thousand each. Course, there's a couple of hundred you got to pay so's you don't spend your life just waiting for them clowns to let your license get approved—

RUTH: You mean graft?

WALTER: [*Frowning impatiently.*] Don't call it that. See there, that just goes to show you what women understand about the world. Baby, don't *nothing* happen for you in this world 'less you pay *somebody* off!

RUTH: Walter, leave me alone! [*She raises her head and stares at him vigorously—then says, more quietly.*] Eat your eggs, they gonna be cold.

WALTER: [*Straightening up from her and looking off.*] That's it. There you are. Man say to his woman: I got me a dream. His woman say: Eat your eggs. [*Sadly, but gaining in power.*] Man say: I got to take hold of this here world, baby! And a woman will say: Eat your eggs and go to work.

[*Passionately now.*] Man say: I got to change my life, I'm choking to death, baby! And his woman say— [*In utter anguish as he brings his fists down on his thighs.*] —Your eggs is getting cold!

RUTH: [*Softly.*] Walter, that ain't none of our money.

WALTER: [*Not listening at all or even looking at her.*] This morning, I was lookin' in the mirror and thinking about it . . . I'm thirty-five years old; I been married eleven years and I got a boy who sleeps in the living room— [*Very, very quietly.*] —and all I got to give him is stories about how rich white people live . . .

RUTH: Eat your eggs, Walter.

WALTER: *Damn my eggs . . . damn all the eggs that ever was!*

RUTH: Then go to work.

WALTER: [*Looking up at her.*] See—I'm trying to talk to you 'bout myself— [*Shaking his head with the repetition.*] —and all you can say is eat them eggs and go to work.

RUTH: [*Wearily.*] Honey, you never say nothing new. I listen to you every day, every night and every morning, and you never say nothing new. [*Shrugging.*] So you would rather *be* Mr. Arnold than be his chauffeur. So—I would *rather* be living in Buckingham Palace.[3] ——

WALTER: That is just what is wrong with the colored woman in this world . . . Don't understand about building their men up and making 'em feel like they somebody. Like they can do something.

RUTH: [*Drily, but to hurt.*] There *are* colored men who do things.

WALTER: No thanks to the colored woman.

RUTH: Well, being a colored woman, I guess I can't help myself none.

[*She rises and gets the ironing board and sets it up and attacks a huge pile of rough-dried clothes, sprinkling them in preparation for the iron-ing and then rolling them into tight fat balls.*]

WALTER: [*Mumbling.*] We one group of men tied to a race of women with small minds.

[*His sister* BENEATHA *enters. She is about twenty, as slim and intense as her brother. She is not as pretty as her sister-in-law, but her lean, almost intellectual face has a handsomeness of its own. She wears a bright-red flannel nightie, and her thick hair stands wildly about her head. Her speech is a mixture of many things; it is different from the rest of the family's insofar as education has permeated her sense of English—and perhaps the Midwest rather than the South has finally—at last—won out in her inflection; but not altogether, because over all of it is a soft slurring*]

3. London residence of the queen of the United Kingdom of Great Britain and Northern Ireland.

and transformed use of vowels which is the decided influence of the Southside. She passes through the room without looking at either RUTH *or* WALTER *and goes to the outside door and looks, a little blindly, out to the bathroom. She sees that it has been lost to the Johnsons. She closes the door with a sleepy vengeance and crosses to the table and sits down a little defeated.*]

BENEATHA: I am going to start timing those people.

WALTER: You should get up earlier.

BENEATHA: [*Her face in her hands. She is still fighting the urge to go back to bed.*] Really—would you suggest dawn? Where's the paper?

WALTER: [*Pushing the paper across the table to her as he studies her almost clinically, as though he has never seen her before.*] You a horrible-looking chick at this hour.

BENEATHA: [*Drily.*] Good morning, everybody.

WALTER: [*Senselessly.*] How is school coming?

BENEATHA: [*In the same spirit.*] Lovely. Lovely. And you know, biology is the greatest. [*Looking up at him.*] I dissected something that looked just like you yesterday.

WALTER: I just wondered if you've made up your mind and everything.

BENEATHA: [*Gaining in sharpness and impatience.*] And what did I answer yesterday morning—and the day before that?

RUTH: [*From the ironing board, like someone disinterested and old.*] Don't be so nasty, Bennie.

BENEATHA: [*Still to her brother.*] And the day before that and the day before that!

WALTER: [*Defensively.*] I'm interested in you. Something wrong with that? Ain't many girls who decide—

WALTER AND BENEATHA: [*In unison.*]—"to be a doctor."

[*Silence.*]

WALTER: Have we figured out yet just exactly how much medical school is going to cost?

RUTH: Walter Lee, why don't you leave that girl alone and get out of here to work?

BENEATHA: [*Exits to the bathroom and bangs on the door.*] Come on out of there, please!

[*She comes back into the room.*]

WALTER: [*Looking at his sister intently.*] You know the check is coming tomorrow.

BENEATHA: [*Turning on him with a sharpness all her own.*] That money belongs to Mama, Walter, and it's for her to decide how she wants to use it. I don't care if she wants to buy a house or a rocket ship or just nail it up somewhere and look at it. It's hers. Not ours—*hers*.

WALTER: [*Bitterly.*] Now ain't that fine! You just got your mother's interest at heart, ain't you, girl? You such a nice girl—but if Mama got that money she can always take a few thousand and help you through school too—can't she?

BENEATHA: I have never asked anyone around here to do anything for me.

WALTER: No! And the line between asking and just accepting when the time comes is big and wide—ain't it!

BENEATHA: [*With fury.*] What do you want from me, Brother—that I quit school or just drop dead, which!

WALTER: I don't want nothing but for you to stop acting holy 'round here. Me and Ruth done made some sacrifices for you—why can't you do something for the family?

RUTH: Walter, don't be dragging me in it.

WALTER: You are in it—Don't you get up and go work in somebody's kitchen for the last three years to help put clothes on her back?

RUTH: Oh, Walter—that's not fair . . .

WALTER: It ain't that nobody expects you to get on your knees and say thank you, Brother; thank you, Ruth; thank you, Mama—and thank you, Travis, for wearing the same pair of shoes for two semesters—

BENEATHA: [*Dropping to her knees.*] Well—I *do*—all right?—thank everybody . . . and forgive me for ever wanting to be anything at all . . . forgive me, forgive me!

RUTH: Please stop it! Your mama'll hear you.

WALTER: Who the hell told you you had to be a doctor? If you so crazy 'bout messing 'round with sick people—then go be a nurse like other women—or just get married and be quiet . . .

BENEATHA: Well—you finally got it said . . . it took you three years but you finally got it said. Walter, give up; leave me alone—it's Mama's money.

WALTER: *He was my father, too!*

BENEATHA: So what? He was mine, too—and Travis' grandfather—but the insurance money belongs to Mama. Picking on me is not going to make her give it to you to invest in any liquor stores— [*Underbreath, dropping into a chair.*] —and I for one say, God bless Mama for that!

WALTER: [*To* RUTH.] See—did you hear? Did you hear!

RUTH: Honey, please go to work.

WALTER: Nobody in this house is ever going to understand me.

BENEATHA: Because you're a nut.

WALTER: Who's a nut?

BENEATHA: You—you are a nut. Thee is mad, boy.

WALTER: [*Looking at his wife and his sister from the door, very sadly.*] The world's most backward race of people, and that's a fact.

BENEATHA: [*Turning slowly in her chair.*] And then there are all those prophets who would lead us out of the wilderness—. [WALTER *slams out of the house.*] —into the swamps!

RUTH: Bennie, why you always gotta be pickin' on your brother? Can't you be a little sweeter sometimes? [*Door opens.* WALTER *walks in.*]

WALTER: [*To* RUTH.] I need some money for carfare.

RUTH: [*Looks at him, then warms; teasing, but tenderly.*] Fifty cents? [*She goes to her bag and gets money.*] Here, take a taxi.

> [WALTER *exits.* MAMA *enters. She is a woman in her early sixties, full-bodied and strong. She is one of those women of a certain grace and beauty who wear it so unobtrusively that it takes a while to notice. Her dark-brown face is surrounded by the total whiteness of her hair, and, being a woman who has adjusted to many things in life and overcome many more, her face is full of strength. She has, we can see, wit and faith of a kind that keep her eyes lit and full of interest and expectancy. She is, in a word, a beautiful woman. Her bearing is perhaps most like the noble bearing of the women of the Hereros of Southwest Africa—rather as if she imagines that as she walks she still bears a basket or a vessel upon her head. Her speech, on the other hand, is as careless as her carriage is precise—she is inclined to slur everything—but her voice is perhaps not so much quiet as simply soft.*]

MAMA: Who that 'round here slamming doors at this hour?

> [*She crosses through the room, goes to the window, opens it, and brings in a feeble little plant growing doggedly in a small pot on the window sill. She feels the dirt and puts it back out.*]

RUTH: That was Walter Lee. He and Bennie was at it again.

MAMA: My children and they tempers. Lord, if this little old plant don't get more sun than it's been getting it ain't never going to see spring again. [*She turns from the window.*] What's the matter with you this morning, Ruth? You looks right peaked. You aiming to iron all them things? Leave some for me. I'll get to 'em this afternoon. Bennie honey, it's too drafty for you to be sitting 'round half dressed. Where's your robe?

BENEATHA: In the cleaners.

MAMA: Well, go get mine and put it on.

BENEATHA: I'm not cold, Mama, honest.

MAMA: I know—but you so thin . . .

BENEATHA: [*Irritably.*] Mama, I'm not cold.

MAMA: [*Seeing the make-down bed as* TRAVIS *has left it.*] Lord have mercy, look at that poor bed. Bless his heart—he tries, don't he?

[*She moves to the bed* TRAVIS *has sloppily made up.*]

RUTH: No—he don't half try at all 'cause he knows you going to come along behind him and fix everything. That's just how come he don't know how to do nothing right now—you done spoiled that boy so.

MAMA: Well—he's a little boy. Ain't supposed to know 'bout housekeeping. My baby, that's what he is. What you fix for his breakfast this morning?

RUTH: [*Angrily.*] I feed my son, Lena!

MAMA: I ain't meddling— [*Underbreath; busy-bodyish.*] I just noticed all last week he had cold cereal, and when it starts getting this chilly in the fall a child ought to have some hot grits or something when he goes out in the cold—

RUTH: [*Furious.*] I gave him hot oats—is that all right!

MAMA: I ain't meddling. [*Pause.*] Put a lot of nice butter on it? [RUTH *shoots her an angry look and does not reply.*] He likes lots of butter.

RUTH: [*Exasperated.*] Lena—

MAMA: [*To* BENEATHA. MAMA *is inclined to wander conversationally sometimes.*] What was you and your brother fussing 'bout this morning?

BENEATHA: It's not important, Mama.

[*She gets up and goes to look out at the bathroom, which is apparently free, and she picks up her towels and rushes out.*]

MAMA: What was they fighting about?

RUTH: Now you know as well as I do.

MAMA: [*Shaking her head.*] Brother still worrying hisself sick about that money?

RUTH: You know he is.

MAMA: You had breakfast?

RUTH: Some coffee.

MAMA: Girl, you better start eating and looking after yourself better. You almost thin as Travis.

RUTH: Lena—

MAMA: Un-hunh?

RUTH: What are you going to do with it?

MAMA: Now don't you start, child. It's too early in the morning to be talking about money. It ain't Christian.

RUTH: It's just that he got his heart set on that store—

MAMA: You mean that liquor store that Willy Harris want him to invest in?

RUTH: Yes—

MAMA: We ain't no business people, Ruth. We just plain working folks.

RUTH: Ain't nobody business people till they go into business. Walter Lee say colored people ain't never going to start getting ahead till they start gambling on some different kinds of things in the world—investments and things.

MAMA: What done got into you, girl? Walter Lee done finally sold you on investing.

RUTH: No. Mama, something is happening between Walter and me. I don't know what it is—but he needs something—something I can't give him anymore. He needs this chance, Lena.

MAMA: [*Frowning deeply.*] But liquor, honey—

RUTH: Well—like Walter say—I spec people going to always be drinking themselves some liquor.

MAMA: Well—whether they drinks it or not ain't none of my business. But whether I go into business selling it to 'em *is*, and I don't want that on my ledger this late in life. [*Stopping suddenly and studying her daughter-in-law.*] Ruth Younger, what's the matter with you today? You look like you could fall over right there.

RUTH: I'm tired.

MAMA: Then you better stay home from work today.

RUTH: I can't stay home. She'd be calling up the agency and screaming at them, "My girl didn't come in today—send me somebody! My girl didn't come in!" Oh, she just have a fit . . .

MAMA: Well, let her have it. I'll just call her up and say you got the flu—

RUTH: [*Laughing.*] Why the flu?

MAMA: 'Cause it sounds respectable to 'em. Something white people get, too. They know 'bout the flu. Otherwise they think you been cut up or something when you tell 'em you sick.

RUTH: I got to go in. We need the money.

MAMA: Somebody would of thought my children done all but starved to death the way they talk about money here late. Child, we got a great big old check coming tomorrow.

RUTH: [*Sincerely, but also self-righteously.*] Now that's your money. It ain't got nothing to do with me. We all feel like that—Walter and Bennie and me—even Travis.

MAMA: [*Thoughtfully, and suddenly very far away.*] Ten thousand dollars—

RUTH: Sure is wonderful.

MAMA: Ten thousand dollars.

RUTH: You know what you should do, Miss Lena? You should take yourself a trip somewhere. To Europe or South America or someplace—

MAMA: [*Throwing up her hands at the thought.*] Oh, child!

RUTH: I'm serious. Just pack up and leave! Go on away and enjoy yourself some. Forget about the family and have yourself a ball for once in your life—

MAMA: [*Drily.*] You sound like I'm just about ready to die. Who'd go with me? What I look like wandering 'round Europe by myself?

RUTH: Shoot—these here rich white women do it all the time. They don't think nothing of packing up they suitcases and piling on one of them big steamships and—swoosh!—they gone, child.

MAMA: Something always told me I wasn't no rich white woman.

RUTH: Well—what are you going to do with it then?

MAMA: I ain't rightly decided. [*Thinking. She speaks now with emphasis.*] Some of it got to be put away for Beneatha and her schoolin'—and ain't nothing going to touch that part of it. Nothing. [*She waits several seconds, trying to make up her mind about something, and looks at* RUTH *a little tentatively before going on.*] Been thinking that we maybe could meet the notes on a little old two-story somewhere, with a yard where Travis could play in the summertime, if we use part of the insurance for a down payment and everybody kind of pitch in. I could maybe take on a little day work again, few days a week—

RUTH: [*Studying her mother-in-law furtively and concentrating on her ironing, anxious to encourage without seeming to.*] Well, Lord knows, we've put enough rent into this here rat trap to pay for four houses by now . . .

MAMA: [*Looking up at the words "rat trap" and then looking around and leaning back and sighing—in a suddenly reflective mood—*] "Rat trap"— yes, that's all it is. [*Smiling.*] I remember just as well the day me and Big Walter moved in here. Hadn't been married but two weeks and wasn't planning on living here no more than a year. [*She shakes her head at the dissolved dream.*] We was going to set away, little by little, don't you know, and buy a little place out in Morgan Park. We had even picked out the house. [*Chuckling a little.*] Looks right dumpy today. But Lord, child, you should know all the dreams I had 'bout buying that house and fixing it up and making me a little garden in the back— [*She waits and stops smiling.*] And didn't none of it happen.

[*Dropping her hands in a futile gesture.*]

RUTH: [*Keeps her head down, ironing.*] Yes, life can be a barrel of disappointments, sometimes.

MAMA: Honey, Big Walter would come in here some nights back then and slump down on that couch there and just look at the rug, and look at me and look at the rug and then back at me—and I'd know he was down then . . . really down. [*After a second very long and thoughtful pause; she is seeing back to times that only she can see.*] And then, Lord, when I lost that baby—little Claude—I almost thought I was going to lose Big Walter too. Oh, that man grieved hisself! He was one man to love his children.

RUTH: Ain't nothin' can tear at you like losin' your baby.

MAMA: I guess that's how come that man finally worked hisself to death like he done. Like he was fighting his own war with this here world that took his baby from him.

RUTH: He sure was a fine man, all right. I always liked Mr. Younger.

MAMA: Crazy 'bout his children! God knows there was plenty wrong with Walter Younger—hard-headed, mean, kind of wild with women— plenty wrong with him. But he sure loved his children. Always wanted them to have something—be something. That's where Brother gets all these notions, I reckon. Big Walter used to say, he'd get right wet in the eyes sometimes, lean his head back with the water standing in his eyes and say, "Seem like God didn't see fit to give the black man nothing but dreams—but He did give us children to make them dreams seem worthwhile." [*She smiles.*] He could talk like that, don't you know.

RUTH: Yes, he sure could. He was a good man, Mr. Younger.

MAMA: Yes, a fine man—just couldn't never catch up with his dreams, that's all.

[BENEATHA *comes in, brushing her hair and looking up to the ceiling, where the sound of a vacuum cleaner has started up.*]

BENEATHA: What could be so dirty on that woman's rugs that she has to vacuum them every single day?

RUTH: I wish certain young women 'round here who I could name would take inspiration about certain rugs in a certain apartment I could also mention.

BENEATHA: [*Shrugging.*] How much cleaning can a house need, for Christ's sakes.

MAMA: [*Not liking the Lord's name used thus.*] Bennie!

RUTH: Just listen to her—just listen!

BENEATHA: Oh, God!

MAMA: If you use the Lord's name just one more time—

BENEATHA: [*A bit of a whine.*] Oh, Mama—

RUTH: Fresh—just fresh as salt, this girl!

BENEATHA: [*Drily.*] Well—if the salt loses its savor[4]—

MAMA: Now that will do. I just ain't going to have you 'round here reciting the scriptures in vain—you hear me?

BENEATHA: How did I manage to get on everybody's wrong side by just walking into a room?

RUTH: If you weren't so fresh—

---

4. See Matthew 5.13: "You are the salt of the earth. But if the salt loses its taste, with what can it be seasoned? It is no longer good for anything but to be thrown out and trampled underfoot."

BENEATHA: Ruth, I'm twenty years old.

MAMA: What time you be home from school today?

BENEATHA: Kind of late. [*With enthusiasm.*] Madeline is going to start my guitar lessons today.

[MAMA *and* RUTH *look up with the same expression.*]

MAMA: Your *what* kind of lessons?

BENEATHA: Guitar.

RUTH: Oh, Father!

MAMA: How come you done taken it in your mind to learn to play the guitar?

BENEATHA: I just want to, that's all.

MAMA: [*Smiling.*] Lord, child, don't you know what to do with yourself ? How long it going to be before you get tired of this now—like you got tired of that little play-acting group you joined last year? [*Looking at* RUTH.] And what was it the year before that?

RUTH: The horseback-riding club for which she bought that fifty-five-dollar riding habit that's been hanging in the closet ever since!

MAMA: [*To* BENEATHA.] Why you got to flit so from one thing to another, baby?

BENEATHA: [*Sharply.*] I just want to learn to play the guitar. Is there anything wrong with that?

MAMA: Ain't nobody trying to stop you. I just wonders sometimes why you has to flit so from one thing to another all the time. You ain't never done nothing with all that camera equipment you brought home—

BENEATHA: I don't flit! I—I experiment with different forms of expression—

RUTH: Like riding a horse?

BENEATHA: —People have to express themselves one way or another.

MAMA: What is it you want to express?

BENEATHA: [*Angrily.*] Me! [MAMA *and* RUTH *look at each other and burst into raucous laughter.*] Don't worry—I don't expect you to understand.

MAMA: [*To change the subject.*] Who you going out with tomorrow night?

BENEATHA: [*With displeasure.*] George Murchison again.

MAMA: [*Pleased.*] Oh—you getting a little sweet on him?

RUTH: You ask me, this child ain't sweet on nobody but herself— [*Under-breath.*] Express herself!

[*They laugh.*]

BENEATHA: Oh—I like George all right, Mama. I mean I like him enough to go out with him and stuff, but—

RUTH: [*For devilment.*] What does *and stuff* mean?

BENEATHA: Mind your own business.

MAMA: Stop picking at her now, Ruth. [*A thoughtful pause, and then a suspicious sudden look at her daughter as she turns in her chair for emphasis.*] What *does* it mean?

BENEATHA: [*Wearily.*] Oh, I just mean I couldn't ever really be serious about George. He's—he's so shallow.

RUTH: Shallow—what do you mean he's shallow? He's *rich*!

MAMA: Hush, Ruth.

BENEATHA: I know he's rich. He knows he's rich, too.

RUTH: Well—what other qualities a man got to have to satisfy you, little girl?

BENEATHA: You wouldn't even begin to understand. Anybody who married Walter could not possibly understand.

MAMA: [*Outraged.*] What kind of way is that to talk about your brother?

BENEATHA: Brother is a flip—let's face it.

MAMA: [*To* RUTH, *helplessly.*] What's a flip?

RUTH: [*Glad to add kindling.*] She's saying he's crazy.

BENEATHA: Not crazy. Brother isn't really crazy yet—he—he's an elaborate neurotic.

MAMA: Hush your mouth!

BENEATHA: As for George. Well. George looks good—he's got a beautiful car and he takes me to nice places and, as my sister-in-law says, he is probably the richest boy I will ever get to know and I even like him sometimes—but if the Youngers are sitting around waiting to see if their little Bennie is going to tie up the family with the Murchisons, they are wasting their time.

RUTH: You mean you wouldn't marry George Murchison if he asked you someday? That pretty, rich thing? Honey, I knew you was odd—

BENEATHA: No I would not marry him if all I felt for him was what I feel now. Besides, George's family wouldn't really like it.

MAMA: Why not?

BENEATHA: Oh, Mama—The Murchisons are honest-to-God-real-*live*-rich colored people, and the only people in the world who are more snobbish than rich white people are rich colored people. I thought everybody knew that. I've met Mrs. Murchison. She's a scene!

MAMA: You must not dislike people 'cause they well off, honey.

BENEATHA: Why not? It makes just as much sense as disliking people 'cause they are poor, and lots of people do that.

RUTH: [*A wisdom-of-the-ages manner. To* MAMA.] Well, she'll get over some of this—

BENEATHA: Get over it? What are you talking about, Ruth? Listen, I'm going to be a doctor. I'm not worried about who I'm going to marry yet—if I ever get married.

MAMA AND RUTH: *If!*

MAMA: Now, Bennie—

BENEATHA: Oh, I probably will . . . but first I'm going to be a doctor, and George, for one, still thinks that's pretty funny. I couldn't be bothered with that. I am going to be a doctor and everybody around here better understand that!

MAMA: [*Kindly.*] 'Course you going to be a doctor, honey, God willing.

BENEATHA: [*Drily.*] God hasn't got a thing to do with it.

MAMA: Beneatha—that just wasn't necessary.

BENEATHA: Well—neither is God. I get sick of hearing about God.

MAMA: Beneatha!

BENEATHA: I mean it! I'm just tired of hearing about God all the time. What has He got to do with anything? Does He pay tuition?

MAMA: You 'bout to get your fresh little jaw slapped!

RUTH: That's just what she needs, all right!

BENEATHA: Why? Why can't I say what I want to around here, like everybody else?

MAMA: It don't sound nice for a young girl to say things like that—you wasn't brought up that way. Me and your father went to trouble to get you and Brother to church every Sunday.

BENEATHA: Mama, you don't understand. It's all a matter of ideas, and God is just one idea I don't accept. It's not important. I am not going out and be immoral or commit crimes because I don't believe in God. I don't even think about it. It's just that I get tired of Him getting credit for all the things the human race achieves through its own stubborn effort. There simply is no blasted God—there is only man and it is he who makes miracles!

[MAMA *absorbs this speech, studies her daughter and rises slowly and crosses to* BENEATHA *and slaps her powerfully across the face. After, there is only silence and the daughter drops her eyes from her mother's face, and* MAMA *is very tall before her.*]

MAMA: Now—you say after me, in my mother's house there is still God. [*There is a long pause and* BENEATHA *stares at the floor wordlessly.* MAMA *repeats the phrase with precision and cool emotion.*] In my mother's house there is still God.

BENEATHA: In my mother's house there is still God.

[*A long pause.*]

MAMA: [*Walking away from* BENEATHA, *too disturbed for triumphant posture. Stopping and turning back to her daughter.*] There are some ideas we ain't going to have in this house. Not long as I am at the head of this family.

BENEATHA: Yes, ma'am.

[MAMA *walks out of the room.*]

RUTH: [*Almost gently, with profound understanding.*] You think you a woman, Bennie—but you still a little girl. What you did was childish—so you got treated like a child.

BENEATHA: I see. [*Quietly.*] I also see that everybody thinks it's all right for Mama to be a tyrant. But all the tyranny in the world will never put a God in the heavens!

[*She picks up her books and goes out.*]

RUTH: [*Goes to* MAMA's *door.*] She said she was sorry.

MAMA: [*Coming out, going to her plant.*] They frightens me, Ruth. My children.

RUTH: You got good children, Lena. They just a little off sometimes—but they're good.

MAMA: No—there's something come down between me and them that don't let us understand each other and I don't know what it is. One done almost lost his mind thinking 'bout money all the time and the other done commence to talk about things I can't seem to understand in no form or fashion. What is it that's changing, Ruth?

RUTH: [*Soothingly, older than her years.*] Now . . . you taking it all too seriously. You just got strong-willed children and it takes a strong woman like you to keep 'em in hand.

MAMA: [*Looking at her plant and sprinkling a little water on it.*] They spirited all right, my children. Got to admit they got spirit—Bennie and Walter. Like this little old plant that ain't never had enough sunshine or nothing—and look at it . . .

[*She has her back to* RUTH, *who has had to stop ironing and lean against something and put the back of her hand to her forehead.*]

RUTH: [*Trying to keep* MAMA *from noticing.*] You . . . sure . . . loves that little old thing, don't you? . . .

MAMA: Well, I always wanted me a garden like I used to see sometimes at the back of the houses down home. This plant is close as I ever got to having one. [*She looks out of the window as she replaces the plant.*] Lord, ain't nothing as dreary as the view from this window on a dreary day, is there? Why ain't you singing this morning, Ruth? Sing that "No Ways Tired." That song always lifts me up so— [*She turns at last to see that* RUTH *has slipped quietly into a chair, in a state of semiconsciousness.*] Ruth! Ruth honey—what's the matter with you . . . Ruth!

[CURTAIN.]

Scene Two

It is the following morning; a Saturday morning, and house cleaning is in progress at the Youngers. Furniture has been shoved hither and yon and MAMA *is giving the kitchen-area walls a washing down.* BENEATHA, *in dungarees, with a handkerchief tied around her face, is spraying insecticide into the cracks in the walls. As they work, the radio is on and a Southside disk-jockey program is inappropriately filling the house with a rather exotic saxophone blues.* TRAVIS, *the sole idle one, is leaning on his arms, looking out of the window.*

TRAVIS: Grandmama, that stuff Bennie is using smells awful. Can I go downstairs, please?

MAMA: Did you get all them chores done already? I ain't seen you doing much.

TRAVIS: Yes'm—finished early. Where did Mama go this morning?

MAMA: [*Looking at* BENEATHA.] She had to go on a little errand.

TRAVIS: Where?

MAMA: To tend to her business.

TRAVIS: Can I go outside then?

MAMA: Oh, I guess so. You better stay right in front of the house, though . . . and keep a good lookout for the postman.

TRAVIS: Yes'm. [*He starts out and decides to give his aunt* BENEATHA *a good swat on the legs as he passes her.*] Leave them poor little old cockroaches alone, they ain't bothering you none.

[*He runs as she swings the spray gun at him both viciously and playfully.* WALTER *enters from the bedroom and goes to the phone.*]

MAMA: Look out there, girl, before you be spilling some of that stuff on that child!

TRAVIS: [*Teasing.*] That's right—look out now!

[*He exits.*]

BENEATHA: [*Drily.*] I can't imagine that it would hurt him—it has never hurt the roaches.

MAMA: Well, little boys' hides ain't as tough as Southside roaches.

WALTER: [*Into phone.*] Hello—Let me talk to Willy Harris.

MAMA: You better get over there behind the bureau. I seen one marching out of there like Napoleon yesterday.

WALTER: Hello, Willy? It ain't come yet. It'll be here in a few minutes. Did the lawyer give you the papers?

BENEATHA: There's really only one way to get rid of them, Mama—

MAMA: How?

BENEATHA: Set fire to this building.

WALTER: Good. Good. I'll be right over.

BENEATHA: Where did Ruth go, Walter?

WALTER: I don't know.

[*He exits abruptly.*]

BENEATHA: Mama, where did Ruth go?

MAMA: [*Looking at her with meaning.*] To the doctor, I think.

BENEATHA: The doctor? What's the matter? [*They exchange glances.*] You don't think—

MAMA: [*With her sense of drama.*] Now I ain't saying what I think. But I ain't never been wrong 'bout a woman neither.

[*The phone rings.*]

BENEATHA: [*At the phone.*] Hay-lo . . . [*Pause, and a moment of recognition.*] Well—when did you get back! . . . And how was it? . . . Of course I've missed you—in my way . . . This morning? No . . . house cleaning and all that and Mama hates it if I let people come over when the house is like this . . . You *have?* Well, that's different . . . What is it—Oh, what the hell, come on over . . . Right, see you then.

[*She hangs up.*]

MAMA: [*Who has listened vigorously, as is her habit.*] Who is that you inviting over here with this house looking like this? You ain't got the pride you was born with!

BENEATHA: Asagai doesn't care how houses look, Mama—he's an intellectual.

MAMA: *Who?*

BENEATHA: Asagai—Joseph Asagai. He's an African boy I met on campus. He's been studying in Canada all summer.

MAMA: What's his name?

BENEATHA: Asagai, Joseph. Ah-sah-guy . . . He's from Nigeria.

MAMA: Oh, that's the little country that was founded by slaves way back . . .

BENEATHA: No, Mama—that's Liberia.

MAMA: I don't think I never met no African before.

BENEATHA: Well, do me a favor and don't ask him a whole lot of ignorant questions about Africans. I mean, do they wear clothes and all that—

MAMA: Well, now, I guess if you think we so ignorant 'round here maybe you shouldn't bring your friends here—

BENEATHA: It's just that people ask such crazy things. All anyone seems to know about when it comes to Africa is Tarzan—

MAMA: [*Indignantly.*] Why should I know anything about Africa?
BENEATHA: Why do you give money at church for the missionary work?
MAMA: Well, that's to help save people.
BENEATHA: You mean save them from *heathenism*—
MAMA: [*Innocently.*] Yes.
BENEATHA: I'm afraid they need more salvation from the British and the French.

[RUTH *comes in forlornly and pulls off her coat with dejection. They both turn to look at her.*]

RUTH: [*Dispiritedly.*] Well, I guess from all the happy faces—everybody knows.
BENEATHA: You pregnant?
MAMA: Lord have mercy, I sure hope it's a little old girl. Travis ought to have a sister.

[BENEATHA *and* RUTH *give her a hopeless look for this grandmotherly enthusiasm.*]

BENEATHA: How far along are you?
RUTH: Two months.
BENEATHA: Did you mean to? I mean did you plan it or was it an accident?
MAMA: What do you know about planning or not planning?
BENEATHA: Oh, Mama.
RUTH: [*Wearily.*] She's twenty years old, Lena.
BENEATHA: Did you plan it, Ruth?
RUTH: Mind your own business.
BENEATHA: It is my business—where is he going to live, on the roof? [*There is silence following the remark as the three women react to the sense of it.*] Gee—I didn't mean that, Ruth, honest. Gee, I don't feel like that at all. I—I think it is wonderful.
RUTH: [*Dully.*] Wonderful.
BENEATHA: Yes—really.
MAMA: [*Looking at* RUTH, *worried.*] Doctor say everything going to be all right?
RUTH: [*Far away.*] Yes—she says everything is going to be fine . . .
MAMA: [*Immediately suspicious.*] "She"—What doctor you went to?

[RUTH *folds over, near hysteria.*]

MAMA: [*Worriedly hovering over* RUTH.] Ruth honey—what's the matter with you—you sick?

[RUTH *has her fists clenched on her thighs and is fighting hard to suppress a scream that seems to be rising in her.*]

BENEATHA: What's the matter with her, Mama?

MAMA: [*Working her fingers in* RUTH's *shoulder to relax her.*] She be all right. Women gets right depressed sometimes when they get her way. [*Speaking softly, expertly, rapidly.*] Now you just relax. That's right . . . just lean back, don't think 'bout nothing at all . . . nothing at all—

RUTH: I'm all right . . .

[*The glassy-eyed look melts and then she collapses into a fit of heavy sobbing. The bell rings.*]

BENEATHA: Oh, my God—that must be Asagai.

MAMA: [*To* RUTH.] Come on now, honey. You need to lie down and rest awhile . . . then have some nice hot food.

[*They exit,* RUTH's *weight on her mother-in-law.* BENEATHA, *herself profoundly disturbed, opens the door to admit a rather dramatic-looking young man with a large package.*]

ASAGAI: Hello, Alaiyo—

BENEATHA: [*Holding the door open and regarding him with pleasure.*] Hello . . . [*Long pause.*] Well—come in. And please excuse everything. My mother was very upset about my letting anyone come here with the place like this.

ASAGAI: [*Coming into the room.*] You look disturbed too . . . Is something wrong?

BENEATHA: [*Still at the door, absently.*] Yes . . . we've all got acute ghettoitis. [*She smiles and comes toward him, finding a cigarette and sitting.*] So—sit down! How was Canada?

ASAGAI: [*A sophisticate.*] Canadian.

BENEATHA: [*Looking at him.*] I'm very glad you are back.

ASAGAI: [*Looking back at her in turn.*] Are you really?

BENEATHA: Yes—very.

ASAGAI: Why—you were quite glad when I went away. What happened?

BENEATHA: You went away.

ASAGAI: Ahhhhhhhh.

BENEATHA: Before—you wanted to be so serious before there was time.

ASAGAI: How much time must there be before one knows what one feels?

BENEATHA: [*Stalling this particular conversation. Her hands pressed together, in a deliberately childish gesture.*] What did you bring me?

ASAGAI: [*Handing her the package.*] Open it and see.

BENEATHA: [*Eagerly opening the package and drawing out some records and the colorful robes of a Nigerian woman.*] Oh, Asagai! . . . You got them for me! . . . How beautiful . . . and the records too! [*She lifts out the robes and runs to the mirror with them and holds the drapery up in front of herself.*]

ASAGAI: [*Coming to her at the mirror.*] I shall have to teach you how to drape it properly. [*He flings the material about her for the moment and stands back to look at her.*] Ah—Oh-pay-gay-day, oh-gbah-mu-shay. [*A Yoruba exclamation for admiration.*] You wear it well . . . very well . . . mutilated hair and all.

BENEATHA: [*Turning suddenly.*] My hair—what's wrong with my hair?

ASAGAI: [*Shrugging.*] Were you born with it like that?

BENEATHA: [*Reaching up to touch it.*] No . . . of course not.

[*She looks back to the mirror, disturbed.*]

ASAGAI: [*Smiling.*] How then?

BENEATHA: You know perfectly well how . . . as crinkly as yours . . . that's how.

ASAGAI: And it is ugly to you that way?

BENEATHA: [*Quickly.*] Oh, no—not ugly . . . [*More slowly, apologetically.*] But it's so hard to manage when it's, well—raw.

ASAGAI: And so to accommodate that—you mutilate it every week?

BENEATHA: It's not mutilation!

ASAGAI: [*Laughing aloud at her seriousness.*] Oh . . . please! I am only teasing you because you are so very serious about these things. [*He stands back from her and folds his arms across his chest as he watches her pulling at her hair and frowning in the mirror.*] Do you remember the first time you met me at school? . . . [*He laughs.*] You came up to me and you said—and I thought you were the most serious little thing I had ever seen—you said: [*He imitates her.*] "Mr. Asagai—I want very much to talk with you. About Africa. You see, Mr. Asagai, I am looking for my *identity!*"

[*He laughs.*]

BENEATHA: [*Turning to him, not laughing.*] Yes—

[*Her face is quizzical, profoundly disturbed.*]

ASAGAI: [*Still teasing and reaching out and taking her face in his hands and turning her profile to him.*] Well . . . it is true that this is not so much a profile of a Hollywood queen as perhaps a queen of the Nile— [*A mock dismissal of the importance of the question.*] But what does it matter? Assimilationism is so popular in your country.

BENEATHA: [*Wheeling, passionately, sharply.*] I am not an assimilationist!

ASAGAI: [*The protest hangs in the room for a moment and* ASAGAI *studies her, his laughter fading.*] Such a serious one. [*There is a pause.*] So—you like the robes? You must take excellent care of them—they are from my sister's personal wardrobe.

BENEATHA: [*With incredulity.*] You—you sent all the way home—for me?

ASAGAI: [*With charm.*] For you—I would do much more . . . Well, that is what I came for. I must go.

BENEATHA: Will you call me Monday?

ASAGAI: Yes . . . We have a great deal to talk about. I mean about identity and time and all that.

BENEATHA: Time?

ASAGAI: Yes. About how much time one needs to know what one feels.

BENEATHA: You never understood that there is more than one kind of feeling which can exist between a man and a woman—or, at least, there should be.

ASAGAI: [*Shaking his head negatively but gently.*] No. Between a man and a woman there need be only one kind of feeling. I have that for you . . . Now even . . . right this moment . . .

BENEATHA: I know—and by itself—it won't do. I can find that anywhere.

ASAGAI: For a woman it should be enough.

BENEATHA: I know—because that's what it says in all the novels that men write. But it isn't. Go ahead and laugh—but I'm not interested in being someone's little episode in America or— [*With feminine vengeance.*] —one of them! [ASAGAI *has burst into laughter again.*] That's funny as hell, huh!

ASAGAI: It's just that every American girl I have known has said that to me. White—black—in this you are all the same. And the same speech, too!

BENEATHA: [*Angrily.*] Yuk, yuk, yuk!

ASAGAI: It's how you can be sure that the world's most liberated women are not liberated at all. You all talk about it too much!

[MAMA *enters and is immediately all social charm because of the presence of a guest.*]

BENEATHA: Oh—Mama—this is Mr. Asagai.

MAMA: How do you do?

ASAGAI: [*Total politeness to an elder.*] How do you do, Mrs. Younger. Please forgive me for coming at such an outrageous hour on a Saturday.

MAMA: Well, you are quite welcome. I just hope you understand that our house don't always look like this. [*Chatterish.*] You must come again. I would love to hear all about— [*Not sure of the name.*] —your country. I think it's so sad the way our American Negroes don't know nothing about Africa 'cept Tarzan and all that. And all that money they pour into these churches when they ought to be helping you people over there drive out them French and Englishmen done taken away your land.

[*The mother flashes a slightly superior look at her daughter upon completion of the recitation.*]

ASAGAI: [*Taken aback by this sudden and acutely unrelated expression of sympathy.*] Yes . . . yes . . .

MAMA: [*Smiling at him suddenly and relaxing and looking him over.*] How many miles is it from here to where you come from?

ASAGAI: Many thousands.

MAMA: [*Looking at him as she would* WALTER.] I bet you don't half look after yourself, being away from your mama either. I spec you better come 'round here from time to time and get yourself some decent home-cooked meals . . .

ASAGAI: [*Moved.*] Thank you. Thank you very much. [*They are all quiet, then—*] Well . . . I must go. I will call you Monday, Alaiyo.

MAMA: What's that he call you?

ASAGAI: Oh—"Alaiyo." I hope you don't mind. It is what you would call a nickname, I think. It is a Yoruba word. I am a Yoruba.

MAMA: [*Looking at* BENEATHA.] I—I thought he was from—

ASAGAI: [*Understanding.*] Nigeria is my country. Yoruba is my tribal origin—

BENEATHA: You didn't tell us what Alaiyo means . . . for all I know, you might be calling me Little Idiot or something . . .

ASAGAI: Well . . . let me see . . . I do not know how just to explain it . . . The sense of a thing can be so different when it changes languages.

BENEATHA: You're evading.

ASAGAI: No—really it is difficult . . . [*Thinking.*] It means . . . it means One for Whom Bread—Food—Is Not Enough. [*He looks at her.*] Is that all right?

BENEATHA: [*Understanding, softly.*] Thank you.

MAMA: [*Looking from one to the other and not understanding any of it.*] Well . . . that's nice . . . You must come see us again—Mr.—

ASAGAI: Ah-sah-guy . . .

MAMA: Yes . . . Do come again.

ASAGAI: Good-bye.

[*He exits.*]

MAMA: [*After him.*] Lord, that's a pretty thing just went out here! [*Insinuatingly, to her daughter.*] Yes, I guess I see why we done commence to get so interested in Africa 'round here. Missionaries my aunt Jenny!

[*She exits.*]

BENEATHA: Oh, Mama! . . .

[*She picks up the Nigerian dress and holds it up to her in front of the mirror again. She sets the headdress on haphazardly and then notices her hair again and clutches at it and then replaces the headdress and frowns at herself. Then she starts to wriggle in front of the mirror as she thinks a Nigerian woman might.* TRAVIS *enters and regards her.*]

TRAVIS: You cracking up?

BENEATHA: Shut up.

[*She pulls the headdress off and looks at herself in the mirror and clutches at her hair again and squinches her eyes as if trying to imagine something. Then, suddenly, she gets her raincoat and kerchief and hurriedly prepares for going out.*]

MAMA: [*Coming back into the room.*] She's resting now. Travis, baby, run next door and ask Miss Johnson to please let me have a little kitchen cleanser. This here can is empty as Jacob's kettle.

TRAVIS: I just came in.

MAMA: Do as you told. [*He exits and she looks at her daughter.*] Where you going?

BENEATHA: [*Halting at the door.*] To become a queen of the Nile!

[*She exits in a breathless blaze of glory.* RUTH *appears in the bedroom doorway.*]

MAMA: Who told you to get up?

RUTH: Ain't nothing wrong with me to be lying in no bed for. Where did Bennie go?

MAMA: [*Drumming her fingers.*] Far as I could make out—to Egypt. [RUTH *just looks at her.*] What time is it getting to?

RUTH: Ten twenty. And the mailman going to ring that bell this morning just like he done every morning for the last umpteen years.

[TRAVIS *comes in with the cleanser can.*]

TRAVIS: She say to tell you that she don't have much.

MAMA: [*Angrily.*] Lord, some people I could name sure is tight-fisted! [*Directing her grandson.*] Mark two cans of cleanser down on the list there. If she that hard up for kitchen cleanser, I sure don't want to forget to get her none!

RUTH: Lena—maybe the woman is just short on cleanser—

MAMA: [*Not listening.*] —Much baking powder as she done borrowed from me all these years, she could of done gone into the baking business!

[*The bell sounds suddenly and sharply and all three are stunned—serious and silent—mid-speech. In spite of all the other conversations and distractions of the morning, this is what they have been waiting for, even* TRAVIS, *who looks helplessly from his mother to his grandmother.* RUTH *is the first to come to life again.*]

RUTH: [*To* TRAVIS.] *Get down them steps, boy!*

[TRAVIS *snaps to life and flies out to get the mail.*]

MAMA: [*Her eyes wide, her hand to her breast.*] You mean it done really come?

RUTH: [*Excited.*] Oh, Miss Lena!

MAMA: [*Collecting herself.*] Well . . . I don't know what we all so excited about 'round here for. We known it was coming for months.

RUTH: That's a whole lot different from having it come and being able to hold it in your hands . . . a piece of paper worth ten thousand dollars . . . [TRAVIS *bursts back into the room. He holds the envelope high above his head, like a little dancer, his face is radiant and he is breathless. He moves to his grandmother with sudden slow ceremony and puts the envelope into her hands. She accepts it, and then merely holds it and looks at it.*] Come on! Open it . . . Lord have mercy, I wish Walter Lee was here!

TRAVIS: Open it, Grandmama!

MAMA: [*Staring at it.*] Now you all be quiet. It's just a check.

RUTH: Open it . . .

MAMA: [*Still staring at it.*] Now don't act silly . . . We ain't never been no people to act silly 'bout no money—

RUTH: [*Swiftly.*] We ain't never had none before—*open it!*

[MAMA *finally makes a good strong tear and pulls out the thin blue slice of paper and inspects it closely. The boy and his mother study it raptly over* MAMA's *shoulders.*]

MAMA: Travis! [*She is counting off with doubt.*] Is that the right number of zeros.

TRAVIS: Yes'm . . . ten thousand dollars. Gaalee, Grandmama, you rich.

MAMA: [*She holds the check away from her, still looking at it. Slowly her face sobers into a mask of unhappiness.*] Ten thousand dollars. [*She hands it to* RUTH.] Put it away somewhere, Ruth. [*She does not look at* RUTH; *her eyes seem to be seeing something somewhere very far off.*] Ten thousand dollars they give you. Ten thousand dollars.

TRAVIS: [*To his mother, sincerely.*] What's the matter with Grandmama—don't she want to be rich?

RUTH: [*Distractedly.*] You go on out and play now, baby. [TRAVIS *exits.* MAMA *starts wiping dishes absently, humming intently to herself.* RUTH *turns to her, with kind exasperation.*] You've gone and got yourself upset.

MAMA: [*Not looking at her.*] I spec if it wasn't for you all . . . I would just put that money away or give it to the church or something.

RUTH: Now what kind of talk is that. Mr. Younger would just be plain mad if he could hear you talking foolish like that.

MAMA: [*Stopping and staring off.*] Yes . . . he sure would. [*Sighing.*] We got enough to do with that money, all right. [*She halts then, and turns and looks at her daughter-in-law hard;* RUTH *avoids her eyes and* MAMA *wipes her hands with finality and starts to speak firmly to* RUTH.] Where did you go today, girl?

RUTH: To the doctor.

MAMA: [*Impatiently.*] Now, Ruth . . . you know better than that. Old Doctor Jones is strange enough in his way but there ain't nothing 'bout him make somebody slip and call him "she"—like you done this morning.

RUTH: Well, that's what happened—my tongue slipped.

MAMA: You went to see that woman, didn't you?

RUTH: [*Defensively, giving herself away.*] What woman you talking about?

MAMA: [*Angrily.*] That woman who—

[WALTER *enters in great excitement.*]

WALTER: Did it come?

MAMA: [*Quietly.*] Can't you give people a Christian greeting before you start asking about money?

WALTER: [*To* RUTH.] Did it come? [RUTH *unfolds the check and lays it quietly before him, watching him intently with thoughts of her own.* WALTER *sits down and grasps it close and counts off the zeros.*] Ten thousand dollars— [*He turns suddenly, frantically to his mother and draws some papers out of his breast pocket.*] Mama—look. Old Willy Harris put everything on paper—

MAMA: Son—I think you ought to talk to your wife . . . I'll go on out and leave you alone if you want—

WALTER: I can talk to her later—Mama, look—

MAMA: Son—

WALTER: WILL SOMEBODY PLEASE LISTEN TO ME TODAY!

MAMA: [*Quietly.*] I don't 'low no yellin' in this house, Walter Lee, and you know it— [WALTER *stares at them in frustration and starts to speak several times.*] And there ain't going to be no investing in no liquor stores. I don't aim to have to speak on that again.

[*A long pause.*]

WALTER: Oh—so you don't aim to have to speak on that again? So you have decided . . . [*Crumpling his papers.*] Well, *you* tell that to my boy tonight when you put him to sleep on the living-room couch . . . [*Turning to* MAMA *and speaking directly to her.*] Yeah—and tell it to my wife, Mama, tomorrow when she has to go out of here to look after somebody else's kids. And tell it to *me*, Mama, every time we need a new pair of curtains and I have to watch *you* go out and work in somebody's kitchen. Yeah, you tell me then!

[WALTER *starts out.*]

RUTH: Where you going?

WALTER: I'm going out!

RUTH: Where?

WALTER: Just out of this house somewhere—

RUTH: [*Getting her coat.*] I'll come too.

WALTER: I don't want you to come!

RUTH: I got something to talk to you about, Walter.

WALTER: That's too bad.

MAMA: [*Still quietly.*] Walter Lee— [*She waits and he finally turns and looks at her.*] Sit down.

WALTER: I'm a grown man, Mama.

MAMA: Ain't nobody said you wasn't grown. But you still in my house and my presence. And as long as you are—you'll talk to your wife civil. Now sit down.

RUTH: [*Suddenly.*] Oh, let him go on out and drink himself to death! He makes me sick to my stomach! [*She flings her coat against him.*]

WALTER: [*Violently.*] And you turn mine too, baby! [RUTH *goes into their bedroom and slams the door behind her.*] That was my greatest mistake—

MAMA: [*Still quietly.*] Walter, what is the matter with you?

WALTER: Matter with me? Ain't nothing the matter with *me!*

MAMA: Yes there is. Something eating you up like a crazy man. Something more than me not giving you this money. The past few years I been watching it happen to you. You get all nervous acting and kind of wild in the eyes—[WALTER *jumps up impatiently at her words.*] I said sit there now, I'm talking to you!

WALTER: Mama—I don't need no nagging at me today.

MAMA: Seem like you getting to a place where you always tied up in some kind of knot about something. But if anybody ask you 'bout it you just yell at 'em and bust out the house and go out and drink somewheres. Walter Lee, people can't live with that. Ruth's a good, patient girl in her way—but you getting to be too much. Boy, don't make the mistake of driving that girl away from you.

WALTER: Why—what she do for me?

MAMA: She loves you.

WALTER: Mama—I'm going out. I want to go off somewhere and be by myself for a while.

MAMA: I'm sorry 'bout your liquor store, son. It just wasn't the thing for us to do. That's what I want to tell you about—

WALTER: I got to go out, Mama—

[*He rises.*]

MAMA: It's dangerous, son.

WALTER: What's dangerous?

MAMA: When a man goes outside his home to look for peace.

WALTER: [*Beseechingly.*] Then why can't there never be no peace in this house then?

MAMA: You done found it in some other house?

WALTER: No—there ain't no woman! Why do women always think there's a woman somewhere when a man gets restless. [*Coming to her.*] Mama—Mama—I want so many things . . .

MAMA: Yes, son—

WALTER: I want so many things that they are driving me kind of crazy . . . Mama—look at me.

MAMA: I'm looking at you. You a good-looking boy. You got a job, a nice wife, a fine boy and—

WALTER: A job. [*Looks at her.*] Mama, a job? I open and close car doors all day long. I drive a man around in his limousine and I say, "Yes, sir; no, sir; very good, sir; shall I take the Drive, sir?" Mama, that ain't no kind of job . . . that ain't nothing at all. [*Very quietly.*] Mama, I don't know if I can make you understand.

MAMA: Understand what, baby?

WALTER: [*Quietly.*] Sometimes it's like I can see the future stretched out in front of me—just plain as day. The future, Mama. Hanging over there at the edge of my days. Just waiting for me—a big, looming blank space—full of *nothing*. Just waiting for *me*. [*Pause.*] Mama—sometimes when I'm downtown and I pass them cool, quiet-looking restaurants where them white boys are sitting back and talking 'bout things . . . sitting there turning deals worth millions of dollars . . . sometimes I see guys don't look much older than me—

MAMA: Son—how come you talk so much 'bout money?

WALTER: [*With immense passion.*] Because it is life, Mama!

MAMA: [*Quietly.*] Oh— [*Very quietly.*] So now it's life. Money is life. Once upon a time freedom used to be life—now it's money. I guess the world really do change . . .

WALTER: No—it was always money, Mama. We just didn't know about it.

MAMA: No . . . something has changed. [*She looks at him.*] You something new, boy. In my time we was worried about not being lynched and getting to the North if we could and how to stay alive and still have a pinch of dignity too . . . Now here come you and Beneatha—talking 'bout things we ain't never even thought about hardly, me and your daddy. You ain't satisfied or proud of nothing we done. I mean that you had a home; that we kept you out of trouble till you was grown; that you don't have to ride to work on the back of nobody's streetcar—You my children—but how different we done become.

WALTER: You just don't understand, Mama, you just don't understand.

MAMA: Son—do you know your wife is expecting another baby? [WALTER *stands, stunned, and absorbs what his mother has said.*] That's what she wanted to talk to you about. [WALTER *sinks down into a chair.*] This ain't for me to be telling—but you ought to know. [*She waits.*] I think Ruth is thinking 'bout getting rid of that child.[5]

WALTER: [*Slowly understanding.*] No—no—Ruth wouldn't do that.

MAMA: When the world gets ugly enough—a woman will do anything for her family. *The part that's already living.*

WALTER: You don't know Ruth, Mama, if you think she would do that.

[RUTH *opens the bedroom door and stands there a little limp.*]

RUTH: [*Beaten.*] Yes I would too, Walter. [*Pause.*] I gave her a five-dollar down payment.

[*There is total silence as the man stares at his wife and the mother stares at her son.*]

MAMA: [*Presently.*] Well— [*Tightly.*] Well—son, I'm waiting to hear you say something . . . I'm waiting to hear how you be your father's son. Be the man he was . . . [*Pause.*] Your wife say she going to destroy your child. And I'm waiting to hear you talk like him and say we a people who give children life, not who destroys them— [*She rises.*] I'm waiting to see you stand up and look like your daddy and say we done give up one baby to poverty and that we ain't going to give up nary another one . . . I'm waiting.

WALTER: Ruth—

MAMA: If you a son of mine, tell her! [WALTER *turns, looks at her and can say nothing. She continues, bitterly.*] You . . . you are a disgrace to your father's memory. Somebody get me my hat.

[CURTAIN.]

5. Abortions were illegal and dangerous in the United States prior to the 1973 *Roe v. Wade* Supreme Court decision.

ACT II

Scene One

Time: Later the same day.
At rise: RUTH *is ironing again. She has the radio going. Presently* BENEATHA'S
bedroom door opens and RUTH's *mouth falls and she puts down the iron in*
fascination.

RUTH: What have we got on tonight!

BENEATHA: [*Emerging grandly from the doorway so that we can see her thor-*
oughly robed in the costume ASAGAI *brought.*] You are looking at what a
well-dressed Nigerian woman wears— [*She parades for* RUTH, *her hair*
completely hidden by the headdress; she is coquettishly fanning herself with
*an ornate oriental fan, mistakenly more like Butterfly*⁶ *than any Nigerian*
that ever was.] Isn't it beautiful? [*She promenades to the radio and, with an*
arrogant flourish, turns off the good loud blues that is playing.] Enough of
this assimilationist junk! [RUTH *follows her with her eyes as she goes to the*
phonograph and puts on a record and turns and waits ceremoniously for the
music to come up. Then, with a shout—] OCOMOGOSIAY!

[RUTH *jumps. The music comes up, a lovely Nigerian melody.* BENEATHA
listens, enraptured, her eyes far away—"back to the past." She begins to
dance. RUTH *is dumbfounded.*]

RUTH: What kind of dance is that?
BENEATHA: A folk dance.
RUTH: [*Pearl Bailey.*]⁷ What kind of folks do that, honey?
BENEATHA: It's from Nigeria. It's a dance of welcome.
RUTH: Who you welcoming?
BENEATHA: The men back to the village.
RUTH: Where they been?
BENEATHA: How should I know—out hunting or something. Anyway, they
are coming back now . . .
RUTH: Well, that's good.
BENEATHA: [*With the record.*]

Alundi, alundi
Alundi alunya
Jop pu a jeepua
Ang gu sooooooooooo

6. Madame Butterfly, a Japanese woman married to and then abandoned by an American man
in the opera *Madama Butterfly* (1904), by the Italian composer Giacomo Puccini (1858–1924).
7. That is, in the manner of the popular African American singer and entertainer (1918–90).

Ai yai yae . . .
Ayehaye—alundi . . .

[WALTER *comes in during this performance; he has obviously been drinking. He leans against the door heavily and watches his sister, at first with distaste. Then his eyes look off—"back to the past"—as he lifts both his fists to the roof, screaming.*]

WALTER: YEAH . . . AND ETHIOPIA STRETCH FORTH HER HANDS AGAIN! . . .[8]

RUTH: [*Drily, looking at him.*] Yes—and Africa sure is claiming her own tonight. [*She gives them both up and starts ironing again.*]

WALTER: [*All in a drunken, dramatic shout.*] Shut up! . . . I'm digging them drums . . . them drums move me! . . . [*He makes his weaving way to his wife's face and leans in close to her.*] In my *heart of hearts—* [*He thumps his chest.*] —I am much warrior!

RUTH: [*Without even looking up.*] In your heart of hearts you are much drunkard.

WALTER: [*Coming away from her and starting to wander around the room, shouting.*] Me and Jomo . . . [*Intently, in his sister's face. She has stopped dancing to watch him in this unknown mood.*] That's my man, Kenyatta.[9] [*Shouting and thumping his chest.*] FLAMING SPEAR! HOT DAMN! [*He is suddenly in possession of an imaginary spear and actively spearing enemies all over the room.*] OCOMOGOSIAY . . . THE LION IS WAKING . . . OWIMOWEH! [*He pulls his shirt open and leaps up on a table and gestures with his spear. The bell rings.* RUTH *goes to answer.*]

BENEATHA: [*To encourage* WALTER, *thoroughly caught up with this side of him.*] OCOMOGOSIAY, FLAMING SPEAR!

WALTER: [*On the table, very far gone, his eyes pure glass sheets. He sees what we cannot, that he is a leader of his people, a great chief, a descendant of Chaka,[1] and that the hour to march has come.*] Listen, my black brothers—

BENEATHA: OCOMOGOSIAY!

WALTER: —Do you hear the waters rushing against the shores of the coastlands—

BENEATHA: OCOMOGOSIAY!

8. See Psalms 68.31: "Princes shall come out of Egypt; Ethiopia shall soon stretch out her hands unto God."
9. Jomo Kenyatta (1893–1978), African political leader and first president of Kenya (1964–78) following its independence from British colonial rule.
1. Zulu chief (1786–1828), also known as "Shaka" and called "The Black Napoleon" for his strategic and organizational genius.

WALTER: —Do you hear the screeching of the cocks in yonder hills beyond where the chiefs meet in council for the coming of the mighty war—

BENEATHA: OCOMOGOSIAY!

WALTER: —Do you hear the beating of the wings of the birds flying low over the mountains and the low places of our land—

[RUTH *opens the door.* GEORGE MURCHISON *enters.*]

BENEATHA: OCOMOGOSIAY!

WALTER: —Do you hear the singing of the women, singing the war songs of our fathers to the babies in the great houses . . . singing the sweet war songs? OH, DO YOU HEAR, MY BLACK BROTHERS!

BENEATHA: [*Completely gone.*] We hear you, Flaming Spear—

WALTER: Telling us to prepare for the greatness of the time— [*To* GEORGE.] Black Brother!

[*He extends his hand for the fraternal clasp.*]

GEORGE: Black Brother, hell!

RUTH: [*Having had enough, and embarrassed for the family.*] Beneatha, you got company—what's the matter with you? Walter Lee Younger, get down off that table and stop acting like a fool . . .

[WALTER *comes down off the table suddenly and makes a quick exit to the bathroom.*]

RUTH: He's had a little to drink . . . I don't know what her excuse is.

GEORGE: [*To* BENEATHA.] Look honey, we're going *to* the theatre—we're not going to be *in* it . . . so go change, huh?

RUTH: You expect this boy to go out with you looking like that?

BENEATHA: [*Looking at* GEORGE.] That's up to George. If he's ashamed of his heritage—

GEORGE: Oh, don't be so proud of yourself, Bennie—just because you look eccentric.

BENEATHA: How can something that's natural be eccentric?

GEORGE: That's what being eccentric means—being natural. Get dressed.

BENEATHA: I don't like that, George.

RUTH: Why must you and your brother make an argument out of everything people say?

BENEATHA: Because I hate assimilationist Negroes!

RUTH: Will somebody please tell me what assimila-who-ever means!

GEORGE: Oh, it's just a college girl's way of calling people Uncle Toms—but that isn't what it means at all.

RUTH: Well, what does it mean?

BENEATHA: [*Cutting* GEORGE *off and staring at him as she replies to* RUTH.] It means someone who is willing to give up his own culture and submerge himself completely in the dominant, and in this case, *oppressive* culture!

GEORGE: Oh, dear, dear, dear! Here we go! A lecture on the African past! On our Great West African Heritage! In one second we will hear all about the great Ashanti empires; the great Songhay civilizations; and the great sculpture of Bénin—and then some poetry in the Bantu— and the whole monologue will end with the word *heritage!* [*Nastily.*] Let's face it, baby, your heritage is nothing but a bunch of raggedy-assed spirituals and some grass huts!

BENEATHA: *Grass huts!* [RUTH *crosses to her and forcibly pushes her toward the bedroom.*] See there . . . you are standing there in your splendid ignorance talking about people who were the first to smelt iron on the face of the earth! [RUTH *is pushing her through the door.*] The Ashanti were performing surgical operations when the English— [RUTH *pulls the door to, with* BENEATHA *on the other side, and smiles graciously at* GEORGE. BENEATHA *opens the door and shouts the end of the sentence defiantly at* GEORGE.] —were still tattooing themselves with blue dragons . . . [*She goes back inside.*]

RUTH: Have a seat, George. [*They both sit.* RUTH *folds her hands rather primly on her lap, determined to demonstrate the civilization of the family.*] Warm, ain't it? I mean for September. [*Pause.*] Just like they always say about Chicago weather: If it's too hot or cold for you, just wait a minute and it'll change. [*She smiles happily at this cliché of clichés.*] Everybody say it's got to do with them bombs and things they keep setting off.[2] [*Pause.*] Would you like a nice cold beer?

GEORGE: No, thank you. I don't care for beer. [*He looks at his watch.*] I hope she hurries up.

RUTH: What time is the show?

GEORGE: It's an eight-thirty curtain. That's just Chicago, though. In New York standard curtain time is eight forty.

[*He is rather proud of this knowledge.*]

RUTH: [*Properly appreciating it.*] You get to New York a lot?

GEORGE: [*Offhand.*] Few times a year.

RUTH: Oh—that's nice. I've never been to New York.

[WALTER *enters. We feel he has relieved himself, but the edge of unreality is still with him.*]

---

2. In the 1950s, people commonly blamed weather fluctuations on atomic testing.

WALTER: New York ain't got nothing Chicago ain't. Just a bunch of hustling people all squeezed up together—being "Eastern."

[*He turns his face into a screw of displeasure.*]

GEORGE: Oh—you've been?

WALTER: *Plenty* of times.

RUTH: [*Shocked at the lie.*] Walter Lee Younger!

WALTER: [*Staring her down.*] Plenty! [*Pause.*] What we got to drink in this house? Why don't you offer this man some refreshment. [*To* GEORGE.] They don't know how to entertain people in this house, man.

GEORGE: Thank you—I don't really care for anything.

WALTER: [*Feeling his head; sobriety coming.*] Where's Mama?

RUTH: She ain't come back yet.

WALTER: [*Looking* MURCHISON *over from head to toe, scrutinizing his carefully casual tweed sports jacket over cashmere V-neck sweater over soft eyelet shirt and tie, and soft slacks, finished off with white buckskin shoes.*] Why all you college boys wear them fairyish-looking white shoes?

RUTH: Walter Lee!

[GEORGE MURCHISON *ignores the remark.*]

WALTER: [*To* RUTH.] Well, they look crazy as hell—white shoes, cold as it is.

RUTH: [*Crushed.*] You have to excuse him—

WALTER: No he don't! Excuse me for what? What you always excusing me for! I'll excuse myself when I needs to be excused! [*A pause.*] They look as funny as them black knee socks Beneatha wears out of here all the time.

RUTH: It's the college *style*, Walter.

WALTER: Style, hell, She looks like she got burnt legs or something!

RUTH: Oh, Walter—

WALTER: [*An irritable mimic.*] Oh, Walter! Oh, Walter! [*To* MURCHISON.] How's your old man making out? I understand you all going to buy that big hotel on the Drive?[3] [*He finds a beer in the refrigerator, wanders over to* MURCHISON, *sipping and wiping his lips with the back of his hand, and straddling a chair backwards to talk to the other man.*] Shrewd move. Your old man is all right, man. [*Tapping his head and half winking for emphasis.*] I mean he knows how to operate. I mean he thinks *big*, you know what I mean, I mean for a *home*, you know? But I think he's kind of running out of ideas now. I'd like to talk to him. Listen, man, I got

---

3. Lake Shore Drive, a scenic thoroughfare along Lake Michigan.

some plans that could turn this city upside down. I mean I think like he does. *Big.* Invest big, gamble big, hell, lose *big* if you have to, you know what I mean. It's hard to find a man on this whole Southside who understands my kind of thinking—you dig? [*He scrutinizes* MURCHISON *again, drinks his beer, squints his eyes and leans in close, confidential, man to man.*] Me and you ought to sit down and talk sometimes, man. Man, I got me some ideas . . .

GEORGE: [*With boredom.*] Yeah—sometimes we'll have to do that, Walter.

WALTER: [*Understanding the indifference, and offended.*] Yeah—well, when you get the time, man. I know you a busy little boy.

RUTH: Walter, please—

WALTER: [*Bitterly, hurt.*] I know ain't nothing in this world as busy as you colored college boys with your fraternity pins and white shoes . . .

RUTH: [*Covering her face with humiliation.*] Oh, Walter Lee—

WALTER: I see you all the time—with the books tucked under your arms—going to your [*British A—a mimic.*] "clahsses." And for what! What the hell you learning over there? Filling up your heads— [*Counting off on his fingers.*] —with the sociology and the psychology—but they teaching you how to be a man? How to take over and run the world? They teaching you how to run a rubber plantation or a steel mill? Naw—just to talk proper and read books and wear white shoes . . .

GEORGE: [*Looking at him with distaste, a little above it all.*] You're all wacked up with bitterness, man.

WALTER: [*Intently, almost quietly, between the teeth, glaring at the boy.*] And you—ain't you bitter, man? Ain't you just about had it yet? Don't you see no stars gleaming that you can't reach out and grab? You happy?—You contented son-of-a-bitch—you happy? You got it made? Bitter? Man, I'm a volcano. Bitter? Here I am a giant—surrounded by ants! Ants who can't even understand what it is the giant is talking about.

RUTH: [*Passionately and suddenly.*] Oh, Walter—ain't you with nobody!

WALTER: [*Violently.*] No! 'Cause ain't nobody with me! Not even my own mother!

RUTH: Walter, that's a terrible thing to say!

[BENEATHA *enters, dressed for the evening in a cocktail dress and earrings.*]

GEORGE: Well—hey, you look great.

BENEATHA: Let's go, George. See you all later.

RUTH: Have a nice time.

GEORGE: Thanks. Good night. [*To* WALTER, *sarcastically.*] Good night, Prometheus.[4]

    [BENEATHA *and* GEORGE *exit.*]

WALTER: [*To* RUTH.] Who is Prometheus?

RUTH: I don't know. Don't worry about it.

WALTER: [*In fury, pointing after* GEORGE.] See there—they get to a point where they can't insult you man to man—they got to go talk about something ain't nobody never heard of!

RUTH: How do you know it was an insult? [*To humor him.*] Maybe Prometheus is a nice fellow.

WALTER: Prometheus! I bet there ain't even no such thing! I bet that simple-minded clown—

RUTH: Walter—

    [*She stops what she is doing and looks at him.*]

WALTER: [*Yelling.*] Don't start!

RUTH: Start what?

WALTER: Your nagging! Where was I? Who was I with? How much money did I spend?

RUTH: [*Plaintively.*] Walter Lee—why don't we just try to talk about it . . .

WALTER: [*Not listening.*] I been out talking with people who understand me. People who care about the things I got on my mind.

RUTH: [*Wearily.*] I guess that means people like Willy Harris.

WALTER: Yes, people like Willy Harris.

RUTH: [*With a sudden flash of impatience.*] Why don't you all just hurry up and go into the banking business and stop talking about it!

WALTER: Why? You want to know why? 'Cause we all tied up in a race of people that don't know how to do nothing but moan, pray and have babies!

    [*The line is too bitter even for him and he looks at her and sits down.*]

RUTH: Oh, Walter . . . [*Softly.*] Honey, why can't you stop fighting me?

WALTER: [*Without thinking.*] Who's fighting you? Who even cares about you?

    [*This line begins the retardation of his mood.*]

RUTH: Well— [*She waits a long time, and then with resignation starts to put away her things.*] I guess I might as well go on to bed . . . [*More or less to*

---

4. In Greek mythology, Prometheus represented the bold creative spirit; defying the gods, he stole fire from Olympus (the locale of the gods) and gave it to humankind. Though successful, he was harshly punished by Zeus.

herself.] I don't know where we lost it . . . but we have . . . [*Then, to him.*]
I—I'm sorry about this new baby, Walter. I guess maybe I better go on
and do what I started . . . I guess I just didn't realize how bad things was
with us . . . I guess I just didn't really realize— [*She starts out to the bedroom and stops.*] You want some hot milk?

WALTER: Hot milk?

RUTH: Yes—hot milk.

WALTER: Why hot milk?

RUTH: 'Cause after all that liquor you come home with you ought to have
something hot in your stomach.

WALTER: I don't want no milk.

RUTH: You want some coffee then?

WALTER: No, I don't want no coffee. I don't want nothing hot to drink.
[*Almost plaintively.*] Why you always trying to give me something to
eat?

RUTH: [*Standing and looking at him helplessly.*] What else can I give you,
Walter Lee Younger?

[*She stands and looks at him and presently turns to go out again. He lifts
his head and watches her going away from him in a new mood which
began to emerge when he asked her "Who cares about you?"*]

WALTER: It's been rough, ain't it, baby? [*She hears and stops but does not turn
around and he continues to her back.*] I guess between two people there
ain't never as much understood as folks generally thinks there is. I mean
like between me and you— [*She turns to face him.*] How we gets to the
place where we scared to talk softness to each other. [*He waits, thinking
hard himself.*] Why you think it got to be like that? [*He is thoughtful,
almost as a child would be.*] Ruth, what is it gets into people ought to be
close?

RUTH: I don't know, honey. I think about it a lot.

WALTER: On account of you and me, you mean? The way things are with
us. The way something done come down between us.

RUTH: There ain't so much between us, Walter . . . Not when you come to
me and try to talk to me. Try to be with me . . . a little even.

WALTER: [*Total honesty.*] Sometimes . . . sometimes . . . I don't even know
how to try.

RUTH: Walter—

WALTER: Yes?

RUTH: [*Coming to him, gently and with misgiving, but coming to him.*]
Honey . . . life don't have to be like this. I mean sometimes people can
do things so that things are better . . . You remember how we used to
talk when Travis was born . . . about the way we were going to live . . .

the kind of house . . . [*She is stroking his head.*] Well, it's all starting to slip away from us . . .

[MAMA *enters, and* WALTER *jumps up and shouts at her.*]

WALTER: Mama, where have you been?

MAMA: My—them steps is longer than they used to be. Whew! [*She sits down and ignores him.*] How you feeling this evening, Ruth?

[RUTH *shrugs, disturbed some at having been prematurely interrupted and watching her husband knowingly.*]

WALTER: Mama, where have you been all day?

MAMA: [*Still ignoring him and leaning on the table and changing to more comfortable shoes.*] Where's Travis?

RUTH: I let him go out earlier and he ain't come back yet. Boy, is he going to get it!

WALTER: Mama!

MAMA: [*As if she has heard him for the first time.*] Yes, son?

WALTER: Where did you go this afternoon?

MAMA: I went downtown to tend to some business that I had to tend to.

WALTER: What kind of business?

MAMA: You know better than to question me like a child, Brother.

WALTER: [*Rising and bending over the table.*] Where were you, Mama? [*Bringing his fists down and shouting.*] Mama, you didn't go do something with that insurance money, something crazy?

[*The front door opens slowly, interrupting him, and* TRAVIS *peeks his head in, less than hopefully.*]

TRAVIS: [*To his mother.*] Mama, I—

RUTH: "Mama I" nothing! You're going to get it, boy! Get on in that bedroom and get yourself ready!

TRAVIS: But I—

MAMA: Why don't you all never let the child explain hisself.

RUTH: Keep out of it now, Lena.

[MAMA *clamps her lips together, and* RUTH *advances toward her son menacingly.*]

RUTH: A thousand times I have told you not to go off like that—

MAMA: [*Holding out her arms to her grandson.*] Well—at least let me tell him something. I want him to be the first one to hear . . . Come here, Travis. [*The boy obeys, gladly.*] Travis— [*She takes him by the shoulder and looks into his face.*] —you know that money we got in the mail this morning?

TRAVIS: Yes'm—

MAMA: Well—what you think your grandmama gone and done with that money?

TRAVIS: I don't know, Grandmama.

MAMA: [*Putting her finger on his nose for emphasis.*] She went out and she bought you a house! [*The explosion comes from* WALTER *at the end of the revelation and he jumps up and turns away from all of them in a fury.* MAMA *continues, to* TRAVIS.] You glad about the house? It's going to be yours when you get to be a man.

TRAVIS: Yeah—I always wanted to live in a house.

MAMA: All right, gimme some sugar then— [TRAVIS *puts his arms around her neck as she watches her son over the boy's shoulder. Then, to* TRAVIS, *after the embrace.*] Now when you say your prayers tonight, you thank God and your grandfather—'cause it was him who give you the house—in his way.

RUTH: [*Taking the boy from* MAMA *and pushing him toward the bedroom.*] Now you get out of here and get ready for your beating.

TRAVIS: Aw, Mama—

RUTH: Get on in there— [*Closing the door behind him and turning radiantly to her mother-in-law.*] So you went and did it!

MAMA: [*Quietly, looking at her son with pain.*] Yes, I did.

RUTH: [*Raising both arms classically.*] Praise God! [*Looks at* WALTER *a moment, who says nothing. She crosses rapidly to her husband.*] Please, honey—let me be glad . . . you be glad too. [*She has laid her hands on his shoulders, but he shakes himself free of her roughly, without turning to face her.*] Oh, Walter . . . a home . . . a home. [*She comes back to* MAMA.] Well—where is it? How big is it? How much it going to cost?

MAMA: Well—

RUTH: When we moving?

MAMA: [*Smiling at her.*] First of the month.

RUTH: [*Throwing back her head with jubilance.*] Praise God!

MAMA: [*Tentatively, still looking at her son's back turned against her and* RUTH.] It's—it's a nice house too . . . [*She cannot help speaking directly to him. An imploring quality in her voice, her manner, makes her almost like a girl now.*] Three bedrooms—nice big one for you and Ruth . . . Me and Beneatha still have to share our room, but Travis have one of his own—and [*With difficulty.*] I figure if the—new baby—is a boy, we could get one of them double-decker outfits . . . And there's a yard with a little patch of dirt where I could maybe get to grow me a few flowers . . . And a nice big basement . . .

RUTH: Walter honey, be glad—

MAMA: [*Still to his back, fingering things on the table.*] 'Course I don't want to make it sound fancier than it is . . . It's just a plain little old house—but it's made good and solid—and it will be *ours*. Walter Lee—it makes a difference in a man when he can walk on floors that belong to *him* . . .

RUTH: Where is it?

MAMA: [*Frightened at this telling.*] Well—well—it's out there in Clybourne Park[5]—

> [RUTH's *radiance fades abruptly, and* WALTER *finally turns slowly to face his mother with incredulity and hostility.*]

RUTH: Where?

MAMA: [*Matter-of-factly.*] Four o six Clybourne Street, Clybourne Park.

RUTH: Clybourne Park? Mama, there ain't no colored people living in Clybourne Park.

MAMA: [*Almost idiotically.*] Well, I guess there's going to be some now.

WALTER: [*Bitterly.*] So that's the peace and comfort you went out and bought for us today!

MAMA: [*Raising her eyes to meet his finally.*] Son—I just tried to find the nicest place for the least amount of money for my family.

RUTH: [*Trying to recover from the shock.*] Well—well—'course I ain't one never been 'fraid of no crackers[6] mind you—but—well, wasn't there no other houses nowhere?

MAMA: Them houses they put up for colored in them areas way out all seem to cost twice as much as other houses. I did the best I could.

RUTH: [*Struck senseless with the news, in its various degrees of goodness and trouble, she sits a moment, her fists propping her chin in thought, and then she starts to rise, bringing her fists down with vigor, the radiance spreading from cheek to cheek again.*] Well—well!—All I can say is—if this is my time in life—*my time*—to say good-bye— [*And she builds with momentum as she starts to circle the room with an exuberant, almost tearfully happy release.*] —to these Goddamned cracking walls!— [*She pounds the walls.*] —and these marching roaches!— [*She wipes at an imaginary army of marching roaches.*] —and this cramped little closet which ain't now or never was no kitchen!* . . . then I say it loud and good, *Hallelujah! and good-bye misery . . . I don't never want to see your ugly face again!* [*She laughs joyously, having practically destroyed the apartment, and flings her arms up and lets them come down happily, slowly, reflectively, over her abdomen, aware for the first time perhaps that the life therein pulses with happiness and not despair.*] Lena?

MAMA: [*Moved, watching her happiness.*] Yes, honey?

RUTH: [*Looking off.*] Is there—is there a whole lot of sunlight?

---

5. On Chicago's Near North Side.
6. Derogatory term for poor whites.

MAMA: [*Understanding.*] Yes, child, there's a whole lot of sunlight.

[*Long pause.*]

RUTH: [*Collecting herself and going to the door of the room* TRAVIS *is in.*] Well—I guess I better see 'bout Travis. [*To* MAMA.] Lord, I sure don't feel like whipping nobody today!

[*She exits.*]

MAMA: [*The mother and son are left alone now and the mother waits a long time, considering deeply, before she speaks.*] Son—you—you understand what I done, don't you? [WALTER *is silent and sullen.*] I—I just seen my family falling apart today . . . just falling to pieces in front of my eyes . . . We couldn't of gone on like we was today. We was going backwards 'stead of forwards—talking 'bout killing babies and wishing each other was dead . . . When it gets like that in life—you just got to do something different, push on out and do something bigger . . . [*She waits.*] I wish you say something, son . . . I wish you'd say how deep inside you you think I done the right thing—

WALTER: [*Crossing slowly to his bedroom door and finally turning there and speaking measuredly.*] What you need me to say you done right for? *You* the head of this family. You run our lives like you want to. It was your money and you did what you wanted with it. So what you need for me to say it was all right for? [*Bitterly, to hurt her as deeply as he knows is possible.*] So you butchered up a dream of mine—you—who always talking 'bout your children's dreams . . .

MAMA: Walter Lee—

[*He just closes the door behind him.* MAMA *sits alone, thinking heavily.*]

[CURTAIN.]

Scene Two

Time: Friday night. A few weeks later.

At rise: Packing crates mark the intention of the family to move. BENEATHA *and* GEORGE *come in, presumably from an evening out again.*

GEORGE: O.K. . . . O.K., whatever you say . . . [*They both sit on the couch. He tries to kiss her. She moves away.*] Look, we've had a nice evening; let's not spoil it, huh? . . .

[*He again turns her head and tries to nuzzle in and she turns away from him, not with distaste but with momentary lack of interest; in a mood to pursue what they were talking about.*]

BENEATHA: I'm *trying* to talk to you.
GEORGE: We always talk.
BENEATHA: Yes—and I love to talk.
GEORGE: [*Exasperated; rising.*] I know it and I don't mind it sometimes . . .
I want you to cut it out, see—The moody stuff, I mean. I don't like it.
You're a nice-looking girl . . . all over. That's all you need, honey, forget
the atmosphere. Guys aren't going to go for the atmosphere—they're
going to go for what they see. Be glad for that. Drop the Garbo[7] routine.
It doesn't go with you. As for myself, I want a nice— [*Groping.*] —simple
[*Thoughtfully.*] —sophisticated girl . . . not a poet— O.K.?

[*She rebuffs him again and he starts to leave.*]

BENEATHA: Why are you angry?
GEORGE: Because this is stupid! I don't go out with you to discuss the nature
of "quiet desperation"[8] or to hear all about your thoughts—because the
world will go on thinking what it thinks regardless—
BENEATHA: Then why read books? Why go to school?
GEORGE: [*With artificial patience, counting on his fingers.*] It's simple. You
read books—to learn facts—to get grades—to pass the course—to get
a degree. That's all—it has nothing to do with thoughts.

[*A long pause.*]

BENEATHA: I see. [*A longer pause as she looks at him.*] Good night, George.

[GEORGE *looks at her a little oddly, and starts to exit. He meets* MAMA
coming in.]

GEORGE: Oh—hello, Mrs. Younger.
MAMA: Hello, George, how you feeling?
GEORGE: Fine—fine, how are you?
MAMA: Oh, a little tired. You know them steps can get you after a day's
work. You all have a nice time tonight?
GEORGE: Yes—a fine time. Well, good night.
MAMA: Good night. [*He exits.* MAMA *closes the door behind her.*] Hello,
honey. What you sitting like that for?
BENEATHA: I'm just sitting.
MAMA: Didn't you have a nice time?
BENEATHA: No.

---

7. Greta Garbo (1905–90), Swedish-born American film star whose sultry, remote, and European femininity was widely imitated.
8. In *Walden* (1854), Henry Thoreau asserts that "the mass of men lead lives of quiet desperation."

MAMA: No? What's the matter?

BENEATHA: Mama, George is a fool—honest. [*She rises.*]

MAMA: [*Hustling around unloading the packages she has entered with. She stops.*] Is he, baby?

BENEATHA: Yes.

[BENEATHA *makes up* TRAVIS' *bed as she talks.*]

MAMA: You sure?

BENEATHA: Yes.

MAMA: Well—I guess you better not waste your time with no fools.

[BENEATHA *looks up at her mother, watching her put groceries in the refrigerator. Finally she gathers up her things and starts into the bedroom. At the door she stops and looks back at her mother.*]

BENEATHA: Mama—

MAMA: Yes, baby—

BENEATHA: Thank you.

MAMA: For what?

BENEATHA: For understanding me this time.

[*She exits quickly and the mother stands, smiling a little, looking at the place where* BENEATHA *just stood.* RUTH *enters.*]

RUTH: Now don't you fool with any of this stuff, Lena—

MAMA: Oh, I just thought I'd sort a few things out.

[*The phone rings.* RUTH *answers.*]

RUTH: [*At the phone.*] Hello—Just a minute. [*Goes to door.*] Walter, it's Mrs. Arnold. [*Waits. Goes back to the phone. Tense.*] Hello. Yes, this is his wife speaking . . . He's lying down now. Yes . . . well, he'll be in tomorrow. He's been very sick. Yes—I know we should have called, but we were so sure he'd be able to come in today. Yes—yes, I'm very sorry. Yes . . . Thank you very much. [*She hangs up.* WALTER *is standing in the doorway of the bedroom behind her.*] That was Mrs. Arnold.

WALTER: [*Indifferently.*] Was it?

RUTH: She said if you don't come in tomorrow that they are getting a new man . . .

WALTER: Ain't that sad—ain't that crying sad.

RUTH: She said Mr. Arnold has had to take a cab for three days . . . Walter, you ain't been to work for three days! [*This is a revelation to her.*] Where you been, Walter Lee Younger? [WALTER *looks at her and starts to laugh.*] You're going to lose your job.

WALTER: That's right . . .

RUTH: Oh, Walter, and with your mother working like a dog every day—

WALTER: That's sad too—Everything is sad.

MAMA: What you been doing for these three days, son?

WALTER: Mama—you don't know all the things a man what got leisure can find to do in this city . . . What's this—Friday night? Well—Wednesday I borrowed Willy Harris' car and I went for a drive . . . just me and myself and I drove and drove . . . Way out . . . way past South Chicago, and I parked the car and I sat and looked at the steel mills all day long. I just sat in the car and looked at them big black chimneys for hours. Then I drove back and I went to the Green Hat. [*Pause.*] And Thursday— Thursday I borrowed the car again and I got in it and I pointed it the other way and I drove the other way—for hours—way, way up to Wisconsin, and I looked at the farms. I just drove and looked at the farms. Then I drove back and I went to the Green Hat. [*Pause.*] And today— today I didn't get the car. Today I just walked. All over the Southside. And I looked at the Negroes and they looked at me and finally I just sat down on the curb at Thirty-ninth and South Parkway and I just sat there and watched the Negroes go by. And then I went to the Green Hat. You all sad? You all depressed? And you know where I am going right now—

[RUTH *goes out quietly.*]

MAMA: Oh, Big Walter, is this the harvest of our days?

WALTER: You know what I like about the Green Hat? [*He turns the radio on and a steamy, deep blues pours into the room.*] I like this little cat they got there who blows a sax . . . He blows. He talks to me. He ain't but 'bout five feet tall and he's got a conked head[9] and his eyes is always closed and he's all music—

MAMA: [*Rising and getting some papers out of her handbag.*] Walter—

WALTER: And there's this other guy who plays the piano . . . and they got a sound. I mean they can work on some music . . . They got the best little combo in the world in the Green Hat . . . You can just sit there and drink and listen to them three men play and you realize that don't nothing matter worth a damn, but just being there—

MAMA: I've helped do it to you, haven't I, son? Walter, I been wrong.

WALTER: Naw—you ain't never been wrong about nothing, Mama.

MAMA: Listen to me, now. I say I been wrong, son. That I been doing to you what the rest of the world been doing to you. [*She stops and he looks up slowly at her and she meets his eyes pleadingly.*] Walter—what you ain't never understood is that I ain't got nothing, don't own nothing, ain't never really wanted nothing that wasn't for you. There ain't noth-

9. Straightened hair.

ing as precious to me . . . . There ain't nothing worth holding on to, money, dreams, nothing else—if it means—if it means it's going to destroy my boy. [*She puts her papers in front of him and he watches her without speaking or moving.*] I paid the man thirty-five hundred dollars down on the house. That leaves sixty-five hundred dollars. Monday morning I want you to take this money and take three thousand dollars and put it in a savings account for Beneatha's medical schooling. The rest you put in a checking account—with your name on it. And from now on any penny that come out of it or that go in it is for you to look after. For you to decide. [*She drops her hands a little helplessly.*] It ain't much, but it's all I got in the world and I'm putting it in your hands. I'm telling you to be the head of this family from now on like you supposed to be.

WALTER: [*Stares at the money.*] You trust me like that, Mama?

MAMA: I ain't never stop trusting you. Like I ain't never stop loving you.

[*She goes out, and* WALTER *sits looking at the money on the table as the music continues in its idiom, pulsing in the room. Finally, in a decisive gesture, he gets up, and, in mingled joy and desperation, picks up the money. At the same moment,* TRAVIS *enters for bed.*]

TRAVIS: What's the matter, Daddy? You drunk?

WALTER: [*Sweetly, more sweetly than we have ever known him.*] No, Daddy ain't drunk. Daddy ain't going to never be drunk again. . . .

TRAVIS: Well, good night, Daddy.

[*The father has come from behind the couch and leans over, embracing his son.*]

WALTER: Son, I feel like talking to you tonight.

TRAVIS: About what?

WALTER: Oh, about a lot of things. About you and what kind of man you going to be when you grow up . . . Son—son, what do you want to be when you grow up?

TRAVIS: A bus driver.

WALTER: [*Laughing a little.*] A what? Man, that ain't nothing to want to be!

TRAVIS: Why not?

WALTER: 'Cause, man—it ain't big enough—you know what I mean.

TRAVIS: I don't know then. I can't make up my mind. Sometimes Mama asks me that too. And sometimes when I tell her I just want to be like you—she says she don't want me to be like that and sometimes she says she does . . .

WALTER: [*Gathering him up in his arms.*] You know what, Travis? In seven years you going to be seventeen years old. And things is going to be very different with us in seven years, Travis . . . One day when you are seventeen I'll come home—home from my office downtown somewhere—

TRAVIS: You don't work in no office, Daddy.

WALTER: No—but after tonight. After what your daddy gonna do tonight, there's going to be offices—a whole lot of offices . . .

TRAVIS: What you gonna do tonight, Daddy?

WALTER: You wouldn't understand yet, son, but your daddy's gonna make a transaction . . . a business transaction that's going to change our lives . . . That's how come one day when you 'bout seventeen years old I'll come home and I'll be pretty tired, you know what I mean, after a day of conferences and secretaries getting things wrong the way they do . . .'cause an executive's life is hell, man— [*The more he talks the farther away he gets.*] And I'll pull the car up on the driveway . . . just a plain black Chrysler, I think, with white walls—no—black tires. More elegant. Rich people don't have to be flashy . . . though I'll have to get something a little sportier for Ruth—maybe a Cadillac convertible to do her shopping in . . . And I'll come up the steps to the house and the gardener will be clipping away at the hedges and he'll say, "Good evening, Mr. Younger." And I'll say, "Hello, Jefferson, how are you this evening?" And I'll go inside and Ruth will come downstairs and meet me at the door and we'll kiss each other and she'll take my arm and we'll go up to your room to see you sitting on the floor with the catalogues of all the great schools in America around you . . . All the great schools in the world. And—and I'll say, all right son—it's your seventeenth birthday, what is it you've decided? . . . Just tell me where you want to go to school and you'll *go.* Just tell me, what it is you want to be—and you'll *be* it . . . Whatever you want to be—Yessir! [*He holds his arms open for* TRAVIS.] You just name it, son . . . [TRAVIS *leaps into them.*] and I hand you the world!

[WALTER'S *voice has risen in pitch and hysterical promise and on the last line he lifts* TRAVIS *high.*]

[BLACKOUT.]

Scene Three

Time: Saturday, moving day, one week later.

Before the curtain rises, RUTH'S *voice, a strident, dramatic church alto, cuts through the silence.*

It is, in the darkness, a triumphant surge, a penetrating statement of expectation: "Oh, Lord, I don't feel no ways tired! Children, oh, glory hallelujah!"

As the curtain rises we see that RUTH *is alone in the living room, finishing up the family's packing. It is moving day. She is nailing crates and tying car-*

tons. BENEATHA *enters, carrying a guitar case, and watches her exuberant sister-in-law.*

RUTH: Hey!

BENEATHA: [*Putting away the case.*] Hi.

RUTH: [*Pointing at a package.*] Honey—look in that package there and see what I found on sale this morning at the South Center. [RUTH *gets up and moves to the package and draws out some curtains.*] Lookahere—hand-turned hems!

BENEATHA: How do you know the window size out there?

RUTH: [*Who hadn't thought of that.*] Oh—Well, they bound to fit something in the whole house. Anyhow, they was too good a bargain to pass up. [RUTH *slaps her head, suddenly remembering something.*] Oh, Bennie—I meant to put a special note on that carton over there. That's your mama's good china and she wants 'em to be very careful with it.

BENEATHA: I'll do it.

[BENEATHA *finds a piece of paper and starts to draw large letters on it.*]

RUTH: You know what I'm going to do soon as I get in that new house?

BENEATHA: What?

RUTH: Honey—I'm going to run me a tub of water up to here . . . [*With her fingers practically up to her nostrils.*] And I'm going to get in it—and I am going to sit . . . and sit . . . and sit in that hot water and the first person who knocks to tell *me* to hurry up and come out—

BENEATHA: Gets shot at sunrise.

RUTH: [*Laughing happily.*] You said it, sister! [*Noticing how large* BENEATHA *is absentmindedly making the note.*] Honey, they ain't going to read that from no airplane.

BENEATHA: [*Laughing herself.*] I guess I always think things have more emphasis if they are big, somehow.

RUTH: [*Looking up at her and smiling.*] You and your brother seem to have that as a philosophy of life. Lord, that man—done changed so 'round here. You know—you know what we did last night? Me and Walter Lee?

BENEATHA: What?

RUTH: [*Smiling to herself.*] We went to the movies. [*Looking at* BENEATHA *to see if she understands.*] We went to the movies. You know the last time me and Walter went to the movies together?

BENEATHA: No.

RUTH: Me neither. That's how long it been. [*Smiling again.*] But we went last night. The picture wasn't much good, but that didn't seem to matter. We went—and we held hands.

BENEATHA: Oh, Lord!

RUTH: We held hands—and you know what?

BENEATHA: What?

RUTH: When we come out of the show it was late and dark and all the stores and things was closed up . . . and it was kind of chilly and there wasn't many people on the streets . . . and we was still holding hands, me and Walter.

BENEATHA: You're killing me.

[WALTER *enters with a large package. His happiness is deep in him; he cannot keep still with his new-found exuberance. He is singing and wiggling and snapping his fingers. He puts his package in a corner and puts a phonograph record, which he has brought in with him, on the record player. As the music comes up he dances over to* RUTH *and tries to get her to dance with him. She gives in at last to his raunchiness and in a fit of giggling allows herself to be drawn into his mood and together they deliberately burlesque an old social dance of their youth.*]

BENEATHA: [*Regarding them a long time as they dance, then drawing in her breath for a deeply exaggerated comment which she does not particularly mean.*] Talk about—olddddddddddd-fashionedddddddd—Negroes!

WALTER: [*Stopping momentarily.*] What kind of Negroes?

[*He says this in fun. He is not angry with her today, nor with anyone. He starts to dance with his wife again.*]

BENEATHA: Old-fashioned.

WALTER: [*As he dances with* RUTH.] You know, when these *New Negroes* have their convention— [*Pointing at his sister.*] —that is going to be the chairman of the Committee on Unending Agitation. [*He goes on dancing, then stops.*] Race, race, race! . . . Girl, I do believe you are the first person in the history of the entire human race to successfully brainwash yourself. [BENEATHA *breaks up and he goes on dancing. He stops again, enjoying his tease.*] Damn, even the N double A C P[1] takes a holiday sometimes! [BENEATHA *and* RUTH *laugh. He dances with* RUTH *some more and starts to laugh and stops and pantomimes someone over an operating table.*] I can just see that chick someday looking down at some poor cat on an operating table before she starts to slice him, saying . . . [*Pulling his sleeves back maliciously.*] "By the way, what are your views on civil rights down there? . . ."

[*He laughs at her again and starts to dance happily. The bell sounds.*]

---

1. National Association for the Advancement of Colored People, civil rights organization founded in 1909.

BENEATHA: Sticks and stones may break my bones but . . . words will never hurt me!

[BENEATHA *goes to the door and opens it as* WALTER *and* RUTH *go on with the clowning.* BENEATHA *is somewhat surprised to see a quiet-looking middle-aged white man in a business suit holding his hat and a briefcase in his hand and consulting a small piece of paper.*]

MAN: Uh—how do you do, miss. I am looking for a Mrs.— [*He looks at the slip of paper.*] Mrs. Lena Younger?

BENEATHA: [*Smoothing her hair with slight embarrassment.*] Oh—yes, that's my mother. Excuse me [*She closes the door and turns to quiet the other two.*] Ruth! Brother! Somebody's here. [*Then she opens the door. The* MAN *casts a curious quick glance at all of them.*] Uh—come in please.

MAN: [*Coming in.*] Thank you.

BENEATHA: My mother isn't here just now. Is it business?

MAN: Yes . . . well, of a sort.

WALTER: [*Freely, the Man of the House.*] Have a seat. I'm Mrs. Younger's son. I look after most of her business matters.

[RUTH *and* BENEATHA *exchange amused glances.*]

MAN: [*Regarding* WALTER, *and sitting.*] Well—My name is Karl Lindner . . .

WALTER: [*Stretching out his hand.*] Walter Younger. This is my wife— [RUTH *nods politely.*] —and my sister.

LINDNER: How do you do.

WALTER: [*Amiably, as he sits himself easily on a chair, leaning with interest forward on his knees and looking expectantly into the newcomer's face.*] What can we do for you, Mr. Lindner!

LINDNER: [*Some minor shuffling of the hat and briefcase on his knees.*] Well—I am a representative of the Clybourne Park Improvement Association—

WALTER: [*Pointing.*] Why don't you sit your things on the floor?

LINDNER: Oh—yes. Thank you. [*He slides the briefcase and hat under the chair.*] And as I was saying—I am from the Clybourne Park Improvement Association and we have had it brought to our attention at the last meeting that you people—or at least your mother—has bought a piece of residential property at— [*He digs for the slip of paper again.*] —four o six Clybourne Street . . .

WALTER: That's right. Care for something to drink? Ruth, get Mr. Lindner a beer.

LINDNER: [*Upset for some reason.*] Oh—no, really. I mean thank you very much, but no thank you.

RUTH: [*Innocently.*] Some coffee?

LINDNER: Thank you, nothing at all.

[BENEATHA *is watching the man carefully.*]

LINDNER: Well, I don't know how much you folks know about our organization. [*He is a gentle man; thoughtful and somewhat labored in his manner.*] It is one of these community organizations set up to look after—oh, you know, things like block upkeep and special projects and we also have what we call our New Neighbors Orientation Committee . . .

BENEATHA: [*Drily.*] Yes—and what do they do?

LINDNER: [*Turning a little to her and then returning the main force to* WALTER.] Well—it's what you might call a sort of welcoming committee, I guess. I mean they, we, I'm the chairman of the committee—go around and see the new people who move into the neighborhood and sort of give them the lowdown on the way we do things out in Clybourne Park.

BENEATHA: [*With appreciation of the two meanings, which escape* RUTH *and* WALTER.] Un-huh.

LINDNER: And we also have the category of what the association calls— [*He looks elsewhere.*] —uh—special community problems . . .

BENEATHA: Yes—and what are some of those?

WALTER: Girl, let the man talk.

LINDNER: [*With understated relief.*] Thank you. I would sort of like to explain this thing in my own way. I mean I want to explain to you in a certain way.

WALTER: Go ahead.

LINDNER: Yes. Well. I'm going to try to get right to the point. I'm sure we'll all appreciate that in the long run.

BENEATHA: Yes.

WALTER: Be still now!

LINDNER: Well—

RUTH: [*Still innocently.*] Would you like another chair—you don't look comfortable.

LINDNER: [*More frustrated than annoyed.*] No, thank you very much. Please. Well—to get right to the point I— [*A great breath, and he is off at last.*] I am sure you people must be aware of some of the incidents which have happened in various parts of the city when colored people have moved into certain areas— [BENEATHA *exhales heavily and starts tossing a piece of fruit up and down in the air.*] Well—because we have what I think is going to be a unique type of organization in American community life—not only do we deplore that kind of thing—but we are trying to do something about it. [BENEATHA *stops tossing and turns with a new and quizzical interest to the man.*] We feel— [*Gaining confi-*

dence in his mission because of the interest in the faces of the people he is talking to.] —we feel that most of the trouble in this world, when you come right down to it— [*He hits his knee for emphasis.*] —most of the trouble exists because people just don't sit down and talk to each other.

RUTH: [*Nodding as she might in church, pleased with the remark.*] You can say that again, mister.

LINDNER: [*More encouraged by such affirmation.*] That we don't try hard enough in this world to understand the other fellow's problem. The other guy's point of view.

RUTH: Now that's right.

[BENEATHA *and* WALTER *merely watch and listen with genuine interest.*]

LINDNER: Yes—that's the way we feel out in Clybourne Park. And that's why I was elected to come here this afternoon and talk to you people. Friendly like, you know, the way people should talk to each other and see if we couldn't find some way to work this thing out. As I say, the whole business is a matter of *caring* about the other fellow. Anybody can see that you are a nice family of folks, hard working and honest I'm sure. [BENEATHA *frowns slightly, quizzically, her head tilted regarding him.*] Today everybody knows what it means to be on the outside of something. And of course, there is always somebody who is out to take the advantage of people who don't always understand.

WALTER: What do you mean?

LINDNER: Well—you see our community is made up of people who've worked hard as the dickens for years to build up that little community. They're not rich and fancy people; just hard-working, honest people who don't really have much but those little homes and a dream of the kind of community they want to raise their children in. Now, I don't say we are perfect and there is a lot wrong in some of the things they want. But you've got to admit that a man, right or wrong, has the right to want to have the neighborhood he lives in a certain kind of way. And at the moment the overwhelming majority of our people out there feel that people get along better, take more of a common interest in the life of the community, when they share a common background. I want you to believe me when I tell you that race prejudice simply doesn't enter into it. It is a matter of the people of Clybourne Park believing, rightly or wrongly, as I say, that for the happiness of all concerned that our Negro families are happier when they live in their *own* communities.

BENEATHA: [*With a grand and bitter gesture.*] This, friends, is the Welcoming Committee!

WALTER: [*Dumfounded, looking at* LINDNER.] Is this what you came marching all the way over here to tell us?

LINDNER: Well, now we've been having a fine conversation. I hope you'll hear me all the way through.

WALTER: [*Tightly.*] Go ahead, man.

LINDNER: You see—in the face of all things I have said, we are prepared to make your family a very generous offer . . .

BENEATHA: Thirty pieces and not a coin less![2]

WALTER: Yeah?

LINDNER: [*Putting on his glasses and drawing a form out of the briefcase.*] Our association is prepared, through the collective effort of our people, to buy the house from you at a financial gain to your family.

RUTH: Lord have mercy, ain't this the living gall!

WALTER: All right, you through?

LINDNER: Well, I want to give you the exact terms of the financial arrangement—

WALTER: We don't want to hear no exact terms of no arrangements. I want to know if you got any more to tell us 'bout getting together?

LINDNER: [*Taking off his glasses.*] Well—I don't suppose that you feel . . .

WALTER: Never mind how I feel—you got any more to say 'bout how people ought to sit down and talk to each other? . . . Get out of my house, man.

[*He turns his back and walks to the door.*]

LINDNER: [*Looking around at the hostile faces and reaching and assembling his hat and briefcase.*] Well—I don't understand why you people are reacting this way. What do you think you are going to gain by moving into a neighborhood where you just aren't wanted and where some elements—well—people can get awful worked up when they feel that their whole way of life and everything they've ever worked for is threatened.

WALTER: Get out.

LINDNER: [*At the door, holding a small card.*] Well—I'm sorry it went like this.

WALTER: Get out.

LINDNER: [*Almost sadly regarding* WALTER.] You just can't force people to change their hearts, son.

[*He turns and puts his card on a table and exits.* WALTER *pushes the door to with stinging hatred, and stands looking at it.* RUTH *just sits and* BENEATHA *just stands. They say nothing.* MAMA *and* TRAVIS *enter.*]

MAMA: Well—this all the packing got done since I left out of here this morning. I testify before God that my children got all the energy of the dead. What time the moving men due?

BENEATHA: Four o'clock. You had a caller, Mama.

2. See Matthew 26.15, in which Judas Iscariot is paid thirty pieces of silver to betray Jesus.

[*She is smiling, teasingly.*]

MAMA: Sure enough—who?

BENEATHA: [*Her arms folded saucily.*] The Welcoming Committee.

[WALTER *and* RUTH *giggle.*]

MAMA: [*Innocently.*] Who?

BENEATHA: The Welcoming Committee. They said they're sure going to be glad to see you when you get there.

WALTER: [*Devilishly.*] Yeah, they said they can't hardly wait to see your face.

[*Laughter.*]

MAMA: [*Sensing their facetiousness.*] What's the matter with you all?

WALTER: Ain't nothing the matter with us. We just telling you 'bout the gentleman who came to see you this afternoon. From the Clybourne Park Improvement Association.

MAMA: What he want?

RUTH: [*In the same mood as* BENEATHA *and* WALTER.] To welcome you, honey.

WALTER: He said they can't hardly wait. He said the one thing they don't have, that they just *dying* to have out there is a fine family of colored people! [*To* RUTH *and* BENEATHA.] Ain't that right!

RUTH AND BENEATHA: [*Mockingly.*] Yeah! He left his card in case—

[*They indicate the card, and* MAMA *picks it up and throws it on the floor—understanding and looking off as she draws her chair up to the table on which she has put her plant and some sticks and some cord.*]

MAMA: Father, give us strength. [*Knowingly—and without fun.*] Did he threaten us?

BENEATHA: Oh—Mama—they don't do it like that anymore. He talked Brotherhood. He said everybody ought to learn how to sit down and hate each other with good Christian fellowship.

[*She and* WALTER *shake hands to ridicule the remark.*]

MAMA: [*Sadly.*] Lord, protect us . . .

RUTH: You should hear the money those folks raised to buy the house from us. All we paid and then some.

BENEATHA: What they think we going to do—eat 'em?

RUTH: No, honey, marry 'em.

MAMA: [*Shaking her head.*] Lord, Lord, Lord . . .

RUTH: Well—that's the way the crackers crumble. Joke.

BENEATHA: [*Laughingly noticing what her mother is doing.*] Mama, what are you doing?

MAMA: Fixing my plant so it won't get hurt none on the way . . .

BENEATHA: Mama, you going to take *that* to the new house?

MAMA: Un-huh—

BENEATHA: That raggedy-looking old thing?

MAMA: [*Stopping and looking at her.*] It expresses *me*.

RUTH: [*With delight, to* BENEATHA.] So there, Miss Thing!

[WALTER *comes to* MAMA *suddenly and bends down behind her and squeezes her in his arms with all his strength. She is overwhelmed by the suddenness of it and, though delighted, her manner is like that of* RUTH *with* TRAVIS.]

MAMA: Look out now, boy! You make me mess up my thing here!

WALTER: [*His face lit, he slips down on his knees beside her, his arms still about her.*] Mama . . . you know what it means to climb up in the chariot?

MAMA: [*Gruffly, very happy.*] Get on away from me now . . .

RUTH: [*Near the gift-wrapped package, trying to catch* WALTER's *eye.*] Psst—

WALTER: What the old song say, Mama . . .

RUTH: Walter—Now?

[*She is pointing at the package.*]

WALTER: [*Speaking the lines, sweetly, playfully, in his mother's face.*]

I got wings . . . you got wings . . .
All God's Children got wings[3] . . .

MAMA: Boy—get out of my face and do some work . . .

WALTER:

When I get to heaven gonna put on my wings,
Gonna fly all over God's heaven . . .

BENEATHA: [*Teasingly, from across the room.*] Everybody talking 'bout heaven ain't going there!

WALTER: [*To* RUTH, *who is carrying the box across to them.*] I don't know, you think we ought to give her that . . . Seems to me she ain't been very appreciative around here.

MAMA: [*Eying the box, which is obviously a gift.*] What is that?

WALTER: [*Taking it from* RUTH *and putting it on the table in front of* MAMA.] Well—what you all think? Should we give it to her?

---

3. Lines from an African American spiritual. Walter's and Beneatha's next lines are also from the song.

RUTH: Oh—she was pretty good today.

MAMA: I'll good you—

[*She turns her eyes to the box again.*]

BENEATHA: Open it, Mama.

[*She stands up, looks at it, turns and looks at all of them, and then presses her hands together and does not open the package.*]

WALTER: [*Sweetly.*] Open it, Mama. It's for you. [MAMA *looks in his eyes. It is the first present in her life without its being Christmas. Slowly she opens her package and lifts out, one by one, a brand-new sparkling set of gardening tools.* WALTER *continues, prodding.*] Ruth made up the note—read it . . .

MAMA: [*Picking up the card and adjusting her glasses.*] "To our own Mrs. Miniver[4]—Love from Brother, Ruth and Beneatha." Ain't that lovely . . .

TRAVIS: [*Tugging at his father's sleeve.*] Daddy, can I give her mine now?

WALTER: All right, son. [TRAVIS *flies to get his gift.*] Travis didn't want to go in with the rest of us, Mama. He got his own. [*Somewhat amused.*] We don't know what it is . . .

TRAVIS: [*Racing back in the room with a large hatbox and putting it in front of his grandmother.*] Here!

MAMA: Lord have mercy, baby. You done gone and bought your grand-mother a hat?

TRAVIS: [*Very proud.*] Open it!

[*She does and lifts out an elaborate, but very elaborate, wide gardening hat, and all the adults break up at the sight of it.*]

RUTH: Travis, honey, what is that?

TRAVIS: [*Who thinks it is beautiful and appropriate.*] It's a gardening hat! Like the ladies always have on in the magazines when they work in their gardens.

BENEATHA: [*Giggling fiercely.*] Travis—we were trying to make Mama Mrs. Miniver—not Scarlett O'Hara![5]

MAMA: [*Indignantly.*] What's the matter with you all! This here is a beauti-ful hat! [*Absurdly.*] I always wanted me one just like it!

[*She pops it on her head to prove it to her grandson, and the hat is ludicrous and considerably oversized.*]

RUTH: Hot dog! Go, Mama!

---

4. Courageous, charismatic title character of a 1942 film starring Greer Garson.
5. Glamorous, headstrong heroine of Margaret Mitchell's 1936 historical novel *Gone with the Wind*; Vivien Leigh played Scarlett in the 1939 film adaptation.

WALTER: [*Doubled over with laughter.*] I'm sorry, Mama—but you look like you ready to go out and chop you some cotton sure enough!

[*They all laugh except* MAMA, *out of deference to* TRAVIS' *feelings.*]

MAMA: [*Gathering the boy up to her.*] Bless your heart—this is the prettiest hat I ever owned— [WALTER, RUTH *and* BENEATHA *chime in—noisily, festively and insincerely congratulating* TRAVIS *on his gift.*] What are we all standing around here for? We ain't finished packin' yet. Bennie, you ain't packed one book.

[*The bell rings.*]

BENEATHA: That couldn't be the movers . . . it's not hardly two good yet—

[BENEATHA *goes into her room.* MAMA *starts for door.*]

WALTER: [*Turning, stiffening.*] Wait—wait—I'll get it.

[*He stands and looks at the door.*]

MAMA: You expecting company, son?
WALTER: [*Just looking at the door.*] Yeah—yeah . . .

[MAMA *looks at* RUTH, *and they exchange innocent and unfrightened glances.*]

MAMA: [*Not understanding.*] Well, let them in, son.
BENEATHA: [*From her room.*] We need some more string.
MAMA: Travis—you run to the hardware and get me some string cord.

[MAMA *goes out and* WALTER *turns and looks at* RUTH. TRAVIS *goes to a dish for money.*]

RUTH: Why don't you answer the door, man?
WALTER: [*Suddenly bounding across the floor to her.*] 'Cause sometimes it hard to let the future begin! [*Stooping down in her face.*]

I got wings! You got wings!
All God's children got wings!

[*He crosses to the door and throws it open. Standing there is a very slight little man in a not too prosperous business suit and with haunted frightened eyes and a hat pulled down tightly, brim up, around his forehead.* TRAVIS *passes between the men and exits.* WALTER *leans deep in the man's face, still in his jubilance.*]

When I get to heaven gonna put on my wings,
Gonna fly all over God's heaven . . .

[*The little man just stares at him.*]

Heaven—

[*Suddenly he stops and looks past the little man into the empty hallway.*] Where's Willy, man?

BOBO: He ain't with me.

WALTER: [*Not disturbed.*] Oh—come on in. You know my wife.

BOBO: [*Dumbly, taking off his hat.*] Yes—h'you, Miss Ruth.

RUTH: [*Quietly, a mood apart from her husband already, seeing* BOBO.] Hello, Bobo.

WALTER: You right on time today . . . Right on time. That's the way! [*He slaps* BOBO *on his back.*] Sit down . . . lemme hear.

[RUTH *stands stiffly and quietly in back of them, as though somehow she senses death, her eyes fixed on her husband.*]

BOBO: [*His frightened eyes on the floor, his hat in his hands.*] Could I please get a drink of water, before I tell you about it, Walter Lee?

[WALTER *does not take his eyes off the man.* RUTH *goes blindly to the tap and gets a glass of water and brings it to* BOBO.]

WALTER: There ain't nothing wrong, is there?

BOBO: Lemme tell you—

WALTER: Man—didn't nothing go wrong?

BOBO: Lemme tell you—Walter Lee. [*Looking at* RUTH *and talking to her more than to* WALTER.] You know how it was. I got to tell you how it was. I mean first I got to tell you how it was all the way . . . I mean about the money I put in, Walter Lee . . .

WALTER: [*With taut agitation now.*] What about the money you put in?

BOBO: Well—it wasn't much as we told you—me and Willy— [*He stops.*] I'm sorry, Walter. I got a bad feeling about it. I got a real bad feeling about it . . .

WALTER: Man, what you telling me about all this for? . . . Tell me what happened in Springfield . . .

BOBO: Springfield.

RUTH: [*Like a dead woman.*] What was supposed to happen in Springfield?

BOBO: [*To her.*] This deal that me and Walter went into with Willy—Me and Willy was going to go down to Springfield and spread some money 'round so's we wouldn't have to wait so long for the liquor license . . . That's what we were going to do. Everybody said that was the way you had to do, you understand, Miss Ruth?

WALTER: Man—what happened down there?

BOBO: [*A pitiful man, near tears.*] I'm trying to tell you, Walter.

WALTER: [*Screaming at him suddenly.*] THEN TELL ME, GODDAM-MIT . . . WHAT'S THE MATTER WITH YOU?

BOBO: Man . . . I didn't go to no Springfield, yesterday.

WALTER: [*Halted, life hanging in the moment.*] Why not?

BOBO: [*The long way, the hard way to tell.*] 'Cause I didn't have no reasons to . . .

WALTER: Man, what are you talking about!

BOBO: I'm talking about the fact that when I got to the train station yesterday morning—eight o'clock like we planned . . . Man—*Willy didn't never show up.*

WALTER: Why . . . where was he . . . where is he?

BOBO: That's what I'm trying to tell you . . . I don't know . . . I waited six hours . . . I called his house . . . and I waited . . . six hours . . . I waited in that train station six hours . . . [*Breaking into tears.*] That was all the extra money I had in the world . . . [*Looking up at* WALTER *with the tears running down his face.*] Man, *Willy is gone.*

WALTER: Gone, what you mean Willy is gone? Gone where? You mean he went by himself. You mean he went off to Springfield by himself—to take care of getting the license— [*Turns and looks anxiously at* RUTH.] You mean maybe he didn't want too many people in on the business down there? [*Looks to* RUTH *again, as before.*] You know Willy got his own ways. [*Looks back to* BOBO.] Maybe you was late yesterday and he just went on down there without you. Maybe—maybe—he's been callin' you at home tryin' to tell you what happened or something. Maybe—maybe—he just got sick. He's somewhere—he's got to be somewhere. We just got to find him—me and you got to find him. [*Grabs* BOBO *senselessly by the collar and starts to shake him.*] We got to!

BOBO: [*In sudden angry, frightened agony.*] What's the matter with you, Walter! *When a cat take off with your money he don't leave you no maps!*

WALTER: [*Turning madly, as though he is looking for* WILLY *in the very room.*] Willy! . . . Willy . . . don't do it . . . Please don't do it . . . Man, not with that money . . . Man, please, not with that money . . . Oh, God . . . Don't let it be true . . . [*He is wandering around, crying out for* WILLY *and looking for him or perhaps for help from God.*] Man . . . I trusted you . . . Man, I put my life in your hands . . . [*He starts to crumple down on the floor as* RUTH *just covers her face in horror.* MAMA *opens the door and comes into the room, with* BENEATHA *behind her.*] Man . . . [*He starts to pound the floor with his fists, sobbing wildly.*] *That money is made out of my father's flesh* . . .

BOBO: [*Standing over him helplessly.*] I'm sorry, Walter . . . [*Only* WALTER'S *sobs reply.* BOBO *puts on his hat.*] I had my life staked on this deal, too . . .

[*He exits.*]

MAMA: [*To* WALTER.] Son— [*She goes to him, bends down to him, talks to his bent head.*] Son . . . Is it gone? Son, I gave you sixty-five hundred dollars. Is it gone? All of it? Beneatha's money too?

WALTER: [*Lifting his head slowly.*] Mama . . . I never . . . went to the bank at all . . .

MAMA: [*Not wanting to believe him.*] You mean . . . your sister's school money . . . you used that too . . . Walter? . . .

WALTER: Yessss! . . . All of it . . . It's all gone . . . [*There is total silence.* RUTH *stands with her face covered with her hands;* BENEATHA *leans forlornly against a wall, fingering a piece of red ribbon from the mother's gift.* MAMA *stops and looks at her son without recognition and then, quite without thinking about it, starts to beat him senselessly in the face.* BENEATHA *goes to them and stops it.*]

BENEATHA: Mama!

[MAMA *stops and looks at both of her children and rises slowly and wanders vaguely, aimlessly away from them.*]

MAMA: I seen . . . him . . . night after night . . . come in . . . and look at that rug . . . and then look at me . . . the red showing in his eyes . . . the veins moving in his head . . . I seen him grow thin and old before he was forty . . . working and working and working like somebody's old horse . . . killing himself . . . and you—you give it all away in a day . . .

BENEATHA: Mama—

MAMA: Oh, God . . . [*She looks up to Him.*] Look down here—and show me the strength.

BENEATHA: Mama—

MAMA: [*Folding over.*] Strength . . .

BENEATHA: [*Plaintively.*] Mama . . .

MAMA: Strength!

[CURTAIN.]

ACT III

An hour later.

At curtain, there is a sullen light of gloom in the living room, gray light not unlike that which began the first scene of Act I. At left we can see WALTER *within his room, alone with himself. He is stretched out on the bed, his shirt out and open, his arms under his head. He does not smoke, he does not cry out, he merely lies there, looking up at the ceiling, much as if he were alone in the world.*

In the living room BENEATHA *sits at the table, still surrounded by the now almost ominous packing crates. She sits looking off. We feel that this is a mood struck perhaps an hour before, and it lingers now, full of the empty sound of profound disappointment. We see on a line from her brother's bedroom the sameness of their attitudes. Presently the bell rings and* BENEATHA *rises without ambition or interest in answering. It is* ASAGAI, *smiling broadly, striding into the room with energy and happy expectation and conversation.*

ASAGAI: I came over . . . I had some free time. I thought I might help with the packing. Ah, I like the look of packing crates! A household in preparation for a journey! It depresses some people . . . but for me . . . it is another feeling. Something full of the flow of life, do you understand? Movement, progress . . . It makes me think of Africa.

BENEATHA: Africa!

ASAGAI: What kind of a mood is this? Have I told you how deeply you move me?

BENEATHA: He gave away the money, Asagai . . .

ASAGAI: Who gave away what money?

BENEATHA: The insurance money. My brother gave it away.

ASAGAI: Gave it away?

BENEATHA: He made an investment! With a man even Travis wouldn't have trusted.

ASAGAI: And it's gone?

BENEATHA: Gone!

ASAGAI: I'm very sorry . . . And you, now?

BENEATHA: Me? . . . Me? . . . Me, I'm nothing . . . Me. When I was very small . . . we used to take our sleds out in the wintertime and the only hills we had were the ice-covered stone steps of some houses down the street. And we used to fill them in with snow and make them smooth and slide down them all day . . . and it was very dangerous you know . . . far too steep . . . and sure enough one day a kid named Rufus came down too fast and hit the sidewalk . . . and we saw his face just split open right there in front of us . . . And I remember standing there looking at his bloody open face thinking that was the end of Rufus. But the ambulance came and they took him to the hospital and they fixed the broken bones and they sewed it all up . . . and the next time I saw Rufus he just had a little line down the middle of his face . . . I never got over that . . .

[WALTER *sits up, listening on the bed. Throughout this scene it is important that we feel his reaction at all times, that he visibly respond to the words of his sister and* ASAGAI.]

ASAGAI: What?

BENEATHA: That that was what one person could do for another, fix him up—sew up the problem, make him all right again. That was the most marvelous thing in the world . . . I wanted to do that. I always thought it was the one concrete thing in the world that a human being could do. Fix up the sick, you know—and make them whole again. This was truly being God . . .

ASAGAI: You wanted to be God?

BENEATHA: No—I wanted to cure. It used to be so important to me. I wanted to cure. It used to matter. I used to care. I mean about people and how their bodies hurt . . .

ASAGAI: And you've stopped caring?

BENEATHA: Yes—I think so.

ASAGAI: Why?

[WALTER *rises, goes to the door of his room and is about to open it, then stops and stands listening, leaning on the door jamb.*]

BENEATHA: Because it doesn't seem deep enough, close enough to what ails mankind—I mean this thing of sewing up bodies or administering drugs. Don't you understand? It was a child's reaction to the world. I thought that doctors had the secret to all the hurts . . . That's the way a child sees things—or an idealist.

ASAGAI: Children see things very well sometimes—and idealists even better.

BENEATHA: I know that's what you think. Because you are still where I left off—you still care. This is what you see for the world, for Africa. You with the dreams of the future will patch up all Africa—you are going to cure the Great Sore of colonialism with Independence—

ASAGAI: Yes!

BENEATHA: Yes—and you think that one word is the penicillin of the human spirit: "Independence!" But then what?

ASAGAI: That will be the problem for another time. First we must get there.

BENEATHA: And where does it end?

ASAGAI: End? Who even spoke of an end? To life? To living?

BENEATHA: An end to misery!

ASAGAI: [*Smiling.*] You sound like a French intellectual.

BENEATHA: No! I sound like a human being who just had her future taken right out of her hands! While I was sleeping in my bed in there, things were happening in this world that directly concerned me—and nobody asked me, consulted me—they just went out and did things—and changed my life. Don't you see there isn't any real progress, Asagai, there is only one large circle that we march in, around and around, each of us with our own little picture—in front of us—our own little mirage that we think is the future.

ASAGAI: That is the mistake.

BENEATHA: What?

ASAGAI: What you just said—about the circle. It isn't a circle—it is simply a long line—as in geometry, you know, one that reaches into infinity. And because we cannot see the end—we also cannot see how it changes. And it is very odd but those who see the changes are called "idealists"— and those who cannot, or refuse to think, they are the "realists." It is very strange, and amusing too, I think.

BENEATHA: You—you are almost religious.

ASAGAI: Yes . . . I think I have the religion of doing what is necessary in the world—and of worshipping man—because he is so marvelous, you see.

BENEATHA: Man is foul! And the human race deserves its misery!

ASAGAI: You see: *you* have become the religious one in the old sense. Already, and after such a small defeat, you are worshipping despair.

BENEATHA: From now on, I worship the truth—and the truth is that people are puny, small and selfish . . .

ASAGAI: Truth? Why is it that you despairing ones always think that only you have the truth? I never thought to see *you* like that. You! Your brother made a stupid, childish mistake—and you are grateful to him. So that now you can give up the ailing human race on account of it. You talk about what good is struggle; what good is anything? Where are we all going? And why are we bothering?

BENEATHA: *And you cannot answer it!* All your talk and dreams about Africa and Independence. Independence and then what? What about all the crooks and petty thieves and just plain idiots who will come into power to steal and plunder the same as before—only now they will be black and do it in the name of the new Independence—You cannot answer that.

ASAGAI: [*Shouting over her.*] I live the answer! [*Pause.*] In my village at home it is the exceptional man who can even read a newspaper . . . or who ever *sees* a book at all. I will go home and much of what I will have to say will seem strange to the people of my village . . . But I will teach and work and things will happen, slowly and swiftly. At times it will seem that nothing changes at all . . . and then again . . . the sudden dramatic events which make history leap into the future. And then quiet again. Retrogression even. Guns, murder, revolution. And I even will have moments when I wonder if the quiet was not better than all that death and hatred. But I will look about my village at the illiteracy

and disease and ignorance and I will not wonder long. And perhaps . . .
perhaps I will be a great man . . . I mean perhaps I will hold on to the
substance of truth and find my way always with the right course . . .
and perhaps for it I will be butchered in my bed some night by the servants of empire . . .

BENEATHA: *The martyr!*

ASAGAI: . . . or perhaps I shall live to be a very old man, respected and
esteemed in my new nation . . . And perhaps I shall hold office and this
is what I'm trying to tell you, Alaiyo; perhaps the things I believe now for
my country will be wrong and outmoded, and I will not understand and
do terrible things to have things my way or merely to keep my power.
Don't you see that there will be young men and women, not British soldiers then, but my own black countrymen . . . to step out of the shadows
some evening and slit my then useless throat? Don't you see they have
always been there . . . that they always will be. And that such a thing as
my own death will be an advance? They who might kill me even . . .
actually replenish me!

BENEATHA: Oh, Asagai, I know all that.

ASAGAI: Good! Then stop moaning and groaning and tell me what you
plan to do.

BENEATHA: Do?

ASAGAI: I have a bit of a suggestion.

BENEATHA: What?

ASAGAI: [*Rather quietly for him.*] That when it is all over—that you come
home with me—

BENEATHA: [*Slapping herself on the forehead with exasperation born of
misunderstanding.*] Oh—Asagai—at this moment you decide to be
romantic!

ASAGAI: [*Quickly understanding the misunderstanding.*] My dear, young
creature of the New World—I do not mean across the city—I mean
across the ocean; home—to Africa.

BENEATHA: [*Slowly understanding and turning to him with murmured
amazement.*] To—to Nigeria?

ASAGAI: Yes! . . . [*Smiling and lifting his arms playfully.*] Three hundred
years later the African Prince rose up out of the seas and swept the
maiden back across the middle passage[6] over which her ancestors
had come—

BENEATHA: [*Unable to play.*] Nigeria?

ASAGAI: Nigeria. Home. [*Coming to her with genuine romantic flippancy.*] I
will show you our mountains and our stars; and give you cool drinks

6. Term denoting the route traveled by slaves transported from Africa to the Americas.

from gourds and teach you the old songs and the ways of our people—
and, in time, we will pretend that— [*Very softly.*] —you have only been
away for a day—

[*She turns her back to him, thinking. He swings her around and takes
her full in his arms in a long embrace which proceeds to passion.*]

BENEATHA: [*Pulling away.*] You're getting me all mixed up—

ASAGAI: Why?

BENEATHA: Too many things—too many things have happened today. I
must sit down and think. I don't know what I feel about anything right
this minute.

[*She promptly sits down and props her chin on her fist.*]

ASAGAI: [*Charmed.*] All right, I shall leave you. No—don't get up. [*Touching her, gently, sweetly.*] Just sit awhile and think . . . Never be afraid to
sit awhile and think. [*He goes to door and looks at her.*] How often I have
looked at you and said, "Ah—so this is what the New World hath
finally wrought . . ."[7]

[*He exits.* BENEATHA *sits on alone. Presently* WALTER *enters from his
room and starts to rummage through things, feverishly looking for
something. She looks up and turns in her seat.*]

BENEATHA: [*Hissingly.*] Yes—just look at what the New World hath
wrought! . . . Just look! [*She gestures with bitter disgust.*] There he is! *Mon-
sieur le petit bourgeois noir*[8]—himself! There he is—Symbol of a Rising
Class! Entrepreneur! Titan of the system! [WALTER *ignores her completely
and continues frantically and destructively looking for something and hurling things to the floor and tearing things out of their place in his search.*
BENEATHA *ignores the eccentricity of his actions and goes on with the monologue of insult.*] Did you dream of yachts on Lake Michigan, Brother? Did
you see yourself on that Great Day sitting down at the Conference Table,
surrounded by all the mighty bald-headed men in America? All halted,
waiting, breathless, waiting for your pronouncements on industry? Waiting for you—Chairman of the Board? [WALTER *finds what he is looking
for—a small piece of white paper—and pushes it in his pocket and puts on
his coat and rushes out without ever having looked at her. She shouts after
him.*] I look at you and I see the final triumph of stupidity in the world!

[*The door slams and she returns to just sitting again.* RUTH *comes
quickly out of* MAMA'S *room.*]

7. Allusion to the biblical exclamation "What hath God wrought!" (Num. 23.23).
8. Mister Black Middle Class (French).

RUTH: Who was that?

BENEATHA: Your husband.

RUTH: Where did he go?

BENEATHA: Who knows—maybe he has an appointment at U.S. Steel.

RUTH: [*Anxiously, with frightened eyes.*] You didn't say nothing bad to him, did you?

BENEATHA: Bad? Say anything bad to him? No—I told him he was a sweet boy and full of dreams and everything is strictly peachy keen, as the ofay[9] kids say!

[MAMA *enters from her bedroom. She is lost, vague, trying to catch hold, to make some sense of her former command of the world, but it still eludes her. A sense of waste overwhelms her gait; a measure of apology rides on her shoulders. She goes to her plant, which has remained on the table, looks at it, picks it up and takes it to the window sill and sits it outside, and she stands and looks at it a long moment. Then she closes the window, straightens her body with effort and turns around to her children.*]

MAMA: Well—ain't it a mess in here, though? [*A false cheerfulness, a beginning of something.*] I guess we all better stop moping around and get some work done. All this unpacking and everything we got to do. [RUTH *raises her head slowly in response to the sense of the line; and* BENEATHA *in similar manner turns very slowly to look at her mother.*] One of you all better call the moving people and tell 'em not to come.

RUTH: Tell 'em not to come?

MAMA: Of course, baby. Ain't no need in 'em coming all the way here and having to go back. They charges for that too. [*She sits down, fingers to her brow, thinking.*] Lord, ever since I was a little girl, I always remembers people saying, "Lena—Lena Eggleston, you aims too high all the time. You needs to slow down and see life a little more like it is. Just slow down some." That's what they always used to say down home—"Lord, that Lena Eggleston is a high-minded thing. She'll get her due one day!"

RUTH: No, Lena . . .

MAMA: Me and Big Walter just didn't never learn right.

RUTH: Lena, no! We gotta go. Bennie—tell her . . . [*She rises and crosses to* BENEATHA *with her arms outstretched.* BENEATHA *doesn't respond.*] Tell her we can still move . . . the notes ain't but a hundred and twenty-five a month. We got four grown people in this house—we can work . . .

MAMA: [*To herself.*] Just aimed too high all the time—

9. White.

RUTH: [*Turning and going to* MAMA *fast—the words pouring out with urgency and desperation.*] Lena—I'll work . . . I'll work twenty hours a day in all the kitchens in Chicago . . . I'll strap my baby on my back if I have to and scrub all the floors in America and wash all the sheets in America if I have to—but we got to move . . . We got to get out of here . . .

[MAMA *reaches out absently and pats* RUTH's *hand.*]

MAMA: No—I sees things differently now. Been thinking 'bout some of the things we could do to fix this place up some. I seen a second-hand bureau over on Maxwell Street[1] just the other day that could fit right there. [*She points to where the new furniture might go.* RUTH *wanders away from her.*] Would need some new handles on it and then a little varnish and then it look like something brand-new. And—we can put up them new curtains in the kitchen . . . Why this place be looking fine. Cheer us all up so that we forget trouble ever came . . . [*To* RUTH.] And you could get some nice screens to put up in your room round the baby's bassinet . . . [*She looks at both of them, pleadingly.*] Sometimes you just got to know when to give up some things . . . and hold on to what you got.

[WALTER *enters from the outside, looking spent and leaning against the door, his coat hanging from him.*]

MAMA: Where you been, son?
WALTER: [*Breathing hard.*] Made a call.
MAMA: To who, son?
WALTER: To The Man.
MAMA: What man, baby?
WALTER: The Man, Mama. Don't you know who The Man is?
RUTH: Walter Lee?
WALTER: *The Man.* Like the guys in the streets say—The Man. Captain Boss—Mistuh Charley . . . Old Captain Please Mr. Bossman . . .
BENEATHA: [*Suddenly.*] Lindner!
WALTER: That's right! That's good. I told him to come right over.
BENEATHA: [*Fiercely, understanding.*] For what? What do you want to see him for!
WALTER: [*Looking at his sister.*] We going to do business with him.
MAMA: What you talking 'bout, son?
WALTER: Talking 'bout life, Mama. You all always telling me to see life like it is. Well—I laid in there on my back today . . . and I figured it out. Life just like it is. Who gets and who don't get. [*He sits down with his*

1. Street market southwest of the Loop.

coat on and laughs.] Mama, you know it's all divided up. Life is. Sure enough. Between the takers and the "tooken." [*He laughs.*] I've figured it out finally. [*He looks around at them.*] Yeah. Some of us always getting "tooken." [*He laughs.*] People like Willy Harris, they don't never get "tooken." And you know why the rest of us do? 'Cause we all mixed up. Mixed up bad. We get to looking 'round for the right and the wrong, and we worry about it and cry about it and stay up nights trying to figure out 'bout the wrong and the right of things all the time . . . And all the time, man, them takers is out there operating, just taking and taking. Willy Harris? Shoot—Willy Harris don't even count. He don't even count in the big scheme of things. But I'll say one thing for old Willy Harris . . . he's taught me something. He's taught me to keep my eye on what counts in this world. Yeah— [*Shouting out a little.*] Thanks, Willy!

RUTH: What did you call that man for, Walter Lee?

WALTER: Called him to tell him to come on over to the show. Gonna put on a show for the man. Just what he wants to see. You see, Mama, the man came here today and he told us that them people out there where you want us to move—well they so upset they willing to pay us not to move out there. [*He laughs again.*] And—and oh, Mama—you would of been proud of the way me and Ruth and Bennie acted. We told him to get out . . . Lord have mercy! We told the man to get out. Oh, we was some proud folks this afternoon, yeah. [*He lights a cigarette.*] We were still full of that old-time stuff . . .

RUTH: [*Coming toward him slowly.*] You talking 'bout taking them people's money to keep us from moving in that house?

WALTER: I ain't just talking 'bout it, baby—I'm telling you that's what's going to happen.

BENEATHA: Oh, God! Where is the bottom! Where is the real honest-to-God bottom so he can't go any farther!

WALTER: See—that's the old stuff. You and that boy that was here today. You all want everybody to carry a flag and a spear and sing some marching songs, huh? You wanna spend your life looking into things and trying to find the right and the wrong part, huh? Yeah. You know what's going to happen to that boy someday—he'll find himself sitting in a dungeon, locked in forever—and the takers will have the key! Forget it, baby! There ain't no causes—there ain't nothing but taking in this world, and he who takes most is smartest—and it don't make a damn bit of difference *how*.

MAMA: You making something inside me cry, son. Some awful pain inside me.

WALTER: Don't cry, Mama. Understand. That white man is going to walk in that door able to write checks for more money than we ever had. It's important to him and I'm going to help him . . . I'm going to put on the show, Mama.

MAMA: Son—I come from five generations of people who was slaves and sharecroppers—but ain't nobody in my family never let nobody pay 'em no money that was a way of telling us we wasn't fit to walk the earth. We ain't never been that poor. [*Raising her eyes and looking at him.*] We ain't never been that dead inside.

BENEATHA: Well—we are dead now. All the talk about dreams and sunlight that goes on in this house. All dead.

WALTER: What's the matter with you all! I didn't make this world! It was give to me this way! Hell, yes, I want me some yachts someday! Yes, I want to hang some real pearls 'round my wife's neck. Ain't she supposed to wear no pearls? Somebody tell me—tell me, who decides which women is suppose to wear pearls in this world. I tell you I am a *man*— and I think my wife should wear some pearls in this world!

[*This last line hangs a good while and* WALTER *begins to move about the room. The word "Man" has penetrated his consciousness; he mumbles it to himself repeatedly between strange agitated pauses as he moves about.*]

MAMA: Baby, how you going to feel on the inside?

WALTER: Fine! . . . Going to feel fine . . . a man . . .

MAMA: You won't have nothing left then, Walter Lee.

WALTER: [*Coming to her.*] I'm going to feel fine, Mama. I'm going to look that son-of-a-bitch in the eyes and say— [*He falters.*] —and say, "All right, Mr. Lindner— [*He falters even more.*] —that's your neighborhood out there. You got the right to keep it like you want. You got the right to have it like you want. Just write the check and—the house is yours." And, and I am going to say— [*His voice almost breaks.*] And you—you people just put the money in my hand and you won't have to live next to this bunch of stinking niggers! . . . [*He straightens up and moves away from his mother, walking around the room.*] Maybe—maybe I'll just get down on my black knees . . . [*He does so;* RUTH *and* BENNIE *and* MAMA *watch him in frozen horror.*] Captain, Mistuh, Bossman. [*He starts crying.*] A-hee-hee-hee! [*Wringing his hands in profoundly anguished imitation.*] Yassss-suh! Great White Father, just gi' ussen de money, fo' God's sake, and we's ain't gwine come out deh and dirty up yo' white folks neighborhood . . .

[*He breaks down completely, then gets up and goes into the bedroom.*]

BENEATHA: That is not a man. That is nothing but a toothless rat.

MAMA: Yes—death done come in this here house. [*She is nodding, slowly, reflectively.*] Done come walking in my house. On the lips of my children.

You what supposed to be my beginning again. You—what supposed to be
my harvest. [*To* BENEATHA.] You—you mourning your brother?

BENEATHA: He's no brother of mine.

MAMA: What you say?

BENEATHA: I said that that individual in that room is no brother of mine.

MAMA: That's what I thought you said. You feeling like you better than he is
today? [BENEATHA *does not answer.*] Yes? What you tell him a minute ago?
That he wasn't a man? Yes? You give him up for me? You done wrote his
epitaph too—like the rest of the world? Well, who give you the privilege?

BENEATHA: Be on my side for once! You saw what he just did, Mama! You
saw him—down on his knees. Wasn't it you who taught me—to despise
any man who would do that. Do what he's going to do.

MAMA: Yes—I taught you that. Me and your daddy. But I thought I taught
you something else too . . . I thought I taught you to love him.

BENEATHA: Love him? There is nothing left to love.

MAMA: There is always something left to love. And if you ain't learned that,
you ain't learned nothing. [*Looking at her.*] Have you cried for that boy
today? I don't mean for yourself and for the family 'cause we lost the
money. I mean for him; what he been through and what it done to him.
Child, when do you think is the time to love somebody the most; when
they done good and made things easy for everybody? Well then, you ain't
through learning—because that ain't the time at all. It's when he's at his
lowest and can't believe in hisself 'cause the world done whipped him so.
When you starts measuring somebody, measure him right, child, measure him right. Make sure you done taken into account what hills and
valleys he come through before he got to wherever he is.

[TRAVIS *bursts into the room at the end of the speech, leaving the door
open.*]

TRAVIS: Grandmama—the moving men are downstairs! The truck just
pulled up.

MAMA: [*Turning and looking at him.*] Are they, baby? They downstairs?

[*She sighs and sits.* LINDNER *appears in the doorway. He peers in and
knocks lightly, to gain attention, and comes in. All turn to look at him.*]

LINDNER: [*Hat and briefcase in hand.*] Uh—hello . . . [RUTH *crosses mechanically to the bedroom door and opens it and lets it swing open freely and
slowly as the lights come up on* WALTER *within, still in his coat, sitting at the
far corner of the room. He looks up and out through the room to* LINDNER.]

RUTH: He's here.

[*A long minute passes and* WALTER *slowly gets up.*]

LINDNER: [*Coming to the table with efficiency, putting his briefcase on the table and starting to unfold papers and unscrew fountain pens.*] Well, I certainly was glad to hear from you people. [WALTER *has begun the trek out of the room, slowly and awkwardly, rather like a small boy, passing the back of his sleeve across his mouth from time to time.*] Life can really be so much simpler than people let it be most of the time. Well—with whom do I negotiate? You, Mrs. Younger, or your son here? [MAMA *sits with her hands folded on her lap and her eyes closed as* WALTER *advances.* TRAVIS *goes close to* LINDNER *and looks at the papers curiously.*] Just some official papers, sonny.

RUTH: Travis, you go downstairs.

MAMA: [*Opening her eyes and looking into* WALTER'S.] No. Travis, you stay right here. And you make him understand what you doing, Walter Lee. You teach him good. Like Willy Harris taught you. You show where our five generations done come to. Go ahead, son—

WALTER: [*Looks down into his boy's eyes.* TRAVIS *grins at him merrily and* WALTER *draws him beside him with his arm lightly around his shoulders.*] Well, Mr. Lindner. [BENEATHA *turns away.*] We called you— [*There is a profound, simple groping quality in his speech.*] —because, well, me and my family [*He looks around and shifts from one foot to the other.*] Well—we are very plain people . . .

LINDNER: Yes—

WALTER: I mean—I have worked as a chauffeur most of my life—and my wife here, she does domestic work in people's kitchens. So does my mother. I mean—we are plain people . . .

LINDNER: Yes, Mr. Younger—

WALTER: [*Really like a small boy, looking down at his shoes and then up at the man.*] And—uh—well, my father, well, he was a laborer most of his life.

LINDNER: [*Absolutely confused.*] Uh, yes—

WALTER: [*Looking down at his toes once again.*] My father almost beat a man to death once because this man called him a bad name or something, you know what I mean?

LINDNER: No, I'm afraid I don't.

WALTER: [*Finally straightening up.*] Well, what I mean is that we come from people who had a lot of pride. I mean—we are very proud people. And that's my sister over there and she's going to be a doctor—and we are very proud—

LINDNER: Well—I am sure that is very nice, but—

WALTER: [*Starting to cry and facing the man eye to eye.*] What I am telling you is that we called you over here to tell you that we are very proud and that this is—this is my son, who makes the sixth generation of our family in this country, and that we have all thought about your offer and

we have decided to move into our house because my father—my
father—he earned it. [MAMA *has her eyes closed and is rocking back and
forth as though she were in church, with her head nodding the amen yes.*]
We don't want to make no trouble for nobody or fight no causes—but
we will try to be good neighbors. That's all we got to say. [*He looks the
man absolutely in the eyes.*] We don't want your money.

[*He turns and walks away from the man.*]

LINDNER: [*Looking around at all of them.*] I take it then that you have
decided to occupy.

BENEATHA: That's what the man said.

LINDNER: [*To* MAMA *in her reverie.*] Then I would like to appeal to you,
Mrs. Younger. You are older and wiser and understand things better
I am sure . . .

MAMA: [*Rising.*] I am afraid you don't understand. My son said we was
going to move and there ain't nothing left for me to say. [*Shaking her
head with double meaning.*] You know how these young folks is nowadays, mister. Can't do a thing with 'em. Good-bye.

LINDNER: [*Folding up his materials.*] Well—if you are that final about it . . .
There is nothing left for me to say. [*He finishes. He is almost ignored by
the family, who are concentrating on* WALTER LEE. *At the door* LINDNER
halts and looks around.] I sure hope you people know what you're doing.

[*He shakes his head and exits.*]

RUTH: [*Looking around and coming to life.*] Well, for God's sake—if the
moving men are here—LET'S GET THE HELL OUT OF HERE!

MAMA: [*Into action.*] Ain't it the truth! Look at all this here mess. Ruth, put
Travis' good jacket on him . . . Walter Lee, fix your tie and tuck your shirt
in, you look just like somebody's hoodlum. Lord have mercy, where is my
plant? [*She flies to get it amid the general bustling of the family, who are
deliberately trying to ignore the nobility of the past moment.*] You all start
on down . . . Travis child, don't go empty-handed . . . Ruth, where did I
put that box with my skillets in it? I want to be in charge of it myself . . .
I'm going to make us the biggest dinner we ever ate tonight . . . Beneatha,
what's the matter with them stockings? Pull them things up, girl . . .

[*The family starts to file out as two moving men appear and begin to
carry out the heavier pieces of furniture, bumping into the family as
they move about.*]

BENEATHA: Mama, Asagai—asked me to marry him today and go to
Africa—

MAMA: [*In the middle of her getting-ready activity.*] He did? You ain't old
enough to marry nobody— [*Seeing the moving men lifting one of her*

chairs precariously.] Darling, that ain't no bale of cotton, please handle it so we can sit in it again. I had that chair twenty-five years . . .

[*The movers sigh with exasperation and go on with their work.*]

BENEATHA: [*Girlishly and unreasonably trying to pursue the conversation.*] To go to Africa, Mama—be a doctor in Africa . . .

MAMA: [*Distracted.*] Yes, baby—

WALTER: Africa! What he want you to go to Africa for?

BENEATHA: To practice there . . .

WALTER: Girl, if you don't get all them silly ideas out your head! You better marry yourself a man with some loot . . .

BENEATHA: [*Angrily, precisely as in the first scene of the play.*] What have you got to do with who I marry!

WALTER: Plenty. Now I think George Murchison—

[*He and* BENEATHA *go out yelling at each other vigorously;* BENEATHA *is heard saying that she would not marry* GEORGE MURCHISON *if he were Adam and she were Eve, etc. The anger is loud and real till their voices diminish.* RUTH *stands at the door and turns to* MAMA *and smiles knowingly.*]

MAMA: [*Fixing her hat at last.*] Yeah—they something all right, my children . . .

RUTH: Yeah—they're something. Let's go, Lena.

MAMA: [*Stalling, starting to look around at the house.*] Yes—I'm coming. Ruth—

RUTH: Yes?

MAMA: [*Quietly, woman to woman.*] He finally come into his manhood today, didn't he? Kind of like a rainbow after the rain . . .

RUTH: [*Biting her lip lest her own pride explode in front of* MAMA.] Yes, Lena.

[WALTER's *voice calls for them raucously.*]

MAMA: [*Waving* RUTH *out vaguely.*] All right, honey—go on down. I be down directly.

[RUTH *hesitates, then exits.* MAMA *stands, at last alone in the living room, her plant on the table before her as the lights start to come down. She looks around at all the walls and ceilings and suddenly, despite herself, while the children call below, a great heaving thing rises in her and she puts her fist to her mouth, takes a final desperate look, pulls her coat about her, pats her hat and goes out. The lights dim down. The door opens and she comes back in, grabs her plant, and goes out for the last time.*]

[CURTAIN.]

1959

JANE MARTIN
Two Monologues from *Talking With* ...

The true identity of the award-winning playwright known as "Jane Martin" has been the subject of widespread speculation and debate since 1982, when her *Talking With* . . . debuted to great acclaim at the sixth annual Humana Festival in Louisville, Kentucky, and then went on to win the 1982 American Theatre Critics Association (ATCA) principal citation for most outstanding script of the season. Composed of eleven monologues by a diverse array of female characters, the play established Martin as a master of the monologue form and earned her comparisons to Flannery O'Connor, thanks not least to its bizarre, even grotesque, and usually obsessive characters, its deft rendering of their distinctive speech patterns, its often darkly religious undertones, and its fascination with physical and psychological violence. In the years since, Martin's work has included two other monologue-based plays, *Vital Signs* (1990) and *Sez She* (2006); comedies such as *Cementville* (1991) and *Criminal Hearts* (1992); the theater satire *Anton in Show Business* (2000), about three Texas actresses who mount a disastrous production of Anton Chekhov's *The Three Sisters;* the parody *Flaming Guns of the Purple Sage* (2001); and the highly topical plays *Keely and Du* (1993), about a working-class rape victim held captive by pro-life terrorists bent on preventing her from having an abortion; *Mr. Bundy* (1998), in which the parents of an eleven-year-old discover that a convicted child molester lives next door; and *Flags* (2005), which focuses on a father's extreme reaction to the death of his soldier-son in Iraq. Prior to 2001, almost all of Martin's plays debuted at the Humana Festival under the direction of its founder, Jon Jory (b. 1938). As a result, and despite the director's demurrals, many believe Jane Martin is in fact either Jory himself or a team of writers that includes him.

The play Talking With . . . *consists of eleven monologues delivered by a diverse array of female characters. We here include two, "Handler" and "French Fries."*

Handler

> *A young woman in a simple, country-print dress. On the floor before her is a handmade wooden box about two feet long and eighteen inches high with a sliding wire screen top.*

CARO: My Dada [Pronounced *"Dád-aw."*] was gonna do this tonight but the Lord froze his face so he sent me. I learned this from my Dada and

he learned it up from great Gran, who took it on from the Reverend Solo-
man Bracewood, who had him a mule ministry[1] 'round these parts way
back when. Dada taught Miss Ellie, my ma, and my brother Jamie . . . he
was in it too, 'fore he went for Detroit.

See, what I got in here is snakes. Lotta people don't like snakes.
Gives it its nature, I guess. This here is water mocs. Jamie, he said they
got the dirtiest, nastiest bite of all . . . well, rattlers is yer biggest. Lotta
venom. You milk you a rattler, you can half fill up a juice glass. Dada
said Jamie should do rattlers, but he never. Did 'heads, copperheads.
Now they're slower and safer but it ain't such a good show. You know
those dang snakes smell like cucumbers? Well, they do. Miss Ellie, she
favored moccasins. Dada too . . . well, Dada he did all kinds, all ways.
Your moccasin now, he's your good ol' boy snake. Flat out mean an' lots
of get up n' go. Heck, they'll chase ya. They will. Ol' Dada he didn't like
Miss Ellie doin' 'em. "You lay off them mocs 'fore they lay you down."
Made Miss Ellie laugh. Lotta handlers think moccasins are slimy.
Couldn't get me to touch one. They'll do rattlers . . . got him a nice dry
feel. Little bit sandpapery. Rattler can find ya in the pitch dark though.
They git on to yer body heat. Snake handlin.' *All* my blood does it. Only
Dada an' me now though. Snake handlin', with the Holiness Church.
Down where I come from we take God pretty serious. If you got the
spirit, snake don't bite. If he bites you, you know you ain't got the spirit.
Makes the difference real clear, don't it?

It's right there in the scripture . . . Mark, Chapter 16, verses 17 and 18,
"And these signs shall follow them that believe. In my name they shall
cast out devils; they shall speak in new tongues; they shall take up ser-
pents; and if they shall drink any deadly thing, it shall not hurt them; they
shall lay hands on the sick and they shall recover." Don't figure it could be
much clearer than that. There's some churches don't use snakes, use
strychnine, powdered poison, same idea though. They mix it with Cherry
kool-ade, sing 'em a hymn, drink it off, and then just stand around waitin'
to see if they fall over. Ain't much of a show. Not like snakes. Dada does
fire but I can't do it. Pours some kerosene in a coke bottle, sticks a rag in
the top and lights it up. Holds that fire under his chin, passes it down the
arm, puts his hand in it, you know, that kind of stuff. He says there's
people do blow torches down to Tennessee. I don't know. Jamie give it a
try 'fore he went to Detroit. Just about burned his ass off. Sorry.

When I handle, I keep 'em in this box. Dada gimme this and some
Heidi[2] doll on my ninth birthday. Sometimes I'll just open up the lid

---

1. That is, he was a traveling preacher who traveled by mule.
2. Protagonist of two Swiss children's books published in 1880 by Johanna Spyri and of many
subsequent films.

and put my foot in or, uh, maybe stick it open side to my chest. There's some lay it to their face. I don't. Scares my eyes. Durin' service we take 'em right out, pass 'em around. It's more dangerous than a single handler. Snake gets to comparin' who got the spirit a whole lot an' who jes got it some. Somebody's jes about bound to come in second. Don't get me wrong now. Y' don't die everytime yer bit. I been bit seven times. Four times by the same serpent. Dada says he got the sweet tooth for me. Dada been bit thirty-two times an' never saw him a doctor. Used to let me kiss him on the marks. Last one got him here.

(*Points to eye.*) Froze him right up. Dada says he'll thaw but I don't know.

Day after Jamie took off Miss Ellie did moccasins standin' in the back of the pickup over to Hard Burley. Shouldn't ought to 'cause her mind weren't there. Coal truck backfired and she got bit. Snake bit her three more times 'fore she hit the ground. Dada layed hands on her but she died anyway. There was ten of us handled right there at the funeral. Snake handlin'.

Snake knows what you feel. You can fool a person but you can't fool a snake. You got the spirit, God locks their jaws. Keeps you safe. Tell you what though . . . I don't believe in a God. Left me. Gone with Miss Ellie. I was handlin' when I knew it sure. Snake was jes comin' on down the line. Marita she yells out, "The Lord. Lord's in me and with me. In me and with me." Noah he was ululatin', talkin' in tongues. Couple of folks was rollin' and singing. Dada was doin' switch grips. Had Miss Ellie's weddin' ring on his little finger. And it came on me, heck, there ain't no God in here. There's just a bunch of shouters gettin' tranced. There ain't no God in here at all. 'Bout that time they layed that serpent to me. Felt fussy. Nasty. Just lookin' for an excuse y'know? An' I was an empty vessel, worse nor a pharasee,[3] grist for the mill. My blood went so cold I coulda crapped ice-cubes. Snake knew. Started to get leverage. So I said, "Snake. You Satan's hand-maiden. You're right, there ain't no God in me. I'm just a woman, but I'm the only woman in my Dada's house and he needs me home. Outta his faith and his need, you lock yer jaws." I let that snake feel a child's pure love and it sponged it up offa my hands and then ol' wiggley went limp. I tranced it. It was a real good service. Didn't nobody handlin' get bit.

(*Takes snake out of the box.*) Yes, you got to believe. Holiness Church is dead right about that. Make me wonder, you know? I git to lookin' at people and wonderin' if they got anything in 'em could lock a serpent's

---

3. In Matthew 23, Jesus represents the Pharisees, a Jewish sect, as "hypocrites" who do not practice as they preach.

jaws. Any power or spirit or love or whatever. I look at 'em and I wonder, could they handle? Tell you what though, you can see it in a face. You can read it. You look me full in the face it don't take me 30 seconds. It's like I was the snake, some ol' pit viper, an' I can read yer heart. Maybe you could handle and maybe you can't, but there's but one sure thing in this world . . . yer empty, yer gonna get bit.

[*Fade out.*]

French Fries

An old woman in a straight-back chair holding a McDonald's cup. She is surrounded by several bundles of newspapers. She wears thick glasses that distort her eyes to the viewer.

ANNA MAE: If I had one wish in my life, why I'd like to live in McDonald's. Right there in the restaurant. 'Stead of in this old place. I'll come up to the brow of the hill, bowed down with my troubles, hurtin' under my load and I'll see that yellow horseshoe, sort of like part of a rainbow, and it gives my old spirit a lift. Lord, I can sit in a McDonald's all day. I've done it too. Walked the seven miles with the sun just on its way, and then sat on the curb till five minutes of seven. First one there and the last to leave. Just like some ol' french fry they forgot.

I like the young people workin' there. Like a team of fine young horses when I was growin' up. All smilin'. Tell you what I really like though is the plastic. God gave us plastic so there wouldn't be no stains on his world. See, in the human world of the earth it all gets scratched, stained, tore up, faded down. Loses its shine. All of it does. In time. Well, God he gave us the idea of plastic so we'd know what the everlasting really was. See if there's plastic then there's surely eternity. It's God's hint.

You ever watch folks when they come on in the McDonald's? They always speed up, almost run the last few steps. You see if they don't. Old Dobbin[1] with the barn in sight. They know it's safe in there and it ain't safe outside. Now it ain't safe outside and you know it.

I've seen a man healed by a Big Mac. I have. I was just sittin' there. Last summer it was. Oh, they don't never move you on. It's a sacred law in McDonald's, you can sit for a hundred years. Only place in the world. Anyway, a fella, maybe thirty-five, maybe forty, come on in there dressed real nice, real bright tie, bran' new baseball cap, nice white socks and he

---

1. Traditional name for a horse, especially a working farm horse.

Laura Saladino in a scene from *Talking with . . .* at Theatre TCU

had him that disease. You know the one I mean, Cerebral Walrus[2] they call it. Anyway, he had him a cock leg. His poor old body had it two speeds at the same time. Now he got him some coffee, with a lid on, and sat him down and Jimmy the tow-head[3] cook knew him, see, and he brought over a Big Mac. Well, the sick fella ate maybe half of it and then he was just sittin', you know, suffering those tremors, when a couple of *ants* come right out of the burger. Now there ain't no ants in McDonald's no way. Lord sent those ants, and the sick fella he looked real sharp at the burger and a bunch *more* ants marched on out nice as you please and his head lolled right over and he pitched himself out of that chair and banged his head on the floor, loud. Thwack! Like a bowling ball dropping. Made you half sick to hear it. We jump up and run over but he was cold out. Well those servin' kids, so cute, they watered him, stuck a touch pepper up his nostril, slapped him right smart, and bang, up he got. Standin' an' blinkin'. "Well, how are you?," we say. An he looks us over, looks right in our eyes, and he say, "I'm fine." And he was. He was fine! Tipped his Cincinnati Reds baseball cap, big "us'-swallowed-the-canary" grin, paraded out of there clean, straight like a pole-bean poplar, walked him a plumb line without no trace of the "walrus." Got outside, jumped up, whooped, hollered, sang him the National Anthem, flagged down a

---

2. Cerebral palsy.   3. Someone with extremely blond, even white, hair.

Circle Line bus, an' rode off up Muhammad Ali Boulevard wavin' an' smilin' like the King of the Pharoahs. Healed by a Big Mac. I saw it.

McDonald's. You ever see anybody die in a McDonald's? No sir. No way. Nobody ever has died in one. Shoot, they die in Burger Kings all the time. Kentucky Fried Chicken's got their own damn ambulances. Noooooooooo, you can't die in a McDonald's no matter how hard you try. It's the spices. Seals you safe in this life like it seals in the flavor. Yesssssss, yes!

I asked Jarrell could I live there. See they close up around ten, and there ain't a thing goin' on in 'em till seven a.m. I'd just sit in those nice swingy chairs and lean forward. Rest my head on those cool, cool, smooth tables, sing me a hymn and sleep like a baby. Jarrell, he said he'd write him a letter up the chain of command and see would they let me. Oh, I got my bid in. Peaceful and clean.

Sometimes I see it like the last of a movie. You know how they start the picture up real close and then back it off steady and far? Well, that's how I dream it. I'm living in McDonald's and it's real late at night and you see me up close, smiling, and then you see the whole McDonald's from the outside, lit up and friendly. And I get smaller and smaller, like they do, and then it's just a light in the darkness, like a star, and I'm in it. I'm part of that light, part of the whole sky, and it's all McDonald's, but part of something even bigger, something fixed and shiny . . . like plastic.

I know. I know. It's just a dream. Just a beacon in the storm. But you got to have a dream. It's our dreams make us what we are.

[*Blackout.*]

1980

ARTHUR MILLER
(1915–2005)
Death of a Salesman

Arthur Miller was born in New York City to a prosperous family whose fortunes were ruined by the Depression, a circumstance that would shape his political outlook and imbue him with a deep sense of social responsibility. Miller studied history, economics, and journalism at the University of Michigan, began writing plays, and joined the Federal Theater Project, a proving ground for some of the best playwrights of the period. He had his first Broadway success, *All My Sons*, in 1947, followed two years later by his Pulitzer Prize–winning masterpiece, *Death of a Salesman*. In 1953, against the backdrop of Senator Joseph McCarthy's anti-Communist "witch-hunts," Miller fashioned another modern parable, his Tony Award–winning *The Crucible*, based on the seventeenth-century Salem witch trials. Among his other works for the stage are the Pulitzer Prize–winner *A View from the Bridge* (1955), *After the Fall* (1964), *Incident at Vichy* (1965), *The Price* (1968), *The Ride Down Mt. Morgan* (1991), *Broken Glass* (1994), and *Resurrection Blues* (2004). In addition, Miller wrote a novel, *Focus* (1945); the screenplay for the film *The Misfits* (1961), which starred his second wife, Marilyn Monroe; *The Theater Essays* (1971), a collection of his writings about dramatic literature; and *Timebends* (1987), his autobiography.

Certain Private Conversations in Two Acts and a Requiem

CHARACTERS

WILLY LOMAN	THE WOMAN	STANLEY
LINDA	CHARLEY	MISS FORSYTHE
BIFF	UNCLE BEN	LETTA
HAPPY	HOWARD WAGNER	
BERNARD	JENNY	

The action takes place in WILLY LOMAN'S *house and yard and in various places he visits in the New York and Boston of today.*

ACT I

A melody is heard, playing upon a flute. It is small and fine, telling of grass and trees and the horizon. The curtain rises.

Before us is the Salesman's house. We are aware of towering, angular shapes behind it, surrounding it on all sides. Only the blue light of the sky falls upon the house and forestage; the surrounding area shows an angry flow of orange. As more light appears, we see a solid vault of apartment houses around the small, fragile-seeming home. An air of the dream clings to the place, a dream rising out of reality. The kitchen at center seems actual enough, for there is a kitchen table with three chairs, and a refrigerator. But no other fixtures are seen. At the back of the kitchen there is a draped entrance, which leads to the living-room. To the right of the kitchen, on a level raised two feet, is a bedroom furnished only with a brass bedstead and a straight chair. On a shelf over the bed a silver athletic trophy stands. A window opens onto the apartment house at the side.

Behind the kitchen, on a level raised six and a half feet, is the boys' bedroom, at present barely visible. Two beds are dimly seen, and at the back of the room a dormer window. (This bedroom is above the unseen living-room.) At the left a stairway curves up to it from the kitchen.

The entire setting is wholly or, in some places, partially transparent. The roof-line of the house is one-dimensional; under and over it we see the apartment buildings. Before the house lies an apron, curving beyond the forestage into the orchestra. This forward area serves as the back yard as well as the locale of all WILLY's imaginings and of his city scenes. Whenever the action is in the present the actors observe the imaginary wall-lines, entering the house only through its door at the left. But in the scenes of the past these boundaries are broken, and characters enter or leave a room by stepping "through" a wall onto the forestage.

From the right, WILLY LOMAN, the Salesman, enters, carrying two large sample cases. The flute plays on. He hears but is not aware of it. He is past sixty years of age, dressed quietly. Even as he crosses the stage to the doorway of the house, his exhaustion is apparent. He unlocks the door, comes into the kitchen, and thankfully lets his burden down, feeling the soreness of his palms. A word-sigh escapes his lips—it might be "Oh, boy, oh, boy." He closes the door, then carries his cases out into the living-room, through the draped kitchen doorway.

LINDA, his wife, has stirred in her bed at the right. She gets out and puts on a robe, listening. Most often jovial, she has developed an iron repression of her exceptions to WILLY's behavior—she more than loves him, she admires him, as though his mercurial nature, his temper, his massive dreams and little cruelties, served her only as sharp reminders of the turbulent longings within him, longings which she shares but lacks the temperament to utter and follow to their end.

LINDA: [Hearing WILLY outside the bedroom, calls with some trepidation.] Willy!

WILLY: It's all right. I came back.

LINDA: Why? What happened? [Slight pause.] Did something happen, Willy?

WILLY: No, nothing happened.

LINDA: You didn't smash the car, did you?

WILLY: [With casual irritation.] I said nothing happened. Didn't you hear me?

LINDA: Don't you feel well?

WILLY: I'm tired to the death. [The flute has faded away. He sits on the bed beside her, a little numb.] I couldn't make it. I just couldn't make it, Linda.

LINDA: [Very carefully, delicately.] Where were you all day? You look terrible.

WILLY: I got as far as a little above Yonkers. I stopped for a cup of coffee. Maybe it was the coffee.

LINDA: What?

WILLY: [*After a pause.*] I suddenly couldn't drive any more. The car kept going off onto the shoulder, y'know?

LINDA: [*Helpfully.*] Oh. Maybe it was the steering again. I don't think Angelo knows the Studebaker.

WILLY: No, it's me, it's me. Suddenly I realize I'm goin' sixty miles an hour and I don't remember the last five minutes. I'm—I can't seem to—keep my mind to it.

LINDA: Maybe it's your glasses. You never went for your new glasses.

WILLY: No, I see everything. I came back ten miles an hour. It took me nearly four hours from Yonkers.

LINDA: [*Resigned.*] Well, you'll just have to take a rest, Willy, you can't continue this way.

WILLY: I just got back from Florida.

LINDA: But you didn't rest your mind. Your mind is overactive, and the mind is what counts, dear.

WILLY: I'll start out in the morning. Maybe I'll feel better in the morning. [*She is taking off his shoes.*] These goddam arch supports are killing me.

LINDA: Take an aspirin. Should I get you an aspirin? It'll soothe you.

WILLY: [*With wonder.*] I was driving along, you understand? And I was fine. I was even observing the scenery. You can imagine, me looking at scenery, on the road every week of my life. But it's so beautiful up there, Linda, the trees are so thick, and the sun is warm. I opened the windshield and just let the warm air bathe over me. And then all of a sudden I'm goin' off the road! I'm tellin' ya, I absolutely forgot I was driving. If I'd've gone the other way over the white line I might've killed somebody. So I went on again—and five minutes later I'm dreamin' again, and I nearly—[*He presses two fingers against his eyes.*] I have such thoughts, I have such strange thoughts.

LINDA: Willy, dear. Talk to them again. There's no reason why you can't work in New York.

WILLY: They don't need me in New York. I'm the New England man. I'm vital in New England.

LINDA: But you're sixty years old. They can't expect you to keep traveling every week.

WILLY: I'll have to send a wire[1] to Portland. I'm supposed to see Brown and Morrison tomorrow morning at ten o'clock to show the line. Goddammit, I could sell them! [*He starts putting on his jacket.*]

---

1. Telegram.

LINDA: [*Taking the jacket from him.*] Why don't you go down to the place tomorrow and tell Howard you've simply got to work in New York? You're too accommodating, dear.

WILLY: If old man Wagner was alive I'da been in charge of New York now! That man was a prince, he was a masterful man. But that boy of his, that Howard, he don't appreciate. When I went north the first time, the Wagner Company didn't know where New England was!

LINDA: Why don't you tell those things to Howard, dear?

WILLY: [*Encouraged.*] I will, I definitely will. Is there any cheese?

LINDA: I'll make you a sandwich.

WILLY: No, go to sleep. I'll take some milk. I'll be up right away. The boys in?

LINDA: They're sleeping. Happy took Biff on a date tonight.

WILLY: [*Interested.*] That so?

LINDA: It was so nice to see them shaving together, one behind the other, in the bathroom. And going out together. You notice? The whole house smells of shaving lotion.

WILLY: Figure it out. Work a lifetime to pay off a house. You finally own it, and there's nobody to live in it.

LINDA: Well, dear, life is a casting off. It's always that way.

WILLY: No, no, some people—some people accomplish something. Did Biff say anything after I went this morning?

LINDA: You shouldn't have criticized him, Willy, especially after he just got off the train. You mustn't lose your temper with him.

WILLY: When the hell did I lose my temper? I simply asked him if he was making any money. Is that a criticism?

LINDA: But, dear, how could he make any money?

WILLY: [*Worried and angered.*] There's such an undercurrent in him. He became a moody man. Did he apologize when I left this morning?

LINDA: He was crestfallen, Willy. You know how he admires you. I think if he finds himself, then you'll both be happier and not fight any more.

WILLY: How can he find himself on a farm? Is that a life? A farmhand? In the beginning, when he was young, I thought, well, a young man, it's good for him to tramp around, take a lot of different jobs. But it's more than ten years now and he has yet to make thirty-five dollars a week!

LINDA: He's finding himself, Willy.

WILLY: Not finding yourself at the age of thirty-four is a disgrace!

LINDA: Shh!

WILLY: The trouble is he's lazy, goddammit!

LINDA: Willy, please!

WILLY: Biff is a lazy bum!

LINDA: They're sleeping. Get something to eat. Go on down.

WILLY: Why did he come home? I would like to know what brought him home.

LINDA: I don't know. I think he's still lost, Willy. I think he's very lost.

WILLY: Biff Loman is lost. In the greatest country in the world a young man with such—personal attractiveness, gets lost. And such a hard worker. There's one thing about Biff—he's not lazy.

LINDA: Never.

WILLY: [*With pity and resolve.*] I'll see him in the morning; I'll have a nice talk with him. I'll get him a job selling. He could be big in no time. My God! Remember how they used to follow him around in high school? When he smiled at one of them their faces lit up. When he walked down the street . . . [*He loses himself in reminiscences.*]

LINDA: [*Trying to bring him out of it.*] Willy, dear, I got a new kind of American-type cheese today. It's whipped.

WILLY: Why do you get American when I like Swiss?

LINDA: I just thought you'd like a change—

WILLY: I don't want a change! I want Swiss cheese. Why am I always being contradicted?

LINDA: [*With a covering laugh.*] I thought it would be a surprise.

WILLY: Why don't you open a window in here, for God's sake?

LINDA: [*With infinite patience.*] They're all open, dear.

WILLY: The way they boxed us in here. Bricks and windows, windows and bricks.

LINDA: We should've bought the land next door.

WILLY: The street is lined with cars. There's not a breath of fresh air in the neighborhood. The grass don't grow any more, you can't raise a carrot in the back yard. They should've had a law against apartment houses. Remember those two beautiful elm trees out there? When I and Biff hung the swing between them?

LINDA: Yeah, like being a million miles from the city.

WILLY: They should've arrested the builder for cutting those down. They massacred the neighborhood. [*Lost.*] More and more I think of those days, Linda. This time of year it was lilac and wisteria. And then the peonies would come out, and the daffodils. What fragrance in this room!

LINDA: Well, after all, people had to move somewhere.

WILLY: No, there's more people now.

LINDA: I don't think there's more people. I think—

WILLY: There's more people! That's what ruining this country! Population is getting out of control. The competition is maddening! Smell the stink from that apartment house! And another one on the other side . . . How can they whip cheese?

[*On* WILLY's *last line,* BIFF *and* HAPPY *raise themselves up in their beds, listening.*]

LINDA: Go down, try it. And be quiet.

WILLY: [*Turning to* LINDA, *guiltily.*] You're not worried about me, are you, sweetheart?

BIFF: What's the matter?

HAPPY: Listen!

LINDA: You've got too much on the ball to worry about.

WILLY: You're my foundation and my support, Linda.

LINDA: Just try to relax, dear. You make mountains out of mole-hills.

WILLY: I won't fight with him anymore. If he wants to go back to Texas, let him go.

LINDA: He'll find his way.

WILLY: Sure. Certain men just don't get started till later in life. Like Thomas Edison, I think. Or B. F. Goodrich. One of them was deaf.[2] [*He starts for the bedroom doorway.*] I'll put my money on Biff.

LINDA: And Willy—if it's warm Sunday we'll drive in the country. And we'll open the windshield, and take lunch.

WILLY: No, the windshields don't open on the new cars.

LINDA: But you opened it today.

WILLY: Me? I didn't. [*He stops.*] Now isn't that peculiar! Isn't that a remark-able—[*He breaks off in amazement and fright as the flute is heard distantly.*]

LINDA: What, darling?

WILLY: That is the most remarkable thing.

LINDA: What, dear?

WILLY: I was thinking of the Chevvy. [*Slight pause.*] Nineteen twenty-eight . . . when I had that red Chevvy—[*Breaks off.*] That funny? I coulda sworn I was driving that Chevvy today.

LINDA: Well, that's nothing. Something must've reminded you.

WILLY: Remarkable. Ts. Remember those days? The way Biff used to simo-nize[3] that car? The dealer refused to believe there was eighty thousand miles on it. [*He shakes his head.*] Heh! [*To* LINDA.] Close your eyes, I'll be right up. [*He walks out of the bedroom.*]

HAPPY: [*To* BIFF.] Jesus, maybe he smashed up the car again!

2. Thomas Alva Edison (1847–1931), American inventor best known for the phonograph and the incandescent lightbulb; Edison's deafness was legendary. Benjamin Franklin Goodrich (1841–88), American industrialist known for the tire company that still bears his name.
3. Polish with car wax. Ts: Ford Model Ts, extraordinarily popular cars manufactured from 1908 to 1928.

LINDA: [*Calling after* WILLY.] Be careful on the stairs, dear! The cheese is on the middle shelf! [*She turns, goes over to the bed, takes his jacket, and goes out of the bedroom.*]

[*Light has risen on the boys' room. Unseen,* WILLY *is heard talking to himself, "Eighty thousand miles," and a little laugh.* BIFF *gets out of bed, comes downstage a bit, and stands attentively.* BIFF *is two years older than his brother,* HAPPY, *well built, but in these days bears a worn air and seems less self-assured. He has succeeded less, and his dreams are stronger and less acceptable than* HAPPY'S. HAPPY *is tall, powerfully made. Sexuality is like a visible color on him, or a scent that many women have discovered. He, like his brother, is lost, but in a different way, for he has never allowed himself to turn his face toward defeat and is thus more confused and hard-skinned, although seemingly more content.*]

HAPPY: [*Getting out of bed.*] He's going to get his license taken away if he keeps that up. I'm getting nervous about him, y'know, Biff?

BIFF: His eyes are going.

HAPPY: No, I've driven with him. He sees all right. He just doesn't keep his mind on it. I drove into the city with him last week. He stops at a green light and then it turns red and he goes. [*He laughs.*]

BIFF: Maybe he's color-blind.

HAPPY: Pop? Why he's got the finest eye for color in the business. You know that.

BIFF: [*Sitting down on his bed.*] I'm going to sleep.

HAPPY: You're not still sour on Dad, are you Biff?

BIFF: He's all right, I guess.

WILLY: [*Underneath them, in the living-room.*] Yes, sir, eighty thousand miles—eighty-two thousand!

BIFF: You smoking?

HAPPY: [*Holding out a pack of cigarettes.*] Want one?

BIFF: [*Taking a cigarette.*] I can never sleep when I smell it.

WILLY: What a simonizing job, heh!

HAPPY: [*With deep sentiment.*] Funny, Biff, y'know? Us sleeping in here again? The old beds. [*He pats his bed affectionately.*] All the talk that went across those two beds, huh? Our whole lives.

BIFF: Yeah. Lotta dreams and plans.

HAPPY: [*With a deep and masculine laugh.*] About five hundred women would like to know what was said in this room.

[*They share a soft laugh.*]

BIFF: Remember that big Betsy something—what the hell was her name—over on Bushwick Avenue?[4]

HAPPY: [*Combing his hair.*] With the collie dog!

BIFF: That's the one. I got you in there, remember?

HAPPY: Yeah, that was my first time—I think. Boy, there was a pig! [*They laugh, almost crudely.*] You taught me everything I know about women. Don't forget that.

BIFF: I bet you forgot how bashful you used to be. Especially with girls.

HAPPY: Oh, I still am, Biff.

BIFF: Oh, go on.

HAPPY: I just control it, that's all. I think I got less bashful and you got more so. What happened, Biff? Where's the old humor, the old confidence? [*He shakes* BIFF's *knee.* BIFF *gets up and moves restlessly about the room.*] What's the matter?

BIFF: Why does Dad mock me all the time?

HAPPY: He's not mocking you, he—

BIFF: Everything I say there's a twist of mockery on his face. I can't get near him.

HAPPY: He just wants you to make good, that's all. I wanted to talk to you about Dad for a long time, Biff. Something's—happening to him. He—talks to himself.

BIFF: I noticed that this morning. But he always mumbled.

HAPPY: But not so noticeable. It got so embarrassing I sent him to Florida. And you know something? Most of the time he's talking to you.

BIFF: What's he say about me?

HAPPY: I can't make it out.

BIFF: What's he say about me?

HAPPY: I think the fact that you're not settled, that you're still kind of up in the air . . .

BIFF: There's one or two things depressing him, Happy.

HAPPY: What do you mean?

BIFF: Never mind. Just don't lay it all to me.

HAPPY: But I think if you just got started—I mean—is there any future for you out there?

BIFF: I tell ya, Hap, I don't know what the future is. I don't know—what I'm supposed to want.

HAPPY: What do you mean?

BIFF: Well, I spent six or seven years after high school trying to work myself up. Shipping clerk, salesman, business of one kind or another. And it's a measly manner of existence. To get on that subway on the hot morn-

---

4. Major thoroughfare in Brooklyn, New York.

ings in summer. To devote your whole life to keeping stock, or making phone calls, or selling or buying. To suffer fifty weeks of the year for the sake of a two-week vacation, when all you really desire is to be outdoors, with your shirt off. And always to have to get ahead of the next fella. And still—that's how you build a future.

HAPPY: Well, you really enjoy it on a farm? Are you content out there?

BIFF: [*With rising agitation.*] Hap, I've had twenty or thirty different kinds of jobs since I left home before the war, and it always turns out the same. I just realized it lately. In Nebraska when I herded cattle, and the Dakotas, and Arizona, and now in Texas. It's why I came home now, I guess, because I realized it. This farm I work on, it's spring there now, see? And they've got about fifteen new colts. There's nothing more inspiring or—beautiful than the sight of a mare and a new colt. And it's cool there now, see? Texas is cool now, and it's spring. And whenever spring comes to where I am, I suddenly get the feeling, my God, I'm not gettin' anywhere! What the hell am I doing, playing around with horses, twenty-eight dollars a week! I'm thirty-four years old. I oughta be makin' my future. That's when I come running home. And now, I get there, and I don't know what to do with myself. [*After a pause.*] I've always made a point of not wasting my life, and everytime I come back here I know that all I've done is to waste my life.

HAPPY: You're a poet, you know that, Biff? You're a—you're an idealist!

BIFF: No, I'm mixed up very bad. Maybe I oughta get married. Maybe I oughta get stuck into something. Maybe that's my trouble. I'm like a boy. I'm not married. I'm not in business, I just—I'm like a boy. Are you content, Hap? You're a success, aren't you? Are you content?

HAPPY: Hell, no!

BIFF: Why? You're making money, aren't you?

HAPPY: [*Moving about with energy, expressiveness.*] All I can do now is wait for the merchandise manager to die. And suppose I get to be merchandise manager? He's a good friend of mine, and he just built a terrific estate on Long Island. And he lived there about two months and sold it, and now he's building another one. He can't enjoy it once it's finished. And I know that's just what I would do. I don't know what the hell I'm workin' for. Sometimes I sit in my apartment—all alone. And I think of the rent I'm paying. And it's crazy. But then, it's what I always wanted. My own apartment, a car, and plenty of women. And still, goddammit, I'm lonely.

BIFF: [*With enthusiasm.*] Listen, why don't you come out West with me?

HAPPY: You and I, heh?

BIFF: Sure, maybe we could buy a ranch. Raise cattle, use our muscles. Men built like we are should be working out in the open.

HAPPY: [*Avidly.*] The Loman Brothers, heh?

BIFF: [*With vast affection.*] Sure, we'd be known all over the counties!

HAPPY: [*Enthralled.*] That's what I dream about, Biff. Sometimes I want to just rip my clothes off in the middle of the store and outbox that goddam merchandise manager. I mean I can outbox, outrun, and outlift anybody in that store, and I have to take orders from those common, petty sons-of-bitches till I can't stand it anymore.

BIFF: I'm tellin' you, kid, if you were with me I'd be happy out there.

HAPPY: [*Enthused.*] See, Biff, everybody around me is so false that I'm constantly lowering my ideals . . .

BIFF: Baby, together we'd stand up for one another, we'd have someone to trust.

HAPPY: If I were around you—

BIFF: Hap, the trouble is we weren't brought up to grub for money. I don't know how to do it.

HAPPY: Neither can I!

BIFF: Then let's go!

HAPPY: The only thing is—what can you make out there?

BIFF: But look at your friend. Builds an estate and then hasn't the peace of mind to live in it.

HAPPY: Yeah, but when he walks into the store the waves part in front of him. That's fifty-two thousand dollars a year coming through the revolving door, and I got more in my pinky finger than he's got in his head.

BIFF: Yeah, but you just said—

HAPPY: I gotta show some of those pompous, self-important executives over there that Hap Loman can make the grade. I want to walk into the store the way he walks in. Then I'll go with you, Biff. We'll be together yet, I swear. But take those two we had tonight. Now weren't they gorgeous creatures?

BIFF: Yeah, yeah, most gorgeous I've had in years.

HAPPY: I get that any time I want, Biff. Whenever I feel disgusted. The only trouble is, it gets like bowling or something. I just keep knockin' them over and it doesn't mean anything. You still run around a lot?

BIFF: Naa. I'd like to find a girl—steady, somebody with substance.

HAPPY: That's what I long for.

BIFF: Go on! You'd never come home.

HAPPY: I would! Somebody with character, with resistance! Like Mom, y'know? You're gonna call me a bastard when I tell you this. That girl Charlotte I was with tonight is engaged to be married in five weeks. [*He tries on his new hat.*]

BIFF: No kiddin'!

HAPPY: Sure, the guy's in line for the vice-presidency of the store. I don't know what gets into me, maybe I just have an overdeveloped sense of competition or something, but I went and ruined her, and furthermore I can't get rid of her. And he's the third executive I've done that to. Isn't that a crummy characteristic? And to top it all, I go to their weddings! [*Indignantly, but laughing.*] Like I'm not supposed to take bribes. Manufacturers offer me a hundred-dollar bill now and then to throw an order their way. You know how honest I am, but it's like this girl, see. I hate myself for it. Because I don't want the girl, and, still, I take it and—I love it!

BIFF: Let's go to sleep.

HAPPY: I guess we didn't settle anything, heh?

BIFF: I just got one idea that I'm going to try.

HAPPY: What's that?

BIFF: Remember Bill Oliver?

HAPPY: Sure, Oliver is very big now. You want to work for him again?

BIFF: No, but when I quit he said something to me. He put his arm on my shoulder, and he said, "Biff, if you ever need anything, come to me."

HAPPY: I remember that. That sounds good.

BIFF: I think I'll go to see him. If I could get ten thousand or even seven or eight thousand dollars I could buy a beautiful ranch.

HAPPY: I bet he'd back you. 'Cause he thought highly of you, Biff. I mean, they all do. You're well liked, Biff. That's why I say to come back here, and we both have the apartment. And I'm tellin' you, Biff, any babe you want . . .

BIFF: No, with a ranch I could do the work I like and still be something. I just wonder though. I wonder if Oliver still thinks I stole that carton of basketballs.

HAPPY: Oh, he probably forgot that long ago. It's almost ten years. You're too sensitive. Anyway, he didn't really fire you.

BIFF: Well, I think he was going to. I think that's why I quit. I was never sure whether he knew or not. I know he thought the world of me, though. I was the only one he'd let lock up the place.

WILLY: [*Below.*] You gonna wash the engine, Biff?

HAPPY: Shh! [BIFF *looks at* HAPPY, *who is gazing down, listening.* WILLY *is mumbling in the parlor.*] You hear that?

[*They listen.* WILLY *laughs warmly.*]

BIFF: [*Growing angry.*] Doesn't he know Mom can hear that?

WILLY: Don't get your sweater dirty, Biff!

[*A look of pain crosses* BIFF's *face.*]

HAPPY: Isn't that terrible? Don't leave again, will you? You'll find a job here. You gotta stick around. I don't know what to do about him, it's getting embarrassing.

WILLY: What a simonizing job!

BIFF: Mom's hearing that!

WILLY: No kiddin', Biff, you got a date? Wonderful!

HAPPY: Go on to sleep. But talk to him in the morning, will you?

BIFF: [*Reluctantly getting into bed.*] With her in the house. Brother!

HAPPY: [*Getting into bed.*] I wish you'd have a good talk with him.

[*The light on their room begins to fade.*]

BIFF: [To himself in bed.] That selfish, stupid . . .

HAPPY: Sh . . . Sleep, Biff.

[*Their light is out. Well before they have finished speaking,* WILLY's *form is dimly seen below in the darkened kitchen. He opens the refrigerator, searches in there, and takes out a bottle of milk. The apartment houses are fading out, and the entire house and surroundings become covered with leaves. Music insinuates itself as the leaves appear.*]

WILLY: Just wanna be careful with those girls, Biff, that's all. Don't make any promises. No promises of any kind. Because a girl, y'know, they always believe what you tell 'em, and you're very young, Biff, you're too young to be talking seriously to girls. [*Light rises on the kitchen.* WILLY, *talking, shuts the refrigerator door and comes downstage to the kitchen table. He pours milk into a glass. He is totally immersed in himself, smiling faintly.*] Too young entirely, Biff. You want to watch your schooling first. Then when you're all set, there'll be plenty of girls for a boy like you. [*He smiles broadly at a kitchen chair.*] That so? The girls pay for you? [*He laughs.*] Boy, you must really be makin' a hit. [WILLY *is gradually addressing—physically—a point offstage, speaking through the wall of the kitchen, and his voice has been rising in volume to that of a normal conversation.*] I been wondering why you polish the car so careful. Ha! Don't leave the hubcaps, boys. Get the chamois to the hubcaps. Happy, use newspaper on the windows, it's the easiest thing. Show him how to do it, Biff! You see, Happy? Pad it up, use it like a pad. That's it, that's it, good work. You're doin' all right, Hap. [*He pauses, then nods in approbation for a few seconds, then looks upward.*] Biff, first thing we gotta do when we get time is clip that big branch over the house. Afraid it's gonna fall in a storm and hit the roof. Tell you what. We get a rope and sling her around, and then we climb up there with a couple of saws and take her down. Soon as you finish the car, boys, I wanna see ya. I got a surprise for you, boys.

BIFF: [*Offstage.*] Whatta ya got, Dad?

WILLY: No, you finish first. Never leave a job till you're finished—remember that. [*Looking toward the "big trees."*] Biff, up in Albany I saw a beautiful hammock. I think I'll buy it next trip, and we'll hang it right between those two elms. Wouldn't that be something? Just swingin' there under those branches. Boy, that would be . . .

[YOUNG BIFF *and* YOUNG HAPPY *appear from the direction* WILLY *was addressing.* HAPPY *carries rags and a pail of water.* BIFF, *wearing a sweater with a block "S," carries a football.*]

BIFF: [*Pointing in the direction of the car offstage.*] How's that, Pop, professional?

WILLY: Terrific. Terrific job, boys. Good work, Biff.

HAPPY: Where's the surprise, Pop?

WILLY: In the back seat of the car.

HAPPY: Boy! [*He runs off.*]

BIFF: What is it, Dad? Tell me, what'd you buy?

WILLY: [*Laughing, cuffs him.*] Never mind, something I want you to have.

BIFF: [*Turns and starts off.*] What is it, Hap?

HAPPY: [*Offstage.*] It's a punching bag!

BIFF: Oh, Pop!

WILLY: It's got Gene Tunney's[5] signature on it!

[HAPPY *runs onstage with a punching bag.*]

BIFF: Gee, how'd you know we wanted a punching bag?

WILLY: Well, it's the finest thing for the timing.

HAPPY: [*Lies down on his back and pedals with his feet.*] I'm losing weight, you notice, Pop?

WILLY: [*To* HAPPY.] Jumping rope is good too.

BIFF: Did you see the new football I got?

WILLY: [*Examining the ball.*] Where'd you get a new ball?

BIFF: The coach told me to practice my passing.

WILLY: That so? And he gave you the ball, heh?

BIFF: Well, I borrowed it from the locker room. [*He laughs confidentially.*]

WILLY: [*Laughing with him at the theft.*] I want you to return that.

HAPPY: I told you he wouldn't like it!

BIFF: [*Angrily.*] Well, I'm bringing it back!

WILLY: [*Stopping the incipient argument, to* HAPPY.] Sure, he's gotta practice with a regulation ball, doesn't he? [*To* BIFF.] Coach'll probably congratulate you on your initiative!

BIFF: Oh, he keeps congratulating my initiative all the time, Pop.

---

5. Tunney (1897–1978) was world heavyweight boxing champion from 1926 to 1928 and retired undefeated.

WILLY: That's because he likes you. If somebody else took that ball there'd be an uproar. So what's the report, boys, what's the report?

BIFF: Where'd you go this time, Dad? Gee we were lonesome for you.

WILLY: [*Pleased, puts an arm around each boy and they come down to the apron.*] Lonesome, heh?

BIFF: Missed you every minute.

WILLY: Don't say? Tell you a secret, boys. Don't breathe it to a soul. Someday I'll have my own business, and I'll never have to leave home anymore.

HAPPY: Like Uncle Charley, heh?

WILLY: Bigger than Uncle Charley! Because Charley is not—liked. He's liked, but he's not—well liked.

BIFF: Where'd you go this time, Dad?

WILLY: Well, I got on the road, and I went north to Providence. Met the mayor.

BIFF: The mayor of Providence!

WILLY: He was sitting in the hotel lobby.

BIFF: What'd he say?

WILLY: He said, "Morning!" And I said, "You got a fine city here, Mayor." And then he had coffee with me. And then I went to Waterbury. Waterbury is a fine city. Big clock city, the famous Waterbury clock. Sold a nice bill there. And then Boston—Boston is the cradle of the Revolution. A fine city. And a couple of other towns in Mass., and on to Portland and Bangor and straight home!

BIFF: Gee, I'd love to go with you sometime, Dad.

WILLY: Soon as summer comes.

HAPPY: Promise?

WILLY: You and Hap and I, and I'll show you all the towns. America is full of beautiful towns and fine, upstanding people. And they know me, boys, they know me up and down New England. The finest people. And when I bring you fellas up, there'll be open sesame for all of us, 'cause one thing, boys: I have friends. I can park my car in any street in New England, and the cops protect it like their own. This summer, heh?

BIFF and HAPPY: [*Together.*] Yeah! You bet!

WILLY: We'll take our bathing suits.

HAPPY: We'll carry your bags, Pop!

WILLY: Oh, won't that be something! Me comin' into the Boston stores with you boys carryin' my bags. What a sensation! [BIFF *is prancing around, practicing passing the ball.*] You nervous, Biff, about the game?

BIFF: Not if you're gonna be there.

WILLY: What do they say about you in school, now that they made you captain?

HAPPY: There's a crowd of girls behind him every time the classes change.

BIFF: [*Taking* WILLY's *hand.*] This Saturday, Pop, this Saturday—just for you, I'm going to break through for a touchdown.

HAPPY: You're supposed to pass.

BIFF: I'm takin' one play for Pop. You watch me, Pop, and when I take off my helmet, that means I'm breakin' out. Then you watch me crash through that line!

WILLY: [*Kisses* BIFF.] Oh, wait'll I tell this in Boston!

[BERNARD *enters in knickers. He is younger than* BIFF, *earnest and loyal, a worried boy.*]

BERNARD: Biff, where are you? You're supposed to study with me today.

WILLY: Hey, looka Bernard. What're you lookin' so anemic about, Bernard?

BERNARD: He's gotta study, Uncle Willy. He's got Regents[6] next week.

HAPPY: [*Tauntingly, spinning* BERNARD *around.*] Let's box, Bernard!

BERNARD: Biff! [*He gets away from* HAPPY.] Listen, Biff, I heard Mr. Birnbaum say that if you don't start studyin' math he's gonna flunk you, and you won't graduate. I heard him!

WILLY: You better study with him, Biff. Go ahead now.

BERNARD: I heard him!

BIFF: Oh, Pop, you didn't see my sneakers! [*He holds up a foot for* WILLY *to look at.*]

WILLY: Hey, that's a beautiful job of printing!

BERNARD: [*Wiping his glasses.*] Just because he printed University of Virginia on his sneakers doesn't mean they've got to graduate him, Uncle Willy!

WILLY: [*Angrily.*] What're you talking about? With scholarships to three universities they're gonna flunk him?

BERNARD: But I heard Mr. Birnbaum say—

WILLY: Don't be a pest, Bernard! [*To his boys.*] What an anemic!

BERNARD: Okay, I'm waiting for you in my house, Biff.

[BERNARD *goes off. The* LOMANS *laugh.*]

WILLY: Bernard is not well liked, is he?

BIFF: He's liked, but he's not well liked.

HAPPY: That's right, Pop.

WILLY: That's just what I mean. Bernard can get the best marks in school, y'understand, but when he gets out in the business world, y'understand,

---

6. Examinations administered to New York State high-school students.

you are going to be five times ahead of him. That's why I thank Almighty God you're both built like Adonises.[7] Because the man who makes an appearance in the business world, the man who creates personal interest, is the man who gets ahead. Be liked and you will never want. You take me, for instance. I never have to wait in line to see a buyer. "Willy Loman is here!" That's all they have to know, and I go right through.

BIFF: Did you knock them dead, Pop?

WILLY: Knocked 'em cold in Providence, slaughtered 'em in Boston.

HAPPY: [*On his back, pedaling again.*] I'm losing weight, you notice, Pop?

[LINDA *enters, as of old, a ribbon in her hair, carrying a basket of washing.*]

LINDA: [*With youthful energy.*] Hello, dear!

WILLY: Sweetheart!

LINDA: How'd the Chevvy run?

WILLY: Chevrolet, Linda, is the greatest car ever built. [*To the boys.*] Since when do you let your mother carry wash up the stairs?

BIFF: Grab hold there, boy!

HAPPY: Where to, Mom?

LINDA: Hang them up on the line. And you better go down to your friends, Biff. The cellar is full of boys. They don't know what to do with themselves.

BIFF: Ah, when Pop comes home they can wait!

WILLY: [*Laughs appreciatively.*] You better go down and tell them what to do, Biff.

BIFF: I think I'll have them sweep out the furnace room.

WILLY: Good work, Biff.

BIFF: [*Goes through wall-line of kitchen to doorway at back and calls down.*] Fellas! Everybody sweep out the furnace room! I'll be right down!

VOICES: All right! Okay, Biff.

BIFF: George and Sam and Frank, come out back! We're hangin' up the wash! Come on, Hap, on the double!

[*He and* HAPPY *carry out the basket.*]

LINDA: The way they obey him!

WILLY: Well, that training, the training. I'm tellin' you, I was sellin' thousands and thousands, but I had to come home.

LINDA: Oh, the whole block'll be at that game. Did you sell anything?

WILLY: I did five hundred gross in Providence and seven hundred gross in Boston.

---

7. In Greek myth Adonis was a beautiful youth.

LINDA: No! Wait a minute, I've got a pencil. [*She pulls pencil and paper out of her apron pocket.*] That makes your commission . . . Two hundred—my God! Two hundred and twelve dollars!

WILLY: Well, I didn't figure it yet, but . . .

LINDA: How much did you do?

WILLY: Well, I—I did—about a hundred and eighty gross in Providence. Well, no—it came to—roughly two hundred gross on the whole trip.

LINDA: [*Without hesitation.*] Two hundred gross. That's . . . [*She figures.*]

WILLY: The trouble was that three of the stores were half closed for inventory in Boston. Otherwise I woulda broke records.

LINDA: Well, it makes seventy dollars and some pennies. That's very good.

WILLY: What do we owe?

LINDA: Well, on the first there's sixteen dollars on the refrigerator—

WILLY: Why sixteen?

LINDA: Well, the fan belt broke, so it was a dollar eighty.

WILLY: But it's brand new.

LINDA: Well, the man said that's the way it is. Till they work themselves in, y'know.

[*They move through the wall-line into the kitchen.*]

WILLY: I hope we didn't get stuck on that machine.

LINDA: They got the biggest ads of any of them!

WILLY: I know, it's a fine machine. What else?

LINDA: Well, there's nine-sixty for the washing machine. And for the vacuum cleaner there's three and a half due on the fifteenth. Then the roof, you got twenty-one dollars remaining.

WILLY: It don't leak, does it?

LINDA: No, they did a wonderful job. Then you owe Frank for the carburetor.

WILLY: I'm not going to pay that man! That goddam Chevrolet, they ought to prohibit the manufacture of that car!

LINDA: Well, you owe him three and a half. And odds and ends, comes to around a hundred and twenty dollars by the fifteenth.

WILLY: A hundred and twenty dollars! My God, if business don't pick up I don't know what I'm gonna do!

LINDA: Well, next week you'll do better.

WILLY: Oh, I'll knock 'em dead next week. I'll go to Hartford. I'm very well liked in Hartford. You know, the trouble is, Linda, people don't seem to take to me.

[*They move onto the forestage.*]

LINDA: Oh, don't be foolish.

WILLY: I know it when I walk in. They seem to laugh at me.

LINDA: Why? Why would they laugh at you? Don't talk that way, Willy.

[WILLY *moves to the edge of the stage.* LINDA *goes into the kitchen and starts to darn stockings.*]

WILLY: I don't know the reason for it, but they just pass me by. I'm not noticed.

LINDA: But you're doing wonderful, dear. You're making seventy to a hundred dollars a week.

WILLY: But I gotta be at it ten, twelve hours a day. Other men—I don't know—they do it easier. I don't know why—I can't stop myself—I talk too much. A man oughta come in with a few words. One thing about Charley. He's a man of few words, and they respect him.

LINDA: You don't talk too much, you're just lively.

WILLY: [*Smiling.*] Well, I figure, what the hell, life is short, a couple of jokes. [*To himself.*] I joke too much! [*The smile goes.*]

LINDA: Why? You're—

WILLY: I'm fat. I'm very—foolish to look at, Linda. I didn't tell you, but Christmas time I happened to be calling on F. H. Stewarts, and a salesman I know, as I was going in to see the buyer I heard him say something about—walrus. And I—I cracked him right across the face. I won't take that. I simply will not take that. But they do laugh at me. I know that.

LINDA: Darling . . .

WILLY: I gotta overcome it. I know I gotta overcome it. I'm not dressing to advantage, maybe.

LINDA: Willy, darling, you're the handsomest man in the world—

WILLY: Oh, no, Linda.

LINDA: To me you are. [*Slight pause.*] The handsomest. [*From the darkness is heard the laughter of a woman.* WILLY *doesn't turn to it, but it continues through* LINDA's *lines.*] And the boys, Willy. Few men are idolized by their children the way you are.

[*Music is heard as behind a scrim, to the left of the house,* THE WOMAN, *dimly seen, is dressing.*]

WILLY: [*With great feeling.*] You're the best there is, Linda, you're a pal, you know that? On the road—on the road I want to grab you sometimes and just kiss the life outa you. [*The laughter is loud now, and he moves into a brightening area at the left, where* THE WOMAN *has come from behind the scrim and is standing, putting on her hat, looking into a "mirror" and laughing.*] 'Cause I get so lonely—especially when business is bad and there's nobody to talk to. I get the feeling that I'll never sell anything again, that I won't make a living for you, or a business, a business for the boys. [*He talks through* THE WOMAN's *subsiding laughter.* THE WOMAN *primps at the "mirror."*] There's so much I want to make for—

THE WOMAN: Me? You didn't make me, Willy. I picked you.

WILLY: [*Pleased.*] You picked me?

THE WOMAN: [*Who is quite proper-looking,* WILLY's *age.*] I did. I've been sitting at that desk watching all the salesmen go by, day in, day out. But you've got such a sense of humor, and we do have such a good time together, don't we?

WILLY: Sure, sure. [*He takes her in his arms.*] Why do you have to go now?

THE WOMAN: It's two o'clock . . .

WILLY: No, come on in! [*He pulls her.*]

THE WOMAN: . . . my sisters'll be scandalized. When'll you be back?

WILLY: Oh, two weeks about. Will you come up again?

THE WOMAN: Sure thing. You do make me laugh. It's good for me. [*She squeezes his arm, kisses him.*] And I think you're a wonderful man.

WILLY: You picked me, heh?

THE WOMAN: Sure. Because you're so sweet. And such a kidder.

WILLY: Well, I'll see you next time I'm in Boston.

THE WOMAN: I'll put you right through to the buyers.

WILLY: [*Slapping her bottom.*] Right. Well, bottoms up!

THE WOMAN: [*Slaps him gently and laughs.*] You just kill me, Willy. [*He suddenly grabs her and kisses her roughly.*] You kill me. And thanks for the stockings. I love a lot of stockings. Well, good night.

WILLY: Good night. And keep your pores open!

THE WOMAN: Oh, Willy!

[THE WOMAN *bursts out laughing, and* LINDA's *laughter blends in.* THE WOMAN *disappears into the dark. Now the area at the kitchen table brightens.* LINDA *is sitting where she was at the kitchen table, but now is mending a pair of her silk stockings.*]

LINDA: You are, Willy. The handsomest man. You've got no reason to feel that—

WILLY: [*Coming out of* THE WOMAN's *dimming area and going over to* LINDA.] I'll make it all up to you, Linda. I'll—

LINDA: There's nothing to make up, dear. You're doing fine, better than—

WILLY: [*Noticing her mending.*] What's that?

LINDA: Just mending my stockings. They're so expensive—

WILLY: [*Angrily, taking them from her.*] I won't have you mending stockings in this house! Now throw them out!

[LINDA *puts the stockings in her pocket.*]

BERNARD: [*Entering on the run.*] Where is he? If he doesn't study!

WILLY: [*Moving to the forestage, with great agitation.*] You'll give him the answers!

BERNARD: I do, but I can't on a Regents! That's a state exam! They're liable to arrest me!

WILLY: Where is he? I'll whip him, I'll whip him!

LINDA: And he'd better give back that football, Willy, it's not nice.

WILLY: Biff! Where is he? Why is he taking everything?

LINDA: He's too rough with the girls, Willy. All the mothers are afraid of him!

WILLY: I'll whip him!

BERNARD: He's driving the car without a license!

[THE WOMAN's *laugh is heard.*]

WILLY: Shut up!

LINDA: All the mothers—

WILLY: Shut up!

BERNARD: [*Backing quietly away and out.*] Mr. Birnbaum says he's stuck up.

WILLY: Get outa here!

BERNARD: If he doesn't buckle down he'll flunk math! [*He goes off.*]

LINDA: He's right, Willy, you've gotta—

WILLY: [*Exploding at her.*] There's nothing the matter with him! You want him to be a worm like Bernard? He's got spirit, personality . . . [*As he speaks,* LINDA, *almost in tears, exits into the living room.* WILLY *is alone in the kitchen, wilting and staring. The leaves are gone. It is night again, and the apartment houses look down from behind.*] Loaded with it. Loaded! What is he stealing? He's giving it back, isn't he? Why is he stealing? What did I tell him? I never in my life told him anything but decent things.

[HAPPY *in pajamas has come down the stairs;* WILLY *suddenly becomes aware of* HAPPY's *presence.*]

HAPPY: Let's go now, come on.

WILLY: [*Sitting down at the kitchen table.*] Huh! Why did she have to wax the floors herself? Everytime she waxes the floors she keels over. She knows that!

HAPPY: Shh! Take it easy. What brought you back tonight?

WILLY: I got an awful scare. Nearly hit a kid in Yonkers. God! Why didn't I go to Alaska with my brother Ben that time! Ben! That man was a genius, that man was success incarnate! What a mistake! He begged me to go.

HAPPY: Well, there's no use in—

WILLY: You guys! There was a man started with the clothes on his back and ended up with diamond mines!

HAPPY: Boy, someday I'd like to know how he did it.

WILLY: What's the mystery? The man knew what he wanted and went out and got it! Walked into a jungle, and comes out, the age of twenty-one, and he's rich! The world is an oyster, but you don't crack it open on a mattress!

HAPPY: Pop, I told you I'm gonna retire you for life.

WILLY: You'll retire me for life on seventy goddam dollars a week? And your women and your car and your apartment, and you'll retire me for life! Christ's sake, I couldn't get past Yonkers today! Where are you guys, where are you? The woods are burning! I can't drive a car!

[CHARLEY *has appeared in the doorway. He is a large man, slow of speech, laconic, immovable. In all he says, despite what he says, there is pity, and now, trepidation. He has a robe over pajamas, slippers on his feet. He enters the kitchen.*]

CHARLEY: Everything all right?

HAPPY: Yeah, Charley, everything's . . .

WILLY: What's the matter?

CHARLEY: I heard some noise. I thought something happened. Can't we do something about the walls? You sneeze in here, and in my house hats blow off.

HAPPY: Let's go to bed, Dad. Come on.

[CHARLEY *signals to* HAPPY *to go.*]

WILLY: You go ahead, I'm not tired at the moment.

HAPPY: [*To* WILLY.] Take it easy, huh? [*He exits.*]

WILLY: What're you doin' up?

CHARLEY: [*Sitting down at the kitchen table opposite* WILLY.] Couldn't sleep good. I had a heartburn.

WILLY: Well, you don't know how to eat.

CHARLEY: I eat with my mouth.

WILLY: No, you're ignorant. You gotta know about vitamins and things like that.

CHARLEY: Come on, let's shoot. Tire you out a little.

WILLY: [*Hesitantly.*] All right. You got cards?

CHARLEY: [*Taking a deck from his pocket.*] Yeah, I got them. Someplace. What is it with those vitamins?

WILLY: [*Dealing.*] They build up your bones. Chemistry.

CHARLEY: Yeah, but there's no bones in a heartburn.

WILLY: What are you talkin' about? Do you know the first thing about it?

CHARLEY: Don't get insulted.
WILLY: Don't talk about something you don't know anything about.

[*They are playing. Pause.*]

CHARLEY: What're you doin' home?
WILLY: A little trouble with the car.
CHARLEY: Oh. [*Pause.*] I'd like to take a trip to California.
WILLY: Don't say.
CHARLEY: You want a job?
WILLY: I got a job, I told you that. [*After a slight pause.*] What the hell are you offering me a job for?
CHARLEY: Don't get insulted.
WILLY: Don't insult me.
CHARLEY: I don't see no sense in it. You don't have to go on this way.
WILLY: I got a good job. [*Slight pause.*] What do you keep comin' in here for?
CHARLEY: You want me to go?
WILLY: [*After a pause, withering.*] I can't understand it. He's going back to Texas again. What the hell is that?
CHARLEY: Let him go.
WILLY: I got nothin' to give him, Charley, I'm clean, I'm clean.
CHARLEY: He won't starve. None a them starve. Forget about him.
WILLY: Then what have I got to remember?
CHARLEY: You take it too hard. To hell with it. When a deposit bottle is broken you don't get your nickel back.
WILLY: That's easy enough for you to say.
CHARLEY: That ain't easy for me to say.
WILLY: Did you see the ceiling I put up in the living-room?
CHARLEY: Yeah, that's a piece of work. To put up a ceiling is a mystery to me. How do you do it?
WILLY: What's the difference?
CHARLEY: Well, talk about it.
WILLY: You gonna put up a ceiling?
CHARLEY: How could I put up a ceiling?
WILLY: Then what the hell are you bothering me for?
CHARLEY: You're insulted again.
WILLY: A man who can't handle tools is not a man. You're disgusting.
CHARLEY: Don't call me disgusting, Willy.

[UNCLE BEN, *carrying a valise and an umbrella, enters the forestage from around the right corner of the house. He is a stolid man, in his sixties, with a mustache and an authoritative air. He is utterly certain of his destiny, and there is an aura of far places about him. He enters exactly as* WILLY *speaks.*]

WILLY: I'm getting awfully tired, Ben.

[BEN's *music is heard.* BEN *looks around at everything.*]

CHARLEY: Good, keep playing; you'll sleep better. Did you call me Ben?

[BEN *looks at his watch.*]

WILLY: That's funny. For a second there you reminded me of my brother Ben.

BEN: I only have a few minutes. [*He strolls, inspecting the place.* WILLY *and* CHARLEY *continue playing.*]

CHARLEY: You never heard from him again, heh? Since that time?

WILLY: Didn't Linda tell you? Couple of weeks ago we got a letter from his wife in Africa. He died.

CHARLEY: That so.

BEN: [*Chuckling.*] So this is Brooklyn, eh?

CHARLEY: Maybe you're in for some of his money.

WILLY: Naa, he had seven sons. There's just one opportunity I had with that man . . .

BEN: I must make a train, William. There are several properties I'm looking at in Alaska.

WILLY: Sure, sure! If I'd gone with him to Alaska that time, everything would've been totally different.

CHARLEY: Go on, you'da froze to death up there.

WILLY: What're you talking about?

BEN: Opportunity is tremendous in Alaska, William. Surprised you're not up there.

WILLY: Sure, tremendous.

CHARLEY: Heh?

WILLY: There was the only man I ever met who knew the answers.

CHARLEY: Who?

BEN: How are you all?

WILLY: [*Taking a pot, smiling.*] Fine, fine.

CHARLEY: Pretty sharp tonight.

BEN: Is Mother living with you?

WILLY: No, she died a long time ago.

CHARLEY: Who?

BEN: That's too bad. Fine specimen of a lady, Mother.

WILLY: [*To* CHARLEY.] Heh?

BEN: I'd hoped to see the old girl.

CHARLEY: Who died?

BEN: Heard anything from Father, have you?

WILLY: [*Unnerved.*] What do you mean, who died?

CHARLEY: [*Taking a pot.*] What're you talkin' about?

BEN: [*Looking at his watch.*] William, it's half-past eight!

WILLY: [*As though to dispel his confusion he angrily stops* CHARLEY's *hand.*] That's my build!

CHARLEY: I put the ace—

WILLY: If you don't know how to play the game I'm not gonna throw my money away on you!

CHARLEY: [*Rising.*] It was my ace, for God's sake!

WILLY: I'm through, I'm through!

BEN: When did Mother die?

WILLY: Long ago. Since the beginning you never knew how to play cards.

CHARLEY: [*Picks up the cards and goes to the door.*] All right! Next time I'll bring a deck with five aces.

WILLY: I don't play that kind of game!

CHARLEY: [*Turning to him.*] You ought to be ashamed of yourself!

WILLY: Yeah?

CHARLEY: Yeah! [*He goes out.*]

WILLY: [*Slamming the door after him.*] Ignoramus!

BEN: [*As* WILLY *comes toward him through the wall-line of the kitchen.*] So you're William.

WILLY: [*Shaking* BEN's *hand.*] Ben! I've been waiting for you so long! What's the answer? How did you do it?

BEN: Oh, there's a story in that.

[LINDA *enters the forestage, as of old, carrying the wash basket.*]

LINDA: Is this Ben?

BEN: [*Gallantly.*] How do you do, my dear.

LINDA: Where've you been all these years? Willy's always wondered why you—

WILLY: [*Pulling* BEN *away from her impatiently.*] Where is Dad? Didn't you follow him? How did you get started?

BEN: Well, I don't know how much you remember.

WILLY: Well, I was just a baby, of course, only three or four years old—

BEN: Three years and eleven months.

WILLY: What a memory, Ben!

BEN: I have many enterprises, William, and I have never kept books.

WILLY: I remember I was sitting under the wagon in—was it Nebraska?

BEN: It was South Dakota, and I gave you a bunch of wild flowers.

WILLY: I remember you walking away down some open road.

BEN: [*Laughing.*] I was going to find Father in Alaska.

WILLY: Where is he?

BEN: At that age I had a very faulty view of geography, William. I discovered after a few days that I was heading due south, so instead of Alaska, I ended up in Africa.

LINDA: Africa!

WILLY: The Gold Coast!

BEN: Principally diamond mines.

LINDA: Diamond mines!

BEN: Yes, my dear. But I've only a few minutes—

WILLY: No! Boys! Boys! [*Young* BIFF *and* HAPPY *appear.*] Listen to this. This is your Uncle Ben, a great man! Tell my boys, Ben!

BEN: Why, boys, when I was seventeen I walked into the jungle, and when I was twenty-one I walked out. [*He laughs.*] And by God I was rich.

WILLY: [*To the boys.*] You see what I been talking about? The greatest things can happen!

BEN: [*Glancing at his watch.*] I have an appointment in Ketchikan Tuesday week.[8]

WILLY: No, Ben! Please tell about Dad. I want my boys to hear. I want them to know the kind of stock they spring from. All I remember is a man with a big beard, and I was in Mamma's lap, sitting around a fire, and some kind of high music.

BEN: His flute. He played the flute.

WILLY: Sure, the flute, that's right!

[*New music is heard, a high, rollicking tune.*]

BEN: Father was a very great and a very wild-hearted man. We would start in Boston, and he'd toss the whole family into the wagon, and then he'd drive the team right across the country; through Ohio, and Indiana, Michigan, Illinois, and all the Western states. And we'd stop in the towns and sell the flutes that he'd made on the way. Great inventor, Father. With one gadget he made more in a week than a man like you could make in a lifetime.

WILLY: That's just the way I'm bringing them up, Ben—rugged, well liked, all-around.

BEN: Yeah? [*To* BIFF.] Hit that, boy—hard as you can. [*He pounds his stomach.*]

BIFF: Oh, no, sir!

BEN: [*Taking boxing stance.*] Come on, get to me! [*He laughs.*]

WILLY: Go to it, Biff! Go ahead, show him!

BIFF: Okay! [*He cocks his fist and starts in.*]

8. That is, in Ketchikan, Alaska, one week from Tuesday.

LINDA: [*To* WILLY.] Why must he fight, dear?

BEN: [*Sparring with* BIFF.] Good boy! Good boy!

WILLY: How's that, Ben, heh?

HAPPY: Give him the left, Biff!

LINDA: Why are you fighting?

BEN: Good boy! [*Suddenly comes in, trips* BIFF, *and stands over him, the point of his umbrella poised over* BIFF's *eye.*]

LINDA: Look out, Biff!

BIFF: Gee!

BEN: [*Patting* BIFF's *knee.*] Never fight fair with a stranger, boy. You'll never get out of the jungle that way. [*Taking* LINDA's *hand and bowing.*] It was an honor and a pleasure to meet you, Linda.

LINDA: [*Withdrawing her hand coldly, frightened.*] Have a nice—trip.

BEN: [*To* WILLY.] And good luck with your—what do you do?

WILLY: Selling.

BEN: Yes. Well . . . . [*He raises his hand in farewell to all.*]

WILLY: No, Ben, I don't want you to think . . . [*He takes* BEN's *arm to show him.*] It's Brooklyn, I know, but we hunt too.

BEN: Really, now.

WILLY: Oh, sure, there's snakes and rabbits and—that's why I moved out here. Why, Biff can fell any one of these trees in no time! Boys! Go right over to where they're building the apartment house and get some sand. We're gonna rebuild the entire front stoop right now! Watch this, Ben!

BIFF: Yes, sir! On the double, Hap!

HAPPY: [*As he and* BIFF *run off.*] I lost weight, Pop, you notice?

[CHARLEY *enters in knickers, even before the boys are gone.*]

CHARLEY: Listen, if they steal any more from that building the watchman'll put the cops on them!

LINDA: [*To* WILLY.] Don't let Biff . . .

[BEN *laughs lustily.*]

WILLY: You shoulda seen the lumber they brought home last week. At least a dozen six-by-tens worth all kinds a money.

CHARLEY: Listen, if that watchman—

WILLY: I gave them hell, understand. But I got a couple of fearless characters there.

CHARLEY: Willy, the jails are full of fearless characters.

BEN: [*Clapping* WILLY *on the back, with a laugh at* CHARLEY.] And the stock exchange, friend!

WILLY: [*Joining in* BEN's *laughter.*] Where are the rest of your pants?

CHARLEY: My wife bought them.

WILLY: Now all you need is a golf club and you can go upstairs and go to sleep. [*To* BEN.] Great athlete! Between him and his son Bernard they can't hammer a nail!

BERNARD: [*Rushing in.*] The watchman's chasing Biff!

WILLY: [*Angrily.*] Shut up! He's not stealing anything!

LINDA: [*Alarmed, hurrying off left.*] Where is he? Biff, dear! [*She exits.*]

WILLY: [*Moving toward the left, away from* BEN.] There's nothing wrong. What's the matter with you?

BEN: Nervy boy. Good!

WILLY: [*Laughing.*] Oh, nerves of iron, that Biff!

CHARLEY: Don't know what it is. My New England man comes back and he's bleedin', they murdered him up there.

WILLY: It's contacts, Charley, I got important contacts!

CHARLEY: [*Sarcastically.*] Glad to hear it, Willy. Come in later, we'll shoot a little casino. I'll take some of your Portland money. [*He laughs at* WILLY *and exits.*]

WILLY: [*Turning to* BEN.] Business is bad, it's murderous. But not for me, of course.

BEN: I'll stop by on my way back to Africa.

WILLY: [*Longingly.*] Can't you stay a few days? You're just what I need, Ben, because I—I have a fine position here, but I—well, Dad left when I was such a baby and I never had a chance to talk to him and I still feel—kind of temporary about myself.

BEN: I'll be late for my train.

[*They are at opposite ends of the stage.*]

WILLY: Ben, my boys—can't we talk? They'd go into the jaws of hell for me, see, but I—

BEN: William, you're being first-rate with your boys. Outstanding, manly chaps!

WILLY: [*Hanging on to his words.*] Oh, Ben, that's good to hear! Because sometimes I'm afraid that I'm not teaching them the right kind of— Ben, how should I teach them?

BEN: [*Giving great weight to each word, and with a certain vicious audacity.*] William, when I walked into the jungle, I was seventeen. When I walked out I was twenty-one. And, by God, I was rich! [*He goes off into darkness around the right corner of the house.*]

WILLY: . . . was rich! That's just the spirit I want to imbue them with! To walk into a jungle! I was right! I was right! I was right!

[BEN *is gone, but* WILLY *is still speaking to him as* LINDA, *in nightgown and robe, enters the kitchen, glances around for* WILLY, *then goes to the door of the house, looks out and sees him. Comes down to his left. He looks at her.*]

LINDA: Willy, dear? Willy?

WILLY: I was right!

LINDA: Did you have some cheese? [*He can't answer.*] It's very late, darling. Come to bed, heh?

WILLY: [*Looking straight up.*] Gotta break your neck to see a star in this yard.

LINDA: You coming in?

WILLY: Whatever happened to that diamond watch fob? Remember? When Ben came from Africa that time? Didn't he give me a watch fob with a diamond in it?

LINDA: You pawned it, dear. Twelve, thirteen years ago. For Biff's radio correspondence course.

WILLY: Gee, that was a beautiful thing. I'll take a walk.

LINDA: But you're in your slippers.

WILLY: [*Starting to go around the house at the left.*] I was right! I was! [*Half to LINDA, as he goes, shaking his head.*] What a man! There was a man worth talking to. I was right!

LINDA: [*Calling after WILLY.*] But in your slippers, Willy!

[WILLY *is almost gone when* BIFF, *in his pajamas, comes down the stairs and enters the kitchen.*]

BIFF: What is he doing out there?

LINDA: Sh!

BIFF: God Almighty, Mom, how long has he been doing this?

LINDA: Don't, he'll hear you.

BIFF: What the hell is the matter with him?

LINDA: It'll pass by morning.

BIFF: Shouldn't we do anything?

LINDA: Oh, my dear, you should do a lot of things, but there's nothing to do, so go to sleep.

[HAPPY *comes down the stairs and sits on the steps.*]

HAPPY: I never heard him so loud, Mom.

LINDA: Well, come around more often; you'll hear him. [*She sits down at the table and mends the lining of* WILLY's *jacket.*]

BIFF: Why didn't you ever write me about this, Mom?

LINDA: How would I write to you? For over three months you had no address.

BIFF: I was on the move. But you know I thought of you all the time. You know that, don't you, pal?

LINDA: I know, dear, I know. But he likes to have a letter. Just to know that there's still a possibility for better things.

BIFF: He's not like this all the time, is he?

LINDA: It's when you come home he's always the worst.

BIFF: When I come home?

LINDA: When you write you're coming, he's all smiles, and talks about the future, and—he's just wonderful. And then the closer you seem to come, the more shaky he gets, and then, by the time you get here, he's arguing, and he seems angry at you. I think it's just that maybe he can't bring himself to—to open up to you. Why are you so hateful to each other? Why is that?

BIFF: [*Evasively.*] I'm not hateful, Mom.

LINDA: But you no sooner come in the door than you're fighting!

BIFF: I don't know why. I mean to change. I'm tryin', Mom, you understand?

LINDA: Are you home to stay now?

BIFF: I don't know. I want to look around, see what's doin'.

LINDA: Biff, you can't look around all your life, can you?

BIFF: I just can't take hold, Mom. I can't take hold of some kind of a life.

LINDA: Biff, a man is not a bird, to come and go with the springtime.

BIFF: Your hair . . . [*He touches her hair.*] Your hair got so gray.

LINDA: Oh, it's been gray since you were in high school. I just stopped dyeing it, that's all.

BIFF: Dye it again, will ya? I don't want my pal looking old. [*He smiles.*]

LINDA: You're such a boy! You think you can go away for a year and . . . You've got to get it into your head now that one day you'll knock on this door and there'll be strange people here—

BIFF: What are you talking about? You're not even sixty, Mom.

LINDA: But what about your father?

BIFF: [*Lamely.*] Well, I meant him too.

HAPPY: He admires Pop.

LINDA: Biff, dear, if you don't have any feeling for him, then you can't have any feeling for me.

BIFF: Sure I can, Mom.

LINDA: No. You can't just come to see me, because I love him. [*With a threat, but only a threat, of tears.*] He's the dearest man in the world to me, and I won't have anyone making him feel unwanted and low and blue. You've got to make up your mind now, darling, there's no leeway anymore. Either he's your father and you pay him that respect, or else you're not to come here. I know he's not easy to get along with—nobody knows that better than me—but . . .

WILLY: [*From the left, with a laugh.*] Hey, hey, Biffo!

BIFF: [*Starting to go out after* WILLY.] What the hell is the matter with him? [HAPPY *stops him.*]

LINDA: Don't—don't go near him!

BIFF: Stop making excuses for him! He always, always wiped the floor with you. Never had an ounce of respect for you.

HAPPY: He's always had respect for—

BIFF: What the hell do you know about it?

HAPPY: [*Surlily.*] Just don't call him crazy!

BIFF: He's got no character—Charley wouldn't do this. Not in his own house—spewing out that vomit from his mind.

HAPPY: Charley never had to cope with what he's got to.

BIFF: People are worse off than Willy Loman. Believe me, I've seen them!

LINDA: Then make Charley your father, Biff. You can't do that, can you? I don't say he's a great man. Willy Loman never made a lot of money. His name was never in the paper. He's not the finest character that ever lived. But he's a human being, and a terrible thing is happening to him. So attention must be paid. He's not to be allowed to fall into his grave like an old dog. Attention, attention must be finally paid to such a person. You called him crazy—

BIFF: I didn't mean—

LINDA: No, a lot of people think he's lost his—balance. But you don't have to be very smart to know what his trouble is. The man is exhausted.

HAPPY: Sure!

LINDA: A small man can be just as exhausted as a great man. He works for a company thirty-six years this March, opens up unheard-of territories to their trademark, and now in his old age they take his salary away.

HAPPY: [*Indignantly.*] I didn't know that, Mom.

LINDA: You never asked, my dear! Now that you get your spending money someplace else you don't trouble your mind with him.

HAPPY: But I gave you money last—

LINDA: Christmas time, fifty dollars! To fix the hot water it cost ninety-seven fifty! For five weeks he's been on straight commission, like a beginner, an unknown!

BIFF: Those ungrateful bastards!

LINDA: Are they any worse than his sons? When he brought them business, when he was young, they were glad to see him. But now his old friends, the old buyers that loved him so and always found some order to hand him in a pinch—they're all dead, retired. He used to be able to make six, seven calls a day in Boston. Now he takes his valises out of the car and puts them back and takes them out again and he's exhausted. Instead of walking he talks now. He drives seven hundred miles, and when he gets there no one knows him anymore, no one welcomes him. And what goes through a man's mind, driving seven hundred miles home without having earned a cent? Why shouldn't he talk to himself? Why? When he has to go to Charley and borrow fifty dollars a week and pretend to me that it's his pay? How long can that go on? How long? You see what I'm sitting here and waiting for? And you tell me he has no character? The man who never worked a day but for your benefit? When does he get the medal for that? Is this his reward—to turn around at the age of sixty-three and find his sons, who he loved better than his life, one a philandering bum—

HAPPY: Mom!

LINDA: That's all you are, my baby! [*To* BIFF.] And you! What happened to the love you had for him? You were such pals! How you used to talk to him on the phone every night! How lonely he was till he could come home to you!

BIFF: All right, Mom. I'll live here in my room, and I'll get a job. I'll keep away from him, that's all.

LINDA: No, Biff. You can't stay here and fight all the time.

BIFF: He threw me out of this house, remember that.

LINDA: Why did he do that? I never knew why.

BIFF: Because I know he's a fake and he doesn't like anybody around who knows!

LINDA: Why a fake? In what way? What do you mean?

BIFF: Just don't lay it all at my feet. It's between me and him—that's all I have to say. I'll chip in from now on. He'll settle for half my paycheck. He'll be all right. I'm going to bed. [*He starts for the stairs.*]

LINDA: He won't be all right.

BIFF: [*Turning on the stairs, furiously.*] I hate this city and I'll stay here. Now what do you want?

LINDA: He's dying, Biff.

[HAPPY *turns quickly to her, shocked.*]

BIFF: [*After a pause.*] Why is he dying?

LINDA: He's been trying to kill himself.

BIFF: [*With great horror.*] How?

LINDA: I live from day to day.

BIFF: What're you talking about?

LINDA: Remember I wrote you that he smashed up the car again? In February?

BIFF: Well?

LINDA: The insurance inspector came. He said that they have evidence. That all these accidents in the last year—weren't—weren't—accidents.

HAPPY: How can they tell that? That's a lie.

LINDA: It seems there's a woman . . . [*She takes a breath as. . . . .*]

{ BIFF: [*Sharply but contained.*] What woman?
LINDA: [*Simultaneously.*] . . . and this woman . . .

LINDA: What?

BIFF: Nothing. Go ahead.

LINDA: What did you say?

BIFF: Nothing. I just said what woman?

HAPPY: What about her?

LINDA: Well, it seems she was walking down the road and saw his car. She says that he wasn't driving fast at all, and that he didn't skid. She says he came to that little bridge, and then deliberately smashed into the railing, and it was only the shallowness of the water that saved him.

BIFF: Oh, no, he probably just fell asleep again.

LINDA: I don't think he fell asleep.

BIFF: Why not?

LINDA: Last month . . . [*With great difficulty.*] Oh, boys, it's so hard to say a thing like this! He's just a big stupid man to you, but I tell you there's more good in him than in many other people. [*She chokes, wipes her eyes.*] I was looking for a fuse. The lights blew out, and I went down the cellar. And behind the fuse box—it happened to fall out—was a length of rubber pipe—just short.

HAPPY: No kidding?

LINDA: There's a little attachment on the end of it. I knew right away. And sure enough, on the bottom of the water heater there's a new little nipple on the gas pipe.

HAPPY: [*Angrily.*] That—jerk.

BIFF: Did you have it taken off?

LINDA: I'm—I'm ashamed to. How can I mention it to him? Every day I go down and take away that little rubber pipe. But, when he comes home, I put it back where it was. How can I insult him that way? I don't know what to do. I live from day to day, boys. I tell you, I know every thought in his mind. It sounds so old-fashioned and silly, but I tell you he put his whole life into you and you've turned your backs on him. [*She is bent over in the chair, weeping, her face in her hands.*] Biff, I swear to God! Biff, his life is in your hands!

HAPPY: [*To* BIFF.] How do you like that damned fool!

BIFF: [*Kissing her.*] All right, pal, all right. It's all settled now. I've been remiss. I know that, Mom. But now I'll stay, and I swear to you, I'll apply myself. [*Kneeling in front of her, in a fever of self-reproach.*] It's just—you see, Mom, I don't fit in business. Not that I won't try. I'll try, and I'll make good.

HAPPY: Sure you will. The trouble with you in business was you never tried to please people.

BIFF: I know, I—

HAPPY: Like when you worked for Harrison's. Bob Harrison said you were tops, and then you go and do some damn fool thing like whistling whole songs in the elevator like a comedian.

BIFF: [*Against* HAPPY.] So what? I like to whistle sometimes.

HAPPY: You don't raise a guy to a responsible job who whistles in the elevator!

LINDA: Well, don't argue about it now.

HAPPY: Like when you'd go off and swim in the middle of the day instead of taking the line around.

BIFF: [*His resentment rising.*] Well, don't you run off? You take off sometimes, don't you? On a nice summer day?

HAPPY: Yeah, but I cover myself!

LINDA: Boys!

HAPPY: If I'm going to take a fade the boss can call any number where I'm supposed to be and they'll swear to him that I just left. I'll tell you something that I hate to say, Biff, but in the business world some of them think you're crazy.

BIFF: [*Angered.*] Screw the business world!

HAPPY: All right, screw it! Great, but cover yourself!

LINDA: Hap, Hap!

BIFF: I don't care what they think! They've laughed at Dad for years, and you know why? Because we don't belong in this nuthouse of a city! We should be mixing cement on some open plain, or—or carpenters. A carpenter is allowed to whistle!

[WILLY *walks in from the entrance of the house, at left.*]

WILLY: Even your grandfather was better than a carpenter. [*Pause. They watch him.*] You never grew up. Bernard does not whistle in the elevator, I assure you.

BIFF: [*As though to laugh* WILLY *out of it.*] Yeah, but you do, Pop.

WILLY: I never in my life whistled in an elevator! And who in the business world thinks I'm crazy?

BIFF: I didn't mean it like that, Pop. Now don't make a whole thing out of it, will ya?

WILLY: Go back to the West! Be a carpenter, a cowboy, enjoy yourself!

LINDA: Willy, he was just saying—

WILLY: I heard what he said!

HAPPY: [*Trying to quiet* WILLY.] Hey, Pop, come on now . . .

WILLY: [*Continuing over* HAPPY's *line.*] They laugh at me, heh? Go to Filene's, go to the Hub, go to Slattery's Boston. Call out the name Willy Loman and see what happens! Big shot!

BIFF: All right, Pop.

WILLY: Big!

BIFF: All right!

WILLY: Why do you always insult me?

BIFF: I didn't say a word. [*To* LINDA.] Did I say a word?

LINDA: He didn't say anything, Willy.

WILLY: [*Going to the doorway of the living-room.*] All right, good night, good night.

LINDA: Willy, dear, he just decided . . .

WILLY: [*To* BIFF.] If you get tired hanging around tomorrow, paint the ceiling I put up in the living-room.

BIFF: I'm leaving early tomorrow.

HAPPY: He's going to see Bill Oliver, Pop.

WILLY: [*Interestedly.*] Oliver? For what?

BIFF: [*With reserve, but trying, trying.*] He always said he'd stake me. I'd like to go into business, so maybe I can take him up on it.

LINDA: Isn't that wonderful?

WILLY: Don't interrupt. What's wonderful about it? There's fifty men in the City of New York who'd stake him. [*To* BIFF.] Sporting goods?

BIFF: I guess so. I know something about it and—

WILLY: He knows something about it! You know sporting goods better than Spalding,[9] for God's sake! How much is he giving you?

BIFF: I don't know, I didn't even see him yet, but—

WILLY: Then what're you talkin' about?

BIFF: [*Getting angry.*] Well, all I said was I'm gonna see him, that's all!

WILLY: [*Turning away.*] Ah, you're counting your chickens again.

BIFF: [*Starting left for the stairs.*] Oh, Jesus, I'm going to sleep!

WILLY: [*Calling after him.*] Don't curse in this house!

BIFF: [*Turning.*] Since when did you get so clean?

HAPPY: [*Trying to stop them.*] Wait a . . .

WILLY: Don't use that language to me! I won't have it!

HAPPY: [*Grabbing* BIFF, *shouts.*] Wait a minute! I got an idea. I got a feasible idea. Come here, Biff, let's talk this over now, let's talk some sense here. When I was down in Florida last time, I thought of a great idea to sell sporting goods. It just came back to me. You and I, Biff—we have a line, the Loman Line. We train a couple of weeks, and put on a couple of exhibitions, see?

WILLY: That's an idea!

HAPPY: Wait! We form two basketball teams, see? Two water-polo teams. We play each other. It's a million dollars' worth of publicity. Two brothers,

9. Albert G. Spalding (1850–1915), American baseball player and sporting-goods manufacturer.

see? The Loman Brothers. Displays in the Royal Palms—all the hotels. And banners over the ring and the basketball court: "Loman Brothers." Baby, we could sell sporting goods!

WILLY: That is a one-million-dollar idea!

LINDA: Marvelous!

BIFF: I'm in great shape as far as that's concerned.

HAPPY: And the beauty of it is, Biff, it wouldn't be like a business. We'd be out playin' ball again . . .

BIFF: [*Enthused.*] Yeah, that's . . .

WILLY: Million-dollar . . .

HAPPY: And you wouldn't get fed up with it, Biff. It'd be the family again. There'd be the old honor, and comradeship, and if you wanted to go off for a swim or somethin'—well, you'd do it! Without some smart cooky gettin' up ahead of you!

WILLY: Lick the world! You guys together could absolutely lick the civilized world.

BIFF: I'll see Oliver tomorrow. Hap, if we could work that out . . .

LINDA: Maybe things are beginning to—

WILLY: [*Wildly enthused, to* LINDA.] Stop interrupting! [*To* BIFF.] But don't wear sport jacket and slacks when you see Oliver.

BIFF: No, I'll—

WILLY: A business suit, and talk as little as possible, and don't crack any jokes.

BIFF: He did like me. Always liked me.

LINDA: He loved you!

WILLY: [*To* LINDA.] Will you stop! [*To* BIFF.] Walk in very serious. You are not applying for a boy's job. Money is to pass. Be quiet, fine, and serious. Everybody likes a kidder, but nobody lends him money.

HAPPY: I'll try to get some myself, Biff. I'm sure I can.

WILLY: I see great things for you kids, I think your troubles are over. But remember, start big and you'll end big. Ask for fifteen. How much you gonna ask for?

BIFF: Gee, I don't know—

WILLY: And don't say "Gee." "Gee" is a boy's word. A man walking in for fifteen thousand dollars does not say "Gee!"

BIFF: Ten, I think, would be top though.

WILLY: Don't be so modest. You always started too low. Walk in with a big laugh. Don't look worried. Start off with a couple of your good stories to lighten things up. It's not what you say, it's how you say it—because personality always wins the day.

LINDA: Oliver always thought the highest of him—

WILLY: Will you let me talk?

BIFF: Don't yell at her, Pop, will ya?

WILLY: [*Angrily.*] I was talking, wasn't I?

BIFF: I don't like you yelling at her all the time, and I'm tellin' you, that's all.

WILLY: What're you, takin' over this house?

LINDA: Willy—

WILLY: [*Turning on her.*] Don't take his side all the time, goddammit!

BIFF: [*Furiously.*] Stop yelling at her!

WILLY: [*Suddenly pulling on his cheek, beaten down, guilt ridden.*] Give my best to Bill Oliver—he may remember me. [*He exits through the living-room doorway.*]

LINDA: [*Her voice subdued.*] What'd you have to start that for? [BIFF *turns away.*] You see how sweet he was as soon as you talked hopefully? [*She goes over to* BIFF.] Come up and say good night to him. Don't let him go to bed that way.

HAPPY: Come on, Biff, let's buck him up.

LINDA: Please, dear. Just say good night. It takes so little to make him happy. Come. [*She goes through the living-room doorway, calling upstairs from within the living-room.*] Your pajamas are hanging in the bathroom, Willy!

HAPPY: [*Looking toward where* LINDA *went out.*] What a woman! They broke the mold when they made her. You know that, Biff?

BIFF: He's off salary. My God, working on commission!

HAPPY: Well, let's face it: he's no hot-shot selling man. Except that sometimes, you have to admit, he's a sweet personality.

BIFF: [*Deciding.*] Lend me ten bucks, will ya? I want to buy some new ties.

HAPPY: I'll take you to a place I know. Beautiful stuff. Wear one of my striped shirts tomorrow.

BIFF: She got gray. Mom got awful old. Gee, I'm gonna go in to Oliver tomorrow and knock him for a—

HAPPY: Come on up. Tell that to Dad. Let's give him a whirl. Come on.

BIFF: [*Steamed up.*] You know, with ten thousand bucks, boy!

HAPPY: [*As they go into the living-room.*] That's the talk, Biff, that's the first time I've heard the old confidence out of you! [*From within the living-room, fading off.*] You're gonna live with me, kid, and any babe you want just say the word . . .

[*The last lines are hardly heard. They are mounting the stairs to their parents' bedroom.*]

LINDA: [*Entering her bedroom and addressing* WILLY, *who is in the bathroom. She is straightening the bed for him.*] Can you do anything about the shower? It drips.

WILLY: [*From the bathroom.*] All of a sudden everything falls to pieces! Goddam plumbing, oughta be sued, those people. I hardly finished putting it in and the thing . . . [*His words rumble off.*]

LINDA: I'm just wondering if Oliver will remember him. You think he might?

WILLY: [*Coming out of the bathroom in his pajamas.*] Remember him? What's the matter with you, you crazy? If he'd've stayed with Oliver he'd be on top by now! Wait'll Oliver gets a look at him. You don't know the average caliber anymore. The average young man today—[*He is getting into bed.*]—is got a caliber of zero. Greatest thing in the world for him was to bum around. [BIFF *and* HAPPY *enter the bedroom. Slight pause.* WILLY *stops short, looking at* BIFF.] Glad to hear it, boy.

HAPPY: He wanted to say good night to you, sport.

WILLY: [*To* BIFF.] Yeah. Knock him dead, boy. What'd you want to tell me?

BIFF: Just take it easy, Pop. Good night. [*He turns to go.*]

WILLY: [*Unable to resist.*] And if anything falls off the desk while you're talking to him—like a package or something—don't you pick it up. They have office boys for that.

LINDA: I'll make a big breakfast—

WILLY: Will you let me finish? [*To* BIFF.] Tell him you were in the business in the West. Not farm work.

BIFF: All right, Dad.

LINDA: I think everything—

WILLY: [*Going right through her speech.*] And don't undersell yourself. No less than fifteen thousand dollars.

BIFF: [*Unable to bear him.*] Okay. Good night, Mom. [*He starts moving.*]

WILLY: Because you got a greatness in you, Biff, remember that. You got all kinds of greatness . . . [*He lies back, exhausted.* BIFF *walks out.*]

LINDA: [*Calling after* BIFF.] Sleep well, darling!

HAPPY: I'm gonna get married, Mom. I wanted to tell you.

LINDA: Go to sleep, dear.

HAPPY: [*Going.*] I just wanted to tell you.

WILLY: Keep up the good work. [HAPPY *exits.*] God . . . remember that Ebbets Field[1] game? The championship of the city?

LINDA: Just rest. Should I sing to you?

WILLY: Yeah. Sing to me. [LINDA *hums a soft lullaby.*] When that team came out—he was the tallest, remember?

LINDA: Oh, yes. And in gold.

---

1. Stadium where the Dodgers, Brooklyn's major-league baseball team, played from 1913 to 1957.

[BIFF *enters the darkened kitchen, takes a cigarette, and leaves the* *house. He comes downstage into a golden pool of light. He smokes, star-* *ing at the night.*]

WILLY: Like a young god. Hercules—something like that. And the sun, the sun all around him. Remember how he waved to me? Right up from the field, with the representatives of three colleges standing by? And the buyers I brought, and the cheers when he came out—Loman, Loman, Loman! God Almighty, he'll be great yet. A star like that, magnificent, can never really fade away!

[*The light on* WILLY *is fading. The gas heater begins to glow through* *the kitchen wall, near the stairs, a blue flame beneath red coils.*]

LINDA: [*Timidly.*] Willy dear, what has he got against you?
WILLY: I'm so tired. Don't talk anymore.

[BIFF *slowly returns to the kitchen. He stops, stares toward the heater.*]

LINDA: Will you ask Howard to let you work in New York?
WILLY: First thing in the morning. Everything'll be all right.

[BIFF *reaches behind the heater and draws out a length of rubber tubing.* *He is horrified and turns his head toward* WILLY'S *room, still dimly lit,* *from which the strains of* LINDA'S *desperate but monotonous humming* *rise.*]

WILLY: [*Staring through the window into the moonlight.*] Gee, look at the moon moving between the buildings!

[BIFF *wraps the tubing around his hand and quickly goes up the stairs.*]

CURTAIN

ACT II

Music is heard, gay and bright. The curtain rises as the music fades away. WILLY, *in shirt sleeves, is sitting at the kitchen table, sipping coffee, his* *hat in his lap.* LINDA *is filling his cup when she can.*

WILLY: Wonderful coffee. Meal in itself.
LINDA: Can I make you some eggs?
WILLY: No. Take a breath.
LINDA: You look so rested, dear.
WILLY: I slept like a dead one. First time in months. Imagine, sleeping till ten on a Tuesday morning. Boys left nice and early, heh?
LINDA: They were out of here by eight o'clock.

WILLY: Good work!

LINDA: It was so thrilling to see them leaving together. I can't get over the shaving lotion in this house!

WILLY: [*Smiling.*] Mmm—

LINDA: Biff was very changed this morning. His whole attitude seemed to be hopeful. He couldn't wait to get downtown to see Oliver.

WILLY: He's heading for a change. There's no question, there simply are certain men that take longer to get—solidified. How did he dress?

LINDA: His blue suit. He's so handsome in that suit. He could be a— anything in that suit!

[WILLY *gets up from the table.* LINDA *holds his jacket for him.*]

WILLY: There's no question, no question at all. Gee, on the way home tonight I'd like to buy some seeds.

LINDA: [*Laughing.*] That'd be wonderful. But not enough sun gets back there. Nothing'll grow any more.

WILLY: You wait, kid, before it's all over we're gonna get a little place out in the country, and I'll raise some vegetables, a couple of chickens . . .

LINDA: You'll do it yet, dear.

[WILLY *walks out of his jacket.* LINDA *follows him.*]

WILLY: And they'll get married, and come for a weekend. I'd build a little guest house. 'Cause I got so many fine tools, all I'd need would be a little lumber and some peace of mind.

LINDA: [*Joyfully.*] I sewed the lining . . .

WILLY: I could build two guest houses, so they'd both come. Did he decide how much he's going to ask Oliver for?

LINDA: [*Getting him into the jacket.*] He didn't mention it, but I imagine ten or fifteen thousand. You going to talk to Howard today?

WILLY: Yeah. I'll put it to him straight and simple. He'll just have to take me off the road.

LINDA: And Willy, don't forget to ask for a little advance, because we've got the insurance premium. It's the grace period now.

WILLY: That's a hundred . . . ?

LINDA: A hundred and eight, sixty-eight. Because we're a little short again.

WILLY: Why are we short?

LINDA: Well, you had the motor job on the car . . .

WILLY: That goddam Studebaker!

LINDA: And you got one more payment on the refrigerator . . .

WILLY: But it just broke again!

LINDA: Well, it's old, dear.

WILLY: I told you we should've bought a well-advertised machine. Charley bought a General Electric and it's twenty years old and it's still good, that son-of-a-bitch.

LINDA: But, Willy—

WILLY: Whoever heard of a Hastings refrigerator? Once in my life I would like to own something outright before it's broken! I'm always in a race with the junkyard! I just finished paying for the car and it's on its last legs. The refrigerator consumes belts like a goddam maniac. They time those things. They time them so when you finally paid for them, they're used up.

LINDA: [Buttoning up his jacket as he unbuttons it.] All told, about two hundred dollars would carry us, dear. But that includes the last payment on the mortgage. After this payment, Willy, the house belongs to us.

WILLY: It's twenty-five years!

LINDA: Biff was nine years old when we bought it.

WILLY: Well, that's a great thing. To weather a twenty-five year mortgage is—

LINDA: It's an accomplishment.

WILLY: All the cement, the lumber, the reconstruction I put in this house! There ain't a crack to be found in it anymore.

LINDA: Well, it served its purpose.

WILLY: What purpose? Some stranger'll come along, move in, and that's that. If only Biff would take this house, and raise a family . . . [He starts to go.] Good-bye, I'm late.

LINDA: [Suddenly remembering.] Oh, I forgot! You're supposed to meet them for dinner.

WILLY: Me?

LINDA: At Frank's Chop House on Forty-eighth near Sixth Avenue.

WILLY: Is that so! How about you?

LINDA: No, just the three of you. They're gonna blow you to a big meal!

WILLY: Don't say! Who thought of that?

LINDA: Biff came to me this morning, Willy, and he said, "Tell Dad, we want to blow him to a big meal." Be there six o'clock. You and your two boys are going to have dinner.

WILLY: Gee whiz! That's really somethin'. I'm gonna knock Howard for a loop, kid. I'll get an advance, and I'll come home with a New York job. Goddammit, now I'm gonna do it!

LINDA: Oh, that's the spirit, Willy!

WILLY: I will never get behind a wheel the rest of my life!

LINDA: It's changing, Willy, I can feel it changing!

WILLY: Beyond a question. G'bye, I'm late. [He starts to go again.]

LINDA: [Calling after him as she runs to the kitchen table for a handkerchief.] You got your glasses?

WILLY: [*Feels for them, then comes back in.*] Yeah, yeah, got my glasses.
LINDA: [*Giving him the handkerchief.*] And a handkerchief.
WILLY: Yeah, handkerchief.
LINDA: And your saccharine?[2]
WILLY: Yeah, my saccharine.
LINDA: Be careful on the subway stairs.

[*She kisses him, and a silk stocking is seen hanging from her hand.*
WILLY *notices it.*]

WILLY: Will you stop mending stockings? At least while I'm in the house.
It gets me nervous. I can't tell you. Please.

[LINDA *hides the stocking in her hand as she follows* WILLY *across the
forestage in front of the house.*]

LINDA: Remember, Frank's Chop House.
WILLY: [*Passing the apron.*[3]] Maybe beets would grow out there.
LINDA: [*Laughing.*] But you tried so many times.
WILLY: Yeah. Well, don't work hard today. [*He disappears around the right
corner of the house.*]
LINDA: Be careful! [*As* WILLY *vanishes,* LINDA *waves to him. Suddenly the
phone rings. She runs across the stage and into the kitchen and lifts it.*]
Hello? Oh, Biff! I'm so glad you called, I just . . . Yes, sure, I just told
him. Yes, he'll be there for dinner at six o'clock, I didn't forget. Listen, I
was just dying to tell you. You know that little rubber pipe I told you
about? That he connected to the gas heater? I finally decided to go down
the cellar this morning and take it away and destroy it. But it's gone!
Imagine? He took it away himself, it isn't there! [*She listens.*] When? Oh,
then you took it. Oh—nothing, it's just that I'd hoped he'd taken it away
himself. Oh, I'm not worried, darling, because this morning he left in
such high spirits, it was like the old days! I'm not afraid anymore. Did
Mr. Oliver see you? . . . Well, you wait there then. And make a nice
impression on him, darling. Just don't perspire too much before you
see him. And have a nice time with Dad. He may have big news too! . . .
That's right, a New York job. And be sweet to him tonight, dear. Be loving to him. Because he's only a little boat looking for a harbor. [*She is
trembling with sorrow and joy.*] Oh, that's wonderful, Biff, you'll save his
life. Thanks, darling. Just put your arm around him when he comes into
the restaurant. Give him a smile. That's the boy . . . Good-bye, dear . . .
You got your comb? . . . That's fine. Good-bye, Biff dear.

2. Artificial sweetener once recommended as a healthy alternative to sugar.
3. Foremost part of the stage, in front of the proscenium arch.

[*In the middle of her speech,* HOWARD WAGNER, *thirty-six, wheels on a small typewriter table on which is a wire-recording machine*[4] *and proceeds to plug it in. This is on the left forestage. Light slowly fades on* LINDA *as it rises on* HOWARD. HOWARD *is intent on threading the machine and only glances over his shoulder as* WILLY *appears.*]

WILLY: Pst! Pst!

HOWARD: Hello, Willy, come in.

WILLY: Like to have a little talk with you, Howard.

HOWARD: Sorry to keep you waiting. I'll be with you in a minute.

WILLY: What's that, Howard?

HOWARD: Didn't you ever see one of these? Wire recorder.

WILLY: Oh. Can we talk a minute?

HOWARD: Records things. Just got delivery yesterday. Been driving me crazy, the most terrific machine I ever saw in my life. I was up all night with it.

WILLY: What do you do with it?

HOWARD: I bought it for dictation, but you can do anything with it. Listen to this. I had it home last night. Listen to what I picked up. The first one is my daughter. Get this. [*He flicks the switch and "Roll out the Barrel" is heard being whistled.*] Listen to that kid whistle.

WILLY: That is lifelike, isn't it?

HOWARD: Seven years old. Get that tone.

WILLY: Ts, ts. Like to ask a little favor if you . . .

[*The whistling breaks off, and the voice of* HOWARD's *daughter is heard.*]

HIS DAUGHTER: "Now you, Daddy."

HOWARD: She's crazy for me! [*Again the same song is whistled.*] That's me! Ha! [*He winks.*]

WILLY: You're very good!

[*The whistling breaks off again. The machine runs silent for a moment.*]

HOWARD: Sh! Get this now, this is my son.

HIS SON: "The capital of Alabama is Montgomery; the capital of Arizona is Phoenix; the capital of Arkansas is Little Rock; the capital of California is Sacramento . . ." [*And on, and on.*]

HOWARD: [*Holding up five fingers.*] Five years old, Willy!

WILLY: He'll make an announcer some day!

HIS SON: [*Continuing.*] "The capital . . ."

HOWARD: Get that—alphabetical order! [*The machine breaks off suddenly.*] Wait a minute. The maid kicked the plug out.

WILLY: It certainly is a—

4. Precursor to the tape recorder.

HOWARD: Sh, for God's sake!

HIS SON: "It's nine o'clock, Bulova watch time.[5] So I have to go to sleep."

WILLY: That really is—

HOWARD: Wait a minute! The next is my wife.

[*They wait.*]

HOWARD'S VOICE: "Go on, say something." [*Pause.*] "Well, you gonna talk?"

HIS WIFE: "I can't think of anything."

HOWARD'S VOICE: "Well, talk—it's turning."

HIS WIFE: [*Shyly, beaten.*] "Hello." [*Silence.*] "Oh, Howard, I can't talk into this . . ."

HOWARD: [*Snapping the machine off.*] That was my wife.

WILLY: That is a wonderful machine. Can we—

HOWARD: I tell you, Willy, I'm gonna take my camera, and my bandsaw, and all my hobbies, and out they go. This is the most fascinating relaxation I ever found.

WILLY: I think I'll get one myself.

HOWARD: Sure, they're only a hundred and a half. You can't do without it. Supposing you wanna hear Jack Benny,[6] see? But you can't be at home at that hour. So you tell the maid to turn the radio on when Jack Benny comes on, and this automatically goes on with the radio . . .

WILLY: And when you come home you . . .

HOWARD: You can come home twelve o'clock, one o'clock, any time you like, and you get yourself a Coke and sit yourself down, throw the switch, and there's Jack Benny's program in the middle of the night!

WILLY: I'm definitely going to get one. Because lots of time I'm on the road, and I think to myself, what I must be missing on the radio!

HOWARD: Don't you have a radio in the car?

WILLY: Well, yeah, but who ever thinks of turning it on?

HOWARD: Say, aren't you supposed to be in Boston?

WILLY: That's what I want to talk to you about, Howard. You got a minute? [*He draws a chair in from the wing.*]

HOWARD: What happened? What're you doing here?

WILLY: Well . . .

HOWARD: You didn't crack up again, did you?

WILLY: Oh, no. No . . .

HOWARD: Geez, you had me worried there for a minute. What's the trouble?

5. Phrase commonly heard on radio programs sponsored by the Bulova Watch Company.
6. Vaudeville, radio, television, and movie star (1894–1974); he hosted America's most popular radio show from 1932 to 1955.

WILLY: Well, tell you the truth, Howard. I've come to the decision that I'd rather not travel anymore.

HOWARD: Not travel! Well, what'll you do?

WILLY: Remember, Christmas time, when you had the party here? You said you'd try to think of some spot for me here in town.

HOWARD: With us?

WILLY: Well, sure.

HOWARD: Oh, yeah, yeah. I remember. Well, I couldn't think of anything for you, Willy.

WILLY: I tell ya, Howard. The kids are all grown up, y'know. I don't need much anymore. If I could take home—well, sixty-five dollars a week, I could swing it.

HOWARD: Yeah, but Willy, see I—

WILLY: I tell ya why, Howard. Speaking frankly and between the two of us, y'know—I'm just a little tired.

HOWARD: Oh, I could understand that, Willy. But you're a road man, Willy, and we do a road business. We've only got a half-dozen salesmen on the floor here.

WILLY: God knows, Howard, I never asked a favor of any man. But I was with the firm when your father used to carry you in here in his arms.

HOWARD: I know that, Willy, but—

WILLY: Your father came to me the day you were born and asked me what I thought of the name of Howard, may he rest in peace.

HOWARD: I appreciate that, Willy, but there just is no spot here for you. If I had a spot I'd slam you right in, but I just don't have a single solitary spot.

[*He looks for his lighter.* WILLY *has picked it up and gives it to him. Pause.*]

WILLY: [*With increasing anger.*] Howard, all I need to set my table is fifty dollars a week.

HOWARD: But where am I going to put you, kid?

WILLY: Look, it isn't a question of whether I can sell merchandise, is it?

HOWARD: No, but it's a business, kid, and everybody's gotta pull his own weight.

WILLY: [*Desperately.*] Just let me tell you a story, Howard—

HOWARD: 'Cause you gotta admit, business is business.

WILLY: [*Angrily.*] Business is definitely business, but just listen for a minute. You don't understand this. When I was a boy—eighteen, nineteen—I was already on the road. And there was a question in my mind as to whether selling had a future for me. Because in those days I had a yearning to go to Alaska. See, there were three gold strikes in one month in Alaska, and I felt like going out. Just for the ride, you might say.

HOWARD: [*Barely interested.*] Don't say.

WILLY: Oh, yeah, my father lived many years in Alaska. He was an adventurous man. We've got quite a little streak of self-reliance in our family. I thought I'd go out with my older brother and try to locate him, and maybe settle in the North with the old man. And I was almost decided to go, when I met a salesman in the Parker House. His name was Dave Singleman. And he was eighty-four years old, and he'd drummed merchandise in thirty-one states. And old Dave, he'd go up to his room, y'understand, put on his green velvet slippers—I'll never forget—and pick up his phone and call the buyers, and without ever leaving his room, at the age of eighty-four, he made a living. And when I saw that, I realized that selling was the greatest career a man could want. 'Cause what could be more satisfying than to be able to go, at the age of eighty-four, into twenty or thirty different cities, and pick up his phone and be remembered and loved and helped by so many different people? Do you know? when he died—and by the way he died the death of a salesman, in his green velvet slippers in the smoker[7] of the New York, New Haven and Hartford, going into Boston—when he died, hundreds of salesmen and buyers were at his funeral. Things were sad on a lotta trains for months after that. [*He stands up.* HOWARD *has not looked at him.*] In those days there was personality in it, Howard. There was respect, and comradeship, and gratitude in it. Today, it's all cut and dried, and there's no chance for bringing friendship to bear—or personality. You see what I mean? They don't know me anymore.

HOWARD: [*Moving away, toward the right.*] That's just the thing, Willy.

WILLY: If I had forty dollars a week—that's all I'd need. Forty dollars, Howard.

HOWARD: Kid, I can't take blood from a stone, I—

WILLY: [*Desperation is on him now.*] Howard, the year Al Smith[8] was nominated, your father came to me and—

HOWARD: [*Starting to go off.*] I've got to see some people, kid.

WILLY: [*Stopping him.*] I'm talking about your father! There were promises made across this desk! You mustn't tell me you've got people to see—I put thirty-four years into this firm, Howard, and now I can't pay my insurance! You can't eat the orange and throw the peel away—a man is not a piece of fruit! [*After a pause.*] Now pay attention. Your father—in

---

7. That is, smoking car on a train.
8. Alfred E. Smith (1873–1944), governor of New York and Democratic presidential nominee who lost to Herbert Hoover in 1928.

1928 I had a big year. I averaged a hundred and seventy dollars a week
in commissions.

HOWARD: [*Impatiently.*] Now, Willy, you never averaged—

WILLY: [*Banging his hand on the desk.*] I averaged a hundred and seventy
dollars a week in the year of 1928! And your father came to me—or
rather, I was in the office here—it was right over this desk—and he
put his hand on my shoulder—

HOWARD: [*Getting up.*] You'll have to excuse me, Willy, I gotta see some
people. Pull yourself together. [*Going out.*] I'll be back in a little while.

[*On* HOWARD's *exit, the light on his chair grows very bright and strange.*]

WILLY: Pull myself together! What the hell did I say to him? My God, I was
yelling at him! How could I! [WILLY *breaks off, staring at the light, which
occupies the chair, animating it. He approaches this chair, standing across
the desk from it.*] Frank, Frank, don't you remember what you told me that
time? How you put your hand on my shoulder, and Frank . . . [*He leans on
the desk and as he speaks the dead man's name he accidentally switches on
the recorder, and instantly.*]

HOWARD's SON: ". . . of New York is Albany. The capital of Ohio is Cincinnati, the capital of Rhode Island is . . ." [*The recitation continues.*]

WILLY: [*Leaping away with fright, shouting.*] Ha! Howard! Howard! Howard!

HOWARD: [*Rushing in.*] What happened?

WILLY: [*Pointing at the machine, which continues nasally, childishly, with the
capital cities.*] Shut it off! Shut it off!

HOWARD: [*Pulling the plug out.*] Look, Willy . . .

WILLY: [*Pressing his hands to his eyes.*] I gotta get myself some coffee. I'll
get some coffee . . .

[WILLY *starts to walk out.* HOWARD *stops him.*]

HOWARD: [*Rolling up the cord.*] Willy, look . . .

WILLY: I'll go to Boston.

HOWARD: Willy, you can't go to Boston for us.

WILLY: Why can't I go?

HOWARD: I don't want you to represent us. I've been meaning to tell you for
a long time now.

WILLY: Howard, are you firing me?

HOWARD: I think you need a good long rest, Willy.

WILLY: Howard—

HOWARD: And when you feel better, come back, and we'll see if we can
work something out.

WILLY: But I gotta earn money, Howard. I'm in no position to—

HOWARD: Where are your sons? Why don't your sons give you a hand?

WILLY: They're working on a very big deal.

HOWARD: This is no time for false pride, Willy. You go to your sons and you tell them that you're tired. You've got two great boys, haven't you?

WILLY: Oh, no question, no question, but in the meantime . . .

HOWARD: Then that's that, heh?

WILLY: All right, I'll go to Boston tomorrow.

HOWARD: No, no.

WILLY: I can't throw myself on my sons. I'm not a cripple!

HOWARD: Look, kid, I'm busy, I'm busy this morning.

WILLY: [*Grasping* HOWARD's *arm.*] Howard, you've got to let me go to Boston!

HOWARD: [*Hard, keeping himself under control.*] I've got a line of people to see this morning. Sit down, take five minutes, and pull yourself together, and then go home, will ya? I need the office, Willy. [*He starts to go, turns, remembering the recorder, starts to push off the table holding the recorder.*] Oh, yeah. Whenever you can this week, stop by and drop off the samples. You'll feel better, Willy, and then come back and we'll talk. Pull yourself together, kid, there's people outside.

[HOWARD *exits, pushing the table off left.* WILLY *stares into space, exhausted. Now the music is heard*—BEN's *music—first distantly, then closer, closer. As* WILLY *speaks,* BEN *enters from the right. He carries valise and umbrella.*]

WILLY: Oh, Ben, how did you do it? What is the answer? Did you wind up the Alaska deal already?

BEN: Doesn't take much time if you know what you're doing. Just a short business trip. Boarding ship in an hour. Wanted to say good-by.

WILLY: Ben, I've got to talk to you.

BEN: [*Glancing at his watch.*] Haven't the time, William.

WILLY: [*Crossing the apron to* BEN.] Ben, nothing's working out. I don't know what to do.

BEN: Now, look here, William. I've bought timberland in Alaska and I need a man to look after things for me.

WILLY: God, timberland! Me and my boys in those grand outdoors!

BEN: You've a new continent at your doorstep, William. Get out of these cities, they're full of talk and time payments and courts of law. Screw on your fists and you can fight for a fortune up there.

WILLY: Yes, yes! Linda, Linda!

[LINDA *enters as of old, with the wash.*]

LINDA: Oh, you're back?

BEN: I haven't much time.

WILLY: No, wait! Linda, he's got a proposition for me in Alaska.

LINDA: But you've got—[*To* BEN.] He's got a beautiful job here.

WILLY: But in Alaska, kid, I could—

LINDA: You're doing well enough, Willy!

BEN: [*To* LINDA.] Enough for what, my dear?

LINDA: [*Frightened of* BEN *and angry at him.*] Don't say those things to him! Enough to be happy right here, right now. [*To* WILLY, *while* BEN *laughs.*] Why must everybody conquer the world? You're well liked, and the boys love you, and someday—[*To* BEN.]—why, old man Wagner told him just the other day that if he keeps it up he'll be a member of the firm, didn't he, Willy?

WILLY: Sure, sure. I am building something with this firm, Ben, and if a man is building something he must be on the right track, mustn't he?

BEN: What are you building? Lay your hand on it. Where is it?

WILLY: [*Hesitantly.*] That's true, Linda, there's nothing.

LINDA: Why? [*To* BEN.] There's a man eighty-four years old—

WILLY: That's right, Ben, that's right. When I look at that man I say, what is there to worry about?

BEN: Bah!

WILLY: It's true, Ben. All he has to do is go into any city, pick up the phone, and he's making his living and you know why?

BEN: [*Picking up his valise.*] I've got to go.

WILLY: [*Holding* BEN *back.*] Look at this boy! [BIFF, *in his high school sweater, enters carrying suitcase.* HAPPY *carries* BIFF's *shoulder guards, gold helmet, and football pants.*] Without a penny to his name, three great universities are begging for him, and from there the sky's the limit, because it's not what you do, Ben. It's who you know and the smile on your face! It's contacts, Ben, contacts! The whole wealth of Alaska passes over the lunch table at the Commodore Hotel, and that's the wonder, the wonder of this country, that a man can end with diamonds here on the basis of being liked! [*He turns to* BIFF.] And that's why when you get out on that field today it's important. Because thousands of people will be rooting for you and loving you. [*To* BEN, *who has again begun to leave.*] And Ben! when he walks into a business office his name will sound out like a bell and all the doors will open to him! I've seen it, Ben, I've seen it a thousand times! You can't feel it with your hand like timber, but it's there!

BEN: Good-by, William.

WILLY: Ben, am I right? Don't you think I'm right? I value your advice.

BEN: There's a new continent at your doorstep, William. You could walk out rich. Rich! [*He is gone.*]

WILLY: We'll do it here, Ben! You hear me? We're gonna do it here!

[*Young* BERNARD *rushes in. The gay music of the Boys is heard.*]

BERNARD: Oh, gee, I was afraid you left already!

WILLY: Why? What time is it?

BERNARD: It's half-past one!

WILLY: Well, come on, everybody! Ebbets Field next stop! Where's the pennants? [*He rushes through the wall-line of the kitchen and out into the living room.*]

LINDA: [*To* BIFF.] Did you pack fresh underwear?

BIFF: [*Who has been limbering up.*] I want to go!

BERNARD: Biff, I'm carrying your helmet, ain't I?

HAPPY: No, I'm carrying the helmet.

BERNARD: Oh, Biff, you promised me.

HAPPY: I'm carrying the helmet.

BERNARD: How am I going to get in the locker room?

LINDA: Let him carry the shoulder guards. [*She puts her coat and hat on in the kitchen.*]

BERNARD: Can I, Biff? 'Cause I told everybody I'm going to be in the locker room.

HAPPY: In Ebbets Field it's the clubhouse.

BERNARD: I meant the clubhouse, Biff!

HAPPY: Biff!

BIFF: [*Grandly, after a slight pause.*] Let him carry the shoulder guards.

HAPPY: [*As he gives* BERNARD *the shoulder guards.*] Stay close to us now.

[WILLY *rushes in with the pennants.*]

WILLY: [*Handing them out.*] Everybody wave when Biff comes out on the field. [HAPPY *and* BERNARD *run off.*] You set now, boy?

[*The music has died away.*]

BIFF: Ready to go, Pop. Every muscle is ready.

WILLY: [*At the edge of the apron.*] You realize what this means?

BIFF: That's right, Pop.

WILLY: [*Feeling* BIFF's *muscles.*] You're comin' home this afternoon captain of the All-Scholastic Championship Team of the City of New York.

BIFF: I got it, Pop. And remember, pal, when I take off my helmet, that touchdown is for you.

WILLY: Let's go! [*He is starting out, with his arm around* BIFF, *when* CHARLEY *enters, as of old, in knickers.*] I got no room for you, Charley.

CHARLEY: Room? For what?

WILLY: In the car.

CHARLEY: You goin' for a ride? I wanted to shoot some casino.

WILLY: [*Furiously.*] Casino! [*Incredulously.*] Don't you realize what today is?

LINDA: Oh, he knows, Willy. He's just kidding you.

WILLY: That's nothing to kid about!

CHARLEY: No, Linda, what's goin' on?

LINDA: He's playing in Ebbets Field.

CHARLEY: Baseball in this weather?

WILLY: Don't talk to him. Come on, come on! [*He is pushing them out.*]

CHARLEY: Wait a minute, didn't you hear the news?

WILLY: What?

CHARLEY: Don't you listen to the radio? Ebbets Field just blew up.

WILLY: You go to hell! [CHARLEY *laughs. Pushing them out.*] Come on, come on! We're late.

CHARLEY: [*As they go.*] Knock a homer, Biff, knock a homer!

WILLY: [*The last to leave, turning to* CHARLEY.] I don't think that was funny, Charley. This is the greatest day of my life.

CHARLEY: Willy, when are you going to grow up?

WILLY: Yeah, heh? When this game is over, Charley, you'll be laughing out of the other side of your face. They'll be calling him another Red Grange.[9] Twenty-five thousand a year.

CHARLEY: [*Kidding.*] Is that so?

WILLY: Yeah, that's so.

CHARLEY: Well, then, I'm sorry, Willy. But tell me something.

WILLY: What?

CHARLEY: Who is Red Grange?

WILLY: Put up your hands. Goddam you, put up your hands! [CHARLEY, *chuckling, shakes his head and walks away, around the left corner of the stage.* WILLY *follows him. The music rises to a mocking frenzy.*] Who the hell do you think you are, better than everybody else? You don't know everything, you big, ignorant, stupid . . . Put up your hands!

[*Light rises, on the right side of the forestage, on a small table in the reception room of* CHARLEY's *office. Traffic sounds are heard.* BERNARD, *now mature, sits whistling to himself. A pair of tennis rackets and an overnight bag are on the floor beside him.*]

WILLY: [*Offstage.*] What are you walking away for? Don't walk away! If you're going to say something say it to my face! I know you laugh at me behind my back. You'll laugh out of the other side of your goddam face after this

---

9. Harold Edward Grange (1903–91), All-American halfback at the University of Illinois from 1923 to 1925; he played professionally for the Chicago Bears.

game. Touchdown! Touchdown! Eighty thousand people! Touchdown! Right between the goal posts.

[BERNARD *is a quiet, earnest, but self-assured young man.* WILLY's *voice is coming from right upstage now.* BERNARD *lowers his feet off the table and listens.* JENNY, *his father's secretary, enters.*]

JENNY: [*Distressed.*] Say, Bernard, will you go out in the hall?

BERNARD: What is that noise? Who is it?

JENNY: Mr. Loman. He just got off the elevator.

BERNARD: [*Getting up.*] Who's he arguing with?

JENNY: Nobody. There's nobody with him. I can't deal with him anymore, and your father gets all upset everytime he comes. I've got a lot of typing to do, and your father's waiting to sign it. Will you see him?

WILLY: [*Entering.*] Touchdown! Touch—[*He sees* JENNY.] Jenny, Jenny, good to see you. How're ya? Workin'? Or still honest?

JENNY: Fine. How've you been feeling?

WILLY: Not much anymore, Jenny. Ha, ha! [*He is surprised to see the rackets.*]

BERNARD: Hello, Uncle Willy.

WILLY: [*Almost shocked.*] Bernard! Well, look who's here! [*He comes quickly, guiltily to* BERNARD *and warmly shakes his hand.*]

BERNARD: How are you? Good to see you.

WILLY: What are you doing here?

BERNARD: Oh, just stopped by to see Pop. Get off my feet till my train leaves. I'm going to Washington in a few minutes.

WILLY: Is he in?

BERNARD: Yes, he's in his office with the accountant. Sit down.

WILLY: [*Sitting down.*] What're you going to do in Washington?

BERNARD: Oh, just a case I've got there, Willy.

WILLY: That so? [*Indicating the rackets.*] You going to play tennis there?

BERNARD: I'm staying with a friend who's got a court.

WILLY: Don't say. His own tennis court. Must be fine people, I bet.

BERNARD: They are, very nice. Dad tells me Biff's in town.

WILLY: [*With a big smile.*] Yeah, Biff's in. Working on a very big deal, Bernard.

BERNARD: What's Biff doing?

WILLY: Well, he's been doing very big things in the West. But he decided to establish himself here. Very big. We're having dinner. Did I hear your wife had a boy?

BERNARD: That's right. Our second.

WILLY: Two boys! What do you know!

BERNARD: What kind of a deal has Biff got?

WILLY: Well, Bill Oliver—very big sporting-goods man—he wants Biff very badly. Called him in from the West. Long distance, carte blanche, special deliveries. Your friends have their own private tennis court?

BERNARD: You still with the old firm, Willy?

WILLY: [*After a pause.*] I'm—I'm overjoyed to see how you made the grade, Bernard, overjoyed. It's an encouraging thing to see a young man really— really—Looks very good for Biff—very—[*He breaks off, then.*] Bernard— [*He is so full of emotion, he breaks off again.*]

BERNARD: What is it, Willy?

WILLY: [*Small and alone.*] What—what's the secret?

BERNARD: What secret?

WILLY: How—how did you? Why didn't he ever catch on?

BERNARD: I wouldn't know that, Willy.

WILLY: [*Confidentially, desperately.*] You were his friend, his boyhood friend. There's something I don't understand about it. His life ended after that Ebbets Field game. From the age of seventeen nothing good ever happened to him.

BERNARD: He never trained himself for anything.

WILLY: But he did, he did. After high school he took so many correspondence courses. Radio mechanics; television; God knows what, and never made the slightest mark.

BERNARD: [*Taking off his glasses.*] Willy, do you want to talk candidly?

WILLY: [*Rising, faces* BERNARD.] I regard you as a very brilliant man, Bernard. I value your advice.

BERNARD: Oh, the hell with the advice, Willy. I couldn't advise you. There's just one thing I've always wanted to ask you. When he was supposed to graduate, and the math teacher flunked him—

WILLY: Oh, that son-of-a-bitch ruined his life.

BERNARD: Yeah, but, Willy, all he had to do was go to summer school and make up that subject.

WILLY: That's right, that's right.

BERNARD: Did you tell him not to go to summer school?

WILLY: Me? I begged him to go. I ordered him to go!

BERNARD: Then why wouldn't he go?

WILLY: Why? Why! Bernard, that question has been trailing me like a ghost for the last fifteen years. He flunked the subject, and laid down and died like a hammer hit him!

BERNARD: Take it easy, kid.

WILLY: Let me talk to you—I got nobody to talk to. Bernard, Bernard, was it my fault? Y'see? It keeps going around in my mind, maybe I did something to him. I got nothing to give him.

BERNARD: Don't take it so hard.

WILLY: Why did he lay down? What is the story there? You were his friend!

BERNARD: Willy, I remember, it was June, and our grades came out. And he'd flunked math.

WILLY: That son-of-a-bitch!

BERNARD: No, it wasn't right then. Biff just got very angry, I remember, and he was ready to enroll in summer school.

WILLY: [*Surprised.*] He was?

BERNARD: He wasn't beaten by it at all. But then, Willy, he disappeared from the block for almost a month. And I got the idea that he'd gone up to New England to see you. Did he have a talk with you then? [WILLY *stares in silence.*] Willy?

WILLY: [*With a strong edge of resentment in his voice.*] Yeah, he came to Boston. What about it?

BERNARD: Well, just that when he came back—I'll never forget this, it always mystifies me. Because I'd thought so well of Biff, even though he'd always taken advantage of me. I loved him, Willy, y'know? And he came back after that month and took his sneakers—remember those sneakers with "University of Virginia" printed on them? He was so proud of those, wore them every day. And he took them down in the cellar, and burned them up in the furnace. We had a fist fight. It lasted at least half an hour. Just the two of us, punching each other down the cellar, and crying right through it. I've often thought of how strange it was that I knew he'd given up his life. What happened in Boston, Willy? [WILLY *looks at him as at an intruder.*] I just bring it up because you asked me.

WILLY: [*Angrily.*] Nothing. What do you mean, "What happened?" What's that got to do with anything?

BERNARD: Well, don't get sore.

WILLY: What are you trying to do, blame it on me? If a boy lays down is that my fault?

BERNARD: Now, Willy, don't get—

WILLY: Well, don't—don't talk to me that way! What does that mean, "What happened?"

[CHARLEY *enters. He is in his vest, and he carries a bottle of bourbon.*]

CHARLEY: Hey, you're going to miss that train. [*He waves the bottle.*]

BERNARD: Yeah, I'm going. [*He takes the bottle.*] Thanks, Pop. [*He picks up his rackets and bag.*] Good-bye, Willy, and don't worry about it. You know, "If at first you don't succeed . . ."

WILLY: Yes, I believe in that.

BERNARD: But sometimes, Willy, it's better for a man just to walk away.

WILLY: Walk away?

BERNARD: That's right.

WILLY: But if you can't walk away?

BERNARD: [*After a slight pause.*] I guess that's when it's tough. [*Extending his hand.*] Good-bye, Willy.

WILLY: [*Shaking* BERNARD's *hand.*] Good-bye, boy.

CHARLEY: [*An arm on* BERNARD's *shoulder.*] How do you like this kid? Gonna argue a case in front of the Supreme Court.

BERNARD: [*Protesting.*] Pop!

WILLY: [*Genuinely shocked, pained, and happy.*] No! The Supreme Court!

BERNARD: I gotta run. 'Bye, Dad!

CHARLEY: Knock 'em dead, Bernard!

[BERNARD *goes off.*]

WILLY: [*As* CHARLEY *takes out his wallet.*] The Supreme Court! And he didn't even mention it!

CHARLEY: [*Counting out money on the desk.*] He don't have to—he's gonna do it.

WILLY: And you never told him what to do, did you? You never took any interest in him.

CHARLEY: My salvation is that I never took any interest in anything. There's some money—fifty dollars. I got an accountant inside.

WILLY: Charley, look . . . [*With difficulty.*] I got my insurance to pay. If you can manage it—I need a hundred and ten dollars. [CHARLEY *doesn't reply for a moment; merely stops moving.*] I'd draw it from my bank but Linda would know, and I . . .

CHARLEY: Sit down, Willy.

WILLY: [*Moving toward the chair.*] I'm keeping an account of everything, remember. I'll pay every penny back. [*He sits.*]

CHARLEY: Now listen to me, Willy.

WILLY: I want you to know I appreciate . . .

CHARLEY: [*Sitting down on the table.*] Willy, what're you doin'? What the hell is goin' on in your head?

WILLY: Why? I'm simply . . .

CHARLEY: I offered you a job. You can make fifty dollars a week. And I won't send you on the road.

WILLY: I've got a job.

CHARLEY: Without pay? What kind of job is a job without pay? [*He rises.*] Now, look kid, enough is enough. I'm no genius but I know when I'm being insulted.

WILLY: Insulted!

CHARLEY: Why don't you want to work for me?

WILLY: What's the matter with you? I've got a job.

CHARLEY: Then what're you walkin' in here every week for?

WILLY: [*Getting up.*] Well, if you don't want me to walk in here—

CHARLEY: I am offering you a job!

WILLY: I don't want your goddam job!

CHARLEY: When the hell are you going to grow up?

WILLY: [*Furiously.*] You big ignoramus, if you say that to me again I'll rap you one! I don't care how big you are! [*He's ready to fight. Pause.*]

CHARLEY: [*Kindly, going to him.*] How much do you need, Willy?

WILLY: Charley, I'm strapped, I'm strapped. I don't know what to do. I was just fired.

CHARLEY: Howard fired you?

WILLY: That snotnose. Imagine that? I named him. I named him Howard.

CHARLEY: Willy, when're you gonna realize that them things don't mean anything? You named him Howard, but you can't sell that. The only thing you got in this world is what you can sell. And the funny thing is that you're a salesman, and you don't know that.

WILLY: I've always tried to think otherwise, I guess. I always felt that if a man was impressive, and well liked, that nothing—

CHARLEY: Why must everybody like you? Who liked J. P. Morgan?[1] Was he impressive? In a Turkish bath he'd look like a butcher. But with his pockets on he was very well liked. Now listen, Willy, I know you don't like me, and nobody can say I'm in love with you, but I'll give you a job because— just for the hell of it, put it that way. Now what do you say?

WILLY: I—I just can't work for you, Charley.

CHARLEY: What're you, jealous of me?

WILLY: I can't work for you, that's all, don't ask me why.

CHARLEY: [*Angered, takes out more bills.*] You been jealous of me all your life, you damned fool! Here, pay your insurance. [*He puts the money in* WILLY's *hand.*]

WILLY: I'm keeping strict accounts.

CHARLEY: I've got some work to do. Take care of yourself. And pay your insurance.

WILLY: [*Moving to the right.*] Funny, y'know? After all the highways and the trains, and the appointments, and the years, you end up worth more dead than alive.

CHARLEY: Willy, nobody's worth nothin' dead. [*After a slight pause.*] Did you hear what I said? [WILLY *stands still, dreaming.*] Willy!

WILLY: Apologize to Bernard for me when you see him. I didn't mean to argue with him. He's a fine boy. They're all fine boys, and they'll end up

---

1. American financier and industrialist John Pierpont Morgan (1837–1913), widely criticized for his business dealings with the U.S. government.

big—all of them. Someday they'll all play tennis together. Wish me luck, Charley. He saw Bill Oliver today.

CHARLEY: Good luck.

WILLY: [*On the verge of tears.*] Charley, you're the only friend I got. Isn't that a remarkable thing? [*He goes out.*]

CHARLEY: Jesus!

[CHARLEY *stares after him a moment and follows. All light blacks out. Suddenly raucous music is heard, and a red glow rises behind the screen at right.* STANLEY, *a young waiter, appears, carrying a table, followed by* HAPPY, *who is carrying two chairs.*]

STANLEY: [*Putting the table down.*] That's all right, Mr. Loman, I can handle it myself. [*He turns and takes the chairs from* HAPPY *and places them at the table.*]

HAPPY: [*Glancing around.*] Oh, this is better.

STANLEY: Sure, in the front there you're in the middle of all kinds a noise. Whenever you got a party, Mr. Loman, you just tell me and I'll put you back here. Y'know, there's a lotta people they don't like it private, because when they go out they like to see a lotta action around them because they're sick and tired to stay in the house by theirself. But I know you, you ain't from Hackensack.[2] You know what I mean?

HAPPY: [*Sitting down.*] So how's it coming, Stanley?

STANLEY: Ah, it's a dog life. I only wish during the war they'd a took me in the Army. I couda been dead by now.

HAPPY: My brother's back, Stanley.

STANLEY: Oh, he come back, heh? From the Far West.

HAPPY: Yeah, big cattle man, my brother, so treat him right. And my father's coming too.

STANLEY: Oh, your father too!

HAPPY: You got a couple of nice lobsters?

STANLEY: Hundred per cent, big.

HAPPY: I want them with the claws.

STANLEY: Don't worry, I don't give you no mice. [HAPPY *laughs.*] How about some wine? It'll put a head on the meal.

HAPPY: No. You remember, Stanley, that recipe I brought you from overseas? With the champagne in it?

STANLEY: Oh, yeah, sure. I still got it tacked up yet in the kitchen. But that'll have to cost a buck apiece anyways.

HAPPY: That's all right.

STANLEY: What'd you, hit a number or somethin'?

---

2. Mainly working-class city in northern New Jersey.

HAPPY: No, it's a little celebration. My brother is—I think he pulled off a big deal today. I think we're going into business together.

STANLEY: Great! That's the best for you. Because a family business, you know what I mean?—that's the best.

HAPPY: That's what I think.

STANLEY: 'Cause what's the difference? Somebody steals? It's in the family. Know what I mean? [*Sotto voce.*[3]] Like this bartender here. The boss is goin' crazy what kinda leak he's got in the cash register. You put it in but it don't come out.

HAPPY: [*Raising his head.*] Sh!

STANLEY: What?

HAPPY: You notice I wasn't lookin' right or left, was I?

STANLEY: No.

HAPPY: And my eyes are closed.

STANLEY: So what's the—?

HAPPY: Strudel's comin'.

STANLEY: [*Catching on, looks around.*] Ah, no, there's no—[*He breaks off as a furred, lavishly dressed* GIRL *enters and sits at the next table. Both follow her with their eyes.*] Geez, how'd ya know?

HAPPY: I got radar or something. [*Staring directly at her profile.*] Oooooooo . . . Stanley.

STANLEY: I think, that's for you, Mr. Loman.

HAPPY: Look at that mouth. Oh, God. And the binoculars.

STANLEY: Geez, you got a life, Mr. Loman.

HAPPY: Wait on her.

STANLEY: [*Going to the* GIRL's *table.*] Would you like a menu, ma'am?

GIRL: I'm expecting someone, but I'd like a—

HAPPY: Why don't you bring her—excuse me, miss, do you mind? I sell champagne, and I'd like you to try my brand. Bring her a champagne, Stanley.

GIRL: That's awfully nice of you.

HAPPY: Don't mention it. It's all company money. [*He laughs.*]

GIRL: That's a charming product to be selling, isn't it?

HAPPY: Oh, gets to be like everything else. Selling is selling, y'know.

GIRL: I suppose.

HAPPY: You don't happen to sell, do you?

GIRL: No, I don't sell.

HAPPY: Would you object to a compliment from a stranger? You ought to be on a magazine cover.

GIRL: [*Looking at him a little archly.*] I have been.

3. In an undertone (Italian).

[STANLEY *comes in with a glass of champagne.*]

HAPPY: What'd I say before, Stanley? You see? She's a cover girl.

STANLEY: Oh, I could see, I could see.

HAPPY: [*To the* GIRL.] What magazine?

GIRL: Oh, a lot of them. [*She takes the drink.*] Thank you.

HAPPY: You know what they say in France, don't you? "Champagne is the drink of the complexion"—Hya, Biff!

[BIFF *has entered and sits with* HAPPY.]

BIFF: Hello, kid. Sorry I'm late.

HAPPY: I just got here. Uh, Miss—?

GIRL: Forsythe.

HAPPY: Miss Forsythe, this is my brother.

BIFF: Is Dad here?

HAPPY: His name is Biff. You might've heard of him. Great football player.

GIRL: Really? What team?

HAPPY: Are you familiar with football?

GIRL: No, I'm afraid I'm not.

HAPPY: Biff is quarterback with the New York Giants.

GIRL: Well, that's nice, isn't it? [*She drinks.*]

HAPPY: Good health.

GIRL: I'm happy to meet you.

HAPPY: That's my name, Hap. It's really Harold, but at West Point they called me Happy.

GIRL: [*Now really impressed.*] Oh, I see. How do you do? [*She turns her profile.*]

BIFF: Isn't Dad coming?

HAPPY: You want her?

BIFF: Oh, I could never make that.

HAPPY: I remember the time that idea would never come into your head. Where's the old confidence, Biff?

BIFF: I just saw Oliver—

HAPPY: Wait a minute. I've got to see that old confidence again. Do you want her? She's on call.

BIFF: Oh, no. [*He turns to look at the* GIRL.]

HAPPY: I'm telling you. Watch this. [*Turning to see the* GIRL.] Honey? [*She turns to him.*] Are you busy?

GIRL: Well, I am . . . but I could make a phone call.

HAPPY: Do that, will you, honey? And see if you can get a friend. We'll be here for a while. Biff is one of the greatest football players in the country.

GIRL: [*Standing up.*] Well, I'm certainly happy to meet you.

HAPPY: Come back soon.

GIRL: I'll try.

HAPPY: Don't try, honey, try hard. [*The* GIRL *exits.* STANLEY *follows, shaking his head in bewildered admiration.*] Isn't that a shame now? A beautiful girl like that? That's why I can't get married. There's not a good woman in a thousand. New York is loaded with them, kid!

BIFF: Hap, look—

HAPPY: I told you she was on call![4]

BIFF: [*Strangely unnerved.*] Cut it out, will ya? I want to say something to you.

HAPPY: Did you see Oliver?

BIFF: I saw him all right. Now look, I want to tell Dad a couple of things and I want you to help me.

HAPPY: What? Is he going to back you?

BIFF: Are you crazy? You're out of your goddam head, you know that?

HAPPY: Why? What happened?

BIFF: [*Breathlessly.*] I did a terrible thing today, Hap. It's been the strangest day I ever went through. I'm all numb, I swear.

HAPPY: You mean he wouldn't see you?

BIFF: Well, I waited six hours for him, see? All day. Kept sending my name in. Even tried to date his secretary so she'd get me to him, but no soap.

HAPPY: Because you're not showin' the old confidence, Biff. He remembered you, didn't he?

BIFF: [*Stopping* HAPPY *with a gesture.*] Finally, about five o'clock, he comes out. Didn't remember who I was or anything. I felt like such an idiot, Hap.

HAPPY: Did you tell him my Florida idea?

BIFF: He walked away. I saw him for one minute. I got so mad I could've torn the walls down! How the hell did I ever get the idea I was a salesman there? I even believed myself that I'd been a salesman for him! And then he gave me one look and—I realized what a ridiculous lie my whole life has been! We've been talking in a dream for fifteen years. I was a shipping clerk.

HAPPY: What'd you do?

BIFF: [*With great tension and wonder.*] Well, he left, see. And the secretary went out. I was all alone in the waiting-room. I don't know what came over me, Hap. The next thing I know I'm in his office—paneled walls, everything. I can't explain it. I—Hap, I took his fountain pen.

HAPPY: Geez, did he catch you?

BIFF: I ran out. I ran down all eleven flights. I ran and ran and ran.

HAPPY: That was an awful dumb—what'd you do that for?

4. That is, a call girl, a prostitute.

BIFF: [*Agonized.*] I don't know, I just—wanted to take something, I don't know. You gotta help me, Hap, I'm gonna tell Pop.

HAPPY: You crazy? What for?

BIFF: Hap, he's got to understand that I'm not the man somebody lends that kind of money to. He thinks I've been spiting him all these years and it's eating him up.

HAPPY: That's just it. You tell him something nice.

BIFF: I can't.

HAPPY: Say you got a lunch date with Oliver tomorrow.

BIFF: So what do I do tomorrow?

HAPPY: You leave the house tomorrow and come back at night and say Oliver is thinking it over. And he thinks it over for a couple of weeks, and gradually it fades away and nobody's the worse.

BIFF: But it'll go on forever!

HAPPY: Dad is never so happy as when he's looking forward to something! [WILLY *enters.*] Hello, scout!

WILLY: Gee, I haven't been here in years!

[STANLEY *has followed* WILLY *in and sets a chair for him.* STANLEY *starts off but* HAPPY *stops him.*]

HAPPY: Stanley!

[STANLEY *stands by, waiting for an order.*]

BIFF: [*Going to* WILLY *with guilt, as to an invalid.*] Sit down, Pop. You want a drink?

WILLY: Sure, I don't mind.

BIFF: Let's get a load on.

WILLY: You look worried.

BIFF: N-no. [*To* STANLEY.] Scotch all around. Make it doubles.

STANLEY: Doubles, right. [*He goes.*]

WILLY: You had a couple already, didn't you?

BIFF: Just a couple, yeah.

WILLY: Well, what happened, boy? [*Nodding affirmatively, with a smile.*] Everything go all right?

BIFF: [*Takes a breath, then reaches out and grasps* WILLY's *hand.*] Pal . . . [*He is smiling bravely, and* WILLY *is smiling too.*] I had an experience today.

HAPPY: Terrific, Pop.

WILLY: That so? What happened?

BIFF: [*High, slightly alcoholic, above the earth.*] I'm going to tell you everything from first to last. It's been a strange day. [*Silence. He looks around, composes himself as best he can, but his breath keeps breaking the rhythm of his voice.*] I had to wait quite a while for him, and—

WILLY: Oliver?

BIFF: Yeah, Oliver. All day, as a matter of cold fact. And a lot of—instances—facts, Pop, facts about my life came back to me. Who was it, Pop? Who ever said I was a salesman with Oliver?

WILLY: Well, you were.

BIFF: No, Dad, I was shipping clerk.

WILLY: But you were practically—

BIFF: [*With determination.*] Dad, I don't know who said it first, but I was never a salesman for Bill Oliver.

WILLY: What're you talking about?

BIFF: Let's hold on to the facts tonight, Pop. We're not going to get any-where bullin' around. I was a shipping clerk.

WILLY: [*Angrily.*] All right, now listen to me—

BIFF: Why don't you let me finish?

WILLY: I'm not interested in stories about the past or any crap of that kind because the woods are burning, boys, you understand? There's a big blaze going on all around. I was fired today.

BIFF: [*Shocked.*] How could you be?

WILLY: I was fired, and I'm looking for a little good news to tell your mother, because the woman has waited and the woman has suffered. The gist of it is that I haven't got a story left in my head, Biff. So don't give me a lecture about facts and aspects. I am not interested. Now what've you got to say to me? [STANLEY *enters with three drinks. They wait until he leaves.*] Did you see Oliver?

BIFF: Jesus, Dad!

WILLY: You mean you didn't go up there?

HAPPY: Sure he went up there.

BIFF: I did. I—saw him. How could they fire you?

WILLY: [*On the edge of his chair.*] What kind of a welcome did he give you?

BIFF: He won't even let you work on commission?

WILLY: I'm out. [*Driving.*] So tell me, he gave you a warm welcome?

HAPPY: Sure, Pop, sure!

BIFF: [*Driven.*] Well, it was kind of—

WILLY: I was wondering if he'd remember you. [*To* HAPPY.] Imagine, man doesn't see him for ten, twelve years and gives him that kind of a welcome!

HAPPY: Damn right!

BIFF: [*Trying to return to the offensive.*] Pop, look—

WILLY: You know why he remembered you, don't you? Because you impressed him in those days.

BIFF: Let's talk quietly and get this down to the facts, huh?

WILLY: [*As though* BIFF *had been interrupting.*] Well, what happened? It's great news, Biff. Did he take you into his office or'd you talk in the waiting-room?

BIFF: Well, he came in, see and—

WILLY: [*With a big smile.*] What'd he say? Betcha he threw his arm around you.

BIFF: Well, he kinda—

WILLY: He's a fine man. [*To* HAPPY.] Very hard man to see, y'know.

HAPPY: [*Agreeing.*] Oh, I know.

WILLY: [*To* BIFF.] Is that where you had the drinks?

BIFF: Yeah, he gave me a couple of—no, no!

HAPPY: [*Cutting in.*] He told him my Florida idea.

WILLY: Don't interrupt. [*To* BIFF.] How'd he react to the Florida idea?

BIFF: Dad, will you give me a minute to explain?

WILLY: I've been waiting for you to explain since I sat down here! What happened? He took you into his office and what?

BIFF: Well—I talked. And—he listened, see.

WILLY: Famous for the way he listens, y'know. What was his answer?

BIFF: His answer was—[*He breaks off, suddenly angry.*] Dad, you're not letting me tell you what I want to tell you!

WILLY: [*Accusing, angered.*] You didn't see him, did you?

BIFF: I did see him!

WILLY: What'd you insult him or something? You insulted him, didn't you?

BIFF: Listen, will you let me out of it, will you just let me out of it!

HAPPY: What the hell!

WILLY: Tell me what happened!

BIFF: [*To* HAPPY.] I can't talk to him!

[*A single trumpet note jars the ear. The light of green leaves stains the house, which holds the air of night and a dream.* YOUNG BERNARD *enters and knocks on the door of the house.*]

YOUNG BERNARD: [*Frantically.*] Mrs. Loman, Mrs. Loman!

HAPPY: Tell him what happened!

BIFF: [*To* HAPPY.] Shut up and leave me alone!

WILLY: No, no. You had to go and flunk math!

BIFF: What math? What're you talking about?

YOUNG BERNARD: Mrs. Loman, Mrs. Loman!

[LINDA *appears in the house, as of old.*]

WILLY: [*Wildly.*] Math, math, math!

BIFF: Take it easy, Pop!

YOUNG BERNARD: Mrs. Loman!

WILLY: [*Furiously.*] If you hadn't flunked you'd've been set by now!

BIFF: Now, look, I'm gonna tell you what happened, and you're going to listen to me.

YOUNG BERNARD: Mrs. Loman!

BIFF: I waited six hours—

HAPPY: What the hell are you saying?

BIFF: I kept sending in my name but he wouldn't see me. So finally he . . .
[*He continues unheard as light fades low on the restaurant.*]

YOUNG BERNARD: Biff flunked math!

LINDA: No!

YOUNG BERNARD: Birnbaum flunked him! They won't graduate him!

LINDA: But they have to. He's gotta go to the university. Where is he? Biff! Biff!

YOUNG BERNARD: No, he left. He went to Grand Central.[5]

LINDA: Grand—You mean he went to Boston!

YOUNG BERNARD: Is Uncle Willy in Boston?

LINDA: Oh, maybe Willy can talk to the teacher. Oh, the poor, poor boy!

[*Light on house area snaps out.*]

BIFF: [*At the table, now audible, holding up a gold fountain pen.*] . . . so I'm washed up with Oliver, you understand? Are you listening to me?

WILLY: [*At a loss.*] Yeah, sure. If you hadn't flunked—

BIFF: Flunked what? What're you talking about?

WILLY: Don't blame everything on me! I didn't flunk math—you did! What pen?

HAPPY: That was awful dumb, Biff, a pen like that is worth—

WILLY: [*Seeing the pen for the first time.*] You took Oliver's pen?

BIFF: [*Weakening.*] Dad, I just explained it to you.

WILLY: You stole Bill Oliver's fountain pen!

BIFF: I didn't exactly steal it! That's just what I've been explaining to you!

HAPPY: He had it in his hand and just then Oliver walked in, so he got nervous and stuck it in his pocket!

WILLY: My God, Biff!

BIFF: I never intended to do it, Dad!

OPERATOR'S VOICE: Standish Arms, good evening!

WILLY: [*Shouting.*] I'm not in my room!

BIFF: [*Frightened.*] Dad, what's the matter? [*He and* HAPPY *stand up.*]

OPERATOR: Ringing Mr. Loman for you!

5. Grand Central Terminal, New York City's principal railway and subway station.

BIFF: [*Horrified, gets down on one knee before* WILLY.] Dad, I'll make good, I'll make good. [WILLY *tries to get to his feet.* BIFF *holds him down.*] Sit down now.

WILLY: No, you're no good, you're no good for anything.

BIFF: I am, Dad, I'll find something else, you understand? Now don't worry about anything. [*He holds up* WILLY's *face.*] Talk to me, Dad.

OPERATOR: Mr. Loman does not answer. Shall I page him?

WILLY: [*Attempting to stand, as though to rush and silence the* OPERATOR.] No, no, no!

HAPPY: He'll strike something, Pop.

WILLY: No, no . . .

BIFF: [*Desperately, standing over* WILLY.] Pop, listen! Listen to me! I'm telling you something good. Oliver talked to his partner about the Florida idea. You listening? He—he talked to his partner, and he came to me . . . I'm going to be all right, you hear? Dad, listen to me, he said it was just a question of the amount!

WILLY: Then you . . . got it?

HAPPY: He's gonna be terrific, Pop!

WILLY: [*Trying to stand.*] Then you got it, haven't you? You got it! You got it!

BIFF: [*Agonized, holds* WILLY *down.*] No, no. Look, Pop. I'm supposed to have lunch with them tomorrow. I'm just telling you this so you'll know that I can still make an impression, Pop. And I'll make good somewhere, but I can't go tomorrow, see?

WILLY: Why not? You simply—

BIFF: But the pen, Pop!

WILLY: You give it to him and tell him it was an oversight!

HAPPY: Sure, have lunch tomorrow!

BIFF: I can't say that—

WILLY: You were doing a crossword puzzle and accidentally used his pen!

BIFF: Listen, kid, I took those balls years ago, now I walk in with his fountain pen? That clinches it, don't you see? I can't face him like that! I'll try elsewhere.

PAGE'S VOICE: Paging Mr. Loman!

WILLY: Don't you want to be anything?

BIFF: Pop, how can I go back?

WILLY: You don't want to be anything, is that what's behind it?

BIFF: [*Now angry at* WILLY *for not crediting his sympathy.*] Don't take it that way! You think it was easy walking into that office after what I'd done to him? A team of horses couldn't have dragged me back to Bill Oliver!

WILLY: Then why'd you go?

BIFF: Why did I go? Why did I go! Look at you! Look at what's become of you!

[*Off left,* THE WOMAN *laughs.*]

WILLY: Biff, you're going to go to that lunch tomorrow, or—
BIFF: I can't go. I've got an appointment!
HAPPY: Biff, for . . . !
WILLY: Are you spiting me?
BIFF: Don't take it that way! Goddammit!
WILLY: [*Strikes* BIFF *and falters away from the table.*] You rotten little louse!
   Are you spiting me?
THE WOMAN: Someone's at the door, Willy!
BIFF: I'm no good, can't you see what I am?
HAPPY: [*Separating them.*] Hey, you're in a restaurant! Now cut it out, both
   of you! [*The* GIRLS *enter.*] Hello, girls, sit down.

   [THE WOMAN *laughs, off left.*]

MISS FORSYTHE: I guess we might as well. This is Letta.
THE WOMAN: Willy, are you going to wake up?
BIFF: [*Ignoring* WILLY.] How're ya, miss, sit down. What do you drink?
MISS FORSYTHE: Letta might not be able to stay long.
LETTA: I gotta get up early tomorrow. I got jury duty. I'm so excited! Were
   you fellows ever on a jury?
BIFF: No, but I been in front of them! [*The* GIRLS *laugh.*] This is my father.
LETTA: Isn't he cute? Sit down with us, Pop.
HAPPY: Sit him down, Biff!
BIFF: [*Going to him.*] Come on, slugger, drink us under the table. To hell
   with it! Come on, sit down, pal.

   [*On* BIFF's *last insistence,* WILLY *is about to sit.*]

THE WOMAN: [*Now urgently.*] Willy, are you going to answer the door!

   [THE WOMAN's *call pulls* WILLY *back. He starts right, befuddled.*]

BIFF: Hey, where are you going?
WILLY: Open the door.
BIFF: The door?
WILLY: The washroom . . . the door . . . where's the door?
BIFF: [*Leading* WILLY *to the left.*] Just go straight down.

   [WILLY *moves left.*]

THE WOMAN: Willy, Willy, are you going to get up, get up, get up, get up?

   [WILLY *exits left.*]

LETTA: I think it's sweet you bring your daddy along.

MISS FORSYTHE: Oh, he isn't really your father!

BIFF: [*At left, turning to her resentfully.*] Miss Forsythe, you've just seen a prince walk by. A fine, troubled prince. A hardworking, unappreciated prince. A pal, you understand? A good companion. Always for his boys.

LETTA: That's so sweet.

HAPPY: Well, girls, what's the program? We're wasting time. Come on, Biff. Gather round. Where would you like to go?

BIFF: Why don't you do something for him?

HAPPY: Me!

BIFF: Don't you give a damn for him, Hap?

HAPPY: What're you talking about? I'm the one who—

BIFF: I sense it, you don't give a good goddam about him. [*He takes the rolled-up hose from his pocket and puts it on the table in front of* HAPPY.] Look what I found in the cellar, for Christ's sake. How can you bear to let it go on?

HAPPY: Me? Who goes away? Who runs off and—

BIFF: Yeah, but he doesn't mean anything to you. You could help him—I can't! Don't you understand what I'm talking about? He's going to kill himself, don't you know that?

HAPPY: Don't I know it! Me!

BIFF: Hap, help him! Jesus . . . help him . . . Help me, help me, I can't bear to look at his face! [*Ready to weep, he hurries out, up right.*]

HAPPY: [*Starting after him.*] Where are you going?

MISS FORSYTHE: What's he so mad about?

HAPPY: Come on, girls, we'll catch up with him.

MISS FORSYTHE: [*As* HAPPY *pushes her out.*] Say, I don't like that temper of his!

HAPPY: He's just a little overstrung, he'll be all right!

WILLY: [*Off left, as* THE WOMAN *laughs.*] Don't answer! Don't answer!

LETTA: Don't you want to tell your father—

HAPPY: No, that's not my father. He's just a guy. Come on, we'll catch Biff, and, honey, we're going to paint this town! Stanley, where's the check! Hey, Stanley!

[*They exit.* STANLEY *looks toward left.*]

STANLEY: [*Calling to* HAPPY *indignantly.*] Mr. Loman! Mr. Loman!

[STANLEY *picks up a chair and follows them off. Knocking is heard off left.* THE WOMAN *enters, laughing.* WILLY *follows her. She is in a black slip; he is buttoning his shirt. Raw, sensuous music accompanies their speech.*]

WILLY: Will you stop laughing? Will you stop?

THE WOMAN: Aren't you going to answer the door? He'll wake the whole hotel.

WILLY: I'm not expecting anybody.

THE WOMAN: Whyn't you have another drink, honey, and stop being so damn self-centered?

WILLY: I'm so lonely.

THE WOMAN: You know you ruined me, Willy? From now on, whenever you come to the office, I'll see that you go right through to the buyers. No waiting at my desk anymore, Willy. You ruined me.

WILLY: That's nice of you to say that.

THE WOMAN: Gee, you are self-centered! Why so sad? You are the saddest, self-centeredest soul I ever did see-saw. [*She laughs. He kisses her.*] Come on inside, drummer boy. It's silly to be dressing in the middle of the night. [*As knocking is heard.*] Aren't you going to answer the door?

WILLY: They're knocking on the wrong door.

THE WOMAN: But I felt the knocking. And he heard us talking in here. Maybe the hotel's on fire!

WILLY: [*His terror rising.*] It's a mistake.

THE WOMAN: Then tell them to go away!

WILLY: There's nobody there.

THE WOMAN: It's getting on my nerves, Willy. There's somebody standing out there and it's getting on my nerves!

WILLY: [*Pushing her away from him.*] All right, stay in the bathroom here, and don't come out. I think there's a law in Massachusetts about it, so don't come out. It may be that new room clerk. He looked very mean. So don't come out. It's a mistake, there's no fire.

[*The knocking is heard again. He takes a few steps away from her, and she vanishes into the wing. The light follows him, and now he is facing* YOUNG BIFF, *who carries a suitcase.* BIFF *steps toward him. The music is gone.*]

BIFF: Why didn't you answer?

WILLY: Biff! What are you doing in Boston?

BIFF: Why didn't you answer? I've been knocking for five minutes, I called you on the phone—

WILLY: I just heard you. I was in the bathroom and had the door shut. Did anything happen home?

BIFF: Dad—I let you down.

WILLY: What do you mean?

BIFF: Dad . . .

WILLY: Biffo, what's this about? [*Putting his arm around* BIFF.] Come on, let's go downstairs and get you a malted.

BIFF: Dad, I flunked math.

WILLY: Not for the term?

BIFF: The term. I haven't got enough credits to graduate.

WILLY: You mean to say Bernard wouldn't give you the answers?

BIFF: He did, he tried, but I only got a sixty-one.

WILLY: And they wouldn't give you four points?

BIFF: Birnbaum refused absolutely. I begged him, Pop, but he won't give me those points. You gotta talk to him before they close the school. Because if he saw the kind of man you are, and you just talked to him in your way, I'm sure he'd come through for me. The class came right before practice, see, and I didn't go enough. Would you talk to him? He'd like you, Pop. You know the way you could talk.

WILLY: You're on. We'll drive right back.

BIFF: Oh, Dad, good work! I'm sure he'll change for you!

WILLY: Go downstairs and tell the clerk I'm checkin' out. Go right down.

BIFF: Yes, sir! See, the reason he hates me, Pop—one day he was late for class so I got up at the blackboard and imitated him. I crossed my eyes and talked with a lithp.

WILLY: [Laughing.] You did? The kids like it?

BIFF: They nearly died laughing!

WILLY: Yeah? What'd you do?

BIFF: The thquare root of thixthy twee is . . . [WILLY bursts out laughing; BIFF joins him.] And in the middle of it he walked in!

[WILLY laughs and THE WOMAN joins in offstage.]

WILLY: [Without hesitation.] Hurry downstairs and—

BIFF: Somebody in there?

WILLY: No, that was next door.

[THE WOMAN laughs offstage.]

BIFF: Somebody got in your bathroom!

WILLY: No, it's the next room, there's a party—

THE WOMAN: [Enters laughing. She lisps this.] Can I come in? There's something in the bathtub, Willy, and it's moving!

[WILLY looks at BIFF, who is staring open-mouthed and horrified at THE WOMAN.]

WILLY: Ah—you better go back to your room. They must be finished painting by now. They're painting her room so I let her take a shower here. Go back, go back . . . [He pushes her.]

THE WOMAN: [Resisting.] But I've got to get dressed, Willy, I can't—

WILLY: Get out of here! Go back, go back . . . [*Suddenly striving for the ordinary.*] This is Miss Francis, Biff, she's a buyer. They're painting her room. Go back, Miss Francis, go back . . .

THE WOMAN: But my clothes, I can't go out naked in the hall!

WILLY: [*Pushing her offstage.*] Get outa here! Go back, go back!

[BIFF *slowly sits down on his suitcase as the argument continues offstage.*]

THE WOMAN: Where's my stockings? You promised me stockings, Willy!

WILLY: I have no stockings here!

THE WOMAN: You had two boxes of size nine sheers for me, and I want them!

WILLY: Here, for God's sake, will you get outa here!

THE WOMAN: [*Enters holding a box of stockings.*] I just hope there's nobody in the hall. That's all I hope. [*To* BIFF.] Are you football or baseball?

BIFF: Football.

THE WOMAN: [*Angry, humiliated.*] That's me too. G'night. [*She snatches her clothes from* WILLY, *and walks out.*]

WILLY: [*After a pause.*] Well, better get going. I want to get to the school first thing in the morning. Get my suits out of the closet. I'll get my valise. [BIFF *doesn't move.*] What's the matter? [BIFF *remains motionless, tears falling.*] She's a buyer. Buys for J. H. Simmons. She lives down the hall—they're painting. You don't imagine—[*He breaks off. After a pause.*] Now listen, pal, she's just a buyer. She sees merchandise in her room and they have to keep it looking just so . . . [*Pause. Assuming command.*] All right, get my suits. [BIFF *doesn't move.*] Now stop crying and do as I say. I gave you an order. Biff, I gave you an order! Is that what you do when I give you an order? How dare you cry! [*Putting his arm around* BIFF.] Now look, Biff, when you grow up you'll understand about these things. You mustn't—you mustn't overemphasize a thing like this. I'll see Birnbaum first thing in the morning.

BIFF: Never mind.

WILLY: [*Getting down beside* BIFF.] Never mind! He's going to give you those points. I'll see to it.

BIFF: He wouldn't listen to you.

WILLY: He certainly will listen to me. You need those points for the U. of Virginia.

BIFF: I'm not going there.

WILLY: Heh? If I can't get him to change that mark you'll make it up in summer school. You've got all summer to—

BIFF: [*His weeping breaking from him.*] Dad . . .

WILLY: [*Infected by it.*] Oh, my boy . . .

BIFF: Dad . . .

WILLY: She's nothing to me, Biff. I was lonely, I was terribly lonely.

BIFF: You—you gave her Mama's stockings! [*His tears break through and he rises to go.*]

WILLY: [*Grabbing for* BIFF.] I gave you an order!

BIFF: Don't touch me, you—liar!

WILLY: Apologize for that!

BIFF: You fake! You phony little fake! You fake!

[*Overcome, he turns quickly and weeping fully goes out with his suitcase.* WILLY *is left on the floor on his knees.*]

WILLY: I gave you an order! Biff, come back here or I'll beat you! Come back here! I'll whip you! [STANLEY *comes quickly in from the right and stands in front of* WILLY. WILLY *shouts at* STANLEY.] I gave you an order . . .

STANLEY: Hey, let's pick it up, pick it up, Mr. Loman. [*He helps* WILLY *to his feet.*] Your boys left with the chippies.[6] They said they'll see you home.

[*A* SECOND WAITER *watches some distance away.*]

WILLY: But we were supposed to have dinner together.

[*Music is heard,* WILLY'S *theme.*]

STANLEY: Can you make it?

WILLY: I'll—sure, I can make it. [*Suddenly concerned about his clothes.*] Do I—I look all right?

STANLEY: Sure, you look all right. [*He flicks a speck off* WILLY'S *lapel.*]

WILLY: Here—here's a dollar.

STANLEY: Oh, your son paid me. It's all right.

WILLY: [*Putting it in* STANLEY'S *hand.*] No, take it. You're a good boy.

STANLEY: Oh, no, you don't have to . . .

WILLY: Here—here's some more, I don't need it anymore. [*After a slight pause.*] Tell me—is there a seed store in the neighborhood?

STANLEY: Seeds? You mean like to plant?

[*As* WILLY *turns,* STANLEY *slips the money back into his jacket pocket.*]

WILLY: Yes. Carrots, peas . . .

STANLEY: Well, there's hardware stores on Sixth Avenue, but it may be too late now.

WILLY: [*Anxiously.*] Oh, I'd better hurry. I've got to get some seeds. [*He starts off to the right.*] I've got to get some seeds, right away. Nothing's planted. I don't have a thing in the ground.

6. Prostitutes, tramps.

[WILLY *hurries out as the light goes down.* STANLEY *moves over to the right after him, watches him off. The other* WAITER *has been staring at* WILLY.]

STANLEY: [*To the* WAITER.] Well, whatta you looking at?

[*The* WAITER *picks up the chairs and moves off right.* STANLEY *takes the table and follows him. The light fades on this area. There is a long pause, the sound of the flute coming over. The light gradually rises on the kitchen, which is empty.* HAPPY *appears at the door of the house, followed by* BIFF. HAPPY *is carrying a large bunch of long-stemmed roses. He enters the kitchen, looks around for* LINDA. *Not seeing her, he turns to* BIFF, *who is just outside the house door, and makes a gesture with his hands, indicating "Not here, I guess." He looks into the living-room and freezes. Inside,* LINDA, *unseen, is seated,* WILLY's *coat on her lap. She rises ominously and quietly and moves toward* HAPPY, *who backs up into the kitchen, afraid.*]

HAPPY: Hey, what're you doing up? [LINDA *says nothing but moves toward him implacably.*] Where's Pop? [*He keeps backing to the right, and now* LINDA *is in full view in the doorway to the living-room.*] Is he sleeping?

LINDA: Where were you?

HAPPY: [*Trying to laugh it off.*] We met two girls, Mom, very fine types. Here, we brought you some flowers. [*Offering them to her.*] Put them in your room, Ma. [*She knocks them to the floor at* BIFF's *feet. He has now come inside and closed the door behind him. She stares at* BIFF, *silent.*] Now what'd you do that for? Mom, I want you to have some flowers—

LINDA: [*Cutting* HAPPY *off, violently to* BIFF.] Don't you care whether he lives or dies?

HAPPY: [*Going to the stairs.*] Come upstairs, Biff.

BIFF: [*With a flare of disgust, to* HAPPY.] Go away from me! [*To* LINDA.] What do you mean, lives or dies? Nobody's dying around here, pal.

LINDA: Get out of my sight! Get out of here!

BIFF: I wanna see the boss.

LINDA: You're not going near him!

BIFF: Where is he? [*He moves into the living-room and* LINDA *follows.*]

LINDA: [*Shouting after* BIFF.] You invite him for dinner. He looks forward to it all day—[BIFF *appears in his parents' bedroom, looks around and exits.*]—and then you desert him there. There's no stranger you'd do that to!

HAPPY: Why? He had a swell time with us. Listen, when I—[LINDA *comes back into the kitchen.*]—desert him I hope I don't outlive the day!

LINDA: Get out of here!

HAPPY: Now look, Mom . . .

LINDA: Did you have to go to women tonight? You and your lousy rotten whores!

[BIFF *re-enters the kitchen.*]

HAPPY: Mom, all we did was follow Biff around trying to cheer him up! [*To* BIFF.] Boy, what a night you gave me!

LINDA: Get out of here, both of you, and don't come back! I don't want you tormenting him anymore. Go on now, get your things together! [*To* BIFF.] You can sleep in his apartment. [*She starts to pick up the flowers and stops herself.*] Pick up this stuff, I'm not your maid anymore. Pick it up, you bum, you! [HAPPY *turns his back to her in refusal.* BIFF *slowly moves over and gets down on his knees, picking up the flowers.*] You're a pair of animals! Not one, not another living soul would have had the cruelty to walk out on that man in a restaurant!

BIFF: [*Not looking at her.*] Is that what he said?

LINDA: He didn't have to say anything. He was so humiliated he nearly limped when he came in.

HAPPY: But, Mom, he had a great time with us—

BIFF: [*Cutting him off violently.*] Shut up!

[*Without another word,* HAPPY *goes upstairs.*]

LINDA: You! You didn't even go in to see if he was all right!

BIFF: [*Still on the floor in front of* LINDA, *the flowers in his hand; with self-loathing.*] No. Didn't. Didn't do a damned thing. How do you like that, heh? Left him babbling in a toilet.

LINDA: You louse. You . . .

BIFF: Now you hit it on the nose! [*He gets up, throws the flowers in the wastebasket.*] The scum of the earth, and you're looking at him!

LINDA: Get out of here!

BIFF: I gotta talk to the boss, Mom. Where is he?

LINDA: You're not going near him. Get out of this house!

BIFF: [*With absolute assurance, determination.*] No. We're gonna have an abrupt conversation, him and me.

LINDA: You're not talking to him! [*Hammering is heard from outside the house, off right.* BIFF *turns toward the noise. Suddenly pleading.*] Will you please leave him alone?

BIFF: What's he doing out there?

LINDA: He's planting the garden!

BIFF: [*Quietly.*] Now? Oh, my God!

[BIFF *moves outside,* LINDA *following. The light dies down on them and comes up on the center of the apron as* WILLY *walks into it. He is carry-*

ing a flashlight, a hoe, and a handful of seed packets. He raps the top of the hoe sharply to fix it firmly, and then moves to the left, measuring off the distance with his foot. He holds the flashlight to look at the seed packets, reading off the instructions. He is in the blue of night.]

WILLY: Carrots . . . quarter-inch apart. Rows . . . one-foot rows. [*He measures it off.*] One foot. [*He puts down a package and measures off.*] Beets. [*He puts down another package and measures again.*] Lettuce. [*He reads the package, puts it down.*] One foot—[*He breaks off as* BEN *appears at the right and moves slowly down to him.*] What a proposition, ts, ts. Terrific, terrific. 'Cause she's suffered, Ben, the woman has suffered. You understand me? A man can't go out the way he came in, Ben, a man has got to add up to something. You can't, you can't—[BEN *moves toward him as though to interrupt.*] You gotta consider, now. Don't answer so quick. Remember, it's a guaranteed twenty-thousand-dollar proposition. Now look, Ben, I want you to go through the ins and outs of this thing with me. I've got nobody to talk to, Ben, and the woman has suffered, you hear me?

BEN: [*Standing still, considering.*] What's the proposition?

WILLY: It's twenty thousand dollars on the barrelhead. Guaranteed, gilt-edged, you understand?

BEN: You don't want to make a fool of yourself. They might not honor the policy.

WILLY: How can they dare refuse? Didn't I work like a coolie to meet every premium on the nose? And now they don't pay off! Impossible!

BEN: It's called a cowardly thing, William.

WILLY: Why? Does it take more guts to stand here the rest of my life ringing up a zero?

BEN: [*Yielding.*] That's a point, William. [*He moves, thinking, turns.*] And twenty thousand—that *is* something one can feel with the hand, it is there.

WILLY: [*Now assured, with rising power.*] Oh, Ben, that's the whole beauty of it! I see it like a diamond, shining in the dark, hard and rough, that I can pick up and touch in my hand. Not like—like an appointment! This would not be another damned-fool appointment, Ben, and it changes all the aspects. Because he thinks I'm nothing, see, and so he spites me. But the funeral—[*Straightening up.*] Ben, that funeral will be massive! They'll come from Maine, Massachusetts, Vermont, New Hampshire! All the old-timers with the strange license plates—that boy will be thunderstruck, Ben, because he never realized—I am known! Rhode Island, New York, New Jersey—I am known, Ben, and he'll see it with his eyes once and for all. He'll see what I am, Ben! He's in for a shock, that boy!

BEN: [*Coming down to the edge of the garden.*] He'll call you a coward.

WILLY: [*Suddenly fearful.*] No, that would be terrible.

BEN: Yes. And a damned fool.

WILLY: No, no, he mustn't, I won't have that! [*He is broken and desperate.*]

BEN: He'll hate you, William.

[*The gay music of the Boys is heard.*]

WILLY: Oh, Ben, how do we get back to all the great times? Used to be so full of light, and comradeship, the sleigh-riding in winter, and the ruddiness on his cheeks. And always some kind of good news coming up, always something nice coming up ahead. And never even let me carry the valises in the house, and simonizing, simonizing that little red car! Why, why can't I give him something and not have him hate me?

BEN: Let me think about it. [*He glances at his watch.*] I still have a little time. Remarkable proposition, but you've got to be sure you're not making a fool of yourself.

[BEN *drifts off upstage and goes out of sight.* BIFF *comes down from the left.*]

WILLY: [*Suddenly conscious of* BIFF, *turns and looks up at him, then begins picking up the packages of seeds in confusion.*] Where the hell is that seed? [*Indignantly.*] You can't see nothing out here! They boxed in the whole goddam neighborhood!

BIFF: There are people all around here. Don't you realize that?

WILLY: I'm busy. Don't bother me.

BIFF: [*Taking the hoe from* WILLY.] I'm saying good-bye to you, Pop. [WILLY *looks at him, silent, unable to move.*] I'm not coming back anymore.

WILLY: You're not going to see Oliver tomorrow?

BIFF: I've got no appointment, Dad.

WILLY: He put his arm around you, and you've got no appointment?

BIFF: Pop, get this now, will you? Everytime I've left it's been a fight that sent me out of here. Today I realized something about myself and I tried to explain it to you and I—I think I'm just not smart enough to make any sense out of it for you. To hell with whose fault it is or anything like that. [*He takes* WILLY'S *arm.*] Let's just wrap it up, heh? Come on in, we'll tell Mom. [*He gently tries to pull* WILLY *to left.*]

WILLY: [*Frozen, immobile, with guilt in his voice.*] No, I don't want to see her.

BIFF: Come on! [*He pulls again, and* WILLY *tries to pull away.*]

WILLY: [*Highly nervous.*] No, no, I don't want to see her.

BIFF: [*Tries to look into* WILLY'S *face, as if to find the answer there.*] Why don't you want to see her?

WILLY: [*More harshly now.*] Don't bother me, will you?

BIFF: What do you mean, you don't want to see her? You don't want them calling you yellow, do you? This isn't your fault; it's me, I'm a bum. Now come inside! [WILLY *strains to get away.*] Did you hear what I said to you?

[WILLY *pulls away and quickly goes by himself into the house.* BIFF *follows.*]

LINDA: [*To* WILLY.] Did you plant, dear?

BIFF: [*At the door, to* LINDA.] All right, we had it out. I'm going and I'm not writing anymore.

LINDA: [*Going to* WILLY *in the kitchen.*] I think that's the best way, dear. 'Cause there's no use drawing it out, you'll just never get along.

[WILLY *doesn't respond.*]

BIFF: People ask where I am and what I'm doing, you don't know, and you don't care. That way it'll be off your mind and you can start brightening up again. All right? That clears it, doesn't it? [WILLY *is silent, and* BIFF *goes to him.*] You gonna wish me luck, scout? [*He extends his hand.*] What do you say?

LINDA: Shake his hand, Willy.

WILLY: [*Turning to her, seething with hurt.*] There's no necessity to mention the pen at all, y'know.

BIFF: [*Gently.*] I've got no appointment, Dad.

WILLY: [*Erupting fiercely.*] He put his arm around . . . ?

BIFF: Dad, you're never going to see what I am, so what's the use of arguing? If I strike oil I'll send you a check. Meantime forget I'm alive.

WILLY: [*To* LINDA.] Spite, see?

BIFF: Shake hands, Dad.

WILLY: Not my hand.

BIFF: I was hoping not to go this way.

WILLY: Well, this is the way you're going. Good-bye. [BIFF *looks at him a moment, then turns sharply and goes to the stairs.* WILLY *stops him with.*] May you rot in hell if you leave this house!

BIFF: [*Turning.*] Exactly what is it that you want from me?

WILLY: I want you to know, on the train, in the mountains, in the valleys, wherever you go, that you cut down your life for spite!

BIFF: No, no.

WILLY: Spite, spite, is the word of your undoing! And when you're down and out, remember what did it. When you're rotting somewhere beside the railroad tracks, remember, and don't you dare blame it on me!

BIFF: I'm not blaming it on you!

WILLY: I won't take the rap for this, you hear?

[HAPPY *comes down the stairs and stands on the bottom step, watching.*]

BIFF: That's just what I'm telling you!

WILLY: [*Sinking into a chair at the table, with full accusation.*] You're trying to put a knife in me—don't think I don't know what you're doing!

BIFF: All right, phony! Then let's lay it on the line. [*He whips the rubber tube out of his pocket and puts it on the table.*]

HAPPY: You crazy—

LINDA: Biff!

[*She moves to grab the hose, but* BIFF *holds it down with his hand.*]

BIFF: Leave it there! Don't move it!

WILLY: [*Not looking at it.*] What is that?

BIFF: You know goddam well what that is.

WILLY: [*Caged, wanting to escape.*] I never saw that.

BIFF: You saw it. The mice didn't bring it into the cellar! What is this supposed to do, make a hero out of you? This supposed to make me sorry for you?

WILLY: Never heard of it.

BIFF: There'll be no pity for you, you hear it? No pity!

WILLY: [*To* LINDA.] You hear the spite!

BIFF: No, you're going to hear the truth—what you are and what I am!

LINDA: Stop it!

WILLY: Spite!

HAPPY: [*Coming down toward* BIFF.] You cut it now!

BIFF: [*To* HAPPY.] The man don't know who we are! The man is gonna know! [*To* WILLY.] We never told the truth for ten minutes in this house!

HAPPY: We always told the truth!

BIFF: [*Turning on him.*] You big blow, are you the assistant buyer? You're one of the two assistants to the assistant, aren't you?

HAPPY: Well, I'm practically—

BIFF: You're practically full of it! We all are! And I'm through with it. [*To* WILLY.] Now hear this, Willy, this is me.

WILLY: I know you!

BIFF: You know why I had no address for three months? I stole a suit in Kansas City and I was in jail. [*To* LINDA, *who is sobbing.*] Stop crying. I'm through with it.

[LINDA *turns away from them, her hands covering her face.*]

WILLY: I suppose that's my fault!

BIFF: I stole myself out of every good job since high school!

WILLY: And whose fault is that?

BIFF: And I never got anywhere because you blew me so full of hot air I could never stand taking orders from anybody! That's whose fault it is!

WILLY: I hear that!

LINDA: Don't, Biff!

BIFF: It's goddam time you heard that! I had to be boss big shot in two weeks, and I'm through with it!

WILLY: Then hang yourself! For spite, hang yourself!

BIFF: No! Nobody's hanging himself, Willy! I ran down eleven flights with a pen in my hand today. And suddenly I stopped, you hear me? And in the middle of that office building, do you hear this? I stopped in the middle of that building and I saw—the sky. I saw the things that I love in this world. The work and the food and time to sit and smoke. And I looked at the pen and said to myself, what the hell am I grabbing this for? Why am I trying to become what I don't want to be? What am I doing in an office, making a contemptuous, begging fool of myself, when all I want is out there, waiting for me the minute I say I know who I am! Why can't I say that, Willy? [*He tries to make* WILLY *face him, but* WILLY *pulls away and moves to the left.*]

WILLY: [*With hatred, threateningly.*] The door of your life is wide open!

BIFF: Pop! I'm a dime a dozen, and so are you!

WILLY: [*Turning on him now in an uncontrolled outburst.*] I am not a dime a dozen! I am Willy Loman, and you are Biff Loman!

[BIFF *starts for* WILLY, *but is blocked by* HAPPY. *In his fury,* BIFF *seems on the verge of attacking his father.*]

BIFF: I am not a leader of men, Willy, and neither are you. You were never anything but a hard-working drummer who landed in the ash can like all the rest of them! I'm one dollar an hour, Willy! I tried seven states and couldn't raise it. A buck an hour! Do you gather my meaning? I'm not bringing home any prizes anymore, and you're going to stop waiting for me to bring them home!

WILLY: [*Directly to* BIFF.] You vengeful, spiteful mut!

[BIFF *breaks from* HAPPY. WILLY, *in fright, starts up the stairs.* BIFF *grabs him.*]

BIFF: [*At the peak of his fury.*] Pop, I'm nothing! I'm nothing, Pop. Can't you understand that? There's no spite in it anymore. I'm just what I am, that's all.

[BIFF's *fury has spent itself, and he breaks down, sobbing, holding on to* WILLY, *who dumbly fumbles for* BIFF's *face.*]

WILLY: [*Astonished.*] What're you doing? What're you doing? [*To* LINDA.] Why is he crying?

BIFF: [*Crying, broken.*] Will you let me go, for Christ's sake? Will you take that phony dream and burn it before something happens? [*Struggling to contain himself, he pulls away and moves to the stairs.*] I'll go in the morning. Put him—put him to bed. [*Exhausted,* BIFF *moves up the stairs to his room.*]

WILLY: [*After a long pause, astonished, elevated.*] Isn't that—isn't that remarkable? Biff—he likes me!

LINDA: He loves you, Willy!

HAPPY: [*Deeply moved.*] Always did, Pop.

WILLY: Oh, Biff! [*Staring wildly.*] He cried! Cried to me. [*He is choking with his love, and now cries out his promise.*] That boy—that boy is going to be magnificent!

[BEN *appears in the light just outside the kitchen.*]

BEN: Yes, outstanding, with twenty thousand behind him.

LINDA: [*Sensing the racing of his mind, fearfully, carefully.*] Now come to bed, Willy. It's all settled now.

WILLY: [*Finding it difficult not to rush out of the house.*] Yes, we'll sleep. Come on. Go to sleep, Hap.

BEN: And it does take a great kind of man to crack the jungle.

[*In accents of dread,* BEN's *idyllic music starts up.*]

HAPPY: [*His arm around* LINDA.] I'm getting married, Pop, don't forget it. I'm changing everything. I'm gonna run that department before the year is up. You'll see, Mom. [*He kisses her.*]

BEN: The jungle is dark but full of diamonds, Willy.

[WILLY *turns, moves, listening to* BEN.]

LINDA: Be good. You're both good boys, just act that way, that's all.

HAPPY: 'Night, Pop. [*He goes upstairs.*]

LINDA: [*To* WILLY.] Come, dear.

BEN: [*With greater force.*] One must go in to fetch a diamond out.

WILLY: [*To* LINDA, *as he moves slowly along the edge of the kitchen, toward the door.*] I just want to get settled down, Linda. Let me sit alone for a little.

LINDA: [*Almost uttering her fear.*] I want you upstairs.

WILLY: [*Taking her in his arms.*] In a few minutes, Linda. I couldn't sleep right now. Go on, you look awful tired. [*He kisses her.*]

BEN: Not like an appointment at all. A diamond is rough and hard to the touch.

WILLY: Go on now. I'll be right up.

LINDA: I think this is the only way, Willy.

WILLY: Sure, it's the best thing.

BEN: Best thing!

WILLY: The only way. Everything is gonna be—go on, kid, get to bed. You look so tired.

LINDA: Come right up.

WILLY: Two minutes. [LINDA *goes into the living-room, then reappears in her bedroom.* WILLY *moves just outside the kitchen door.*] Loves me. [*Wonderingly.*] Always loved me. Isn't that a remarkable thing? Ben, he'll worship me for it!

BEN: [*With promise.*] It's dark there, but full of diamonds.

WILLY: Can you imagine that magnificence with twenty thousand dollars in his pocket?

LINDA: [*Calling from her room.*] Willy! Come up!

WILLY: [*Calling into the kitchen.*] Yes! Yes. Coming! It's very smart, you realize that, don't you, sweetheart? Even Ben sees it. I gotta go, baby. 'Bye! 'Bye! [*Going over to* BEN, *almost dancing.*] Imagine? When the mail comes he'll be ahead of Bernard again!

BEN: A perfect proposition all around.

WILLY: Did you see how he cried to me? Oh, if I could kiss him, Ben!

BEN: Time, William, time!

WILLY: Oh, Ben, I always knew one way or another we were gonna make it, Biff and I!

BEN: [*Looking at his watch.*] The boat. We'll be late. [*He moves slowly off into the darkness.*]

WILLY: [*Elegiacally, turning to the house.*] Now when you kick off, boy, I want a seventy-yard boot, and get right down the field under the ball, and when you hit, hit low and hit hard, because it's important, boy. [*He swings around and faces the audience.*] There's all kinds of important people in the stands, and the first thing you know . . . [*Suddenly realizing he is alone.*] Ben! Ben, where do I . . . ? [*He makes a sudden movement of search.*] Ben, how do I . . . ?

LINDA: [*Calling.*] Willy, you coming up?

WILLY: [*Uttering a gasp of fear, whirling about as if to quiet her.*] Sh! [*He turns around as if to find his way; sounds, faces, voices, seem to be swarming in upon him and he flicks at them, crying.*] Sh! Sh! [*Suddenly music, faint and high, stops him. It rises in intensity, almost to an unbearable scream. He goes up and down on his toes, and rushes off around the house.*] Shhh!

LINDA: Willy? [*There is no answer.* LINDA *waits.* BIFF *gets up off his bed. He is still in his clothes.* HAPPY *sits up.* BIFF *stands listening.*] [*With real fear.*] Willy, answer me! Willy! [*There is the sound of a car starting and moving away at full speed.*] No!

BIFF: [*Rushing down the stairs.*] Pop!

[*As the car speeds off, the music crashes down in a frenzy of sound, which becomes the soft pulsation of a single cello string.* BIFF *slowly returns to his bedroom. He and* HAPPY *gravely don their jackets.* LINDA *slowly walks out of her room. The music has developed into a dead march. The leaves of day are appearing over everything.* CHARLEY *and* BERNARD, *somberly dressed, appear and knock on the kitchen door.* BIFF *and* HAPPY *slowly descend the stairs to the kitchen as* CHARLEY *and* BERNARD *enter. All stop a moment when* LINDA, *in clothes of mourning, bearing a little bunch of roses, comes through the draped doorway into the kitchen. She goes to* CHARLEY *and takes his arm. Now all move toward the audience, through the wall-line of the kitchen. At the limit of the apron,* LINDA *lays down the flowers, kneels, and sits back on her heels. All stare down at the grave.*]

REQUIEM[7]

CHARLEY: It's getting dark, Linda.

[LINDA *doesn't react. She stares at the grave.*]

BIFF: How about it, Mom? Better get some rest, heh? They'll be closing the gate soon.

[LINDA *makes no move. Pause.*]

HAPPY: [*Deeply angered.*] He had no right to do that. There was no necessity for it. We would've helped him.

CHARLEY: [*Grunting.*] Hmmm.

BIFF: Come along, Mom.

LINDA: Why didn't anybody come?

CHARLEY: It was a very nice funeral.

LINDA: But where are all the people he knew? Maybe they blame him.

CHARLEY: Naa. It's a rough world, Linda. They wouldn't blame him.

LINDA: I can't understand it. At this time especially. First time in thirty-five years we were just about free and clear. He only needed a little salary. He was even finished with the dentist.

CHARLEY: No man only needs a little salary.

LINDA: I can't understand it.

BIFF: There were a lot of nice days. When he'd come home from a trip; or on Sundays, making the stoop; finishing the cellar; putting on the new porch; when he built the extra bathroom; and put up the garage. You know something, Charley, there's more of him in that front stoop than in all the sales he ever made.

CHARLEY: Yeah. He was a happy man with a batch of cement.

LINDA: He was so wonderful with his hands.

BIFF: He had the wrong dreams. All, all, wrong.

HAPPY: [*Almost ready to fight* BIFF.] Don't say that!

7. Mass for the repose of departed souls; also a musical setting for such a mass.

BIFF: He never knew who he was.

CHARLEY: [*Stopping* HAPPY's *movement and reply. To* BIFF.] Nobody dast blame this man. You don't understand: Willy was a salesman. And for a salesman, there is no rock bottom to the life. He don't put a bolt to a nut, he don't tell you the law or give you medicine. He's a man way out there in the blue, riding on a smile and a shoeshine. And when they start not smiling back—that's an earthquake. And then you get yourself a couple of spots on your hat, and you're finished. Nobody dast blame this man. A salesman is got to dream, boy. It comes with the territory.

BIFF: Charley, the man didn't know who he was.

HAPPY: [*Infuriated.*] Don't say that!

BIFF: Why don't you come with me, Happy?

HAPPY: I'm not licked that easily. I'm staying right in this city, and I'm gonna beat this racket! [*He looks at* BIFF, *his chin set.*] The Loman Brothers!

BIFF: I know who I am, kid.

HAPPY: All right, boy. I'm gonna show you and everybody else that Willy Loman did not die in vain. He had a good dream. It's the only dream you can have—to come out number-one-man. He fought it out here, and this is where I'm gonna win it for him.

BIFF: [*With a hopeless glance at* HAPPY, *bends toward his mother.*] Let's go, Mom.

LINDA: I'll be with you in a minute. Go on, Charley. [*He hesitates.*] I want to, just for a minute. I never had a chance to say good-bye. [CHARLEY *moves away, followed by* HAPPY. BIFF *remains a slight distance up and left of* LINDA. *She sits there, summoning herself. The flute begins, not far away, playing behind her speech.*] Forgive me, dear. I can't cry. I don't know what it is, but I can't cry. I don't understand it. Why did you ever do that? Help me, Willy, I can't cry. It seems to me that you're just on another trip. I keep expecting you. Willy, dear, I can't cry. Why did you do it? I search and search and I search, and I can't understand it, Willy. I made the last payment on the house today. Today, dear. And there'll be nobody home. [*A sob rises in her throat.*] We're free and clear. [*Sobbing more fully, released.*] We're free. [BIFF *comes slowly toward her.*] We're free . . . We're free . . .

[BIFF *lifts her to her feet and moves out up right with her in his arms.* LINDA *sobs quietly.* BERNARD *and* CHARLEY *come together and follow them, followed by* HAPPY. *Only the music of the flute is left on the darkening stage as over the house the hard towers of the apartment buildings rise into sharp focus.*]

CURTAIN

1949

ARTHUR MILLER (1915–2005)
From "Arthur Miller Interview" (2001)*

MILLER: [. . .] a lot of people give a lot of their lives to a company or even the government, and when they are no longer needed, when they are used up, they're tossed aside. [. . .] Willie Loman's situation is even more common now than it was then [1949]. A lot of people are eliminated earlier from the productive life in this society than they used to be.

. . .

MILLER: That play [*Death of a Salesman*] is several inventions which have been pilfered over the years by other writers. It is new in the sense that, first of all, there is very little or no waste. The play begins with its action, and there are no transitions. It is a kind of frontal attack on the conditions of this man's life, without any piddling around with techniques. The basic technique is very straightforward. It is told like a dream. In a dream, we are simply confronted with various loaded symbols, and where one is exhausted, it gives way to another. In *Salesman*, there is the use of a past in the present. It has been mistakenly called flashbacks, but there are no flashbacks in that play. It is a concurrence of a past with the present, and that's a bit different.

. . .

[INTERVIEWER]: [. . .] I heard that after you saw *Streetcar* [*Named Desire*], you rewrote the play you were working on at the time, *Inside of His Head*, and that turned into *Death of a Salesman*. What did you see in *Streetcar* that changed your vision of your own play?

MILLER: [. . .] What it did was to validate the use of language the way *Salesman* used language. [. . .] Willie Loman isn't talking street talk; Willie Loman's talk is very formed and formal, very often. [. . .] That was the decision I made: to lift him into the area where one could deal with his ideas and his feelings and make them applicable to the whole human race. I'm using slang in the play and different kinds of speech, but it is basically a formed, very aware use of the English language. Of course, Tennessee [Williams] was similarly a fundamentally formal writer, and he was not trying to write the way people speak on the street.

*"Arthur Miller Interview." Interview by William R. Ferris. *National Endowment for the Humanities*, www.neh.gov/about/awards/jefferson-lecture/arthur-miller-interview. Originally published in *Humanities Magazine*, Mar.–Apr. 2001.

WILLIAM SHAKESPEARE
(1554–1616)
Hamlet

Considering the great and well-deserved fame of his work, surprisingly little is known of William Shakespeare's life. Between 1585 and 1592, he left his birthplace of Stratford-upon-Avon for London to begin a career as playwright and actor. No dates of his professional career are recorded, however, nor can the order in which he composed his plays and poetry be determined with certainty. By 1594, he had established himself as a poet with two long works—*Venus and Adonis* and *The Rape of Lucrece*; his more than 150 sonnets are supreme expressions of the form. His matchless reputation, though, rests on his works for the theater. Shakespeare produced perhaps thirty-five plays in twenty-five years, proving himself a master of every dramatic genre: tragedy (in works such as *Macbeth, Hamlet, King Lear,* and *Othello*); historical drama (for example, *Richard III* and *Henry IV*); comedy (*A Midsummer Night's Dream, Twelfth Night, As You Like It,* and many more); and romance or "tragicomedy" (in plays such as *The Tempest* and *Cymbeline*). Without question, Shakespeare is the most quoted, discussed, and beloved writer in English literature.

CHARACTERS

CLAUDIUS, *King of Denmark*
HAMLET, *son of the former king and*
    nephew to the present king
POLONIUS, *Lord Chamberlain*
HORATIO, *friend of Hamlet*
LAERTES, *son of Polonius*
VOLTEMAND ⎫
CORNELIUS ⎪
ROSENCRANTZ ⎬ *courtiers*
GUILDENSTERN ⎪
OSRIC ⎪
A GENTLEMAN ⎭
A PRIEST

MARCELLUS ⎱ *officers*
BERNARDO ⎰
FRANCISCO, *a soldier*
REYNALDO, *servant to Polonius*
PLAYERS
TWO CLOWNS, *gravediggers*
FORTINBRAS, *Prince of Norway*
A NORWEGIAN CAPTAIN
ENGLISH AMBASSADORS
GERTRUDE, *Queen of Denmark, and*
    mother of Hamlet
OPHELIA, *daughter of Polonius*
GHOST OF HAMLET'S FATHER

LORDS, LADIES, OFFICERS, SOLDIERS, SAILORS, MESSENGERS, AND ATTENDANTS

SCENE: *The action takes place in or near the royal castle of Denmark at Elsinore.*

ACT I

Scene 1

A guard station atop the castle. Enter BERNARDO *and* FRANCISCO, *two sentinels.*

BERNARDO: Who's there?
FRANCISCO: Nay, answer me. Stand and unfold yourself.
BERNARDO: Long live the king!
FRANCISCO: Bernardo?
5 BERNARDO: He.
FRANCISCO: You come most carefully upon your hour.
BERNARDO: 'Tis now struck twelve. Get thee to bed, Francisco.
FRANCISCO: For this relief much thanks. 'Tis bitter cold,
    And I am sick at heart.
BERNARDO: Have you had quiet guard?
10 FRANCISCO: Not a mouse stirring.
BERNARDO: Well, good night.
    If you do meet Horatio and Marcellus,
    The rivals[1] of my watch, bid them make haste.

[*Enter* HORATIO *and* MARCELLUS.]

FRANCISCO: I think I hear them. Stand, ho! Who is there?
HORATIO: Friends to this ground.
15 MARCELLUS: And liegemen to the Dane.[2]
FRANCISCO: Give you good night.
MARCELLUS: O, farewell, honest soldier!
    Who hath relieved you?
FRANCISCO: Bernardo hath my place.
    Give you good night.   [*Exit* FRANCISCO.]
MARCELLUS: Holla, Bernardo!
BERNARDO: Say—
    What, is Horatio there?
HORATIO: A piece of him.
20 BERNARDO: Welcome, Horatio. Welcome, good Marcellus.
HORATIO: What, has this thing appeared again tonight?
BERNARDO: I have seen nothing.
MARCELLUS: Horatio says 'tis but our fantasy,

1. Companions.
2. The "Dane" is the king of Denmark, who is also called "Denmark," as in line 48 of this scene. In line 61 a similar reference is used for the king of Norway.

And will not let belief take hold of him
Touching this dreaded sight twice seen of us. 25
Therefore I have entreated him along
With us to watch the minutes of this night,
That if again this apparition come,
He may approve[3] our eyes and speak to it.
HORATIO: Tush, tush, 'twill not appear.
BERNARDO: Sit down awhile, 30
And let us once again assail your ears,
That are so fortified against our story,
What we have two nights seen.
HORATIO: Well, sit we down.
And let us hear Bernardo speak of this.
BERNARDO: Last night of all, 35
When yond same star that's westward from the pole[4]
Had made his course t' illume that part of heaven
Where now it burns, Marcellus and myself,
The bell then beating one—

   [*Enter* GHOST.]

MARCELLUS: Peace, break thee off. Look where it comes again. 40
BERNARDO: In the same figure like the king that's dead.
MARCELLUS: Thou art a scholar; speak to it, Horatio.
BERNARDO: Looks 'a[5] not like the king? Mark it, Horatio.
HORATIO: Most like. It harrows me with fear and wonder.
BERNARDO: It would be spoke to.
MARCELLUS: Speak to it, Horatio. 45
HORATIO: What art thou that usurp'st this time of night
Together with that fair and warlike form
In which the majesty of buried Denmark
Did sometimes march? By heaven I charge thee, speak.
MARCELLUS: It is offended.
BERNARDO: See, it stalks away. 50
HORATIO: Stay. Speak, speak. I charge thee, speak. [*Exit* GHOST.]
MARCELLUS: 'Tis gone and will not answer.
BERNARDO: How now, Horatio! You tremble and look pale.
Is not this something more than fantasy?
What think you on't? 55
HORATIO: Before my God, I might not this believe
Without the sensible[6] and true avouch
Of mine own eyes.

3. Confirm the testimony of.   4. Polestar.   5. He.   6. Perceptible.

MARCELLUS: It is not like the king?
HORATIO: As thou art to thyself.
60   Such was the very armor he had on
When he the ambitious Norway combated.
So frowned he once when, in an angry parle,[7]
He smote the sledded Polacks on the ice.
'Tis strange.
65   MARCELLUS: Thus twice before, and jump[8] at this dead hour,
With martial stalk hath he gone by our watch.
HORATIO: In what particular thought to work I know not,
But in the gross and scope of mine opinion,
This bodes some strange eruption to our state.
70   MARCELLUS: Good now, sit down, and tell me he that knows,
Why this same strict and most observant watch
So nightly toils the subject[9] of the land,
And why such daily cast of brazen cannon
And foreign mart for implements of war;
75   Why such impress of shipwrights, whose sore task
Does not divide the Sunday from the week.
What might be toward that this sweaty haste
Doth make the night joint-laborer with the day?
Who is't that can inform me?
HORATIO: That can I.
80   At least, the whisper goes so. Our last king,
Whose image even but now appeared to us,
Was as you know by Fortinbras of Norway,
Thereto pricked on by a most emulate pride,
Dared to the combat; in which our valiant Hamlet
85   (For so this side of our known world esteemed him)
Did slay this Fortinbras; who by a sealed compact
Well ratified by law and heraldry,
Did forfeit, with his life, all those his lands
Which he stood seized of,[1] to the conqueror;
90   Against the which a moiety competent[2]
Was gagèd[3] by our king; which had returned
To the inheritance of Fortinbras,
Had he been vanquisher; as, by the same covenant
And carriage of the article designed,
95   His fell to Hamlet. Now, sir, young Fortinbras,
Of unimprovèd mettle hot and full,

---

7. Parley.   8. Precisely.   9. People.   1. Possessed.   2. Portion of similar value.   3. Pledged.

Hath in the skirts of Norway here and there
Sharked up a list of lawless resolutes
For food and diet to some enterprise
That hath a stomach in't; which is no other,   100
As it doth well appear unto our state,
But to recover of us by strong hand
And terms compulsatory, those foresaid lands
So by his father lost; and this, I take it,
Is the main motive of our preparations,   105
The source of this our watch, and the chief head
Of this post-haste and romage[4] in the land.
BERNARDO: I think it be no other but e'en so.
Well may it sort[5] that this portentous figure
Comes armèd through our watch so like the king   110
That was and is the question of these wars.
HORATIO: A mote[6] it is to trouble the mind's eye.
In the most high and palmy state of Rome,
A little ere the mightiest Julius fell,
The graves stood tenantless, and the sheeted dead   115
Did squeak and gibber in the Roman streets;
As stars with trains of fire, and dews of blood,
Disasters in the sun; and the moist star,
Upon whose influence Neptune's empire stands,[7]
Was sick almost to doomsday with eclipse.   120
And even the like precurse[8] of feared events,
As harbingers preceding still the fates
And prologue to the omen coming on,
Have heaven and earth together demonstrated
Unto our climatures[9] and countrymen.   125

[*Enter* GHOST.]

But soft, behold, lo where it comes again!
I'll cross it[1] though it blast me.—Stay, illusion.

[*It spreads (its) arms.*]

---

4. Stir.   5. Chance.   6. Speck of dust.
7. Neptune was the Roman sea god; the "moist star" is the moon.   8. Precursor.   9. Regions.
1. Horatio means either that he will move across the ghost's path in order to stop the ghost or
that he will make the sign of the cross to gain power over the ghost. The stage direction that
follows is somewhat ambiguous. "It" seems to refer to the ghost, but the movement would be
appropriate to Horatio.

If thou hast any sound or use of voice,
Speak to me.
130   If there be any good thing to be done,
That may to thee do ease, and grace to me,
Speak to me.
If thou art privy to thy country's fate,
Which happily foreknowing may avoid,
135   O, speak!
Or if thou hast uphoarded in thy life
Extorted treasure in the womb of earth,
For which, they say, you spirits oft walk in death,

[*The cock crows.*]

Speak of it. Stay, and speak. Stop it, Marcellus.
140 MARCELLUS: Shall I strike at it with my partisan?[2]
HORATIO: Do, if it will not stand.
BERNARDO: 'Tis here.
HORATIO: 'Tis here.
MARCELLUS: 'Tis gone.   [*Exit* GHOST.]
We do it wrong, being so majestical,
To offer it the show of violence;
145   For it is as the air, invulnerable,
And our vain blows malicious mockery.
BERNARDO: It was about to speak when the cock crew.
HORATIO: And then it started like a guilty thing
Upon a fearful summons. I have heard
150   The cock, that is the trumpet to the morn,
Doth with his lofty and shrill-sounding throat
Awake the god of day, and at his warning,
Whether in sea or fire, in earth or air,
Th' extravagant and erring[3] spirit hies
155   To his confine; and of the truth herein
This present object made probation.[4]
MARCELLUS: It faded on the crowing of the cock.
Some say that ever 'gainst that season comes
Wherein our Savior's birth is celebrated,
160   This bird of dawning singeth all night long,
And then, they say, no spirit dare stir abroad,
The nights are wholesome, then no planets strike,
No fairy takes,[5] nor witch hath power to charm,

2. Halberd.   3. Errant, wandering out of bounds.   4. Proof.   5. Enchants.

So hallowed and so gracious is that time.
HORATIO: So have I heard and do in part believe it.   165
　　But look, the morn in russet mantle clad
　　Walks o'er the dew of yon high eastward hill.
　　Break we our watch up, and by my advice
　　Let us impart what we have seen tonight
　　Unto young Hamlet, for upon my life   170
　　This spirit, dumb to us, will speak to him.
　　Do you consent we shall acquaint him with it,
　　As needful in our loves, fitting our duty?
MARCELLUS: Let's do't, I pray, and I this morning know
　　Where we shall find him most conveniently.   [*Exeunt.*] 175

Scene 2

A chamber of state. Enter KING CLAUDIUS, QUEEN GERTRUDE, HAMLET,
POLONIUS, LAERTES, VOLTEMAND, CORNELIUS *and other members of the
court.*

KING: Though yet of Hamlet our dear brother's death
　　The memory be green, and that it us befitted
　　To bear our hearts in grief, and our whole kingdom
　　To be contracted in one brow of woe,
　　Yet so far hath discretion fought with nature   5
　　That we with wisest sorrow think on him,
　　Together with remembrance of ourselves.
　　Therefore our sometime sister, now our queen,
　　Th' imperial jointress[6] to this warlike state,
　　Have we, as 'twere with a defeated joy,   10
　　With an auspicious and a dropping eye,
　　With mirth in funeral, and with dirge in marriage,
　　In equal scale weighing delight and dole,
　　Taken to wife; nor have we herein barred
　　Your better wisdoms, which have freely gone   15
　　With this affair along. For all, our thanks.
　　Now follows that you know young Fortinbras,
　　Holding a weak supposal of our worth,
　　Or thinking by our late dear brother's death
　　Our state to be disjoint and out of frame,   20
　　Colleaguèd with this dream of his advantage,
　　He hath not failed to pester us with message

6. Widow who holds a *jointure* or life interest in the estate of her deceased husband.

Importing the surrender of those lands
Lost by his father, with all bonds of law,
25 To our most valiant brother. So much for him.
Now for ourself, and for this time of meeting,
Thus much the business is: we have here writ
To Norway, uncle of young Fortinbras—
Who, impotent and bedrid, scarcely hears
30 Of this his nephew's purpose—to suppress
His further gait[7] herein, in that the levies,
The lists, and full proportions are all made
Out of his subject; and we here dispatch
You, good Cornelius, and you, Voltemand,
35 For bearers of this greeting to old Norway,
Giving to you no further personal power
To business with the king, more than the scope
Of these dilated[8] articles allow.
Farewell, and let your haste commend your duty.
40 CORNELIUS: ⎫ In that, and all things will we show our duty.
VOLTEMAND: ⎭
KING: We doubt it nothing, heartily farewell.
　　　　　　　　　[*Exeunt* VOLTEMAND *and* CORNELIUS.]
And now, Laertes, what's the news with you?
You told us of some suit. What is't, Laertes?
You cannot speak of reason to the Dane
45 And lose your voice. What wouldst thou beg, Laertes,
That shall not be my offer, not thy asking?
The head is not more native to the heart,
The hand more instrumental[9] to the mouth,
Than is the throne of Denmark to thy father.
What wouldst thou have, Laertes?
50 LAERTES:　　　　　　　　　　　My dread lord,
Your leave and favor to return to France,
From whence, though willingly, I came to Denmark
To show my duty in your coronation,
Yet now I must confess, that duty done,
55 My thoughts and wishes bend again toward France,
And bow them to your gracious leave and pardon.
KING: Have you your father's leave? What says Polonius?
POLONIUS: He hath, my lord, wrung from me my slow leave
By laborsome petition, and at last

---

7. Progress.　8. Fully expressed.　9. Serviceable.

Upon his will I sealed my hard consent.   60
I do beseech you give him leave to go.
KING: Take thy fair hour, Laertes. Time be thine,
And thy best graces spend it at thy will.
But now, my cousin[1] Hamlet, and my son—
HAMLET: [*Aside*.] A little more than kin, and less than kind.   65
KING: How is it that the clouds still hang on you?
HAMLET: Not so, my lord. I am too much in the sun.
QUEEN: Good Hamlet, cast thy nighted color off,
And let thine eye look like a friend on Denmark.
Do not for ever with thy vailèd lids[2]   70
Seek for thy noble father in the dust.
Thou know'st 'tis common—all that lives must die,
Passing through nature to eternity.
HAMLET: Ay, madam, it is common.
QUEEN: If it be,
Why seems it so particular with thee?   75
HAMLET: Seems, madam? Nay, it is. I know not "seems."
'Tis not alone my inky cloak, good mother,
Nor customary suits of solemn black,
Nor windy suspiration of forced breath,
No, nor the fruitful river in the eye,   80
Nor the dejected havior[3] of the visage,
Together with all forms, moods, shapes of grief,
That can denote me truly. These indeed seem,
For they are actions that a man might play,
But I have that within which passes show—   85
These but the trappings and the suits of woe.
KING: 'Tis sweet and commendable in your nature, Hamlet,
To give these mourning duties to your father,
But you must know your father lost a father,
That father lost, lost his, and the survivor bound   90
In filial obligation for some term
To do obsequious[4] sorrow. But to persever
In obstinate condolement is a course
Of impious stubbornness. 'Tis unmanly grief.
It shows a will most incorrect to[5] heaven,   95
A heart unfortified, a mind impatient,
An understanding simple and unschooled.

---

1. "Cousin" is used here as a general term of kinship. 2. Lowered eyes. 3. Appearance.
4. Suited for funeral obsequies. 5. Unsubmissive toward.

For what we know must be, and is as common
As any the most vulgar thing to sense,
Why should we in our peevish opposition
Take it to heart? Fie, 'tis a fault to heaven,
A fault against the dead, a fault to nature,
To reason most absurd, whose common theme
Is death of fathers, and who still hath cried,
From the first corse[6] till he that died today,
"This must be so." We pray you throw to earth
This unprevailing woe, and think of us
As of a father, for let the world take note
You are the most immediate[7] to our throne,
And with no less nobility of love
Than that which dearest father bears his son
Do I impart toward you. For your intent
In going back to school in Wittenberg,
It is most retrograde[8] to our desire,
And we beseech you, bend you to remain
Here in the cheer and comfort of our eye,
Our chiefest courtier, cousin, and our son.
QUEEN: Let not thy mother lose her prayers, Hamlet.
I pray thee stay with us, go not to Wittenberg.
HAMLET: I shall in all my best obey you, madam.
KING: Why, 'tis a loving and a fair reply.
Be as ourself in Denmark. Madam, come.
This gentle and unforced accord of Hamlet
Sits smiling to my heart, in grace whereof,
No jocund health that Denmark drinks today
But the great cannon to the clouds shall tell,
And the king's rouse the heaven shall bruit[9] again,
Respeaking earthly thunder. Come away.

[*Flourish. Exeunt all but* HAMLET.]

HAMLET: O, that this too too solid flesh would melt,
Thaw, and resolve itself into a dew,
Or that the Everlasting had not fixed
His canon[1] 'gainst self-slaughter. O God, God,
How weary, stale, flat, and unprofitable
Seem to me all the uses of this world!
Fie on't, ah, fie, 'tis an unweeded garden
That grows to seed. Things rank and gross in nature

6. Corpse.   7. Next in line.   8. Contrary.   9. Echo. *Rouse:* carousal.   1. Law.

Possess it merely.[2] That it should come to this,
But two months dead, nay, not so much, not two.
So excellent a king, that was to this
Hyperion to a satyr,[3] so loving to my mother,   140
That he might not beteem[4] the winds of heaven
Visit her face too roughly. Heaven and earth,
Must I remember? Why, she would hang on him
As if increase of appetite had grown
By what it fed on, and yet, within a month—   145
Let me not think on't. Frailty, thy name is woman—
A little month, or ere those shoes were old
With which she followed my poor father's body
Like Niobe,[5] all tears, why she, even she—
O God, a beast that wants discourse of reason   150
Would have mourned longer—married with my uncle,
My father's brother, but no more like my father
Than I to Hercules.[6] Within a month,
Ere yet the salt of most unrighteous tears
Had left the flushing in her gallèd eyes,   155
She married. O, most wicked speed, to post
With such dexterity to incestuous sheets!
It is not, nor it cannot come to good.
But break my heart, for I must hold my tongue.

[*Enter* HORATIO, MARCELLUS, *and* BERNARDO.]

HORATIO: Hail to your lordship!
HAMLET: I am glad to see you well.   160
     Horatio—or I do forget myself.
HORATIO: The same, my lord, and your poor servant ever.
HAMLET: Sir, my good friend, I'll change that name with you.
     And what make you from[7] Wittenberg, Horatio?
     Marcellus?   165
MARCELLUS: My good lord!
HAMLET: I am very glad to see you. [*To* BERNARDO.] Good even, sir.—
     But what, in faith, make you from Wittenberg?

---

2. Entirely.   3. Hyperion, a Greek god, stands here for beauty in contrast to the monstrous
satyr, a lecherous creature, half man and half goat.   4. Permit.
5. In Greek mythology, Niobe was turned to stone after a tremendous fit of weeping over the
death of her fourteen children, a misfortune brought about by her boasting over her fertility.
6. The demigod Hercules was noted for his strength and the series of spectacular labors that he
accomplished.   7. What are you doing away from? *Change*: exchange.

HORATIO: A truant disposition, good my lord.

170 HAMLET: I would not hear your enemy say so,
    Nor shall you do my ear that violence
    To make it truster of your own report
    Against yourself. I know you are no truant.
    But what is your affair in Elsinore?
175   We'll teach you to drink deep ere you depart.

HORATIO: My lord, I came to see your father's funeral.

HAMLET: I prithee do not mock me, fellow-student,
    I think it was to see my mother's wedding.

HORATIO: Indeed, my lord, it followed hard upon.

180 HAMLET: Thrift, thrift, Horatio. The funeral-baked meats
    Did coldly furnish forth the marriage tables.
    Would I had met my dearest[8] foe in heaven
    Or ever I had seen that day, Horatio!
    My father—methinks I see my father.

HORATIO: Where, my lord?

185 HAMLET: In my mind's eye, Horatio.

HORATIO: I saw him once, 'a was a goodly king.

HAMLET: 'A was a man, take him for all in all,
    I shall not look upon his like again.

HORATIO: My lord, I think I saw him yesternight.

190 HAMLET: Saw who?

HORATIO: My lord, the king your father.

HAMLET: The king my father?

HORATIO: Season your admiration[9] for a while
    With an attent ear till I may deliver[1]
    Upon the witness of these gentlemen
    This marvel to you.

195 HAMLET: For God's love, let me hear!

HORATIO: Two nights together had these gentlemen,
    Marcellus and Bernardo, on their watch
    In the dead waste and middle of the night
    Been thus encountered. A figure like your father,
200   Armèd at point exactly, cap-a-pe,[2]
    Appears before them, and with solemn march
    Goes slow and stately by them. Thrice he walked
    By their oppressed and fear-surprisèd eyes
    Within his truncheon's[3] length, whilst they, distilled
205   Almost to jelly with the act of fear,

---

8. Bitterest.   9. Moderate your wonder.   1. Relate. *Attent*: attentive.
2. From head to toe. *Exactly*: completely.   3. Baton of office.

Stand dumb and speak not to him. This to me
In dreadful secrecy impart they did,
And I with them the third night kept the watch,
Where, as they had delivered, both in time,
Form of the thing, each word made true and good,   210
The apparition comes. I knew your father.
These hands are not more like.

HAMLET: But where was this?

MARCELLUS: My lord, upon the platform where we watch.

HAMLET: Did you not speak to it?

HORATIO: My lord, I did,
But answer made it none. Yet once methought   215
It lifted up it head and did address
Itself to motion, like as it would speak;
But even then the morning cock crew loud,
And at the sound it shrunk in haste away
And vanished from our sight.

HAMLET: 'Tis very strange.   220

HORATIO: As I do live, my honored lord, 'tis true,
And we did think it writ down in our duty
To let you know of it.

HAMLET: Indeed, sirs, but
This troubles me. Hold you the watch tonight?

ALL: We do, my lord.

HAMLET: Armed, say you?

ALL: Armed, my lord.   225

HAMLET: From top to toe?

ALL: My lord, from head to foot.

HAMLET: Then saw you not his face.

HORATIO: O yes, my lord, he wore his beaver[4] up.

HAMLET: What, looked he frowningly?

HORATIO: A countenance more in sorrow than in anger.   230

HAMLET: Pale or red?

HORATIO: Nay, very pale.

HAMLET: And fixed his eyes upon you?

HORATIO: Most constantly.

HAMLET: I would I had been there.

HORATIO: It would have much amazed you.

HAMLET: Very like.
Stayed it long?   235

HORATIO: While one with moderate haste might tell[5] a hundred.

---

4. Hinged face protector. 5. Count.

BOTH: Longer, longer.

HORATIO: Not when I saw't.

HAMLET: His beard was grizzled, no?

HORATIO: It was as I have seen it in his life,
    A sable silvered.

240 HAMLET: I will watch tonight.
    Perchance 'twill walk again.

HORATIO: I warr'nt it will.

HAMLET: If it assume my noble father's person,
    I'll speak to it though hell itself should gape
    And bid me hold my peace. I pray you all,

245   If you have hitherto concealed this sight,
    Let it be tenable[6] in your silence still,
    And whatsomever else shall hap tonight,
    Give it an understanding but no tongue.
    I will requite your loves. So fare you well.

250   Upon the platform 'twixt eleven and twelve
    I'll visit you.

ALL: Our duty to your honor.

HAMLET: Your loves, as mine to you. Farewell.   [*Exeunt all but* HAMLET.]
    My father's spirit in arms? All is not well.
    I doubt[7] some foul play. Would the night were come!

255   Till then sit still, my soul. Foul deeds will rise,
    Though all the earth o'erwhelm them, to men's eyes.   [*Exit.*]

Scene 3

The dwelling of POLONIUS. *Enter* LAERTES *and* OPHELIA.

LAERTES: My necessaries are embarked. Farewell.
    And, sister, as the winds give benefit
    And convoy is assistant,[8] do not sleep,
    But let me hear from you.

OPHELIA: Do you doubt that?

5 LAERTES: For Hamlet, and the trifling of his favor,
    Hold it a fashion and a toy in blood,
    A violet in the youth of primy[9] nature,
    Forward, not permanent, sweet, not lasting,
    The perfume and suppliance of a minute,
    No more.

OPHELIA: No more but so?

6. Held.   7. Suspect.   8. Means of transport is available.   9. Of the spring.

LAERTES: Think it no more.   10
For nature crescent[1] does not grow alone
In thews and bulk, but as this temple[2] waxes
The inward service of the mind and soul
Grows wide withal. Perhaps he loves you now,
And now no soil nor cautel[3] doth besmirch   15
The virtue of his will, but you must fear,
His greatness weighted,[4] his will is not his own,
For he himself is subject to his birth.
He may not, as unvalued persons do,
Carve for himself, for on his choice depends   20
The safety and health of this whole state,
And therefore must his choice be circumscribed
Unto the voice[5] and yielding of that body
Whereof he is the head. Then if he says he loves you,
It fits your wisdom so far to believe it   25
As he in his particular act and place
May give his saying deed, which is no further
Than the main voice of Denmark goes withal.
Then weigh what loss your honor may sustain
If with too credent[6] ear you list his songs,   30
Or lose your heart, or your chaste treasure open
To his unmastered importunity.
Fear it, Ophelia, fear it, my dear sister,
And keep you in the rear of your affection,
Out of the shot and danger of desire.   35
The chariest[7] maid is prodigal enough
If she unmask her beauty to the moon.
Virtue itself scapes not calumnious strokes.
The canker[8] galls the infants of the spring
Too oft before their buttons[9] be disclosed,   40
And in the morn and liquid dew of youth
Contagious blastments[1] are most imminent.
Be wary then; best safety lies in fear.
Youth to itself rebels, though none else near.
OPHELIA: I shall the effect of this good lesson keep   45
As watchman to my heart. But, good my brother,
Do not as some ungracious pastors do,
Show me the steep and thorny way to heaven,

---

1. Growing.   2. Body. *Thews*: muscles.   3. Deceit.   4. Rank considered.   5. Assent.
6. Credulous. *List*: listen to.   7. Most circumspect.   8. Cankerworm.   9. Buds.   1. Blights.

Whiles like a puffed and reckless libertine
50   Himself the primrose path of dalliance treads
And recks not his own rede.[2]

LAERTES: O, fear me not.

[*Enter* POLONIUS.]

I stay too long. But here my father comes.
A double blessing is a double grace;
Occasion smiles upon a second leave.
55 POLONIUS: Yet here, Laertes? Aboard, aboard, for shame!
The wind sits in the shoulder of your sail,
And you are stayed for. There—my blessing with thee,
And these few precepts in thy memory
Look thou character.[3] Give thy thoughts no tongue,
60   Nor any unproportioned thought his act.
Be thou familiar, but by no means vulgar.
Those friends thou hast, and their adoption tried,
Grapple them unto thy soul with hoops of steel;
But do not dull[4] thy palm with entertainment
65   Of each new-hatched, unfledged comrade. Beware
Of entrance to a quarrel, but being in,
Bear't that th' opposèd[5] may beware of thee.
Give every man thy ear, but few thy voice;[6]
Take each man's censure, but reserve thy judgment.
70   Costly thy habit as thy purse can buy,
But not expressed in fancy; rich not gaudy,
For the apparel oft proclaims the man,
And they in France of the best rank and station
Are of a most select and generous chief[7] in that.
75   Neither a borrower nor a lender be,
For loan oft loses both itself and friend,
And borrowing dulls th' edge of husbandry.
This above all, to thine own self be true,
And it must follow as the night the day
80   Thou canst not then be false to any man.
Farewell. My blessing season this in thee!
LAERTES: Most humbly do I take my leave, my lord.
POLONIUS: The time invests you. Go, your servants tend.[8]
LAERTES: Farewell, Ophelia, and remember well
What I have said to you.

2. Heeds not his own advice.   3. Write.   4. Make callous.
5. Conduct it so that the opponent.   6. Approval.   7. Eminence.   8. Await.

OPHELIA: 'Tis in my memory locked,   85
  And you yourself shall keep the key of it.
LAERTES: Farewell.   [*Exit.*]
POLONIUS: What is't, Ophelia, he hath said to you?
OPHELIA: So please you, something touching the Lord Hamlet.
POLONIUS: Marry, well bethought.   90
  'Tis told me he hath very oft of late
  Given private time to you, and you yourself
  Have of your audience been most free and bounteous.
  If it be so—as so 'tis put on me,
  And that in way of caution—I must tell you,   95
  You do not understand yourself so clearly
  As it behooves my daughter and your honor.
  What is between you? Give me up the truth.
OPHELIA: He hath, my lord, of late made many tenders
  Of his affection to me.   100
POLONIUS: Affection? Pooh! You speak like a green girl,
  Unsifted in such perilous circumstance.
  Do you believe his tenders, as you call them?
OPHELIA: I do not know, my lord, what I should think.
POLONIUS: Marry, I will teach you. Think yourself a baby   105
  That you have ta'en these tenders for true pay
  Which are not sterling. Tender yourself more dearly,
  Or (not to crack the wind of the poor phrase,
  Running it thus) you'll tender me a fool.
OPHELIA: My lord, he hath importuned me with love   110
  In honorable fashion.
POLONIUS: Ay, fashion you may call it. Go to, go to.
OPHELIA: And hath given countenance[9] to his speech, my lord,
  With almost all the holy vows of heaven.
POLONIUS: Ay, springes[1] to catch woodcocks. I do know,   115
  When the blood burns, how prodigal the soul
  Lends the tongue vows. These blazes, daughter,
  Giving more light than heat, extinct in both
  Even in their promise, as it is a-making,
  You must not take for fire. From this time   120
  Be something scanter of your maiden presence.
  Set your entreatments[2] at a higher rate
  Than a command to parle. For Lord Hamlet,
  Believe so much in him that he is young,
  And with a larger tether may he walk   125

---

9. Confirmation.   1. Snares.   2. Negotiations before a surrender.

Than may be given you. In few, Ophelia,
Do not believe his vows, for they are brokers,[3]
Not of that dye which their investments[4] show,
But mere implorators[5] of unholy suits,
130   Breathing like sanctified and pious bawds,
The better to beguile. This is for all:
I would not, in plain terms, from this time forth
Have you so slander any moment leisure
As to give words or talk with the Lord Hamlet.
135   Look to't, I charge you. Come your ways.
OPHELIA: I shall obey, my lord.   [*Exeunt.*]

Scene 4

The guard station. Enter HAMLET, HORATIO *and* MARCELLUS.

HAMLET: The air bites shrewdly;[6] it is very cold.
HORATIO: It is a nipping and an eager[7] air.
HAMLET: What hour now?
HORATIO: I think it lacks of twelve.
MARCELLUS: No, it is struck.
HORATIO: Indeed? I heard it not.
5   It then draws near the season
Wherein the spirit held his wont to walk.

[*A flourish of trumpets, and two pieces go off.*]

What does this mean, my lord?
HAMLET: The king doth wake tonight and takes his rouse,
Keeps wassail, and the swagg'ring up-spring reels,
10   And as he drains his draughts of Rhenish[8] down,
The kettledrum and trumpet thus bray out
The triumph of his pledge.
HORATIO: Is it a custom?
HAMLET: Ay, marry, is't,
But to my mind, though I am native here
15   And to the manner born, it is a custom
More honored in the breach than the observance.
This heavy-headed revel east and west
Makes us traduced and taxed of other nations.
They clepe[9] us drunkards, and with swinish phrase

3. Panderers.   4. Garments.   5. Solicitors.   6. Sharply.   7. Keen.
8. Rhine wine. *Up-spring*: a German dance.   9. Call.

Soil our addition,[1] and indeed it takes   20
From our achievements, though performed at height,
The pith and marrow of our attribute.[2]
So oft it chances in particular men,
That for some vicious mole of nature in them,
As in their birth, wherein they are not guilty   25
(Since nature cannot choose his origin),
By their o'ergrowth of some complexion,
Oft breaking down the pales[3] and forts of reason,
Or by some habit that too much o'er-leavens
The form of plausive[4] manners—that these men,   30
Carrying, I say, the stamp of one defect,
Being nature's livery or fortune's star,
His virtues else, be they as pure as grace,
As infinite as man may undergo,
Shall in the general censure take corruption   35
From that particular fault. The dram of evil
Doth all the noble substance often doubt[5]
To his own scandal.

[*Enter* GHOST.]

HORATIO: Look, my lord, it comes.
HAMLET: Angels and ministers of grace defend us!
Be thou a spirit of health or goblin damned,   40
Bring with thee airs from heaven or blasts from hell,
Be thy intents wicked or charitable,
Thou com'st in such a questionable[6] shape
That I will speak to thee. I'll call thee Hamlet,
King, father, royal Dane. O, answer me!   45
Let me not burst in ignorance, but tell
Why thy canonized[7] bones, hearsèd in death,
Have burst their cerements;[8] why the sepulchre
Wherein we saw thee quietly inurned
Hath oped his ponderous and marble jaws   50
To cast thee up again. What may this mean
That thou, dead corse, again in complete steel[9]
Revisits thus the glimpses of the moon,
Making night hideous, and we fools of nature
So horridly to shake our disposition   55
With thoughts beyond the reaches of our souls?

1. Reputation.   2. Honor.   3. Barriers.   4. Pleasing.   5. Extinguish.   6. Prompting question.
7. Buried in accordance with church canons.   8. Gravecloths.   9. Armor.

Say, why is this? Wherefore? What should we do?

[GHOST *beckons*.]

HORATIO: It beckons you to go away with it,
   As if it some impartment[1] did desire
   To you alone.
60 MARCELLUS: Look with what courteous action
   It waves you to a more removèd[2] ground.
   But do not go with it.
HORATIO: No, by no means.
HAMLET: It will not speak; then I will follow it.
HORATIO: Do not, my lord.
HAMLET: Why, what should be the fear?
65 I do not set my life at a pin's fee,[3]
   And for my soul, what can it do to that,
   Being a thing immortal as itself?
   It waves me forth again. I'll follow it.
HORATIO: What if it tempt you toward the flood, my lord,
70 Or to the dreadful summit of the cliff
   That beetles[4] o'er his base into the sea,
   And there assume some other horrible form,
   Which might deprive your sovereignty of reason[5]
   And draw you into madness? Think of it.
75 The very place puts toys of desperation,[6]
   Without more motive, into every brain
   That looks so many fathoms to the sea
   And hears it roar beneath.
HAMLET: It wafts me still.
   Go on. I'll follow thee.
MARCELLUS: You shall not go, my lord.
80 HAMLET: Hold off your hands.
HORATIO: Be ruled. You shall not go.
HAMLET: My fate cries out
   And makes each petty artere in this body
   As hardy as the Nemean lion's nerve.[7]
   Still am I called. Unhand me, gentlemen.
85 By heaven, I'll make a ghost of him that lets[8] me.
   I say, away! Go on. I'll follow thee.   [*Exeunt* GHOST *and* HAMLET.]

1. Communication.   2. Beckons you to a more distant.   3. Price.   4. Juts out.
5. Rational power. *Deprive*: take away.   6. Desperate fancies.
7. The Nemean lion was a mythological monster slain by Hercules as one of his twelve labors.
Artere: artery.   8. Hinders.

HORATIO: He waxes desperate with imagination.
MARCELLUS: Let's follow. 'Tis not fit thus to obey him.
HORATIO: Have after. To what issue will this come?
MARCELLUS: Something is rotten in the state of Denmark.   90
HORATIO: Heaven will direct it.
MARCELLUS: Nay, let's follow him.   [*Exeunt.*]

Scene 5

Near the guard station. Enter GHOST *and* HAMLET.

HAMLET: Whither wilt thou lead me? Speak. I'll go no further.
GHOST: Mark me.
HAMLET: I will.
GHOST: My hour is almost come,
    When I to sulph'rous and tormenting flames
    Must render up myself.
HAMLET: Alas, poor ghost!
GHOST: Pity me not, but lend thy serious hearing   5
    To what I shall unfold.
HAMLET: Speak. I am bound to hear.
GHOST: So art thou to revenge, when thou shalt hear.
HAMLET: What?
GHOST: I am thy father's spirit,
    Doomed for a certain term to walk the night,   10
    And for the day confined to fast in fires,
    Till the foul crimes done in my days of nature[9]
    Are burnt and purged away. But that I am forbid
    To tell the secrets of my prison house,
    I could a tale unfold whose lightest word   15
    Would harrow up thy soul, freeze thy young blood,
    Make thy two eyes like stars start from their spheres,
    Thy knotted and combinèd[1] locks to part,
    And each particular hair to stand an end,
    Like quills upon the fretful porpentine.[2]   20
    But this eternal blazon[3] must not be
    To ears of flesh and blood. List, list, O, list!
    If thou didst ever thy dear father love—
HAMLET: O God!
GHOST: Revenge his foul and most unnatural murder.   25
HAMLET: Murder!

9. That is, while I was alive.   1. Tangled.   2. Porcupine.   3. Description of eternity.

GHOST: Murder most foul, as in the best it is,
    But this most foul, strange, and unnatural.
HAMLET: Haste me to know't, that I, with wings as swift
30   As meditation or the thoughts of love,
    May sweep to my revenge.
GHOST: I find thee apt.
    And duller shouldst thou be than the fat weed
    That rots itself in ease on Lethe[4] wharf,—
    Wouldst thou not stir in this. Now, Hamlet, hear.
35   'Tis given out that, sleeping in my orchard,
    A serpent stung me. So the whole ear of Denmark
    Is by a forgèd process[5] of my death
    Rankly abused. But know, thou noble youth,
    The serpent that did sting thy father's life
    Now wears his crown.
40 HAMLET: O my prophetic soul!
    My uncle!
GHOST: Ay, that incestuous, that adulterate beast,
    With witchcraft of his wits, with traitorous gifts—
    O wicked wit and gifts that have the power
45   So to seduce!—won to his shameful lust
    The will of my most seeming virtuous queen.
    O Hamlet, what a falling off was there,
    From me, whose love was of that dignity
    That it went hand in hand even with the vow
50   I made to her in marriage, and to decline[6]
    Upon a wretch whose natural gifts were poor
    To those of mine! The virtue, as it never will be moved,
    But virtue, as it never will be moved,
    Though lewdness court it in a shape of heaven,
55   So lust, though to a radiant angel linked,
    Will sate itself in a celestial bed
    And prey on garbage.
    But soft, methinks I scent the morning air.
    Brief let me be. Sleeping within my orchard,
60   My custom always of the afternoon,
    Upon my secure hour thy uncle stole,
    With juice of cursed hebona[7] in a vial,

---

4. When drunk, the waters of the Lethe, one of the rivers of the classical underworld, induced forgetfulness. The "fat weed" is the asphodel that grew there; some texts have "roots" for "rots."
5. False report. 6. Sink. 7. A poison.

And in the porches of my ears did pour
The leperous distilment, whose effect
Holds such an enmity with blood of man   65
That swift as quicksilver it courses through
The natural gates and alleys of the body,
And with a sudden vigor it doth posset[8]
And curd, like eager[9] droppings into milk,
The thin and wholesome blood. So did it mine,   70
And a most instant tetter barked about[1]
Most lazar-like[2] with vile and loathsome crust
All my smooth body.
Thus was I sleeping by a brother's hand
Of life, of crown, of queen at once dispatched,   75
Cut off even in the blossoms of my sin,
Unhouseled, disappointed, unaneled,[3]
No reck'ning made, but sent to my account
With all my imperfections on my head.
O, horrible! O, horrible, most horrible!   80
If thou hast nature in thee, bear it not.
Let not the royal bed of Denmark be
A couch of luxury[4] and damnèd incest.
But howsomever thou pursues this act,
Taint not thy mind, nor let thy soul contrive   85
Against thy mother aught. Leave her to heaven,
And to those thorns that in her bosom lodge
To prick and sting her. Fare thee well at once.
The glowworm shows the matin[5] to be near,
And gins to pale his uneffectual fire.   90
Adieu, adieu, adieu. Remember me.   [*Exit.*]
HAMLET: O all you host of heaven! O earth! What else?
    And shall I couple hell? O, fie! Hold, hold, my heart,
    And you, my sinews, grow not instant old,
    But bear me stiffly up. Remember thee?   95
    Ay, thou poor ghost, whiles memory holds a seat
    In this distracted globe.[6] Remember thee?
    Yea, from the table[7] of my memory
    I'll wipe away all trivial fond[8] records,
    All saws of books, all forms, all pressures past   100

---

8. Coagulate.   9. Acid. *Curd*: curdle.   1. Covered like bark. *Tetter*: a skin disease.   2. Leperlike.
3. The ghost means that he died without the customary rites of the church, that is, without
receiving the Sacrament, without confession, and without Extreme Unction.   4. Lust.
5. Morning.   6. Skull.   7. Writing tablet.   8. Foolish.

That youth and observation copied there,
And thy commandment all alone shall live
Within the book and volume of my brain,
Unmixed with baser matter. Yes, by heaven!
105   O most pernicious woman!
O villain, villain, smiling, damnèd villain!
My tables—meet it is I set it down
That one may smile, and smile, and be a villain.
At least I am sure it may be so in Denmark.
110   So, uncle, there you are. Now to my word:[9]
It is "Adieu, adieu. Remember me."
I have sworn't.

[*Enter* HORATIO *and* MARCELLUS.]

HORATIO: My lord, my lord!
MARCELLUS: Lord Hamlet!
HORATIO: Heavens secure him!
HAMLET: So be it!
115   MARCELLUS: Illo, ho, ho,[1] my lord!
HAMLET: Hillo, ho, ho, boy! Come, bird, come.
MARCELLUS: How is't, my noble lord?
HORATIO: What news, my lord?
HAMLET: O, wonderful!
HORATIO: Good my lord, tell it.
HAMLET: No, you will reveal it.
HORATIO: Not I, my lord, by heaven.
120   MARCELLUS: Nor I, my lord.
HAMLET: How say you then, would heart of man once think it?
    But you'll be secret?
BOTH: Ay, by heaven, my lord.
HAMLET: There's never a villain dwelling in all Denmark
    But he's an arrant knave.
125   HORATIO: There needs no ghost, my lord, come from the grave
    To tell us this.
HAMLET: Why, right, you are in the right,
    And so without more circumstance at all
    I hold it fit that we shake hands and part,
    You, as your business and desire shall point you,
130   For every man hath business and desire
    Such as it is, and for my own poor part,

9. For my motto.   1. A falconer's cry.

Look you, I'll go pray.

HORATIO: These are but wild and whirling words, my lord.

HAMLET: I am sorry they offend you, heartily;
    Yes, faith, heartily.

HORATIO: There's no offence, my lord.   135

HAMLET: Yes, by Saint Patrick, but there is, Horatio,
    And much offence too. Touching this vision here,
    It is an honest ghost, that let me tell you.
    For your desire to know what is between us,
    O'ermaster't as you may. And now, good friends,   140
    As you are friends, scholars, and soldiers,
    Give me one poor request.

HORATIO: What is't, my lord? We will.

HAMLET: Never make known what you have seen tonight.

BOTH: My lord, we will not.

HAMLET: Nay, but swear't.

HORATIO: In faith,   145
    My lord, not I.

MARCELLUS: Nor I, my lord, in faith.

HAMLET: Upon my sword.

MARCELLUS: We have sworn, my lord, already.

HAMLET: Indeed, upon my sword, indeed.

    [GHOST *cries under the stage.*]

GHOST: Swear.

HAMLET: Ha, ha, boy, say'st thou so? Art thou there, truepenny?[2]
    Come on. You hear this fellow in the cellarage.[3]   150
    Consent to swear.

HORATIO: Propose the oath, my lord.

HAMLET: Never to speak of this that you have seen,
    Swear by my sword.

GHOST: [*Beneath.*] Swear.

HAMLET: Hic et ubique?[4] Then we'll shift our ground.   155
    Come hither, gentlemen,
    And lay your hands again upon my sword.
    Swear by my sword
    Never to speak of this that you have heard.

GHOST: [*Beneath.*] Swear by his sword.   160

HAMLET: Well said, old mole! Canst work i' th' earth so fast?
    A worthy pioneer![5] Once more remove, good friends.

---

2. Trusty old fellow.   3. Below.   4. Here and everywhere? (Latin).   5. Soldier who digs trenches.

HORATIO: O day and night, but this is wondrous strange!

HAMLET: And therefore as a stranger give it welcome.

165 There are more things in heaven and earth, Horatio,
Than are dreamt of in your philosophy.
. But come.
Here as before, never, so help you mercy,
How strange or odd some'er I bear myself

170 (As I perchance hereafter shall think meet
To put an antic⁶ disposition on),
That you, at such times, seeing me, never shall,
With arms encumbered⁷ thus, or this head-shake,
Or by pronouncing of some doubtful phrase,

175 As "Well, we know," or "We could, and if we would"
Or "If we list to speak," or "There be, and if they might"
Or such ambiguous giving out, to note
That you know aught of me—this do swear,
So grace and mercy at your most need help you.

180 GHOST: [Beneath.] Swear.   [They swear.]

HAMLET: Rest, rest, perturbèd spirit! So, gentlemen,
With all my love I do commend me to you,
And what so poor a man as Hamlet is
May do t'express his love and friending⁸ to you,

185 God willing, shall not lack. Let us go in together,
And still your fingers on your lips, I pray.
The time is out of joint. O cursèd spite
That ever I was born to set it right!
Nay, come, let's go together.   [Exeunt.]

ACT II

Scene 1

The dwelling of POLONIUS. *Enter* POLONIUS *and* REYNALDO.

POLONIUS: Give him this money and these notes, Reynaldo.

REYNALDO: I will, my lord.

POLONIUS: You shall do marvellous wisely, good Reynaldo,
Before you visit him, to make inquire⁹
Of his behavior.

5 REYNALDO: My lord, I did intend it.

POLONIUS: Marry, well said, very well said. Look you, sir.

---

6. Mad.   7. Folded.   8. Friendship.   9. Inquiry.

Enquire me first what Danskers[1] are in Paris,
And how, and who, what means, and where they keep,[2]
What company, at what expense; and finding
By this encompassment[3] and drift of question   10
That they do know my son, come you more nearer
Than your particular demands[4] will touch it.
Take you as 'twere some distant knowledge of him,
As thus, "I know his father and his friends,
And in part him." Do you mark this, Reynaldo?   15
REYNALDO: Ay, very well, my lord.
POLONIUS: "And in part him, but," you may say, "not well,
But if't be he I mean, he's very wild,
Addicted so and so." And there put on him
What forgeries you please; marry, none so rank[5]   20
As may dishonor him. Take heed of that.
But, sir, such wanton, wild, and usual slips
As are companions noted and most known
To youth and liberty.
REYNALDO: As gaming, my lord.
POLONIUS: Ay, or drinking, fencing, swearing,   25
Quarrelling, drabbing[6]—you may go so far.
REYNALDO: My lord, that would dishonor him.
POLONIUS: Faith, no, as you may season it in the charge.[7]
You must not put another scandal on him,
That he is open to incontinency.[8]   30
That's not my meaning. But breathe his faults so quaintly[9]
That they may seem the taints of liberty,[1]
The flash and outbreak of a fiery mind,
A savageness in unreclaimèd[2] blood,
Of general assault.[3]
REYNALDO: But, my good lord—   35
POLONIUS: Wherefore should you do this?
REYNALDO: Ay, my lord,
I would know that.
POLONIUS: Marry, sir, here's my drift,
And I believe it is a fetch of warrant.[4]
You laying these slight sullies on my son,
As 'twere a thing a little soiled wi' th' working,   40
Mark you,

1. Danes.   2. Live.   3. Indirect means.   4. Direct questions.   5. Foul. *Forgeries*: lies.
6. Whoring.   7. Soften the accusation.   8. Sexual excess.   9. With delicacy.
1. Faults of freedom.   2. Untamed.   3. Touching everyone.   4. Permissible trick.

Your party in converse,[5] him you would sound,
Having ever seen in the prenominate[6] crimes
The youth you breathe[7] of guilty, be assured
45 He closes with you in this consequence,
"Good sir," or so, or "friend," or "gentleman,"
According to the phrase or the addition
Of man and country.

REYNALDO: Very good, my lord.

POLONIUS: And then, sir, does 'a this—'a does—What was I about to say?
50   By the mass, I was about to say something.
Where did I leave?

REYNALDO: At "closes in the consequence."

POLONIUS: At "closes in the consequence"—ay, marry,
He closes thus: "I know the gentleman.
55   I saw him yesterday, or th' other day,
Or then, or then, with such, or such, and as you say,
There was 'a gaming, there o'ertook in's rouse,
There falling out at tennis," or perchance
"I saw him enter such a house of sale,"
60   Videlicet,[8] a brothel, or so forth.
See you, now—
Your bait of falsehood takes this carp of truth,
And thus do we of wisdom and of reach,[9]
With windlasses and with assays of bias,[1]
65   By indirections find directions out;
So by my former lecture and advice
Shall you my son. You have me, have you not?

REYNALDO: My lord, I have.

POLONIUS: God b'wi' ye; fare ye well.

REYNALDO: Good my lord.

70 POLONIUS: Observe his inclination in yourself.

REYNALDO: I shall, my lord.

POLONIUS: And let him ply[2] his music.

REYNALDO: Well, my lord.

POLONIUS: Farewell.   [*Exit* REYNALDO.]

[*Enter* OPHELIA.]

How now, Ophelia, what's the matter?

OPHELIA: O my lord, my lord, I have been so affrighted!

5. Conversation.   6. Already named.   7. Speak.   8. Namely.   9. Ability.   1. Indirect tests.
2. Practice.

POLONIUS: With what, i' th' name of God?   75
OPHELIA: My lord, as I was sewing in my closet,[3]
    Lord Hamlet with his doublet all unbraced,[4]
    No hat upon his head, his stockings fouled,
    Ungartered and down-gyvèd[5] to his ankle,
    Pale as his shirt, his knees knocking each other,   80
    And with a look so piteous in purport
    As if he had been loosèd out of hell
    To speak of horrors—he comes before me.
POLONIUS: Mad for thy love?
OPHELIA: My lord, I do not know,
    But truly I do fear it.
POLONIUS: What said he?   85
OPHELIA: He took me by the wrist, and held me hard,
    Then goes he to the length of all his arm,
    And with his other hand thus o'er his brow,
    He falls to such perusal of my face
    As 'a would draw it. Long stayed he so.   90
    At last, a little shaking of mine arm,
    And thrice his head thus waving up and down,
    He raised a sigh so piteous and profound
    As it did seem to shatter all his bulk,[6]
    And end his being. That done, he lets me go,   95
    And with his head over his shoulder turned
    He seemed to find his way without his eyes,
    For out adoors he went without their helps,
    And to the last bended[7] their light on me.
POLONIUS: Come, go with me. I will go seek the king.   100
    This is the very ecstasy of love,
    Whose violent property fordoes[8] itself,
    And leads the will to desperate undertakings
    As oft as any passion under heaven
    That does afflict our natures. I am sorry.   105
    What, have you given him any hard words of late?
OPHELIA: No, my good lord, but as you did command
    I did repel[9] his letters, and denied
    His access to me.
POLONIUS: That hath made him mad.
    I am sorry that with better heed and judgment   110

---

3. Chamber.   4. Unlaced. *Doublet*: jacket.   5. Fallen down like fetters.   6. Body.   7. Directed.
8. Destroys. *Property*: character.   9. Refuse.

I had not quoted¹ him. I feared he did but trifle,
And meant to wrack² thee; but beshrew my jealousy.
By heaven, it is as proper to our age
To cast beyond ourselves in our opinions
115   As it is common for the younger sort
To lack discretion. Come, go we to the king.
This must be known, which being kept close, might move
More grief to hide than hate to utter love.
Come.   [*Exeunt.*]

Scene 2

A public room. Enter KING, QUEEN, ROSENCRANTZ *and* GUILDENSTERN.

KING: Welcome, dear Rosencrantz and Guildenstern.
Moreover that³ we much did long to see you,
The need we have to use you did provoke
Our hasty sending. Something have you heard
5   Of Hamlet's transformation—so call it,
Sith⁴ nor th' exterior nor the inward man
Resembles that it was. What it should be,
More than his father's death, that thus hath put him
So much from th' understanding of himself,
10   I cannot deem of. I entreat you both
That, being of so young days⁵ brought up with him,
And sith so neighbored⁶ to his youth and havior,
That you vouchsafe your rest here in our court
Some little time, so by your companies
15   To draw him on to pleasures, and to gather
So much as from occasion you may glean,
Whether aught to us unknown afflicts him thus,
That opened lies within our remedy.
QUEEN: Good gentlemen, he hath much talked of you,
20   And sure I am two men there are not living
To whom he more adheres. If it will please you
To show us so much gentry⁷ and good will
As to expend your time with us awhile
For the supply and profit of our hope,
25   Your visitation shall receive such thanks
As fits a king's remembrance.

---

1. Observed.   2. Harm.   3. In addition to the fact that.   4. Since.   5. From childhood.
6. Closely allied.   7. Courtesy.

ROSENCRANTZ: Both your majesties
    Might, by the sovereign power you have of us,
    Put your dread pleasures more into command
    Than to entreaty.
GUILDENSTERN: But we both obey,
    And here give up ourselves in the full bent[8]   30
    To lay our service freely at your feet,
    To be commanded.
KING: Thanks, Rosencrantz and gentle Guildenstern.
QUEEN: Thanks, Guildenstern and gentle Rosencrantz.
    And I beseech you instantly to visit   35
    My too much changed son. Go, some of you,
    And bring these gentlemen where Hamlet is.
GUILDENSTERN: Heavens make our presence and our practices
    Pleasant and helpful to him!
QUEEN: Ay, amen!
                  [*Exeunt* ROSENCRANTZ *and* GUILDENSTERN.]

    [*Enter* POLONIUS.]

POLONIUS: Th' ambassadors from Norway, my good lord,   40
    Are joyfully returned.
KING: Thou still[9] hast been the father of good news.
POLONIUS: Have I, my lord? I assure you, my good liege,
    I hold my duty as I hold my soul,
    Both to my God and to my gracious king;   45
    And I do think—or else this brain of mine
    Hunts not the trail of policy[1] so sure
    As it hath used to do—that I have found
    The very cause of Hamlet's lunacy.
KING: O, speak of that, that do I long to hear.   50
POLONIUS: Give first admittance to th' ambassadors.
    My news shall be the fruit[2] to that great feast.
KING: Thyself do grace to them, and bring them in.   [*Exit* POLONIUS.]
    He tells me, my dear Gertrude, he hath found
    The head and source of all your son's distemper.   55
QUEEN: I doubt it is no other but the main,
    His father's death and our o'erhasty marriage.
KING: Well, we shall sift[3] him.

    [*Enter Ambassadors* (VOLTEMAND *and* CORNELIUS) *with* POLONIUS.]

8. Completely.   9. Ever.   1. Statecraft.   2. Dessert.   3. Examine.

Welcome, my good friends,
Say, Voltemand, what from our brother Norway?

60 VOLTEMAND: Most fair return of greetings and desires.
Upon our first,[4] he sent out to suppress
His nephew's levies, which to him appeared
To be a preparation 'gainst the Polack,
But better looked into, he truly found

65 It was against your highness, whereat grieved,
That so his sickness, age, and impotence
Was falsely borne in hand, sends out arrests[5]
On Fortinbras, which he in brief obeys,
Receives rebuke from Norway, and in fine,

70 Makes vow before his uncle never more
To give th' assay[6] of arms against your majesty.
Whereon old Norway, overcome with joy,
Gives him three thousand crowns in annual fee,
And his commission to employ those soldiers,

75 So levied as before, against the Polack,
With an entreaty, herein further shown,   [*Gives* CLAUDIUS *a paper.*]
That it might please you to give quiet pass[7]
Through your dominions for this enterprise,
On such regards of safety and allowance
As therein are set down.

80 KING: It likes[8] us well,
And at our more considered time[9] we'll read,
Answer, and think upon this business.
Meantime we thank you for your well-took[1] labor.
Go to your rest; at night we'll feast together.
Most welcome home!   [*Exeunt* AMBASSADORS.]

85 POLONIUS: This business is well ended.
My liege and madam, to expostulate[2]
What majesty should be, what duty is,
Why day is day, night night, and time is time,
Were nothing but to waste night, day, and time.

90 Therefore, since brevity is the soul of wit,
And tediousness the limbs and outward flourishes,[3]
I will be brief. Your noble son is mad.
Mad call I it, for to define true madness,

---

4. That is, first appearance. 5. Orders to stop. *Falsely borne in hand*: deceived.   6. Trial.
7. Safe conduct. 8. Pleases. 9. Time for more consideration. 1. Successful. 2. Discuss.
3. Adornments.

What is't but to be nothing else but mad?
But let that go.
QUEEN: More matter with less art.   95
POLONIUS: Madam, I swear I use no art at all.
That he is mad, 'tis true: 'tis true 'tis pity,
And pity 'tis 'tis true. A foolish figure,
But farewell it, for I will use no art.
Mad let us grant him, then, and now remains   100
That we find out the cause of this effect,
Or rather say the cause of this defect,
For this effect defective comes by cause.
Thus it remains, and the remainder thus.
Perpend.[4]   105
I have a daughter—have while she is mine—
Who in her duty and obedience, mark,
Hath given me this. Now gather, and surmise.
[*Reads*] *the letter.*
"To the celestial, and my soul's idol, the most beautified Ophelia."—
That's an ill phrase, a vile phrase, "beautified" is a vile phrase. But you   110
shall hear. Thus:
"In her excellent white bosom, these, etc."
QUEEN: Came this from Hamlet to her?
POLONIUS: Good madam, stay awhile. I will be faithful.

        "Doubt thou the stars are fire,   115
            Doubt that the sun doth move;
        Doubt truth to be a liar;
            But never doubt I love.

O dear Ophelia, I am ill at these numbers.[5] I have not art to reckon
my groans, but that I love thee best, O most best, believe it. Adieu.   120
        Thine evermore, most dear lady,
            whilst this machine[6] is to him, Hamlet."
This in obedience hath my daughter shown me,
And more above, hath his solicitings,
As they fell out by time, by means, and place,   125
All given to mine ear.
KING: But how hath she
Received his love?
POLONIUS: What do you think of me?
KING: As of a man faithful and honorable.

4. Consider.   5. Verses.   6. Body.

POLONIUS: I would fain prove so. But what might you think,
130   When I had seen this hot love on the wing.
        (As I perceived it, I must tell you that,
        Before my daughter told me), what might you,
        Or my dear majesty your queen here, think,
        If I had played the desk or table-book,
135   Or given my heart a winking, mute and dumb,
        Or looked upon this love with idle sight,[7]
        What might you think? No, I went round[8] to work,
        And my young mistress thus I did bespeak:
        "Lord Hamlet is a prince out of thy star.[9]
140   This must not be." And then I prescripts[1] gave her,
        That she should lock herself from his resort,
        Admit no messengers, receive no tokens.
        Which done, she took[2] the fruits of my advice;
        And he repelled, a short tale to make,
145   Fell into a sadness, then into a fast,
        Thence to a watch, thence into a weakness,
        Thence to a lightness, and by this declension,
        Into the madness wherein now he raves,
        And all we mourn for.
KING: Do you think 'tis this?
150 QUEEN: It may be, very like.
POLONIUS: Hath there been such a time—I would fain know that—
        That I have positively said "'Tis so,"
        When it proved otherwise?
KING: Not that I know.
POLONIUS: [Pointing to his head and shoulder.] Take this from this, if this
        be otherwise.
155   If circumstances lead me, I will find
        Where truth is hid, though it were hid indeed
        Within the centre.[3]
KING: How may we try it further?
POLONIUS: You know sometimes he walks four hours together
        Here in the lobby.
QUEEN: So he does, indeed.
160 POLONIUS: At such a time I'll loose[4] my daughter to him.
        Be you and I behind an arras[5] then.

---

7. Polonius means that he would have been at fault if, having seen Hamlet's attention to Ophelia, he had winked at it or not paid attention, an "idle sight," and if he had remained silent and kept the information to himself, as if it were written in a "desk" or "table-book."   8. Directly.
9. Beyond your sphere.   1. Orders.   2. Followed.   3. Of the earth.   4. Let loose.   5. Tapestry.

Mark the encounter. If he love her not,
And be not from his reason fall'n thereon,
Let me be no assistant for a state,
But keep a farm and carters.
KING: We will try it.   165

[*Enter* HAMLET *reading a book.*]

QUEEN: But look where sadly the poor wretch comes reading.
POLONIUS: Away, I do beseech you both away,
    I'll board[6] him presently.   [*Exeunt* KING *and* QUEEN.]
                    O, give me leave.
    How does my good Lord Hamlet?
HAMLET: Well, God-a-mercy.   170
POLONIUS: Do you know me, my lord?
HAMLET: Excellent well, you are a fishmonger.
POLONIUS: Not I, my lord.
HAMLET: Then I would you were so honest a man.
POLONIUS: Honest, my lord?   175
HAMLET: Ay, sir, to be honest as this world goes, is to be one man picked
    out of ten thousand.
POLONIUS: That's very true, my lord.
HAMLET: For if the sun breed maggots in a dead dog, being a god kissing
    carrion[7]—Have you a daughter?   180
POLONIUS: I have, my lord.
HAMLET: Let her not walk i' th' sun. Conception is a blessing, but as your
    daughter may conceive—friend, look to't.
POLONIUS: How say you by that? [*Aside.*] Still harping on my daughter. Yet
    he knew me not at first. 'A said I was a fishmonger. 'A is far gone. And 185
    truly in my youth I suffered much extremity for love. Very near this. I'll
    speak to him again.—What do you read, my lord?
HAMLET: Words, words, words.
POLONIUS: What is the matter, my lord?
HAMLET: Between who?   190
POLONIUS: I mean the matter that you read, my lord.
HAMLET: Slanders, sir; for the satirical rogue says here that old men have
    grey beards, that their faces are wrinkled, their eyes purging thick amber
    and plumtree gum, and that they have a plentiful lack of wit, together
    with most weak hams[8]—all which, sir, though I most powerfully and   195

---

6. Accost.
7. Reference to the belief that maggots were produced spontaneously by the action of sunshine
on carrion.   8. Limbs.

potently believe, yet I hold it not honesty to have it thus set down, for yourself, sir, shall grow old as I am, if like a crab you could go backward.

POLONIUS: [*Aside.*] Though this be madness, yet there is method in't.— Will you walk out of the air, my lord?

200 HAMLET: Into my grave?

POLONIUS: [*Aside.*] Indeed, that's out of the air. How pregnant sometime his replies are! a happiness that often madness hits on, which reason and sanity could not so prosperously be delivered of. I will leave him, and suddenly contrive the means of meeting between him and my daughter.—My

205 honorable lord. I will most humbly take my leave of you.

HAMLET: You cannot take from me anything that I will more willingly part withal—except my life, except my life, except my life.

[*Enter* GUILDENSTERN *and* ROSENCRANTZ.]

POLONIUS: Fare you well, my lord.

HAMLET: These tedious old fools!

210 POLONIUS: You go to seek the Lord Hamlet. There he is.

ROSENCRANTZ: [*To* POLONIUS.] God save you, sir!   [*Exit* POLONIUS.]

GUILDENSTERN: My honored lord!

ROSENCRANTZ: My most dear lord!

HAMLET: My excellent good friends! How dost thou, Guildenstern?

215   Ah, Rosencrantz! Good lads, how do you both?

ROSENCRANTZ: As the indifferent[9] children of the earth.

GUILDENSTERN: Happy in that we are not over-happy;
On Fortune's cap we are not the very button.[1]

HAMLET: Nor the soles of her shoe?

220 ROSENCRANTZ: Neither, my lord.

HAMLET: Then you live about her waist, or in the middle of her favors?

GUILDENSTERN: Faith, her privates we.

HAMLET: In the secret parts of Fortune? O, most true, she is a strumpet.[2]
What news?

225 ROSENCRANTZ: None, my lord, but that the world's grown honest.

HAMLET: Then is doomsday near. But your news is not true. Let me question more in particular. What have you, my good friends, deserved at the hands of Fortune, that she sends you to prison hither?

GUILDENSTERN: Prison, my lord?

230 HAMLET: Denmark's a prison.

ROSENCRANTZ: Then is the world one.

9. Ordinary.   1. That is, on top.
2. Prostitute. Hamlet is indulging in characteristic ribaldry. Guildenstern means that they are "privates" = ordinary citizens, but Hamlet takes him to mean "privates" = sexual organs and "middle of her favors" = waist = sexual organs.

HAMLET: A goodly one, in which there are many confines, wards[3] and
dungeons. Denmark being one o' th' worst.

ROSENCRANTZ: We think not so, my lord.

HAMLET: Why then 'tis none to you; for there is nothing either good or   235
bad, but thinking makes it so. To me it is a prison.

ROSENCRANTZ: Why then your ambition makes it one. 'Tis too narrow for
your mind.

HAMLET: O God, I could be bounded in a nutshell and count myself a
king of infinite space, were it not that I have bad dreams.   240

GUILDENSTERN: Which dreams indeed are ambition; for the very substance of the ambitious is merely the shadow of a dream.

HAMLET: A dream itself is but a shadow.

ROSENCRANTZ: Truly, and I hold ambition of so airy and light a quality
that it is but a shadow's shadow.   245

HAMLET: Then are our beggars bodies, and our monarchs and outstretched
heroes the beggars' shadows. Shall we to th' court? for, by my fay,[4] I
cannot reason.

BOTH: We'll wait upon you.

HAMLET: No such matter. I will not sort[5] you with the rest of my servants;   250
for to speak to you like an honest man, I am most dreadfully attended.
But in the beaten way of friendship, what make you at Elsinore?

ROSENCRANTZ: To visit you, my lord; no other occasion.

HAMLET: Beggar that I am, I am even poor in thanks, but I thank you; and
sure, dear friends, my thanks are too dear a halfpenny.[6] Were you not   255
sent for? Is it your own inclining? Is it a free visitation? Come, come,
deal justly with me. Come, come, nay speak.

GUILDENSTERN: What should we say, my lord?

HAMLET: Anything but to th' purpose. You were sent for, and there is a
kind of confession in your looks, which your modesties have not craft   260
enough to color. I know the good king and queen have sent for you.

ROSENCRANTZ: To what end, my lord?

HAMLET: That you must teach me. But let me conjure you by the rights of
our fellowship, by the consonancy of our youth, by the obligation of our
ever preserved love, and by what more dear a better proposer can   265
charge you withal, be even and direct[7] with me whether you were sent
for or no.

ROSENCRANTZ: [*Aside to* GUILDENSTERN.] What say you?

HAMLET: [*Aside.*] Nay, then, I have an eye of you.—If you love me, hold
not off.

GUILDENSTERN: My lord, we were sent for.

3. Cells.   4. Faith.   5. Include.   6. Not worth a halfpenny.   7. Straightforward.

HAMLET: I will tell you why; so shall my anticipation prevent your discovery,[8] and your secrecy to the king and queen moult no feather. I have
270   of late—but wherefore I know not—lost all my mirth, forgone all custom of exercises; and indeed it goes so heavily with my disposition, that this goodly frame the earth seems to me a sterile promontory, this most excellent canopy the air, look you, this brave o'er-hanging firmament, this majestical roof fretted[9] with golden fire, why it appeareth nothing to me
275   but a foul and pestilent congregation of vapors. What a piece of work is a man, how noble in reason, how infinite in faculties, in form and moving, how express[1] and admirable in action, how like an angel in apprehension, how like a god: the beauty of the world, the paragon of animals. And yet to me, what is this quintessence of dust? Man delights not me, nor
280   woman neither, though by your smiling you seem to say so.

ROSENCRANTZ: My lord, there was no such stuff in my thoughts.

HAMLET: Why did ye laugh, then, when I said "Man delights not me"?

ROSENCRANTZ: To think, my lord, if you delight not in man, what lenten entertainment the players shall receive from you. We coted[2] them on
285   the way, and hither are they coming to offer you service.

HAMLET: He that plays the king shall be welcome—his majesty shall have tribute of me; the adventurous knight shall use his foil and target; the lover shall not sigh gratis; the humorous[3] man shall end his part in peace; the clown shall make those laugh whose lungs are tickle o' th' sere;[4]
290   and the lady shall say her mind freely, or the blank verse shall halt for't. What players are they?

ROSENCRANTZ: Even those you were wont to take such delight in, the tragedians of the city.

HAMLET: How chances it they travel? Their residence, both in reputation
295   and profit, was better both ways.

ROSENCRANTZ: I think their inhibition comes by the means of the late innovation.

HAMLET: Do they hold the same estimation they did when I was in the city? Are they so followed?

300 ROSENCRANTZ: No, indeed, are they not.

HAMLET: How comes it? Do they grow rusty?

ROSENCRANTZ: Nay, their endeavor keeps in the wonted pace; but there is, sir, an eyrie of children, little eyases,[5] that cry out on the top of question,[6]
305   and are most tyrannically clapped for't. These are now the fashion, and so

---

8. Disclosure.   9. Ornamented with fretwork.   1. Well built.   2. Passed. *Lenten*: scanty.
3. Eccentric. *Foil and target*: sword and shield.   4. Easily set off.   5. Little hawks.
6. With a loud, high delivery.

berattle the common stages (so they call them) that many wearing rapiers are afraid of goose quills[7] and dare scarce come thither.[8]

HAMLET: What, are they children? Who maintains 'em? How are they escoted?[9] Will they pursue the quality no longer than they can sing? Will they not say afterwards, if they should grow themselves to common players (as it is most like, if their means are no better), their writers do them wrong to make them exclaim against their own succession?[1] 310

ROSENCRANTZ: Faith, there has been much todo on both sides; and the nation holds it no sin to tarre[2] them to controversy. There was for a while no money bid for argument,[3] unless the poet and the player went to cuffs[4] in the question. 315

HAMLET: Is't possible?

GUILDENSTERN: O, there has been much throwing about of brains.

HAMLET: Do the boys carry it away?

ROSENCRANTZ: Ay, that they do, my lord. Hercules and his load too.[5]

HAMLET: It is not very strange, for my uncle is King of Denmark, and those 320 that would make mouths[6] at him while my father lived give twenty, forty, fifty, a hundred ducats apiece for his picture in little.[7] 'Sblood, there is something in this more than natural, if philosophy could find it out.

[*A flourish.*]

GUILDENSTERN: There are the players.

HAMLET: Gentlemen, you are welcome to Elsinore. Your hands. Come then, 325 th' appurtenance of welcome is fashion and ceremony. Let me comply with you in this garb, lest my extent[8] to the players, which I tell you must show fairly outwards should more appear like entertainment[9] than yours. You are welcome. But my uncle-father and aunt-mother are deceived.

GUILDENSTERN: In what, my dear lord? 330

HAMLET: I am but mad north-north-west; when the wind is southerly I know a hawk from a handsaw.[1]

[*Enter* POLONIUS.]

POLONIUS: Well be with you, gentlemen.

---

7. Pens of satirical writers.
8. The passage refers to the emergence at the time of the play of theatrical companies made up of children from London choir schools. Their performances became fashionable and hurt the business of the established companies. Hamlet says that if they continue to act ("pursue the quality") when they are grown, they will find that they have been damaging their own future careers. 9. Supported. 1. Future careers. 2. Urge. 3. Paid for a play plot. 4. Blows.
5. During one of his labors Hercules assumed for a time the burden of the Titan Atlas, who supported the heavens on his shoulders. Also a reference to the effect on business at Shakespeare's theater, the Globe. 6. Sneer. 7. Miniature. 8. Fashion. *Comply with*: welcome. 9. Cordiality.
1. A "hawk" is a plasterer's tool; Hamlet may also be using "handsaw" = hernshaw = heron.

HAMLET: Hark you, Guildenstern—and you too—at each ear a hearer.
335   That great baby you see there is not yet out of his swaddling clouts.[2]
ROSENCRANTZ: Happily he is the second time come to them, for they say
    an old man is twice a child.
HAMLET: I will prophesy he comes to tell me of the players. Mark it.—You
    say right, sir, a Monday morning, 'twas then indeed.
340   POLONIUS: My lord, I have news to tell you.
HAMLET: My lord, I have news to tell you. When Roscius was an actor in
    Rome[3]—
POLONIUS: The actors are come hither, my lord.
HAMLET: Buzz, buzz.
345   POLONIUS: Upon my honor—
HAMLET: Then came each actor on his ass—
POLONIUS: The best actors in the world, either for tragedy, comedy, his-
    tory, pastoral, pastoral-comical, historical-pastoral, tragical-historical,
    tragical-comical historical-pastoral, scene individable, or poem unlim-
350   ited. Seneca cannot be too heavy nor Plautus too light. For the law of
    writ and the liberty, these are the only men.[4]
HAMLET: O Jephtha, judge of Israel, what a treasure hadst thou![5]
POLONIUS: What a treasure had he, my lord?
HAMLET: Why—

355   "One fair daughter, and no more,
        The which he loved passing well."

POLONIUS: [Aside.] Still on my daughter.
HAMLET: Am I not i' th' right, old Jephtha?
POLONIUS: If you call me Jephtha, my lord, I have a daughter that I love
360   passing well.
HAMLET: Nay, that follows not.
POLONIUS: What follows then, my lord?
HAMLET: Why—

        "As by lot, God wot"

365   and then, you know,

        "It came to pass, as most like it was."

2. Wrappings for an infant.   3. Roscius was the most famous actor of classical Rome.
4. Seneca and Plautus were Roman writers of tragedy and comedy, respectively. The "law of
writ" refers to plays written according to such rules as the classical unities, the "liberty" to
those written otherwise.
5. To ensure victory, Jephtha promised to sacrifice the first creature to meet him on his return.
Unfortunately, his only daughter outstripped his dog and was the victim of his vow. The biblical
story is told in Judges 11.

The first row of the pious chanson[6] will show you more, for look where
my abridgement[7] comes.

[*Enter the* PLAYERS.]

You are welcome, masters; welcome, all.—I am glad to see thee well.—
Welcome, good friends.—O, old friend! Why, thy face is valanced[8]   370
since I saw thee last. Com'st thou to beard me in Denmark?—What,
my young lady and mistress? By'r lady, your ladyship is nearer to heaven
than when I saw you last by the altitude of a chopine.[9] Pray God your
voice, like a piece of uncurrent gold, be not cracked within the ring.—
Masters, you are all welcome. We'll e'en to't like French falconers, fly at   375
anything we see. We'll have a speech straight. Come give us a taste of
your quality,[1] come a passionate speech.

FIRST PLAYER: What speech, my good lord?

HAMLET: I heard thee speak me a speech once, but it was never acted, or
if it was, not above once, for the play, I remember, pleased not the mil-   380
lion; 'twas caviary to the general.[2] But it was—as I received it, and others whose judgments in such matters cried in the top of[3] mine—an
excellent play, well digested[4] in the scenes, set down with as much
modesty as cunning. I remember one said there were no sallets[5] in the
lines to make the matter savory, nor no matter in the phrase that might
indict the author of affectation, but called it an honest method, as   385
wholesome as sweet, and by very much more handsome than fine. One
speech in't I chiefly loved. 'Twas Æneas' tale to Dido, and thereabout of
it especially where he speaks of Priam's slaughter.[6] If it live in your
memory, begin at this line—let me see, let me see:

"The rugged Pyrrhus, like th' Hyrcanian beast"[7]—   390

'tis not so; it begins with Pyrrhus—

"The rugged Pyrrhus, he whose sable arms,
Black as his purpose, did the night resemble
When he lay couchéd in th' ominous horse,[8]

---

6. Song. *Row*: stanza.   7. That which cuts short by interrupting.   8. Fringed (with a beard).
9. Reference to the contemporary theatrical practice of using boys to play women's parts. The
company's "lady" has grown in height by the size of a woman's thick-soled shoe ("chopine")
since Hamlet saw him last. The next sentence refers to the possibility, suggested by his growth,
that the young actor's voice may soon begin to change.   1. Trade.
2. Caviar to the masses (i.e., pearls before swine).   3. Were weightier than.   4. Arranged.
5. Spicy passages.
6. Aeneas, fleeing with his band from fallen Troy (Ilium), arrives in Carthage, where he tells
Dido, the queen of Carthage, of Troy's fall. Here he is describing the death of Priam, the aged
king of Troy, at the hands of Pyrrhus, the son of the slain Achilles.   7. Tiger.
8. That is, the Trojan horse.

395   Hath now this dread and black complexion smeared
        With heraldry more dismal; head to foot
        Now is he total gules, horridly tricked[9]
        With blood of fathers, mothers, daughters, sons,
        Baked and impasted with the parching[1] streets,
400   That lend a tyrannous and a damnèd light
        To their lord's murder. Roasted in wrath and fire,
        And thus o'er-sizèd with coagulate[2] gore,
        With eyes like carbuncles, the hellish Pyrrhus
        Old grandsire Priam seeks."

405 So proceed you.

POLONIUS: Fore God, my lord, well spoken, with good accent and good
    discretion.

FIRST PLAYER: "Anon he finds him[3]
        Striking too short at Greeks. His antique[4] sword,
410   Rebellious[5] to his arm, lies where it falls,
        Repugnant to command. Unequal matched,
        Pyrrhus at Priam drives, in rage strikes wide.
        But with the whiff and wind of his fell sword
        Th' unnervèd father falls. Then senseless[6] Ilium,
415   Seeming to feel this blow, with flaming top
        Stoops[7] to his base, and with a hideous crash
        Takes prisoner Pyrrhus' ear. For, lo! his sword,
        Which was declining[8] on the milky head
        Of reverend Priam, seemed i' th' air to stick.
420   So as a painted tyrant Pyrrhus stood,
        And like a neutral to his will and matter,[9]
        Did nothing.
        But as we often see, against some storm,
        A silence in the heavens, the rack[1] stand still,
425   The bold winds speechless, and the orb below
        As hush as death, anon the dreadful thunder
        Doth rend the region; so, after Pyrrhus' pause,
        A rousèd vengeance sets him new awork,[2]
        And never did the Cyclops' hammers fall
430   On Mars's armor, forged for proof eterne,[3]

---

9. Adorned. *Total gules*: completely red.   1. Burning. *Impasted*: crusted.
2. Clotted. *O'er-sizèd*: glued over.   3. That is, Pyrrhus finds Priam.
4. Which he used when young.   5. Refractory.   6. Without feeling.   7. Falls.   8. About to fall.
9. Between his will and the fulfillment of it.   1. Clouds.   2. To work.
3. Mars, as befits a Roman war god, had armor made for him by the blacksmith god Vulcan and
his assistants, the Cyclopes. It was suitably impenetrable (of "proof eterne").

With less remorse than Pyrrhus' bleeding sword
Now falls on Priam.
Out, out, thou strumpet, Fortune! All you gods,
In general synod take away her power,
Break all the spokes and fellies[4] from her wheel,   435
And bowl the round nave[5] down the hill of heaven
As low as to the fiends."

POLONIUS: This is too long.

HAMLET: It shall to the barber's with your beard.—Prithee say on. He's for
a jig,[6] or a tale of bawdry, or he sleeps. Say on; come to Hecuba.[7]   440

FIRST PLAYER: "But who, ah woe! had seen the moblèd[8] queen—"

HAMLET: "The moblèd queen"?

POLONIUS: That's good. "Moblèd queen" is good.

FIRST PLAYER: "Run barefoot up and down, threat'ning the flames
With bisson rheum, a clout[9] upon that head   445
Where late the diadem stood, and for a robe,
About her lank and all o'er-teemèd loins,
A blanket, in the alarm of fear caught up—
Who this had seen, with tongue in venom steeped,
'Gainst Fortune's state[1] would treason have pronounced.   450
But if the gods themselves did see her then,
When she saw Pyrrhus make malicious sport
In mincing[2] with his sword her husband's limbs,
The instant burst of clamor that she made,
Unless things mortal move them not at all,   455
Would have made milch[3] the burning eyes of heaven,
And passion in the gods."

POLONIUS: Look whe'r[4] he has not turned his color, and has tears in's eyes.
Prithee no more.

HAMLET: 'Tis well. I'll have thee speak out the rest of this soon.—Good   460
my lord, will you see the players well bestowed?[5] Do you hear, let them
be well used, for they are the abstract[6] and brief chronicles of the time;
after your death you were better have a bad epitaph than their ill report
while you live.

POLONIUS: My lord, I will use them according to their desert.

---

4. Parts of the rim.   5. Hub. *Bowl*: roll.   6. A comic act.
7. Hecuba was the wife of Priam and queen of Troy. Her "loins" are described below as
"o'erteemèd" because of her unusual fertility. The number of her children varies in different
accounts, but twenty is a safe minimum.   8. Muffled (in a hood).
9. Cloth. *Bisson rheum*: blinding tears.   1. Government.   2. Cutting up.
3. Tearful (literally, milk-giving).   4. Whether.   5. Provided for.   6. Summary.

465 HAMLET: God's bodkin, man, much better. Use every man after his desert, and who shall 'scape whipping? Use them after your own honor and dignity. The less they deserve, the more merit is in your bounty. Take them in.

POLONIUS: Come, sirs.

HAMLET: Follow him, friends. We'll hear a play tomorrow.

[Aside to FIRST PLAYER.]

470 Dost thou hear me, old friend, can you play "The Murder of Gonzago"?

FIRST PLAYER: Ay, my lord.

HAMLET: We'll ha't tomorrow night. You could for a need study a speech of some dozen or sixteen lines which I would set down and insert in't, could you not?

FIRST PLAYER: Ay, my lord.

475 HAMLET: Very well. Follow that lord, and look you mock him not.

[Exeunt POLONIUS and PLAYERS.]

My good friends, I'll leave you till night. You are welcome to Elsinore.

ROSENCRANTZ: Good my lord.   [Exeunt ROSENCRANTZ and GUILDENSTERN.]

HAMLET: Ay, so God b'wi'ye. Now I am alone.

O, what a rogue and peasant slave am I!

480 Is it not monstrous that this player here,
But in a fiction, in a dream of passion,
Could force his soul so to his own conceit⁷
That from her working all his visage wanned;⁸
Tears in his eyes, distraction in his aspect⁹

485 A broken voice, and his whole function suiting
With forms to his conceit? And all for nothing,
For Hecuba!
What's Hecuba to him or he to Hecuba,
That he should weep for her? What would he do

490 Had he the motive and the cue for passion
That I have? He would drown the stage with tears,
And cleave the general ear with horrid speech,
Make mad the guilty, and appal the free,
Confound the ignorant, and amaze indeed

495 The very faculties of eyes and ears.
Yet I,
A dull and muddy-mettled rascal, peak¹
Like John-a-dreams, unpregnant² of my cause,

---

7. Imagination.   8. Grew pale.   9. Face.   1. Mope. *Muddy-mettled*: dull-spirited.
2. Not quickened by. *John-a-dreams*: a man dreaming.

And can say nothing; no, not for a king
Upon whose property and most dear life   500
A damned defeat was made. Am I a coward?
Who calls me villain, breaks my pate across,
Plucks off my beard and blows it in my face,
Tweaks me by the nose, gives me the lie i' th' throat
As deep as to the lungs? Who does me this?   505
Ha, 'swounds, I should take it; for it cannot be
But I am pigeon-livered and lack gall[3]
To make oppression bitter, or ere this
I should 'a fatted all the region kites[4]
With this slave's offal. Bloody, bawdy villain!   510
Remorseless, treacherous, lecherous, kindless[5] villain!
O, vengeance!
Why, what an ass am I! This is most brave,
That I, the son of a dear father murdered,
Prompted to my revenge by heaven and hell,   515
Must like a whore unpack[6] my heart with words,
And fall a-cursing like a very drab,
A scullion![7] Fie upon't! foh!
About, my brains. Hum—I have heard
That guilty creatures sitting at a play,   520
Have by the very cunning of the scene
Been struck so to the soul that presently
They have proclaimed[8] their malefactions;
For murder, though it have no tongue, will speak
With most miraculous organ. I'll have these players   525
Play something like the murder of my father
Before mine uncle. I'll observe his looks.
I'll tent him to the quick. If 'a do blench,[9]
I know my course. The spirit that I have seen
May be a devil, and the devil hath power   530
T' assume a pleasing shape, yea, and perhaps
Out of my weakness and my melancholy,
As he is very potent with such spirits,
Abuses me to damn me. I'll have grounds
More relative[1] than this. The play's the thing   535
Wherein I'll catch the conscience of the king.   [*Exit.*]

---

3. Bitterness. 4. Birds of prey of the area. 5. Unnatural. 6. Relieve.
7. In some versions of the play, the word "stallion," a slang term for prostitute, appears in place
of "scullion." 8. Admitted. 9. Turn pale. *Tent*: try. 1. Conclusive.

ACT III

Scene 1

A room in the castle. Enter KING, QUEEN, POLONIUS, OPHELIA, ROSEN-
CRANTZ *and* GUILDENSTERN.

KING: And can you by no drift of conference[2]
    Get from him why he puts on this confusion,
    Grating so harshly all his days of quiet
    With turbulent[3] and dangerous lunacy?
5 ROSENCRANTZ: He does confess he feels himself distracted,
    But from what cause 'a will by no means speak.
GUILDENSTERN: Nor do we find him forward to be sounded,[4]
    But with a crafty madness keeps aloof
    When we would bring him on to some confession
    Of his true state.
10 QUEEN: Did he receive you well?
ROSENCRANTZ: Most like a gentleman.
GUILDENSTERN: But with much forcing of his disposition.[5]
ROSENCRANTZ: Niggard of question, but of our demands[6]
    Most free in his reply.
QUEEN: Did you assay[7] him
15   To any pastime?
ROSENCRANTZ: Madam, it so fell out that certain players
    We o'er-raught[8] on the way. Of these we told him,
    And there did seem in him a kind of joy
    To hear of it. They are here about the court,
20   And as I think, they have already order
    This night to play before him.
POLONIUS: 'Tis most true,
    And he beseeched me to entreat your majesties
    To hear and see the matter.[9]
KING: With all my heart, and it doth much content me
25   To hear him so inclined.
    Good gentlemen, give him a further edge,
    And drive his purpose[1] into these delights.
ROSENCRANTZ: We shall, my lord. [*Exeunt* ROSENCRANTZ *and* GUILDENSTERN.]
KING: Sweet Gertrude, leave us too,

---

2. Line of conversation.   3. Disturbing.   4. Questioned. *Forward:* eager.   5. Mood.
6. To our questions.   7. Tempt.   8. Passed.   9. Performance.   1. Sharpen his intention.

For we have closely sent for Hamlet hither,
That he, as 'twere by accident, may here   30
Affront[2] Ophelia.
Her father and myself (lawful espials[3])
Will so bestow ourselves that, seeing unseen,
We may of their encounter frankly judge,
And gather by him, as he is behaved,   35
If 't be th' affliction of his love or no
That thus he suffers for.
QUEEN: I shall obey you.—
And for your part, Ophelia, I do wish
That your good beauties be the happy cause
Of Hamlet's wildness. So shall I hope your virtues   40
Will bring him to his wonted[4] way again,
To both your honors.
OPHELIA: Madam, I wish it may.   [*Exit* QUEEN.]
POLONIUS: Ophelia, walk you here.—Gracious,[5] so please you,
We will bestow ourselves.—[*To* OPHELIA.] Read on this book,
That show of such an exercise may color[6]   45
Your loneliness.—We are oft to blame in this,
'Tis too much proved, that with devotion's visage
And pious action we do sugar o'er
The devil himself.
KING: [*Aside.*]   O, 'tis too true.
How smart a lash that speech doth give my conscience!   50
The harlot's cheek, beautied with plast'ring[7] art,
Is not more ugly to the thing that helps it
Than is my deed to my most painted word.
O heavy burden!
POLONIUS: I hear him coming. Let's withdraw, my lord.   55
                              [*Exeunt* KING *and* POLONIUS.]

[*Enter* HAMLET.]

HAMLET: To be, or not to be, that is the question:
Whether 'tis nobler in the mind to suffer
The slings and arrows of outrageous fortune,
Or to take arms against a sea of troubles,
And by opposing end them. To die, to sleep—   60
No more; and by a sleep to say we end

2. Confront. 3. Justified spies. 4. Usual. 5. Majesty. 6. Explain. *Exercise*: act of devotion.
7. Thickly painted.

The heartache, and the thousand natural shocks
That flesh is heir to. 'Tis a consummation
Devoutly to be wished—to die, to sleep—
65   To sleep, perchance to dream, ay there's the rub;
For in that sleep of death what dreams may come
When we have shuffled off this mortal coil[8]
Must give us pause—there's the respect[9]
That makes calamity of so long life.
70   For who would bear the whips and scorns of time,
Th' oppressor's wrong, the proud man's contumely,[1]
The pangs of despised love, the law's delay,
The insolence of office, and the spurns[2]
That patient merit of th' unworthy takes,
75   When he himself might his quietus[3] make
With a bare bodkin? Who would fardels[4] bear,
To grunt and sweat under a weary life,
But that the dread of something after death,
The undiscovered country, from whose bourn[5]
80   No traveller returns, puzzles the will,
And makes us rather bear those ills we have
Than fly to others that we know not of?
Thus conscience does make cowards of us all;
And thus the native[6] hue of resolution
85   Is sicklied o'er with the pale cast of thought,
And enterprises of great pitch and moment[7]
With this regard their currents turn awry
And lose the name of action.—Soft you now,
The fair Ophelia.—Nymph, in thy orisons[8]
Be all my sins remembered.
90   OPHELIA: Good my lord,
How does your honor for this many a day?
HAMLET: I humbly thank you, well, well, well.
OPHELIA: My lord, I have remembrances of yours
That I have longèd long to re-deliver.
I pray you now receive them.
95   HAMLET: No, not I,
I never gave you aught.
OPHELIA: My honored lord, you know right well you did,

---

8. Turmoil.   9. Consideration.   1. Insulting behavior.   2. Rejections.   3. Settlement.
4. Burdens. *Bodkin:* dagger.   5. Boundary.   6. Natural.   7. Importance. *Pitch:* height.
8. Prayers.

And with them words of so sweet breath composed
As made the things more rich. Their perfume lost,
Take these again, for to the noble mind   100
Rich gifts wax[9] poor when givers prove unkind.
There, my lord.

HAMLET: Ha, ha! are you honest?[1]

OPHELIA: My lord?

HAMLET: Are you fair?   105

OPHELIA: What means your lordship?

HAMLET: That if you be honest and fair, your honesty should admit no
discourse to your beauty.

OPHELIA: Could beauty, my lord, have better commerce[2] than with honesty?

HAMLET: Ay, truly, for the power of beauty will sooner transform honesty   110
from what it is to a bawd than the force of honesty can translate beauty
into his likeness. This was sometimes a paradox, but now the time
gives it proof. I did love you once.

OPHELIA: Indeed, my lord, you made me believe so.

HAMLET: You should not have believed me, for virtue cannot so inoculate[3] 115
our old stock but we shall relish of it. I loved you not.

OPHELIA: I was the more deceived.

HAMLET: Get thee to a nunnery.[4] Why wouldst thou be a breeder of sinners? I am myself indifferent[5] honest, but yet I could accuse me of such
things that it were better my mother had not borne me: I am very proud, 120
revengeful, ambitious, with more offences at my beck[6] than I have
thoughts to put them in, imagination to give them shape, or time to act
them in. What should such fellows as I do crawling between earth and
heaven? We are arrant[7] knaves all; believe none of us. Go thy ways to a
nunnery. Where's your father?   125

OPHELIA: At home, my lord.

HAMLET: Let the doors be shut upon him, that he may play the fool
nowhere but in's own house. Farewell.

OPHELIA: O, help him, you sweet heavens!

HAMLET: If thou dost marry, I'll give thee this plague for thy dowry: be   130
thou as chaste as ice, as pure as snow, thou shalt not escape calumny.
Get thee to a nunnery, farewell. Or if thou wilt needs marry, marry a
fool, for wise men know well enough what monsters[8] you make of
them. To a nunnery, go, and quickly too. Farewell.

OPHELIA: Heavenly powers, restore him!   135

---

9. Become.   1. Chaste.   2. Intercourse.   3. Change by grafting.
4. Hamlet uses "nunnery" in two senses, the second as a slang term for brothel.   5. Moderately.
6. Command.   7. Thorough.   8. Horned because cuckolded.

HAMLET: I have heard of your paintings, too, well enough. God hath given you one face, and you make yourselves another. You jig, you amble, and you lisp;[9] you nickname God's creatures, and make your wantonness your ignorance.[1] Go to, I'll no more on't, it hath made me mad. I say we
140 will have no more marriage. Those that are married already, all but one, shall live. The rest shall keep as they are. To a nunnery, go.   [*Exit.*]

OPHELIA: O, what a noble mind is here o'erthrown!
The courtier's, soldier's, scholar's, eye, tongue, sword,
Th' expectancy and rose[2] of the fair state,
145 The glass of fashion and the mould[3] of form,
Th' observed of all observers, quite quite down!
And I of ladies most deject and wretched,
That sucked the honey of his music[4] vows,
Now see that noble and most sovereign reason
150 Like sweet bells jangled, out of time and harsh;
That unmatched form and feature of blown[5] youth
Blasted with ecstasy. O, woe is me
T' have seen what I have seen, see what I see!

[*Enter* KING *and* POLONIUS.]

KING: Love! His affections do not that way tend,
155 Nor what he spake, though it lacked form a little,
Was not like madness. There's something in his soul
O'er which his melancholy sits on brood,[6]
And I do doubt the hatch and the disclose[7]
Will be some danger; which to prevent,
160 I have in quick determination
Thus set it down: he shall with speed to England
For the demand of our neglected tribute.
Haply the seas and countries different,
With variable objects, shall expel
165 This something-settled matter in his heart
Whereon his brains still beating puts him thus
From fashion of himself. What think you on't?

POLONIUS: It shall do well. But yet do I believe
The origin and commencement of his grief
170 Sprung from neglected love.—How now, Ophelia?
You need not tell us what Lord Hamlet said,

---

9. Walk and talk affectedly.
1. Hamlet means that women call things by pet names and then blame the affectation on ignorance.   2. Ornament. *Expectancy*: hope.   3. Model. *Glass*: mirror.   4. Musical.
5. Full-blown.   6. That is, like a hen.   7. Result. *Doubt*: fear.

We heard it all.—My lord, do as you please,
But if you hold it fit, after the play
Let his queen-mother all alone entreat him
To show his grief. Let her be round[8] with him,   175
And I'll be placed, so please you, in the ear[9]
Of all their conference. If she find him not,[1]
To England send him; or confine him where
Your wisdom best shall think.
KING: It shall be so.
Madness in great ones must not unwatched go.   [*Exeunt.*]   180

Scene 2

A public room in the castle. Enter HAMLET *and three of the* PLAYERS.

HAMLET: Speak the speech, I pray you, as I pronounced it to you, trippingly
on the tongue; but if you mouth it as many of our players do, I had as lief
the town-crier spoke my lines. Nor do not saw the air too much with your
hand thus, but use all gently, for in the very torrent, tempest, and as I may
say, whirlwind of your passion, you must acquire and beget a temperance   5
that may give it smoothness. O, it offends me to the soul to hear a robustious periwig-pated[2] fellow tear a passion to tatters, to very rags, to split
the ears of the groundlings, who for the most part are capable of[3] nothing
but inexplicable dumb shows and noise. I would have such a fellow
whipped for o'erdoing Termagant. It out-herods Herod.[4] Pray you avoid it.   10
FIRST PLAYER: I warrant your honor.
HAMLET: Be not too tame neither, but let your own discretion be your
tutor. Suit the action to the word, the word to the action, with this special observance, that you o'erstep not the modesty of nature; for anything so o'erdone is from[5] the purpose of playing, whose end both at   15
the first, and now, was and is, to hold as 'twere the mirror up to nature,
to show virtue her own feature, scorn her own image, and the very age
and body of the time his form and pressure.[6] Now this overdone, or
come tardy off, though it makes the unskilful[7] laugh, cannot but make
the judicious grieve, the censure[8] of the which one must in your allow-   20
ance o'erweigh a whole theatre of others. O, there be players that I have

---

8. Direct.   9. Hearing.   1. Does not discover his problem.   2. Bewigged. *Robustious*: noisy.
3. That is, capable of understanding. *Groundlings*: the spectators who paid least and had to stand.
4. Termagant, a "Saracen" deity, and the biblical Herod were stock characters in popular drama
noted for the excesses of sound and fury used by their interpreters.   5. Contrary to.
6. Shape.   7. Ignorant.   8. Judgment.

seen play—and heard others praise, and that highly—not to speak it profanely, that neither having th' accent of Christians, nor the gait of Christian, pagan, nor man, have so strutted and bellowed that I have
25   thought some of nature's journeymen[9] had made men, and not made them well, they imitated humanity so abominably.

FIRST PLAYER: I hope we have reformed that indifferently[1] with us, sir.

HAMLET: O, reform it altogether. And let those that play your clowns speak no more than is set down for them, for there be of them that will them-
30   selves laugh, to set on some quantity of barren[2] spectators to laugh too, though in the meantime some necessary question of the play be then to be considered. That's villainous, and shows a most pitiful ambition in the fool that uses it. Go, make you ready.   [*Exeunt* PLAYERS.]

[*Enter* POLONIUS, GUILDENSTERN, *and* ROSENCRANTZ.]

How now, my lord? Will the king hear this piece of work?
35 POLONIUS: And the queen too, and that presently.

HAMLET: Bid the players make haste.   [*Exit* POLONIUS.]
Will you two help to hasten them?

ROSENCRANTZ: Ay, my lord.   [*Exeunt they two.*]

HAMLET: What, ho, Horatio!

[*Enter* HORATIO.]

40 HORATIO: Here, sweet lord, at your service.

HAMLET: Horatio, thou art e'en as just a man
As e'er my conversation coped[3] withal.

HORATIO: O my dear lord!

HAMLET: Nay, do not think I flatter,
For what advancement may I hope from thee,
45   That no revenue hast but thy good spirits
To feed and clothe thee? Why should the poor be flattered?
No, let the candied tongue lick absurd pomp,
And crook the pregnant[4] hinges of the knee
Where thrift[5] may follow fawning. Dost thou hear?
50   Since my dear soul was mistress of her choice
And could of men distinguish her election,
S'hath sealed thee for herself, for thou hast been
As one in suff'ring all that suffers nothing,
A man that Fortune's buffets and rewards
55   Hast ta'en with equal thanks; and blest are those
Whose blood and judgment are so well commingled

---

9. Inferior craftsmen. 1. Somewhat. 2. Dullwitted. 3. Encountered. 4. Quick to bend.
5. Profit.

That they are not a pipe[6] for Fortune's finger
To sound what stop[7] she please. Give me that man
That is not passion's slave, and I will wear him
In my heart's core, ay, in my heart of heart,   60
As I do thee. Something too much of this.
There is a play tonight before the king.
One scene of it comes near the circumstance
Which I have told thee of my father's death.
I prithee, when thou seest that act afoot,   65
Even with the very comment[8] of thy soul
Observe my uncle. If his occulted[9] guilt
Do not itself unkennel[1] in one speech,
It is a damnèd ghost that we have seen,
And my imaginations are as foul   70
As Vulcan's stithy. Give him heedful note,[2]
For I mine eyes will rivet to his face,
And after we will both our judgments join
In censure of his seeming.[3]
HORATIO: Well, my lord.
If 'a steal aught the whilst this play in playing,   75
And 'scape detecting, I will pay[4] the theft.

[*Enter Trumpets and Kettledrums,* KING, QUEEN, POLONIUS, OPHELIA,
ROSENCRANTZ, GUILDENSTERN, *and other* LORDS *attendant.*]

HAMLET: They are coming to the play. I must be idle.
    Get you a place.
KING: How fares our cousin Hamlet?
HAMLET: Excellent, i' faith, of the chameleon's dish. I eat the air, promise
    crammed. You cannot feed capons[5] so.   80
KING: I have nothing with this answer, Hamlet. These words are not mine.
HAMLET: No, nor mine now. [*To* POLONIUS.] My lord, you played once i' th'
    university, you say?
POLONIUS: That did I, my lord, and was accounted a good actor.
HAMLET: What did you enact?   85
POLONIUS: I did enact Julius Cæsar. I was killed i' th' Capitol; Brutus
    killed me.[6]

6. Musical instrument.   7. Note. *Sound:* play.   8. Keenest observation.   9. Hidden.
1. Break loose.   2. Careful attention. *Stithy:* smithy.   3. Manner.   4. Repay.
5. Castrated male chickens fattened for slaughter; also a term for fool. *Chameleon's dish:* reference to a popular belief that the chameleon subsisted on a diet of air. Hamlet has deliberately misunderstood the king's question.
6. Julius Caesar's assassination by Brutus and others is the subject of another play by Shakespeare.

HAMLET: It was a brute part of him to kill so capital a calf there. Be the players ready?

90 ROSENCRANTZ: Ay, my lord, they stay upon your patience.[7]

QUEEN: Come hither, my dear Hamlet, sit by me.

HAMLET: No, good mother, here's metal more attractive.

POLONIUS: [To the KING.] O, ho! do you mark that?

HAMLET: Lady, shall I lie in your lap?

[Lying down at OPHELIA's feet.]

95 OPHELIA: No, my lord.

HAMLET: I mean, my head upon your lap?

OPHELIA: Ay, my lord.

HAMLET: Do you think I meant country matters?[8]

OPHELIA: I think nothing, my lord.

100 HAMLET: That's a fair thought to lie between maids' legs.

OPHELIA: What is, my lord?

HAMLET: Nothing.

OPHELIA: You are merry, my lord.

HAMLET: Who, I?

105 OPHELIA: Ay, my lord.

HAMLET: O God, your only jig-maker![9] What should a man do but be merry? For look you how cheerfully my mother looks, and my father died within's two hours.

OPHELIA: Nay, 'tis twice two months, my lord.

110 HAMLET: So long? Nay then, let the devil wear black, for I'll have a suit of sables. O heavens! die two months ago, and not forgotten yet? Then there's hope a great man's memory may outlive his life half a year, but by'r lady 'a must build churches then, or else shall 'a suffer not thinking on, with the hobby-horse, whose epitaph is "For O, for O, the hobby-horse is forgot!"[1]

The trumpets sound. Dumb Show follows. Enter a KING *and a* QUEEN *very lovingly; the* QUEEN *embracing him and he her. She kneels, and makes show of protestation unto him. He takes her up, and declines[2] his head upon her neck. He lies him down upon a bank of flowers; she, seeing him asleep, leaves him. Anon come in another man, takes off his crown, kisses it, pours poison in the sleeper's ears, and leaves him. The*

7. Leisure. *Stay:* wait.

8. Presumably, rustic misbehavior, but here and elsewhere in this exchange Hamlet treats Ophelia to some ribald double meanings.   9. Writer of comic scenes.

1. In traditional games and dances one of the characters was a man represented as riding a horse. The horse was made of something like cardboard and was worn about the "rider's" waist.

2. Lays.

QUEEN *returns, finds the* KING *dead, makes passionate action. The* POI-
SONER *with some three or four come in again, seem to condole with her.
The dead body is carried away. The* POISONER *woos the* QUEEN *with
gifts; she seems harsh awhile, but in the end accepts love.* [*Exeunt.*]

OPHELIA: What means this, my lord? 115
HAMLET: Marry, this is miching mallecho;[3] it means mischief.
OPHELIA: Belike this show imports the argument[4] of the play.

[*Enter* PROLOGUE.]

HAMLET: We shall know by this fellow. The players cannot keep counsel;
they'll tell all.
OPHELIA: Will 'a tell us what this show meant? 120
HAMLET: Ay, or any show that you will show him. Be not you ashamed to
show, he'll not shame to tell you what it means.
OPHELIA: You are naught, you are naught. I'll mark[5] the play.
PROLOGUE: *For us, and for our tragedy,*
Here stooping to your clemency, 125
We beg your hearing patiently. [*Exit.*]

HAMLET: Is this a prologue, or the posy[6] of a ring?
OPHELIA: 'Tis brief, my lord.
HAMLET: As woman's love.

[*Enter the* PLAYER KING *and* QUEEN.]

PLAYER KING: *Full thirty times hath Phœbus' cart gone round* 130
Neptune's salt wash and Tellus' orbèd ground,
And thirty dozen moons with borrowed sheen[7]
About the world have times twelve thirties been,
Since love our hearts and Hymen did our hands
Unite comutual in most sacred bands.[8] 135
PLAYER QUEEN: *So many journeys may the sun and moon*
Make us again count o'er ere love be done!
But woe is me, you are so sick of late,
So far from cheer and from your former state,
That I distrust[9] you. Yet though I distrust, 140

---

3. Sneaking crime (from the Spanish *malhecho*, "evil deed").
4. Plot. *Imports*: explains.   5. Attend to. *Naught*: obscene.   6. Motto engraved inside.
7. Light.
8. The speech contains several references to Greek mythology. Phoebus was the sun god, and
his chariot or "cart" is the sun. The "salt wash" of Neptune is the ocean; Tellus was an earth
goddess, and her "orbed ground" is the Earth, or globe. Hymen was the god of marriage. *Comutual*: mutually.   9. Fear for.

Discomfort you, my lord, it nothing must.
For women's fear and love hold quantity,[1]
In neither aught, or in extremity.[2]
Now what my love is proof hath made you know,
145   And as my love is sized,[3] my fear is so.
Where love is great, the littlest doubts are fear;
Where little fears grow great, great love grows there.

PLAYER KING: Faith, I must leave thee, love, and shortly too;
My operant powers their functions leave[4] to do.
150   And thou shalt live in this fair world behind,
Honored, beloved, and haply one as kind
For husband shalt thou—

PLAYER QUEEN: O, confound the rest!
Such love must needs be treason in my breast.
In second husband let me be accurst!
155   None wed the second but who killed the first.[5]

HAMLET: That's wormwood.[6]

PLAYER QUEEN: The instances[7] that second marriage move
Are base respects[8] of thrift, but none of love.
A second time I kill my husband dead,
160   When second husband kisses me in bed.

PLAYER KING: I do believe you think what now you speak,
But what we do determine oft we break.
Purpose is but the slave to memory,
Of violent birth, but poor validity;
165   Which now, like fruit unripe, sticks on the tree,
But fall unshaken when they mellow be.
Most necessary 'tis that we forget
To pay ourselves what to ourselves is debt.
What to ourselves in passion we propose,
170   The passion ending, doth the purpose lose.
The violence of either grief or joy
Their own enactures[9] with themselves destroy.
Where joy most revels, grief doth most lament;
Grief joys, joy grieves, on slender accident.
175   This world is not for aye,[1] nor 'tis not strange
That even our loves should with our fortunes change;
For 'tis a question left us yet to prove,

1. Agree in weight.   2. Without regard to too much or too little.   3. In size.
4. Cease. *Operant powers:* active forces.
5. Though there is some ambiguity, she seems to mean that the only kind of woman who would remarry is one who has killed or would kill her first husband.   6. Bitter medicine.   7. Causes.
8. Concerns.   9. Actions.   1. Eternal.

Whether love lead fortune, or else fortune love.
The great man down, you mark his favorite flies;
The poor advanced makes friends of enemies;   180
And hitherto doth love on fortune tend,
For who not needs shall never lack a friend,
And who in want a hollow[2] friend doth try,
Directly seasons him[3] his enemy.
But orderly to end where I begun,   185
Our wills and fates do so contrary run
That our devices[4] still are overthrown;
Our thoughts are ours, their ends none of our own.
So think thou wilt no second husband wed,
But die thy thoughts when thy first lord is dead.   190

PLAYER QUEEN: *Nor earth to me give food, nor heaven light,*
Sport and repose lock from me day and night,
To desperation turn my trust and hope,
An anchor's cheer[5] in prison be my scope,
Each opposite that blanks[6] the face of joy   195
Meet what I would have well, and it destroy,
Both here and hence[7] pursue me lasting strife,
If once a widow, ever I be wife!

HAMLET: If she should break it now!

PLAYER KING: 'Tis deeply sworn. Sweet, leave me here awhile.   200
My spirits grow dull, and fain I would beguile
The tedious day with sleep.   [*Sleeps.*]

PLAYER QUEEN: *Sleep rock thy brain,*
And never come mischance between us twain!   [*Exit.*]

HAMLET: Madam, how like you this play?

QUEEN: The lady doth protest too much, methinks.   205

HAMLET: O, but she'll keep her word.

KING: Have you heard the argument? Is there no offence in't?

HAMLET: No, no, they do but jest, poison in jest; no offence i' th' world.

KING: What do you call the play?

HAMLET: "The Mouse-trap." Marry, how? Tropically.[8] This play is the image   210
of a murder done in Vienna. Gonzago is the duke's name; his wife, Bap-
tista. You shall see anon. 'Tis a knavish piece of work, but what of that?
Your majesty, and we that have free souls, it touches us not. Let the galled
jade wince, our withers are unwrung.[9]

---

2. False.   3. Ripens him into.   4. Plans.   5. Anchorite's (hermit's) food.   6. Blanches.
7. In the next world.   8. Figuratively.
9. A "galled jade" is a horse, particularly one of poor quality, with a sore back. The "withers" are
the ridge between a horse's shoulders; "unwrung withers" are not chafed by the harness.

[*Enter* LUCIANUS.]

215   This is one Lucianus, nephew to the king.

OPHELIA: You are as good as a chorus, my lord.

HAMLET: I could interpret between you and your love, if I could see the
puppets dallying.

OPHELIA: You are keen, my lord, you are keen.

220 HAMLET: It would cost you a groaning to take off mine edge.

OPHELIA: Still better, and worse.

HAMLET: So you mistake your husbands.—Begin, murderer. Leave thy dam-
nable faces and begin. Come, the croaking raven doth bellow for revenge.

LUCIANUS: *Thoughts black, hands apt, drugs fit, and time agreeing,*
225   *Confederate season,*[1] *else no creature seeing,*
        Thou mixture rank, of midnight weeds collected,
        With Hecate's ban thrice blasted, thrice infected,[2]
        Thy natural magic[3] *and dire property*
        On wholesome life usurp immediately.   [Pours the poison in his ears.]

230 HAMLET: 'A poisons him i' th' garden for his estate. His name's Gonzago.
The story is extant, and written in very choice Italian. You shall see
anon how the murderer gets the love of Gonzago's wife.

OPHELIA: The king rises.

HAMLET: What, frighted with false fire?

235 QUEEN: How fares my lord?

POLONIUS: Give o'er the play.

KING: Give me some light. Away!

POLONIUS: Lights, lights, lights!   [*Exeunt all but* HAMLET *and* HORATIO.]

HAMLET:

        Why, let the strucken deer go weep,
240   The hart ungallèd[4] play.
        For some must watch while some must sleep;
            Thus runs the world away.

Would not this, sir, and a forest of feathers[5]—if the rest of my fortunes
turn Turk with me—with two Provincial roses on my razed shoes, get
245 me a fellowship in a cry of players?[6]

HORATIO: Half a share.

---

1. A helpful time for the crime.   2. Hecate was a classical goddess of witchcraft.
3. Native power.   4. Uninjured.   5. Plumes.
6. Hamlet asks Horatio if "this" recitation, accompanied with a player's costume, including
plumes and rosettes on shoes that have been slashed for decorative effect, might not entitle
him to become a shareholder in a theatrical company in the event that Fortune goes against
him ("turn Turk"). *Cry:* company.

HAMLET: A whole one, I.

> For thou dost know, O Damon dear,[7]
>> This realm dismantled was
>> Of Jove himself, and now reigns here   250
>> A very, very—peacock.

HORATIO: You might have rhymed.

HAMLET: O good Horatio, I'll take the ghost's word for a thousand pound. Didst perceive?

HORATIO: Very well, my lord.   255

HAMLET: Upon the talk of the poisoning.

HORATIO: I did very well note[8] him.

HAMLET: Ah, ha! Come, some music. Come, the recorders.[9]

> For if the king like not the comedy.
> Why then, belike he likes it not, perdy.[1]   260

Come, some music.

[*Enter* ROSENCRANTZ *and* GUILDENSTERN.]

GUILDENSTERN: Good my lord, vouchsafe me a word with you.

HAMLET: Sir, a whole history.

GUILDENSTERN: The king, sir—

HAMLET: Ay, sir, what of him?   265

GUILDENSTERN: Is in his retirement marvellous distempered.[2]

HAMLET: With drink, sir?

GUILDENSTERN: No, my lord, with choler.[3]

HAMLET: Your wisdom should show itself more richer to signify this to the doctor, for for me to put him to his purgation[4] would perhaps plunge   270 him into more choler.

GUILDENSTERN: Good my lord, put your discourse into some frame,[5] and start not so wildly from my affair.

HAMLET: I am tame, sir. Pronounce.

GUILDENSTERN: The queen your mother, in most great affliction of spirit,   275 hath sent me to you.

HAMLET: You are welcome.

GUILDENSTERN: Nay, good my lord, this courtesy is not of the right breed. If it shall please you to make me a wholesome[6] answer, I will do your

---

7. Damon was a common name for a young man or a shepherd in pastoral poetry. Jove was the chief god of the Romans. Readers may supply for themselves the rhyme referred to by Horatio.
8. Observe.   9. Wooden, end-blown flutes.   1. That is, *par Dieu* (French for "by God").
2. Vexed. *Retirement*: place to which he has retired.   3. Bile (anger).
4. Treatment with a laxative.   5. Order. *Discourse*: speech.   6. Reasonable.

280   mother's commandment. If not, your pardon and my return[7] shall be
the end of my business.

HAMLET: Sir, I cannot.

ROSENCRANTZ: What, my lord?

HAMLET: Make you a wholesome answer; my wit's diseased. But, sir, such
285   answer as I can make, you shall command, or rather, as you say, my
mother. Therefore no more, but to the matter. My mother, you say—

ROSENCRANTZ: Then thus she says: your behavior hath struck her into
amazement and admiration.[8]

HAMLET: O wonderful son, that can so stonish a mother! But is there no
290   sequel at the heels of his mother's admiration? Impart.[9]

ROSENCRANTZ: She desires to speak with you in her closet[1] ere you go to
bed.

HAMLET: We shall obey, were she ten times our mother. Have you any
further trade[2] with us?

295   ROSENCRANTZ: My lord, you once did love me.

HAMLET: And do still, by these pickers and stealers.[3]

ROSENCRANTZ: Good my lord, what is your cause of distemper? You do
surely bar the door upon your own liberty, if you deny your griefs to
your friend.

HAMLET: Sir, I lack advancement.

300   ROSENCRANTZ: How can that be, when you have the voice of the king
himself for your succession in Denmark?

HAMLET: Ay, sir, but "while the grass grows"—the proverb[4] is something
musty.

[Enter the PLAYERS with recorders.]

O, the recorders! Let me see one. To withdraw with you[5]—why do you
305   go about to recover the wind of me, as if you would drive me into a toil?[6]

GUILDENSTERN: O my lord, if my duty be too bold, my love is too
unmannerly.

HAMLET: I do not well understand that. Will you play upon this pipe?[7]

GUILDENSTERN: My lord, I cannot.

310   HAMLET: I pray you.

GUILDENSTERN: Believe me, I cannot.

HAMLET: I do beseech you.

GUILDENSTERN: I know no touch of it,[8] my lord.

---

7. That is, to the queen.   8. Wonder.   9. Tell me.   1. Bedroom.   2. Business.   3. Hands.
4. The proverb ends "the horse starves."   5. Let me step aside.
6. The simile refers to hunting. Hamlet asks why Guildenstern is attempting to get windward of
him, as if he would drive him into a net.   7. Recorder.   8. Have no ability.

HAMLET: It is as easy as lying. Govern these ventages[9] with your fingers and thumb, give it breath with your mouth, and it will discourse most   315
eloquent music. Look you, these are the stops.[1]

GUILDENSTERN: But these cannot I command to any utt'rance of harmony. I have not the skill.

HAMLET: Why, look you now, how unworthy a thing you make of me! You would play upon me, you would seem to know my stops, you would   320
pluck out the heart of my mystery, you would sound[2] me from my lowest note to the top of my compass;[3] and there is much music, excellent voice, in this little organ, yet cannot you make it speak. 'Sblood, do you think I am easier to be played on than a pipe? Call me what instrument you will, though you can fret[4] me, you cannot play upon me.   325

[*Enter* POLONIUS.]

God bless you, sir!

POLONIUS: My lord, the queen would speak with you, and presently.[5]

HAMLET: Do you see yonder cloud that's almost in shape of a camel?

POLONIUS: By th' mass, and 'tis like a camel indeed.

HAMLET: Methinks it is like a weasel.   330

POLONIUS: It is backed like a weasel.

HAMLET: Or like a whale.

POLONIUS: Very like a whale.

HAMLET: Then I will come to my mother by and by. [*Aside.*] They fool me to the top of my bent.[6]—I will come by and by.   335

POLONIUS: I will say so.   [*Exit.*]

HAMLET: "By and by" is easily said. Leave me, friends.   [*Exeunt all but* HAMLET.]

   'Tis now the very witching time of night,
When churchyards yawn, and hell itself breathes out
Contagion to this world. Now could I drink hot blood,   340
And do such bitter business as the day
Would quake to look on. Soft, now to my mother.
O heart, lose not thy nature; let not ever
The soul of Nero[7] enter this firm bosom.
Let me be cruel, not unnatural;   345
I will speak daggers to her, but use none.
My tongue and soul in this be hypocrites—

9. Holes. *Govern:* cover and uncover.   1. Windholes.   2. Play.   3. Range.
4. "Fret" is used in a double sense, to annoy and to play a guitar or similar instrument using the "frets" or small bars on the neck.   5. At once.   6. Treat me as an utter fool.
7. The Roman emperor Nero, known for his excesses, was believed responsible for the death of his mother.

How in my words somever she be shent,[8]
To give them seals[9] never, my soul, consent!   [Exit.]

Scene 3

A room in the castle. Enter KING, ROSENCRANTZ, *and* GUILDENSTERN.

KING: I like him not,[1] nor stands it safe with us
   To let his madness range.[2] Therefore prepare you.
   I your commission will forthwith dispatch,
   And he to England shall along with you.
5   The terms of our estate[3] may not endure
   Hazard so near's as doth hourly grow
   Out of his brows.
GUILDENSTERN: We will ourselves provide,[4]
   Most holy and religious fear it is
   To keep those many many bodies safe
10   That live and feed upon your majesty.
ROSENCRANTZ: The single and peculiar[5] life is bound
   With all the strength and armor of the mind
   To keep itself from noyance,[6] but much more
   That spirit upon whose weal[7] depends and rests
15   The lives of many. The cess[8] of majesty
   Dies not alone, but like a gulf[9] doth draw
   What's near it with it. It is a massy[1] wheel
   Fixed on the summit of the highest mount,
   To whose huge spokes ten thousand lesser things
20   Are mortised and adjoined,[2] which when it falls,
   Each small annexment, petty consequence,
   Attends[3] the boist'rous ruin. Never alone
   Did the king sigh, but with a general groan.
KING: Arm you, I pray you, to this speedy voyage,
25   For we will fetters put about this fear,
   Which now goes too free-footed.
ROSENCRANTZ: We will haste us.
            [*Exeunt* ROSENCRANTZ *and* GUILDENSTERN.]

[*Enter* POLONIUS.]

POLONIUS: My lord, he's going to his mother's closet.

8. Shamed.   9. Fulfillment in action.   1. Distrust him.   2. Roam freely.
3. Condition of the state.   4. Equip (for the journey).   5. Individual.   6. Harm.   7. Welfare.
8. Cessation.   9. Whirlpool.   1. Massive.   2. Attached.   3. Joins in.

Behind the arras I'll convey[4] myself
To hear the process. I'll warrant she'll tax him home,[5]
And as you said, and wisely was it said,   30
'Tis meet that some more audience than a mother,
Since nature makes them partial, should o'erhear
The speech, of vantage.[6] Fare you well, my liege.
I'll call upon you ere you go to bed,
And tell you what I know.

KING: Thanks, dear my lord. [*Exit* POLONIUS.]   35
O, my offence is rank, it smells to heaven;
It hath the primal eldest curse[7] upon't,
A brother's murder. Pray can I not,
Though inclination be as sharp as will.
My stronger guilt defeats my strong intent,   40
And like a man to double business[8] bound,
I stand in pause where I shall first begin,
And both neglect. What if this cursèd hand
Were thicker than itself with brother's blood,
Is there not rain enough in the sweet heavens   45
To wash it white as snow? Whereto serves mercy
But to confront the visage of offence?
And what's in prayer but this twofold force,
To be forestallèd[9] ere we come to fall,
Or pardoned being down?[1] Then I'll look up.   50
My fault is past, But, O, what form of prayer
Can serve my turn? "Forgive me my foul murder"?
That cannot be, since I am still possessed
Of those effects[2] for which I did the murder—
My crown, mine own ambition, and my queen.   55
May one be pardoned and retain th' offence?[3]
In the corrupted currents of this world
Offence's gilded[4] hand may shove by justice,
And oft 'tis seen the wicked prize itself
Buys out the law. But 'tis not so above.   60
There is no shuffling; there the action[5] lies
In his true nature, and we ourselves compelled,
Even to the teeth and forehead of[6] our faults,
To give in evidence. What then? What rests?[7]

4. Station.   5. Sharply. *Process*: proceedings.   6. From a position of vantage.   7. That is, of Cain.
8. Two mutually opposed interests.   9. Prevented (from sin).   1. Having sinned.   2. Gains.
3. That is, benefits of the offense.   4. Bearing gold as a bribe.   5. Case at law.
6. Face-to-face with.   7. Remains.

65   Try what repentance can. What can it not?
      Yet what can it when one cannot repent?
      O wretched state! O bosom black as death!
      O limèd[8] soul, that struggling to be free
      Art more engaged! Help, angels! Make assay.
70   Bow, stubborn knees, and heart with strings of steel,
      Be soft as sinews of the new-born babe.
      All may be well.   [*He kneels.*]

      [*Enter* HAMLET.]

HAMLET: Now might I do it pat,[9] now 'a is a-praying,
      And now I'll do't—and so 'a goes to heaven,
75   And so am I revenged. That would be scanned.[1]
      A villain kills my father, and for that,
      I, his sole son, do this same villain send
      To heaven.
      Why, this is hire and salary, not revenge.
80   'A took my father grossly, full of bread,[2]
      With all his crimes broad blown, as flush[3] as May;
      And how his audit stands who knows save heaven?
      But in our circumstance and course of thought
      'Tis heavy with him; and am I then revenged
85   To take him in the purging of his soul,
      When he is fit and seasoned[4] for his passage?
      No.
      Up, sword, and know thou a more horrid hent.[5]
      When he is drunk, asleep, or in his rage,
90   Or in th' incestuous pleasure of his bed,
      At game a-swearing, or about some act
      That has no relish[6] of salvation in't—
      Then trip him, that his heels may kick at heaven,
      And that his soul may be as damned and black
95   As hell, whereto it goes. My mother stays.
      This physic[7] but prolongs thy sickly days.   [*Exit.*]
KING: [*Rising.*] My words fly up, my thoughts remain below.
      Words without thoughts never to heaven go.   [*Exit.*]

---

8. Caught as with birdlime.   9. Easily.   1. Deserves consideration.
2. In a state of sin and without fasting.   3. Vigorous. *Broad blown*: full blown.   4. Ready.
5. Opportunity.   6. Flavor.   7. Medicine.

Scene 4

The Queen's chamber. Enter QUEEN *and* POLONIUS.

POLONIUS: 'A will come straight. Look you lay home to[8] him.
Tell him his pranks have been too broad[9] to bear with,
And that your grace hath screen'd[1] and stood between
Much heat and him. I'll silence me even here.
Pray you be round with him.   5
HAMLET: [*Within.*] Mother, mother, mother!
QUEEN: I'll warrant you. Fear[2] me not.
Withdraw, I hear him coming.

[POLONIUS *goes behind the arras. Enter* HAMLET.]

HAMLET: Now, mother, what's the matter?
QUEEN: Hamlet, thou hast thy father much offended.   10
HAMLET: Mother, you have my father much offended.
QUEEN: Come, come, you answer with an idle tongue.
HAMLET: Go, go, you question with a wicked tongue.
QUEEN: Why, how now, Hamlet?
HAMLET: What's the matter now?
QUEEN: Have you forgot me?
HAMLET: No, by the rood,[3] not so.   15
You are the queen, your husband's brother's wife,
And would it were not so, you are my mother.
QUEEN: Nay, then I'll set those to you that can speak.
HAMLET: Come, come, and sit you down. You shall not budge.
You go not till I set you up a glass[4]   20
Where you may see the inmost part of you.
QUEEN: What wilt thou do? Thou wilt not murder me?
Help, ho!
POLONIUS: [*Behind.*] What, ho! help!
HAMLET: [*Draws.*] How now, a rat?   25
Dead for a ducat, dead!

[*Kills* POLONIUS *with a pass through the arras.*]

POLONIUS: [*Behind.*] O, I am slain!
QUEEN: O me, what hast thou done?
HAMLET: Nay, I know not.
Is it the king?

8. Be sharp with.   9. Outrageous.   1. Acted as a fire screen.   2. Doubt.   3. Cross.   4. Mirror.

30   QUEEN: O, what a rash and bloody deed is this!
   HAMLET: A bloody deed!—almost as bad, good mother,
       As kill a king and marry with his brother.
   QUEEN: As kill a king?
   HAMLET: Ay, lady, it was my word.   [*Parting the arras.*]
       Thou wretched, rash, intruding fool, farewell!
35   I took thee for thy better. Take thy fortune.
       Thou find'st to be too busy[5] is some danger.—
       Leave wringing of your hands. Peace, sit you down
       And let me wring your heart, for so I shall
       If it be made of penetrable stuff,
40   If damnèd custom have not brazed it[6] so
       That it be proof and bulwark against sense.[7]
   QUEEN: What have I done that thou dar'st wag thy tongue
       In noise so rude against me?
   HAMLET: Such an act
       That blurs the grace and blush of modesty,
45   Calls virtue hypocrite, takes off the rose
       From the fair forehead of an innocent love.
       And sets a blister[8] there, makes marriage-vows
       As false as dicers' oaths. O, such a deed
       As from the body of contraction[9] plucks
50   The very soul, and sweet religion makes
       A rhapsody of words. Heaven's face does glow
       O'er this solidity and compound mass[1]
       With heated visage, as against the doom[2]—
       Is thought-sick at the act.
   QUEEN: Ay me, what act
55   That roars so loud and thunders in the index?[3]
   HAMLET: Look here upon this picture[4] and on this,
       The counterfeit presentment of two brothers.
       See what a grace was seated on this brow:
       Hyperion's curls, the front[5] of Jove himself,
60   An eye like Mars, to threaten and command,
       A station like the herald Mercury[6]
       New lighted[7] on a heaven-kissing hill—
       A combination and a form indeed
       Where every god did seem to set his seal,[8]

---

5. Officious.   6. Plated it with brass.   7. Feeling. *Proof*: armor.   8. Brand.
9. The marriage contract.   1. Meaningless mass (Earth).   2. Judgment Day.
3. Table of contents.   4. Portrait.   5. Forehead.   6. In Roman mythology, Mercury served as
the messenger of the gods. *Station*: bearing.   7. Newly alighted.   8. Mark of approval.

To give the world assurance of a man.   65
This was your husband. Look you now what follows.
Here is your husband, like a mildewed ear
Blasting his wholesome brother. Have you eyes?
Could you on this fair mountain leave to feed,
And batten[9] on this moor? Ha! have you eyes?   70
You cannot call it love, for at your age
The heyday in the blood is tame, it's humble,
And waits upon the judgment, and what judgment
Would step from this to this? Sense sure you have
Else could you not have motion, but sure that sense   75
Is apoplexed[1] for madness would not err,
Nor sense to ecstasy was ne'er so thralled
But it reserved some quantity[2] of choice
To serve in such a difference. What devil was't
That thus hath cozened you at hoodman-blind?[3]   80
Eyes without feeling, feeling without sight,
Ears without hands or eyes, smelling sans[4] all,
Or but a sickly part of one true sense
Could not so mope.[5] O shame! where is thy blush?
Rebellious hell,   85
If thou canst mutine[6] in a matron's bones,
To flaming youth let virtue be as wax
And melt in her own fire. Proclaim no shame
When the compulsive ardor gives the charge,[7]
Since frost itself as actively doth burn,   90
And reason panders[8] will.
QUEEN: O Hamlet, speak no more!
Thou turn'st my eyes into my very soul;
And there I see such black and grainèd[9] spots
As will not leave their tinct.[1]
HAMLET: Nay, but to live
In the rank sweat of an enseamèd[2] bed,   95
Stewed in curruption, honeying and making love
Over the nasty sty—
QUEEN: O, speak to me no more!
These words like daggers enter in my ears;
No more, sweet Hamlet.
HAMLET: A murderer and a villain,

---

9. Feed greedily. 1. Paralyzed. 2. Power. 3. Blindman's buff. *Cozened*: cheated.
4. Without. 5. Be stupid. 6. Commit mutiny. 7. Attacks. 8. Pimps for. 9. Ingrained.
1. Lose their color. 2. Greasy.

100   A slave that is not twentieth part the tithe[3]
        Of your precedent lord, a vice of kings,[4]
        A cutpurse[5] of the empire and the rule,
        That from a shelf the precious diadem stole
        And put it in his pocket—
105 QUEEN: No more.

        [*Enter* GHOST.]

HAMLET: A king of shreds and patches—
        Save me and hover o'er me with your wings,
        You heavenly guards! What would your gracious figure?
QUEEN: Alas, he's mad.
110 HAMLET: Do you not come your tardy[6] son to chide,
        That lapsed in time and passion lets go by
        Th' important acting of your dread command?
        O, say!
GHOST: Do not forget. This visitation
115   Is but to whet thy almost blunted purpose.
        But look, amazement on thy mother sits.
        O, step between her and her fighting soul!
        Conceit[7] in weakest bodies strongest works.
        Speak to her, Hamlet.
HAMLET: How is it with you, lady?
120 QUEEN: Alas, how is't with you,
        That you do bend[8] your eye on vacancy,
        And with th' incorporal air do hold discourse?
        Forth at your eyes your spirits wildly peep,
        And as the sleeping soldiers in th' alarm,
125   Your bedded hairs like life in excrements[9]
        Start up and stand an end. O gentle son,
        Upon the heat and flame of thy distemper
        Sprinkle cool patience. Whereon do you look?
HAMLET: On him, on him! Look you how pale he glares.
130   His form and cause conjoined,[1] preaching to stones,
        Would make them capable.[2]—Do not look upon me,
        Lest with this piteous action you convert
        My stern effects.[3] Then what I have to do
        Will want true color—tears perchance for blood.

---

3. One-tenth.
4. The "Vice," a common character in the popular drama, was a clown or buffoon. *Precedent lord*: first husband.   5. Pickpocket.   6. Slow to act.   7. Imagination.   8. Turn.
9. Nails and hair.   1. Working together.   2. Of responding.   3. Deeds.

QUEEN: To whom do you speak this? 135
HAMLET: Do you see nothing there?
QUEEN: Nothing at all, yet all that is I see.
HAMLET: Nor did you nothing hear?
QUEEN: No, nothing but ourselves.
HAMLET: Why, look you there. Look how it steals away. 140
    My father, in his habit[4] as he lived!
    Look where he goes even now out at the portal.   [*Exit* GHOST.]
QUEEN: This is the very coinage[5] of your brain.
    This bodiless creation ecstasy[6]
    Is very cunning[7] in.
HAMLET: Ecstasy? 145
    My pulse as yours doth temperately keep time,
    And makes as healthful music. It is not madness
    That I have uttered. Bring me to the test,
    And I the matter will re-word, which madness
    Would gambol[8] from. Mother, for love of grace, 150
    Lay not that flattering unction[9] to your soul,
    That not your trespass but my madness speaks.
    It will but skin and film the ulcerous place
    Whiles rank corruption, mining[1] all within,
    Infects unseen. Confess yourself to heaven, 155
    Repent what's past, avoid what is to come.
    And do not spread the compost on the weeds,
    To make them ranker. Forgive me this my virtue,
    For in the fatness of these pursy[2] times
    Virtue itself of vice must pardon beg, 160
    Yea, curb[3] and woo for leave to do him good.
QUEEN: O Hamlet, thou hast cleft my heart in twain.
HAMLET: O, throw away the worser part of it,
    And live the purer with the other half.
    Good night—but go not to my uncle's bed. 165
    Assume a virtue, if you have it not.
    That monster custom[4] who all sense doth eat
    Of habits devil, is angel yet in this,
    That to the use of actions fair and good
    He likewise gives a frock or livery 170
    That aptly[5] is put on. Refrain tonight,
    And that shall lend a kind of easiness

---

4. Clothing.   5. Invention.   6. Madness.   7. Skilled.   8. Shy away.   9. Ointment.
1. Undermining.   2. Bloated.   3. Bow.   4. Habit.   5. Easily.

To the next abstinence; the next more easy;
For use almost can change the stamp of nature,
175   And either curb the devil, or throw him out
With wondrous potency. Once more, good night,
And when you are desirous to be blest,
I'll blessing beg of you. For this same lord
I do repent; but heaven hath pleased it so,
180   To punish me with this, and this with me,
That I must be their scourge and minister.
I will bestow[6] him and will answer well
The death I gave him. So, again, good night.
I must be cruel only to be kind.
185   Thus bad begins and worse remains behind.
One word more, good lady.

QUEEN: What shall I do?

HAMLET: Not this, by no means, that I bid you do:
Let the bloat[7] king tempt you again to bed,
Pinch wanton[8] on your cheek, call you his mouse,
190   And let him, for a pair of reechy[9] kisses,
Or paddling in your neck with his damned fingers,
Make you to ravel[1] all this matter out,
That I essentially am not in madness,
But mad in craft. 'Twere good you let him know,
195   For who that's but a queen, fair, sober, wise,
Would from a paddock, from a bat, a gib,[2]
Such dear concernings hide? Who would so do?
No, in despite of sense and secrecy,
Unpeg the basket on the house's top,
200   Let the birds fly, and like the famous ape,
To try conclusions, in the basket creep
And break your own neck down.[3]

QUEEN: Be thou assured, if words be made of breath
And breath of life, I have no life to breathe
205   What thou hast said to me.

HAMLET: I must to England; you know that?

QUEEN: Alack,
I had forgot. 'Tis so concluded on.

HAMLET: There's letters sealed, and my two school-fellows,

---

6. Dispose of.   7. Bloated.   8. Lewdly.   9. Foul.   1. Reveal.   2. Tomcat. *Paddock*: toad.
3. Apparently a reference to a now-lost fable in which an ape, finding a basket containing a cage of
birds on a housetop, opens the cage. The birds fly away. The ape, thinking that if he were in the
basket he too could fly, enters, jumps out, and breaks his neck.

Whom I will trust as I will adders fanged,
They bear the mandate; they must sweep[4] my way   210
And marshal me to knavery. Let it work,
For 'tis the sport to have the enginer
Hoist with his own petard;[5] and't shall go hard
But I will delve[6] one yard below their mines
And blow them at the moon. O, 'tis most sweet   215
When in one line two crafts directly meet.
This man shall set me packing.
I'll lug the guts into the neighbor room.
Mother, good night. Indeed, this counsellor
Is now most still, most secret, and most grave,   220
Who was in life a foolish prating knave.
Come sir, to draw toward an end with you.
Good night, mother.
                    [*Exit the* QUEEN. *Then exit* HAMLET *tugging* POLONIUS.]

ACT IV

Scene 1

A room in the castle. Enter KING, QUEEN, ROSENCRANTZ *and*
GUILDENSTERN.

KING: There's matter in these sighs, these profound heaves,
    You must translate;[7] 'tis fit we understand them.
    Where is your son?
QUEEN: Bestow this place on us a little while.
                    [*Exeunt* ROSENCRANTZ *and* GUILDENSTERN.]
    Ah, mine own lord, what have I seen tonight!   5
KING: What, Gertrude? How does Hamlet?
QUEEN: Mad as the sea and wind when both contend
    Which is the mightier. In his lawless fit,
    Behind the arras hearing something stir,
    Whips out his rapier, cries "A rat, a rat!"   10
    And in this brainish apprehension[8] kills
    The unseen good old man.

4. Prepare. *Mandate*: command.
5. The "enginer," or engineer, is a military man who is here described as being blown up by a
bomb of his own construction ("hoist with his own petard"). The military imagery continues in
the succeeding lines where Hamlet describes himself as digging a countermine or tunnel beneath
the one Claudius is digging to defeat Hamlet. In line 216, the two tunnels unexpectedly meet.
6. Dig.   7. Explain.   8. Insane notion.

KING: O heavy deed!
     It had been so with us had we been there.
     His liberty is full of threats to all—
15   To you yourself, to us, to every one.
     Alas, how shall this bloody deed be answered?
     It will be laid to us, whose providence[9]
     Should have kept short, restrained, and out of haunt,[1]
     This mad young man. But so much was our love,
20   We would not understand what was most fit;
     But, like the owner of a foul disease,
     To keep it from divulging, let it feed
     Even on the pith of life. Where is he gone?
QUEEN: To draw apart the body he hath killed,
25   O'er whom his very madness, like some ore
     Among a mineral of metals base,
     Shows itself pure: 'a weeps for what is done.
KING: O Gertrude, come away!
     The sun no sooner shall the mountains touch
30   But we will ship him hence, and this vile deed
     We must with all our majesty and skill
     Both countenance and excuse. Ho, Guildenstern!

[Enter ROSENCRANTZ and GUILDENSTERN.]

     Friends both, go join you with some further aid.
     Hamlet in madness hath Polonius slain,
35   And from his mother's closet hath he dragged him.
     Go seek him out; speak fair, and bring the body
     Into the chapel. I pray you haste in this.
                    [Exeunt ROSENCRANTZ and GUILDENSTERN.]
     Come, Gertrude, we'll call up our wisest friends
     And let them know both what we mean to do
40   And what's untimely done;
     Whose whisper o'er the world's diameter,
     As level as the cannon to his blank,[2]
     Transports his poisoned shot—may miss our name,
     And hit the woundless air. O, come away!
45   My soul is full of discord and dismay.   [Exeunt.]

9. Prudence.   1. Away from public gatherings.   2. Mark. *Level:* direct.

Scene 2

A passageway. Enter HAMLET.

HAMLET: Safely stowed.
ROSENCRANTZ *and* GUILDENSTERN: [*Within.*] Hamlet! Lord Hamlet!
HAMLET: But soft, what noise? Who calls on Hamlet?
    O, here they come.

[*Enter* ROSENCRANTZ, GUILDENSTERN, *and* OTHERS.]

ROSENCRANTZ: What have you done, my lord, with the dead body?   5
HAMLET: Compounded it with dust, whereto 'tis kin.
ROSENCRANTZ: Tell us where 'tis, that we may take it thence
    And bear it to the chapel.
HAMLET: Do not believe it.
ROSENCRANTZ: Believe what?   10
HAMLET: That I can keep your counsel and not mine own. Besides, to be
    demanded of a sponge—what replication[3] should be made by the son of
    a king?
ROSENCRANTZ: Take you me for a sponge, my lord?
HAMLET: Ay, sir, that soaks up the king's countenance,[4] his rewards, his
    authorities. But such officers do the king best service in the end. He   15
    keeps them like an apple in the corner of his jaw, first mouthed to
    be last swallowed. When he needs what you have gleaned, it is but
    squeezing you and, sponge, you shall be dry again.
ROSENCRANTZ: I understand you not, my lord.
HAMLET: I am glad of it. A knavish speech sleeps in a foolish ear.   20
ROSENCRANTZ: My lord, you must tell us where the body is, and go with us
    to the king.
HAMLET: The body is with the king, but the king is not with the body.
    The king is a thing—
GUILDENSTERN: A thing, my lord!   25
HAMLET: Of nothing. Bring me to him. Hide fox, and all after.[5] [*Exeunt.*]

Scene 3

A room in the castle. Enter KING.

KING: I have sent to seek him, and to find the body.
    How dangerous is it that this man goes loose!

---

3. Answer. *Demanded of*: questioned by.   4. Favor.
5. Apparently a reference to a children's game like hide-and-seek.

Yet must not we put the strong law on him.
He's loved of the distracted[6] multitude,
5   Who like not in their judgment but their eyes,
And where 'tis so, th' offender's scourge[7] is weighed,
But never the offence. To bear all smooth and even,
This sudden sending him away must seem
Deliberate pause.[8] Diseases desperate grown
10   By desperate appliance are relieved,
Or not at all.

[*Enter* ROSENCRANTZ, GUILDENSTERN, *and all the rest.*]

How now! what hath befall'n?
ROSENCRANTZ: Where the dead body is bestowed, my lord,
We cannot get from him.
KING: But where is he?
ROSENCRANTZ: Without, my lord; guarded, to know[9] your pleasure.
KING: Bring him before us.
15   ROSENCRANTZ: Ho! bring in the lord.

[*They enter with* HAMLET.]

KING: Now, Hamlet, where's Polonius?
HAMLET: At supper.
KING: At supper? Where?
HAMLET: Not where he eats, but where 'a is eaten. A certain convocation
20   of politic[1] worms are e'en at him. Your worm is your only emperor for
diet. We fat all creatures else to fat us, and we fat ourselves for maggots. Your fat king and your lean beggar is but variable service—two
dishes, but to one table. That's the end.
KING: Alas, alas!
25   HAMLET: A man may fish with the worm that hath eat of a king, and eat of
the fish that hath fed of that worm.
KING: What dost thou mean by this?
HAMLET: Nothing but to show you how a king may go a progress through
the guts of a beggar.
30   KING: Where is Polonius?
HAMLET: In heaven. Send thither to see. If your messenger find him not
there, seek him i' th' other place yourself. But if, indeed, you find him
not within this month, you shall nose[2] him as you go up the stairs into
the lobby.
KING: [*To* ATTENDANTS.] Go seek him there.

---

6. Confused.   7. Punishment.   8. That is, not an impulse.   9. Await.
1. Scheming. *Convocation*: gathering.   2. Smell.

HAMLET: 'A will stay till you come.   [*Exeunt* ATTENDANTS.] 35
KING: Hamlet, this deed, for thine especial safety—
    Which we do tender, as we dearly³ grieve
    For that which thou hast done—must send thee hence
    With fiery quickness. Therefore prepare thyself.
    The bark is ready, and the wind at help,   40
    Th' associates tend, and everything is bent
    For England.
HAMLET: For England?
KING: Ay, Hamlet.
HAMLET: Good.
KING: So it is, if thou knew'st our purposes.
HAMLET: I see a cherub that sees them. But come, for England!
    Farewell, dear mother.   45
KING: Thy loving father, Hamlet.
HAMLET: My mother. Father and mother is man and wife, man and wife is
    one flesh. So, my mother. Come, for England.   [*Exit.*]
KING: Follow him at foot;⁴ tempt him with speed aboard.
    Delay it not; I'll have him hence tonight.   50
    Away! for everything is sealed and done
    That else leans on th' affair. Pray you make haste.
                                        [*Exeunt all but the* KING.]
    And, England, if my love thou hold'st at aught—
    As my great power thereof may give thee sense,⁵
    Since yet thy cicatrice⁶ looks raw and red   55
    After the Danish sword, and thy free awe
    Pays homage to us—thou mayst not coldly set⁷
    Our sovereign process,⁸ which imports at full
    By letters congruing⁹ to that effect
    The present death of Hamlet. Do it, England,   60
    For like the hectic¹ in my blood he rages,
    And thou must cure me. Till I know 'tis done,
    Howe'er my haps, my joys were ne'er begun.   [*Exit.*]

Scene 4

Near Elsinore. Enter FORTINBRAS *with his army.*

FORTINBRAS: Go, captain, from me greet the Danish king.
    Tell him that by his license Fortinbras

---

3. Deeply. *Tender:* consider.   4. Closely.
5. Of its value.   6. Wound scar.   7. Set aside.   8. Mandate.   9. Agreeing.   1. Chronic fever.

Craves the conveyance[2] of a promised march
Over his kingdom. You know the rendezvous.
5   If that his majesty would aught with us,
We shall express our duty in his eye,[3]
And let him know so.

CAPTAIN: I will do't, my lord.

FORTINBRAS: Go softly on.   [*Exeunt all but the* CAPTAIN.]

[*Enter* HAMLET, ROSENCRANTZ, GUILDENSTERN, *and* OTHERS.]

HAMLET: Good sir, whose powers are these?
10   CAPTAIN: They are of Norway, sir.
HAMLET: How purposed, sir, I pray you?
CAPTAIN: Against some part of Poland.
HAMLET: Who commands them, sir?
CAPTAIN: The nephew to old Norway, Fortinbras.
15   HAMLET: Goes it against the main[4] of Poland, sir,
Or for some frontier?
CAPTAIN: Truly to speak, and with no addition,[5]
We go to gain a little patch of ground
That hath in it no profit but the name.
20   To pay five ducats,[6] five, I would not farm it;
Nor will it yield to Norway or the Pole
A ranker rate should it be sold in fee.[7]
HAMLET: Why, then the Polack never will defend it.
CAPTAIN: Yes, it is already garrisoned.
25   HAMLET: Two thousand souls and twenty thousand ducats
Will not debate the question of this straw.
This is th' imposthume[8] of much wealth and peace,
That inward breaks, and shows no cause without
Why the man dies. I humbly thank you, sir.
CAPTAIN: God b'wi'ye, sir.   [*Exit.*]
30   ROSENCRANTZ: Will't please you go, my lord?
HAMLET: I'll be with you straight. Go a little before.
                              [*Exeunt all but* HAMLET.]
How all occasions do inform against me,
And spur my dull revenge! What is a man,
If his chief good and market[9] of his time
35   Be but to sleep and feed? A beast, no more.
Sure he that made us with such large discourse,[1]
Looking before and after, gave us not

2. Escort.   3. Presence.   4. Central part.   5. Exaggeration.   6. That is, in rent.
7. Outright. *Ranker*: higher.   8. Abscess.   9. Occupation.   1. Ample reasoning power.

That capability and godlike reason
To fust[2] in us unused. Now, whether it be
Bestial oblivion, or some craven scruple   40
Of thinking too precisely on th' event[3]—
A thought which, quartered, hath but one part wisdom
And ever three parts coward—I do not know
Why yet I live to say "This thing's to do,"
Sith[4] I have cause, and will, and strength, and means,   45
To do't. Examples gross as earth exhort me.
Witness this army of such mass and charge,[5]
Led by a delicate and tender prince,
Whose spirit, with divine ambition puffed,
Makes mouths at[6] the invisible event,   50
Exposing what is mortal and unsure
To all that fortune, death, and danger dare,
Even for an eggshell. Rightly to be great
Is not to stir without great argument,
But greatly to find quarrel in a straw   55
When honor's at the stake. How stand I then,
That have a father killed, a mother stained,
Excitements of my reason and my blood,
And let all sleep, while to my shame I see
The imminent death of twenty thousand men   60
That for a fantasy and trick of fame
Go to their graves like beds, fight for a plot
Whereon the numbers cannot try the cause,
Which is not tomb enough and continent
To hide the slain?[7] O, from this time forth,   65
My thoughts be bloody, or be nothing worth!   [*Exit.*]

Scene 5

A room in the castle. Enter QUEEN, HORATIO *and a* GENTLEMAN.

QUEEN: I will not speak with her.
GENTLEMAN: She is importunate, indeed distract.
    Her mood will needs to be pitied.
QUEEN: What would she have?
GENTLEMAN: She speaks much of her father, says she hears

---

2. Grow musty.   3. Outcome.   4. Since.   5. Expense.   6. Scorns.
7. The plot of ground involved is so small that it cannot contain the number of men involved in
fighting or furnish burial space for the number of those who will die.

5   There's tricks i' th' world, and hems, and beats her heart,
Spurns enviously at straws,[8] speaks things in doubt
That carry but half sense. Her speech is nothing,
Yet the unshapèd use of it doth move
The hearers to collection;[9] they yawn at it,
10   And botch the words up fit to their own thoughts,
Which, as her winks and nods and gestures yield them,
Indeed would make one think there might be thought,
Though nothing sure, yet much unhappily.

HORATIO: 'Twere good she were spoken with, for she may strew
15   Dangerous conjectures in ill-breeding minds.

QUEEN: Let her come in.   [*Exit* GENTLEMAN.]
    [*Aside.*] To my sick soul, as sin's true nature is,
    Each toy seems prologue to some great amiss.[1]
    So full of artless jealousy is guilt,
20   It spills itself in fearing to be spilt.

[*Enter* OPHELIA *distracted.*]

OPHELIA: Where is the beauteous majesty of Denmark?

QUEEN: How now, Ophelia!

OPHELIA:

    [*Sings.*]

    How should I your true love know
      From another one?
25   By his cockle hat and staff,[2]
      And his sandal shoon.[3]

QUEEN: Alas, sweet lady, what imports this song?

OPHELIA: Say you? Nay, pray you mark.

    [*Sings.*]

    He is dead and gone, lady,
30   He is dead and gone;
    At his head a grass-green turf,
      At his heels a stone.

    O, ho!

QUEEN: Nay, but Ophelia—

OPHELIA: Pray you mark.

---

8. Takes offense at trifles.   9. An attempt to order.   1. Catastrophe. *Toy:* trifle.
2. A cockle hat, one decorated with a shell, indicated that its wearer had made a pilgrimage to the shrine of St. James at Compostela in Spain. The staff also marked the carrier as a pilgrim.
3. Shoes.

[*Sings.*]

White his shroud as the mountain snow—

[*Enter* KING.]

QUEEN: Alas, look here, my lord.   35

OPHELIA:

[*Sings.*]

Larded all with sweet flowers;
Which bewept to the grave did not go
With true-love showers.

KING: How do you, pretty lady?

OPHELIA: Well, God dild you! They say the owl was a baker's daughter.[4] 40
Lord, we know what we are, but know not what we may be. God be
at your table!

KING: Conceit[5] upon her father.

OPHELIA: Pray let's have no words of this, but when they ask you what it
means, say you this:

[*Sings.*]

Tomorrow is Saint Valentine's day,   45
All in the morning betime,
And I a maid at your window,
To be your Valentine.

Then up he rose, and donn'd his clo'es,
And dupped[6] the chamber-door,   50
Let in the maid, that out a maid
Never departed more.

KING: Pretty Ophelia!

OPHELIA: Indeed, without an oath, I'll make an end on't.

[*Sings.*]

By Gis[7] and by Saint Charity,   55
Alack, and fie for shame!
Young men will do't, if they come to't;
By Cock,[8] they are to blame.
Quoth she "before you tumbled me,
You promised me to wed."   60

---

4. Reference to a folktale about a young woman transformed into an owl when she failed to
offer generosity to Jesus, who had asked for bread in her father's shop. *Dild:* yield, repay.
5. Thought.   6. Opened.   7. Jesus.   8. Corruption of "God," with a sexual pun.

He answers:

"So would I'a done, by yonder sun,
An thou hadst not come to my bed."

KING: How long hath she been thus?
65 OPHELIA: I hope all will be well. We must be patient, but I cannot choose
but weep to think they would lay him i' th' cold ground. My brother
shall know of it, and so I thank you for your good counsel. Come, my
coach! Good night, ladies, good night. Sweet ladies, good night, good
night.   [*Exit.*]
KING: Follow her close; give her good watch, I pray you.
                              [*Exeunt* HORATIO *and* GENTLEMAN.]
70   O, this is the poison of deep grief; it springs
       All from her father's death, and now behold!
       O Gertrude, Gertrude!
       When sorrows come, they come not single spies,
       But in battalions: first, her father slain;
75   Next, your son gone, and he most violent author
       Of his own just remove; the people muddied,[9]
       Thick and unwholesome in their thoughts and whispers
       For good Polonius' death; and we have done but greenly[1]
       In hugger-mugger[2] to inter him; poor Ophelia
80   Divided from herself and her fair judgment,
       Without the which we are pictures, or mere beasts;
       Last, and as much containing as all these,
       Her brother is in secret come from France,
       Feeds on his wonder, keeps himself in clouds,
85   And wants not buzzers to infect his ear
       With pestilent speeches of his father's death,
       Wherein necessity, of matter beggared,[3]
       Will nothing stick our person to arraign[4]
       In ear and ear.[5] O my dear Gertrude, this,
90   Like to a murd'ring piece,[6] in many places
       Gives me superfluous death.   [*A noise within.*]
QUEEN: Alack, what noise is this?
KING: Attend!
       Where are my Switzers?[7] Let them guard the door.
       What is the matter?
95 MESSENGER: Save yourself, my lord.

9. Disturbed.   1. Without judgment.   2. Haste.   3. Short on facts.   4. Accuse. *Stick*: hesitate.
5. From both sides.   6. Weapon designed to scatter its shot.   7. Swiss guards.

The ocean, overpeering of his list,[8]
Eats not the flats with more impiteous[9] haste
Than young Laertes, in a riotous head,[1]
O'erbears your officers. The rabble call him lord,
And as the world were now but to begin,   100
Antiquity forgot, custom not known,
The ratifiers and props of every word,
They cry "Choose we, Laertes shall be king."
Caps, hands, and tongues, applaud it to the clouds,
"Laertes shall be king, Laertes king."   105
QUEEN: How cheerfully on the false trail they cry![2]

[*A noise within.*]

O, this is counter,[3] you false Danish dogs!
KING: The doors are broke.

[*Enter* LAERTES, *with* OTHERS.]

LAERTES: Where is this king?—Sirs, stand you all without.
ALL: No, let's come in.
LAERTES: I pray you give me leave.   110
ALL: We will, we will.
LAERTES: I thank you. Keep[4] the door.   [*Exeunt his followers.*]
                    O thou vile king,
Give me my father!
QUEEN: Calmly, good Laertes.
LAERTES: That drop of blood that's calm proclaims me bastard,
Cries cuckold to my father, brands the harlot   115
Even here between the chaste unsmirchèd brow
Of my true mother.
KING: What is the cause, Laertes,
That thy rebellion looks so giant-like?
Let him go, Gertrude. Do not fear[5] our person.
There's such divinity doth hedge a king   120
That treason can but peep to[6] what it would,
Acts little of his will. Tell me, Laertes.
Why thou art thus incensed. Let him go, Gertrude.
Speak, man.
LAERTES: Where is my father?
KING: Dead.

---

8. Towering above its limits.   9. Pitiless.   1. With an armed band.   2. As if following the scent.
3. Backward.   4. Guard.   5. Fear for.   6. Look at over or through a barrier.

QUEEN: But not by him.

125 KING: Let him demand[7] his fill.

LAERTES: How came he dead? I'll not be juggled with.
    To hell allegiance, vows to the blackest devil,
    Conscience and grace to the profoundest pit!
    I dare damnation. To this point I stand,
130   That both the worlds I give to negligence,[8]
    Let come what comes, only I'll be revenged
    Most throughly for my father.

KING: Who shall stay you?

LAERTES: My will, not all the world's.
    And for my means, I'll husband[9] them so well
    They shall go far with little.

135 KING: Good Laertes,
    If you desire to know the certainty
    Of your dear father, is't writ in your revenge
    That, swoopstake,[1] you will draw both friend and foe,
    Winner and loser?

LAERTES: None but his enemies.

140 KING: Will you know them, then?

LAERTES: To his good friends thus wide I'll ope my arms,
    And like the kind life-rend'ring pelican,[2]
    Repast them with my blood.

KING: Why, now you speak
    Like a good child and a true gentleman.
145   That I am guiltless of your father's death,
    And am most sensibly in grief for it,
    It shall as level[3] to your judgment 'pear
    As day does to your eye.

[A noise within: "Let her come in."]

LAERTES: How now? What noise is that?

[Enter OPHELIA.]

150   O, heat dry up my brains! tears seven times salt
    Burn out the sense and virtue[4] of mine eye!
    By heaven, thy madness shall be paid with weight
    Till our scale turn the beam. O rose of May,
    Dear maid, kind sister, sweet Ophelia!
155   O heavens, is't possible a young maid's wits

_____

7. Question.   8. Disregard. *Both the worlds:* that is, this world and the next.   9. Manage.
1. Sweeping the board.   2. The pelican was believed to feed her young with her own blood.
3. Plain.   4. Function. *Sense:* feeling.

Should be as mortal as an old man's life?
Nature is fin[5] in love, and where 'tis fine
It sends some precious instances of itself
After the thing it loves.[6]

OPHELIA:

[*Sings.*]

They bore him barefac'd on the bier;   160
  Hey non nonny, nonny, hey nonny;
And in his grave rain'd many a tear—

Fare you well, my dove!

LAERTES: Hadst thou thy wits, and didst persuade revenge,
  It could not move thus.   165

OPHELIA: You must sing "A-down, a-down, and you call him a-down-a." O,
  how the wheel becomes it! It is the false steward, that stole his master's
  daughter.[7]

LAERTES: This nothing's more than matter.

OPHELIA: There's a rosemary, that's for remembrance. Pray you, love,
  remember.
  And there is pansies, that's for thoughts.   170

LAERTES: A document[8] in madness, thoughts and remembrance fitted.

OPHELIA: There's fennel for you, and columbines. There's rue for you, and
  here's some for me. We may call it herb of grace a Sundays. O, you must
  wear your rue with a difference. There's a daisy. I would give you some
  violets, but they withered all when my father died. They say 'a made a
  good end.   175

[*Sings.*]

For bonny sweet Robin is all my joy.

LAERTES: Thought and affliction, passion, hell itself,
  She turns to favor[9] and to prettiness.

OPHELIA:

[*Sings.*]

And will 'a not come again?
And will 'a not come again?   180

5. Refined.
6. Laertes means that Ophelia, because of her love for her father, gave up her sanity as a token
of grief at his death.
7. The "wheel" refers to the "burden" or refrain of a song, in this case "A-down, a-down, and you
call him a-down-a." The ballad to which she refers was about a false steward. Others have suggested that the "wheel" is either the Wheel of Fortune, a spinning wheel to whose rhythm such
a song might have been sung, or a kind of dance movement performed by Ophelia as she sings.
8. Lesson.   9. Beauty.

No, no, he is dead,
Go to thy death-bed,
He never will come again.

His beard was as white as snow,
185   All flaxen was his poll;[1]
He is gone, he is gone,
And we cast away moan:
God-a-mercy on his soul!

And of all Christian souls, I pray God. God b'wi'you. [*Exit.*]
190 LAERTES: Do you see this, O God?
KING: Laertes, I must commune with your grief,
Or you deny me right. Go but apart,
Make choice of whom your wisest friends you will,
And they shall hear and judge 'twixt you and me.
195   If by direct or by collateral[2] hand
They find us touched,[3] we will our kingdom give,
Our crown, our life, and all that we call ours,
To you in satisfaction; but if not,
Be you content to lend your patience to us,
200   And we shall jointly labor with your soul
To give it due content.
LAERTES: Let this be so.
His means of death, his obscure funeral—
No trophy, sword, nor hatchment,[4] o'er his bones,
No noble rite nor formal ostentation[5]—
205   Cry to be heard, as 'twere from heaven to earth,
That I must call't in question.
KING: So you shall;
And where th' offence is, let the great axe fall.
I pray you go with me.   [*Exeunt.*]

Scene 6

Another room in the castle. Enter HORATIO *and a* GENTLEMAN.

HORATIO: What are they that would speak with me?
GENTLEMAN: Sea-faring men, sir. They say they have letters for you.
HORATIO: Let them come in.   [*Exit* GENTLEMAN.]

1. Head.   2. Indirect.   3. By guilt.   4. Coat of arms.   5. Pomp.

I do not know from what part of the world
I should be greeted, if not from Lord Hamlet.   5

[*Enter* SAILORS.]

SAILOR: God bless you, sir.
HORATIO: Let him bless thee too.
SAILOR: 'A shall, sir, an't please him. There's a letter for you, sir—it came
from th' ambassador that was bound for England—if your name be
Horatio, as I am let to know[6] it is.   10
HORATIO: [*Reads.*] "Horatio, when thou shalt have overlooked[7] this, give
these fellows some means[8] to the king. They have letters for him. Ere
we were two days old at sea, a pirate of very warlike appointment[9] gave
us chase. Finding ourselves too slow of sail, we put on a compelled
valor, and in the grapple I boarded them. On the instant they got clear 15
of our ship, so I alone became their prisoner. They have dealt with me
like thieves of mercy, but they knew what they did; I am to do a good
turn for them. Let the king have the letters I have sent, and repair thou
to me with as much speed as thou wouldest fly death. I have words to
speak in thine ear will make thee dumb; yet are they much too light for 20
the bore of the matter.[1] These good fellows will bring thee where I am.
Rosencrantz and Guildenstern hold their course for England. Of them I
have much to tell thee. Farewell.
                          He that thou knowest thine, Hamlet."
Come, I will give you way[2] for these your letters,
And do't the speedier that you may direct me   25
To him from whom you brought them.   [*Exeunt.*]

Scene 7

Another room in the castle. Enter KING *and* LAERTES.

KING: Now must your conscience my acquittance seal,[3]
    And you must put me in your heart for friend,
    Sith you have heard, and with a knowing ear,
    That he which hath your noble father slain
    Pursued my life.
LAERTES: It well appears. But tell me   5
    Why you proceeded not against these feats,

---

6. Informed.   7. Read through.   8. Access.   9. Equipment.
1. Figure of speech from gunnery, referring to shot that is too small for the size of the weapons
to be fired.   2. Means of delivery.   3. Grant me innocent.

So criminal and so capital in nature,
As by your safety, greatness, wisdom, all things else,
You mainly were stirred up.

KING: O, for two special reasons,
10   Which may to you, perhaps, seem much unsinewed,[4]
But yet to me th' are strong. The queen his mother
Lives almost by his looks, and for myself—
My virtue or my plague, be it either which—
She is so conjunctive[5] to my life and soul
15   That, as the star moves not but in his sphere,[6]
I could not but by her. The other motive,
Why to a public count[7] I might not go,
Is the great love the general gender[8] bear him,
Who, dipping all his faults in their affection,
20   Work like the spring that turneth wood to stone,[9]
Convert his gyves[1] to graces; so that my arrows,
Too slightly timbered[2] for so loud a wind,
Would have reverted to my bow again,
But not where I had aimed them.

25   LAERTES: And so have I a noble father lost,
A sister driven into desp'rate terms,
Whose worth, if praises may go back again,
Stood challenger on mount of all the age
For her perfections. But my revenge will come.

30   KING: Break not your sleeps for that. You must not think
That we are made of stuff so flat and dull
That we can let our beard be shook with danger,
And think it pastime. You shortly shall hear more.
I loved your father, and we love our self,
35   And that, I hope, will teach you to imagine—

[Enter a MESSENGER with letters.]

How now? What news?

MESSENGER: Letters, my lord, from Hamlet.
These to your majesty; this to the queen.

KING: From Hamlet! Who brought them?

MESSENGER: Sailors, my lord, they say. I saw them not.

---

4. Weak.   5. Closely joined.
6. Reference to the Ptolemaic cosmology, in which planets and stars were believed to revolve in crystalline spheres concentrically about the Earth.   7. Reckoning.   8. Common people.
9. Certain English springs contain so much lime that a log placed in one of them for a length of time will be covered in limestone.   1. Fetters.   2. Shafted.

They were given me by Claudio; he received them 40
Of him that brought them.
KING: Laertes, you shall hear them.—
Leave us.   [*Exit* MESSENGER.]
[*Reads.*] "High and mighty, you shall know I am set naked on your
kingdom. Tomorrow shall I beg leave to see your kingly eyes; when I
shall, first asking your pardon thereunto, recount the occasion of my 45
sudden and more strange return.
        Hamlet."
What should this mean? Are all the rest come back?
Or is it some abuse,[3] and no such thing?
LAERTES: Know you the hand?
KING: 'Tis Hamlet's character.[4] "Naked"! 50
And in a postscript here, he says "alone."
Can you devise[5] me?
LAERTES: I am lost in it, my lord. But let him come.
It warms the very sickness in my heart
That I shall live and tell him to his teeth 55
"Thus didest thou."
KING: If it be so, Laertes—
As how should it be so, how otherwise?—
Will you be ruled by me?
LAERTES: Ay, my lord,
So you will not o'errule me to a peace.
KING: To thine own peace. If he be now returned, 60
As checking at[6] his voyage, and that he means
No more to undertake it, I will work him
To an exploit now ripe in my device,
Under the which he shall not choose but fall;
And for his death no wind of blame shall breathe 65
But even his mother shall uncharge[7] the practice
And call it accident.
LAERTES: My lord, I will be ruled;
The rather if you could devise it so
That I might be the organ.[8]
KING: It falls right.
You have been talked of since your travel much, 70
And that in Hamlet's hearing, for a quality
Wherein they say you shine. Your sum of parts

3. Trick.   4. Handwriting.   5. Explain it to.   6. Turning aside from.   7. Not accuse.
8. Instrument.

Did not together pluck such envy from him
As did that one, and that, in my regard,
Of the unworthiest siege.[9]

75 LAERTES: What part is that, my lord?
KING: A very riband in the cap of youth,
      Yet needful too, for youth no less becomes
      The light and careless livery that it wears
      Than settled age his sables and his weeds,[1]
80   Importing health and graveness. Two months since
      Here was a gentleman of Normandy.
      I have seen myself, and served against, the French,
      And they can[2] well on horseback, but this gallant
      Had witchcraft in't. He grew unto his seat,
85   And to such wondrous doing brought his horse,
      As had he been incorpsed and demi-natured
      With the brave beast. So far he topped my thought
      That I, in forgery[3] of shapes and tricks,
      Come short of what he did.[4]
LAERTES: A Norman was't?
90 KING: A Norman.
LAERTES: Upon my life, Lamord.
KING: The very same.
LAERTES: I know him well. He is the brooch indeed
      And gem of all the nation.
KING: He made confession[5] of you,
95   And gave you such a masterly report
      For art and exercise in your defence,[6]
      And for your rapier most especial,
      That he cried out 'twould be a sight indeed
      If one could match you. The scrimers[7] of their nation
100   He swore had neither motion, guard, nor eye,
      If you opposed them. Sir, this report of his
      Did Hamlet so envenom with his envy
      That he could nothing do but wish and beg
      Your sudden coming o'er, to play with you.
      Now out of this—
105 LAERTES: What out of this, my lord?

9. Lowest rank.   1. Dignified clothing.   2. Perform.   3. Imagination.
4. The gentleman referred to was so skilled in horsemanship that he seemed to share one body
with the horse ("incorpsed"). The king further extends the compliment by saying that he appeared
like the mythical centaur, a creature who was man from the waist up and horse from the waist
down, therefore "demi-natured."   5. Gave a report.   6. Skill in fencing.   7. Fencers.

KING: Laertes, was your father dear to you?
    Or are you like the painting of a sorrow,
    A face without a heart?
LAERTES: Why ask you this?
KING: Not that I think you did not love your father,
    But that I know love is begun by time,   110
    And that I see in passages of proof,[8]
    Time qualifies the spark and fire of it.
    There lives within the very flame of love
    A kind of wick or snuff that will abate it,
    And nothing is at a like goodness still,   115
    For goodness, growing to a plurisy,[9]
    Dies in his own too much.[1] That we would do,
    We should do when we would; for this "would" changes,
    And hath abatements and delays as many
    As there are tongues, are hands, are accidents,   120
    And then this "should" is like a spendthrift's sigh
    That hurts by easing. But to the quick of th' ulcer[2]—
    Hamlet comes back; what would you undertake
    To show yourself in deed your father's son
    More than in words?
LAERTES: To cut his throat i' th' church.   125
KING: No place indeed should murder sanctuarize;[3]
    Revenge should have no bounds. But, good Laertes,
    Will you do this? Keep close within your chamber.
    Hamlet returned shall know you are come home.
    We'll put on those shall praise your excellence,   130
    And set a double varnish on the fame
    The Frenchman gave you, bring you in fine[4] together,
    And wager on your heads. He, being remiss,[5]
    Most generous, and free from all contriving,
    Will not peruse[6] the foils, so that with ease,   135
    Or with a little shuffling, you may choose
    A sword unbated,[7] and in a pass of practice
    Requite him for your father.
LAERTES: I will do't,
    And for that purpose I'll anoint my sword.
    I bought an unction of a mountebank   140

---

8. Tests of experience.   9. Fullness.   1. Excess.
2. Heart of the matter. *Spendthrift's sigh*: a sigh was believed to draw a drop of blood from the
heart and thus to "hurt" by "easing" sadness.   3. Provide sanctuary for murder.   4. In short.
5. Careless.   6. Examine.   7. Not blunted.

So mortal that but dip a knife in it,
Where it draws blood no cataplasm[8] so rare,
Collected from all simples[9] that have virtue
Under the moon, can save the thing from death
145   That is but scratched withal. I'll touch my point
With this contagion, that if I gall[1] him slightly,
It may be death.

KING: Let's further think of this,
Weigh what convenience both of time and means
May fit us to our shape. If this should fail,
150   And that our drift look[2] through our bad performance,
'Twere better not assayed. Therefore this project
Should have a back or second that might hold
If this did blast in proof.[3] Soft, let me see.
We'll make a solemn wager on your cunnings—
155   I ha't.
When in your motion you are hot and dry—
As make your bouts more violent to that end—
And that he calls for drink, I'll have prepared him
A chalice for the nonce, whereon but sipping,
160   If he by chance escape your venomed stuck,[4]
Our purpose may hold there.—But stay, what noise?

[*Enter* QUEEN.]

QUEEN: One woe doth tread upon another's heel,
So fast they follow. Your sister's drowned, Laertes.
LAERTES: Drowned? O, where?
165   QUEEN: There is a willow grows aslant the brook
That shows his hoar leaves in the glassy stream.
Therewith fantastic garlands did she make
Of crowflowers, nettles, daisies, and long purples
That liberal shepherds give a grosser[5] name,
170   But our cold[6] maids do dead men's fingers call them.
There on the pendent boughs her coronet weeds
Clamb'ring to hang, an envious[7] sliver broke,
When down her weedy trophies and herself
Fell in the weeping brook. Her clothes spread wide,
175   And mermaid-like awhile they bore her up,

---

8. Poultice.   9. Herbs.   1. Scratch.   2. Intent become obvious.   3. Fail when tried.   4. Thrust.
5. Coarser. The "long purples" are purple orchises, a type of orchid known as "dog's cullions"
(testicles) or "goat's cullions." *Liberal*: vulgar.   6. Chaste.   7. Malicious.

Which time she chanted snatches of old tunes,
As one incapable[8] of her own distress,
Or like a creature native and indued[9]
Unto that element. But long it could not be
Till that her garments, heavy with their drink,   180
Pulled the poor wretch from her melodious lay
To muddy death.
LAERTES: Alas, then she is drowned?
QUEEN: Drowned, drowned.
LAERTES: Too much of water hast thou, poor Ophelia,
And therefore I forbid my tears; but yet   185
It is our trick; nature her custom holds,
Let shame say what it will. When these are gone,
The woman will be out. Adieu, my lord.
I have a speech o' fire that fain would blaze
But that this folly drowns it.   [*Exit.*]
KING: Let's follow, Gertrude.   190
How much I had to do to calm his rage!
Now fear I this will give it start again;
Therefore let's follow.   [*Exeunt.*]

ACT V

Scene 1

A churchyard. Enter two CLOWNS.[1]

CLOWN: Is she to be buried in Christian burial when she wilfully seeks
    her own salvation?
OTHER: I tell thee she is. Therefore make her grave straight. The crowner
    hath sat on her,[2] and finds it Christian burial.
CLOWN: How can that be, unless she drowned herself in her own defence?   5
OTHER: Why, 'tis found so.
CLOWN: It must be "se offendendo";[3] it cannot be else. For here lies the
    point: if I drown myself wittingly, it argues an act, and an act hath
    three branches—it is to act, to do, to perform; argal,[4] she drowned herself
    wittingly.
OTHER: Nay, but hear you, Goodman Delver.   10

---

8. Unaware.   9. Habituated.   1. Rustics; unsophisticated peasants.
2. Held an inquest. *Crowner:* coroner.   3. Error for *se defendendo*, in self-defense.
4. "Ergo," therefore.

CLOWN: Give me leave. Here lies the water; good. Here stands the man; good. If the man go to this water and drown himself, it is, will he, nill he, he goes—mark you that. But if the water come to him and drown him, he drowns not himself. Argal, he that is not guilty of his own
15   death shortens not his own life.

OTHER: But is this law?

CLOWN: Ay, marry, is't; crowner's quest[5] law.

OTHER: Will you ha' the truth on't? If this had not been a gentlewoman, she should have been buried out o' Christian burial.

20   CLOWN: Why, there thou say'st. And the more pity that great folk should have count'nance[6] in this world to drown or hang themselves more than their even-Christen.[7] Come, my spade. There is no ancient gentlemen but gard'ners, ditchers, and grave-makers. They hold up Adam's profession.

OTHER: Was he a gentleman?

25   CLOWN: 'A was the first that ever bore arms.

OTHER: Why, he had none.

CLOWN: What, art a heathen? How dost thou understand the Scripture? The Scripture says Adam digged. Could he dig without arms? I'll put another question to thee. If thou answerest me not to the purpose, confess thyself—

30   OTHER: Go to.

CLOWN: What is he that builds stronger than either the mason, the shipwright, or the carpenter?

OTHER: The gallows-maker, for that frame outlives a thousand tenants.

CLOWN: I like thy wit well, in good faith. The gallows does well. But how
35   does it well? It does well to those that do ill. Now thou dost ill to say the gallows is built stronger than the church. Argal, the gallows may do well to thee. To't again,[8] come.

OTHER: Who builds stronger than a mason, a shipwright, or a carpenter?

CLOWN: Ay tell me that, and unyoke.[9]

40   OTHER: Marry, now I can tell.

CLOWN: To't.

OTHER: Mass, I cannot tell.

CLOWN: Cudgel thy brains no more about it, for your dull ass will not mend his pace with beating. And when you are asked this question
45   next, say "a grave maker." The houses he makes lasts till doomsday. Go, get thee in, and fetch me a stoup[1] of liquor.   [*Exit* OTHER CLOWN.]

---

5. Inquest.   6. Approval.   7. Fellow Christians.   8. Guess again.   9. Finish the matter.
1. Mug.

[*Enter* HAMLET *and* HORATIO *as* CLOWN *digs and sings.*]

    In youth, when I did love, did love,
      Methought it was very sweet,
    To contract the time for-a my behove,[2]
      O, methought there-a was nothing-a meet.[3]   50

HAMLET: Has this fellow no feeling of his business, that 'a sings in grave-making?
HORATIO: Custom hath made it in him a property of easiness.
HAMLET: 'Tis e'en so. The hand of little employment hath the daintier sense.
CLOWN:

      [*Sings.*]

    But age, with his stealing steps,
      Hath clawed me in his clutch,   55
    And hath shipped me into the land,
      As if I had never been such.

    [*Throws up a skull.*]

HAMLET: That skull had a tongue in it, and could sing once. How the knave jowls[4] it to the ground, as if 'twere Cain's jawbone, that did the first murder! This might be the pate of a politician, which this ass now 60 o'erreaches;[5] one that would circumvent God, might it not?
HORATIO: It might, my lord.
HAMLET: Or of a courtier, which could say, "Good morrow, sweet lord! How does thou, sweet lord?" This might be my Lord Such-a-one, that praised my Lord Such-a-one's horse, when 'a meant to beg it, might it not? 65
HORATIO: Ay, my lord.
HAMLET: Why, e'en so, and now my Lady Worm's, chapless,[6] and knock'd about the mazzard with a sexton's spade. Here's fine revolution,[7] an we had the trick to see't. Did these bones cost no more the breeding but to play at loggets with them?[8] Mine ache to think on't. 70
CLOWN:

      [*Sings.*]

    A pick-axe and a spade, a spade,
      For and a shrouding sheet:

2. Advantage. *Contract*: shorten.
3. The gravedigger's song is a free version of "The aged lover renounceth love" by Thomas, Lord Vaux, published in *Tottel's Miscellany* (1557).   4. Hurls.   5. Gets the better of.
6. Lacking a lower jaw.   7. Skill. *Mazzard*: head.
8. "Loggets" were small pieces of wood thrown as part of a game.

> O, a pit of clay for to be made
> For such a guest is meet.

[*Throws up another skull.*]

75 HAMLET: There's another. Why may not that be the skull of a lawyer? Where be his quiddities now, his quillets, his cases, his tenures, and his tricks? Why does he suffer this mad knave now to knock him about the sconce[9] with a dirty shovel, and will not tell him of his action of battery? Hum! This fellow might be in's time a great buyer of land, with his stat-
80 utes, his recognizances, his fines, his double vouchers, his recoveries. Is this the fine[1] of his fines, and the recovery of his recoveries, to have his fine pate full of fine dirt? Will his vouchers vouch him no more of his purchases, and double ones too, than the length and breadth of a pair of indentures?[2] The very conveyances of his lands will scarcely lie in this
85 box, and must th' inheritor himself have no more, ha?[3]
HORATIO: Not a jot more, my lord.
HAMLET: Is not parchment made of sheepskins?
HORATIO: Ay, my lord, and of calves' skins too.
HAMLET: They are sheep and calves which seek out assurance in that. I
90 will speak to this fellow. Whose grave's this, sirrah?
CLOWN: Mine, sir.

[*Sings.*]

> O, a pit of clay for to be made
> For such a guest is meet.

HAMLET: I think it be thine indeed, for thou liest in't.
95 CLOWN: You lie out on't, sir, and therefore 'tis not yours. For my part, I do not lie in't, yet it is mine.
HAMLET: Thou dost lie in't, to be in't and say it is thine. 'Tis for the dead, not for the quick;[4] therefore thou liest.
CLOWN: 'Tis a quick lie, sir; 'twill away again from me to you.
100 HAMLET: What man dost thou dig it for?
CLOWN: For no man, sir.
HAMLET: What woman, then?
CLOWN: For none neither.
HAMLET: Who is to be buried in't?
105 CLOWN: One that was a woman, sir; but, rest her soul, she's dead.

---

9. Head.   1. End.   2. Contracts.
3. In this speech Hamlet reels off a list of legal terms relating to property transactions.
4. Living.

HAMLET: How absolute the knave is! We must speak by the card,[5] or equivocation will undo us. By the Lord, Horatio, this three years I have took note of it, the age is grown so picked[6] that the toe of the peasant comes so near the heel of the courtier, he galls his kibe.[7] How long hast thou been a grave-maker?

CLOWN: Of all the days i' th' year, I came to't that day that our last King Hamlet overcame Fortinbras.   110

HAMLET: How long is that since?

CLOWN: Cannot you tell that? Every fool can tell that. It was that very day that young Hamlet was born—he that is mad, and sent into England.

HAMLET: Ay, marry, why was he sent into England?   115

CLOWN: Why, because 'a was mad. 'A shall recover his wits there; or, if 'a do not, 'tis no great matter there.

HAMLET: Why?

CLOWN: 'Twill not be seen in him there. There the men are as mad as he.

HAMLET: How came he mad?   120

CLOWN: Very strangely, they say.

HAMLET: How strangely?

CLOWN: Faith, e'en with losing his wits.

HAMLET: Upon what ground?

CLOWN: Why, here in Denmark. I have been sexton here, man and boy,   125
thirty years.

HAMLET: How long will a man lie i' th' earth ere he rot?

CLOWN: Faith, if 'a be not rotten before 'a die—as we have many pocky[8] corses now-a-days that will scarce hold the laying in—'a will last you some eight year or nine year. A tanner will last you nine year.   130

HAMLET: Why he more than another?

CLOWN: Why, sir, his hide is so tanned with his trade that 'a will keep out water a great while; and your water is a sore decayer of your whoreson dead body. Here's a skull now hath lien[9] you i' th' earth three and twenty years.

HAMLET: Whose was it?   135

CLOWN: A whoreson mad fellow's it was. Whose do you think it was?

HAMLET: Nay, I know not.

CLOWN: A pestilence on him for a mad rogue! 'A poured a flagon of Rhenish on my head once. This same skull, sir, was, sir, Yorick's skull, the king's jester.

HAMLET: [*Takes the skull.*] This?   140

---

5. Exactly. *Absolute*: precise.   6. Refined.   7. Rubs a blister on his heel.
8. Corrupted by syphilis.   9. Lain. *Whoreson*: bastard (not literally).

CLOWN: E'en that.

HAMLET: Alas, poor Yorick! I knew him, Horatio—a fellow of infinite jest,
of most excellent fancy. He hath bore me on his back a thousand times,
and now how abhorred in my imagination it is! My gorg[1] rises at it. Here
145 hung those lips that I have kissed I know not how oft. Where be your
gibes now, your gambols, your songs, your flashes of merriment that were
wont to set the table on a roar? Not one now to mock your own grinning?
Quite chap-fall'n?[2] Now get you to my lady's chamber, and tell her, let
her paint an inch thick, to this favor[3] she must come. Make her laugh
150 at that. Prithee, Horatio, tell me one thing.

HORATIO: What's that, my lord?

HAMLET: Dost thou think Alexander looked o' this fashion i' th' earth?

HORATIO: E'en so.

HAMLET: And smelt so? Pah!   [Throws down the skull.]

155 HORATIO: E'en so, my lord.

HAMLET: To what base uses we may return, Horatio! Why may not imagination trace the noble dust of Alexander till 'a find it stopping a bung-hole?[4]

HORATIO: 'Twere to consider too curiously[5] to consider so.

HAMLET: No, faith, not a jot, but to follow him thither with modesty[6] enough,
160 and likelihood to lead it. Alexander died, Alexander was buried, Alexander
returneth to dust; the dust is earth; of earth we make loam; and why of
that loam whereto he was converted might they not stop a beerbarrel?

Imperious Cæsar, dead and turned to clay,
Might stop a hole to keep the wind away.
165 O, that that earth which kept the world in awe
Should patch a wall t'expel the winter's flaw![7]

But soft, but soft awhile! Here comes the king,
The queen, the courtiers.

[Enter KING, QUEEN, LAERTES, and the Corse with a PRIEST and LORDS
attendant.]

Who is this they follow?
And with such maimèd[8] rites? This doth betoken
170 The corse they follow did with desperate hand
Fordo its own life. 'Twas of some estate.[9]
Couch[1] we awhile and mark.   [Retires with HORATIO.]

LAERTES: What ceremony else?[2]

---

1. Throat.   2. Lacking a lower jaw.   3. Appearance.   4. Used as a cork in a cask.   5. Precisely.
6. Moderation.   7. Gusty wind.   8. Shortened.   9. Rank. Fordo: destroy.   1. Conceal ourselves.
2. More.

HAMLET: That is Laertes, a very noble youth. Mark.

LAERTES: What ceremony else?   175

PRIEST: Here obsequies have been as far enlarged[3]
    As we have warranty. Her death was doubtful,
    And but that great command o'ersways the order,[4]
    She should in ground unsanctified been lodged
    Till the last trumpet. For charitable prayers,   180
    Shards, flints, and pebbles, should be thrown on her.
    Yet here she is allowed her virgin crants,[5]
    Her maiden strewments,[6] and the bringing home
    Of bell and burial.

LAERTES: Must there no more be done?

PRIEST: No more be done.   185
    We should profane the service of the dead
    To sing a requiem and such rest to her
    As to peace-parted souls.

LAERTES: Lay her i' th' earth,
    And from her fair and unpolluted flesh
    May violets spring! I tell thee, churlish priest,   190
    A minist'ring angel shall my sister be
    When thou liest howling.[7]

HAMLET: What, the fair Ophelia!

QUEEN: Sweets to the sweet. Farewell!   [*Scatters flowers.*]
    I hoped thou shouldst have been my Hamlet's wife.
    I thought thy bride-bed to have decked, sweet maid,   195
    And not t' have strewed thy grave.

LAERTES: O, treble woe
    Fall ten times treble on that cursèd head
    Whose wicked deed thy most ingenious sense[8]
    Deprived thee of! Hold off the earth awhile,
    Till I have caught her once more in mine arms. [*Leaps into the grave.*] 200
    Now pile your dust upon the quick and dead,
    Till of this flat a mountain you have made
    T' o'er-top old Pelion or the skyish head
    Of blue Olympus.[9]

---

3. Extended.   4. Usual rules.   5. Wreaths.   6. Flowers strewn on the grave.   7. In Hell.
8. Lively mind.
9. The rivalry between Laertes and Hamlet in this scene extends even to their rhetoric. Pelion and Olympus, mentioned here by Laertes, and Ossa, mentioned below by Hamlet, are Greek mountains noted in mythology for their height. Olympus was the reputed home of the gods, and the other two were piled one on top of the other by the Giants in an attempt to reach the top of Olympus and overthrow the gods.

HAMLET: [*Coming forward.*] What is he whose grief
205   Bears such an emphasis, whose phrase of sorrow
    Conjures[1] the wand'ring stars, and makes them stand
    Like wonder-wounded hearers? This is I,
    Hamlet the Dane.

[HAMLET *leaps into the grave and they grapple.*]

LAERTES: The devil take thy soul!
HAMLET: Thou pray'st not well.
210   I prithee take thy fingers from my throat,
    For though I am not splenitive[2] and rash,
    Yet have I in me something dangerous,
    Which let thy wisdom fear. Hold off thy hand.
KING: Pluck them asunder.
215 QUEEN: Hamlet! Hamlet!
ALL: Gentlemen!
HORATIO: Good my lord, be quiet.

[*The* ATTENDANTS *part them, and they come out of the grave.*]

HAMLET: Why, I will fight with him upon this theme
    Until my eyelids will no longer wag.[3]
220 QUEEN: O my son, what theme?
HAMLET: I loved Ophelia. Forty thousand brothers
    Could not with all their quantity of love
    Make up my sum. What wilt thou do for her?
KING: O, he is mad, Laertes.
225 QUEEN: For love of God, forbear[4] him.
HAMLET: 'Swounds, show me what th'owt do.
    Woo't[5] weep, woo't fight, woo't fast, woo't tear thyself,
    Woo't drink up eisel,[6] eat a crocodile?
    I'll do't. Dost come here to whine?
230   To outface[7] me with leaping in her grave?
    Be buried quick with her, and so will I.
    And if thou prate of mountains, let them throw
    Millions of acres on us, till our ground,
    Singeing his pate against the burning zone,[8]
235   Make Ossa like a wart! Nay, an thou'lt mouth,
    I'll rant as well as thou.
QUEEN: This is mere madness

---

1. Casts a spell on.   2. Hot tempered.   3. Move.   4. Bear with.   5. Will you.   6. Vinegar.
7. Get the best of.   8. Sky in the torrid zone.

And thus awhile the fit will work on him.
Anon, as patient as the female dove
When that her golden couplets⁹ are disclosed,
His silence will sit drooping.
HAMLET: Hear you, sir.
What is the reason that you use me thus?   240
I loved you ever. But it is no matter.
Let Hercules himself do what he may,
The cat will mew, and dog will have his day.   [*Exit.*]
KING: I pray thee, good Horatio, wait upon¹ him.

[*Exit* HORATIO.]

[*To* LAERTES.] Strengthen your patience in our last night's speech.   245
We'll put the matter to the present push.²—
Good Gertrude, set some watch over your son.—
This grave shall have a living monument.
An hour of quiet shortly shall we see;
Till then in patience our proceeding be.   [*Exeunt.*]   250

Scene 2

A hall or public room. Enter HAMLET *and* HORATIO.

HAMLET: So much for this, sir; now shall you see the other.
You do remember all the circumstance?
HORATIO: Remember it, my lord!
HAMLET: Sir, in my heart there was a kind of fighting
That would not let me sleep. Methought I lay   5
Worse than the mutines in the bilboes.³ Rashly,
And praised be rashness for it—let us know,
Our indiscretion sometime serves us well,
When our deep plots do pall; and that should learn⁴ us
There's a divinity that shapes our ends,   10
Rough-hew them how we will—
HORATIO: That is most certain.
HAMLET: Up from my cabin,
My sea-gown scarfed⁵ about me, in the dark
Groped I to find out them, had my desire,
Fingered their packet, and in fine⁶ withdrew   15
To mine own room again, making so bold,

9. Pair of eggs.   1. Attend.   2. Immediate trial.   3. Stocks. *Mutines*: mutineers.   4. Teach.
5. Wrapped.   6. Quickly. *Fingered*: stole.

My fears forgetting manners, to unseal
Their grand commission; where I found, Horatio—
Ah, royal knavery!—an exact[7] command,
20   Larded[8] with many several sorts of reasons,
Importing Denmark's health, and England's too,
With, ho! such bugs and goblins in my life,[9]
That on the supervise,[1] no leisure bated,
No, not to stay the grinding of the axe,
My head should be struck off.
25 HORATIO: Is't possible?
HAMLET: Here's the commission; read it at more leisure.
But wilt thou hear now how I did proceed?
HORATIO: I beseech you.
HAMLET: Being thus benetted[2] round with villainies,
30   Ere I could make a prologue to my brains,
They had begun the play. I sat me down,
Devised a new commission, wrote it fair.[3]
I once did hold it, as our statists[4] do,
A baseness to write fair, and labored much
35   How to forget that learning; but sir, now
It did me yeoman's service.[5] Wilt thou know
Th' effect[6] of what I wrote?
HORATIO: Ay, good my lord.
HAMLET: An earnest conjuration from the king,
As England was his faithful tributary,[7]
40   As love between them like the palm might flourish,
As peace should still her wheaten garland wear
And stand a comma 'tween their amities[8]
And many such like as's of great charge,[9]
That on the view and knowing of these contents,
45   Without debatement[1] further more or less,
He should those bearers put to sudden death,
Not shriving-time allowed.[2]
HORATIO: How was this sealed?
HAMLET: Why, even in that was heaven ordinant,[3]
I had my father's signet in my purse,
50   Which was the model of that Danish seal,
Folded the writ up in the form of th' other,

---

7. Precisely stated.   8. Garnished.   9. Such dangers if I remained alive.
1. As soon as the commission was read.   2. Caught in a net.   3. Legibly. *Devised*: made.
4. Politicians.   5. Served me well.   6. Contents.   7. Vassal.   8. Link friendships.   9. Import.
1. Consideration.   2. Without time for confession.   3. Operative.

Subscribed it, gave't th' impression,[4] placed it safely,
The changeling[5] never known. Now, the next day
Was our sea-fight, and what to this was sequent[6]
Thou knowest already.   55
HORATIO: So Guildenstern and Rosencrantz go to't.
HAMLET: Why, man, they did make love to this employment.
    They are not near my conscience; their defeat[7]
    Does by their own insinuation grow.
    'Tis dangerous when the baser nature comes   60
    Between the pass and fell[8] incensèd points
    Of mighty opposites.
HORATIO: Why, what a king is this!
HAMLET: Does it not, think thee, stand me now upon—
    He that hath killed my king and whored my mother,
    Popped in between th' election and my hopes,   65
    Thrown out his angle[9] for my proper life,
    And with such coz'nage[1]—is't not perfect conscience
    To quit[2] him with this arm? And is't not to be damned
    To let this canker of our nature come
    In further evil?   70
HORATIO: It must be shortly known to him from England
    What is the issue[3] of the business there.
HAMLET: It will be short;[4] the interim is mine.
    And a man's life's no more than to say "one."
    But I am very sorry, good Horatio,   75
    That to Laertes I forgot myself;
    For by the image of my cause I see
    The portraiture of his. I'll court his favors.
    But sure the bravery[5] of his grief did put me
    Into a tow'ring passion.
HORATIO: Peace; who comes here?   80

[*Enter* OSRIC.]

OSRIC: Your lordship is right welcome back to Denmark.
HAMLET: I humbly thank you, sir. [*Aside to* HORATIO.] Dost know this
    water-fly?
HORATIO: [*Aside to* HAMLET.] No, my good lord.
HAMLET: [*Aside to* HORATIO.] Thy state is the more gracious, for 'tis a vice 85
    to know him. He hath much land, and fertile. Let a beast be lord of

---

4. With the seal.   5. Replacement.   6. Followed.   7. Death. *Are not near*: do not touch.
8. Cruel. *Pass*: thrust.   9. Fishhook.   1. Trickery.   2. Repay.   3. Outcome.   4. Soon.
5. Exaggerated display.

beasts, and his crib shall stand at the king's mess. 'Tis a chough,[6] but as I say, spacious in the possession of dirt.

OSRIC: Sweet lord, if your lordship were at leisure, I should impart a thing
90   to you from his majesty.

HAMLET: I will receive it, sir, with all diligence of spirit. Put your bonnet to his right use. 'Tis for the head.[7]

OSRIC: I thank your lordship, it is very hot.

HAMLET: No, believe me, 'tis very cold; the wind is northerly.

95   OSRIC: It is indifferent[8] cold, my lord, indeed.

HAMLET: But yet methinks it is very sultry and hot for my complexion.[9]

OSRIC: Exceedingly, my lord; it is very sultry, as 'twere—I cannot tell how. My lord, his majesty bade me signify to you that 'a has laid a great wager on your head. Sir, this is the matter—

100   HAMLET: I beseech you, remember.   [*Moves him to put on his hat.*]

OSRIC: Nay, good my lord; for my ease, in good faith. Sir, here is newly come to court Laertes; believe me, an absolute[1] gentleman, full of most excellent differences of very soft society and great showing.[2] Indeed, to speak feelingly of him, he is the card or calendar of gentry, for you shall
105   find in him the continent[3] of what part a gentleman would see.

HAMLET: Sir, his definement[4] suffers no perdition in you, though I know to divide him inventorially would dozy th' arithmetic of memory, and yet but yaw[5] neither in respect of his quick sail. But in the verity of extolment, I take him to be a soul of great article, and his infusion[6] of such
110   dearth and rareness as, to make true diction of him, his semblage is his mirror,[7] and who else would trace him, his umbrage,[8] nothing more.

OSRIC: Your lordship speaks most infallibly of him.

HAMLET: The concernancy,[9] sir? Why do we wrap the gentleman in our more rawer breath?[1]

115   OSRIC: Sir?

HORATIO: Is't not possible to understand in another tongue? You will to't, sir, really.

HAMLET: What imports the nomination[2] of this gentleman?

OSRIC: Of Laertes?

120   HORATIO: [*Aside.*] His purse is empty already. All's golden words are spent.

HAMLET: Of him, sir.

---

6. Jackdaw.   7. Osric has evidently removed his hat in deference to the prince.   8. Moderately.
9. Temperament.   1. Perfect.   2. Good manners. *Excellent differences*: qualities.
3. Sum total. *Calendar*: measure.   4. Description.
5. Steer wildly. *Dozy*: daze. *Divide him inventorially*: examine bit by bit.   6. Nature. *Article*: scope.
7. That is, his likeness ("semblage") is (only) his own mirror image; he is unrivaled. *Diction*: telling.   8. Shadow. *Trace*: keep pace with.
9. Meaning. (Hamlet is mocking Osric's affected speech.)   1. Cruder words.   2. Naming.

OSRIC: I know you are not ignorant—

HAMLET: I would you did, sir; yet, in faith, if you did, it would not much
approve me. Well, sir.

OSRIC: You are not ignorant of what excellence Laertes is— 125

HAMLET: I dare not confess that, lest I should compare[3] with him in excellence; but to know a man well were to know himself.

OSRIC: I mean, sir, for his weapon; but in the imputation[4] laid on him by
them, in his meed he's unfellowed.[5]

HAMLET: What's his weapon? 130

OSRIC: Rapier and dagger.

HAMLET: That's two of his weapons—but well.

OSRIC: The king, sir, hath wagered with him six Barbary horses, against the
which he has impawned,[6] as I take it, six French rapiers and poniards,
with their assigns, as girdle, hangers,[7] and so. Three of the carriages, 135
in faith, are very dear to fancy,[8] very responsive to the hilts, most delicate carriages, and of very liberal conceit.[9]

HAMLET: What call you the carriages?

HORATIO: [*Aside to* HAMLET.] I knew you must be edified by the margent[1]
ere you had done. 140

OSRIC: The carriages, sir, are the hangers.

HAMLET: The phrase would be more germane to the matter if we could
carry a cannon by our sides. I would it might be hangers till then. But
on! Six Barbary horses against six French swords, their assigns, and
three liberal conceited carriages; that's the French bet against the Danish. 145
Why is this all impawned, as you call it?

OSRIC: The king, sir, hath laid, sir, that in a dozen passes between yourself
and him he shall not exceed you three hits; he hath laid on twelve for
nine, and it would come to immediate trial if your lordship would
vouchsafe the answer. 150

HAMLET: How if I answer no?

OSRIC: I mean, my lord, the opposition of your person in trial.

HAMLET: Sir, I will walk here in the hall. If it please his majesty, it is the
breathing time[2] of day with me. Let the foils be brought, the gentleman
willing, and the king hold his purpose; I will win for him an I can. If 155
not, I will gain nothing but my shame and the odd hits.

OSRIC: Shall I deliver you so?

HAMLET: To this effect, sir, after what flourish your nature will.

OSRIC: I commend my duty to your lordship.

---

3. That is, compare myself.   4. Reputation.   5. Unequaled in his excellence   6. Staked.
7. Sword belts. *Assigns:* appurtenances.   8. Finely designed.
9. Elegant design. *Delicate:* well adjusted.   1. Marginal gloss.   2. Time for exercise.

160 HAMLET: Yours, yours. [*Exit* OSRIC.] He does well to commend it himself;
there are no tongues else for's turn.
HORATIO: This lapwing runs away with the shell on his head.[3]
HAMLET: 'A did comply, sir, with his dug[4] before 'a sucked it. Thus has he,
and many more of the same bevy that I know the drossy age dotes on,
165 only got the tune of the time; and out of an habit of encounter, a king
of yesty[5] collection which carries them through and through the most
fanned and winnowed opinions; and do but blow them to their trial,
the bubbles are out.

[*Enter a* LORD.]

LORD: My lord, his majesty commended him to you by young Osric, who
170 brings back to him that you attend[6] him in the hall. He sends to know if
your pleasure hold to play with Laertes, or that you will take longer time.
HAMLET: I am constant to my purposes; they follow the king's pleasure. If
his fitness speaks, mine is ready; now or whensoever, provided I be so
able as now.
175 LORD: The king and queen and all are coming down.
HAMLET: In happy time.
LORD: The queen desires you to use some gentle entertainment[7] to Laertes
before you fall to play.
HAMLET: She well instructs me.   [*Exit* LORD.]
180 HORATIO: You will lose this wager, my lord.
HAMLET: I do not think so. Since he went into France I have been in continual practice. I shall win at the odds. But thou wouldst not think how
ill[8] all's here about my heart. But it's no matter.
HORATIO: Nay, good my lord—
185 HAMLET: It is but foolery, but it is such a kind of gaingiving[9] as would perhaps trouble a woman.
HORATIO: If your mind dislike anything, obey it. I will forestall their repair[1]
hither, and say you are not fit.
HAMLET: Not a whit, we defy augury. There is special providence in the
190 fall of a sparrow. If it be now, 'tis not to come; if it be not to come, it
will be now; if it be not now, yet it will come. The readiness is all. Since
no man of aught he leaves knows, what is't to leave betimes? Let be.

[*A table prepared. Enter* TRUMPETS, DRUMS, *and* OFFICERS *with cushions;*
KING, QUEEN, OSRIC *and* ATTENDANTS *with foils, daggers, and* LAERTES.]

3. The lapwing was thought to be so precocious that it could run immediately after being
hatched, even, as here, with bits of the shell still on its head.
4. Mother's breast. *Comply*: deal formally.   5. Yeasty.   6. Await.   7. Cordiality.   8. Uneasy.
9. Misgiving.   1. Coming.

KING: Come, Hamlet, come and take this hand from me.

[*The* KING *puts* LAERTES' *hand into* HAMLET's.]

HAMLET: Give me your pardon, sir. I have done you wrong,
But pardon 't as you are a gentleman.   195
This presence[2] knows, and you must needs have heard,
How I am punished with a sore distraction.
What I have done
That might your nature, honor, and exception,[3]
Roughly awake, I here proclaim was madness.   200
Was 't Hamlet wronged Laertes? Never Hamlet.
If Hamlet from himself be ta'en away,
And when he's not himself does wrong Laertes,
Then Hamlet does it not, Hamlet denies it.
Who does it then? His madness. If't be so,   205
Hamlet is of the faction that is wronged;
His madness is poor Hamlet's enemy.
Sir, in this audience,
Let my disclaiming from[4] a purposed evil
Free[5] me so far in your most generous thoughts   210
That I have shot my arrow o'er the house
And hurt my brother.

LAERTES: I am satisfied in nature,
Whose motive in this case should stir me most
To my revenge. But in my terms of honor   215
I stand aloof, and will no reconcilement
Till by some elder masters of known honor
I have a voice[6] and precedent of peace
To keep my name ungored.[7] But till that time
I do receive your offered love like love,   220
And will not wrong it.

HAMLET: I embrace it freely,
And will this brother's wager frankly[8] play.
Give us the foils. Come on.

LAERTES: Come, one for me.   225

HAMLET: I'll be your foil, Laertes. In mine ignorance
Your skill shall, like a star i' th' darkest night,
Stick fiery off[9] indeed.

LAERTES: You mock me, sir.

HAMLET: No, by this hand.   230

2. Company.   3. Resentment.   4. Denying of.   5. Absolve.   6. Authority.   7. Unshamed.
8. Freely.   9. Shine brightly.

KING: Give them the foils, young Osric. Cousin Hamlet,
    You know the wager?
HAMLET: Very well, my lord;
    Your Grace has laid the odds o' th' weaker side.
235 KING: I do not fear it, I have seen you both;
    But since he is bettered[1] we have therefore odds.
LAERTES: This is too heavy; let me see another.
HAMLET: This likes me well. These foils have all a[2] length?

    [*They prepare to play.*]

OSRIC: Ay, my good lord.
240 KING: Set me the stoups of wine upon that table.
    If Hamlet give the first or second hit,
    Or quit in answer of[3] the third exchange,
    Let all the battlements their ordnance fire.
    The king shall drink to Hamlet's better breath,
245   And in the cup an union[4] shall he throw,
    Richer than that which four successive kings
    In Denmark's crown have worn. Give me the cups,
    And let the kettle[5] to the trumpet speak,
    The trumpet to the cannoneer without,
250   The cannons to the heavens, the heaven to earth,
    "Now the king drinks to Hamlet." Come, begin—

    [*Trumpets the while.*]

    And you, the judges, bear a wary eye.
HAMLET: Come on, sir.
LAERTES: Come, my lord.

    [*They play.*]

255 HAMLET: One.
LAERTES: No.
HAMLET: Judgment?
OSRIC: A hit, a very palpable hit.

    [*Drums, trumpets, and shot. Flourish; a piece goes off.*]

LAERTES: Well, again.
260 KING: Stay, give me drink. Hamlet, this pearl is thine.
    Here's to thy health. Give him the cup.
HAMLET: I'll play this bout first; set it by awhile.

---

1. Reported better.   2. The same. *Likes*: suits.   3. Repay.   4. Pearl.   5. Kettledrum.

Come.

[*They play.*]

Another hit; what say you?

LAERTES: A touch, a touch, I do confess't.   265

KING: Our son shall win.

QUEEN: He's fat,[6] and scant of breath.

Here, Hamlet, take my napkin, rub thy brows.

The queen carouses to thy fortune, Hamlet.

HAMLET: Good madam!   270

KING: Gertrude, do not drink.

QUEEN: I will, my lord; I pray you pardon me.

KING: [*Aside.*] It is the poisoned cup; it is too late.

HAMLET: I dare not drink yet, madam; by and by.

QUEEN: Come, let me wipe thy face.   275

LAERTES: My lord, I'll hit him now.

KING: I do not think't.

LAERTES: [*Aside.*] And yet it is almost against my conscience.

HAMLET: Come, for the third, Laertes. You do but dally.

I pray you pass[7] with your best violence;   280

I am afeard you make a wanton of me.[8]

LAERTES: Say you so? Come on.

[*They play.*]

OSRIC: Nothing, neither way.

LAERTES: Have at you now!

[LAERTES *wounds* HAMLET: *then, in scuffling, they change rapiers, and* HAMLET *wounds* LAERTES.]

KING: Part them. They are incensed.   285

HAMLET: Nay, come again.

[*The* QUEEN *falls.*]

OSRIC: Look to the queen there, ho!

HORATIO: They bleed on both sides. How is it, my lord?

OSRIC: How is't, Laertes?

LAERTES: Why, as a woodcock to mine own springe,[9] Osric.   290

I am justly killed with mine own treachery.

HAMLET: How does the queen?

KING: She swoons to see them bleed.

6. Out of shape.   7. Attack.   8. Trifle with me.   9. Snare.

QUEEN: No, no, the drink, the drink! O my dear Hamlet!
295   The drink, the drink! I am poisoned.   [*Dies.*]
HAMLET: O, villainy! Ho! let the door be locked.
     Treachery! seek it out.
LAERTES: It is here, Hamlet. Hamlet, thou art slain;
     No med'cine in the world can do thee good.
300   In thee there is not half an hour's life.
     The treacherous instrument is in thy hand,
     Unbated[1] and envenomed. The foul practice
     Hath turned itself on me. Lo, here I lie,
     Never to rise again. Thy mother's poisoned.
305   I can no more. The king, the king's to blame.
HAMLET: The point envenomed too?
     Then, venom, to thy work.   [*Hurts the* KING.]
ALL: Treason! treason!
KING: O, yet defend me, friends. I am but hurt.[2]
310 HAMLET: Here, thou incestuous, murd'rous, damnèd Dane,
     Drink off this potion. Is thy union here?
     Follow my mother.

     [*The* KING *dies.*]

LAERTES: He is justly served.
     It is a poison tempered[3] by himself.
315   Exchange forgiveness with me, noble Hamlet.
     Mine and my father's death come not upon thee,
     Nor thine on me!   [*Dies.*]
HAMLET: Heaven make thee free of[4] it! I follow thee.
     I am dead, Horatio. Wretched queen, adieu!
320   You that look pale and tremble at this chance,[5]
     That are but mutes or audience to this act,
     Had I but time, as this fell sergeant Death
     Is strict in his arrest,[6] O, I could tell you—
     But let it be. Horatio, I am dead:
325   Thou livest; report me and my cause aright
     To the unsatisfied.[7]
HORATIO: Never believe it.
     I am more an antique Roman than a Dane.
     Here's yet some liquor left.
330 HAMLET: As th'art a man,
     Give me the cup. Let go. By heaven, I'll ha't.

---

1. Unblunted.   2. Wounded.   3. Mixed.   4. Forgive.   5. Circumstance.   6. Summons to court.
7. Uninformed.

O God, Horatio, what a wounded name,
Things standing thus unknown, shall live behind me!
If thou didst ever hold me in thy heart,
Absent thee from felicity awhile,   335
And in this harsh world draw thy breath in pain,
To tell my story.

[*A march afar off.*]

                What warlike noise is this?
OSRIC: Young Fortinbras, with conquest come from Poland,
  To th' ambassadors of England gives   340
  This warlike volley.[8]
HAMLET: O, I die, Horatio!
The potent poison quite o'er-crows[9] my spirit.
I cannot live to hear the news from England,
But I do prophesy th' election[1] lights   345
On Fortinbras. He has my dying voice.[2]
So tell him, with th' occurrents,[3] more and less,
Which have solicited[4]—the rest is silence.   [*Dies.*]
HORATIO: Now cracks a noble heart. Good night, sweet prince,
And flights of angels sing thee to thy rest!   350

[*March within.*]

Why does the drum come hither?

[*Enter* FORTINBRAS, *with the* AMBASSADORS *and with drum, colors,*
and ATTENDANTS.]

FORTINBRAS: Where is this sight?
HORATIO: What is it you would see?
If aught of woe or wonder, cease your search.
FORTINBRAS: This quarry cries on havoc.[5] O proud death,   355
What feast is toward[6] in thine eternal cell
That thou so many princes at a shot
So bloodily hast struck?
AMBASSADORS: The sight is dismal;
And our affairs from England come too late.   360

---

8. The staging presents some difficulties here. Unless Osric is clairvoyant, he must have left the
stage at some point and returned. One possibility is that he might have left to carry out Hamlet's
order to lock the door (line 296) and returned when the sound of the distant march is heard.
9. Overcomes.   1. (Of a new king for Denmark.)   2. Support.   3. Circumstances.
4. Brought about this scene.   5. The game killed in the hunt proclaims a slaughter.
6. In preparation.

The ears are senseless[7] that should give us hearing
To tell him his commandment is fulfilled,
That Rosencrantz and Guildenstern are dead.
Where should we have our thanks?

365 HORATIO: Not from his mouth,
Had it th' ability of life to thank you.
He never gave commandment for their death.
But since, so jump[8] upon this bloody question,
You from the Polack wars, and you from England,
370 Are here arrived, give orders that these bodies
High on a stage be placèd to the view,
And let me speak to th' yet unknowing world
How these things came about. So shall you hear
Of carnal, bloody, and unnatural acts;
375 Of accidental judgments, casual[9] slaughters;
Of deaths put on by cunning and forced cause;
And, in this upshot,[1] purposes mistook
Fall'n on th' inventors' heads. All this can I
Truly deliver.

380 FORTINBRAS: Let us haste to hear it,
And call the noblest to the audience.[2]
For me, with sorrow I embrace my fortune.
I have some rights of memory[3] in this kingdom,
Which now to claim my vantage[4] doth invite me.

385 HORATIO: Of that I shall have also cause to speak,
And from his mouth whose voice will draw on more.
But let this same be presently performed,
Even while men's minds are wild, lest more mischance
On plots and errors happen.

390 FORTINBRAS: Let four captains
Bear Hamlet like a soldier to the stage,
For he was likely, had he been put on,[5]
To have proved most royal; and for his passage
The soldier's music and the rite of war
395 Speak loudly for him.
Take up the bodies. Such a sight as this
Becomes the field,[6] but here shows much amiss.
Go, bid the soldiers shoot.

[*Exeunt marching. A peal of ordnance shot off.*]

c. 1600

---

7. Without sense of hearing.   8. Exactly.   9. Brought about by apparent accident.   1. Result.
2. Hearing.   3. Succession   4. Position.   5. Elected king.   6. Battlefield.

SOPHOCLES
(496?–406 BCE)
Antigone[1]

Sophocles lived at a time when Athens and Greek civilization were at the peak of their power and influence. He not only served as a general under Pericles and played a prominent role in the city's affairs but also was arguably the greatest of the Greek tragic playwrights, winning the annual dramatic competition about twenty times, a feat unmatched by even his great contemporaries, Aeschylus and Euripides. An innovator, Sophocles fundamentally changed the nature of dramatic performance by adding a third actor, enlarging the chorus, and introducing the use of painted scenery. Aristotle held that Sophocles's *Oedipus the King* (c. 429 BCE) was the perfect tragedy and used it as his model when he discussed the nature of tragedy in his *Poetics*. Today only seven of Sophocles's tragedies survive—the Oedipus trilogy (*Oedipus the King, Oedipus at Colonus,* and *Antigone*), *Philoctetes, Ajax, Trachiniae,* and *Electra*—though he is believed to have written as many as 123 plays.

CHARACTERS

ANTIGONE   HAEMON
ISMENE   TEIRESIAS
CHORUS OF THEBAN ELDERS   A MESSENGER
CREON   EURYDICE
A SENTRY   SECOND MESSENGER

The two sisters ANTIGONE *and* ISMENE *meet in front of the palace gates in Thebes.*

ANTIGONE: Ismene, my dear sister,
  whose father was my father, can you think of any
  of all the evils that stem from Oedipus[2]
  that Zeus does not bring to pass for us, while we yet live?

1. Translated by David Grene.
2. In Greek legend, Oedipus became king of Thebes by inadvertently fulfilling the prophecy that he was destined to kill his father and marry his mother (as depicted in Sophocles's *Oedipus the King*); for these offenses against nature and the gods, Creon sent Oedipus, along with his daughters Antigone and Ismene, into exile at Colonus. Oedipus's sons, Eteocles and Polyneices, agreed to take turns ruling Thebes. But when Eteocles refused to give up the throne at the end of his first allotted year, Polyneices gathered an "Argive army" (line 17) and attacked the city.

5   No pain, no ruin, no shame, and no dishonor
        but I have seen it in our mischiefs,
        yours and mine.
        And now what is the proclamation that they tell of
        made lately by the commander, publicly,
10   to all the people? Do you know it? Have you heard it?
        Don't you notice when the evils due to enemies
        are headed towards those we love?

ISMENE: Not a word, Antigone, of those we love,
        either sweet or bitter, has come to me since the moment
15   when we lost our two brothers,
        on one day, by their hands dealing mutual death.
        Since the Argive[3] army fled in this past night,
        I know of nothing further, nothing
        of better fortune or of more destruction.

20 ANTIGONE: I knew it well; that is why I sent for you
        to come outside the palace gates
        to listen to me, privately.

ISMENE: What is it? Certainly your words
        come of dark thoughts.

25 ANTIGONE: Yes, indeed; for those two brothers of ours, in burial
        has not Creon honored the one, dishonored the other?
        Eteocles, they say he has used justly
        with lawful rites and hid him in the earth
        to have his honor among the dead men there.
30   But the unhappy corpse of Polyneices
        he has proclaimed to all the citizens,
        they say, no man may hide
        in a grave nor mourn in funeral,
        but leave unwept, unburied, a dainty treasure
35   for the birds that see him, for their feast's delight.
        That is what, they say, the worthy Creon
        has proclaimed for you and me—for me, I tell you—
        and he comes here to clarify to the unknowing
        his proclamation; he takes it seriously;
40   for whoever breaks the edict death is prescribed,
        and death by stoning publicly.
        There you have it; soon you will show yourself
        as noble both in your nature and your birth,
        or yourself as base, although of noble parents.

3. From Argos, a rival Greek city-state.

ISMENE: If things are as you say, poor sister, how   45
    can I better them? how loose or tie the knot?
ANTIGONE: Decide if you will share the work, the deed.
ISMENE: What kind of danger is there? How far have your thoughts gone?
ANTIGONE: Here is this hand. Will you help it to lift the dead man?
ISMENE: Would you bury him, when it is forbidden the city?   50
ANTIGONE: At least he is my brother—and yours, too,
    though you deny him. *I* will not prove false to him.
ISMENE: You are so headstrong. Creon has forbidden it.
ANTIGONE: It is not for him to keep me from my own.
ISMENE: O God!   55
    Consider, sister, how our father died,
    hated and infamous; how he brought to light
    his own offenses; how he himself struck out
    the sight of his two eyes;
    his own hand was their executioner.   60
    Then, mother and wife, two names in one, did shame
    violently on her life, with twisted cords.
    Third, our two brothers, on a single day,
    poor wretches, themselves worked out their mutual doom.
    Each killed the other, hand against brother's hand.   65
    Now there are only the two of us, left behind,
    and see how miserable our end shall be
    if in the teeth of law we shall transgress
    against the sovereign's decree and power.
    You ought to realize we are only women,   70
    not meant in nature to fight against men,
    and that we are ruled, by those who are stronger,
    to obedience in this and even more painful matters.
    I do indeed beg those beneath the earth
    to give me their forgiveness,   75
    since force constrains me,
    that I shall yield in this to the authorities.
    Extravagant action is not sensible.
ANTIGONE: I would not urge you now; nor if you wanted
    to act would I be glad to have you with me.   80
    Be as you choose to be; but for myself
    I myself will bury him. It will be good
    to die, so doing. I shall lie by his side,
    loving him as he loved me; I shall be
    a criminal—but a religious one.   85
    The time in which I must please those that are dead

is longer than I must please those of this world.
For there I shall lie forever. You, if you like,
can cast dishonor on what the gods have honored.

90 ISMENE: I will not put dishonor on them, but
to act in defiance of the citizenry,
my nature does not give me means for that.

ANTIGONE: Let that be your excuse. But I will go
to heap the earth on the grave of my loved brother.

95 ISMENE: How I fear for you, my poor sister!

ANTIGONE: Do not fear for me. Make straight your own path to destiny.

ISMENE: At least do not speak of this act to anyone else;
bury him in secret; I will be silent, too.

ANTIGONE: Oh, oh, no! shout it out. I will hate you still worse

100   for silence—should you not proclaim it,
to everyone.

ISMENE: You have a warm heart for such chilly deeds.

ANTIGONE: I know I am pleasing those I should please most.

ISMENE: *If* you can do it. But you are in love

105   with the impossible.

ANTIGONE: No. When I can no more, then I will stop.

ISMENE: It is better not to hunt the impossible
at all.

ANTIGONE: If you will talk like this I will loathe you,

110   and you will be adjudged an enemy—
justly—by the dead's decision. Let me alone
and my folly with me, to endure this terror.
No suffering of mine will be enough
to make me die ignobly.

115 ISMENE: Well, if you will, go on.
Know this; that though you are wrong to go, your friends
are right to love you.

CHORUS: Sun's beam, fairest of all
that ever till now shone

120   on seven-gated Thebes;
O golden eye of day, you shone
coming over Dirce's stream;[4]
You drove in headlong rout
the whiteshielded man from Argos,

125   complete in arms;
his bits rang sharper
under your urging.

---

4. River near Thebes.

Polyneices brought him here
against our land, Polyneices,
roused by contentious quarrel;   130
like an eagle he flew into our country,
with many men-at-arms,
with many a helmet crowned with horsehair.

He stood above the halls, gaping with murderous lances,
encompassing the city's   135
seven-gated mouth[5]
But before his jaws would be sated
with our blood, before the fire,
pine fed, should capture our crown of towers,
he went hence—   140
such clamor of war stretched behind his back,
from his dragon foe, a thing he could not overcome.

For Zeus, who hates the most
the boasts of a great tongue,
saw them coming in a great tide,   145
insolent in the clang of golden armor.
The god struck him down with hurled fire,
as he strove to raise the victory cry,
now at the very winning post.

The earth rose to strike him as he fell swinging.   150
In his frantic onslaught, possessed, he breathed upon us
with blasting winds of hate.
Sometimes the great god of war was on one side,
and sometimes he struck a staggering blow on the other;
the god was a very wheel horse[6] on the right trace.   155

At seven gates stood seven captains,
ranged equals against equals, and there left
their brazen suits of armor
to Zeus, the god of trophies.
Only those two wretches born of one father and mother   160
set their spears to win a victory on both sides;
they worked out their share in a common death.

Now Victory, whose name is great, has come
to Thebes of many chariots

5. Thebes was known throughout the ancient world for having seven gateways through the
walls protecting the city.
6. Strongest and ablest horse in a team pulling a vehicle, harnessed nearest the front wheels
"on the right trace."

165   with joy to answer her joy,
    to bring forgetfulness of these wars;
    let us go to all the shrines of the gods
    and dance all night long.
    Let Bacchus lead the dance,
170   shaking Thebes to trembling.

    But here is the king of our land,
    Creon,[7] son of Menoeceus;
    in our new contingencies with the gods,
    he is our new ruler.
175   He comes to set in motion some design—
    what design is it? Because he has proposed
    the convocation of the elders.
    He sent a public summons for our discussion.

CREON: Gentlemen: as for our city's fortune,
180   the gods have shaken her, when the great waves broke,
    but the gods have brought her through again to safety.
    For yourselves, I chose you out of all and summoned you
    to come to me, partly because I knew you
    as always loyal to the throne—at first,
185   when Laïus[8] was king, and then again
    when Oedipus saved our city and then again
    when he died and you remained with steadfast truth
    to their descendants,
    until they met their double fate upon one day,
190   striking and stricken, defiled each by a brother's murder.
    Now here I am, holding all authority
    and the throne, in virtue of kinship with the dead.
    It is impossible to know any man—
    I mean his soul, intelligence, and judgment—
195   until he shows his skill in rule and law.
    I think that a man supreme ruler of a whole city,
    if he does not reach for the best counsel for her,
    but through some fear, keeps his tongue under lock and key,
    him I judge the worst of any;
200   I have always judged so; and anyone thinking
    another man more a friend than his own country,
    I rate him nowhere. For my part, God is my witness,
    who sees all, always, I would not be silent

---

7. Brother of Jocasta, mother and wife of Oedipus; he became king of Thebes after the deaths of Oedipus's sons.
8. Father of Oedipus.

if I saw ruin, not safety, on the way
towards my fellow citizens. I would not count   205
any enemy of my country as a friend—
because of what I know, that she it is
which gives us our security. If she sails upright
and we sail on her, friends will be ours for the making.
In the light of rules like these, I will make her greater still.   210

In consonance with this, I here proclaim
to the citizens about Oedipus' sons.
For Eteocles, who died this city's champion,
showing his valor's supremacy everywhere,
he shall be buried in his grave with every rite   215
of sanctity given to heroes under earth.
However, his brother, Polyneices, a returned exile,
who sought to burn with fire from top to bottom
his native city, and the gods of his own people;
who sought to taste the blood he shared with us,   220
and lead the rest of us to slavery—
I here proclaim to the city that this man
shall no one honor with a grave and none shall mourn.
You shall leave him without burial; you shall watch him
chewed up by birds and dogs and violated.   225
Such is my mind in the matter; never by me
shall the wicked man have precedence in honor
over the just. But he that is loyal to the state
in death, in life alike, shall have my honor.
CHORUS: Son of Menoeceus, so it is your pleasure   230
to deal with foe and friend of this our city.
To use any legal means lies in your power,
both about the dead and those of us who live.
CREON: I understand, then, you will do my bidding.
CHORUS: Please lay this burden on some younger man.   235
CREON: Oh, watchers of the corpse I have already.
CHORUS: What else, then, do your commands entail?
CREON: That you should not side with those who disagree.
CHORUS: There is none so foolish as to love his own death.
CREON: Yes, indeed those are the wages, but often greed   240
has with its hopes brought men to ruin.

[*The* SENTRY *whose speeches follow represents a remarkable experiment
in Greek tragedy in the direction of naturalism of speech. He speaks
with marked clumsiness, partly because he is excited and talks almost*

colloquially. But also the royal presence makes him think apparently that he should be rather grand in his show of respect. He uses odd bits of archaism or somewhat stale poetical passages, particularly in catch phrases. He sounds something like lower-level Shakespearean characters, e.g., Constable Elbow, with his uncertainty about benefactor and malefactor.]

SENTRY: My lord, I will never claim my shortness of breath
　　　is due to hurrying, nor were there wings in my feet.
　　　I stopped at many a lay-by in my thinking;
245　　I circled myself till I met myself coming back.
　　　My soul accosted me with different speeches.
　　　"Poor fool, yourself, why are you going somewhere
　　　when once you get there you will pay the piper?"
　　　"Well, aren't you the daring fellow! stopping again?
250　　and suppose Creon hears the news from someone else—
　　　don't you realize that you will smart for that?"
　　　I turned the whole matter over. I suppose I may say
　　　"I made haste slowly" and the short road became long.
　　　However, at last I came to a resolve:
255　　I must go to you; even if what I say
　　　is nothing, really, still I shall say it.
　　　I come here, a man with a firm clutch on the hope
　　　that nothing can betide him save what is fated.
CREON: What is it then that makes you so afraid?
260 SENTRY: No, I want first of all to tell you my side of it.
　　　I didn't do the thing; I never saw who did it.
　　　It would not be fair for me to get into trouble.
CREON: You hedge, and barricade the thing itself.
　　　Clearly you have some ugly news for me.
265 SENTRY: Well, you know how disasters make a man
　　　hesitate to be their messenger.
CREON: For God's sake, tell me and get out of here!
SENTRY: Yes, I *will* tell you. Someone just now
　　　buried the corpse and vanished. He scattered on the skin
270　　some thirsty dust; he did the ritual,
　　　duly, to purge the body of desecration.
CREON: What! Now who on earth could have done that?
SENTRY: I do not know. For there was there no mark
　　　of axe's stroke nor casting up of earth
275　　of any mattock; the ground was hard and dry,
　　　unbroken; there were no signs of wagon wheels.
　　　The doer of the deed had left no trace.

But when the first sentry of the day pointed it out,
there was for all of us a disagreeable
wonder. For the body had disappeared;   280
not in a grave, of course; but there lay upon him
a little dust as of a hand avoiding
the curse of violating the dead body's sanctity.
There were no signs of any beast nor dog
that came there; he had clearly not been torn.   285
There was a tide of bad words at one another,
guard taunting guard, and it might well have ended
in blows, for there was no one there to stop it.
Each one of us was the criminal but no one
manifestly so; all denied knowledge of it.   290
We were ready to take hot bars in our hands
or walk through fire,⁹ and call on the gods with oaths
that we had neither done it nor were privy
to a plot with anyone, neither in planning
nor yet in execution.   295
At last when nothing came of all our searching,
there was one man who spoke, made every head
bow to the ground in fear. For we could not
either contradict him nor yet could we see how
if we did what he said we would come out all right.   300
His word was that we must lay information
about the matter to yourself; we could not cover it.
This view prevailed and the lot of the draw chose me,
unlucky me, to win that prize. So here
I am. I did not want to come,   305
and you don't want to have me. I know that.
For no one likes the messenger of bad news.
CHORUS: My lord: I wonder, could this be God's doing?
This is the thought that keeps on haunting me.
CREON: Stop, before your words fill even me with rage,   310
that you should be exposed as a fool, and you so old.
For what you say is surely insupportable
when you say the gods took forethought for this corpse.
Is it out of excess of honor for the man,
for the favors that he did them, they should cover him?   315
This man who came to burn their pillared temples,

9. Ancient legal custom in which an accused person was required to undergo a "trial by ordeal,"
such as walking through fire; if the resulting injuries were not serious, the person was thought
to be innocent and therefore divinely protected.

their dedicated offerings—and this land
and laws he would have scattered to the winds?
Or do you see the gods as honoring
320 criminals? This is not so. But what I am doing
now, and other things before this, some men disliked,
within this very city, and muttered against me,
secretly shaking their heads; they would not bow
justly beneath the yoke to submit to me.
325 I am very sure that these men hired others
to do this thing. I tell you the worse currency
that ever grew among mankind is money. This
sacks cities, this drives people from their homes,
this teaches and corrupts the minds of the loyal
330 to acts of shame. This displays
all kinds of evil for the use of men,
instructs in the knowledge of every impious act.
Those that have done this deed have been paid to do it,
but in the end they will pay for what they have done.

335 It is as sure as I still reverence Zeus—
know this right well—and I speak under oath—
if you and your fellows do not find this man
who with his own hand did the burial
and bring him here before me face to face,
340 your death alone will not be enough for me.
You will hang alive till you open up this outrage.
That will teach you in the days to come from what
you may draw profit—safely—from your plundering.
It's not from anything and everything
345 you can grow rich. You will find out
that ill-gotten gains ruin more than they save.
SENTRY: Have I your leave to say something—or should
    I just turn and go?
CREON: Don't you know your talk is painful enough already?
350 SENTRY: Is the ache in your ears or in your mind?
CREON: Why do you dissect the whereabouts of my pain?
SENTRY: Because it is he who did the deed who hurts your
    mind. I only hurt your ears that listen.
CREON: I am sure you have been a chatterbox since you were born.
355 SENTRY: All the same, I did not do this thing.
CREON: You might have done this, too, if you sold your soul.
SENTRY: It's a bad thing if one judges and judges wrongly.

CREON: You may talk as wittily as you like of judgment.
    Only, if you don't bring to light those men
    who have done this, you will yet come to say   360
    that your wretched gains have brought bad consequences.
SENTRY: [*Aside.*] It were best that he were found, but whether
    the criminal is taken or he isn't—
    for that chance will decide—one thing is certain,
    you'll never see me coming here again.   365
    I never hoped to escape, never thought I could.
    But now I have come off safe, I thank God heartily.
CHORUS: Many are the wonders, none
    is more wonderful than what is man.
    This it is that crosses the sea   370
    with the south winds storming and the waves swelling,
    breaking around him in roaring surf.
    He it is again who wears away
    the Earth, oldest of gods, immortal, unwearied,
    as the ploughs wind across her from year to year   375
    when he works her with the breed that comes from horses.

    The tribe of the lighthearted birds he snares
    and takes prisoner the races of savage beasts
    and the brood of the fish of the sea,
    with the close-spun web of nets.   380
    A cunning fellow is man. His contrivances
    make him master of beasts of the field
    and those that move in the mountains.
    So he brings the horse with the shaggy neck
    to bend underneath the yoke;   385
    and also the untamed mountain bull;
    and speech and windswift thought
    and the tempers that go with city living
    he has taught himself, and how to avoid
    the sharp frost, when lodging is cold   390
    under the open sky
    and pelting strokes of the rain.
    He has a way against everything,
    and he faces nothing that is to come
    without contrivance.   395
    Only against death
    can he call on no means of escape;
    but escape from hopeless diseases
    he has found in the depths of his mind.
    With some sort of cunning, inventive   400

beyond all expectation
he reaches sometimes evil,
and sometimes good.

If he honors the laws of earth,
405   and the justice of the gods he has confirmed by oath,
high is his city; no city
has he with whom dwells dishonor
prompted by recklessness.
He who is so, may he never
410   share my hearth!
may he never think my thoughts!

Is this a portent sent by God?
I cannot tell.
I know her. How can I say
415   that this is not Antigone?
Unhappy girl, child of unhappy Oedipus,
what is this?
Surely it is not you they bring here
as disobedient to the royal edict,
420   surely not you, taken in such folly.
SENTRY: She is the one who did the deed;
we took her burying him. But where is Creon?
CHORUS: He is just coming from the house, when you most need him.
CREON: What is this? What has happened that I come
425   so opportunely?
SENTRY: My lord, there is nothing
that a man should swear he would never do.
Second thoughts make liars of the first resolution.
I would have vowed it would be long enough
430   before I came again, lashed hence by your threats.
But since the joy that comes past hope, and against all hope,
is like no other pleasure in extent,
I have come here, though I break my oath in coming.
I bring this girl here who has been captured
435   giving the grace of burial to the dead man.
This time no lot chose me; this was my jackpot,
and no one else's. Now, my lord, take her
and as you please judge her and test her; I
am justly free and clear of all this trouble.
440 CREON: This girl—how did you take her and from where?
SENTRY: She was burying the man. Now you know all.
CREON: Do you know what you are saying? Do you mean it?

SENTRY: She is the one; I saw her burying
    the dead man you forbade the burial of.
    Now, do I speak plainly and clearly enough?   445
CREON: How was she seen? How was she caught in the act?
SENTRY: This is how it was. When we came there,
    with those dreadful threats of yours upon us,
    we brushed off all the dust that lay upon
    the dead man's body, heedfully   450
    leaving it moist and naked.
    We sat on the brow of the hill, to windward,
    that we might shun the smell of the corpse upon us.
    Each of us wakefully urged his fellow
    with torrents of abuse, not to be careless   455
    in this work of ours. So it went on,
    until in the midst of the sky the sun's bright circle
    stood still; the heat was burning. Suddenly
    a squall lifted out of the earth a storm of dust,
    a trouble in the sky. It filled the plain,   460
    ruining all the foliage of the wood
    that was around it. The great empty air
    was filled with it. We closed our eyes, enduring
    this plague sent by the gods. When at long last
    we were quit of it, why, then we saw the girl.   465

    She was crying out with the shrill cry
    of an embittered bird
    that sees its nest robbed of its nestlings
    and the bed empty. So, too, when she saw
    the body stripped of its cover, she burst out in groans,   470
    calling terrible curses on those that had done that deed;
    and with her hands immediately
    brought thirsty dust to the body; from a shapely brazen
    urn, held high over it, poured a triple stream
    of funeral offerings; and crowned the corpse.   475
    When we saw that, we rushed upon her and
    caught our quarry then and there, not a bit disturbed.
    We charged her with what she had done, then and the first time.
    She did not deny a word of it—to my joy,
    but to my pain as well. It is most pleasant   480
    to have escaped oneself out of such troubles
    but painful to bring into it those whom we love.
    However, it is but natural for me

to count all this less than my own escape.
485 CREON: You there, that turn your eyes upon the ground,
do you confess or deny what you have done?
ANTIGONE: Yes, I confess; I will not deny my deed.
CREON: [To the SENTRY.] You take yourself off where you like.
You are free of a heavy charge.
490 Now, Antigone, tell me shortly and to the point,
did you know the proclamation against your action?
ANTIGONE: I knew it; of course I did. For it was public.
CREON: And did you dare to disobey that law?
ANTIGONE: Yes, it was not Zeus that made the proclamation;
495 nor did Justice, which lives with those below, enact
such laws as that, for mankind. I did not believe
your proclamation had such power to enable
one who will someday die to override
God's ordinances, unwritten and secure.
500 *They* are not of today and yesterday;
they live forever; none knows when first they were.
These are the laws whose penalties I would not
incur from the gods, through fear of any man's temper.

I know that I will die—of course I do—
505 even if you had not doomed me by proclamation.
If I shall die before my time, I count that
a profit. How can such as I, that live
among such troubles, not find a profit in death?
So for such as me, to face such a fate as this
510 is pain that does not count. But if I dared to leave
the dead man, my mother's son, dead and unburied,
that would have been real pain. The other is not.
Now, if you think me a fool to act like this,
perhaps it is a fool that judges so.
515 CHORUS: The savage spirit of a savage father
shows itself in this girl. She does not know
how to yield to trouble.
CREON: I would have you know the most fanatic spirits
fall most of all. It is the toughest iron,
520 baked in the fire to hardness, you may see
most shattered, twisted, shivered to fragments.
I know hot horses are restrained
by a small curb. For he that is his neighbor's slave cannot
be high in spirit. This girl had learned her insolence
525 before this, when she broke the established laws.

But here is still another insolence
in that she boasts of it, laughs at what she did.
I swear I am no man and she the man
if she can win this and not pay for it.
No; though she were my sister's child or closer   530
in blood than all that my hearth god acknowledges
as mine, neither she nor her sister should escape
the utmost sentence—death. For indeed I accuse her,
the sister, equally of plotting the burial.
Summon her. I saw her inside, just now,   535
crazy, distraught. When people plot
mischief in the dark, it is the mind which first
is convicted of deceit. But surely I hate indeed
the one that is caught in evil and then makes
that evil look like good.   540
ANTIGONE: Do you want anything
    beyond my taking and my execution?
CREON: Oh, nothing! Once I have that I have everything.
ANTIGONE: Why do you wait, then? Nothing that you say
    pleases me; God forbid it ever should.   545
    So my words, too, naturally offend you.
    Yet how could I win a greater share of glory
    than putting my own brother in his grave?
    All that are here would surely say that's true,
    if fear did not lock their tongues up. A prince's power   550
    is blessed in many things, not least in this,
    that he can say and do whatever he likes.
CREON: You are alone among the people of Thebes
    to see things in that way.
ANTIGONE: No, these do, too,   555
    but keep their mouths shut for the fear of you.
CREON: Are you not ashamed to think so differently
    from them?
ANTIGONE: There is nothing shameful in honoring my brother.
CREON: Was not he that died on the other side your brother?   560
ANTIGONE: Yes, indeed, of my own blood from father and mother.
CREON: Why then do you show a grace that must be impious
    in *his* sight?
ANTIGONE: *That* other dead man
    would never bear you witness in what you say.   565
CREON: Yes he would, if you put him only on equality
    with one that was a desecrator.
ANTIGONE: It was his brother, not his slave, that died.

CREON: He died destroying the country the other defended.
570 ANTIGONE: The god of death demands these rites for both.
CREON: But the good man does not seek an *equal* share only,
with the bad.
ANTIGONE: Who knows
if in that other world this is true piety?
CREON: My enemy is still my enemy, even in death.
575 ANTIGONE: My nature is to join in love, not hate.
CREON: Go then to the world below, yourself, if you
must love. Love *them*. When I am alive no woman shall rule.
CHORUS: Here before the gates comes Ismene
shedding tears for the love of a brother.
580 A cloud over her brow casts shame
on her flushed face, as the tears wet
her fair cheeks.
CREON: You there, who lurked in my house, viper-like—
secretly drawing its lifeblood; I never thought
585 that I was raising two sources of destruction,
two rebels against my throne. Come tell me now,
will you, too, say you bore a hand in the burial
or will you swear that you know nothing of it?
ISMENE: I did it, yes—if she will say I did it
590 I bear my share in it, bear the guilt, too.
ANTIGONE: Justice will not allow you what you refused
and I will have none of your partnership.
ISMENE: But in your troubles I am not ashamed
to sail with you the sea of suffering.
595 ANTIGONE: Where the act was death, the dead are witnesses.
I do not love a friend who loves in words.
ISMENE: Sister, do not dishonor me, denying me
a common death with you, a common honoring
of the dead man.
600 ANTIGONE: Don't die with me, nor make your own
what you have never touched. I that die am enough.
ISMENE: What life is there for me, once I have lost you?
ANTIGONE: Ask Creon; all your care was on his behalf.
ISMENE: Why do you hurt me, when you gain nothing by it?
605 ANTIGONE: I am hurt by my own mockery—if I mock you.
ISMENE: Even now—what can I do to help you still?
ANTIGONE: Save yourself; I do not grudge you your escape.
ISMENE: I cannot bear it! Not even to share your death!
ANTIGONE: Life was your choice, and death was mine.

ISMENE: You cannot say I accepted that choice in silence.   610
ANTIGONE: You were right in the eyes of one party, I in the other.
ISMENE: Well then, the fault is equally between us.
ANTIGONE: Take heart; you are alive, but my life died
    long ago, to serve the dead.
CREON: Here are two girls; I think that one of them   615
    has suddenly lost her wits—the other was always so.
ISMENE: Yes, for, my lord, the wits that they are born with
    do not stay firm for the unfortunate.
    They go astray.
CREON: Certainly yours do,
    when you share troubles with the troublemaker.   620
ISMENE: What life can be mine alone without her?
CREON: Do not
    speak of *her*. *She* isn't, anymore.
ISMENE: Will you kill your son's wife to be?[1]
CREON: Yes, there are other fields for him to plough.
ISMENE: Not with the mutual love of him and her.   625
CREON: I hate a bad wife for a son of mine.
ANTIGONE: Dear Haemon, how your father dishonors you.
CREON: There is too much of you—and of your marriage!
CHORUS: Will you rob your son of this girl?
CREON: Death—it is death that will stop the marriage for me.   630
CHORUS: Your decision it seems is taken: she shall die.
CREON: Both you and I have decided it. No more delay.

    [*He turns to the* SERVANTS.]

    Bring her inside, you. From this time forth,
    these must be women, and not free to roam.
    For even the stout of heart shrink when they see   635
    the approach of death close to their lives.
CHORUS: Lucky are those whose lives
    know no taste of sorrow.
    But for those whose house has been shaken by God
    there is never cessation of ruin;   640
    it steals on generation after generation
    within a breed. Even as the swell
    is driven over the dark deep
    by the fierce Thracian winds
    I see the ancient evils of Labdacus' house[2]   645

1. Antigone, betrothed to Creon's son Haemon.
2. Theban royal lineage that included Labdacus; his son, Laïus; and his grandson, Oedipus.

are heaped on the evils of the dead.
No generation frees another, some god
strikes them down; there is no deliverance.
Here was the light of hope stretched
650   over the last roots of Oedipus' house,
and the bloody dust due to the gods below
has mowed it down—that and the folly of speech
and ruin's enchantment of the mind.

Your power, O Zeus, what sin of man can limit?
655   All-aging sleep does not overtake it,
nor the unwearied months of the gods; and you,
for whom time brings no age,
you hold the glowing brightness of Olympus.

For the future near and far,
660   and the past, this law holds good:
nothing very great
comes to the life of mortal man
without ruin to accompany it.
For Hope, widely wandering, comes to many of mankind
665   as a blessing,
but to many as the deceiver,
using light-minded lusts;
she comes to him that knows nothing
till he burns his foot in the glowing fire.
670   With wisdom has someone declared
a word of distinction:
that evil seems good to one whose mind
the god leads to ruin,
and but for the briefest moment of time
675   is his life outside of calamity.
Here is Haemon, youngest of your sons.
Does he come grieving
for the fate of his bride to be,
in agony at being cheated of his marriage?
680 CREON: Soon we will know that better than the prophets.
My son, can it be that you have not heard
of my final decision on your betrothed?
Can you have come here in your fury against your father?
Or have I your love still, no matter what I do?
685 HAEMON: Father, I am yours; with your excellent judgment
you lay the right before me, and I shall follow it.
No marriage will ever be so valued by me

as to override the goodness of your leadership.

CREON: Yes, my son, this should always be
in your very heart, that everything else   690
shall be second to your father's decision.
It is for this that fathers pray to have
obedient sons begotten in their halls,
that they may requite with ill their father's enemy
and honor his friend no less than he would himself.   695
If a man have sons that are no use to him,
what can one say of him but that he has bred
so many sorrows to himself, laughter to his enemies?
Do not, my son, banish your good sense
through pleasure in a woman, since you know   700
that the embrace grows cold
when an evil woman shares your bed and home.
What greater wound can there be than a false friend?
No. Spit on her, throw her out like an enemy,
this girl, to marry someone in Death's house.   705
I caught her openly in disobedience
alone out of all this city and I shall not make
myself a liar in the city's sight. No, I will kill her.
So let her cry if she will on the Zeus of kinship;
for if I rear those of my race and breeding   710
to be rebels, surely I will do so with those outside it.
For he who is in his household a good man
will be found a just man, too, in the city.
But he that breaches the law or does it violence
or thinks to dictate to those who govern him   715
shall never have my good word.
The man the city sets up in authority
must be obeyed in small things and in just
but also in their opposites.
I am confident such a man of whom I speak   720
will be a good ruler, and willing to be well ruled.
He will stand on his country's side, faithful and just,
in the storm of battle. There is nothing worse
than disobedience to authority.
It destroys cities, it demolishes homes;   725
it breaks and routs one's allies. Of successful lives
the most of them are saved by discipline.
So we must stand on the side of what is orderly;
we cannot give victory to a woman.

730   If we must accept defeat, let it be from a man;
        we must not let people say that a woman beat us.
CHORUS: We think, if we are not victims of Time the Thief,
        that you speak intelligently of what you speak.
HAEMON: Father, the natural sense that the gods breed
735   in men is surely the best of their possessions.
        I certainly could not declare you wrong—
        may I never know how to do so!—Still there might
        be something useful that some other than you might think.
        It is natural for me to be watchful on your behalf
740   concerning what all men say or do or find to blame.
        Your face is terrible to a simple citizen;
        it frightens him from words you dislike to hear.
        But what *I* can hear, in the dark, are things like these:
        the city mourns for this girl; they think she is dying
745   most wrongly and most undeservedly
        of all womenkind, for the most glorious acts.
        Here is one who would not leave her brother unburied,
        a brother who had fallen in bloody conflict,
        to meet his end by greedy dogs or by
750   the bird that chanced that way. Surely what she merits
        is golden honor, isn't it? That's the dark rumor
        that spreads in secret. Nothing I own
        I value more highly, father, than your success.
        What greater distinction can a son have than the glory
755   of a successful father, and for a father
        the distinction of successful children?
        Do not bear this single habit of mind, to think
        that what you say and nothing else is true.
        A man who thinks that he alone is right,
760   or what he says, or what he *is* himself,
        unique, such men, when opened up, are seen
        to be quite empty. For a man, though he be wise,
        it is no shame to learn—learn many things,
        and not maintain his views too rigidly.
765   You notice how by streams in wintertime
        the trees that yield preserve their branches safely,
        but those that fight the tempest perish utterly.
        The man who keeps the sheet[3] of his sail tight
        and never slackens capsizes his boat

---

3. Rope attached to the corner of a sail to hold it at the proper angle to the wind.

and makes the rest of his trip keel uppermost.   770
Yield something of your anger, give way a little.
If a much younger man, like me, may have
a judgment, I would say it were far better
to be one altogether wise by nature, but,
as things incline not to be so, then it is good   775
also to learn from those who advise well.
CHORUS: My lord, if he says anything to the point,
you should learn from him, and you, too, Haemon,
learn from your father. Both of you
have spoken well.   780
CREON: Should we that are my age learn wisdom
from young men such as he is?
HAEMON: Not learn injustice, certainly. If I am young,
do not look at my years but what I do.
CREON: Is what you do to have respect for rebels?
HAEMON: I   785
would not urge you to be scrupulous
towards the wicked.
CREON: Is *she* not tainted by the disease of wickedness?
HAEMON: The entire people of Thebes says no to that.
CREON: Should the city tell me how I am to rule them?   790
HAEMON: Do you see what a young man's words these are of yours?
CREON: Must I rule the land by someone else's judgment
rather than my own?
HAEMON: There is no city
possessed by one man only.
CREON: Is not the city thought to be the ruler's?   795
HAEMON: You would be a fine dictator of a desert.
CREON: It seems this boy is on the woman's side.
HAEMON: If you are a woman—my care is all for you.
CREON: You villain, to bandy words with your own father!
HAEMON: I see your acts as mistaken and unjust.   800
CREON: Am I mistaken, reverencing my own office?
HAEMON: There is no reverence in trampling on God's honor.
CREON: Your nature is vile, in yielding to a woman.
HAEMON: You will not find me yield to what is shameful.
CREON: At least, your argument is all for her.   805
HAEMON: Yes, and for you and me—and for the gods below.
CREON: You will never marry her while her life lasts.
HAEMON: Then she must die—and dying destroy another.
CREON: Has your daring gone so far, to threaten me?

810 HAEMON: What threat is it to speak against empty judgments?
    CREON: Empty of sense yourself, you will regret
       your schooling of me in sense.
    HAEMON: If you were not
       my father, I would say you are insane.
    CREON: You woman's slave, do not try to wheedle me.
815 HAEMON: You want to talk but never to hear and listen.
    CREON: Is that so? By the heavens above you will not—
       be sure of that—get off scot-free, insulting,
       abusing me.

       [*He speaks to the* SERVANTS.]

                   You people bring out this creature,
       this hated creature, that she may die before
820   his very eyes, right now, next her would-be husband.
    HAEMON: Not at my side! Never think that! She will not
       die by my side. But you will never again
       set eyes upon my face. Go then and rage
       with such of your friends as are willing to endure it.
825 CHORUS: The man is gone, my lord, quick in his anger.
       A young man's mind is fierce when he is hurt.
    CREON: Let him go, and do and think things superhuman.
       But these two girls he shall not save from death.
    CHORUS: Both of them? Do you mean to kill them both?
830 CREON: No, not the one that didn't do anything.
       You are quite right there.
    CHORUS: And by what form of death do you mean to kill her?
    CREON: I will bring her where the path is loneliest,
       and hide her alive in a rocky cavern there.
835   I'll give just enough of food as shall suffice
       for a bare expiation, that the city may avoid pollution.
       In that place she shall call on Hades, god of death,
       in her prayers. That god only she reveres.
       Perhaps she will win from him escape from death
840   or at least in that last moment will recognize
       her honoring of the dead is labor lost.
    CHORUS: Love undefeated in the fight,
          Love that makes havoc of possessions,
          Love who lives at night in a young girl's soft cheeks,
845   Who travels over sea, or in huts in the countryside—
          there is no god able to escape you

nor anyone of men, whose life is a day only,
and whom you possess is mad.

You wrench the minds of just men to injustice,
to their disgrace; this conflict among kinsmen   850
it is you who stirred to turmoil.
The winner is desire. She gleaming kindles
from the eyes of the girl good to bed.
Love shares the throne with the great powers that rule.
For the golden Aphrodite[4] holds her play there   855
and then no one can overcome her.

Here I too am borne out of the course of lawfulness
when I see these things, and I cannot control
the springs of my tears
when I see Antigone making her way   860
to her bed—but the bed
that is rest for everyone.

ANTIGONE: You see me, you people of my country,
as I set out on my last road of all,
looking for the last time on this light of this sun—   865
never again. I am alive but Hades who gives sleep to everyone
is leading me to the shores of Acheron,[5]
though I have known nothing of marriage songs
nor the chant that brings the bride to bed.
My husband is to be the Lord of Death.   870

CHORUS: Yes, you go to the place where the dead are hidden,
but you go with distinction and praise.
You have not been stricken by wasting sickness;
you have not earned the wages of the sword;
it was your own choice and alone among mankind   875
you will descend, alive,
to that world of death.

ANTIGONE: But indeed I have heard of the saddest of deaths—
of the Phrygian stranger,[6] daughter of Tantalus,
whom the rocky growth subdued, like clinging ivy.   880
The rains never leave her, the snow never fails,
as she wastes away. That is how men tell the story.
From streaming eyes her tears wet the crags;
most like to her the god brings me to rest.

4. Goddess of love and beauty.   5. River in Hades.
6. Niobe, whose children were slain because of her boastfulness and who was herself turned
into a stone on Mount Sipylus. Her tears became the mountain's streams.

885 CHORUS: Yes, but she was a god, and god born,
and you are mortal and mortal born.
Surely it is great renown
for a woman that dies, that in life and death
her lot is a lot shared with demigods.

890 ANTIGONE: You mock me. In the name of our fathers' gods
why do you not wait till I am gone to insult me?
Must you do it face to face?
My city! Rich citizens of my city!
You springs of Dirce, you holy groves of Thebes,
895 famed for its chariots! I would still have you as my witnesses,
with what dry-eyed friends, under what laws
I make my way to my prison sealed like a tomb.
Pity me. Neither among the living nor the dead
do I have a home in common—
900 neither with the living nor the dead.

CHORUS: You went to the extreme of daring
and against the high throne of Justice
you fell, my daughter, grievously.
But perhaps it was for some ordeal of your father
905 that you are paying requital.

ANTIGONE: You have touched the most painful of my cares—
the pity for my father, ever reawakened,
and the fate of all of our race, the famous Labdacids;
the doomed self-destruction of my mother's bed
910 when she slept with her own son,
my father.
What parents I was born of, God help me!
To them I am going to share their home,
the curse on me, too, and unmarried.
915 Brother, it was a luckless marriage you made,
and dying killed my life.

CHORUS: There *is* a certain reverence for piety.
But for him in authority,
he cannot see that authority defied;
920 it is your own self-willed temper
that has destroyed you.

ANTIGONE: No tears for me, no friends, no marriage. Brokenhearted
I am led along the road ready before me.
I shall never again be suffered
925 to look on the holy eye of the day.

But my fate claims no tears—
no friend cries for me.

CREON: [*To the* SERVANTS.] Don't you know that weeping and wailing before death
would never stop if one is allowed to weep and wail?
Lead her away at once. Enfold her   930
in that rocky tomb of hers—as I told you to.
There leave her alone, solitary,
to die if she so wishes
or live a buried life in such a home;
we are guiltless in respect of her, this girl.   935
But living above, among the rest of us, this life
she shall certainly lose.

ANTIGONE: Tomb, bridal chamber, prison forever
dug in rock, it is to you I am going
to join my people, that great number that have died,   940
whom in their death Persephone[7] received.
I am the last of them and I go down
in the worst death of all—for I have not lived
the due term of my life. But when I come
to that other world my hope is strong   945
that my coming will be welcome to my father,
and dear to you, my mother, and dear to you,
my brother deeply loved. For when you died,
with my own hands I washed and dressed you all,
and poured the lustral offerings on your graves.   950
And now, Polyneices, it was for such care of your body
that I have earned these wages.
Yet those who think rightly will think I did right
in honoring you. Had I been a mother
of children, and my husband been dead and rotten,   955
I would not have taken this weary task upon me
against the will of the city. What law backs me
when I say this? I will tell you:
If my husband were dead, I might have had another,
and child from another man, if I lost the first.   960
But when father and mother both were hidden in death
no brother's life would bloom for me again.

7. Abducted by Pluto (known to the Greeks as Hades), god of the underworld, who made her his queen.

That is the law under which I gave you precedence,
my dearest brother, and that is why Creon thinks me
965   wrong, even a criminal, and now takes me
by the hand and leads me away,
unbedded, without bridal, without share
in marriage and in nurturing of children;
as lonely as you see me; without friends;
970   with fate against me I go to the vault of death
while still alive. What law of God have I broken?
Why should I still look to the gods in my misery?
Whom should I summon as ally? For indeed
because of piety I was called impious.
975   If this proceeding is good in the gods' eyes
I shall know my sin, once I have suffered.
But if Creon and his people are the wrongdoers
let their suffering be no worse than the injustice
they are meting out to me.

980 CHORUS: It is the same blasts, the tempests of the soul,
    possess her.

  CREON: Then for this her guards,
    who are so slow, will find themselves in trouble.

  ANTIGONE: [*Cries out.*] Oh, that word has come
    very close to death.

985 CREON: I will not comfort you
    with hope that the sentence will not be accomplished.

  ANTIGONE: O my father's city, in Theban land,
    O gods that sired my race,
    I am led away, I have no more stay.
990   Look on me, princes of Thebes,
    the last remnant of the old royal line;
    see what I suffer and who makes me suffer
    because I gave reverence to what claims reverence.

  CHORUS: Danae suffered, too, when, her beauty lost, she gave
995   the light of heaven in exchange for brassbound walls,
    and in the tomb-like cell was she hidden and held;
    yet she was honored in her breeding, child,
    and she kept, as guardian, the seed of Zeus
    that came to her in a golden shower.[8]

---

8. Danae was locked away because it was prophesized that her son would kill her father. Zeus entered her cell as a shower of gold, impregnated her, and thus fathered Perseus, the child who fulfilled the prophecy.

But there is some terrible power in destiny   1000
and neither wealth nor war
nor tower nor black ships, beaten by the sea,
can give escape from it.

The hot-tempered son of Dryas,[9] the Edonian king,
in fury mocked Dionysus,   1005
who then held him in restraint
in a rocky dungeon.
So the terrible force and flower of his madness
drained away. He came to know the god
whom in frenzy he had touched with his mocking tongue,   1010
when he would have checked the inspired women
and the fire of Dionysus,
when he provoked the Muses[1] that love the lyre.
By the black rocks, dividing the sea in two,
are the shores of the Bosporus, Thracian Salmydessus.[2]   1015
There the god of war who lives near the city
saw the terrible blinding wound
dealt by his savage wife
on Phineus' two sons.[3]
She blinded and tore with the points of her shuttle,   1020
and her bloodied hands, those eyes
that else would have looked on her vengefully.
As they wasted away, they lamented
their unhappy fate that they were doomed
to be born of a mother cursed in her marriage.   1025
She traced her descent from the seed
of the ancient Erechtheidae.
In far-distant caves she was raised
among her father's storms, that child of Boreas[4]
quick as a horse, over the steep hills,   1030
a daughter of the gods.
But, my child, the long-lived Fates[5]
bore hard upon her, too.

---

9. Stricken with madness by Dionysus.   1. Nine sister goddesses of poetry, music, and the arts.
2. City in the land of Thrace, in ancient times erroneously believed to lie on the Bosporus, the strait separating Europe and Asia at the outlet of the Black Sea.
3. King Phineus's second wife blinded the children of his first wife, whom Phineus had imprisoned in a cave.
4. God of the cold north wind, who sometimes took the form of a stallion.
5. Supernatural forces, usually represented as three old women, who determine the quality and length of life.

[*Enter* TEIRESIAS, *the blind prophet, led by a* BOY.]

TEIRESIAS: My lords of Thebes, we have come here together,
1035   one pair of eyes serving us both. For the blind
    such must be the way of going, by a guide's leading.
CREON: What is the news, my old Teiresias?
TEIRESIAS: I will tell you; and you, listen to the prophet.
CREON: Never in the past have I turned from your advice.
1040 TEIRESIAS: And so you have steered well the ship of state.
CREON: I have benefited and can testify to that.
TEIRESIAS: Then realize you are on the razor edge
    of danger.
CREON: What can that be? I shudder to hear those words.
1045 TEIRESIAS: When you learn the signs recognized by my art
    you will understand.
    I sat at my ancient place of divination
    for watching the birds, where every bird finds shelter;
    and I heard an unwonted voice among them;
1050   they were horribly distressed, and screamed unmeaningly.
    I knew they were tearing each other murderously;
    the beating of their wings was a clear sign.
    I was full of fear; at once on all the altars,
    as they were fully kindled, I tasted the offerings,
1055   but the god of fire refused to burn from the sacrifice,
    and from the thighbones a dark stream of moisture
    oozed from the embers, smoked and sputtered.
    The gall bladder burst and scattered to the air
    and the streaming thighbones lay exposed
1060   from the fat wrapped round them—
    so much I learned from this boy here,
    the fading prophecies of a rite that failed.
    This boy here is my guide, as I am others'.
    This is the city's sickness—and your plans are the cause of it.
1065   For our altars and our sacrificial hearths
    are filled with the carrion meat of birds and dogs,
    torn from the flesh of Oedipus' poor son.
    So the gods will not take our prayers or sacrifice
    nor yet the flame from the thighbones, and no bird
1070   cries shrill and clear, so glutted
    are they with fat of the blood of the killed man.
    Reflect on these things, son. All men
    can make mistakes; but, once mistaken,

a man is no longer stupid nor accursed
who, having fallen on ill, tries to cure that ill,   1075
not taking a fine undeviating stand.
It is obstinacy that convicts of folly.
Yield to the dead man; do not stab him—
now he is gone—what bravery is this,
to inflict another death upon the dead?   1080
I mean you well and speak well for your good.
It is never sweeter to learn from a good counselor
than when he counsels to your benefit.
CREON: Old man, you are all archers, and I am your mark.
I must be tried by your prophecies as well.   1085
By the breed of you I have been bought and sold
and made a merchandise, for ages now.
But I tell you: make your profit from silver-gold
from Sardis[6] and the gold from India
if you will. But this dead man you shall not hide   1090
in a grave, not though the eagles of Zeus should bear
the carrion, snatching it to the throne of Zeus itself.
Even so, I shall not so tremble at the pollution
to let you bury him.
                    No, I am certain
no human has the power to pollute the gods.   1095
They fall, you old Teiresias, those men,
—so very clever—in a bad fall whenever
they eloquently speak vile words for profit.
TEIRESIAS: I wonder if there's a man who dares consider—
CREON: What do you mean? What sort of generalization   1100
is this talk of yours?
TEIRESIAS: How much the best of possessions is the ability
to listen to wise advice?
CREON: As I should imagine that the worst
injury must be native stupidity.   1105
TEIRESIAS: Now that is exactly where your mind is sick.
CREON: I do not like to answer a seer with insults.
TEIRESIAS: But you do, when you say my prophecies are lies.
CREON: Well,
    the whole breed of prophets certainly loves money.   1110
TEIRESIAS: And the breed that comes from princes loves to take
advantage—base advantage.

6. Capital of the ancient kingdom of Lydia, part of modern-day Turkey, and an important trading
center, famed for its wealth.

CREON: Do you realize
    you are speaking in such terms of your own prince?
TEIRESIAS: I know. But it is through me you have saved the city.
1115 CREON: You are a wise prophet, but what you love is wrong.
TEIRESIAS: You will force me to declare what should be hidden
    in my own heart.
CREON: Out with it—
    but only if your words are not for gain.
TEIRESIAS: They won't be for *your* gain—that I am sure of.
1120 CREON: But realize you will not make a merchandise
    of my decisions.
TEIRESIAS: And you must realize
    that you will not outlive many cycles more
    of this swift sun before you give in exchange
    one of your own loins bred, a corpse for a corpse,
1125   for you have thrust one that belongs above
    below the earth, and bitterly dishonored
    a living soul by lodging her in the grave;
    while one that belonged indeed to the underworld
    gods you have kept on this earth without due share
1130   of rites of burial, of due funeral offerings,
    a corpse unhallowed. With all of this you, Creon,
    have nothing to do, nor have the gods above.
    These acts of yours are violence, on your part.
    And in requital the avenging Spirits
1135   of Death itself and the gods' Furies shall
    after *your* deeds, lie in ambush for you, and
    in their hands you shall be taken cruelly.
    Now, look at this and tell me I was bribed
    to say it! The delay will not be long
1140   before the cries of mourning in your house,
    of men and women. All the cities will stir in hatred
    against you, because their sons in mangled shreds
    received their burial rites from dogs, from wild beasts
    or when some bird of the air brought a vile stink
1145   to each city that contained the hearths of the dead.
    These are the arrows that archer-like I launched—
    you vexed me so to anger—at your heart.
    You shall not escape their sting. You, boy,
    lead me away to my house, so he may discharge
1150   his anger on younger men; so may he come to know

to bear a quieter tongue in his head and a better
mind than that now he carries in him.
CHORUS: That was a terrible prophecy, my lord.
The man has gone. Since these hairs of mine grew white
from the black they once were, he has never spoken   1155
a word of a lie to our city.
CREON: I know, I know.
My mind is all bewildered. To yield is terrible.
But by opposition to destroy my very being
with a self-destructive curse must also be reckoned   1160
in what is terrible.
CHORUS: You need good counsel, son of Menoeceus,
and need to take it.
CREON: What must I do, then? Tell me; I shall agree.
CHORUS: The girl—go now and bring her up from her cave,   1165
and for the exposed dead man, give him his burial.
CREON: That is really your advice? You would have me yield.
CHORUS: And quickly as you may, my lord. Swift harms
sent by the gods cut off the paths of the foolish.
CREON: Oh, it is hard; I must give up what my heart   1170
would have me do. But it is ill to fight
against what must be.
CHORUS: Go now, and do this;
do not give the task to others.
CREON: I will go,   1175
just as I am. Come, servants, all of you;
take axes in your hands; away with you
to the place you see, there.
For my part, since my intention is so changed,
as I bound her myself, myself will free her.   1180
I am afraid it may be best, in the end
of life, to have kept the old accepted laws.
CHORUS: You of many names,[7] glory of the Cadmeian
bride, breed of loud thundering Zeus;
you who watch over famous Italy;   1185
you who rule where all are welcome in Eleusis;
in the sheltered plains of Deo—
O Bacchus that dwells in Thebes,

---

7. Refers to Dionysus, known also as Bacchus (especially to the later Romans); son of Zeus
and Semele, a mortal princess of Thebes. As god of wine, Dionysus presided over frenzied
rites known as Bacchanals.

the mother city of Bacchanals,
1190   by the flowing stream of Ismenus,
in the ground sown by the fierce dragon's teeth.

You are he on whom the murky gleam of torches glares,
above the twin peaks of the crag
where come the Corycean nymphs
1195   to worship you, the Bacchanals;
and the stream of Castalia has seen you, too;
and you are he that the ivy-clad
slopes of Nisaean hills,
and the green shore ivy-clustered,
1200   sent to watch over the roads of Thebes,
where the immortal Evoe chant[8] rings out.

It is Thebes which you honor most of all cities,
you and your mother both,
she who died by the blast of Zeus' thunderbolt.
1205   And now when the city, with all its folk,
is gripped by a violent plague,
come with healing foot, over the slopes of Parnassus,[9]
over the moaning strait.
You lead the dance of the fire-breathing stars,
1210   you are master of the voices of the night.
True-born child of Zeus, appear,
my lord, with your Thyiad attendants,
who in frenzy all night long
dance in your house, Iacchus,
1215   dispenser of gifts.

MESSENGER: You who live by the house of Cadmus and Amphion,[1]
hear me. There is no condition of man's life
that stands secure. As such I would not
praise it or blame. It is chance that sets upright;
1220   it is chance that brings down the lucky and the unlucky,
each in his turn. For men, that belong to death,
there is no prophet of established things.
Once Creon was a man worthy of envy—
of my envy, at least. For he saved this city
1225   of Thebes from her enemies, and attained
the throne of the land, with all a king's power.
He guided it right. His race bloomed

8. Come forth, come forth!
9. Mountain in central Greece sacred to Apollo, Dionysus, and the Muses; Apollo's shrine, Delphi, lies at the foot of Parnassus.   1. A name for Thebes.

with good children. But when a man forfeits joy
I do not count his life as life, but only
a life trapped in a corpse. 1230
Be rich within your house, yes greatly rich,
if so you will, and live in a prince's style.
If the gladness of these things is gone, I would not
give the shadow of smoke for the rest,
as against joy. 1235

CHORUS: What is the sorrow of our princes
of which you are the messenger?

MESSENGER: Death; and the living are guilty of their deaths.

CHORUS: But who is the murderer? Who the murdered? Tell us.

MESSENGER: Haemon is dead; the hand that shed his blood 1240
was his very own.

CHORUS: Truly his own hand? Or his father's?

MESSENGER: His own hand, in his anger
against his father for a murder.

CHORUS: Prophet, how truly you have made good your word! 1245

MESSENGER: These things are so; you may debate the rest.
Here I see Creon's wife Eurydice
approaching. Unhappy woman!
Does she come from the house as hearing about her son
or has she come by chance? 1250

EURYDICE: I heard your words, all you men of Thebes, as I
was going out to greet Pallas[2] with my prayers.
I was just drawing back the bolts of the gate
to open it when a cry struck through my ears
telling of my household's ruin. I fell backward 1255
in terror into the arms of my servants; I fainted.
But tell me again, what is the story? I
will hear it as one who is no stranger to sorrow.

MESSENGER: Dear mistress, I will tell you, for I was there,
and I will leave out no word of the truth. 1260
Why should I comfort you and then tomorrow
be proved a liar? The truth is always best.
I followed your husband, at his heels, to the end of the plain
where Polyneices' body still lay unpitied,
and torn by dogs. We prayed to Hecate, goddess 1265
of the crossroads, and also to Pluto[3]

---

2. Athena, goddess of wisdom.
3. King of the underworld, known to the Greeks as Hades. *Hecate*: goddess of witchcraft.

that they might restrain their anger and turn kind.
And him we washed with sacred lustral water
and with fresh-cut boughs we burned what was left of him
1270 and raised a high mound of his native earth;
then we set out again for the hollowed rock,
death's stone bridal chamber for the girl.
Someone then heard a voice of bitter weeping
while we were still far off, coming from that unblest room.
1275 The man came to tell our master Creon of it.
As the king drew nearer, there swarmed about him
a cry of misery but no clear words.
He groaned and in an anguished mourning voice
cried "Oh, am I a true prophet? Is this the road
1280 that I must travel, saddest of all my wayfaring?
It is my son's voice that haunts my ear. Servants,
get closer, quickly. Stand around the tomb
and look. There is a gap there where the stones
have been wrenched away; enter there, by the very mouth,
1285 and see whether I recognize the voice of Haemon
or if the gods deceive me." On the command
of our despairing master we went to look.
In the furthest part of the tomb we saw her, hanging
by her neck. She had tied a noose of muslin on it.
1290 Haemon's hands were about her waist embracing her,
while he cried for the loss of his bride gone to the dead,
and for all his father had done, and his own sad love.
When Creon saw him he gave a bitter cry,
went in and called to him with a groan: "Poor son!
1295 what have you done? What can you have meant?
What happened to destroy you? Come out, I pray you!"
The boy glared at him with savage eyes, and then
spat in his face, without a word of answer.
He drew his double-hilted sword. As his father
1300 ran to escape him, Haemon failed to strike him,
and the poor wretch in anger at himself
leaned on his sword and drove it halfway in,
into his ribs. Then he folded the girl to him,
in his arms, while he was conscious still,
1305 and gasping poured a sharp stream of bloody drops
on her white cheeks. There they lie,
the dead upon the dead. So he has won
the pitiful fulfillment of his marriage

within death's house. In this human world he has shown
how the wrong choice in plans is for a man   1310
his greatest evil.
CHORUS: What do you make of this? My lady is gone,
without a word of good or bad.
MESSENGER: I, too,
am lost in wonder. I am inclined to hope
that hearing of her son's death she could not   1315
open her sorrow to the city, but chose rather
within her house to lay upon her maids
the mourning for the household grief. Her judgment
is good; she will not make any false step.
CHORUS: I do not know. To me this over-heavy silence   1320
seems just as dangerous as much empty wailing.
MESSENGER: I will go in and learn if in her passionate
heart she keeps hidden some secret purpose.
You are right; there is sometimes danger in too much silence.
CHORUS: Here comes our king himself. He bears in his hands   1325
a memorial all too clear;
it is a ruin of none other's making,
purely his own if one dare to say that.
CREON: The mistakes of a blinded man
are themselves rigid and laden with death.   1330
You look at us the killer and the killed
of the one blood. Oh, the awful blindness
of those plans of mine. My son, you were so young,
so young to die. You were freed from the bonds of life
through no folly of your own—only through mine.   1335
CHORUS: I think you have learned justice—but too late.
CREON: Yes, I have learned it to my bitterness. At this moment
God has sprung on my head with a vast weight
and struck me down. He shook me in my savage ways;
he has overturned my joy, has trampled it,   1340
underfoot. The pains men suffer
are pains indeed.
SECOND MESSENGER: My lord, you have troubles and a store besides;
some are there in your hands, but there are others
you will surely see when you come to your house.   1345
CREON: What trouble can there be beside these troubles?
SECOND MESSENGER: The queen is dead. She was indeed true mother
of the dead son. She died, poor lady,
by recent violence upon herself.

1350 CREON: Haven of death, you can never have enough.
        Why, why do you destroy me?
        You messenger, who have brought me bitter news,
        what is this tale you tell?
        It is a dead man that you kill again—
1355   what new message of yours is this, boy?
        Is this new slaughter of a woman
        a doom to lie on the pile of the dead?
      CHORUS: You can see. It is no longer
        hidden in a corner.

      [*By some stage device, perhaps the so-called eccyclema,*[4] *the inside of
      the palace is shown, with the body of the dead* QUEEN.]

1360 CREON: Here is yet another horror
        for my unhappy eyes to see.
        What doom still waits for me?
        I have but now taken in my arms my son,
        and again I look upon another dead face.
1365   Poor mother and poor son!
      SECOND MESSENGER: She stood at the altar, and with keen whetted knife
        she suffered her darkening eyes to close.
        First she cried in agony recalling the noble fate of Megareus,[5]
        who died before all this,
1370   and then for the fate of this son; and in the end
        she cursed you for the evil you had done
        in killing her sons.
      CREON: I am distracted with fear. Why does not someone
        strike a two-edged sword right through me?
1375   I am dissolved in an agony of misery.
      SECOND MESSENGER: You were indeed accused
        by her that is dead
        of Haemon's and of Megareus' death.
      CREON: By what kind of violence did she find her end?
1380 SECOND MESSENGER: Her own hand struck her to the entrails
        when she heard of her son's lamentable death.
      CREON: These acts can never be made to fit another
        to free me from the guilt. It was I that killed her.
        Poor wretch that I am, I say it is true!
1385   Servants, lead me away, quickly, quickly.
        I am no more a live man than one dead.

      4. Wheeled platform rolled forward onto the stage to depict interior scenes; often used in trag-
      edies to reveal dead bodies.   5. Another son of Creon who died defending Thebes.

CHORUS: What you say is for the best—if there be a best
    in evil such as this. For the shortest way
    is best with troubles that lie at our feet.
CREON: O, let it come, let it come,   1390
    that best of fates that waits on my last day.
    Surely best fate of all. Let it come, let it come!
    That I may never see one more day's light!
CHORUS: These things are for the future. We must deal
    with what impends. What in the future is to care for   1395
    rests with those whose duty it is
    to care for them.
CREON: At least, all that *I* want
    is in that prayer of mine.
CHORUS: Pray for no more at all. For what is destined   1400
    for us, men mortal, there is no escape.
CREON: Lead me away, a vain silly man
    who killed you, son, and you, too, lady.
    I did not mean to, but I did.
    I do not know where to turn my eyes   1405
    to look to, for support.
    Everything in my hands is crossed. A most unwelcome fate
    has leaped upon me.
CHORUS: Wisdom is far the chief element in happiness
    and, secondly, no irreverence towards the gods.   1410
    But great words of haughty men exact
    in retribution blows as great
    and in old age teach wisdom.

THE END

c. 441 BCE

Writing about Literature

When it comes to the study of literature, reading and writing are closely interrelated—even mutually dependent—activities. The quality of whatever we write about literature depends entirely on the quality of our work as readers. Conversely, our reading isn't truly complete until we've tried to capture our sense of the literature in writing so as to make it intelligible, persuasive, and meaningful to other people. We read literature much more actively and attentively when we both integrate informal writing into the reading process—pausing periodically to mark important or confusing passages, to jot down significant facts, to describe the impressions and responses the text provokes—and when we envision our reading of literature as preparation for writing about it in a more sustained and formal way. The actual process of writing, conversely, requires re-reading and rethinking, testing our first impressions and initial hypotheses.

As we've suggested from the beginning of this book, literature itself is a vast conversation in which we participate most fully only when we engage with other readers. Writing allows us the opportunity—and even imposes on us the obligation—to do just that: In writing we respond not only to what other readers have actually said or written about the work but also to how we imagine other readers *might* realistically see it. By considering other readers' points of view and working to persuade them to accept alternative ways of interpreting a literary work, we ourselves learn new ways of seeing.

Writing about literature can take any number of forms, ranging from the very informal and personal to the very formal and public. Your instructor may well ask you to try your hand at more than one form. However, the essay is by far the most common and complex form that writing about literature—or **literary criticism**—takes. As a result, the following chapters will focus primarily on the essay.

Whether they require an essay, a response paper, or something else, however, assignments in literature courses often come equipped with a warning that goes something like this: "DO NOT SIMPLY RESTATE THE FACTS, PARAPHRASE, OR SUMMARIZE." We thus start here with a brief chapter (ch. 17) explaining what paraphrase, summary, and description are and how you can use them to move from response to essay.

Chapter 18, "The Literature Essay," reviews the five basic elements of all literature essays before turning, briefly, to two specific types—the comparative essay and the in-class exam essay. The chapter's goal is to give you a vivid sense of what you want to end up with at the end of the essay-writing process.

Chapter 19, "The Writing Process," focuses on how you get there, providing tips on every stage of essay development, from interpreting an assignment and generating a thesis to editing, proofreading, and manuscript formatting.

Chapter 20, "The Literature Research Essay," introduces the most common types of literature research and the key steps and strategies involved in writing research essays, from identifying and evaluating sources to responsibly and effectively integrating source material into your essay.

Whether they involve research or not, *all* essays about literature require responsible and effective quotation and citation; these are discussed in a separate chapter, "Quotation, Citation, and Documentation" (ch. 21).

Finally, this section concludes with a sample research essay (ch. 22) annotated to point out some of the features and strategies discussed in earlier chapters.

17 BASIC MOVES: PARAPHRASE, SUMMARY, AND DESCRIPTION

In literature courses, writing assignments often come equipped with a warning that goes something like this: "DO NOT SIMPLY RESTATE THE FACTS, PARAPHRASE, OR SUMMARIZE." It's a warning you ignore at your peril: *paraphrase*, *summary*, and *description* are each specific ways of "simply restating the facts," and a paper for a literature course will rarely pass muster if it does only that. Such papers must make arguments *about* facts and their significance, using statements of fact like those that make up paraphrases, summaries, and descriptions in order to substantiate and develop debatable claims about the literary text. (For more on factual statements versus debatable claims, see 18.1.2.)

As this suggests, however, any literature paper will need to include *some* paraphrase, description, and/or summary, since effective arguments must be based on, supported by, and developed with statements of fact. As important, paraphrase, summary, and description can be effective ways to *start* the writing process, helping you to discover potential paper topics and even debatable claims of the sort that drive literature essays.

In later chapters, we'll discuss and demonstrate ways to use paraphrase, summary, and description within literature essays of various types. The rest of this chapter simply defines and models these three basic, nonargumentative forms of writing about literature and discusses how you can use them to move from initial response to more formal, argumentative writing.

17.1 PARAPHRASE

17.1.1 What It Is

To paraphrase a statement is to restate it in your own words. Since the goal of paraphrase is to represent a statement fully and faithfully, a paraphrase tends to be at least as long as the original.

Below are paraphrases of sentences from a work of fiction (Jane Austen's *Pride and Prejudice*), a poem (W. B. Yeats's ALL THINGS CAN TEMPT ME), and a literature essay of the sort that could also be a secondary source in a literature research essay (George L. Dillon's "Styles of Reading").

Three Examples of Paraphrase

ORIGINAL SENTENCE	PARAPHRASE
It is a truth universally acknowledged that a single man in possession of a good fortune must be in want of a wife.	Everyone knows that a wealthy bachelor wants to get married.
All things can tempt me from this craft of verse: One time it was a woman's face, or worse— The seeming needs of my fool-driven land;	Anything can distract me from writing poetry, from a pretty girl to a foolish political cause.
[. . .] making order out of Emily's life is a complicated matter, since the narrator recalls the details through a nonlinear filter.	It's difficult to figure out when things happen to Emily because the narrator doesn't relate events in chronological order.

17.1.2 How to Use It

- Paraphrasing ensures and demonstrates that you understand what you've read. It can be especially helpful when authors' diction and syntax or their logic seems especially difficult, complex, or "foreign" to you. This is why paraphrase can be especially useful when reading and responding to a poem (see "Poetry: Reading, Responding, Writing") and when taking notes on secondary sources (see 20.3.2).
- Paraphrasing can direct your attention to nuances of tone or potentially significant details in any literary text, especially when you pay attention to anything you have difficulty paraphrasing. For example, paraphrasing Austen's sentence (above) might call your attention to the multiple—and thus difficult to paraphrase—meanings of phrases such as *a good fortune* and *in want of*.
- By drawing your attention to such details, paraphrasing can help you begin to generate the kind of interpretive questions an essay might explore. For example, the Austen paraphrase might lead you to ask, *What does* Pride and Prejudice *define as "a good fortune"? Does the novel illustrate different definitions? Does it endorse one definition over another?*

On the use of paraphrase in literature essays, see 18.1.4 (on evidence), 18.2.2 (on in-class exam essays), and 20.4.2 (on incorporating secondary source material into the literature research essay).

17.2 SUMMARY

17.2.1 What It Is

A summary is a fairly succinct restatement or overview—in your own words—of the content of an entire literary text or other source or a significant portion thereof. A summary of a literary work is generally called a *plot summary* because it focuses on the **action** or **plot**. Though a summary should be significantly shorter than the original, it can be any length you need it to be. (For more on plot summary, see ch. 1.)

Different readers—or even the same reader on different occasions and with different purposes in mind—will almost certainly summarize the same text or source in dramatically different ways. Summarizing entails selection and emphasis. As a result, any summary reflects a particular point of view and may even begin to imply a possible interpretation or argument. When writing a summary, you should try to be as objective as possible. Nevertheless, your summary will reflect a particular understanding and attitude, which is actually why it's useful.

Here are three quite different one-sentence summaries of HAMLET.

1. In the process of avenging his uncle's murder of his father, a young prince kills his uncle, himself, and many others.
2. A young Danish prince avenges the murder of his father, the king, by his uncle, who has usurped the throne, but the prince himself is killed, as are others, and a well-led foreign army has no trouble successfully invading the troubled state.
3. When a young prince hears, from the ghost of his murdered father, that his uncle, who has married the prince's mother, is the father's murderer, the prince devotes himself to learning the truth and avenging the wrong, feigning madness, acting erratically, causing the suicide of his beloved and the deaths of numerous others including, ultimately, himself.

17.2.2 How to Use It

Because even the most objective summary implies a point of view, summarizing a literary work may help you begin to figure out just what your particular point of view is or at least what aspects of the work strike you as most important and potentially worthy of analysis, especially if you compare your summary to that of another reader (as in the exercise in ch. 1) or try out different ways of summarizing the same work yourself. The second *Hamlet* summary above, for example, suggests a more political interpretation of the play than either of the other two summaries, by emphasizing the political roles of the various characters, the fact that the crime in the play involves two distinctly political crimes (usurpation and regicide), and the fact that the play ends with a foreign invasion.

On the use of summary in literature essays, see 18.1.4 (on evidence), 18.1.5 (on introductions), 18.2.2 (on in-class exam essays), and 20.4.2 (on incorporating secondary source material into the literature research essay).

17.3 DESCRIPTION

17.3.1 What It Is

Whereas both summary and paraphrase focus on content, a description of a literary text focuses more on its form, style, or structure, or any particular aspect thereof.

Below are two such descriptions, one of the rhyme scheme of Thomas Hardy's THE RUINED MAID, the other of Susan Glaspell's TRIFLES.

"The Ruined Maid"

A dialogue between "the ruined maid," 'Melia, and another woman from her hometown, Hardy's 24-line poem consists of six four-line stanzas. Each stanza consists of two rhyming couplets and ends with the same two words ("said she") and thus with the same (long *e*) rhyme sound. In stanzas 2 through 5, the first couplets each feature different rhymes ("socks/docks," "thou/now," "bleak/cheek," "dream/seem"). But in the first and last stanza they have the same rhyme and even the same final word ("crown/Town," "gown/Town"). As these examples illustrate, most of the end rhymes involve one-syllable words. But in four out of six stanzas, line 3 instead ends with a polysyllabic word (rhyming with "she") in which the rhyming syllable is set off from the first syllables by a dash: "prosperi-ty" (line 3), "compa-ny" (11), "la-dy" (15), "melancho-ly" (19).

Trifles

Trifles is a one-act play featuring only five characters, two women (Mrs. Hale and Mrs. Peters) and three men (the Sheriff, the County Attorney, and Mr. Hale). The play begins with all the characters entering the stage together, and a man (the County Attorney) is the first to speak. The play strictly observes the three classical or dramatic unities—of time, of place, and of action: it all unfolds in one setting (the kitchen of a remote midwestern farmhouse) and over the course of about one hour (on a very cold winter morning), exactly the same amount of time it takes to watch the play. Though the play isn't formally divided into scenes, and its action is continuous, it is broken up into about eight informal segments by the exits and re-entrances of the male characters, who usually (but not always) come and go as a group. The two female characters remain on the stage the entire time. The play ends with all the characters except one (Mr. Hale) onstage and with a woman (Mrs. Hale) speaking the last word.

17.3.2 How to Use It

Responding actively to a text and preparing to write about it require paying close attention to form, style, and structure, as well as content. Describing a text or some aspect of it (its **imagery**, **rhyme scheme**, or **meter**; plotting or point of view; divisions into **stanzas**, acts and scenes, or chapters; and so on) is a useful way to make sure that you are paying that kind of attention, identifying the sort of details whose significance you might explore in an essay. To move from description to argument begins with asking, "How do these details relate to each other?" "How do they individually and collectively contribute to the text's effect and meaning?"

On the use of description in literature essays, see 18.1.4 (on evidence) and 18.1.5 (on introductions).

THE LITERATURE ESSAY

The literature essay is a distinct subgenre of writing with unique elements and conventions. Just as you come to a poem, play, or short story with a specific set of expectations, so will readers approach your essay *about* a poem, play or story. They will be looking for particular elements, anticipating that the work will unfold in a certain way. This chapter explains and explores those elements so as to give you a clear sense of what an effective essay about literature looks like and how it works, along with concrete advice about how to craft your own.

A literature essay has particular elements and a particular form because it serves a specific purpose. Like any essay, it is a relatively short written composition that articulates, supports, and develops one major idea or claim. Like any work of expository prose, it aims to explain something complex—in this case at least one literary work—so that a reader may gain a new and deeper understanding. Explaining in this case entails both *analysis* (breaking the work down into its constituent parts and showing how they work together to form a meaningful whole) and *argument* (working to convince someone that the analysis is valid). Your essay needs to show your readers a particular way to understand the work, to interpret or read it. That interpretation or reading starts with your own personal response. But your essay also needs to persuade its readers that your interpretation is reasonable and enlightening—that though it is distinctive and new, it is more than merely idiosyncratic or subjective.

18.1 ELEMENTS OF THE LITERATURE ESSAY

To achieve its purpose, a literature essay must incorporate five elements: an effective *tone*; a compelling *thesis* and *motive*; ample, appropriate *evidence*; and a coherent *structure*. Though these five elements are essential to essays of any kind, each needs to take a specific shape in literature essays. The goal of this section is to give you a clear sense of that shape.

18.1.1 Tone (and Audience)

Although your reader or audience isn't an element *in* your essay, tone is. And tone and audience are closely interrelated. In everyday life, the tone we adopt has everything to do with whom we're talking to and what situation we're in. We talk very differently to our parents than to our best friends. And in different situations we talk to the same person in different ways, depending in part on what response we want to elicit. What tone do you adopt with your best friend when you need a favor? when you want advice? when you want him to take your advice? In each situation, you act on your knowledge of who your audience is, what information they already have, and what their response is likely to be. But you also try to adopt a tone that will encourage your listener to respond in a specific way. In writing, as in life, your sense of audience shapes your tone, even as you use tone to shape your audience's response.

So who is your audience? When you write an essay for class, the obvious answer is your instructor. But in an important sense, that's the wrong answer. Although your instructor could literally be the only person besides you who will ever read your essay, you write about literature to learn how to write for a general audience of peers—people a lot like you who are sensible and educated and who will appreciate having a literary work explained so that they can understand it more fully. Picture your readers as people with at least the same educational background. Assume they have some experience in reading literature and some familiarity with the basic literary terminology outlined in this book. (You should not feel the need to explain what a stanza is or to define the term *in medias res*.) But assume, too, that your readers have read the specific literary work(s) only once, have not yet closely analyzed the work(s), and have not been privy to class discussions.

Above all, don't think of yourself as writing for only one reader and especially one reader who already sees the text as you do. Remember that the purpose of your essay is to *persuade* multiple readers with differing outlooks and opinions to see the text your way. That process begins with persuading those readers that you deserve their time, their attention, and their respect. The tone of your paper should be serious and straightforward, respectful toward your readers and the literary work. But its approach and vocabulary, while formal enough for academic writing, should be lively enough to capture and hold the interest of busy, distracted readers. Demonstrate *in* your essay the stance you want readers to take *toward* your essay: Earn careful attention and respect by demonstrating care, attentiveness, and respect; encourage your readers to keep an open mind by doing the same; engage your readers by demonstrating genuine engagement with the text, the topic, and the very enterprise of writing.

WAYS OF SETTING THE RIGHT TONE

• *Write about literature in the present tense.*
Convincing your readers that you are a knowledgeable student of literature whose ideas they should respect requires not only correctly using—
without feeling the need to explain—basic literary terms such as *stanza*
and *in medias res* but also following other long-established conventions.
Writing in present tense is one such convention, and it has two very practical advantages. One, it helps you avoid confusing tense shifts. Simply put,
you can more clearly indicate *when* in a text something happens by simply
specifying, "When X first visits Y" or "In the first stanza," and so on than
you can by switching tenses. Two, present tense actually makes logical
sense if you think about it: Though each time you pick up a story, poem,
or play, your interpretation of the work might be different, the work itself
isn't. Similarly, though in reading we experience a text as unfolding in
time, it actually doesn't: Everything in the text simply, always *is*. Thus,
yesterday, today, and tomorrow, Shakespeare's Ophelia goes mad, "A & P"
asks what it means to grow up, John Donne (the implied author) depicts our
relationship with God as a lifelong struggle, and so on.
      That said, things do get a bit tricky when you write about contexts as
well as texts or about *actual* versus *implied authors*. Notice, for example,
how the following sentence moves from past to present tense as it moves
from a statement about the actual author to one about the text: "In perhaps the same year, Dickinson wrote 'The Bible is an antique Volume,' which
shows a mix of skepticism and optimism." Again, this switch (from past to
present tense) makes logical sense: The actual author Emily Dickinson
wrote this poem in the historical past, even as the poem *shows* now what
it always has and always will (if we accept this writer's interpretation of
it). By the same logic, the same tenses would be appropriate if we revised
the sentence so as to make Emily Dickinson, the implied author, rather
than her poem the subject of its second half: "In perhaps the same year,
Dickinson wrote 'The Bible is an antique Volume,' a poem in which she
expresses a mix of skepticism and optimism." (On implied versus actual
authors, see ch. 2.)

• *Use the word "I" carefully.*
On the one hand, many instructors have no problem with your using "I"
when context makes that appropriate and effective; and used well, the
first person can create a real sense of engagement and of "presence," of
a distinctive mind at work. On the other hand, however, you should be
aware that many instructors strongly object to any use of the word "I"
simply because inexperienced writers so often use it inappropriately and
ineffectively. Since the job of a literature essay is to use evidence to
persuade readers to accept an interpretation of the work that is generally

and objectively, not just personally or subjectively, valid and meaningful, resorting to "I feel" or "I think" can defeat that purpose. Sometimes such phrases can even be a sign that you've gotten way off track, perhaps substituting expressions of feeling for actual argument or dwelling more on your thoughts about an issue the text explores than on your thoughts about the text and the thoughts *it* communicates about that issue (as in the last example in 18.1.2 below). Generally speaking, if everything that follows a phrase like "I feel" or "I think" makes sense and has merit and relevance on its own, cut to the chase by cutting the phrase.

18.1.2 Thesis

A thesis is to an essay what a **theme** is to a short story, play, or poem: the governing idea or claim. Yet where a literary work implies at least one theme and often more, any essay about a literary work needs to have only one thesis that is explicitly stated in about one to three sentences somewhere in the introduction, usually at or near its end. Like a theme, as we have defined that term in earlier chapters, your thesis must be debatable—a claim that all readers won't automatically accept. It's a proposition you *can* prove with evidence from the literary text, yet it's one you *have* to prove, that isn't obviously true or merely factual.

Though it's unlikely that any of that is news to you, even experienced writers sometimes find themselves flummoxed when it comes to figuring out just what makes for a debatable claim or thesis about literature. To clarify, we juxtapose below two sets of sentences. On the left are inarguable statements—ones that are merely factual or descriptive and thus might easily find a home in a paraphrase, summary, or description (see ch. 17). On the right are debatable claims about the same topic or fact of the type that might work very well as the thesis of a literature essay.

FACTUAL STATEMENT	THESIS
"The Story of an Hour" explores the topic of marriage.	"The Story of an Hour" poses a troubling question: Does marriage inevitably encourage people to "impose [their] private will upon a fellow-creature" (par. 14)?
"Cathedral" features a character with a physical handicap.	By depicting an able-bodied protagonist who discovers his own emotional and spiritual shortcomings through an encounter with a physically handicapped person, "Cathedral" invites us to question traditional definitions of "disability."

(continued)

FACTUAL STATEMENT	THESIS
"London" has three discrete stanzas that each end with a period; two-thirds of the lines are end-stopped.	In "London," William Blake uses various formal devices to suggest the unnatural rigidity of modern urban life.
Creon and Antigone are both similar and different.	Antigone and Creon share the same fatal flaw: Each recognizes only one set of obligations. In the end, however, the play presents Antigone as more admirable.

All of the thesis statements above are arguable because each implicitly answers a compelling interpretive question to which multiple, equally reasonable answers seem possible—for instance, *What is the key similarity between Antigone and Creon? Which character's actions and values does the play as a whole ultimately champion?* or, *What exactly does Blake demonstrate about modern urban life?* But they share other traits as well. All are clear and emphatic. All use *active verbs* to capture what the text and/or its implied author does (*poses, invites, uses, presents* versus *has, is, tries to*). And each entices us to read further by implying further interpretive questions—*What "set of obligations" do Antigone and Creon each "recognize"? Given how alike they are, what makes Antigone more admirable than Creon?* or, *According to Blake, what specifically is "unnatural" and "rigid" about modern urban life?* (Note, by the way, that the arguable claim in the Blake example *isn't* that he "uses various formal devices to suggest" something: *All* authors do that. Instead, the arguable claim has to do with *what* he suggests through formal devices.)

An effective thesis enables the reader to enter the essay with a clear sense that its writer has something to prove and what that is, and it inspires readers with the desire to see the writer prove it. We want to understand how the writer arrived at this view, to test whether it's valid, and to see how the writer will answer the other questions the thesis has generated in our minds. A good thesis captures readers' interest and shapes their expectations. In so doing, it also makes specific promises to readers that the rest of the essay must fulfill.

At the same time, an arguable claim about literature is not one-sided or narrow-minded. A thesis needs to stake out a position, but a position can and should admit complexity. Literature, after all, tends to focus more on exploring problems, conflicts, and questions than on offering easy solutions, resolutions, and answers. Its goal is to complicate and enrich, not to simplify, our way of looking at the world. The best essays about literature and the theses that drive them often do the same. As some of the sample thesis statements above demonstrate, for example, a good thesis can be a claim about just what the key question or conflict explored in a text is rather than about how that question is answered or that conflict resolved. Though an essay with this sort of thesis wouldn't be complete unless it ultimately considered possible answers and resolutions, it doesn't have to *start* there.

INTERPRETATION VERSUS EVALUATION (OR WHY IS A LITERATURE ESSAY *NOT* A REVIEW)

All the sample theses above involve *interpretive* claims—claims about how a literary text works, what it says, how one should understand it. Unless your instructor suggests otherwise, this is the kind of claim you need for a thesis in a literature essay.

Yet it's useful to remember that in reading and writing about literature we often make (and debate) a different type of claim—the *evaluative*. Evaluation entails assessment, and evaluative claims about literature tend to be of two kinds. The first involves aesthetic assessment and/or personal preference— whether a text (or a part or element thereof) succeeds, or seems to you "good," in artistic terms or whether you personally "like" it. This kind of claim features prominently in movie and book reviews, but literature essays are not reviews. Where the thesis of a review of Raymond Carver's CATHEDRAL, for example, might be that "Carver's story fails as a story because of its lack of action and unlikeable narrator" or that "'Cathedral' does a great job of characterizing its narrator-protagonist," a better thesis for a literature essay might be something like that of Bethany Qualls's "A Narrator's Blindness in Raymond Carver's 'Cathedral'" (see "Fiction: Reading, Responding, Writing"): "Through his words even more than his actions the narrator unwittingly shows us why nothing much happens to him by continually demonstrating his utter inability to connect with others or to understand himself." In other words, where reviewers are mainly concerned with answering the question of *whether* a text "works," literary critics focus primarily on showing *how* it does so and with what effects. Likewise, though personal preferences may well influence your choice of which texts to write about, such preferences shouldn't be the primary focus of your essay— who, after all, can really argue with your personal preferences?

The second kind of evaluative claim involves moral, philosophical, social, or political judgment—whether an idea or action is wise or good, valid or admirable, something you "agree with." Both interpretive and evaluative claims involve informed opinion (which is why they are debatable). But whereas interpretive claims of the kind literary critics tend to privilege aim to elucidate the opinions and values expressed or enacted *in* and *by* a text or its characters, evaluative claims of this second type instead assess the validity *of* those opinions and values, often by comparison with one's own. Our sample thesis statement about ANTIGONE, for example, is a claim about which character *the play presents* as more admirable, not about which character the essay writer herself admires more.

The latter kind of claim is far from irrelevant or unimportant. One major reason why we read and write about literature is because it encourages us to

grapple with real moral, social, and political issues of the kind we *should* develop informed opinions about. The question is simply one of emphasis: In a literature essay, the literature itself must be your primary focus, not your personal experience with or opinions about the issues it raises or the situations it explores.

Your main job in a literature essay is to thoughtfully explore *what* the work communicates and *how* it does so. Making an interpretive claim your thesis ensures that you keep your priorities straight. Once you have done that job thoroughly and well in the body of your essay, *then* you can consider evaluative questions in your conclusion (see "End: The Conclusion," in 18.1.5).

The poem "Ulysses" demonstrates that traveling and meeting new people are important parts of life. The speaker argues that staying in one place for too long is equivalent to substituting the simple act of breathing for truly living. I very much agree with the speaker's argument because I also believe that travel is one of life's most valuable experiences. Traveling allows you to experience different cultures, different political systems, and different points of view. It may change your way of thinking or make you realize that people all over the world are more similar than they are different.

This paragraph might be the kernel of a good conclusion to an essay that develops the thesis that "'Ulysses' demonstrates that traveling and meeting new people are important parts of life." Unfortunately, however, this paragraph actually appeared at the beginning of a student paper so full of similar paragraphs that it simply never managed to be *about* ULYSSES at all. Unfortunately, too, then, this paragraph demonstrates one of the reasons why some instructors forbid you to use the word "I" at all in literature essays (see 18.1.1).

18.1.3 Motive ("Although . . . I Think . . .")

One reason inexperienced writers might be tempted to emphasize evaluation over interpretation is that evaluative claims sometimes *seem* more debatable. It isn't always apparent, in other words, why there is anything useful or revelatory, even arguable or debatable, about a claim like "*Antigone* presents Antigone's form of over-simplification as more admirable than Creon's" or "Emily Dickinson questions traditional Christian doctrines." In the work of professional literary critics, however, such claims seem compelling because they are never presented in a vacuum but rather as what they truly are—a response to other actual or potential claims about the text. Such a presentation provides a *motive* for the reader of such an essay just as it does its writer.

Boil any good literature essay down to its essence, in other words, and you'll end up with a sentence that goes something like this (even though such a sentence never appears in the essay):

Although they say / I used to think / someone might reasonably think _____ about this text, I say / now think _____ because _____.

An effective essay doesn't just state a thesis ("I say/now think . . .") and prove it by providing reasons and evidence ("because . . ."); it also interests us in that thesis by framing it as a response to some other actual or potential thesis— something that "they" actually "say" about a text; that you "used to think" about it, perhaps on a first, casual reading; or that some reader *might* reasonably think or say.[1] In a literature research essay, "they" may well be published literary critics. But you don't have to have read any published work on a literary text to discover alternative readings to which to respond: If you have discussed a text in class, you have heard plenty of statements made and questions raised about it, all of which are fodder for response. If you've read and re-read a work carefully, your view of it has almost certainly evolved, ensuring that you yourself have a "naive reading" to compare to your more enlightened one. Finally, to write effectively about a text you inevitably have to imagine other possible interpretations, and, again, those *potential* readings are also ones you can "take on" in your essay.

Below, an introduction to one student writer's essay on Emily Dickinson appears first; below that are two different ways of paraphrasing the "Although . . . , I think" statement that introduction implies.

When cataloguing Christian poets, it might be tempting to place Emily Dickinson between Dante and John Donne. She built many poems around biblical quotations, locations, and characters. She meditated often on the afterlife, prayer, and trust in God. Yet Dickinson was also intensely doubtful of the strand of Christianity that she inherited. In fact, she never became a Christian by the standards of her community in nineteenth-century Amherst, Massachusetts. Rather, like many of her contemporaries in Boston, Dickinson recognized the tension between traditional religious teaching and modern ideas. And these tensions between hope and doubt, between tradition and modernity animate her poetry. In "Some keep the Sabbath going to church—," "The Brain—is wider than the Sky—," "Because I could not stop for Death—," and "The Bible is an antique Volume," the poet uses traditional religious terms and biblical allusions. But she does so in order both to criticize traditional doctrines and practices and to articulate her own unorthodox beliefs.

1. *Although someone might reasonably think* of Emily Dickinson as a conventionally religious poet, *I think* she only uses traditional religious terms and biblical allusions to criticize traditional doctrines and practices and to articulate her own unorthodox beliefs.
2. *Although someone might reasonably think* of Emily Dickinson as either a conventionally religious poet or as an intensely doubtful one, *I think* she is both: Her poetry enacts a tension between traditional religious teaching and the hope it inspires and modern doubt.

1. For a more extensive discussion of this approach to writing, see Gerald Graff and Cathy Birkenstein's *"They Say/I Say": The Moves That Matter in Academic Writing*, 3rd ed., W. W. Norton, 2014.

The introduction above is an especially useful example because it demonstrates three things you need to keep in mind in articulating motive:

1. *Crafting a strong motive requires giving real substance to the argument you respond to,* taking it seriously enough that your readers do, too. Notice how the introduction above does that by actually listing a few good reasons why it might be entirely reasonable for a reader to think of Emily Dickinson either as a religious poet or as a skeptical one before making the claim that she is both. Simply put, you lose credibility from the get-go rather than generating interest in your thesis if you seem to be building a "straw man" just so you can knock him down.

2. *"Responding" to another point of view doesn't have to mean disagreeing with it.* Instead, you might

   • agree with, but complicate or qualify, the original claim

     Although my classmates might be right to suggest that Miss Emily is heroic, I think she needs to be seen specifically as a tragic heroine.

   • present your thesis as a middle way between two extreme alternatives (as in the sample introduction above); or

   • as in any conversation, change the subject by turning attention to something previously or easily ignored

     Though our class discussion about "A Rose for Emily" focused exclusively on Miss Emily, we shouldn't ignore her father, since he makes Miss Emily what she is.

3. *"Although . . . I think . . . because . . ." is a useful sentence to use as you plan or summarize an argument, not a sentence that should actually appear in an essay,* in part because it creates problems with tone (see 18.1.1).

18.1.4 Evidence

Showing readers that your interpretation and argument are valid requires ample, appropriate evidence. And the appropriateness and quality of your evidence will depend on how you prepare and present it. Simply speaking, the term *evidence* refers to facts. But a fact by itself isn't really evidence for anything, or rather—as lawyers well know—any one fact can be evidence for many things. Like lawyers, literary critics turn a fact into evidence by interpreting it, drawing an inference from it, giving the reader a vivid sense of why and how the fact demonstrates a specific claim. You need, then, both to present concrete facts and to actively interpret them. *Show* readers why and how each fact matters.

KINDS OF LITERARY EVIDENCE: QUOTATION, PARAPHRASE, SUMMARY, DESCRIPTION

Quotations are an especially important form of evidence in literature essays. Any essay about literature that contains no quotations is likely to be weak. Readers of such an essay may doubt whether its writer has a thorough knowledge of the literary work or has paid adequate attention to details. And certain kinds of claims—about a character's motivations, a speaker's **tone**, a narrator's attitude toward a character, and so on—just can't be truly substantiated or developed *without* recourse to quotations.

At the same time, inexperienced writers sometimes make the mistake of thinking quotations are the *only* form of evidence in literature essays. They aren't. In fact, because a quotation will lead your reader to expect commentary on, and interpretation of, its language, you should quote directly from the text only when the actual wording is significant. Otherwise, keep attention on the facts that really matter by simply paraphrasing, describing, or summarizing. (For a discussion and examples of paraphrase, summary, and description, see ch. 17.)

In this paragraph, note how the student writer simply summarizes and paraphrases (in bold) when the key facts are what happens (who does what to whom when) and what the "gist" of a character's remarks are, but she quotes when the specific wording is the key evidence. Notice, too, how the writer turns quotations into evidence by both introducing and following each with interpretive commentary (in italics) to create what some writing experts call a "quotation sandwich." (For more on effective quotation, see ch. 21.)

At this point in the novel, Tess is so conflicted about what to do that she can't decide or do anything at all. **Only after asking her to marry him several times and repeatedly wondering aloud why Tess is hesitating does Angel finally get her to say yes or no. Even after agreeing to be his bride, Tess refuses to set a date, and it is Angel who finally, weeks later, suggests December 31.** Once Tess agrees, *the narrator describes this more as a matter of totally letting go than of finally taking charge:* "carried along upon the wings of the hours, without the sense of a will," she simply "drifted into . . . passive responsiveness to all things her lover suggested" (221; ch. 32). *Tess has given up agency and responsibility, letting events take whatever course they will rather than exerting her will,* even though—or maybe because—she is so terrified about the direction they will take.

Through its form, the poem demonstrates that division can increase instead of lessen meaning, as well as love. On the one hand, just as the poem's content stresses the power of the love among *three people,* so the poem's form also stresses "threeness" as well as "twoness." **It is** after all **divided into *three* distinctly numbered stanzas, and each stanza consists of *three* sentences.** On the other hand, **every *sentence* is "divided equally twixt two" *lines,*** just as the speaker's "passion" is divided equally between two men. Formally, then, the poem mirrors the kinds of division it describes. Sound and especially rhyme reinforce this pattern since **the two lines that make up one sentence usually rhyme with each other to form a couplet. The only lines that don't conform to this pattern come at the beginning of the second stanza where we instead have alternating rhyme—*is* (line 7) rhymes with *miss* (9), *mourn* (8) rhymes with *scorn* (10).** But here, again, form reinforces content since these lines describe how the speaker "miss[es]" one man when the other is "by," a sensation she arguably reproduces in us as we read by ensuring we twice "miss" the rhyme that the rest of the poem leads us to expect.

Description (in bold) provides the evidence in this paragraph from the essay on Aphra Behn's ON HER LOVING TWO EQUALLY that appears earlier in this book ("Poetry: Reading, Responding, Writing").

18.1.5 Structure

Like an effective short story, poem, or play, your essay needs to have a beginning (or introduction), a middle (or body), and an ending (or conclusion). Each of these parts plays its own unique and vital role in creating a coherent, persuasive, and satisfying whole.

BEGINNING: THE INTRODUCTION

Your essay's beginning, or introduction, needs to draw readers in and prepare them for what's to come by not only articulating your thesis and your motive but also providing any basic information—about the author, the topic, the text, or its contexts—readers will need to understand and appreciate your argument. At the very least, you need to specify the title of the work you're writing about and the author's full name. Very short (one-sentence) plot summaries or descriptions of the text can also be useful, but they should be "slanted" so as to emphasize the aspects of the text you'll be most concerned with. (On summary and description, see ch. 17.)

Below are the first few sentences of two different essays on HAMLET. Notice how each uses plot summary to establish motive and build up to a thesis. Though we don't yet know exactly what each thesis will be, each summary is slanted to give readers a pretty clear sense of the essay's general topic and of the kind of thesis it's heading toward.

1. It would be easy to read William Shakespeare's *Hamlet* as a play dealing with exclusively personal issues and questions—"to be or not to be," am I really crazy?, did Mommy really love Daddy?, do I love Mommy too much? What such a reading ignores is the play's political dimension: Hamlet isn't just any person; he's the Prince of Denmark. The crime he investigates isn't just any old murder or even simple fratricide: by killing his brother, who is also Hamlet's father and Denmark's rightful king, Claudius commits regicide only in order to usurp the throne—a throne Hamlet is supposed to inherit. Thanks to their actions, the tragedy ends not only with the decimation of Denmark's entire royal family, including the prince himself, but also with a successful foreign invasion that we—and all of the characters—have been warned about from the beginning.

2. As everyone knows, William Shakespeare's *Hamlet* depicts a young man's efforts to figure out both whether his uncle murdered his father and what to do about it. What everyone may not have thought about is this: does it matter that the young man is a prince? that his uncle is now king? or even that the action takes place in ancient Denmark rather than in modern America? Ultimately, it does not. Though the play's setting and its characters' political roles and responsibilities might add an extra layer of interest, they shouldn't distract us from the universal and deeply personal questions the play explores.

Like the sentences in these partial introductions, each and every sentence in your introduction should *directly* contribute to your effort to spark readers' interest, articulate your thesis and motive, or provide necessary background information. Avoid sentences that are only "filler," especially vapid (hence boring and uninformative) generalizations or "truisms" about literature or life such as "Throughout human history, people have struggled with the question . . ."; "Literature often portrays conflicts"; "This story deals with many relevant issues"; or "In life, joy and sorrow often go together." To offer up one more truism worth keeping in mind in crafting introductions, "you only get one chance to make a first impression," and generalizations, truisms, and clichés seldom make a good one.

MIDDLE: THE BODY

As in any essay, the middle, or body, of your literature essay is where you do the essential work of supporting and developing your thesis by presenting and analyzing evidence. Each body paragraph needs to articulate, support, and develop *one* specific claim—a debatable idea directly related to the thesis, but smaller and more specific. This claim should be stated fairly early in the paragraph in a *topic sentence*. (If your paragraphs open with factual statements, you may have a problem.) And every sentence in the paragraph should help prove and elaborate on that claim. Indeed, each paragraph ideally should build from an initial, general statement of the claim to the more complex form of it that you develop by presenting and analyzing evidence. In this way, each paragraph functions a bit like a miniature essay with its own thesis, body, and conclusion.

Your essay as a whole should develop logically, just as each paragraph does. To ensure that happens, you need to do the following:

- Order your paragraphs so that each builds on the last, with one idea following another in a *logical* sequence. The goal is to lay out a clear path for the reader. Like any path, it should go somewhere. Don't just prove your point; develop it.
- Present each idea/paragraph so that the logic behind the order is clear. Try to start each paragraph with a sentence that functions as a bridge, transporting the reader from one claim to the next. The reader shouldn't have to leap.

The specific sorts of topic and transition sentences you need will depend in part on the kind of literature essay you're writing. Later in this and other chapters, we'll demonstrate what they tend to look like in comparative essays, for example. But your thesis should always be your main guide.

Below are the thesis and topic sentences from the student essay on Raymond Carver's "Cathedral" that appears earlier in this book ("Fiction: Reading, Responding, Writing"). Notice that just as the thesis is a claim about the narrator, so, too, are all the topic sentences and that the writer begins with what she acknowledges to be the most "evident" or obvious claim.

Thesis: Through his words even more than his actions the narrator unwittingly demonstrates his utter inability to connect with others or to understand himself.

Topic Sentences:

1. The narrator's isolation is most evident in the distanced way he introduces his own story and the people in it.

2. At least three times the narrator himself notices that this habit of not naming or really acknowledging people is significant.

3. Also reinforcing the narrator's isolation and dissatisfaction with it are the awkward euphemisms and clichés he uses, which

emphasize how disconnected he is from his own feelings and how uncomfortable he is with other people's.

4. Once the visit actually begins, the narrator's interactions and conversations with the other characters are even more awkward.

5. Despite Robert's best attempt to make a connection with the narrator, the narrator resorts to labels again.

6. There is hope for the narrator at the end as he gains some empathy and forges a bond with Robert over the drawing of a cathedral.

7. However, even at the very end it isn't clear just whether or how the narrator has really changed.

END: THE CONCLUSION

In terms of their purpose (not their content), conclusions are introductions in reverse. Whereas introductions draw readers away from their world and into your essay, conclusions send them back. Introductions work to convince readers that they should read the essay; conclusions work to show them why and how the experience was worthwhile. You should approach conclusions, then, by thinking about what specific sort of lasting impression you want to create. What can you give readers to take with them as they journey back into the "real world"?

In literature essays, effective conclusions often consider at least one of the following three things:

1. *Implications*—What picture of your author's work or worldview does your argument imply? Alternatively, what might your argument suggest about some real-world issue or situation? Implications don't have to be earth-shattering. It's unlikely that your reading of August Wilson's FENCES will rock your readers' world. But your argument about this play should in some small but worthwhile way change how readers see Wilson's work or provide some new insight into some topic that work explores—how racism works, or how difficult it is for people to adjust to changes in the world around us, or how a parent or spouse might go wrong, and so on. If your essay has not, to this point, dealt with theme, now is a good time to do so. If you have not mentioned the author's name since the introduction, do so now; often, making the implied or actual author the subject of at least some of your sentences is one way to ensure that you are moving from argument to implications.

2. *Evaluation*—Though, as we've stressed, literature essays need to focus primarily on interpretation, conclusions are a good place to move from

interpretation to evaluation. In a sense, careful interpretation earns you the right to do some thoughtful evaluation. What might your specific interpretation of the text reveal about its literary quality or effectiveness? Alternatively, to what extent and how exactly do you agree or disagree with the author's conclusions about a particular issue? How, for example, might your own view of how racism works compare to the view implied in *Fences*? (For more on evaluative and/versus interpretive claims, see 18.1.2.)

3. *Areas of ambiguity or unresolved questions*—Are there any remaining puzzles or questions that your argument or the text itself doesn't resolve or answer? Or might your argument suggest a new question or puzzle worth investigating?

Above all, don't merely repeat what you've already said. If your essay has done its job to this point, and especially if your essay is relatively short, your readers may well feel bored or even insulted if they get a mere summary. You should certainly clarify anything that needs clarifying, but you should also go further. The best essays are rounded wholes in which conclusions do, in a sense, circle back to the place where they started. But the best essays remind readers of where they began only in order to give them a more palpable sense of how far they've come and why it matters. Your conclusion is your chance to ensure that readers *don't* leave your essay wondering, "Okay. So what?"

In its original state, this conclusion to Bethany Qualls's essay on Raymond Carver's "Cathedral" might beg the "So what?" question. Yet notice what happens when we add just three more sentences that try to answer that question. (Qualls's essay appears at the end of "Fiction: Reading, Responding, Writing.")

It's possible that not feeling "inside anything" (par. 135) could be a feeling of freedom from his own habits of guardedness and insensitivity, his emotional "blindness." But even with this final hope for connection, for the majority of the story the narrator is a closed, judgmental man who isolates himself and cannot connect with others. The narrator's view of the world is one filled with misconceptions that the visit from Robert starts to slowly change, yet it is not clear what those changes are, how far they will go, or whether they will last. **Living with such a narrator for the length even of a short story and the one night it describes can be a frustrating experience. But in the end that might be Raymond Carver's goal: by making us temporarily see the world through the eyes of its judgmental narrator, "Cathedral" forces us to do what the narrator himself has a hard time doing. The question is, will that change us?**

18.2 COMMON ESSAY TYPES

All literature essays have the same basic purpose and the same five elements. Yet they come in almost infinite varieties, each of which handles those elements somewhat differently and thus also poses somewhat different writing challenges. In the next chapter, for example, we discuss a few literature essay topics so common that they virtually define distinct types or subgenres of the literature essay (19.1.3). The rest of this chapter, however, concentrates exclusively on two especially common and in some ways especially challenging essay types—the comparative essay and the in-class exam essay.

18.2.1 The Comparative Essay

As we have emphasized throughout this book, comparison is a fundamental part of all reading: We develop our expectations about how a poem, play, or story will unfold in part by consciously or unconsciously comparing it to other poems, plays, and stories we've read; we get a sense of just who a character is by comparing her to other characters in the same story or play; and so on. Not surprisingly, then, one of the most common types of essays assigned in literature classes is one that considers similarities and differences within a work, between two works, or among several. One might, for example, write an essay comparing different characters' interpretations of Georgianna's birthmark in Nathaniel Hawthorne's THE BIRTH-MARK or one comparing the use of symbolism in this Hawthorne story to that in Edwidge Danticat's A WALL OF FIRE RISING.

The key challenges involved in writing effective comparison essays are achieving the right balance between comparison and contrast, crafting an appropriate thesis, and effectively structuring the body of the essay.

COMPARISON AND/VERSUS CONTRAST

"Comparison-contrast" is a label commonly applied to comparison essays, but it's a somewhat misleading one: Though some comparative essays give greater stress to similarities, others to differences (or contrast), *all* comparison has to pay at least some attention to both. Contrast is thus *always* part of comparison.

Where the emphasis falls in your essay will depend partly on your assignment, so be sure that you scrutinize it carefully and understand what it requires of you. An assignment that asks you to "explain how and why children feature prominently in Romantic literature" by "analyzing the work of at least two Romantic poets," for example, encourages you to pay more attention to similarities so as to demonstrate understanding of a single "Romantic" outlook. Conversely, an assignment asking you to "contrast Wordsworth and Coleridge" and describe "the major differences in their poetry" obviously emphasizes contrast. Again, however, even an assignment that stresses differences requires you first to establish some similarities as a ground for contrast, even as an assignment that stresses similarities requires you to acknowledge the differences that make the similarities meaningful.

If the assignment gives you leeway, your particular topic and thesis will determine the relative emphasis you give to similarities and differences. In "Out-Sonneting Shakespeare: An Examination of Edna St. Vincent Millay's Use of the Sonnet Form" (ch. 15), for example, student writer Melissa Makolin makes her case for the distinctiveness and even radicalism of Millay's sonnets both by contrasting them to those of Shakespeare and by demonstrating the similarities between two sonnets by Shakespeare, on the one hand, and by Millay, on the other. But one could easily imagine an essay that instead demonstrated Millay's range by emphasizing the differences between her two sonnets, perhaps by building a thesis out of Makolin's claim that one poem is about "impermanent lust," the other "eternal love."

THE COMPARATIVE ESSAY THESIS

Like any essay, a comparative essay needs a thesis—*one* argumentative idea that embraces all the things (texts, characters, etc.) being compared. If you're like most of us, you may well be tempted to fall back on a statement along the lines of "These things are similar but different." Sadly, that won't cut it as a thesis. It isn't arguable (what two or more things *aren't* both similar and different?), nor is it specific enough to give your comparison direction and purpose: What such a thesis promises is less a coherent argument than a series of seemingly random, only loosely related observations about similarities and differences, desperately in search of a point.

At the end of the introduction to his comparative essay, student writer Charles Collins first articulates his main claim about each of the two short stories he will compare and then offers *one* overarching thesis statement.

> In "The Birth-Mark," the main character, Aylmer, views his wife's birthmark as a flaw in her beauty, as well as a symbol of human imperfection, and tries to remove it. In "the Thing in the Forest," the protagonists, Penny and Primrose, react to the Thing both as a real thing and as a symbol. The characters' interpretation of these things is what creates conflict, and the stories are both shaped by the symbolic meanings that the characters ascribe to those things.

COMPARATIVE ESSAY STRUCTURES

In structuring the body of a comparative essay, you have two basic options, though it's also possible to combine these two approaches. Make sure to choose the option that best suits your particular texts, topics, and thesis rather than simply fall back on whichever structure feels most familiar or easy to you. Your structure and your thesis should work together to create a coherent essay that illuminates something about the works that can only be seen through comparison.

The Block Method

The first option tends to work best both for shorter essays and for essays, of any length, in which you want to stress differences at least as much as similarities. As its common label, "the block method," implies, this approach entails dividing your essay into "blocks" or sections that each lay out your entire argument about one of the things you're comparing. Charles Collins's essay comparing two stories, for example, is divided roughly in half: His first three body paragraphs analyze one story ("The Birth-Mark"), the last four body paragraphs another story ("The Thing in the Forest"). To knit the two halves of the essay together into one whole, however, Collins begins the second "block" with a paragraph that discusses both stories. Such transitions are crucial to making the "block" method work.

This paragraph of Collins's essay serves as a transition between the two halves or "blocks" of his essay, the first on "The Birth-Mark," the second on "The Thing in the Forest."

> The symbolism in "The Birth-Mark" is fairly straightforward. The characters openly acknowledge the power of the symbol, and the narrator of the story clearly states what meaning Aylmer finds in it. In "The Thing in the Forest" what the thing represents is not as clear. Penny and Primrose, the story's main characters, do not view the Thing as symbolic, as Aylmer does the birthmark. Neither the narrator nor the characters directly say why the Thing is important to Penny and Primrose or even whether the Thing they see in the forest is the monster, the Loathly Worm, that they later read about in the book at the mansion. . . .

In addition to strong, meaty transition paragraphs, effective use of the block method also requires that you

- *make each block or section of your essay match the others* in terms of the issues it takes up or the questions it answers, so as to maintain clear points of comparison. In Collins's essay, for example, each "block" answers the same questions with regard to each of the two stories and main characters being compared: whether or not the characters in a story see something as a symbol, what it ultimately comes to symbolize to them or to the reader, and how the characters' response to the symbol shapes their behavior.
- *order and present the blocks so that each builds on the last*: Though your blocks should match, their order shouldn't be random; rather,

each block should *build* on the one that came before, just as should paragraphs/topic sentences in any essay. In Collins's essay, for example, the discussion of "The Birth-Mark" comes first because his argument is that symbolism here is more "straightforward" or simple than it is in "The Thing in the Forest," and the transition homes in on that difference. As in many essays, then, the movement here is from the most to the least obvious and simple points.

The Point-by-Point or Side-by-Side Method
The second method of structuring a comparative essay requires you to integrate your discussions of the things—texts or characters, for example—that you are comparing. Each section of your essay (which might be one paragraph or two) should begin with a topic sentence that refers to all the things you're comparing rather than exclusively to one.

Below is a paragraph from a student essay comparing Samuel Taylor Coleridge's FROST AT MIDNIGHT and Matthew Arnold's DOVER BEACH using the "point-by-point method." Like every other body paragraph in this essay, this one discusses both poems and their speakers.

Differently but equally disturbed by the thoughts and emotions stirred by the natural scene before them, both speakers turn to the past, without finding much consolation in it. In Coleridge's poem, that past is specific and personal: What the speaker remembers are his schooldays, a time when he was just as bored and lonely and just as trapped inside his own head as he is now. Then, as now, he "gazed upon the" fire and "watch[ed] that fluttering" ash (lines 25–26), feeling no more connection then to his "stern precepto[r]" than he does now to his sleeping baby (37). In Arnold's poem, the past the speaker thinks of is more distant and historical. What he remembers are lines by Sophocles written thousands of years ago and thousands of miles away. But in his case, too, the past just seems to offer more of the same rather than any sort of comfort or relief. Just as he now—standing by a "distant northern sea" (20)—hears in the waves "[t]he eternal note of sadness" (14), so "Sophocles long ago"—"on the Aegean"—"[h]eard" in them "the turbid ebb and flow / Of human misery" (15–16, 18).

Below are the thesis and outline for another point-by-point comparison essay, this one analyzing two short stories—Franz Kafka's A HUNGER ARTIST and Flannery O'Connor's "Everything That Rises Must Converge." In the essay itself, each numbered section consists of two paragraphs, the first (a) discussing O'Connor's protagonist, the second (b) Kafka's.

Thesis: "A Hunger Artist" and "Everything That Rises Must Converge" depict changing worlds in which the refusal to adapt amounts to a death sentence.

Outline:

1. Both Julian's mother and the hunger artist live in rapidly changing worlds in which they don't enjoy the status they once did.

   a) Julian's mother's world: the civil rights movement and economic change > loss of status

   b) hunger artist's world: declining "interest in professional fasting" > loss of status

2. Rather than embracing such changes, both the artist and the mother resist them.

   a) Julian's mother: verbally expressed nostalgia, refusal to even *see* that things are changing

   b) the hunger artist: nostalgia expressed through behavior, does see that things are changing

3. Both characters take pride in forms of self-sacrifice that they see as essential to upholding "old-world" standards.

   a) Julian's mother: sacrifices for him, upholding family position and honor

   b) hunger artist: sacrifices for himself, upholding traditions of his art

4. Both characters nonetheless die as a result of their unwillingness to adapt.

   a) Julian's mother

   b) hunger artist

5. The endings of both stories create uncertainty about how we are to judge these characters and their attitudes.

   a) Julian's mother: Julian's last words and the story's create more sympathy for the mother

   b) hunger artist: his last words and description of the panther that replaces him make him less sympathetic

18.2.2 The Essay Test

Essays you are required to write for in-class exams do not fundamentally differ from those you write outside of class. Obviously, however, having to generate an essay on the spot presents peculiar challenges. Below, we offer some general tips before discussing the two basic types of in-class essay exams.

GENERAL TIPS

• *Carefully review instructions.*
Though instructors rarely provide actual exam questions in advance, they usually do give you some indication of how many questions you'll have to answer, what kind of questions they will be, and how much they will each count. Whether you get such instructions before or during the exam, take the time to consider them carefully before you start writing. Make sure you understand exactly what is expected of you, and ask your instructor about anything that seems the least confusing or ambiguous. You don't want to produce a great essay on a Shakespeare sonnet only to discover that your essay was supposed to compare two Shakespeare sonnets. Nor do you want to spend 75 percent of your time on the question worth 25 points and 25 percent on the question worth 75 points.

• *Glean all the information you can from sample questions.*
In lieu of or in addition to instructions, instructors will sometimes provide sample questions in advance of an exam. Read rightly, such questions can give you a lot of information about what you need to be able to do on the exam. If presented with the sample question "What are three characteristic features of short stories by Flannery O'Connor, and what is their combined effect?," for example, you should come to the exam prepared not only to write an essay addressing this specific question but also or alternatively an essay addressing either a different question about the assigned O'Connor stories (i.e., same texts, different topic) or a similar question about other authors that you read multiple works by (i.e., same topic, different texts).

• *Anticipate questions or topics and strategize about how to use what you know.*
Whether or not an instructor actually gives you sample questions, exam questions rarely, if ever, come entirely out of the blue. Instead they typically emerge directly out of class lectures and discussions. As important, even questions that do ask you to approach a text in what seems like a new way can still be answered effectively by drawing upon the facts and ideas discussed in class. Keeping good notes and reviewing them as you prepare for the exam should thus help you both to anticipate the sorts of topics you'll be asked to address and to master the information and ideas well enough so that you can use what you know in responding even to unanticipated questions.

• *Review and brainstorm with classmates.*
Just as discussing a work in class can broaden and deepen your understanding of it, so reviewing with classmates can help you see different ways of understanding and organizing the material and the information and ideas discussed in class. Compare notes, certainly, but also discuss and brainstorm. What sorts of questions might your classmates anticipate?

• *Read questions carefully and make sure you answer them.*
Once you have the actual exam questions, read them carefully before you start writing. Make sure you understand exactly what the question asks you to do, and—again—ask your instructor to clarify anything confusing or ambiguous.
    Don't ignore any part of a question, but do put your emphasis where the question itself does. Let's suppose your question is, "What does Dickinson seem to mean by 'Telling all the truth but telling it slant'? How might she do just that in her poetry? How might Dickinson's personal experience or historical milieu have encouraged her to approach things this way?" An essay in answer to this question that didn't say anything at all about biographical or historical context or speculate at all about how one or the other shaped Dickinson's notion of truth telling would be less than complete. Yet the question allows you to consider only *one* of these two contexts rather than both. More important, it asks you to devote most of your essay to analyzing *at least two poems* ("poetry") rather than discussing context. A good strategy might thus be to consider context only in your introduction and/or conclusion.

• *Be specific.*
One key difference between good exam essays and so-so or poor ones is the level and kind of detail they provide: One thing an exam is testing is whether you have actually read and really know the material; another is how well you can draw on facts to make an argument rather than simply regurgitating general ideas expressed in class. In response to the question above, for example, noodling on in a general way about Dickinson's use of dashes or metaphor will only take you so far—and not nearly far enough to score well. In answering this question, you should mention the titles of at least two specific poems and carefully explain precisely how each of them tells the truth slantwise or helps us understand what Dickinson means by slantwise truth. For example: "In the poem that actually begins 'Tell all the truth but tell it slant,' Dickinson suggests that to successfully convey the truth, you have to do it in a roundabout way. People need to be eased into the truth; if it comes all at once, it's too much. She even compares that kind of direct truth-telling to being struck by lightning." (See below for further discussion of specificity and how to achieve it in closed- versus open-book exams.)

• *Allow time to review and reconsider your essays.*
Though you're obviously pressed for time in an exam, leave yourself at least a few minutes to read over your essay before you have to hand it in. In addition to correcting actual mistakes, look for places where you could use more concrete evidence or make tighter, clearer connections between one point or claim and another.

CLOSED- VERSUS OPEN-BOOK EXAMS

How you prepare for exam essays and how those essays will be judged will depend, in part, on whether your exam is "open-book" or "closed-book"— whether, in other words, you are allowed to consult the literary texts and perhaps even your notes about them during the exam itself.

At first glance, open-book exams seem much easier, and in some ways they are. Having the literary text(s) in front of you ensures that you don't have to rely entirely on memory to conjure up factual evidence: You can double-check characters' names, see what a poem's rhyme scheme is, actually quote the text, and so on. The fact that you *can* do all that also means, however, that you need to: Instructors rightly expect more concrete and specific evidence, including quotations, in open-book exam essays. The bar, in short, is higher.

At the same time, there's a danger of spending so much time during the exam looking back through the text that you don't have adequate time to craft your argument about it. Here, good preparation can help. If you know which texts you're likely to be asked about on the exam, make sure that you mark them up in advance, highlighting especially telling passages (including those discussed in class), making notations about **rhyme scheme** and **meter**, and so on, so that you can marshal your evidence faster during the exam. Just make sure that you consult with your instructor in advance about what, if any, notes you are allowed to write in the book you bring with you to the exam.

If the exam is closed-book, your instructor won't be looking for quite the same level of detail when it comes to evidence, but that doesn't mean you don't need any. To prepare for a closed-book exam, you will need to do some memorizing: Knowing a text word-for-word is rarely required or helpful, but it is essential that you master the basic facts about it such as **genre**, title, author, characters' names; have a general sense of its **plot**, structure, and form; and can recall any facts about context that were stressed in class. In your essay, you will need to make good use of paraphrase, summary, and description (see ch. 17).

Below are two versions of a paragraph from an essay written for a closed-book exam. Without consulting the texts, the essayist cannot actually quote them. What the essayist can do is paraphrase an important piece of dialogue and summarize key episodes. What makes the second version better than the first is its much greater specificity about action, timing, characters, and dialogue—who says and does what to whom, when, and in what story.

1. O'Connor's stories often involve moments of extreme violence, like what happens to the old ladies in "Everything That Rises Must Converge" and "A Good Man Is Hard to Find." A character even says it would be a good thing if we were threatened with violence all the time.

2. O'Connor's stories often end with moments of extreme violence. At the end of "Everything That Rises Must Converge," after Julian's mother's gives a little boy a penny, his mother reacts to what she sees as condescension by whacking Julian's mother in the head with her purse. "A Good Man Is Hard to Find" ends with the Misfit shooting the grandmother point-blank after she has had to watch and listen as each of her family members is dragged off into the woods and shot. Afterward, the Misfit even suggests that the grandmother would have been a better person if she'd been threatened with that kind of violence all the time.

19 THE WRITING PROCESS

Doing anything well requires both knowing what you're trying to achieve and having some strategies for how to go about it. Where "The Literature Essay" chapter (ch. 18) focuses mainly on the *what*, this chapter focuses more on the *how*. In practice, of course, the writing process will vary from writer to writer and from assignment to assignment. No one can give you a recipe. What we instead do here is present you with a menu of strategies to try out and adapt to your particular tendencies as a writer and to the requirements of specific writing occasions and assignments.

As you do so, keep in mind that writing needn't be a solitary enterprise. Ultimately, your essay must be your own work. That is absolutely essential; anything else is plagiarism. But most writers—working in every genre and discipline, at every level—get inspiration, guidance, and feedback from others throughout the writing process, and so can you. Use class discussions to generate and test out topics and theses. Ask your instructor to clarify assignments or to discuss your ideas. Have classmates, friends, or roommates critique your drafts. In writing about literature, as in reading it, we get a much better sense of what our own ideas are and how best to convey them by considering others' impressions.

19.1 GETTING STARTED

19.1.1 Scrutinizing the Assignment

For student essayists, as for most professional ones, the writing process usually begins with an assignment. Though assignments vary, all impose restrictions. These are designed not to hinder your creativity but to direct it into productive channels, ensuring you hone particular skills, try out different approaches, and avoid common pitfalls.

Your first task as a writer is thus to scrutinize your assignment. Make sure that you fully understand what you are being asked to do (and not do), and ask questions about anything unclear or puzzling.

Almost all assignments restrict the length of an essay by imposing word or page limits. Keep those limits in mind as you consider potential topics, making sure to choose a topic you can handle in the space allowed. In three pages, you cannot thoroughly analyze all the characters in August Wilson's FENCES. But you might within that limit say something significant about some specific aspect of a character or of characterization—perhaps how Troy Maxson's approach to parenting relates to the way he was parented or how Wilson's inclusion of the final scene, set after Troy's death, affects our interpretation of his character.

Many assignments impose further restrictions, often indicating the texts and/or topics your essay should explore. As a result, any assignment will shape whether and how you tackle later steps such as "Choosing a Text" or "Identifying Topics."

Below are several representative essay assignments, each of which imposes a particular set of restrictions.

Choose any story in this anthology and write an essay analyzing how and why its protagonist changes.

This assignment dictates your topic and main question. It also provides you with the kernel of a thesis: *In [story title], [protagonist's name] goes from being a* _____ *to a* _____. OR *By the end of [story title], [protagonist's name] has learned that* _____. Though the assignment lets you choose your story, it limits you to those in which the protagonist changes or learns a lesson of some kind.

Write an essay analyzing one of the following sonnets: "Nuns Fret Not," "In an Artist's Studio," or "In the Park." Be sure to consider how the poem's form contributes to its meaning.

This assignment limits your choice of texts to three. It also requires that your essay address the effects of the poet's choice to use the sonnet form. Notice, though, that the assignment doesn't require that this be the main topic of your essay, but instead leaves you free to pursue any topic related to the poem's meaning.

Write an essay exploring the significance of references to eyes and vision in *A Midsummer Night's Dream.* What, through them, does the play suggest about the power and the limitations of human vision?

This assignment is more restrictive, indicating both text and topic. At the same time, it requires you to narrow the topic and formulate a specific thesis.

Write an essay comparing at least two poems by any one author in your anthology.

This assignment specifies the type of essay you must write (a comparison essay) and limits your choice of texts. Yet it leaves you the choice of which author to focus on, how many and which poems to analyze, what topic to explore, and what relative weight to give to similarities and differences.

(continued)

Explain how and why children feature prominently in Romantic literature by analyzing the work of at least two Romantic poets.

This assignment is more restrictive, specifying the type of essay (comparison), the topic (depictions of children), and the kinds of texts (Romantic poems), while also encouraging you to focus mainly on similarities so as to define a single Romantic outlook on children and childhood.

19.1.2 Choosing a Text

If your assignment allows you to choose which text to write about, try letting your initial impressions or "gut reactions" guide you. Do that, and your first impulse may be to choose a text that you immediately like or "get." Perhaps its language resembles your own; it depicts speakers, characters, or situations you easily relate to; or it explores issues you care deeply about. Following that first impulse can be a good strategy. Writing an engaging essay requires *being* engaged, and we all find it easier to engage with texts, authors, characters, and so on that we "like" immediately.

Paradoxically, however, writers often discover that they have little interesting or new to say about such a text. Perhaps they're too emotionally invested to analyze it closely or to imagine alternative ways to read it, or maybe its meaning seems so obvious that there's no puzzle or problem to drive an argument. Often, then, it can actually be more productive to choose a work that provokes the opposite reaction—that initially puzzles or even frustrates or angers you, one whose characters seem alien or whom you don't "like," one that investigates an issue you haven't thought much about, or one that articulates a theme you don't agree with. Sometimes such negative first reactions can have surprisingly positive results when it comes to writing. When you have to dig deeper, you sometimes discover more. And your own initial response might also provide you with the kernel of a good motive (see 18.1.3).

So, too, might the responses of your classmates. If you are writing about a text you've discussed in class, in other words, you might also or instead start with your "gut responses" to that discussion. Were you surprised by anything your classmates claimed about the text? Or did you strongly agree or disagree with any of your classmate's interpretations? Especially in hindsight, was anything *not* said or discussed in class that you think should have been?

19.1.3 Generating Topics

When an assignment allows you to create your own topic, you are more likely to build a lively and engaging essay from a particular insight or question that captures your attention and makes you want to say something, solve a problem, or stake out a position. The best essays originate in an individual response to a text and focus on a genuine question about it. Even when an instructor assigns you a topic, your essay's effectiveness will largely depend on whether you have made the topic your own, turning it into a real question to which you discover your own answer.

Often we refer to "finding" a topic, as if there are a bevy of topics "out there" just waiting to be plucked like ripe fruit off the topic tree. In at least two ways, that's true. For one thing, as we read a literary work, certain topics often do jump out and say, "Hey, look at me! I'm a topic!" A title alone may have that effect: *What "lesson" seems to be learned in "The Lesson"? Why is Keats so fixated on that darn nightingale; what does it symbolize for him? Or what the heck is an "ode" anyway, and how might it matter that Keats's poem is an "Ode to a Nightingale"?*

For another thing, certain general topics can be adapted to fit many different literary works. In fact, that's just another way of saying that there are certain common types (even subgenres) of literary essays, just as there are of short stories, plays, and poems. Here are a few especially common topics:

- the significance of a seemingly insignificant aspect or element of a work—a word or group of related words, an image or image-cluster, a minor character, a seemingly small incident or action, and so on. (This topic is appealing in part because it practically comes with a built-in motive: "Although a casual reader would likely ignore X . . .")
- the outlook or worldview of a single character or **speaker** (or of a group of characters) and its consequences
- the changes a major character or speaker undergoes over the course of a literary work (What is the change? When, how, and why does it occur?)
- the precise nature and wider significance of an internal or external **conflict** and its ultimate resolution

Especially when you're utterly befuddled about where to begin, it can be very useful to keep in mind such generic topics or essay types and to use them as starting points. But remember that they are just starting points. You always have to adapt and narrow a generic topic such as "imagery" or "character change" in order to produce an effective essay. In practice, then, no writer simply "finds" a topic; she *makes* one.

Here are some other techniques that might help you generate topics. (And generating *topics*, giving yourself a choice, is often a good idea.)

- *Analyze your initial response.*
  If you've chosen a text you feel strongly about, start with those responses. Try to describe your feelings and trace them to their source. Be as specific as possible. What moments, aspects, or elements of the text most affected you? How and why exactly? Try to articulate the question

behind your feelings. Often, strong responses result when a work either challenges or affirms an expectation, assumption, or conviction that you bring *to* it. Think about whether and how that's true in your case. Define the specific expectation, assumption, or conviction. How, where, and why does the text challenge it? fulfill or affirm it? Which of your responses and expectations are objectively valid, likely to be shared by other readers?

- *Think through the elements.*

Start with a list of elements and work your way through them, identifying anything that might be especially unique, interesting, or puzzling about the text in terms of each element. What stands out about the **tone**, the speaker, the **situation**, and so on? Come up with a statement about each. Look for patterns among your statements. Also, think about the questions your statements imply or ignore.

- *Pose motive questions.*

In articulating a motive in your essay's introduction, your concern is primarily with your readers, your goal to give *them* a substantive reason to find your thesis new and interesting and your essay thus worth reading. But you can also work your way toward a topic and even, eventually, a thesis, by considering motive-related questions. Keep in mind the basic "*Although they say/I used to think/someone might reasonably think . . . , I say/now think . . .*" statement and turn it into questions:

—What element(s) or aspect(s) of this work might a casual reader misinterpret? Or which might you have misinterpreted on a first reading? Or which did your classmates seem to misinterpret?

—What potentially significant element(s) or aspect(s) of this work were ignored entirely in class discussion? Or which might you have ignored on a first reading? Or which might any reasonable person ignore?

—What aspect(s) or element(s) of this work have your classmates disagreed among themselves about or maybe even taken extreme positions on? Or which have you seen in very different ways as you've read and thought about the work?

—What interesting paradox(es), contradiction(s), or tension(s) do you see in the work?

19.1.4 Formulating a Question and a Thesis

Before you begin writing an essay on any topic, you need to come up with a thesis or hypothesis—an arguable statement about the topic. Quite often, topic and thesis occur to you simultaneously: You might well decide to write about a topic precisely because you've got something specific to say about it. At other times, that's not the case: The topic comes much

more easily than the thesis. In this event, it helps to formulate a specific question about the topic and to develop a specific answer. That answer will be
your thesis.

Again, remember that your question and thesis should focus on something specific, yet they need to be generally valid, involving more than your
personal feelings. One way to move from an initial, subjective response to
an arguable thesis is to freewrite, as in the example below. Don't worry what
form your writing takes or how good it is: Just write.

> I really admire Bartleby. But why? What in the story encourages me to
> admire him? Well, he sticks to his guns and insists on doing only what
> he "prefers" to do. He doesn't just follow orders. That makes him really
> different from all the other characters in the story, especially the narra-
> tor. And also from a lot of people I know, even me. He's a nonconformist.
> Do I think other readers should feel the same way? Maybe, but maybe
> not. After all, his refusal to conform does cause problems for everyone
> around him. And it doesn't do him a lot of good either. Plus, he would be
> really annoying in real life. I wouldn't want to work in the same office.
> And even if you admire him, you can't really care about him because he
> doesn't seem to care much about anybody else. Or even about himself?
> Maybe that's the point. Through Bartleby, Melville explores both how
> rare and important and how dangerous nonconformity can be.

However you arrive at your thesis or however strongly you believe in it,
you should still think of it for now as a working hypothesis—a claim that's
provisional, still open to rethinking and revision.

19.2 PLANNING

Once you've formulated a tentative thesis and, ideally, a motive ("Although . . . ,
I think . . ."), you need to work on the ". . . because" part of the equation,
which means both (1) figuring out how to structure your argument, articulating and ordering your claims or sub-ideas; and (2) identifying the evidence
you need to prove and develop each of those claims.

Start by looking closely at your thesis. As in almost every phase of writing,
it helps to temporarily fill your readers' shoes: Try to see your thesis and the
promises it makes from their point of view. What will they need to be shown,
and in what order? If a good thesis shapes readers' expectations, it can also
guide you, as a writer.

A good thesis usually implies not only what the essay's claims should be but
also how they should be ordered. For instance, a thesis that focuses on the
development of a character implies that the first body paragraphs will explain

what that character is initially like and that later paragraphs will explore when, how, and why that character changes. Working wholly from the thesis and this rough sense of structure, generate an outline, either listing each claim (to create a *sentence outline*) or each topic to be covered (to create a *topic outline*). Though a sentence outline is far more helpful, you may find that at this stage you can only identify topics.

Take, for example, the Bartleby thesis developed in the last section (19.1.4)—Through Bartleby, Melville explores both how rare and important, and how dangerous, nonconformity can be. From it, we can generate the following outline, which begins with two clear claims/sentences and then simply describes two other topics that will need to be covered:

1. <u>Claim</u>: Bartleby is a nonconformist.
2. <u>Claim</u>: Bartleby's nonconformity makes him very different from every other character in the story, especially the narrator.
3. <u>Topic</u>: positive aspects or consequences of Bartleby's nonconformity.
4. <u>Topic</u>: negative aspects or consequences of Bartleby's nonconformity—how it's dangerous.

At this stage, in other words, it's clear that our Bartleby essay needs first to show *that* and *how* Bartleby refuses to conform (1) and then to show *that* and *how* such nonconformity differentiates him from other characters (2). Not only are these the most obvious and least debatable claims, but they also lay the essential groundwork for the rest: Questions about why or how Bartleby's nonconformity might be negative or positive (3–4) only make sense once you establish that there is nonconformity and show what it looks like. To further refine the first half of the outline or to draft the first half of the essay, all its hypothetical writer needs to do is review the story and her notes about it to identify appropriate evidence. Her discoveries will also determine whether she can fully develop each of these claims in just one paragraph or whether she might need two.

The shape of the second half of the essay is less clear and will demand more work. In reviewing the story and her notes, the writer would need to come up with claims about what the positive and negative aspects or consequences of Bartleby's nonconformity are. Ultimately she might even need to rethink the order in which she discusses these topics. Since whatever comes last in an essay should usually be not only the most complicated and debatable point but also the one that gets most emphasis as we build toward a conclusion, this writer would need to figure out where she thinks the story puts the most emphasis—the value of nonconformity (3) or its dangers (4).

As this example demonstrates, just as your thesis can guide you to an outline, so an outline can show you exactly what you need to figure out and what evidence you need to look for as you move toward a draft. The more detailed your outline, the easier drafting tends to be. But the truth is that sometimes we can only figure out what our actual claims or ideas are by trying to write them out, which might mean moving straight from a rough outline to a draft rather than further refining the outline before drafting.

As you begin to gather evidence, however, it is important that you let the evidence guide you, as well as your outline. As you look back at the text, you may well discover facts that are relevant to the thesis but that don't seem to relate directly to any of the claims or topics you've articulated. In that case, you may need to insert a new topic into the outline. Additionally, you may find (and should in fact actively look for) facts that challenge your argument. Test and reassess your claims against those facts and adjust them accordingly. Don't ignore inconvenient truths.

19.3 DRAFTING

If you've put time and care into getting started and planning, you may already be quite close to a first draft. If you've instead jumped straight into writing, you may have to move back and forth between composing and some of the steps described in earlier sections of this chapter.

Either way, remember that first drafts are called *rough drafts* for a reason. Think of yourself as a painter "roughing out" a sketch in preparation for the more detailed painting to come. At this stage, try not to worry about grammar, punctuation, and mechanics. Concentrate on the argument—articulating your ideas and proving them.

Sometimes the best way to start is simply to copy your thesis and outline into a new document. Forget about introducing your thesis, and just go right to work on your first body paragraph. Sometimes, however, you'll find that starting with the introduction helps: Having to draw readers in and set up your thesis and motive can give you a clearer sense of where you're going and why.

However you start, you will almost certainly feel frustrated at times. Stick to it. If you become truly stuck, try explaining your point to another person or getting out an actual piece of paper and a pen and *writing* for a few minutes before returning to your computer and your draft. If all else fails, make a note about what needs to go in the spot you can't get through. Then move on and come back to that spot once you've written the next paragraph. Whatever it takes, stay with your draft until you've at least got a middle, or body, that you're relatively satisfied with. Then take a break.

Later or—better yet, tomorrow—come back, look at the draft with a fresh eye, and take another shot, attaching a conclusion and (if necessary) an introduction, filling in any gaps, crafting smooth(er) transitions within and between paragraphs, deleting anything that now seems irrelevant (or, better yet, copying it into a separate "outtakes" document just in case you figure out later how to make it relevant). Do your utmost to create a relatively satisfying whole. Now pat yourself on the back and take another break.

19.4 REVISING

Revision is one of the most important and difficult tasks for any writer. It's a crucial stage in the writing process, yet one that is all too easy to ignore or mismanage. The difference between a so-so essay and a good one, between a good essay and a great one, often depends entirely on effective revision. Give yourself time to revise more than once. As you do so, develop revision strategies that work for you. The investment in time and effort will pay rich dividends on this essay and on future ones.

The essential thing is not to confuse *revising* with *editing and proofreading*. We've devoted separate sections of this chapter to each of these steps because they *are* entirely different processes. Where editing and proofreading focus mainly on sentence-level matters (grammar, punctuation, spelling, and so on), revision is about the whole essay, "the big picture." Revision entails assessing and improving both (1) the essay's working parts or elements and (2) your overall argument. Doing these two things well requires *not* getting distracted by small grammatical errors, spelling mistakes, and so on.

Before considering in depth what it means to assess the elements and enrich the argument, here are a few general tips about how to approach revision:

- *Think like readers.* Effective revision requires you to temporarily play the role of reader, as well as writer, of your essay. Take a step back from your draft, doing your utmost to see it from a more objective, even skeptical standpoint. Revision demands *re-vision*—looking again, seeing anew.
- *Get input from real readers.* This is an especially good time to involve other people in your writing process. Copy the "Assessing the Elements" checklist below and have a friend or classmate use it to critique your draft.
- *Think strengths and weaknesses, not right and wrong.* In critiquing your own draft or someone else's, it helps to think less in absolute terms (right and wrong, good and bad) than in terms of strengths and weaknesses—specific elements and aspects that work well and those that need some work.
- *Work with a hard copy.* Computers are a godsend when it comes to making revisions. But because they only allow us to look at one or two pages of an essay at a time, they actually make it harder to see the essay as a whole and to assess the effects of the changes they make it so easy for us to make. During the revision process, then, move away from the computer sometimes. Print out hard copies so that you can see your essay as a whole and mark it up, identifying problems that you can return to the computer to fix.

19.4.1 Assessing the Elements

The first step in revision is to make sure that all the working parts of your essay are, indeed, working. To help with that process, run through the following checklist to identify the strengths and weaknesses of your draft—or ask someone else to do so. Try to answer each question with ruthless honesty.

Whenever you can't justify a check, remember that you and/or your readers need to identify the specific problems in order to solve them—If information is missing from the introduction, *what information?* If every sentence in the introduction isn't serving a clear purpose, *which sentence* is the problem? And so on.

Thesis and Motive
☐ Is there *one* claim that effectively controls the essay?
☐ Is the claim debatable?
☐ Does the claim demonstrate real thought? Does it truly illuminate the text and topic?
☐ Does the writer *show* us that (and why) the thesis is new and worthwhile by suggesting an actual or potential alternative view?

Structure

BEGINNING/INTRODUCTION
☐ Does the introduction provide readers all—and only—the information they need about the author, text, context, and topic?
☐ Does the introduction imply a clear, substantive, debatable but plausible thesis? Is it clear which claim is the thesis?
☐ Does every sentence either help to articulate the thesis and motive or to provide essential information?

MIDDLE/BODY
☐ Does each paragraph clearly state one debatable claim? Does everything in the paragraph directly relate to, and help support and develop, that claim?
☐ Is each of those claims clearly related to (but different from) the thesis?
☐ Are the claims logically ordered?
☐ Is that logic clear? Is each claim clearly linked to those that come before and after? Are there any logical "leaps" that readers might have trouble following?
☐ Does each claim/paragraph clearly build on the last one? Does the argument move forward, or does it seem more like a list or a tour through a museum of interesting but unrelated observations?
☐ Do any key claims or logical steps in the argument seem to be missing?

ENDING/CONCLUSION
☐ Does the conclusion give readers the sense that they've gotten somewhere and that the journey has been worthwhile?

☐ Does it indicate the implications of the argument, consider relevant evaluative questions, or discuss questions that remain unanswered?

Evidence
☐ Is there ample, appropriate evidence for each claim?
☐ Are the appropriateness and significance of each fact—its relevance to the claim—perfectly clear?
☐ Are there any weak examples or inferences that aren't reasonable? Are there moments when readers might reasonably ask, "But couldn't that fact instead mean this?"
☐ Are all the relevant facts considered? What about facts that might complicate or contradict any of the claims? Are there moments when readers might reasonably think, "But what about X?"
☐ Is each piece of evidence clearly presented? Do readers have all the contextual information they need to understand a quotation, for example?
☐ Is each piece of evidence gracefully presented? Are quotations varied by length and presentation? Are they ever too long? Are there any unnecessary block quotations, or block quotations that require additional analysis? (On responsible and effective quotation, see 21.1–2.)
☐ Are there any unnecessary quotations—instances when the writer should instead simply paraphrase, summarize, or describe?

Tone
☐ Does the writer establish and maintain an effective tone—do any moments in, or aspects of, the essay make its writer seem anything other than serious, credible, engaged, and engaging? respectful toward the text(s) and a range of readers?
☐ Does the writer correctly and consistently use literary terminology?
☐ Does the writer ever assume too much or too little readerly knowledge or interest?

COMMON PROBLEMS AND TIPS

Though you want to pay attention to everything on this "assessing the elements" checklist, certain types of problems are common in early drafts. Here are three:

- *mismatch between thesis or argument or between introduction and body*
  Sometimes an early draft ends up being a way to discover what you really want to say. As a result, you may find that the thesis of your draft—or even your entire introduction—no longer truly fits or introduces the argument you've ended up making. If so, you will need to rework the thesis and introduction. Then work your way back through the essay, making sure that each claim or topic sentence fits the new thesis.

- *the list or "museum tour" structure*
  In a draft, writers sometimes present each claim as if it were just an item on a list (*First, second,* and so on) or as a stop on a tour of potentially interesting but unrelated topics (*And this is also important . . .*). But presenting your material in this way fails to help you and your readers make logical connections between ideas. It may also prevent your argument from developing. Sometimes it can even be a sign that you've ceased arguing entirely, falling into mere plot summary or description rather than articulating real *ideas* at all. Check to see if number-like words or phrases appear prominently at the beginning of your paragraphs or if your paragraphs could be put into a different order without fundamentally changing what you're saying. Sometimes solving this problem will require wholesale rethinking and reorganizing—a process that should probably start with crafting a meatier, more specific thesis. But sometimes all that's required is adding or reworking topic sentences. Again, make sure that there is a clearly stated, *debatable* claim at the beginning of each paragraph; that each claim relates to the thesis but does not simply restate it; and that each claim *builds* logically on the one before.

- *missing sub-ideas*
  When you take a step back from your draft, you may discover that you've skipped a logical step in your argument—that the claim you make in, say, body paragraph 3 actually depends on, or makes sense only in light of, a more basic claim that you took for granted. In the second half of an essay about how a character changes, for example, you might suggest that there is something significant about the character being decisive, but decisiveness only counts as change—and thus your point about decisiveness relates to your thesis—if the first part of your essay has demonstrated that the character is initially *indecisive*. Whatever the missing idea is, you'll need to create and insert a new paragraph that articulates, supports, and develops it.

19.4.2 Enriching the Argument

The first step of the revision process is all about ensuring that your essay does the best possible job of making your argument. But revision is also an opportunity to go further—to think about ways in which your overall argument might be made more thorough and complex. In drafting an essay our attention is often and rightly focused on emphatically staking out a particular position and proving its validity. This is the fundamental task of any essay, and you certainly don't want to do anything at this stage to compromise that. At the same time, you do want to make sure that you haven't purchased clarity at the cost of oversimplification by, for example, ignoring facts that might undermine or complicate your claims, alternative interpretations of the evidence you do present, or alternative claims or points of view. Remember, you have a better chance of persuading readers to accept your argument if you show them that it's based on a thorough, open-minded exploration of the text and topic. Don't invent unreasonable or irrelevant complications or counterarguments. Do try to assess your argument objectively and honestly, perhaps testing it against the text one more time. Think like a skeptical reader rather than a writer: Are there moments where such a reader might reasonably disagree with your argument? Are there places where *two* interpretations might be equally plausible? Have you ignored or glossed over any questions that a reasonable reader might expect an essay on this topic to address?

Such questions are ones you should *always* ask in revision. But they are especially crucial if you finish your draft only to discover that it is significantly shorter than the assignment requires. Inexperienced writers of literature essays often run out of things to say too quickly because they simply don't keep asking relevant questions (*How? Why?*) or make enough allowance for alternative answers.

19.5 EDITING AND PROOFREADING

Once you've gotten the overall argument in good shape, *then* it's time focus on the small but crucial stuff—words and sentences. Your prose should not only convey your ideas to your readers but also demonstrate how much you care about your essay. Flawless prose can't disguise or make up for a vapid or illogical argument. But faulty, flabby, boring prose can destroy a potentially persuasive and thoughtful one. Don't sabotage all your hard work by failing to correct misspelled words, grammatical problems, misquotations, incorrect citations, and typographical errors. Little oversights make all the difference when it comes to clarity and credibility. Readers care more about careful work. Especially when you are writing about literature, the art of language, *your* language matters.

When it comes to words and sentences, each writer has particular strengths and weaknesses. Likewise every writer tends to be overly fond of certain phrases and sentence structures, which become monotonous and ineffective if overused. With practice, you will learn to watch out for the kinds of mistakes and repetitions to which you are most prone. Then you can develop your own personalized editing checklist. But below is one to start with.

Sentences
☐ Does each one read clearly and crisply?
☐ Are they varied in length, structure, and syntax?
☐ Is the phrasing direct rather than roundabout?
☐ Are tenses appropriate and consistent?

TIPS

- Try using the Find function to search for every preposition (especially *of* and *in*) and every *to be* verb. Since these can lead to confusing or roundabout phrasing, weed out as many as you can.
- Try reading your paper aloud or having a friend read it aloud to you. Mark places where you or your friend stumble, and listen for sentences that are hard to get through or understand.

Words

☐ Have you used any words whose meaning you're not sure of?

☐ Is terminology correct and consistent?

☐ Is a "fancy" word or phrase ever used where a simpler one might do?

☐ Are there unnecessary words or phrases?

☐ Do metaphors and other figures of speech make literal sense?

☐ Are verbs active and precise?

☐ Are pronoun references always clear and correct?

☐ Do subjects and verbs always agree?

Punctuation and Mechanics

☐ Are all words spelled correctly? (Double-check your auto-correct and spell-check: these can create new errors in the process of correcting others.)

☐ Are all titles formatted correctly? (See the section following this checklist.)

☐ Is every quotation accurate and punctuated correctly (See ch. 21.)?

Citation and Documentation (See ch. 21.)

☐ Is the source of each quotation, as well as any fact or idea drawn from sources, clearly indicated through parenthetical citation?

☐ Do parenthetical citations correctly coordinate with the list of works cited?

☐ Are both all parenthetical citations and all entries in the list of works cited formatted correctly?

Titles

Formatting titles correctly in both the body of your essay and your list of works cited is essential to your clarity, as well as to your self-presentation as a knowledgeable and careful writer: Bartleby the Scrivener is a character; "Bartleby, the Scrivener" is a short story. "Interpreter of Maladies" is also a short story, but *Interpreter of Maladies* is a book. To make sure you get this right, here is a quick review:

- *Italicize* the titles of all books and other "stand-alone" works, including
  —novels and novellas (*To Kill a Mockingbird, Heart of Darkness*)
  —collections and anthologies of short stories, essays, or poems (*Interpreter of Maladies, The Norton Introduction to Literature*)

—long poems that could be or have been published as books (*The Odyssey, Paradise Lost, Goblin Market*)
—plays (*Hamlet, A Raisin in the Sun*)
—periodicals, including newspapers, magazines, and scholarly journals (*USA Today, People, College English*)
—Web sites, blogs, and databases (*Google Books, Gawker, JSTOR*)
—movies and television programs or series (*The Fault in Our Stars, Orange Is the New Black*)

- Put quotation marks around the titles of works that are part of such "stand-alone" works, including
  —short stories ("Interpreter of Maladies," "A Rose for Emily")
  —poems ("Daddy," "Ode to a Nightingale")
  —essays and articles in periodicals ("A Narrator's Blindness in Raymond Carver's 'Cathedral'"; "When We Dead Awaken: Writing as Re-Vision"; "Chicago Fiddles While Trumbull Park Burns")
  —parts of Web sites (e.g., Web pages, blog posts)
  —episodes of a television series

19.6 FINISHING UP

19.6.1 Crafting a Title

Your essay isn't truly complete until you give it a title. A good title both informs and interests. Inform readers by telling them both the work(s) you will analyze ("The Road Not Taken" or "two poems by Robert Frost") and something about your topic ("Symbolism," "Nonconformity"). To interest them, try using one of the following:

- an especially vivid and relevant word or a short phrase from the literary work ("'They Have Eaten Me Alive': Motherhood in 'In the Park' and 'Daystar'")
- a bit of wordplay ("Wordsworth and the Art of Artlessness")
- a bit of both ("'Untrodden Ways': Wordsworth and the Art of Artlessness").

Do not put your own title in quotation marks, but do correctly format any titles that appear in your title.

19.6.2 Formatting Your Essay

Unless your instructor provides specific instructions on how to format your essay, follow these guidelines, adapted from *The MLA Style Center: Writing Resources from the Modern Language Association* (style.mla.org/formatting-papers) and demonstrated in the sample research essay in chapter 22.

- Choose a readable 11- or 12-point font; set your page margins at 1 inch; and double-space throughout. Do not add extra lines between paragraphs or before or after block quotations. Indent the first line of each paragraph ½ inch. An entire block quotation should be indented ½ inch. (For more on formatting quotations, see 21.1.)
- Do not include a title page. Instead, in the top left corner of the first page, type your name, your instructor's name, the course number, and the date, each on a separate line. Then center your title on the next line. (Do not put your own title in quotation marks.)
- Number every page consecutively, and put your last name and the page number in the upper right corner ½ inch below the top of the page and aligned with the right margin. (Do not put any punctuation between your name and the page number.)
- Begin your list of works cited on a new page, *after* the last page of your essay. Center the words *Works Cited* at the top of the page. (Do not put quotation marks around or italicize these words.) Indent the second and subsequent lines of each works cited entry ½ inch. (For more on formatting the list of works cited, see 21.3.2.)

20 THE LITERATURE RESEARCH ESSAY

Whenever we read, discuss, and write about literature, our primary concern is always the text. But literature speaks to and about the real world even when it depicts an entirely unreal one. Both texts and our readings of them are inevitably shaped by, and intervene in, particular contexts. Literary research is simply a way to learn more about those contexts. In a literature research essay we bring what we learn to bear to illuminate the work in a new way.

On the one hand, writing a research essay may at first seem like a daunting task. Research adds a few more steps to the writing process, so you will need to give yourself more time. And those steps require you to draw on and develop skills somewhat different from those involved in crafting essays that focus exclusively on the literary text. Were this not the case, no one would ask you to write a research essay.

On the other hand, however, a literature research essay is still a literature essay. Its core elements are the same, as is its basic purpose—to articulate and develop a debatable, interpretive claim about at least one literary work. As a result, this kind of essay requires many of the same skills and strategies you've already begun to develop. And though you will need to add a few new steps, the process of writing a literature research essay still involves getting started, planning, drafting, revising, editing, and finishing up—exactly the same dance whose rhythms you've already begun to master.

The only distinctive thing about a research essay is that it requires you to draw on sources in addition to the literary text itself. Though that adds to your burden in some ways, it can actually lighten it in others. Think of such sources not as another ball you have to juggle but as another tool you get to add to your tool belt: You're still being asked to build a cabinet, but now you get to use a hammer *and* an electric drill. This chapter will help you make the best use of these powerful tools.

20.1 TYPES OF ESSAYS AND SOURCES

The three most common types of literature research essay are those described below. But though we treat these types separately here for clarity's sake, many literature research essays are in fact hybrids of one sort or another. An essay on Emily Dickinson by student writer Richard Gibson is a case in point: It analyzes three poems by Emily Dickinson by drawing on literary criticism, biographical materials, and studies of Dickinson's historical and cultural context. Should your assignment allow, your essay, too, could combine two or more of these approaches. Either way, it's useful to remember that your secondary sources probably will.

20.1.1 Critical Contexts

Whenever we write a literature essay, we engage in conversation with other readers about the meaning and significance of a literary work. Effective argumentation always depends on anticipating how other readers are likely to respond to, and interpret, that work. Almost all texts and authors are also the subject of actual public conversations, often extending over many years and involving all the numerous scholarly readers who have published their readings of the work. A "critical contexts" research essay is an opportunity both to investigate this conversation and to contribute to it.

For this kind of essay, your secondary sources will be work by literary scholars on the specific text you're writing about; on an author's body of work; or on a relevant genre or body of literature (e.g., *The Development of the Sonnet: An Introduction* or *"Reading the Wind": The Literature of the Vietnam War*). The latter, more general sorts of sources may be especially crucial if you are researching a relatively recent work about which little literary criticism has yet been published. In that case, too, you may want to consult book reviews; just remember that it's reviewers' *interpretive* claims you're most interested in, not their evaluation of the work. (On interpretation versus evaluation, see 18.1.2.)

20.1.2 Biographical Contexts

If literature *only* reflected, and gave us insight into, its author's psyche, it ultimately wouldn't be that interesting: Good poets, fiction writers, and playwrights write about and for others, not just themselves. Nonetheless, authors are real people whose unique experience and outlook shape both what they write and how. A "biographical contexts" research essay is a chance to learn more about an author's life, work, and ideas and to explore how these might have shaped or be reflected in the text. Sources for this sort of project will likely include biographies (secondary sources) and essays, letters, and other nonfiction prose by the author (primary sources).

20.1.3 Historical and Cultural Contexts

Every literary work is both shaped by and speaks to the circumstances, events, and debates peculiar to its historical and cultural context, though some literary works speak of their times by depicting other times. The purpose of a "cultural and historical contexts" essay is to explore the interconnections between a text and the context it was either written in or depicts. Sources useful for this sort of essay might include studies of a relevant historical period or literary movement (secondary sources) or documents dating from that period or written by others involved in that movement (primary sources). (For an example of an historical and cultural context essay by a student writer, see ch. 22.)

20.2 WHAT SOURCES DO

Unless your instructor indicates otherwise, *your* argument about the literary text should be the focus of your essay, and sources should function simply as tools that you use to deepen and enrich your argument about the literary text. They shouldn't substitute for it. Your essay should never simply repeat or report on what other people have already said.

Sources, in other words, are *not* the source of your ideas. Instead, to paraphrase writing expert Gordon Harvey's *Writing with Sources* (Hackett, 1998), they are the source of

- *argument* or *debatable claim*—other readers' views and interpretations of a text, author, topic, literary movement, period, and so on, which "you support, criticize, or develop";
- *information*—facts about an author's life; about the work's composition, publication, or reception; about the era during, or about which, the author wrote; about movements in which the author participated; and so on.
- *concept*—general terms or theoretical frameworks that you borrow and apply to your author or text. (You might, for example, use concepts drawn from Sigmund Freud's theories of psychological development to interpret Sylvia Plath's poem DADDY.)

Any one source will in fact likely offer you more than one of these things. Nonetheless, the distinction between argument or debatable claim, on the one hand, and information or factual statement, on the other, is crucial. As you read a source, you must discriminate between the two.

When drawing on sources in your essay, remember, too, that an argument about the text, no matter how well informed, isn't the same as evidence. Only facts can serve that function. Suppose, for example, you are writing an essay on "Daddy." You claim that the speaker adopts two voices, that of her child self and that of her adult self—a claim also made in a secondary source. You cannot prove this claim to be true merely by saying that the source makes the same claim. Like any debatable claim, this one must be backed up with evidence from the primary text.

In this situation, however, you must indicate that a source has made the same claim that you do in order to accomplish three things:

- give the source credit for having this idea before you did (to avoid even the appearance of plagiarism; see 20.4.1);
- encourage readers to see you as a knowledgeable, trustworthy writer who has done your research and taken the time to explore, digest, and fairly represent others' views;
- demonstrate that your opinion isn't merely idiosyncratic because another informed, even "expert," reader agrees with you.

Were you to disagree with the source's claim, it would be just as important and helpful to your argument to acknowledge that disagreement in order to demonstrate the originality of your own interpretation, while also, again, encouraging readers to see you as a knowledgeable, careful writer.

You will need to cite sources throughout your essay whenever you make a claim that resembles, complements, or contradicts the claim of another source; rely on information or concepts from a source; or paraphrase, quote, or summarize anything in a source. Especially in a critical contexts essay, you should also at least consider using sources to establish motive (see below).

20.2.1 Source-Related Motives

Not all research essays use sources to articulate motive. However, doing so is one way both to ensure and to demonstrate that your own ideas are the focus of your essay and that your essay contributes to a literary critical conversation rather than just reporting on it or repeating what others have already said. In these essays, in other words, your "Although . . ." statement (as outlined in 18.1.3) may refer to sources—actual "theys" and what they "say." Indeed, whether you ultimately use sources to articulate a motive or not, keeping motive-related questions in mind as you read sources is nonetheless a very good idea, for reasons we'll detail in the next section of this chapter. Here are the three most common source-related motives:

1. Sources offer different opinions about a particular issue in the text, thus suggesting that there is still a problem or puzzle worth investigating. (Your argument might agree with one side or the other or offer a "third way.")

Almost all interpreters of [*Antigone*] have agreed that the play shows Creon to be morally defective [. . .]. The situation of Antigone is more controversial. Hegel assimilated her defect to Creon's; some more recent writers uncritically hold her up as a blameless heroine. Without entering into an exhaustive study of her role in the tragedy, I should like to claim (with the support of an increasing number of recent critics) that there is at least some justification for the Hegelian assimilation—though the criticism needs to be focused more clearly and specifically than it is in Hegel's brief remarks.

In these sentences from *The Fragility of Goodness*, Martha C. Nussbaum summarizes an ongoing debate about *Antigone* and then positions her argument as contributing to that debate by supporting and developing one of the two usual positions.

2. A source or sources make(s) a faulty claim that needs to be wholly or partly challenged or clarified.

Modern critics who do not share Sophocles' conviction about the paramount duty of burying the dead and who attach more importance than he did to the claims of political authority have tended to underestimate the way in which he justifies Antigone against Creon.

In this sentence from the introduction to *Sophoclean Tragedy*, Maurice Bowra makes a generalization about the stance taken by "[m]odern critics" that his essay will challenge. (Subsequent sentences provide more details about that stance.)

While I find Smith's article thoughtful and intriguing, and while I agree with much feminist criticism of Vietnam War literature, this essay proposes that the work of Tim O'Brien, particularly *The Things They Carried*, stands apart from the genre as a whole. O'Brien is much more self-consciously aware of gender issues and critical of traditional gender dichotomies than are the bulk of U.S. writers about the Vietnam War.

In "Tim O'Brien and Gender: A Defense of *The Things They Carried*," Susan Farrell does the opposite of what Bowra does. Having first summarized the arguments of one specific critic (Smith), she now (in this sentence) articulates her contrary view.

3. Sources neglect a significant aspect or element of the text, or a source or sources make(s) a claim that needs to be further developed or applied in a new way (perhaps to a text other than the one the sources actually discuss).

Tim O'Brien's 1990 book of interlocked stories, *The Things They Carried*, garnered one rave review after another, reinforcing O'Brien's already established position as one of the most important veteran writers of the Vietnam War. The Penguin paperback edition serves up six pages of superlative blurbs like "consummate artistry," "classic," "the best American writer of his generation," "unique," and "master work." [. . .] Yet, O'Brien—and his reviewers—seem curiously unself-conscious about this book's obsession with an ambivalence about representations of masculinity and femininity, particularly in the five stories originally published during the 1980s in *Esquire*.

Here, in "'The Things Men Do': The Gendered Subtext in Tim O'Brien's *Esquire* Stories," Lorrie Smith suggests not that others' claims are wrong but that they simply miss something that her essay will investigate.

(In ch. 22, you'll find a research essay on Alice Munro's BOYS AND GIRLS that combines versions of the first and third kinds of source-related motives described above.)

20.3 THE RESEARCH PROCESS

20.3.1 Finding Authoritative Secondary Sources

Regardless of your author, text, or topic, you will almost certainly find a wealth of sources to consult. The conversation about literature and its contexts occurs online and in print, in periodicals and in books. Your instructor may well give you specific guidance about which sorts of sources you need to use. If not, it's usually best to consult at least some print sources or sources that appear in both print and digital form (e.g., the scholarly journals housed in databases such as *JSTOR* or *Academic Search Premier*). Citing only one kind of source— books but not articles, online but not print—may cast doubt on the thoroughness of your research; you want your reader to know that you sought out the *best* sources, not just the most easily available ones.

Whatever their form, it is crucial that your secondary sources be authoritative ones, since the credibility and persuasiveness of your research essay will depend on that of your sources: At the very least, you do not want to look like someone who doesn't know the difference or care enough to figure it out. Learning how to identify authoritative sources is one of the rationales for research essay assignments. "Evaluating sources" thus initially means evaluating their credibility and importance. At this stage, concentrate on whether the opinions expressed and information provided in a source are worthy of serious consideration, not on whether you agree with them. Save that question for later.

As a general rule and with the exception of a general dictionary, *you should not rely on or cite any source that is not attributed to a named author.* This includes (but is not limited to) *Wikipedia* and Web sites such as *Schmoop* and *SparkNotes*. Because these will likely be the first things a general *Google* search turns up and because they are almost certainly familiar to you, it's tempting to rely on them. Avoid the temptation. Though much of the information on such sites is correct and useful, much of it isn't. As important, the very virtue of such sites—the fact that they are designed for, and mainly written by, nonexperts—makes them inappropriate as sources for a research essay, since the goal of such an essay is to familiarize yourself with and to enter a conversation among acknowledged experts.

In these terms, the most valuable sources tend to be books published by academic and university presses and articles published in scholarly or professional journals (rather than magazines or newspapers). This isn't mere snobbishness or narcissism: Such work appears in print or online only after a rigorous peer-review process. As a result, you and your readers can trust that these publications have been judged worthwhile by more than one acknowledged expert.

Rather than heading straight to *Google* and searching the entire web, then, try starting instead with your library's Web site. In addition to the catalog, you will here find a wealth of specialized reference works, bibliographies, and databases. Which of these are available to you will depend on your library. But here are two especially common and helpful resources to start with:

- *Oxford Encyclopedia of American Literature* and *Oxford Encyclopedia of British Literature:* Both include signed entries by recognized experts on major authors, texts, and topics. Each entry ends with a short annotated bibliography. In addition to being a source, such an entry will thus lead you to other sources that one expert regards as the most important on the subject. In a sense, this person has already done some of your research for you.
- *MLA International Bibliography,* the "go-to" source for identifying all scholarly work—books, articles, and book chapters—on any author, work, or topic. The virtue and (for your purposes) potential limitation of this bibliography is its inclusiveness: You can generally trust that sources included in the bibliography are, indeed, scholarly, published mainly by academic presses or in scholarly journals. MLA does not, however, discriminate among those sources in terms of quality, importance, and so on.

Once you have identified potentially useful articles and books, you may be able to access some of them online. Many full-text scholarly articles are accessible via subscription databases such as *JSTOR, Project Muse*, and *Academic Search Premier*. Your library may have "e-book" versions of some of the books you are interested in, while other, especially older books can be found on the Web: In addition to *Google Books*, try *Hathi Trust* and *Internet Archive*. Again, however, do not neglect any important source simply because you actually have to go to the library to look at it; this includes books only *partly* viewable on *Google*.

Look for the most up-to-date sources but don't automatically discount older ones. You should consult recent sources in order to get the most up-to-date information on your topic and a sense of what scholars today consider the most significant, debatable interpretive questions and claims. But be aware that in literary studies (and the humanities generally), newer work doesn't always entirely supersede older work, as it tends to do in the sciences. Twenty-first-century scholars, for example, still cite and debate the arguments about ANTIGONE made well over a hundred years ago by German philosopher Georg Wilhelm Friedrich Hegel (1770–1831).

Once you find an especially good source, its bibliography will lead you to others. Test sources against one another: If multiple reliable sources agree about a given fact, you can probably assume it's accurate; if they all cite a particular article or book, you know it's a key contribution to the conversation.

20.3.2 Reading and Taking Notes

Once you've acquired or accessed your sources, it's a good idea to skim each one. (In the case of a book, concentrate on the introduction and on the chapter that seems most relevant.) Focus at this point on assessing the relevance of each source to your topic. Or, if you're working your way toward a topic, look for things that spark your interest. Either way, try to get a rough sense of the overall conversation—of the issues and topics that come up again and again across the various sources.

Once you've identified the most pertinent sources, it's time to begin reading more carefully and taking notes. For each source, make sure that you note down all the bibliographical information that you will ultimately need to cite the source correctly. (For details, see the guide to citation in ch. 21.) Your notes for each source will likely include four things: summary, paraphrase, quotation, and your own comments and thoughts. To avoid confusion (even plagiarism), it's crucial that you develop your own system for clearly differentiating each of these from the other. Whenever you write down, type out, or paste in two or more consecutive words from a source, you should place these words in quotation marks so that you will later recognize them as direct quotations; make sure to quote with absolute accuracy; and record the page where the quotation is found (if the source is paginated). Keep such quotations to a minimum. In lieu of extensive quotations, try to summarize and paraphrase as much as possible. You can't decide how to use the source or whether you agree with its argument unless you've first understood it, and you can usually best understand and test your understanding through summary and paraphrase. You might, for example, either start or conclude your notes with a one- or two-sentence summary of the author's overall argument, perhaps using the "Although . . . I think . . . because" rubric. Paraphrase especially important points, making sure to note the page on which each appears. (For more on paraphrase, summary, and description, see ch. 17 and 20.4.2 below.)

20.3.3 Synthesizing

It can be very useful to complete the note-taking process by writing a summary that synthesizes all of your secondary sources. Your goal is to show how all the arguments fit together to form one coherent conversation. (Like any conversation, however, a scholarly one usually considers multiple topics.) Doing so will require that you both define the main questions at issue in the conversation and indicate what stance each source takes on each question— where and how their opinions coincide and differ. If you tend to be a visual learner, you might also try diagraming the conversation somehow.

If you read even one or two essays about *Antigone*, for example, you may quickly realize that the main questions that preoccupy scholars are (1) *What is the exact nature of the conflict between Antigone and Creon, or what two conflicting worldviews do they represent?* and (2) *How is that conflict resolved? Which, if either, of the two characters and worldviews does the play ultimately endorse?* A synthetic summary of these sources (i.e., one that combines or "synthesizes" them) would explain how each critic answers each of these questions.

This kind of summary can be especially helpful when you haven't yet identified a specific essay topic or crafted a thesis because it may help you to see gaps in the conversation, places where you can enter and contribute. If you have identified a topic or thesis, a synthetic summary is still useful to identifying points of agreement and disagreement and to articulating motive (20.2). Indeed, students required to write synthetic summaries by their instructors often end up using it as the kernel of their introduction.

20.4 WRITING WITH SOURCES
20.4.1 Using Sources Responsibly and Avoiding Plagiarism

Both the clarity and the credibility of any research essay depend on responsible use of sources. And using sources responsibly entails accurately representing them, clearly discriminating between their ideas and words and your own, giving credit where credit is due. Since ideas, words, information, and concepts not directly and clearly attributed to a source will be taken as your own, any lack of clarity on that score amounts to *plagiarism*. Representing anyone else's ideas or data as your own, even if you state them in your own words, is plagiarism—whether you do so intentionally or unintentionally; whether the ideas or data comes from a published book or article, another student's paper, the Internet, or any other source. Plagiarism is among the most serious of offenses within academe because it amounts both to taking credit for someone else's hard labor and to stealing ideas—the resource most precious to this community and its members. That's why the punishments for plagiarism are severe—including failure, suspension, and expulsion, for students; the loss of a job, for teachers who are also researchers.

To avoid both the offense and its consequences, you must always

- *put quotation marks around any quotation from a source* (a quotation being any two or more consecutive words or any one especially distinctive word, label, or concept) *or indent it to create a "block quotation"*;
- *credit a source whenever you take from it any of the following*:
  —*a quotation* (as described above);
  —*a nonfactual or debatable claim* (an idea, opinion, interpretation, evaluation, or conclusion) stated in your own words;
  —*a distinctive concept or term*;
  —*a fact or piece of data that isn't common knowledge*; or
  —*a distinctive way of organizing factual information.*

To clarify, a fact counts as "common knowledge"—and therefore doesn't need to be credited to a source—whenever you can find it in multiple reputable sources, none of which seriously question its validity. It is common knowledge, for instance, that Sherman Alexie is Native American, that he was born in 1966, and that he published a collection of short stories titled *Ten Little Indians*. No source can "own" or get credit for these facts. However, a source can still "own" a particular way of arranging or presenting such facts. If you begin your essay by stating—in your own words—a series of facts about Alexie's life in exactly the same order they appear in a specific source, then you would need to acknowledge that source. When in doubt, cite. (For guidance about *how* to do so, see both 20.4.2 below and ch. 21.)

20.4.2 Integrating Secondary Source Material into Your Essay

The responsible use of sources depends as much on how you integrate ideas, facts, and words from sources into your essay as on how effectively you use a citation and documentation system like that outlined in chapter 21. Indeed, in this (the MLA) system, where a citation belongs and what it looks like depend entirely on what information you provide about the source in your text.

Research essays can refer to secondary sources in a number of ways. You may

- *briefly allude to them:*

    Many critics, including Maurice Bowra and Bernard Knox, see Creon as morally inferior to Antigone.

- *summarize or paraphrase their contents:*

    According to Maurice Bowra, Creon's arrogance is his downfall. However prideful Antigone may occasionally seem, Bowra insists that Creon is genuinely, deeply, and consistently so (1586).

- *quote them directly:*

    Maurice Bowra reads Creon as the prototypical "proud man"; where Antigone's arrogance is only "apparent," says Bowra, Creon's is all too "real" (1586).

Choose whichever strategy suits your purpose in a particular context. But keep the number and length of quotations from secondary sources to a minimum. This is *your* essay. Your ideas about the text are its primary focus. And you should use your own words whenever possible, even when you are describing or articulating what you must clearly acknowledge to be someone else's ideas or facts.

USING SIGNAL PHRASES

Whether you are quoting, summarizing, or paraphrasing a source, always introduce source material with a "signal phrase." Usually, this should include the author's name. You might also include the author's title or any information about the author or source that affects its credibility or clarifies the relationship between the source's argument and your own. Titles can be especially helpful when you cite more than one source by the same author.

Oyin Ogunba, himself a scholar of Yoruban descent, suggests that many of Wole Soyinka's plays attempt to capture the mood and rhythm of traditional Yoruban festivals (8).	Since most of the authors cited in a literature research essay should be scholars, calling them that is usually redundant and unhelpful. Here, however, the phrase "scholar of Yoruban descent" implies that the author is doubly authoritative, since he writes about a culture he knows through experience and study.

(continued)

As historian R. K. Webb observes, "Britain is a country in miniature" (1).

In a literature research essay, most scholars you cite will be literary critics. If they aren't and it matters, identify their discipline.

In his study of the Frankenstein myth, Chris Baldick claims that "[m]ost myths, in literate societies at least, prolong their lives not by being retold at great length, but by being alluded to" (3)—a claim that definitely applies to the Hamlet myth.

Notice how crucial this signal phrase is to making clear that its author is applying a source's claim about one thing (myths in general and the Frankenstein myth in particular) to another, entirely different thing (the Hamlet myth). Such clarity is key both to accurately representing the source and to establishing the author's own originality.

If your summary goes on for more than a sentence or two, keep using signal phrases to remind readers that you're still summarizing others' ideas rather than stating your own.

The ways of interpreting Emily's decision to murder Homer are numerous. [. . .] For simple clarification, they can be summarized along two lines. One group finds the murder growing out of Emily's demented attempt to forestall the inevitable passage of time—toward her abandonment by Homer, toward her own death, and toward the steady encroachment of the North and the New South on something loosely defined as the "tradition" of the Old South. Another view sees the murder in more psychological terms. It grows out of Emily's complex relationship to her father, who, by elevating her above all of the eligible men of Jefferson, insured that to yield what one commentator called the "normal emotions" associated with desire, his daughter had to "retreat into a marginal world, into fantasy" (O'Connor 416).

In this paragraph from his essay "'We All Said, "She Will Kill Herself"': The Narrator/Detective in William Faulkner's 'A Rose for Emily,'" Lawrence R. Rodgers heads into a general summary of other critics' arguments by announcing that it's coming ("*For simple clarification, they can be summarized . . .*"). Then, as he begins summarizing each view, he reminds us that it is a "view," that he's still articulating others' ideas, not his own. Notice that he only quotes "one commentator" among the many to whom he refers; the others are indicated in a footnote.

For the sake of interest and clarity, vary the content and placement of signal phrases, and always choose the most accurate verb. (*Says*, for example, implies that words are spoken, not written.) Here is a list of verbs you might find useful to describe what sources do.

acknowledges	considers	explains	investigates	sees
affirms	contends	explores	maintains	shows
argues	demonstrates	finds	notes	speculates
asks	describes	identifies	observes	states
asserts	discusses	illustrates	points out	stresses
claims	draws attention	implies	remarks	suggests
comments	to	indicates	reminds us	surmises
concludes	emphasizes	insists	reports	writes

21 QUOTATION, CITATION, AND DOCUMENTATION

The bulk of any literature essay you write should consist of your own ideas expressed in your own words. Yet you can develop your ideas and persuade readers to accept them only if you present and analyze evidence. In literature essays of every kind, quotations are an especially privileged kind of evidence, though paraphrase, summary, and description play key roles (see ch. 17 and 18.1.4). Likewise, a literature research essay, which must make use of other primary and secondary sources, typically quotes selectively from these as well (see 20.4.2). In all literature essays, then, your clarity, credibility, and persuasiveness greatly depend on two things: (1) how responsibly, effectively, and gracefully you present, differentiate, and move between others' words and ideas and your own; and (2) how careful you are to let readers know exactly where they can find each quotation and each fact or idea that you paraphrase from a source. This chapter addresses the question of *how* to quote, cite, and document sources of all kinds. (For a discussion of *when* to do so, see 18.1.4 and 20.4.1.)

Rules for quoting, citing, and documenting sources can seem daunting and even, at times, arcane or trivial. Why the heck should it matter whether you put a word in brackets or parentheses, or where in a sentence your parentheses appears? By demonstrating mastery of such conventions, you assert your credibility as a member of the scholarly community. But such conventions also serve an eminently practical purpose: They provide you a system for conveying a wealth of important information clearly, concisely, and unobtrusively, with the least distraction to you and your reader.

As you probably know, there are many such systems. And different disciplines, publications, and even individual instructors prefer or require different ones. In English and other humanities disciplines, however, the preferred system is that developed by the Modern Language Association (MLA) and laid out in the *MLA Handbook* (8th ed., 2016) and *The MLA Style Center: Writing Resources from the Modern Language Association* (style.mla.org). All the rules presented in this chapter accord with, and draw heavily upon, these sources, which we encourage you to consult for more extensive and detailed guidance than we can provide here.

21.1 THE RULES OF RESPONSIBLE QUOTING

When it comes to quoting, there are certain rules that you must follow in order to be responsible both to your sources and to the integrity of your own prose. Additionally, there are certain strategies that, though not required, will do much to make your argument more clear, engaging, and persuasive. The next section of this chapter (21.2) discusses strategies; this one concentrates on the rules, starting with the cardinal principles of responsible quotation before turning first to those rules specific to the genres of prose, poetry, and drama and then to those rules that aren't genre-specific.

21.1.1 Cardinal Principles

Three requirements so crucial to your credibility that you should regard them as cardinal principles rather than simple rules are these:

1. *A quotation means any two or more consecutive words or any one especially distinctive word or label that appears in a source.*

   Representation as O'Brien practices it in this book is not a mimetic act but a "game," as Iser also calls it in a more recent essay, "The Play of the Text," a process of acting things out. . . .

   In this sentence from "The Undying Uncertainty of the Narrator in Tim O'Brien's *The Things They Carried*," Steven Kaplan puts the word *game* in quotation marks because it is a key concept defined in distinctive ways in his source.

2. *Except in the very few cases and specific ways outlined in the rest of this section, you must reproduce each quotation exactly as it appears in a source,* including every word and preserving original spelling, punctuation, capitalization, italics, spacing, and so on.

ORIGINAL SOURCE	INCORRECT VS. CORRECT QUOTATION
[MRS. PETERS *sits down. The two women sit there not looking at one another, but as if peering into something and at the same time holding back. When they talk now it is in the manner of feeling their way over strange ground, as if afraid of what they are saying, but as if they cannot help saying it.*]	**Incorrect:** After they discover the dead bird and the men leave the room, Mrs. Peters and Mrs. Hale simply "sit there not looking at each other," compelled to speak but also "afraid of what they are saying." **Correct:** After they discover the dead bird and the men leave the room, Mrs. Peters and Mrs. Hale simply *"sit there not looking at one another,"* compelled to speak but also *"afraid of what they are saying."*

3. *No change to a quotation, however much it accords with the rules out-lined below, is acceptable if it in any way distorts the original meaning of the quoted passage.*

21.1.2 Genre-Specific Rules

Because prose, poetry, and drama each work somewhat differently, there are special rules governing how to quote texts in each of these genres. This section spells out the rules specific to prose (both fiction and nonfiction), poetry, and drama; the next section covers rules applicable to all genres.

PROSE (FICTION OR NONFICTION)

- When a quotation from a single paragraph of a prose source takes up no more than four lines of your essay, put it in quotation marks.

  Georgiana's birthmark becomes "a frightful object" only because "Aylmer's somber imagination" turns it into one, "selecting it as the symbol of his wife's liability to sin, sorrow, decay, and death."

- When a prose quotation takes up more than four lines of your essay or includes a paragraph break, indent it ½ inch from the left margin to create a *block quotation*. Do not enclose the quotation in quotation marks, since these are implied by the formatting. On the rare occasions you quote more than one paragraph reproduce any paragraph break that occurs within the quotation by indenting the first line an additional ¼ inch.

  Georgiana's birthmark becomes "a frightful object" only because "Aylmer's somber imagination" turns it into a "symbol" of

  > the fatal flaw of humanity which Nature, in one shape or another, stamps ineffaceably on all her productions, either to imply that they are temporary and finite, or that their perfection must be wrought by toil and pain. The crimson hand expressed the ineludible gripe in which mortality clutches the highest and purest of earthly mould, degrading them into kindred with the lowest, and even with the very brutes, like whom their visible frames return to dust.

POETRY

- When quoting three or fewer lines of poetry, put the quotation in quotation marks, and use a slash mark (/) with a space on either side to indicate any line break that occurs in the quotation, and a double slash mark (//) to indicate a stanza break.

Before Milton's speaker can question his "Maker" for allowing him to go blind, "Patience" intervenes "to prevent / That murmur."

◦ **When quoting more than three lines, indent the quotation ½ inch from the left margin to create a *block quotation*.** Do not enclose the quotation in quotation marks, since these are implied by the formatting, but do reproduce original line and stanza breaks and the spatial arrangement of the original lines, including indentation.

Midway through the poem, the speaker suddenly shifts to second-person, for the first time addressing the drowned girl directly and almost affectionately as he also begins to imagine her as a living person rather than a dead corpse:

> Little adulteress,
> before they punished you
>
> you were flaxen-haired,
> undernourished, and your
> tar-black face was beautiful.

◦ **When a block quotation begins in the middle of a line of verse, indent the partial line as much as you need to in order to approximate its original positioning.**

The speaker first demonstrates both his knowledge of persimmons and his understanding of precision by telling us exactly what ripe fruits look and smell like and then, step by careful step,

> How to eat:
> put the knife away, lay down newspaper.
> Peel the skin tenderly, not to tear the meat.
> Chew the skin, suck it,
> and swallow. Now, eat
> the meat of the fruit

◦ **If you omit one or more lines in the middle of a block quotation, indicate the omission with a line of spaced periods approximately the same length as a complete line of the quoted poem.**

About another image on the urn, the speaker has more questions than answers:

> Who are these coming to the sacrifice?
>   To what green altar, O mysterious priest,
> Lead'st thou that heifer lowing at the skies,
>   And all her silken flanks with garlands dressed?
> What little town by river or sea shore,
> . . . .
>   Is emptied of its folk, this pious morn?

DRAMA

- With one exception (covered in the next rule), a quotation from a play is governed by the same rules as outlined above under "Prose," if the quotation is in prose; under "Poetry," if in verse.
- Regardless of its length, if a quotation from a play includes dialogue between two or more characters, indent it ½ inch from the left margin to create a *block quotation*. Begin each character's speech with the character's name in capital letters followed by a period; indent the second and subsequent lines an additional ¼ inch. If a speech is in verse, you must also follow the applicable rules outlined in the "Poetry" section above, by, for example, reproducing original line breaks (as in the second example below).

1. As soon as the men exit, the women start talking about the men and undoing what the men just did:

   > MRS. HALE. I'd hate to have men coming into my kitchen, snooping around and criticizing. [*She arranges the pans under the sink which the* LAWYER *had shoved out of place.*]
   > MRS. PETERS. Of course it's no more than their duty.

2. Antigone and Ismene's initial exchange climaxes with Antigone declaring her sister an "enemy," even as Ismene declares herself one of Antigone's loving "friends":

   > ANTIGONE. If you will talk like this I will loathe you,
   >   and you will be adjudged an enemy—
   >   justly—by the dead's decision. Let me alone
   >   and my folly with me, to endure this terror.
   >   No suffering of mine will be enough
   >   to make me die ignobly.
   > ISMENE. Well, if you will, go on.
   >   Know this; that though you are wrong to go, your friends
   >   are right to love you.

21.1.3 General Rules and Strategies

Unlike the rules covered in the last section, the ones laid out here apply regardless of whether you are quoting prose, poetry, or drama.

GRAMMAR, SYNTAX, TENSE, AND THE USE OF BRACKETS

- Quotations need not be complete sentences and may go anywhere in your sentence.

1. The narrator says of Mr. Kapasi, "In his youth he'd been a devoted scholar of foreign languages" who "dreamed of being an interpreter for diplomats and dignitaries."

2. "In his youth a devoted scholar of foreign languages," says the narrator, Mr. Kapasi once "dreamed of being an interpreter for diplomats and dignitaries."

○ Every sentence that includes a quotation and every quotation you present as if it is a sentence must—like every other sentence in your essay—observe all the usual rules of grammar, syntax, and consistency of tense. (In terms of these rules, words inside quotation marks don't operate any differently than do words outside of quotation marks.)

1. The woman in all the portraits is idealized. "Not as she is, but as she fills his dream."	Sentence 1 includes a quotation that is treated as a sentence but isn't one. Sentence 2 corrects that problem by using a colon to make the quoted fragment part of the preceding sentence. Yet the fragment still contains a pronoun (*his*) that lacks any clear referent in the sentence, making sentence 3 a better fix.
2. The woman in all the portraits is idealized: "Not as she is, but as she fills his dream."	
3. The woman in all the paintings is idealized, portrayed by the artist "[n]ot as she is, but as she fills his dream."	
4. As Joy waits for Manley's arrival, "She looked up and down the empty highway and had the furious feeling that she had been tricked, that he had only meant to make her walk to the gate after the idea of him" rather than the reality.	The fact that fiction typically uses past tense, while we write about it in present tense, often creates confusing tense shifts like that in sentence 4. Usually, partial paraphrase is a good solution: As in sentence 5, quote only the most essential words from the passage, remembering that what those words are will depend on the point you want to make.
5. As Joy waits for Manley's arrival, she becomes "furious," convinced that he has "tricked" her and only "meant to make her walk to the gate after the idea of him" rather than the reality.	

○ When necessary to the grammar of your sentence or the intelligibility of your quotation, you may add words to the latter or make minor changes to words within it, but you must enclose your alterations in brackets ([]) to let readers know that they *are* alterations. (In example 3 above, for example, the first letter of the word "not" appears in brackets because a capital "N" has been changed to a lower-case "n.")

As Joy waits for Manley's arrival, "She look[s] up and down the empty highway and ha[s] the furious feeling that she ha[s] been tricked, that he had only meant to make her walk to the gate after the idea of him."	This sentence demonstrates how changing verb endings and putting the new ones in brackets can be an easy way to solve tense shift problems of the kind found in example 4 above.
The woman in all the portraits is idealized, represented "[n]ot as she is, but as she fills his [the painter's] dream."	If a pronoun reference in a quotation is unclear, one fix is to put the noun to which the pronoun refers in brackets after the pronoun, as in this sentence. For an alternative fix, see example 3 above.
As Mays explains, a writer "can assume that their reader will recognize the traditional meanings of these ["traditional"] symbols," but "invented symbols" work differently.	In this sentence, the phrase "these symbols" refers to something outside the quoted sentence. The added and thus bracketed word *traditional* appears in quotation marks because it, too, comes directly from the same source.

> TIP: Though such alterations are permissible, they are often so much less effective than other techniques that some of them (including changes to verb endings) are not actually mentioned in the *MLA Handbook*. Used too often, this technique can become very distracting and put you at risk of appearing as if you're "fiddling" with sources. As a result, look for other fixes whenever possible.

OMISSIONS AND ELLIPSES

○ A quotation that is obviously a sentence fragment need not be preceded or followed by an ellipsis (. . .). But you must use an ellipsis whenever
   —your quotation appears to be a complete sentence but actually isn't one in the source (as in the first and last sentences in the example below),
   —you omit words from the middle of a quoted sentence (as in the second sentence in the example below), or
   —you omit one or more sentences between quoted sentences (as between the second and third sentences in the example below).

When the ellipsis coincides with the end of your sentence, add a period followed by an ellipsis with a space before and between each ellipsis dot. A space follows the final ellipsis dot only if a new sentence follows (as in the first sentence below).

The narrator says of Mr. Kapasi,
> In his youth he'd been a devoted scholar of foreign languages. . . . He had dreamed of being an interpreter for diplomats and dignitaries, . . . settling

disputes of which he alone could understand both sides. . . . Now only a handful of European phrases remained in his memory, scattered words for things like saucers and chairs. . . . Sometimes he feared that his children knew better English than he did, just from watching television.

> NOTE: If you omit the end of a sentence *and* one or more of the sentences that immediately follow it, the four dots are sufficient; you do not need two ellipses.

○ If the quoted source uses an ellipsis, put your ellipsis in brackets to distinguish between the two. [NOTE: Throughout this book, we have instead put *every* added ellipsis in brackets.]

As an excited Ruth explains, the prospect of receiving a check is "a whole lot different from having it come and being able to hold it in your hands . . . a piece of paper worth ten thousand dollars." "[. . .] I wish Walter Lee was here!," she exclaims.	The first (unbracketed) ellipsis here occurs in the original source; the second (bracketed) ellipsis doesn't.

OTHER ACCEPTABLE CHANGES TO QUOTATIONS: *SIC* AND *EMPHASIS ADDED*

○ If a quotation includes what is or might seem to your reader an error of fact or of grammar, spelling, and so on, you may signal to the reader that you haven't introduced the error yourself through misquotation by putting the word *sic* (Latin for "thus" or "so") next to the error. Put parentheses around *sic* if it comes *after* the quotation (as in the first example below), brackets if it appears *within* the quotation (as in the second example). Do not use *sic* if context makes it obvious that the error isn't yours or isn't truly an error, as in the case of texts featuring archaic spelling, dialect, and so on.

1. Shaw admitted, "Nothing can extinguish my interest in Shakespear" (sic). 2. In the preface to *Shakes Versus Shav: A Puppet Play* (1949), Shaw avows, "Nothing can extinguish my interest in Shakespear [sic]. It began when I was a small boy. . . ."	In sentence 1 (from the *MLA Handbook*) parentheses work because nothing has been added *into* the quotation; the second, slightly modified version requires brackets. Either way, the word *sic* appears next to the misspelled word and is not italicized.
3. Charley gets to the heart of the matter when he asks Willy, "when're you gonna realize that them things don't mean anything?"	*Sic* would be inappropriate here, since it's clear this quotation accurately reproduces the character's speech patterns.

(*continued*)

4. The Misfit firmly rejects the idea that he should pray, insisting, "I don't want no hep" (sic), "I'm doing all right by myself."	In this case, though use of the word *hep* (for *help*) is entirely characteristic of the character's speech, it could so easily look like a typo, that the word *sic* seems helpful.

○ On the relatively rare occasions when you need to emphasize a specific word or phrase within a quotation, you may put it in italics and indicate this change by putting the words *emphasis added* in parentheses after the quotation, ideally at the end of the clause or sentence.

Avowing that men "must help them [women] to stay in that beautiful world of their own, *lest ours get worse*" (emphasis added), Marlow acknowledges that men have a selfish interest in preserving women's innocence and idealism.

PUNCTUATING QUOTATIONS

○ Though you must always reproduce original punctuation *within* a quotation, you may *end it* with whatever punctuation your sentence requires, and this is the one change you do not need to indicate with brackets.

Whether portrayed as "queen," "saint," or "angel," the same "nameless girl" appears in "all his canvases."	In the poem quoted here, no commas appear after the words *queen* and *angel*, but the syntax of the sentence requires they be added. Similarly, the comma that appears after the word *canvases* in the poem is here replaced by a period.
The narrator tells us that Mr. Kapasi's "job was a sign of his failings," for "[i]n his youth he'd been a devoted scholar of foreign languages" who "dreamed of being an interpreter for diplomats and dignitaries."	Here, a comma replaces the original period after *failings*, and a period replaces the original comma after *dignitaries.*

○ Commas and periods belong *inside* the closing quotation mark (as in the above examples). All other punctuation marks belongs *outside* the closing quotation mark if they are your additions, inside if they are not.

1. Wordsworth calls nature a "homely Nurse"; she has "something of a Mother's Mind."
2. What exactly does Lili mean when she tells Guy, "You are here to protect me if anything happens"?
3. Bobby Lee speaks volumes about the grandmother when he says, "She was a talker, wasn't she?"

○ When your indented, block quotation includes a quotation, put the latter in double quotation marks (" ").

Written just four years after *A Raisin in the Sun*'s debut, Martin Luther King, Jr.'s "Letter from Birmingham Jail" stresses the urgency of the situation of African Americans like himself and the Youngers by comparing it to those of Africans like Joseph Asagai and white Americans like Karl Lindner:

> We have waited for more than 340 years for our constitutional and God-given rights. The nations of . . . Africa are moving with jetlike speed toward gaining political independence, but we still creep at horse-and-buggy pace toward gaining a cup of coffee at a lunch counter. Perhaps it is easy for those who have never felt the stinging darts of segregation to say, "Wait."

○ When a shorter (non-block) quotation includes a quotation, put the latter in single quotation marks (' ').

1. As Martin Luther King, Jr., insisted in 1963, "it is easy for those who have never felt the stinging darts of segregation" or the "degenerating sense of 'nobodiness'" it instills, "to say, 'Wait,'" be patient, your time will come.

2. In a poem less about Hard Rock himself than about the way he is perceived by his fellow inmates, it makes sense that many words and lines take the form of unattributed quotations, as in the unforgettable opening, "Hard Rock was 'known not to take no shit / From nobody.'"

○ When your quotation consists *entirely* of words that appear within quotation marks in the source, use double quotation marks, while making sure that you introduce the quotation in a way that makes the special status of these words and their provenance clear.

1. "[K]nown not to take no shit / From nobody," as his fellow inmates put it, Hard Rock initially appears almost superhuman.

2. The Misfit's response is as shocking as it is simple: "I don't want no hep," "I'm doing all right by myself."

3. In an introductory note quoted by Alvarez, Plath describes the poem's speaker as "a girl with an Electra complex" whose "father died while she thought he was God."

21.2 STRATEGIES FOR EFFECTIVE QUOTING

○ Though it is not a rule that all of your quotations must appear inside one of your sentences, your clarity will be enormously enhanced if you treat it like one, making the connection between quotation and inference as seamless as possible.

1. Smith is highly critical of O'Brien's portrayal of Martha. "Like other women in the book, she represents all those back home who will never understand the warrior's trauma."

2. Smith is highly critical of O'Brien's portrayal of Martha: "Like other women in the book, she represents all those back home who will never understand the warrior's trauma."

3. Smith is highly critical of O'Brien's portrayal of Martha, claiming that, "[l]ike other women in the book," Martha "represents all those back home who will never understand the warrior's trauma."

Example 1 includes a quotation that isn't part of any sentence. Example 2 corrects that problem with a colon, but the reader still has to pause to figure out that it's Smith who's being quoted here and that the quotation refers to Martha. Sentence 3 thus offers a better solution.

○ Avoid drawing attention to your evidence as evidence with "filler" phrases such as *This statement is proof that . . . ; This phrase is significant because . . . ; This idea is illustrated by . . . ; There is good evidence for this. . . .* Show *why* facts are meaningful or interesting rather than first or only saying *that* they are.

INEFFECTIVE QUOTATION	EFFECTIVE QUOTATION
Wordsworth calls nature a "homely Nurse" and says that she has "something of a Mother's mind" (lines 81, 79). This diction supports the idea that he sees nature as a healing, maternal force. He is saying that nature heals and cares for us.	Personifying nature as a "homely Nurse" with "something of a Mother's Mind," Wordsworth depicts nature as healing and nurturing the humans it also resembles. OR A "homely Nurse" with "something of a Mother's Mind," nature, implies Wordsworth, both heals and nurtures the humans it also resembles.
Tennyson advocates decisive action, even as he highlights the forces that often prohibited his contemporaries from taking it. This is suggested by the lines "Made weak by time and fate, but strong in will, / To strive, to seek, to find, and not to yield" (lines 69–70).	Tennyson advocates forceful action, encouraging his contemporaries "To strive, to seek to find, and not to yield" (line 70). Yet he recognizes that his generation is more tempted to "yield" than earlier ones because they have been "Made weak by time and fate" (69).

○ On the one hand, make sure that you provide readers the information they need to understand the quotation and to appreciate its relevance to your argument. Quite often, contextual information—for instance, about who's speaking to whom and in what situation—is crucial to a quotation's meaning. On the other hand, keep such contextual information to a minimum and put the emphasis on the words that really matter and on your inferences about why and how they matter.

1. Strong as Mama is, she and Walter share a similar, traditional vision of gender roles: "I'm telling you to be the head of this family . . . like you supposed to be"; "the colored woman" should be "building their men up and making 'em feel like they somebody."

2. Strong as Mama is, she shares Walter's traditional vision of gender roles. When she urges him "to be the head of this family from now on like you supposed to be," she affirms that her son is the family's rightful leader—not her daughter, not her daughter-in-law, not even herself, despite her seniority in terms of age. Implicitly, she's also doing what Walter elsewhere says "the colored woman" should do—"building their men up and making 'em feel like they somebody."

Example 2 is more effective because it offers crucial information about who is speaking to whom ("*When Lena tells Walter*," "*Walter elsewhere says*") and includes inferences ("*she affirms that her son is the family's rightful leader . . .*"; "*Implicitly, she's also doing*"). Purely contextual information is, however, stated briefly and early, in subordinate clauses.

3. Julian expresses disgust for the class distinctions so precious to his mother: "Rolling his eyes upward, he put his tie back on. 'Restored to my class,' he muttered."

4. Julian professes disgust for the class distinctions so precious to his mother. At her request, he puts back on his tie, but he can't do so without "[r]olling his eyes" and making fun (at least under his breath) of the idea that he is thereby "[r]estored to [his] class."

Again, example 4 improves on example 3 by providing missing information ("*At her request*") and yet paraphrasing and subordinating what is only information ("*he puts back on his tie*").

○ Lead your readers into long, especially block, quotations with a clear sense of just what in the quotation they should be paying attention to and why. Follow it up with at least a sentence or more of analysis/ inferences, perhaps repeating especially key words and phrases from the long quotation.

Whereas the second stanza individualizes the dead martyrs, the third considers the characteristics they shared with each other and with all those
who dedicate themselves utterly to any one cause:

> Hearts with one purpose alone
> Through summer and winter seem
> Enchanted to a stone
> To trouble the living stream. (lines 41–44)

Whereas all other "living" people and things are caught up in the "stream"
of change represented by the shift of seasons, those who fill their "hearts
with one purpose alone" become as hard, unchanging, and immoveable as
stone.

○ Be aware that even though long, especially block quotations can be
effective, they should be used sparingly and strategically. All too easily,
they can create information overload or confusion for readers, making it hard to see what is most significant and why. When you quote
only individual words or short phrases, weaving them into your sentences in the ways demonstrated earlier in this section, you and your
readers can more easily stay focused on what's significant and on *why*
and *how* it is.

○ Vary the length of quotations and the way you present them, using a
variety of strategies. It can be very tempting to fall into a pattern—
always, for example, choosing quotations that are at least a sentence
long and attaching them to your sentence with a colon. But overusing
any one technique can easily render your essay monotonous and
might even prompt readers to focus more on the (repetitive) way you
present evidence than on the evidence and argument themselves. To
demonstrate, here are two sets of sentences that present the very same
material in varying ways.

1. According to Wordsworth, nature is a "homely Nurse" with "something
   of a Mother's Mind"; it heals and nurtures the humans it also resembles.

2. A "homely Nurse" with "something of a Mother's Mind," nature, suggests
   Wordsworth, both heals and nurtures the humans it also resembles.

3. Personifying nature as a "homely Nurse" with "something of a Mother's
   Mind," Wordsworth depicts nature as healing and nurturing the humans
   it also resembles.

4. Healing and nurturing the humans it also resembles, Wordsworth's nature
   is a "homely Nurse" with "something of a Mother's Mind."

1. Howe insists that the poem's "personal-confessional element . . . is simply too obtrusive," "strident and undisciplined," to allow a reader to interpret "Daddy" "as a dramatic presentation, a monologue spoken by a
   disturbed girl not necessarily to be identified with Sylvia Plath," espe-

cially given the resemblances between "events" described in the poem and those that actually occurred in Plath's life.

2. "Daddy," argues Howe, cannot be read "as a dramatic presentation, a monologue spoken by a disturbed girl not necessarily to be identified with Sylvia Plath"; its "personal-confessional element . . . is simply too obtrusive," too "strident and undisciplined," he reasons, while the "events of the poem" too closely correspond to "the events of her life."

21.3 CITATION AND DOCUMENTATION

In addition to indicating which words, facts, and ideas in your essay derive from someone else's work, you need to let your readers know where each can be found. You want to enable readers not only to "check up" on you but also to follow in your footsteps and build on your work. After all, you hope that your analysis of a text will entice readers to re-read certain passages from the text in a different way or to consult sources that you've made sound interesting. This is another way your essay contributes to keeping the conversation about literature going. And this is where citation and documentation come into play.

In the MLA system, parenthetical citations embedded in your essay are keyed to an alphabetized list of works cited that follows your essay. By virtue of both their content and placement, parenthetical citations help you to quickly and unobtrusively indicate *what* you have derived from *which* source and *where* in that source your readers can find that material. The list of works cited communicates the information about the source that your readers need both to find it themselves and, in the meantime, to begin evaluating for themselves its relevance, credibility, currency, and so on *without* having to find it.

To demonstrate how this works, here is a typical sentence with parenthetical citation, followed by the coordinating works-cited entry:

In-Text Citation

In one critic's view, "Ode on a Grecian Urn" explores "what great art means" not to the ordinary person, but "to those who create it" (Bowra 148).

Placed at the end of the sentence and beginning with the word *Bowra* (sans quotation marks or italics) and the number 148, this parenthetical citation tells us that the last name of the "critic" the sentence mentions and quotes is *Bowra*, that the source of the quotations is something he authored, and that the quotations come from page 148 of that source. To find out more, we have to turn to the list of works cited and look for an entry, like the following, that begins with the name *Bowra*.

Works Cited Entry

Bowra, C. M. *The Romantic Imagination.* Oxford UP, 1950.

This coordinating works-cited entry gives us Bowra's complete name as it appears in the source and indicates its title, publisher, and date of publication.

That our explanations of this sample parenthetical citation and works-cited entry take up much more space than the citation and entry themselves demonstrates the value of the MLA system. What it also demonstrates is the importance of both the placement and content of each citation and entry: Where the parenthetical citation falls in a sentence is key to clearly indicating what is being "sourced"; what the parenthetical citation and works cited include and in what order are all key to ensuring that the citation leads us seamlessly to *one* source in the works cited and tells us where precisely to look in that source.

The exact content and placement of each parenthetical citation and works-cited entry will thus depend on a host of factors. The next sections explain how this works.

21.3.1 Parenthetical Citation

THE STANDARD PARENTHETICAL CITATION: CONTENT AND PLACEMENT

Because lists of works cited are organized primarily by author, the standard MLA parenthetical citation looks just like, and appears in the same place as, the ones in the sample sentences above and below. It includes an author's name and a page number or numbers with nothing but a space in between. (Do not write *page* or *p.,* for example, or insert a comma.) The citation comes at the end of a sentence—*inside* the period (because it is part of the sentence in which you borrow from a source) and *outside* any quotation marks within the sentence (since it is *not* part of an actual quotation; it is not *in* the source but provides information *about* the source). In keeping with the rules for punctuating quotations laid out earlier in this chapter (21.1.3), you omit any final punctuation mark within your quotation, as in the second example below.

1. Most domestic poems of the 1950s foreground the parent-child relationship (Axelrod 1093).

2. As a character in one of the most famous works of Southern fiction memorably declares of the South, "I dont hate it" (Faulkner 378).

When citing a work from an anthology, refer to the author of the work, not the anthology editor, and make sure to create a corresponding entry in your list of works cited. Below is an example of this kind of citation, as well as the corresponding works-cited entry.

In-Text Citation

By the end of an initiation story, its protagonist may well have to confront "how hard the world" usually is (Updike 443).

Works Cited Entry

Updike, John. "A & P." *The Norton Introduction to Literature*, edited by Kelly J. Mays, portable 12th ed., W. W. Norton, 2017, pp. 437-43.

The next two sections detail the variations on the standard MLA parenthetical citation format, starting with variations in *where* the citation goes before turning to variations in *what* it includes.

VARIATIONS IN PLACEMENT

- In the case of a block quotation, the parenthetical citation should immediately *follow* (not precede) the punctuation mark that ends the quotation.

  According to the narrator,
    The job was a sign of his failings. In his youth he'd been a devoted scholar of foreign languages, the owner of an impressive collection of dictionaries. He had dreamed of being an interpreter for diplomats and dignitaries, resolving conflicts between people and nations, settling disputes of which he alone could understand both sides. (Lahiri 351)

- If a sentence either incorporates material from multiple sources (as in the first example below) or refers both to something from a source and to your own idea (as in the second example), put the appropriate parenthetical citation in midsentence next to the material to which it refers. Ideally, you should insert the citation before a comma or semicolon, since it will be less obtrusive that way. But your first priority should be clarity about which material comes from which source (see the third example below).

  1. Critics describe Caliban as a creature with an essentially "unalterable natur[e]" (Garner 458), "incapable of comprehending the good or of learning from the past" (Peterson 442), "impervious to genuine moral improvement" (Wright 451).
  2. If Caliban is truly "incapable of . . . learning from the past" (Peterson 442), then how do we explain the changed attitude he seems to demonstrate at the play's end?
  3. Tanner (7) and Smith (viii) have looked at works from a cultural perspective.

- If, in a single paragraph, you make several *uninterrupted* references to the same source and especially to the same passage in a source, you may save the parenthetical citation until after the last such reference, as in the following example from Susan Farrell's "Tim O'Brien and Gender: A Defense of *The Things They Carried*."

Smith connects a 1980s backlash against the feminist movement to the misogyny she reads in Vietnam War literature, a misogyny which she describes as "very visible," as seemingly "natural and expected." In popular presentations, Smith argues, the "Vietnam War is being reconstructed as a site where white American manhood—figuratively as well as literally wounded during the war and assaulted by the women's movement for twenty years—can reassert its dominance in the social hierarchy" ("Back" 115).

VARIATIONS IN CONTENT: IDENTIFYING THE SOURCE

The standard MLA parenthetical citation may contain the author's name and the relevant page number(s). But variations are the rule when it comes to content. In this section, we deal with variations in how a citation indicates *which* source you refer to; the next section instead covers variations in how you indicate *where* in the source borrowed material can be found.

Your parenthetical citation should include something besides or in addition to one author's name whenever you do the following:

○ *Name the author(s) in your text.*
Parenthetical citations should include only information that isn't crucial to the intelligibility and credibility of your argument. Yet in nine cases out of ten, information about *whose* ideas, data, or words you are referring to is crucial. As a result, you should try whenever possible to indicate this in your text, usually via a *signal phrase* (as described in 20.4.2). When you do so, your parenthetical citation usually need only include location information such as page number(s).

1. In Maurice Bowra's view, "Ode on a Grecian Urn" explores "what great art means" not to the ordinary person, but "to those who create it" (148).
2. As Faulkner's Quentin Compson memorably declares of the South, "I dont hate it" (378).

In literature essays, parenthetical citations containing the name of the author whose work you are analyzing should be relatively rare.

○ *Cite a source with multiple authors.*
If the source has two authors, and they are not named in your text, the parenthetical citation should include both last names (as in the example below). If the source has three or more authors, include the first author's name followed by the words *et al.* (abbreviated Latin for "and others").

Surprisingly, "it seems not to have been primarily the coarseness and sexuality of *Jane Eyre* which shocked Victorian reviewers" so much as its "rebellious feminism" (Gilbert and Gubar 338).

○ *Cite multiple works by the same author or an anonymous work.*
In either of these cases, you will need to indicate the title of your source. If possible, do so in your text, putting only location information in the parenthetical citation (as in the first example below). Otherwise, your parenthetical citation must include a shortened version of the title (as in the second example below). If your parenthetical citation also needs to include the author's name(s), this comes first, followed by a comma, the shortened title, and the location information (as in the third example below).

1. Like Joy, in O'Connor's "Good Country People," the protagonist of her story "Everything that Rises Must Converge" takes enormous pride in his intellect, even believing himself "too intelligent to be a success" (500).
2. Many of O'Connor's most faulty characters put enormous stock in their intellects, one even secretly believing himself "too intelligent to be a success" ("Everything" 500).
3. Intellectuals fare poorly in much Southern fiction. When we learn that the protagonist of one short story secretly believes himself "too intelligent to be a success," we can be pretty sure that he's in for a fall (O'Connor, "Everything" 500).

Be sure to format shortened titles just as you do full titles, either putting them in quotation marks or italicizing them as appropriate (see 19.5).

○ *Cite multiple authors with the same last name.*
In this case, you should ideally indicate the author's full name in the text so that your parenthetical citation need only include location information. Otherwise, the parenthetical citation should begin with the author's first initial followed by a period, followed by his or her last name and the location information (as in the first example below). If your authors share the same first initial, however, you will need to include a first name instead of initial (as in the second example).

1. As one of Joyce's fellow writers points out, "To be absolutely faithful to what one sees and hears and not to speculate on what may lie behind it . . . is a creed that produces obvious limitations" (F. O'Connor 188).
2. As one of Flannery O'Connor's fellow short story writers points out, "To be absolutely faithful to what one sees and hears and not to speculate on what may lie behind it . . . is a creed that produces obvious limitations" (Frank O'Connor 188).

○ *Cite multiple authors simultaneously.*
In this case, include all the citations within a single set of parentheses, separating them with semicolons.

Many scholars attribute Caliban's bestiality to a seemingly innate inability to learn or change (Garner 438; Peterson 442; Wright 451).

○ *Quote a source quoted in another source.*
You should quote from an original source whenever possible. But on the rare occasions when you quote something quoted in another source, indicate the original source in your text. Then start your parenthetical citation with the abbreviation *qtd. in* followed by the name of the second-hand source's author and the location information.

In an introductory note to "Daddy" that Plath wrote for a radio program that never aired, she describes the poem's speaker as "a girl with an Electra complex" whose "father died while she thought he was God" and whose "case is complicated by the fact that her father was also a Nazi and her mother very possibly part Jewish" (qtd. in Alvarez 1080).

VARIATIONS IN CONTENT: INDICATING A LOCATION WITHIN THE SOURCE

Though page numbers are usually the only means we use to identify where in a source a reader can find the ideas, information, or words we cite, there are exceptions. Indeed, exceptions are unusually frequent in literature essays. The most important reason for this is that literary texts tend to be available in different editions, so it's helpful to give readers the information they need to locate material in the text regardless of the edition they use.

When it comes to the question of how to do so, there is frankly a good deal of ambiguity and "wiggle room" in the MLA guidelines. Thus, as we explain below, different instructors may interpret some of these guidelines differently or simply prefer that you use one method rather than another.

Your parenthetical citation will generally need to include location information other than, or in addition to, a page number whenever you cite any of the following:

○ *Poetry*
When citing poetry, it is customary to refer to line (not page) number(s) and to indicate that you are doing so by including the word *line* or *lines*, as appropriate, in your first such parenthetical citation. Though MLA guidelines stipulate that later parenthetical citations include only the line number (as in the example below), some instructors prefer that the word *line* or *lines* appear in every poem-related parenthetical citation.

In a poem less about Hard Rock himself than about the way he is perceived by his fellow inmates, it makes sense that many words and lines take the form of unattributed quotations, as in the unforgettable opening, "Hard Rock was 'known not to take no shit / From nobody' " (lines 1-2), or "Yeah, remember when he / Smacked the captain with his dinner tray?" (17-18).

○ *Play with more than one act or scene*
At least when it comes to canonical plays, MLA guidelines call for omitting page numbers entirely and referring only to act, scene, and/or line numbers as appropriate, always using arabic numerals (*1, 2,* etc.) and separating each with a period (as in the first example below). Some instructors, however, prefer that you use roman numerals (*I, II, i, ii,* etc.) for acts and scenes (as in the second example below).

1. "I know not 'seems,' " Hamlet famously declares (1.2.76).
2. "I know not 'seems,' " Hamlet famously declares (I.ii.76).

○ *Commonly studied work of fiction or nonfiction prose*
Parenthetical citations of this kind should always include page numbers unless your instructor indicates otherwise. But you may also need or want to include additional location information. In this case, the page number comes first, followed by a semicolon and the other information. Use common abbreviations to indicate what this information is (e.g., *vol.* for *volume, bk.* for *book, sec.* for *section*), and give it in arabic numerals (*1, 2,* etc.), even if the text uses roman numerals (*I, II,* etc.). (The second example below is quoted directly from the *MLA Handbook.*)

1. "I learned," explains Frankenstein's creature, "that the possessions most esteemed by your fellow-creatures were, high and unsullied descent united with riches" (96; vol. 2, ch. 5).
2. In *A Vindication of the Rights of Woman,* Mary Wollstonecraft recollects many "women who, not led by degrees to proper studies, and not permitted to choose for themselves, have indeed been overgrown children" (185; ch. 13, sec. 2).

When you cite prose works from an anthology like this one, in which paragraphs are numbered, your instructor may allow or even require you to cite paragraph numbers, using the appropriate abbreviation (*par.*). If you include both page and paragraph number, insert a semicolon after the page number (as in the first example below). If your parenthetical citations don't include page, as well as paragraph, numbers, your instructor may also allow you to omit the abbreviation *par.* from the second and subsequent such citations (as in the second example).

1. When they meet years later in the supermarket, Roberta's "lovely and summery and rich" appearance leaves the narrator not only "dying to know" how this transformation came about but also resentful of Roberta and people like her: "Everything is so easy for them," she thinks (147; par. 68).

2. Though "dying to know" just how Roberta came to be so "lovely and summery and rich" since they last met (par. 68), all the narrator initially asks is, "How long you been here?" (69).

○ *Sacred text*
When citing sacred texts such as the Bible or the Qur'an, indicate either in your text or in your parenthetical citation the title, editor, or translator of the edition you're using on the first occasion you cite it. Then include in your parenthetical citation(s) the book, chapter, and verse (or their equivalent), separated by periods, unless you have indicated these in your text. (Either way, do not include page numbers.) Abbreviate the names of the books of the Bible, but don't put these abbreviations in quotation marks or italicize them. (The second example below is quoted directly from the *MLA Handbook*.)

1. *The New English Bible* version of the verse reads, "In the beginning of creation, when God made heaven and earth, the earth was without form and void, with darkness over the face of the abyss, and a mighty wind that swept over the surface of the waters" (Gen. 1.1-2).
2. In one of the most vivid prophetic visions in the Bible, Ezekiel saw "what seemed to be four living creatures," each with the faces of a man, a lion, an ox, and an eagle (*New Jerusalem Bible*, Ezek. 1.5-10). John of Patmos echoes this passage when describing his vision (Rev. 4.6-8).

○ *An entire source, a source without page numbers, a source that is only one page long, or an entry in a dictionary or other source organized alphabetically*
When you refer in a blanket way to an entire source rather than to something particular in it, to a source that has no pages or page numbers, to a source that is only one page long or has unnumbered pages, or to an entry in a dictionary or other work organized alphabetically, your parenthetical citation will include no page numbers. If you refer to something specific in a source lacking pages or page numbers but having other numbered divisions such as sections or paragraphs, do include these, using appropriate abbreviations (e.g., *sec.*, *par.*), and make sure to add a comma after the author's name or, if the author is unknown, after the title of the work. Otherwise, if you clearly identify such a source (by author and/or title) in your text, you won't need a parenthetical citation at all (as in the first and second examples below). If you don't clearly identify the source in your text, your citation will include only author's name(s) and/or a shortened title (as in the third and fourth examples).

1. Many critics, including Maurice Bowra, see Creon as morally inferior to Antigone.
2. The entry for *Lord Weary's Castle* in *The Oxford Companion to American Literature*, for example, takes the "[m]ajor works" it includes to be the elegy

"The Quaker Graveyard in Nantucket," the Jonathan Edwards-inspired "Mr. Edwards and the Spider," and the war poem "Christmas Eve Under Hooker's Statue."

3. Where some critics see the play as siding unequivocally with Antigone (Bowra), others see it as more ambivalent and/or ambiguous on this score (Nussbaum).

4. According to *The Oxford Companion to American Literature*, the elegy "The Quaker Graveyard in Nantucket" is among the three "[m]ajor works" in Lowell's *Lord Weary's Castle* (*"Lord Weary's Castle"*).

OTHER VARIATIONS IN CONTENT: *SIC* AND *EMPHASIS ADDED*

When a parenthetical citation intervenes between the end of a quotation that you need to follow up with the words *sic* or *emphasis added* (for the reasons outlined in 21.1.3), it's usually advisable to put *sic* in brackets within the quotation, next to the error to which it applies (as in the second example below), but to put *emphasis added* at the end of the parenthetical citation, preceding it with a semicolon (as in the second example).

1. Shaw admitted, "Nothing can extinguish my interest in Shakespear [sic]" (1).

2. Avowing that men "must help them [women] to stay in that beautiful world of their own, *lest ours get worse*" (1196; emphasis added), Marlow acknowledges that men have a selfish interest in preserving women's innocence and idealism.

21.3.2 The List of Works Cited

Your list of works cited must include all, and only, the sources that you cite in your essay, providing full publication information about each. This section explains both how to format and organize the list and how to put together each entry in it.

FORMATTING THE LIST

Your list of works cited should begin on a separate page after the conclusion of your essay. Center the heading *Works Cited* (without quotation marks or italics) at the top of the first page, and double space throughout.

The first line of each entry should begin at the left margin; the second and subsequent lines should be indented ½ inch.

Your list should be alphabetized, ignoring articles (such as *A, An, The*) in entries that begin with a title.

If your list includes multiple works by the same author, begin the first entry with the author's name, and each subsequent entry with three hyphens followed by a period. Alphabetize these entries by title, again ignoring articles (*A, An, The*).

Works Cited

Broyles, William. "Why Men Love War." *Esquire,* Nov. 1984, pp. 55-65.

Clarke, Michael Tavel. " 'I Feel Close to Myself': Solipsism and U.S. Imperialism in Tim O'Brien's *The Things They Carried.*" *College Literature,* vol. 40, no. 2, Spring 2013, pp. 130-54. *Project Muse,* doi:10.1353/lit.2013.0018.

O'Brien, Tim. *Going After Cacciato.* Dell Publishing, 1978.

---. *The Things They Carried.* Houghton Mifflin, 1990.

Smith, Lorrie N. " 'The Things Men Do': The Gendered Subtext in Tim O'Brien's *Esquire* Stories." *Critique,* vol. 36, no. 1, Fall 1994, pp. 16-40. *Taylor & Francis Online,* doi:10.1080/00111619.1994.9935239.

FORMATTING INDIVIDUAL ENTRIES—GENERAL GUIDELINES

All information in a works-cited entry should come from the source itself and appear as it does in the source. Many if not most sources cited today are produced or experienced as part of larger wholes—or what MLA calls containers. If you cite a poem from this or any other anthology, for example, the poem is your source, the anthology its container. Works-cited entries may consist of as many as nine "core elements," each of which should be included when it is relevant and available. In general, they must appear in the following order: author, title of source, title of container, other contributors, version, number, publisher, publication date, and location. Some other elements are recommended, but not required: in this book, for instance, dates of access for online sources have been omitted. For further details on required and optional elements, please consult the *MLA Handbook* (8th ed., 2016) and *The MLA Style Center* (style.mla.org).

Below we offer only a few formatting guidelines applicable to all works-cited entries, along with model entries for especially common types of sources.

○ *Names*

Reproduce the names of authors, editors, and so on as they appear *in* the source—on a book's title page; at the beginning or end of a journal, magazine, or newspaper article; and so on. If initials are used, use them. If there are multiple authors or editors, list them in the order the source does, using the following format when they appear at the beginning of your entry:

2 names   Lastname, Firstname, and Firstname Lastname.
3+names   Lastname, Firstname, et al.

If the author is unknown, begin your entry with the title.

○ *Publishers*

Shorten publishers' names by doing the following:

○ Omit business words and abbreviations (*Company* or *Co., Inc.*): instead of *W. W. Norton & Co.,* type *W. W. Norton.*

○ With university presses, abbreviate *University* to *U* and *Press* to *P:* shorten *University of Chicago Press* to *U of Chicago P,* *Harvard University Press* to *Harvard UP.*

○ *Dates*

For a book's publication date, use the most recent year on the title or copyright page; for a Web source, use copyright date or the date of the most recent update. Abbreviate the names of all months except May, June, and July.

○ *Page numbers*

If you cite an article from a magazine or newspaper that isn't printed on consecutive pages, include only the first page number and a plus sign (+).

FORMATTING INDIVIDUAL ENTRIES FOR DIFFERENT TYPES OF SOURCES

This section explains how to format works-cited entries for the types of sources most frequently cited in literature essays. For other types of sources, consult the *MLA Handbook.*

1. *Book with an author or authors*

○ *Print book*

Author's Lastname, Firstname. *Book Title.* Publisher, Year of publication.

O'Brien, Tim. *Going After Cacciato.* Dell Publishing, 1978.

○ *Print book on the Web*

Author's Lastname, Firstname. *Book Title.* Publisher, Year of publication. *Web Site Title,* URL or DOI.

Melville, Herman. *Moby-Dick: or, The Whale.* Harper and Brothers, 1851. *Google Books,* books.google.com/books/about/Moby_Dick.html?id=J _yoAgAAQBAJ.

○ *E-book*

Author's Lastname, Firstname. *Book Title.* E-book or Kindle ed. [if any], Publisher, Year of Publication.

Lahiri, Jhumpa. *Interpreter of Maladies.* E-book, Houghton Mifflin Harcourt, 1999.

○ *E-book in database*

Author's Lastname, Firstname. *Book Title.* Publisher, Year of publication. *Database Title,* URL or DOI.

Boyle, Elizabeth, and Anne-Marie Evans, editors. *Reading America: New Perspectives on the American Novel.* Cambridge Scholars, 2008. *ProQuest Ebrary,* site.ebrary.com.ezproxy.library.unlv.edu/lib/unlv/detail.action ?docID=10655216&p00=reading+America.

2. *Anthology or other book with editor(s) rather than author(s)*
Format your entry as indicated for a book (1), but after the (last) author's name or the abbreviation *et al.*, insert a comma and the word *editor* or *editors*.

> Kitchen, Judith, and Mary Paumier Jones, editors. *In Short: A Collection of Brief Creative Nonfiction.* W. W. Norton, 1996.

> Rowell, Charles Henry, editor. *Angles of Ascent: A Norton Anthology of Contemporary African American Poetry.* W. W. Norton, 2013.

3. *Book with author(s) and editor(s) or translator(s)*
If what you cite or emphasize in your essay is the book itself, format your entry as indicated for a book (1), but insert between the book title and publication information the words *edited by* or *translated by*; the first and last names of the editor(s) and/or translator(s); and a period.

> Kafka, Franz. *The Metamorphosis.* Translated by Joyce Crick, edited by Ritchie Robertson, E-book, Oxford UP, 2009.

> Keats, John. *Letters of John Keats to His Family and Friends.* Edited by Sidney Colvin, Macmillan, 1891. *Google Books,* books.google.com/books/about /Letters_of_John_Keats_to_his_family_and.html?id=ULlZnQEACAAJ.

If what you cite or emphasize in your essay is the work of the editor or translator, your entry should instead start with that person's name, followed by a comma and the word *editor* or *translator* (no capitalization), followed by the title of the book and the author.

> Colvin, Sidney, editor. *Letters of John Keats to His Family and Friends.* By John Keats, Macmillan, 1891. *Google Books,* books.google.com/books/about /Letters_of_John_Keats_to_his_family_and.html?id=ULlZnQEACAAJ.

> Crick, Joyce, translator. *The Metamorphosis.* By Franz Kafka, edited by Ritchie Robertson, E-book, Oxford UP, 2009.

4. *Graphic narrative or book with author(s) and illustrator(s)*
If the book is written and illustrated by the same person or people, format the entry as you would for any other book (1). Otherwise, your entry will take one of the two forms below, depending upon whether your essay most emphasizes the work of the author(s) or the illustrator(s).

> Crumb, R., illustrator. *American Spendor: Bob and Harv's Comics.* By Harvey Pekar, Four Walls Eight Windows, 1996.

> Pekar, Harvey. *American Splendor: Bob and Harv's Comics.* Illustrated by R. Crumb, Four Walls Eight Windows, 1996.

5. Sacred text

> *Text Title.* Editor's Firstname Lastname, editor [if any]. Publisher, Year of publication.

> *The New English Bible with the Apocrypha.* Oxford UP, 1971.

6. Book in an edition other than the first

Format your entry as indicated for a book (1) or anthology (2), but insert the edition information, followed by a comma, just *before* the publication information. Identify the edition in whatever way the book's title page does, but abbreviate (e.g., *3rd ed.* for *Third edition*, *Rev. ed.* for *Revised edition*).

> Drabble, Margaret, editor. *The Oxford Companion to English Literature.* Rev. ed., Oxford UP, 1998.

7. Book in a series

Format your entry as indicated for a book (1) or anthology (2). Then, at the end, add the series title, followed by a period.

> Joyce, James. *A Portrait of the Artist as a Young Man.* Oxford UP, 2001. Oxford World's Classics.

> Stein, Karen F. *Margaret Atwood Revisited.* Twayne Publishers, 1999. Twayne's World Authors.

8. Introduction, preface, foreword, or afterword to a book

Start your entry with the name of the author of the introduction, preface, and so on. If that author is not the same as the author of the book itself, your entry should look like this:

> Part Author's Lastname, Firstname. Introduction, Preface, or Foreword. *Book Title*, by Book Author's Firstname Lastname, Publisher, Year of publication, Page numbers.

> O'Prey, Paul. Introduction. *Heart of Darkness,* by Joseph Conrad, Penguin, 1983, pp. 7-24.
> Meynell, Viola. Introduction. *Moby-Dick or The Whale,* by Herman Melville, Oxford UP, 1921. *Hathi Trust,* catalog.hathitrust.org/Record/001910361.

If the author of the part of the book you're citing is also the book's editor, and the book has no author, your entry should look like this:

> Author's Lastname, Firstname. Introduction, Preface, or Foreword. *Book Title*, edited by Editor's Lastname, Publisher, Year of publication, Page numbers.

> Rowell, Charles Henry. Preface. *Angles of Ascent: A Norton Anthology of Contemporary African American Poetry,* edited by Rowell, W. W. Norton, 2013, pp. xxiii–xxvii.

If the introduction, foreword, and so on has a title, format your entry as indicated above, but insert the title (in quotation marks) between its author's name and the word *Introduction, Preface,* and so on.

> Ozick, Cynthia. "Portrait of the Essay as a Warm Body." Introduction. *The Best American Essays 1998,* edited by Ozick, Houghton Mifflin, 1998, pp. xv–xxi.

9. *Work(s) in an anthology*

If you cite only one work from an anthology, your entry should look like this:

> Author's Lastname, Firstname. "Title of Work" or *Title of Work. Title of Anthology,* edited by Editor's Firstname Lastname, Publisher, Year of publication, Page numbers.

> Sanchez, Sonia. "A Poem for My Father." *Angles of Ascent: A Norton Anthology of Contemporary African American Poetry,* edited by Charles Henry Rowell, W. W. Norton, 2013, p. 70.

If you cite multiple works from the same anthology, create an entry for the anthology itself, following the guidelines for an anthology (2). Then create shortened entries like the following for each individual work:

> Author's Lastname, Firstname. "Title of Work" or *Title of Work.* Anthology Editor's Lastname, Page numbers.

> Dove, Rita. "Heroes." Rowell, pp. 215-16.

> Jackson, Major. "Some Kind of Crazy." Rowell, pp. 351-52.

> Sanchez, Sonia. "A Poem for My Father." Rowell, p. 70.

10. *Entry or article in a well-known general reference work (e.g., encyclopedia, dictionary)*

○ *Print*

> Author's Lastname, Firstname [if any]. "Title of Article." *Title of Reference Work,* edited by Editor's Firstname Lastname [if any], Edition [if any], Year of publication, Page numbers.

> "Histrionics." *Merriam-Webster's Collegiate Dictionary,* 11th ed., 2003, p. 590.

○ *Web*

> Author's Lastname, Firstname [if any]. "Title of Article." *Title of Reference Work,* edited by Editor's Firstname Lastname [if any], Edition [if any], Publisher, Date published or last updated, URL.

> Yoshida, Atsuhiko. "Epic." *Encyclopaedia Britannica,* Encyclopaedia Britannica, 19 Mar. 2014, www.britannica.com/art/epic.

> "Fable, n." *OED Online,* Oxford UP, Dec. 2014, www.oed.com/view/Entry67384.

11. **Entry or article in a lesser-known or specialized reference work**

○ *Print*

Author's Lastname, Firstname. "Title of Article." *Title of Reference Work*, edited by Editor's Firstname Lastname, Edition number [if other than first], Volume number [if more than one], Publisher, Year of publication, Page numbers.

Sullivan, Erin. "Humours." *The Oxford Companion to Shakespeare,* edited by Michael Dobson and Stanley Wells, 2nd ed., Oxford UP, 2015, p. 170.

○ *Database*

Author's Lastname, Firstname. "Title of Article." *Title of Reference Work*, edited by Editor's Firstname Lastname, Edition number [if other than first], Volume number [if more than one], Publisher, Year of publication. *Database Title*, URL.

Carter, Steven R. "Lorraine Hansberry's *A Raisin in the Sun*." *The Oxford Encyclopedia of American Literature*, edited by Jay Parini and Philip W. Leininger, Oxford UP, 2004. *Oxford Reference*, www.oxfordreference.com/view/10.1093/acref/9780195156539.001.0001/acref-9780195156539-e-0106.

○ *Web*

Author's Lastname, Firstname. "Title of Article." *Title of Reference Work*, edited by Editor's Firstname Lastname. Publisher or Sponsoring Institution, Date of publication or last update, URL.

Wicks, Robert. "Friedrich Nietzsche." *Stanford Encyclopedia of Philosophy*, edited by Edward N. Zalta. Metaphysics Research Lab, Center for the Study of Language and Information, Stanford U, 29 Apr. 2011, plato.stanford.edu/entries/nietzsche.

12. **Article in a journal**

○ *Print journal*

Author's Lastname, Firstname. "Title of Article." *Title of Journal*, Volume number, Issue number, Month or Season Year of publication, Page numbers.

Clarke, Michael Tavel. " 'I Feel Close to Myself': Solipsism and U.S. Imperialism in Tim O'Brien's *The Things They Carried*." *College Literature*, vol. 40, no. 2, Spring 2013, pp. 130-54.

○ *Journal in database*

Author's Lastname, Firstname. "Title of Article." *Title of Journal*, Volume number, Issue number, Month or Season Year of publication, Page numbers. *Database Title*, URL or DOI.

Clarke, Michael Tavel. "'I Feel Close to Myself': Solipsism and U.S. Imperialism in Tim O'Brien's *The Things They Carried.*" *College Literature*, vol. 40, no. 2, Spring 2013, pp. 130-54. *Project Muse*, doi:10.1353/lit.2013.0018.

○ *Web-only journal*

Author's Lastname, Firstname. "Title of Article." *Title of Journal*, Volume number, Issue number, Month or Season Year of publication, Page numbers [if any], URL or DOI.

Joneson, Devan. "Mythic Mentor Figures and Liminal Sacred Spaces in *Doctor Who* and *Battlestar Galactica.*" *Inquire: Journal of Comparative Literature*, vol. 3, no. 1, March 2013, inquire.streetmag.org/articles/113.

13. *Article in a magazine or on a magazine Web site*
For publication date, give day, month, and year of publication if appropriate and available; otherwise, give month and year.

○ *Print magazine*

Author's Lastname, Firstname. "Title of Article." *Title of Magazine*, Day Month Year of publication, Page numbers.

Alexie, Sherman. "When the Story Stolen Is Your Own." *Time*, 6 Feb. 2006, p. 72.

○ *Magazine in database*

Author's Lastname, Firstname. "Title of Article." *Title of Magazine*, Day Month Year of Publication, Page numbers. *Database Title*, URL or DOI.

Alexie, Sherman. "When the Story Stolen Is Your Own." *Time*, 6 Feb. 2006, p. 72. *Academic Search Premier*, connection.ebscohost.com/c/essays /19551314/when-story-stolen-your-own.

○ *Web-only magazine or magazine Web site*

Author's Lastname, Firstname. "Title of Article." *Web Site Title*, Day Month Year of publication, Page numbers [if any], URL.

Alston, Joshua. "Puffy Combs Revives 'Raisin.'" *Newsweek*, 24 Feb. 2008, www.newsweek.com/puffy-combs-revives-raisin-93493.

O'Rourke, Meghan. "Poetry's Lioness: Defending Sylvia Plath from Her Detractors." *Slate*, 28 Oct. 2003, www.slate.com/articles/arts/culturebox /2003/10/poetrys_lioness.html.

14. *Article in a newspaper or on a newspaper Web site*
If the title doesn't include the city of publication, add that information in brackets after the title (as in the "Database" example below).

○ *Print newspaper*

Author's Lastname, Firstname. "Title of Article." *Title of Newspaper,* Day Month Year of publication, Page numbers.

Feeney, Mark. "Gabriel Garcia Marquez, 87; Nobel Winner Popularized Magical Realism." *The Boston Globe,* 18 Apr. 2014, p. B12.

○ *Newspaper in database*

Author's Lastname, Firstname. "Title of Article." *Title of Newspaper,* Day Month Year of publication, Page numbers. *Database Title,* URL or DOI.

Malvern, Jack. "Globe Offers Shakespeare on Demand." *The Times* [London], 4 Nov. 2014, p. 3. *EBSCOhost Newspaper Source Plus,* ezproxy.library .unlv.edu/login?url=http://search.ebscohost.com/login.aspx?direct =true&db=n5h&AN=7EH92164329&site=ehost-live.

○ *Newspaper Web site*

Author's Lastname, Firstname. "Title of Article." *Title of Newspaper,* Day Month Year of publication, URL.

Wren, Celia. "Family Bonds, Music Play Together in Quiara Alegria Hudes's 'Water by the Spoonful.'" *The Washington Post,* 28 Feb. 2014, www .washingtonpost.com/entertainment/theater_dance/family-bonds -music-play-together-in-quiara-alegria-hudess-water-by-the-spoonful /2014/02/27/941f00de-9b38-11e3-8112-52fdf646027b_story.html.

15. *Review*

Follow the same guidelines as indicated above for an article in a journal (12), magazine (13), or newspaper (14), but between the title of the review (if any) and the title of the periodical insert the following:

Review of *Title of Work being Reviewed,* by Work Author's Firstname Lastname.

Bunting, Josiah. "Vietnam, Carried On: Tim O'Brien's Intense Collection of Soldiers' Memoirs." Review of *The Things They Carried,* by Tim O'Brien. *The Washington Post,* 23 Apr. 1990, p. B3. *National Newspapers Expanded,* ezproxy.library.unlv.edu/login?url=http://search.proquest.com/docview /408042877?accountid=3611.

Marks, Peter. "'Water by the Spoonful' Dispenses Measured Fury." Review of *Water by the Spoonful,* by Quiara Alegria Hudes. *The Washington Post,* 10 Mar. 2014, www.washingtonpost.com/entertainment/theater _dance/water-by-the-spoonful-dispenses-measured-fury/2014/03/10 /840c1a68-a887-11e3-8a7b-c1c684e2671f_story.html.

Review of *The Bluest Eye,* by Toni Morrison. *Kirkus Reviews,* 1 Oct. 1970.

16. *Interview*

If the interview appears in a book or periodical, your entry will need all of the usual bibliographical information for that kind of source, but it should begin like this:

> Interviewee's Lastname, Firstname. "Title of Interview [if any]." Interview by Interviewer's Firstname Lastname [if known but not indicated in title].

> Collins, Billy. "Pushing Poetry to Lighten Up—And Brighten Up." Interview. *Newsweek*, 8 July 2001, www.newsweek.com/pushing-poetry-lighten -and-brighten-154859.

> Knight, Etheridge. "A MELUS Interview: Etheridge Knight." Interview by Steven C. Tracy. *MELUS*, vol. 12, no. 2, Summer 1985, pp. 7-23. *JSTOR*, www.jstor.org/stable/467427.

For broadcast (television or radio) interviews, format your entry like this:

> Interviewee's Lastname, Firstname. Interview. *Title of Program*. Network, Station, Day Month Year.

> Gates, Henry Louis, Jr. Interview. *Fresh Air*. NPR, WNYC, 9 Apr. 2002.

17. *Republished work*

Give the most recent publication information in whatever format is appropriate for that kind of source. Then insert *Originally published in* followed by the original publication information.

> Komunyakaa, Yusef. "The Body Is Our First Music: Interview with Tony Barnstone and Michael Garabedian." *Blue Notes: Essays, Interviews, and Commentaries*, edited by Radiclani Clytus, U of Michigan P, 2000, pp. 107-25. Originally published in *Poetry Flash*, no. 227, June-July 1998.

> Larkin, Philip. "A Conversation with Ian Hamilton." *Further Requirements: Interviews, Broadcasts, Statements and Book Reviews*, edited by Anthony Thwaite, Faber and Faber, 2001, pp. 19-26. Originally published in *London Magazine*, Nov. 1946.

> Stevenson, R. L. "A Gossip on Romance." *A Victorian Art of Fiction: Essays on the Novel in British Periodicals 1870-1900*, Garland, 1979, pp. 187-99. Originally printed in *Longman's Magazine*, Nov. 1882, pp. 69-79.

18. *Entire Web site*

If the Web site has an author, begin with his or her name. If it instead has an editor, compiler, or director, rather than an author, begin with that person's name, followed by a comma and the appropriate description.

> Lastname, Firstname. *Title of Web Site*. Publisher, Date posted or last updated, URL.

Eaves, Morris, et al., editors. *The William Blake Archive.* 1996-2014, www
.blakearchive.org/blake/.

19. Work from a Web site

Author's Lastname, Firstname. "Title of Work." *Title of Web Site,* edited by Editor's
Firstname Lastname [if any], Publisher. Date posted or last updated, URL.

Viscomi, Joseph. "Illuminated Printing." *The William Blake Archive,* edited
by Morris Eaves et al., 1996-2014, www.blakearchive.org/exist/blake/
archive/biography.xq?b=illum&targ_div=d1.

20. Film

If your essay emphasizes the whole work, your entry should begin
with the title and conclude like this:

Distributor, Date.

In between these, include the names of whatever contributors to the
film are most pertinent, preceding each with the appropriate description (e.g., *directed by, performance by, produced by*). You may also or
instead indicate the author of the screenplay preceded by the words
Screenplay by. Elements should be separated by commas.

A Raisin in the Sun. Screenplay by Lorraine Hansberry, directed by Daniel
Petrie, performances by Sidney Poitier, Claudia McNeil, and Ruby Dee,
Columbia, 1961.

If your essay emphasizes the contribution of a particular individual
(e.g., the screenwriter or director), start your entry with that person's
name; a comma; his or her title; and a period.

Hansberry, Lorraine, adapter. *A Raisin in the Sun,* by Lorraine Hansberry,
directed by Daniel Petrie, performances by Sidney Poitier, Claudia
McNeil, and Ruby Dee, Columbia, 1961.

Petrie, Daniel, director. *A Raisin in the Sun.* Screenplay by Lorraine Hansberry,
performances by Sidney Poitier, Claudia McNeil, and Ruby Dee, Columbia,
1961.

21. Videorecording (DVD, etc.)

Format your entry as indicated above for a film (20), but insert the
film's original year of release and a period immediately after the title;
end your entry with the year of release of the version consulted.

A Raisin in the Sun. 1961. Screenplay by Lorraine Hansberry, directed by
Daniel Petrie, performances by Sidney Poitier, Claudia McNeil, and
Ruby Dee, Columbia, 2000.

SAMPLE RESEARCH ESSAY

The following research essay analyzes Alice Munro's short story Boys and
Girls. As you will see, the essay gives some consideration to the story's biographical and historical contexts, drawing on interviews with Munro and a
sociological study of Canadian farm families. Yet the essay is primarily a critical contexts essay, as we define that term in chapter 20. In addition to considering the critical conversation about this specific short story, however, this
essay examines another critical conversation, one about the initiation-story
genre in general. The essay's literary critical secondary sources thus include
three scholarly articles that focus exclusively on "Boys and Girls," as well as two
articles that make arguments about the initiation story by instead analyzing a
range of other stories. Diverse as are the sources and contexts this essay considers, however, notice that its thesis is an original, debatable interpretive claim
about the literary text (Munro's story) and that the body of the essay supports
and develops that claim by presenting and analyzing evidence from the text.

Roberts 1

Sarah Roberts
Prof. Jernigan
English 204
15 February 2017

"Only a Girl"? Gendered Initiation in Alice Munro's
"Boys and Girls"

In 1960, an article in the *Journal of Aesthetics and Art Criticism*
asked a question still worth asking over fifty years later, "What is an
initiation story?" That article, by Mordecai Marcus, points out that
literary critics frequently "used the term 'initiation' to describe a theme
and a type of story" but that they didn't all use or define it exactly the
same way. Marcus defines it as a story that "show[s] its young protagonist
experiencing a significant change of knowledge about the world or
himself, or a change of character, or of both," which "must point

Roberts establishes a motive for her essay by first presenting two competing scholarly arguments about the initiation story genre, then indicating that she will be both "siding" with the second of these and expanding on it by considering a story the source does not. (Only because her essay will apply and test that source's claims does Roberts need to spell them out in such detail at the end of her opening paragraph.)

Roberts here prepares readers for the consideration of biographical and historical context later in the essay but makes the story and its critical contexts her main focus.

Here, Roberts briefly alludes to the three contributions to the second critical conversation her essay engages with—that about

or lead him towards an adult world" (222). For him, the only significant difference between initiation stories has to do with their endings. He divides them into three types, depending on how far and "decisively" into that "adult world" their protagonists travel by the end (223). Published fifteen years after Marcus's essay, however, Elaine Ginsberg's "The Female Initiation Theme in American Fiction" (1975) suggests that it matters more what gender the story's protagonist is, at least in American fiction. According to her, "the female initiation story is rare in American literature," the first really "legitimat[e]" ones appearing only in the twentieth century (27, 31). Further, she argues those twentieth-century stories follow a pattern that is distinct in at least five ways: (1) "young girls are always introduced to a heterosexual world, in which relationships between men and women . . . are the most important," "a world in which men are always present, always important, and always more free and independent" (31, 37); (2) they "seem to see their future roles as women almost always in relation to men" (31, 36); (3) their "initiation process" involves both "sexual experience" and (4) "dropping" the attributes like boyish "clothing" or "names" that make them "androgynous creatures" at the beginning of the story; and (5) they never seem "to be aided or guided by an older" person of the same sex, as boys in initiation stories are (31). As a result, according to Ginsberg, the "sense of disillusionment, disappointment, and regret is perhaps the most significant characteristic of the female initiate in American literature" (35).

Whether Ginsberg is right about all of American literature, her argument does offer a way to think about a story she doesn't consider, Canadian Nobel Prize-winner Alice Munro's "Boys and Girls." Published in 1968, "Boys and Girls" appeared in *Dance of the Happy Shades*, Munro's first book and the event that basically initiated her career as an author. On the one hand, "Boys and Girls" is clearly a female initiation story. Its narrator is a woman remembering events that happened around the time she was eleven, and it ends with her admitting that "[m]aybe" she truly is "only a girl" (par. 65, 64). Her initiation mostly does follow the pattern Ginsberg outlines in a way that draws on Munro's personal experience and reflects that of other Canadian farm families. On the other hand, however, Munro's

Roberts 3

story does all that even better because it also depicts, as Reingard M. Nischik, Marlene Goldman, and Heliane Ventura show, another character and another initiation—that of the protagonist's younger brother, Laird. As Goldman puts it, the story "highlights the almost invisible societal forces which shape children, in this case, *the narrator and her brother Laird*, into gendered adults" (emphasis added). Rather than being either a male or female initiation story, "Boys and Girls" is both.

Like the heroines in the female initiation stories that Ginsberg discusses, Munro's protagonist starts out as an "androgynous creatur[e]" (31). But in Munro's story, that androgyny doesn't have anything to do with the protagonist's clothes or her name. In "Boys and Girls," clothes and names aren't very important. On the Ontario fox farm where it is set, horses and "foxes all ha[ve] names" (par. 8), but only two human characters in the story do, Laird and "the hired man," Henry Bailey (par. 2). The only pieces of clothing described are a school dress the protagonist wants and her mother makes for her (par. 17), some dresses her mother once wore and describes to her (par. 10), and the aprons both her mother and her father wear when she sees them talking together outside the barn one night (par. 12–13).

Instead of clothes or names, what really makes adult men and women different in the story is, as all the story's critics notice, the kind of work they do, where they do it, and whom they do it with. What makes the outdoor meeting between the parents so "odd" is that the mother does "not often come out of the house" or get much exercise, as the "bumpy" shape and pale color of her legs show. Her workplace is the house and especially the "hot dark kitchen," where she cans and cooks the family's food. The father instead works "out of doors" (par. 13), even if outdoors includes the barn and the fox pens he builds outside it and even if, to the mother's disgust, he has to do the "pelting . . . in the house" in winter (par. 2). Also, the mother performs her work alone and isn't paid for it, but the father gets paid enough for the furs he sells "to the Hudson's Bay Company or the Montreal Fur Traders" to hire Henry Bailey to help him (par. 1).

"Boys and Girls" specifically (rather than the initiation story generally).

Since Roberts's thesis is a claim about Munro's story, so, too, is the topic sentence of each body paragraph, starting with this one. At the same time, she clearly indicates how that claim relates to that of her source (Ginsberg).

Because Roberts's claim here has to do only with *which* "pieces of clothing" are "described" and *whom* they belong to, not *how* they are described, she simply summarizes rather than quotes. Yet parenthetical citations ensure that her readers can find the specific moments in the text to which she refers.

Roberts can simply refer to "the story's critics" here because her introduction has already indicated who they are.

Roberts is careful to spell out the *inference* that makes the fact (the mother's legs are "bumpy" and "pale") evidence for the claim (she "does not 'often come out of the house' or get much exercise").

Here, Roberts is careful to state her claim in her own words, while indicating that it is one also already made by one of her sources (Ventura).

The narrator's androgyny, then, has to do with two things. One is the way she moves across these male and female places and activities, as Ventura observes, too (83). In the kitchen, she is "given jobs to do" like "peeling peaches . . . or cutting up onions" with her mother (par. 13). Outdoors, her "job" includes getting the foxes water and raking up the grass between their pens after her father cuts it (par. 7, 10). But in terms of her androgyny, the second and just as important thing is how close she is to her brother. The narrator and Laird are so much a unit early on in the story that the narrator slips practically automatically from "I" to "we." After she introduces Laird, Henry Bailey, and her mother in the story's second paragraph, when she says in the next one, "*We* admired him [Henry] for this performance" and "It was . . . always possible that" he "might be [laughing] at *us*," it's not exactly clear who "we" or "us" means until she starts the next paragraph by saying, "After *we* had been sent to bed" (emphasis added). And this paragraph is all about the bedroom that she and her brother share, their shared fears about it, and the "rules" they both follow to make themselves feel safe (par. 4). As Goldman argues, this room is the only place in the story that isn't either clearly "male" or "female," its "unfinished state" symbolizing "the undifferentiated consciousness of the children" at this point in the story.

Roberts doesn't need to include a parenthetical citation here only because the source is unpaginated and its author's name is mentioned in a signal phrase ("As Goldman argues").

What's strange about this, however, is that even though they share so much, Laird is actually treated differently. He helps out when it comes to outdoor work like watering the foxes, but there's never any hint that he helps out in the house. There is a difference between boy and girl in terms of the work they do from the very beginning, even if it's not a difference the narrator or the story's critics point out. What two critics (Ventura and Nischik) do point out is another difference, that unlike the narrator, Laird gets a name, and his name is Scottish for "landowner": ". . . Laird is a potential laird, the male heir to the family" (Ventura 82).

Roberts's signal phrase indicates that two sources make the same observation, even though she only quotes one source. To specify which of the two sources she quotes, Roberts repeats its author's name in her parenthetical citation.

In these ways, the story seems to accurately reflect the reality of life on Canadian family farms through the 1950s and 1960s. As Munro, who grew up on one, insists in one interview, because "what's going on" on those farms, "chiefly, is [or was] making enough to live on," "everybody has to work and be useful to the family" ("Interview" 183). Based on her study of ten farm families (in Saskatchewan instead of Ontario), sociologist June Corman describes that work as "distinctly gendered." While men had legal "title to the land" and "retained control of the agricultural income-producing work" in which "women . . . were not extensively involved," women "laboured . . . to make home made essentials instead of buying consumer goods so farm income could be used to pay down . . . debt" (70). Furthermore, she argues, "This structured gendered division of labour had implications for their . . . children": "From childhood onward girls learned" both "the skills required of farm wives" and "at least a minimal amount of skills related to grain and livestock production." But boys worked exclusively with their fathers and learned "agricultural skills but . . . not . . . domestic knowledge" (71). Farm families required equal work from all members of the family but not the same work.

At the same time that she reflects this reality about Canadian farm life, Munro's choice to focus specifically on a fox farm like the one she grew up on takes on importance in terms of how female and male worlds are characterized in the story. It's not entirely clear in the story that men are truly any more "free and independent" than women are, as Ginsberg suggests is true in a lot of female initiation stories (37), since both the mother and the father are "enslaved by the farm, harassed by [their] work" (Ventura 85). But Goldman does seem right to say that men's work in this story is all about controlling other wild and even dangerous creatures. "Alive, the foxes inhabited a world my father made for them," the narrator explains (par. 7). Here, they "prow[l] up and down" inside "sturdy pens" that are "surrounded by a high guard fence"with a "padlocked" gate that no one but the narrator's father is ever brave enough to go into (par. 9, 7). And, as Goldman points out, the fox pen does sort of resemble "[t]he dark, hot, stifling kitchen [that] imprisons the narrator's mother and threatens to imprison the narrator."

Maybe as a result of his power and bravery, the protagonist—as Nischik, Ventura, and Goldman all notice—clearly sees her father's work and world as superior to her mother's. She "hate[s]" the kitchen, whose "bumpy linoleum" resembles her mother's

Roberts here specifies the basis for the source's claims (a "study of ten," Saskatchewan "farm families") and the author's key credential ("sociologist").

Rather than letting her source get the last word in her paragraph, Roberts summarizes the key point in her own words.

Roberts transitions from one paragraph/ claim to another by restating the main idea of the last paragraph in the first part of this sentence and then, in the second part, stating the claim developed in this paragraph.

"lumpy legs," and sees housework as so "endless, dreary and peculiarly depressing" that she runs away as soon as she can (par. 13). But her father's "world," especially the pens he creates, seems to her "tidy and ingenious" (par. 7). And his work seems to her so "tirelessly inventive" (par. 7) and "ritualistically important" (par. 13) that she always helps him "willingly . . . and with a feeling of pride" (par. 10).

The adults around her reinforce that feeling. The only time her father praises her, he does it by calling her a "man" (par. 10), even specifically his "new hired man." In saying that, he compares her to Henry Bailey, which is interesting, but more important, he communicates the same message about the jobs of men and women and their unequal worth that the salesman does when he responds to the father by saying, "I thought it was only a girl." Paired with the word *only*, the word *girl*, as the narrator thinks later, becomes a label "always touched . . . with reproach and disappointment" or even "a joke on [her]" that the real hired man, Henry, especially, finds funny (par. 21). The label also gets associated with prohibitions as much as confinement. When the narrator's grandmother (the last of only three female characters total) arrives on the scene, the only thing we hear from her are commands about the things girls shouldn't do—"slam doors," sit with their knees apart, ask questions (par. 22).

The narrator *is* thus, in a way, "aided or guided by an older" person of the same sex, as boys in initiation stories are, according to Ginsberg (31). But that aid isn't positive. In fact, the girl actually sees her mother as her "enemy" because she thinks her mother is the one "plotting" to imprison her in the house and the lesser adult role it implies (par. 17). She sees that her mother is "kinder than [her] father" and "love[s] her" enough to stay up all night making the "difficult" dress she wants for school. But she still sides with her father and even likes his dismissive attitude toward her mother when they talk about her in the yard: "I was pleased by the way he stood listening [to her], politely as he would to a salesman or a stranger, but with an air of wanting to get on with his real work" (par. 15), she says, "I did not expect my father to pay any attention to what she said" (par. 18).

Roberts needs quotations in this paragraph because her claim is about how the narrator "sees" things, something she can only prove by showing us how the narrator describes them. Notice, though, how only the most relevant language is quoted.

Roberts 7

Goldman identifies a parallel between the protagonist's attitudes to her mother and the foxes. As Goldman puts it, just as she earlier in the story "does not comprehend that the hostility she sees in the foxes' 'malevolent faces' . . . is a response to their enforced captivity," so she now interprets "her mother's behaviour . . . not as an expression of frustration and disappointment, or loneliness, but as a manifestation of innate wickedness and petty tyranny. . . ." What Goldman doesn't say is that we learn about these other possible interpretations, however, because the adult narrator *does* see them. When the narrator says, "*It did not occur to me* that she could be lonely, or jealous" (par. 17; emphasis added), it's obvious that it *does* occur to her *now,* as an adult.

In this way, too, the story actually seems to reflect and bend reality, but in this case the reality of Munro's personal life instead of Canadian farm families'. Munro biographer Hallvard Dahlie claims that many Munro stories include "unfulfilled and despairing mothers" like Munro's real mother, a former teacher who "expended her energies during the formative years of the three Laidlaw children in the nurturing of a family under conditions of deprivation and hardship" (qtd. in Nischik). In interviews, Munro often mentions her mother in a way that implies her attitude toward her mother changed in the same way her narrator-protagonist's does. She told *The New Yorker* that her "mother . . . is still a main figure in my life because her life was so sad and unfair and she so brave, but also because she was determined to make me into the Sunday-school-recitation little girl I was, from the age of seven or so, fighting not to be" ("On 'Dear'"). She told *The Paris Review,* "The tenderness I feel now for my mother, I didn't feel for a long time" ("Alice"). At the same time, Munro leaves out of "Boys and Girls" one of the things that made her real-life mother's life particularly "sad and unfair," which was the fact that she had Parkinson's disease. By not giving her fictional mother that kind of illness or even a name, for that matter, Munro makes her more like all women, just as she makes her story about boys versus girls (period) by not giving the protagonist what she had in real life—a sister and a brother.

Because Roberts found the quotation from one source (Hallvard Dahlie's biography of Munro) in another (Nischik's article), she puts the essential information about the original source in a signal phrase ("Munro biographer Hallvard Dahlie claims . . ."), then uses the parenthetical citation to tell us which of her sources it was quoted in ("qtd. in Nischik").

Because Roberts doesn't mention the titles of these sources in a signal phrase, she needs parenthetical citations. The latter don't include page numbers only because these sources are unpaginated.

Roberts doesn't cite a source for the fact that Munro's mother had Parkinson's, two daughters, and a son because this is common knowledge.

Roberts 8

In the story, the protagonist's full initiation into womanhood doesn't really involve a change in her relationship to her mother. (Late in the story she does think about confiding in her, but she doesn't [par. 51].) Instead, it involves changes in the way she relates to her father, animals, and her brother. That change begins with the scene where she and Laird secretly witness their father and Henry shooting the horse, Mack. We can tell that what she sees disturbs her partly because her legs shake and partly because she suddenly mentions a memory of Laird that makes her feel "the sadness of unexorcized guilt" (par. 37). But the question is why, since she and her brother have watched their father killing and skinning other animals and, unlike their mother, weren't bothered by that or the gross smells it produced (par. 2)? Or, as she herself explains,

> I did not have any great feeling of horror and opposition, such as a city child might have had. I was used to see-ing the death of animals as a necessity by which we lived. Yet I felt a little ashamed, and there was a new wariness, a sense of holding-off, in my attitude to my father and his work. (par. 43)

By putting the narrator's characterizations of Mack's and Flora's different reactions to their imprisonment in parentheses, Roberts substantiates her claim about the narrator's detailed descriptions, while staying focused on this paragraph's main topic—the narrator's *feelings about* the horses.

There are many possible reasons for her reaction, but one might be that even before this point the girl begins to identify with the horses in a way she never does with the foxes. It is when—in her life and in the story—she is beginning to feel most pressured about being a girl and first expresses a wish to remain "free" that she remembers to mention how the foxes were fed at all and to describe, in detail, the two particular horses, Mack and Flora, and the different ways they respond to their similarly unfree situation (par. 22). (Mack is "slow and easy to handle"; Flora rears and kicks at people and fences [par. 20, 23].) That identification might explain why she might suddenly have a new "wariness" of her father and his work after seeing one of the horses killed (par. 43).

That feeling might be compounded, too, by the way Henry behaves, especially the fact that he laughs about Mack being shot in the same ways he's already laughed at her more than once in the story (par. 2, 21). But her sense of being "ashamed" about the shooting seems to come from seeing how she in a way acted like

Roberts 9

him long ago when she endangered her little brother's life just "for excitement" (par. 43, 37). As Goldman argues,

> Bailey's laughter [when "the horse kicks its legs in the air"] is particularly unnerving because it fully exposes his delight in power based on sheer inequality.
>
> The narrator recognizes this as an abuse of power . . . as a result of her own experience. She, too, lorded power over an innocent victim. . . .

It doesn't seem surprising, then, that when the narrator has the chance to save Flora ten days later, even just temporarily, she just does it without "mak[ing] any decision" or even "understand[ing] why" (par. 48, 50). By doing that, in Ventura's words, "the girl vicariously achieves her own temporary liberation" (84), and, in Goldman's words, "she radically breaks from her male-identified position." As the narrator points out, she disobeys her father for the very first time in her life and in a way she knows will change their relationship forever (par. 50). Rather than helping him as she's always wanted to do before, she "make[s] more work for" him by letting Flora go (par. 50). Worse, she knows that once he figures out what she's done he won't "trust me any more," but "would know that I was not entirely on his side. I was on Flora's side . . ." (par. 50). Her change of "side[s]," though, isn't complete or recognized by other people until dinner. When the truth about how she let Flora go is revealed, her father responds in a way that "absolved and dismissed [her] for good" by repeating the words the salesman used earlier, "She's only a girl" (par. 64). More important, the narrator doesn't "protest . . . , even in [her] heart" (par. 65). Like Mack and unlike the foxes and Flora, she now silently accepts her fate.

Just as important, though, is the way she separates herself from her brother. At the exact same time that the narrator permanently separates herself from her father, by letting Flora out, she also separates herself from Laird in a way that seems ironic, given that it was in a way sympathy with Laird or guilt about him that started the change in her in the first place. At any rate, when Henry and her father go off to get Flora, Laird goes with them, but the narrator doesn't. When she says, "I shut the gate after they were all gone,"

Here, as throughout the essay, Roberts never substitutes the claim of a source for the textual evidence necessary to substantiate and develop it.

To reinforce her claim about the narrator's development over the course of the story and connect the earlier parts of her essay with the later ones, Roberts briefly alludes to evidence and a point she made earlier.

it seems like the first time in the story that Henry, the father, and Laird become a "they" that doesn't include her (par. 49). At least it seems like a far cry from the "we" she and Laird are early in the story. Importantly, though, it isn't really true that, as Ventura claims, the narrator "is not allowed aboard the bouncing truck" because she, unlike Laird, never actually asks to go (86). That change in her relationship to Laird is confirmed by the way, in between Flora's escape and the dinner that ends the story, the narrator mentions their bedroom one more time. In addition to decorating her part of the room, she "planned to put up some kind of barricade between [her] bed and Laird's, to keep my section separate from his" (par. 52).

As Goldman argues, though, Laird's very different initiation and behavior are significant:

> As they lift him into the truck, the little boy becomes a man: he joins the hunting party. Upon his return, he brandishes the streak of blood on his arm. . . . [T]he mark of blood and the domination of the Other continues to function as a crucial element in the rites of manhood. The boy cements his alliance with the father on the basis of their mutual triumph over nature.

In fact, that "alliance" isn't "cemented" until that night, when Laird, "look[ing] across the table at" her "proudly, distinctly" tells her secret to everyone (par. 56). In a weird way, he reverses the roles they each play in the memory that sparks her change—now he's the powerful one who leaves her figuratively hanging.

Here, though, is where the male and female initiations in this one story differ in a way that totally accords with Ginsberg's argument. Laird becomes a man in relationship to other men, grown-ups of his own gender, but in a way that has nothing to do with actual sex. Like the protagonists of most female initiation stories, according to Ginsberg, however, the protagonist of this one "seem[s] to see [her] future rol[e] as [a] wom[a]n . . . in relation to men" in a way that involves "sexual experience" (31). We see this in the stories she tells herself at night. Where the stories she makes up at the beginning of the story are all adventure stories in which she does things like shoot animals (just as Laird actually ends up doing by the end of this story), the stories she makes up at the end of the story are more like romances featuring boys she knows from school or one of her male teachers (par. 52).

If we go back to Marcus's question, "What is an initiation story?," then, "Boys and Girls" shows us that Ginsberg is right to say that the answer can depend most on whether the story features boys, girls, or "boys and girls." Or at least it once did, because here is where it might matter that Munro's story was published in 1968 and is set much earlier. In interviews, Munro expresses the idea that things were, in real life, changing even in her generation, which is also, as Nischik points out, her protagonist's. "If I had been a farm girl of a former generation," she says in one interview, "I wouldn't have had a chance" to go to college or be a writer, for example." Instead, her only option would have been to become a farm wife like her own mother or her protagonist's mother. "But in the generation that I was, there were scholarships. Girls were not encouraged to get them, but you could. I could imagine, from an early age, that I would be a writer" ("Interview" 183). Even if her protagonist never explicitly imagines herself some day being a writer, she is writing stories in her head every night. And that doesn't change over the course of the story, even if the kinds of stories she tells do. Even if at the end of the story the protagonist ends up accepting the idea that she is "only a girl" and not saying anything, the fact that she keeps telling herself stories and that she is, in fact, narrating her story to us as an adult suggests that the end of the story *isn't* the end of the story. Girls don't have to grow up to be "only" one thing after all. They can grow up to tell both their stories and their brothers. They can even win Nobel Prizes for it.

Roberts opens her conclusion by referring us back to the "frame" she established in the beginning— the different views of two sources (Marcus and Ginsberg).

Works Cited

Corman, June. "The 'Good Wife' and Her Farm Husband: Changing Household Practices in Rural Saskatchewan." *Canadian Woman Studies*, vol. 24, no. 4, Summer/Fall 2005, pp. 68-74. *GenderWatch*, ezproxy.library.unlv.edu/login?url=http://search.proquest.com /docview/217447689?accountid=3611.

Ginsberg, Elaine. "The Female Initiation Theme in American Fiction." *Studies in American Fiction*, vol. 3, no. 1, Spring 1975, pp. 27-37. *Periodicals Archive Online*, ezproxy.library.unlv.edu/login?url=http:// search.proquest.com/docview/1297894583?accountid=3611.

Goldman, Marlene. "Penning in the Bodies: The Construction of Gendered Subjects in Alice Munro's 'Boys and Girls.'" *Studies in Canadian Literature*, vol. 15, no. 1, 1990, journals.lib.unb.ca/index.php/SCL/article /view/8112.

Marcus, Mordecai. "What Is an Initiation Story?" *The Journal of Aesthetics and Art Criticism*, vol. 19, no. 2, Winter 1960, pp. 221-28. *JSTOR*, doi:10.2307/428289.

Munro, Alice. "Alice Munro, The Art of Fiction No. 137." Interview by Jeanne McCulloch and Mona Simpson. *The Paris Review*, no. 131, Summer 1994, www.theparisreview.org/interviews/1791/the-art-of-fiction-no -137-alice-munro.

---. "Boys and Girls." *The Norton Introduction to Literature*, edited by Kelly J. Mays, portable 12th ed., W. W. Norton, 2017, pp. 400-12.

---. "An Interview with Alice Munro." Interview by Lisa Dickler Awano. *Virginia Quarterly Review*, vol. 89, no. 2, Spring 2013, pp. 180-84. *Academic Search Main Edition*, ezproxy.library.unlv.edu/login?url =http://search.ebscohost.com/login.aspx?direct=true&db=asm &AN=87119387&site=ehost-live.

---. "On 'Dear Life': An Interview with Alice Munro." Interview by Deborah Treisman. *The New Yorker*, 20 Nov. 2012, www.newyorker.com /books/page-turner/on-dear-life-an-interview-with-alice-munro.

Nischik, Reingard M. "(Un-)Doing Gender: Alice Munro, 'Boys and Girls' (1964)." *Contemporary Literary Criticism*, edited by Lawrence J. Trudeau, vol. 370, Gale, 2015. *Literature Resource Center*, go.galegroup .com/ps/i.do?id=GALE%7CH1100118828&v=2.1&u=unlv_main&it=r&p =LitRC&sw=w&asid=1ec18259fbc8af3aecfc233e918cf0e8. Originally published in *The Canadian Short Story*, edited by Nischik, Camden House, 2007, pp. 203-18.

Ventura, Heliane. "Alice Munro's 'Boys and Girls': Mapping out Boundaries." *Commonwealth*, no. 15, Autumn 1992, pp. 80-87.

Critical Approaches

F

ew human abilities are more remarkable than the ability to read and interpret literature. A computer program or a database can't perform the complex process of reading and interpreting—not to mention writing about—a literary text, although computers can easily exceed human powers of processing codes and information. Readers follow the sequence of printed words and as if by magic re-create a scene between characters in a novel or play, or they respond to the almost inexpressible emotional effect of a poem's figurative language. Experienced readers can pick up on a multitude of literary signals all at once. With rereading and some research, readers can draw on information such as the author's life or the time period when this work and others like it were first published. Varied and complex as the approaches to literary criticism may be, they are not difficult to learn. For the most part schools of criticism and theory have developed to address questions that any reader can begin to answer.

There are essentially three participants in what could be called the literary exchange or interaction: the *text*, the *source* (the *author* and other factors that produce the text), and the *receiver* (the *reader* and other aspects of *reception*). All the varieties of literary analysis concern themselves with these aspects of the literary exchange in varying degrees and with varying emphases. Although each of these elements has a role in any form of literary analysis, systematic studies of literature and its history have defined approaches or methods that focus on the different elements and circumstances of the literary interaction. The first three sections below—"Emphasis on the Text," "Emphasis on the Source," and "Emphasis on the Receiver"—describe briefly those schools or modes of literary analysis that have concentrated on one of the three participants while de-emphasizing the others. These different emphases, plainly speaking, are habits of asking different kinds of questions. Answers or interpretations will vary according to the questions we ask of a literary work. In practice the range of questions can be—and to some extent *should* be—combined whenever we develop a literary interpretation. Such questions can always generate the thesis or argument of a critical essay.

Although some approaches to literary analysis treat the literary exchange (text, source, receiver) in isolation from the world surrounding that exchange (the world of economics, politics, religion, cultural tradition, and sexuality—in other words, the world in which we live), most contemporary modes of analysis acknowledge the importance of that world to the literary exchange.

These days, even if literary scholars want to focus on the text or its source or receiver, they will often incorporate some of the observations and methods developed by theorists and critics who have turned their attention toward the changing world surrounding the formal conventions of literature, the writing process and writer's career, and the reception or response to literature. We describe the work of such theorists and critics in the fourth section below, "Historical and Ideological Criticism."

Before expanding on the kinds of critical approaches within these four categories, let's consider one example in which questions concerning the text, source, and receiver, as well as a consideration of historical and ideological questions, would contribute to a richer interpretation of a text. To begin as usual with preliminary questions about the *text*: What is "First Fight. Then Fiddle."? Printed correctly on a separate piece of paper, the text would tell us at once that it is a poem because of its form: rhythm, repeating word sounds, lines that leave very wide margins on the page. Because you are reading this poem in this book, you know even more about its form (in this way, the publication *source* gives clues about the *text*). By putting it in a section with other poetry, we have told you it is a poem worth reading, rereading, and thinking about. (What other ways do you encounter poems, and what does the medium in which a poem is presented tell you about it?)

You should pursue other questions focused on the text. What *kind* of poem is it? Here we have helped you, especially if you are not already familiar with the sonnet form, by grouping this poem with other sonnets (in The Sonnet: An Album). Classifying "First Fight. Then Fiddle." as a sonnet might then prompt you to interpret the ways that this poem is or is not like other sonnets. Well and good: You can check off its fourteen lines of (basically) iambic pentameter and note its somewhat unusual rhyme scheme and meter in relation to the rules of Italian and English sonnets. But *why* does this experiment with the sonnet form matter?

To answer questions about the purpose of form, you need to answer some basic questions about *source*, such as *When* was this sonnet written and published? *Who* wrote it? *What* do you know about Gwendolyn Brooks, about 1949, about African American women and/or poets in the United States at that time? A short historical and biographical essay answering such questions might help put the "sonnetness" of "First Fight. Then Fiddle." in context. But assembling all the available information about the source and original context of the poem, even some sort of documented testimony from Brooks about her intentions or interpretation of it, would still leave room for other questions leading to new interpretations.

What about the *receiver* of "First Fight. Then Fiddle."? Even within the poem a kind of audience exists. This sonnet seems to be a set of instructions addressed to "you." (Although many sonnets are addressed by a speaker, "I," to an auditor, "you," such address rarely sounds like a series of military commands, as it does here.) This internal audience is not of course to be confused with real people responding to the poem, and it is the latter who are its *receivers*. How did readers respond to it when it was first published? Can you find any published reviews, or any criticism of this sonnet published in studies of Gwendolyn Brooks?

Questions about the receiver, like those about the author and other sources, readily connect with questions about historical and cultural context. Would a reader or someone listening to this poem read aloud respond differently in the years after World War II than in an age of global terrorism? Does it make a difference if the audience addressed by the speaker inside the poem is imagined as a group of African American men and women or as a group of European American male commanders? (The latter question could be regarded as an inquiry involving the text and the source as well as the receiver.) Does a reader need to identify with any of the particular groups the poem fictitiously addresses, or would any reader, from any background, respond to it the same way? Even the formal qualities of the text could be examined through historical lenses: The sonnet form has been associated with prestigious European literature, and with themes of love and mortality, since the Renaissance. It is significant that a twentieth-century African American poet chose *this* traditional form to twist "threadwise" into a poem about conflict.

The above are only some of the worthwhile questions that might help illuminate this short, intricate poem. (We will develop a few more thoughts about it in illustrating different approaches to the text and to the source.) Similarly, the complexity of critical approaches far exceeds our four categories. While a great deal of worthwhile scholarship and criticism borrows from a range of theories and methods, below we give necessarily simplified descriptions of various critical approaches that have continuing influence. We cannot trace a history of the issues involved, or the complexity and controversies within these movements. Instead think of what follows as a road map to the terrain of literary analysis. Many available resources describe the entire landscape of literary analysis in more precise detail. If you are interested in learning more about these or any other analytical approaches, consult the works listed in the bibliography at the end of this chapter.

EMPHASIS ON THE TEXT

This broad category encompasses approaches that de-emphasize questions about the author/source or the reader/reception in order to focus on the work itself. In a sense any writing about literature presupposes recognition of form, in that it deems the object of study to *be* a literary work that belongs to a genre or subgenre of literature, as Brooks's poem belongs with sonnets. Moreover, almost all literary criticism notes some details of style or structure, some *intrinsic* features such as the relation between dialogue or narration, or the pattern of rhyme and meter. But *formalist* approaches go further by foregrounding the design of the text itself above all or most other considerations.

Some formalists, reasonably denying the division of content from form (since the form is an aspect of the content or meaning), have more controversially excluded any discussion of *extrinsic* or contextual (versus textual) matters such as the author's biography or questions of psychology, sociology, or history. This has led to accusations that formalism, in avoiding relevance to actual authors and readers or to the world of economic power or social change, also avoids political issues or commitments. Some historical or ideological critics have therefore argued that formalism supports the powers that be, since it precludes protest. Conversely, some formalists charge that any extrinsic—that is, historical, political, ideological, as well as biographical or psychological—interpretations of literature reduce the text to a set of more or less cleverly encoded messages or propaganda. A formalist might maintain that the inventive wonders of art exceed any practical function it serves. In practice, influential formalists have generated modes of *close reading* that balance attention to form, significance, and social context, with some acknowledgment of the political implications of literature. In the early twenty-first century the formalist methods of close reading remain influential, especially in classrooms. Indeed, *The Norton Introduction to Literature* adheres to these methods in its presentation of elements and interpretation of form.

New Criticism

One strain of formalism, loosely identified as the New Criticism, dominated literary studies from approximately the 1920s to the 1970s. New Critics rejected both of the approaches that prevailed then in the relatively new field of English studies: the dry analysis of the development of the English language, and the misty-eyed appreciation and evaluation of "Great Works." Generally, New Criticism minimizes consideration of both the source and the receiver, emphasizing instead the intrinsic qualities of a unified literary work. Psychological or historical information about the author, the intentions or feelings of authors or readers, and any philosophical or socially relevant "messages" derived from the work all are out of bounds in a New Critical reading. The text in a fundamental way refers to itself: Its medium is its message. Although interested in ambiguity and irony as well as figurative language, a New Critical reader considers the organic unity of the unique work. Like an organism, the work develops in a synergetic relation of parts to whole.

A New Critic might, for example, publish an article titled "A Reading of 'First Fight. Then Fiddle.'" (The method works best with **lyric** or other short forms because it requires painstaking attention to details such as metaphors or alliteration.) Little if anything would be said of Gwendolyn Brooks or the poem's relation to Modernist poetry. The critic's task is to give credit to the poem, not the poet or the period, and if it is a good poem, then—implicitly— it can't be merely "about" World War II or civil rights. New Criticism presumes that a good literary work symbolically embodies universal human themes and may be interpreted objectively on many levels. These levels may be related more by tension and contradiction than harmony, yet that relation demonstrates the coherence of the whole.

Thus the New Critic's essay might include some of the following observations. The title—which reappears as half of the first line—consists of a pair of two-word imperative sentences, and most statements in the poem paraphrase these two sentences, especially the first of them, "First fight." Thus an alliterative two-word command, "Win war" (line 12), follows a longer version of such a command: "But first to arms, to armor" (9). Echoes of this sort of exhortation appear throughout. We, as audience, begin to feel "bewitch[ed], bewilder[ed]" (4) by a buildup of undesirable urgings, whether at the beginning of a line ("Be deaf," 11) or the end of a line ("Be remote," 7; "Carry hate," 9) or in the middle of a line ("Rise bloody," 12). It's hardly what we would want to do. Yet the speaker makes a strong case for the practical view that a society needs to take care of defense before it can "devote" itself to "silks and honey" (6–7), that is, the soft and sweet pleasures of art. But what kind of culture would place "hate / In front of . . . harmony" and try to ignore "music" and "beauty" (9–11)? What kind of people are only "remote / A while from malice and from murdering" (6–7)? A society of warlike heroes would rally to this speech. Yet on rereading, many of the words jar with the tone of heroic battle cry.

The New Critic examines not only the speaker's style and words but also the order of ideas and lines in the poem. Ironically, the poem defies the speaker's command; it fiddles first, and then fights, as the octave (first eight lines) concern art, and the sestet (last six) concern war. The New Critic might be delighted by the irony that the two segments of the poem in fact unite, in that their topics—octave on how to fiddle, sestet on how to fight—mirror each other. The beginning of the poem plays with metaphors for music and art as means of inflicting "hurting love" (line 3) or emotional conquest, that is, ways to "fight." War and art are both, as far as we know, universal in all human societies. The poem, then, is an organic whole that explores timeless concerns.

Later critics have pointed out that New Criticism, despite its avoidance of extrinsic questions, had a political context of its own. The affirmation of unity for the artwork and humanities in general should be regarded as a strategy adapted during the Cold War as a counterbalance to the politicization of art in fascist and communist regimes. New Criticism also provided a program for literary reading that is accessible to beginners regardless of their social background, which was extremely useful at a time when more women, minorities, and members of the working class than ever before were entering college. By the 1970s these same groups had helped generate two sources of opposition to New Criticism's ostensible neutrality and transparency: critical studies that emphasized the politics of social differences (e.g., feminist criticism), and theoretical approaches, based on linguistics, philosophy, and political theory, that effectively distanced nonspecialists once more.

Structuralism

Whereas New Criticism was largely a British and American phenomenon, structuralism and its successor, poststructuralism, derive primarily from French theorists. Strains of structuralism also emerged in the Soviet Union and in Prague. Each of these movements was drawn to scientific objectivity and at the same time wary of political commitment. Politics, after all, had been the rallying cry for censorship of science, art, and inquiry throughout centuries and in recent memory.

Structuralist philosophy, however, was something rather new. Influenced by the French linguist Ferdinand de Saussure (1857–1913), structuralists sought an objective system for studying the principles of language. Saussure distinguished between individual uses of language, such as the sentences you or I might have just spoken or written (*parole*), and the sets of rules of English or any language (*langue*). Just as a structuralist linguist would study the interrelations of signs in the *langue* rather than the variations in specific utterances in *parole*, a structuralist critic of literature or culture would study shared systems of meaning, such as genres or myths that pass from one country or period to another, rather than a certain poem in isolation (the favored subject of New Criticism).

Another structuralist principle derived from Saussure is the emphasis on the arbitrary association between a word and what it is said to signify—that is, between the *signifier* and the *signified*. The word "horse," for example, has no divine, natural, or necessary connection to that four-legged, domesticated mammal, which is named by other combinations of sounds and letters in other languages. Any language is a network of relations among such arbitrary signifiers, just as each word in the dictionary must be defined using other words in that dictionary. Structuralists largely attribute the meanings of words to rules of differentiation from other words. Such differences may be phonetic (as among the words "cat" and "bat" and "hat") or they may belong to conceptual associations (as among the words "dinky," "puny," "tiny," "small," "miniature," "petite," "compact"). Structuralist thought has particularly called attention to the way that opposites or dualisms such as "night" and "day" or "feminine" and "masculine" define each other through their differences from each other rather than in direct reference to objective reality. For example, the earth's motion around the sun produces changing exposure to sunlight daily and seasonally, but by linguistic convention we call it "night" between, let's say, 8 p.m. and 5 a.m., no matter how light it is. (We may differ in opinions about "evening" or "dawn." But our "day" at work may begin or end in the dark.) The point is that arbitrary labels divide what in fact is continuous.

Structuralism's linguistic insights have greatly influenced literary studies. Like New Criticism, structuralism shows little interest in the creative
process or in authors, their intentions, or their circumstances. Similarly,
structuralism discounts the idiosyncrasies of particular readings; it takes texts
to represent interactions of words and ideas that stand apart from individual
human identities or sociopolitical commitments. Structuralist approaches have
applied less to lyric poetry than to myths, narratives, and cultural practices,
such as sports or fashion. Although structuralism tends to affirm a universal
humanity just as New Critics do, its work in comparative mythology and
anthropology challenged the absolute value that New Criticism tended to
grant to time-honored canons of great literature.

The structuralist would regard a text not as a self-sufficient icon but as
part of a network of conventions. A structuralist essay on "First Fight. Then
Fiddle." might ask why the string is plied with the "feathery sorcery" (line 2)
of the "bow" (7). These words suggest the art of a Native American trickster
or primitive sorcerer, while at the same time the instrument is a disguised
weapon: a stringed bow with feathered arrows (the term "muzzle" is a similar
pun, suggesting an animal's snout and the discharging end of a gun). Or is
the fiddle—a violin played in musical forms such as bluegrass—a metaphor
for popular art or folk resistance to official culture? In many folk tales a hero
is taught to play the fiddle by the devil or tricks the devil with a fiddle or
similar instrument. Further, a structuralist reading might attach great significance to the sonnet form as a paradigm that has shaped poetic expression for centuries. The classic "turn" or reversal of thought in a sonnet may
imitate the form of many narratives of departure and return, separation and
reconciliation. Brooks's poem repeats in the numerous short reversing
imperatives, as well as in the structure of octave versus sestet, the eternal
oscillation between love and death, creation and destruction.

Poststructuralism

By emphasizing the paradoxes of dualisms and the ways that language con-
structs our awareness, structuralism planted the seeds of its own destruction or, rather, deconstruction. Dualisms (e.g., masculine/feminine, mind/
body, culture/nature) cannot be separate-but-equal; rather, they take effect
as differences of power in which one dominates the other. Yet as the German philosopher of history Georg Wilhelm Friedrich Hegel (1770–1831)
insisted, the relations of the dominant and subordinate, of master and slave
readily invert themselves. The master is dominated by his need for the slave's
subordination; the possession of subordinates defines his mastery. As
Brooks's poem implies, each society reflects its own identity through an
opposing "they," in a dualism of civilized/barbaric. The instability of the
speaker's position in this poem (is he or she among the conquerors or the
conquered?) is a model of the instability of roles throughout the human

world. There is no transcendent ground—except on another planet, perhaps—from which to measure the relative positions of the polar opposites on Earth. Roland Barthes (1915–80) and others, influenced by the radical movements of the 1960s and the increasing complexity of culture in an era of mass consumerism and global media, extended structuralism into more profoundly relativist perspectives.

Poststructuralism is the broad term used to designate the philosophical position that attacks the objective, universalizing claims of most fields of knowledge since the eighteenth century. Poststructuralists, distrusting the optimism of a positivist philosophy that suggests the world is knowable and explainable, ultimately doubt the possibility of certainties of any kind, since language signifies only through a chain of other words rather than through any fundamental link to reality. This argument derives from structuralism, yet it also criticizes structuralist universalism and avoidance of political issues. *Ideology* is a key conceptual ingredient in the poststructuralist argument against structuralism. Ideology is a slippery term that can broadly be defined as a socially shared set of ideas that shape behavior; often it refers to the values that legitimate the ruling interests in a society, and in many accounts it is the hidden code that is officially denied. (We discuss kinds of "ideological" criticism later.) Poststructuralist theory has played a part in a number of critical schools introduced below, not all of them focused on the text. But in literary criticism, poststructuralism has marshaled most forces under the banner of deconstruction.

Deconstruction

Deconstruction insists on the logical impossibility of knowledge that is not influenced or biased by the words used to express it. Deconstruction also claims that language is incapable of representing any sort of reality directly. As practiced by its most famous proponent, the French philosopher Jacques Derrida (1930–2004), deconstruction endeavors to trace the way texts imply the contradiction of their explicit meanings. The deconstructionist delights in the sense of dizziness as the grounds of conviction crumble away; *aporia*, or irresolvable doubt, is the desired, if fleeting, end of an encounter with a text. Deconstruction threatens *humanism*, or the worldview that is centered on human values and the self-sufficient individual, because it denies that there is an ultimate, solid reality on which to base truth or the identity of the self. All values and identities are constructed by the competing systems of meaning, or *discourses*. This is a remarkably influential set of ideas that you will meet again as we discuss other approaches.

The traditional concept of the author as creative origin of the text comes under fire in deconstructionist criticism, which emphasizes instead the creative power of language or the text, and the ingenious work of the critic in detecting gaps and contradictions in writing. Thus, like New Criticism, deconstruction disregards the author and concentrates on textual close reading, but unlike New Criticism, it features the role of the reader as well. Moreover, the text need not be respected as a pure and coherent icon. Deconstructionists might "read" many kinds of writing and representation in other media in much the same way that they might read Milton's *Paradise Lost*, that is, irreverently. Indeed, when deconstruction erupted in university departments of literature, traditional critics and scholars feared the breakdown of the distinctions between literature and criticism and between literature and many other kinds of texts. Many attacks on literary theory have particularly lambasted deconstructionists for apparently rejecting all the reasons to care about literature in the first place and for writing in a style so flamboyantly obscure that no one but specialists can understand. Yet in practice Derrida and others have carried harmony before them, to paraphrase Brooks; their readings can delight in the play of figurative language, thereby enhancing rather than debunking the value of literature.

A deconstructionist might read "First Fight. Then Fiddle." in a manner somewhat similar to the New Critic's, but with even more focus on puns and paradoxes and on the poem's resistance to organic unity. For instance, the two alliterative commands, "fight" and "fiddle," might be opposites, twins, or inseparable consequences of each other. The word "fiddle" is tricky. Does it suggest that art is trivial? Does it allude to a dictator who "fiddles while Rome burns," as the saying goes? Someone who "fiddles" is not performing a grand, honest, or even competent act: One fiddles with a hobby, with the books, with car keys in the dark. The artist in this poem defies the orthodoxy of the sonnet form, instead making a kind of harlequin patchwork out of different traditions, breaking the rhythm, intermixing endearments and assaults.

To the deconstructionist the recurring broken antitheses of war and art, art and war cancel each other out. The very metaphors undermine the speaker's summons to war. The command "Be deaf to music and to beauty blind," which takes the form of a *chiasmus*, or X-shaped sequence (adjective, noun; noun, adjective), is a kind of miniature version of this chiasmic poem. (We are supposed to follow a sequence, fight then fiddle, but instead reverse that by imagining ways to do violence with art or to create beauty through destruction.) The poem, a lyric written but imagined as spoken or sung, puts the senses and the arts under erasure; we are somehow not to hear music (by definition audible), not to see beauty (here a visual attribute). "Maybe not too late" comes rather too late: At the end of the poem it will be too late to start over, although "having first to civilize a space / Wherein to play your violin with grace" (lines 12–14) comes across as a kind of beginning. These comforting lines form the only heroic couplet in the poem, the only two lines that run smoothly from end to end. (All the other lines have **caesuras**, **enjambments**, or balanced pairs of concepts, as in "from malice and from murdering" [8].) But the violence behind "civilize," the switch to the high-art term "violin," and the use of the Christian term "grace" suggest that the pagan erotic art promised at the outset, the "sorcery" of "hurting love" that can "bewitch," will be suppressed.

Like other formalisms, deconstruction can appear apolitical or conservative because of its skepticism about the referential connection between literature and the world of economics, politics, and other social forms. Yet poststructuralist linguistics provides a theory of *difference* that clearly pertains to the rankings of status and power in society, as in earlier examples of masculine/feminine, master/slave. The *Other*, the negative of the norm, is always less than an equal counterpart. Deconstruction has been a tool for various poststructuralist thinkers—including the historian Michel Foucault (1926–84), the feminist theorist and psychoanalyst Julia Kristeva (b. 1941), and the psychoanalytic theorist Jacques Lacan (1901–81).

Narrative Theory

Before concluding the discussion of text-centered approaches, we should mention the schools of narratology and narrative theory that have shaped study of the novel and other kinds of narrative. Criticism of fiction has been in a boom period since the 1950s, but the varieties of narrative theory per se have had more limited effect than the approaches we have discussed above. Since the 1960s different analysts of the forms and techniques of narrative, most notably the Chicago formalists and the structuralist narratologists, have developed terminology for the various interactions of author, implied author, narrator, and characters; of plot and the treatment of time in the selection and sequence of scenes; of voice, point of view, or focus and other aspects of fiction. As formalisms, narrative theories tend to exclude the author's biography, individual reader response, and the historical context of the work or its actual reception.

Narratology began by presenting itself as a structuralist science; its branches have grown from psychoanalytic theory or extended to reader-response criticism. In recent decades studies of narrative technique and form have responded to Marxist, feminist, and other ideological criticism that insists on the political contexts of literature. One important influence on this shift has been the revival of the work of the Russian literary theorist Mikhail Bakhtin (1895–1975), which considers the novel as a *dialogic* form that pulls together the many discourses and voices of a culture and its history. Part of the appeal of Bakhtin's work has been the fusion of textual close reading with attention to material factors such as economics and class, and a sense of the open-endedness and contradictoriness of writing (in the spirit of deconstruction more than of New Criticism). Like other Marxist-trained European formalists, Bakhtin sought to place the complex literary modes of communication in the light of politics and history.

EMPHASIS ON THE SOURCE

As the examples above suggest, a great deal can be drawn from a text without any reference to its source or its author. For millennia many anonymous works were shared in oral or manuscript form, and even after printing spread in Europe few thought it necessary to know the author's name or anything about him or her. Yet criticism from its beginnings in ancient Greece has been interested in the designing intention "behind" the text. Even when no evidence remained about the author, a legendary personality has sometimes been invented to satisfy readers' curiosity. From the legend of blind Homer to the latest debates about biographical evidence and portraits of William Shakespeare, literary criticism has been accompanied by interest in the author's life.

Biographical Criticism

This approach reached its height in an era when humanism prevailed in literary studies (roughly the 1750s to the 1960s). At this time there was widely shared confidence in the ideas that art and literature were the direct expressions of the artist's or writer's genius and that criticism of great works supported veneration of the great persons who created them. The lives of some famous writers became the models that aspiring writers emulated. Criticism at times was skewed by social judgments of personalities, as when John Keats was put down as a "Cockney" poet, that is, London-bred and lower-class. Many writers have struggled to get their work taken seriously because of mistaken biographical criticism. Women or minorities have at times used pseudonyms or published anonymously to avoid having their work put down or having it read only through the expectations, negative or positive, of what a woman or person of color might write. Biographical criticism can be diminishing in this respect. Others have objected to reading literature as a reflection of the author's personality. Such critics have supported the idea that the highest literary art is pure form, untouched by gossip or personal emotion. In this spirit some early twentieth-century critics as well as Modernist writers such as T. S. Eliot, James Joyce, and Virginia Woolf tried to dissociate the text from the personality or political commitments of the author. (The theories of these writers and their actual practices did not always coincide.)

In the early twentieth century, psychoanalytic interpretations placed the text in light of the author's emotional conflicts, and other interpretations relied heavily on the author's stated intentions. (Although psychoanalytic criticism entails more than analysis of the author, we will introduce it as an approach that primarily concerns the human source[s] of literature; it usually has less to say about the form and receiver of the text.) Author-based readings can be reductive. All the accessible information about a writer's life cannot definitively explain the writings. As a young man D. H. Lawrence might have hated his father and loved his mother, but all men who hate their fathers and love their mothers do not write fiction as powerful as Lawrence's. Indeed, Lawrence himself cautioned that we should "trust the tale, not the teller." Any kind of criticism benefits to some extent, however, from being informed by knowledge of the writer's life and career. Certain critical approaches, devoted to recognition of separate literary traditions, make sense only in light of supporting biographical evidence. Studies that concern traditions such as Irish literature, Asian American literature, or literature by Southern women require reliable information about the writers' birth and upbringing and even some judgment of the writers' intentions to write *as* members of such traditions. (We discuss feminist, African American, and other studies of distinct literatures in the "Historical and Ideological Criticism" section that follows, although such studies recognize the biographical "source" as a starting point.)

A reading of "First Fight. Then Fiddle." can become rather different when we know more about Gwendolyn Brooks. An African American, she was raised in Chicago in the 1920s. These facts begin to provide a context for her work. Some of the biographical information has more to do with her time and place than with her race and sex. Brooks began in the 1940s to associate with Harriet Monroe's magazine, *Poetry*, which had been influential in promoting Modernist poetry. Brooks early received acclaim for books of poetry that depict the everyday lives of poor, urban African Americans; in 1950 she was the first African American to win a Pulitzer Prize. In 1967 she became an outspoken advocate for the Black Arts movement, which promoted a separate tradition rather than integration into the aesthetic mainstream. But even before this political commitment, her work never sought to "pass" or to distance itself from the reality of racial difference, nor did it become any less concerned with poetic tradition and form when she published it through small, independent black presses in her "political" phase.

It is reasonable, then, to read "First Fight. Then Fiddle.," published in 1949, in relation to the role of a racial outsider mastering and adapting the forms of a dominant tradition. Perhaps Brooks's speaker addresses an African American audience in the voice of a revolutionary, calling for violence to gain the right to express African American culture. Perhaps the lines "the music that they wrote / Bewitch, bewilder. Qualify to sing / Threadwise" (lines 3–5) suggest the way that the colonized may transform the empire's music rather than the other way around. Ten years before the poem was published, a famous African American singer, Marian Anderson, had more than "qualif[ied] to sing" opera and classical concert music, but had still encountered the color barrier in the United States. Honored throughout Europe as the greatest living contralto, Anderson was barred in 1939 from performing at Constitution Hall in Washington, D.C., because of her race. Instead she performed at the Lincoln Memorial on Easter Sunday to an audience of seventy-five thousand people. It was not easy to find a "space" in which to practice her art. Such a contextual reference, whether or not intended, relates biographically to Brooks's role as an African American woman wisely reweaving classical traditions "threadwise" rather than straining them into "hempen" (5) ropes. Beneath the manifest reference to the recent world war, this poem refers to the segregation of the arts in America. (Questions of source and historical context often interrelate.)

Besides readings that derive from biographical and historical information, there are still other ways to read aspects of the *source* rather than the *text* or the *receiver*. The source of the work extends beyond the life of the person who wrote it to include not only the writer's other works but also the circumstances of contemporary publishing; contemporary literary movements; the history of the composition, editing, and publication of this particular text, with all the variations; and other contributing factors. While entire schools of literary scholarship have been devoted to each of these matters, any analyst of a particular work should bear in mind what is known about the circumstances of writers at that time, the material conditions of the work's first publication, and the means of dissemination ever since. It makes a difference in our interpretation to know that a certain sonnet circulated in manuscript in a small courtly audience or that a particular novel was serialized in a weekly journal cheap enough for the masses to read it.

Psychoanalytic Criticism

With the development of psychology and psychoanalysis toward the end of the nineteenth century, many critics were tempted to apply psychological theories to literary analysis. Symbolism, dreamlike imagery, emotional rather than rational logic, and a pleasure in language all suggested that literature profoundly evoked a mental and emotional landscape, often one of disorder or abnormality. From mad poets to patients speaking in verse, imaginative literature might be regarded as a representation of shared irrational structures within all *psyches* (i.e., souls) or selves. While psychoanalytic approaches have developed along with structuralism and poststructuralist linguistics and philosophy, they rarely focus on textual form. Rather, they attribute latent or hidden meaning to unacknowledged desires in some person, usually the author or source behind the character in a narrative or drama. A psychoanalytic critic can also focus on the response of readers and, in recent decades, usually accepts the influence of changing social history on the structures of sexual desire represented in the work. Nevertheless, psychoanalysis has typically aspired to a universal, unchanging theory of the mind and personality, and criticism that applies it has tended to emphasize the authorial source.

FREUDIAN CRITICISM

For most of the twentieth century, the dominant school of psychoanalytic critics was the Freudian, based on the work of Sigmund Freud (1856–1939). Many of its practitioners assert that the meaning of a literary work exists not on its surface but in the psyche (some would even claim, in the neuroses) of the author. Classic psychoanalytic criticism read works as though they were the recorded dreams of patients; interpreted the life histories of authors as keys to the works; or analyzed characters as though they, like real people, have a set of repressed childhood memories. (In fact, many novels and most plays leave out information about characters' development from infancy through adolescence, the period that psychoanalysis especially strives to reconstruct.)

A well-known Freudian reading of *Hamlet*, for example, insists that Hamlet suffers from an Oedipus complex, a Freudian term for a group of repressed desires and memories that corresponds with the Greek myth that is the basis of Sophocles's play *Oedipus the King*. In this view Hamlet envies his uncle because the son unconsciously wants to sleep with his mother, who was the first object of his desire as a baby. The ghost of Hamlet Sr. may then be a manifestation of Hamlet's unconscious desire or of his guilt for wanting to kill his father, the person who has a right to the desired mother's body. Hamlet's madness is not just acting but the result of this frustrated desire; his cruel mistreatment of Ophelia is a deflection of his disgust at his mother's being "unfaithful" in her love for him. Some Freudian critics stress the author's psyche and so might read *Hamlet* as the expression of Shakespeare's own Oedipus complex. In another mode psychoanalytic critics, reading imaginative literature as symbolic fulfillment of unconscious wishes much as an analyst would interpret a dream, look for objects, spaces, or actions that appear to relate to sexual anatomy or activity. Much as if tracing out the extended metaphors of an erotic poem by John Donne or a blues or Motown lyric, the Freudian reads containers, empty spaces, or bodies of water as female; tools, weapons, towers or trees, trains or planes as male.

JUNGIAN AND MYTH CRITICISM

Just as a Freudian assumes that all human psyches have similar histories and structures, the Jungian critic assumes that we all share a universal or collective unconscious (just as each has a racial and an individual unconscious). According to Carl Gustav Jung (1875–1961) and his followers, the unconscious harbors universal patterns and forms of human experiences, or **archetypes**. We can never know these archetypes directly, but they surface in art in an imperfect, shadowy way, taking the form of archetypes—the snake with its tail in its mouth, rebirth, the mother, the double, the descent into hell. In the classic quest narrative, the hero struggles to free himself (the gender of the pronoun is significant) from the Great Mother to become a separate, self-sufficient being (combating a demonic antagonist), surviving trials to gain the reward of union with his ideal other, the feminine anima. In a related school of *archetypal criticism*, influenced by Northrop Frye (1912–91), the prevailing myth follows a seasonal cycle of death and rebirth. Frye proposed a system for literary criticism that classified all literary forms in all ages according to a cycle of genres associated with the phases of human experience from birth to death and the natural cycle of seasons (e.g., Spring/Romance).

These approaches have been useful in the study of folklore and early literatures as well as in comparative studies of various national literatures. While most myth critics focus on the hero's quest, there have been forays into feminist archetypal criticism. These emphasize variations on the myths of Isis and Demeter, goddesses of fertility or seasonal renewal, who take different forms to restore either the sacrificed woman (Persephone's season in the underworld) or the sacrificed man (Isis's search for Osiris and her rescue of their son, Horus). Many twentieth-century poets were drawn to the heritage of archetypes and myths. Adrienne Rich's "Diving into the Wreck," for example, self-consciously rewrites a number of gendered archetypes, with a female protagonist on a quest into a submerged world.

Most critics today, influenced by poststructuralism, have become wary of universal patterns. Like structuralists, Jungians and archetypal critics strive to compare and unite the ages and peoples of the world and to reveal fundamental truths. Rich, as a feminist poet, suggests that the "book of myths" is an eclectic anthology that needs to be revised. Claims of universality tend to obscure the detailed differences among cultures and often appeal to some idea of *biological determinism*. Such determinism diminishes the power of individuals to design alternative life patterns and even implies that no literature can really surprise us.

LACANIAN CRITICISM

As it has absorbed the indeterminacies of poststructuralism under the influence of thinkers such as Jacques Lacan and Julia Kristeva, psychological criticism has become increasingly complex. Few critics today are direct Freudian analysts of authors or texts, and few maintain that universal archetypes explain the meaning of a tree or water in a text. Yet psychoanalytic theory continues to inform many varieties of criticism, and most new work in this field is affiliated with Lacanian psychoanalysis. Lacan's theory unites poststructuralist linguistics with Freudian theory. The Lacanian critic, like a deconstructionist, focuses on the text that defies conscious authorial control, foregrounding the powerful interpretation of the critic rather than the author or any other reader. Accepting the Oedipal paradigm and the unconscious as the realm of repressed desire, Lacanian theory aligns the development and structure of the individual human *subject* with the development and structure of language. To simplify a purposefully dense theory: The very young infant inhabits the Imaginary, in a preverbal, undifferentiated phase dominated by a sense of union with the Mother. Recognition of identity begins with the Mirror Stage, ironically with a disruption of a sense of oneness. For when one first looks into a mirror, one begins to recognize a split or difference between one's body and the image in the mirror. This splitting prefigures a sense that the *object* of desire is Other and distinct from the subject. With difference or the splitting of subject and object comes language and entry into the Symbolic Order, since we use words to summon the absent object of desire (as a child would cry "Mama" to bring her back). But what language signifies most is the lack of that object. The imaginary, perfectly nurturing Mother would never need to be called.

As in the biblical Genesis, the Lacanian "genesis" of the subject tells of a loss of paradise through knowledge of the difference between subject and object or Man and Woman (eating of the Tree of the Knowledge of Good and Evil leads to the sense of shame that teaches Adam and Eve to hide their nakedness). In Lacanian theory the Father governs language or the Symbolic Order; the Word spells the end of a child's sense of oneness with the Mother. Further, the Father's power claims omnipotence, the possession of male prerogative symbolized by the Phallus, which is not the anatomical difference between men and women but the idea or construction of that difference. Thus it is language or culture rather than nature that generates the difference and inequality between the sexes. Some feminist theorists have adopted aspects of Lacanian psychoanalytic theory, particularly the concept of *the gaze*. This concept notes that the masculine subject is the one who looks, whereas the feminine object is to be looked at.

Another influential concept is *abjection*. The Franco-Bulgarian psychoanalyst Julia Kristeva's theory of abjection most simply reimagines the infant's blissful sense of union with the mother and the darker side of such possible union. To return to the mother's body would be death, as metaphorically we are buried in Mother Earth. Yet according to the theory, people both desire and dread such loss of boundaries. A sense of self or *subjectivity* and hence of independence and power depends on resisting abjection. The association of the maternal body with abjection or with the powerlessness symbolized by the female's Lack of the Phallus can help explain negative cultural images of women. Many narrative genres seem to split the images of women between an angelic and a witchlike type. Lacanian or Kristevan theory has been well adapted to film criticism and to fantasy and other popular forms favored by structuralism or archetypal criticism.

Psychoanalytic literary criticism today—as distinct from specialized discussion of Lacanian theory, for example—treads more lightly than in the past. In James Joyce's "Araby," a young Dublin boy, orphaned and raised by an aunt and uncle, likes to haunt a back room in the house; there the "former tenant, . . . a priest, had died" (par. 2). (Disused rooms at the margins of houses resemble the unconscious, and a dead celibate "father" suggests a kind of failure of the Law, conscience, or in Freudian terms, superego.) The priest had left behind a "rusty bicycle-pump" in the "wild garden" with "a central apple tree" (these echoes of the garden of Eden suggesting the impotence of Catholic religious symbolism). The boy seems to gain consciousness of a separate self—or his subjectivity is constructed—through his gaze upon an idealized female object, Mangan's sister, whose "name was like a summons to all my foolish blood" (par. 4). Though he secretly watches and follows her, she is not so much a sexual fantasy as a beautiful art object (par. 9). He retreats to the back room to think of her in a kind of ecstasy that resembles masturbation. Yet it is not masturbation: It is pre-adolescent, dispersed through all orifices—the rain feels like "incessant needles . . . playing in the sodden beds"; and it is sublimated, that is, repressed and redirected into artistic or religious forms rather than directly expressed by bodily pleasure: "All my senses seemed to desire to veil them-selves" (par. 6).

It is not in the back room but on the street that the girl finally speaks to the hero, charging him to go on a quest to Araby. After several trials the hero carrying the talisman arrives in a darkened hall "girdled at half its height by a gallery," an underworld or maternal space that is also a deserted temple (par. 25). The story ends without his grasping the prize to carry back, the "chalice" or holy grail (symbolic of female sexuality) that he had once thought to bear "safely through a throng of foes" (par. 5).

Such a reading seems likely to raise objections that it is overreading: *You're seeing too much in it; the author didn't mean that.* This has been a popular reaction to psychoanalysis for over a hundred years, but it is only a heightened version of a response to many kinds of criticism. This sample reading pays close attention to the text, but does not really follow a formal approach because its goal is to explain the psychological implications or resonance of the story's details. We have mentioned nothing about the author, though we could have used this reading to forward a psychoanalytic reading of Joyce's biography.

EMPHASIS ON THE RECEIVER

In some sense critical schools develop in reaction to the excesses of other critical schools. By the 1970s, in a time of political upheaval that placed a high value on individual expression, a number of critics felt that the various routes toward objective criticism had proved to be dead ends. New Critics, structuralists, and psychoanalytic or myth critics had sought objective, sci-entific systems that disregarded changing times, political issues, or the read-er's personal response. New Critics and other formalists tended to value a literary canon made up of works that were regarded as complete, unchang-ing objects to be interpreted according to ostensibly timeless standards.

Reader-Response Criticism

Among critics who challenge New Critical assumptions, reader-response critics regard the work not as what is printed on the page but as what is experienced temporally through each act of reading. According to such critics, the reader effectively performs the text into existence the way a musician performs music from a score. Reader-response critics ask not what a work means but what a work does to and through a reader. Literary texts especially leave gaps that experienced readers fill according to expectations or conventions. Individual readers differ, of course, and gaps in a text provide space for different readings or interpretations. Some of these lacunae are temporary—such as the withholding of the murderer's name until the end of a mystery novel—and are closed by the text sooner or later, though each reader will in the meantime fill them differently. But other lacunae are permanent and can never be filled with certainty; they result in a degree of uncertainty or indeterminacy in the text.

The reader-response critic observes the expectations aroused by a text, how they are satisfied or modified, and how the reader comprehends the work when all of it has been read, and when it is reread in whole or in part. Such criticism attends to the reading habits associated with different genres and to the shared assumptions of a cultural context that seem to furnish what is left unsaid in the text.

Beyond theoretical formulations about reading, there are other approaches to literary study that concern the receiver rather than the text or source. A critic might examine specific documents of a work's reception, from contemporary reviews to critical essays written across the generations since the work was first published. Sometimes we have available diaries or autobiographical evidence about readers' encounters with particular works. Just as there are histories of publishing and of the book, there are histories of literacy and reading practices. Poetry, fiction, and drama often directly represent the theme of reading as well as writing. Many published works over the centuries have debated the benefits and perils of reading works such as sermons or novels. Different genres and particular works construct different classes or kinds of readers in the way they address them or supply what they are supposed to want. Some scholars have found quantitative measures for reading, from sales and library lending rates to questionnaires.

Finally, the role of the reader or receiver in the literary exchange has been portrayed from a political perspective. Literature helps shape social identity, and social status shapes access to different kinds of literature. Feminist critics adapted reader-response criticism, for example, to note that girls often do not identify with many American literary classics as boys do, and thus girls do not simply accept the stereotype of women as angels, temptresses, or scolds who should be abandoned for the sake of all-male adventures. Studies of African American literature and other ethnic literatures have often featured discussion of literacy and of the obstacles for readers who cannot find their counterparts within the texts or who encounter negative stereotypes of their group. Thus, as we will discuss below, most forms of historical and ideological criticism include some consideration of the reader.

HISTORICAL AND IDEOLOGICAL CRITICISM

The approaches to the text, the author, and the reader outlined above may each take some note of historical contexts, including changes in formal conventions, the writer's milieu, or audience expectations. In the nineteenth century, historical criticism took the obvious facts that a work is created in a specific historical and cultural context and that the author is a part of that context as reasons to treat literature as a reflection of society. Twentieth-century formalists rejected the *reflectivist* model of art in the old historical criticism, that is, the assumption that literature and other arts straightforwardly express the collective spirit of the society at a given time. But as we have remarked, formalist rules for isolating the work of art from social and historical context met resistance in the last decades of the twentieth century. In a revival of historical approaches, critics have replaced the reflectivist model with a *constructivist* model, whereby literature and other cultural discourses are seen to help construct social relations and roles rather than merely reflect them. In other words, art is not just the frosting on the cake but an integral part of the recipe's ingredients and instructions. A society's ideology, its system of representations (ideas, myths, images), is inscribed in literature and other cultural forms, which in turn help shape identities and social practices.

Since the 1980s, historical approaches have regained great influence in literary studies. Some critical schools have been insistently *materialist*, that is, seeking causes more in concrete conditions such as technology, production, and distribution of wealth. Such criticism usually owes an acknowledged debt to Marxism. Other historical approaches have been influenced to a degree by Marxist critics and cultural theorists, but work within the realm of ideology, textual production, and interpretation, using some of the methods and concerns of traditional literary history. Still others emerge from the civil rights movement and the struggles for recognition of women and racial, ethnic, and sexual constituencies.

Feminist studies, African American studies, gay and lesbian studies, and studies of the cultures of different immigrant and ethnic populations within and beyond the United States have each developed along similar theoretical lines. These schools, like Marxist criticism, adopt a constructivist position: Literature is not simply a reflection of prejudices and norms; it also helps define social identities, such as what it means to be an African American woman. Each of these schools has moved through stages of first claiming *equality* with the literature dominated by white Anglo American men, then affirming the *difference* of their own separate culture, and then theoretically *questioning the terms and standards* of such comparisons. At a certain point in the thought process, each group rejects *essentialism*, the notion of innate or biological bases for the differences between the sexes, races, or other groups. This rejection of essentialism is usually called the constructivist position, in a somewhat different but related sense to our definition above. Constructivism maintains that identity is socially formed rather than biologically determined. Differences of anatomical sex, skin color, first language, parental ethnicity, and eventual sexual preferences have great impact on how one is classified, brought up, and treated socially, and on one's subjectivity or conception of identity. Constructivists maintain that these differences, however, are more constructed by ideology and the resulting behaviors than by any natural programming.

Marxist Criticism

The most insistent and vigorous historical approach through the twentieth century to the present has been Marxism, based on the work of Karl Marx (1818–83). With roots in nineteenth-century historicism, Marxist criticism was initially reflectivist. Economics, the underlying cause of history, was thus the *base*, and culture, including literature and the other arts, was the *superstructure*, an outcome or reflection of the base. Viewed from the Marxist perspective, the literary works of a period were economically determined; they would *reflect* the state of the struggle between classes in any place and time. History enacted recurrent three-step cycles, a pattern that Hegel had defined as *dialectic* (Hegel was cited above on the interdependence of master and slave). Each socioeconomic phase, or *thesis*, is counteracted by its *antithesis*, and the resulting conflict yields a *synthesis*, which becomes the ensuing *thesis*, and so on. As with early Freudian criticism, early Marxist criticism was often preoccupied with labeling and exposing illusions or deceptions. A novel might be read as a thinly disguised defense of the power of bourgeois industrial capital; its appeal on behalf of the suffering poor might be dismissed as an effort to fend off class rebellion.

As a rationale for state control of the arts, Marxism was abused in the Soviet Union and in other totalitarian states. In the hands of sophisticated critics, however, Marxism has been richly rewarding. Various schools that unite formal close reading and political analysis developed in the early twentieth century under Soviet communism and under fascism in Europe, often in covert resistance. These schools in turn have influenced critical movements in North America; New Criticism, structuralist linguistics, deconstruction, and narrative theory have each borrowed from European Marxist critics.

Most recently, a new mode of Marxist theory has developed, largely guided by the thinking of Walter Benjamin (1892–1940) and Theodor Adorno (1903–69) of the Frankfurt School in Germany, Louis Althusser (1918–90) in France, and Raymond Williams (1921–98) in Britain. This work has generally tended to modify the base/superstructure distinction and to interrelate public and private life, economics and culture. Newer Marxist interpretation assumes that the relation of a literary work to its historical context is *overdetermined*—the relation has multiple determining factors rather than a sole cause or aim. This thinking similarly acknowledges that neither the source nor the receiver of the literary interaction is a mere tool or victim of the ruling powers or state. Representation of all kinds, including literature, always has a political dimension, according to this approach; conversely, political and material conditions such as work, money, or institutions depend on representation.

Showing some influence of psychoanalytic and poststructuralist theories, recent Marxist literary studies examine the effects of ideology by focusing on the works' gaps and silences: Ideology may be conveyed in what is repressed or contradicted. In many ways Marxist criticism has adapted to the conditions of consumer rather than industrial capitalism and to global rather than national economies. The worldwide revolution that was to come when the proletariat or working classes overthrew the capitalists has never taken place; in many countries industrial labor has been swallowed up by the service sector, and workers reject the political Left that would seem their most likely ally. Increasingly, Marxist criticism has acknowledged that the audience of literature may be active rather than passive, just as the text and source may be more than straightforward instructions for toeing a given political line. Marxist criticism has been especially successful with the novel, since that genre more than drama or short fiction is capable of representing numerous people from different classes as they develop over a significant amount of time.

Feminist Criticism

Like Marxist criticism and the schools discussed below, feminist criticism derives from a critique of a history of oppression, in this case the history of women's inequality. Feminist criticism has no single founder like Freud or Marx; it has been practiced to some extent since the 1790s, when praise of women's cultural achievements went hand in hand with arguments that women were rational beings deserving equal rights and education. Contemporary feminist criticism emerged from a "second wave" of feminist activism, in the 1960s and 1970s, associated with the civil rights and anti-war movements. One of the first disciplines in which women's activism took root was literary criticism, but feminist theory and women's studies quickly became recognized methods across the disciplines.

Feminist literary studies began by denouncing the misrepresentation of women in literature and affirming the importance of women's writings, before quickly adopting the insights of poststructuralist theory; yet the early strategies continue to have their use. At first, feminist criticism in the 1970s, like early Marxist criticism, regarded literature as a reflection of patriarchal society's sexist base; the demeaning images of women in literature were symptoms of a system that had to be overthrown. Feminist literary studies soon began, however, to claim the *equal* but distinctive qualities of writings by women and men. Critics such as Elaine Showalter (b. 1941), Sandra M. Gilbert (b. 1936), and Susan Gubar (b. 1944) explored canonical works by women, relying on close reading with some aid from historical and psychoanalytic methods.

Yet by the 1980s it was widely recognized that a New Critical method would leave most of the male-dominated canon intact and most women writers still in obscurity, because many women had written in different genres and styles, on different themes, and for different audiences than had male writers. To affirm the *difference* of female literary traditions, some feminist studies claimed women's innate or universal affinity for fluidity and cycle rather than solidity and linear progress. Others concentrated on the role of the mother in human psychological development. According to this argument, girls, not having to adopt a gender role different from that of their first object of desire, the mother, grow up with less rigid boundaries of self and a relational rather than judgmental ethic.

The dangers of these intriguing generalizations soon became apparent. If the reasons for women's differences from men were biologically based or were due to universal archetypes, there was no solution to women's oppression, which many cultures worldwide had justified in terms of biological reproduction or archetypes of nature. At this point in the debate, feminist literary studies intersected with poststructuralist linguistic theory in *questioning the terms and standards* of comparison. French feminist theory, articulated most prominently by Hélène Cixous (b. 1937) and Luce Irigaray (b. 1932), deconstructed the supposed archetypes of gender written into the founding discourses of Western culture. We have seen that deconstruction helps expose the power imbalance in every dualism. Thus man is to woman as culture is to nature or mind is to body, and in each case the second term is held to be inferior or Other. The language and hence the worldview and social formations of our culture, not nature or eternal archetypes, constructed woman as Other. This insight was helpful in avoiding essentialism or biological determinism.

Having reached a theoretical criticism of the terms on which women might claim equality or difference from men in the field of literature, feminist studies also confronted other issues in the 1980s. Deconstructionist readings of gender difference in texts by men as well as women could lose sight of the real world, in which women are paid less and are more likely to be victims of sexual violence. With this in mind, some feminist critics pursued links with Marxist or African American studies; gender roles, like those of class and race, were interdependent systems for registering the material consequences of people's differences. It no longer seemed so easy to say what the term "women" referred to, when the interests of different kinds of women had been opposed to each other. African American women asked if feminism was really their cause, when white women had so long enjoyed power over both men and women of their race. In a classic Marxist view, women allied with men of their class rather than with women of other classes. It became more difficult to make universal claims about women's literature, as the horizon of the college-educated North American feminists expanded to recognize the range of conditions of women and of literature worldwide. Feminist literary studies have continued to consider famous and obscure women writers; the way women and gender are portrayed in writings by men as well as women; feminist issues concerning the text, source, or receiver in any national literature; theoretical and historical questions about the representation of differences such as gender, race, class, and nationality, and the way these differences shape each other.

Gender Studies and Queer Theory

From the 1970s, feminists sought recognition for lesbian writers and lesbian culture, which they felt had been even less visible than male homosexual writers and gay culture. Concurrently, feminist studies abandoned the simple dualism of male/female, part of the very binary logic of patriarchy that seemed to cause the oppression of women. Thus feminists recognized a zone of inquiry, the study of gender, as distinct from historical studies of women, and increasingly they included masculinity as a subject of investigation. As gender studies turned to interpretation of the text in ideological context regardless of the sex or intention of the author, it incorporated the ideas of Michel Foucault's *History of Sexuality* (1976). Foucault helped show that there was nothing natural, universal, or timeless in the constructions of sexual difference or sexual practices. Foucault also introduced a history of the concept of homosexuality, which had once been regarded in terms of taboo acts and in the later nineteenth century became defined as a disease associated with a personality type. Literary scholars began to study the history of sexuality as a key to the shifts in modern culture that had also shaped literature.

By the 1980s gender had come to be widely regarded as a discourse that imposed binary social norms on human beings' diversity. Theorists such as Donna Haraway (b. 1944) and Judith Butler (b. 1956) insisted further that sex and sexuality have no natural basis; even the anatomical differences are representations from the moment the newborn is put in a pink or blue blanket. Moreover, these theorists claimed that gender and sexuality are *performative* and malleable positions, enacted in many more than two varieties. From cross-dressing to surgical sex changes, the alternatives chosen by real people have influenced critical theory and generated both writings and literary criticism about those writings. Perhaps biographical and feminist studies face new challenges when identity seems subject to radical change and it is less easy to determine the sex of an author.

Gay and lesbian literary studies have included practices that parallel those of feminist criticism. At times critics identify oppressive or positive representations of homosexuality in works by men or women, gay, lesbian, or straight. At other times critics seek to establish the equivalent stature of a work by a gay or lesbian writer or, because these identities tended to be hidden in the past, to reveal that a writer *was* gay or lesbian. Again stages of *equality* and *difference* have yielded to a *questioning of the terms of difference*, in this case what has been called queer theory. The field of queer theory hopes to leave everyone guessing rather than to identify gay or lesbian writers, characters, or themes. One of its founding texts, *Between Men* (1985), by Eve Kosofsky Sedgwick (1950–2009), drew on structuralist insight into desire as well as anthropological models of kinship to show that, in canonical works of English literature, male characters form "homosocial" (versus homosexual) bonds through their rivalry for and exchange of a woman. Queer theory, because it rejects the idea of a fixed identity or innate or essential gender, likes to discover resistance to heterosexuality in unexpected places. Queer theorists value gay writers such as Oscar Wilde, but they also find queer implications regardless of the author's acknowledged identity. This approach emphasizes not the surface signals of the text but the subtler meanings an audience or receiver might detect. It encompasses elaborate close reading of many varieties of literary work; characteristically, a leading queer theorist, D. A. Miller (b. 1948), has written in loving detail about both Jane Austen and Broadway musicals.

African American and Ethnic Literary Studies

Critics sought to define an African American literary tradition as early as the turn of the twentieth century. A period of literary success in the 1920s, known as the Harlem Renaissance, produced some of the first classic essays on writings by African Americans. Criticism and histories of African American literature tended to ignore and dismiss women writers, while feminist literary histories, guided by Virginia Woolf's classic *A Room of One's Own* (1929), neglected women writers of color. Only after feminist critics began to succeed in the academy and African American studies programs were established did the whiteness of feminist studies and the masculinity of African American studies become glaring; both fields have for some time corrected this narrowness of vision, in part by learning from each other. The study of African American literature followed the general pattern that we have noted, first striving to claim equality, on established aesthetic grounds, of works such as Ralph Ellison's magnificent *Invisible Man* (1952). Then in the 1960s the Black Arts or Black Aesthetic emerged. Once launched in the academy, however, African American studies has been devoted less to celebrating an essential racial difference than to tracing the historical construction of a racial Other and a subordinated literature. The field sought to recover neglected genres such as slave narratives and traced common elements in fiction or poetry to the conditions of slavery and segregation. By the 1980s, feminist and poststructuralist theory had an impact in the work of some African American critics such as Henry Louis Gates Jr. (b. 1950), Houston A. Baker Jr. (b. 1943), and Hazel V. Carby (b. 1948), while others objected that the doubts raised by "theory" stood in the way of political commitment. African Americans' cultural contributions to America have gained much more recognition than before. New histories of American culture have been written with the view that racism is not an aberration but inherent to the guiding narratives of national progress. Many critics now regard race as a discourse with only slight basis in genetics but with weighty investments in ideology. This poststructuralist position coexists with scholarship that takes into account the race of the author or reader or that focuses on African American characters or themes.

In recent years a series of fields has arisen in recognition of the literatures of other American ethnic groups, large and small: Asian Americans, Native Americans, Latinos, and Chicanos. Increasingly, such studies avoid romanticizing an original, pure culture or assuming that these literatures by their very nature undermine the values and power of the dominant culture. Instead, critics emphasize the *hybridity* of all cultures in a global economy. The contact and intermixture of cultures across geographical borders and languages (translations, "creole" speech made up of native and acquired languages, dialects) may be read as enriching literature and art, despite being caused by economic exploitation. In method and in aim these fields have much in common with African American studies, though each cultural and historical context is very different. Each field deserves the separate study that we cannot offer here.

Not so very long ago, critics might have been charged with a fundamental misunderstanding of the nature of literature if they pursued matters considered the business of sociologists, matters—such as class, race, and gender—that seemed extrinsic to the text. The rise of the above-noted fields has made it standard practice that a critic will address questions about class, race, and gender to place a text, its source, and its reception in historical and ideological context. One brief example might illustrate the way Marxist, feminist, queer, and African American criticism can contribute to a literary reading.

Tennessee Williams's *A Streetcar Named Desire* was first produced in 1947 and won the Pulitzer Prize in 1948. Part of its acclaim was likely due to its fashionable blend of naturalism and symbolism: The action takes place in a shabby tenement on an otherworldly street, Elysian Fields—in an "atmosphere of decay" laced with "lyricism," as Williams's stage directions put it (1.1). After the Depression and World War II, American audiences welcomed a turn away from world politics into the psychological core of human sexuality. This turn to ostensibly individual conflict was a kind of alibi for at least two sets of issues that Williams and the middle-class theatergoers in New York and elsewhere sought to avoid. First are racial questions that relate to ones of gender and class: What is the play's attitude to race, and what is Williams's attitude? Biography seems relevant, though not the last word on what the play means. Williams's family had included slaveholding cotton growers, and he chose to spend much of his adult life in the South, which he saw as representing a beautiful but dying way of life. He was deeply attached to women in his family who might be models for the brilliant, fragile, cultivated Southern white woman, Blanche DuBois. Blanche ("white" in French), representative of a genteel, feminine past that has gambled, prostituted, dissipated itself, speaks some of the most eloquent lines in the play when she mourns the faded Delta plantation society. Neither the playwright nor his audience wished to deal with segregation in the South, a region that since the Civil War had stagnated as a kind of agricultural working class in relation to the dominant North—which had its racism, too.

The play scarcely notices race. The main characters are white. The cast includes a "Negro Woman" as servant, and a blind Mexican woman who offers artificial flowers to remember the dead, but these figures seem more like props or symbols than fully developed characters. Instead, racial difference is transposed as ethnic and class difference in the story of a working-class Pole intruding into a family clinging to French gentility. Stella warns Blanche that she lives among "heterogeneous types" and that Stanley is "a different species" (1.1). The play thus transfigures contemporary anxieties about miscegenation, as the virile (black) man dominates the ideal white woman and rapes the spirit of the plantation South. A former soldier who works in a factory, Stanley represents as well the defeat of the old, agricultural economy by industrialization.

The second set of issues that neither the playwright nor his audience confronts directly is the disturbance of sexual and gender roles that would in later decades lead to movements for women's and gay rights. It was well known in New Orleans at least that Williams was gay. In the 1940s he lived with his lover, Pancho Rodriguez y Gonzales, in the French Quarter. Like many homosexual writers in other eras, Williams recasts homosexual desire in heterosexual costume. Blanche, performing femininity with a kind of camp excess, might be a fading queen pursuing and failing to capture younger men. Stanley, hypermasculine, might caricature the object of desire of both men and women as well as the anti-intellectual, brute force in postwar America. His conquest of women (he had "the power and pride of a richly feathered male bird among hens" [1.1]) appears to be biologically determined. By the same token it seems natural that Stanley and his buddies go out to work and that their wives become homemakers in the way now seen as typical of the 1950s. In this world, artists, homosexuals, or unmarried working women like Blanche would be both vulnerable and threatening. Blanche after all has secret pleasures—drinking and sex—that Stanley indulges in openly. Blanche is the one who is taken into custody by the medical establishment, which in this period diagnosed homosexuality as a form of insanity.

New Historicism

Three interrelated schools of historical and ideological criticism have been important innovations in the past two decades. These are part of the swing of the pendulum away from formal analysis of the text and toward historical analysis of context. New historicism has less obvious political commitments than Marxism, feminism, or queer theory, but it shares their interest in the power of discourse to shape ideology. Old historicism, in the 1850s–1950s, confidently told a story of civilization's progress from the point of view of a Western nation; a historicist critic would offer a close reading of the plays of Shakespeare and then locate them within the prevailing Elizabethan "worldview." "New Historicism," labeled in 1982 by Stephen Greenblatt (b. 1943), rejected the technique of plugging samples of a culture into a history of ideas. Influenced by poststructuralist anthropology, New Historicism tried to offer a multilayered impression or "thick description" of a culture at one moment in time, including popular as well as elite forms of representation. As a method, New Historicism belongs with those that deny the unity of the text, defy the authority of the source, and license the receiver—much like deconstructionism. Accordingly, New Historicism doubts the accessibility of the past, insisting that all we have is discourse. One model for New Historicism was the historiography of Michel Foucault, who insisted on the power of discourses, that is, not only writing but all structuring myths or ideologies that underlie social relations. The New Historicist, like Foucault, is interested in the transition from the external powers of the state and church in the feudal order to modern forms of power. The rule of the modern state and middle-class ideology is enforced insidiously by systems of surveillance and by each individual's internalization of discipline (not unlike Freud's idea of the superego).

No longer so "new," the New Historicists have had a lasting influence on a more narrative and concrete style of criticism even among those who espouse poststructuralist and Marxist theories. A New Historicist article begins with an anecdote, often a description of a public spectacle, and teases out the many contributing causes that brought disparate social elements together in that way. It usually applies techniques of close reading to forms that would not traditionally have received such attention. Although it often concentrates on events several hundred years ago, in some ways it defies historicity, flouting the idea that a complete objective impression of the entire context could ever be achieved.

Cultural Studies

Popular culture often gets major attention in the work of New Historicists. Yet today most studies of popular culture would acknowledge their debt instead to cultural studies, as filtered through the now-defunct Center for Contemporary Cultural Studies, founded in 1964 by Stuart Hall (1932–2014) and others at the University of Birmingham in England. Method, style, and subject matter may be similar in New Historicism and cultural studies: Both attend to historical context, theoretical method, political commitment, and textual analysis. But whereas the American movement shares Foucault's paranoid view of state domination through discourse, the British school, influenced by Raymond Williams and his concept of "structures of feeling," emphasizes the possibility that ordinary people, the receivers of cultural forms, may resist dominant ideology. The documents examined in a cultural-studies essay may be recent, such as artifacts of tourism at Shakespeare's birthplace, rather than sixteenth-century maps. Cultural studies today influences history, sociology, communications and media, and literature departments; its studies may focus on television, film, romance novels, and advertising, or on museums and the art market, sports and stadiums, New Age religious groups, or other forms and practices.

The questions raised by cultural studies would encourage a critic to place a poem like Marge Piercy's "Barbie Doll" in the context of the history of that toy, a doll whose slender, impossibly long legs, tiptoe feet (not unlike the bound feet of Chinese women of an earlier era), small nose, and torpedo breasts epitomized a 1950s ideal for the female body. A critic influenced by cultural studies might align the poem with other works published around 1973 that express feminist protest concerning cosmetics, body image, consumption, and the objectification of women, while she or he would draw on research into the founding and marketing of Mattel toys. The poem reverses the Sleeping Beauty story: This heroine puts herself into the coffin rather than waking up. The poem omits any hero—Ken?—who would rescue her. "Barbie Doll" protests the pressure a girl feels to fit into a heterosexual plot of romance and marriage; no one will buy her if she is not the right toy or accessory.

Indeed, accessories such as "GE stoves and irons" (line 3) taught girls to plan their lives as domestic consumers, and Barbie's lifestyle is decidedly middle-class and suburban (everyone has a house, car, pool, and lots of handbags). The whiteness of the typical "girlchild" (1) goes without saying. Although Mattel produced Barbie's African American friend, Christie, in 1968, Piercy's title makes the reader imagine Barbie, not Christie. In 1997 Mattel issued Share a Smile Becky, a friend in a wheelchair, as though in answer to the humiliation of the girl in Piercy's poem, who feels so deformed, in spite of her "strong arms and back, / abundant sexual drive and manual dexterity" (8–9), that she finally cripples herself. The icon, in short, responds to changing ideology. Perhaps responding to generations of objections like Piercy's, Barbies over the years have been given feminist career goals, yet women's lives are still plotted according to physical image.

In this manner a popular product might be "read" alongside a literary work. The approach would be influenced by Marxist, feminist, gender, and ethnic studies, but it would not be driven by a desire to destroy Barbie as sinister, misogynist propaganda. Piercy's kind of protest against indoctrination has gone out of style. Girls have found ways to respond to such messages and divert them into stories of empowerment. Such at least is the outlook of cultural studies, which usually affirms popular culture. A researcher could gather data on Barbie sales and could interview girls or videotape their play in order to establish the actual effects of the dolls. Whereas traditional anthropology examined non-European or preindustrial cultures, cultural studies may direct its "field work," or ethnographic research, inward, at home. Nevertheless, many contributions to cultural studies rely on methods of textual close reading or Marxist and Freudian literary criticism developed in the mid-twentieth century.

Postcolonial Criticism and Studies of World Literature

In the middle of the twentieth century, the remaining colonies of the European nations struggled toward independence. French-speaking Frantz Fanon (1925–61) of Martinique was one of the most compelling voices for the point of view of the colonized or exploited countries, which like the feminine Other had been objectified and denied the right to look and talk back. Edward Said (1935–2003), in *Orientalism* (1978), brought a poststructuralist analysis to bear on the history of colonization, illustrating the ways that Western culture feminized and objectified the East. Postcolonial literary studies developed into a distinct field in the 1990s in light of globalization and the replacement of direct colonial power with international corporations and "NGOs" (nongovernmental agencies such as the World Bank). In general this field cannot share the optimism of some cultural studies, given the histories of slavery and economic exploitation of colonies and the violence committed in the name of civilization's progress. Studies by Gayatri Chakravorty Spivak (b. 1942) and Homi K. Bhabha (b. 1949) have further mingled Marxist, feminist, and poststructuralist theory to reread both canonical Western works and the writings of marginalized peoples. Colonial or postcolonial literatures may include works set or published in countries during colonial rule or after independence, or they may feature texts produced in the context of international cultural exchange, such as a novel in English by a woman of Chinese descent writing in Malaysia.

Like feminist studies and studies of African American or other literatures, the field is inspired by recovery of neglected works, redress of a systematic denial of rights and recognition, and increasing realization that the dualisms of opposing groups reveal interdependence. In this field the stage of difference came early, with the celebrations of African heritage known as *Négritude*, but the danger of that essentialist claim was soon apparent: The Dark Continent or wild island might be romanticized and idealized as a source of innate qualities of vitality long repressed in Enlightened Europe. Currently, most critics accept that the context for literature in all countries is hybrid, with immigration and educational intermixing. Close readings of texts are always linked to the author's biography and literary influences and placed within the context of contemporary international politics as well as colonial history. Many fiction writers, from Salman Rushdie to Jhumpa Lahiri, make the theme of cultural mixture or hybridity part of their work, whether in a pastiche of Charles Dickens or a story of an Indian family growing up in New Jersey and returning as tourists to their supposed "native" land. Poststructuralist theories of trauma, and theories of the interrelation of narrative and memory, provide explanatory frames for interpreting writings from Afghanistan to Zambia.

Studies of postcolonial culture retain a clear political mission that feminist and Marxist criticism have found difficult to sustain. Perhaps this is because the scale of the power relations is so vast, between nations rather than the sexes or classes within those nations. Imperialism can be called an absolute evil, and the destruction of local cultures a crime against humanity. Today some of the most exciting literature in English emerges from countries once under the British Empire, and all the techniques of criticism will be brought to bear on it. If history is any guide, in later decades some critical school will attempt to read the diverse literatures of the early twenty-first century in pure isolation from authorship and national origin, as self-enclosed form. The themes of hybridity, indeterminacy, trauma, and memory will be praised as universal. It is even possible that readers' continuing desire to revere authors as creative geniuses in control of their meanings will regain respectability among specialists. The elements of the literary exchange—text, source, and receiver—are always there to provoke questions that generate criticism, which in turn produces articulations of the methods of that criticism. It is an ongoing discussion well worth participating in.

BIBLIOGRAPHY

For good introductions to the issues discussed here, see the following books, from which we have drawn in this overview. Some of these provide bibliographies of the works of critics and schools mentioned above.

Alter, Robert. *The Pleasure of Reading in an Ideological Age.* W. W. Norton, 1996. Originally published as *The Pleasures of Reading: Thinking about Literature in an Ideological Age,* 1989.

Barnet, Sylvan, and William E. Cain. *A Short Guide to Writing about Literature.* 10th ed., Longman, 2005.

Barry, Peter. *Beginning Theory: An Introduction to Literary and Cultural Theory.* 2nd ed., Manchester UP, 2002.

Bressler, Charles E. *Literary Criticism: An Introduction to Theory and Practice.* 3rd ed., Prentice Hall, 2003.

Culler, Jonathan. *Literary Theory: A Very Short Introduction.* Oxford UP, 1997.

Davis, Robert Con, and Ronald Schleifer. *Contemporary Literary Criticism: Literary and Cultural Studies.* 4th ed., Addison Wesley Longman, 1999.

During, Simon. *Cultural Studies: A Critical Introduction.* Routledge, 2005.

---. *The Cultural Studies Reader.* Routledge, 1999.

Eagleton, Mary, editor. *Feminist Literary Theory: A Reader.* 2nd ed., Blackwell, 1996.

Eagleton, Terry. *Literary Theory: An Introduction.* 2nd rev. ed., U of Minnesota P, 1996.

Groden, Michael, and Martin Kreiswirth. *The Johns Hopkins Guide to Literary Theory and Criticism.* Johns Hopkins UP, 1994.

Hawthorn, Jeremy. *A Glossary of Contemporary Literary Theory.* 3rd ed., Arnold, 1998.

Leitch, Vincent B. *American Literary Criticism from the Thirties to the Eighties.* Columbia UP, 1989.

---, et al. *The Norton Anthology of Theory and Criticism.* 2nd ed., W. W. Norton, 2010.

Lentricchia, Frank. *After the New Criticism.* U of Chicago P, 1981.

Macksey, Richard, and Eugenio Donato, editors. *The Structuralist Controversy: The Languages of Criticism and the Sciences of Man.* Johns Hopkins UP, 2007.

Moi, Toril. *Sexual-Textual Politics.* Routledge, 1985.

Murfin, Ross, and Supryia M. Ray. *The Bedford Glossary of Critical and Literary Terms.* Bedford, 1997.

Piaget, Jean. *Structuralism.* Translated and edited by Chaninah Maschler, Basic Books, 1970.

Selden, Raman, and Peter Widdowson. *A Reader's Guide to Contemporary Literary Theory.* 3rd ed., U of Kentucky P, 1993.

Stevens, Anne H. *Literary Theory and Criticism: An Introduction.* Broadview Press, 2015.

Todorov, Tzvetan. *Mikhail Bakhtin: The Dialogic Principle.* Translated by Wlad Godzich, U of Minnesota P, 1984.

Turco, Lewis. *The Book of Literary Terms.* UP of New England, 1999.

Veeser, Harold, editor. *The New Historicism.* Routledge, 1989.

---. *The New Historicism Reader.* Routledge, 1994.

Warhol, Robyn R., and Diane Price Herndl. *Feminisms.* 2nd ed., Rutgers UP, 1997.

Wolfreys, Julian. *Literary Theories: A Reader and Guide.* Edinburgh UP, 1999.

Glossary

Boldface words within definitions are themselves defined in the glossary.

action any event or series of events depicted in a literary work; an event may be verbal as well as physical, so that saying something or telling a story within the story may be an event. *See also* **climax, complication, falling action, inciting incident, plot,** *and* **rising action.**

allegory a literary work in which **characters, actions,** and even **settings** have two connected levels of meaning. Elements of the literal level signify (or serve as symbols for) a figurative level that often imparts a lesson or moral to the reader. One of the most famous English-language allegories is John Bunyan's *Pilgrim's Progress,* in which a character named Christian has to make his way through obstacles such as the Valley of Humiliation to get to the Celestial City.

alliteration the repetition of usually initial consonant sounds through a sequence of words—for example, "While I *n*odded, *n*early *n*apping" in Edgar Allan Poe's "The Raven."

allusion a brief, often implicit and indirect reference within a literary text to something outside the text, whether another text (e.g., the Bible, a **myth,** another literary work, a painting, or a piece of music) or any imaginary or historical person, place, or thing. Many of the footnotes in this book explain allusions found in literary selections.

amphitheater a theater consisting of a stage area surrounded by a semicircle of tiered seats.

analogy like a **metaphor,** a representation of one thing or idea by something else; in this case, often a simpler explanation that gets at the gist of the more complicated example (e.g., "the brain is like a computer").

anapestic referring to a metrical form in which each **foot** consists of two unstressed syllables followed by a stressed one—for example, "There are mán- | y who sáy | that a dóg | has his dáy" (Dylan Thomas, "The Song of the Mischievous Dog"). A single foot of this type is called an *anapest.*

antagonist a **character** or a nonhuman force that opposes or is in **conflict** with the **protagonist.**

antihero a **protagonist** who is in one way or another the very opposite of a traditional **hero.** Instead of being courageous and determined, for instance, an antihero might be timid, hypersensitive, and indecisive to the point of paralysis. Antiheroes are especially common in modern literary works; examples might include the **speaker** of T. S. Eliot's "The Love Song of J. Alfred Prufrock" or the **protagonist** of Franz Kafka's *The Metamorphosis.*

apostrophe a figure of speech in which a **speaker** or **narrator** addresses an abstraction, an object, or a dead or absent person. An example occurs at the end of Melville's "Bartleby, the Scrivener." "Ah, Bartleby! Ah, Humanity!"

archetype a **character,** ritual, **symbol,** or **plot** pattern that recurs in the **myth** and literature of many cultures; examples include the scapegoat or trickster (character type), the rite of passage (ritual), and the quest or descent into the underworld (plot pattern). The term and our contemporary understanding of it derive from the work of psychologist Carl Jung (1875–1961), who argued that archetypes emerge from—and give us a clue to the workings of—the "collective unconscious," a reservoir of memories and impulses that all humans share but aren't consciously aware of.

arena stage a stage design in which the audience is seated all the way around the acting area; actors make their entrances and exits through the auditorium.

assonance the repetition of vowel sounds in a sequence of words with different endings—for example, "The death of the poet was kept from his poems" in W. H. Auden's "In Memory of W. B. Yeats."

aubade a poem in which the coming of dawn is either celebrated or denounced as a nuisance, as in John Donne's "The Sun Rising."

auditor an imaginary listener within a literary work, as opposed to the actual reader or audience outside the work.

author the *actual* or *real author* of a work is the historical person who actually wrote it and the focus of biographical criticism, which interprets a work by drawing on facts about the author's life and career. The *implied author* is the vision of the author's personality and outlook implied by the work as a whole. Thus when we make a claim about the author that relies solely on evidence from the work rather than from other sources, our subject is the implied author; for example, "In *Dubliners*, James Joyce heavily criticizes the Catholic church."

author time *see* time.

autobiography *see* biography.

ballad a verse narrative that is, or originally was, meant to be sung. Ballads were originally a folk creation, transmitted orally from person to person and age to age and characterized by relatively simple diction, meter, and rhyme scheme; by stock imagery; and by repetition; and often by a refrain (a recurrent phrase or series of phrases). An example is "Sir Patrick Spens."

ballad stanza a common stanza form, consisting of a quatrain that alternates four-foot and three-foot lines; lines 1 and 3 are unrhymed iambic tetrameter (four feet), and lines 2 and 4 are rhymed iambic trimeter (three feet), as in "Sir Patrick Spens."

bildungsroman literally, "education novel" (German), a novel that depicts the intellectual, emotional, and moral development of its protagonist from childhood into adulthood; also sometimes called an

apprenticeship novel. This type of novel tends to envision character as the product of environment, experience, nurture, and education (in the widest sense) rather than of nature, fate, and so on. Charlotte Brontë's *Jane Eyre* is a famous example.

biography a work of nonfiction that recounts the life of a real person. If the person depicted in a biography is also its author, then we instead use the term *autobiography*. An autobiography that focuses only on a specific aspect of, or episode in, its author's life is a *memoir*.

blank verse the metrical verse form most like everyday human speech; blank verse consists of unrhymed lines in iambic pentameter. Many of Shakespeare's plays are in blank verse, as is John Milton's *Paradise Lost* and Alfred Tennyson's *Ulysses*.

caesura a short pause within a line of poetry; often but not always signaled by punctuation. Note the two caesuras in this line from Poe's "The Raven": "Once upon a midnight dreary, while I pondered, weak and weary."

canon the range of works that a consensus of scholars, teachers, and readers of a particular time and culture consider "great" or "major."

carpe diem literally, "seize the day" in Latin, a common theme of literary works that emphasize the brevity of life and the need to make the most of the present. Andrew Marvell's poem "To His Coy Mistress" is a well-known example.

central consciousness a character whose inner thoughts, perceptions, and feelings are revealed by a *third-person* limited narrator who does not reveal the thoughts, perceptions, or feelings of other characters.

character an imaginary personage who acts, appears, or is referred to in a literary work. *Major* or *main characters* are those that receive most attention, *minor characters* least. *Flat characters* are relatively simple, have a few dominant traits, and tend to be predictable. Conversely, *round characters* are complex and multifaceted and act in a way that readers might not expect but accept as possible. *Static characters* do not change; *dynamic characters* do. *Stock characters* represent familiar types that recur frequently in literary works, especially of a particular **genre** (e.g., the "mad scientist" of horror fiction and film or the fool in Renaissance, especially Shakespearean, drama).

characterization the presentation of a fictional personage. A term like "a good character" can, then, be ambiguous—it may mean that the personage is virtuous or that he or she is well presented regardless of his or her characteristics or moral qualities. In fiction, *direct characterization* occurs when a narrator explicitly tells us what a character is like. *Indirect characterization* occurs when a character's traits are revealed implicitly, through his or her speech, behavior, thoughts, appearance, and so on.

chorus a group of actors in a drama who comment on and describe the **action**. In classical Greek theater, members of the chorus often wore masks and relied on song, dance, and recitation to make their commentary.

classical unities as derived from Aristotle's *Poetics*, the three principles of structure that require a play to have one **plot** (*unity of action*) that occurs in one place (*unity of place*) and within one day (*unity of time*); also called the *dramatic unities*. Susan Glaspell's *Trifles* and Sophocles's *Antigone* observe the classical unities.

climax the third part of **plot**, the point at which the **action** stops rising and begins falling or reversing; also called *turning point* or (following Aristotle) *peripeteia*. *See also* **crisis**.

closet drama *see* **drama**.

colloquial diction *see* **diction**.

comedy a broad category of literary, especially dramatic, works intended primarily to entertain and amuse an audience. Comedies take many different forms, but they share three basic characteristics: (1) the values that are expressed and that typically cause **conflict** are determined by the general opinion of society (as opposed to being universal and beyond the control of humankind, as in **tragedy**); (2) **characters** in comedies are often defined primarily in terms of their social identities and roles and tend to be *flat* or *stock characters*

rather than highly individualized or *round* ones; (3) comedies conventionally end happily with an act of social reintegration and celebration such as marriage. William Shakespeare's *A Midsummer Night's Dream* is a famous example.

The term *high* or *verbal comedy* may refer either to a particular type of comedy or to a sort of humor found within any literary work that employs subtlety and wit and usually represents high society. Conversely, *low* or *physical comedy* is a type of either comedy or humor that involves burlesque, horseplay, and the representation of unrefined life. *See also* **farce**.

coming-of-age story *see* **initiation story**.

complication in plot, an **action** or event that introduces a new **conflict** or intensifies the existing one, especially during the **rising action** phase of plot.

conclusion also called *resolution*, the fifth and last phase or part of **plot**, the point at which the situation that was destabilized at the beginning becomes stable once more and the **conflict** is resolved.

concrete poetry poetry in which the words on the page are arranged to look like an object; also called *shaped verse*. George Herbert's "Easter Wings," for example, is arranged to look like two pairs of wings.

conflict a struggle between opposing forces. A conflict is *external* when it pits a **character** against something or someone outside himself or herself—another character or characters or something in nature or society. A conflict is *internal* when the opposing forces are two drives, impulses, or parts of a single character.

connotation what is suggested by a word, apart from what it literally means or how it is defined in the dictionary. *See also* **denotation**.

consonance the repetition of certain consonant sounds in close proximity, such as mish-mash. Especially prominent in Middle English poetry, such as *Beowulf*.

controlling metaphor *see* **metaphor**.

convention in literature, a standard or traditional way of presenting or expressing something, or a traditional or characteristic feature of a particular literary **genre** or subgenre. Division into lines and **stanzas** is a convention of poetry. Conventions of the type of poem known as the **epic** include a **plot** that begins *in medias res* and frequent use of **epithets** and extended **similes**.

cosmic irony *see* irony.

couplet two consecutive lines of verse linked by **rhyme** and **meter**; the meter of a *heroic couplet* is **iambic pentameter**.

crisis in plot, the moment when the conflict comes to a head, often requiring the character to make a decision; sometimes the crisis is equated with the **climax** or *turning point* and sometimes it is treated as a distinct moment that precedes and prepares for the climax.

criticism *see* literary criticism.

cycle *see* sequence.

dactylic referring to the metrical pattern in which each **foot** consists of a stressed syllable followed by two unstressed ones—for example, "Fláshed all their/sábres bare" (Tennyson, "Charge of the Light Brigade"). A single foot of this type is called a *dactyl*.

denotation a word's direct and literal meaning, as opposed to its **connotation**.

dénouement literally, "untying" (as of a knot) in French; a **plot**-related term used in three ways: (1) as a synonym for **falling action**, (2) as a synonym for **conclusion** or resolution, and (3) as the label for a phase following the conclusion in which any loose ends are tied up.

destabilizing event *see* inciting incident.

deus ex machina literally, "god out of the machine" (Latin); any improbable, unprepared-for plot contrivance introduced late in a literary work to resolve the **conflict**. The term derives from the ancient Greek theatrical practice of using a mechanical device to lower a god or gods onto the stage to resolve the conflicts of the human characters.

dialogue (1) usually, words spoken by **characters** in a literary work, especially as opposed to words that come directly from the **narrator** in a work of fiction; (2) more rarely, a literary work that consists mainly or entirely of the speech of two or more characters; examples include Thomas Hardy's poem "The Ruined Maid" and Plato's treatise *Republic*.

diction choice of words. Diction is often described as either *informal* or *colloquial* if it resembles everyday speech, or as *formal* if it is instead lofty, impersonal, and dignified. Tone is determined largely through diction.

discriminated occasion a specific, discrete moment portrayed in a fictional work, often signaled by phrases such as "At 5:05 in the morning . . . ," "It was about dusk, one evening during the supreme madness of the carnival season . . . ," or "the day before Maggie fell down. . . ."

drama a literary **genre** consisting of works in which **action** is performed and all words are spoken before an audience by an actor or actors impersonating the **characters**. (Drama typically lacks the **narrators** and **narration** found in fiction.) *Closet drama*, however, is a subgenre of drama that has most of these features yet is intended to be read, either silently by a single reader or out loud in a group setting. *Verse drama* is drama written in verse rather than prose.

dramatic irony *see* irony.

dramatic monologue a type or subgenre of poetry in which a **speaker** addresses a silent **auditor** or auditors in a specific situation and setting that is revealed entirely through the speaker's words; this kind of poem's primary aim is the revelation of the speaker's personality, views, and values. For example, Alfred Tennyson's "Ulysses" consists of an aged Ulysses's words to the mariners whom he hopes to convince to return to sea with him; most of Robert Browning's best-known poems, such as "My Last Duchess," are dramatic monologues.

dramatic poem a poem structured so as to present a **scene** or series of scenes, as in a work of drama. *See also* **dramatic monologue**.

dramatic unities *see* classical unities.

dramatis personae literally, "persons of the drama" (Latin); the list of **characters** that appears either in a play's program or at the top of the first page of the written play.

dynamic character *see* character.

elegy (1) since the Renaissance, usually a formal lament on the death of a particular person, but focusing mainly on the speaker's efforts to come to terms with his or her grief; (2) more broadly, any **lyric** in sorrowful mood that takes death as its primary subject. An example is W. H. Auden's "In Memory of W. B. Yeats."

end-stopped line a line of verse that contains or concludes a complete clause and usually ends with a punctuation mark. *See also* **enjambment**.

English sonnet *see* **sonnet**.

enjambment in poetry, the technique of running over from one line to the next without stop, as in the following lines by William Wordsworth: "My heart leaps up when I behold / A rainbow in the sky." The lines themselves would be described as *enjambed*.

epic a long **narrative poem** that celebrates the achievements of mighty **heroes** and **heroines**, usually in founding a nation or developing a culture, and uses elevated language and a grand, high style. Other epic **conventions** include a beginning **in medias res**, an invocation of the muse, a journey to the underworld, battle scenes, and a scene in which the hero arms himself for battle. Examples include *Beowulf* and Homer's *Iliad*. A *mock epic* is a form of **satire** in which epic language and conventions are used to depict **characters**, **actions**, and **settings** utterly unlike those in conventional epics, usually (though not always) with the purpose of ridiculing the social milieu or types of people portrayed in the poem. A famous example is Alexander Pope's *The Rape of the Lock*.

epigram a very short, usually witty verse with a quick turn at the end.

epigraph a quotation appearing at the beginning of a literary work or of one section of such a work; not to be confused with **epigram**.

epilogue (1) in fiction, a short section or chapter that comes after the **conclusion**, tying up loose ends and often describing what happens to the characters after the resolution of the **conflict**; (2) in drama, a short speech, often addressed directly to the audience, delivered by a **character** at the end of a play.

epiphany a sudden revelation of truth, often inspired by a seemingly simple or commonplace event. The term, originally from Christian theology, was first popularized by the Irish fiction writer James Joyce, though Joyce also used the term to describe the individual short stories collected in his book *Dubliners*.

episode a distinct **action** or series of actions within a **plot**.

epistolary novel *see* **novel**.

epithet a characterizing word or phrase that precedes, follows, or substitutes for the name of a person or thing, such as *slain civil rights leader* Martin Luther King Jr., or Zeus, *the god of trophies*; not to be confused with **epitaph**. **Epics** conventionally make frequent use of epithets.

epitaph an inscription on a tombstone or grave marker; not to be confused with epigram, epigraph, or epithet.

eponymous having a name used in the title of a literary work. For example, Lemuel Gulliver is the eponymous **protagonist** of Jonathan Swift's *Gulliver's Travels*.

expectation like **foreshadowing**, a set up for something believed to occur later on in a work of literature.

exposition the first phase or part of **plot**, which sets the scene, introduces and identifies **characters**, and establishes the situation at the beginning of a story or play. Additional exposition is often scattered throughout the work.

extended metaphor *see* **metaphor**.

external conflict *see* **conflict**.

external narration or narrator *see* **narrator**.

fable an ancient type of short **fiction**, in verse or prose, illustrating a **moral** or satirizing human beings. The **characters** in a fable are often animals that talk and act like human beings. The fable is sometimes treated as a specific type of folktale and sometimes as a fictional subgenre in its own right. An example is Aesop's "The Two Crabs."

fairy tale *see* **tale**.

falling action the fourth of the five phases or parts of **plot**, in which the **conflict** or conflicts move toward resolution.

fantasy a genre of literary work featuring strange settings and characters and often involving magic or the supernatural; though closely related to horror and science fiction, fantasy is typically less concerned with the macabre or with science and technology. J. R. R. Tolkien's *The Hobbit* is a well-known example.

farce a literary work, especially drama, characterized by broad humor, wild antics, and often slapstick, pratfalls, or other physical humor. *See also* **comedy**.

fiction any narrative, especially in prose, about invented or imagined **characters** and **action**. Today, we tend to divide fiction into three major subgenres based on length—the **short story**, **novella**, and **novel**. Older, originally oral forms of short fiction include the **fable**, **legend**, **parable**, and **tale**. Fictional works may also be categorized not by their length but by their handling of particular elements such as **plot** and **character**. Detective and science fiction, for example, are subgenres that include both novels and novellas such as Frank Herbert's *Dune* and short stories such as Edgar Allan Poe's "The Murders at the Rue Morgue" or Isaac Asimov's "I, Robot." *See also* **gothic fiction**, **historical fiction**, **nonfiction**, and **romance**.

figurative language language that uses figures of speech.

figure of speech any word or phrase that creates a "figure" in the mind of the reader by effecting an obvious change in the usual meaning or order of words, by comparing or identifying one thing with another; also called a *trope*. **Metaphor**, **simile**, **metonymy**, **overstatement**, **oxymoron**, and **understatement** are common figures of speech.

first-person narrator *see* **narrator**.

flashback a plot-structuring device whereby a scene from the fictional past is inserted into the fictional present or is dramatized out of order.

flashforward a plot-structuring device whereby a scene from the fictional future is inserted into the fictional present or is dramatized out of order.

flat character *see* **character**.

focus the visual component of **point of view**, the point from which people, events, and other details in a story are viewed; also called *focalization*. *See also* **voice**.

foil a **character** that serves as a contrast to another.

folktale *see* **tale**.

foot the basic unit of poetic **meter**, consisting of any of various fixed patterns of one to three stressed and unstressed syllables. A foot may contain more than one word or just one syllable of a multisyllabic word. In **scansion**, breaks between feet are usually indicated with a vertical line or slash mark, as in the following example (which contains five feet): "One com- | mon note | on ei- | ther lyre | did strike" (Dryden, "To the Memory of Mr. Oldham"). *For specific examples of metrical feet, see* **anapestic**, **dactylic**, **iambic**, **pyrrhic**, **spondee**, and **trochaic**.

foreshadowing a hint or clue about what will happen at a later moment in the **plot**.

formal diction *see* **diction**.

frame narrative *see* **narrative**.

free verse poetry characterized by varying line lengths, lack of traditional **meter**, and nonrhyming lines.

Freytag's pyramid a diagram of **plot** structure first created by the German novelist and critic Gustav Freytag (1816–95).

general setting *see* **setting**.

genre a type or category of works sharing particular formal or textual features and **conventions**; especially used to refer to the largest categories for classifying literature—**fiction**, **poetry**, **drama**, and **nonfiction**. A smaller division within a genre is usually known as a *subgenre*, such as **gothic fiction** or **epic poetry**.

gothic fiction a subgenre of **fiction** conventionally featuring plots that involve secrets, mystery, and the supernatural (or the seemingly supernatural) and large, gloomy, and usually antiquated (especially medieval) buildings as settings. Examples include Horace Walpole's *The Castle of Otranto* and Edgar Allan Poe's "The Fall of the House of Usher."

haiku a poetic form, Japanese in origin, that consists of seventeen syllables arranged in three unrhymed lines of five, seven, and five syllables, respectively.

hero/heroine a character in a literary work, especially the leading male/female **character**, who is especially virtuous, usually larger than life, sometimes almost godlike. *See also* **antihero**, **protagonist**, and **villain**.

heroic couplet *see* couplet.

hexameter a line of poetry with six **feet**: "She comes, | she comes | again, | like ring | dove frayed | and fled" (Keats, *The Eve of St. Agnes*). *See* **alexandrine**.

high (verbal) comedy *see* comedy.

historical fiction a subgenre of fiction, of whatever length, in which the temporal **setting**, or plot time, is significantly earlier than the time in which the work was written (typically, a period before the birth of the author). Conventionally, such works describe the atmosphere and mores of the setting in vivid detail and explore the influence of historical factors on the **characters** and **action**; though focusing mainly on invented or imaginary characters and events, historical fiction sometimes includes some characters and action based on actual historical personages and events. The *historical novel* is a type of historical fiction pioneered by nineteenth-century Scottish writer Walter Scott in works such as *Rob Roy* and *Ivanhoe*.

hyperbole *see* **overstatement**. (*See also* **understatement**.)

iambic referring to a metrical form in which each **foot** consists of an unstressed syllable followed by a stressed one; this type of foot is an *iamb*. The most common poetic meter in English is *iambic pentameter*—a metrical form in which most lines consist of five iambs: "One cóm- | mon nóte | on éi- | ther lýre | did stríke" (John Dryden, "To the Memory of Mr. Oldham").

image/imagery broadly defined, any sensory detail or evocation in a work; more narrowly, the use of **figurative language** to evoke a feeling, to call to mind an idea, or to describe an object. Imagery may be described as *auditory*, *tactile*, *visual*, or *olfactory* depending on which sense it primarily appeals to—hearing, touch, vision, or smell. An *image* is a particular instance of imagery.

implied author *see* author.

inciting incident an action that sets a **plot** in motion by creating **conflict**; also called *destabilizing event*.

informal diction *see* diction.

initiation story a kind of **short story** in which a **character**—often a child or young person—first learns a significant,

usually life-changing truth about the universe, society, people, or himself or herself; also called a *coming-of-age story*. James Joyce's "Araby" is a notable example.

in medias res "in the midst of things" (Latin); refers to opening a **plot** in the middle of the **action**, and then filling in past details by means of **exposition** and/or **flashback**.

interior monologue *see* monologue.

internal conflict *see* conflict.

internal narration or **narrator** *see* narrator.

intrusive narration or **narrator** *see* narrator.

inversion a change in normal **syntax** such as putting a verb before its subject. Common in poetry, the technique is also famously used by *Star Wars*' Yoda, as in "when 900 years old you reach, look as good, you will not."

irony a situation or statement characterized by a significant difference between what is expected or understood and what actually happens or is meant. *Verbal irony* occurs when a word or expression in context means something different from, and usually the opposite of, what it appears to mean; when the intended meaning is harshly critical or satiric, verbal irony becomes *sarcasm*. *Situational irony* occurs when a character holds a position or has an expectation that is reversed or fulfilled in an unexpected way. When there is instead a gap between what an audience knows and what a character believes or expects, we have *dramatic irony*; when this occurs in a **tragedy**, dramatic irony is sometimes called *tragic irony*. Finally, the terms *cosmic irony* and *irony of fate* are sometimes used to refer to situations in which situational irony is the result of fate, chance, the gods, or some other superhuman force or entity.

Italian sonnet *see* sonnet.

legend a type of **tale** conventionally set in the real world and in either the present or historical past, based on actual historical people and events and offering an exaggerated or distorted version of the truth about those people and events. American examples might include stories featuring Davy Crockett or Johnny Appleseed or the story about George Washington chopping down the cherry tree. British examples are the legends of King Arthur or Robin Hood.

limerick a light or humorous **poem** or subgenre of poems consisting of mainly **anapestic** lines of which the first, second, and fifth lines are of three **feet**; the third and fourth lines are of two feet; and the **rhyme scheme** is *aabba*.

limited narrator *see* **narrator**.

limited point of view *see* **point of view**.

lines in a poem, a discrete organization of words; the length and shape of a line can communicate meaning in a poem, and can be a formal element characterizing a poem, such as the fourteen lines that make up a **sonnet**.

literary criticism the mainly interpretive (versus evaluative) work written by readers of literary texts, especially professional ones (who are thus known as *literary critics*). It is "criticism" not because it is negative or corrective but rather because those who write criticism ask probing, analytical, "critical" questions about the works they read.

litotes a form of **understatement** in which one negates the contrary of what one means. Examples from common speech include "Not bad" (meaning "good") and "a novelist of no small repute" (meaning "a novelist with a big reputation"), and so on.

low (physical) comedy *see* **comedy**.

lyric originally, a poem meant to be sung to the accompaniment of a lyre; now, any relatively short poem in which the **speaker** expresses his or her thoughts and feelings in the first person rather than recounting a **narrative** or portraying a dramatic situation.

magic realism a type of **fiction** that involves the creation of a fictional world in which the kind of familiar, plausible **action** and **characters** one might find in more straightforwardly realist fiction coexist with utterly fantastic ones straight out of **myths** or dreams. This style of **realism** is associated especially with modern Latin American writers such as Gabriel García Márquez and Jorge Luis Borges. But the label is also sometimes applied to works by other con-

temporary writers from around the world, including Italo Calvino and Salman Rushdie.

major (main) character *see* **character**.

memoir *see* **biography**.

metafiction a subgenre of works that playfully draw attention to their status as **fiction** in order to explore the nature of fiction and the role of authors and readers.

metaphor a **figure of speech** in which two unlike things are compared implicitly—that is, without the use of a signal such as the word *like* or *as*—as in "Love is a rose, but you better not pick it." *See also* **simile**.

An *extended metaphor* is a detailed and complex metaphor that stretches across a long section of a work. If such a metaphor is so extensive that it dominates or organizes an entire literary work, especially a poem, it is called a *controlling metaphor*. In Linda Pastan's "Marks," for example, the controlling metaphor involves the use of "marks" or grades to talk about the speaker's performance of her familial roles. A *mixed metaphor* occurs when two or more usually incompatible metaphors are entangled together so as to become unclear and often unintentionally humorous, as in "Her blazing words dripped all over him."

meter the more or less regular pattern of stressed and unstressed syllables in a line of poetry. This is determined by the kind of **foot** (iambic or dactylic, for example) and by the number of feet per line (e.g., five feet = pentameter, six feet = hexameter).

metonymy a **figure of speech** in which the name of one thing is used to refer to another associated thing. When we say, "The White House has promised to veto the bill," for example, we use the White House as a metonym for the president and his administration. **Synecdoche** is a specific type of metonymy.

minor character *see* **character**.

mock epic *see* **epic**.

monologue (1) a long speech, usually in a play but also in other **genres**, spoken by one person and uninterrupted by the speech of anyone else, or (2) an entire work consisting of this sort of speech. In fiction, an *interior monologue* takes place entirely within the mind of a character rather than being spoken aloud. A **soliloquy** is a particular type of monologue occurring in drama, while a **dramatic monologue** is a type of poem.

moral a rule of conduct or a maxim for living (that is, a statement about how one should live or behave) communicated in a literary work. Though **fables** often have morals such as "Don't count your chickens before they hatch," more modern literary works instead tend to have **themes**.

motif a recurrent device, formula, or situation within a literary work. For example, the sound of the breaking harp string is a motif of Anton Chekhov's play *The Cherry Orchard*.

motive the animating impulse for an action, the reason why something is done or attempted.

myth (1) originally and narrowly, a **narrative** explaining how the world and humanity developed into their present form and, unlike a folktale, generally considered to be true by the people who develop it. Many, though not all, myths feature supernatural beings and have a religious significance or function within their culture of origin. Two especially common types of myth are the *creation myth*, which explains how the world, human beings, a god or gods, or good and evil came to be (e.g., the myth of Adam and Eve), and the *explanatory myth*, which explains features of the natural landscape or natural processes or events (e.g., "How the Leopard Got His Spots"); (2) more broadly and especially in its adjectival form (*mythic*), any narrative that obviously seeks to work like a myth in the first and more narrow sense, especially by portraying experiences or conveying truths that it implies are universally valid regardless of culture or time.

narration (1) broadly, the act of telling a story or recounting a **narrative**; (2) more narrowly, the portions of a narrative attributable to the **narrator** rather than words spoken by **characters** (that is, **dialogue**).

narrative a story, whether fictional or true and in prose or verse, related by a **narrator** or narrators (rather than acted out onstage, as in drama). A *frame narrative* is a narrative that recounts and thus "frames" the telling of another narrative or story. An example is Samuel Taylor Coleridge's "The Rime of the Ancient Mariner," in which an anonymous third-person narrator recounts how an old sailor comes to tell a young wedding guest the story of his adventures at sea.

narrative poem a poem in which a **narrator** tells a story.

narrator someone who recounts a **narrative** or tells a story. Though we usually instead use the term **speaker** when referring to poetry as opposed to prose fiction, *narrative poems* include at least one speaker who functions as a narrator. *See also* **narrative**.

A narrator or narration is said to be *internal* when the narrator is a **character** within the work, telling the story to an equally fictional **auditor** or listener; internal narrators are usually first- or second-person narrators (*see below*). A narrator or narration is instead said to be *external* when the narrator is not a character.

A *first-person narrator* is an internal narrator who consistently refers to himself or herself using the first-person pronouns *I* or *we*. A *second-person narrator* consistently uses the second-person pronoun *you* (a very uncommon technique). A *third-person narrator* uses third-person pronouns such as *she, he, they, it,* and so on; third-person narrators are almost always external narrators. Third-person narrators are said to be *omniscient* (literally, "all-knowing") when they describe the inner thoughts and feelings of multiple characters; they are said to be *limited* when they relate the thoughts, feelings, and perceptions of only one character (the **central consciousness**). If a work encourages us to view a narrator's account of events with suspicion, the narrator (usually first-person) is called *unreliable*. An *intrusive narrator* is a third-person narrator who occasionally disrupts his or her narrative to speak directly to the reader or audience in what is sometimes called *direct address*.

narrator time *see* time.

nonfiction a work or **genre** of prose works that describe actual, as opposed to imaginary or fictional, **characters** and events.

Subgenres of nonfiction include **biography**, **memoir**, and the **essay**. *See also* **fiction**.

novel a long work of **fiction** (approximately 40,000+ words), typically published (or at least publishable) as a stand-alone book; though most novels are written in **prose**, those written as poetry are called *verse novels*. A novel (as opposed to a **short story**) conventionally has a complex **plot** and, often, at least one **subplot**, as well as a fully realized **setting** and a relatively large number of **characters**. One important novelistic subgenre is the *epistolary novel*—a novel composed entirely of letters written by its characters. Another is the **bildungsroman**.

novella a work of prose fiction that falls somewhere in between a **short story** and a **novel** in terms of length, scope, and complexity. Novellas can be, and have been, published either as books in their own right or as parts of books that include other works. Franz Kafka's *The Metamorphosis* is an example.

octameter a line of poetry with eight **feet**: "Once u- | pon a | midnight | dreary | while I | pondered | weak and | weary."

octave eight lines of verse linked by a pattern of end rhymes, especially the first eight lines of an Italian, or Petrarchan, **sonnet**. *See also* **sestet**.

ode a **lyric** poem characterized by a serious topic and formal tone but without a prescribed formal pattern in which the speaker talks about, and often to, an especially revered person or thing. Examples include John Keats's odes and Percy Bysshe Shelley's "Ode to the West Wind."

oeuvre all of the works verifiably written by one author.

omniscient narrator *see* **narrator**.

omniscient point of view *see* **point of view**.

onomatopoeia a word capturing or approximating the sound of what it describes; *buzz* is a good example.

orchestra in classical Greek theater, a semicircular area used mostly for dancing by the **chorus**.

ottava rima literally, "octave (eighth) rhyme" (Italian); a verse form consisting of eight-line **stanzas** with an *abababcc*

rhyme scheme and **iambic** meter (usually **pentameter**). W. B. Yeats's "Sailing to Byzantium" is written in ottava rima.

overplot especially in Shakespearean drama, a **subplot** that resembles the main plot but stresses the political implications of the depicted action and situation.

overstatement exaggerated language; also called *hyperbole*.

oxymoron a **figure of speech** that combines two apparently contradictory elements, as in *wise fool*.

parable a short work of **fiction** that illustrates an explicit **moral** but that, unlike a **fable**, lacks fantastic or anthropomorphic characters. Especially familiar examples are the stories attributed to Jesus in the Bible—about the prodigal son, the good Samaritan, and so on.

parody any work that imitates or spoofs another work or **genre** for comic effect by exaggerating the style and changing the content of the original; parody is a subgenre of **satire**. Examples include *Scary Movie*, which parodies horror films; *The Colbert Report*, which spoofs conservative talk shows; and Tom Stoppard's *Real Inspector Hound*, a parody of detective fiction and drama.

particular setting *see* **setting**.

pastoral literature a work or category of works—whether fiction, poetry, drama, or nonfiction—describing and idealizing the simple life of country folk, usually shepherds who live a painless life in a world full of beauty, music, and love. An example is Christopher Marlowe's "The Passionate Shepherd to His Love."

pentameter a line of poetry with five **feet**: "Nuns fret | not at | their con- | vent's nar- | row room."

persona the voice or figure of the **author** who tells and structures the work and who may or may not share the values of the actual author. *See also* **author**.

personification a **figure of speech** that involves treating something nonhuman, such as an abstraction, as if it were a person by endowing it with humanlike qualities, as in "Death entered the room."

Petrarchan sonnet *see* **sonnet**.

plot the arrangement of the **action**. The five main parts or phases of plot are exposition, rising action, climax or turning point, falling action, and conclusion or resolution. *See also* subplot, overplot.

plot summary a brief recounting of the principal action of a work of fiction, drama, or narrative poetry, usually in the same order in which the action is recounted in the original work rather than in chronological order.

plot time *see* time.

poetry one of the three major genres of imaginative literature, which has its origins in music and oral performance and is characterized by controlled patterns of rhythm and syntax (often using meter and rhyme); compression and compactness and an allowance for ambiguity; a particularly concentrated emphasis on the sensual, especially visual and aural, qualities and effects of words and word order; and especially vivid, often figurative language.

point of view the perspective from which people, events, and other details in a work of fiction are viewed; also called focus, though the term *point of view* usually includes both focus and voice. See narrator.

prop in drama, an object used on the stage.

proscenium arch an arch over the front of a stage; the proscenium serves as a "frame" for the action onstage.

prose the regular form of spoken and written language, measured in sentences rather than lines, as in poetry.

protagonist the most neutral and broadly applicable term for the main character in a work, whether male or female, heroic or not heroic. *See also* antagonist, antihero, and hero/heroine.

psychological realism *see* realism.

pyrrhic a rarely used metrical foot consisting of two unstressed syllables.

quatrain a four-line unit of verse, whether an entire poem, a stanza, or a group of four lines linked by a pattern of rhyme (as in an English or Shakespearean sonnet).

reader time *see* time.

realism (1) generally, the practice in literature, especially fiction and drama, of attempting to describe nature and life as they are without idealization and with attention to detail, especially the everyday life of ordinary people. *See also* verisimilitude.

Just as notions of how life and nature differ widely across cultures and time periods, however, so do notions of what is "realistic." Thus, there are many different kinds of realism. *Psychological realism* refers, broadly, to any literary attempt to accurately represent the workings of the human mind and, more specifically, to the practice of a particular group of late-nineteenth- and early-twentieth-century writers including Joseph Conrad, Henry James, James Joyce, and Virginia Woolf, who developed the stream of consciousness technique of depicting the flow of thought. *See also* magic realism.

(2) more narrowly and especially when capitalized, a mid- to late-nineteenth-century literary and artistic movement, mainly in the U.S. and Europe, that championed realism in the first, more general sense, rejected what its proponents saw as the elitism and idealism of earlier literature and art, and emphasized settings, situations, action, and (especially middle- and working-class) characters ignored or belittled in earlier literature and art. Writers associated with the movement include Gustave Flaubert and Emile Zola (in France), George Eliot and Thomas Hardy (in Britain), and Theodore Dreiser (in the United States).

resolution *see* conclusion.

rhetoric the art and scholarly study of effective communication, whether in writing or speech. Many literary terms, especially those for figures of speech, derive from classical and Renaissance rhetoric.

rhyme repetition or correspondence of the terminal sounds of words ("How now, brown cow?"). The most common type, *end rhyme*, occurs when the last words in two or more lines of a poem rhyme with each other. *Internal rhyme* occurs when a word *within* a line of poetry rhymes with another word in the same or adjacent lines, as in "The Dew drew quivering and chill" (Emily Dickinson). An *eye rhyme* or *sight rhyme* involves words that don't actually rhyme but look like they do because of their similar spelling ("cough" and "bough"). *Off, half, near,* or *slant rhyme* is rhyme that is slightly "off" or only approximate, usually because words' final consonant sounds correspond, but not the vowels that proceed them ("phases" and "houses"). When two syllables rhyme and the last is unstressed or unaccented, they create a *feminine rhyme* ("ocean" and "motion"); *masculine rhyme* involves only a single stressed or accented syllable ("cat" and "hat"). See also **rhyme scheme**.

rhyme scheme the pattern of **end rhymes** in a poem, often noted by small letters, such as *abab* or *abba*.

rhythm the modulation of weak and strong (or stressed and unstressed) elements in the flow of speech. In most poetry written before the twentieth century, rhythm was often expressed in **meter**; in prose and in **free verse**, rhythm is present but in a much less predictable and regular manner.

rising action the second of the five phases or parts of **plot**, in which events complicate the **situation** that existed at the beginning of a work, intensifying the initial **conflict** or introducing a new one.

romance (1) originally, a long medieval narrative in verse or prose written in one of the Romance languages (French, Spanish, Italian, etc.) and depicting the quests of knights and other chivalric heroes and the vicissitudes of *courtly love*; also known as *chivalric romance*; (2) later and more broadly, any literary work, especially a long work of prose fiction, characterized by a nonrealistic and idealizing use of the imagination; (3) commonly today, works of prose fiction aimed at a mass, primarily female, audience and focusing on love affairs (as in *Harlequin Romance*).

round character see **character**.

sarcasm see **irony**.

satire a literary work—whether fiction, poetry, or drama—that holds up human failings to ridicule and censure. Examples include Jonathan Swift's novel *Gulliver's Travels* and Stanley Kubrick's film *Dr. Strangelove*.

scansion the process of analyzing (and sometimes also marking) verse to determine its **meter**, line by line.

scapegoat in a work of literature, the character or characters that take the blame for others' actions; usually an innocent party or only tangentially responsible, their punishment lets others off the hook.

scene a section or subdivision of a play or narrative that presents continuous **action** in one specific **setting**.

second-person narrator see **narrator**.

sequence (1) the ordering of **action** in a fictional **plot**; (2) a closely linked series or *cycle* of individual literary works, especially short stories or poems, designed to be read or performed together, as in the **sonnet** sequences of William Shakespeare and Edna St. Vincent Millay.

sestet six lines of verse linked by a pattern of **rhyme**, as in the last six lines of the Italian, or Petrarchan, **sonnet**. See also **octave**.

sestina an elaborate verse structure written in **blank verse** that consists of six **stanzas** of six lines each followed by a three-line stanza. The final words of each line in the first stanza appear in variable order in the next five stanzas and are repeated in the middle and at the end of the three lines in the final stanza. Elizabeth Bishop's "Sestina" is an example.

set the design, decoration, and scenery of the stage during a play; not to be confused with **setting**.

setting the time and place of the **action** in a work of fiction, poetry, or drama. The *spatial setting* is the place or places in which action unfolds, the *temporal setting* is the time. (Temporal setting is thus the same as *plot* **time**.) It is sometimes also helpful to distinguish between *general setting*—the general time and place in which all the action unfolds—and *particular settings*—the times and places in which individual **episodes** or **scenes** take place. The film version of *Gone with the Wind*, for example, is generally set in Civil War–era Georgia, while its opening scene takes place on the porch of Tara, Scarlett O'Hara's family home, before the war begins.

Shakespearean sonnet see **sonnet**.

shaped verse see **concrete poetry**.

short short story see **short story**.

short story a relatively short work of prose fiction (approximately 500 to 10,000 words) that, according to Edgar Allan Poe, can be read in a single sitting of two hours or less and works to create "a single effect." Two types of short story are the initiation story and the *short short story*. (Also sometimes called *microfiction*, a short short story is, as its name suggests, a short story that is especially brief; examples include Linda Brewer's "20/20" and Jamaica Kincaid's "Girl.")

simile a figure of speech involving a direct, explicit comparison of one thing to another, usually using the words *like* or *as* to draw the connection, as in "My love is like a red, red rose." An *analogy* is an extended simile. *See also* **metaphor**.

situation the basic circumstances depicted in a literary work, especially when the story, play, or poem begins or at a specific later moment in the **action**. In John Keats's "Ode to a Nightingale," for example, the situation involves a man (the **speaker**) sitting under a tree as he listens to a nightingale's song.

situational irony *see* irony.

skene a low building in the back of the stage area in classical Greek theaters. It represented the palace or temple in front of which the **action** took place.

soliloquy a monologue in which the **character** in a play is alone onstage and thinking out loud, as in the famous Hamlet speech that begins "To be or not to be."

sonnet a fixed verse form consisting of fourteen lines usually in **iambic pentameter**. An *Italian sonnet* consists of eight rhyme-linked lines (an **octave**) plus six rhyme-linked lines (a **sestet**), often with either an *abbaabba cdecde* or *abbacddc defdef* **rhyme scheme**. This type of sonnet is also called the *Petrarchan sonnet* in honor of the Italian poet Petrarch (1304–74). An *English* or *Shakespearean sonnet* instead consists of three **quatrains** (four-line units) and a **couplet** and often rhymes *abab cdcd efef gg*.

spatial setting *see* setting.

speaker (1) the person who is the voice of a poem; (2) anyone who speaks **dialogue** in a work of fiction, poetry, or drama.

Spenserian stanza a stanza consisting of eight lines of **iambic pentameter** (five feet) followed by a ninth line of iambic **hexameter** (six feet). The rhyme scheme is *ababbcbcc*. The stanza form takes its name from Edmund Spenser (ca. 1552–99), who used it in *The Faerie Queene*.

spondee a metrical **foot** consisting of a pair of stressed syllables ("Déad sét").

stage directions the words in the printed text of a play that inform the director, crew, actors, and readers how to stage, perform, or imagine the play. Stage directions are not spoken aloud and may appear at the beginning of a play, before any scene, or attached to a line of dialogue; they are often set in italics. The place and time of the action, the design of the set itself, and at times the characters' actions or tone of voice are given through stage directions and interpreted by the group of people who put on a performance.

stanza a section of a poem, marked by extra line spacing before and after, that often has a single pattern of **meter** and/or **rhyme**. Conventional stanza forms include **ballad stanza**, **Spenserian stanza**, **ottava rima**, and **terza rima**. *See also* **verse paragraph**.

static character *see* character.

stock character *see* character.

stream of consciousness a type of third-person **narration** that replicates the thought processes of a **character** without much or any intervention by a **narrator**. The term was originally coined by the nineteenth-century American psychologist William James (brother of novelist Henry James) to describe the workings of the human mind and only later adopted to describe the type of narration that seeks to replicate this process. The technique is closely associated with twentieth-century fiction writers of *psychological* **realism** such as Virginia Woolf, James Joyce, and William Faulkner, who were all heavily influenced by early psychologists such as William James and Sigmund Freud.

style a distinctive manner of expression; each author's style is expressed through his or her **diction**, **rhythm**, **imagery**, and so on.

subgenre *see* genre.

subplot a secondary **plot** in a work of fiction or drama. *See also* **overplot** and **underplot**.

symbol a person, place, thing, or event that figuratively represents or stands for something else. Often the thing or idea represented is more abstract and general, and the symbol is more concrete and particular. A *traditional symbol* is one that recurs frequently in (and beyond) literature and is thus immediately recognizable to those who belong to a given culture. In Western literature and culture, for example, the rose and snake traditionally symbolize love and evil, respectively. Other symbols such as the scarlet letter in Nathaniel Hawthorne's *The Scarlet Letter* instead accrue their complex meanings only within a particular literary work; these are sometimes called *invented symbols*.

symbolic poem a poem in which the use of symbols is so pervasive and internally consistent that the reference to the outside world being symbolized becomes secondary. William Blake's "The Sick Rose" and W. B. Yeats's "Second Coming" are examples.

synecdoche a type of **metonymy** in which the part is used to name or stand in for the whole, as when we refer to manual laborers as *hands* or say *wheels* to mean a car.

syntax word order; the way words are put together to form phrases, clauses, and sentences.

tale a brief **narrative** with a simple **plot** and **characters**, an ancient and originally oral form of storytelling. Unlike **fables**, tales typically don't convey or state a simple or single **moral**. An especially common type of tale is the *folktale*, the **conventions** of which include a formulaic beginning and ending ("Once upon a time . . . ," ". . . And so they lived happily ever after."); a **setting** that is not highly particularized in terms of time or place; *flat* and often *stock characters*, animal or human; and fairly simple **plots**. Though the term *fairy tale* is often and broadly used as a synonym for *folktale*, it more narrowly and properly designates a specific type of folktale featuring fairies or other fantastic creatures such as pixies or ogres.

temporal setting *see* **setting**.

terza rima literally, "third rhyme" (Italian); a verse form consisting of three-line **stanzas** in which the second line of each stanza rhymes with the first and third of

the next. Percy Bysshe Shelley's "Ode to the West Wind" is written in terza rima.

tetrameter a line of poetry with four feet: "The Grass | divides | as with | a comb" (Emily Dickinson).

theme (1) broadly and commonly, a topic explored in a literary work (e.g., "the value of all life"); (2) more narrowly and properly, the insight about a topic communicated in a work (e.g., "All living things are equally precious"). Most literary works have multiple themes, though some people reserve the term *theme* for the central or main insight and refer to others as *subthemes*. Usually, a theme is implicitly communicated by the work as a whole rather than explicitly stated in it, though fables are an exception. *See also* moral.

thesis the central debatable claim articulated, supported, and developed in an essay or other work of expository prose.

third-person narrator *see* **narrator**.

thrust stage a stage design that allows the audience to sit around three sides of the major acting area.

time in literature, at least four potentially quite different time frames are at issue: (1) *author time*, when the author originally created or published a literary text; (2) *narrator time*, when the **narrator** in a work of fiction supposedly narrated the story; (3) *plot time*, when the **action** depicted in the work supposedly took place (in other words, the work's temporal **setting**); and (4) *reader* (or *audience*) *time*, when an actual reader reads the work or an actual audience sees it performed.

In some cases, author, narrator, plot, and reader time will be roughly the same— if, for example, in 2008 you were to read Sherman Alexie's "Flight Patterns," a story published in 2003; set some time after September 11, 2001; and presumably narrated not long after the action ends. But in some cases, some or all of these time frames might differ. Walter Scott's novel *Rob Roy*, for example, was written and published in the early nineteenth century (1817); this is its author time. But the novel (a work of **historical fiction**) is set one hundred years earlier (1715); this is its plot time. The novel's narrator is a **character** supposedly writing down the story of his youthful adventures in his old age and long after the deaths of many of the principal characters; this is the narrator time. Were you to read the novel today, reader time would be almost two hundred years later than author time and almost three hundred years later than plot time.

tone the attitude a literary work takes toward its subject, especially the way this attitude is revealed through **diction**.

traditional symbol *see* **symbol.**

tragedy a work, especially of drama, in which a **character** (traditionally a good and noble person of high rank) is brought to a disastrous end in his or her confrontation with a superior force (fortune, the gods, human nature, universal values), but also comes to understand the meaning of his or her deeds and to accept an appropriate punishment. In some cases, the **protagonist**'s downfall can be direct result of a fatal but common character flaw. Examples include Sophocles's *Antigone*, William Shakespeare's *Hamlet*, and Wole Soyinka's *Death and the King's Horseman*.

trimeter a line of poetry with three **feet**: "Little | lamb, who | made thee?" (Blake).

trochaic referring to a metrical form in which the basic **foot** is a *trochee*—a metrical foot consisting of a stressed syllable followed by an unstressed one ("Hómer").

trope *see* **figure of speech.**

turning point *see* **climax.**

underplot a particular type of **subplot,** especially in Shakespeare's plays, that is a parodic or highly romantic version of the main plot. A good example would be the subplot in *A Midsummer Night's Dream* that features the character Bottom. *See also* **overplot.**

understatement language that makes its point by self-consciously downplaying its real emphasis, as in "Final exams aren't exactly a walk in the park"; **litotes** is one form of understatement. *See also* **overstatement.**

unity of action *see* **classical unities.**

unity of place *see* **classical unities.**

unity of time *see* **classical unities.**

unlimited point of view *see* **point of view.**

unreliable narrator *see* **narrator.**

verbal irony *see* **irony.**

verisimilitude from the Latin phrase *veri similes* ("like the truth"); the internal truthfulness, lifelikeness, and consistency of the world created within any literary work when we judge that world on its own terms rather than in terms of its correspondence to the real world. Thus, even a work that contains utterly fantastic or supernatural **characters** or **actions** (and doesn't aim at **realism**) may very well achieve a high degree of verisimilitude.

verse drama *see* **drama.**

verse novel *see* **novel.**

verse paragraph though sometimes used as a synonym for **stanza,** this term technically designates passages of verse, often beginning with an indented line, that are unified by topic (as in a prose paragraph) rather than by **rhyme** or **meter.**

villain a **character** who not only opposes the **hero** or **heroine** (and is thus an **antagonist**) but also is characterized as an especially evil person or "bad guy."

villanelle a verse form consisting of nineteen lines divided into six **stanzas**—five tercets (three-line stanzas) and one quatrain (four-line stanza). The first and third lines of the first tercet rhyme with each other, and this rhyme is repeated through each of the next four tercets and in the last two lines of the concluding quatrain. The villanelle is also known for its repetition of select lines. An example is Dylan Thomas's "Do Not Go Gentle into That Good Night."

voice the verbal aspect of **point of view,** the acknowledged or unacknowledged source of a story's words; the **speaker;** the "person" telling the story and that person's particular qualities of insight, attitude, and verbal style. *See also* **focus.**

Permissions Acknowledgments

PHOTO CREDITS

Fiction

Page 2 'Speed Bump', used with the permission of Dave Coverly and the Cartoonist Group. All rights reserved.; p. 11: Bettmann/Corbis; p. 21: Sean Gallup/Getty Images; p. 33: Sophie Bassouls/Corbis; p. 59: DOONESBURY ©1985 G. B. Trudeau. Reprinted with permission of UNIVERSAL UCLICK. All rights reserved.; p. 66: Sophie Bassouls/Corbis; p. 94: Christopher Felver/Corbis; p. 115: Bettmann/Corbis; p. 122: Rue des Archives/The Granger Collection; p. 127: Jeremy Bembaron/Corbis; p. 130: reproduced by courtesy of Charles Dickens Museum, London; p. 138: Christopher Felver/Corbis; p. 156: Gary Hannabarger/Corbis; p. 169: Bettmann/Corbis; p. 171: The Art Archive at Art Resource, NY; p. 186: Christopher Felver/Corbis; p. 203: © Heinemann (Photo by Melissa Cooperman); p. 213: (left to right, top to bottom) www.chinesenames.org; picerella/iStockphoto; Michael Brown/Dreamstime; Lftan/Dreamstime; p. 219: Granger Collection; p. 234: AP Photo/Gino Domenico; p. 254: Bettmann/Corbis; p. 275: Bettmann/Corbis; p. 279: Courtesy of Vintage/RandomHouse; p. 287: Granger Collection; p. 289: AP Photo/Eric Miller; p. 308: Everett Collection Inc/Alamy; p. 316: Corbis; p. 330: Hulton-Deutsch Collection/Corbis; p. 336: Hulton Archive/Getty Images; p. 344: Nancy Kaszerman/Zuma/Corbis; p. 362: Colita/Corbis; p. 368: Library of Congress; p. 400: AP Photo/Paul Hawthorne; p. 412: Photograph by Ralph Morrissey. Reprinted by the courtesy of the Morrissey Collection and the Photographic Archives, Vanderbilt University, Nashville, Tennessee; p. 426: Christopher Felver/Corbis; p. 433: Ralph Orlowski/Getty Images; p. 437: Francine Fleischer/Corbis; p. 444: Bettmann/Corbis; p. 455: Ulf Andersen/Getty Images.

Poetry

Page 475: Time Life Pictures/Pix Inc./The LIFE Picture Collection/Getty Images; p. 533: David Shankbone/Flickr/CC BY 2.0; p. 607: Alice James Books/MCT/via Getty Images; p. 666: Ink on paper from 'Black, Grey and White: A Book of Visual Sonnets' (Veer Books). ©David Miller; p. 751: (Auden): Corbis; (Bashō): Asian Art & Archaeology/Corbis; (Bishop): Bettmann/Corbis; p. 752: (Blake): Bettmann/Corbis; (Brooks): AP Photo; (Browning): Bettmann/Corbis; (Cofer): © Heinemann 2011(Photo by Melissa Cooperman); p. 753: (Coleridge): Bettmann/Corbis; (Billy Collins): AP Photo/Gino Domenico; (Martha Collins): courtesy Martha Collins/photo by Doug Macomber; p. 754 (Cullen): Bettmann/Corbis; (cummings): Bettmann/ Corbis; (Dickinson): Everett Collection Inc/Alamy; p. 755: (Donne): Bettmann/Corbis; (Dunbar): Corbis; (Espada): David Shankbone/Flickr/CC BY 2.0; p. 756: (Frost): E.O. Hoppe/Corbis; (Grimké): Moorland-Spingarn Research Center, Howard University; (Hayden): Pach Brothers/Corbis; p. 757: (Heaney): Christopher Felver/Corbis; (Hopkins): Granger Collection; (Hughes): National Portrait Gallery, Smithsonian Institution/Art Resource; (Keats): Portrait by Joseph Severn. Reprinted by courtesy of the National Portrait Gallery, London.; p. 758: (Knight): Judy Ray; (Larkin): TopFoto/The Image Works; p. 759: (McKay): Corbis; (Millay): Underwood & Underwood/Corbis; (Mora): Cheron Bayna Ryan; (Olds): Christopher Felver/Corbis; p. 760: (Owen): Hulton-Deutsch Collection/Corbis (Parker): AP Photo; (Pastan): Margaretta K. Mitchell; (Plath): Courtesy of the Sylvia Plath Collection, Mortimer Rare Book Room, Smith College; p. 761: (Pope): Culture Club/Hulton Archives/Getty Images; (Pound): E.O. Hoppe/Corbis; (Rich): Jason Langer/ Glasshouse Images; p. 762: (Ryan): Christopher Felver/Corbis; (Shakespeare): Chris Hellier/ Corbis; p. 763: (Stevens): Bettmann/Corbis; (Su): Courtesy Adrienne Su/ Photo by Guy Freeman; (Tennyson): Bettmann/Corbis; p. 764: (Trethewey): AP Photo/Rogelio V. Solis; (Whitman): Library of Congress; (Wilbur): Oscar White/Corbis p. 765: (Williams): Lisa Larsen/The LIFE Picture Collection/Getty Images; (Wordsworth): Hulton-Deutsch Collection/Corbis; (Yeats): Bettmann/Corbis; p. 766: (Young): Melanie Dunea/CPI.

Drama

Page 767: Sam Falk/The New York Times/Redux; p. 771: AP Photo; p. 812: Bettmann/Corbis; p. 873: AP Photo/Ted S. Warren; p. 936: Bettmann/Corbis; p. 938: Bettmann/Corbis; p. 1017: Theatre TCU Laura Saladino (pictured) Directed by Blake Robertson Photo by Amy Peterson; p. 1018: Interfoto/Alamy; p. 1101: Chris Hellier/Corbis; p. 1211: Bettmann/Corbis.

TEXT CREDITS

Fiction

JAMES BALDWIN: "Sonny's Blues" copyright © 1957 by James Baldwin was originally published in *Partisan Review*. Copyright renewed. Collected in GOING TO MEET THE MAN, published by Vintage Books. Reprinted by arrangement with the James Baldwin Estate.

TONI CADE BAMBARA: "The Lesson" from GORILLA, MY LOVE by Toni Cade Bambara, copyright © 1972 by Toni Cade Bambara. Used by permission of Random House, an imprint and division of Penguin Random House LLC. All rights reserved. Any third party use of this material, outside of this publication, is prohibited. Interested parties must apply directly to Penguin Random House LLC for permission.

LINDA BREWER: "20/20" from MICRO FICTION: AN ANTHOLOGY OF REALLY SHORT STORIES, ed. by Jerome Stern. Reprinted by permission of the author.

RAYMOND CARVER: "Cathedral" from CATHEDRAL by Raymond Carver, copyright © 1981, 1982, 1983 by Raymond Carver. Used by permission of Alfred A. Knopf, an imprint of the Knopf Doubleday Publishing Group, a division of Penguin Random House LLC. All rights reserved. Any third party use of this material, outside of this publication, is prohibited. Interested parties must apply directly to Penguin Random House LLC for permission.

JUDITH ORTIZ COFER: "Volar" from THE YEAR OF OUR REVOLUTION. Copyright © 1998 by Arte Publico Press-University of Houston. Reprinted with permission of the publisher.

EDWIDGE DANTICAT: "A Wall of Fire Rising" from KRIK? KRAK! by Edwidge Danticat, copyright © 1991, 1955 by Edwidge Danticat. Used by permission of Soho Press, Inc. All rights reserved.

JUNOT DÍAZ: "Wildwood 1982-1985" from THE BRIEF WONDROUS LIFE OF OSCAR WAO, copyright © 2007 by Junot Díaz. Used by permission of Riverhead, an imprint of Penguin Publishing Group, a division of Penguin Random House LLC.

LOUISE ERDRICH: "Love Medicine" from LOVE MEDICINE (new and expanded version) by Louise Erdrich. Copyright © 1984, 1993 by Louise Erdrich. Reprinted by arrangement with Henry Holt and Company, LLC. All rights reserved.

WILLIAM FAULKNER: "A Rose for Emily" from COLLECTED STORIES OF WILLIAM FAULKNER by William Faulkner. Copyright © 1950 by Random House, Inc., and renewed 1977 by Jill Faulkner Summers. Reprinted by permission of W.W. Norton and Company

GABRIEL GARCÍA MÁRQUEZ: "A Very Old Man With Enormous Wings" from LEAF STORM AND OTHER STORIES by Gabriel García Márquez, trans. by Gregory Rabassa. Copyright © 1971 by Gabriel Garcia Marquez. Reprinted by permission of HarperCollins Publishers.

ERNEST HEMINGWAY: "Hills Like White Elephants" is reprinted with the permission of Scribner, a division of Simon & Schuster, Inc., from MEN WITHOUT WOMEN by Ernest Hemingway. Copyright © 1927 by Charles Scribner's Sons. Copyright © renewed 1955 by Ernest Hemingway. All rights reserved.

FRANZ KAFKA: "A Hunger Artist" from THE COMPLETE STORIES, copyright © 1946, 1947, 1948, 1949, 1954, 1958, 1971 by Schocken Books, an imprint of the Knopf Doubleday Group, a division of Random House LLC. Used by permission of Schocken Books, an imprint of the Knopf Doubleday Publishing Group, a division of Penguin Random House LLC. All rights reserved. . Any third party use of this material, outside of this publication, is prohibited. Interested parties must apply directly to Penguin Random House LLC for permission.

YASUNARI KAWABATA: "The Grasshopper and the Bell Cricket" from PALM-OF-THE-HAND STORIES by Yasunari Kawabata. Translated by Lane Dunlop and J. Martin Holman. Translation copyright © 1988 by Lane Dunlop and J. Martin Holman. Reprinted by permission of North Point Press, a division of Farrar, Straus & Giroux, LLC.

JAMAICA KINCAID: "Girl" from AT THE BOTTOM OF THE RIVER by Jamaica Kincaid. Copyright © 1983 by Jamaica Kincaid. Reprinted by permission of Farrar, Straus & Giroux, LLC.

JHUMPA LAHIRI: "Interpreter of Maladies" from INTERPRETER OF MALADIES. Copyright © 1999 by Jhumpa Lahiri. Reprinted by permission of Houghton Mifflin Harcourt Publishing Company. All rights reserved.

TONI MORRISON: "Recitatif," copyright © 2015 by Toni Morrison. Used by permission. All rights reserved.

ALICE MUNRO: "Boys and Girls" from DANCE OF THE HAPPY SHADES: AND OTHER STORIES by Alice Munro is reprinted by permission of the author. Copyright © 1968 by Alice Munro.

JOYCE CAROL OATES: "Where Are You Going, Where Have You Been?" from HIGH LONE-SOME: NEW AND SELECTED STORIES 1966-2006, pp.267-283. Copyright © 2006 by Ontario Review, Inc. Reprinted by permission of HarperCollins Publishers.

FLANNERY O'CONNOR: "A Good Man is Hard to Find" is reprinted from A GOOD MAN IS HARD TO FIND AND OTHER STORIES by permission of Houghton Mifflin Harcourt Publishing Company. Copyright © 1955 by Flannery O'Connor and renewed 1983 by Regina O'Connor. All rights reserved.

TILLIE OLSEN: "I Stand Here Ironing" from TELL ME A RIDDLE, reprinted by permission of the University of Nebraska Press. Copyright © 1956 by Tillie Olsen. Rights outside North America by permission of The Frances Goldin Literary Agency. Copyright © 1961 by Tillie Olsen.

MARJANE SATRAPI: "The Shabbat" from PERSEPOLIS: THE STORY OF A CHILD-HOOD by Marjane Satrapi, trans. by Mattias Ripa & Blake Ferris, translation copyright © 2003 by L'Association, Paris, France. Used by permission of Pantheon Books, an imprint of the Knopf Doubleday Publishing Group, a division of Penguin Random House LLC. All rights reserved. Any third party use of this material, outside of this publication, is prohibited. Interested parties must apply directly to Penguin Random House LLC for permission.

Poetry

HELEN CHASIN: "The Word *Plum*" from COMING CLOSE AND OTHER POEMS by Helen Chasin. Copyright © 1968 by Helen Chasin. Reprinted by permission of Yale University Press.

KELLY CHERRY: "Alzheimer's" from DEATH AND TRANSFIGURATION. Copyright © 1997. Reprinted by permission of Louisiana State University Press.

LUCILLE CLIFTON: "cream of wheat" from THE COLLECTED POEMS OF LUCILLE CLIFTON, 1965-2019. Copyright © 2008 by Lucille Clifton. Reprinted with the permission of The Permissions Company, Inc., on behalf of BOA Editions Ltd., www.boaeditions.org.

JUDITH ORTIZ COFER: "The Latin Deli: An Ars Poetica" by Judith Ortiz Cofer is reprinted with permission from the publisher of "The Americas Review." Copyright © 1992 Arte Publico Press-University of Houston.

BILLY COLLINS: "Sonnet," copyright © 2001 by Billy Collins, from SAILING ALONE AROUND THE ROOM. "Divorce" from BALLISTICS, copyright © 2008 by Billy Collins. Used by permission of Random House, an imprint and division of Penguin Random House LLC. All rights reserved. Any third party use of this material, outside of this publication, is prohibited. Interested parties must apply directly to Penguin Random House LLC for permission. "Introduction to Poetry" from THE APPLE THAT ASTONISHED PARIS. Copyright © 1988, 1996 by Billy Collins. Reprinted with the permission of The Permissions Company, Inc. on behalf of the University of Arkansas Press, www.uapress.com

MARTHA COLLINS: "Lies" from SOME THINGS WORDS CAN DO (Sheep Meadow Press, 1998). Copyright © 1998 by Martha Collins. Reprinted by permission of the author.

COUNTEE CULLEN: "Yet Do I Marvel" from COLOR. Copyright © 1925 by Harper & Bros., New York. Renewed 1952 by Ida M. Cullen. "From the Dark Tower" from COPPER SUN. Copyright © 1927 by Harper & Bros., New York. Renewed 1954 by Ida M. Cullen.. Copyrights held by Amistad Research Center, Tulane University, administered by Thompson and Thompson, Brooklyn, NY.

E. E. CUMMINGS: "next to of course god america I" copyright 1926, 1954, © 1991 by the Trustees for the E.E. Cummings Trust. Copyright © 1985 by George James Firmage. "Buffalo Bill's," copyright 1923, 1951, © 1991 by the Trustees for the E.E. Cummings Trust. Copyright © 1976 by George James Firmage. "in Just-," copyright 1923, 1951, © 1991 by the Trustees for the E.E. Cummings Trust. Copyright © 1976 by George James Firmage. "I(a," copyright © 1958, 1986, 1991 by the Trustees for the E.E. Cummings Trust. From COMPLETE POEMS: 1904-1962 by E.E. Cummings, edited by George J. Firmage. Used by permission of Liveright Publishing Corporation.

LYDIA DAVIS: "Head, Heart" from THE COLLECTED STORIES OF LYDIA DAVIS. Copyright © 2009 by Lydia Davis. Reprinted by permission of Farrar, Straus and Giroux, LLC.

WALTER DE LA MARE: "Slim Cunning Hands" from THE COMPLETE POEMS OF WALTER DE LA MARE. Reprinted by permission of the Literary Trustees of Walter de la Mare and the Society of Authors as their representative.

JAMES DICKEY: "The Leap" from POEMS, 1957-1967. Copyright © 1964 and © 1967 by Wesleyan University Press. Reprinted by permission of the publisher.

EMILY DICKINSON: Poems by Emily Dickinson are reprinted by permission of the publishers and the Trustees of Amherst College from THE POEMS OF EMILY DICKINSON, Thomas H. Johnson, ed., Cambridge, Mass.: The Belknap Press of Harvard University Press. Copyright © 1951, 1955, 1979, 1983 by the President and Fellows of Harvard College and from THE POEMS OF EMILY DICKINSON: READING EDITION, Ralph W. Franklin, ed., Cambridge, Mass.: The Belknap Press of Harvard University Press. Copyright © 1998, 1999 by the President and Fellows of Harvard College. Copyright © 1951, 1955, 1979,

1983 by the President and Fellows of Harvard College. Reprinted by permission of the publishers and the Trustees of Amherst College.

RITA DOVE: "Daystar" from THOMAS AND BEULAH (Carnegie-Melllon University Press, 1986). Copyright © 1986 by Rita Dove. Reprinted by permission of the author.

T. S. ELIOT: "The Love Song of J. Alfred Prufrock" from COLLECTED POEMS 1909-1962 by T.S. Eliot is reprinted by permission of the publisher, Faber & Faber Ltd.

MARTÍN ESPADA: "Litany at the Tomb of Frederick Douglass" from THE TROUBLE BALL by Martín Espada. Copyright © 2011 by Martín Espada. Used by permission of W.W. Norton & Company, Inc. "Of the Threads that Connect the Stars" first published in *Ploughshares*, Spring 2013, is reprinted by permission of the author. Copyright © 2013 by Martín Espada.

KENNETH FEARING: "Dirge" from COMPLETE POEMS by Kenneth Fearing is reprinted by the permission of Russell & Volkening, Inc. as agents for the author. Copyright © 1934 by Kenneth Fearing, renewed in 1972 by the Estate of Kenneth Fearing.

ROBERT FROST: "Range-Finding," "Stopping by Woods on a Snowy Evening," "The Road Not Taken," "Home Burial," and "Design" from the book THE POETRY OF ROBERT FROST edited by Edward Connery Lathem. Copyright © 1923, 1930, 1939, 1969 by Henry Holt and Company, copyright © 1944, 1951, 1958 by Robert Frost, copyright © 1967 by Lesley Frost Ballantine. Reprinted by permission of Henry Holt and Company, LLC.

ANGELINA GRIMKÉ: "Tenebris" from SELECTED WORKS OF ANGELINA GRIMKE, Angelina Grimké Papers, Moorland-Springarn Research Center, Howard University.

GWEN HARWOOD: "In the Park" from SELECTED POEMS by Gwen Harwood, ed. by Gregory Kratzmann (2001). Reproduced with permission of Penguin Random House Australia.

ROBERT HAYDEN: "A Letter from Phillis Wheatley," copyright © 1978 by Robert Hayden. "Those Winter Sundays." Copyright © 1966 by Robert Hayden. From COLLECTED POEMS OF ROBERT HAYDEN, edited by Frederick Glaysher. Used by permission of Liveright Publishing Corporation.

SEAMUS HEANEY: "Digging," and "Punishment" from OPENED GROUND: SELECTED POEMS 1966-1996 by Seamus Heaney. Copyright © 1998 by Seamus Heaney. Reprinted by permission of Farrar, Straus & Giroux, LLC and Faber & Faber Ltd.

ANTHONY HECHT: "The Dover Bitch" from COLLECTED EARLIER POEMS by Anthony Hecht, copyright © 1990 by Anthony E. Hecht. Used by permission of Alfred A. Knopf, an imprint of the Knopf Doubleday Publishing Group, a division of Penguin Random House LLC. All rights reserved. Any third party use of this material, outside of this publication, is prohibited. Interested parties must apply directly to Penguin Random House LLC for permission.

LANGSTON HUGHES: "Ballad of the Landlord," "Harlem (2)," "I, Too," from THE COLLECTED POEMS OF LANGSTON HUGHES by Langston Hughes, ed. by Arnold Rampersad with David Roessel, Associate Editor, copyright © 1994 by the Estate of Langston Hughes. Used by permission of Alfred A. Knopf, an imprint of the Knopf Doubleday Publishing Group, a division of Penguin Random House LLC. All rights reserved. Any third party use of this material, outside of this publication, is prohibited. Interested parties must apply directly to Penguin Random House LLC for permission.

RANDALL JARRELL: "The Death of the Ball Turret Gunner" from THE COMPLETE POEMS by Randall Jarrell. Copyright © 1969 by Randall Jarrell, renewed 1997 by Mary von S. Jarrell. Reprinted by permission of Farrar Straus & Giroux. LLC

X. J. KENNEDY: "In a Prominent Bar in Secaucus One Day" from IN A PROMINENT BAR IN SECAUCUS: NEW AND SELECTED POEMS, 1955-2007, p. 11-12. Copyright © 2007 X.J. Kennedy. Reprinted with permission of The Johns Hopkins University Press.

GALWAY KINNELL: "Blackberry Eating" from THREE BOOKS by Galway Kinnell. Copyright © 1993 by Galway Kinnell. Reprinted by permission of Houghton Mifflin Harcourt Publishing Company. All Rights Reserved.

ETHERIDGE KNIGHT: "Eastern Guard Tower," "Hard Rock Returns to Prison from the Hospital for the Criminal Insane," "[The falling snow flakes]," and "[Making jazz swing in]" from THE ESSENTIAL ETHERIDGE KNIGHT, copyright © 1986. Reprinted by permission of the University of Pittsburgh Press.

MAXINE KUMIN: "Woodchucks" from SELECTED POEMS 1960-1990 by Maxine Kumin. Copyright © 1972, 1997 by Maxine Kumin. Used by permission of W.W. Norton & Company, Inc.

PHILIP LARKIN: "Church Going" from THE COMPLETE POEMS OF PHILIP LARKIN, ed. by Archie Burnett. Copyright © 2012 by the Estate of Philip Larkin. Introduction copyright © 2012 by Archie Burnett. Reprinted by permission of Farrar, Straus and Giroux, LLC and Faber & Faber Ltd. Excerpts from "A Conversation with Ian Hamilton" from "An Interview with John Haffenden" published in FURTHER REQUIREMENTS: INTERVIEWS, BROADCASTS, STATEMENTS AND BOOK REVIEWS, by Philip Larkin, ed. by Anthony Thwaite (Faber & Faber 2001) are reprinted by permission of The Society of Authors as the Literary Representative of the Estate of Philip Larkin.

LI-YOUNG LEE: "Persimmons" from ROSE. Copyright © 1986 by Li-Young Lee. Reprinted with the permission of The Permissions Company, Inc. on behalf of BOA Editions, Ltd., www.boaeditions.org

PATRICIA LOCKWOOD: "What Is the Zoo for What?" first published in The New Yorker, Oct. 28, 2013 is reprinted by permission of the author.

AMIT MAJMUDAR: "Dothead" originally published in The New Yorker, Aug. 1, 2011. Copyright © 2011 by Amit Majmudar. Reprinted by permission of Georges Borchardt, Inc. on behalf of the author.

CLAUDE MCKAY: "The White House" and "The Harlem Dancer" by Claude McKay are reprinted courtesy of the Literary Estate for the Works of Claude McKay.

EDNA ST. VINCENT MILLAY: "Woman have loved before as I have now," © 1931, 1958 "I, being born a woman and distressed," "What lips my lips have kissed," and "I will put Chaos in fourteen lines" from COLLECTED POEMS. Copyright 1923, 1928, 1931, 1054 © 1955, 1958, 1982 by Edna St. Vincent Millay and Norma Millay Ellis. Reprinted with the permission of The Permissions Company, Inc. on behalf of Holly Peppe, Literary Executor, The Millay Society, www.millay.org

PAT MORA: "Sonrisas" from BORDERS by Pat Mora is reprinted with permission from the publisher (© 1986 Arte Publico Press-Univ. of Houston). "Elena" from CHANTS by Pat Mora is reprinted with permission from the publisher (© 1994 Arte Publico Press-University of Houston). "Gentle Communion from COMMUNION by Pat Mora Is reprinted with permission from the publisher (© 1991 Arte Publico Press- University of Houston).

HARRYETTE MULLEN: "Dim Lady" from SLEEPING WITH THE DICTIONARY by Harryette Mullen, copyright © 2002 by the Regents of the University of California is reprinted by permission of the University of California Press.

HOWARD NEMEROV: "The Vacuum" from THE COLLECTED POEMS OF HOWARD NEMEROV. Copyright © 1977 by Howard Nemerov. Reprinted by permission of the Estate of Howard Nemerov.

FRANK O'HARA: "[Lana Turner has collapsed]" from LUNCH POEMS (1964) is reprinted by permission of City Lights Books.

Drama

Index of Authors

Aesop
  The Two Crabs, 249
Alvarez, Julia
  "Poetry Makes Nothing
    Happen"?, 685
Anonymous
  The Elephant in the
    Village of the Blind, 14
Anonymous
  Sir Patrick Spens, 686
Anonymous
  [There was a young girl
    from St. Paul], 623
Anonymous
  The Twenty-Third Psalm,
    589
Arnold, Matthew
  Dover Beach, 530
Atwood, Margaret
  Death of a Young Son by
    Drowning, 515
Auden, W. H.
  In Memory of W. B. Yeats,
    687
  Musée des Beaux Arts, 689
  [Stop all the clocks, cut
    off the telephone], 556

Baldwin, James
  Sonny's Blues, 66
Bambara, Toni Cade
  Authors on Their Work,
    286
  The Lesson, 279
Bashō
  [A village without
    bells—], 690
  [This road—], 690
Behn, Aphra
  On Her Loving Two
    Equally, 493

Bishop, Elizabeth
  Exchanging Hats, 522
  Sestina, 661
Blake, William
  The Chimney Sweeper,
    692
  The Lamb, 690
  London, 554
  The Sick Rose, 598
  The Tyger, 691
Borson, Roo
  After a Death, 606
Boss, Todd
  My Love for You Is So
    Embarrassingly, 585
Bradstreet, Anne
  To My Dear and Loving
    Husband, 625
Brewer, Linda
  20/20, 17
Brooks, Gwendolyn
  First Fight. Then Fiddle.,
    676
  We Real Cool, 521
Browning, Elizabeth
  Barrett
  How Do I Love Thee?,
    672
Browning, Robert
  My Last Duchess, 692
  Soliloquy of the Spanish
    Cloister, 511
Burns, Robert
  A Red, Red Rose, 584

Calvino, Italo
  from Invisible Cities, 166
Carver, Raymond
  Cathedral, 33
Chasin, Helen
  The Word Plum, 613

Chekhov, Anton
  The Lady with the Dog,
    171
Cherry, Kelly
  Alzheimer's, 541
Chopin, Kate
  The Story of an Hour, 287
Cleghorn, Sarah
  [The golf links lie so near
    the mill], 566
Clifton, Lucille
  cream of wheat, 521
Cofer, Judith Ortiz
  The Latin Deli: An Ars
    Poetica, 542
  Volar, 203
Coleridge, Samuel Taylor
  Frost at Midnight, 639
  Kubla Khan, 694
  Metrical Feet, 620
Collins, Billy
  Authors on Their Work,
    480, 516
  Divorce, 488
  Introduction to Poetry, 695
  Sonnet, 677
Collins, Martha
  Lies, 567
Constable, Henry
  [My lady's presence makes
    the roses red], 668
Crane, Stephen
  The Open Boat, 254
Cullen, Countee
  Yet Do I Marvel, 696
Cummings, E. E.
  [Buffalo Bill's], 663
  [in Just-], 696
  [l(a], 663
  [next to of course god
    america i], 520

Danticat, Edwidge
  A Wall of Fire Rising,
    234
Davis, Lydia
  Head, Heart, 478
de la Mare, Walter
  Slim Cunning Hands,
    568
Díaz, Junot
  Wildwood, 455
Dickey, James
  The Leap, 593
Dickinson, Emily
  [*A narrow Fellow in the
    Grass*], 699
  [*Because I could not stop
    for Death*—], 583
  [*I dwell in Possibility*–],
    697
  [*I stepped from Plank to
    Plank*], 698
  [*My Life had stood*— a
    Loaded Gun*—], 698
  [*Tell all the truth but tell
    it slant*—], 699
  [*The Sky is low*–*the
    Clouds are mean*],
    488
  [*Wild Nights*- *Wild
    Nights!*], 700
Donne, John
  [*Batter my heart,
    three-personed God*],
    590
  The Canonization, 700
  [*Death, be not proud*],
    702
  The Flea, 527
  Song, 702
  *A Valediction: Forbidding
    Mourning*, 703
Dove, Rita
  Daystar, 525
Dunbar, Paul Laurence
  Sympathy, 555
  We Wear the Mask, 704

Eliot, T. S.
  *The Love Song of J.
    Alfred Prufrock*, 705

Erdrich, Louise
  Love Medicine, 289
Espada, Martín
  Authors on Their Work,
    533
  *Litany at the Tomb of
    Frederick Douglass*,
    532
  *Of the Threads That
    Connect the Stars*, 560

Faulkner, William
  A Rose for Emily, 308
Fearing, Kenneth
  Dirge, 614
Frost, Robert
  Design, 675
  Home Burial, 709
  Range-Finding, 675
  The Road Not Taken,
    602
  *Stopping by Woods on a
    Snowy Evening*, 712

Gilman, Charlotte Perkins
  The Yellow Wallpaper,
    316
Glaspell, Susan
  Trifles, 771
Grimké, Angelina
  Tenebris, 713
Grimm, Jacob and Wilhelm
  The Shroud, 60

Hansberry, Lorraine
  A Raisin in the Sun, 936
Hardy, Thomas
  The Ruined Maid, 483
Harwood, Gwen
  In the Park, 676
Hawthorne, Nathaniel
  The Birth-Mark, 219
Hayden, Robert
  *A Letter from Phillis
    Wheatley*, 490
  Those Winter Sundays,
    559
Heaney, Seamus
  Digging, 713
  Punishment, 636

Hecht, Anthony
  The Dover Bitch, 539
Hemingway, Ernest
  *Hills Like White
    Elephants*, 122
Herbert, George
  Easter Wings, 664
Hopkins, Gerard Manley
  God's Grandeur, 714
  Pied Beauty, 573
  Spring and Fall, 628
  The Windhover, 715
Hughes, Langston
  Ballad of the Landlord,
    519
  Harlem, 715
  I, Too, 716

Ibsen, Henrik
  A Doll House, 812

Jarrell, Randall
  *The Death of the Ball
    Turret Gunner*, 590
Jonson, Ben
  On My First Son, 716
Joyce, James
  Araby, 330

Kafka, Franz
  A Hunger Artist, 336
Kawabata, Yasunari
  *The Grasshopper and the
    Bell Cricket*, 275
Keats, John
  To Autumn, 718
  *On First Looking into
    Chapman's Homer*, 4
  Ode on a Grecian Urn,
    717
  Ode to a Nightingale,
    599
Kennedy, X. J.
  *In a Prominent Bar in
    Secaucus One Day*,
    509
Kincaid, Jamaica
  Girl, 127
Kinnell, Galway
  Blackberry Eating, 635

Knight, Etheridge
[*Eastern guard tower*],
720
*Hard Rock Returns to
Prison from the
Hospital for the
Criminal Insane*, 720
[*Making jazz swing in*],
720
[*The falling snow flakes*],
720
Kumin, Maxine
Woodchucks, 549

Lahiri, Jhumpa
Interpreter of Maladies,
344
Larkin, Philip
Authors on Their Work,
649
Church Going, 647
Lee, Li-Young
Persimmons, 534
Lockwood, Patricia
*What Is the Zoo for
What*, 587

Majmudar, Amit
Dothead, 586
Marlowe, Christopher
*The Passionate Shepherd
to His Love*, 537
Márquez, Gabriel García
*A Very Old Man with
Enormous Wings*, 362
Martin, Jane
Two Monologues from
Talking With . . . ,
1013
Marvell, Andrew
To His Coy Mistress, 528
McKay, Claude
The Harlem Dancer, 721
The White House, 722
Melville, Herman
Bartleby, the Scrivener,
368
Millay, Edna St. Vincent
[*I, being born a woman
and distressed*], 674

[*I will put Chaos into
fourteen lines*], 674
[*What lips my lips have
kissed, and where, and
why*], 673
[*Women have loved before
as I love now*], 673
Miller, Arthur
Authors on Their Work,
1100
Death of a Salesman, 1018
Milton, John
[*When I consider how my
light is spent*], 670
Mora, Pat
Elena, 722
Gentle Communion, 723
Sonrisas, 633
Morrison, Toni
Authors on Their Work,
155
Recitatif, 138
Mullen, Harryette
Dim Lady, 677
Munro, Alice
Boys and Girls, 400

Nemerov, Howard
The Vacuum, 603

Oates, Joyce Carol
*Where Are You Going,
Where Have You
Been?*, 94
O'Connor, Flannery
*A Good Man Is Hard to
Find*, 412
O'Hara, Frank
Poem, 486
Olds, Sharon
Authors on Their Work,
516
Last Night, 556
Sex without Love, 572
The Victims, 641
Olsen, Tillie
I Stand Here Ironing,
426
Ortiz, Simon J.
My Father's Song, 558

Owen, Wilfred
Dulce et Decorum Est,
627

Parker, Dorothy
A Certain Lady, 518
One Perfect Rose, 597
Pastan, Linda
*To a Daughter Leaving
Home*, 526
love poem, 724
Marks, 582
Piercy, Marge
Barbie Doll, 724
Plath, Sylvia
Daddy, 725
Lady Lazarus, 727
Poe, Edgar Allan
The Cask of Amontillado,
115
The Raven, 730
Pope, Alexander
from *The Rape of the
Lock*, 612
Sound and Sense, 615
Pope, Jessie
The Call, 626
Pound, Ezra
*The River-Merchant's
Wife: A Letter*, 733
In a Station of the Metro,
733
Powell, Lynn
Kind of Blue, 579

Raleigh, Sir Walter
*The Nymph's Reply to the
Shepherd*, 538
Randall, Dudley
Ballad of Birmingham,
734
Rich, Adrienne
Aunt Jennifer's Tigers,
550
Authors on Their Work,
551
At a Bach Concert, 735
Diving into the Wreck,
603
History, 736

Robinson, Edwin Arlington
Richard Cory, 482
Roethke, Theodore
My Papa's Waltz, 569
Rossetti, Christina
In an Artist's Studio, 672
Ryan, Kay
Blandeur, 574
Repulsive Theory, 557

Satrapi, Marjane
from Persepolis, 21
Sedaris, David
Jesus Shaves, 433
Shakespeare, William
Hamlet, 1101
[Let me not to the marriage of true minds], 670
[Like as the waves make towards the pebbled shore], 628
[My mistress' eyes are nothing like the sun], 669
[Not marble, nor the gilded monuments], 669
[Shall I compare thee to a summer's day?], 589
[That time of year thou mayst in me behold], 580
[Th'expense of spirit in a waste of shame], 644
Shelley, Percy Bysshe
Ode to the West Wind, 645
Ozymandias, 737
Shuttleworth, Ciara
Sestina, 662
Snodgrass, W. D.
Leaving the Motel, 547
Sophocles
Antigone, 1211
Springsteen, Bruce
Nebraska, 489
Stallings, A. E.
Shoulda, Woulda, Coulda, 575

Stevens, Wallace
Anecdote of the Jar, 737
The Emperor of Ice-Cream, 738
Su, Adrienne
Authors on Their Work, 554
Escape from the Old Country, 543
On Writing, 553

Tan, Amy
A Pair of Tickets, 186
Taylor, Jane
The Star, 624
Tennyson, Alfred Lord
from The Charge of the Light Brigade, 623
Tears, Idle Tears, 739
Ulysses, 739
Thomas, Dylan
Do Not Go Gentle into That Good Night, 659
Trethewey, Natasha
Myth, 660
Pilgrimage, 540
Turner, Brian
Authors on Their Work, 607
Jundee Ameriki, 606

Updike, John
Authors on Their Work, 443
A & P, 437

Walcott, Derek
A Far Cry from Africa, 741
Wallace, David Foster
Good People, 156
Waller, Edmund
Song, 596
Welty, Eudora
Why I Live at the P.O., 444
Wheatley, Phillis
On Being Brought from Africa to America, 487

Whitman, Walt
Beat! Beat! Drums!, 629
Facing West from California's Shores, 742
[I celebrate myself, and sing myself], 519
I Hear America Singing, 643
A Noiseless Patient Spider, 743
Wilbur, Richard
Terza Rima, 657
The Beautiful Changes, 578
Love Calls Us to the Things of This World, 743
Williams, William Carlos
The Dance, 744
The Red Wheelbarrow, 574
This Is Just to Say, 574
Wilson, August
Authors on Their Work, 935
Fences, 873
Wordsworth, William
[A slumber did my spirit seal], 745
[I wandered lonely as a cloud], 485
Nuns Fret Not, 671
She Dwelt among the Untrodden Ways, 517
[The world is too much with us], 745

Yeats, W. B.
All Things Can Tempt Me, 745
Easter 1916, 746
The Lake Isle of Innisfree, 748
Leda and the Swan, 749
The Second Coming, 749
Young, Kevin
Ode to Pork, 630

Index of Titles and First Lines

1-2-3 was the number he played but today the number came 3-2-1, 614

20/20 (Brewer), 17

About suffering they were never wrong, 689

After a Death (Borson), 606

A little black thing among the snow:, 692

All Things Can Tempt Me (Yeats), 745

All things can tempt me from this craft of verse:, 745

All we need is fourteen lines, well, thirteen now, 677

A love poem risks becoming a ruin, 553

Alzheimer's (Cherry), 541

[*A narrow Fellow in the Grass*] (Dickinson), 699

Anecdote of the Jar (Stevens), 737

Antigone (Sophocles), 1211

Anyone can get it wrong, laying low, 567

A & P (Updike), 437

Applauding youths laughed with young prostitutes, 721

Araby (Joyce), 330

A slumber did my spirit seal, 745

A sudden blow: the great wings beating still, 749

As virtuous men pass mildly away, 703

At a Bach Concert (Rich), 735

At the VA hospital in Long Beach, California, 606

Aunt Jennifer's Tigers (Rich), 550

Aunt Jennifer's tigers prance across a screen, 550

[*A village without bells—*] (Bashō), 690

A wind is ruffling the tawny pelt, 741

Ballad of Birmingham (Randall), 734

Ballad of the Landlord (Hughes), 519

Barbie Doll (Piercy), 724

Bartleby, the Scrivener (Melville), 368

[*Batter my heart, three-personed God*] (Donne), 590

Beat! Beat! Drums! (Whitman), 629

Beat! beat! drums!—Blow! bugles! blow!, 629

The Beautiful Changes (Wilbur), 578

[*Because I could not stop for Death—*] (Dickinson), 583

Bent double, like old beggars under sacks, 627

Between my finger and my thumb, 713

The Birth-Mark (Hawthorne), 219

Blackberry Eating (Kinnell), 635

Blandeur (Ryan), 574

Boys and Girls (Munro), 400

[*Buffalo Bill's*] (Cummings), 663

The Call (Pope), 626

Call the roller of big cigars, 738

The Cask of Amontillado (Poe), 115

Cathedral (Carver), 33

A Certain Lady (Parker), 518

The Charge of the Light Brigade (Tennyson), 623

The Chimney Sweeper (Blake), 692

Church Going (Larkin), 647

Come live with me and be my love, 537

Coming by evening through the wintry city, 735

cream of wheat (Clifton), 521

Daddy (Plath), 725

The Dance (Williams), 744

Daystar (Dove), 525

Dear Obour, 490

[*Death, be not proud*] (Donne), 702

Death of a Salesman (Miller), 1018

Death of a Young Son by Drowning (Atwood), 515

The Death of the Ball Turret Gunner (Jarrell), 590

Design (Frost), 675

Did you ever see stars? asked my father with a cackle. He was not, 560

Digging (Heaney), 713

Dim Lady (Mullen), 677
Dirge (Fearing), 614
Diving into the Wreck (Rich), 603
Divorce (Collins), 488
A Doll House (Ibsen), 812
Do Not Go Gentle into That Good Night (Thomas), 659
Dothead (Majmudar), 586
Dover Beach (Arnold), 530
The Dover Bitch (Hecht), 539
Dulce et Decorum Est (Owen), 627

Easter 1916 (Yeats), 746
[Eastern guard tower] (Knight), 720
Easter Wings (Herbert), 664
Elena (Mora), 722
The Elephant in the Village of the Blind (Anonymous), 14
The Emperor of Ice-Cream (Stevens), 738
Escape from the Old Country (Su), 543
Even the long-dead are willing to move, 723
Exchanging Hats (Bishop), 522

Facing West from California's Shores (Whitman), 742
A Far Cry from Africa (Walcott), 741
Farewell, thou child of my right hand, and joy;, 716
Fences (Wilson), 873
First Fight. Then Fiddle. (Brooks), 676
First fight. Then fiddle. Ply the slipping string, 676
First having read the book of myths, 603
The Flea (Donne), 527
For God's sake hold your tongue and let me love!, 700
From my mother's sleep I fell into the State, 590
Frost at Midnight (Coleridge), 639

Gassing the woodchucks didn't turn out right, 549
Gentle Communion (Mora), 723
Girl (Kincaid), 127
Glory be to God for dappled things—, 573
Go, and catch a falling star, 702
God's Grandeur (Hopkins), 714
[The golf links lie so near the mill] (Cleghorn), 566

A Good Man Is Hard to Find (O'Connor), 412
Good People (Wallace), 156
grand . . . would you mind terribly, my groundling, 585
The Grasshopper and the Bell Cricket (Kawabata), 275
Gr-r-r—there go, my heart's abhorrence!, 511

Had we but world enough, and time, 528
Half a league, half a league, 623
Hamlet (Shakespeare), 1101
Hard Rock Returns to Prison from the Hospital for the Criminal Insane (Knight), 720
Hard Rock was "known not to take no shit, 720
Harlem (Hughes), 715
The Harlem Dancer (McKay), 721
He, who navigated with success, 515
Head, Heart (Davis), 478
Heart weeps, 478
He disappeared in the dead of winter:, 687
Here, the Mississippi carved, 540
He saw her from the bottom of the stairs, 709
He stands at the door, a crazy old man, 541
Hills Like White Elephants (Hemingway), 122
History (Rich), 736
Home Burial (Frost), 709
How Do I Love Thee? (Browning), 672
How do I love thee? Let me count the ways., 672
How do they do it, the ones who make love, 572
How strongly does my passion flow, 493
A Hunger Artist (Kafka), 336

I, Too (Hughes), 716
I, too, sing America, 716
[I, being born a woman and distressed] (Millay), 674
I ask them to take a poem, 695
I can feel the tug, 636
I caught this morning morning's minion, king-, 715

[*I celebrate myself, and sing myself*]
  (Whitman), 519
I doubt not God is good, well-meaning,
  kind, 696
[*I dwell in Possibility–*] (Dickinson), 697
If all the world and love were young, 538
If ever two were one, then surely we, 625
If it please God, 574
I found a dimpled spider, fat and white, 675
I have done it again, 727
I have eaten, 574
I have met them at close of day, 746
I Hear America Singing (Whitman), 643
I hear America singing, the varied carols I
  hear, 643
I know what the caged bird feels, alas!, 555
I live in a doorway, 633
I love to go out in late September, 635
I met a traveler from an antique land, 737
In An Artist's Studio (Rossetti), 672
In a Station of the Metro (Pound), 733
In Brueghel's great picture, The Kermess,
  744
I never had to make one, 543
[*in Just-*] (cummings), 696
In Memory of W. B. Yeats (Auden), 687
In Prominent Bar in Secaucus One Day
  (Kennedy), 509
In sixth grade Mrs. Walker, 534
Interpreter of Maladies (Lahiri), 344
In the Park (Harwood), 676
In this great form, as Dante proved
  in Hell, 657
Introduction to Poetry (Collins), 695
Invisible Cities (Calvino), 166
In Xanadu did Kubla Khan, 694
I placed a jar in Tennessee, 737
I saw her standin' on her front lawn, 489
I Stand Here Ironing (Olsen), 426
[*I stepped from Plank to Plank*] (Dickin-
  son), 698
It little profits that an idle king, 739
[*I wandered lonely as a cloud*] (Words-
  worth), 485
I wander through each chartered street,
  554
I want to write you, 724
I was asleep while you were dying, 660
I will arise and go now, and go to
  Innisfree, 748

[*I will put Chaos into fourteen lines*]
  (Millay), 674
I wouldn't be here, 630

Jesus Shaves (Sedaris), 433
Jundee Ameriki (Turner), 606

Kind of Blue (Powell), 579
Kubla Khan (Coleridge), 694

[*l(a*] (cummings), 663
Lady Lazarus (Plath), 727
The Lady with the Dog (Chekhov), 171
The Lake Isle of Innisfree (Yeats), 748
The Lamb (Blake), 690
Lana Turner has collapsed!, 486
Landlord, landlord, 519
Last Night (Olds), 556
The Latin Deli: An Ars Poetica (Cofer), 542
The Leap (Dickey), 593
Leaving the Motel (Snodgrass), 547
Leda and the Swan (Yeats), 749
The Lesson (Bambara), 279
Lesson for a Boy, 620
[*Let me not to the marriage of true minds*]
  (Shakespeare), 670
A Letter from Phillis Wheatley (Hayden),
  490
Let us go then, you and I, 705
Lies (Collins), 567
[*Like as the waves make towards the
  pebbled shore*] (Shakespeare), 628
Listening to a poem on the radio, 685
Litany at the Tomb of Frederick Douglass
  (Espada), 532
Little has been made, 557
London (Blake), 554
Lord, who createdst man in the wealth
  and store, 664
Love Calls Us to the Things of This World
  (Wilbur), 743
Love Medicine (Erdrich), 289
love poem (Pastan), 724
The Love Song of J. Alfred Prufrock
  (Eliot), 705

[*Making jazz swing in*] (Knight), 720
Márgarét, áre you gríeving, 628
Mark but this flea, and mark in this,
  527

Marks (Pastan), 582
Metrical Feet (Coleridge), 620
"Mother dear, may I go downtown, 734
Much have I traveled in the realms of gold, 4
Musée des Beaux Arts (Auden), 689
My Father's Song (Ortiz), 558
My heart aches, and a drowsy numbness pains, 599
My honeybunch's peepers are nothing like neon. Today's, 677
My husband gives me an A, 582
[*My lady's presence makes the roses red*] (Constable), 668
My Last Duchess (Browning), 692
[*My Life had stood— a Loaded Gun—*] (Dickinson), 698
My Love for You Is So Embarrassingly (Boss), 585
[*My mistress' eyes are nothing like the sun*] (Shakespeare), 669
My Papa's Waltz (Roethke), 569
My Spanish isn't enough, 722
Myth (Trethewey), 660

Nebraska (Springsteen), 489
The next day, I am almost afraid, 556
[*next to of course god america i*] (cummings), 520
A Noiseless Patient Spider (Whitman), 743
Not Delft or, 579
[*Not marble, nor the gilded monuments*] (Shakespeare), 669
Nuns Fret Not (Wordsworth), 671
Nuns fret not at their convent's narrow room, 671
The Nymph's Reply to the Shepherd (Raleigh), 538

O, my luve's like a red, red rose, 584
Ode on a Grecian Urn (Keats), 717
Ode to a Nightingale (Keats), 599
Ode to Pork (Young), 630
Ode to the West Wind (Shelley), 645
Of the Threads That Connect the Stars (Espada), 560
Oh, I can smile for you, and tilt my head, 518

"O 'Melia, my dear, this does everything crown!, 483
On Being Brought from Africa to America (Wheatley), 487
Once, two spoons in bed, 488
Once I am sure there's nothing going on, 647
Once upon a midnight dreary, while I pondered, weak and weary, 730
One face looks out from all his canvases, 672
One Perfect Rose (Parker), 597
1-2-3 was the number he played but today the number came 3-2-1, 614
One wading a Fall meadow finds on all sides, 578
On First Looking into Chapman's Homer (Keats), 4
On Her Loving Two Equally (Behn), 493
On My First Son (Jonson), 716
On Writing (Su), 553
The Open Boat (Crane), 254
O rose, thou art sick, 598
O wild West Wind, thou breath of Autumn's being, 645

A Pair of Tickets (Tan), 186
The Passionate Shepherd to His Love (Marlowe), 537
Persepolis (Satrapi), 21
Persimmons (Lee), 534
Pied Beauty (Hopkins), 573
Pilgrimage (Trethewey), 540
Poem (O'Hara), 486
"*Poetry Makes Nothing Happen*"? (Alvarez), 685
Presiding over a formica counter, 542
Punishment (Heaney), 636

A Raisin in the Sun (Hansberry), 936
Range-Finding (Frost), 675
The Rape of the Lock (Pope), 612
The Raven (Poe), 730
Recitatif (Morrison), 138
A Red, Red Rose (Burns), 584
The Red Wheelbarrow (Williams), 574
Repulsive Theory (Ryan), 557
Richard Cory (Robinson), 482
The River-Merchant's Wife: A Letter (Pound), 733

The Road Not Taken (Frost), 602
A Rose for Emily (Faulkner), 308
The Ruined Maid (Hardy), 483

Season of mists and mellow
    fruitfulness, 718
The Second Coming (Yeats), 749
Seeing that there's no other way, 606
September rain falls on the house, 661
Sestina (Bishop), 661
Sestina (Shuttleworth), 662
Sex without Love (Olds), 572
[Shall I compare thee to a summer's day?]
    (Shakespeare), 589
She Dwelt among the Untrodden Ways
    (Wordsworth), 517
She sits in the park. Her clothes are out of
    date., 676
She wanted a little room for thinking:,
    525
Shoulda, Woulda, Coulda (Stallings), 575
Should I simplify my life for you?, 736
The Shroud (Grimm), 60
The Sick Rose (Blake), 598
A single flow'r he sent me, since we met,
    597
Sir Patrick Spens (Anonymous), 686
[The Sky is low—the Clouds are mean]
    (Dickinson), 488
Slim Cunning Hands (de la Mare), 568
Slim cunning hands at rest, and cozening
    eyes—, 568
Soliloquy of the Spanish Cloister
    (Browning), 511
so much depends, 574
Song (Donne), 702
Song (Waller), 596
Sonnet (Collins), 677
Sonny's Blues (Baldwin), 66
Sonrisas (Mora), 633
So there stood Matthew Arnold and
    this girl, 539
Sound and Sense (Pope), 615
Spring and Fall (Hopkins), 628
The Star (Taylor), 624
Stopping by Woods on a Snowy Evening
    (Frost), 712
The Story of an Hour (Chopin), 287
Sundays too my father got up early, 559
Sympathy (Dunbar), 555

Talking With . . . (Martin), 1013
Tears, Idle Tears (Tennyson), 739
Tears, idle tears, I know not what they
    mean, 739
[Tell all the truth but tell it slant—]
    (Dickinson), 699
Tenebris (Grimké), 713
Terza Rima (Wilbur), 657
That's my last Duchess painted on the
    wall, 692
[That time of year thou mayst in me behold]
    (Shakespeare), 580
The apparition of these faces in the
    crowd, 733
The battle rent a cobweb diamond-strung,
    675
The eyes open to a cry of pulleys, 743
[The falling snow flakes] (Knight), 720
The frost performs its secret ministry, 639
The house is so quiet now, 603
The king sits in Dumferling toune, 686
The mood made him tense—, 575
The only thing I have of Jane MacNaugh-
    ton, 593
There is a tree, by day, 713
[There was a young girl from St. Paul]
    (Anonymous), 623
The sea is calm tonight, 530
The whiskey on your breath, 569
The word plum is delicious, 613
[The world is too much with us]
    (Wordsworth), 745
[Th'expense of spirit in a waste of shame]
    (Shakespeare), 644
This girlchild was born as usual, 724
This Is Just to Say (Williams), 574
This is the longitude and latitude of the
    impossible;, 532
[This road—] (Bashō), 690
Those Winter Sundays (Hayden), 559
Thou still unravished bride of quietness,
    717
To a Daughter Leaving Home (Pastan), 526
To Autumn (Keats), 718
To His Coy Mistress (Marvell), 528
To My Dear and Loving Husband
    (Bradstreet), 625
Trifles (Glaspell), 771
Turning and turning in the widening gyre,
    749

'Twas mercy brought me from my Pagan
  land, 487
The Twenty-Third Psalm (Anonymous),
  589
20/20 (Brewer), 17
'Twinkle , twinkle, little star, 624
The Two Crabs (Aesop), 249
Two roads diverged in a yellow wood, 602
The Tyger (Blake), 691
Tyger! Tyger! burning bright, 691

Ulysses (Tennyson), 739
Unfunny uncles who insist, 522

The Vacuum (Nemerov), 603
A Valediction: Forbidding Mourning
  (Donne), 703
A Very Old Man with Enormous Wings
  (Márquez), 362
The Victims (Olds), 641
Volar (Cofer), 203

A Wall of Fire Rising (Danticat), 234
Wanting to say things, 558
Well, yes, I said, my mother wears a dot,
  586
We Real Cool (Brooks), 521
We Wear the Mask (Dunbar), 704
We wear the mask that grins and lies,
  704
What happens to a dream deferred?, 715
What Is the Zoo for What (Lockwood), 587
[What lips my lips have kissed, and where,
  and why] (Millay), 673

Whenever Richard Cory went down
  town, 482
[When I consider how my light is spent]
  (Milton), 670
When I taught you, 526
When Mother divorced you, we were glad.
  She took it and, 641
Where Are You Going, Where Have You
  Been? (Oates), 94
While my hair was still cut straight across
  my forehead, 733
The White House (McKay), 722
Whose woods these are I think I know,
  712
Who's for the trench—, 626
Why I Live at the P.O. (Welty), 444
[Wild Nights- Wild Nights!] (Dickinson),
  700
Wildwood (Díaz), 455
The Windhover (Hopkins), 715
[Women have loved before as I love now]
  (Millay), 673
Woodchucks (Kumin), 549
The Word Plum (Chasin), 613
The word "zoo" is a zoo for the zoo, 587
The world is charged with the grandeur of
  God, 714

The Yellow Wallpaper (Gilman), 316
Yet Do I Marvel (Cullen), 696
You do not do, you do not do, 725
Your door is shut against my tightened
  face, 722
You/used, 662

Index of Literary Terms

action, 57, 478, 498, 770, 803, 1252
allegory, 215, 216
alliteration, 480, 499, 609, 612, 809
allusion, 216, 530, 552, 585, 809
amphitheater, 805
analogy, 584, 636
anapestic meter, 500, 619, 622
antagonist, 16, 769, 801
antihero, 132
apostrophe, 497
archetype, 133, 166, 215
arena stage, 805
assonance, 612
auditor, 112, 489, 497, 524, 539
author, 31
author time, 164

ballad, 482, 500, 658
ballad stanza, 500, 658
bildungsroman, 6
biography, 6, 32
blank verse, 500, 658

caesura, 622
canon, 1
carpe diem, 527
central consciousness, 111
character, 6, 16, 131, 478, 497, 800
characterization, 134, 769
chorus, 802
classical unities, 807
climax, 62, 804
comedy, 65, 770
complication, 62
conclusion, 63, 804
concrete poetry, 664
conflict, 15, 59, 165, 479, 498, 803, 1282
connotation, 568
consonance, 612
controlling metaphor, 581, 590, 809
convention, 7, 65

couplet, 500, 611, 618
crisis, 62
criticism, 5
cycle, 804

dactylic meter, 619
denotation, 567, 592
dénouement, 63
descriptive lyric, 487
destabilizing event, 62
deus ex machina, 63
diction, 478, 655
discriminated occasion, 59
drama, 6, 768
dramatic irony, 809
dramatic monologue, 489, 511
dramatic poem, 481
dynamic character, 133

echo, 612
elegy, 481
endstopped, 499
English sonnet, 667
enjambment, 499, 622
epic, 7, 65, 482, 532
epilogue, 63
epiphany, 62
episode, 58
epistolary novel, 6
epitaph, 568
epithet, 497, 638
expectation, 769
exposition, 61, 769, 800, 803
extended metaphor, 581
external conflict, 59, 794, 803
external narration/narrator, 111

fable, 249
fairy tale, 31, 166, 249
falling action, 62, 804
falling meter, 619
fantasy, 164
farce, 770

fiction, 6, 12
figurative language, 169, 215
figure of speech, 16, 215, 479, 569,
   578, 809
first-person narration, 111–112
flashback, 58
flashforward, 58
flat character, 133
focus, 110
foil, 132, 801
folktale, 31, 166, 249
foot, 618
foreshadowing, 58, 167
formal diction, 110
free verse, 609, 659
Freytag's pyramid, 61

general setting, 164
genre, 1, 16, 800, 1277
gothic fiction, 6
graphic fiction, 20

haiku, 659
hero/heroine, 131, 801
heroic couplet, 658
hexameter, 657
historical fiction, 6, 32, 164

iambic meter, 619, 621, 656, 667
image/imagery, 16, 170, 216, 655,
   770, 1254
implied author, 113–114
inciting incident, 62, 804
in medias res, 58, 1256
internal conflict, 59–60, 794, 802
internal narration, 111
inversion, 494
irony, 111, 216, 250, 484, 809
Italian sonnet, 667

limerick, 623, 659
limited narrator, 111
lines, 479
literary criticism, 5, 1248
lyric, 514, 633
lyric poem, 481

magic realism, 164
major (main) character, 132
memoir, 6, 32

metaphor, 5, 216, 488, 580, 809
meter, 499, 552, 609, 655, 809,
   1254, 1277
metonymy, 216, 479
minor character, 132–133
monologue, 809
moral, 251
myth, 215, 585

narration, 110–114
narrative, 30
narrative poem, 481
narrator, 16, 110, 478, 509, 800
nonfiction, 6, 32
novel, 6, 31
novella, 6, 31

octameter, 620
octave, 667
ode, 484, 500
omniscient narrator, 111
omniscient point of view, 111
onomatopoeia, 612
orchestra, 805
oxymoron, 216

palindrome, 659
paraphrase, 479
parody, 7
pastoral literature, 7, 537
pentameter, 656
personification, 217, 479, 582, 809
Petrarchan sonnet, 667
plot, 6, 16, 57, 478, 498, 770, 1252,
   1277
plot summary, 64
plot time, 164
poetry, 6
point of view, 110
prop, 807
proscenium stage, 805
prose, 6, 16, 31, 32
protagonist, 16, 769, 801
pyrrhic meter, 619

resolution, 804
rhetoric, 216
rhyme, 480, 499, 609, 655
rhyme scheme, 610, 656, 667,
   1254, 1277

rhythm, 478
rising action, 62, 804
rising meter, 619
romance, 6, 65, 482
round character, 133

sarcasm, 216
satire, 6
scansion, 620
scapegoat, 134
second-person narration, 112–113
sequence, 804
sestet, 667
sestina, 659
set, 807
setting, 6, 16, 164, 481, 497, 524, 546,
    655, 770, 806
Shakespearean sonnet, 667
short short story, 32
short story, 6, 31
simile, 5, 217, 584, 636
situation, 481, 498, 524, 546, 655,
    1283
skene, 805
sonnet, 481, 500, 655, 667
spatial setting, 524
speaker, 497, 509, 524, 546, 655, 1282
Spenserian stanza, 657
spondaic meter, 619
stage direction, 769, 801
stanza, 479, 635, 655–656, 1254
static character, 133
stock character, 133
style, 16, 110, 770

subgenre, 6
subplot, 58, 804
symbol, 16, 214, 217, 592, 809
symbolic poem, 598
synecdoche, 217
syntax, 478, 493, 571

tale, 30–31
temporal setting, 164, 524
terza rima, 656
tetrameter, 658
theme, 16, 57, 165, 249, 498, 546, 644,
    655, 770, 810, 1258
third-person narration, 111
thrust stage, 805
time, 164
tone, 16, 110, 488, 493, 546, 633, 655,
    668, 770, 1263, 1283
topic, 546
traditional symbol, 214, 595
tragedy, 65, 770, 809
trochaic meter, 619, 622
trope, 215
turning point, 62, 804

unity of time, 807
unlimited point for view, 111
unreliable narrator, 112

verbal irony, 216, 809
verse drama, 483
villain, 131, 801
villanelle, 659
voice, 110